CORPORATE INSOLVENCY LAW

SECOND EDITION

The first edition of *Corporate Insolvency Law* proposed a fundamentally revised concept of insolvency law – one intended to serve to corporate as well as broader social ends. This second edition takes on board a host of changes that have subsequently reshaped insolvency law and practice, such as the consolidation of the rescue culture in the UK, the arrival of the 'pre-packaged' administration and the broad replacement of administrative receivership with administration. It also considers the implications of recent and dramatic changes in the provision (and trading) of credit, the movement of an increasing amount of 'insolvency work' towards the pre-formal insolvency stage of corporate affairs and the explosion, on the insolvency scene, of a new cadre of specialists in corporate turnaround. Looking to the future, Vanessa Finch argues that changes of approach are needed if insolvency law is to develop with coherence and purpose and she offers a framework for such an approach.

VANESSA FINCH is a Professor of Law at the London School of Economics and Political Science, where she teaches Corporate Insolvency Law and Corporate Accountability at undergraduate and master's levels.

CORPORATE INSOLVENCY LAW

Perspectives and Principles

SECOND EDITION

VANESSA FINCH

CAMBRIDGE
UNIVERSITY PRESS

CAMBRIDGE UNIVERSITY PRESS
Cambridge, New York, Melbourne, Madrid, Cape Town,
Singapore, São Paulo, Delhi, Tokyo, Mexico City

Cambridge University Press
The Edinburgh Building, Cambridge CB2 8RU, UK

Published in the United States of America by
Cambridge University Press, New York

www.cambridge.org
Information on this title: www.cambridge.org/9780521701822

First edition 2002
Second edition 2009

A catalogue record for this publication is available from the British Library

Library of Congress Cataloguing in Publication data
Finch, Vanessa.
Corporate insolvency law : perspectives and principles / Vanessa Finch. – 2nd ed.
p. cm.
Includes index.
ISBN 978-0-521-87810-4
1. Bankruptcy – Great Britain. 2. Business failures – Law and legislation – Great
Britain. I. Title.
KD2139.F558 2009
346.4107′8–dc22
2009007333

ISBN 978-0-521-87810-4 Hardback
ISBN 978-0-521-70182-2 Paperback

To Rob
and in memory of D.F.G. and M.A.G.

CONTENTS

ACKNOWLEDGEMENTS

I would like to thank all my colleagues at the London School of Economics who have helped me with this second edition and who have made the Law Department such a stimulating environment in which to research law in its broader contexts.

Particular thanks go to Rob Baldwin of LSE for reading drafts, to Adrian Walters of Nottingham Law School for his helpful suggestions and to Eyal Geva for research assistance. Finally, I thank Luke, Olivia and Nat for their encouragement and forbearance during the production of this edition.

TABLE OF CASES

TABLE OF STATUTES AND OTHER INSTRUMENTS

ABBREVIATIONS

ABFA	Asset Based Finance Association
ABS	asset-backed security
ACCA	Association of Chartered Certified Accountants
AR	administrative receiver
ARA	Assets Recovery Agency
BAPCPA	Bankruptcy Abuse Prevention and Consumer Protection Act 2005
BBAA	British Business Angels Association
BCCI	Bank of Credit and Commerce International
BERR	Department of Business Enterprise and Regulatory Reform
BVCA	British Venture Capital Association
CA	Companies Act 2006
CBI	Confederation of British Industry
CDDA	Company Directors' Disqualification Act 1986
CDO	collateralised debt obligation
CDS	credit default swap
CFA	conditional fee arrangement
CIB	Companies Investigation Branch
CLRSG	Company Law Review Steering Group
CVA	Company Voluntary Arrangement
CVL	Creditors' Voluntary Liquidation
DIP	debtor in possession
DTI	Department of Trade and Industry
EA	Enterprise Act 2002
EAT	Employment Appeal Tribunal
ECHR	European Court of Human Rights
ECJ	European Court of Justice
EEC	European Economic Community
EHYA	European High Yield Association
EIB	European Investment Bank

ERA	Employment Rights Act 1996
ESRC	Economic and Social Research Council
ETO	economic, technical or organisational
FIRS	Forensic Insolvency Recovery Service
FSA	Financial Services Authority
FSB	Federation of Small Businesses
FSMA	Financial Services and Markets Act 2000
HMRC	Her Majesty's Revenue and Customs
HP	hire purchase
HRA	Human Rights Act 1998
IA	Insolvency Act 1986
IBR	independent business review
ICAEW	Institute of Chartered Accountants of England and Wales
ICAI	Institute of Chartered Accountants in Ireland
ICAS	Institute of Chartered Accountants in Scotland
IFT	Institute for Turnaround
ILA	Insolvency Lawyers' Association
IOD	Institute of Directors
IP	insolvency practitioner
IPA	Insolvency Practitioners' Association
IPC	Insolvency Practices Council
IR	Inland Revenue; Insolvency Rules
IRWP	Insolvency Review Working Party
IS	Insolvency Service
ISA	Insolvency Services Account
IVA	Individual Voluntary Arrangement
JIC	Joint Insolvency Committee
JIEB	Joint Insolvency Examining Board
JIMU	Joint Insolvency Monitoring Unit
LPA	Law of Property Act 1925
LS	Law Society
LSS	Law Society of Scotland
MBO	management buyout
NAO	National Audit Office
NBAN	National Business Angel Network
NI	national insurance
NIF	National Insurance Fund
OFT	Office of Fair Trading

OR	Official Receiver
PAYE	pay as you earn
PCA	Parliamentary Commissioner for Administration
PIK	payment in kind note
PIL	public interest liquidation
PIP	practitioner in possession
PIU	Public Interest Unit
PMSI	purchase money security interest
PPF	Pension Protection Fund
QFC	qualifying floating charge
QFCH	qualifying floating charge holder
R3	Association of Business Recovery Professionals
RBS	Royal Bank of Scotland
ROT	retention of title
RPB	recognised professional body
SBS	Small Business Service
SFLGS	Small Firms Loan Guarantee Scheme
SIP	Statement of Insolvency Practice
SMEs	small and medium enterprises
SPI	Society of Practitioners in Insolvency
SPV	special purpose vehicle
SSP	statutory super-priority
STP	Society of Turnaround Professionals
TMA	Turnaround Management Association
TP	turnaround professional
TQM	total quality management
TUPE	Transfer of Undertakings (Protection of Employment)
UCC	Uniform Commercial Code
UNCITRAL	United Nations Commission on International Trade Law
VAS	Voluntary Arrangements Service

Introduction to the second edition

This book sets out to offer a critical appraisal of modern corporate insolvency law rather than a description of existing statutory rules and case law on the subject. It will nevertheless attempt to set out rules and procedures of corporate insolvency law in sufficient detail to facilitate understanding of the framework and operation of this area of law.

A critical approach is seen as essential here on the grounds that it is impossible to evaluate areas of the law, suggest reforms or develop the law with a sense of purpose unless there is clarity concerning the objectives and values sought to be furthered, the feasibility of operating certain procedures and the efficiency with which given rules or processes can be applied on the ground.

Insolvency is an area of law of increasing importance not merely in its own right but because it impinges on a host of other sectors such as company, employment, tort, environmental, pension and banking law. It is essential, therefore, that the development of insolvency law proceeds with a sense of purpose. If this is lacking, this area of law is liable to be marked by inconsistencies of reasoning and failures of policy, with the result that related legal sectors will also be adversely affected.

The book's aims are threefold. The first is to outline the law on corporate insolvency (as at 31 May 2008) and the procedures and enforcement mechanisms used in giving effect to that law. Corporate insolvency law will be seen as raising important social, political and moral issues rather than viewed merely as a device for maximising returns for creditors. Questions of stakeholding, community interests and the concerns of employees and the public as well as creditors will thus be discussed.

The second aim is to set out a theoretical framework for corporate insolvency law that will establish benchmarks for evaluating that law and any proposed reforms. Those benchmarks will be applied throughout the volume. It will be consistently asked whether the laws and processes under discussion will serve the variety of values and ends suggested at the start of the book.

A third objective is to move beyond an appraisal of current laws and processes and to consider whether new approaches to insolvency

1

institutions and rules are called for: in other words, to see whether improvements have to be sought by adopting new perspectives; by changing approaches in response to developments in commercial and credit markets; and by challenging the assumptions that underpin present corporate insolvency regimes. The focus here is on domestic corporate insolvency law. Space does not allow an appraisal of the European Council Regulation on Insolvency Proceedings[1] or of international and cross-border issues[2] as individual topics (these are areas that have been dealt with specifically by others, though mention will be made of non-UK or international insolvency laws and processes that are of relevance to questions under discussion).[3]

Since the first edition of this book was published in 2002, a number of important changes have taken place both within corporate insolvency

---

[1] Council Regulation (EC) 1346/2000 of 29 May 2000, OJ 2000 No. L160/1, 30 June 2000, pp. 0001–0013, amended in 2005 by Council Regulation (EC) 603/2005 and in 2006 by Council Regulation (EC) 694/2006. See further I. Fletcher, 'Reflections on the EC Regulation on Insolvency Proceedings – Parts 1 and 2' (2005) 18 *Insolvency Intelligence* 49 and 68; Fletcher, *Insolvency in Private International Law: National and International Approaches* (2nd edn, Oxford University Press, Oxford, 2005) ch. 7; G. Moss and C. Paulus, 'The European Insolvency Regulation – The Case for Urgent Reform' (2006) 19 *Insolvency Intelligence* 1; P. J. Omar, *European Insolvency Law* (Ashgate Publishing, Aldershot, 2004) chs. 3, 5, 6–10; M. Virgos and F. Garcimartin, *The European Insolvency Regulation: Law and Practice* (Kluwer, The Hague, 2004); K. Dawson, 'Cross Border Insolvency: The EC Regulation and the UNCITRAL Model Law' in K. Gromek Broc and R. Parry (eds.), *Corporate Rescue: An Overview of Recent Developments* (2nd edn, Kluwer, London, 2006).

[2] See, for example, P. Omar (ed.) *International Insolvency Law: Themes and Perspectives* (Ashgate Publishing, Aldershot, 2008); J. Townsend, 'International Co-operation in Cross Border Insolvency: *Hill Insurance*' (2008) 71 MLR 811; J. Bannister, 'Universality Upheld: The House of Lords' Decision in *McGrath* v. *Riddell* Considered' (2008) 232 *Sweet & Maxwell's Company Law Newsletter* 1; H. Anderson, 'Legal Update – The Ruling in *McGrath* v. *Riddell and Others* [2008] UKHL 21' (2008) *Recovery* (Summer) 9; Fletcher, *Insolvency in Private International Law*; Fletcher, *The Law of Insolvency* (3rd edn, Sweet & Maxwell, London, 2002) ch. 31; Fletcher, '"Better Late than Never": The UNCITRAL Model Law Enters into Force in GB' (2006) 19 *Insolvency Intelligence* 86; Fletcher, 'The Quest for a Global Insolvency Law: A Challenge for Our Time' in M. Freeman (ed.), 55 *Current Legal Problems* (Oxford University Press, Oxford, 2002) pp. 427–45; UNCITRAL Model Law on Cross-Border Insolvency; Cross-Border Insolvency Regulations 2006 (SI 2006/1030); Dawson, 'Cross Border Insolvency'; J. Westbrook, 'Global Insolvencies in a World of Nation States' in A. Clarke (ed.), *Current Issues in Insolvency Law* (Stevens, London, 1991).

[3] For a discussion of key features of the insolvency systems in a selection of European jurisdictions see, for example, C. Laughton, 'Review of European Corporate Insolvency Regimes Part 1' (2004) *Recovery* (Autumn) 16; 'Part 2' (2005) *Recovery* (Summer) 20; B. Wessels, 'Europe Deserves a New Approach to Insolvency Proceedings' (2007) 4 *European Company Law* 253; E. Geva, 'National Policy Objectives from an EU Perspective: UK Corporate Rescue and the European Insolvency Regulation' (2007) 8 EBOR 605.

law and in the business and credit worlds. As will be detailed further in chapter 1, the rescue culture has become further embedded within the UK insolvency culture so that an increased stress is placed on dealing with insolvency risks at the earliest stages of corporate difficulties. Part of this process involves the greater use of 'pre-packaged' arrangements that deal with problems well in advance of entry into any formal insolvency procedure. New types of specialist adviser now play a role in such negotiations and they supplement the work done by the insolvency practitioners who formerly dominated this area of activity.

Legal procedures have also changed markedly, with the Enterprise Act 2002 largely replacing administrative receivership with a revised administration process; offering greater protection for unsecured creditors (by means of a 'prescribed part' fund); and removing the Crown's status as a preferential creditor. For their part, the courts have contributed to change by deciding such landmark cases as *Spectrum Plus* and *Leyland DAF*, which have impacted significantly on financing possibilities.

As will also be discussed in more detail below, the credit crisis of 2007–8 has highlighted the extent to which debt arrangements have shifted remarkably in recent years – and in ways that present dramatic new challenges for those involved with insolvency processes and with corporate rescue. Borrower-to-lender relationships have become vastly more complex and less transparent than was traditionally the case and creditors' incentives to intervene in, or monitor, management were reduced (most markedly in the lead up to the credit crisis) as it became ever easier to deal with insolvency risks by trading in packages of debt rather than by instigating reforms within the corporation. Such changes in the debt markets have involved significant adjustments in the roles played by different parties and organisations. The major banks, for instance, can no longer be assumed to lie at the heart of the credit supply or managerial discipline processes and greater attention has to be paid to the implications of financing by means of such sources as the bond markets and hedge funds.

These and further changes both bring insolvency law into increasingly close contact with other areas of law and make the study of insolvency laws and processes more interesting than at any time before. It is clearer than ever that insolvency law and procedure is of relevance not merely to insolvent and distressed companies but also to those companies that are concerned to manage their financial risks according to best practice.

The framing structure of this volume remains as found in the first edition except that a new chapter 10 has been added in order to discuss the advent of the 'pre-packaged' administration. Many additions and revisions have, however, been included in this new edition. It is hoped that these will assist in both updating the discussion and in reorienting it towards the many new challenges that insolvency law now confronts.

Part I of the book deals with agendas and objectives. Chapter 1 discusses the principal concerns of corporate insolvency law and considers the set of major issues that confront corporate insolvency law. Chapter 2 examines the values and aims sought to be furthered in this area. It is this chapter that identifies the benchmarks already referred to.

Part II is concerned with the financial and institutional context within which corporate insolvency laws and processes play a role. The problems with which corporate insolvency law has to come to grips cannot be fully understood without an appreciation of the legal regimes that govern corporate structures and borrowing. Chapter 3, accordingly, examines corporate borrowing, its continuing development and the rapid movement towards more complex and fragmented credit structures and markets. Other matters dealt with are the nature of security interests, fixed and floating charges, and different types of creditor. Chapter 4 looks at the nature and causes of corporate failure and the ways in which the law decides that a company is 'insolvent', and chapter 5 moves to the administrative framework and the role of insolvency practitioners, the Insolvency Service and turnaround professionals.

Corporate insolvency law is not merely concerned with the death and burial of companies. Important issues are whether corporate difficulties should be treated as terminal and whether it is feasible to mount rescue operations. Part III reviews processes for attempting to avert corporate death and liquidation. Chapter 6 considers the challenge of corporate rescue, the reasons for attempting rescue, the development of the UK's focus on rescue and rescue proceedings and approaches in other jurisdictions (including the US Chapter 11 strategy). It discusses the nature and implications of the recent shift towards seeing corporate troubles as matters to be anticipated rather than reacted to. Chapter 7 deals with rescue mechanisms (such as negotiated settlements) that avoid resort to formal insolvency procedures as provided under insolvency legislation. Chapters 8, 9, 10 and 11 consider different aspects of the formal rescue procedures: administrative receivership; administration; and company voluntary arrangements (including schemes of arrangement). Chapter 9 has been substantially rewritten since the first edition in order to take account of the Enterprise Act 2002 and its establishment of a new administration procedure. Chapter 10 is new to this edition and develops the discussion of administration by examining the emergence of the 'pre-packaging' process and the use of negotiations and agreements that anticipate resort to this procedure. Chapter 12 offers an overview and evaluation of rescue procedures and reviews proposed improvements.

Part IV is concerned with the process of liquidating companies. Chapter 13 deals with gathering in the assets of an insolvent company, the nature and scope of the winding-up process, the liquidator's role, the special issues raised by corporate groups and the parts played by the courts, directors and creditors in liquidation. Chapter 14 focuses on the *pari passu* principle and its place in the process of distributing assets. Chapter 15 discusses devices that are intended to gain, or have the effect of gaining, priority and bypass the *pari passu* principle.

When a corporate failure occurs, this may have a dramatic impact on the lives, interests and employment prospects of a number of parties. It is important to understand the nature of these potential effects in considering how corporate insolvency law should be developed. Part V thus looks at the repercussions of insolvency. Chapter 16 reviews the implications of a corporate collapse for company directors, considers the incentives under which directors operate in times of crisis and also assesses rationales underpinning the law's treatment of directors in this context. Chapter 17 looks to employees and asks how and why their interests should be considered when companies are in mortal peril. Further issues are whether employees should be seen as having interests other than financial ones and the extent to which efficiency considerations should be tempered with reference to other objectives, such as security of employment.

Finally, chapter 18, the Conclusion, offers more general observations.

PART I

Agendas and objectives

1

The roots of corporate insolvency law

In a society that facilitates the use of credit by companies[1] there is a degree of risk that those who are owed money by a firm will suffer because the firm has become unable to pay its debts on the due date. If a number of creditors were owed money and all pursued the rights and remedies available to them (for example, contractual rights; rights to enforce security interests; rights to set off the debt against other obligations; proceedings for delivery, foreclosure or sale) a chaotic race to protect interests would take place and this might produce inefficiencies and unfairness. Huge costs would be incurred in pursuing individual creditors' claims competitively[2] and (since in an insolvency there are insufficient assets to go round) those creditors who enforced their claim with most vigour and expertise would be paid but naïve latecomers would not.

A main aim of insolvency law is to replace this free-for-all with a legal regime in which creditors' rights and remedies are suspended and a process established for the orderly collection and realisation of the debtors' assets and the fair distribution of these according to creditors' claims. Part of the drama of insolvency law flows, accordingly, from its potentially having to unpack and reassemble what were seemingly concrete and clear legal rights.

Corporate insolvency law, with which this book is concerned, is now a quite separate body of law from personal bankruptcy law although these have shared historical roots. Those roots should be noted, since the shape of modern corporate insolvency law is as much a product of past history and accidents of development as of design.

---

[1] See Cork Report: *Report of the Review Committee on Insolvency Law and Practice* (Cmnd 8558, 1982) ch. 1; see ch. 3 below.
[2] T. H. Jackson, *The Logic and Limits of Bankruptcy Law* (Harvard University Press, Cambridge, Mass., 1986) chs. 1, 2; see ch. 2 below.

Development and structure

The earliest insolvency laws in England and Wales were concerned with individual insolvency (bankruptcy) and date back to medieval times.[3] Early common law offered no collective procedure for administering an insolvent's estate but a creditor could seize either the body of a debtor or his effects – but not both. Creditors, moreover, had to act individually, there being no machinery for sharing expenses. When the person of the debtor was seized, detention in person at the creditor's pleasure was provided for. Insolvency was thus seen as an offence little less criminal than a felony. From Tudor times onwards, insolvency has been driven by three distinct forces: impulsions to punish bankrupts; wishes to organise administration of their assets so that competing creditors are treated fairly and efficiently; and the hope that the bankrupt would be allowed to rehabilitate himself.[4] Early insolvency law was dominated by punitive approaches and it was not until the early eighteenth century that notions of rehabilitation gained force. The idea that creditors might act collectively was recognised in 1542 with the enactment of the first English Bankruptcy Act which dealt with absconding debtors and empowered any aggrieved party to procure seizure of the debtor's property, its sale and distribution to creditors 'according to the quantity of their debts'.[5] This statute did not, however, provide for rehabilitation in so far as it did not discharge the bankrupt's liability for claims that were not fully paid.

Elizabethan legislation of 1570 then drew an important distinction between traders and others, including within the definition of a bankrupt only traders and merchants: those who earned their living by 'buying and selling'.[6] Non-traders could thus not be declared bankrupt. As for

---

[3] On the history of insolvency law see Cork Report ch. 2, paras. 26–34; D. Milman, *Personal Insolvency Law, Regulation and Policy* (Ashgate, Aldershot, 2005) pp. 5–12; I. F. Fletcher, *The Law of Insolvency* (3rd edn, Sweet & Maxwell, London, 2002) pp. 6 ff.; B. G. Carruthers and T. C. Halliday, *Rescuing Business: The Making of Corporate Bankruptcy Law in England and the United States* (Clarendon Press, Oxford, 1998); G. R. Rubin and D. Sugarman (eds.), *Law, Economy and Society: Essays in the History of English Law* (Professional Books, Abingdon, 1984) pp. 43–7; W. R. Cornish and G. de N. Clark, *Law and Society in England 1750–1950* (Sweet & Maxwell, London, 1989) ch. 3, part II; V. M. Lester, *Victorian Insolvency* (Oxford University Press, Oxford, 1996).

[4] See Cornish and Clark, *Law and Society*, p. 231.

[5] Stat. 34 & 35 Hen. 8, c. 4, s. 1; see Fletcher, *Law of Insolvency*, p. 7; W. J. Jones, 'The Foundations of English Bankruptcy: Statutes and Commissions in the Early Modern Period' (1979) 69(3) *Transactions of American Philosophical Society* 69.

[6] J. Cohen, 'History of Imprisonment for Debt and its Relation to the Development of Discharge in Bankruptcy' (1982) 3 *Journal of Legal History* 153–6.

distribution, this statute again provided for equal distribution of assets among creditors.

Discharge of a bankrupt's existing liabilities came into the law in the early eighteenth century when a 1705 statute relieved traders of liability for existing debts. This restriction of discharge to traders prompted a good deal of litigation throughout the eighteenth and early nineteenth centuries and an expansion of the definition of a trader. On why bankruptcy should have been restricted to the trader, contemporary and modern commentators[7] have followed Blackstone[8] in referring to the risks that traders run of becoming unable to pay debts without any fault of their own and to the trading necessity of allowing merchants to discharge debts. It can be pointed out that long before a general law of incorporation arrived (in the mid-nineteenth century), bankruptcy served as almost a surrogate form of limited liability which needed to be restricted to those undertaking mercantile endeavours and risks. The bankruptcy legislation, moreover, provided the only means by which eighteenth- and early-nineteenth-century traders might limit their liabilities.

The state of the law was, however, deficient in many respects. Non-traders were still subject to the severities of common law enforcement procedures by means of seizures and impoundings of property and persons. These processes were non-collective and debtors might be imprisoned at the behest of single creditors without regard to the interests of others. An important difference between the bankruptcy laws available to traders and the insolvency schemes for non-traders was that whereas the bankrupt's liabilities to creditors could be discharged on surrender of assets (even if these assets were insufficient to satisfy his entire debt), the insolvent non-trader was still obliged to repay the remainder of his judgment debt even though he had suffered seizure of his goods or served his term of imprisonment. Even traders could not apply of their own accord to be made bankrupt and, although discharge was possible after 1705, the law criminalised bankrupt traders and punished them severely, with the death penalty available in cases of

---

[7] Crompton, *Practice Common-placed: Or, the Rules and Cases of the Practice in the Courts of King's Bench and Common Pleas*, LXVII (3rd edn, 1786); J. Dunscombe, 'Bankruptcy: A Study in Comparative Legislation' (1893) 2 *Columbia University Studies in Political Science* 17–18.

[8] W. Blackstone, *Commentaries on the Laws of England* (8th edn, Clarendon Press, Oxford, 1765–9) vol. II, no. 5: Cohen, 'History of Imprisonment', pp. 160–2; Cornish and Clark, *Law and Society*, p. 232; Cork Report, p. 33.

fraud.[9] The bankruptcy system, moreover, was liable to manipulation by creditors and laid open to the 'eighteenth century penchant for malign administration'.[10] Nor was it the case that all traders were in practice brought within bankruptcy proceedings. The Erskine Commission of 1840 noted that the common law insolvency processes were frequently being used for small traders whose creditors were owed too little to justify bankruptcy proceedings (two-thirds of those before the Insolvent Debtors Court in 1839 were traders).[11]

Pressure for reform grew alongside dissatisfaction with the confinement of bankruptcy to traders. During the nineteenth century, attitudes towards trade credit and risk of default changed. A depersonalisation of business and credit was encouraged by Parliament's enactment of the Joint Stock Companies Act 1844 together with notions that credit might be raised on an institutional basis and capital through stocks rather than both of these dealt with as matters of individual standing.[12] Such changed attitudes rendered increasingly questionable Blackstone's view that it was not justifiable for any person other than a trader to 'encumber himself with debts of any considerable value'.[13] The distinction between traders and non-traders was finally abolished in 1861 when bankruptcy proceedings became available for non-traders. Soon afterwards the Debtors Act 1869 abolished imprisonment for debt.

The origins of corporate insolvency law are to be found in the nineteenth-century development of the company. The key statute was the Joint Stock Companies Act 1844 which established the company as a distinct legal entity, although it retained unlimited liability for the shareholders. From 1844 onwards corporate insolvency was dealt with by means of special statutory provisions[14] and the modern limited liability company emerged in 1855, to be followed seven years later by the first modern company law statute containing detailed winding-up provisions.[15] Only from 1855 onwards, therefore, was the concept of the limited liability of members for the debts incurred by the company established in law. Members of incorporated companies could limit

---

[9] See Cork Report, paras. 37–8; Fletcher, *Law of Insolvency*, pp. 8–9.

[10] Cornish and Clark, *Law and Society*, p. 232.   [11] Ibid., p. 234.

[12] On depersonalisation of business and credit in the USA see Rubin and Sugarman, *Law, Economy and Society*, pp. 43–4.

[13] Blackstone, vol. II, no. 5, p. 473.

[14] See e.g. Companies Winding Up Act 1844; Joint Stock Companies Act 1856; Companies Act 1862; Companies (Consolidation) Act 1908; Companies Acts of 1929, 1948 and 1985.

[15] Limited Liability Act 1855; Companies Act 1862.

their personal liability, thus creating a distinction between corporate and individual insolvency. The House of Lords in *Salomon's* case[16] confirmed that a duly formed company was a separate legal person from its members and that consequently even a one-man company's debts were self-contained and distinct. The growth of a specialised corpus of law and procedures dealing with corporate insolvency was manifest in the dedicated statutes already noted but it was also encouraged when issues relating to such matters became the exclusive jurisdiction of the Chancery Court in 1862.[17]

Thus the law dealing with company insolvencies developed independently from the law on the bankruptcy of individuals. By the late nineteenth century two separate bodies of law governed individual and corporate insolvency matters and these were dealt with by different courts, under different procedural rules[18] and offering different substantive remedies. A degree of cross-influence between personal bankruptcy and corporate insolvency is discernible, however, and a number of principles and provisions of personal bankruptcy have been made applicable to company liquidation.[19]

Such a bifurcation of approaches produced, during the first half of the twentieth century, a confused tangle of insolvency laws that was both difficult to operate and prone to manipulation by the unscrupulous. Various committees were set up to look at particular aspects of the law dealing with credit, security and debt[20] but it was the mid-1970s before the deficiencies in insolvency law were attended to at the governmental level. In 1975, Justice issued a report[21] pointing to a number of serious deficiencies in the law of bankruptcy and making a number of reform proposals, some of which were adopted in the Insolvency Act of 1976, a short piece of legislation that was passed to remedy a number of the most serious defects pending broader review. Further pressure to reassess insolvency law flowed from the UK's accession to membership of the EEC. This demanded that the UK negotiate with other Member States concerning a draft EEC Bankruptcy Convention. In order to secure advice for the Department of Trade, an advisory committee was

---

[16] *Salomon v. A. Salomon & Co. Ltd* [1897] AC 22.
[17] Companies Act 1862 s. 81. [18] See Fletcher, *Law of Insolvency*, p. 12.
[19] See H. Rajak, *Insolvency Law: Theory and Practice* (Sweet & Maxwell, London, 1993) p. 3 (citing as examples Companies Act 1985 ss. 612–13, 615).
[20] See the Crowther Committee (Cmnd 4596, 1968–71) and the Payne Committee (Cmnd 3909, 1965–9).
[21] Justice, *Bankruptcy* (London, 1975).

appointed in 1973 under the chairmanship of Mr Kenneth Cork, as he then was. The resultant report[22] stressed that a comprehensive review of insolvency was required, not only in order to participate in negotiations with other EEC Member States, but also because the state of the law demanded this. Thus prompted, Edmund Dell MP, the Labour Government's Secretary of State for Trade, appointed a Review Committee on Insolvency Law and Practice in January 1977, with Kenneth Cork again serving as chairman. The Committee was asked to review, examine and make recommendations on: the law and practice relating to 'insolvency, bankruptcy, liquidation and receiverships';[23] the possibility of formulating a comprehensive insolvency system; the extent to which existing procedures should be harmonised and integrated; and less formal procedures as alternatives to bankruptcy and company winding-up proceedings. The Cork Committee was not, however, asked to conduct a review of credit and security laws or remedies for debt enforcement, nor was provision made for the Committee to undertake an extended programme of research into the causes of company failure.[24]

The Cork Report[25] in final form was published in June 1982 at a time when the rate of business failures was at a record level.[26] The 460-page document provided a sustained critique of contemporary law and practice and a set of recommendations constituting the foundations of modern insolvency law. The report argued for fundamental reforms, and central recommendations were, *inter alia*: that a unified insolvency code replace the array of statutes that made up two distinct branches of the law; that a unified system of insolvency courts be created to administer the law; and that a range of new procedures be introduced as alternatives to outright bankruptcy or winding up, which would deal

---

[22] Report of the Cork Advisory Committee (Cmnd 6602, 1976).

[23] Cork Report, p. 3. On the background to, and implementation of, Cork see Carruthers and Halliday, *Rescuing Business*, pp. 112–23.

[24] For criticism on this point, see J. H. Farrar, 'Company Insolvency and the Cork Recommendations' (1983) 4 Co. Law. 20.

[25] Cork Report. In 1979 the Cork Committee issued an interim report to the Minister, published in July 1980 as *Bankruptcy: Interim Report of the Insolvency Law Review Committee* (Cmnd 7968, 1980). The Government also produced a Green Paper: *Bankruptcy: A Consultative Document* (Cmnd 7967, 1980). This contained proposals for the privatisation of insolvency procedures which were attacked by commentators (see I. F. Fletcher (1981) 44 MLR 77) and subsequently dropped.

[26] The rate of failure increased by over 35 per cent: see D. Hare and D. Milman, 'Corporate Insolvency: The Cork Committee Proposals I' (1983) 127 Sol. Jo. 230.

with individual cases on their merits. On particular matters of substance concerning corporate insolvency, the Cork Committee's key recommendations included steps to deal with abusive practices. These involved recommendations that private insolvency practitioners should be professionally regulated to ensure adequate standards of competence and integrity; that creditors be given a greater voice in the choice of the liquidator; and that new penalties and constraints be placed on errant directors. Cork also proposed reforms designed to increase the survival chances of firms in difficulties. He had informed the press, on the establishment of his committee, that many more companies could be saved if outside administrators could be brought into companies before the time when a bank would formally appoint a receiver and in circumstances when the company lacked a loan structure allowing the appointment of receivers.[27] The Cork Report, in due course, introduced the concept of the 'administrator' into corporate insolvency procedures with the function of managing a company's business during a period of grace in the hope of reorganising the company and restoring it to profitability. The report, furthermore, favoured a movement towards greater creditor participation with an increased role for creditor committees and strengthened access to information for such committees.

A special concern of Cork was the plight of the unsecured creditor, who generally received nothing at the end of the day. This concern was reflected in the recommendations that virtually all preferential claims[28] be abolished and that funding representing 10 per cent of all net realisations of assets subject to a floating charge be made available for distribution among ordinary unsecured creditors.[29] This fund was also designed to be utilised to provide liquidators with the financial resources to investigate company affairs and to take the actions that Cork proposed should be taken against delinquent directors.

The broad philosophy of Cork – as far as it related to corporate insolvency – represented a movement towards stricter control of errant directors but also in favour of an increasing emphasis on rehabilitation of the company. Cork might have thought that existing law dealt with individual bankrupts (perhaps sole traders) in an excessively punitive

---

[27] See K. Cork, *Cork on Cork: Sir Kenneth Cork Takes Stock* (Macmillan, London, 1988) ch. 10, pp. 184–203.

[28] See pp. 604–14 below.

[29] On the Enterprise Act 2002 reform implementing a similar 'prescribed part' see ch. 3 below.

and stigmatic manner,[30] but the Committee was determined to remedy the law's perceived leniency in dealing with directors who abused the privilege of limited liability. In doing so, Cork aimed to bolster standards of commercial morality and to encourage the fulfilment of financial obligations.

As for rehabilitation, the Cork Committee aimed to devise an insolvency regime that would facilitate rescues rather than just process failures.[31] Sir Kenneth Cork was to reflect on this philosophy in the autobiography he published six years after his seminal report. He wrote:

> through publication of the Cork Report, I have ... put forward our principle that business is a national asset and, that being so, all insolvency schemes must be aimed at saving businesses. I have been at pains to stress that when a business becomes insolvent it provides an occasion for a change of ownership from incompetent hands to people who not only have the wherewithal but also hopefully the competence, the imagination and the energy to save the business. Before the 1985 Act every insolvent business went into liquidation or receivership automatically. It was the kiss of death for them and the creator of unemployment ... [W]ith the concept of the administrator and voluntary arrangements taking its place in Britain's insolvency law, the chances look bright for more and more businesses being saved in the years that lie ahead ...[32]

The Cork Report thus not merely provided the most comprehensive and rational review of English company insolvency rules ever undertaken but also flagged a historic movement away from punitive towards rehabilitative objectives.

The Report was not, however, to be instantly transposed into legislative form. It was not even made the subject of a formal debate in either House of Parliament.[33] Four years passed before legislation delivered the unified code of insolvency law that Cork had advocated. This came with the Insolvency Act 1986. That statute was preceded by a 1984 White Paper[34] and the Insolvency Act 1985, which together dealt with a variety of important aspects of insolvency but neither implemented the main body of Cork nor brought together in one Act all the statutory provisions relating to bankruptcy and those dealing with corporate insolvency. The Insolvency Act 1986 offered such an aggregation of measures dealing with the bankruptcy

---

[30] See Cork, *Cork on Cork*, ch. 10. [31] See Cork Report, para. 1502.

[32] Cork, *Cork on Cork*, ch. 10, pp. 202–3.

[33] For an account of governmental and legislative developments in the wake of the Cork Report, see Fletcher, *Law of Insolvency*, pp. 16–20.

[34] *A Revised Framework for Insolvency Law* (Cmnd 9175, 1984).

of individuals and the insolvency of companies. It consolidated the Insolvency Act 1985 and the insolvency provisions of the Companies Act 1985 (except in relation to the disqualification of directors).[35]

The Cork Report recommendations produced a sea change in English corporate insolvency and, as noted, can be seen as the foundations of modern corporate insolvency regimes. The Cork Committee had been established by a Labour Government but its recommendations were given legislative effect by Margaret Thatcher's Conservative administration. The membership of the committee was, however, characterised by strong professional and practitioner rather than political representation.[36] The Cork Report set out to be systematic, pragmatic and balanced: as seen in its efforts to recognise the interests of secured creditors (especially banks) and those of unsecured, trade creditors. The Cork approach to floating charges, for instance, was to acknowledge their effect in prejudicing weaker creditors' interests but to stop short of alienating the banks by proposing abolition of such charges.[37] As for the Insolvency Act 1986, this can be seen as strongly shaped by both professional and political factors. As Carruthers and Halliday put it:

> [I]t is inconceivable that the [1986 Act] can be understood without comprehension of the powerful ideological undercurrents that variously sought to champion reorganisation, privatise bankruptcy administration, professionalise insolvency practice and discipline company directors. While professionals and their technical interests were persuasive in the English reforms, the particular cost of the insolvency reforms, and the very fact of the parliamentary passage, testified to the affinity between professional agendas and wider party ideology.[38]

As will be seen in subsequent chapters, however, the Cork Report was not implemented to the letter by the 1986 Act and, although the different branches of insolvency law were harmonised to a degree, the long-established distinction between corporate insolvency and personal bankruptcy law and procedures survived the passing of the Act. Sir Kenneth, moreover, was to be deeply concerned that the Government was selective in its approach to his recommendations, saying in his autobiography: 'They

---

[35] See Company Directors' Disqualification Act 1986. A few provisions of the Companies Act 2006 are relevant to insolvency and survive the Insolvency Act 1986: CA 2006 ss. 754, 895–900, 993 (see chs. 11 and 16 below).

[36] See Carruthers and Halliday, *Rescuing Business*, pp. 124–5.   [37] See chs. 3 and 15 below.

[38] Carruthers and Halliday, *Rescuing Business*, p. 148. On the politics of Cork and the committee's membership see ibid., pp. 124–49.

ended up by doing the very thing we asked them not to. They picked bits and pieces out of it so that they finished with a mish-mash of old and new.'[39]

What was reflected in the 1986 Act, however, was the (already noted) aim of Cork to produce a set of rules capable of practical implementation. Thus, in the Act there can be seen two strong threads of concern: to establish formal legal procedures for business rescue and the orderly realisation and distribution of assets and to erect a regulatory framework that would prevent commercial malpractice and abuse of the insolvency procedures themselves.

The operation of the Insolvency Act 1986 is a central concern of the chapters that follow. This piece of legislation has been through the fire of the 1989–93 economic recession and has been subject to review in a number of respects.[40] The Enterprise Act 2002 effected a number of highly significant changes – most notably in largely replacing administrative receivership with the more inclusive arrangements of a revised administration process; in providing a 'prescribed part' fund for unsecured creditors; and in ending the Crown's status as preferential creditor. The courts have also played their role in effecting change – with cases such as *Spectrum Plus* and *Leyland DAF* that have served either to change incentives to use different financing arrangements or to prompt the Government to make a legislative response on an issue.

In recent years, moreover, a number of dramatic changes have altered the landscape of corporate insolvency law and have transformed the assumptions that underpin the law and key processes of insolvency beyond those obtaining during the passing of the 1986 Act. Commercially and politically, there has, for instance, been a consolidation of the rescue culture within the UK and a new emphasis on managing insolvency risks proactively rather than after troubles have become crises. In comparison with the seventies and eighties, much more work on corporate problems is now carried out before any insolvency procedure is entered into. The 'pre-packaged'

---

[39] Cork, *Cork on Cork*, p. 197; White Paper, *A Revised Framework for Insolvency Law* (1984).

[40] See DTI/Insolvency Service, *Company Voluntary Arrangements and Administration Orders: A Consultative Document* (October 1993). See also DTI/IS, *Revised Proposals for a New Company Voluntary Arrangement Procedure* (April 1995); DTI/IS, *A Review of Company Rescue and Business Reconstruction Mechanisms* (1999); DTI/IS, *A Review of Company Rescue and Business Reconstruction Mechanisms: Report by the Review Group* (2000); Justice, *Insolvency Law: An Agenda for Reform* (London, 1994); DTI/IS, *Productivity and Enterprise: Insolvency – A Second Chance* (Cm 5234, 2001); Company Law Review Steering Group, *Modern Company Law for a Competitive Economy: Final Report* (DTI, London, 2001). Key amending legislation since 1986 has included the Insolvency Acts of 1994 and 2000, the Enterprise Act 2002 and the Companies Act 2006.

administration, for instance, is rapidly growing in popularity and involves agreements that are drawn up in advance of entry into administration. The insolvency practitioners who carried out most of the insolvency work in the wake of Cork have now been joined by new ranks of specialist advisers, 'turnaround professionals' and others who are concerned to assist in reconstruction and rescue operations. The banks themselves are equipped as never before with departments that are dedicated to the provision of 'intensive care' for troubled companies. Procedures have also become more collective in nature – notably since the Enterprise Act 2002 reforms.

The world of credit has, however, also changed dramatically in the last decade or so and this has created challenges for companies and their insolvency advisers that could hardly have been envisaged by the Cork Committee or the drafters of the Insolvency Act 1986. In the global world of the 'new capitalism', credit has become a commodity that is traded across the world in ever more complex packages of debt. This emergence of the credit derivative markets impacts on insolvency processes and corporate rescues in a number of ways – notably by rendering relationships between lenders and borrowers more distant and less transparent than formerly and by making it much easier for creditors to handle insolvency risks by resort to credit or loan default swaps rather than by exerting influence over the relevant corporate managers. Thus, on the one hand, the banks have become better equipped than ever before to monitor managerial performance and to assist companies with rescue efforts, but, on the other, they have embraced new market opportunities and incentives to shed their debt problems by trading in debt products. In the world of Cork and the 1986 Act, the major banks were assumed to play roles in relation to the provision of credit and managerial discipline that cannot be taken for granted in a world where they have often become facilitators of credit rather than main creditors and where corporations that seek finance will as readily look to bond markets and hedge funds as to banks.

Such developments have left the corporate insolvency stage occupied by a number of actors operating a variety of procedures in carrying out certain key tasks. To provide a basis for further discussion it may be helpful to outline these procedures and players.

Corporate insolvency procedures

There are five main statutory procedures that may come into play when a company is in trouble. Four of these are provided for in the Insolvency Act 1986, the fifth by the Companies Act 1985.

Administrative receivership

Before the coming into operation of the Enterprise Act 2002, a creditor who had lent money to a company and secured this by means of a floating charge over the whole or substantially the whole of the company's assets[41] could appoint an administrative receiver (AR). This individual had to be an insolvency practitioner (IP)[42] and could take control of all assets subject to the security, so that he would effectively control the company. His primary duty was to his appointor and to realise the security[43] and, after deducting his remuneration and expenses and paying prior-ranking creditors, he would pay the proceeds to his appointor up to the amount of the secured debt and pay any balance to subsequent ranking creditors, the company or its liquidator, if one had been appointed.

The Enterprise Act 2002 largely replaced receivership with administration and prohibited (subject to certain exceptions)[44] the use of administrative receivership by the holders of floating charges. The general enforcement of floating charges thus falls to be carried out through the administration process – in which the administrator differs from the traditional receiver in having a duty to act, not in the interests of the appointor, but in the interests of the creditors as a whole. Receivership is not, however, wholly dead. Creditors with qualifying floating charges created before the Enterprise Act 2002, or those with charges that fall within the exceptions now set out in the Insolvency Act 1986, may still appoint administrative receivers and 'ordinary' receivers can still be appointed by debenture holders and by the courts.[45]

Although 'ordinary' receivers may be appointed by the court, these appointments are comparatively rare. Where the option is available to them, lenders (normally banks) prefer to appoint receivers in pursuance of express powers contained in their security. Indeed, receivership historically is a creation of equity and is merely a method by which a secured

---

[41] See Insolvency Act 1986 s. 29(2); see also ch. 8 below.

[42] See Insolvency Act 1986 s. 230(2); see also ch. 5 below.

[43] On security and methods of borrowing generally, see ch. 3 below.

[44] See Enterprise Act 2002 s. 250 inserting s. 72A–72G into the Insolvency Act 1986 and Sch. 2A. See further ch. 8 below.

[45] The AR must be distinguished from other types of receiver appointed over a *specific* part of the company's assets, for example Law of Property Act 1925 receivers. Such a receiver can be removed or replaced with little formality (the AR can only be removed by the court), he has no management powers and his task is to collect an income and apply it to keep down outgoings and mortgage interest.

creditor enforces his security. 'Ordinary' receivership is a private contractual remedy requiring no recourse to the court. Administrative
receivership, however, has more of the *appearance* of a collective insolvency proceeding.[46]

Administration

This was a court-based procedure, first introduced by the Insolvency Act
1985 following the Cork Committee's recommendations and emphasis
on the benefits that could flow from having a corporate insolvency
procedure that was designed specifically for corporate rescue rather
than asset realisation; one, moreover, that focused on the interests of
unsecured creditors and of the company itself rather than those of a
specific secured creditor.[47]

Revisions to the administration procedure (as now detailed in the
Insolvency Act 1986, Schedule B1) were introduced by the Enterprise
Act 2002 so as to provide a more streamlined process. Since the 2002 Act,
a company can be put into administration by the court (on application by
the company, its directors or one or more creditors); out of court on the
application of a holder of a qualifying floating charge; or out of court on
application by the company or its directors. The court must be satisfied
that the company is, or is likely to be, unable to pay its debts before
making an order appointing an administrator – except if the application
is from the holder of a qualifying floating charge. After the changes of the
2002 Act, the administrator (in brief terms)[48] is obliged to act with the
objective of (a) rescuing the company as a going concern or (b) achieving
a better than winding-up outcome for creditors as a whole or (c) realising
property to distribute to one or more secured or preferential creditors.
Objective (a) must be pursued unless this is not reasonably practicable or
if (b) would offer a better result for creditors as a whole. Aim (c) is only to
be pursued if (a) and (b) are impracticable. This appointee has the power
on behalf of the company to do all things necessary for the management
of the affairs, business and property of the company.

---

[46] The Insolvency Act 1986 tends to treat it as such: see Insolvency Act 1986 ss. 388(1)(a),
230–7 (office holder), 42–3 and Sch. 1, paras. 44–5; but see F. Oditah, 'Assets and the
Treatment of Claims in Insolvency' (1992) 108 LQR 459 at 460–1.

[47] See Cork Report, ch. 6, paras. 29–33, and ch. 9. Cork's view was that the potential benefit
of rescue via a receiver/manager should also be available to cases where there was no
floating charge.

[48] See ch. 9 below for details.

The most significant feature of administration is that it imposes a freeze (moratorium) on all legal proceedings and creditor actions against the company, including the enforcement of security, while the administrator seeks to achieve the purpose(s) for which the administration order was granted.[49] The position of secured creditors is thus less protected than in receivership or liquidation as the freeze includes (unless the administrator or court consents) a prohibition on any action to enforce any security or any rights under hire purchase (HP), chattel leasing, conditional sale and retention of title agreements. In addition, the administrator can sell property free of security constituted by floating charges and (with the court's consent) fixed charges and free of any rights of third parties under HP agreements or other agreements mentioned above.[50] An administrative receiver cannot be appointed when the company is in administration and an AR in office must vacate.[51] No winding up can take place while the administrator is in control, but administration is often followed by liquidation.[52] As soon as reasonably practicable after appointment, and after a maximum of eight weeks (or such longer period as the court allows), the administrator must produce a statement of proposals for achieving the objectives of the administration and send this to all creditors of whose addresses he is aware.[53] Proposals must then be submitted for approval to a creditors' meeting. Once approved, the administrator must manage the company in accordance with those proposals unless he, or any interested party, applies to the court for variation or discharge of the administration order. Administration is, at least initially, a temporary measure and an administrator will automatically vacate office one year from the commencement of the administration unless this period is extended by the court or with the consent of creditors.[54]

Winding up/liquidation

Liquidation is a procedure of last resort. It involves a liquidator being appointed to take control of the company and to collect, realise and distribute its assets to creditors according to their legal priority. Once the

---

[49] An interim moratorium applies pending the disposal of an administration order application or the coming into effect of an out-of-court appointment of an administrator: Insolvency Act 1986 Sch. B1, para. 44.

[50] In each case the security will attach to the proceeds of sale and the administrator, when dealing with fixed charges, must account for any shortfall between those proceeds and the market value at the time of sale.

[51] Sch. B1, paras. 43(6A), 41(1).   [52] See Sch. B1, para. 42(2)(3) and ch. 13 below.

[53] Sch. B1, para. 49(4).   [54] Sch. B1, paras. 76–8.

process has been completed, the company is dissolved: liquidators have no powers to carry on the company's business except for the purpose of winding up.[55] There are two routes to liquidating an insolvent company: a creditors' voluntary liquidation and a compulsory liquidation.[56] The former process involves a resolution of the shareholders to put the company into voluntary liquidation, followed by a creditors' meeting to appoint a liquidator and establish a liquidation committee whose members are principally creditors' representatives. The liquidation committee has a supervisory role over the liquidator, while he collects in and realises the company's assets, ascertains claims, distributes dividends to creditors and investigates the causes of the company's failure. The creditors' voluntary liquidation is the most frequently used of the insolvency procedures.

Compulsory liquidation is liquidation by order of the court and is the only method by which a creditor can initiate winding up. A winding-up petition can be presented by a creditor, the directors, the company shareholders and, in certain circumstances, the Department of Trade and Industry (DTI). The petition to the court has to be based on one or more specific grounds stated in section 122 of the Insolvency Act 1986, including the inability of the company to pay its debts. If a winding-up order is made, the Official Receiver[57] becomes liquidator, unless and until the creditors' meeting appoints an insolvency practitioner in his place (i.e. if the company's assets are sufficient to pay the liquidator's remuneration and expenses). Generally compulsory liquidation is subjected to a greater degree of court control than a creditors' voluntary liquidation, but in both methods interested parties can apply to the court to determine questions arising in the winding up or to confirm, reverse or nullify the liquidator's decisions.

Formal arrangements with creditors

Companies in distress may be able to negotiate settlements on a variety of terms and such agreements may operate within a statutory format or informally and contractually between the company, its lenders and possibly even general creditors.[58] These agreements may defer payments

---

[55] Insolvency Act 1986 Sch. 4, para. 5.

[56] Companies may also be wound up by the BERR or FSA in the public interest, e.g. to stop enterprises trading where they engage in practices that defraud customers and swindle the vulnerable: see ch. 13 below.

[57] The Official Receiver is not to be confused with a receiver or administrative receiver appointed by a secured creditor.

[58] See ch. 7 below.

or postpone collection (a moratorium); they may agree to pay sums less than those due (a composition); or to pay a designated sum where there is doubt about the quantum or enforceability of a claim (a compromise). Formal, statutory arrangements or compromises may be made principally under section 895 of the Companies Act 2006 and 'compositions in satisfaction of [the company's] debts or a scheme of arrangement of its affairs', termed 'company voluntary arrangements' (CVAs), can be made under section 2 of the Insolvency Act 1986. (Arrangements by way of reconstruction can be undertaken by liquidators in a voluntary winding up under section 110 of the Insolvency Act 1986, while sections 165–7 and Schedule 4 of the Insolvency Act 1986 allow liquidators with the appropriate sanction to make compromises or arrangements with creditors but only according to creditors' strict legal rights.)

Small and medium-sized companies may find a CVA useful, since it is generally less complex, time-consuming and costly than alternative procedures. CVAs under section 1 of the Insolvency Act 1986 cannot, however, be undertaken when the company is in winding up and, indeed, do not even require a company to be insolvent. The use of this option will depend on the company's precise position and the attitude of its creditors. Using a CVA allows a company to reach an arrangement with its creditors under the supervision of an insolvency practitioner. The CVA must, however, be approved by requisite majorities at shareholder (50 per cent by value) and creditors' (75 per cent by value) meetings and it does not bind creditors without notice of the meetings nor those with unliquidated/unascertained claims nor secured or preferential creditors without their agreement. The Insolvency Act 2000 introduced a moratorium of twenty-eight days into a CVA procedure for small companies.[59] The effect of the moratorium is *inter alia* to offer a company protection against petitions for winding up or administration orders, winding-up resolutions, appointments of receivers and other steps to enforce security or repossess goods – though a moratorium cannot be filed for if an administration order is already in force, the company is being wound up or a receiver has been appointed.

Schemes of arrangement under the Companies Act 2006 s. 895 are an alternative formal method. Here the court sanctions a scheme duly approved by the requisite majority of creditors of each class at separately convened meetings, and once the scheme has been so approved, *all* the creditors are

---

[59] See now Insolvency Act 1986 Sch. 1A and ch. 11 below.

bound. The section 895 scheme is, however, more cumbersome than a CVA and the latter process is, therefore, likely to be used in preference.

The players

The insolvency procedures described above involve a number of institutions or actors and (leaving aside the turnaround specialists and other specialists who usually come into play before the operation of the above procedures) these can be outlined as follows:

Administrators

Administrators carry out administration orders under the Insolvency Act 1986[60] and must be qualified insolvency practitioners. An administrator possesses a wide range of powers, including the power to sell company property, is an officer of the court and can apply to the court for directions. [61]

Administrative receivers

Administrative receivers are usually appointed out of court by debenture holders under an express power contained in the debenture. Such a receiver is defined by section 29(2) of the Insolvency Act 1986 as 'a receiver or manager of the whole (or substantially the whole) of a company's property appointed by and on behalf of the holders of any debentures of the company, secured by a charge, which, as created, was a floating charge, or by such charge and one or more other securities'. As noted above, the holder of a qualifying floating charge can, after the coming into effect of the Enterprise Act 2002, only appoint an administrative receiver if the charge predated the Act or falls within an exception to the Act's prohibition on the appointment of administrative receivers by floating charge holders. The administrative receiver is the company's agent and must be a qualified insolvency practitioner;[62] he is an office holder;[63] he has broader statutory powers than an ordinary receiver;[64] and he enjoys the protection of section 44 of the Insolvency Act 1986 (as amended by the Insolvency Act 1994) concerning liability in respect of new contracts and contracts of employment which he adopts.[65]

---

[60] Insolvency Act 1986 Sch. B1.   [61] See ch. 9 below.
[62] Insolvency Act 1986 ss. 45(2), 230(2).   [63] Ibid., ss. 230–7.
[64] Ibid., ss. 42, 43 and Sch. 1.   [65] See ch. 8 below.

Receivers

Receivers are appointed by creditors with a charge over particular assets or assets given in security pursuant to powers in a debenture and the Law of Property Act 1925. They may also (more rarely) be appointed by the court and, as such, are officers of the court and accountable to it rather than subject to the directions of the creditor in whose interest they have been appointed. Receivers are always in practice made agents of the company. A number of provisions of the Insolvency Act 1986 apply to receivership generally: for example, prohibiting the appointment of bodies corporate or undischarged bankrupts as receivers.[66]

Liquidators

Liquidators differ from receivers in so far as they act primarily in the interest of unsecured creditors and members whereas receivers look to the interests of the secured creditor who appointed them.[67] Liquidators are statutory creatures and are appointed by the company or by the court, usually on an unsecured creditor's petition. Like administrative receivers and administrators, liquidators must be qualified insolvency practitioners.

Company voluntary arrangement (CVA) supervisors

As previously noted, Part I of the Insolvency Act 1986 and Part I of the Insolvency Rules 1986 provide a statutory framework for voluntary arrangements between companies and their creditors. Central to the CVA is the issuing of a directors' written proposal to creditors. This should identify the insolvency practitioner[68] who has agreed to take responsibility for the CVA ('the nominee'). The nominee will obtain statements of affairs from the directors, require further information from company officers and report to the court. The nominee will summon a meeting of the company and all known creditors to gain approval of the scheme. If obtained, it is the responsibility of the nominee, who becomes now 'the supervisor', to see that the CVA is put into effect. The

---

[66] Insolvency Act 1986 ss. 30, 32.

[67] See Hoffmann J in *Re Potters Oils Ltd (No. 2)* [1986] 1 WLR 201; and ch. 12 below.

[68] In the CVA procedure for small companies introduced by the Insolvency Act 2000 there is no requirement that a nominee/supervisor be an IP: see Insolvency Act 2000 s. 4(4) introducing a new s. 389A to the Insolvency Act 1986 to allow persons to act if authorised by a body recognised by the Secretary of State.

supervisor can apply to the court for directions;[69] petition for a winding up; or ask for administration of the company. On completing the CVA the supervisor must make a final report within twenty-eight days to creditors and members.

The tasks of corporate insolvency law

Corporate insolvency law has a number of key tasks to perform (for example, to distribute the assets). In outlining these we should distinguish between descriptions of core jobs and statements of the broader objectives or values that a set of insolvency laws and procedures might seek to further (for example, fairness and efficiency). To list tasks provides very limited assistance in deciding what corporate insolvency laws should seek to achieve through carrying them out, just as composing a list of garden tasks for the autumn tells us little about *why* we are gardening. Selecting 'key' tasks does, moreover, make certain assumptions about the appropriate purposes of corporate insolvency law. It is useful, nevertheless, to note the key tasks that are frequently referred to in practice and in commentaries so that an image of the corporate insolvency law agenda can be conveyed. Chapter 2 will return to the theme of objectives and values to be furthered in carrying out (and in rethinking) such tasks.

The tasks can be set out thus:

- To lay down rules governing the distribution of the assets of an insolvent company, including rules protecting the pool of assets available to creditors.
- To provide for management of companies in times of crisis.
- To facilitate the recovery of companies in times of financial crisis and to stimulate the rehabilitation of insolvent companies and businesses as going concerns.
- To balance the interests of different groupings and to protect the interests of the public and of employees in the face of financial failures or management malpractices.
- To encourage good management of companies by imposing sanctions on directors who are responsible for financial collapses where there has been malpractice and by providing for the investigation of the causes of corporate failure.
- To dissolve companies when necessary.

---

[69] Insolvency Act 1986 s. 7(4).

Conclusions

Corporate insolvency law has developed enormously during the last century and the Cork Report is a conspicuous highlight in that development. Cork and its statutory aftermath, however, have not supplied complete answers. In one sense this is inevitable since laws have to develop and adapt to social and economic changes. In another sense, however, current approaches to corporate insolvency law have yet to come fully to grips with certain challenges that have to be faced if corporate insolvency law is to develop in a manner that contributes appropriately to the (business) life of the nation. Three challenges are of central importance. The first is to see corporate insolvency law as a complete process: not merely as a set of rules but as a system of institutions, rules, procedures, implementation processes and practical effects. This demands that, in developing corporate insolvency law, there is an awareness of implications on the ground and of impacts on the resilience of enterprises as well as on credit and employment relationships. The second challenge is to develop clarity in setting out the general purposes of corporate insolvency law and in effecting balances between different competing interests. The third is to develop an insolvency law that is attuned to the changing realities of the business environment and, in particular, to the dynamics of credit markets.

Cork, in many ways, did not provide a fully satisfactory basis for meeting these challenges directly in so far as the Committee collected limited research and evidence on the effects of different insolvency procedures and because Cork offered a start but not a finish in outlining the objectives of insolvency law. On the particular challenges of the new markets Cork cannot be blamed for failing to anticipate the nature and implications of the global credit derivatives markets and there is work to be done by the current generation. This book seeks to take matters further in relation to these three different challenges: by taking on board the available research evidence on the workings of insolvency procedures; by looking to objectives and values; and by continuing to examine how corporate insolvency processes, seen as a whole, can meet those objectives within the context of new commercial and credit conditions.

2

Aims, objectives and benchmarks

Openness concerning the aims and objectives of corporate insolvency law is necessary if evaluations of proposals, or even existing regimes, are to be made. Without such transparency it is possible only to describe legal states of affairs or to make prescriptions on the basis of unstated premises. As will be argued in this chapter, however, it may not be possible to set down in convincing fashion a single rationale or end for corporate insolvency law. A number of objectives can be identified and these may have to be traded off against each other. It is, nevertheless, feasible to view legal developments with these objectives in mind and to argue about trade-offs once the natures of these objectives have been stipulated.

This chapter will suggest an approach that allows and explains such trade-offs but it begins by reviewing a number of competing visions of the insolvency process that are to be found in the legal literature. A starting point in looking for the objectives of modern English corporate insolvency law is the statement of aims contained in the Cork Committee Report of 1982.[1]

Cork on principles

The Cork Committee produced a set of 'aims of a good modern insolvency law'.[2] It is necessary, however, to draw from a number of areas of the Cork Report in order to produce a combined statement of objectives relevant to corporate insolvency.[3] Drawing thus, and paraphrasing, produces the following exposition of aims:

(a) to underpin the credit system and cope with its casualties;
(b) to diagnose and treat an imminent insolvency at an early, rather than a late, stage;

[1] *Report of the Review Committee on Insolvency Law and Practice* (Cmnd 8558, 1982). This chapter builds on V. Finch, 'The Measures of Insolvency Law' (1997) 17 OJLS 227.
[2] Para. 198.
[3] See paras. 191–8, 203–4, 232, 235, 238–9. See also R. M. Goode, *Principles of Corporate Insolvency Law* (3rd edn, Sweet & Maxwell, London, 2005) ch. 3, where Goode sets out ten principles of corporate insolvency law as established by legislation and the general law.

(c) to prevent conflicts between individual creditors;

(d) to realise the assets of the insolvent which should properly be taken to satisfy debts with the minimum of delay and expense;

(e) to distribute the proceeds of realisations amongst creditors fairly and equitably, returning any surplus to the debtor;[4]

(f) to ensure that the processes of realisation and distribution are administered honestly and competently;

(g) to ascertain the causes of the insolvent's failure and, if conduct merits criticism or punishment, to decide what measures, if any, require to be taken; to establish an investigative process sufficiently full and competent to discourage undesirable conduct by creditors and debtors; to encourage settlement of debts; to uphold business standards and commercial morality; and to sustain confidence in insolvency law by effectively uncovering assets concealed from creditors, ascertaining the validity of creditors' claims and exposing the circumstances attending failure;[5]

(h) to recognise and safeguard the interests not merely of insolvents and their creditors but of society and other groups in society who are affected by the insolvency, for instance not only the interests of directors, shareholders and employees but also those of suppliers, those whose livelihoods depend on the enterprise and the community;[6]

(i) to preserve viable commercial enterprises capable of contributing usefully to national economic life;[7]

(j) to offer a framework of insolvency law commanding respect and observance, yet sufficiently flexible to cope with change, and which is also:
   (i) seen to produce practical solutions to commercial and financial problems,
   (ii) simple and easily understood,
   (iii) free from anomalies and inconsistencies,
   (iv) capable of being administered efficiently and economically;

(k) to ensure due recognition and respect abroad for English insolvency proceedings.

---

[4] On the importance of fairness to creditors given the mandatory, collective nature of proceedings, see also para. 232.

[5] See para. 198(h) and amplification in paras. 235 and 238.

[6] See para. 198(i) and amplification in paras. 203–4.

[7] See para. 198(j) and amplification in para. 204.

Cork's statement of aims was largely endorsed in the subsequent 1984 Government White Paper.[8] It is noteworthy, however, that the DTI objectives for insolvency legislation, as stated in the White Paper, expanded on Cork by stressing the need to provide a statutory framework to encourage companies to pay careful attention to their financial circumstances so as to recognise difficulties at an early stage and before the prejudicing of creditor interests. The White Paper, moreover, differed in emphasis from Cork in so far as its statement of objectives focused on the interests of creditors and express mention was not made of broader, non-creditor concerns.[9]

Subsequent legislation[10] gave substantial but not complete effect to Cork's recommendations and, notably, reflected two major strands of Cork's corporate insolvency law reform policy: namely those of providing a regulatory framework to prevent commercial malpractice or the abuse of insolvency procedures themselves,[11] and of providing a formal legal procedure for business rescue.[12] What that legislation (and subsequent legislation) did not do, however, was to lay down a formal statement of the purposes of insolvency law or a set of objectives.[13]

[8] *A Revised Framework for Insolvency Law* (Cmnd 9175, 1984). The 2005 United Nations Commission on International Trade Law (UNCITRAL), *Legislative Guide on Insolvency Law* (United Nations, New York, 2005) p. 14 suggests that an effective insolvency law should: (a) provide certainty in the market; (b) maximise value of assets; (c) balance liquidation and reorganisation; (d) ensure equitable treatment of similarly situated creditors; (e) provide for timely, efficient and impartial resolution of insolvency; (f) preserve the insolvency estate for distribution to creditors; (g) ensure transparency, predictability and good information flows; and (h) recognise existing creditors' rights and establish clear rules on the ranking of claims.

[9] *Revised Framework.*, para. 2. Contrast the UNCITRAL *Legislative Guide on Insolvency Law*, the advice of which aims at 'achieving a balance between the need to address the debtor's financial difficulty as quickly and efficiently as possible and the interests of the various parties concerned with that financial difficulty, principally creditors and other parties with a stake in the debtor's business, as well as public policy concerns'.

[10] Insolvency Acts 1985 and 1986; Company Directors' Disqualification Act 1986. See further I. F. Fletcher, 'Genesis of Modern Insolvency Law: An Odyssey of Law Reform' [1989] JBL 365; J. H. Farrar, 'Company Insolvency and the Cork Recommendations' (1983) 4 Co. Law. 20.

[11] See e.g. Company Directors' Disqualification Act 1986 ss. 2–12; Insolvency Act 1986 ss. 214, 238–41, 230(2), 390–2; Insolvency Practitioners (Recognised Professional Bodies) Order 1986 (SI 1986/1764).

[12] See Insolvency Act 1986 ss. 8–27 (Administration). After the reforms of the Enterprise Act 2002, see now Insolvency Act 1986 Sch. B1.

[13] Insolvency legislation thus differs materially from typical regulatory statutes which tend to lay down objectives: see e.g. the Communications Act 2003; Utilities Act 2000; Water Act 2003; Environment Act 1995.

Does Cork's expression of aims offer a sustainable and useful statement of objectives for a modern insolvency law? It has not been beyond
criticism. The Justice Report of 1994[14] noted that Cork had failed to
formulate a limited number of core principles to which others might be
treated as subservient and that, as a result, no sense of direction could be
discerned.[15]

Some notable attempts have been made to provide single or dominant
rationales for corporate insolvency processes and a variety of visions will
now be reviewed before an alternative approach is suggested.[16]

Visions of corporate insolvency law

Creditor wealth maximisation and the creditors' bargain

A number of US commentators, inspired by the law and economics
movement,[17] have argued that the proper function of insolvency law
can be seen in terms of a single objective: to maximise the collective
return to creditors.[18] Thus, according to Jackson,[19] insolvency law is best
seen as a 'collectivized debt collection device' and as a response to the
'common pool' problem created when diverse 'co-owners' assert rights
against a common pool of assets. Jackson, moreover, has stated that
insolvency law should be seen as a system designed to mirror the agreements one would expect creditors to arrive at were they able to negotiate

---

[14] Justice, *Insolvency Law: An Agenda for Reform* (London, 1994).

[15] Ibid., paras. 3.7–3.8.

[16] On distinguishing 'traditionalist' insolvency scholars (who see insolvency law as unrelated to 'healthy-state' corporate behaviour) from 'proceduralists' (who 'worry intensely
about how rules in bankruptcy affect behaviour elsewhere') see D. Baird, 'Bankruptcy's
Uncontested Axioms' (1998) 108 Yale LJ 573.

[17] See e.g. T. H. Jackson, *The Logic and Limits of Bankruptcy Law* (Harvard University
Press, Cambridge, Mass., 1986); D. G. Baird, 'The Uneasy Case for Corporate
Reorganisations' (1986) 15 *Journal of Legal Studies* 127. For a refined creditors' bargain
theory see T. H. Jackson and R. Scott, 'On the Nature of Bankruptcy: An Essay on
Bankruptcy Sharing and the Creditors' Bargain' (1989) 75 Va. L Rev. 155. For an
extensive collection of key law and economics readings see J. S. Bhandari and
L. A. Weiss (eds.), *Corporate Bankruptcy: Economic and Legal Perspectives* (Cambridge
University Press, Cambridge, 1996).

[18] See e.g. Jackson, *Logic and Limits of Bankruptcy Law*; D. G. Baird and T. Jackson,
'Corporate Reorganisations and the Treatment of Diverse Ownership Interests: A
Comment on Adequate Protection of Secured Creditors in Bankruptcy' (1984) 51 U
Chic. L Rev. 97.

[19] See Jackson, *Logic and Limits of Bankruptcy Law*, chs. 1 and 2.

such agreements *ex ante* from behind a Rawlsian 'veil of ignorance'.[20] This 'creditors' bargain' theory is argued to justify the compulsory, collectivist regime of insolvency law on the grounds that were company creditors free to agree forms of enforcement of their claims on insolvency they would agree to collectivist arrangements rather than procedures of individual action or partial collectivism. Jackson sees the collectivist, compulsory system as attractive to creditors in reducing strategic costs, increasing the aggregate pool of assets, and as administratively efficient. It follows from the above argument that the protection of the non-creditor interests of other victims of corporate decline, such as employees, managers and members of the community, is not the role of insolvency law.[21] Keeping firms in operation is thus not seen as an independent goal of insolvency law.

In the creditor wealth maximisation approach all policies and rules are designed to ensure that the return to creditors as a group is maximised. Insolvency law is thus concerned with maximising the value of a given pool of assets, not with how the law should allocate entitlements to the pool. Accordingly effect should only be given to existing pre-insolvency rights, and new rights should not be created. Variation of existing rights is only justified when those rights interfere with group advantages associated with creditors acting in concert.

The creditor wealth maximisation vision has been highly influential and has been put into legislative effect in some jurisdictions. Thus the German Bankruptcy Code of 1999 (*Insolvenzordnung*) aims to establish a system that will enhance market exchange processes and rationalise debt collection rather than supersede market processes.[22] It is a vision, however, that has been subject to extensive criticism, some of which has been phrased in the strongest terms.[23] Major concerns have focused, firstly, on insolvency being seen as a debt collection process for the

---

[20] Ibid., p. 17; J. Rawls, *A Theory of Justice* (Harvard University Press, Cambridge, Mass., 1971); Rawls, *The Liberal Theory of Justice: A Critical Examination of the Principal Doctrines in 'A Theory of Justice'* (Clarendon Press, Oxford, 1973). For further discussion see pp. 38–40 below. See also the discussion in A. Duggan, 'Contractarianism and the Law of Corporate Insolvency' (2005) 42 Canadian Bus. LJ 463.

[21] See Jackson, *Logic and Limits of Bankruptcy Law*, p. 25.

[22] See C. Schiller and E. Braun, 'The New Insolvency Code' in J. Reuvid and R. Millar (eds.), *Doing Business with Germany* (Kogan Page, London, 1999). (At the time of writing, a bill to amend the insolvency code has been passed by the German Parliament.)

[23] See e.g. D. G. Carlson, 'Thomas Jackson has written an unremittingly dreadful book', in 'Philosophy in Bankruptcy (Book Review)' (1987) 85 Mich. L Rev. 1341; see also V. Countryman, 'The Concept of a Voidable Preference in Bankruptcy' (1985) 38 Vand.

benefit of creditors. This, it has been said,[24] fails to recognise the legitimate interests of many who are not defined as contract creditors: for instance, managers, suppliers, employees, their dependants and the community at large.[25] Creditor wealth maximisation, moreover, fails to focus on the non-efficiency objectives that are often recognised in legislation.[26] To see insolvency as in essence a sale of assets for creditors (what might be termed a 'fire sale' image), moreover, fails both to treat insolvency as a problem of business failure and to place value on assisting firms to stay in business. Thus, it has been argued that to explain why the law might give firms breathing space or reorganise them in order to preserve jobs requires resort to other values in addition to economic ones. The economic approach, as exemplified by Jackson, is alleged to demonstrate only that its own economic value is incapable of recognising non-economic values, such as moral, political, social and personal considerations.[27]

The idea, moreover, that a troubled company constitutes a mere pool of assets can also be criticised. Such a firm can be seen not purely as a lost cause but as an organic enterprise with a degree of residual potential: 'Unlike mere property, a corporation, whether in or out of bankruptcy, has potential. A corporation can continue as an enterprise: as an enterprise, it can change its personality and, perhaps more importantly, whether the corporation continues and how it changes its personality

L Rev. 713, 823–5, 827; J. L. Westbrook, 'A Functional Analysis of Executory Contracts' (1989) 74 Minn. L Rev. 227, 251 n. 114, 337; T. A. Sullivan, E. Warren and J. L. Westbrook, *As We Forgive Our Debtors: Bankruptcy and Consumer Credit in America* (Oxford University Press, New York, 1989) p. 256.

[24] See D. R. Korobkin, 'Contractarianism and the Normative Foundations of Bankruptcy Law' (1993) 71 Texas L Rev. 541, 555; E. Warren, 'Bankruptcy Policy' (1987) 54 U Chic. L Rev. 775, 787–8.

[25] See K. Gross, 'Taking Community Interests into Account in Bankruptcy: An Essay' (1994) 72 Wash. ULQ 1031.

[26] See D. R. Korobkin, 'The Role of Normative Theory in Bankruptcy Debates' (1996–7) 82 Iowa L Rev. 75, 86.

[27] See D. R. Korobkin, 'Rehabilitating Values: A Jurisprudence of Bankruptcy' (1991) 91 Colum. L Rev. 717, 762. Certain economic approaches may, of course, favour a particular corporate reorganisation and job preservation arrangement because this maximises social wealth: though in other circumstances there may, on this basis, be arguments for allowing jobs to move into new, more efficient and profitable contexts. (Jackson, in contrast, seeks to maximise creditor wealth.) On wealth maximisation as an ethical basis see generally R. Posner, 'Utilitarianism, Economics and Legal Theory' (1979) 8 *Journal of Legal Studies* 103, but cf. R. M. Dworkin, 'Is Wealth a Value?' (1980) 9 *Journal of Legal Studies* 191; Dworkin, *A Matter of Principle* (Clarendon Press, Oxford, 1986) chs. 12, 13.

affects people in ways that are not only economic.'[28] Insolvency law, indeed, has for some time on both sides of the Atlantic recognised that the rehabilitation of the firm is a legitimate factor to take on board in insolvency decision-making.[29]

Does it make sense, in any event, to point to a common pool of assets to which creditors have a claim before insolvency? Unless credit is secured, it is arguably extended on the basis that repayments will be made from income and not from a sale of fixed assets. Income, moreover, cannot be said normally to be produced by the assets themselves but, in the case of an enterprise, from 'an organisational set-up consisting of owners, management, employees plus a functioning network of relations with the outside world, particularly with customers, suppliers and, under modern conditions, with various government agencies'.[30] It is, indeed, insolvency law itself that creates an estate or pool of assets and this undermines any assertion that insolvency processes should maximise the value of a pre-existing pool of assets and should not disturb pre-insolvency entitlements.

The idea that insolvency law can be justified in a contractarian fashion with reference to a creditors' bargain has also come under heavy fire.[31] The creditors' bargain restricts participation to contract creditors. In this sense the veil of ignorance used by Jackson is transparent since the agreeing parties know their status in insolvency. It is not surprising that in an *ex ante* position such creditors would agree to maximise the value of assets available for distribution to themselves.[32] Jackson, moreover, focuses exclusively on voluntary and bargaining creditors, while assuming a perfect market, and leaves out of account other types of creditor, for whom there is no market at all.

---

[28] Korobkin, 'Rehabilitating Values', p. 745. See also Warren, 'Bankruptcy Policy', p. 798.

[29] See Korobkin, 'Rehabilitating Values', pp. 749 and 751. On the UK, see S. Hill, 'Company Voluntary Arrangements' (1990) 6 IL&P 47; Cork Report, paras. 29–33 (re administration); H. Rajak 'Company Rescue' (1993) 4 IL&P 111; Insolvency Service, *Company Voluntary Arrangements and Administration Orders: A Consultative Document* (DTI, 1993); *Revised Proposals for a New Company Voluntary Arrangement Procedure* (DTI, 1995); *A Review of Company Rescue and Business Reconstruction Mechanisms* (DTI, 1999); *A Review of Company Rescue and Business Reconstruction Mechanisms: Report by the Review Group* (DTI, 2000).

[30] See A. Flessner, 'Philosophies of Business Bankruptcy Law: An International Overview' in J. S. Ziegel (ed.), *Current Developments in International and Comparative Corporate Insolvency Law* (Clarendon Press, Oxford, 1994) p. 19.

[31] See Carlson, 'Philosophy in Bankruptcy', p. 1355: 'even less than a hollow tautology'.

[32] See Korobkin, 'Contractarianism and the Normative Foundations', p. 555. See also Gross, 'Community Interests', p. 1044.

The circular nature of the bargain has been exposed by critics. Creditors in the bargain are assumed to be de-historicised and equal. The creditors' bargain model explains the rule of creditor equality only by presupposing what it sets out to prove.[33] In real life, in contrast, creditors differ in their knowledge, skill, leverage and costs of litigating. The assumption that powerful creditors (e.g. secured creditors) would agree to collectivise their claims to the pool alongside their weaker brethren is highly questionable. It is more likely that what parties will agree to will inevitably mirror those disparities in rights, authority and practical leverage that shape their perspectives.[34] Jackson's solution to this problem is to suggest that secured creditors should receive from the pool no less than what they would be entitled to outside insolvency. This is the equality of *Animal Farm*, though, and is inconsistent with the homogeneity of creditors originally posited. To assume, moreover, that all creditors have purely economic interests is also questionable. Thus, for instance, employee creditors who face displacement costs that are separate from their claims for back wages might not agree to creditor equality because they could well consider that such costs should be reflected in a higher priority for their back-wages claims. They might, additionally, consider that their claims on assets morally outrank those of secured creditors and for this reason also insist on priority for wage claims.[35]

A further major weakness of the creditor wealth maximisation vision is its alleged lack of honesty on distributional issues.[36] The collectivism advocated by Jackson is treated as neutral but it begs distributional questions. By purporting merely to enforce pre-insolvency rights Jackson presupposes the defensibility of the state-determined collection scheme without further argument; by this process distributive elements are worked into his theory via the back door. The inappropriateness of transplanting the system of state allocation of rights becomes clearer on noting the very different functions of

---

[33] See Carlson, 'Philosophy in Bankruptcy', pp. 1348–9; Korobkin, 'Rehabilitating Values', pp. 736–7.

[34] See Korobkin, 'Contractarianism and the Normative Foundations', p. 552.

[35] See Carlson, 'Philosophy in Bankruptcy', p. 1353. It might be argued from an economic perspective that employees could be expected to compensate for employment insecurities by demanding that these be reflected in higher wage packets. Inequalities of employer/employee bargaining positions and information levels are factors, *inter alia*, however that make such expectations unrealistic: see e.g. A. I. Ogus, *Regulation: Legal Form and Economic Theory* (Oxford University Press, Oxford, 1994) pp. 38–41; S. Breyer, *Regulation and Its Reform* (Harvard University Press, Cambridge, Mass., 1982); K. Van Wezel Stone, 'Policing Employment Contracts Within the Nexus-of-Contracts Firm' (1993) 43 U Toronto LJ 353.

[36] See Warren, 'Bankruptcy Policy', esp. pp. 790, 802, 808.

the respective bodies of law. Whereas pre-insolvency state entitlements are designed with an eye to ongoing contractual relationships, it is arguably the very purpose of a (federal) insolvency system to apportion the losses of a debtor's default in a new and different situation when a variety of factors impinge on decisions as to where losses should fall.

If, indeed, it is proper for insolvency law to look beyond pre-insolvency rights, this again strikes at the heart of the creditors' bargain thesis. It can be said, in the first instance, that insolvency does and should recognise the interests of parties who lack formal legal rights in the pre-insolvency scenario,[37] not least because parties with formal legal rights never bear the complete costs of a business failure. Thus, creditors may suffer in an insolvency but those without formal legal rights may also be prejudiced: not only, as already noted, employees who will lose jobs and suppliers who will lose customers, but also tax authorities whose prospective entitlements may be diminished and neighbouring traders whose business environments may be devalued. A danger of the creditor wealth maximisation vision is that it fails adequately to value the continuation of business relationships that have not been formalised in contracts and may, indeed, omit from consideration those who suffer the greatest hardships in the context of financial distress.[38]

A second point concerns those parties with various pre-insolvency legal rights. The argument that insolvency law should only give effect to these pre-insolvency rights can be countered by asserting that a core and proper function of insolvency law is to pursue different distributional objectives than are implied in the body of pre-insolvency rights; that insolvency law does so by adopting a base-line rule on equality – *pari passu* – and by then making considered exceptions to that rule. It is insolvency law's application to the turbulence of financial crisis, as distinct from the calm waters that mark pre-insolvency contracts, that can be said to justify the intrusion of a number of value judgements concerning relative priorities of various liabilities and the order in which groups of liabilities should be discharged.[39]

---

[37] See E. Warren, 'Bankruptcy Policymaking in an Imperfect World' (1993) 92 Mich. L Rev. 336 at 356.

[38] See Korobkin, 'Contractarianism and the Normative Foundations', p. 581.

[39] See Warren, 'Bankruptcy Policy', p. 778; Warren, 'Bankruptcy Policymaking', pp. 353–4. On preferential status generally see Cork Report, chs. 32, 33; D. Milman, 'Priority Rights on Corporate Insolvency' in A. Clarke (ed.), *Current Issues in Insolvency Law* (Stevens & Sons, London, 1991) p. 57; S. S. Cantlie, 'Preferred Priority in Bankruptcy' in J. Ziegel (ed.), *Current Developments in International and Comparative Corporate Insolvency Law* (Clarendon Press, Oxford, 1994) p. 413.

A broad-based contractarian approach

A vision of insolvency law that attempts to overcome the restrictions of creditor wealth maximisation is a broader contractarianism. The version discussed here is the Rawlsian scheme of Donald Korobkin.[40] Whereas Jackson seeks to justify insolvency law with reference to the rules that contract creditors would agree to from behind the veil of ignorance, Korobkin places behind the veil not merely contract creditors but representatives of all those persons who are potentially affected by a company's decline, including employees, managers, owners, tort claimants, members of the community, etc. These people choose the principles of insolvency law from behind a strict veil, ignorant of their legal status, position within the company or other factors that might lead them to advance personal interests. They would, however, foresee that the financial distress of companies would affect a wide variety of individuals and groups occupying various positions and differing in their ability to affect the actions and decisions of the companies in distress.

Korobkin argues that the parties in such a position of choice would opt for two principles to govern insolvencies.[41] First, a 'principle of inclusion' would provide that all parties affected by financial distress would be eligible to press their demands. Second, a principle of 'rational planning' would determine whether and to what extent persons would be able to enforce legal rights and exert leverage. It would seek to promote the greatest part of the most important aims (the 'maximisation of aims') and would involve formulating the most rational, long-term plan as a means of realising the 'good' for the business enterprise. It would require an outcome that would 'maximumly satisfy the aims' but, in reflection of Rawls' difference principle, would mandate that persons in the worst-off positions in the context of financial distress should be protected over those occupying better-off positions. For such purposes persons in worst-off positions would be those relatively powerless to promote their aims, yet with the most to lose on the frustration of those aims.

---

[40] See Korobkin, 'Contractarianism and the Normative Foundations'. See also Rawls, *A Theory of Justice*. For an argument that the economic approach is compatible with Rawlsian social justice see R. Rasmussen, 'An Essay on Optimal Bankruptcy Rules and Social Justice' (1994) U Illinois L Rev. 1 (an approach perhaps throwing light on the distributional limitations of Rawls' theory of justice). See also R. Mokal, 'The Authentic Consent Model: Contractarianism, Creditors' Bargain and Corporate Liquidation' (2001) 21 *Legal Studies* 400; Mokal, *Corporate Insolvency Law: Theory and Application* (Oxford University Press, Oxford, 2005) ch. 3.

[41] Korobkin, 'Contractarianism and the Normative Foundations', pp. 575–89.

Korobkin argues that application of his contractarian approach would produce laws corresponding in fundamental ways to the kind of insolvency system encountered in the USA.[42] His approach, like that of Rawls,[43] however, is open to question on a number of fronts. First, the particular choices of principle made from behind the veil of ignorance depend on a particular concept of the person: it is not possible to strip the individual completely yet conclude that he or she would choose, for instance, the difference principle.[44] Risk-averse and risk-neutral individuals might produce very different principles of justice. It is not clear why an individual behind the veil might not prefer a regime marked by low-cost credit and low protection for vulnerable parties to one with high costs of credit and high levels of protection.

This introduces a second difficulty as encountered in Rawls: the extent to which diminutions in justice may be traded off against gains on other fronts, such as in wealth. Advocates of creditor wealth maximisation might object to Korobkin's scheme on the grounds that principles of insolvency law designed by a veiled and highly inclusive group are liable to be so protective of so many interests, and as a result so uncertain, that the effects on the cost of credit would be catastrophic. Korobkin's answer would be that such effects would be anticipated by those behind the veil.[45] The device of the veil, however, does not in itself explain, in a convincing fashion, important distributional issues, such as how to judge

---

[42] In this, the approach differs markedly from other proposed regime designs that have been called 'contractualist' and which suggest that businesses might elect *ex ante* for a system in which they are free to bargain in advance for a set of rules to govern their rights in the event of bankruptcy and in which such bargains would override the federal rules of bankruptcy: see e.g. B. E. Adler, 'Financial and Political Theories of American Corporate Bankruptcy' (1993) 45 Stanford L Rev. 311; L. A. Bebchuk, 'A New Approach to Corporate Reorganisations' (1988) 101 Harv. L Rev. 775; R. Rasmussen, 'Debtor's Choice: A Menu Approach to Corporate Bankruptcy' (1992) 71 Texas L Rev. 51; and for a critique of these (questioning their economic efficiency contentions) see E. Warren and J. Westbrook, 'Contracting Out of Bankruptcy: An Empirical Intervention' (2005) 118 Harv. L Rev 1197.

[43] On Rawls see e.g. N. Daniels (ed.), *Reading Rawls: Critical Studies on Rawls' 'A Theory of Justice'* (Stanford University Press, Stanford, 1989); R. Nozick, *Anarchy, State and Utopia* (Blackwell, Oxford, 1974) pp. 183–231; R. Wolff, *Understanding Rawls* (Princeton University Press, Princeton, N. J., 1977).

[44] In F. H. Bradley's words, 'a theoretical attempt to isolate what cannot be isolated', quoted in M. Loughlin, *Public Law and Political Theory* (Clarendon Press, Oxford, 1992) p. 96. See also M. J. Sandel, *Liberalism and the Limits of Justice* (Cambridge University Press, Cambridge, 1982) pp. 93–4.

[45] Korobkin ('Contractarianism and the Normative Foundations', pp. 583–4) notes that parties in a bankruptcy choice situation (behind the veil) are aware of the 'difficulty of

trade-offs between fairness or justice and wealth creation. Such matters are governed by the concept of human nature built into the system rather than the veil.[46] If such trade-offs are ruled out it can be objected that the protection offered by a just rule is of very limited value if individuals lack the resources required to take advantage of that rule. The distinction, moreover, between principles of fairness or justice and principles governing the allocation of other goods such as wealth is also problematic.[47]

It might be further objected that the contractarian approach fails to explain how agreements can be reached behind the veil as to who in a potential insolvency is most vulnerable and thus should enjoy priority of protection over those occupying less threatened positions. Korobkin acknowledges the difficulties of comparing positions in terms of vulnerability, and these are indeed real.[48] He suggests that vulnerability be measured in terms of the product of the potential loss to, and the degree of influence exercised by, an individual. There is no reason, however, why such an approach would be accepted by all parties behind the veil. Many may think that such benchmarking distorts the system in favour of those who already possess advantages and so have much to lose. A final difficulty is whether agreement could be expected on the relative valuations of, say, rights to secure or continued employment, as opposed to particular sums of money owed by parties to others. As a guide to the practical development of insolvency law contractarianism may indeed be considerably flawed by its indeterminacy.

The communitarian vision

In contrast with the emphasis on private rights contained within the creditor wealth maximisation approach, the communitarian countervision sees insolvency processes as weighing the interests of a broad range of different constituents. It accordingly countenances the redistribution of values so that, on insolvency, high-priority claimants may to some extent give way to others, including the community at large, in

---

actual decision-making' and would be attracted to a rational plan based on Rawls' difference principle for this reason.

[46] Notably the concept of human nature that is assumed to attract parties behind the veil of ignorance to Rawls' difference principle rather than to more high-risk principles that are less protective of the most vulnerable.

[47] See P. P. Craig, *Public Law and Democracy in the United Kingdom and the United States of America* (Clarendon Press, Oxford, 1990) pp. 262–3.

[48] Korobkin, 'Contractarianism and the Normative Foundations', p. 584 and his n. 198.

sharing the value of an insolvent firm.[49] A concern to protect community interests may, furthermore, militate in favour of insolvency laws that compel companies and their creditors to bear the costs of financial failure (for example, environmental cleaning costs) rather than shift those to third parties or taxpayers.[50]

Communitarianism thus challenges the premise that serves as the basis for the traditional economic model, namely that individuals should be seen as selfish, rational calculators. An important aspect of communitarianism is the centrality that is given to distributional concerns.[51] Redistribution is seen, not as an aberration from the protection of creditors' rights, but as a core and unavoidable function of insolvency law: 'bankruptcy is simply a ... scheme designed to distribute the costs amongst those at risk'.[52]

It follows from the concerns of communitarianism that insolvency law should look to the survival of organisations as well as to their orderly liquidation. In this respect, the Cork Committee's[53] statement of aims incorporates aspects of communitarianism in stressing not merely that insolvency affects interests in society beyond insolvents and their creditors, but that the insolvency process should provide means to preserve viable commercial enterprises capable of contributing to the economic life of the country.[54] To creditor wealth maximisers the communitarian vision is objectionable in so far as it clouds insolvency law by departing from creditor right enforcement and taking on issues – for example,

---

[49] See Warren, 'Bankruptcy Policy' and 'Bankruptcy Policymaking'; Gross, 'Community Interests'; Gross, *Failure and Forgiveness: Rebalancing the Bankruptcy System* (Yale University Press, New Haven, 1997). See also *Report of the Commission on the Bankruptcy Laws of the US*, Pt 1, HR Doc. No. 137, 93d Cong., 1st Sess. 85 (1973), discussing the 'overriding community goals and values' of bankruptcy.

[50] See e.g. K. R. Heidt, 'The Automatic Stay in Environmental Bankruptcies' (1993) 67 *American Bankruptcy Law Journal* 69; L. Manolopoulos, 'Note – A Congressional Choice: The Question of Environmental Priority in Bankrupt Estates' (1990) 9 *UCLA Journal of Environmental Law and Policy* 73. But see C. S. Lavargna, 'Government-Sponsored Enterprises are "Too Big to Fail": Balancing Public and Private Interests' (1993) 44(5) Hastings LJ 991.

[51] See Warren, 'Bankruptcy Policy'. See also E. Warren and J. L. Westbrook, *The Law of Debtors and Creditors: Text, Cases and Problems* (Little, Brown, Boston, 1986) pp. 3–7, 219–26.

[52] Warren, 'Bankruptcy Policy', p. 790.

[53] See Cork Report, paras. 191–8, 203–4, 232, 235, 238–9. On Cork's communitarianism see A. Keay and P. Walton, *Insolvency Law: Corporate and Personal* (2nd edn, Jordans, Bristol, 2008) p. 27.

[54] Cork Report, para. 198(i) and (j).

protections for workers – which more properly should be dealt with by allocating pre-insolvency rights – for example, rights to employment security, fair dismissal and compensation on redundancy.[55] In response, communitarians might urge, first, that there is no reason why issues arising in insolvency should be governed by rules or agreements formulated without regard to insolvency and, second, that it is perfectly proper to advert to communitarian issues in both pre-insolvency and insolvency law.[56]

The breadth of concerns encompassed within communitarianism gives rise in itself to problems of indeterminacy. It may be objected that corporatist visions of the company have difficulty in defining the public good and offer 'simply a mask behind which corporate managers exercise unrestrained social and economic power'.[57] Similarly, communitarianism can be said to lack the degree of focus necessary for the design of insolvency law because of the breadth of interests to which it refers. As Schermer has argued, 'it is impossible to delineate the community … There are an infinite number of community interests at stake in each bankruptcy and their boundaries are limitless…[A]lmost anyone, from local employee to a distant supplier, can claim some remote loss to the failure of a once viable local business.'[58]

The problem is not so much that community interests cannot be identified but that there are so many potential interests in every insolvency and that selection of interests worthy of legal protection is liable to give rise to considerable contention. How, moreover, can selected interests be weighed? How might a court balance the community's interest in maintaining employment against potential environmental damage? Doubts, furthermore, have been expressed about the feasibility of redistributing funds in an insolvency.[59] Insolvency law might be designed in

---

[55] B. Adler, 'A World Without Debt' (1994) 72 Wash. ULQ 811 at 826; compare D. G. Baird, 'Loss Distribution, Forum Shopping and Bankruptcy: A Reply to Warren' (1987) 54 U Chic. L Rev. 815 with Warren, 'Bankruptcy Policy'.

[56] To argue that it is proper for insolvency law in some circumstances to look to communitarian issues and, if necessary, to adjust some prior rights is not, of course, to declare open season on adjusting any laws or rights that happen to arise in an insolvency, however tangentially.

[57] M. Stokes, 'Company Law and Legal Theory' in W. Twining (ed.), *Legal Theory and Common Law* (Blackwell, Oxford, 1986) pp. 155–83 at p. 180.

[58] B. S. Schermer, 'Response to Professor Gross: Taking the Interests of the Community into Account in Bankruptcy' (1994) 72 Wash. ULQ 1049 at 1051.

[59] W. Bowers, 'Rehabilitation, Redistribution or Dissipation: The Evidence of Choosing Among Bankruptcy Hypotheses' (1994) 72 Wash. ULQ 955 at 964.

order to dilute the legal rights of secured creditors and redistribute the associated wealth to other parties, but (transaction costs permitting) prospective secured lenders may well alter the terms and tariffs of their respective deals so as to contract around the legal alterations. There is some evidence from US studies that such circumvention has been encountered.[60]

A final objection to communitarianism urges that insolvency judges are not necessarily well placed to decide what should, or should not, be deemed a community problem, or what should be in the community's best interest,[61] and that this involves judges in politically fraught decision-making and encourages policy ad hocery. In defence, however, communitarians might respond that judges inevitably and in all sectors of the law advert to public and community interests, that an insolvency law solely for creditor protection is objectionably narrow and that if community interests impinge on judicial decisions they should be dealt with openly and fully.

The forum vision

Rather than seeing the insolvency process in terms of substantive objectives it may be conceptualised in procedural terms, its essence being to establish a forum within which all interests affected by business failure, whether directly monetary or not, can be voiced.[62] The enterprise is seen as comprising not merely the physical assets and stock of business but the focus of interests and concerns of all participants in the company's financial distress. The law's function, in turn, is seen as establishing space. It 'creates conditions for an ongoing debate in which, by expressing ... conflicting and incommensurable values, participants work towards defining and re-defining the fundamental aims of the enterprise. Through the medium of bankruptcy discourse, the enterprise realises its potential as a fully dimensional personality.'[63] Not only interested parties can engage in this discourse. To some it, most significantly, allows extra-legal resources and expertise to be brought into play so as to construct the domain to be legally regulated. Thus accountants play an important part in defining the onset of insolvency and in advising on responses: 'Before corporate failure can be internalised within the legal system, it has first to

---

[60] See citation in ibid., p. 959.   [61] Schermers, 'Response to Professor Gross', p. 1051.
[62] See Flessner, 'Philosophies of Business Bankruptcy Law'.
[63] Korobkin, 'Rehabilitating Values', p. 772.

be represented and calculated as an economic event by means of the calculative technologies of accountancy.'[64]

Such a vision may throw light on an important role to be played by insolvency law but it necessarily falls short of offering guidance on matters of substance. As, moreover, with other theories of legitimation through providing means of representation,[65] difficult issues remain concerning the amount of representation to be offered to different parties; the 'right' balance between provisions for representation and efficiency in decision- and policy-making; and the extent to which representation should be reinforced with legal rights.

The ethical vision

According to Philip Shuchman, insolvency laws fail to rest on an adequate philosophical foundation in so far as the formal rules of insolvency disregard issues of greatest moral concern.[66] He argues that the situation of the debtor, the moral worthiness of the debt and the size, situation and intent of the creditor should be taken into account in laying the foundations for insolvency law. Judgements in such matters would not be based upon intuitions but on utilitarian principles. Thus the criteria to be employed would be 'present and prospective need, desert and the moral and philanthropic worth, and the importance of the underlying transaction ... [I]n the context of bankruptcy it is assumed that interpersonal comparisons of utility are significant and that social states can be ordered according to the sum of utilities of individuals; further, that the choice of any given arrangement ordinarily ought to be some sort of aggregation of individual preferences.'[67]

Shuchman, therefore, argues that a distinction should be drawn between debts that have arisen out of contracts that personally benefit the creditor and debts flowing from involuntary acts or loans between friends. He would, accordingly, have judges or administrators base

---

[64] P. Miller and M. Power, 'Calculating Corporate Failure' in Y. Dezalay and D. Sugarman (eds.), *Professional Competition and Professional Power: Lawyers, Accountants and the Social Construction of Markets* (Routledge, London, 1995) pp. 51–76 at p. 58.

[65] See R. B. Stewart, 'The Reformation of American Administrative Law' (1975) 99(2) Harv. L Rev. 1667 and, generally, C. Pateman, *Participation and Democratic Theory* (Cambridge University Press, London, 1970).

[66] P. Shuchman, 'An Attempt at a "Philosophy of Bankruptcy"' (1973) 21 UCLA L Rev. 403. See also J. Kilpi, *The Ethics of Bankruptcy* (Routledge, London, 1998).

[67] Shuchman, 'An Attempt', p. 447.

decisions on such matters as priorities on ethically relevant realities. He would resist blind acceptance of pre-petition creditors being equal.

Whether it is realistic to expect to find ethical principles to underpin all insolvency law can be questioned,[68] as indeed might the possibility of any group of individuals or judges coming to agree on the substance of such principles.[69] The boundaries, moreover, of relevant ethical principles (and the border between ethical principle and prejudice, distaste or disgust)[70] cannot be established uncontentiously. To rely upon the judiciary to evaluate the moral needs and deserts of creditors and the moral worthiness of debts, and to incorporate such evaluations within insolvency law, places a large degree of faith in their own moral judgement (not to say the existence of an identifiable and agreed set of moral predicates) and their determination and ability to develop a consistent and coherent body of law on this basis. Such a system might also have considerable and detrimental effects on the availability and cost of credit in so far as creditors' bargains would be placed in the shadow of legal uncertainty. Creditor wealth maximisers might, finally, add that questions of consistency between bodies of law arise, and argue that if non-insolvency law generally declines to take on board the virtuous (or disreputable) motives of those involved in legal transactions then insolvency law should do likewise.[71]

The multiple values/eclectic approach

In stark contrast to approaches offering a single, economic rationale, as exemplified by the creditor wealth maximisation vision, is the notion that insolvency law serves a series of values that cannot be organised into neat priorities. Thus Warren offers what she calls a 'dirty, complex, elastic, inter-connected' view of insolvency law from which neither outcomes can be predicted nor all the factors relevant to a policy decision can necessarily be fully articulated.[72] Whereas the economic account can explain insolvency law only as a device to maximise creditor wealth, not distribute fairly, a value-based account is said to understand

---

[68] See Carlson, 'Philosophy in Bankruptcy', p. 1389.
[69] See the exchange between H. L. A. Hart, *Law, Liberty and Morality* (Oxford University Press, Oxford, 1963) and P. Devlin, *The Enforcement of Morals* (Oxford University Press, London, 1965).
[70] See R. M. Dworkin, *Taking Rights Seriously* (Duckworths, London, 1977) ch. 10.
[71] See Jackson, *Logic and Limits of Bankruptcy Law*, ch. 1.
[72] Warren, 'Bankruptcy Policy', p. 811.

insolvency law's 'economic and non-economic dimensions and the principle of fairness as a moral, political, personal and social value'.[73]

Multiple values/eclectic approaches as exemplified by Warren and Korobkin see insolvency processes as attempting to achieve such ends as distributing the consequences of financial failure among a wide range of actors; establishing priorities between creditors; protecting the interests of future claimants; offering opportunities for continuation, reorganisation, rehabilitation; providing time for adjustments; serving the interests of those who are not technically creditors but who have an interest in continuation of the business (e.g. employees with scant pro-spect of re-employment, customers, suppliers, neighbouring property owners and state tax authorities); and protecting the investing public, jobs, the public and community interests. Such approaches incorporate communitarian philosophies and take on board distributive rationales, placing value, for instance, on relative ability to bear costs; the incentive effect on pre-insolvency transactions; the need to treat like creditors alike; and the aim of compelling shareholders to bear the lion's share of the costs of failure.

Further goals can be added by making reference to the Cork Committee's own statement of aims – a clear example of the multiple values approach.[74] Thus, as already noted, Cork emphasised the role of insolvency law in reinforcing the demands of commercial morality and encouraging debt settlement,[75] and also stressed deterrent and distribu-tive ends in urging that insolvency should seek to ascertain the causes of failure and consider whether conduct merited punishment.

The multiple values approach, moreover, is broad enough to encom-pass the forum vision. Thus, in putting forward his own value-based approach, Korobkin posits the worth, *inter alia*, of insolvency law's providing a forum for the representation of views: 'under the value-based account, bankruptcy law has the distinct function of creating conditions for a discourse in which values of participants may be

---

[73] Korobkin, 'Rehabilitating Values', p. 781.

[74] See Cork Report, para. 198. For an overview of multiple aims and essential features of an insolvency system see E. Flaschen and T. DeSieno, 'The Development of Insolvency Law as Part of the Transition from a Centrally Planned to a Market Economy' (1992) 26 *International Lawyer* 667 at 668–71.

[75] See also G. Triantis, 'Mitigating the Collective Action Problem of Debt Enforcement through Bankruptcy Law: Bill C-22 and its Shadow' (1992) 20 Canadian Bus. LJ 242, who argues that while bankruptcy law may be valuable to resolve the collective action problem and to secure efficiency, an additional objective should be to promote efficient 'private workouts' in the shadow of bankruptcy law. (See also Baird's reply, pp. 261–8.)

rehabilitated into an informed and coherent vision of what the estate as enterprise shall exist to do'.[76]

What is the case for a multiple values approach? Warren argues that a policy focusing on the values to be protected in an insolvency distribution and on the effective implementation of those values assists decision-makers even if it does not dictate specific answers. It illuminates the critical, normative and empirical questions and involves inquiries into the range of relevant issues such as who may be hurt by a business failure; how they may be hurt; whether the hurt can be avoided and at what cost; who is helped by the failure; whether aid to those helped offsets the injury to those hurt; who can effectively evaluate the risks of failure; who may have contributed to the failure and how; whether the contribution to failure serves useful goals; and who can best bear the costs of failure and who expected to bear those costs.[77]

Such an approach is thus said to highlight the empirical assumptions underlying insolvency decisions to ask tough and specific questions by coming to grips with the 'difficult and complex tapestry' of empirical presumptions and normative concerns.[78] It honestly acknowledges that judgements are made in balancing numbers of values in insolvency decision-making. Answers may not be complete but are said to be more fully reasoned than those resulting from single rationale approaches.[79]

Eclecticism, nevertheless, gives rise to not inconsiderable problems. In the first instance, little assistance is offered to decision-makers on the management of tensions and contradictions between different values or on the way that trade-offs between various ends should be effected. Questions, moreover, are easily begged in choosing which values to invoke or emphasise.[80] Nor do core principles emerge to guide decisions on such trade-offs or to establish weightings: this, as noted, was a concern that the 1994 Justice Report expressed with regard to the Cork statement of aims.[81]

The open-textured nature of eclecticism can be a problem in some multi-value schemes. Unless particular values are identified with

---

[76] Korobkin, 'Rehabilitating Values', p. 781.   [77] Warren, 'Bankruptcy Policy', p. 796.

[78] Ibid., p. 797.   [79] Korobkin, 'Rehabilitating Values', p. 787.

[80] See G. E. Frug, 'The Ideology of Bureaucracy in American Law' (1984) 97 Harv. L Rev. 1277 at 1379.

[81] *Insolvency Law: An Agenda for Reform*, paras. 3.7–3.8.

precision, appeals can be made to an open-ended menu[82] of purposes and it is difficult to decide when to rule out appeals on the basis that they invoke irrelevant values or aims. (Cork, it should be conceded, does offer a list, as we have seen.) Eclecticism runs the danger of seeing all arguments as valid and, as a result, guidance for practical decision-making is lacking and confusion results. If an identification of the objectives of insolvency law is desired so as to provide a framework within which judges and legislators can act, then the multi-value/eclectic, even more than the communitarian, approach is guilty of settling untrammelled discretions on such individuals and allowing them freely to choose from and combine an indeterminately long list of vaguely stated ingredients.

The nature of measuring

The above visions or approaches to insolvency emphasise different facets of corporate insolvency law's role. What fails to emerge from the review undertaken, however, is any complete view of the appropriate measures of insolvency law. Creditor wealth maximisation was narrow in its exclusive concerns with creditors' interests and pre-insolvency rights and in its conception of the insolvent company as a pool of assets. The broad-based contractarian approach begged questions concerning the nature of persons behind the veil of ignorance and failed to explain trade-offs of fairness or justice versus efficiency or between different kinds of interests worthy of protection. The communitarian vision escaped the narrowness of creditor wealth maximisation but encountered problems of indeterminacy. The forum vision made much of procedural concerns but shed little light on the substantive ends to be pursued by insolvency law or processes. The ethical vision gave rise to difficulties concerning the possibility of locating agreement as to ethical content and to establishing the boundaries of relevant ethical concerns. How ethical aspects of decisions on insolvency interacted with other, say legal, principles remained in doubt. Finally, the eclectic approach, again, gave rise to problems of indeterminacy and of contradictions and tensions between different ends.

---

[82] For a view that insolvency law should offer a 'menu of options' and allow firms to choose the optimal rules for their own, perhaps idiosyncratic, requirements, see Rasmussen, 'Debtor's Choice' and Rasmussen, 'The Ex Ante Effects of Bankruptcy Reform on Investment Incentives' (1994) 72 Wash. ULQ 1159.

To advance the search for measures in the light of such competing, yet contestable, visions, it is necessary to examine further the purpose of a quest for benchmarks and in doing so to answer two questions. What precisely is being measured? Is it possible to justify insolvency law or processes given present approaches? A response to these issues can be made by examining a well-known treatment of justification in company law and by suggesting that it can be built upon to develop an approach that has relevance for the insolvency arena.

A framework for analysing the fundamental rules of company law has been offered by focusing on the question of how corporate managerial power is legitimated. This issue is said to be a 'unifying theme of company law'.[83] Mary Stokes' argument, in brief, is as follows. If economic power, derived from private property, is to be legitimated within the framework of a liberal society, it is necessary to show that there are restraints preventing it from becoming a threat to liberty or a challenge to state power. Two strategies are contained within the fabric of the law to attempt this demonstration: first, it is posited that the economic power at issue is not sufficiently concentrated to be a threat; second, such economic power is seen as subject to constraints imposed by the competitive market. Unfortunately both strands of argument are afflicted with deficiencies. The growth of the corporate enterprise has allowed concentrations of economic power; and the separation of ownership from control has produced managers' powers that are unrestrained by the market (much economic power indeed has come to be exercised not within markets but within corporate bureaucracies).

Company law can be said to have offered a response to the problem of corporate managerial power by explaining why discretion was conferred on corporate managers and by demonstrating that such discretionary power was subject to checks and controls. The justification for discretion was based by some on a contractual view of the company.[84] Thus, the owners might legitimately contract with managers to establish the latter

---

[83] Stokes, 'Company Law and Legal Theory', p. 155.

[84] On the contractual view see J. E. Parkinson, *Corporate Power and Responsibility: Issues in the Theory of Company Law* (Clarendon Press, Oxford, 1993) pp. 25–32 and Parkinson, 'The Contractual Theory of the Company and the Protection of Non-Shareholder Interests' in D. Feldman and F. Meisel (eds.), *Corporate and Commercial Law: Modern Developments* (Lloyd's of London Press, London, 1996); W. W. Bratton, 'The "Nexus of Contracts Corporation": A Critical Appraisal' (1989) 74 Cornell L Rev. 408 at 415–23; M. C. Jensen and W. H. Meckling, 'Theory of the Firm: Managerial Behaviour, Agency Costs and Ownership Structure' (1976) 3 *Journal of Financial Economics* 305; F. H. Easterbrook and D. R. Fischel, 'The Corporate Contract' (1989) 89 Colum. L Rev.

as agents. As companies grew, though, the artificiality of a contractarian analysis became apparent. A 'natural entity' view of the corporation was seen by others to be more appropriate.[85] This saw the company as a living organism with the managers as the brain and the shareholders as passive suppliers of capital. The natural entity view gave rise to a further way of justifying the vesting of discretionary power in managers: it was the expertise and competence of managers that legitimated their discretion. The boundaries of such expertise and appropriate deference to it were nevertheless difficult to delineate.

As for legitimation through checks on arbitrariness, the traditional legal model offered two mechanisms: accountability to shareholders through internal company controls and directorial duties to act in the best interest of shareholders. (The latter duties legitimated discretions by compelling directors to aim at profit maximisation.) Both mechanisms proved flawed and the law's quest to legitimate the power of corporate management failed.[86]

In response to this failure two strategies might be advocated within the traditional approach: either managers could be made more responsible to the market or new legal steps could be taken to ensure management in the interest of shareholders. Both of these strategies would constitute tinkering. It would be better, argued Stokes, to recognise the misguided nature of attempts to control through markets or the ordering of power in the company and to adopt a new perspective on legitimating managerial power.[87] This new approach would accept the separation of ownership and control and break free from the contractual conception of the company. It might build on a corporatist model of the company and see

---

1416; E. F. Fama, 'Agency Problems and the Theory of the Firm' (1980) 88(1) *Journal of Political Economy* 288; Symposium, 'Contractual Freedoms in Corporate Law' (1988) 89 Colum. L Rev. 1385; H. Butler, 'The Contractual Theory of the Corporation' (1989) 11 Geo. Mason UL Rev. 99.

[85] See Stokes, 'Company Law and Legal Theory', p. 164. See also further discussion in S. W. Mayson, D. French and C. L. Ryan, *Mayson, French and Ryan on Company Law* (24th edn, Oxford University Press, Oxford, 2007) ch. 5. Another problem of using a contractual conception to legitimate managerial power was that this view conflicted with the case-law theory of the company as a body distinct and separate from its shareholders.

[86] Notably because in large public companies the dispersion of shareholding undermined shareholder control and managers, in reality, wielded power free from either shareholder constraint or the courts, who displayed deference to managerial expertise. (Dispersed shareholding produced a lack of control over managers because of low information levels and low incentives to enforce duties against directors: see V. Finch, 'Company Directors: Who Cares About Skill and Care?' (1992) 55 MLR 179.)

[87] Stokes, 'Company Law and Legal Theory', pp. 173–7.

its interests not merely as those of shareholders but as involving both public and private dimensions; see directors as expert public servants balancing a variety of claims by various groups in the community and doing so with reference to public policy not private cupidity; and see the company as an organic body unifying the interests of participants in harmonious purpose. Managerial power would be legitimated as giving expression to the common purposes of shareholders, creditors, employees and the community.

Stokes' argument, in short, is thus that current strategies for legitimating managerial power should be seen as unnecessarily tied to traditional contractarian views of the company and as inadequate; and that the values involved in the corporatist and democratic ideals of the company should be embraced in rethinking rationales for legitimation.

The importance of the argument outlined lies in its critique of the assumptions that underpin traditionalist approaches to the legitimation of managerial power and in its stressing that the public dimension of corporate power demands measures reflecting community and democratic rather than simply private values. Against Stokes it can be countered, however, that reservations about narrow contractarianism and endorsement of the communitarian/democratic approach do not necessarily mean that arguments for legitimation based on contractarian assumptions lack all validity. Here the question is whether traditionalist arguments for legitimation are 'fundamentally misguided'[88] in the sense that they are positive deceptions or whether they are criticisable as telling only part of the story. The communitarian/democratic vision may be completely at odds with the contractarian vision but it may be that legitimating arguments from both camps may cumulate: that adding a communitarian perspective means that corporate managerial power is capable of legitimation to some degree with reference both to controls exercised over managers by the market and to controls operating through representative arrangements corresponding to the democratic ideal. Legitimating arguments such as those based on expertise and accountability can thus be seen as having cumulative force in spite of being flawed in various ways. Indeed, arguments derived from the communitarian/democratic vision are themselves not problem free. (How much representation of which interests is appropriate? How should such representation best be achieved?)

---

[88] Ibid., p. 174.

To consider a series of legitimating arguments and point serially to the limitations of each one, and to conclude that legitimation cannot result, may be to misportray legitimation as a chain of arguments as strong as its weakest link rather than as a cable able to bear strain according to the collective power of its (albeit imperfect) strands.[89]

A further problem may arise if legitimation is seen exclusively as restraint, as all about the limitation of discretionary powers. Subjection to control and accountability may be necessary for legitimation but these factors may themselves be insufficient to guarantee it. Those attributing legitimacy may also demand that the system enables and encourages the protection of substantive outcomes effectively and they may also recognise the legitimacy of genuinely expert management.[90]

An 'explicit values' approach to insolvency law

What lessons does the above discussion provide for those seeking measures and benchmarks for insolvency law? Indeed, whereabouts in the insolvency sphere is the power requiring legitimation? Company law was said to be about the legitimation of corporate managerial power in the hands of directors. Insolvency is more complex because it is the tendency of English insolvency law to take power out of the hands of management and place it, according to various circumstances, with different parties such as creditors, insolvency practitioners[91] and the courts themselves. It

---

[89] It might be argued that the strands analogy breaks down where individual strands oppose rather than lie parallel (e.g. employee versus creditor interests). The point, however, is that values may be placed on items in spite of such tensions. Employee and creditor interests are thus valued in spite of the trade-offs which often have to be made between them.

[90] On restraint versus enabling models of influence ('red light v. green light' approaches) see C. Harlow and R. Rawlings, *Law and Administration* (2nd edn, Butterworths, London, 1997) chs. 2 and 3. On legitimation in general see D. Beetham, *The Legitimation of Power* (Macmillan, London, 1991); Frug, 'Ideology of Bureaucracy'; R. Baldwin and C. McCrudden (eds.), *Regulation and Public Law* (Weidenfeld & Nicolson, London, 1987) ch. 3; R. Baldwin, *Rules and Government* (Oxford University Press, Oxford, 1995) ch. 3; Baldwin, *Understanding Regulation* (Oxford University Press, Oxford, 1999) ch. 6.

[91] For example, as administrative receivers, administrators and liquidators. Contrast the US concept of 'debtor in possession' in Chapter 11 of the Uniform Commercial Code: see J. L. Westbrook, 'A Comparison of Bankruptcy Reorganisation in the US with Administration Procedure in the UK' (1990) 6 IL&P 86; Bank of England Occasional Paper, 'Company Reorganisation: A Comparison of Practice in the US and the UK' (1983); R. Broude, 'How the Rescue Culture Came to the United States and the Myths that Surround Chapter 11' (2001) 16 IL&P 194.

is thus the broad insolvency process in all its dimensions and with its variety of actors that requires legitimation.

A second issue concerns the basis for requiring legitimation. It cannot be assumed that since corporate managerial power in a going concern requires legitimation, insolvency regimes and powers automatically require legitimation. Insolvency processes do, however, impinge strongly upon the public interest in so far as decisions are made about the lives or deaths of enterprises and those decisions affect livelihoods and communities. Insolvency processes also have dramatic import for private rights in so far as, for instance, pre-insolvency property rights and securities can be frozen and individual efforts to enforce other legal rights constrained. On both public and private interest grounds, accordingly, the powers involved in insolvency processes can be seen as calling for strong justification. This, in turn, militates in favour of justifications that have aspects which can be democratically secured (as is appropriate in so far as the public interest is involved) and which involve respect for individual rights (since private interests are at issue).[92] The attribution of legitimacy can accordingly be seen against a vision of the insolvency process that is broad enough to encompass legitimating arguments that are based on communitarian approaches as well as expressive of concerns that creditors' interests be protected. How tensions and trade-offs between different legitimating rationales can be resolved remains, of course, an issue to which we shall return below.

To argue thus, it may be responded, is all very well where insolvency processes have both public and private dimensions, but in relation to some aspects of insolvency there are real disputes as to whether arrangements should be seen as an integral part of the insolvency process and not just as a matter of private debt collection or contracting. (Administrative receivership and types of 'contractual' arrangements such as *ipso facto* clauses in contracts give rise to such issues.)[93] Private

---

[92] Actors in insolvency processes may, of course, carry out some functions that are oriented towards private interests and some that look to public considerations: thus liquidators both collect and realise assets for distribution to creditors and report directorial 'unfitness' to the Disqualification Unit of the Insolvency Service as part of the disqualification process. See further S. Wheeler, 'Directors' Disqualification: Insolvency Practitioners and the Decision-making Process' (1995) 15 *Legal Studies* 283.

[93] E.g. hire purchase agreements made to terminate on the insolvency of the hirer: see further D. Prentice, 'Contracts and Corporate Insolvency Proceedings', paper given at SPTL Seminar on Insolvency Proceedings, Oxford, September 1995. For US treatment of agreements designed to operate only on bankruptcy see Bankruptcy Code 1978 (as amended) s. 365(a)(1) and (b)(1).

contracting, indeed, can be seen as shading into the province of insolvency law so that clear boundaries do not exist.

Such a lack of clear boundaries should not, however, be seen as fatal to the enterprise of measuring insolvency processes. Persons of different political persuasions might be expected to disagree as to the aspects of insolvency processes that require legitimation by democratically secured rather than private rights based arguments. The point is that if legitimation is seen in terms of rationales that reflect both democratic (public) and private rights roots, clarity will be given to evaluations and the extent to which, for example, present arrangements in an area depend on contractarian justifications will be manifest. To explore modes of measuring or legitimating insolvency law is not to suppose homogeneity of political philosophies.

As for the array of rationales that can be used to legitimate powers impinging upon public interests and private rights, these have been identified by Stokes, Frug and others[94] and, moreover, are limited in number. As Frug has commented: 'we have adopted only a limited number of ways to reassure ourselves'[95] about the exercise of powers. The rationales can be described as: firstly, formalist, which justifies with reference to the efficient implementation of a statutory or shareholders' mandate; secondly, expertise-based, which sees managers as worthy of trust due to their expertise and professionalism; thirdly, control-based, which looks to the restrictions imposed on discretions by courts, markets and others; and, fourthly, pluralist, which adverts to the degree of amenability of processes to representations from the public about how corporate affairs should be conducted.[96]

The justifications of insolvency processes can similarly be seen as dependent not merely on the efficient pursuit of mandates but also on the degree of expertise exercised by relevant actors, the adequacy of control and accountability schemes and the procedural fairness that is shown in dealing with affected parties' interests.

---

[94] See Stokes, 'Company Law and Legal Theory'; Frug, 'Ideology of Bureaucracy'. See also B. Sutton (ed.), *The Legitimate Corporation* (Blackwell, Oxford, 1993).

[95] Frug, 'Ideology of Bureaucracy', p. 1281. The description of rationales that follows in the text paraphrases and reorganises Frug in so far as judicial review is joined with market and other forms of control.

[96] See also Baldwin and McCrudden, *Regulation and Public Law*, ch. 3, who, in the public law context, employ the headings: legislative mandate; accountability; due process; expertise; and efficiency.

A final message to be drawn from a discussion of corporate power and its legitimation is that individual justificatory arguments may prove contentious and possess limitations (for example, the proper boundaries for expertise cannot be set without argument) but they may nevertheless possess force and may be combined with other arguments. To argue thus, it should be clear, is at odds with Frug's well-known attack on the traditional bases for legitimating corporate or bureaucratic power. Frug identifies the four models of legitimation already noted but argues that these fail to legitimate corporate power and stresses that combining them together 'only shifts the problem of making a subjective/objective distinction away from any particular model and locates it, instead, in the boundaries between different models'.[97] For Frug each model fails to provide an objective justification for corporate/bureaucratic power, one free from contention. Linking the different models 'allows people to believe that although the device they are considering at any particular moment is empty, one of the others surely is better [and] helps theorists convince themselves (and us) that the internal difficulties of each particular story of bureaucratic legitimacy are unimportant'.[98]

The limitation of Frug's argument, however, lies in his fundamental idea of justification: in the notion that, without a basis in some objectivity, legitimating arguments lack force. If, as I have already contended, legitimation can be argued for cumulatively so that the justificatory cable is strong in spite of its flawed strands, there is far less of a problem in combining rationales of legitimation. The exercise of power can thus be seen as capable of being rendered acceptable not on the grounds that it is 'objective in some way'[99] but because it is supportable by a thread of different arguments based on a limited number of identifiable rationales that are invoked on a collective basis.[100]

Measuring the legitimacy of an insolvency process, decision or law, it should be made clear, differs from merely expressing a political opinion on the topic. Persons of opposing political persuasions – with divergent views on the just society – might differ radically in their views on dealing with a troubled enterprise. One individual might favour immediate closure, payment of creditors and reliance on reinvestment to create

[97] Frug, 'Ideology of Bureaucracy', p. 1378.   [98] Ibid., p. 1379.   [99] Ibid., p. 1380.
[100] As Korobkin has argued, there are no 'clear winners' in arguments based on competing values, but: 'much of the purpose of a full debate is to compare the relative strengths and weaknesses of plausible arguments, not to find a clear winner': see Korobkin, 'Role of Normative Theory', pp. 108–9.

jobs. Another might stress the importance of allowing time for reorganisation because of the high premium he or she places on continuity of employment and avoidance of the external costs that closure might occasion.[101] An exchange of such political views would not, however, amount to a discussion of the legitimacy of the proposed move. To debate legitimacy, as conceived here, involves a stepping back and reference, not to personal preferences or visions, but to values enjoying broad acceptance as consistent with the underpinnings of democratic liberalism. The four key values referred to build on Frug: thus 'efficiency' looks to the securing of democratically mandated ends at lowest cost; 'expertise' refers to the allocation of decision and policy functions to properly competent persons; 'accountability' looks to the control of insolvency participants by democratic bodies or courts or through the openness of processes and their amenability to representations; and 'fairness' considers issues of justice and propensities to respect the interests of affected parties by allowing such parties access to, and respect within, decision and policy processes.[102]

To be clear, these are, accordingly, not offered as values plucked from the sky but as values that would be endorsed by parties of differing political persuasions – provided that those parties endorse democratic liberalism – albeit in their own precise terms. Such a 'values' argument[103] thus proceeds to normativity from the factual assumption that certain values are broadly accepted and by asserting that it is, therefore, right that insolvency regimes should be designed and operated to serve those values. Such an approach does not offer the certainty or the authority that flows from a single theoretical vision of the just insolvency system but it is on much safer practical ground. It is inconceivable that all persons can be persuaded to share the same single theoretical vision (we will never all be Rawlsians or Jacksonians) but it is far safer to assert that we all share an acceptance of certain values: for instance, those served by pursuing democratically mandated ends without waste or by operating procedures that are accountable, open and fair to affected

---

[101] See L. J. Rusch, 'Bankruptcy Reorganisation Jurisprudence: Matters of Belief, Faith and Hope' (1994) 55 Montana L Rev. 16, arguing that competing theories of bankruptcy law reduce to competing 'beliefs and values' which cannot be shown to be true or false (discussed in Korobkin, 'Role of Normative Theory').

[102] Such a notion of justice, accordingly, has procedural and substantive aspects – whether a process accords respect to an interest can be seen as a procedural issue but defining who constitutes an 'interested party' raises substantive issues.

[103] On 'values' approaches see Korobkin, 'Role of Normative Theory' pp. 104–11.

parties.[104] As Korobkin has pointed out, such 'value' arguments are not completely authoritative – they do not attempt to set out an authoritative basis upon which to justify or act – but: 'they have a certain kind of normative force, in that they identify what we value and cite coherent reasons to adopt a particular critical claim'. In essence they allow the proposer of a course of action to say: 'We should do X because this course will serve the values we all acknowledge' rather than: 'We should do X because this course will serve my vision of the just society, which you should all accept.'

What, though, of the difficulty, noted above, of tensions and trade-offs between different legitimating values or rationales? Surely some such rationales will pull in opposite directions? How, moreover, will the above justificatory principles influence the concrete decisions to be confronted by insolvency law, for example whether English insolvency law might introduce some variant of debtor in possession?

The answer to these questions is that clarity concerning the measures of insolvency law can be seen as clarity concerning the values that can be served by such laws. Such clarity, however, does not produce cut and dried answers on whether particular trade-offs between, for instance, protections for secured creditors and for employees are desirable or not. The rightness or wrongness of particular trade-offs can only be argued for by giving weightings or priorities to the protection of different values or interests. Such weightings and priorities presuppose substantive visions of the just society and, accordingly, persons of different political persuasions might be expected to differ on the 'right' balancing of different interests in insolvency.

The approach to evaluation offered here may produce no fine-tuned answers on either procedural or substantive issues (to demand such answers would be to ask for conversion to a particular ethical or political vision). The approach, nevertheless, does have force in identifying the values and rationales that can be accorded currency in debates on insolvency law. It can, accordingly, be termed an 'explicit values' rather than a multiple value vision of insolvency processes. The explicit values perspective brings the advantage of making clear the need for and nature of trade-offs. Thus, in discussing whether a variant of debtor in possession ought to be introduced into English insolvency law, an assessment

---

[104] We can thus all agree that processes should be fair (procedurally and substantively) even though we might, at the end of the day, disagree on the details, e.g. concerning the parties whose interests entitle them to participation in a process.

would be made of the support that such a measure would merit under the various legitimating headings made explicit above. Relevant questions would be: is this a process that allows Parliament's will to be effected without waste of resources? Can appropriate expertise be applied in such processes? Are levels of accountability acceptable? Can the proposed processes be deemed fair as giving due access to and respect for the interests of affected parties? The issue of trade-offs would, nevertheless, remain, but final political judgements would be made with a transparency that would be lacking were reference not made to the array of values or rationales described here.

That transparency, it must be conceded, cannot be complete. Such a state of affairs could only be achieved by persuading all parties to agree to a single vision of the just insolvency regime as derived from a single vision of the just society.[105] This sort of agreed vision would form a basis for clarity on, for example, the level of expertise that is appropriate in a process or how, precisely, we can delineate acceptable standards of access or qualifying interests. It is not, however, an agreed vision liable to be encountered in the real world. What the 'explicit values' approach offers, accordingly, is something more realistic but less neat. It offers no ideal vision aimed at universal subscription but a means of bringing a degree of clarity to evaluative discussions while accepting that we may all differ in our conceptions of the just society or the just distribution of rights in insolvency. It explains how, with such differing conceptions, and in the

---

[105] LoPucki has spoken of a debate between bankruptcy scholars as involving the 'Paradigm Dominance Game' which aims not to solve problems but 'to get everyone thinking about the problem in one's own frame of reference and talking about it in one's own language': see L. M. LoPucki, 'Reorganisation Realities, Methodological Realities, and the Paradigm Dominance Game' (1994) 72 Wash. ULQ 1307, 1310; and Korobkin, 'Role of Normative Theory'. For an essay in promulgating a single vision see Mokal's 'Authentic Consent Model' (in *Corporate Insolvency Law* ch. 3) which adapts Rawlsian principles for 'analysing and justifying' the body of corporate insolvency law. Sceptics are liable, however, to ask why any non-Rawlsian should be expected to buy into such a vision and are liable to object that Mokal's use of a Dramatic Ignorance device is question-begging because the Rawlsian consent position is set up on the basis of prior and key assumptions of a contentious nature – notably regarding the political conception of the person (an 'ideal of the individual') and the 'legal and political culture of society'. For further concerns regarding this approach see Duggan, 'Contractarianism and the Law of Corporate Insolvency', pp. 463–81 and Goode, *Principles of Corporate Insolvency Law*, p. 48, who criticises those who espouse variants of the creditors' bargain theory on the grounds that: 'most of them assume an original position in which the various players and the bargain they make act in an economically rational manner according to a single set of criteria. This may be an elegant model but has no necessary connection with fact.'

face of mandates that are less than certain, we can still have meaningful debates on insolvency processes or reforms – and can do so in examining how different values are collectively served. It accepts that there are no knock-down arguments in such debates, only those of greater or lesser persuasive power.

Assessing the legitimacy of insolvency processes or decisions is not, however, the same thing as assessing the formal legitimacy of an insolvency law or statute. As noted, one benchmark for processes or decisions is the extent to which a statutory mandate is efficiently implemented. Where a clear mandate exists this, indeed, provides a very compelling yardstick for measuring an insolvency decision or process, and some aspects of insolvency processes do involve agents in implementing quite clear, almost mechanical, tasks as set down in statutes: for example, the liquidator's statutory duty in voluntary winding up to distribute *pari passu*.[106] To the extent that such clear mandates are lacking – and it is not always possible to produce a clear prescription as opposed to a conferring of discretions, or a listing of factors to be taken into account or a stipulation of proper purposes for action[107] – there is all the more need to legitimate with reference to the expertise, accountability and fairness justifications. Put another way, it is because mandates are often unclear that justifications based on expertise, accountability and fairness come into play. In such circumstances, these procedural rationales have a value that is freestanding and possessing of legitimating force within a democracy – and this is why they are not merely aspects of the mandate. To take the examples of accountability and fairness, it can be argued that if a procedure is appropriately open, controlled, amenable to access and respectful of affected interests, this allows the public and affected parties a degree of representation that, in a democracy, compensates for vagueness in the mandate by allowing them to shape the mandate in its application.

It might, of course, be objected that, without a single agreed notion of the just society, it is as impossible to say what procedural fairness amounts to as it is to give content to the notion of substantive fairness. The real world challenge is, however, not to sell a concept of justice to the

---

[106] See Insolvency Act 1986 s. 107.

[107] See e.g. the Insolvency Act 1986 Sch. B1, paras. 3(1), (2), (3), (4) regarding the administrator's functions. On strong versus weak discretions see Dworkin, *Taking Rights Seriously*, pp. 31–9, 68–71. On discretion in fact finding see D. J. Galligan, *Discretionary Powers: A Legal Study of Official Discretion* (Clarendon Press, Oxford, 1986) pp. 34–7.

general population but to find what coherence we can in a world of different visions and preferences – to explain how we can debate insolvency (or other) processes when we hold divergent views concerning justice, fairness, accountability and so on.[108] The contention here is that we can engage in such debates, and find a level of coherence in these, by using common benchmarks or reference points. In the case of procedural fairness, for instance, parties can – necessarily in a broad church manner – agree that this demands that persons or firms with affected interests should be allowed an access to processes that implies a respect for their interests. The fact that people with different visions of justice will disagree at the end of the day on the weighting of various interests is not, on such a view, fatal to a debate that makes reference to a series of democratically valued (but elastic) yardsticks.

Would it not be circular, however, to evaluate an insolvency law by asking (*inter alia*) whether it implements a statutory mandate? If a judicial application of a statute is at issue then circularity is avoided since it makes sense to ask if, in a particular instance, a judge's ruling derives legitimacy from its clear implementation of Parliament's will as expressed in a statute (again there may or may not be a clear expression of the mandate available). What of an actual or proposed statutory provision? Does reference to the implementation of a statutory mandate involve circularity? This may not necessarily be the case. Where there is a clear policy or practice laid down then it may be claimed that Parliament's will is being effected and there is a high degree of legitimacy involved, though it will still be possible to consider whether a reform of the provision would be supportable on grounds other than mandate implementation. If, however, the provision at issue merely confers discretion (while, perhaps, laying down factors for consideration) it can be contended that there is not so much an expression of Parliament's voice as a delegation on the substantive issue. The legitimacy of any decision or act taken in implementation of such a provision would accordingly fall to be judged with reference to a series of rationales since the mandate justification only renders the others irrelevant where there is absolute clarity of the mandate.

Does this mean that an insolvency law is worthy of support provided that it has proper statutory form? Again this is not necessarily the case. It

---

[108] See also Korobkin's argument that different kinds of insolvency theory can be thought of as doing different jobs – for example explaining events, offering predictions or providing normative prescriptions. (Korobkin, 'Role of Normative Theory' at p. 96.)

means that a very high level of democratic legitimacy is assured to a statutory insolvency provision provided that the statutory mandate is absolutely clear (a rare event). Where it is not possible to lay down a statutory provision that dictates a result with clarity, the other benchmarks come into play and reference can be made to expertise, accountability and fairness considerations in evaluating the provision and its anticipated effects.

The implication of this argument, it might be contended, is that if Parliament decrees something (anything) on insolvency with a clear voice then this is hardly challengeable. The response is that it is difficult to deny the democratic authority of our democracy's most authoritative voice but that evaluation by the hypothetical or proposed reform method noted above is still possible. In the vast majority of instances, where Parliament does not dictate a result but leaves issues and discretions open (or indeed in debating proposed legislation), evaluations may be made with reference to the array of legitimating rationales: asking, for example, of a proposed insolvency provision, whether it will produce results that are supportable according to expertise, accountability and fairness as well as the mandate rationales. Such evaluations may be made of and by the various actors involved in the insolvency processes: for example, judges, administrators, nominees under voluntary arrangements and liquidators.[109]

Where, though, does this leave economic efficiency in the wealth maximisation sense as a benchmark for insolvency regimes?[110] The

---

[109] Liquidators may implement statutory mandates mechanically in distributing assets *pari passu*, but discretion is involved in their 'policing' functions (e.g. whether to initiate proceedings under *inter alia* the Insolvency Act 1986 ss. 214, 238 or 239) and in their reporting 'unfit' directorial conduct to the Disqualification Unit: see Wheeler, 'Directors' Disqualification', pp. 300–1.

[110] Economists use 'efficiency' in a number of senses and it is as well to be clear about these. The notion of *allocative efficiency* is commonly used in two ways. A situation is *Pareto efficient* if the welfare of one individual cannot be improved without reducing the welfare of any other member of society. In contrast, a situation is *Kaldor–Hicks efficient* if those who gain could in principle compensate those who have been harmed by a position and still be better off. (This efficiency can also be referred to as cost–benefit analysis, wealth maximisation, allocative efficiency or simply efficiency.) *Technical efficiency* (or *transaction cost efficiency*) is concerned with achieving desired results with the minimum use of resources and costs and the minimum wastage of effort. *Dynamic efficiency* refers to the capacity of a given system to innovate and survive in a changing and uncertain environment. In this book the word 'efficiency' will be used to denote *technical efficiency*, and 'economic efficiency' will refer to efficiency in the Kaldor–Hicks/wealth maximisation/cost–benefit sense. On efficiency concepts and

wealth maximisation argument was criticised above as offering little assistance on distributional matters.[111] We have seen that clear mandates are rare in the insolvency field and it is not advisable, in the absence of clear mandates, to leap to wealth maximisation itself as the next best statement of substantive objectives. Wealth maximisation, accordingly, will be treated, in this volume, as having no freestanding value as an objective of insolvency processes. Note will, nevertheless, be taken of influential debates concerning the economic efficiency/wealth maximising (hereafter 'economic efficiency') effects of certain processes – since, on a given issue, elective bodies may – or may not – be inclined to pursue such economic efficiency objectives.[112]

As for matters of technical efficiency (hereafter 'efficiency'), it is possible to respond to economists' concerns regarding the minimising of transaction costs and to treat these as ancillary to discussions of democratically legitimate objectives (or mandates) and questions of expertise, accountability and fairness. This can be done by considering whether the processes at issue avoid unnecessary transaction costs – an approach that allows existing legal provisions and procedures to be evaluated but also offers some scope for evaluating proposals. A basis for criticising a legislative proposal (for instance a clause in a Bill) might,

---

corporate law see A. Ogus and C. Veljanovski, *Readings in the Economics of Law and Regulation* (Oxford University Press, Oxford, 1984), pp. 19–20; Ogus, *Regulation*, pp. 23–5; Law Commission, *Company Directors: Regulating Conflicts of Interests and Formulating a Statement of Duties*, LCCP 153, SLCDP 105 (TSO, London, 1998) part III; S. Deakin and A. Hughes, 'Economics and Company Law Reform: A Fruitful Analysis?' (1999) 20 Co. Law. 212; Deakin and Hughes, 'Economic Efficiency and the Proceduralisation of Company Law' [1999] CfiLR 169; J. Armour, 'Share Capital and Creditor Protection: Efficient Rules for a Modern Company Law' (2000) 63 MLR 355.

[111] See note 36 above, accompanying text, and, notably, Dworkin, 'Is Wealth a Value?'. A key reason why principles of wealth maximisation offer no basis for guiding distributional decisions is that this would involve circularity – judgements regarding the actions that would maximise total wealth can only be made by making prior assumptions about the distributions of wealth in society. See e.g. R. Coase, 'The Problem of Social Cost' (1960) 3 J Law and Econ. 1; A. Kronman, 'Wealth Maximisation as a Normative Principle' (1980) 9 *Journal of Legal Studies* 227.

[112] The economic efficiency or otherwise of a process or institution is thus seen as contingently relevant – when, for instance, statutory objectives aim for such economic efficiency. In the absence of a link to a mandate, economic efficiency is not treated here as a factor of independent value. This treatment of economic efficiency contrasts with that accorded to, say, accountability which is seen as having a value independent of the mandate – indeed as a counterbalance to any lack of clarity in the mandate. On the value of considering economic efficiency as one of a number of evaluative criteria see A. Keay, 'Directors' Duties to Creditors: Contractarian Concerns Relating to Efficiency and Over-Protection of Creditors' (2003) 66 MLR 665, 678.

accordingly, be that, given the objectives being pursued by Parliament (as derived from a reading of the Bill as a whole), the clause in question would set up a mode of achieving those objectives that is not lowest cost. To criticise on this basis is not so much to set one's own objectives above those of Parliament as to assume that Parliament wishes its aims to be achieved without waste of resources. Arguments might similarly be mounted that a certain interpretation of a statutory provision is undesirable because it is not consistent with lowest-cost ways of achieving Parliament's overall objectives as expressed in the given statute as a whole.

Conclusions

In looking for the measures of insolvency law, a series of different visions of insolvency is encountered and, although these visions may be flawed, they can be seen as incorporating a number of important legitimating rationales for insolvency processes. There is more to measuring such processes, it has been noted, than stipulating a series of substantive outcomes (e.g. preserving viable enterprises). Procedural concerns are relevant also. Measuring, as put forward here, thus looks to the whole breadth of insolvency processes and the cumulative force of arguments deriving from a variety of visions: making reference to technical efficiency *in producing appropriate outcomes*; expertise; accountability; and fairness.

How does this advance matters beyond the substantive and procedural aims set down, for instance, by Cork?[113] First, the approach arrived at here offers an explanation of what is involved in assessing insolvency processes and, in addition, throws light on the different kinds of legitimating argument that are contained within such lists of aims as Cork offers. Second, it might be complained that the present approach is as lacking in precise benchmarks as the eclectic or communitarian visions, but it has been possible to identify and make explicit a number of different rationales for justifying insolvency processes: namely efficiency, expertise, accountability and fairness. Trade-offs between different rationales do remain a problem but, unless a single vision of the just society is assumed, the absence of easy answers has to be accepted when dealing with processes whose essence is the balancing of multiple objectives.

---

[113] Cork Report, paras. 191–8, 203–4, 232, 238–9.

What has been offered here has been an approach to measuring that takes on board the public and private, the procedural and substantive, and the contractarian and democratic dimensions of insolvency. As already noted, acceptance that both the public and private dimensions of insolvency law are to be reflected in legitimation involves an acceptance, in turn, that legitimation may be derived from both the propensity of insolvency laws and decisions to further communitarian interests and the potential of such laws and decisions to protect pre-existing rights. The approach offered in this book – the explicit values approach – holds that an identifiable list of justifications has relevance in assessing the legitimacy of insolvency processes. The list is limited rather than open-ended (as was a problem with eclectic and communitarian visions) in so far as relevant legitimating arguments are organised under the four headings noted and arguments not falling under such headings are accordingly not to be treated as relevant for purposes of legitimation.

Such an approach, in turn, implies a particular approach to insolvency procedures. Dealing with explicit values in the above manner exposes the trade-offs between different values that have to be made in designing and applying insolvency processes. A variety of interests will accordingly have to enter consideration in a host of procedures. Such processes must respect the interests of, and the roles to be played in, insolvency by a range of parties affected by insolvency: not merely creditors (secured and unsecured) but employees, company directors, shareholders, suppliers, customers and other 'commercial dependants' of the company. The broad public interest must also enter deliberations as a valid concern and procedural inclusivity should be seen in access to information, broad inputs into key decisions and in holding parties to account. This is not to argue that customers, for instance, should have the same access to information and processes as creditors; it is to suggest that reasonable access for customers should not be denied in insolvency procedures on the grounds that customers have no recognisable interest in insolvency. The interests of affected or potentially affected parties should be procedurally recognised where the costs of doing so are reasonable. In some particular contexts, of course, rights of reasonable access may involve excessive costs through creating legal uncertainties that cannot be resolved and in those contexts restrictions will be appropriate. Such matters will be considered in the chapters that follow.

Does an explicit values approach supply the 'fundamental or core principles' that the 1994 Justice Report advocated as guides to the 'true essence of the insolvency process'? It does not offer a cut-and-dried series of primary principles to which others can be seen as subservient. The list of values set out here does, however, provide a core in the sense of a framework offering guidance in the development of insolvency rules and arrangements. It adds, for instance, to the arrangements of objectives set down by the Cork Committee by placing those objectives within a frame of concerns established according to the four particular rationales serving to justify insolvency rules. Those rationales provide a context for Cork's objectives rather than leaving them as aims apparently plucked from the sky. The linking or cumulation of rationales also reminds us that objectives, such as are set out by Cork, do have to be weighed and traded against each other.

An explicit list of rationales, furthermore, offers a checklist to be dealt with by judges and decision-makers when dealing with insolvency issues. These actors may thus be invited not to reason with reference to a single or dominant vision of insolvency but to deal with points relevant to each of the four kinds of justificatory argument noted. Trade-offs between different ends and justifications are thus to be argued for in particular contexts and cannot be preordained according to set rules. Such argumentation should, however, be carried out explicitly and it is this structured transparency that will be the best guarantee of insolvency laws and processes that display a sense of direction.

For the purposes of this book, the rationales of *efficiency, expertise, accountability* and *fairness* provide benchmarks with which to evaluate both current and proposed arrangements. Such benchmarks can be applied not merely to substantive laws and informal rules but also to institutional structures and to those processes that are used to apply insolvency laws and rules on the ground. Throughout the chapters that follow, these benchmarks will be applied and, in particular contexts, attempts will be made to explain the balances and trade-offs that are involved between particular values or rationales. This book, however, sets out not merely to evaluate laws, processes and reforms. As indicated in the Introduction, it also aims to rethink perspectives. The ensuing chapters will, accordingly, apply the above benchmarks but will also consider whether improvements in corporate insolvency laws and processes have to come through new approaches and by adopting perspectives that challenge the underpinning assumptions of current corporate insolvency systems.

PART II

The context of corporate insolvency law: financial and institutional

3

Insolvency and corporate borrowing

The issues attending corporate insolvency law are closely linked to those surrounding corporate borrowing. It is the creation of credit that gives rise to the debtor–creditor relationship and makes insolvency possible in the first place.[1] Credit can be obtained by companies in a variety of ways, as we will see in this chapter, and the various modes of obtaining debt bring with them different arrangements for dealing with repayments. These arrangements will be relevant when dealing with companies that can no longer repay all their creditors.

To ask whether the legal framework of corporate insolvency law is acceptable demands, accordingly, some examination of the arrangements that the law recognises for obtaining credit in order to raise corporate capital. If corporations or creditors in an insolvency face problems that arise from the multiplicity and complexity of arrangements for obtaining credit and the ensuing difficulty of resolving the respective claims of different types of creditor, the best way to reform insolvency arrangements might well be to rationalise the legal methods available for raising capital and obtaining credit rather than to tinker with the insolvency rules that apply to the various credit devices.[2]

Insolvency arrangements can be assessed with reference to the factors outlined in chapter 2 but the link with credit should always be borne in mind and companies should be seen in both their healthy and their troubled contexts. It would be undesirable, for instance, to reform and improve insolvency arrangements if the result was to prejudice mechanisms for providing healthy companies with the credit arrangements that they need for effective action in the marketplace. The arrangements that best meet the needs of healthy, trading companies, it should be recognised, are not those that necessarily produce the smoothest-operating insolvency regimes and,

---

[1] See *Report of the Review Committee on Insolvency Law and Practice* (Cmnd 8558, 1982) ('Cork Report') ch. 1, especially para. 10, on credit as the 'lifeblood of the modern industrialised economy' and 'the cornerstone of the trading community'.

[2] See Cork Report, para. 1628 for acknowledgement of this connection.

in designing credit arrangements (with their attendant insolvency implications), the objective should be to maximise the sum of benefits to those involved with both healthy and troubled companies. (Here 'benefits' refers to procedural and democratic as well as financial advantages.) It may be the case that companies need a wide range of flexible credit arrangements and insolvency law has to cope accordingly.

This chapter will consider the main methods by which companies can borrow money and will explore the insolvency law implications of different credit arrangements. The emphasis of the chapter will rest on the benchmark of economic efficiency since it is necessary to respond to a considerable body of debate on credit arrangements which has focused heavily on that yardstick. As was noted in chapter 2, however, it is essential to place economic efficiency debates in their proper, limited, context by considering questions of expertise, accountability and fairness. These matters, accordingly, will be returned to in parts III and IV of the book. The discussion here asks how the legal structure of each mode of obtaining credit contributes to the supply of funds for a healthy company and whether that structure fosters economic efficiency by allowing insolvencies to be dealt with at lowest cost. (The needs of healthy, trading companies will be dealt with briefly since this is not a book dealing centrally with corporate financing.) At this stage, it should be noted, it is the formal legal structure of financing arrangements that is the primary object of attention. Later chapters will broaden the discussion to consider in more detail how such arrangements are put into effect.

Arrangements for obtaining credit will be examined individually in this chapter but it will then be necessary to consider whether, as a package, the available legal arrangements perform well in relation to both healthy and troubled companies. It is conceivable, after all, that each device may perform adequately in its own right but that collectively they may prove economically inefficient because they give rise to legal confusions and uncertainties. We begin by looking at the parties involved in, and the incidence of, borrowing before considering in more detail the particular routes available for the financing of corporate activity.

Creditors, borrowing and debtors

Companies in England can raise capital through issuing equity – by selling shares[3] – but they are also able to borrow from a wide variety of

---

[3] Space here does not allow a discussion of strategies for raising equity capital, on which see G. Arnold, *The Handbook of Corporate Finance* (Pearson Education, London, 2005)

individuals and institutions.[4] A first kind of creditor is the institutional lender. This is exemplified by the high street clearing bank that plays an important role in offering companies not merely loans but flexible finance in the form of overdrafts.[5] Other types of institution are the accepting houses: a number of merchant banks which usually offer term loans for periods of five years or more. The merchant banks have traditionally been associated with the supply of venture capital: money used in relation to high-risk activities, for example to start up ventures or to effect rescues and, in reflection of higher than average risks, tending to be accompanied by demands for higher than average returns or shares in the enterprise, or both.

A second kind of commonly encountered lender is the trade creditor,[6] the individual or firm who supplies goods or services to the company but who does not require immediate payment. Such creditors will often transfer goods to a company and await payment at a later date but they may also offer goods in return for a bill of exchange (in the form, for example, of a post-dated cheque) or in accordance with leasing or hire purchase terms. These latter arrangements allow companies to spread the costs of purchasing an item (for example, a new piece of machinery) over a proportion, or all, of the asset's lifetime.[7]

A third type of creditor is the wealthy individual who may be persuaded to put money into a venture. The term 'business angel' has developed to refer to individuals who perform venture capital roles, usually offering loans and, in return for these, combining repayment

---

ch. 17. It should be noted, however, that much activity goes on outside the world of the stock exchange. As Arnold notes: 'There are over one million limited liability companies in the UK and only 0.2 percent of them have shares traded on the recognized exchanges. For decades there has been a perceived financing gap for small and medium-sized firms which has to a large extent been filled by the rapidly growing venture capital/private equity capital industry' (p. 453). See further pp. 82–3, 85–7 below.

[4] See generally G. Fuller, *Corporate Borrowing: Law and Practice* (Jordans, Bristol, 2006); Bank of England, *Finance for Small Firms*, Eleventh Report (Bank of England, April 2004) ('Bank of England 2004'); A. Cosh and A. Hughes, *British Enterprise in Transition* (ESRC Centre for Business Research, Cambridge, 2000) ('Cosh and Hughes 2000'), especially ch. 5; Cosh and Hughes, *British Enterprise: Thriving or Surviving?* (ESRC Centre for Business Research, Cambridge, 2007) ('Cosh and Hughes 2007').

[5] On bank loans see Fuller, *Corporate Borrowing*, ch. 2.

[6] Though note that sale credit does not in law constitute a loan (in the sense of providing free funds to conduct business). In legal terms it is seen as the contractual deferment of a price obligation: see R. M. Goode, *Commercial Law* (3rd edn, Penguin Books, London, 2004) pp. 578–81.

[7] Other (unsecured) creditors include landlords (rent arrears), utility suppliers and those with provable debts against a company in liquidation.

conditions with the taking of an equity stake in the debtor company.[8] There is now a trade association for business angels: the British Business Angels Association (BBAA), which aims to promote business angel finance subject to its own code of conduct for members.

Governmental agencies comprise a fourth group of creditors.[9] Thus the Government has deployed three main types of fund in order to stimulate the growth of private capital. These are Regional Venture Capital Funds (which by 2006 had committed over £250 million);[10] the UK High Technology Fund (supporting 216 small high technology businesses by the end of 2005) and Early Growth Funds (distributing early growth funding on a regional basis).

In 2000 the Government set up the Small Business Service (SBS) which, in 2007, was renamed the 'Enterprise Directorate'. This is a unit within the Department for Business Enterprise and Regulatory Reform (BERR) and is given policy responsibility for the Government's invest-ments in a range of business support tools – including Business Link, Enterprise Insight and access to finance funds. Such funds can be used to stimulate private sector funding as is the case with the Small Firms Loan Guarantee Scheme (SFLGS). This is a joint venture between BERR and a number of participating lenders and, under this scheme, government guarantees against default can be used to encourage lenders to fund small firms that lack the assets to cover a security.

At the European level, the European Investment Bank (EIB) operates as a non-profit-making body and is a source of venture capital as well as medium- and long-term loans to companies of all sizes.[11] The Inland Revenue also constitutes a creditor (often an involuntary one)[12] in so far

---

[8] See further p. 82 below.

[9] See NAO, *Supporting Small Business* (HC 962 Session 2005–6, London, May 2006) ('NAO 2006'); HM Treasury and Small Business Service, *Bridging the Finance Gap* (London, 2003); J. Tucker and J. Lean, 'Small Firm Finance and Public Policy' (2003) 10 *Journal of Small Business and Enterprise Development* 50–61.

[10] See NAO 2006, p. 24.

[11] The European Commission decided to adopt a Fourth Multinational Programme for SMEs for the five years from January 2001 with a budget of €450 million: see EU Commission, *Enterprise and Industry, Multinational Programme for SMEs 2001–6* (europa website). For an overview of funding opportunities available to European SMEs see European Commission, Enterprise Directorate-General, *EU Support Programmes for SMEs*, 2005.

[12] See Cork Report, paras. 1409–50. The Crown's preferential status for moneys owed on PAYE or NI has now been abolished: see Enterprise Act 2002 s. 251.

as companies may owe tax payments, though in some cases they may have negotiated schedules for such payments.[13]

A further type of creditor is the holder of a document issued by the company which acknowledges indebtedness and which usually (but not necessarily) involves a charge on the assets of the company. Under the Companies Act 2006 a 'debenture' includes debenture stock and bonds[14] and company debentures can also be referred to as 'loan stock'. A debenture is a document given in exchange for money lent to the company and debentures and debenture stock can be offered for sale to the public.[15] The debenture holder is a creditor of the company and the latter agrees to repay the holder the principal sum by a future date and to pay, each year, a stated rate of interest in return for use of the funds. The use of loan stock, particularly by larger companies, will be returned to below.[16]

Another major category of corporate creditor is the employee. In so far as employees have carried out work and are entitled contractually to wages and other benefits as yet unpaid, they constitute creditors of the firm. Shareholders, moreover, may also be creditors in that they may be owed money in their capacity as shareholders (such as dividends). Similarly, consumers of the company's products and other corporate customers may provide credit to the company where they pay in advance for goods or services – practices common in the mail order, travel, furniture retail and building sectors.[17] Those who prepay are almost invariably unsecured creditors where the supplying company becomes insolvent before delivery. They are, however, important creditors for many firms.[18] Cork noted that 'In many cases, advance payments are an essential part of the trader's working capital.'[19]

---

[13] Local authorities can also be (unsecured) creditors for rate arrears and council taxes: see further D. Milman and C. Durrant, *Corporate Insolvency: Law and Practice* (3rd edn, Sweet & Maxwell, London, 1999) ch. 10.

[14] Companies Act 2006 s. 738; see further Fuller, *Corporate Borrowing*, ch. 17.

[15] See B. M. Hannigan, *Company Law* (Lexis Nexis/Butterworths, London, 2003) ch. 23.

[16] See pp. 91–3 below.

[17] See Office of Fair Trading (OFT), *The Protection of Consumer Prepayments: A Discussion Paper* (1984); Cork Report, para. 1052: 'the customer who pays in advance for goods or services to be supplied later extends credit just as surely as the trader who supplies in advance goods or services to be paid for later. There is no essential difference.' See chs. 14 and 15 below.

[18] The OFT has estimated there to be at least 15 million prepayment transactions each year (OFT, *Protection of Consumer Prepayments*, para. 2.12).

[19] Cork Report, para. 1050.

Finally, there is a class of involuntary creditor that should not be forgotten. This is the individual or firm who is owed money because they are entitled to payment from the company in accordance with a court order. Thus victims of corporate torts may be treated as corporate creditors and will have participatory rights in an insolvency.

How to borrow

Credit arrangements are complex and, as will be discussed below, are exploding in complexity. It is, therefore, useful before proceeding further to map out the main legal methods – or building blocks – of borrowing. This will give a picture of the array of options that are open to companies seeking funds. It should be repeated first, however, that not all ways of raising money involve credit. As we will see below, companies can raise finance through the sale of equity shares – a process in which money is put into the company in return for dividends and a hoped-for increase in share value. These shareholders are not creditors of the company, who have rights *against* the company, but owners of the company with rights *in* it.[20]

Credit can be obtained in four main ways: by offering security; by seeking an unsecured loan; by using a sale as a *de facto* security arrangement; and by resort to a third-party guarantee.

Security

When borrowing companies offer security to lenders this may prove attractive to the latter because, *inter alia*, it reduces their loan risks by giving them privileged claims to repayment in the event of the borrowing company's insolvency.[21] The normal rule in a corporate insolvency is

---

[20] Capital in modern company law is used to cover not only share capital provided by the proprietors but also the loan capital provided by the creditors. On shareholders viewed as owners of the company see, for example, H. Butler, 'The Contractual Theory of the Corporation' (1989) 11 Geo. Mason UL Rev. 99. On different characterisations of the nature of a shareholder's interest see E. Ferran, *Company Law and Corporate Finance* (Oxford University Press, Oxford, 1999) pp. 131–3.

[21] On varieties of security see generally Fuller, *Corporate Borrowing*, ch. 6; A. L. Diamond, *A Review of Security Interests in Property* (DTI, HMSO, London, 1989) ('Diamond Report'). Note the lack of rationality in the use of the term 'security' in England, i.e. the lack of distinction between the security agreement which creates the security and the property securing the obligation: see R. Cranston, *Principles of Banking Law* (2nd edn, Oxford University Press, Oxford, 2002) p. 399. On the effect of security in general see Cork Report, p. 12.

supposedly that all unsecured creditors are treated on an equal footing –
pari passu – and share in insolvency assets *pro rata* according to their
pre-insolvency entitlements or sums they are owed.[22] Security avoids the
effect of *pari passu* distribution by creating rights that have priority over
the claims of unsecured creditors.[23]

Security can arise either consensually or through operation of the law.
There are four forms of consensual security in English law: the pledge;
the contractual lien; the mortgage; and the equitable charge. Pledges
involve the creditor taking possession of the debtor's assets (goods or
documents of title to goods) and retaining these as security until payment of the debt. The early common law demanded actual transfer of
possession to the creditor but the development of the doctrine of constructive possession obviated the need for this.[24] Where a contractual
lien is used to obtain credit, the borrower gives the creditor, by contract, a
power to detain goods already in the creditor's possession for non-
security reasons and to use these as security for payment. This position
might arise, for instance, where the creditor possesses an item of machinery in order to carry out maintenance work. A lien differs from a pledge
in conveying a power to detain the goods rather than sell them on default
by the borrower.[25]

A mortgage of chattels transfers ownership to the creditor as security
on a condition (express or implied) that there shall be reconveyance to
the debtor once the secured sum has been repaid. In the case of land,
however, a mortgage interest can be hived off from a fee simple so that
land mortgages do not involve complete transfers of ownership and both
mortgagor and mortgagee have concurrent legal estates (fee simple
possession) and they can be applied to all classes of asset, tangible and
intangible. They are, accordingly, of enormous utility to borrowers.

---

[22] On *pari passu* see chs. 14 and 15 below; D. Milman, 'Priority Rights on Corporate
Insolvency' in A. Clarke (ed.), *Current Issues in Insolvency Law* (Stevens & Sons,
London, 1991).

[23] See Cork Report, ch. 35, paras. 149–97; Goode, *Commercial Law*, part IV.

[24] See I. Snaith, *The Law of Corporate Insolvency* (Waterlow, London, 1990) pp. 12–13, 24–8.

[25] See Goode, *Commercial Law*, p. 585; but see *Re Hamlet International plc* [1998] 2 BCLC
164, where a contractual possessory lien over goods, granted by a customer to a
company, coupled with a contractual right entitling the company to sell such goods to
pay sums owed to it by the customer, did *not* constitute a charge registrable under the
Companies Act 1985 s. 395 (see now Companies Act 2006 s. 860). On registration of
company charges generally see H. Beale, M. Bridge, L. Gullifer and E. Lomnicka, *The Law
of Personal Property Security* (Oxford University Press, Oxford, 2007).

The use of an equitable charge allows debtors to agree that certain specific items of their property will be available as security for loans. Such a charge does not involve a transfer of ownership or possession; instead it gives the creditor a right to have the designated asset sold to discharge the debt. The equitable charge may be fixed on a particular asset or may be floating. With fixed charges the debtor may dispose of the asset only with the creditor's consent (or by repaying the debt). The floating charge hovers over a stipulated class of assets in which the debtor has present or future interest. The debtor is, however, free to deal with particular assets within the class while the charge remains floating, that is until the point when the charge crystallises and fixes on all the assets then in the fund.[26]

As for security arising through operation of the law ('non-consensual security'), this may be anticipated by the potential corporate debtor and used as a way of establishing a credit arrangement. The main forms of security thus arising are the lien, the statutory charge, the non-contractual right of set-off, the equitable right to trace and procedural securities.[27]

Liens, as noted, give persons in possession of the property of others for the purposes of work a right of retention until the work at issue has been paid for. Liens may arise through the operation of the common law,[28] equity[29] or statute.[30] A statutory charge gives the chargee a right to apply to the court for an order of sale where a debt has not been paid.[31] Both law and equity allow mutual debts between parties to be set off.[32] Equitable tracing allows a person whose asset has been wrongfully

---

[26] Or on assets of the specified description subsequently acquired by the debtor: see Goode, *Commercial Law*, p. 587. Crystallisation arises on the occurrence of a number of events, e.g. the commencement of the winding up of the company, the chargee appointing a receiver under the terms of the charging document or the chargee taking possession of the assets. Crystallisation will also occur where an administrator is appointed by a qualifying floating charge holder under the Insolvency Act 1986 Sch. B1, paras. 2(b), 14.

[27] See generally Snaith, *Law of Corporate Insolvency*, ch. 6; Goode, *Commercial Law*, pp. 619–23.

[28] Some general liens may extend to all goods in the lienee's possession whether the sum payable relates to work done on those goods or other work. Thus solicitors, bankers and others enjoy these liens: see Goode, *Commercial Law*, p. 619.

[29] Which does not require possession, as with the vendor of the land's lien to secure the purchase price.

[30] See also the maritime lien: Goode, *Commercial Law*, p. 621; D. Jackson, 'Foreign Maritime Liens in English Courts: Principle and Policy' [1981] 3 LMCLQ 335.

[31] E.g. the Legal Aid Act 1988 s. 16(6) gave the Law Society a charge on money and property recovered in proceedings by a legally aided litigant to secure payment of Law Society costs.

[32] See ch. 14 below.

disposed of by another to assert a claim to the proceeds received in exchange for it. Finally, procedural securities may operate at law so that a company making a claim through the legal process can apply to have certain of its opponent's assets taken into the custody of the court as security for satisfaction of the claim at issue or, *inter alia*, an order for costs.[33]

Unsecured loans

A company can seek a loan without offering security but in such an arrangement the lender bears the risk that if the debtor company becomes insolvent its own debt will be satisfied after the secured creditors have been paid. The unsecured creditor, moreover, has no enforceable interest in the debtor's property prior to bankruptcy or winding up, only a right to sue for money owed and to enforce a court judgment against the debtor.

Like a secured loan, an unsecured loan may constitute 'loan credit' – the loan of money – or it may be 'sale credit' – where goods or services are supplied to the debtor but payment of the price for these is allowed to be delayed. In practice, however, sale credit in the normal course of trade is more likely to be unsecured than secured. Companies, moreover, may seek either fixed-sum or revolving credit.[34] With the former the debtor takes a fixed amount for a stated period but with revolving credit there is an ongoing facility to draw varying sums within agreed limits.

Quasi-security

Companies can enter into a number of legal relationships that, on their face, appear to be sale arrangements but which operate in practice as security devices.[35] These arrangements may merit the close attention of insolvency lawyers since they can be seen as having roles both in supplementing and in circumventing legal rules and principles covering corporate insolvency. They may, for example, not require registration and the assets involved may not be caught in the insolvency net. The main

---

[33] See Goode, *Commercial Law*, pp. 622–3; D. Milman, 'Security for Costs: Principles and Pragmatism in Corporate Litigation' in B. Rider (ed.), *The Realm of Company Law* (Kluwer, London, 1998) ch. 9. See also ch. 13 below.

[34] See Goode, *Commercial Law*, p. 581. On 'running account credit' see Consumer Credit Act 1974 s. 10(1) (as amended by Consumer Credit Act 2006).

[35] See F. Oditah, *Legal Aspects of Receivables Financing* (Sweet & Maxwell, London, 1991) p. 11; M. G. Bridge, 'Form, Substance and Innovation in Personal Property Security Law' [1992] JBL 1.

devices are reservations of title;[36] hire purchase agreements; sale and lease back; sale and repurchase; and discounting of receivables.[37] The key aspect of these agreements is that the debtor company is able to raise funds by allowing ownership to rest with the 'creditor' rather than offering security, and the 'creditor' avoids having to compete for insolvency assets with other creditors because he or she holds title or has not passed title in the assets at issue to the insolvent company.

With reservations of title, for instance, the goods will be sent to the 'debtor' company by the seller, 'creditor' A, but ownership, it will be stipulated, will not pass until the full price has been paid. If the debtor company becomes insolvent, the goods, whose title remained with A, do not form part of the insolvency assets.[38] In a sale and lease back a similar effect is achieved by the debtor selling an asset to the creditor in return for a sum of money and continuing to use the asset (for example, a warehouse) by leasing it back under a hire or hire purchase agreement.[39] The creditor retains the title throughout and the warehouse does not form part of the insolvency assets or estate. Sale and repurchase offers another variation in which the company sells goods to the debtor company for a price to be paid in instalments. The agreement states that where the debtor defaults, A may repurchase the goods after deducting the amount outstanding from the purchase price. Finally, discounting of receivables (or factoring) involves the purchase of invoiced receivables (sums due under outstanding invoices) at less than their face value. The

---

[36] Surveys reveal that the majority of suppliers employ retention of title clauses in their conditions of sale. J. Spencer, 'The Commercial Realities of Reservation of Title Clauses' [1989] JBL 220, 221 surveyed fifty suppliers and found that 59 per cent of respondents said they used such clauses. Wheeler examined fifteen receiverships and liquidations and found that 92 per cent of suppliers of goods had 'some sort of reservation of title provision': see S. Wheeler, *Reservation of Title Clauses* (Oxford University Press, Oxford, 1991) p. 5.

[37] See Goode, *Commercial Law*, p. 609; Oditah, *Legal Aspects*, pp. 32–5, 50–5; A. Hewitt, 'Asset Finance' (2003) 43 *Bank of England Quarterly Bulletin* 207. See also Goode, *Commercial Law*, pp. 605 ff. on the imposition of conditions on the right to withdraw a deposit and contractual set-off. On charges over credit balances see *Re BCCI (No. 8)* [1997] 3 WLR 909; R. M. Goode, 'Charge-Backs and Legal Fictions' (1998) 114 LQR 178; G. McCormack, 'Charge-Backs and Commercial Certainty in the House of Lords' [1998] CfiLR 111; E. Mujih, 'Legitimising Charge-Backs' [2001] Ins. Law. 3.

[38] See generally Wheeler, *Reservation of Title Clauses*; I. Davies, *Effective Retention of Title* (Fourmat, London, 1991); G. McCormack, *Reservation of Title* (2nd edn, Sweet & Maxwell, London, 1995). See also ch. 15 below.

[39] See J. Ulph, 'Sale and Lease-back Agreements in a World of Title Relativity: *Michael Gerson (Leasing) Ltd* v. *Wilkinson and State Securities Ltd*' (2001) 64 MLR 481.

assignor whose receivables are so discounted receives immediate cash to the extent of the purchase price. The financier deducts an administration charge in addition to the 'discount', which, by being calculated on a daily yield basis, produces a sum equivalent to interest on the amount advanced to the assignor.[40] The company thus receives a cash sum earlier than would have been the case had it waited for its debtors to settle their accounts.

As will be discussed below, however, it is not easy to characterise many quasi-security arrangements and the courts may face difficulties in deciding whether a transaction is, for legal and insolvency purposes, a loan secured by a mortgage or charge, a sale or an outright assignment.[41]

Third-party guarantees

Often a loan from a creditor such as a bank will be 'guaranteed'[42] by a third party – which may be an individual director of the debtor company but could also be a parent or subsidiary company within a group. The Government itself may also act as a guarantor and the UK offers a good deal of credit insurance to exporters through the Export Credits Guarantee Department, which, *inter alia*, guarantees bills of exchange purchased by banks. Guarantees may relate to specific transactions or operate on a continuing basis and relate to a flow of transactions.[43]

The guarantor undertakes to answer for the default of the principal but guarantors can only be sued after the principal debtor's default. Usually the undertaking of the guarantor is to meet the monetary liability arising out of the default, but a guarantor may also assume a secondary liability for performance as stipulated in the contract agreed by the principal. The guarantor is not liable for any amount in excess of that recoverable from the principal debtor and, if the guarantee is given at the request of the debtor, the guarantor has an implied contractual right to be indemnified by the debtor against all liabilities incurred.[44]

---

[40] See Oditah, *Legal Aspects*, p. 34.   [41] Ibid., pp. 35–40.

[42] If A owes B a financial obligation, then instead of, or in addition to, taking a charge on A's property, B may take a contract with a third party, C, under which C promises to meet A's obligation to B if A fails to do so (C being the 'guarantor'). See further R. M. Goode, *Legal Problems of Credit and Security* (3rd edn, Sweet & Maxwell, London, 2003).

[43] See Fuller, *Corporate Borrowing*, ch. 11.

[44] In an insurance arrangement, in contrast, the insurer protects the covered party and there is no right of indemnity against the defaulter: see R. M. Goode, 'Surety and On-Demand Performance Bonds' [1988] JBL 87, 88–9.

Debtors and patterns of borrowing

The above discussion gives an idea of the main sources and credit devices available to borrowers but not of the patterns of borrowing that tend to be encountered in companies. Such patterns are liable to vary according to a number of factors such as the company's needs, size, commercial sector and plans but, bearing this in mind, some generalisations can be made. In doing so it is helpful to distinguish the practices of small and medium enterprises (SMEs) from those of larger companies.

Certain research on SMEs[45] reveals that small businesses tend to rely heavily on internal funds for both operating and investment purposes.[46] Internal sources of finance thus seem to be more attractive than external borrowing. Around 38 per cent of SMEs would appear to seek external finance in a given two-year period, however,[47] with a greater proportion of borrowing by firms of above-average growth rate.[48] Of the SMEs surveyed by Cosh and Hughes for 2002–4, 81 per cent of those who had sought finance externally went to their bank;[49] 38 per cent had sought credit from hire purchase or leasing businesses; 19 per cent went to partners or share-holders; 15 per cent approached factoring businesses; 14 per cent went to venture capitalists; 6 per cent looked to trade customers and around 20 per cent had sought to raise funds by other routes (namely through private individuals or other sources).[50] As for the amount of finance raised by SMEs, the same survey revealed that banks provided 56.9 per cent of this;

---

[45] See Cosh and Hughes 2007; Bank of England 2004. See also J. Freedman and M. Godwin, 'Incorporating the Micro Business: Perceptions and Misperceptions' in A. Hughes and D. Storey (eds.), *Finance and the Small Firm* (Routledge, London, 1994); S. Fraser, *Finance for Small and Medium Enterprises* (Warwick University Centre for Small and Medium Enterprises, 2004) ('Fraser 2004').

[46] See Cosh and Hughes 2007, p. 50; figures for 2004 indicate that the total of external funds sought in 2004 was £1.4 billion.

[47] Ibid. (years 2002–4); Cosh and Hughes 2000 (for years 1997–9). See, however, Fraser 2004 and the survey indicating that 80 per cent of SMEs had used one or more sources of external finance in the previous three years.

[48] See Cosh and Hughes 2007, p. 51. In recent years SMEs have become less reliant on external finance: the 38 per cent figure for SMEs seeking external finance in 2002–4 is down from 65 per cent in 1987–90.

[49] On the advantages of borrowing from banks (expertise, purity of interests, access to advice, interests in stable markets and resources etc.) see B. G. Carruthers and T. C. Halliday, *Rescuing Business: The Making of Corporate Bankruptcy Law in England and the United States* (Clarendon Press, Oxford, 1998) ch. 4.

[50] Cosh and Hughes 2007, pp. 51–3, noting that, compared to the 1997–9 survey, there had been a slight increase in resort to banks and a significant increase in approaches to venture capital firms.

hire purchase/leasing firms, 15.9 per cent; partners and shareholders, 6.5 per cent; factoring businesses, 5.5 per cent; other sources, 7.3 per cent; other private individuals, 2.6 per cent; venture capitalists, 4.4 per cent and trade customers, 0.9 per cent. These figures show a decline in bank finance compared to a similar 1997–9 analysis (from 61.2 per cent to 56.9 per cent), a doubling of factoring (from 2.6 to 5.5 per cent); a more than tripling of venture capital funding (from 1.3 to 4.4 per cent); and a drop in hire purchase/leasing sources (from 22.7 per cent to 15.9 per cent).

Banks thus remain the main providers of credit for SMEs, with more borrowing by term lending than through overdrafts. In the early 1990s the Bank of England expressed concern at the dependence of small businesses on overdraft facilities for purposes other than working capital: for example, to finance long-term business expansion.[51] There has been, since that time, a drift away from overdraft borrowing in favour of term loans. Term lending in 2003 amounted to over £38.9 billion and borrowing on overdrafts was around £9.1 billion. By the end of 2003, overdrafts made up only 23 per cent of small firms' borrowings compared to 25 per cent at the end of 2002.[52] The Bank of England has, nevertheless, acknowledged that the overdraft will 'always be important to small businessmen as a flexible source of working capital'.[53]

Certain kinds of borrowing seem, additionally, to be size dependent. Findings reported in 2007 suggested that micro-companies use venture capital, HP/leasing and factoring significantly less frequently than larger firms and resort to banks more often.[54]

A significant source of SME working capital has been factoring and invoice discounting and, as noted, financing through factoring more than doubled between 1997–9 and 2002–4.[55] An area of modest uptake

---

[51] See Bank of England, *Finance for Small Firms*, Sixth Report (Bank of England, 1999) ('Bank of England 1999') p. 17.

[52] Bank of England 2004, p. 11.

[53] Bank of England 1999, p. 18. In 2002–3 the overall level of overdraft lending rose marginally on the previous year: see Bank of England 2004, p. 11.

[54] See Cosh and Hughes 2007, p. 55.

[55] Ibid., pp. 53–5. Factoring, as noted above, is the purchase by the factor and the sale by a company of book debts on a continuing basis, usually for immediate cash. The sales accounting functions are then provided by the factor who manages the sales ledger and the collection of accounts under the terms agreed by the seller. The factor may assume the credit risk for accounts within agreed limits (non-recourse) or this risk may be retained by the seller. Invoice discounting is the purchase by the discounter and the sale by the company of book debts for immediate cash. The sales accounting functions are retained by the seller and the facility is usually provided on a confidential basis. See Hewitt, 'Asset Finance'. Fraser (2004) suggests that more than half of SMEs use invoice

from SMEs, however, is equity financing, where the evidence is that around 6 per cent of external financing to small businesses in the 2002–4 period involved equity[56] and earlier work suggested that only a third of businesses were even prepared to consider equity financing.[57] There are reasons why smaller enterprises face constraints in using equity to raise finance.[58] First, markets may be reluctant to supply funds in return for equity because they see a willingness to give up equity as a sign of either the equity seller's low confidence in levels of anticipated returns or their having exhausted their ability to raise debt finance. Second, raising equity may be expensive for smaller firms, compared to their larger brethren, because the transaction costs will be relatively high for small investments. Third, investors will want to research the risks involved but, for smaller investments, the costs of such research will be proportionately higher than with larger deals and this may prove off-putting – as may the higher risks posed by smaller companies.

Funding in the UK by the venture capital/private equity industry grew by 28 per cent in 2005 to £6.8 billion (from £5.3 billion in 2004)[59] though figures for 2002–4 suggest that venture capital supplied only 4.4 per cent of total SME finance from external sources.[60] Of total informal venture capital investment, business angel activity, on official figures, makes up only a small proportion.[61] Raising funds through the provision of venture capital often involves investments in high-risk ventures (typically with new companies) and the investor will usually demand a significant equity stake in the enterprise. The expected return is accordingly of capital gain rather than merely income from dividends. Venture capital is frequently used as a

---

discounting and two in five use factoring. In 2008, £16.4 billion was advanced against invoices in the UK: see n. 244 below.

[56] Cosh and Hughes 2007, p. 56.

[57] British Chamber of Commerce, *Small Firm Survey No. 24: Finance* (July 1997).

[58] See Cosh and Hughes 2007, p. 48.

[59] See British Venture Capital Association (BVCA) Annual Report 2006 (London, May 2006).

[60] See Cosh and Hughes 2007.

[61] In 1998–9 around £20 million was invested by business angels in UK companies: Bank of England 2001, p. 5. In 2005 about £29 million was invested in 180 businesses by participating members of the trade association: see BVCA Annual Report 2006. The amount of informal lending by business angels is, however, difficult to quantify since most such angels act anonymously. One estimate is that the UK has 18,000 business angels investing around £500 million annually: see C. Mason and R. Harrison, 'Public Policy and the Development of the Informal Venture Capital Market' in K. Cowling (ed.), *Industrial Policy in Europe: Theoretical Perspectives and Practical Proposals* (Routledge, London, 1999). See also A. Belcher, *Corporate Rescue* (Sweet & Maxwell, London, 1997) pp. 133–4.

source of finance for management buyouts (MBOs) and may well involve the supply of business skills as well as funds.[62]

Credit arrangements such as overdrafts, bank loans, trade credit, leasing and hire purchase can be resorted to by firms of all sizes. Large companies, however, are able, in addition, to secure credit by making use of the capital markets and trading in a huge variety of financial instruments and forms of debt.[63] Thus, use can be made, *inter alia*, of bonds, loan stock, syndicated loans, mezzanine finance, notes and securitisation. A bond[64] involves a contract in which the bondholder lends money to a company and the company agrees to make a series of interest payments ('coupons') until the bond matures – commonly in between seven and thirty years' time. They are usually secured by either fixed or floating charges against the firm's assets. Bonds are tradeable in secondary markets in a variety of arrangements and larger, creditworthy companies are able to use not only domestic bond markets but the foreign bond and the Eurobond markets. Foreign bonds are bonds that are denominated in the country of issue where the issuer is non-resident[65] and Eurobonds (or 'international bonds') are bonds that are traded outside the country of the denominated currency. 'Syndicated loans' are bank loans that spread credit provision across a number of banks, with the originating bank usually managing that syndicate. These loans are normally tradeable in a secondary market. 'Mezzanine' debt offers a high risk / high return mix and may be either secured or unsecured but it will rank below senior loans. It constitutes hybrid financing when it offers lenders a mix of debt and equity and is described as subordinated, intermediate or low grade because it ranks for payment below straight debt but above equity.[66] It is a device that is useful to companies when bank borrowing limits are reached and the firm cannot, or is unwilling to, issue further equity. The term 'mezzanine finance' has, in recent years, tended to be used to refer to high yield / high risk debt that is private rather than gained through a publicly traded bond. Such privately based financing has grown rapidly over the last twenty years and has proved especially attractive to fast-growing companies in the communications and media sectors.[67]

---

[62] See Belcher, *Corporate Rescue*, pp. 131–3.

[63] For a concise outline see Arnold, *Handbook of Corporate Finance*.

[64] The terms 'bond' and 'loan stock' are often used interchangeably.

[65] So that in Japan, bonds issued by non-Japanese companies and denominated in yen (for example, for interest and capital payments) are foreign bonds: see Arnold, *Handbook of Corporate Finance*, p. 430.

[66] Ibid., p. 415. [67] Ibid., p. 416.

Mezzanine financing also has a role in corporate rescues when the creditors of a troubled company may be persuaded to raise leveraging and to effect recapitalisation by accepting a mixture of shares and mezzanine finance – where the high returns attaching to the latter reflect the high risks involved in advancing credit to the firm. 'Junk bonds' involve high risk / high return characteristics and their use has grown dramatically in the USA since the 1980s.[68] The high-yield bond market is, however, yet to develop to the same extent in Europe.

Turning to notes, a medium-term note undertakes to pay the holder a specified sum on the maturity date and interest in the meantime. Such notes are unsecured and may vary widely in terms. A medium-term note programme may provide for the issuing of further bonds under the same documentation (though with a variety of terms and conditions) and this avoids the costs of producing new papers for each stand-alone note (or bond).[69] Finally, note should be taken of securitisation. This involves the marketing of repackaged debt – as where a mortgage lender bundles together its claims to repayment and sells these 'asset-backed securities' to participants in the credit market. This increases liquidity (by replacing long-term assets with cash) but it places a new distance between the borrower and the lender and this may have implications for the monitoring of management and for potential rescues in times of trouble.[70] These matters will be returned to below in discussing the significance of those developments that can be called 'the new capitalism'[71] and in the examination (in part III) of rescue strategies and processes.

Equity and security

Bearing in mind the above fundamentals of borrowing, it is time to consider in more detail how corporate activities can be financed by either equity or credit means and to explore the ways in which different devices serve the needs of healthy and of troubled companies.

---

[68] Where over $100 billion of new issues are now introduced annually. Ibid., p. 415.

[69] Ibid., p. 441. 'Commercial paper' involves shorter terms than the usual medium-term note and promises to the holder that a sum will be paid in a few days and the consideration for the loan is set out by giving the amount paid on redemption a higher value than that of the money advanced for the paper. A high credit rating on the borrower's part is usually required as there is routinely no security involved.

[70] On securitisation see further Fuller, *Corporate Borrowing*, pp. 124–8. See also pp. 133–5 below.

[71] See pp. 133–40 below.

Equity shares

Companies, as noted, can raise funds through the sale of shares either on a flotation or by a subsequent issue. The purchasers of shares have interests in the company and the money they put into the company can be used to buy assets with which to earn profits. If shareholders wish to take their money out of the company, they must sell their shares or force the company into liquidation. The former course of action is more common and relatively easy when the shares are quoted on a stock exchange. If the company is liquidated, the assets of the company are sold, liabilities and insolvency claims are met and the remaining funds are paid out to equity shareholders. These shareholders, as a group, are the last to have their claims met (all other interested parties, be they debenture holders, unsecured creditors or employees, have priority). The ordinary shareholders in a company thus take the greatest risks but they benefit from profits when the firm is successful and if, as is usual, the company is a limited liability company, in times of trouble they are liable only to the amount unpaid on their shares.

The rationale for financing through share capital is that this provides a financial basis for corporate activity: one that, on establishing the company, provides a platform for both commencing operations and seeking funds through non-equity routes such as loans. Whether a going concern raises funds through equity capital or, say, bank borrowing depends on the relative costs. In the case of equity capital, the company management must offer investors at least the annual rate of return that those investors would expect to earn in the market on a share bearing the equivalent level of risk. If a company cannot earn this rate of return it will find it difficult to attract new funds because potential investors will look elsewhere in the marketplace.

If it is assumed that markets are competitive and that a company is able to offer a competitive rate of return to investors, there should be no difficulty in raising equity capital through share sales. This, however, demands such conditions as frictionless exchanges (without transaction costs, taxes or entry/exit constraints); rational behaviour by all players in the market; many buyers and sellers; and a free flow of full, costless information to all parties.

It has been asserted that some institutions, such as the Bank of England, view the equity route as an effective way to raise finance.[72] This may be true in the case of large, established companies, but, as noted

---

[72] W. Hutton, *The State We're In* (Vintage, London, 1996) p. 145.

above, smaller firms may find it much more difficult to finance through equity due to the relatively high transaction and risk appraisal costs in their small-scale offerings. When firms are new, moreover, the market may prefer to look to those with a known record and reputation.

Taxation regimes may also make financing through equity shares less attractive than through loans.[73] If funds are raised through borrowing, the interest paid on a loan can be deducted before payable corporation tax is calculated. Such a deduction will not apply in the case of the rate of return that has to be earned in order to satisfy investors. Loan capital may, as a result, prove cheaper than equity financing and there may accordingly be a bias towards borrowing rather than equity financing. In regard to small businesses it may be the case that investors are reluctant to purchase equity (for reasons discussed above) but, in addition, businesses may be slow to seek financing through equity. Three reasons mooted for such low uptake are the lack of understanding of equity finance among small businesses, the desire of many UK entrepreneurs to avoid sacrificing any degree of ownership, independence or control, even if this could produce higher profits,[74] and a set of cultural factors found in the UK. On the last point, the Bank of England has suggested that a 'fear of failure' may deter business owners from seeking venture capital.[75] To these reasons may be added a fourth: the failure of banks to offer competitively priced equity financing. The Cruickshank review[76] of March 2000 highlighted a number of key barriers to entry in the SME equity markets (including asymmetric information), confirmed the existence of an equity gap for firms which aim to raise between £100,000 and £500,000, and criticised the Small Firms Loan Guarantee Scheme for not

---

[73] For discussion see J. Samuels, F. Wilkes and R. Brayshaw, *Management of Company Finance* (6th edn, International Thompson Business Press, London, 1995) pp. 443, 540–9; Arnold, *Handbook of Corporate Finance*, p. 455.

[74] See Bank of England 2001, p. 44; White Paper, *Our Competitive Future: Building the Knowledge Driven Economy* (Cm 4176, December 1998) para. 2.27. See also P. Poutziouris, F. Chittenden and N. Michaelas, *The Financial Development of Smaller Private and Public SMEs* (Manchester Business School, Manchester, 1999), who reported that only 25 per cent of private companies said that they would consider a flotation on the stock exchange as a way of raising funds for expansion. On the reluctance of US owner-managers to relinquish control see R. Scott, 'A Relational Theory of Secured Financing' (1986) 86 Colum. L Rev. 901, 914; M. C. Jensen and W. H. Meckling, 'Theory of the Firm: Managerial Behaviour, Agency Costs and Ownership Structure' (1976) 3 *Journal of Financial Economics* 305.

[75] Bank of England 2001, p. 44.

[76] D. Cruickshank, *Competition in UK Banking: A Report to the Chancellor of the Exchequer* (HMSO, London, 2000).

addressing these market imperfections. The evidence nevertheless indicates that small businesses will only consider equity finance after internal sources and debt finance have been exhausted. Equity finance, in any event, is seldom used for raising sums of less than £30,000.[77]

From the above there emerge two messages for insolvency lawyers: first, that how shareholders are dealt with in an insolvency will depend very much on the efficiency with which creditors' interests are processed within an insolvency and, second, that there are scant grounds for assuming that corporate financing through the equity route does or will ever do away with a system of credit that can deal efficiently with the needs of both going concerns and companies in trouble.

Secured loan financing

Companies can borrow funds by offering security or by seeking an unsecured loan. The essence of a security interest is that it gives the holder a proprietary claim over assets in order to secure payment of a debt. In contrast, the unsecured creditor will have lent funds to the debtor but will have a personal claim to sue for payment of the debt and the power to use legal processes to enforce any judgment against the debtor. A security interest may, as noted above, be consensual – where it results from the agreement of the parties – or non-consensual – where it arises through the operation of law. Consensual securities include pledges, mortgages, charges and contractual liens. Non-consensual securities can be divided into liens, statutory charges, equitable rights of set-off, equitable rights to trace and procedural securities.[78] It should be emphasised that charges can be equitable or legal. Equitable charges do not involve the transfer of possession or ownership that gives creditors the right to have a designated asset appropriated to discharge their debt. An equitable charge is thus a mere encumbrance and does not involve any conveyance or assignment at law: it can exist only in equity or by statute.

Security may involve establishing real rights over one, some or all of the debtor's assets (a real security) or rights of recourse from a third party who has guaranteed payment to the lender in the event of the debtor's

---

[77] There may, however, be substantial barriers to entry into the public equity markets in the form of fees charged by investment bankers, securities buyers and accountants, and these costs may not be justified where financing needs are modest: see Scott, 'Relational Theory', p. 916.

[78] See further Ferran, *Company Law and Corporate Finance*, ch. 15.

default (a personal security).[79] In this section we consider why security is asked for by creditors and the extent to which the existing legal framework for security serves the needs of healthy and of troubled companies.

Creditors are interested in security as a means of reducing the default risks they face. Before taking security or other protective measures they will be concerned about their position in insolvency and more particularly about the ways in which the shareholders and managers of the company may transfer wealth away from lenders and dilute their potential claims. A number of fears may loom large in their minds.[80] A first worry is that excessive dividend payments may be made, thereby reducing the value of the firm.[81] Second, excessive borrowing may occur when new debt is raised – which may affect the claims of prior debt or, if subordinate, may increase the insolvency risk of all creditors by changing the level of gearing and thus the risks associated with capital structure.[82] Third, assets may be taken outside the company and out of the reach of creditors in an insolvency.[83] Fourth, asset substitutions may occur in a way that alters the risk profile of the firm and disadvantages the creditor (for example, where a move from tangible fixed assets to

[79] See further Snaith, *Law of Corporate Insolvency*, chs. 2–6. Since 1981 the UK Government has, as noted, operated a government-guaranteed loan scheme designed to encourage bankers to lend to small and medium-sized companies that have exhausted normal financing channels. The Government guarantees the banker that, in the event of a default, the Government will repay 75 per cent of outstanding sums. Personal security from the borrower will not be taken but business assets will be expected to be offered as security. The guarantor may or may not go beyond guaranteeing payments and undertake liability for performance of non-monetary obligations. See generally Goode, *Commercial Law*, ch. 30.

[80] See J. Day and P. Taylor, 'The Role of Debt Contracts in UK Corporate Governance' (1998) 2 *Journal of Management and Governance* 171; C. Smith and J. Warner, 'On Financial Contracting: An Analysis of Bond Covenants' (1979) 7 *Journal of Financial Economics* 117; M. Barclay and C. Smith, 'The Priority Structure of Corporate Liabilities' (1995) 50 *Journal of Finance* 899; G. Triantis, 'Financial Slack Policy and the Law of Secured Transactions' (2000) 29 *Journal of Legal Studies* 35. On agency costs generally see Jensen and Meckling, 'Theory of the Firm'.

[81] I.e. if cash flows are directed to dividends rather than investment or the repayment of debt or if assets are sold (for example, by sale and lease-back arrangements) and the proceeds paid in dividends thereby reduce the value of assets available to creditors on break up: see Day and Taylor, 'Role of Debt Contracts', p. 176.

[82] Ibid., pp. 176–7.

[83] On asset dilution see Smith and Warner, 'On Financial Contracting', p. 118; G. Triantis, 'Secured Debt under Conditions of Imperfect Information' (1992) 21 *Journal of Legal Studies* 225, 235.

intangibles takes place).[84] Fifth, underinvestment may occur where managers forgo investments that would benefit lenders[85] (they may, alternatively, engage in inefficient strategies because their central aim is to preserve managerial jobs). Finally, managers may engage in excessive risk-taking.[86] They may borrow money for stated purposes but divert those funds towards use on projects presenting higher financial risks – projects the creditor would not have funded at the given interest rates or perhaps at all.

In responding to these potential problems, creditors can seek security; obtain price protection by trading debts, where possible; spread risks by diversifying; shorten repayment periods;[87] and use covenants in debt contracts.[88] The clauses of the latter can, for instance, be used to restrict levels of dividends or asset disposals or levels of debt.

A major reason for taking security,[89] in this risk-laden context, is thus to establish claims that, on distribution of the insolvent company's assets, will rank above the claims of unsecured creditors. Creditors may also take security in order to gain access to information. This can be achieved by using the threat of realising the security to obtain access to company decision-making. The creditor can thus become privy to managerial decisions, may even be represented on the board[90] and may engage in informed monitoring in order to protect their security.[91] Security may, in addition, give the creditor a right of pursuit so that where the debtor disposes of property that is subject to a charge, a claim may be advanced

---

[84] See R. Green and E. Talmor, 'Asset Substitution and the Agency Costs of Debt Financing' (1986) 10 *Journal of Banking Law* 391; M. Miller, 'Wealth Transfers in Bankruptcy: Some Illustrative Examples' (1977) 41 *Law and Contemporary Problems* 39.

[85] See S. Myers, 'Determinants of Corporate Borrowing' (1977) 5 *Journal of Financial Economics* 147.

[86] See L. Bebchuk and J. Fried, 'The Uneasy Case for the Priority of Secured Claims in Bankruptcy' (1996) 105 Yale LJ 857, 873–5; Triantis, 'Secured Debt under Conditions of Imperfect Information', pp. 237–8.

[87] See B. Cheffins, *Company Law: Theory, Structure and Operation* (Clarendon Press, Oxford, 1997) p. 74.

[88] See Day and Taylor, 'Role of Debt Contracts'.

[89] See R. M. Goode, 'Is the Law Too Favourable to Secured Creditors?' (1983–4) 8 Canadian Bus. LJ 53. See also Diamond Report (1989). Security may also be attractive to creditors because it gives powers of enforcement (fear of which often leads debtors to give priority of performance to secured creditors); it allows the secured creditor to prevent seizure of secured assets by other creditors; and it may also allow pursuit where the secured assets are sold to another party. See Diamond Report, pp. 9–10.

[90] See further V. Finch, 'Company Directors: Who Cares About Skill and Care?' (1992) 55 MLR 179, 189–95.

[91] On monitoring see pp. 95–9, 102–6, 121 below.

against the proceeds of that disposition. The creditor may also seek
security in order to increase their influence over the market behaviour
of the debtor. A charge, for instance, may be so all-embracing as to give
the charge holder what amounts in practice to an exclusive right to
supply the debtor with credit in that potential second financiers will be
deterred from lending by the breadth of the existing charge. A creditor
may, furthermore, take security as an alternative to expending resources
on gaining such information as will allow him or her to quantify the
financial risk involved in lending. Both the taking of security and the
collection and analysis of information provide ways to limit and calculate
risks, but in some circumstances the former route may be preferred to the
latter on the grounds that it involves lower costs and greater certainty.
Finally, a creditor (A) may fear that if it is unsecured, some other, more
aggressive, unsecured creditors will act too quickly against the debtor
company when it faces hard times and that this may prejudice the
company's survival and the repayment of the debt owed to creditor A.
Creditor A may thus be motivated to seek security in order to discourage
or protect against such precipitate action by unsecured creditors.

Bearing in mind the above attractions of security, it might be asked:
why do not all creditors always demand security when advancing goods
or money?[92] A first reason is that the costs of negotiating security may be
excessive given the financial risk involved. Thus, where a trade creditor
advances, say, a small stock of timber to a building firm for later
payment, the sums involved may not justify the costs of drawing up a
security agreement.[93] Other reasons for not taking security may be the
unfamiliarity of the small trade creditor with legal arrangements; the
custom of informality within trading relationships; the timescales being
worked to (with a large number of items being supplied at a high
frequency); and the anticipated high costs of monitoring security
arrangements.[94]

Finally, the relative bargaining positions of the debtor and creditor
may come into play and large corporate debtors with unimpeachable
creditworthiness may insist on loans without security. If both parties are
rational and informed, however, even the most powerful debtor is likely

---

[92] See Carruthers and Halliday, *Rescuing Business*, p. 163.
[93] Supplies may, however, be delivered under retention of title clauses: see pp. 125–7 and
ch. 15 below.
[94] See Carruthers and Halliday, *Rescuing Business*, pp. 305–6; Cheffins, *Company Law*,
p. 82.

to be presented with a choice by the creditor: between a certain interest rate in combination with security and a higher interest rate without security. The rational creditor will set the difference in rates after calculating the extra risks of non-repayment that a lack of security brings. In choosing which of the options to accept, the debtor will calculate whether the extra interest attending the unsecured loan is a greater cost than is involved in negotiating security and implementing a security agreement. The interest difference will tend to be smaller with a large, reputable firm and a short-term loan than with a small, newly established firm seeking a long-term loan. (The extra risk to the unsecured creditor is smaller and more easily calculated in the former instance.) The costs of the interest difference will, in all cases, rise with the size of the loan. The expenses to the debtor of negotiating and implementing the security will perhaps vary to a lesser degree according to the size and reputation of the firm and would be unlikely to rise in a manner directly proportional to the size of the loan or security (the costs of drawing up the legal documents will seldom vary directly with the sum at issue). Overall, then, one would expect security to be demanded most often by creditors who are dealing with small firms with poor or non-assessable reputations and who seek large sums over long terms.

Fixed charge financing

A fixed charge attaches, as soon as it is created, to a particular property and the holder of the charge has an immediate security over that property. In a corporate insolvency the holders of fixed charges are the first to be paid out of the insolvency estate. A company that raises money by offering the security of a fixed charge may, moreover, not sell or otherwise deal with the property at issue without the consent of the charge holder. The floating charge, in contrast, attaches to a designated class of assets in which the debtor has, or may have in the future, an interest.[95] The debtor, in the case of a floating charge, may deal with any of the property subject to the charge in the ordinary course of business.

The most common fixed charge securities created by companies are legal mortgages over land. Equitable mortgages can also be given over land or equitable interests in land and a fixed charge on chattels can be made by a company but this has to be registered in the Companies Registry. Intangible property, such as shares in another company, can also be the subject of a fixed charge.

---

[95] See pp. 92–4, 117–20 and ch. 15 below; Goode, *Commercial Law*, ch. 25.

Floating charges

The floating charge, as noted, attaches to a class of a company's assets, both present and future, rather than to a stipulated item of property.[96] The assets covered are of a kind that in the ordinary course of business are changing from time to time and it is contemplated that until some step is taken by those interested in the charge, the company may carry on business in the ordinary way and dispose of all or any of those assets in the course of that business.[97] Central to the floating charge, accordingly, is the notion of crystallisation. The company is free to deal with the property charged until an event occurs that converts the charge into a fixed charge over the relevant assets in the hands of the company at the time. The events that the law treats as crystallising the floating charge are the winding up of the company, the appointment of a receiver, the appointment of an administrator[98] and the cessation of the company's business. Parties to a charge can, on some authorities, also agree contractually that a floating charge created by a debenture may be crystallised automatically on the occurrence of an expressly stated crystallising event.[99]

Floating charges are commonly given over the whole of the undertaking of the borrowing company but the company, nevertheless, may deal with or dispose of such property without the approval of, or even consultation with, the charge holder. The floating charge, as a device, raises serious issues of fairness, notably as regards the balance between the protection it offers to secured creditors and the resultant exposure of the ordinary, unsecured creditor. Such matters, however, will be returned to in chapter 15; here the focal question is economic efficiency.

---

[96] See *Illingworth* v. *Houldsworth* [1904] AC 355; *Robson* v. *Smith* [1895] 2 Ch 118; *Re Yorkshire Woolcombers' Association Ltd* [1903] 2 Ch 284; Cork Report, paras. 102–10. See generally S. Worthington, *Proprietary Interests in Commercial Transactions* (Clarendon Press, Oxford, 1996) ch. 4; Ferran, *Company Law and Corporate Finance*, pp. 507–17; R. Grantham, 'Refloating a Floating Charge' [1997] CfiLR 53; D. Milman and D. Mond, *Security and Corporate Rescue* (Hodgsons, Manchester, 1999) pp. 50–2; Carruthers and Halliday, *Rescuing Business*, pp. 195–210; J. Getzler and J. Payne (eds.), *Company Charges: Spectrum and Beyond* (Oxford University Press, Oxford, 2006).

[97] On freedom to deal in the 'ordinary course of business' see Etherton J in *Ashborder BV* v. *Green Gas Power Ltd* [2005] BCC 634, esp. para. 634.

[98] Under the Insolvency Act 1986 Sch. B1, paras. 2(b), 14; see further Goode, *Commercial Law*, pp. 681–6.

[99] See Goode, *Commercial Law*, pp. 683–4; *Re Brightlife Ltd* [1987] Ch 200; Cork Report, paras. 1575–80.

Why security? The economic efficiency case

Does the law's providing for security lead to an economically efficient use of resources?[100] Here again it is necessary to consider the position in relation to both healthy and troubled companies. In answering the question it will be assumed, in the first instance, that security is offered under a system of full priority – in which security interests prevail over unsecured claims in insolvency. An extended debate has been carried out in the USA on the economic efficiency case for security[101] and a number of commentators from a law and economics background have pointed to a series of advantages of security, notably that it helps companies to raise new capital and it is conducive to economically efficient lending by reducing creditors' investigation and monitoring costs.

Security facilitates the raising of capital   A system of security, with priority, is frequently said to permit the financing of desirable activities that otherwise would not be funded.[102] Thus, where a firm has a low credit rating but gains the opportunity to enter into a profitable activity subject to moderate levels of risk, it may be able to obtain funds by granting security when it would be unable to obtain unsecured loans. From the creditor's point of view, the benefit of a security with priority reduces the risks of lending and such risk reduction will be reflected in a lower interest rate. A strong priority system, furthermore, assures the creditor that the security enjoyed will not be diluted by the debtor's obtaining more loans by offering further security.[103]

---

[100] This discussion draws on V. Finch, 'Security, Insolvency and Risk: Who Pays the Price?' (1999) 62 MLR 633.

[101] See, for example, T. H. Jackson and A. T. Kronman, 'Secured Financing and Priorities Among Creditors' (1979) 88 Yale LJ 1143; R. Barnes, 'The Efficiency Justification for Secured Transactions: Foxes with Soxes and Other Fanciful Stuff' (1993) 42 Kans. L Rev. 13; J. White, 'Efficiency Justifications for Personal Property Security' (1984) 37 Vand. L Rev. 473; W. Bowers, 'Whither What Hits the Fan? Murphy's Law, Bankruptcy Theory and the Elementary Economics of Loss Distribution' (1991) 26 Ga. L Rev. 27; F. Buckley, 'The Bankruptcy Priority Puzzle' (1986) 72 Va. L Rev. 1393; S. Schwarcz, 'The Easy Case for the Priority of Secured Claims in Bankruptcy' (1997) 47 Duke LJ 425; L. LoPucki, 'The Unsecured Creditor's Bargain' (1994) 80 Va. L Rev. 1887; Triantis, 'Financial Slack Policy'; C. Hill, 'Is Secured Debt Efficient?' (2002) 80 Texas L Rev. 1117; J. Westbrook, 'The Control of Wealth in Bankruptcy' (2004) 82 Texas L Rev. 795.

[102] See, for example, S. Harris and C. Mooney, 'A Property Based Theory of Security Interests: Taking Debtors' Choices Seriously' (1994) 80 Va. L Rev. 2021 at 2033, 2037; R. Stulz and H. Johnson, 'An Analysis of Secured Debt' (1985) 14 *Journal of Financial Economics* 501, 515–20.

[103] Priority assured by registration: see Companies Act 2006 Part 25; *Boyle & Birds' Company Law* (6th edn, Jordans, Bristol, 2007) ch. 10. In the USA priority is secured

The fixed charge may encourage institutions such as banks to advance funds to companies but the disadvantage of such a charge, in efficiency terms, is that it restricts the freedom of the company's management to deal with the assets charged in the ordinary course of business. This might not present great difficulty where the company's main asset is land, but where the bulk of assets is represented by machinery, equipment, trading stock and receivables[104] such constraints might inhibit business flexibility at some cost. As for the fixed charge and insolvencies, enforcement issues are relatively simple, assisted by the requirement that such charges be registered.[105]

Turning to the floating charge, the efficiency rationale is that it allows the creation of security on the entire property of the borrowing company and so provides companies with an easy and effective way to raise money by offering considerable security to the lender. At the same time it involves minimum interference in company operations and management. For bankers, the floating charge offers an attractive way to secure loans. It gives them a broad spread of security together with priority over unsecured creditors of the company (commonly trade creditors or customers).[106] Any provider of finance to a company may ask for the security of a floating charge but such charges are normally encountered in the case of banks lending by overdraft or term loan and the purchasers of debentures in the loan stock market. (Such lenders will usually combine fixed charge security over stipulated assets such as land or buildings with a floating charge over the rest of the company's assets and undertaking.)[107]

The Cork Report noted[108] in 1982 that the use of the floating charge was so widespread that the greater part of the loan finance obtained by companies, particularly finance obtained from banks, involved floating charge security and that the majority of materials and stock in trade of the corporate sector was subject to such charges.[109]

under Article 9 UCC by filing: see Bridge, 'Form, Substance and Innovation'; Bridge, 'The Law Commission's Proposals for the Reform of Corporate Security Interests' in Getzler and Payne, *Company Charges*, pp. 269–70; Bridge, 'How Far Is Article 9 Exportable? The English Experience' (1996) 27 Canadian Bus. LJ 196.

[104] See pp. 128–9 below; Oditah, *Legal Aspects*.
[105] See e.g. *Boyle & Birds' Company Law*, ch. 10.
[106] But not with regard to the 'prescribed part' of funds under the Insolvency Act 1986 s. 176A: see pp. 108–10 below.
[107] The fixed charge will give priority over preferential creditors: see ch. 14 below.
[108] Cork Report, para. 104.
[109] In the three banks studied by Franks and Sussman more than 80 per cent of all client companies involved in the rescue study had a floating charge held by the bank and the

As indicated, security offers a way to reduce loan costs by reducing the risks faced by lenders: if the company does meet trouble, the lender with security has a better chance of recovery than would be the case if all creditors drew from the same pool.[110] Such considerations are at their strongest where the form of security offers a level of risk reduction that is quantifiable. In the case of the floating charge there are, however, uncertainties inherent in the device and the relevant law (to be discussed below) which reduce the degree to which such quantification is possible.[111]

Security reduces investigation and monitoring costs A further reason why security is claimed both to encourage lending and to produce economically efficient lending is, as noted, that it can offer the creditor a far more economical means of managing the risks of lending than is potentially provided by an investigation into the creditworthiness of the debtor.[112] The creditor granted a security that covers the amount of the loan is thus well positioned to extend credit at an appropriate interest rate but is not obliged to calculate the probability of default or the

overall security value over the main bank debt averaged 99 per cent: see J. Franks and O. Sussman, 'The Cycle of Corporate Distress, Rescue and Dissolution: A Study of Small and Medium Size UK Companies', IFA Working Paper 306 (2000) p. 3. In a further study of 542 distressed private SMEs ('Financial Distress and Bank Restructuring of Small to Medium Size UK Companies' (2005) 9 *Review of Finance* 65) Franks and Sussman found that 'in almost every case the bank was the prime lender ... Virtually all of the banks' loans were secured by either a fixed or floating charge or – often – both': 'The Economics of English Insolvency: Recent Developments' in Getzler and Payne, *Company Charges*, p. 257. On limitations on the attractiveness of the floating charge post-Enterprise Act 2002 see ch. 9 below.

[110] R3's 12th Survey, *Corporate Insolvency in the United Kingdom* (R3, London, 2004), indicated that in 2002–3 (before the reforms of the Enterprise Act 2002) the overall returns from CVAs were 50% to secured creditors, 17% to unsecured creditors and 100% to preferential creditors; from administrative receivership the returns were 49.9% to secured creditors, 5.4% to unsecured creditors and 37.4% to preferential creditors; from liquidations (compulsory and creditors' voluntary) they were 53.4% to secured creditors, 10% to unsecured creditors and 50.2% to preferential creditors; from administration they were 53% to secured creditors, 6.3% to unsecured creditors and 17% to preferential creditors. Franks and Sussman ('Cycle of Corporate Distress') reported that recovery rates for banks were 77% compared with 'close to zero' for trade creditors and 27% for preferential creditors and that, regarding the SMEs surveyed ('Economics of English Insolvency'), the banks recovered on 'average around 75% (median of 94%) of the face value of their debt' with 'other creditors, such as trade creditors, recovering very little, about 3%, unless their loans are secured against specific collateral'.

[111] See pp. 117–20 below.

[112] See Bebchuk and Fried, 'Uneasy Case', p. 914; Buckley, 'Bankruptcy Priority Puzzle', pp. 1421–2.

expected value of its share of the borrower's assets in insolvency.[113] What the taking of security does not rule out, however, is the need to calculate the probability that corporate managers will devalue that security by such practices as asset substitution.

Security has also been said to reduce the risks of lending by encouraging broadly beneficial monitoring. Security, it is thus argued, can help to counter the tendency to produce overall efficiency losses when a firm's shareholders and managers pursue certain activities in an attempt to maximise shareholder returns but in doing so increase the expected losses to creditors as a whole by a greater amount than the expected shareholder gains.[114] Monitoring provides a response to such risks. Thus the creditor with security can seek to acquire information from the company in order to determine the probability of, say, asset substitution and, in doing so, may bring pressure on the company in a manner that encourages fiscally prudent behaviour.[115] Such a secured creditor may accordingly demand the production of periodic financial statements and may go so far as to place a representative on the debtor company's board.[116] This creditor may react to such information by adjusting its estimation of risk and changing the interest rate charged or even adjusting the period of the loan to demand early repayment.[117] In more interventionist mode, the creditor may take the additional precaution of imposing contractual limitations on the kinds of conduct or dealings that the debtor may engage in. Where the security exists but is incomplete (or where a secured creditor is reluctant to enforce security because

---

[113] This point assumes that the lender is not concerned about the resource or reputational costs of having to enforce their security.

[114] Bebchuk and Fried, 'Uneasy Case', p. 874.

[115] On security being taken for 'active' rather than 'passive' reasons see Scott, 'Relational Theory', p. 950: 'the function of secured credit is conceived within the industry as enabling the creditor to influence debtor actions prior to the onset of business failure. This conception is markedly different in effect from the traditional vision of collateral as a residual asset claim upon default and insolvency.'

[116] See Finch, 'Company Directors', pp. 189–95. On creditor monitoring and corporate governance see G. Triantis and R. Daniels, 'The Role of Debt in Interactive Corporate Governance' (1995) 83 Calif. L Rev. 1073. On creditor control over financially embarrassed corporations see S. Gilson and M. Vetsuypens, 'Creditor Control in Financially Distressed Firms: Empirical Evidence' (1994) 72 Wash. ULQ 1005.

[117] Another option may be to purchase insurance to cover losses arising from default: see Cheffins, *Company Law*, p. 75. Yet a further strategy for the creditor is to reduce risks by diversification in the lending portfolio. As noted, however, a creditor's incentive to monitor will reduce as the number of its debtors increases and the average loan sum diminishes.

of high transaction costs or reputational concerns) it might be expected that restrictions on management might, as noted, deal with limits on dividend payments, the maximum gearing of the company and the disposition of assets. Such clauses, however, can only offer incomplete protection for creditors since anticipating the kind of conduct that may prejudice their interests can be extremely difficult and it may be costly to draft such terms and to monitor and enforce compliance.[118] Competition in the loan market may, furthermore, limit the creditors' ability to impose such constraints: the average trade creditor, for instance, does not normally attempt to draft contracts on a transaction-specific basis. Normal trading arrangements may involve sums of money that are too small and timescales that are too short to justify extensive contractual stipulations.[119] The dilution of assets may also be subject to legal restriction[120] but those in control of a firm may still enjoy consider-able discretion in deciding whether to transfer assets to shareholders and, without the probability of sustained monitoring and enforcement, legal restrictions may offer only weak deterrence.

At this point it is worth considering when a creditor will possess an incentive to monitor a debtor's behaviour.[121] Here the key is the balance between monitoring costs and the size of the loan. Monitoring will be worthwhile if it costs less than the anticipated gain in risk reduction where the latter is calculated by multiplying the diminution in the probability of non-recovery that monitoring will produce and the size of the potential non-payment. It follows that small loans will justify only modest levels of monitoring.

Security is said to be liable to reduce the overall costs of creditor monitoring where a number of creditors have different levels of pre-existing information and monitoring costs.[122] Some creditors (for

---

[118] See generally Day and Taylor, 'Role of Debt Contracts'; Smith and Warner, 'On Financial Contracting'.

[119] See V. Finch, 'Creditors' Interests and Directors' Obligations' in S. Sheikh and W. Rees (eds.), *Corporate Governance and Corporate Control* (Cavendish, London, 1995) pp. 133–4; Bebchuk and Fried, 'Uneasy Case', pp. 886–7.

[120] See Companies Act 2006 ss. 641, 645, 646, 648–53; Second Council Directive 77/91/EEC of 13 December 1976, OJ 1997, No. L26/1; Insolvency Act 1986 ss. 238, 239, 423. See also P. L. Davies, 'Legal Capital in Private Companies in Great Britain' (1998) 8 *Die Aktien Gesellschaft* 346.

[121] See Jackson and Kronman, 'Secured Financing', pp. 1160–1. See further J. Armour, 'Should We Redistribute in Insolvency?' in Getzler and Payne, *Company Charges*, pp. 208–12.

[122] Jackson and Kronman, 'Secured Financing', pp. 1160–1; Scott, 'Relational Theory', pp. 930–1.

example, trade creditors) with continuing and day-to-day relationships with their debtors may enjoy low monitoring costs and may reduce their lending risks by utilising their stock of knowledge on debtor credit-worthiness. Where such monitoring serves to encourage financially prudent management this will benefit the whole body of creditors.[123] Other creditors, such as banks, may not possess such bodies of information and it may be cheaper for them to reduce risks by taking security than by detailed monitoring.[124] Providing potential creditors with the choice of secured or unsecured loans thus may encourage economically efficient lending by allowing creditors to choose the lowest-cost ways of reducing risks and so of lending. The end result, it is suggested by proponents of security, will be a reduction of total monitoring and lending costs.[125]

A further suggested economic efficiency offered by security is the opportunity for creditors to develop an expertise in monitoring a parti-cular asset or type of asset and, accordingly, to limit monitoring costs by avoiding the need to monitor the total array of the company's financial activities.[126] Finally, it can be argued that, at least in some circumstances, the granting of security can serve to demarcate monitoring functions in a manner that proves more economically efficient than regimes in which many creditors all replicate monitoring efforts. Thus, where security is fixed over a key asset and control of this will benefit all creditors by fostering prudent management more broadly, there is an avoidance of duplicated monitoring and the markets will reward monitors and non-monitors appropriately by compensating secured monitors with prior interests in the debtor's assets and by allowing unsecured non-monitors to charge low interest rates that do not have to reflect monitoring costs. The overall efficiency arises because even if such 'key asset' arrangements are not the norm, the opportunity of offering security allows the market to choose such arrangements where they lower costs all round.

Would such monitoring efficiencies not be achieved in the absence of security? Would the parties involved not simply negotiate the

---

[123] See Triantis and Daniels, 'Role of Debt', p. 1080.
[124] See, however, ibid., pp. 1082–8, where banks are seen as playing the 'principal role in controlling managerial slack'; Scott, 'Relational Theory'.
[125] See, for example, Jackson and Kronman, 'Secured Financing'.
[126] See D. G. Baird and T. Jackson, *Cases, Problems and Materials on Security Interests in Personal Property* (Foundation Press, Mineola, N.Y., 1987) pp. 324–8; White, 'Efficiency Justifications'; Armour, 'Should We Redistribute in Insolvency?', p. 211.

contractual arrangements that best allow them to reduce risks?[127] The argument for security here is that it provides lower transaction costs than other arrangements.[128] This is argued to be the case not least because any attempts by creditors to negotiate priority relationships between themselves would be beset by free-rider and hold-out problems, especially where a firm's creditors are numerous.[129]

The efficiency case against security

The incentive to finance economically efficiently   The core objection to the provision of security is that when corporate debtor A arranges a secured loan with creditor B this may prejudice the interests of non-involved third parties C, D and E and may create incentives to corporate economic inefficiency. Such an arrangement has the effect of transferring insolvency value from C, D and E to B because C, D and E are not in a position to adjust their claims against A or the interest rates they charge.[130] This inability to adjust may occur for a number of reasons. The creditor may be involuntary, as where a party is injured by the company and is a tort claimant with an unsecured claim against the company. Such involuntary creditors cannot adjust their claims to reflect the creation of a security interest.[131]

The inability to adjust may also be a practical rather than a legal matter. Thus, voluntary creditors with small claims against the firm (for example, trade creditors, employees and customers) may not have interests of a size that would justify the expenses involved in adjusting the terms of their loans with the company and in negotiating these changes with the company. Such expenses, indeed, might be considerable and would involve expenditure to gain information on the company's level of secured debt, its likelihood of insolvency, its expected insolvency value and the extent of its own unsecured loan.[132] In practice, small

---

[127] See Jackson and Kronman, 'Secured Financing', p. 115; Day and Taylor, 'Role of Debt Contracts'.

[128] Compare with A. Schwartz, 'A Theory of Loan Priorities' (1989) 18 *Journal of Legal Studies* 209.

[129] See S. Levmore, 'Monitors and Freeriders in Commercial and Corporate Settings' (1982) 92 Yale LJ 49, 53–5; Scott, 'Relational Theory', pp. 909–11; Armour, 'Should We Redistribute in Insolvency?', pp. 212–15.

[130] See Bebchuk and Fried, 'Uneasy Case', pp. 882–7.

[131] See LoPucki, 'Unsecured Creditor's Bargain', pp. 1898–9; J. Scott, 'Bankruptcy, Secured Debt and Optimal Capital Structure' (1977) 32 *Journal of Financial Law* 2–3; P. Shupack, 'Solving the Puzzle of Secured Transactions' (1989) 41 Rutgers L Rev. 1067, 1094–5.

[132] Bebchuk and Fried, 'Uneasy Case', p. 885.

creditors may suffer from a degree of competition in the marketplace that rules out the negotiation of arrangements that adequately reflect risks.[133] If a small supplier of, say, tiles for roofing work is considering adjusting the terms on which credit is offered, that supplier may anticipate that competing small tile firms, who are ill-informed and cavalier concerning risks, may be willing to offer terms that undercut it in the market. The supplier will, accordingly, feel that it cannot adjust and, indeed, that resources spent on evaluating the need for adjustment (and its rational extent) would be wasted.

Trade creditors tend not to look to the risks posed by individual debtors but will charge uniform interest rates to their customers. It could be argued, nevertheless, that those trade creditors who are successful are those who build into their prices an interest rate element that, in a broad-brush manner, reflects averaged-out insolvency risks. They may, for instance, adjust their prices periodically until they produce an acceptable return on investment.[134] The effect is to compensate, at least over a period of time, for difficulties of adjustment. This, it could be contended, is economically efficient because, within reasonable bounds, even small, unsecured creditors manage to attune rates to reflect average risks.

A first difficulty with this argument, however, is that it assumes a level of stability in the trade sector and leaves out of account those trade creditors who have gone out of business through their failures to adjust, perhaps in their early weeks and years. These lost enterprises involve costs to society. The argument also leaves out of account those ill-informed and involuntary parties who cannot adjust by averaging processes or by learning from the market. Many trade creditors, for example, will operate in dispersed, changing markets in which learning is difficult, the process of matching prices to risks may take a long time and may be delayed, distorted or prevented by changes of actors and the arrival in the market of numbers of unsophisticated operators who fail adequately to consider risks. As LoPucki concludes: 'With a constant flow of new suckers and poor information flows, there is no *a priori* reason why the markets for unsecured credit cannot persistently underestimate the risk, resulting in a permanent subsidy to borrowers.'[135]

---

[133] See J. Hudson, 'The Case Against Secured Lending' (1995) 15 *International Review of Law and Economics* 47.

[134] See Buckley, 'Bankruptcy Priority Puzzle', pp. 1410–11 and cf. LoPucki, 'Unsecured Creditor's Bargain', pp. 1955–8.

[135] LoPucki, 'Unsecured Creditor's Bargain', p. 1956; Armour, 'Should We Redistribute in Insolvency?', pp. 212–15.

Second, those who do adjust by 'averaging' approaches to pricing credit may be adjusting to economically inefficient distributions of risk. Thus, if risks are placed disproportionately on the shoulders of those who can only adjust by averaging methods, the heavy-risk bearers are liable to be the unsecured creditors who are least able to manage, absorb and survive financial risks and shocks. Even if rough adjustment by averaging was able to compensate for the sum, in pounds sterling, of the expected insolvency losses, small trade creditors would be unlikely to take on board the potential shock effect on their company of a debtor's insolvency. They are like ships' officers who can calculate the expected size of a hull fracture but not whether it will be above or below the waterline. There is an efficiency case for placing risks on those best able to calculate their precise extent, best able to survive them and most likely to avoid the further costs of shock: in short to place risks where they can be managed at lowest cost. The loading of risks on 'averaging' adjusters is not consistent with that approach.

Finally, the loading of risks onto small, unsecured creditors may cause competitive distortions that are economically inefficient. To give a simplified example, suppose a debtor company is in the house construction business and is considering whether to fit traditional timber or aluminium double-glazed windows in its new houses. It may buy timber windows on credit from a small, efficient carpentry company that does not demand security or aluminium frames from a multinational double-glazing firm whose lawyers insist on security. If the carpentry company adjusts its prices to reflect its high default risks (by a rule of thumb method) and *by virtue of so doing* charges more for windows than the multinational firm, the contractor will obtain the window frames on account from the multinational firm, in spite of the carpentry company having been the more efficient manufacturer. The allocation of risks has produced the distorted, and economically inefficient, purchasing decision.

Creditors, similarly, who grant unsecured loans on fixed interest rates will be in no position to adjust to the creation of new security interests by corporate debtor A. The resultant effect of such non-adjustment is that debtor A, in deciding to encumber further assets, knows that a group of creditors will not adjust their terms or rates. It is thus in a position to 'sell' some of its insolvency value to the secured creditor in return for a reduced interest rate.[136]

Such a favouring of the secured creditor will prove economically inefficient in so far as corporate decision-makers will have incentives to

---

[136] Bebchuk and Fried, 'Uneasy Case', p. 887.

act so as to increase value to shareholders and secured creditors even if such increases are less than the losses to non-adjusting creditors in the form of diminutions in their expectations on insolvency.[137] A system of full priority, moreover, will give debtor company A an incentive to create a security so as to transfer value away from non-adjusting creditors in circumstances where the effect is to reduce the total value to be captured by all creditors on an insolvency.

As for the decision-making incentives of corporate managers, a further economic inefficiency may arise in so far as biases in favour of secured creditors may lead both to an excessive resort to secured loans (a resort encouraged by the 'subsidy' from non-adjusting creditors) and to excessively risky decision-taking. Excessive risk taking is liable to occur because a corporate manager, in calculating the risks attaching to any decision, will give insufficient weight to the interests of unsecured creditors. Thus, in balancing the company's potential gains versus losses in any given transaction, the prospect of having to repay non-adjusting creditors less than the full sum borrowed will distort the decision.[138] In social terms, the bearing of excessive risks by unsecured creditors may be especially undesirable since these creditors are frequently small and less able to survive losses than larger creditors, such as banks, who tend to be secured.[139]

Investigation and monitoring   The argument that security encourages information-gathering practices that conduce to economic efficiency can be pressed too far. It has been contended that security benefits all creditors in so far as the ability to gain credit on the basis of security evidences in itself a degree of creditworthiness.[140] A major proponent of

---

[137] On the extent to which different non-adjusting creditors are hurt by the creation of a new security interest see ibid., pp. 894–5; LoPucki, 'Unsecured Creditor's Bargain', pp. 1896–1916. For discussion of the point that numbers of 'non-adjusting' creditors may be too small to be significant see Armour, 'Should We Redistribute in Insolvency?', pp. 214–15.

[138] Bebchuk and Fried, 'Uneasy Case', p. 934; M. White, 'Public Policy Toward Bankruptcy' (1980) 11 *Bell Journal of Economics* 550. Security with priority thus exacerbates those distortions associated with limited liability: see Bebchuk and Fried, 'Uneasy Case', pp. 899–90; H. Hansman and R. Krackman, 'Towards Unlimited Shareholder Liability for Corporate Torts' (1991) 100 Yale LJ 1879; D. Leebron, 'Limited Liability, Tort Victims and Creditors' (1991) 91 Colum. L Rev. 1565.

[139] See Hudson, 'Case Against Secured Lending', p. 61.

[140] A. Schwartz, 'Security Interests and Bankruptcy Priorities: A Review of Current Theories' (1981) 10 *Journal of Legal Studies* 1.

this signalling theory has, however, himself come to question it on the grounds that bad debtors may be both willing and able to mimic the signals of good debtors.[141] Other counter-arguments to the signalling hypothesis are that the security interest may not in reality offer a clear signal since borrowing on a secured, rather than on an unsecured, basis is usually the preference (sometimes the insistence) of the creditor rather than the debtor company, and that the offering of security signals not so much the creditworthiness of the debtor as the nervousness of the relevant lender.[142] It is also doubtful whether any signalling gains out-weigh the costs of secured lending.[143] Other commentators, moreover, have questioned the value of signalling on the grounds that firms may seek credit as much to help with short-term cash flow problems as to finance programmes of capital expansion. Signals relating to the former, rather than the latter, may be of little value to the array of prospective creditors.[144]

The claim that security leads to economically efficient monitoring can also be treated with some caution. The notion that monitoring by a secured creditor will bring spill-over benefits to the advantage of cred-itors as a whole can be responded to by noting that those benefits are liable to be insignificant where creditors are concerned to ensure that there is no dilution of their particular security rather than to encourage good decision-making generally in relation to the company's affairs. This point can be deployed, indeed, to turn the monitoring argument on its head. If security fixes on particular assets, it may offer a disincentive to monitor generally and, even where a specific item of equipment is monitored, the creditor may not examine whether it is being used productively. If, moreover, most small to medium-sized firms possess only one creditor who is sufficiently sophisticated to be able to monitor at all rigorously (as US evidence suggests),[145] the tendency for that creditor

---

[141] Schwartz, 'Theory of Loan Priorities', p. 244.

[142] H. Kripke, 'Law and Economics: Measuring the Economic Efficiency of Commercial Law in a Vacuum of Fact' (1985) 133 U Pa. L Rev. 929, 969–70; M. G. Bridge, 'The *Quistclose* Trust in a World of Secured Transactions' (1992) 12 OJLS 333, 337.

[143] Scott, 'Relational Theory', p. 907, urges that proponents of security have not offered convincing reasons why security offers a means of overcoming informational barriers that is preferable to other mechanisms, such as the development of commercial reputa-tions or long-term financial relationships. See also C. J. Goetz and R. E. Scott, 'Principles of Relational Contracts' (1981) 67 Va. L Rev. 1089, 1099–1111.

[144] See Hudson, 'Case Against Secured Lending', p. 54.

[145] See M. Peterson and R. Rajan, 'The Benefits of Lending Relationships: Evidence from Small Business Data' (1994) 49 *Journal of Finance* 3, 16.

to be the secured creditor means that any inclination to monitor may be easily exaggerated. It can further be objected that it is rash to assume that those in possession of security are well positioned to monitor management behaviour. There may, indeed, be circumstances in which unsecured, but well-informed, trade creditors may be better placed to monitor.[146]

Other factors may also militate against monitoring by secured creditors. They may have little interest in improving the profitability of their debtor company, since, unlike shareholders, they will not enjoy a proportion of profits but face a fixed rate of return.[147] Creditors who lend to a large number of debtors may be reluctant to devote resources to detailed monitoring of each of their debtor companies, and lending institutions may lack the expertise and specialised trade knowledge necessary for assessing managerial performance effectively.[148] Creditors, moreover, may be ill-disposed to monitor because they may consider that a corporate insolvency may result from causes other than mismanagement[149] and that monitoring at best offers only partial protection against insolvency. The creditor may be interested in security principally as a means of limiting the financial consequences to them of insolvency rather than as a mechanism allowing them to intervene in order to prevent corporate disaster.

Close inspection should also be made of the argument that security provides an economically efficient way for different creditors to co-ordinate their monitoring activities and avoid inefficient duplications of effort. If, as noted, small and medium-sized firms tend not to borrow from more than one creditor who is capable of monitoring, there is little need for such co-ordination and its value, accordingly, may be easily overstated.[150] The notion, moreover, that one creditor will benefit from the monitoring signals sent out by another creditor has to be treated with care.[151] Thus, a large creditor such as a bank may end a relationship with

---

[146] Bridge, '*Quistclose* Trust', p. 339; cf. Triantis and Daniels, 'Role of Debt'; Scott, 'Relational Theory'. Nor should it be assumed that monitoring is inevitably beneficial: this will not be the case where the negative effects of monitoring activity (for example, interference and managerial resources expended on responding to monitors) exceed positive effects as exemplified by increased pressures to act prudently.

[147] F. H. Easterbrook and D. R. Fischel, 'Voting in Corporate Law' (1983) 26 *Journal of Law and Economics* 395, 403.

[148] See Finch, 'Company Directors'; Cheffins, *Company Law*, pp. 75–6.

[149] See discussion in ch. 4 below.

[150] See Bebchuk and Fried, 'Uneasy Case', p. 917.

[151] See Triantis and Daniels, 'Role of Debt', pp. 1090–1103.

a debtor and so may send out a signal, but the action may have been taken for reasons unrelated to any assessment of managerial performance (the bank may have negotiated an unfavourable agreement). A bank may, in another context, appear to be happy with management but in reality it is content with its security; it may give distorted signals because it has taken discreet steps to increase its security or shift risks; or a bank may have negotiated policy concessions with the debtor that, again, are unknown to other creditors. Nor can it be assumed that different classes of creditors have common interests that lend harmony to their monitoring efforts. When the debtor company is healthy there may be a degree of commonality in their desires to reduce managerial slackness but when the debtor firm approaches troubled times the different classes of creditors will have divergent interests and misinformation and concealment may infect the monitoring and signalling processes.[152]

Incentives to monitor may, moreover, be undermined by free-rider and uncertainty problems.[153] Thus, in the case of the floating charge, monitoring is liable to be expensive because such a charge commonly covers the entire undertaking of the debtor and this may mean that monitoring in order to detect misbehaviour or calculate risks could involve scrutinising the whole business. It is not possible, as with a fixed charge, to keep an eye on the stipulated asset alone. The competitors of a creditor who spends time and money on monitoring will be able, at little cost, to benefit from such scrutinising and any resultant signalling (for example, through observed adjustments in the interest rates charged by the monitoring creditor). The competitors, accordingly, will be able to undercut the creditor on, for example, the pricing of loans.[154] This free-rider problem gives the initial creditor a disincentive to monitor the debtor's misbehaviour and to compensate for the higher risks that non-monitoring brings by imposing higher rates of interest. The overall effect is that the floating charge may offer a relatively expensive method of securing finance.

Legal difficulties may also compound the problems of those creditors who are secured by floating charges and who wish to lower risks (and interest rates) by monitoring. Close monitoring may render the creditor liable to a wrongful trading charge on the basis of their operating as a

---

[152] Ibid., p. 1111.
[153] See generally Levmore, 'Monitors and Freeriders', pp. 53–5; Scott, 'Relational Theory'.
[154] See Levmore, 'Monitors and Freeriders', pp. 53–5; Scott, 'Relational Theory'.

shadow director.[155] The legal uncertainty attending this issue will again operate as a disincentive to keep rates down by monitoring.

Improving on security and full priority

The above discussion reveals that it is not possible to state in general terms whether the law's providing security will ensure economically efficient outcomes.[156] The key issue is whether the distortions and incentives to inefficiency that are caused by security and priority will, in the specific context, be outweighed by the resultant gains. Individual circumstances, accordingly, have to be considered and the case for security may differ greatly according to variations in such matters as the balance between sophisticated and non-expert creditors; the duration and sizes of loans; the types of companies seeking loans; the numbers of non-adjusting creditors; and the transaction costs involved in negotiating unsecured loans and contractual schemes of priority.

At this point it is necessary to consider whether arrangements other than security and full priority are likely, in some circumstances, to involve a more economically efficient use of resources. A host of suggestions has been put forward[157] but here attention will focus on the most prominently advocated proposals.

Abolition of security   Abolishing security would place all creditors on an equal footing in relation to the post-insolvency distribution of assets and no secured creditor advantages would be provided for.[158] It is to be expected, however, that powerful lenders, such as banks, would collaborate with corporate debtors to circumvent the abolition of security by devising arrangements that would offer them *de facto* priority over less sophisticated lenders. The company seeking finance would have an incentive to enter into such arrangements for the same reason that it would grant security, namely to transfer insolvency value from unsecured creditors to the major lender in order to obtain a loan or a better

---

[155] See Oditah, *Legal Aspects*, p. 17; Insolvency Act 1986 ss. 214, 217(7), 251; *Ex parte Copp* [1989] BCLC 13; *Re PFTZM Ltd* [1995] BCC 280; *Secretary of State for Trade and Industry* v. *Deverell* [2000] 2 WLR 907. On shadow directors see ch. 16 below.

[156] See Westbrook, 'Control of Wealth in Bankruptcy' and his conclusion (p. 842) that the 'efficiency of security' debate is 'inconclusive' and 'also incomplete because the benefits and costs of control in its various aspects have been almost entirely ignored'.

[157] LoPucki, 'Unsecured Creditor's Bargain'; S. Knippenberg, 'The Unsecured Creditor's Bargain: An Essay in Reply, Reprisal or Support' (1994) 80 Va. L Rev. 1967; Bebchuk and Fried, 'Uneasy Case'; Hudson, 'Case Against Secured Lending'.

[158] Hudson, 'Case Against Secured Lending', pp. 57–8.

rate of interest. Firms might thus 'sell' fixed assets to the banks in lease-back arrangements incorporating options to buy the assets back for a very low price when the lease terminates.[159]

Systems of security with priority may, however, provide a lower-cost method of achieving such priority regimes than arrangements depending on the negotiation of ad hoc contracts.[160] This is because, with the former, the legal system is providing ready-made, 'off the shelf' contract rules based on common assumptions about the parties' motives. Transaction costs are reduced because these ready-made arrangements specify the legal consequences of typical bargains.[161] Lower transaction costs in this context can, however, be said to encourage the offering of security and this may increase the extent to which certain creditors suffer from the negative consequences of priority regimes (for example, transfers of insolvency value from non-adjusting, unsecured creditors; biases in investment; excessive risk taking; reduced monitoring incentives). Again the key balance is between the efficiency gains flowing from lower transaction costs versus the efficiency losses from the negative consequences listed.

Fixed fraction regimes   Transfers of value from non-adjusting creditors can be limited by legal stipulations that a given percentage of secured creditors' claims shall be treated as unsecured[162] or that a percentage of the security's net realisable assets shall be made available for distribution among the ordinary unsecured creditors.[163] The Cork Committee proposed a 10 per cent fund in 1982 and section 252 of the

---

[159] Ibid., p. 58; F. Black, 'Bank Funds in an Efficient Market' (1975) *Journal of Financial Economics* 323.

[160] Jackson and Kronman, 'Secured Financing', p. 1157; White, 'Efficiency Justifications'.

[161] See C. J. Goetz and R. E. Scott, 'Liquidated Damages, Penalties and the Just Compensation Principle: Some Notes on an Enforcement Model and a Theory of Efficient Breach' (1977) 77(4) Colum. L Rev. 554, 588; G. Calabresi and A. Melamed, 'Property Rules, Liability Rules and Inalienability: One View of the Cathedral' (1972) 85 Harv. L Rev. 1089.

[162] In which case the secured creditors participate *pari passu* with unsecured creditors in the fund available to unsecured parties: see Bebchuk and Fried, 'Uneasy Case', pp. 909–11.

[163] See Cork Report, paras. 1538–41. Cork's 10 per cent fund applied to floating charges only, not fixed, and an upper limit was to be applied so that unsecured creditors would not receive a greater percentage of debts than the holders of floating charges. Note that the 10 per cent fund needs to be set in the context of a package of revisions proposed by the Cork Committee: see chs. 8, 13 and 15 below. See also DTI White Paper, *Productivity and Enterprise: Insolvency – A Second Chance* (Cm 5234, 2001) ('White Paper, 2001') para. 2.19.

Enterprise Act 2002 inserted a new section 176A into the Insolvency Act 1986 which built on this proposal. The new section applies where a floating charge relates to the property of a company which has gone into liquidation, administration, provisional liquidation or receivership. The section demands that the office holder shall make a 'prescribed part' of the company's net property[164] available for the satisfaction of unsecured debts and shall not distribute this part to the holder of a floating charge unless it exceeds the sum needed to satisfy those unsecured debts. The quantum of the 'prescribed part' (also referred to as the 'ring-fenced sum') is established by Order[165] and has been fixed at 50 per cent of net property where that net property is less than £10,000.[166]

The extent to which a 'prescribed part' rule avoids the problems associated with transfers from non-adjusting, unsecured creditors depends on the percentage of the secured claim that is treated as unsecured. The larger the percentage, the more the problems are avoided, but the less the value of any security taken, the greater the risk that powerful creditors will 'write around' such a rule and resort to alternative modes of achieving the effects of security. As has been pointed out,[167] the effect of a redistribution may be to encourage creditors to take different kinds of security and the consequence of this may be to render unsecured creditors collectively worse off as a result of the prescribed part rules. This may happen because, on the one hand, unsecured creditors will receive a relatively small increase in their expected payout from the prescribed

---

[164]   I.e. the amount of the company's property which would be available, but for s. 176A, to satisfy the claims of floating charge holders: s. 176A(6) IA 1986. In the case of *Permacell Finesse Ltd (in liquidation)* [2008] BCC 208 His Honour Judge Purle QC held that, on a correct interpretation of s. 176A(2)(b) IA 1986, the floating charge holder cannot prove for a share of the prescribed part in respect of its shortfall: noted D. Offord, (2008) 21 *Insolvency Intelligence* 30. See also *Re Airbase (UK) Ltd, Thorniley* v. *Revenue and Customs Commissioner* [2008] BCC 213: noted A. Walters, 'Statutory Redistribution of Floating Charge Assets: Victory (Again) to Revenue and Customs' (2008) 29 Co. Law. 129. See further ch. 15 below.

[165]   To be made by Statutory Instrument and subject to annulment by resolution of either House of Parliament: Insolvency Act 1986 s. 176A(8).

[166]   See Insolvency Act 1986 (Prescribed Part) Order 2003 (SI 2003/2097): 50% of net property where that net property is less than £10,000; above £10,000, then 50% of the first £10,000 in value and 20% of the excess, up to an overall limit of £600,000. The establishment of the prescribed part under s. 176A is seen by some as a *quid pro quo* for the abolition of the Crown's preferential status as a creditor (in the Enterprise Act 2002 s. 251). Ring fencing will not occur, however, unless the company's net realisation-making property is more than the prescribed minimum and unless the office holder thinks the cost of a distribution is not disproportionate to the benefits (IA 1986 s. 176A(3)).

[167]   Armour, ''Should We Redistribute in Insolvency?', p. 223.

part but, on the other hand, if the prescribed part rules encourage a fragmentation of capital structures, this may stand in the way of effective rescues and increase the probabilities of default (which will be the major cause of unsecured creditors' losses). Given such points, Armour raises the question whether it might be desirable to extend the prescribed part policy so that the prescription applies to all security rather than simply to floating charges.[168]

A 'prescribed part' rule, moreover, benefits the group of unsecured creditors as a whole, not merely non-adjusters. This means that unsecured creditors who are able to adjust terms and rates will enjoy a windfall benefit from the 'prescribed part' fund and that not all of such a fund will be available for non-adjusters. A virtue of the 'prescribed part' approach does, however, reside in its certainty. The creditor who takes a floating security knows that, when making an advance, the security is only worth a set percentage of what would otherwise be its expected value. This is unlikely to reduce their willingness to lend significantly (at least where percentages allocated to the unsecured creditors' fund are modest) since interest rates can be adjusted accordingly.[169] If the negative effects of a 'prescribed part' regime on secured lending are likely to be less than the positive gains to unsecured creditors, the case for the device is strong.

A 'prescribed part' fund might also be argued to conduce to efficiency through more rigorous enforcement against corporate managers and the insolvency estate. This is the 'fighting fund' vision which sees the significance of the 'prescribed part' in terms of its providing financial resources to insolvency practitioners so as to allow their 'hot pursuit' of debtors attempting to hide monies or creditors trying to smuggle out assets before they enter into the estate.[170] The overall effect of pursuit, and its possibility, would, on this view, be greater deterrence of aberrant behaviour by corporate directors, a likely increase in the fund of assets

---

[168] Ibid. Armour notes two practical problems in such an extension of the prescription: avoidance strategies relying on asset transfer rather than securities would still be possibilities and a broader prescribed part rule would, unless targeted at non-adjusting creditors, give adjusting unsecured creditors an opportunity to free-ride at secured creditors' expense (pp. 223–4).

[169] The Cork Report took the view that a reduction in willingness to lend could be discounted as a real possibility (ch. 36, paras. 1534–49); Goode, 'Is the Law Too Favourable to Secured Creditors?', p. 67.

[170] See Carruthers and Halliday, *Rescuing Business*, pp. 341–2. See also debates in Standing Committee E, HC, vol. 78, 30 April 1985, cols. 156–8. On funding litigation see ch. 13 below.

available for all creditors and, as a result, a greater chance of unsecured creditors gaining some real return. Economically inefficient insolvency wealth transfers might, accordingly, be reduced as well as insolvency procedures rendered more effective generally.

There is a counter argument, however, from the proponents of the 'concentrated creditor' theory.[171] This theory urges that the use of the floating charge can generate significant and worthwhile efficiencies notably because concentrating a firm's debt finance in the hands of a relatively small number of creditors can reduce total monitoring and decision-making costs. It follows from the concentrated creditor theory that a negative aspect of the 'prescribed part' provisions is that, in so far as they may deter the use of the floating charge, and, as a result, produce a dispersing of credit holdings, they are likely to undermine the advantages of concentration.[172]

Insurance requirements   Fixed fraction or 'prescribed part' regimes, as noted, look to unsecured creditors as a group and avoid distinguishing between adjusters and non-adjusters within that group. Where, however, classes of non-adjusters can be identified, it is possible to compensate these through insurance. It has been argued that companies ought to be compelled to purchase liability insurance against tort claims to the extent that these claims cannot be met from assets.[173] This would control the adverse effects of limited liability: its restricting the compensation available for tort victims, its externalising risks to those victims and its extracting a subsidy from them.[174] Damage awards, in such a scheme, would be met, first, out of any normal liability insurance possessed by the company. To the extent that such insurance proved inadequate, the claim would be made on the assets of the company in the normal way and,

---

[171]   See J. Armour and S. Frisby, 'Rethinking Receivership' (2001) 21 OJLS 73. For further discussion of the theory see ch. 8 below.

[172]   See Armour, 'Should We Redistribute in Insolvency?', p. 215. On the dispersion or 'fragmentation' of credit arrangements see pp. 133–40 and S. Frisby, *Report to the Insolvency Service: Insolvency Outcomes* (Insolvency Service, London, 26 June 2006).

[173]   See B. Pettet, 'Limited Liability: A Principle for the 21st Century?' in M. Freeman and R. Halson (eds.) (1995) 48 *Current Legal Problems* 125.

[174]   Ibid., pp. 147–8; Hansmann and Krackman, 'Towards Unlimited Shareholder Liability'; P. Halpern, M. Trebilcock and M. Turnbull, 'An Economic Analysis of Limited Liability in Corporation Law' (1980) 30 U Toronto LJ 117; F. H. Easterbrook and D. R. Fischel, *The Economic Structure of Corporate Law* (Harvard University Press, Cambridge, Mass., 1991) p. 113; C. D. Stone, 'The Place of Enterprise Liability in the Control of Corporate Conduct' (1980) 90 Yale LJ 1.

finally, if the assets were exhausted and the claim remained, the 'overtop insurance' would cut in and provide funds.[175] Such an insurance regime would not only offer a response to the problems of limited liability, it would also cover the claims of unpaid tort creditors in corporate insolvencies. This insurance route possesses an important advantage over proposals to defer other creditors (including secured creditors) to tort claimants in insolvency.[176] Giving tort victims higher priority in insolvency would act as a considerable deterrent to those institutions considering offering secured loans to a company since they would be faced with the risk of giving way to huge tort claims in the queue for insolvency payouts. In contrast, an insurance requirement would constitute a general business expense that would prove unthreatening to potential creditors. Such a requirement might operate concurrently with a 'prescribed part' fund and tort victims could be excluded from participation in that fund.

The problems of moral hazard that are often linked to insurance would be controlled not merely by the usual premium adjustments that would follow claims but also by the requirement that 'overtop insurance' would come into play only after corporate assets were exhausted.[177] It should be noted, however, that although insurance would provide compensation to tort victims, it would control, not eliminate, moral hazards. Corporate managers would not be fully deterred from tortious actions since risks would be shifted through the insurance mechanisms: in 'overtop' cases the insurer would meet a proportion of the tort costs. Nor can it be assumed that insurers will monitor managerial performance and act in ways that will ensure non-tortious conduct. The extent to which they will do this is liable to turn on such factors as the particular market's propensity to reward a strategy of monitoring.[178] The costs of monitoring have to be reflected in premium adjustments but competitors may undercut the monitor's prices and so deter such watchfulness.

---

[175] Pettet, 'Limited Liability', p. 157.

[176] See, for example, Leebron, 'Limited Liability', pp. 1643–50.

[177] On insurance and moral hazard see S. Shavell, 'On Liability and Insurance' (1982) 13 *Bell Journal of Economics* 120; Shavell, *Economic Analysis of Accident Law* (Harvard University Press, Cambridge, Mass., 1987); R. Rabin, 'Deterrence and the Tort System' in M. Friedman (ed.), *Sanctions and Rewards in the Legal System* (University of Toronto Press, Toronto, 1989).

[178] See V. Finch, 'Personal Accountability and Corporate Control: The Role of Directors' and Officers' Liability Insurance' (1994) 57 MLR 880; C. Holderness, 'Liability Insurers as Corporate Monitors' (1990) 10 *International Review of Law and Economics* 115; P. Cane (ed.), *Atiyah's Accidents, Compensation and the Law* (7th edn, Cambridge University Press, Cambridge, 2006).

The insurance 'solution' would also be limited in a number of other respects. Insurance cover will not always be available to any given company or operation. Where, for instance, companies are small and high-risk, and where moral hazard problems are severe, there may be an absence of willing insurers.[179] Insurance policies, moreover, will have ceilings on the quantum of cover together with a variety of clauses excluding liability on different grounds or allowing policies to be terminated on short notice. It cannot, accordingly, be assumed that all tort victims will be fully compensated for losses.[180]

These cautions concerning insurance do not mean that this is a device of insignificant utility in dealing with tort victims. They do, however, suggest that reforms of this kind should be treated as partial, not complete, answers.[181]

Information requirements   Transfers of insolvency wealth from non-adjusting to secured creditors would be avoided, it could be argued, if unsecured creditors were given such information concerning a debtor as would allow them to fix interest rates and loan terms in a manner truly reflecting risks.[182] One option, accordingly, is to oblige companies seeking credit to identify, when contracting with any potential creditor, any security then operating.[183] Relevant details of such securities might also be demanded: for example, information on whether they cover genuine new value or whether they are to provide current working capital.[184] In the USA it has been proposed that secured creditors who seek to place unsecured creditors in a subordinate position would have to take

---

[179] See Halpern, Trebilcock and Turnbull, 'An Economic Analysis'; Finch, 'Personal Accountability and Corporate Control', pp. 892–4.

[180] See G. Huberman, D. Mayers and C. Smith, 'Optimal Insurance Policy Indemnity Schedules' (1983) 14 *Bell Journal of Economics* 415.

[181] For arguments, *inter alia*, that tort victims' interests are well protected in the UK 'through systems of mandatory insurance for the most empirically significant categories of tort claim, coupled with the Third Parties (Rights Against Insurers) Act 1930', see Armour, 'Should We Redistribute in Insolvency?', p. 214.

[182] See Diamond Report, para. 8.1.5: 'My general approach is based on the notion that the law should make it easier rather than harder for parties to a security agreement … to achieve their objective and the interests of third parties are best served not by prohibiting others from doing what they seek to do but by making information on what has been done readily available and affording them protection against risks that they should not have to face.'

[183] Actual information rather than making creditors rely on the constructive notice of the charges registered in the register of charges as per Companies Act 2006 ss. 860–5, 876.

[184] See Hudson, 'Case Against Secured Lending', p. 58.

reasonable steps to convey their intentions to the unsecured creditors. To this end, the suggestion is that the Article 9 filing system be modified to serve the information needs of all creditors affected by the terms of a security agreement.[185]

There are limitations, however, to the informational solution. Any regime requiring 'reasonable' information-giving would prompt a good deal of litigation and the legal uncertainties involved in reasonableness testing would increase overall credit costs. The supply of information might assist those unsecured creditors who are currently ill-informed and, as a result, are unable to adjust terms and interest rates to cope with securities granted to others; it would not, however, assist creditors who cannot adjust because they are involuntary. (It has been suggested that in the USA at least a quarter of the debt of financially distressed companies is owed to reluctant creditors: tort and product liability victims, government agencies, tax authorities and parties not in the business of extending credit or seeking credit relationships.)[186]

Another limitation of the information approach is that it does little, without further stipulation, to prevent future transfers of value from current unsecured creditors to new secured creditors. When prospective unsecured creditors are given notice of present securities they may adjust accordingly but once the adjustment is made there is vulnerability to any future granting of security.

A further shortcoming of the information approach is that unsecured creditors have to be able to use the information they receive. As already noted, however, the financial sums involved in many loans may, individually, be too small to justify the time and money expended in adjusting loan terms, the constraints of time, contractual terms and competition may rule out adjustment, and the expertise of the unsecured creditor may be insufficient for such purposes.[187] It has been suggested that competent unsecured creditors may well use the information on security that is

---

[185] See LoPucki, 'Unsecured Creditor's Bargain', p. 1948; S. Block-Lieb, 'The Unsecured Creditor's Bargain: A Reply' (1994) 80 Va. L Rev. 1989, 2013.

[186] See LoPucki, 'Unsecured Creditor's Bargain', pp. 1896–7; T. A. Sullivan, E. Warren and J. L. Westbrook, *As We Forgive Our Debtors: Bankruptcy and Consumer Credit in America* (Oxford University Press, New York, 1989) pp. 18, 294. On protecting involuntary creditors see also B. Adler, 'Financial and Political Theories of American Corporate Bankruptcy' (1993) 45 Stanford L Rev. 311; Leebron, 'Limited Liability'; M. Roe, 'Commentary on "On the Nature of Bankruptcy": Bankruptcy, Priority and Economics' (1989) 75 Va. L Rev. 219; C. Painter, 'Note: Tort Creditor Priority in the Secured Credit System: Asbestos Times, the Worst of Times' (1984) 36 Stanford L Rev. 1045.

[187] See Knippenberg, 'Unsecured Creditor's Bargain', pp. 1984–5.

made available and the less competent will free-ride in a manner that allows the price of credit to reflect the existence of security.[188] This, however, is an 'optimistic' view[189] and it cannot be assumed that unsophisticated creditors will find a more streetwise creditor to free-ride on, that the untutored will be justified in spending resources researching the existence of the more knowledgeable, or that there will be markets that will provide such tutoring and guidance on appropriate levels of credit pricing.

No secured lending on existing assets   Unsecured creditors would be protected from dilution of their interests in insolvency if the law provided for security only on non-corporate assets (for example, the houses of the directors/shareholders of the company) or on new capital value (where the security attaches to the new machinery or buildings that are purchased with the loan).[190] In such cases there would be no depletion of the company's assets to the detriment of unsecured creditors in an insolvency and unsecured creditors would be protected even against the granting of new securities. Companies would still be able to raise capital for new projects but such a legal regime would not allow corporate managers to use corporate assets to secure short-term working capital or loans necessary for tiding the company over lean times and cash flow problems. A serious concern, accordingly, might be that any restriction on the capacity of firms to survive difficult times might lead to more frequent insolvencies and overall inefficiency.

An adjustable priority rule   An adjustable priority rule would limit economically inefficient transfers of insolvency value by not making the claims of non-adjusting creditors subordinate to secured claims. Secured claims would, in insolvency, be treated as unsecured to the extent that other creditors' claims are non-adjusting and the extra amount received by non-adjusting creditors would come at the expense of the secured claims. Adjusting unsecured creditors would receive what they would have received under a rule of full priority.[191] It would not be feasible to

---

[188] See Block-Lieb, 'Unsecured Creditor's Bargain: A Reply', pp. 2014–15; cf. Schwartz, 'Security Interests and Bankruptcy Priorities', p. 36.

[189] See Block-Lieb, 'Unsecured Creditor's Bargain: A Reply', p. 2014; Levmore, 'Monitors and Freeriders'; Scott, 'Relational Theory'. Free-riding may, of course, reduce the incentive of the competent creditor to spend resources on processing information.

[190] See Hudson, 'Case Against Secured Lending', p. 60. On purchase money security interests see the discussion in ch. 15 below.

[191] See Bebchuk and Fried, 'Uneasy Case', pp. 905–8.

implement such a regime by seeking to identify in particular instances which creditors had in fact adjusted to each security interest, but it has been suggested that a number of classes of non-adjusting creditors can be identified and reference could be made to these in fixing priorities.[192] The main classes of non-adjusting creditors to be protected might thus include: creditors who extended credit before the creation of the security interest and who lack an adjustment mechanism in their loan contract; and creditors such as employees and customers who are not in the loan business, were not able to consider the security interest when contracting and did not negotiate credit terms with the debtor.[193]

An adjustable priority rule might be less certain than a fixed fraction/ 'prescribed part' rule but it would offer superior protection to non-adjusters. Compared to full priority the adjustable priority rule increases the secured creditor's exposure to risk (security would only offer incomplete protection) and transaction costs would increase in so far as secured creditors would have an incentive to acquire such information about the borrower as would allow them to set interest rates at levels reflecting the more complex and greater risks faced.

Would incentives to offer secured loans be diminished? In relation to tort creditors it has been argued that the prospect of adjusted priorities might alarm prospective creditors considerably because of their potential exposure to risk and the difficulty of quantifying it. Tort creditors may, for these reasons, best be dealt with through insurance mechanisms as discussed. The tax authorities might also be left out of account in an adjusted priority regime since the Inland Revenue is well positioned to spread its risks of non-payment across the taxation system and it may be appropriate to cost a proportion of failed collections into that system.[194] The remaining non-adjusters might be included in an adjustable priority mechanism, however, since they are not unduly threatening to secured lenders. Such a mechanism does weaken security protections but if those giving loans and taking security are sophisticated creditors they will adjust their interest rates, or amounts of security taken, to reflect the increased risks they face and, accordingly, incentives to lend on security may not be reduced materially. The cost of secured credit may increase

---

[192] Ibid., p. 908.
[193] Not included in the list of non-adjusters are tort victims and governmental creditors such as tax authorities. The former might be dealt with by insurance as considered above.
[194] Note that the Enterprise Act 2002 s. 251 largely abolished the preferential status of the Crown as creditor: see further ch. 14 below.

but this is the effect of restricting the economically inefficient transfer of insolvency wealth from non-adjusting to secured creditors. The reduction of such transfers that would result from an adjustable priority rule might, indeed, be expected to limit the incidence of overinvestment in risky activities that is a shortcoming associated with the full priority rule.[195]

Would economically efficient activities be impeded by an adjustable priority rule? This might happen when the efficiency gains of the activity (for example, the increases in wealth produced by an investment in new machinery) are less than the transfer of value to non-adjusting creditors (that is, the boost to the value of non-adjusting claims that flows from the new secured investment). Such circumstances, it has been suggested, will be encountered only rarely and, in any event, may be countered by non-adjusting creditors agreeing mutually beneficial compromises with secured creditors to allow economically efficient investments and activities to take place.[196]

Secured creditors might pursue another course, however, which would weaken the role of an adjustable priority rule. They might enter into sale and lease-back arrangements so as to achieve the effects of security but escape the contribution to non-adjusting creditors involved in the adjustable priority rule. The assets at issue would be sold to the 'creditor' and leased back by the 'debtor'. On the debtor's insolvency the assets would not form part of the insolvency assets and, accordingly, would not be covered by the adjustable priority rule. Such a strategy, it has been said, would be resisted by the courts in the USA, who might consider an arrangement a secured loan even if labelled a 'lease', and would look for a real economic difference between a lease arrangement and a secured loan if it was to be acknowledged as a lease for insolvency purposes.[197] The English courts may be somewhat behind those in the USA in looking to the substance and function of arrangements rather than their form, but it can be argued that they are moving in this direction[198] and are

[195] See Bebchuk and Fried, 'Uneasy Case', pp. 918–19.
[196] Ibid., p. 920; Triantis, 'Secured Debt Under Conditions of Imperfect Information', pp. 248–9.
[197] See Bebchuk and Fried, 'Uneasy Case', p. 927; J. White, 'The Recent Erosion of the Secured Creditor's Rights Through Cases, Rules and Statutory Changes in Bankruptcy Law' (1983) 53 Miss. LJ 389, 420; F. Oditah and A. Zacaroli, 'Chattel Leases and Insolvency' [1997] CfiLR 29.
[198] See Bridge, 'Form, Substance and Innovation'.

increasingly likely to resist the use of sale-based devices that are designed to avoid the rules governing security.[199]

Rethinking the floating charge The floating charge gives a creditor security over present and future assets and commonly covers the entire undertaking of the borrowing company. Its usefulness to companies seeking funds and its attractiveness to creditors has been noted above but attention must be turned to the floating charge's overall efficiency effects. A first matter is the value of a charge that, whatever its label or details, allows companies to trade freely but gives security over all their present and future assets. (The usefulness of such a charge to companies seeking funds has been noted, as has its attractiveness to creditors.) The Cork Committee found the floating charge to be too much a part of the UK financial structure, and too useful, to consider its abolition.[200] The Crowther and Diamond Reports also favoured the availability of such a charge,[201] and the benefits of such charges to companies are so large that abolition is unlikely to enter the policy agenda of a UK government.[202]

The floating charge type of device does, however, give grounds for concern for another reason. It is a mechanism peculiarly conducive to the transfer of insolvency value from unsecured to secured creditors. The charge floats over the assets of the company and, accordingly, its existence ensures to a greater extent than would otherwise be the case that, on insolvency, unsecured creditors are paid out of working capital. The floating charge is an arrangement that might have been designed to allow large lenders to exploit their dominant bargaining positions and to work

---

[199] On the use of other 'devices' to jump the priority queue see ch. 15 below.

[200] See Cork Report, ch. 36, para. 1531; ch. 2, para. 110. In 2001, however, the DTI White Paper (on *Productivity and Enterprise*) proposed measures to ensure the use of collective insolvency procedures instead of administrative receivership, including restriction of the floating charge holder's right to appoint an administrative receiver (White Paper, 2001). Such changes (and the reform of administration) were effected by the Enterprise Act 2002: see chs. 8 and 9 below.

[201] See *Report of the Committee on Consumer Credit* (Lord Crowther, Chair) (Cmnd 4596, HMSO, 1971) ('Crowther Report') para. 5.7.77; Diamond Report, para. 8.1.5.

[202] Especially since the floating charge survives the Law Commission Final Report on *Company Security Interests* (Law Com. No. 296, Cm 6654, 2005) and the reforms of the Companies Act 2006. Some commentators, though, have questioned the need for a device unreplicated in a number of jurisdictions: see Hudson, 'Case Against Secured Lending', p. 61; R. M. Goode, 'The Exodus of the Floating Charge' in D. Feldman and F. Meisel (eds.), *Corporate and Commercial Law: Modern Developments* (Lloyd's of London Press, London, 1996); Goode, 'The Case for Abolition of the Floating Charge' in Getzler and Payne, *Company Charges*.

with the debtor companies so as to transfer wealth from unsecured creditors. The value of the charge to companies and lenders has thus to be weighed against its negative effects on unsecured creditors, and all possible steps have to be taken to reduce such effects or their consequences.[203]

A second worry is that the floating charge, as presently established in English law, is not the most economically efficient mechanism that can be devised to allow companies to combine borrowing on shifting assets with unrestricted commercial operation. A particular difficulty is, as noted above, the uncertainty of the unsystematised law governing its use. As Goode has argued:

> principles and rules extracted with effort from a huge body of case law are no substitute for a modern personal property security statute in which all transactions intended to serve a security function are brought together in a uniform system of regulation with rules of attachment, perfection and priorities being determined by legislative policy rather than by conceptual reasoning.[204]

Uncertainty attends such matters as the criteria applicable in distinguishing between fixed and floating charges (which are subject to different priority rules in relation to preferential claims on a winding up or the appointment of a receiver). On this distinction legal confusion has resulted, *inter alia*, from a good deal of litigation on the validity of claims to proceeds on the buyer's liquidation and from confusion on such points as whether charges on book debts and their proceeds are to be treated as fixed or floating.[205]

Such legal complexities and uncertainties impose considerable transaction costs on debtor companies and creditors and, in turn, lead to inefficiently high credit costs and business expenses.[206] Further uncertainties compound the position. A key weakness of the floating charge, from the holder's perspective, is that there is a risk of subordination to

---

[203] See the discussion of fixed fraction/'prescribed part' regimes, information requirements and adjustable priority rules above.

[204] Goode, 'Exodus of the Floating Charge', p. 201.

[205] See, for example, the contributions in Getzler and Payne, *Company Charges* and the further discussion in ch. 9 below. For discussion of possible limitations on the attractiveness of the floating charge post-Enterprise Act 2002 see also ch. 9 below. On uncertainties attending automatic crystallisation clauses see *Boyle and Birds' Company Law*, pp. 347–50.

[206] See Diamond Report, para. 1.8.

subsequent secured and execution creditors.[207] This means that the security offered by the floating charge is exposed to potential dilution and risks accordingly cannot be assessed. Certain devices (such as negative pledge clauses) can offer floating charge holders some protection against dilution but that protection is not complete.[208] Quasi-security arrangements such as hire purchase contracts may also dilute the value of the floating charge.

Other ways of classifying securities might, it is arguable, prove more satisfactory. Thus it has been suggested that a classification of security might be based on differences in purpose and function, as in Article 9 of the USA's Uniform Commercial Code, rather than the particular form of transaction selected or the location of the legal title.[209] Creditors would be able to take security over all or any part of the debtors' existing or future property, and such issues as perfection requirements (filing or possession) and priority rules would be laid down as matters of legislative policy.

The main advantages of such an approach are said to include its eradication of the uncertainties that arise from the need to distinguish floating from fixed charges.[210] The Article 9 approach still allows debtor

---

[207] A floating charge will be deferred to any subsequent fixed legal or equitable charge created by the company over its assets: *Wheatley* v. *Silkstone and Haigh Moor Coal Co.* (1885) 29 Ch D 715; *Robson* v. *Smith* [1895] 2 Ch 118; and if debts due to the company are subject to a floating charge, the interest of the floating charge holder will be subject to any lien or set-off that the company creates with respect to the charged assets prior to crystallisation. If a creditor has levied and completed execution the debenture holders cannot compel him to restore the money, nor, until the charge has crystallised, can he be restrained from levying execution: *Evans* v. *Rival Granite Quarries* [1910] 2 KB 979.

[208] *Brunton* v. *Electrical Engineering Corp.* [1892] 1 Ch 434; *Robson* v. *Smith* [1895] 2 Ch 118; *English & Scottish Mercantile Investment Co. Ltd* v. *Brunton* [1892] 2 QB 700; *Re Castell & Brown Ltd* [1898] 1 Ch 315; *Re Valletort Sanitary Steam Laundry* [1903] 2 Ch 654.

[209] See Goode, 'Exodus of the Floating Charge' and 'Case for Abolition of the Floating Charge'; Bridge, 'Form, Substance and Innovation' and 'How Far Is Article 9 Exportable?'; R. M. Goode and L. Gower, 'Is Article 9 of the Uniform Commercial Code Exportable? An English Reaction' in J. Ziegel and W. Foster (eds.), *Aspects of Comparative Commercial Law* (Oceana, Montreal, 1969); R. Cuming, 'The Internationalization of Secured Financing Law: The Spreading Influence of the Concepts UCC, Article 9 and its Progeny' in R. Cranston (ed.), *Making Commercial Law: Essays in Honour of Roy Goode* (Clarendon Press, Oxford, 1997); Cuming, 'Canadian Bankruptcy Law: A Secured Creditor's Haven' in J. Ziegel (ed.), *Current Developments in International and Comparative Corporate Insolvency Law* (Clarendon Press, Oxford, 1994). For a view that urges caution in adopting the Article 9 approach see G. McCormack, 'Personal Property Security Law Reform in England and Canada' [2002] JBL 113.

[210] See Goode, 'Exodus of the Floating Charge'.

companies to deal with assets in the ordinary course of business while permitting immediate attachment of the security interest. Priority rules established in legislation would determine the circumstances in which such interests will be overreached by subsequent dealings. The argument thus goes beyond a call to rationalise case law; it urges that the fixed–floating distinction has involved a huge waste of time and expense and that this can be avoided by a unified concept of security.[211]

The counter-argument is that much might be done to clarify the law on floating charges and, in any event, it is easy to exaggerate the extent to which a purposive approach to classifying security will produce a case law that is more predictable and rational than one that emphasises formal origins.[212] Closer attention might, in a purposive approach, be paid to issues of fairness between creditors but that is not to say that efficiency and certainty would necessarily be increased by assessing priority on the basis of broad considerations of function, fairness and practicality. Article 9 jurisdictions have encountered particular difficulties, for instance in separating functional securities from short-term rentals.[213] On balance it can be concluded that there are strong arguments for removing unnecessary uncertainties from the English floating charge framework but it would be rash to assume that alternative approaches as seen in the USA will produce dramatically lower levels of legal contention.

Unsecured loan financing

Companies in the UK tend to rely heavily on short-term financing, far more so than companies in continental Europe, for instance, who make more use of longer-term loans. This short-term financing is usually provided by way

---

[211] See further Law Commission, *Registration of Security Interests: Company Charges and Property other than Land* (Law Com. Consultation Paper No. 164, 2002), *Company Security Interests* (Law Com. Consultative Report No. 176, 2004), *Company Security Interests* (Law Com. No. 296, Cm 6654, 2005); Goode, 'Case for Abolition of the Floating Charge'; Bridge, 'Law Commission Proposals for the Reform of Corporate Security Interests'; the Law Commission's Draft Company Security Regulations 2006; and ch. 15 below.

[212] On formative versus purposive judicial approaches in the competition field see P. P. Craig, 'The Monopolies and Mergers Commission, Competition and Administrative Rationality' in R. Baldwin and C. McCrudden (eds.), *Regulation and Public Law* (Weidenfeld & Nicolson, London, 1987), esp. pp. 210–14 (Article 85 demands a purposive approach).

[213] See Bridge, 'Form, Substance and Innovation'. On fairness issues see ch. 15 below.

of unsecured loans in the form of bank overdrafts, trade credit, bills of exchange, acceptance credits and deferred tax payments.[214]

As noted above, efficiency may not always demand that security be taken for a loan. The costs of creating a security arrangement may not be justified by the sums or risks involved in a transaction and a series of transactions may be progressing with such frequency that there is no opportunity or interval for the negotiation of security.[215]

Flexibility of financing may also be required for maximising wealth creation and this may be catered for by such unsecured borrowing as is offered by clearing bank overdrafts. When sums borrowed are no longer required, the overdraft regime allows them to be repaid quickly. Overdrafts are, moreover, comparatively cheap because the risks to the lender are less than are involved with term loans (advances on overdraft are legally repayable on demand, though banks usually undertake notice periods of, say, six or twelve months) and the loan interest is a tax deductible expense.[216] The ongoing nature of corporate overdrafts may, moreover, lead to continuing relationships between a company and its bank. This relationship will often place the bank in a good position to monitor the company's general strategy, to gain information on managerial decision-making and to assess risks of default. The bank can accordingly request forecasts, monitor financial statements on a monthly basis and watch movements in the overdraft balance on a day-to-day basis.[217] This monitoring and informational position may offer the bank a more economically efficient means of limiting risks than is achievable through the process of negotiating security.

For the company, the downside of the overdraft is that if an overdraft loan is recalled (as it may be on short notice) the firm has to be in a position to repay. This can be difficult where, for instance, the money has been used to purchase fixed assets and the company may be forced to dispose of such assets quickly and for considerable loss if it is to make repayment. Overdraft lending, moreover, may be vulnerable to broad political changes or currents of financial thought. Thus, when governments require banks to restrict lending, overdrafts may be a primary target and companies may face swift curtailments in the availability or extent of their overdrafts.[218]

---

[214] On trade finance and unsecured loans see Cranston, *Principles of Banking Law*, ch. 14.

[215] See Cheffins, *Company Law*, p. 82; Bebchuk and Fried, 'Uneasy Case', pp. 886–7.

[216] Samuels *et al.*, *Management of Company Finance*.   [217] Cheffins, *Company Law*, p. 70.

[218] Triantis and Daniels, 'Role of Debt'; Scott, 'Relational Theory'; Cheffins, *Company Law*, p. 75.

From the early 1990s onwards, the major clearing banks and the Bank of England were, as noted, concerned at the reliance of small companies on overdraft facilities for the purposes of financing long-term business expansion.[219] These worries were prompted by feelings that such use of overdrafts evidenced both a lack of financial planning and an excessive reliance on funds liable to be subject to recall at short notice. The banks were also attempting to come to grips with the high levels of bad debts experienced at the end of the 1980s, with Third World debt problems and with a recession in industrialised countries. The banks' response, as noted above, was to seek to move debtor companies away from overdraft borrowing and into term loans.

The unsecured overdraft is likely, however, to remain the first choice mode of raising short-term flexible finance for most companies. Its flexibility brings a considerable efficiency for the borrower because interest is charged only on the outstanding balance. Any cash flowing into the company will reduce almost instantly the balance of the advance and so the interest that has to be paid.[220] Alternative sources of finance, in contrast, usually involve a fixed sum to be repaid over a fixed term and interest has to be paid on the full sum for the full term.

Other forms of unsecured credit, such as those mentioned above, bring benefits that can be similar to those offered with overdrafts. Thus, the unsecured loans involved in trade credit arrangements offer low transaction costs, they allow credit agreements to be tailored to the particular transacting parties and they make use of information derived from trade relationships (on, for example, creditworthiness) as a way of reducing risks in a manner that is swifter and more economically efficient than resort to security.[221] It should not be assumed, however, that a trade creditor will always be well positioned to assess the broad competence of their debtor's management. A trade creditor's expertise in a specific sector may, for instance, be of limited value in assessing corporate debtor performance in a completely different sphere of operation.[222] Where, of course, the value of a transaction is so small that a trade creditor would

---

[219] See Bank of England, *Finance for Small Firms*, Fifth Report (Bank of England, 1998) p. 17.

[220] Samuels *et al.*, *Management of Company Finance*, p. 561.

[221] J. MacNeil, 'Economic Analysis of Contractual Relations' in P. Burrows and C. Veljanovski (eds.), *The Economic Approach to Law* (Butterworths, London, 1981); B. Klein, 'Vertical Integration, Appropriable Rents and the Competitive Contracting Process' (1978) 21 *Journal of Law and Economics* 297.

[222] See Finch, 'Company Directors', p. 191.

not rationally engage in the expense of monitoring the debtor,[223] the unsecured loan may still prove more economically efficient than taking security: the trade creditor may simply charge an interest rate that they hope will cover the risks of default.

Unsecured loans can assist wealth creation in another way – by assisting in the flow of money. To take an example, a supplier of machinery, in sending goods to a customer overseas, may accept a bill of exchange in the form of a cheque post-dated to a time after the arrival of the goods at their destination. The buyer of the goods can thus delay payment of the bill until the goods arrive but the seller can obtain cash immediately after dispatch by discounting the bill of exchange, by presenting it to a bank which buys it while charging a percentage discount. Use of the bill of exchange thus assists both the buyer and the seller and avoids delays in the use of funds.

For healthy companies, accordingly, unsecured loans provide a valuable means of acting economically efficiently in the marketplace. This efficiency derives not merely from the low transaction costs involved but also from utilising the monitoring and information-collecting capacities of creditors for the purposes of risk reduction and, in turn, for lowering the cost of credit.

All is not rosy in the garden, however, since a lack of security can lead to inefficiencies in the flow of cash between traders. Without security trade creditors are poorly placed to demand payments of outstanding debts. A secured creditor faced with non-payment has recourse to the charged assets and has rights (curtailed after the Enterprise Act 2002 reforms) to appoint a receiver or to apply to court for orders of foreclosure or sale.[224] Such a response is not open to the unsecured trade creditor, and late payment of debts has been seen as a major problem over the last two decades.[225]

---

[223] See, however, the discussion at pp. 99–102, 107–10, 114–17 above relating to non-adjusting unsecured creditors.

[224] Usually the debenture contains provisions enabling the loan creditor or trustee to appoint an administrative receiver without resort to the court and in practice this was the most common remedy. The Enterprise Act 2002 has largely abolished the right to appoint administrative receivers in so far as charges created after the coming into force of the legislation on 15 September 2003 are concerned: see now the Insolvency Act 1986 s. 72A. Section 72B of the Insolvency Act 1986 (as amended by the Enterprise Act 2002 s. 250) provides for exceptional cases where floating charge holders may still appoint administrative receivers: see further ch. 8 below.

[225] For a discussion of the impact of late payments on companies and of statutory measures to combat late payment see ch. 4 below.

Do unsecured loan arrangements, as they stand, however, conduce to economically efficient insolvency procedures? Here attention must be paid to the position of unsecured creditors in an insolvency and the way that this may affect their behaviour and expenses of doing business. When there is a corporate insolvency, secured creditors can remove their secured assets at will, if able to utilise receivership, free from any notion of *pari passu*.[226] Other suppliers of credit can also prevent their 'debts' from falling into the fund of corporate assets available for distribution: noteworthy here are 'creditors' who have used 'self-help' devices such as retention of title clauses or trust mechanisms.[227] Unsecured creditors will see such 'creditors' escape the insolvency net but, in addition, the unsecured creditors must join the back of the queue for payment from the corpus of assets, a queue headed by the holders of fixed charges, followed by insolvency practitioners who incur expenses acting as office holders, then those with preferential debts (for example, sums owed to employees for remuneration)[228] and then holders of floating charges. Only shareholders and certain deferred debts[229] come after the unsecured creditors. Satisfaction of such prior claims means that unsecured creditors' hopes of recovering anything of substance in the winding-up process are usually dashed.[230] Nor, furthermore, could the unsecured creditor expect any assistance in the form of altruism from receivers who collected from the company's assets for fixed and floating charge holders.[231] Receivers are primarily concerned with generating funds for their debenture holders and this obligation takes precedence even over possible damage to the company's and unsecured creditors' interests.[232] The Enterprise Act 2002 reforms have, however, attempted to redress the balance of power from the institution of receivership and floating charge holder towards

---

[226] Note that a qualifying floating charge holder now has to resort to administration rather than receivership. See Insolvency Act 1986 Sch. B1, paras. 43, 44. On the *pari passu* principle of distribution see chs. 14 and 15 below.

[227] See ch. 15 below.   [228] See ch. 14 below.   [229] See Insolvency Act 1986 s. 74(1)(f).

[230] See Cork Report, paras. 1480 ff.: for unsecured creditors corporate liquidation is usually 'an empty formality' because 'in all too many cases insolvency results in the distribution of the proceeds among the preferential and secured creditors, with little, or nothing, for the ordinary unsecured creditors'. Note, however, that the introduction of the 'ring-fenced' sum in IA 1986 s. 176A may give unsecured creditors some economic interest in a corporate insolvency.

[231] See ch. 8 below. See V. Finch, 'Directors' Duties: Insolvency and the Unsecured Creditor' in A. Clarke (ed.), *Current Issues in Insolvency Law* (Stevens, London, 1991).

[232] *Gomba Holdings UK Ltd and Others* v. *Homan and Bird* [1986] 1 WLR 1301 at 1305; *Downsview Nominees Ltd* v. *First City Corporation Ltd* [1993] 2 WLR 86. Unsecured creditors *per se* are owed no duty by the receiver: *Lathia* v. *Dronsfield Bros. Ltd* [1987] BCLC 321. See ch. 8 below.

unsecured creditors. As noted above, the Act largely abolished the institu-tion of administrative receivership and stipulated that qualifying floating charge holders[233] can instead appoint an administrator out of court. The administrator owes a duty to consider all creditors' interests.[234]

Whether such a regime may be deemed unfair to the unsecured creditor is among those matters to be considered in chapters 14 and 15 but, for now, it should be asked why inefficiency may be produced. A first inefficiency may arise where there are unnecessary transaction costs: where, for instance, the legal costs faced by the unsecured creditors and creditors overall are higher than they should be because the relevant law is subject to avoidable and unnecessary uncertainties. (This is a matter to be returned to below when the processes for managing insolvency have been explored further.)

The second inefficiency of concern here takes us back to the balance between secured and unsecured creditors that was discussed above. Where unsecured creditors are unable to adjust to the granting of security there is liable to be a transfer of insolvency wealth to the secured creditor and unsecured creditors will bear excessive amounts of risk.[235] This leads to the inefficiencies noted above, which need not be reviewed again here.

Ownership-based (quasi-security) financing

As already noted, companies can raise funds or gain the use of goods by using sale arrangements in a manner that substitutes for security. Since the celebrated *Romalpa* decision,[236] trade suppliers of goods on credit have frequently used 'retention of title' clauses to stipulate that owner-ship of the goods shall not pass until payment for the goods has been received.[237] Surveys suggest that the majority of suppliers employ such

---

[233] See IA 1986 Sch. B1, para. 14. It is only the qualifying floating charge holder (QFC) that can appoint an administrator out of court under para. 14. The holders of other charges will have to apply for a court order. See further ch. 9 below.

[234] See for example IA 1986 Sch. B1, paras. 3(1), 3(4).

[235] See LoPucki, 'Unsecured Creditor's Bargain', p. 1899; Hudson, 'Case Against Secured Lending'; Leebron, 'Limited Liability'.

[236] *Aluminium Industrie Vaassen BV* v. *Romalpa Aluminium Ltd* [1976] 1 WLR 676. Note that prior to this decision, although title retention clauses were common on the continent, they were rare in the UK. (The plaintiff in the *Romalpa* case was a Dutch company, using its standard terms of supply.)

[237] Or, indeed, until all sums due from the purchasing company (e.g. in respect of previous supplies) have been satisfied: *Armour* v. *Thyssen Edelstahlwerke AG* [1990] 3 WLR 810.

clauses in their conditions of sale.[238] Retention of ownership operates in substance as security, but a 'simple' retention of title arrangement is not treated by English law as a security arrangement and, accordingly, there is no requirement of registration, as with a company charge or a bill of sale, in order for such a clause to be valid against third parties.[239]

The value to the creditor/owner of retention of title is that on the insolvency of the debtor company the assets at issue do not belong at law to the company, cannot be claimed by the insolvency practitioner and are not available for distribution among the creditors. The creditors of an insolvent company cannot make any claim against goods that are owned by others but are in the possession, control or custody of the company.[240] Powerful trade suppliers of goods are thus well placed to use their bargaining power to avoid the severe consequences, on a corporate insolvency, of status as unsecured creditors.

For a trade creditor, such as a supplier of goods and materials, a retention of title clause may prove more attractive than the taking of

---

[238] Spencer, 'Commercial Realities of Reservation of Title Clauses', surveyed fifty suppliers and found 59 per cent of respondents used such clauses (p. 221); Wheeler, *Reservation of Title Clauses*, examined fifteen receiverships and liquidations and found 92 per cent of suppliers of goods had 'some sort of reservation of title provision' (p. 5).

[239] In a 'simple' retention of title clause the 'security' applies to the goods as supplied but a 'complex' retention of title clause seeks to apply to goods even when they have been altered or changed. The thrust of case law is that whereas simple clauses do not constitute charges, complex ones are regarded as charges and are registrable. For discussion of the case for definitions of 'complex' and 'simple' see J. de Lacy 'Corporate Insolvency and Retention of Title Clauses: Developments in Australia' [2001] Ins. Law. 64. The CLRSG document, *Modern Company Law for a Competitive Economy: Final Report* (DTI, London, 2001) ('CLRSG, *Final Report*, 2001') ch. 12, advocated a regime of notice filing which would link priority to the relative timing of registration. Simple retention of title clauses would not be registrable (para. 12.60). The Law Commission commenced a project of reform of the law of security interests following reference from the CLRSG and endorsed the approach of legislation along the lines of Article 9 of the US Uniform Commercial Code in its Consultation Paper No. 164 (2002) and in its Consultative Report Law Com. No. 176 (2004). In the Final Report on *Company Security Interests* (Law Com. No. 296, 2005) the Law Commission retreated, however, and simple retention of title clauses were not advocated to be covered by the proposed new system of electronic notice filing for companies. See further Goode, 'Case for Abolition of the Floating Charge'; G. McCormack, 'The Law Commission and Company Security Interests – A Climbdown' (2005) 18 *Sweet & Maxwell Company Law Newsletter*; Company Security Regulations 2006; and ch. 15 below. See also D. Milman, 'Company Law Review: Company Charges' [2001] Ins. Law. 180; G. McCormack, 'Retention of Title and the EC Late Payment Directive' [2001] 1 JCLS 501 on the obligation on Member States to recognise contractually agreed-upon 'simple' ROT clauses in contracts for the sale of goods. See pp. 130–3 below.

[240] See Snaith, *Law of Corporate Insolvency*, p. 197.

security (for example, a floating charge) because the latter may be seen as an expensive and cumbersome resort to a legal framework; because retaining title, in comparison, involves a simple standard contractual term not requiring general disclosure; because the customer, when approached for security, might refuse and look elsewhere for supply (fearing that offering security signals a lack of creditworthiness or financial instability to others in the market); and because requests for security might drive customers away, in so far as such requests are seen as hostile actions evidencing a lack of goodwill and trust.[241]

A hire purchase agreement keeps the title to the relevant asset with the seller until the end of the stipulated hire period and is often used as a source of medium-term credit for the purchase of plant and equipment. The hire purchase company supplies the equipment which can be used immediately by the hiree who will make a series of regular payments (including an interest charge) and, after repayment, will become the owner by exercising a right to purchase for a nominal sum. Legal title does not pass to the hiree until payments under the agreement have been completed. The hirer, again, retains a secure position regarding any insolvency of the hiree, provided that the value of the asset at issue remains higher than the repayment sum outstanding and does so for the duration of the agreement. The hiree, in turn, enjoys the use of the equipment and only has to make an initial payment rather than the full purchase price. Hire purchase tends to be an expensive form of finance but the hiree company can claim tax relief on the interest element in the payments made and in regard to any investment allowances.

Leasing operates like hire purchase but at the end of the period of the lease the ownership of the asset still remains with the lessor. It is an arrangement that has grown in popularity for four reasons.[242] First, the company may not have the funds to purchase a large asset, or, if it does, it may have a more profitable use for the cash. Second, leasing may provide tax advantages where investment allowances can be secured or where the lessor pays a higher marginal tax rate than the lessee (less tax will be collectable than would have been the case with a purchase). Third, leasing allows equipment to be updated flexibly and transfers the risks associated with technologically advanced fields to the lessor. Similarly, where a company is ill-positioned to calculate asset depreciation rates, it can transfer risks to the lessor. Finally, if leased assets can be kept off the balance sheet (for example, by classification

---

[241] See Wheeler, *Reservation of Title Clauses*, pp. 38–9.
[242] Samuels *et al.*, *Management of Company Finance*, pp. 586–7.

as operating leases) a company can show a higher return on assets in its accounts than would have been possible had the asset been purchased.

Factoring and invoice discounting involve a company raising funds by selling receivables, such as debts owed to the company, to a financial intermediary who will offer the company a cash percentage of their face value.[243] (Factoring, in the alternative, may operate by the advance of a sum on the security of the receivables.) The company will obtain funds more rapidly than would have been the case had payment from the customer been awaited.

Factoring and invoice discounting have become increasingly important to UK companies. The growth rate of invoice financing exceeded the growth in the GDP in every year from 1987 to 2003 (except 1991) and in 2008 members of the Asset Based Finance Association (ABFA) made advances against invoices of £16.4 billion.[244] It is, indeed, the need for finance that leads companies to use factors and invoice discounters. These are devices of particular value to small, fast-growing companies who experience late payment problems and wish to release funds tied up with debtors for use as working capital. Resort to factoring and invoice discounting allows a business to grow in line with its sales and can also be especially useful when a company has exhausted its overdraft facilities and is not in a position to raise new equity. Sales of receivables, moreover, do not have to be registered and borrowing ratios are unaffected.[245] Sale and lease-back allows funds to be raised by a company selling assets to a financial intermediary but it also allows the company to continue using the assets by leasing them back. The company thus secures funds and only has to pay out rental charges (which are tax deductible) and a sale and lease-back may be preferred by the company to a mortgage because the latter will adversely affect the debt to equity ratio of the company since it appears as a debt on the balance sheet.[246]

---

[243] Factors in general will advance up to 80 per cent of invoice value: see Bank of England 1998, p. 28.

[244] Up 15 per cent on 2007: see ABFA, *Economic Report* (ABFA, London, 2008). Invoice financing grew by over 300 per cent between 1993 and 2002; see Hewitt, 'Asset Finance' pp. 210–11.

[245] See Snaith, *Law of Corporate Insolvency*, p. 220. See generally Oditah, *Legal Aspects.*

[246] See Samuels *et al.*, *Management of Company Finance*, p. 584. Variants on sale and lease-back are sale of stock/inventory or assignments of work in progress, where the company, in the former case, sells its stock, e.g. of bonded whisky, to a bank, receives funds and has an option to repurchase on maturation (of the whisky) at a price reflecting the initial sale price plus interest. During the period of maturation the bank owns the whisky and the company has funds for investment in further projects: see further ibid., pp. 452–3.

A significant advantage of such asset-based financing is that it offers financiers an attractive security – namely ownership of the assets, receivables or leased equipment. Such arrangements also allow financiers to gain value from their specialist knowledge regarding the assets at issue and they are amenable to use by the new, growing business that lacks the track records or the security that is often required by the traditional lender.[247] Devices such as leasing, moreover, take advantage of tax allowances (on, for instance, new equipment purchases). It has been argued, furthermore, that the House of Lords' decision in *Re Spectrum Plus Ltd*[248] will encourage resort to asset-based financing methods such as factoring. The decision makes it 'more difficult, if not impossible' for banks to establish charges over book debts in a manner that renders them fixed rather than floating 'without micro-managing the debtor's company's dealings' in those book debts[249] and, as a result of the concomitant demotion in the priority of charges over book debts, companies are likely to find asset-based receivables finance to be available at lower prices than overdrafts that are secured by a floating charge.[250] Balancing such considerations that favour the use of asset financing is the fact that this mode of raising money can prove to be relatively expensive for small firms who may find the arrangement fees that are charged to be high in relation to the sums advanced.

The broad efficiency case for the above quasi-security devices is that they provide ways to supply the financing that healthy trading companies need during their various stages of development. They are part of the flexible menu of financial devices that the market provides to trading companies and which help to increase cash flows. It could thus be argued that the growing use of financing methods such as factoring is strong evidence of their utility.

When attention is turned to the insolvency context, however, there are a number of efficiency concerns to be noted.[251] A first caution is that quasi-security devices may produce transfers of insolvency wealth away from those unsecured creditors who cannot adjust to the use by others of such devices. The result may be the production of those inefficiencies that were discussed above in relation to security: thus, for instance,

---

[247] See Hewitt, 'Asset Finance'.   [248] [2005] 1 UKHL 41; [2005] 2 AC 680.
[249] Armour, 'Should We Redistribute in Insolvency?', p. 202.
[250] Ibid., pp. 224–5; D. Prentice, 'Bargaining in the Shadow of the Enterprise Act 2002' (2004) 5 EBOR 153. See further the discussion in ch. 9 below.
[251] See Diamond Report; Crowther Report. On the use of other 'devices' to jump the priority queue see ch. 15 below.

companies may have an excessive incentive to rely on unsecured credit and their managers may be under-deterred from making high-risk decisions that affect the interests of unsecured creditors. Many submissions to the Cork Committee, furthermore, argued that on the continent of Europe the wide use of reservation of title clauses had 'virtually emasculated' insolvency procedures as an effective remedy for unsecured creditors since there was generally nothing left in the estate for them.[252] Quasi-security devices tend to be contracted for by the larger, better-placed companies who would otherwise be unsecured, and the effect is to exploit this superior positioning and produce distortions in the pricing of credit. This last point can, perhaps, be overstated because the costs of inserting a retention of title clause into a supply contract may be small (standardised contracting reduces costs in this respect), but there are, nevertheless, suppliers of certain types of goods who cannot retain title effectively and who may, as a result, have to bear undue expected insolvency costs. As the Cork Committee noted in relation to retention of title clauses: 'Fuel supplied to heat furnaces or fodder supplied for livestock disappears on consumption and paint applied to the fabric of a factory becomes attached to the realty; the supplier of credit is necessarily left with an unsecured claim in the insolvency of the customer.'[253]

A second objection to the use of quasi-security is that it undermines many of the efficiencies that are associated with the system of secured priorities. Security, with priority, can be said to reduce the price of credit by reducing risks to lenders. They anticipate, when they are given security, that the protection they enjoy will not be diluted in value by subsequent actions of the debtor.[254] If, however, the debtor looks to

---

[252] Cork Report, para. 1624.

[253] Ibid., para. 1619. On the English courts' reluctance to recognise extensions of ROTs into the manufactured product or its proceeds (i.e. without its being registered as a charge) see ch. 15 below. See also *Chaigley Farms Ltd* v. *Crawford, Kaye & Greyshire Ltd* [1996] BCC 957 but cf. *Armour* v. *Thyssen* [1991] 2 AC 339. See further J. de Lacy, 'Processed Goods and Retention of Title Clauses' [1997] 10 *Palmer's In Company*; de Lacy, 'Corporate Insolvency and Retention of Title Clauses'; G. Lightman and G. Moss, *The Law of Administrators and Receivers of Companies* (4th edn, Thomson/Sweet & Maxwell, London, 2007) ch. 17.

[254] As the essence of a floating charge is that the company is free to deal with its assets in the ordinary course of business, it has been held that this includes being able to create fixed charges on assets within the class covered by the floating charge, having priority over the floating charge, in order to secure borrowing in the ordinary course of the company's business: see *Wheatley* v. *Silkstone and Haigh Moor Coal Co.* (1885) 29 Ch D 715. In view of the court's recognition (in *Re Automatic Bottle Makers Ltd* [1926] Ch 412) of the possibility of creating a second floating charge over a *part* of the assets covered by a

quasi-security and shifts its asset pattern so as to rely more heavily on the use of assets that are leased or subject to hire purchase agreements, retentions of title or other sale-based security devices, the protection offered to the secured creditor will be diminished. Fewer assets within the new pattern will enter the insolvent estate and the holder of, say, a floating charge will have a call on a slimmer body of assets. The efficiency loss is caused by the uncertainty faced by the secured creditors: if they cannot assess the level of protection that their security will offer they either will not lend or will cost into the price of credit the increased level of risk that they face. Uncertainty thus increases credit costs.

A third objection continues the theme of uncertainty. In so far as quasi-securities do not have to be registered, there is a lack of information available to creditors, secured and unsecured, concerning the position of a company's indebtedness. The trade creditor, for instance, may deal with a customer who displays large warehouses with stocked shelves to the world but the title to these assets and stock may belong to a third party and the information relating to this position may well be unavailable to that trade creditor. This possibility will be anticipated by the rational trade creditor who will increase the cost of supply to reflect the unknown risks faced; but, again, uncertainty increases credit costs economically inefficiently.

The need for more information on quasi-security was recognised by the Crowther and Diamond Committees, which both argued in favour of a new register of 'security interests' which, for Diamond, would include 'not only mortgages, charges and security in the strict sense but also any other transfer or retention of any interest in or rights over property other than land which secures the payment of money or the performance of any other obligation'.[255] The Company Law Review Steering Group advocated a system of notice-filing in 2001 as did the Law Commission

---

first floating charge and with priority over the first charge, it has now become standard practice to include in a contract of floating charge a 'negative pledge' clause, prohibiting the company from creating any charge over the assets covered by the floating charge with priority over the floating charge. On the question of establishing knowledge or notice of such a clause (thereby depriving a subsequent chargee of protection), see Hannigan, *Company Law*, p. 690.

[255] Diamond Report, para. 9.3.2 (proposals that, *inter alia*, would cover retentions of title and hire purchase agreements and certain leasing arrangements). See Cork Report, para. 1639, which also argues that clauses reserving title that were not duly registered should be void against a liquidator, trustee, administrator or any other creditor. For support of the Diamond approach and a comparative view see de Lacy, 'Corporate Insolvency and Retention of Title Clauses'.

to varying degrees in 2002, 2004 and 2005.[256] Registrable charges in the proposed Law Commission regime would have included floating charges, all charges on goods and complex retention of title clauses (where the title protecting the indebtedness shifts from one good to another on transformation), but not simple retention of title clauses where the seller merely retains title on transfer. The consultation exercise on the Law Commission's proposals gained no consensus of support, however, and the Companies Act 2006 made no significant changes to the existing rules on the registration of company charges and retention of title clauses.

The above problems are compounded by legal uncertainties. Insolvency lawyers, like any others, will always succeed to an extent in rendering the application of laws uncertain: if necessary they will argue about the relevant facts as much as the applicable laws.[257] There are degrees of uncertainty, however, and costs to companies will increase where the law is excessively complex or uncertain. The problem associated with quasi-security is that the law is fragmented, it treats essentially similar transactions in very different ways and causes unnecessary legal complications.[258] As Diamond concluded: 'The complexity and uncertainty of the law leads to expense and delay and hinders legitimate business activities ... The variations in the different legal rules cause problems in determining priorities between competing interests and give rise to fortuitous differences in insolvency.'[259] On reservations of title in particular, another commentator suggested that the formal law was 'uncertain in its application in almost every area. The most basic level of law in simple reservation of title clauses is open to differing interpretations.'[260]

---

[256] CLRSG, *Final Report*, 2001, ch. 12, para. 12.12; Law Commission, *Registration of Security Interests* (Law Com. Consultation Paper No. 164, 2002), *Company Security Interests* (Law Com. Consultative Report No. 176, 2004), *Company Security Interests* (Law Com. No. 296, Cm 6654, 2005).

[257] See Wheeler, *Reservation of Title Clauses*, pp. 34–6.

[258] The findings of the Diamond Report, para. 1.8(c), and the Cork Report, para. 1627, noted how consultee after consultee had made a 'cry for certainty' to avoid the prospect of 'interminable and expensive litigation'. Note, also, Cork's response that, given *inter alia* the 'illogical and complex' law relating to security in respect of goods, 'nothing that we propose in relation to insolvency law can prevent this': para. 1628.

[259] Diamond Report, paras. 1.8(d)–(e). On suggested solutions to these difficulties and Diamond's proposals for a 'new law on security interests to replace the multitude of different rules we have now' see ch. 15 below.

[260] Wheeler, *Reservation of Title Clauses*, p. 34. It is now, as noted, accepted that a simple retention of title (as opposed to a complex one) is effective: see A. Hicks, 'Reservation of Title: Latest Developments' [1992] JBL 398.

Finally, it could be cautioned that quasi-securities not only queer the pitch for security mechanisms but they may also fail to work well themselves. In the case of retention of title clauses, it has been suggested that even claimants with the strongest cases face a formidable series of obstacles to recovery, that those insolvency practitioners who act as administrative receivers or liquidators enjoy huge expertise and 'repeat player' advantages over claimants and that the overall result is that only 15 per cent of claimants succeed in recovery.[261] It is, accordingly, conceivable that, as presently operated, a device such as the retention of title clause achieves the worst of both worlds: it is perceived (wrongly) as a huge threat by holders of floating charges and this escalates credit costs, but the device fails, at the end of the long and legally uncertain day, to deliver real protection to the quasi-secured creditor.

The 'new capitalism' and the credit crisis

Over the last twenty years the above building blocks of borrowing may not have altered but the modes of arranging corporate financing on the basis of these foundations have changed radically. In the world of the so-called 'new capitalism'[262] borrowing relationships, credit arrangements and involved actors have all mutated dramatically and there has been a movement from 'managerial capitalism into global financial capitalism'.[263] The developments comprising this movement should be noted here since they are of considerable significance for insolvency law – not least because they involve an explosive fragmentation of debt.

The first such development has been the massive growth in the use of financial derivatives, and, notably, in credit derivatives.[264] The latter are

---

[261] Wheeler, *Reservation of Title Clauses*, p. 178. See also Spencer, 'Commercial Realities of Reservation of Title Clauses', in whose survey half of respondents said that their clauses had been challenged by receivers or liquidators. In practice the insolvency practitioner not only will consider whether the wording of the ROT clause establishes a prima facie claim but also will be influenced by the bargaining position of the supplier: see *Leyland DAF Ltd* v. *Automotive Products plc* [1993] BCC 389; A. Belcher and W. Beglan, 'Jumping the Queue' [1997] JBL 1 at 17–19.

[262] See e.g. M. Wolf, 'The New Capitalism', *Financial Times*, 19 June 2007.

[263] Ibid. This section builds on V. Finch, 'Corporate Rescue in a World of Debt' [2008] JBL 756.

[264] The total volume of outstanding credit derivatives contracts stood at £31,300 billion at the end of 2007 – a near doubling on 2006 figures – and an indication that the 2007–8 credit crunch had not halted the rise of the credit derivative market. That market is ten times the size it was in 2004: see G. Tett and P. Davies, 'Upsurge in Credit Derivatives Defies Fears', *Financial Times*, 16 April 2008. See also G. Tett, 'Should Atlas Still Shrug? The Threat that Lurks behind the Growth of Complex Debt Deals', *Financial Times*,

derivative contracts that transfer defined credit risks in a credit product or bundle of credit products to a counterparty – a market participant or the capital market itself. The trading of credit risk is a process that has been advanced by the growth of structured financing techniques and the securitisation of such risks.[265] Securitisation is the process involving the rendering of a credit derivative into an investment product – as where a bank places loans in a special purpose vehicle (SPV)[266] which then issues new securities such as bonds – allowing investors to buy credit-linked notes and to gain credit exposure to an entity or group of entities.[267] The credit product itself might be the risk interest in a loan or a generic credit risk, such as an insolvency risk.[268]

Complex structuring may take place when securitisation involves an SPV issuing an asset-backed security (ABS) secured over a wide range of assets, loans and receivables or issuing a collateralised debt obligation (CDO) involving a portfolio of bonds, loans and swaps.[269] Buyers, in such markets, are able to purchase exposure to particular risks; bundles

---

15 January 2007, noting that global liquidity is made up of 75% derivatives, 13% securitised debt, 11% broad money and 1% bank funds. The volume of high-risk traded debt has risen sharply in recent years. In 2003 £500 million of bonds with a CCC credit rating were issued but this had risen to £2.2 billion in 2005: see G. Tett, 'High Risk Debt Issuance has Grown Sharply', *Financial Times*, 4 December 2006. On derivatives see further J. Benjamin, *Financial Law* (Oxford University Press, Oxford, 2007) ch. 4.

[265] See generally Fuller, *Corporate Borrowing*, ch. 7; V. Selvam, 'Recharacterisation in "True Sale" Securitizations' [2006] JBL 637; J. K. Thompson, *Securitization* (OECD, Paris, 1995); L. R. Lupica, 'Asset Securitization: The Unsecured Creditor's Perspective' (1998) 76 Texas L Rev. 595; J. Flood, 'Rating, Dating and the Informal Regulation and the Formal Ordering of Financial Transactions' in M. B. Likosky (ed.), *Privatising Development* (Martinus Nijhoff, Netherlands, 2005) p. 147.

[266] The use of a special purpose vehicle (SPV) involves use of a paper company where a bank places other mortgages or assets to remove them from its balance sheet. On SPVs see further N. Frome and K. Gibbons, '*Spectrum* – An End to the Conflict or the Signal for a New Campaign?' in Getzler and Payne, *Company Charges*, pp. 122–9, 132.

[267] See G. Aggarwal, 'Securitisation – An Overview' (2006) 3 Int. Corp. Rescue 285. In a securitisation the underlying assets are a pool of assets producing regular cash flows. Another type of asset-backed security is the repackaging, in which the underlying assets are a pool of bonds and a swap arrangement (under which the investor agrees to pay cash flows from bank bonds back to the bank in return for a different set of cash flows): see Fuller, *Corporate Borrowing*, pp. 108–9.

[268] See V. Kothari, *Credit Derivatives and Synthetic Securitisation* (Vinod Kothari, India, 2002).

[269] In 2002 the then head of the Financial Services Authority, Sir Howard Davies, warned the City that synthetic CDOs were being described by some investment bankers as 'the most toxic element of the financial markets today': see J. Treanor, 'Toxic Shock: How the Banking Industry Created a Global Crisis', *The Guardian*, 8 April 2008, noting estimates that in 2007 about a third of the £300 billion CDOs sold contained US sub-prime mortgage loans.

of risks of different types; or an index of credit risks, covering risks in a generalised, diversified index of names. They are, additionally, able to trade in tranches representing risks of different levels or slices of risk in a given market (e.g. the first 3 per cent of risk and so on).[270]

A second important development has been the exponential growth of the hedge fund and the private equity group[271] as vehicles for making investments in companies (especially troubled companies).[272] These funds are largely unregulated entities that invest in a wide variety of domains and often use high levels of leveraging and complex financial arrangements in order to increase their returns.[273] They are prominent in credit derivative trades – which are in the main unregulated and offer opportunities for short trades in credit that are not permitted by the bond market. In such a world 'the whole landscape of leveraged lending has changed'[274] with resort to complex mixes of asset classes, bonds, derivatives, loans and equities and the use of newly devised and tailor-made

---

[270] Fuller, *Corporate Borrowing*, pp. 116–18.

[271] Rod Selkirk, Head of the British Venture Capital Association, has described the difference between the hedge fund and the private equity group as follows: hedge fund investors are experts in trading in public securities and derivatives whereas in private equity the expertise lies in investing in companies and management teams: see P. Smith, 'Private Equity Groups are "Distinct From Hedge Funds"', *Financial Times*, 27 November 2006. The term 'private equity' encompasses investment types ranging from venture capital focused on financing early stage businesses to leveraged buyouts that employ debt to buy more mature companies. The growth equity segment of the private equity industry (a fast-growing sector focused on supporting the expansion of established growth companies) typically employs little or no leverage. For an outline of the private equity industry see D. Walker, *Guidelines for Disclosure and Transparency in Private Equity* (BVCA, London, 20 November 2007) pp. 7–11.

[272] Hedge funds and non-bank credit investment groups held over 50 per cent of all lending to higher-risk European companies in March 2007 – pushing banks into a minor role. This offers a dramatic contrast with the position as recently as 2005 when banks represented three-quarters of the market: see 'Hedge Funds are Moving in on Banks' Territory', *Financial Times*, 25 April 2007. On the challenges of regulating hedge funds see H. McVea, 'Hedge Funds and the New Regulatory Agenda' (2007) 7 *Legal Studies* 709–39. On the Hedge Fund Working Group's 2008 report laying out voluntary standards for the industry see J. Mackintosh, 'Big Hedge Funds Agree Voluntary Code of Practice', *Financial Times*, 23 January 2008; A. Hill, 'Hedge Funds Insure Against the Risk of More Rules', *Financial Times*, 23 January 2008.

[273] See T. Hurst, 'Hedge Funds in the 21st Century' (2007) 28 Co. Law. 228, estimating that 'several hundred' funds hold around US $1.3 trillion in assets and account for 40–50 per cent of all market trading activity. Private equity is now said to own businesses employing around one in six of UK private sector workers: see J. Pickard and P. Smith, 'Myners Warns of Risks from the Growth of Private Equity', *Financial Times*, 21 February 2007.

[274] See G. Tett, 'Deals Galore in a World Awash with Cheap Money', *Financial Times*, 27 September 2006.

instruments such as payment in kind notes (PIKs) and 'hybrid financing' deals using highly structured CDOs and ABSs. Low interest rates have encouraged such heavily leveraged approaches in recent years as has the dramatic globalisation of the credit derivatives market.

A third change has taken place in the traditional role of the bank – which has shifted from that of primary lender to that of 'originator and distributor'.[275] Instead of arranging loans and retaining these on their own books, the banks have moved towards arranging and then selling on the loans and loan risks to other investors.[276] The change has been from commercial long-term lending and durable client relationships towards investment banking and arm's-length trading. When companies encounter difficulties in this new world they are increasingly likely to turn not to commercial banks but to hedge funds and private equity funds or to other sources of 'alternative capital'.

The sanguine view of such developments is that such active financial trading swiftly identifies and attacks pockets of inefficiency and imposes rigorous market disciplines on managers; that it places economically inefficient operations in the hands of those who can extract value most efficiently; and that it allows capital to flow easily around the world to those places where it will work best.[277]

Sceptics, however, focused on a number of concerns even before the credit crisis of 2007–8.[278] The first was that the system leads to risk taking that is unsustainable. It does so, they fear, because lending standards tend to loosen as credit derivative markets encourage banks to believe, excessively optimistically, that they can use credit derivatives to offset the risks of loans. This, it is thought, leads such banks to lend more to companies than they would otherwise do – and at lower rates to higher-risk borrowers.[279] Such a problem is allegedly compounded because the credit

---

[275] See J. Gapper, 'Now Banks Must Relearn their Craft', *Financial Times*, 30 July 2007.

[276] As noted, the use of a special purpose vehicle (SPV) removes loans from its balance sheet.

[277] See Wolf, 'New Capitalism'.

[278] See, for example, F. Partnoy and D. Skeel, 'Credit Derivatives: Playing a Dangerous Game', *Financial Times*, 17 July 2006. In April 2008 the Governor of the Bank of England commented on the failure of the major banks to create incentives for their staff that are conducive to the reasonable control of risks.

[279] The Finance Director of Northern Rock argued early in 2007 that securitising its loans had reduced its risks and allowed it in turn to make more loans: see Tett, 'Should Atlas Still Shrug?' Months later Northern Rock was experiencing a liquidity crisis and was approaching the Bank of England for a £13 billion loan as lender of last resort. On the 2008 collapse of Lehmans with an estimated $400 billion CDS debt on its books see *Financial Times*, Editorial, 16 October 2008.

derivatives market reduces the incentives for banks to monitor corporate behaviour and managerial performance.[280] This tends to take out of play those institutions that, traditionally, are best placed to monitor directorial prudence. A related worry is that the investors in sold-on risks – often the pension and insurance funds – are unlikely to carry out such monitoring as they have no hands-on relationship with the corporate borrower. The upshot pointed to is that this involves a moral hazard on the part of borrowers who are not subject to rigorous financial disciplining. In sum, both lenders and borrowers are excessively encouraged to bear risks and this increases threats to solvency.[281]

A second fear relates to the systemic risks involved with credit derivatives. The new concern is that the regulatory challenges of controlling such a complex global credit market are extremely severe and that the monetary tools of central banks do not work well to control credit conditions.[282] This has for some time given rise to worries regarding the stability of the system and in turn for the welfare of companies – who may face liquidity crises that are driven by global factors beyond their control. As for risk spreading and systemic risks, the traditional view is that dispersing risks encourages resilience and financial stability. In the wake of the credit crisis of 2007–8, the charge is that opacities within the derivatives system made it difficult, in the pre-crisis period, to trace risks and risk bearers so that concentrations developed in a manner that made the general system highly vulnerable to shocks.[283] Another problem encountered was that of contagion, a process in

---

[280] See F. Partnoy and D. Skeel, 'The Promises and Perils of Credit Derivatives' (U. Pa. Law School Working Paper 125, 2006): the banks that financed Enron laid off $8 billion of risk. See also the evidence of the Governor of the Bank of England to the House of Commons Treasury Select Committee on 29 April 2008 regarding the failure of the banks to create incentives for their staff that are conducive to the reasonable control of risks: reported in G. Duncan and G. Gilmore, 'Mervyn King: Banks Paying Price for their Greed', *The Times*, 30 April 2008.

[281] See e.g. J. Plender, 'The Credit Business is More Perilous than Ever', *Financial Times*, 13 October 2006.

[282] On the challenges of regulating hedge funds see Financial Services Authority, 'Hedge Funds: A Discussion of Risk and Regulatory Engagement' (FSA Discussion Paper 05/4, London, June 2005). On the Bank of England and the Financial Services Authority's difficulties in controlling the 2007 Northern Rock crisis see Editorial: 'All Are Losers in the Rock Blame Game', *Financial Times*, 10 October 2007. See further G. Walker, 'Subprime Loans, Inter-bank Markets and Financial Support' (2008) 29 Co. Law. 22.

[283] On the causes of the credit crisis see e.g. R. Tomasic, 'Corporate Rescue, Governance and Risk-taking in Northern Rock' (2008) 29 Co. Law. 297; Technical Committee of the International Organisation of Securities Commissions, *Report on the Subprime Crisis: Final Report* (May 2008), www.iosco.org/library/pubdocs/pdf/ioscoPD273.pdf.

which ill-informed parties afflicted whole areas of investment. When unmonitored expansions of credit were encouraged by low interest rates, when there were high levels of leverage and speculative trading, when there was unprecedented demand for high-risk subordinated loans, and when information flows were impeded by hugely complex contractual fragmentations, crashes resulted when 'the music stopped' on the risk shifting.[284]

The third general concern – again expressed before the 2007–8 crisis and repeated following it – relates to information flows and levels of transparency. The intricacies of credit derivative arrangements and the sophistication of the various vehicles for credit structuring mean that the relevant contracts are difficult to understand and it is extremely hard for regulators to ensure that processes are transparent and conducive to the supply of full and accurate information on risks.[285] This is an area lacking standardised performance information.[286] Investors, accordingly, may be poorly placed to evaluate the risks that are associated with opaquely packaged products.[287] Such opacity may underpin the propensity of the risk-shifting process to move risk into the hands of investors who are ill-equipped to handle it.[288] As has been commented: 'The theory is that risk would be shifted to those best able to bear it. The practice seems to have been that it was shifted onto those least able to understand it.'[289] A further effect is that investors in the company tend to

---

[284] See P. Smit and G. Tett, 'Buyout Deals Raise Alarm on Debt Levels', *Financial Times*, 20 June 2006; Hurst, 'Hedge Funds'; G. Tett, 'Credit Turmoil Shows Not All Innovation Has Been Beneficial', *Financial Times*, 11 September 2007.

[285] See E. Ferran, 'Regulation of Private Equity-Backed Leveraged Buy-out Activity in Europe', ECGI Working Paper 84/2007; J. Harris, 'International Regulation of Hedge Funds: Can the Will Find a Way?' (2007) 28 Co. Law. 277. On FSA consideration of proposals to give companies powers to compel hedge funds to declare secret stakes see J. Mackintosh, 'Secret Hedge Fund Stakes Could be Flushed Out', *Financial Times*, 11 October 2007.

[286] See R. Pozen, 'Reporting Standards for Hedge Funds must be Raised', *Financial Times*, 12 January 2006.

[287] On deficiencies in the performance of credit ratings agencies see S. Jones, G. Tett and P. Davies, 'CPDOs Expose Ratings Flaw at Moodys', *Financial Times* 21 May 2008; P. Davies and G. Tett, 'Moody's Talks of Ratings Reform', *Financial Times*, 18 September 2007. On the difficulties of valuing credit derivative transactions see D. Summa, 'Credit Derivatives: An Untested Market' (2006) 3 Int. Corp. Rescue 249. See also Flood, 'Rating, Dating', pp. 157–64 on the effects of the 'pernicious complexity' of securitisations and the questionable credibility of the ratings agencies' evaluations.

[288] See G. Tett, 'Credit Trading Shows Not All Innovation Has Been Beneficial', *Financial Times*, 11 September 2007.

[289] M. Wolf, 'Questions and Answers on a Sadly Predictable Debt Crisis', *Financial Times*, 5 September 2007.

find it difficult to adjust their credit terms when they do not know whether a lender – for example, the company's bank – has hedged its position with derivatives.[290] The more general worry for those concerned with corporate financial health is that intrinsically volatile systems that involve poor transparency and appreciation of risk can, and, in 2008 did, lead to financial instabilities, excessively risky managerial strategies and solvency crises.[291]

A final worry relating to insolvency risks is the possibility that the popularity of derivatives may impede recoveries in times of corporate trouble because the hedge funds or other holders of credit will enforce debts rapidly against defaulters. In the world of the 'new capital' the troubled company may have no friendly ear at the bank to turn to and creditors who have purchased derivatives may possess few motivations to explore turnaround possibilities. They may even have incentives to encourage corporate default and actively to enforce the terms of the loan agreement even where this destroys corporate value.[292] These are matters to be returned to in chapter 7 below when discussing informal rescue strategies and practices.

It is perhaps too early to draw conclusions on the full effects of the new capitalism. This is not least because regulatory responses to the 2007–8 credit crisis are yet to fully emerge. Even in early 2008, however, steps were in train, for instance, to improve the transparency with which the hedge and private equity funds operate.[293] It remains to be seen whether regulators will institute radical new steps that are designed to reduce the complexity and opacity of credit derivatives and credit markets. Possibilities being canvassed in late 2008 included: the creation of a

---

[290] Ibid.

[291] On the difficulties of using mathematical models to predict the performance of the securitised credit markets see A. Gangahar and K. Burgess, 'Hedge Funds Brace for More Pain', *Financial Times*, 13 August 2007. On some hedge funds' ill-suited risk management policies and weak operational controls leading, *inter alia*, to misstatements of the net asset value (NAV) of the fund see M. Penner, 'Hedge Funds: Risk Management and Valuation "Red Flags"' (2007) *Recovery* (Winter) 30.

[292] See Partnoy and Skeel, 'Promises and Perils', p. 22.

[293] In January 2008 the hedge fund industry's Hedge Fund Working Group (HFWG), representing leading hedge fund managers based mainly in the UK and chaired by Sir Andrew Large, announced that agreement had been reached on voluntary standards intended to codify best practice for the industry: see Mackintosh, 'Big Hedge Funds Agree Voluntary Code of Practice'. (The HFWG was loosely modelled on the committee drawing up a voluntary code for the private equity industry under Sir David Walker, which published *Guidelines for Disclosure and Transparency in Private Equity* on 20 November 2007.)

'clearing house' that would give investors more security by removing counterparty risk; moving towards a system of more standardised financial products rather than bespoke deals; regulatory reforms to demand that derivative contracts be disclosed in a detailed manner; and classifying those institutions that write credit default swaps as insurance groups – and thus subjecting them to increased oversight.[294] What can be said now is that the fragmentation of credit that has resulted from its securitisation has raised new issues of efficiency, expertise, accountability and fairness. It is often said that the credit derivatives market is conducive to efficiency in both the technical and economic senses – in lowering the transaction costs involved in the investment process and in ensuring that money flows to the locations of most productive use. After the 2007–8 crisis, newly urgent questions, however, have arisen concerning the quality and quantity of information that such markets generate and whether this can ensure efficiency in either of the above senses. Further issues relate to the resilience of the regime of 'new capitalism' and its potential to offer a stable environment for lowest-cost or economically efficient investment. Expertise, accountability and fairness are similarly all values that require the provision of foundational information flows. Without these it is difficult for informed expert judgements to be made, for controlling bodies to hold to account and for affected parties' interests to be respected through the granting of representational rights that are underpinned with access to relevant data.

Conclusions

The above discussion has reviewed the main mechanisms by which companies can finance their operations. Even a non-exhaustive view, however, indicates the range of legal instruments that are available for the financing of companies. Also made clear is the complexity of the trade-offs that have to be borne in mind in assessing the legal structures of financing. The needs of healthy companies as well as troubled companies have to be considered; the balance between credit and other financing arrangements has to be evaluated; and the needs of companies of different sizes and profiles have to enter the analysis. The purpose of this chapter has not been to evaluate the UK banking system and its

---

[294] See G. Tett, P. Davies and A. Van Duyn, 'A New Formula? Complex Finance Contemplates a More Fettered Future', *Financial Times*, 1 October 2008.

ability to service industry.[295] It has been to map out the legal framework of borrowing and to consider whether this is, in structural terms, conducive to the economically efficient meeting of healthy and troubled companies' needs.

A number of general conclusions can be drawn at this stage. First, it is clear that, at least in some contexts, there may be significant dangers of economically inefficient transfers of insolvency wealth from unsecured creditors to secured creditors or to those availing themselves of quasi-security devices. The nature of any efficiency loss will, as noted, depend on a number of context-specific factors: for instance, the number of different kinds of creditors that supply financing to a firm; the levels of risks being run by the company; the types of transaction being engaged in; the levels of transaction costs involved; and the nature of the competition in the various credit markets to which the company can turn. Where such transfers of insolvency wealth occur, they may prejudice healthy companies' needs (corporate decisions on financial risks may, for example, be taken with distorted weightings being given to the interests of different creditors). Transfers of this kind may also affect the needs of troubled companies in so far as decisions as to the lives or deaths of troubled companies – decisions which affect different creditor groups in different ways – may also be made with unbalanced views of the interests of different creditor classes. Not only that, but corporate managers may possess incentives to subsidise their company's secured loans by taking their unsecured credit from those unsecured creditors who are least well informed about risks, least able to adjust loan terms, least protected in insolvency and least likely to be capable of absorbing financial shocks.

It may also be concluded that certain courses of action have the potential to reduce economically inefficient insolvency wealth transfers. Procedures could be adopted so as to allow unsecured creditors to become more fully informed about the risks they are running. The value of informational steps should not, however, be exaggerated. They do not assist unsecured creditors who are involuntary or cannot adjust because of lack of resources, paucity of time or expertise, competitive pressures or other reasons. This does not mean, however, that there is no case for assisting those who can be put in a position to adjust and for

---

[295] For an outspoken view see Hutton, *The State We're In*. See also the White Paper, *Our Competitive Future: Building the Knowledge Driven Economy* (Cm 4176, December 1998), para 2.21; Cruickshank, *Competition in UK Banking*.

adopting measures such as the registration of quasi-securities. Similarly, measures designed to increase information flows and transparency in credit arrangements will reduce economically inefficient wealth transfers but may also assist creditors in their monitoring of debtors and the encouragement of efficiency in decision-making. This will be of value to healthy as well as troubled companies.

As for involuntary, unsecured creditors who cannot adjust, other steps might be taken to reduce wealth transfers away from such a group. 'Prescribed part' rules as found in section 176A of the Insolvency Act 1986 are blunt instruments (they benefit all unsecured creditors) but they are known quantities which allow attendant risks to be calculated and which are unlikely to reduce the availability of secured credit. The 'prescribed part' regime may accordingly not impede trading materially but will provide funds of assistance in capturing insolvency assets and may reduce insolvency-driven inefficiencies. A step that might be taken is to introduce compulsory insurance against tort liabilities. This could reduce economically inefficient subsidies from a particular group of involuntary, non-adjusting unsecured creditors.

The above review also suggests that the collectivity of financing arrangements and the array of legal devices encountered in England is likely, in its present form, to impose unnecessary costs on both healthy and troubled companies. Where the financial markets supply a wide range of devices for obtaining finance and credit this might be thought to be consistent with the needs of healthy companies. Companies presented with such wide choices are thus able to select the types of, say, credit which will prove least costly to them given their size, profile, sector, financial plans, transaction patterns and so on. It is one thing, however, to provide a range of clearly identifiable modes of acquiring funds and another to present companies with a patchwork of legal devices that is so confused that they may have difficulty in identifying the kinds of borrowing relationships that they are considering or even have entered into. Where the legal gateways to borrowing are unnecessarily confused and uncertain, unnecessary transaction costs are again produced for both healthy and troubled companies.

We have seen, moreover, that just as confusion attends the legal categories of borrowing, it also permeates the system of priorities, so that the benefits of clear ranking are undermined by the capacity of 'creditors' to employ such quasi-security devices as retention of title clauses and thereby to bypass priority mechanisms. The costs of credit will inevitably rise as such uncertainties increase risks.

Addressing the confusions that are found in the range of credit arrangements demands that attention be given to the legal frameworks that establish the different credit devices. It also demands that thought be given to the application of these frameworks on the ground and the possibility of devising credit arrangements that not only are set up with clear legal frameworks but are operated in the business world in an efficient, fair, accountable and transparent manner. During the rest of this book such matters will be a central concern.

4

Corporate failure

This chapter looks at what constitutes corporate failure, who decides that a company has failed and why some companies fail. From the insolvency lawyer's point of view it is important to understand the nature and causes of corporate decline so that the potential of insolvency law to prevent or process failure can be assessed and so that insolvency law can be shaped in a way that, so far as possible, does not contribute to undesirable failures or prove deficient (substantively or procedurally) in processing failed companies.

The purpose of insolvency law is not, however, to save all companies from failure.[1] The economy is made up of a vast number of firms, each engaged in marketing and product innovations that are designed to improve competitive positions and each being challenged in the market by other firms. Business life involves taking risks and dealing with crises, and the price of progress is that only those able to compete successfully for custom will survive.[2] An efficient, competitive marketplace will thus drive some companies to the wall because those companies should not be in business: they may be operated in a lazy, uncompetitive manner, their products may no longer be wanted by consumers and managerial weaknesses may be placing their creditors' interests at unacceptable risk. The role of insolvency law in such cases is not to take the place of the market's selective functions but to give troubled companies the opportunity to turn their affairs around where it is probable that this will produce overall benefits or, where this is not probable, to end the life of the company efficiently, expertly, accountably and fairly.

It can also be argued, however, that insolvency laws and processes should be able to look beyond the immediate position of the company

---

[1] Where companies enter insolvency procedures orientated towards rescue (e.g. administration and Company Voluntary Arrangement) 79 per cent of cases result in some sort of rescue and, in 62 per cent of these, the rescue is of the entire business: see the R3 Twelfth Survey of Corporate Insolvency in the UK (2004) ('R3 Twelfth Survey') p. 30.

[2] See M. White, 'The Corporate Bankruptcy Decision' (1989) 3 *Journal of Economic Perspectives* 129.

and should be sufficiently accessible to democratic influence to allow consideration of factors beyond the narrow confines of the firm or the strictly economic. Corporate failures may lead to the breaking up of teams with experience and expertise; to wasted resources and to run-on effects such as the unemployment of staff; harm to customers and suppliers; general impoverishment of communities and losses of confidence in commercial, financial, banking and political systems. A large corporate insolvency may, for instance, not only produce job losses and harm to the community, but also prejudice the availability of commercial credit as banks are shocked into newly restrictive lending policies. An insolvency often spreads ripples that extend considerably beyond the troubled firm.

What is failure?

Companies routinely encounter difficult times and survive them.[3] Some firms, however, undergo formal or informal rescue procedures before regaining health and others may end up in liquidation. R3 reported in 2004 that 21 per cent of businesses survived insolvency and continued to operate in one form or another and administration procedures resulted in 66 per cent job preservation.[4] In 2005 the number of companies liquidated per quarter ran at between 3,000 and 3,400.[5] To talk of 'troubled' or 'failing' companies is accordingly to refer in a broadbrush fashion to companies encountering a variety of problems and in different stages of decline or regeneration. More precision can be brought to such discussions by distinguishing between companies that are in distress and companies that are insolvent.

---

[3] Of new companies, 80 per cent of VAT-registered businesses are still going after two years, falling to 70 per cent after three years: see J. Guthrie, 'How the Old Corporate Tortoise Wins the Race', *Financial Times*, 15 February 2007.

[4] R3 Twelfth Survey, p. 4.

[5] BERR Statistics and Analysis Directorate figures. Insolvencies in the recession of the early 1990s peaked at just under 25,000 per annum in 1992. The corporate restructuring company Begbies Traynor reported in October 2008 that stricter lending criteria and the inability to secure funding meant that a 'staggering' 4,566 companies faced critical problems: see J. Grant, 'Businesses in Distress Double', *Financial Times*, 20 October 2008. After a poll of 2,073 of its members in October 2008, R3 was reported as predicting that small and medium-sized company insolvencies were set to rise by a 'catastrophic' 41 per cent by the end of 2009 compared with where they were at the end of 2007: see J. Grant, 'Insolvency Rate to Rise 41% by End of 2009', *Financial Times*, 4 November 2008.

Distressed companies are those that encounter financial crises that cannot be resolved without a sizeable recasting of the firm's operations or structures.[6] Such distress may be seen in terms of default, where the company has failed to make a significant payment of principal or interest to a creditor.[7] Alternatively, distress can be seen in terms of financial ratios. Thus, calculations based on a company's accounts can be used to reveal profitability ratios, liquidity ratios and longer-term solvency ratios.[8] Assessing whether a company is in distress may involve reference to these ratios individually or collectively, but the central issue is whether the company is revealed to be in such a state of crisis that drastic action is required.[9]

A company is insolvent for the purpose of the law if it is unable to pay its debts.[10] No legal consequences attach to a firm, however, simply by virtue of its insolvent state. Such consequences only follow the institution of a formal proceeding such as a winding up or the appointment of an administrator or administrative receiver. There is, moreover, no single

---

[6] C. Foster, *Financial Statement Analysis* (2nd edn, Prentice-Hall, Englewood Cliffs, N.J., 1986) p. 61; A. Belcher, *Corporate Rescue* (Sweet & Maxwell, London, 1997) ch. 3. The R3 Twelfth Survey (p. 30) revealed that 21 per cent of businesses entering a rescue procedure experienced a break-up sale of assets. For a spectrum of potential indicators of distress see R. Morris, *Early Warning Indicators of Corporate Failure* (Ashgate/ICCA, London 1997); see also J. Day and P. Taylor, 'Financial Distress in Small Firms: The Role Played by Debt Covenants and Other Monitoring Devices' [2001] Ins. Law. 97.

[7] In Belcher's terms a 'default proper' as opposed to a 'technical default' of a loan term, which relates not to principal and interest payments but to other issues, e.g. retention by the firm of a minimum level of net worth.

[8] Profitability ratios address the firm's effectiveness using available resources, liquidity ratios speak to its capacity to pay its debts in the short term and longer term, solvency ratios consider the firm's capital structure and its ability to meet longer-term financial commitments (see Belcher, *Corporate Rescue*, p. 40). Ratios are often used in attempts to predict insolvency: on which see ibid., ch. 4; E. I. Altman, 'Financial Ratios, Discriminant Analysis and the Prediction of Corporate Failure' (1968) 23 *Journal of Finance* 589; J. Pesse and D. Wood, 'Issues in Assessing MDA Models of Corporate Failure: A Research Note' (1992) 24 *British Accounting Review* 33; R. Taffler, 'Forecasting Company Failure in the UK Using Discriminant Analysis and Financial Ratio Data' (1982) *Journal of Royal Statistical Society*, Series A, 342.

[9] Wruck defines financial distress as 'a situation where cash flow is insufficient to cover current obligations. These obligations can include unpaid debts to suppliers and employees, actual or potential damages from litigation and missed principal or interest payments': K. Wruck, 'Financial Distress, Reorganisation and Organisational Efficiency' (1990) 27 *Journal of Financial Economics* 419 at 421.

[10] See R. M. Goode, *Principles of Corporate Insolvency Law* (3rd edn, Sweet & Maxwell, London, 2005) ch. 4; *Boyle and Birds' Company Law* (6th edn, Jordans, Bristol, 2007) pp. 846–8; A. Keay and P. Walton, *Insolvency Law: Corporate and Personal* (2nd edn, Jordans, Bristol, 2008) ch. 2.

legal definition of inability to pay debts. Within the Insolvency Act 1986 and other insolvency-related statutes there are a number of tests of insolvency and these relate to the purposes of different legislative provisions. The two main reference points regarding the inability to pay debts are the 'cash flow' and the 'balance sheet' tests.[11] The cash flow test is set out in section 123(1)(e) of the Insolvency Act 1986 and, according to this, a company is insolvent when it is unable to pay its debts as they fall due.[12] (The fact that the firm's assets exceed its liabilities is irrelevant.)[13] The courts, moreover, will pay regard to the firm's actual conduct so that insolvency will be assumed if the company is not in fact paying its debts as they fall due.[14] A further issue is whether future debts can be considered as part of the cash flow test. This was discussed in the *Cheyne Finance* decision[15] in which Briggs J said that, although Parliament had removed the requirement to include contingent and prospective liabilities in framing what is now section 123(1)(e), it had added the words 'as they fall due' which merely replaced 'one futurity requirement with another' and, accordingly, future debts could play a role in the cash flow test.[16]

Insolvency under this test is a ground for a winding-up order[17] or an administration order[18] or for setting aside transactions at undervalue, preferences and floating charges given other than for specified forms of new value.[19]

The balance sheet or asset test of section 123(2) of the Insolvency Act 1986 considers whether the company's assets are insufficient to discharge its liabilities, 'taking into account its contingent and prospective

---

[11] See Goode, *Principles of Corporate Insolvency Law*, pp. 85–9. Note that the Insolvency Act 1986 s. 123(1)(a) and (b) provides two specific alternative methods of establishing inability to pay debts to facilitate the proof of insolvency (i.e. for creditors) for the purposes of winding up or administration proceedings.

[12] The difficulty with the cash flow test is that 'its meaning is vague and imprecise and determining whether a person or company is, on a particular day, insolvent, is often difficult'. Keay and Walton, *Insolvency Law*, p. 16.

[13] See *Cornhill Insurance plc* v. *Improvement Services Ltd* [1986] 1 WLR 114.

[14] Ibid.   [15] *Re Cheyne Finance plc* [2008] BCC 199.

[16] See K. Baird and P. Sidle, 'Cash Flow Insolvency' (2008) 21 *Insolvency Intelligence* 40; T. Bugg, 'Cheyne Finance' (2008) *Recovery* (Spring) 10. The *Cheyne Finance* case concerned the contractual drafting of an insolvency event of default clause, not a petition presented on grounds of cash flow insolvency, and Briggs J's comments are, strictly, *obiter*. It is arguable, however, that the courts are likely to apply common approaches to the cash flow test when deciding either petition or default clause cases: see Baird and Sidle at p. 41.

[17] Insolvency Act 1986 s. 122(1)(f).   [18] Insolvency Act 1986 Sch. B1, paras. 11, 111(1).

[19] Insolvency Act 1986 ss. 238–42 and 245, especially ss. 240(2) and 245(4).

liabilities'. This may involve assessing the value of assets and judging the amount the asset would raise in the market; though a difficulty arises through the Act's failure to indicate whether valuations should be made on the basis of a 'going concern' or 'break-up' sale. Particular difficulties may arise where there is no established market value for the commodity. The test, furthermore, gives rise to potential problems in so far as there is no statutory definition of prospective liabilities. Standard accounting practice treats contingent liabilities more subtly than section 123(2) and that section does not include any particular basis for measuring assets and liabilities.[20] The balance sheet test is also one of the tests prescribed for the purpose of grounds for winding up,[21] administration[22] or the avoidance of transactions at undervalue,[23] preferences[24] and certain floating charges.[25] It is also a test relevant in considering the disqualification of directors[26] and is the one test used in identifying insolvent liquidation for the purposes of assessing directorial liabilities for wrongful trading.[27]

Defining insolvency at law is further complicated by the use of further tests in statutes other than the Insolvency Act 1986. Thus, under the Company Directors' Disqualification Act 1986, a company becomes insolvent for the purposes of potential directorial disqualification if its assets are insufficient for the payment of its debts and other liabilities together with the expenses of winding up, or when it goes into liquidation or when an administration order is made or an administrative receiver is appointed.[28] Under the Employment Rights Act 1996, and for purposes concerning employee rights to payment from the National Insurance Fund on an employer's insolvency and the employee's job termination, the employer is deemed insolvent when a winding-up order or administration order has been made; a resolution for voluntary winding up has been passed with respect to the company; a receiver or manager has been appointed; possession has been taken by holders of debentures secured by floating charges; or any property that is the subject

---

[20] See Belcher, *Corporate Rescue*, pp. 46–7. Prospective and contingent liabilities must be taken into account according to *Re A Company (No. 006794 of 1983)* [1986] BCC 261.

[21] Inability to pay debts for the purposes of winding-up orders can also be assessed in ways independent of insolvency: see Goode, *Principles of Corporate Insolvency Law*, p. 90.

[22] Insolvency Act 1986 Sch. B1, paras. 11, 111(1).

[23] Ibid., ss. 238, 240(2).   [24] Ibid., ss. 239, 240(2).   [25] Ibid., ss. 245, 245(4).

[26] Company Directors' Disqualification Act (CDDA) 1986 s. 6(2).

[27] Insolvency Act 1986 s. 214.   [28] CDDA 1986 s. 6(2).

of a charge and a voluntary arrangement has been approved under Part I of the Insolvency Act 1986.[29]

Finally, for the purposes of a member's voluntary winding up under section 89 of the Insolvency Act 1986, the company's directors must make a declaration of solvency but reference is not made to the cash flow or balance sheet tests. The issue is whether the company will be able to pay its debts in full, together with interest at the official rate, within such period (not exceeding twelve months from the commencement of the winding up) to be stipulated in the declaration.

Insolvency law thus defines 'insolvency' in different ways for different purposes.[30] Legal definitions, moreover, are not the only measures for corporate failure. If economic criteria are employed, a company might be said to be failing if it cannot realise a rate of return on invested capital that, bearing in mind the risks involved, is significantly greater than prevailing market rates on similar investments. Such failure would not necessarily lead to 'legal' insolvency but, if lasting in nature, this is a possibility. Alternatively, a failure to produce appropriate financial returns might result in corporate financial distress or investor-driven changes in the company's staffing and strategies.

Who defines insolvency?

A corporate insolvency can involve a number of concerned parties. These include creditors, shareholders, group subsidiaries,[31] directors and managers of the company, employees, suppliers and customers. A host of professional advisers will also have a role to play and these may include financial and management consultants, lawyers, bankers and accountants.

As seen above, there is no simple objective point in corporate affairs when the law states that the company is insolvent. The law creates opportunities for action rather than laying down consequences for stipulated states of affairs. Different tests are applied for different purposes and there are judgements involved in assessing each test. Thus, the question of whether a firm fails on the cash flow test of ability to pay debts depends on a set of constructions. As Miller and Power have put it: 'Corporate

---

[29] See Goode, *Principles of Corporate Insolvency Law*, p. 92.

[30] Thus we have seen that the Insolvency Act 1986 confines the term 'insolvency' to a formal insolvency proceeding: Insolvency Act 1986 ss. 240(3), 247(1). The phrase 'unable to pay its debts' embodies the concept of a *state* of insolvency: see Goode, *Principles of Corporate Insolvency Law*, p. 84.

[31] See ch. 13 below.

failure is itself constituted out of an assemblage of calculative technologies, expert claims and modes of judgment.'[32] Not only different parties but also different professionals will possess distinctive ways of perceiving and constructing corporate events and of deciding how to respond to these. Accountants invariably have a choice of ways to portray a company's performance in both healthy and troubled times.[33] There is a variety of ways, moreover, to deal with financial challenges and distress so that insolvency becomes as much a negotiable or technical issue for the accountant as an objective one.[34] The law, on this view, can be seen as overlaid on the facts as established by the accountants, so that 'the calculative technologies of accountancy trigger legal processes and provide the knowledge of those processes that law comes to administer after the event'.[35] The accountants can thus be seen as straddling the corporate process and not only providing auditing, consultancy and other services for healthy companies, but also dominating the legally created market for insolvency administration and the extra-legal market for corporate rescue. In these roles, the accountants carry out regulatory, advisory and managerial functions. The law says little in detail about the economic substance of corporate failure (it prefers to set down procedures for dealing with vaguely defined circumstances) and, because this is the case, it creates a 'legal space in which such matters can be negotiated'.[36] The legal process thus becomes highly dependent on extra-legal expertise: on the portrayals of corporate affairs that are presented by the accountancy and economic professionals who appear before the courts and pull the triggers created by the insolvency legislation.[37] Central to such endeavours are the ratio analyses that have 'transformed the nature of corporate failure and opened it up to a new regime of judgment and assessment'.[38] The conception of

---

[32] P. Miller and M. Power, 'Calculating Corporate Failure' in Y. Dezalay and D. Sugarman (eds.), *Professional Competition and Professional Power: Lawyers, Accountants and the Social Construction of Markets* (Routledge, London, 1995).

[33] On the weak role of accountants and auditors in securing information for assessing corporate health, from an Australian perspective, see F. Clarke, G. Dean and K. Oliver, *Corporate Collapse: Accounting, Regulatory and Ethical Failure* (rev. edn, Cambridge University Press, Cambridge, 2003) ch. 17.

[34] Miller and Power, 'Calculating Corporate Failure', p. 54.   [35] Ibid., p. 56.

[36] Ibid., p. 58; though see the portrayals of insolvency practitioner work as obfuscatory rather than negotiatory in S. Wheeler, *Reservation of Title Clauses* (Oxford University Press, Oxford, 1991).

[37] On the role of insolvency professionals in shaping insolvency processes see ch. 5 below.

[38] Miller and Power, 'Calculating Corporate Failure', p. 59. For a classic multi-variant analysis looking at the ratios of working capital to total assets; retained earnings to total assets; earnings before interest and losses to total assets; market value of equity to book

economic viability, in turn, becomes a matter of debate over accountants' calculative technologies so that, at the end of the day, the accountants play as much of a role in constructing the events of insolvency as do lawyers, judges or involved parties.

The message for insolvency lawyers is that insolvency law, to be understood, has to be seen as a tool in the hands of different professionals, one that is manipulated in different ways by those groupings. The resultant processes are consequently not fully captured by images of legal definition and the mechanical transposition of insolvency law into practice.

Why companies fail

Companies can be said, in the main, to fail through either internal deficiencies (such as poor management) or pressures exerted by external factors (such as global credit crises).[39] This section reviews the causes of failure and the concluding section considers the potential impact of insolvency law on these respective causes.

value of long-term debts and sales to total assets, see E. I. Altman, *Corporate Bankruptcy in America* (D. C. Heath, London, 1971).

[39] The R3 Twelfth Survey, p. 26, indicated that the three most frequently cited primary reasons for failure were: loss of market; loss of finance; and managerial failings (fraud; over-optimism in planning; imprudent accounting; erosion of margins; product obsolescence/technical failure; over-gearing). The normal risks of entrepreneurship have been said to cause 63 per cent of European business failures: see R. Meuwissen, G. Mertens and L. Bollen, *Classification and Analysis of Major European Business Failures* (Accounting, Auditing and Information Management Research Centre and RSM Erasmus University, Maastricht/Rotterdam, October 2005) (hereafter 'Maastricht Report 2005'). For a study of clothing companies and media/marketing companies in distress see Day and Taylor, 'Financial Distress in Small Firms', p. 107. On corporate failure see C. F. Pratten, *Company Failure* (Institute of Chartered Accountants in England and Wales, London, 1991); C. Campbell and B. Underdown, *Corporate Insolvency in Practice: An Analytical Approach* (Chapman, London, 1991); H. D. Platt, *Why Companies Fail: Strategies for Detecting, Avoiding, and Profiting from Bankruptcy* (Lexington Books, Lexington, Mass., 1985); J. Argenti, *Corporate Collapse: The Causes and Symptoms* (McGraw-Hill, London, 1976). Insolvency practitioners tend to put most corporate failures down to mismanagement of one kind or another. A 1991 Harrison Willis survey of 200 IPs listed the top ten reasons for failure as: (1) poor management; (2) poor management information; (3) high gearing; (4) poor financial controls; (5) high interest rates; (6) poor cash flow/cash management; (7) slow response to changing markets; (8) excessive overheads/spending; (9) lack of strategic plan; (10) poor communication with banks: see Cork Gully Discussion Paper No. 1 (London, June 1991) p. 2.

Internal factors

Poor financial controls[40]

The immediate cause of failure in a company is a lack of cash available to pay bills when they are due. A common cause of corporate decline, accordingly, is failure to take adequate steps to control cash flows. In the normal course of business a company's current bank account is liable to fluctuate from deficit to surplus levels as it issues funds to purchase materials, pays its work forces, produces its goods and then awaits the inflow of funds through payment of customers' bills. (Such fluctuations may be compounded where the firm's business is seasonal in nature.) Managing cash flows involves the collection of relevant information and the organisation of this: normally the charting out of anticipated cash receipts and disbursements on a weekly or monthly basis. Planning cash flows will involve consulting with lenders, negotiating appropriate credit lines and presenting potential lenders with projected cash flows, plans for product or market development and, amongst other things, programmes for cost control. Such planning has to cope with a number of situations that can decrease liquidity. These situations include: trading losses that reduce cash flows and assets relative to liabilities; bad debts or other write-offs; needed investments in expansion; and falls in the value of assets (which reduce the company's ability to raise cash by granting security).[41]

The firm's managers will aim to make arrangements with the firm's bankers and other creditors so that funds are available to bridge the gaps between deficit and surplus and to continue funding production, marketing and sales activities. At the same time, the firm has to remain able to pay its own debts as they fall due. Funds, accordingly, must be negotiated to allow such obligations to be met. Where the firm's creditors are no longer willing to lend (perhaps because they have lost confidence in the firm's management), or where loan arrangements have not been negotiated, the firm may find it difficult to keep operating or to pay its debts unless it has taken other steps to deal with cash flow problems, such as maintaining a level of cash reserves sufficient to sustain itself between the troughs and peaks.

---

[40] Poor financial controls are dealt with separately here from mismanagement but may be seen as a particular form of managerial failure: see Platt, *Why Companies Fail.*

[41] See Pratten, *Company Failure,* p. 8. The use of credit management procedures and services (e.g. the use of business information reports, credit insurance and debt collection services) can minimise the risk of a company failing due to poor cash flow: see T. Byrne, 'Credit Management and Cash Flow in Businesses' (2007) *Recovery* (Spring) 38.

Over-dependence on short-term financing may, in turn, lead to financial difficulties. Thus, where a firm resorts to overdraft financing in order to fund long-term investment plans, it becomes highly vulnerable. If the bank withdraws the overdraft facility the firm may not have time to obtain alternative funding before it enters difficulties.[42] Lack of control over current assets is a further major cause of corporate failure. When assets are purchased on credit they have to be used in a manner that allows interest payments to be paid and a profit made. If assets are unused or wasted, a company will be in financial trouble unless other activities can carry the losses. Managers must invest in assets such as equipment so as to meet market demands, but they must be wary of possible market changes that will reduce or remove the potential profitability of their equipment. Assets, accordingly, must be managed so that, overall, a firm has sufficient flexibility to cope with market changes. Attention has to be paid to the balance between long-term fixed asset costs (funds tied up with, say, machines) and variable cost items (e.g. labour and fuel costs which are more easily adjusted than fixed asset costs). Long-term assets (e.g. steel production plants) can be highly profitable but they carry greater risks than variable cost items due to their inflexibility, particularly if they are specialist in nature and there is no ready market providing a means to realise their value by sale. If the balance of a firm's investment is tilted too far in the direction of long-term fixed costs, its ability to cope with slow markets diminishes and failure may result.

Similarly, problems may arise where the company operates with 'high gearing': arrangements that involve a high proportion of fixed interest commitments or fixed interest capital in relation to the firm's total assets (i.e. all fixed and current assets). With high gearing a firm devotes a high proportion of its gross profits to the servicing of loan capital. It accordingly becomes highly vulnerable to changes in market conditions and interest rates.[43] Poor control of gearing may thus cause firms to fail when general economic, or particular market, conditions deteriorate or when

---

[42] The Bank of England has in the past expressed unease at the dependence of small UK businesses (highlighted by the recession of the early 1990s) on overdraft facilities to finance anything from working capital to long-term investment projects: see Bank of England, *Finance for Small Firms*, Sixth Report (1999), p. 28.

[43] On high gearing, the vulnerability of the corporate sector and the rise of private equity transactions see ch. 3 above; and Bank of England, *Financial Stability Review* (Bank of England, 2005) p. 14.

there is a credit squeeze[44] and there is some evidence that companies with high gearing are more likely to move into crisis than those with low gearing.[45]

Inadequate financing is a further cause of failure. This may occur when the company fails to raise sufficient funds by debt or equity means to render its operation profitable. If funds, for instance, suffice for production purposes but do not provide adequately for marketing and sales activities, the company is unlikely to make ends meet. Over-expansion and over-trading may also produce severe problems when a firm increases its volume of business more quickly than it is able to raise the funds necessary to finance such operations properly.[46]

Mismanagement

Most English company directors are untrained and unqualified.[47] Poor management, moreover, has been said to account for around a third of company insolvencies.[48] One survey has suggested that in 46 per cent of

---

[44] On the speed with which credit shocks can occur and the aftermath of the US sub-prime mortgage market crisis see Bank of England, *Financial Stability Review* (Bank of England, 2007), ch. 1; *Shocks to the UK Financial System* (Bank of England, 2007). See also G. Walker, 'Sub-prime Loans, Inter-bank Markets and Financial Support' (2008) 29 Co. Law. 22.

[45] See R. Hamilton, B. Halcroft, K. Pond and Z. Liew, 'Back from the Dead: Survival Potential in Administrative Receiverships' (1997) 13 IL&P 78, 80. Companies with cyclical markets and high gearing will be especially vulnerable – and such markets tend to be found in certain sectors, for instance, computer software, automotive, non-food retailing, construction and media.

[46] Over-expansion is the most frequent corporate weakness identified by J. Stein, 'Rescue Operations in Business Crises' in K. J. Hopt and G. Teubner (eds.), *Corporate Governance and Directors' Liabilities: Legal, Economic, and Sociological Analyses on Corporate Social Responsibility* (De Gruyter, Berlin, 1985) p. 380.

[47] An IOD report published in 1998 indicated that directors had become more professional since the beginning of that decade but that there were still 'shortcomings' in their behaviour (65 per cent of respondents had 'prepared themselves' for their boardroom role compared with just 10 per cent in 1990; the proportion of respondents taking training courses had also increased from 8 per cent to 27 per cent; but while 61 per cent of respondents – mainly senior directors of small to medium-sized companies – said directors should have a formal induction to the board, only 6 per cent had had such an induction themselves: IOD, *Sign of the Times* (IOD, London, 1998)).

[48] The SPI Twelfth Survey reported in 2004 that 32 per cent of company failure factors could be put down primarily to bad management. The notion of mismanagement can, however, be drawn sufficiently widely to produce far higher figures. See, for example, Campbell and Underdown, *Corporate Insolvency*, pp. 1–3: 'Companies become insolvent when their management fails to develop adequate long term strategic plans to deal with problems of profitability and cash flow.' (The most frequent managerial failings noted in the SPI Twelfth Survey were excessive overheads, engaging in new ventures/expansions/

cases, companies fail because of matters primarily in the control of the management and that in almost a quarter of cases businesses would have been rescuable if directors had sought the right advice earlier.[49] Some commentators have cautioned, however, that mismanagement often provides a more convincing explanation of *which* firms in a trade fail than of the *number* of firms that fail (which may be dictated by the nature of the market, the product and the role of available economies of scale).[50] One aspect of poor management already discussed is an inability to establish adequate financial controls, and poor information collection and use is very often associated with poor financial controls. Lack of cost information is a major failing since successful corporate operation demands that managers possess knowledge concerning the profitability of the firm's different activities. It is essential to know, for instance, if the price at which a product is being sold is producing profits for the company. Selling at a price below cost will soon lead to failure. Other informational deficiencies may involve the lack of cash flow forecasts, the absence of budgetary control data and the non-availability of figures on the values of company assets.[51] Information, moreover, must flow properly through the firm and poor lines of communication have been said to be one of the main causes of failure.[52] 'Creative accounting' techniques can disguise the true state of financial affairs in a company or can delay the emergence of accurate information about the firm. Such techniques, accordingly, can contribute to mismanagement generally and can reduce the company's ability to respond successfully to market and other pressures.[53] They can also lead managers, investors and bankers to expand corporate operations more rapidly, and at higher risk, than the true state of affairs merits. Creative accounting techniques may also camouflage

acquisitions, lack of information, over-optimism in planning and erosion of margins.) The prevalence of family-run businesses in the UK has been cited as a cause of poor management: see N. Bloom, *Inherited Family Firms and Management Practices* (Centre for Economic Performance, LSE, London, 2006). See also p. 158 below.

[49] See R3 Ninth Survey (2001), p. 2. In the case of larger companies with over £5 million turnover R3 suggested that nearly half could have been rescued if the right advice had been sought (ibid., p. 3).

[50] See Platt, *Why Companies Fail*, p. 6.

[51] Argenti, *Corporate Collapse*, pp. 26–7, 30–3, 94–5.

[52] Ibid., p. 30 (reporting the assessment of Mr Kenneth Cork, as he then was).

[53] On creative accounting and whether auditors should control this more rigorously, see Pratten, *Company Failure*, pp. 50–1; Clarke, Dean and Oliver, *Corporate Collapse*, ch. 2. On auditing as a preoccupation and an end in itself rather than an effective management tool see M. Power, *The Audit Society: Rituals of Verification* (Oxford University Press, Oxford, 1997) ch. 6.

the firm's true levels of debt or inflate profit and asset figures and, as a result, managers may be led to raise the gearing of the company in a dangerous manner.

It has been suggested that accountants in auditing and advisory roles might play a stronger role in ensuring that accurate information is available on a company's financial position and in warning of dangers.[54] Moves on two fronts might thus be considered: methods of reporting to management and shareholders could be rethought; and accountants' training might be revised so as to improve their managerial advisory role.[55] On the first front, however, it should not be assumed that auditing strategies and assumptions can be revised to reveal the 'true position' of a company. Uncertainties in markets and future prospects will always mean that such items as asset valuations contain elements of uncertainty. What can, perhaps, be done is to map out the location and extent of uncertainties in as clear a way as possible.[56] A further key issue is whether auditors can make reliable assessments of the degree to which a company is at risk.[57] Auditors suffer from a number of limitations in judging corporate prospects, not least their restricted knowledge of managers' forthcoming strategies and decisions in a changing marketplace. There

---

[54] See, for example, Pratten, *Company Failure*, p. 48 and references to press reports therein. For doubts as to whether the present audit model is capable of identifying and dealing effectively with managers determined to perpetrate fraud see Maastricht Report 2005. The credit crisis of 2008 was reported as prompting auditors to hold 'unusually early discussions' with companies over year-end results focusing on their financing and ability to continue as a going concern, while the UK accounts watchdog, the Financial and Reporting Review Panel, warned that scrutiny in 2008 would be focused on banks, retailers, commercial property, leisure and house builders where it perceived the biggest risks to viability lay: see J. Hughes, 'Auditors Seek Early Scrutiny', *Financial Times*, 14 August 2008.

[55] Pratten, *Company Failure*, p. 50.

[56] See, for example, Power, *Audit Society*, p. 144: 'The issue is rather a question of organisational design capable of building in "moral competence" and of providing regulated fora of openness around these competences.'

[57] Pratten, *Company Failure*, p. 57. See M. Power, *Organised Uncertainty: Designing a World of Risk Management* (Oxford University Press, Oxford, 2007) where it is argued that the rise of risk management has also coincided with an intensification of auditing and control processes. On the accountancy profession's concern at the 'expectations gap' – the difference between what audits do achieve and what it is thought they achieve, or should achieve – see the *Report of the Committee on the Financial Aspects of Corporate Governance* (Cadbury Committee) (December 1992) paras. 2.1 and 5.4; J. Freedman, 'Accountants and Corporate Governance: Filling a Legal Vacuum?' (1993) *Political Quarterly* 285.

are dangers, moreover, that overt auditors' warnings of risk might themselves contribute to corporate troubles.

As for training and advice, accountants might focus more on such topics as the causes of corporate failure, the requirements of success and the economics of pricing. They might, accordingly, strengthen their roles in advising corporate managers during the ongoing process of corporate decision-making. This, in turn, might be expected to improve information use and managerial decision-making more generally. The result could, for instance, be greater managerial awareness of the dangers involved in creative accounting or in failing to develop accurate costing figures.

Managers may also prove deficient by failing to respond to changes in the company's environment.[58] Thus, when key personnel depart from a company or markets or technologies move in new directions, a company's managers must be capable of developing new staffing arrangements and new products and strategies to keep the firm competitive.[59] Appropriate information and research and development systems are likely to be necessary if such lack of responsiveness is to be avoided. Being responsive, moreover, may demand that managers counter their natural inclinations to over-commit to strategies that they have set in train. It has been argued that corporate decision-makers tend to be psychologically biased in a number of ways that make it difficult to exit from losing strategies.[60] One suggested bias involves an excessive focus on sunk costs and moneys already committed to a project. This produces a tendency, even when projections are bleak, to throw good money after bad in an effort to justify or make good on the past investment. A second bias favours adhering to initial estimations of potential gains and involves a slowness to adjust these to changes in market conditions. These biases, it is contended, affect the timing of decisions both to pull out of ill-fated projects and to seek help when the company meets more general financial difficulties.

---

[58] Campbell and Underdown, *Corporate Insolvency*, p. 18.

[59] Loss of an established competitive advantage has been said to be 'generally fatal' because it is so difficult to regain a competitively supreme position: see J. Kay, 'Fallen Companies Rarely Make It Back to the Top' *Financial Times*, 16 November 2007.

[60] See J. Horn, D. Lovallo and S. Viguerie, 'Learning to Let Go: Making Better Exit Decisions' (2006) 2 *McKinsey Quarterly* 64–75. 'More often, evidence in support of management strategies is overvalued while evidence against it is undervalued ... Under threat, management becomes hyper-resistant to change': J. Baum, 'The Value of a Failing Grade', *Financial Times, Mastering Risk*, 9 September 2005. Joel Baum argues, however, that failure may, in fact, be a more valuable learning experience than success.

A further managerial failing may involve leaving the company particularly vulnerable to changes in the market or the broader environment: as where an excessive dependence on a particular supplier contract or customer is allowed to build up and inadequate provision is made for the departure of that supplier or customer.

Managers may fail simply because they lack appropriate skills.[61] They may be brilliant engineers but poor financial directors. Lack of identification with the company's interests may be another managerial failing. This may range from a targeting of personal rather than corporate objectives through to practices of defrauding the company for the purpose of making illegal personal gains.[62] Fraudsters may, for example, forge cheques in their own favour or steal the stock of the company. Directors may engage in extravagant lifestyles at the firm's expense, employees may turn their backs on corporate interests and parent or associate companies may milk successful businesses of their profits, put no investment back into those businesses but use the proceeds to fund other operations within a group. All of these forms of conduct, illegal and legitimate, may drive a firm into failure.

In the case of small businesses, it has been suggested that a fifth of all failures are attributable to marketing errors.[63] A company's managers may have conducted inadequate research into markets and competitors, they may have failed to set up effective organisations for marketing or may have adopted weak sales strategies. Managers of small firms may, indeed, have a general tendency to focus on product development and give too little attention to marketing.[64]

---

[61] It has been argued, on the basis of a survey of over 730 medium-sized companies in the UK, France, Germany and the USA, that when managers are chosen from the members of the owning family the company tends to be poorly managed – and especially so if the CEO is selected by primogeniture. The reasons given in explanation are that this narrows the available pool of managerial talent drastically and that inherited rights to manage tend to reduce levels of effort. See Bloom, *Inherited Family Firms*.

[62] The Maastricht/Erasmus study of 2005 suggested that 37 per cent of European business failures involve fraudulent or unethical behaviour by managers or employees (see Maastricht Report 2005, p. 8), but, for a view that fraud-induced failures are, in fact, rare, see Pratten, *Company Failure*, p. 6; K. Cork, *Cork on Cork: Sir Kenneth Cork Takes Stock* (Macmillan, London, 1988).

[63] See M. Gaffney, 'Small Firms Really Can Be Helped' (1983) *Management Accounting* (February).

[64] See Campbell and Underdown, *Corporate Insolvency*, p. 21. An analysis of sixty major failures in the European Union over the last twenty-five years concluded that failed companies tended to fall into four categories: the basically unhealthy; those with over-ambitious management; those failing to adapt to change; and those afflicted by dominant managers and fraudulent or unethical behaviour: see Maastricht Report 2005.

Managers may perform their own tasks competently but they may prove to be poor leaders. Poor management may thus lead to inadequacies of supervision, morale and productivity. As a result, the company may operate with high costs, low productivity and diminishing levels of profit. The governance structure of a company may also prove conducive to mismanagement.[65] This may be the case with notable frequency in certain circumstances: where, for instance, a single individual dominates a company;[66] where there is an imbalance on the board (between, for example, financial and technical experts); or where there is a lack of representation on the board (e.g. of accountants). Where procedures for briefing managers and board members are inadequate this, again, may lead to defective control mechanisms and poor decision-making in the company.

As for the characteristics of those managers that are associated with corporate failure, Stein has suggested that the following traits tend to be exhibited by insolvency-prone managers.[67] First, all bad managers tend to be 'out of touch with reality', a condition in which they possess little consciousness of risks. This propensity tends to be found together with high levels of technical knowledge and a willingness to learn on the technological front, or else with high ability in marketing and sales. The area of risk tending to be neglected by such managers is that associated with growth and over-expansion. Second, bad managers tend to be very strong willed, autocratic, unwilling to delegate and able to impose themselves on their business partners and co-workers.[68] Such

---

[65] See C. Daley and C. Dalton, 'Bankruptcy and Corporate Governance: The Impact of Board Composition and Structure' (1994) 37 *Academy of Management Journal* 1603.

[66] See Argenti's discussion of Rolls Royce's troubles in the early 1970s: *Corporate Collapse*, ch. 5.

[67] Stein, 'Rescue Operations in Business Crises'. In 1996 the business information group CN published research indicating that nearly 4,000 company directors (four times as many as had previously been thought) had been associated with more than ten company failures: *Financial Times*, 28 October 1996. (CN reported that of the 2.6 million UK company directors on its database, 952,432 (or 37 per cent) had been associated with one or more failures in the previous seven years and one in twelve directors was a 'serial failure' associated with at least two collapses.)

[68] A relevant portrait emerged when, in 2007, two directors of Independent Insurance were convicted of conspiracy to defraud (after the company plummeted from stock market darling to insolvency). The former Chief Executive's own QC said, in mitigation, that 'corporate arrogance' had been fostered by his client's belief that the company was 'his baby' and that with brilliance had come 'an overbearing, unreasonable dominance, a management style that was simply unacceptable': see M. Peel, 'Former Insurance Executives Face Jail', *Financial Times*, 24 October 2007.

dominance tends to be underpinned by their high abilities with regard to technical or sales issues and their uncritical attitude to growth. Almost all such individuals possess 'remarkable stress tolerance'[69] and the high level of their assertiveness often translates into ambitious plans for corporate dominance of the market. In around half of such individuals there is a tendency to personal high living.

A different sort of manager is, according to Stein, also associated with corporate failure and this is labelled the 'improvident' manager. This individual tends to act in an ill-informed, 'blind' fashion in pursuit of favourable opportunities to advance in the market and tends not to carry out the necessary studies on the sustainability of an expansion or the financial underpinnings required for such a development.

Mismanagement, moreover, may be seen in the shape of single aberrant acts as well as in ongoing weaknesses. Corporate managers may make catastrophic mistakes or fail to deal with particular problems and, in doing so, may place the company in peril. A decision, for instance, may be taken to move the firm's business into a market sector in which the firm is unable to compete, or a huge investment may be put into the production of a poor product. Corporate managers may also embark on a project so large that its failure will place the survival of the company at risk.[70] Such managers may err, again, by buying other companies that are weak, over-priced and whose acquisition cannot be turned to advantage.[71] Thus, a manager looking for growth will often acquire another company by paying a premium and will hope to find synergies and methods of cutting costs. Frequently, though, difficulties arise because the buying company's directors have overestimated their understandings of the targeted firm, because the information systems of the companies are incompatible or because the expected synergies are not yielded when market realities are faced.[72] Failure to deal with a key technological change may also constitute a managerial error that renders the firm's survival uncertain. Most products become obsolete as technologies advance, substitutes come on the scene or consumers' tastes change, and companies that fail to adapt in a suitable manner may go out of business.

---

[69] Stein, 'Rescue Operations in Business Crises', p. 390.

[70] See the discussion of the Rolls Royce RB211 project in Argenti, *Corporate Collapse*, ch. 5.

[71] An example of this was British and Commonwealth's acquisition of Atlantic Computers in the 1980s: see Pratten, *Company Failure*, p. 34. See also Campbell and Underdown, *Corporate Insolvency*, p. 23.

[72] See M. Skapinker, 'The Growing Pains Faced by New Parents', *Financial Times*, 24 January 2005.

External factors

External pressures routinely place companies under stress. Astute managerial teams tend to cope with such stresses and their companies usually survive. Such pressures, however, can lead lesser managers to fail. In the extreme, some external shocks may be so severe that even the most skilled managers cannot save the company.

Changing markets and economic conditions are factors that almost invariably impinge on corporate activities.[73] A business may fail because a demand swing is too severe for it to respond successfully: where, for example, consumers change a preference rapidly from one fashion design to another. The prices of raw materials may escalate in an unpredictable manner and to a degree that makes a company's product or price unattractive to consumers. A major competitor may attack the company's market with a level of commitment and aggression that pulls the financial carpet from beneath the company's feet, and economic cycles (often compounded by drops in investor confidence) may produce slumps that are so severe and sustained that the company fails. Since 1970 the economy has been subjected to a series of shocks which have caused problems for many companies. These shocks have included the oil price rises of 1973–4 and 1979–81, the wage explosions of 1973–4 and 1978–80,[74] and the credit squeeze of the early 1990s and the credit crisis of 2007–8.

Some trade sectors (notably manufacturing and construction)[75] are more prone to failure and insolvency than others and the seasonality encountered in some sectors can place severe stresses on corporate solvency. The seasonality of the toy industry, with its focus on Christmas sales and discounting at other times of the year, has been said to explain the sector's long history of corporate failures.[76]

---

[73] On instability of the global financial system, international market shifts, macroeconomic factors and recessions as causes of corporate failure see Bank of England, *Financial Stability Review*, 2008 (Issue 24) Summary (Bank of England, London, 2008); *Financial Stability Review*, 2007, ch. 1 and *Financial Stability Review*, 2005; K. Dyson and S. Wilks, 'The Character and Economic Content of Industrial Crisis' in Dyson and Wilks (eds.), *Industrial Crisis: A Comparative Study of the State and Industry* (Blackwell, Oxford, 1985).

[74] Pratten, *Company Failure*, p. 4.

[75] The R3 Twelfth Survey suggested that the service sector is the most prone to insolvency and accounts for 49 per cent of cases.

[76] SPI, Eighth Survey, *Company Insolvency in the United Kingdom* (SPI, London, 1999) p. 9.

Overseas producers can provide severe price competition and this has been identified as the probable cause of decline in UK manufacturing industries in such sectors as cars, motor cycles, machine tools, paper and textiles.[77] Nor do pressures come only from markets. Governments and regulatory bodies may take actions that precipitate failures. The British Government's high interest rate policy produced a surge of company failures in the second half of 1990, so that the number of companies entering receivership during those six months matched the figure for the whole of the preceding year. Companies also suffered shocks from high sterling exchange rates in 1980–1 and 1990–1, as well as from credit explosions in 1972–3 and 1986–9, and from the credit crisis in 2008.[78] Rapid inflation made matters worse for companies during the 1970s, early 1980s and in 1990. Recessions resulted in 1974–5, 1980–1 and 1990–1.[79] Adapting to such changes is particularly difficult for companies when the shocks cannot be predicted. Firms that relied on long-term fixed price contracts during the early 1970s were especially hard pressed by inflation.

Where companies operate with high levels of gearing and tight repayment schedules they will be particularly vulnerable to changes in overdraft costs when, as at the start and end of the 1980s, there are dramatic increases in the minimum lending rate.[80] If governments impose squeezes on credit, lenders will tend to ration credit and give priority to those firms that are considered the best risks. These are unlikely to be new or small firms or those with existing problems, and, accordingly, the proportion of loans going to established large firms will tend to rise when money is tight. Small firms tend to be less capable of surviving such credit shortages than large firms. So, overall, the result tends to be a rise in the number of small firm failures.[81] Governments may even precipitate

---

[77] See Campbell and Underdown, *Corporate Insolvency*, p. 19.

[78] On the credit crisis and financial instability of 2007/8 see further Bank of England, *Financial Stability Report – Issue 24* (2008); Bank of England News Release, *Financial Stability Report: Rebuilding Confidence in the Financial System* (28 October 2008); Bank of England and HM Treasury, *Financial Stability and Depositor Protection: Further Consultation* (Cm 7436) (July 2008), pp. 7–9; Technical Committee of the International Organization of Securities Commissions (IOSCO), *Report on the Subprime Crisis – Final Report* (May 2008) (www.iosco.org).

[79] Pratten, *Company Failure*, p. 4. In 2008 the Bank of England stated that a 'global economic turndown' was underway: see Bank of England News Release, *Financial Stability Report: Rebuilding Confidence in the Financial System*.

[80] See Campbell and Underdown, *Corporate Insolvency*, p. 19.

[81] See R3 Twelfth Survey, p. 5. In September 2008, Richard Roberts, head of small/medium-sized enterprise analysis at Barclays, forecast that 'We will probably see the [business]

corporate failures more directly when, for example, they withdraw or decline further financial aid, as occurred in January 1971 when the Government decided not to support Rolls Royce further in the RB211 engine affair[82] and, in October 2001, when anticipated state subsidies were not forthcoming and Railtrack was put into administration.

Regulators, be they agencies, government departments or European bodies, may impose critical stresses on companies by a number of routes. It is commonly complained by industry that the costs of complying with regulations are a burden (particularly for small businesses)[83] and, on occasion, such costs can break the camel's back.[84] In response, however, it can be said that competent managers will generally be able to cope with regulatory burdens, and that if regulation kills firms because the managers of those firms are incompetent, or because regulation outlaws a product central to the company's output, those firms should go to the wall because they are either uncompetitive or Parliament's voice demands that they cease business.[85] If regulators, for instance, enforce statutory rules prohibiting, say, the production of eggs in battery cages, and if battery producers fail to adapt by employing other processes, the effect will be to drive those producers out of business in accordance with the legislative will.

Regulators, however, may produce unjustifiable failures where they regulate badly. They may, for example, vacillate in their demands, delay licensing approvals unnecessarily and impose excessive costs on businesses. A failure to regulate may also produce insolvencies where, for instance, effective regulation is necessary to sustain consumer confidence in a product. The BSE crisis of 1996–9 demonstrated that regulatory deficiencies relating to animal foodstuffs can produce dramatic levels of corporate failure in the farming industry. Deregulation can also precipitate failure by breaking down the entry barriers that have protected enterprises and allowed relatively inefficient operators to survive. Where, moreover, there is a rush of new entrants into a competitive industry there may naturally follow a period in which the less efficient are weeded out. Rates of failure can be expected to rise where the costs of entry and exit to a newly deregulated sector are high.

Government taxation policies can also bring marginal companies to the point of failure and industrial relations problems can break companies. If production is stopped by a prolonged strike the consequences for a firm may be severe. Where the company's own workforce is involved in an industrial dispute the firm's managers may have some control over events and may have to shoulder some blame for mismanagement. If, however, the dispute is between employers and workers at a key supplier or customer, there may be little that even the most competent managers can do.[86]

Unexpected calamities may also threaten companies. These may range from natural disasters, such as earthquakes that destroy essential firm assets, to the illegal acts of humans, for example the criminal behaviour of a financial fraudster or an arsonist who burns down a firm's premises. Devastating losses may also result from new legal liabilities: thus a court decision rendering tobacco companies liable to governmental bodies for the cost of treating lung cancer sufferers might precipitate a series of corporate failures. Penalty clauses in contracts may produce similar effects where companies fail to deliver finished products on time.[87]

---

[86] See J. R. Lingard, *Corporate Rescues and Insolvencies* (2nd edn, Butterworths, London, 1989) p. 3.

[87] See Argenti, *Corporate Collapse*, p. 91 on the role of penalty clauses in the Rolls Royce failure of 1971; Cork, *Cork on Cork*.

Where a company trades with other companies, the latter may cause failure involuntarily: where, for example, they owe debts and fail to settle these before or after their own failures. The actions of a firm's creditors or investors may also bring about a downfall. Mention has already been made of the effects that a bank's withdrawal of an overdraft facility may have. Lenders may withdraw credit through lack of confidence in a firm's management, or as a result of government action (a credit squeeze), or because of instability in the global financial system (a credit crunch), or for reasons internal to the creditor itself, such as a new policy of shifting from overdraft to fixed-term lending. Similarly, investors in a company may take precipitate action for a number of reasons. They may lose confidence in the firm's business or its management and the shares may drop to a point that triggers a crisis of confidence in the company's creditors who then start pressing their claims. This process may spiral and bring about a company's collapse.[88]

Late payment of debts

Special mention should be made of the late payment issue. Many large firms use the process of delaying settling the invoices of small suppliers as a means of extracting credit from those suppliers.[89] Indeed, the evidence suggests that the problem of late payment is predominantly one of larger debtor companies failing to pay smaller suppliers – with the worst payers being in the construction, manufacturing, pharmaceuticals and retail sectors.[90] Late payments of this kind may present small firms with considerable cash flow problems[91] and such firms tend to be both ill-equipped to absorb financial shocks and poorly positioned to chase large debtors.[92] In 2007 three-quarters of respondents to a Forum of Private

[88] Pratten, *Company Failure*, p. 11.

[89] A 2004 survey by the Better Payment Practice Group suggested that more than one in ten companies were happy to pay their bills late: see J. Moules, 'One in Ten Companies Happy to Pay Bills Late', *Financial Times*, 13 October 2004.

[90] See DTI Consultation Paper, *Improving the Payment Culture* (DTI, July 1997) p. 11 and research by the Institute of Credit Management reported in D. Oakley, 'Chart of Shame Lists Time Taken to Settle Bills', *Financial Times*, 4 March 2008.

[91] Lloyds TSB figures released in 1998 suggested that delay in receiving payment was the single biggest worry for small businesses: *Guardian*, 27 October 1998. The Federation of Small Businesses suggested in 1997 that late payment accounted for 5,000 of the 40,000 small UK company failures of 1995 (*Financial Times*, 29 January 1997).

[92] SMEs in the UK have been said to spend in total over 11 million hours a week chasing unpaid invoices: see J. Moules, 'Cheque in the Post Takes Up 11m Hours a Week', *Financial Times*, 24 May 2005. An Institute of Directors survey of SME concerns found that late payment was the most frequently cited problem: see J. Eaglesham, 'Labour's "Fluffy Talk" on Business Problem', *Financial Times*, 13 August 2007.

Business survey cited late payment as a 'considerable threat to my business's viability'.[93]

In 1998 a statutory response to the problem of late payments came with the passing of the Late Payment of Commercial Debts (Interest) Act. This was added to by the Late Payment of Commercial Debts Regulations 2002 to make up a body of legislation that allows businesses and the public sector to claim interest (at reference rate plus 8 per cent)[94] on payments more than thirty days late and owed by businesses, large or small, or other organisations.[95] A right of pursuit in the courts is given to claimants, but the Act allows collection agents to be used or the sale of interest to a third party such as a factoring firm.

Such a statute was intended to assist in changing the commercial culture that endorses late payment as a means of obtaining credit from companies in weak bargaining positions,[96] but has it worked?[97] In 2004 a series of surveys suggested that the 1998 legislation had failed to curb the problem of late payments. In February 2004 Experian, the business information group, surveyed 30,000 firms and found that companies

---

[93] See Eaglesham, 'Labour's "Fluffy Talk" on Business Problem'.

[94] At the start of a six-month period the official dealing rate of the Bank of England (the base rate) will be made a fixed 'reference rate' for the subsequent six months. Thus for the period 1 July to 31 December 2008 the reference rate was 5.0% making the interest rate 13.0% (reference rate plus 8%).

[95] From 1 November 2000, small businesses have also been able to claim from other small businesses as well as from large businesses and the public sector. From 1 November 2002 all businesses and the public sector were entitled to claim on debts incurred after that date. See also the Council Directive on Late Payment of Commercial Debts (2000/35, 29 June 2000) published OJ 2000 No. L2000/35; G. McCormack, 'Retention of Title and the EC Late Payment Directive' [2001] 1 JCLS 501. On the 1998 Act see S. Baister, 'Late Interest on Debts' (1999) Insolvency Bulletin 5. Reasonable debt recovery costs have been claimable by all business owners and managers since 7 August 2002: Late Payment of Commercial Debt Regulations 2002. The compensation entitlement varies in accordance with the size of the debt: for unpaid debts of £10,000 and over the creditor pays £100.00; for unpaid debts of £1,000 to £9,999.99 the creditor pays £70.00 and for unpaid debts of up to £999.99 the creditor pays £40.00. The entitlement to compensation for debt recovery costs does not affect the claimant's other rights and the claimant may still go to court to recover specific fees and charges paid to specialist firms or advisers if felt necessary: see Small Business Service, Users' Guide to Late Payment (DTI, London, 2002).

[96] Under the revised legislation SMEs can ask a representative body to challenge grossly unfair contract terms used by their customers which do not provide a substantial remedy for late payment of commercial debts. A Code of Practice on payments was launched by BERR in December 2008.

[97] This section builds on V. Finch, 'Late Payment of Debt: Re-thinking the Response' (2005) 18 Insolvency Intelligence 38.

waited an average of fifty-eight days for settlement of invoices. This was half a day longer than in 1998, when the Late Payment of Commercial Debts (Interest) Act was passed. Payment delays in the UK averaged twenty-seven days beyond agreed payment terms, compared to ten days in France, seventeen in Germany and twenty-one in Italy. The payment record of larger companies had worsened markedly from 1998, with the average payment period increasing by six days to seventy-eight-and-a-half days. A month earlier, a survey by the Royal Bank of Scotland revealed that the cash flows of two-thirds of small businesses had been disrupted by late payment and two-fifths of these had taken legal action to recover money owed to them.[98] Later research by MacIntyre Hudson in May 2004 was even more pessimistic about the impact of the 1998 Act. It reported that only 43 per cent of owner-managers were even aware of the 1998 legislation and only 3 per cent had actually used this against their debtors. A mere 2 per cent said that the Act had helped them to overcome the problem of bad debt. In 2007 there were further protests that the legislation and regulations had failed.[99] A survey of 600 companies during that year suggested that, if anything, late payment had become a worse problem in the last ten years.[100] An Intrum Justitia ranking of 2007 placed Britain as the fifth worst European country out of twenty-two for delays in commercial payments – with an average of over forty days to achieve payment in the UK compared to twenty-two in Norway.[101] In early 2008 the average payment time for all plcs was forty-four days and a series of interviewees told the *Financial Times* that the late payment problem had grown materially worse in the difficult trading conditions of 2007 onwards.[102]

Why has the Act been so muted in effect? A major reason is that many companies, especially small ones, have proved reluctant to be seen to be taking aggressive action against a powerful trading partner. As Eddie Morrison of Bank of Scotland Corporate Banking said: 'Many

---

[98] See J. Guthrie, 'Legislation Has Failed to Curb Late Payments', *Financial Times*, 18 February 2004. In July 2004 Experian reported that the average payment period had risen again to fifty-nine-and-a-half days: see J. Moules, 'Legislation Fails to Curb Late Payment Problems', *Financial Times*, 28 July 2004.

[99] See J. Eaglesham, 'Act Has Failed Say Credit Experts', *Financial Times*, 13 August 2007.

[100] Ibid. See also A. Bounds, 'Rise in Legal Action on Unpaid Bills', *Financial Times*, 2 December 2008.

[101] In 2005 Intrum Justitia placed the UK seventh in Europe for promptness of payments: J. Moules, 'Significant Fall in Late Payment Risk', *Financial Times*, 23 June 2005.

[102] See Oakley, 'Chart of Shame Lists Time Taken to Settle Bills'; 'Stalling Tactics Help Companies Bolster Profits', *Financial Times*, 4 March 2008.

owner-managers would view levying a late payment charge on a client as commercial suicide.'[103] A significant proportion of small businesses told MacIntyre Hudson that using the legislation 'involved too much hassle'[104] and many smaller businesses will fear the cost and disruption involved in formal enforcement action.

It might be argued that the Act could be made more effective by providing that statutory interest should be *automatically* applicable without going to court, that companies should be entitled to *generous* costs when they enforce[105] or that the response to late payments could be reinforced by the institution of a new, cheap summary legal procedure for collecting late payments without the need to resort to using a lawyer. Such reforms may be desirable but they would not remove the fear of prejudicing business relationships that is the common inhibitor of enforcement.

What hope lies in other strategies? One possibility is a more effective information disclosure, or 'naming and shaming' strategy. Current arrangements here seem unnecessarily weak. All plcs and their large private subsidiaries have a statutory duty to disclose in their annual returns the average period they take to pay debts[106] but such disclosures may be poor indicators of tardiness beyond creditors', as opposed to debtors', notions of agreed payment dates. (Some debtors, for instance, may see payments as being late from the time a reminder or final demand is sent. This contrasts with creditors who will look to agreed dates for payment.) It is, moreover, straying beyond agreed dates, as understood by creditors, that is so important to smaller firms since this is what creates crippling uncertainties regarding cash flows. Most companies, furthermore, do not comply with the rules and make the due disclosures in the annual accounts. The FSB has suggested that only around 30 per cent of plcs comply with the disclosure obligations[107] and has called on Companies House to enforce such requirements more rigorously. Companies House, however, has been quoted as saying that: 'It is up to the accounting bodies

---

[103] See *Financial Times*, 21 January 2004.   [104] See *Financial Times*, 31 May 2004.

[105] Although the 2002 Regulations now allow all businesses to claim reasonable debt recovery costs there is an overall limit of £100 for each late payment, on a sliding scale. See p. 166 above.

[106] See Companies Act 1985 (Directors' Report) (Statement of Payment Practice) Regulations 1997 which amended CA 1985 s. 234 and Sch. 7, Part VI, requiring directors to report details of their payment practices to suppliers as well as the average time it takes them to pay their average debt.

[107] See J. Guthrie, 'Small Businesses Take Swipe at Bad Payers', *Financial Times*, 18 February 2004.

to enforce disclosure. It is nothing to do with us.'[108] For its part, the then DTI, through its Better Payment Practice Group, reportedly brought pressure to bear on the accounting bodies and reminded auditors of the duty to disclose payment periods in their annual returns. More action on this front would be required not only to produce compliance with disclosure requirements but also to ensure that average settlement times are not distorted by debtor conceptions of due dates.[109]

Disclosure-based controls can also be brought into effect by non-governmental bodies. The FSB, for instance, has been publishing a private-sector payment performance table since 1999.[110] The compilers of the FSB league tables, however, have to rely on disclosures by late payers in annual returns to Companies House. Such disclosures are, as noted, patchy, though, and it is likely that the poorest payers will not rank amongst the most assiduous suppliers of this kind of information. A way forward would be for the FSB to co-ordinate a blacklist based not on debtor confessions with all the attendant dangers of distortion and non-disclosure, but on creditor-supplied information that is subjected to a verification process prior to publication. This could operate through recording of creditor complaints about debtor companies and assistance in funding such a regime might be provided by BERR.

An alternative approach would be to rely on factoring. In such a system, the creditor would sell the debt to an intermediary factoring firm that would offer an immediate cash advance on the value of the outstanding invoice.[111] The factoring firm would then take advantage of the interest terms provided for in the 1998 Act and the sum passed on to the creditor would correspond to the interest-enhanced payment. The factoring firm's fee might be chargeable, by law, to the debtor over and above the invoiced sum plus statutory interest. Such a system might

---

[108] Ibid.

[109] In June 2007 ministers decided effectively to disband the Better Payment Practice Group as part of the downgrading of the small business service. This 'gives out the wrong signals to the business community. Late payment (is) the factor causing the most significant negative impact on smaller companies, yet government have withdrawn support and reduced funding on the very initiatives aimed at tackling this growing problem.' Miles Templeman, director-general of the IOD, cited in Eaglesham, 'Labour's "Fluffy Talk" on Business Problem'.

[110] The FSB Payment League Tables are now compiled by the Credit Management Research Centre, Leeds University Business School.

[111] In a factoring arrangement money is released against unpaid sales invoices. Up to 90 per cent of the value of the outstanding customer payment is advanced to the business within twenty-four hours of the invoice being raised. See further ch. 3 above.

improve recovery but, again, many small businesses might be reluctant to use this approach for fear of prejudicing a relationship with a supplier or powerful business partner.

A third possible way forward would be to take actions to encourage smaller companies to play the credit game more astutely. The routine use of prompt payment discounts might be put forward as a solution here but it may be difficult for many firms to use discounts productively because co-ordination between small firms would be required. Where such firms compete, the company offering an early payment discount to a powerful debtor may, in effect, be cutting its margins in the face of the large debtor company's propensity to delay payment.

Similarly, it could be proposed that smaller companies should be encouraged to avoid dependency on a large creditor so that they can discontinue their trading relationships with late payers. This, however, may not be possible in many sectors and such a strategy might lead to a lack of competitiveness with firms that are willing to accept greater risks of late payment.

What, however, smaller firms can perhaps do at low cost is to state more routinely and clearly the date on which any invoice is payable.[112] Such creditors, moreover, might be advised to research the creditworthiness of their debtors more thoroughly before advancing goods or funds. On this front there are growing opportunities. Increasingly, payment periods are being factored into company credit scores by credit ratings agencies. Thus, a Dun and Bradstreet (D & B) comprehensive reference will give data on a firm's average payment behaviour (days beyond terms) that is based on an analysis of trade payment experiences post-invoicing.[113] A company's payment trend will be compared to the industry trend in a D & B report and a breakdown given of value bands of invoice against numbers of days late in settling. The effect of such data distribution may be that late payers will eventually all suffer from lower credit scores and the effects could be multiple. Their ability to obtain credit at lowest cost rates may be pre-judiced and potential trade creditors will be able to identify poor payers – provided that they can afford to pay for a reference and the transaction justifies an investigation into payment records.

---

[112] Evidence also shows that more small businesses are stating at the time the contract is made that they will exercise their right if payment is late. This is usually emphasised on all invoices and letters seeking payment. Better Payment Practice Campaign, *Late Payment Legislation and Interest Calculator* (www.payontime.co.uk).

[113] D & B state that they collect and analyse more than a million trade payment experiences involving European businesses each year.

Credit insurers also provide information of relevance here. A creditor can subscribe to the services of a credit insurer and obtain, on a web-based pay-as-you-go basis, a credit opinion on a trading partner – actual or potential. This opinion will be based on a number of factors including an analysis of payment records. Such a service is inexpensive: an opinion on a UK firm is likely to cost under £10. What the opinion will not do, however, is give a precise disclosure of payment record as opposed to a cumulative opinion based on the whole basket of measures. The danger here is that a poor paying record might be disguised by stronger performance on other fronts.

Cultural change in larger companies has, as noted, also been canvassed as a way to counteract late payments. The problem here, however, is that many large companies may see late-paying as a badge of their strength in the marketplace. (Around one in ten companies have admitted that they would pay their customers late even if their own bills were settled promptly.)[114] Senior corporate staff may, quite understandably, see their main obligation to be the maximising of shareholder value and they may estimate that a policy of late-paying will serve such objectives.[115] They may, indeed, reject arguments that prompt payment is in their own corporate interest because it makes for better business relationships, it enhances reputations, it creates goodwill and encourages better after-sales service. This is a point to be borne in mind in considering the potential of 'naming and shaming' disclosure controls. It implies that such controls may have a primary value in alerting small firms to late payers rather than in shaming larger firms into behaving more honourably.

To summarise, there are good reasons for thinking that the 1998 Act will impact only modestly on late payments. It may be excessively naïve to believe that large corporations can successfully be shamed into paying invoices promptly. Nor can small firms be expected to enforce their rights to prompt payment against powerful companies with never a thought for comebacks.

Conclusions: failures and corporate insolvency law

In concluding on the internal and external causes of corporate failure, it should not be assumed that single causes or single patterns of causes are

---

[114] Better Payment Practice Group Survey, October 2004 (www.payontime.co.uk/news/10.html).

[115] For a sustained portrait of the corporation as amoral calculator see J. Bakan, *The Corporation: The Pathological Pursuit of Profit and Power* (Constable, London, 2004).

to be encountered when numbers of failures are analysed. Collapses generally result from the operation of a number of causes, and involve both external pressures and various internal failings. Argenti has suggested that three prevalent types of corporate failure are encountered in the business world.[116] These types or 'trajectories' of failure are those associated with small companies, the 'high rollers' and the large companies. For small companies the typical failure involves never rising above a poor level of performance and surviving only for a short period.[117] In such companies the proprietor often possesses great determination and knowledge of a trade but lacks basic financial and business skills and is managerially incapable of leading the firm through troubled times. Where the company is new, moreover, it is vulnerable to recessions, high interest rates and other pressures because it has had little time to establish accumulated profits or secure contracts with customers and suppliers.[118] High rollers make up only a small percentage of companies and tend to be led by colourful, flamboyant characters who are attractive to investors. As with small firms that fail, however, the leaders of high rolling firms tend to lack managerial skills. There is a propensity to allow enthusiasm to produce over-trading which, when manifest, leads the firm's bankers to refuse advances and precipitates failure.

With large companies that collapse, the management teams involved are usually professional but the long-established companies that encounter trouble tend to lose touch with their markets or grow slow and

---

[116] Argenti, *Corporate Collapse*, ch. 8. In 1844 the Select Committee on Joint Stock Companies divided 'bubble companies' into three categories: those founded on unsound calculations and which could not succeed; those so ill-constituted as to render mismanagement probable; and those faulty or fraudulent in their object: see *Farrar's Company Law* (4th edn, Butterworths, London, 1998) p. 622; Campbell and Underdown, *Corporate Insolvency*, pp. 23–5.

[117] See R. Cressy, *Why Do Most Firms Die Young?* (Kluwer, Netherlands, 2005). The SPI Eighth Survey suggested that 28 per cent of insolvent companies fail between the ages of five and ten years; 22 per cent between three and four years; 19 per cent between one and two years and 5 per cent after less than one year (SPI Eighth Survey, p. 8). The R3 Ninth Survey revealed an increase in the age of failed businesses, with 18 per cent aged two years or less and 43 per cent less than four years old (figures for the previous survey were 24 per cent and 46 per cent respectively). The first year failure rate had dropped from 5 per cent to 3 per cent between the Eighth and Ninth Surveys. See also Guthrie, 'How the Old Corporate Tortoise Wins the Race'. New companies exploiting new products seem to be particularly prone to failure: see Pratten, *Company Failure*, p. 3.

[118] See J. Hudson, 'Characteristics of Liquidated Companies' (Mimeo, University of Bath, 1982). Hudson's study found that the most dangerous period for companies involved in creditors' voluntary liquidations and compulsory liquidation lay between their second and ninth years.

inefficient.[119] *En route* to failure, such companies tend to experience an initial downturn, a plateau and then a collapse. Large companies, however, will tend to possess greater resilience than small firms because they have larger reserves of assets that can be used to reorganise and they have greater negotiating power when approaching bankers and governments for assistance in attempting a turnaround.[120]

Can corporate insolvency law contribute to the avoidance of undesirable corporate failures and the unwanted consequences of failure? In some respects, the law can be seen as largely irrelevant. It can offer very little assistance where external factors such as global financial crises, new foreign competitors, catastrophic trade disputes or natural disasters drive companies out of business. In other regards, however, the nature of insolvency law can impinge on corporate failure or success. First, it can do so in relation to the costs that such laws impose on healthy and on troubled companies. If, for instance, uncertainties attend the security and priority systems established by law, credit costs will be unnecessarily high, international competitiveness will be prejudiced and companies will face undesirable financial turbulence and stresses. If transaction costs are higher than they should be (because firms have to spend large sums on advisers in order to organise their credit and priority arrangements) then, again, unwarranted pressure is placed on companies and this may in some cases produce failure.

Insolvency law can also impact on the main internal causes of failure that have been discussed above: deficiencies of financial control and management. The extent of this impact should not be exaggerated, however. Corporate managers cannot be assumed to be wholly rational and mechanical followers of legal rules.[121] A host of legal processes and rules nevertheless provides a framework of incentives for company managers.

Deficiencies of financial control are discouraged by the law in so far as failure to keep adequate records may be grounds for disqualifying a person from holding office as a company director on the basis that there has been general misconduct in the affairs of the company or

---

[119] 'Simply put, a run of success can be dangerous. Outstanding companies often succumb to crises because their leaders were innovative years ago but continue to favour strategies and activities based on past success, which do not always translate well after changes in the business and consumer environment.' Baum, 'The Value of a Failing Grade', p. 8.

[120] See ch. 7 below and the 'London Approach'.

[121] For an argument that corporate insolvency law can make only a marginal contribution to the efficiency of corporate management see 'The Fourth Annual Leonard Sainer Lecture – The Rt Hon. Lord Hoffmann', reprinted in (1997) 18 Co. Law. 194. See also V. Finch, 'Company Directors: Who Cares about Skill and Care?' (1992) 55 MLR 179.

unfitness on the part of the director.[122] The rules on directorial disqualification and the system of investigation[123] may also affect corporate
failures in another way. A number of individuals, if unregulated, are
likely to operate numbers of companies in cynical anticipation of their
failure and employ phoenix operations to enrich themselves at the cost of
creditors. The success with which insolvency law controls such phoenix
operations may affect the incidence of corporate failure.[124]

Managerial standards in companies may also be influenced by the
regimes of monitoring that the law establishes and encourages.[125] The
provisions of insolvency law are relevant here in so far as these establish
the regimes of security and priority that offer creditors specific sets of
incentives to review the actions of corporate managers. Thus, for
instance, the strong position in which current insolvency law places
secured creditors gives creditors with fixed charges very few incentives
to monitor corporate affairs beyond looking to see that the assets that are
the subjects of their charges are not alienated or wasted.[126] The amount
of information that creditors may possess, and which allows them to
monitor corporate behaviour, is again dictated in large part by insolvency law. When, for example, administrators are appointed by debenture holders, the information to be supplied to the administrator by
company officers and the arrangements for reporting to creditors and
creditors' meetings are governed by the Insolvency Act.[127]

---

[122] See Company Directors' Disqualification Act 1986 ss. 2–3, 6–9. On disqualification see
ch. 16 below; A. Walters and M. Davis-White QC, *Directors' Disqualification and
Bankruptcy Restrictions* (Thomson/Sweet & Maxwell, London, 2005); V. Finch,
'Disqualifying Directors: Issues of Rights, Privileges and Employment' (1993) Ins. LJ
35; Finch, 'Disqualification of Directors: A Plea for Competence' (1990) 53 MLR 385.

[123] See P. L. Davies, *Gower and Davies' Principles of Modern Company Law* (8th edn,
Thomson/Sweet & Maxwell, London, 2008) ch. 18; Finch, 'Company Directors',
pp. 195–7.

[124] See Insolvency Act 1986 s. 216, the purpose of which is to contribute towards the
eradication of the 'phoenix syndrome', whereby companies are successively allowed to
run down to the point of winding up, only to rise phoenix-like from the ashes as a new
company formed and managed by an almost identical group of persons and utilising a
company name similar to that under which the former company was trading. See
further Company Law Review Steering Group (CLRSG), *Modern Company Law for a
Competitive Economy: Completing the Structure* (November 2000) ch. 13; CLRSG,
Modern Company Law for a Competitive Economy: Final Report (July 2001) ch. 15.

[125] See generally Finch, 'Company Directors'.

[126] See Stein, 'Rescue Operations in Business Crises', p. 394.

[127] Insolvency Act 1986 Sch. B1, paras. 47, 49–51. See ch. 9 below. The terms of debentures
routinely give creditors rights to consultation and information on such matters as the
value of assets subject to floating charges and borrowing levels: see ch. 3 above.

The regimes of personal liability for directors that are established at law may, again, create incentives to manage in a particular way. The rules on wrongful trading, for instance, and the possibilities of actions for misfeasance may provide deterrents to errant directors.[128] In the case of misfeasance actions, these may be brought by shareholders or creditors against past or present company officers who breach any fiduciary or other duty owed to the company,[129] and insolvency law's priority regimes dictate shareholders' and creditors' own incentives to pursue directors. Shareholders are unlikely to act if they will not recover sufficient funds from a director to pay creditors in full before taking their own share, and unsecured creditors are unlikely to pursue actions unless the company's available funds will pay the creditors in full before them.[130]

Insolvency law may also affect the levels of skill that corporate managers have to exhibit and this will have an effect on failure levels. The relatively low standard historically expected from directors' duties of skill and care has now been augmented by the adoption (in the Companies Act 2006's statutory statement) of a similar definition to that contained in section 214(4) of the Insolvency Act 1986.[131] The deterrence element in the wrongful trading provisions themselves is provided by requirements of reasonable diligence and the courts' capacity to order personal contributions to corporate assets where directors fail to show that they have taken proper care.[132] Company law may, furthermore, choose to require a variety of different levels of competence, training and professionalism from directors and this is likely to bear on the propensity of a given company to fail.[133]

---

[128] Under Insolvency Act 1986 ss. 214 and 212. On the effectiveness of s. 214 as, *inter alia*, a deterrent, see ch. 16 below.

[129] See F. Oditah, 'Misfeasance Proceedings against Company Directors' [1992] LMCLQ 207; L. Doyle (1994) 7 *Insolvency Intelligence* 25, 35. See ch. 16 below.

[130] On funding and incentives for liquidators' actions against directors see chs. 13 and 16 below.

[131] See CA 2006 s. 174(2): a director must display the care, skill and diligence that would be exercised by a reasonably diligent person with both (a) the general knowledge, skill and experience that can reasonably be expected of a person carrying out the same functions as the director in relation to that company and (b) the general knowledge, skill and experience that the director actually has. See also Finch, 'Company Directors'; *Norman v. Theodore Goddard* [1991] BCLC 1028; *Re D'Jan of London Ltd* [1994] 1 BCLC 561; CLRSG, *Modern Company Law for a Competitive Economy* (March 2000) ch. 3, (November 2000) ch. 13, *Final Report* (July 2001) pp. 42–5. See further ch. 16 below.

[132] See *Re Produce Marketing Consortium Ltd* [1989] 5 BCC 569; D. Prentice, 'Creditors' Interest and Directors' Duties' (1990) 10 OJLS 265; Finch, 'Company Directors'; see also ch. 16 below.

[133] On directorial levels of care and professionalism, see Finch, 'Company Directors' and ch. 16 below.

If it is accepted that one cause of corporate failure is the taking of unjustifiable risks by directors then insolvency law has relevance beyond the imposition of duties of care and personal liabilities for breach of these. Insolvency law affects the balance of risk bearing in the company. If, as suggested in chapter 3, unsecured creditor interests and risks are underrepresented in corporate affairs because of the present framework of insolvency law, it follows that corporate decisions are liable to under-value such interests, that excessively risk-laden decisions will be taken and that an unjustifiable number of failures will occur. The expected costs to unsecured creditors will not be internalised by the company or fully recognised by corporate managers.

Corporate failure through excessively high gearing may again be influenced by the insolvency/corporate law regime. Thus, it might be argued that the law places many creditors in a position from which they are not able to judge with accuracy the financial position of a prospective borrower and the risks involved in a loan. Company law, for instance, does not at present demand that retentions of title be registered and lenders who are ignorant of a debt applicant's true position may be inclined to grant credit in circumstances that would not have prompted a loan if relevant knowledge had been to hand. The overall effect of poor information may be that firms find it too easy to operate with high gearing. Excessive gearing will also tend to be accompanied by high levels of interest because creditors will demand high returns in order to reflect the high risks that poor information imposes on them. This combination of high gearing and high interest payment levels leads, in turn, to high prospects of corporate failure.

Finally, insolvency law affects levels of corporate failure because it creates the set of incentives that holds sway in the processes for ending corporate lives. Undesirable failures may be caused where certain parties possess incentives to call a halt to corporate activity at times when this is not in the general interest of involved parties. If, for example, the law on wrongful trading operates with a particular level of severity it will give directors of troubled companies a particular motivation to cease business operations at any given time in the process of corporate difficulties.[134] An excessively severe wrongful trading law could thus lead to premature closures of companies which might have revived but have not been given a chance of

---

[134] But see A. Walters, 'Enforcing Wrongful Trading: Substantive Problems and Practical Disincentives' in B. Rider (ed.), *The Corporate Dimension: An Exploration of Developing Areas of Company and Commercial Law: Published in Honour of Professor A. J. Boyle* (Jordans, Bristol, 1998) ch. 9 and discussion in ch. 16 below.

turnaround because the directors have been fearful of the consequences to them of trading on. Similarly, the regime of priorities gives certain creditors incentives to act where this is in their own interests but not those of others. Thus, one of the considerations behind the reforms effected by the Enterprise Act 2002 was that, under the former regime of administrative receivership, banks secured with floating charges could be inclined to appoint a receiver in circumstances where it would overwhelmingly serve the interests of unsecured creditors and shareholders to have an adminis-trator appointed specifically to promote the survival of the company and its undertaking.[135]

Nor do all dangers stem from premature curtailments of corporate activity. When the company faces insolvency and when creditors' interests would best be served by an orderly running down of the business, it may be the case that directors will be pulled in the direction of continued trading by their interest in preserving their employment and business standing. Wherever directors do continue to trade in these circumstances, there is a prospect that the company will descend into a more damaging failure than would otherwise have been the case and the additional loss will fall not on the directors but on the company's creditors.[136]

Insolvency law also sets out timescales and procedures to be adopted when companies are in trouble. Levels of corporate failures can be affected by the use or non-use of cooling-off periods and moratoria, as encountered in the Chapter 11 procedures found in the USA.[137] The variety of rehabilitation procedures offered by insolvency law can also affect the possibilities of failures and recoveries.

In many respects then, insolvency law, like company law, can affect a company's chances of survival or failure in difficult times. Insolvency law can also impinge on overall levels of success or failure. It is important, accordingly, to bear in mind the reasons why companies do fail when the challenges facing insolvency law are considered. Attention should be paid, for instance, to those areas of greatest contribution to failure, of greatest imposition of transaction costs and greatest impediment to recovery programmes. What insolvency law (and indeed company law) should, as a general rule, seek to avoid is loading risks and stresses on those points in corporate life where companies are at their most vulnerable.

---

[135] See chs. 8 and 9 below; DTI/Insolvency Service White Paper, *Productivity and Enterprise: Insolvency – A Second Chance* (Cm 5234, 2001) ch. 2.

[136] See P. L. Davies, 'Legal Capital in Private Companies in Great Britain' (1998) 8 *Die Aktien Gesellschaft* 346.

[137] See ch. 6 below.

Insolvency practitioners and turnaround professionals

Corporate insolvency processes are not mere bodies of rules: they are elaborate procedures in which legal and administrative, formal and informal rules, policies and practices are put into effect by different actors. Those actors, in turn, have cultural, institutional, disciplinary and professional backgrounds which influence their work.[1] They also operate under the influence of a variety of economic, career and other incentives and are subject to a host of constraints ranging from legal duties and professional obligations to client and own-firm expectations. The Cork Report, in an oft-quoted statement, urged that the success of any insolvency system is very largely dependent upon those who administer it,[2] and socio-legal scholars have emphasised how insolvency law is not applied in a mechanical way but is manoeuvred around or manipulated by means of administrative structures 'designed and imposed by dominant actors'.[3]

This chapter looks at how insolvency law and turnaround processes are made operational by those actors who dominate such procedures: the insolvency practitioners (IPs) and turnaround professionals (TPs). In accordance with the discussion in chapter 2, it will be asked whether present practitioner and professional regimes can be supported as efficient, expert,

---

[1] On the roles of accountants and lawyers in insolvency see J. Flood and E. Skordaki, *Insolvency Practitioners and Big Corporate Insolvencies*, ACCA Research Report 43 (ACCA, London, 1995). See also V. Finch, 'Control and Co-ordination in Corporate Rescue' (2005) 25 *Legal Studies* 374.

[2] See *Report of the Review Committee on Insolvency Law and Practice* (Cmnd 8558, 1982) ('Cork Report') para. 732. The Government, moreover, saw insolvency practice as a key to the entire Cork reforms: see the account in B. G. Carruthers and T. C. Halliday, *Rescuing Business: The Making of Corporate Bankruptcy Law in England and the United States* (Clarendon Press, Oxford, 1998) p. 437. On the emergence of the insolvency practitioner profession see ibid., chs. 8–11, and Flood and Skordaki, *Insolvency Practitioners*, ch. 3.

[3] See S. Wheeler, 'Capital Fractionalised: The Role of Insolvency Practitioners in Asset Distribution' in M. Cain and C. B. Harrington (eds.), *Lawyers in a Post Modern World: Translation and Transgression* (Open University Press, Buckingham, 1994) pp. 85–104; Wheeler, *Reservation of Title Clauses* (Oxford University Press, Oxford, 1991).

fair and accountable. This will demand examinations of both the ways that these actors carry out their tasks and the ways that they are regulated.[4]

Insolvency practitioners

Four separate insolvency procedures for companies all involve IPs: Company Voluntary Arrangements (CVAs); administration orders; administrative receiverships;[5] and liquidations. These all differ markedly in their characteristics and in their approaches to the balancing of interests.

CVAs are in essence agreements between companies, their shareholders and their creditors for the satisfaction of corporate debts or for schemes of arrangement of the companies' affairs. Subject to protection for secured creditors[6] and preferential creditors,[7] the parties to the agreement are free to agree almost any terms. Party involvement in the agreement is, moreover, governed by statute: thus a proposal for a CVA needs the approval of 75 per cent of the company's unsecured creditors and over 50 per cent of its shareholders.[8] The CVA, if approved, is

---

[4] See Insolvency Regulation Working Party (IRWP), *Insolvency Practitioner Regulation – Ten Years On* (DTI, 1998) ('IRWP Consultation Document'); IRWP, *A Review of Insolvency Practitioner Regulation* (DTI, 1999) ('IRWP Review'). The IRWP had, as members, representatives of each of the professional bodies that authorise insolvency practitioners, as well as the DTI/BERR Insolvency Service, with the Association of Business Recovery Professionals (R3) (formerly the Society of Practitioners of Insolvency) in attendance. See further V. Finch, 'Insolvency Practitioners: Regulation and Reform' [1998] JBL 334.

[5] The Enterprise Act 2002 largely replaced the administrative receivership regime with the new administration process: see EA 2002 s. 250, Insolvency Act 1986 Sch. B1, s. 72A. See also ch. 8 below. The general prohibition on appointing administrative receivers that was introduced by the 2002 Act applies to holders of 'qualifying floating charges' (see now Insolvency Act 1986 s. 72A) but is subject to six exceptions relating to capital markets, public/private partnerships, utilities, project finance, certain financial markets and registered social landlords/housing authorities: see ss. 72B–72G of the IA 1986 Sch. 2A as modified by the IA 1986 (Amendment) (Administrative Receivership and Capital Market Arrangements) Order 2003 (SI 2003/1468). Transactions that predate the implementation of the EA 2002 (15 September 2003) will still allow holders of qualifying floating charges both to appoint administrative receivers and to block the appointment of an administrator.

[6] See Insolvency Act 1986 s. 4(3).　　[7] Ibid., s. 4(4).

[8] Both percentages calculated in value. See Insolvency Rules 1986 rr. 1.17–1.20. On CVAs under the Insolvency Act 2000 and generally see ch. 11 below; S. Hill, 'Company Voluntary Arrangements' (1990) 6 IL&P 47; DTI/Insolvency Service, *Company Voluntary Arrangements and Administration Orders: A Consultative Document* (October 1993); Insolvency Service, *Revised Proposals for a New Company Voluntary Arrangement Procedure* (1995); J. Flood, R. Abbey, E. Skordaki and P. Aber, *The Professional Restructuring of Corporate Rescue: Company Voluntary Arrangements and the London Approach*, ACCA Research Report 45 (ACCA, London, 1995).

binding on all those who were entitled to vote at the creditors' meeting[9] and the company may continue to trade. An IP will be involved in giving effect to the terms of the CVA[10] but, in doing so, he or she can be seen to be implementing what is in essence a private contractual agreement insulated from public interest concerns.

Administration was originally provided for by the Insolvency Act 1986[11] but it was a formal procedure and required a court order. The reforms of the Enterprise Act 2002 inaugurated a new corporate administration regime, which will be discussed in chapter 9 below. In the 'new' administration procedures the rescue of the company as a going concern is the priority[12] and the administrator has to sustain a company's business while plans are made for its future.[13] The administrator can thus be involved in the day-to-day management of the company as well as in formulating rescue plans. A company is protected from creditors' demands when under an administration order and it can continue to trade[14] but proposals for rescue have to be agreed by creditors.

The Cork Report[15] anticipated that in rescue operations an administrator might take on board society's interests and employment considerations when deciding whether to sustain a business. The Insolvency Act 1986, however, makes no mention of such factors and the administrator looks no further than to the interests of creditors viewed solely as creditors.

Administrative receivers (ARs) are appointed without court involvement by debenture holders who hold security over the whole (or

---

[9] Or would have been so entitled if they had notice of the meeting: Insolvency Act 1986 s. 5 (2)(b).

[10] The IP will in practice usually have been involved in the drawing up of the proposals. On the significance attached by major creditors to the professional reputation of the IP involved see D. Milman and F. Chittenden, *Corporate Rescue: CVAs and the Challenge of Small Companies*, ACCA Research Report 44 (ACCA, London, 1995). Note that the Insolvency Service expects authorisation of the first 'voluntary arrangement practitioners' in 2008 (via s. 389(a) Insolvency Act 1986) (re persons who are not IPs): see IS *Annual Report* 2006–7.

[11] See Insolvency Act 1986 ss. 8–27. CVAs were also introduced by the Insolvency Act 1986 ss. 1–7.

[12] See Insolvency Act 1986 Sch. B1, para. 3(1).

[13] See Insolvency Act 1986 s. 8(3) for the specific purposes for which an administration order can be made.

[14] On the moratorium see Insolvency Act 1986 Sch. B1, paras. 42–4; M. G. Bridge, 'Company Administrators and Secured Creditors' (1991) 107 LQR 394. See also ch. 9 below.

[15] Para. 498.

substantially the whole) of the company's assets.[16] The IP acting as an AR has a central function of realising company assets in order to meet the claims of the debenture holder and, in so doing, he or she can continue the business and can sell it as a going concern. On such a sale the AR distributes funds received to the creditors in due order of priority. The responsibility of the receiver is to the creditor who requested the appointment and not to the company or other creditors.[17] In essence this is, accordingly, a creditors' remedy that does not demand that the AR pays any heed to the wishes or interests of the company or to its directors, shareholders, other creditors (other than minimal obligations to report) or the interests of employees or the broader public.

Liquidators are appointed in signification of the end of a company and are responsible for collecting-in the company's assets, realising them and distributing the proceeds to the company's creditors. If there is a surplus, this can go to the shareholders. In compulsory liquidation a winding-up petition is made to the court and, if granted, the court orders that the company be wound up. In a creditors' voluntary liquidation the shareholders resolve initially to put the company into liquidation and the creditors effectively take control away from the shareholders at the subsequent creditors' meeting when they appoint a liquidator.[18] The IP, acting in both types of liquidation, looks to the interests of all creditors but also acts in the public interest in so far as he is under a duty to report directorial unfitness to the Disqualification Unit of the BERR's Insolvency Service as part of the disqualification process of the Company Directors' Disqualification Act 1986 (CDDA).[19]

---

[16] See Insolvency Act 1986 s. 29(2). But see note 5 above on the curtailment of administrative receivership by the Enterprise Act 2002 and see further ch. 8 below. On receivers generally see I. F. Fletcher, *The Law of Insolvency* (3rd edn, Sweet & Maxwell, London, 2002) ch. 14; Cork Report, ch. 8; R. M. Goode, *Principles of Corporate Insolvency Law* (3rd edn, Sweet & Maxwell, London, 2005) ch. 9; J. S. Ziegel, 'The Privately Appointed Receiver and the Enforcement of Security Interests: Anomaly or Superior Solution?' in Ziegel (ed.), *Current Developments in International and Comparative Corporate Insolvency Law* (Clarendon Press, Oxford, 1994).

[17] See *Lathia* v. *Dronsfield Bros. Ltd* [1987] BCLC 321.

[18] Insolvency Act 1986 ss. 99, 100, 166. On liquidation generally see ch. 13 below.

[19] See S. Wheeler, 'Directors' Disqualification: Insolvency Practitioners and the Decision-making Process' (1995) 15 *Legal Studies* 283. On directors' disqualification generally see ch. 16 below; A. Walters and M. Davis-White QC, *Directors' Disqualification and Bankruptcy Restrictions* (Thomson/Sweet & Maxwell, London, 2005); V. Finch, 'Disqualifying Directors: Issues of Rights, Privileges and Employment' (1993) Ins. LJ 35; Finch, 'Disqualification of Directors: A Plea for Competence' (1990) 53 MLR 385.

IPs may be involved in the above four procedures[20] but other actors also have roles to play. Thus the Official Receiver (OR), an appointee of the Secretary of State, has important investigatory functions to perform when acting in cases of liquidation.[21]

The evolution of the administrative structure

Over the last two centuries accountants have sought to dominate insolvency work and have striven with some success.[22] For most of the second half of the nineteenth century many accountancy firms earned the vast majority of their fees from insolvency practice and it was, indeed, this work that boosted not only accountants' incomes but also their professional organisation.[23] Accountants throughout this period consistently emphasised their superior professional expertise to lawyers in the insolvency field. By the time that the Cork Committee deliberated, however, a number of worries had arisen, notably regarding the qualifications of those persons engaged in insolvency work.[24] The Cork Report itself was concerned that arrangements prior to the date of its inquiry were open to abuse and did not command public confidence.[25] The Report accepted the case for a scheme of IP regulation operating under ministerial control and covering all persons, other than the OR, who hold office as liquidators, trustees in bankruptcy, administrative receivers, administrators or supervisors of voluntary arrangements. The regime envisaged by Cork anticipated that IPs would be provided by the private sector but would be required to be members of an officially recognised and regulated professional body capable of exercising disciplinary supervision over an individual acting as an IP. In the case of IPs who did not belong to a recognised professional body (RPB), these would be licensed

---

[20] Corporate insolvency procedures do not, of course, exhaust the work of IPs. They are also involved in the personal side of insolvency (bankruptcy) as nominees and supervisors of IVAs and as trustees in bankruptcy. See Finch, 'Insolvency Practitioners', pp. 353–4; Fletcher, *Law of Insolvency*, chs. 3, 4, 7; D. Milman, *Personal Insolvency Law, Regulation and Policy* (Ashgate, Aldershot, 2005).

[21] Especially in compulsory liquidation: Insolvency Act 1986 s. 136. The OR is a civil servant and officer of the court. There are currently thirty-five OR offices in England and Wales: see Insolvency Service website, www.insolvency.gov.uk (visited 15 January 2008)

[22] See Flood and Skordaki, *Insolvency Practitioners*, ch. 3; C. Napier and C. Noke, 'Accounting and Law: An Historical Overview of an Uneasy Relationship' in M. Bromwich and A. G. Hopwood (eds.), *Accounting and the Law* (Institute of Chartered Accountants in England and Wales, London, 1992).

[23] Flood and Skordaki, *Insolvency Practitioners*, p. 10.   [24] Cork Report, ch. 15.

[25] See generally Fletcher, *Law of Insolvency*, ch. 2; I. Snaith with assistance of F. Cownie, *The Law of Corporate Insolvency* (Waterlow, London, 1990) ch. 10; Cork Report, para. 756.

individually by the (then) DTI (now BERR) with a view to ensuring proper levels of competence, skill and integrity.

The Insolvency Act 1986 gives legislative effect to the Cork vision and restricts action as an office holder in any designated insolvency proceeding to persons qualified under the 1986 Act.[26] Qualification is achieved by the methods advocated by the Cork Report, namely membership of, and authorisation by, an RPB or licensing directly by the Secretary of State. Acting as an IP in any designated proceeding when not qualified to do so constitutes a criminal offence.[27]

There are now eight RPBs which may grant authorisation.[28] This will only be forthcoming for individuals, not firms, and only on demonstrating, through professional examinations, a prescribed level of technical knowledge and expertise in accountancy and law. Since 1990 all applicants to become qualified IPs have been required to pass an examination organised centrally by the Joint Insolvency Examining Board (JIEB), whichever RPB they belong to. They must also be able to demonstrate a minimum level of appropriate experience. Those who apply for qualification to the Secretary of State rather than to an RPB must generally pass the JIEB examination, though a discretion to make exceptions exists.[29] There are now 1,700 IPs in the UK who are authorised and regulated by the Secretary of State directly or by an RPB.[30]

---

[26] See Insolvency Act 1986 Pt XIII and the Insolvency Practitioners Regulations 2005 (SI 2005/524) and IA 1986 s. 390. Major changes to the rules governing the authorisation and responsibilities owed by IPs were made by the 2005 Regulations: for example, Regulation 6 gives criteria for determining whether a candidate for authorisation is a fit and proper person; Regulation 7 gives requirements as to requisite experience and training; Regulation 11 gives details on annual returns for authorised persons to the Secretary of State. See Regulation 10, Sch. 2, Part 2 concerning the need for IPs to lodge a bond in the form of a security or caution. See further L. S. Sealy and D. Milman, *Annotated Guide to the Insolvency Legislation 2006/7* (10th edn, Thomson/Sweet & Maxwell, London, 2007) vol. I, p. 429. Excluded from the qualification requirement are ORs and receivers appointed by the court or by holders of fixed charges. On the lack of equivalence of rules relating to IPs and ORs see G. Pettit, 'A Level Playing Field?' (2007) *Recovery* (Autumn) 3.

[27] Insolvency Act 1986 s. 389. For authorisation personally from the Secretary of State or from a 'competent authority' see IA 1986 s. 392 and the Insolvency Practitioners Regulations 2005 (SI 2005/524).

[28] The Association of Chartered Certified Accountants (ACCA), the Insolvency Practitioners' Association (IPA) and the Institute of Chartered Accountants in England and Wales (ICAEW); the Institute of Chartered Accountants in Ireland; the Institute of Chartered Accountants in Scotland; and the Law Societies of England and Wales, of Northern Ireland and of Scotland.

[29] See IRWP Consultation Document, pp. 13–14.

[30] See IS *Annual Report* 2005–6: figures as of 1 January 2006.

On insolvency matters the Secretary of State's functions are exercised through the Insolvency Service (IS), which is an executive agency of the BERR. It is headed by a chief executive, the Inspector General, and employs around 2,150 staff.[31] The IS is responsible for, amongst other things, advising on the form and effectiveness of insolvency legislation, ensuring that the RPBs regulate their members properly with suitable rules that are effectively enforced and authorising and regulating Secretary of State authorised IPs.[32] The Secretary of State issues a Framework Document setting down objectives for the IS and, as well as monitoring the RPBs, the IS runs a twice-yearly 'licensing forum' for discussion of authorisation and regulatory issues with the RPBs.

The bulk of RPB-authorised IPs are accountants, with the dominant membership coming from the Institute of Chartered Accountants of England and Wales (ICAEW). Many of these are not full-time IPs but are general accountancy practitioners, some with audit and investment business clients.[33]

The RPBs act as self-regulators in so far as they exercise control over their own qualified members, but the system constitutes governmentally monitored self-regulation since the IS supervises the regulatory process, conducts regular visits to each of the RPBs and seeks to ensure that standards are maintained. For their part, the RPBs operate a variety of control measures designed to control and correct misconduct. A range of disciplinary penalties applies to members and includes the sanction of expulsion from membership – which, for an RPB-authorised practitioner, will produce automatic revocation of authorisation.

The RPBs have, since 1994, carried out monitoring visits to all IPs.[34] There are differences in style and form of regulation among the eight RPBs (each,

---

[31] IS *Annual Report* 2006–7. Prior to 1 April 2006 the Companies Investigation Branch (CIB) was part of the main DTI (now BERR) but it is now under the auspices of the Insolvency Service. Figures given by the IS since 2005–6 thus include CIB personnel.

[32] The IS also takes, *inter alia*, disqualification proceedings against unfit directors (1,200 disqualification orders/undertakings were secured in 2006–7: IS *Annual Report* 2006–7) and carries out, through its ORs, the functions of liquidators in compulsory liquidations and trustees in bankruptcy. The IS also monitors, on a day-to-day basis, those IPs directly authorised by the Secretary of State. The IRWP Review (p. 22) recommends that this monitoring function ought to be contracted out to a professional body so as to leave the IS to concentrate on its functions as a regulator of the RPBs' regulatory activities.

[33] On the historical evolution of the dominance of the accountancy profession over insolvency work see Flood and Skordaki, *Insolvency Practitioners*, ch. 3.

[34] In January 2005 the ICAEW and the IPA took their monitoring back in-house (on abolition of the Joint Insolvency Monitoring Unit). On resultant changes in their

for instance, has its own complaints mechanism) and these reflect variations in traditions as well as powers of intervention. A degree of consistency of approach derives, however, from the RPBs' common subjection to a memorandum of understanding with the Secretary of State[35] and to monitoring by reference to common standards required and approved by the IS.

Establishment of the Society for Practitioners in Insolvency (SPI), a multi-disciplinary trade association, paved the way for lawyers and accountants to develop a shared professional perspective on insolvency work.[36] Around 80 per cent of all IPs belong to this body, now known as R3 (the Association of Business Recovery Professionals),[37] and its activities include assisting with training, continuing professional education and ethical issues as well as the issuing of guidance notes.

Harmonisation of the RPBs' approaches is assisted, in particular, by the RPBs' system of best practice guidance. Statements of Insolvency Practice (SIPs) are issued under procedures agreed between the insolvency regulatory authorities (the RPBs and the IS) acting through the Joint Insolvency Committee (JIC), a co-ordinating forum.[38] SIPs, the status of which is now 'required practice',[39] are commissioned by the JIC, produced by R3, approved by the JIC and adopted by the regulatory authorities within each of their own regulatory regimes.[40] Differences of regulation do, nevertheless, remain within the overall system. The IS, working within a statutory framework, has, for instance, no sanction against its IPs other than removal of authorisation. The eight RPBs can

---

monitoring see further M. Chapman, 'The Insolvency Service's View of Regulation' (2005) *Recovery* (Winter) 24, 25 and further pp. 200–2 below.

[35] The memorandum covers authorisation, handling of complaints, monitoring activities, best practice and exchange of information between RPBs.

[36] See Flood and Skordaki, *Insolvency Practitioners*, p. 37.

[37] On 28 January 2000 the SPI renamed itself R3: the Association of Business Recovery Professionals.

[38] The JIC meets four times a year and acts as a forum for discussion of insolvency issues and professional and ethical standards and includes representatives from each of the RPBs and the IS. (R3 has observer status.) The JIC is also the profession's principal source of contact with the Insolvency Practices Council, a body established to provide an additional public interest input into standard setting in the profession.

[39] In 2004 the status of SIPs changed from 'best practice' to 'required practice'. See further Chapman, 'Insolvency Service's View of Regulation', p. 24.

[40] See *Joint Insolvency Committee Annual Report* 2006, p. 2. Statements of Insolvency Practice (SIPs) have been issued on a number of topics, including liquidators' investigations into the affairs of an insolvent company, records of meetings in formal insolvency proceedings and remuneration of insolvency office holders. On remuneration see pp. 186–8 below.

make their own regulations and impose their own penalties and the RPBs responsible for solicitors have statutory powers of intervention.

Further harmonisation of approach is encouraged by the Insolvency Ethical Guide which was published by the IS and introduced in January 2004. It operates as a standardising measure across all insolvency practitioners, regardless of the particular authorising body. During 2006 and 2007 the JIC engaged in the process of revising a draft Insolvency Code of Ethics for putting out to further consultation.

Evaluating the structure

Efficiency

In 2004 57 per cent of respondents to a survey of R3 members stated that the regime for regulation did not work efficiently.[41] Frequently made criticisms are said to be that regulators have not established an information and monitoring system that would underpin effective regulation – and that this is because of insufficiencies of time, money, organisation, co-ordination and clarity of objectives.[42] Such internal concerns have been echoed from outside the profession where criticisms of IP performance have focused on the charges made for services rendered and the value for money that has been supplied.[43] Matters came to prominence in 1997 when, in three large insolvencies, accountants acting as IPs charged huge fees but recovered little for creditors. The three accounting firms handling the administration of the Maxwell empire reported fees of nearly £35 million and the receivers to the Robert Maxwell estate, accountants Buchler Phillips, recovered £1.672 million, but their bills, together with those of solicitors Nabarro Nathanson, came to £1.628 million, leaving only £44,000 for creditors.[44] In *Mirror Group Newspapers plc* v. *Maxwell*[45] Ferris J described the fee claim as 'profoundly shocking', adding: 'If the amounts claimed are allowed in full, this receivership will have produced substantial rewards for the receivers

---

[41] L. Verrill, 'The R3 Regulation Survey' (2004) *Recovery* (Autumn) 27.

[42] See G. Rumney and R. Smith, 'Sorting Out the Bad Apples' (2005) *Recovery* (Winter) 36.

[43] Press comments on IPs' fees have used terms such as 'obscene', 'vultures' and 'vampires': see Flood and Skordaki, *Insolvency Practitioners*, p. 23.

[44] See 'Insolvency Experts in Firing Line over Fees', *Financial Times*, 1 August 1997. The collapse of the Bank of Credit and Commerce International (BCCI) yielded fees of over $169.2m for Touche Ross, and the administrators of Polly Peck International charged (with legal fees) nearly £25m.

[45] [1998] BCC 324.

and their lawyers and nothing at all for the creditors of the estate. I find it shameful that a court receivership should produce this result in relation to an order of more than £1.5 million.'[46]

Mr Justice Ferris noted increased concern at the generally perceived high level of costs in insolvency cases and other judges had already spoken out on the subject. Mr Justice Lightman expressed concern in a November 1995 lecture to the Insolvency Lawyers' Association[47] and, returning to the topic in 1998, he noted the 'visceral disquiet' in the press on the subject.[48]

How then should charging levels be approached? At present, those who have power to fix the remuneration of office holders fall into two categories. In the first, there are liquidation committees, creditors' committees, general bodies of creditors, or (in some cases) those persons appointing the office holder. In the second, there is the court, which may act in exercise of an original jurisdiction or in an appellate capacity.[49] In the case of most IPs, who act as receivers, their fees are fixed by the debenture holders (usually the banks) and are based on time and expenses.[50] In liquidations, IPs may charge a percentage of the value of assets realised or distributed, or they may bill by time, bearing in mind also any complexities, exceptional responsibilities and so forth.[51] The creditors' committees authorise remuneration. This has given rise to the criticism that, in a professionally comfortable arrangement, accountants,

---

[46] Mr Justice Ferris passed the issue to a taxing officer, Master Hurst, whose judgment was delivered in April 1999: see *Mirror Group Newspapers* v. *Maxwell and Others* [1999] BCC 684. Buchler Phillips was awarded 99 per cent of its claim and no wrongdoing was found in its conduct. Blame was laid on the way Maxwell had organised his business: 'Many assets which on the face of it appeared to be the personal property of Mr Maxwell were either worthless or, because of the immensely complex financial labyrinth which he had constructed, could not ultimately be recovered as personal property.' See J. Kelly, 'The Recovery Position', *Financial Times*, 22 April 1999.

[47] See Mr Justice Lightman, 'The Challenges Ahead' [1996] JBL 113.

[48] See Mr Justice Lightman, 'Office Holders' Charges: Cost, Control and Transparency' (1998) 11 *Insolvency Intelligence* 1. See also Mr Justice Lightman, 'Office Holders: Evidence, Security and Independence' [1997] CfiLR 145.

[49] See Report of Mr Justice Ferris' Working Party on *The Remuneration of Office Holders and Certain Related Matters* (London, 1998) ('Ferris Report').

[50] Under the Insolvency Regulations 1994 (SI 1994/2507) Regulation 36A, as inserted by the Insolvency (Amendment) Regulations 2005 (SI 2005/512), an IP is obliged, on request in writing by a creditor, director, contributory or individual, to supply free of charge, and within twenty-eight days, a statement setting out, *inter alia*, the number of hours spent on a case, and the hourly rate charged for staff.

[51] See also Regulation 36A, note 50 above.

sitting in creditors' committees, are left to authorise the payment levels of their fellow accountants.[52]

The criteria governing the judicial fixing and approval of insolvency appointees' remuneration are set out in a 2004 Practice Statement[53] that was produced in the wake of continuing judicial concern regarding the level of fees claimed by some office holders.[54] The Practice Statement applies, *inter alia*, to liquidators, provisional liquidators, special managers, administrators, trustees in bankruptcy, licensed IPs and interim receivers. It covers applications to court for the approval of remuneration levels and also to challenges of remunerations that have already been fixed. The objective is to ensure that remuneration is fair, reasonable and commensurate with the nature and extent of the work properly carried out. The guiding principles to be considered include the value of the service rendered, the fairness and reasonableness of the amounts claimed, the balance between the complexity of the work done and the value of assets dealt with. The appointee must give an account of the work charged for that breaks it down into individual tasks, and explains why particular tasks were undertaken; why they were undertaken by particular individuals; and why they were carried out in the given manner. The amount of time charged for must be justified,[55] the charge rates for the appointee and his or her staff must be detailed and an account must be given of the likely achievements that the work undertaken will further. The court may, in addition, appoint an assessor or a Costs Judge to produce a report on the claimed remuneration.[56]

---

[52] See Flood and Skordaki, *Insolvency Practitioners*, p. 23. For details of an R3-funded study of IP remuneration see D. Milman, 'Remuneration: Researching the Fourth R' (2000) *Recovery* (August) 18.

[53] Practice Statement: The Fixing and Approval of the Remuneration of Appointees (2004). See *Civil Procedure* (The White Book) (Sweet & Maxwell, London) vol. 2 at 3E–114 ff.

[54] The Ferris Report of 1998 urged that all parties (courts or other bodies) should look to the same criteria when fixing remuneration and that the aim should be to provide IPs with 'reasonable', not 'minimal', remuneration. For comments see K. Theobold, 'The Ferris Report' (1998) 14 IL&P 300; Lightman, 'Office Holders' Charges'; the Hon. Mr Justice Ferris, 'Insolvency Remuneration: Translating Adjectives into Action' [1999] Ins. Law. 48. For analysis and criticism of the 2004 Practice Statement see S. Baister, 'Remuneration, the Insolvency Practitioner and the Courts' [2006] IL&P 50.

[55] The courts will want to see time charged in six-minute units: see *Jacob and Ruddock* v. *UIC Insurance Company Limited* [2006] BCC 167; *Re Independent Insurance Co. Ltd (in provisional liquidation) (No. 2)* [2003] 1 BCLC 640; R3 *Technical Bulletin*, Issue 78, December 2006.

[56] For judicial views on the merits of appointing assessors rather than Costs Judges, see Ferris J in *Re Independent Insurance Co. Ltd (in provisional liquidation) (No. 2)* [2003] 1 BCLC 640. An important role of the assessor may be to advise the judge on fee levels: see

The costs of the IS have in the past also been the subject of criticism.[57] Before April 2004 fees raised by the IS were paid to the (then) DTI (now BERR) and there was no direct relationship between the fees charged and the cost of the function they related to. This meant that fees raised for one function might be used to cross-subsidise other actions. Since April 2004, though, fees have been set to recover costs and a system of average costs per process has been applied.[58]

Criticism has furthermore attached in the past to the use made of the Insolvency Services Account (ISA)[59] – the account into which creditors' money, as realised by trustees in bankruptcy and liquidators, must be paid. In 1996–7 this account generated banking fees of £16 million and a £37 million surplus investment income, but did not pay more than a low rate of interest (subject to tax) to creditors. The overall effect, said critics, was to penalise creditors – most strikingly in those years when the investment account produced a surplus.[60]

The Cork Committee received strong and widespread criticism of the ISA regime,[61] particularly with regard to the low rate of return on compulsory deposits. The requirement that an IP deposit surplus funds in the ISA was also attacked as providing an incentive for liquidators to protract proceedings and delay the submission of accounts. Cork urged that the administration of insolvency was a public service and should be paid for out of general taxation rather than funded by creditors. The existing system, said Cork, was costly, time-consuming and unfair[62] and,

---

G. Moss, 'Independent Assessor Helps To Set "Independent" Fees' (2003) 16 *Insolvency Intelligence* 61. On IP remuneration generally see also Baister, 'Remuneration, the Insolvency Practitioner and the Courts', who notes, *inter alia*, that contested applications relating to costs are on the increase, citing as an example *Re Cabletel Installations Ltd* [2005] BPIR 28. See also S. Fennell and S. Dingles, 'Working with Companies in Financial Difficulties – Will You Be Paid?' (2006) 19 *Insolvency Intelligence* 49; C. Swain, 'He Who Pays the Piper Calls the Tune? Administrators' Remuneration under the New Administration Regime' (2006) 19 *Insolvency Intelligence* 33; M. Mulligan and J. Tribe, 'The Remuneration of Office Holders in Corporate Insolvency – Liquidators, Administrators and Administrative Receivers: Part 1' (2003) 3 Ins. Law. 101.

[57] See H. Anderson, 'A Fair Share of the Company Failures Cake', *Financial Times*, 7 April 1998.

[58] See IS *Annual Report* 2006–7 p. 13.   [59] See Anderson, 'Fair Share'.

[60] See Justice, *Insolvency Law: An Agenda for Reform* (Justice, London, 1994) paras. 5.7–5.11; Cork Report, ch. 17, paras. 847–55. In 1991–2 the IS paid a surplus of £5 million to the (then) DTI (*Financial Times*, 2 September 1992) and in 1992–3 the surplus was £9 million: Justice, *Insolvency Law*. Net income from the Insolvency Services Investment Account in the years 1995–6 and 1996–7 was £45 million and £31.4 million respectively.

[61] Cork Report, paras. 847–55.

[62] Ibid., p. 201. For further criticism see Justice, *Insolvency Law*.

instead, liquidators should be obliged to deposit funds in an interest-bearing account. As an alternative to public funding of the IS, Cork recommended that there should be a levy on the registration of new companies.[63]

The rationale for use of the ISA was, moreover, undermined by the 1986 Insolvency Act. Historically the ISA was used to prevent unscrupulous practitioners misappropriating funds but the 1986 Act set up a licensing and bonding system[64] that offered protection from, and compensation for, such abuse. The Government took these points in its 2001 White Paper[65] when it concluded that paying the bulk of the interest generated on insolvency funds into government coffers could no longer be justified.[66] Action has since been taken so that, after 1 April 2004, moneys from voluntary liquidations do not have to be paid into the ISA (though the requirement remains for compulsory liquidations)[67] and under the 2004 Regulations, deposits earn interest at a 'competitive' rate that can be varied by the Secretary of State.[68] Additionally, with effect from 6 April 2008, unclaimed dividends in administrations and administrative receiverships can be paid into the ISA.[69]

---

[63] Cork Report, p. 201.

[64] IPs must obtain and deposit with their authorising RPB (or the Secretary of State) a bond issued by an insurance company by which it makes itself jointly and severally liable with the IP for the proper performance of his duties: Insolvency Act 1986 s. 390(3); Insolvency Practitioners Regulations 2005, Regulation 10, Sch. 2, Part 2. The bond must be for the general sum of £250,000 and for additional specific sums in accordance with the prescribed limit applicable to particular cases in which the IP is to act. (The amount of required cover is calculated by reference to the value of the assets of the insolvent with a minimum of £5,000 and a maximum of £5 million.) See further G. Todd and S. Todd, 'Insolvency Practitioners have to be Bonded – Is it as Simple as it Seems?' (2006) 19 *Insolvency Intelligence* 129.

[65] DTI/Insolvency Service, *Productivity and Enterprise: Insolvency – A Second Chance* (Cm 5234, July 2001).

[66] Ibid., para. 1.51.

[67] See Insolvency Act 1986 s. 415A (as inserted by Enterprise Act 2002 s. 270); Insolvency Practitioners and Insolvency Services Account (Fees) Order 2003 (SI 2003/3363) as amended by the Insolvency Practitioners and Insolvency Services Account (Fees) (Amendment) Order 2008 (SI 2008/3), Insolvency (Amendment) Regulations 2004 (SI 2004/472), Insolvency Proceedings (Fees) Order 2004 (SI 2004/593). Liquidators of voluntary liquidations may still pay into the ISA if they wish. For cases commenced before 1 April 2004 (to which earlier fees orders still apply) see further the Insolvency Proceedings (Fees) (Amendment) Order 2006 (SI 2006/561).

[68] See Enterprise Act 2002 s. 271. The rate of interest from 10 July 2007 was 7 per cent.

[69] See the Insolvency (Amendment) Regulations 2008 (SI 2008/670).

Expertise

When the Cork Committee considered the qualifications of IPs, it noted that the absence of some 'minimal qualification' was much criticised.[70] The Committee then stressed that 'a certain degree of knowledge and experience' was essential for the IPs to discharge their functions adequately. They needed to be familiar with the relevant law on debtor–creditor relations; the organisation and proceedings of courts dealing with insolvency; the investigation of business dealings and transactions of insolvent debtors; the pursuit and recovery of assets fraudulently disposed of; voidable preferences; and the distribution of assets to creditors. The IP, moreover, had to be capable of taking complete control of a business of some size and complexity and of carrying it on to sell as a going concern or to make other proposals for its continuance as an economic unit.[71]

The Cork Report, as noted, served as a foundation for the systems of entry screening, qualification and monitoring that have been described above. It can be argued that the current regime's reliance on professional control through different 'home' RPBs encourages a breadth of expertise in IPs.[72] Thus, accountancy and lawyer-based IPs are required to display qualities of general professional expertise in a manner that would, perhaps, not be the case if IPs were regulated as a discrete, more narrowly defined, profession.

Questions have, nevertheless, been raised about the scope of IPs' skills. A 1995 analysis of CVAs asked whether IPs are the right people to carry out these arrangements since, by training, they know best 'how to kill companies'.[73] IPs have, in the past, been found to possess a limited knowledge of CVAs,[74] and it was suggested that the 'going concern' departments of the major accountancy firms might be better equipped to engage in corporate rescues than the IPs who are actually involved with insolvencies.[75] The statistics historically revealed that receiverships and liquidations were

---

[70] Cork Report, para. 735.

[71] On IPs' 'vital' use of due diligence to find the value of a company and any aspects enhancing its worth see C. Parr, 'Due Diligence: Seek and You Shall Find' (2008) *Recovery* (Spring) 42.

[72] See IRWP Review, pp. 35–6. IPs may also receive expert assistance from specialists. Thus, it is said that members of the Non-Administrative Receivers Association (NARA) can provide IPs with advice in relation to fixed-charge receiverships: see D. Smith, 'Partners in Insolvency' (2007) *Recovery* (Autumn) 7.

[73] See Flood *et al.*, *Professional Restructuring*, p. 17.

[74] See L. Gee, *How Effective are Voluntary Arrangements?* (Levy Gee, London, 1994).

[75] Flood *et al.*, *Professional Restructuring*, p. 17.

popular in comparison with administrations and CVAs, and Flood *et al.* argued that a senior accountant captured the essence of the IP vision of insolvency work in saying 'We are debt collectors.'[76] As will be argued below,[77] however, in the last decade there has been a revision of insolvency roles so that participants in corporate and insolvency processes are encouraged to see corporate decline as a matter to be anticipated and prevented rather than responded to after the event and, in this development, turnaround professionals have gained a new prominence.[78] Furthermore, the reforms of the Enterprise Act 2002 attempted to foster a 'rescue culture' by replacing the regime of administrative receivership with provisions that give pride of place to the new administration process. The control of this reformed rescue procedure lies principally in the hands of IPs.[79] Thus the training, expertise and approach of IPs may now increasingly be orientated towards including managerial skills so as to encourage them to give proper weight to rescue in reviewing options for troubled companies. As one IP described it: 'the emphasis has shifted from "pathology" to "preventative medicine"… "managing change" has become a critical new discipline'.[80] The law may set up a variety of insolvency procedures but here we see that the machineries of implementation can have a very considerable role in shaping insolvency processes on the ground.

A concern voiced in recent years is not so much that IPs lack skills but that, within the insolvency process, there is often an imbalance of skills in favour of IPs. This topic, however, will be considered in dealing with fairness.

Fairness

Does the present regime of implementing insolvency processes ensure fairness to affected parties?[81] If IPs are allowed to act where conflicts of

---

[76] Ibid.   [77] See pp. 221 ff. and chs. 6–9 below.

[78] See further V. Finch, 'The Recasting of Insolvency Law' (2005) 68 MLR 713. In 2001 R3 established a Society of Turnaround Professionals and this organisation has contributed to the development of a rescue culture: see 'Turnaround Talk' (2001) *Recovery* (September). See further V. Finch, 'Doctoring in the Shadows of Insolvency' [2005] JBL 690; pp. 221 ff. below.

[79] See further V. Finch, 'Control and Co-ordination in Corporate Rescue'.

[80] See L. Hornan, 'The Changing Face of Insolvency Practice' (2005) (March) *International Accountant* 24 at 24. See further ch. 6, pp. 221 ff. below.

[81] This section of the chapter builds on V. Finch, 'Controlling the Insolvency Professionals' [1999] Ins. Law. 228. As for fairness to regulated IPs, the R3 survey of 2004 suggested that 62 per cent of responding members thought that the regime did not operate fairly: see Verrill, 'R3 Regulation Survey'.

interest arise, there is a potential for unfairness or bias, and insolvency processes have the capacity to throw up a plethora of conflicts of interests for IPs. The latter, and their firms, for instance, may have ongoing links with different companies or creditors who are involved in various ways in an insolvency; relationships with the directors of individual companies may create conflicts; personal interests and other appointments held may be relevant; the IP's firm may have financial interests present or future that are potentially affected by advice or decisions relating to a troubled company; and the quantity of work or remuneration that an IP receives may be affected by actions or recommendations made.

It is, accordingly, necessary to consider how the present system controls such conflicts. The Insolvency Act 1986 does not expressly prevent an IP from acting where there is a conflict, but in considering whether a person is fit and proper to act as an IP, the Secretary of State[82] must take into account whether, in any case, the applicant has acted as an IP but has failed fully to disclose to persons who might reasonably be expected to be affected circumstances where there is, or appears to be, a conflict of interest between his so acting and any interest of his own (personal, financial or otherwise) without having received appropriate consent.[83] The Secretary of State must also consider whether the insolvency practice of the applicant is, has been, or will be carried on with the independence, integrity and professional skills appropriate.[84]

These provisions do not apply to the RPBs who also authorise persons to act as IPs, but the RPBs and the BERR do issue guidance on conflicts of interest.[85] The Secretary of State's 'Code of Conduct'[86] warns practitioners to be vigilant about potential conflicts of interest between their IP work and any personal, professional or financial commitments which might impair their objectivity or appear to do so. Specifically prohibited in the Code is acting as a liquidator after having acted as an administrative

---

[82] The Insolvency Practitioner Regulations 2005 specify the matters to be taken into account by the Secretary of State in determining whether a person is fit and proper to hold an IP licence (Regulation 4). Section 419 of the Insolvency Act 1986 empowers the Secretary of State to make regulations prohibiting persons from acting as IPs where conflicts of interest may arise.

[83] Insolvency Practitioner Regulations 2005 Regulation 4(f).

[84] See Insolvency Practitioner Regulations 2005 Regulation 4(e).

[85] See generally H. Anderson, 'Insolvency Practitioners: Professional Independence and Conflict of Interest' in A. Clarke (ed.), Current Issues in Insolvency Law (Stevens, London, 1991) pp. 1–25.

[86] See IS, Guidance to Professional Conduct and Ethics for Persons Authorized by the Secretary of State as IPs, www.insolvency.gov.uk/guidanceleaflets/conductethics/conductethics.htm (visited 11 January 2008).

receiver, and the appointment of auditors as liquidators or administrative receivers, except in the case of a members' voluntary liquidation, where it is beyond reasonable doubt that the company is solvent and that all debts can be satisfied within a twelve-month period. Similar rules are issued by the accountancy bodies in a combined approach through the ICAEW, and the ICAEW's Statement on Insolvency Practice[87] expresses rules on accepting appointments along similar lines to the Secretary of State's Code of Conduct. A key notion is that of the 'material professional relationship'. This arises where 'material'[88] work is being carried out, or has been carried out, during the previous three years, and means that an IP who is a member of a recognised accountancy body should not act as an IP in relation to a company if they, or their partners, have been auditors to that company or if they have carried out one or more 'significant'[89] assignments within three years of the onset of the company's insolvency. (Such requirements do not, however, rule out an IP acting in a members' voluntary liquidation as long as he has given 'careful consideration' to all the implications of acceptance in the particular case and is satisfied that the directors' declaration of solvency is likely to be substantiated by events.)[90]

The courts, for their part, have stressed that IPs must consider not only their own personal or professional interests and connections but also whether persons with whom they are associated have held appointments that would lead to a lack of independence. Harman J has stated that it would be most unlikely (but not totally impossible) that a director could ever be a proper liquidator of a company.[91] In *Re Lowestoft Traffic Services*

---

[87] See ICAEW, Guide to Professional Ethics 2006, sec. 220 (Conflict of Interest); Statement on Insolvency Practice 1.202 (revised September 1998 and reformatted August 2001). For solicitors see Solicitors' Code of Conduct Rules 2007, Rule 3 (Conflict of Interest) and *The Guide to the Professional Conduct of Solicitors* (Insolvency Practice) (8th edn, Law Society, 1999 as amended): see Guide Online, SRA, www.lawsociety.org.uk/professional/conduct/guideonline (visited January 2008). The IPA's *Guide to Professional Conduct and Ethics* will be replaced with a new Ethics Code with effect from 1 January 2009. The new code aims to encourage its members to balance the need to preserve client confidentiality with a need to be transparent in dealing with all parties involved in an insolvency: see J. Grant, 'Balanced Code', *Financial Times*, 4 November 2008.

[88] As defined in ICAEW, Insolvency Practice, paras. 7.0 and 7.1. See also IS, *Guidance to Professional Conduct and Ethics*, Annex of Particular Circumstances, Group A(i).

[89] See ICAEW, Insolvency Practice, para. 7.0(ii): 'where a practice or person has carried out one or more assignments, whether of a continuing nature or not, of such overall significance or in such circumstances that a member's objectivity in carrying out a subsequent insolvency appointment might or reasonably could be seen to be prejudiced'.

[90] See ICAEW, Insolvency Practice, para. 10.0.

[91] See *Re Corbenstoke Ltd (No. 2)* [1989] 5 BCC 767.

Co. Ltd[92] Hoffmann J stated that the public interest required that a liquidator should not only be independent, but also be seen to be independent, and he displaced a liquidator from office following considerable creditor disquiet at the appointment.[93] Conflicts of interest, moreover, arise where an IP holds a number of appointments and acts for more than one company involved in an insolvency: where, for example, a group is liquidated and the IP acts as liquidator for the parent company and the subsidiary companies. The courts have, however, tended to adopt an accepting attitude to such conflicts, seeing them as inevitable and routinely handled by experienced IPs.[94] The ICAEW Statement on Insolvency Practice acknowledges the possibility of conflicts but states that it would be 'impracticable' for a series of different IPs to act.[95] Where a direct conflict may arise, the courts may work around this by allowing IPs to secure the appointment of independent persons to deal with specific issues of conflict. Thus, in *Re Maxwell Communications Corp.*[96] Hoffmann J declined to appoint an additional administrator where the existing administrators had acted for Robert Maxwell personally. He considered the conflicts to be only distant possibilities and able to be dealt with by allowing the existing administrators an area of discretion.

As for powers of control, the courts may remove liquidators,[97] administrative receivers,[98] administrators,[99] supervisors of CVAs[100] and voluntary liquidators.[101] Parties aggrieved by the acts of liquidators may apply to the courts to reverse or modify these,[102] although the courts are generally reluctant to interfere in the administration of insolvency.[103]

---

[92] [1986] BCLC 81; [1986] 2 BCC 98.

[93] The liquidator had been appointed at a creditors' meeting where the chairman (a director) had used proxy voting to outvote the creditors, who favoured another IP. See also *Re Rhine Film Corporation (UK) Ltd* [1986] 2 BCC 98.

[94] See Dillon LJ in the Court of Appeal in *Re Esal (Commodities) Ltd* [1988] 4 BCC 475.

[95] See ICAEW, Insolvency Practice, para. 22.0; Anderson, 'Insolvency Practitioners', p. 14.

[96] [1992] BCLC 465, 469. [97] Insolvency Act 1986 s. 172.

[98] Ibid., s. 45. [99] Ibid., Sch. B1, para. 88. [100] Ibid., s. 7(5).

[101] Ibid., s. 108. See *Re Keypack Homecare Ltd* [1987] BCLC 409. Liquidators may still be removed in some cases without the court being involved: see Insolvency Act 1986 ss. 171–2.

[102] Insolvency Act 1986 ss. 168(5), 112(1).

[103] See *Re Hans Place Ltd* [1993] BCLC 768; *Re Edennote Ltd* [1996] 2 BCLC 389. The passing of the Human Rights Act 1998 opened the possibility of judicial oversight – covering the actions of ORs and possibly also those of IPs carrying out functions of a public nature. Challenges based on the protection of property rights (Article 1 of the First Protocol) or privacy (Article 8 of the Convention) may, for example, be made in the courts: see A. Arora, 'The Human Rights Act 1998: Some Implications for Commercial Law and Practice' (2001) 3 *Finance and Credit Law* 1; R. Tateossian,

Creditors, or members of the company, who are aggrieved by the actions of an administrator may similarly apply to the court under the 1986 Act.[104] IPs also owe common law duties of care and good faith to the company,[105] and liquidators in compulsory windings up and administrators are considered to be officers of the court and obliged to act honourably.[106] It should not be forgotten, furthermore, that under the Human Rights Act 1998 and Article 6 of the European Convention on Human Rights, 1950, there is a right, *inter alia*, to an independent and impartial tribunal. Where, accordingly, IPs act as office holders and determine rights, conflicts of interests may be pointed to and human rights issues raised.[107]

The Enterprise Act 2002 restricted the right of the floating charge holder to appoint an administrative receiver but, before that Act was passed, there were fears that harmful conflicts of interest were involved when investigating accountants were appointed as receivers.[108] A common business occurrence was that a bank, with concerns about the viability of a debtor company, would appoint accountants, often IPs, to investigate and report on the company's financial situation and prospects.[109] If these investigators reported that it was possible to save the company, and devise an action plan for the bank accordingly, they would

'Briefing' (2000) 2 *Finance and Credit Law* 5; N. Pike, 'The Human Rights Act 1998 and its Impact on Insolvency Practitioners' [2001] Ins. Law. 25. See also J. Ulph and T. Allen, 'Transactions at an Undervalue, Purchasers and the Impact of the Human Rights Act 1998' [2004] JBL 1 and ch. 13 below.

[104] See Insolvency Act 1986 Sch. B1, para. 74 – arguing that the administrator is acting, has acted, or is proposing to act in a way which (would) unfairly harm(s) their interests: see ch. 9 below. On liquidation, liquidators and administrative receivers can be found liable for breaches of duty (or 'misfeasance') under the Insolvency Act 1986 s. 212 and administrators can be similarly liable for misfeasance/breach of duty under para. 75 of Sch. B1 of the Insolvency Act 1986 (it is not now necessary regarding administrators for the company to be in liquidation): see chs. 8, 9 and 12 below.

[105] *Re AMF International Ltd (No. 2)* [1996] 2 BCLC 9; *Re Home and Colonial Insurance Co. Ltd* [1930] 1 Ch 102; *Re Windsor Steam Coal Co. (1901) Ltd* [1929] 1 Ch 151; *Pulsford* v. *Devenish* [1903] 2 Ch 625.

[106] See Insolvency Act 1986 Sch. B1, para. 5. Administrators are subject to the rule in *Ex parte James, Re Condon* (1874) 9 Ch App 609. See further I. Dawson, 'The Administrator, Morality and the Court' [1996] JBL 437.

[107] See W. Trower, 'Human Rights: Article 6 – The Reality and the Myth' [2001] Ins. Law. 48.

[108] See Flood and Skordaki, *Insolvency Practitioners*, pp. 16–17. Note, of course, that only *administrative* receivers have to be IPs: Insolvency Act 1986 s. 388(1).

[109] Such investigating accountants may also be called in by directors of the company who seek reassurance that it is proper to continue trading. The directors may be concerned about future liability under the Insolvency Act 1986 s. 214, 'wrongful' trading: see ch. 16 below.

receive fees for the investigation and planning tasks. If, on the other hand, the investigators advised the bank that the safest way to secure repayment of funds was to appoint a receiver, there was a high probability that the investigating firm of accountants would pick up the lucrative receivership work that ensued.[110] This was because they could argue that the investigating accountants were already familiar with the company's books, figures and position and because the bank was usually the largest secured creditor and was likely to be well placed to insist on the appointment of the receiver of its choice. The investigators were subject to real conflicts of interests: they were in a position to report on the company's viability but had a chance of privileged access to work and to assets. They were likely to ensure that the bank (which was effectively the investigating firm's real client) obtained as much of the insolvency assets as possible. The real danger was that such conflicts could produce biased advice to creditors and might exacerbate the existing propensity of large secured creditors to look to their own, not the company's or body of creditors', interests and to end the lives of companies before they had been given a reasonable opportunity of recovery. No independent ombudsman reviewed complaints on these matters and there was no compensation scheme. The regime was characterised as 'the Chaps regulating the Chaps'[111] but concerns on this front are, in the wake of the Enterprise Act 2002 reforms, of more historical than practical interest.[112]

Conflicts of interest may not, however, be the only sources of unfairness within the administration of insolvency regimes. Unfairness may arise where the parties involved in transactions are ill-matched in terms of information, expertise or power. Such inequalities may mean that the interests of certain parties are not fairly represented in the procedures or in the outcomes of insolvency processes. Socio-legal commentators on insolvency have thus emphasised the extent to which the rules on insolvency, which may speak loudly of fairness, are manipulated by

---

[110] Conflicts of interest appear stark where the investigation has been carried out for no fee and the only way the accountant can recover costs is by appointment as receiver: see J. Wilding, 'Instructing Investigating Accountants' (1994) 7 *Insolvency Intelligence* 3 (who states that 'in nearly all cases if the bank decides to appoint a receiver subsequent to an investigation, then it is the investigating accountant who will be appointed').

[111] See G. McCormack, 'Receiverships and the Rescue Culture' [2000] 2 CFILR 229, 245; P. Sikka, 'Turkeys Don't Vote for Christmas, Do They?' (1999) *Insolvency Bulletin* 5 (June); J. Cousins, A. Mitchell, P. Sikka, C. Cooper and P. Arnold, *Insolvency Abuse: Regulating the Insolvency Service* (Association for Accounting and Business Affairs, 2000).

[112] On Enterprise Act 2002 reforms see chs. 8 and 9 below.

experts to the advantage of their clients, or even themselves.[113] Wheeler's examination of the enforcement of retention of title clauses revealed that small trade creditors, who sought the protection of such clauses, were confronted in the enforcement process by the IPs who tended to act for large, secured creditors (in receiverships) or for the body of creditors (in liquidations) and who constituted the 'dominant actors' in the process. This domination flowed from their *de facto* positions as the possessors of the assets at issue; their superior knowledge concerning the assets and their utility to the company; their superior financial capacity and legal competence; and the familiarity with insolvency processes that flowed from their status as repeat players in the insolvency game. On this account, IPs used this superiority to protect the source of their fee income – the insolvency estate – from diminution by, amongst others, the holders of retention of title clauses. The procedures that were encountered were not properly 'negotiations': they were 'defence strategies' put up by the IPs.[114] What the IPs did was erect barrier upon barrier so as to defeat claims on the estate. They would thus 'fob-off' claimants; insert delays into processes; demand answers to never-ending lists of questions; employ bluffing; and confront the claimant with a mass of legal and administrative technicalities.[115] The overall picture, therefore, is neither of negotiations between matched parties, nor of independent fair-minded officials holding the ring between different interests. It is of highly trained practitioners acting for the economically powerful and gaining the advantage over less well-resourced parties.

What can be done to reduce such unfairness? In relation to conflicts of interest it has been suggested that concerned parties should be able to have recourse to a professional tribunal or an arbitration body.[116] There might, accordingly, be an appeal body established by the licensing bodies of IPs, and directors, creditors, employees or others aggrieved at the appointment of, say, a receiver, might put their case to such a body without recourse to the courts. The basis for complaint would be that the relevant provision of the professional code of conduct had not been followed and the arbitrator would be able to rule on compliance with the code. An ombudsman could also be established[117] by the profession and investigatory as well as

---

[113] See Wheeler, 'Capital Fractionalised'; Wheeler, *Reservation of Title Clauses*; Carruthers and Halliday, *Rescuing Business*.

[114] Wheeler, *Reservation of Title Clauses*, p. 96.

[115] Only 24 per cent of suppliers used lawyers in the study discussed in ibid., p. 101.

[116] See Lord Montague of Oxford in HL Debates, vol. 596, col. 940, 26 January 1999.

[117] See Justice, *Insolvency Law*, para. 5.19.

reporting powers might be exercised by such a person. The case for such an arrangement is considered in the next section.

Accountability

The accountability of IPs is provided for, in the main, by the self-regulatory regimes outlined above.[118] Attention should be paid to those concerns that are traditionally expressed in relation to self-regulatory mechanisms.[119] These include the tendency of such mechanisms to exclude 'outsiders' from policy- and rule-making processes; the lack of accountability of self-regulators to the public rather than to members;[120] the tendency of self-regulators to favour members' interests rather than those of the public; their generally poor record of rule enforcement; their anti-competitive effects (for example, through the imposition of excessive restrictions on access); their low levels of procedural transparency, information disclosure and reason giving; and the failure of voluntary schemes of self-regulation to control those persons who are both most likely to cause mischief and least likely to participate in such schemes.[121]

Criticisms of IP regulation echo the above points in some respects, with advocates of independent regulation stressing the protectionism and lack of objectivity of self-regulation.[122]

---

[118] As noted, IPs are held accountable in some respects by statute (see Insolvency Act 1986 s. 212, Sch. B1, para. 75 (misfeasance)), statutory obligations to file periodic returns at the Companies Registry, and the Insolvency Practitioners Regulations 2005. For a review of IP regulation by the IP regulators see IRWP Review. (This section of the chapter builds on Finch, 'Controlling the Insolvency Professionals' and 'Insolvency Practitioners'.)

[119] See generally R. Baldwin and M. Cave, *Understanding Regulation* (Oxford University Press, Oxford, 1999) ch. 10; J. Black, 'Constitutionalising Self-Regulation' (1996) 59 MLR 24; Blach, 'Decentring Regulation' (2001) 54 *Current Legal Problems* 103–47; C. Graham, 'Self-regulation' in G. Richardson and H. Genn (eds.), *Administrative Law and Government Action* (Clarendon Press, Oxford, 1994); C. Parker, *The Open Corporation: Effective Self-Regulation and Democracy* (Cambridge University Press, Cambridge, 2002); D. Sinclair, 'Self-regulation Versus Command and Control' (1997) 20 *Law & Policy* 529; V. Finch, 'Corporate Governance and Cadbury: Self-regulation and Alternatives' [1994] JBL 51.

[120] See Justice, *Insolvency Law*, p. 27.

[121] On the 'consensual paradox' and the tendency of voluntary mechanisms to regulate those least in need of regulating while failing to control those who most need to be restrained, see R. Baldwin, 'Health and Safety at Work: Consensus and Self-regulation' in R. Baldwin and C. McCrudden (eds.), *Regulation and Public Law* (Weidenfeld & Nicolson, London, 1987) p. 153.

[122] See H. Anderson, 'The Case for a Profession', *Financial Times*, 17 February 1998.

Some lay involvement is found, however, in the IPs' complaints procedure. Complaints against IPs are generally handled by the RPBs and the process is regulatory rather than remedial – it is concerned with maintaining professional standards as opposed to providing redress.[123] Typically cases are investigated by an assessor from the RPB, progressed to an investigating committee or panel or, if serious, to a disciplinary panel. An appeal from a disciplinary panel lies to an appeal tribunal and it is these tribunals that have considerable lay input. Sanctions include withdrawals of licence, suspensions, reprimands, fines, costs awards and exclusion from membership.[124] The RPBs report annually to the IS with figures on complaints handling but some commentators have argued that there should be greater and more easily accessible information on what classes of complaint are being (or have been) investigated by the RPBs – with one source disclosing rulings and actions taken.[125]

The quality of RPB monitoring and enforcement has, in the past, been brought into serious question. In 1993 the IS conducted an inspection of around fifty-five IPs and found that half of these were failing seriously to meet their statutory requirements. Ten per cent of those inspected generated very serious disciplinary problems which led to the withdrawal of licences and criminal prosecutions.[126] Pressure from the DTI (as it then was) led, as a result, to the establishment of a Joint Insolvency Monitoring Unit (JIMU) by the RPBs and to a regime of regular, random inspections. This regime of regular inspections still continues despite the abolition of JIMU at the end of 2004, but is now conducted in-house by the RPBs. The head of IP regulation at the IS noted in 2005 that these new monitoring arrangements can involve differences in approach[127] but that overall compliance with principles of good regulation and enforcement

---

[123] See generally A. Walters and M. Seneviratne, *Complaints Handling in the Insolvency Practitioner Profession: A Report for the Insolvency Practices Council* (IPC, London, 2008) and, on purposes, see p. 52.

[124] Ibid.

[125] Rumney and Smith, 'Sorting Out the Bad Apples', argue that the absence of such an information source is a 'glaring omission' in current arrangements (p. 37).

[126] A. Jack, 'Insolvency Regime to be Tightened', *Financial Times*, 22 January 1993. To conclude that the above problems stemmed from self-regulation might, however, be unfounded. The (then) DTI, in the same period, found many serious regulatory breaches among the 150 IPs that it regulated directly and disciplinary action (including deregulation) also resulted.

[127] Chapman, 'Insolvency Service's View of Regulation', p. 25, stating that, for example, the ICAEW has moved to a 'holistic approach' while the IPA has adopted an approach which 'focuses on qualitative outcomes'.

made such differences 'less important'.[128] The IS also monitors the complaints systems of the RPBs during three-yearly monitoring visits.

In their 2007–8 review of IP complaints handling, Walters and Seneviratne suggested that the public might think it odd that 1,700 IPs were subject to eight different complaints mechanisms. The review noted that lawyer-IPs were subject to the independent oversight of an ombudsman but accountant-IPs were not and that directly licensed IPs were not subject to an RPB-administered disciplinary apparatus. Walters and Seneviratne concluded: 'It is clear beyond peradventure that the insolvency regulators' complaints procedures are out of step with comparable procedures in the legal profession.'[129]

A series of general concerns about the IP regulatory system had already been identified when, ten years into the current IP regulatory regime, the Insolvency Review Working Party (IRWP) issued a Consultation Document. Major worries were the absence of systematic external review of the IS as an authorising body[130] and the absence of a greater degree of external involvement both in the writing and enforcement of rules and in monitoring the degree to which the authorising bodies act in the public interest. Other issues were the lack of flexibility, particularly on sanctioning techniques, found in the IS authorisation regime[131] and the scope of the work covered by the regulatory regime. (The IRWP noted that questions had arisen concerning both the need for an IP to be in control of some matters that are regulated but are not insolvency matters and also whether some activities currently carried out by unregulated individuals – for example, non-administrative receivers – should be incorporated into the insolvency regime.) A further problem was said to be posed by unscrupulous 'ambulance chasers' who targeted persons in financial distress and provided them with poor advice at an extortionate price. The complex, fragmentary nature of the regulatory regime for IPs was also a concern as was the absence of a single regulator for an insolvency profession. A plurality of regulators leads, on some accounts, to confusion when members of the public seek the relevant complaints authority, to duplication of resources and to unnecessarily high costs as well as differences in regulatory style and inconsistencies of regulatory response. The 'part-time' nature of much IP work was another worry with the absence of a dedicated

---

[128] See ibid. The principles offered are proportionality, accountability, consistency, transparency and targeting.
[129] Walters and Seneviratne, *Complaints Handling*, p. 79.   [130] IRWP Review, p. 15.
[131] Ibid., p. 15. A point echoed by Walters and Seneviratne, *Complaints Handling*, p. 79.

regulatory system under which only full-time professionals would be allowed to act. Final problem areas were identified in the liability of IPs to disciplinary action under two regimes – for example, as solicitor as well as IP – and the 'practitioner-led' nature of insolvency regulation.

Reforming IP regulation

Proposals for reforming IP regulation have ranged from the radical to the modest and the major options can be dealt with under four headings: insolvency as a discrete profession; an independent regulatory agency; departmental regulation; and fine-tuning profession-led regulation.[132]

Insolvency as a discrete profession

It might be argued that many IPs engage in insolvency work as their primary role and that they should be controlled by a single professional body. Against such a suggestion, however, it can be said that the majority of IPs are in general practice as either accountants or lawyers and that there is benefit in having the relevant RPBs monitoring and regulating the full range of their members' activities, not just insolvency; that the interweaving of insolvency and general practice work, notably the use, in insolvency work, of general practice infrastructures and staff support mechanisms, calls for such 'full-range' control.[133] In order to establish a discrete insolvency profession it would, moreover, be difficult to avoid demanding that all IPs be full-time insolvency workers. Such a requirement, it could be cautioned, would lead to a thinning of the ranks of IPs, a reduction in the breadth of experience of the average IP and an undesirable narrowing of the range of practitioners available to debtors, creditors or others. It is the part-time nature of much IP work, it can be said, that ensures that there are sufficient IPs in practice to meet demand when insolvency peaks and to offer choice to the public.[134]

---

[132] For proposals see IRWP Consultation Document; Justice, *Insolvency Law*; IRWP Review. Not under discussion here is a return to the pre-Cork world that placed unqualified debtor/creditor appointees in charge of insolvency processes, a position that the Cork Committee viewed as incapable of sustaining public confidence.

[133] The IRWP Review (p. 35) contends that co-operation with regulators is likely to be higher where regulation is by professional peer group rather than a body distanced from the home profession and that more rigorous regulation is likely to be provided by a peer group 'with its own reputation and self-interest at stake'.

[134] See IRWP Consultation Document, p. 27.

Establishing an insolvency profession might thus enhance account-ability in one respect and diminish it in another. It would provide one body to be held responsible for regulation in the sector and would offer a focus for public attention. It would, on the other hand, offer little assurance that the public interest was being considered more properly in self-regulatory decision- or policy-making than under the present system. It would, moreover, replace dual scrutiny (as IP and as accoun-tant or lawyer) with single scrutiny by the insolvency regulatory agency. If there is seen to be value in having specialist scrutiny of work done *qua* accountant or lawyer during insolvency processes then abandoning dual scrutiny may materially weaken accountability in spite of the capacity of a specialised profession to develop particular expertise in insolvency work. Transparency of regulation might be expected to be unaffected by professionalising insolvency practice in itself though the consistency brought by a move to a single professional body could have some enhancing effect. As for efficiency and effectiveness, the move to a less flexible single profession might prove detrimental if a move to full-time professionalisation prejudiced the production of a cadre of qualified IPs from which clients could choose.

On balance, the enhanced focus offered by a single profession does not seem to compensate for the losses involved in such a reform, notably the ensuing narrowing of experience that would be offered by the average IP, the shrinking of the body of IPs and the loss of dual scrutiny.[135]

An independent regulatory agency

An alternative to the 'single profession' approach would be retention of dual controls (by the IP regulator and the 'home' RPB) but with IP regulation given over to a single independent agency. At present, insol-vency practitioners (IPs) number around 1,700[136] yet are regulated by eight recognised professional bodies (RPBs). It is not surprising, there-fore, that calls for rationalisation are regular.[137] More remarkable is how many professionals seem to accept the case for rationalisation. In the

---

[135] The IRWP Review (not unsurprisingly) also concluded that regulation through the present professional RPB should be retained (p. 36).

[136] See note 30 above; Walters and Seneviratne, *Complaints Handling*.

[137] See V. Finch, 'Regulating Insolvency Practitioners: Rationalisation on the Agenda' (2005) 18 *Insolvency Intelligence* 17.

autumn of 2004 an R3 survey of members revealed that 79 per cent of respondents believed that there should be a single regulator.[138]

Why did nearly four out of five respondents favour a single regulator? The R3 returns suggest that what advocates of reform were looking for was an increase in the efficiency of regulation and an increase in fairness.[139] What most of them did not favour was a shift from self-regulation to governmental regulation – 69 per cent favoured self-regulation and less than half thought that public perceptions of regulation would be improved by external regulation.

Other professions have been through the mill of regulatory reform and it is worth reviewing the case for a single IP regulatory agency in the context of other movements towards 'single regulator' regimes.[140] The best known of these movements produced the Financial Services Authority (FSA) in November 2001 when it took over the functions of nine different regulatory bodies. More recently, there have been debates about the case for a single legal services regulator and the Clementi Report of 2004 reviewed a number of institutional reforms that ranged in radicalism and included a single regulator option.[141]

In the financial services and legal sectors a number of concerns and rationales have underpinned debates about regulatory reform and it may be useful to assess whether these have resonance in insolvency. With regard to legal services it was argued at the time of the Clementi Review that seven concerns about the regulatory system provided a platform for reform.[142] Those concerns related to, first, the *complaints system*, and in particular the failings of the solicitors' complaints system. A second worry was a perception that *self-regulation* was suspect because it no longer commanded public confidence, or (on a harder-line view) because it was inherently flawed. A third issue concerned what has been dubbed 'the regulatory maze' – the institutional complexity of a regulatory system in which more than twenty regulators exercised a diversity of

---

[138] See Verrill, 'R3 Regulation Survey', p. 27. (Though 59 per cent of R3 members stated that none of the existing regulatory bodies was best qualified for the role of single regulator.)

[139] As noted, 57 per cent of respondents pointed to room for improvement on efficiency and 62 per cent on fairness: ibid.

[140] For an account of changes in professional self-regulation see M. Moran, *The British Regulatory State* (Oxford University Press, Oxford, 2003) pp. 79–86.

[141] D. Clementi, *Review of the Regulatory Framework for Legal Services in England and Wales* (DCA, London, December 2004) ('Clementi Report').

[142] See R. Baldwin, M. Cave and K. Malleson, 'Regulating Legal Services – Time for the Big Bang?' (2004) 67 MLR 787.

sometimes overlapping regulatory functions.[143] A fourth point that critics made was that the regulatory system left considerable areas of service provision uncontrolled – that there were *'regulatory gaps'* that could prejudice consumer interests. A fifth issue was *whether the regulatory system could cope* with new ways of providing services, new business structures and multi-disciplinary partnerships, or whether it locked providers into old-fashioned structures. *Accountability and transparency* were a sixth anxiety and concerns centred on issues such as public involvement in regulatory decisions and policies and the adequacy of information flows for consumers. A final issue was the efficacy of various *price control mechanisms* and their effect in limiting the cost of legal services.[144]

In the financial services sector, the drive towards control by a single regulator agency has been said to have centred around five failings of the pre-FSA regime.[145] The first weakness was that, due to the changes in products, it had become difficult to regulate according to the function being carried out. This meant that the *boundaries between regulators* no longer reflected the economic reality of the industry.[146] It was argued, secondly, that the *proliferation* of existing regulators (nine in number) did not achieve the economies of scale that were obtainable with a single regulator. Similarly, it was contended that *economies of scope* were not being achieved as a single regulator could deal with cross-sector issues more efficiently than a multiplicity of regulators. A fourth criticism of the pre-FSA regime was that it failed to offer a *single, coherent regulatory approach* or philosophy – one that might much more easily be provided

---

[143] See Clementi Report, pp. 1–10.

[144] In January 2006 the Law Society formally split into three distinct bodies, each with its own Chief Executive: the Law Society, the Legal Complaints Service (LCS) and the Solicitors Regulation Authority (SRA). The Legal Services Act 2007 set up the Office for Legal Complaints to administer an ombudsman scheme that will deal with all consumer complaints regarding legal services. The Legal Services Board was set up by the 2007 Act as a single independent oversight regulator with the responsibility of supervising approved regulators. For arguments that the RPBs controlling IPs should not combine regulatory and representative roles and that there should be a clearer distinction between the functions of R3 and the RPBs see G. Jones, 'RPBs and Conflict' (2007) *Recovery* (Spring) 3.

[145] See C. Briault, *The Rationale of a Single National Financial Services Regulator* (FSA Occasional Paper, Series 2, London, May 1999); Briault, *Revisiting the Rationale for a Single National Financial Services Regulator* (FSA Occasional Paper, Series 2, London, February 2002).

[146] See M. Taylor, *Peak Practice: How to Reform the UK's Regulatory System* (Centre for the Study of Financial Innovation, London, 1996) p. 4.

by a unitary regulator. Finally, as in legal services, it was argued that a multi-agency regime did not offer the levels of *accountability and transparency* that a single agency could develop.

In the insolvency context it is clear that a number of the above concerns have been voiced by various parties and that, on some fronts, responses are already being implemented. Thus, regulatory proliferation and institutional complexity are problems that have been acted on in so far as the Joint Insolvency Committee (JIC) and the Insolvency Practices Council (IPC) were put in place following the 'Ten Years On' review of insolvency regulation of 1998.[147] These two bodies have taken numerous steps that are designed to encourage consistency of approach across regulators, to make regulation more efficient and to make regulatory processes simpler and speedier. Concerns about accountability and transparency have also been responded to in so far as the IPC offers increased public oversight of the profession. It remains the case, however, that R3 members and others are still worried about regulatory efficiency, fairness and complexity.[148]

That said, the case for independent regulation seems to have little support among R3 members who, as noted, strongly endorse self-regulation and who doubt whether external regulation will improve the profession's image. Here there seems a contrast with experience in the solicitors' profession where, at least on complaints issues, many commentators and participants allege that in the years up to 2004 there was a collapse of confidence in self-regulation.[149] It may well be the case that insolvency practitioners are prepared to argue that they have at no time suffered the kinds of attacks on self-regulation that solicitors have experienced during the last decade.

Might, however, a new insolvency regulatory agency produce a more efficient and coherent regulatory regime than alternative arrangements? On efficiency, it might be objected that creating an independent agency could *increase* regulatory costs for a number of reasons. First, the existing RPBs rely to a considerable extent on regulatory services that are

---

[147] IRWP Consultation Document; see further Finch, 'Insolvency Practitioners'. On the JIC see p. 185 above. The IPC was created in 2000 and comprises a team of five lay members and three professional advisers. It examines ethical and professional standards in the insolvency profession and puts proposals to the RPBs and, in so doing, meets with public interest groups and takes part in dialogues with the JIC, the IS, the RPBs and R3. Its chairman at the time of writing is Mr Geoffrey Fitchew.

[148] See Finch, 'Controlling the Insolvency Professionals'; Verrill, 'R3 Regulation Survey'.

[149] See Clementi Report, p. 2 and the consequent changes referred to above.

volunteered by members and the JIC operates, in turn, on the goodwill of the licensing bodies for staffing and accommodation. Such volunteered services are cost free to those involved in insolvency services. It is true that, at the end of the day, professional costs under such a system will be borne by the general users of accounting or legal services (many of whom will be subsidising insolvency regulatory work), but the effect is to produce low-cost controls that would be difficult to match in a fully costed, unsubsidised and independent regime.[150] A second fear could be that a new independent agency might tend to put up costs by regulating in an excessively restrictive manner.[151] Under the present system, the RPBs exert control with reference to the standards of acceptable professional conduct. These may be formulated in broad terms, non-legalistically.[152] An independent regulator, exerting control not through professional codes and standards but through enforceable rules, is more likely to become enmeshed in legalism and the minutiae of compliance.[153] The fear is that this would, again, tend to increase costs, would demand that IPs devote more time to compliance work and would be likely to reduce the general efficiency of insolvency regimes.

The responding argument is that a move from control by professional standards to control via rules could be expected to lead to greater transparency and increased assurance to the public and that this more than justifies the modest addition in costs that may be involved. It might also be contended that a dedicated agency would be better positioned to keep its eye on how IPs perform in relation to insolvency matters than would be the case with a professional body concerned also with a host of other affairs.

Turning to coherence, proponents of a single agency would argue that it is likely to be better placed than current regulators to develop a single, transparent and consistent set of regulatory policies and processes. In response, though, it might be replied that a single *self-regulatory* body might offer such coherence and openness and that rationalisations and harmonisations can provide these gains without losing the advantages of professionally based regulation. It has been contended, moreover (notably by the Chairman of the JIC),[154] that the JIC benefits from the diverse backgrounds of the licensing bodies, as it can draw on their experience in

---

[150] This is not to say that ending such subsidies might not prove attractive to some members.

[151] See generally E. Bardach and R. A. Kagan, *Going by the Book: The Problem of Regulatory Unreasonableness* (Temple University Press, Philadelphia, 1982).

[152] See J. Black, *Rules and Regulators* (Clarendon Press, Oxford, 1997) ch. 1.   [153] Ibid.

[154] See letter from Ian Walker, (2004) *Recovery* (Autumn) 29.

other regulated areas, that the successful innovations (as well as the pit-falls) that have been experienced in other areas can be learned from, and that such cross-fertilisation would not be available with one regulator.

Would accountability and fairness be enhanced by a single indepen-dent regulator? An independent regulatory agency might, on the one hand, be seen as 'another unelected quango' but it would be accountable by the usual methods to ministers, to Parliament and its select commit-tees, to consumer representative organisations and, through disclosures, to the public more generally. It would thus be more accountable on a broad basis than a self-regulatory body answering only to its member-ship. An independent regulator would not offer the same degree of accountability as a departmental regulator headed by a minister (who would answer directly to Parliament) but there is a case for establishing regulation at a distance from the Government since the latter may be involved in insolvency as a creditor. Fairness would for this reason be better furthered by an independent rather than a departmental regulator.

Fairness might also be served in so far as a single independent reg-ulator might be perceived as holding the ring more evenly both between different regulated practitioners and between practitioners and their clients or the public. Here it should be noted that fairness may be a particular concern in insolvency processes: first, because a variety of interests have to be served in particularly difficult circumstances; and, second, because many insolvency processes involve a public interest which merits fair treatment like any other.[155]

It could be argued that fairness might be served by institutional steps short of establishing an independent regulatory agency. An insolvency ombudsman might play an important role in ensuring that parties involved in insolvency are treated fairly and without maladministra-tion.[156] The case for such a body will be returned to below but it should be noted at this stage that arguments for an ombudsman may apply to independent and departmental as well as to self-regulatory systems. The rationale for an independent agency is not weakened, in turn, by any assumption concerning the establishing of an ombudsman, since the need for fairness is applied across 'first instance' insolvency processes independently of any machinery for redress that is created.

To summarise, the case for an independent regulator is largely based on its potential to produce improvements in coherence, clarity,

---

[155] See Finch, 'Controlling the Insolvency Professionals'.
[156] See Justice, *Insolvency Law*, para. 5.19.

consistency and fairness. Significant questions arise, however, concerning its added cost and potential to result in more legalistic, narrower and more restrictive regulation than is optimal.

Departmental regulation

The regulation of IPs might be given over completely to the IS of the BERR with the RPBs relinquishing their supervisory role.[157] In terms of accountability, this could be claimed to offer an improved arrangement. At present, the chief executive of the IS (the Inspector General) is responsible for the day-to-day operations of the service. The minister for Employment Relations and Postal Affairs sets the IS a number of published targets and performance against these is monitored by the IS's Steering and Directing Boards. Members of Parliament can write to the Inspector General of the IS on operational issues and the Inspector General is accountable to, and reports to, the BERR ministers on the progress and performance of the IS with regard to its performance targets[158] and the IS, in addition, acts in pursuit of the standards set down under the Insolvency Service Charter.[159] Work targets, and figures representing the extent to which these are achieved, are published by the IS in its Annual Reports.[160] The Parliamentary Commissioner for Administration (PCA) also has the right to investigate and report on the actions of the IS (though functions of Official Receivers as officers of the court are beyond PCA jurisdiction). Such mechanisms might not offer an unquestionably satisfactory regime of accountability[161] but they offer more democratic input (via ministers) than is available with RPBs and they manifest a commitment to the public interest.

---

[157] Not under discussion here is a system in which all IPs would be civil servants provided and authorised by BERR. Such a regime would constitute nationalisation of the private practitioner-led machinery now encountered and is unlikely to appeal to the major political parties. Departmental provision of all IPs would give rise to difficulties (notably the BERR's ability to meet variation in demand for such services – a capacity offered by the private marketplace that would be hard to match) even if costs were passed onto users of insolvency services.

[158] See IS, Annual Report 2007/8, p. 7.

[159] BERR, London, 2008.

[160] See, for example, the Annual Report 2007/8.

[161] For discussion see N. Lewis, 'The Citizens' Charter and Next Steps: A New Way of Governing?' (1993) *Political Quarterly* 316; R. Baldwin, 'The Next Steps: Ministerial Responsibility and Government by Agency' [1988] 51 MLR 622; G. Drewry, 'Forward from FMI: The Next Steps' [1988] PL 505; Drewry, 'Next Steps: The Pace Falters' [1990] PL 322.

Like the proposal for independent agency regulation, departmental control offers a unified scheme able to formulate, and work to, a single set of objectives but it is open to the same objections concerning duplications of jurisdictions, costs and jeopardy. As for expertise, the IS, unlike a new agency, would be able to draw on over a decade of experience in the field (though both would be able to buy in expertise from the body of existing specialists).

Departmental regulation may address public interest concerns more openly than resort to a mixture of private RPBs but, as noted above, a departmental system does not offer the same impartiality as an independent agency. The bias that outsiders may fear when viewing a departmental regime is that of leaning towards the preferences of the Government in power. In some regulated sectors where valuable franchises or contracts are handed out this may be a special concern.[162] Insolvency regulation involves no allocation of such valuables but it usually demands that assets be distributed and government departments, moreover, may be involved as creditors of firms or individuals involved in an insolvency or bankruptcy. It is important, therefore, that IPs should be seen to be acting in a professionally independent manner, free from conflicts of interest.[163] Overall, then, departmental regulation rates generally lower than independent regulation as far as perceived fairness is concerned.

Fine-tuning profession-led regulation

The IP regulatory regime now in operation incorporates a large element of self-regulation in so far as most IPs are members of the RPB that supervises them (albeit under IS oversight). Self-regulatory regimes, in general, are said to possess a number of virtues:[164] those regulating tend to be specialists in the relevant area; they have excellent access to information at low cost and are in constant touch with developments in the profession; they know which regulatory demands will be seen as reasonable and liable to be complied with readily; they can monitor behaviour easily and in a variety of ways; they tend to know 'where the bodies are buried'; and they can investigate matters in a less formal way than external regulators. They can, furthermore, employ general

---

[162] As, for example, in the television, radio or rail sectors.
[163] See Anderson, 'Insolvency Practitioners'; Lightman, 'Office Holders'.
[164] See p. 199 above.

professional standards and requirements to achieve results and influence cultures rather than rely on enforcing detailed rules;[165] they are financed by practitioners; and they are highly adaptable to changes in the economic, legal and social environments.

Such claims can be made in various forms and with different degrees of conviction for the current IP regulation regime and, rather than move to radical change, it may be preferable to fine-tune that regime. It is worth considering five main suggestions. The first of these is that the existing regulatory bodies should be further co-ordinated, rationalised or amalgamated.

Numerous commentators, including Phil Wallace, Chairman of the IPC Committee at the ICAEW,[166] have argued that eight RPBs is too many for the number of IPs (currently 1,700). Here there seems a strong *prima facie* case for reform and a first question is whether amalgamation of RPBs can be accomplished so as to offer a simpler structure, but one that retains some of the advantages of diversity in 'home background'. A second issue is whether amalgamations short of establishing a single self-regulatory body would produce a coherence of policy and a consistency of process that outweighs the supposed advantages of diversity. A further key issue is whether public participation in processes and policies can be ensured at sufficient levels to ensure public confidence in the self-regulatory system.

On current co-ordination, it has been noted above that the RPBs already do co-ordinate in a number of respects. They are bound, for example, by a memorandum of understanding with the Secretary of State and they operate with a Joint Insolvency Examination Board. To continue with the present regime and encourage further emphasis on co-operation and consistency (for instance, by making joint insolvency monitoring mandatory across RPB- and IS-authorised IPs) would require no new structures and would offer dual control by ensuring that lawyer and accountant IPs would remain regulated both as IPs and as lawyers or accountants (such control being beneficial where it is difficult to tease apart IP and home professional work).

---

[165] On 'interpretive communities' and the way that shared interpretations can be achieved without resort to further, detailed, specifications by means of rules see Black, *Rules and Regulators*, pp. 30–7; S. Fish, *Doing What Comes Naturally: Change, Rhetoric and the Practice of Theory in Literary and Legal Studies* (Clarendon Press, Oxford, 1989).

[166] See 'Regulatory Harmonisation'.

It may be argued that co-ordination would still leave too many authorising bodies for under 2,000 IPs; that this would be both inefficient and confusing to the general public or affected parties who may have a complaint about an IP and who would be uncertain about where to pursue this. The inefficiency point, as already noted, however, may be overstated, since it may be efficient to build on existing professional mechanisms for such a small number of IPs rather than to set up new regimes. Complaints issues, moreover, may be addressed by combining a co-ordination strategy for regulation with a unification policy for complaints: by establishing, for example, an Insolvency Ombudsman (a proposal returned to below).

Rationalisations and amalgamations might be employed to reduce the number of RPBs or to create a unified system without resort to an independent regulatory agency. The broad difficulty with both strategies is that, whereas control via existing professional bodies reduces potential 'problems' of dual discipline and double jeopardy, strategies of rationalisation and amalgamation introduce this issue in a new form. This point is, however, turned on its head if dual discipline is seen as a virtue. Less contentious is the suggestion that dealing with questions of dual control is liable to increase overall regulatory costs.

One means of amalgamating would be to establish a single sub-contracted body by agreement between the authorising bodies and to delegate functions of monitoring to this while retaining the responsibility for disciplining and sanctioning IPs in the home professions. As the Consultation Document notes, however,[167] an agreement would give rise to potential confusions and conflicts of functions and responsibilities. It would also court the danger of confusing lines of accountability. At present the RPBs are overseen by the Secretary of State. Establishing a sub-contracted body under the umbrella of the authorising bodies would mean that individual RPBs would not exercise control over it and the Secretary of State's monitoring would be placed at a further distance.

A second way to improve the current regime would be to harness the monitoring capacity of the accountancy or solicitors' firm and to authorise firms as well as individuals as IPs. One advantage would be that transfers of work between different IPs might be made administratively simpler and cheaper. It could also be said that clients tend to see themselves as dealing with firms, not individuals, and to see responsibility for good or poor performance as attaching to the firm. The reality

---

[167] IRWP Consultation Document, p. 29.

of much IP work, moreover, is that the IP uses the resources of the home firm, that the efficiency or otherwise of the insolvency work done may depend as much on the general professional performance of the firm and its employees as on the activities of the relevant individual. Regulating the firm would make it explicit that the support structure and internal controls of the firm are essential to the work of the IP and themselves require regulation.[168]

To regulate firms expressly would give them an incentive to ensure that their IPs operate to high standards. The firms, moreover, are far better placed than the RPBs or any external regulators to gain information on how IPs are doing their job, to review performance periodically and to remedy or sanction instances of under-performance. To attach IP functions to firms would mean that any qualified IP within the firms might carry out insolvency functions. This might involve some loss of personalisation within insolvency processes, since there would be no guarantee that individual X (rather than firm Y) would carry out the functions at issue. A move to regulate at firm level would, however, improve scrutiny of the context within which IPs operate and would do so without removing responsibility from the individual IP.

A third proposed improvement to the present machinery (and, as noted, a potential addition to a 'single regulator' or a departmental regime) would involve the establishment of an Insolvency Ombudsman. This idea has been put forward by a number of parties, including the Cork Committee and Justice.[169] An Ombudsman would handle complaints relating to individual cases rather than deal with general issues and the ombudsman process would only come into play after other alternative routes were exhausted (at present each RPB has its own complaints procedure). The Ombudsman might take a variety of different actions, including requiring organisations to correct matters, referring issues back to an organisation for reconsideration, facilitating conciliation between parties and making awards.

Creating an Ombudsman would offer a central location for complaints and a better and simpler public profile for insolvency complaints mechanisms. Establishing such a post has, however, been opposed by

---

[168] Ibid., p. 19.

[169] See Cork Report, paras. 1772–3; Justice, *Insolvency Law*, p. 25. Ombudsmen are now found in other professional fields. Thus, for example, there is a Legal Services Ombudsman as well as Ombudsmen in the insurance/unit trust, banking, building society and pension sectors. See R. James, *Private Ombudsmen and Public Law* (Ashgate, Dartmouth, 1997).

the IRWP on the grounds that it is doubtful whether an extra tier of complaints procedure is needed when, at present, all RPBs already operate mechanisms; that the extra costs involved might be considerable and would have to be borne by those affected by insolvency; that delays could be caused since such an Ombudsman might have a heavy workload and office holders might not be able to complete the insolvency procedure until the complaint has been finally resolved; and finally that an 'expectations gap'[170] might be created in so far as affected parties might anticipate the provision of effective remedies and do so in an unrealistic manner.[171] The IRWP also doubted whether the Ombudsman device could readily be applied in the insolvency area where there was the absence of a customer or client relationship.[172]

The last two of the above arguments may be the weakest: the possibility of an expectations gap would, on such an approach, remove the case for most systems of scrutiny, review or appeal yet there may be real value in many instances in providing a means of scrutinising the propriety and efficiency of administrative processes, especially where there are likely to be parties dissatisfied with the substantive outcomes of decisions. Nor is it clear why the value of an Ombudsman depends on the existence of a client relationship. Provided that aggrieved parties can be identified, the Ombudsman will have a role in investigating maladministration.

The value of a new complaints system would lie in the handling of complaints outside the RPBs. At present some RPB complaints mechanisms involve reference to independent assessors who scrutinise the handling and determination of complaints, but not all do so. (Even if a separate Ombudsman is not established, each authorising body should be compelled to operate a mechanism in which either complaints are decided by independent assessors or complaints decisions are reviewed by such assessors.)[173] An Ombudsman might also, however, take a broader view of the insolvency process than a body focusing on the behaviour of a particular member practitioner. In insolvency proceedings there is a lack of a speedy and cheap way for a creditor or group of creditors to challenge the conduct of an IP, and the position of a debtor is

---

[170] On the 'expectations gap' in the accountancy sector see J. Freedman, 'Accountants and Corporate Governance: Filling a Legal Vacuum?' (1993) *Political Quarterly* 285. See also *Report of the Committee on the Financial Aspects of Corporate Governance* (Cadbury Committee) (December 1992) paras. 2.1 and 5.4; V. Finch, 'Board Performance and Cadbury on Corporate Governance' [1992] JBL 581.

[171] See IRWP Consultation Document, ch. 5.   [172] See IRWP Review, p. 37.

[173] See IRWP Consultation Document, p. 33.

even weaker.[174] Matters can be raised by a multiplicity of routes: through the courts under the Insolvency Act 1986[175] or by resort to the relevant professional body. A host of parties may also be involved: solicitors, estate agents, accountants and other advisers. To make the services of an Ombudsman available to creditors and debtors or other aggrieved parties would provide a mechanism for cutting through such complexities and for appraising the respective responsibilities and performances of a range of professionals in a way not linked to a particular RPB's perspective. Such an Ombudsman might also be given a general power to make (non-binding) recommendations to the Secretary of State on issues relating to insolvency processes.

A fourth reform that is consistent with both the retention of self-regulation and improved accountability would involve establishing a new independent oversight body, but leaving the RPBs to regulate.[176] At present there is a limited form of oversight offered by the Insolvency Practices Council (IPC). This body comprises a majority of lay members and exercises a number of functions: it keeps under review the appropriateness of IPs' professional and ethical standards; puts proposals to the bodies devising professional and ethical standards for IPs; recommends issues to those bodies for consideration; and considers whether standards, once adopted, are properly observed and enforced.[177]

The IPC's first chair was appointed in December 1999 and it came into being in the spring of 2000.[178] The IPC is not designed to operate independently of the existing regulatory regime but to be a body linked to present mechanisms.[179] The IRWP Review rejected the notion of setting up an 'overriding body' to oversee current structures. It did so on the grounds that the IS offers public accountability through its link to

---

[174] See Justice, *Insolvency Law*, p. 25.

[175] See *inter alia* Insolvency Act 1986 s. 6; Sch. B1, paras. 74, 75.

[176] The legal and the accountancy professions offer examples of recent movements towards independent oversight. The Legal Services Board was set up by the Legal Services Act 2007 as an independent oversight agency and the Accountancy Foundation was set up in 2002 as an independent regulator of the accountancy profession. The Foundation's functions are now carried out by the Professional Oversight Board (POB), a part of the Financial Reporting Council. (The POB exercises powers delegated by the Secretary of State under Pt 11 of the Companies Act 1989 in accordance with the Companies Act 1989 s. 46: see Companies Act 2006, Pt 42, s. 1252.)

[177] On the origins of the IPC see IRWP Consultation Document.

[178] The IPC is made up of an independent chairman with five lay members to provide a majority and three IPs: see p. 206 above.

[179] IRWP Review, pp. 45–6.

the Secretary of State and through its role in overseeing the RPBs: 'it would not be a sensible task for any new body, set up to reflect the public interest in insolvency regulation, to second guess what the DTI and the IS are already doing'.[180] The Review also recommended that the IS should be released, so far as possible, from the duty it has to monitor practitioners directly authorised by the Secretary of State 'so that it can concentrate wholly on its high level function as a regulator of regulators'.[181]

Such proposals, however, seem strongly to have reflected the hold that current institutional arrangements had on IRWP affections and, again, fail wholly to convince. The public input being proposed is as modest as it is possible to imagine. The IPC does not draft standards, it merely makes suggestions to R3, which will continue with the drafting of standards. Indeed, the Review specified that the IPC's remit 'would not extend to the operational activities or responsibilities' of RPBs or the IS.[182] The IRWP's opposition to a more powerful, more independent insolvency oversight board was based on the view that such an accountability mechanism would 'obscure'[183] the ministerial accountability to Parliament that operated *via* the IS. The Review did, however, concede that the (proposed) IPC:

> would be a more appropriate forum for continuing interface with the general public than the Service can be ... At present when the IS reacts to concerns from the general public ... [i]t does so as part of what might be termed the 'ministerial post bag' process. The new Council, by contrast, would provide a dedicated (and a visible) contact point for raising such concerns.[184]

---

[180] Ibid., p. 43.   [181] Ibid., p. 7.

[182] Ibid., p. 48. See Sikka, 'Turkeys Don't Vote for Christmas', p. 7, who comments: 'The IPC will, however, be a toothless tiger unable to intervene in any specific or live case ... [T]he IRWP proposals would not dampen down public anxieties about self regulation, insolvency practices, the absence of an Ombudsman or a compensation scheme.' There is evidence, however, that the IPC will go public in attacking malpractice and tackling issues of creditor and public concern. The IPC's Annual Reports of 2004, 2005 and 2006, for example, expressed strong concern about possible misselling of IVAs to debtors on low incomes and made various recommendations to IPs. The 2006 Annual Report also focused on concerns in the corporate insolvency sector regarding the growth of 'pre-packs' (see ch. 10 below) and regarding cutbacks in the work of the IS in investigating the reports made by IPs on the conduct of directors of insolvent companies (see ch. 16 below). The IPC's Annual Report 2000 stated, however, that the IPC was 'not an Ombudsman', it could not adjudicate on individual cases, but it was 'anxious to learn about general areas of concern' (p. 2).

[183] IRWP Review, p. 50.   [184] Ibid., p. 49.

Such an awareness of the failings of accountability through the IS and the minister might have led the IRWP to the view that a focused, independent oversight board might have a role to play in supplementing any accountability through the IS, but unfortunately it did not.

There is, it seems, a case for an independent Insolvency Review Board that would exercise oversight of the overarching kind that the IRWP rejected. Such a board would be independent of the RPBs and the IS and would identify areas where, in the public interest, standards and guidance should be produced, modified or enhanced; provide an interface with the public; publish an Annual Report to the Secretary of State and the RPBs; and offer a forum for constant review of the insolvency regulatory system. It would provide a visible contact point for the voicing of public concerns. It might be objected that the co-ordinating role of such a body can be fulfilled by the JIC and IPC and so it would have no purpose. What this option would, however, offer is an added element of accountability through the independence of its supervision. It might also resolve the difficulty that the Insolvency Service both regulates some practitioners and also acts in some ways as a 'regulator of regulators'. Independent oversight would allow these functions to be teased apart and would strengthen public input into standard-setting which is currently vulnerable to accusations of weakness. The Board would not become involved in complaints handling in relation to individual cases. It would be IP-funded and its members might come from consumer groups, professional organisations, employee, business and management groups and the judiciary. They should have an understanding of insolvency but only a small minority (if any) should be IPs.

A special reason for establishing such a board is the fragmented nature of existing responsibility for insolvency procedures.[185] The BERR has the major responsibility now but that Department is ill-positioned to take a detached view of the area since it is routinely involved in many aspects of procedures. There is also some diffusion of responsibility between the BERR, the Department for Constitutional Affairs and other government departments (for example, where particular issues such as the family home or the employment implications of insolvency processes are raised). An Insolvency Review Board would have broad strategic relevance and offer a level of policy co-ordination that is at present lacking. Insolvency is an area peculiarly marked out by fragmented responsibility and diversity of inputs: therein lies the special case for a co-ordinating

---

[185] See Justice, *Insolvency Law*, p. 28.

body. The argument for such an institution seems strong in all scenarios of reform, except, perhaps, those involving the setting up of an independent regulatory agency for insolvency which could carry out such functions as might be allocated to an Insolvency Review Board.[186]

In order to counter the case for an IRB, the existing regulators might have to show that the present structure provides sufficient public oversight into the profession. It might also be necessary to establish that there is, in the insolvency field, no tension between regulatory and representative functions as is allegedly encountered in legal services regulation. That said, it can be noted that concerns about complaints and fairness have not been shown to be as acute in the insolvency arena as in the legal services field and, accordingly, there may be a lesser onus to improve external supervision.

A fifth proposal for reform is precautionary rather than remedial in nature and stems from the Select Committee on Social Security's report of 1993 on the work of the Maxwell insolvency practitioners.[187] The suggestion is that there should be a system of independent monitoring of the progress of all insolvencies over a certain value. When originally made, the proposal met with a cool response from the Conservative Government,[188] which argued that the task of monitoring insolvency processes should be left with creditors since it was their interests that were paramount; that it was unclear that independent monitoring would add significantly to creditors' efforts; and that the Government was not disposed to increase the costs associated with insolvency by instituting additional regulation. The counter-view, however, is that creditors cannot be assumed always to be sufficiently well informed, expert and well placed to be entrusted with protecting public and private interests in insolvency processes and that, even if creditors were well informed, expert and well placed, their commitment to protecting the broad public, as opposed to their own private, interests could by no means be taken for granted. Such involvement of the public interest is likely to occur in very large cases of insolvency – as the Maxwell episode demonstrated – and there seems a strong case for allocating a monitoring task in these cases to an Insolvency Ombudsman or an Insolvency Review Board, as discussed below.

To summarise, there are a number of ways in which the accountability of IPs might be improved. Persuasive arguments, for instance, point towards

---

[186] On the case for an independent regulatory agency to replace the RPBs and the IS, see Finch, 'Insolvency Practitioners', pp. 343–4.

[187] See Justice, *Insolvency Law*, p. 8.

[188] For the Government response to the Report see Cm 2415, 1993.

the increased external scrutiny that an Ombudsman or Insolvency Review Board would bring. The case for radical institutional reform in the shape of a new regulatory agency, a new discrete profession or an expanded and exclusive role for the IS, seems, in contrast, not to be made out.

Accountability can also be developed through open and accessible processes. An important question, therefore, is whether the procedures adopted by IPs are transparent and amenable to inputs from affected parties. Those procedures will be dealt with in later chapters and, accordingly, will not be reviewed here. What should be considered at this point, however, is whether IPs are, because of their institutional make-up, predisposed to encourage or obstruct accessibility and transparency. On this point it can be argued that professionals, at least when they act for a client, tend to put client interests before accessibility or transparency, and, in doing so, will rapidly take refuge behind professional status, knowledge and expertise. When IPs act as receivers for debenture holders, for instance, there is evidence that they are slow to volunteer information to other parties (who might reduce the insolvency fund available for the client or for fee payment) and that they may exploit their positions or expertise and knowledge by deliberately 'muddying the waters'.[189] Within the different context of liquidation – where the IP owes duties to all creditors – there tends to be a relatively greater degree of openness and willingness to impart information.[190] Even in liquidation procedures, however, institutional factors may lead to a lack of transparency and poor access. Thus, it has been argued that IPs have been strongly concerned, in the 1980s and 1990s, to build up their professional status and that, if creditors' meetings in insolvent liquidation are observed: 'What is revealed is that IPs, as an emerging professional group, use the meeting space to establish, within their own group, power and territory and that creditors, in whose interests the meeting is being held, are, in fact, marginalised and relegated to the role of audience.'[191] Trade creditors, it is argued, are likely to be particularly disadvantaged as IPs tend, at such meetings, to direct their comments

---

[189] See Wheeler, *Reservation of Title Clauses*, p. 107; see also ibid., pp. 65, 89–90. Again note must be taken of the Enterprise Act 2002 and the substantial replacement of administrative receivership with administration – the collective orientation of which might be expected to shift IPs towards a more inclusive approach to their functions than is seen in their stances as portrayed in Wheeler's work.

[190] Ibid., p. 76.

[191] S. Wheeler, 'Empty Rhetoric and Empty Promises: The Creditors' Meeting' (1994) 21 *Journal of Law and Society* 350, 351.

towards fellow professionals (often IPs representing large creditors). The trade creditors become 'largely a silent observing body only' and cannot participate in any active sense.[192] Overall the creditors' meeting can be seen as a series of 'almost private exchanges between the dominant professional actors'.[193] The tendency to exclude 'outsiders' was noted above in outlining common criticism of self-regulatory mechanisms, and here we find echoes in Wheeler's account of the IPs' work at the creditors' meeting. It reinforces the fear that where professionals are involved with non-experts and non-repeat players, there is unlikely to be transparency and wide accessibility.

Conclusions on insolvency practitioners

Could greater efficiency, expertise, fairness and accountability be achieved by turning away from professional self-regulation and implementing insolvency laws through other mechanisms? Few would argue for a move back to the pre-Cork era in which any person, whether qualified or not, could be appointed as a receiver or liquidator.[194] Implementation through a cadre of court officials or specialist civil servants might, however, be considered.[195] It should be borne in mind that:

> The institutional locus of [insolvency] work has substantial concern for all parties. It determines the relative weight of public and private interests. It affects what motivations underlie the behaviour of professionals ... how insulated will be the market from governmental intervention and what mechanisms, such as inspection or self-regulation, governments will initiate or support in order to ensure a public or political interest is served.[196]

The professional or disciplinary bases of those applying insolvency laws can, in turn, shape processes so that different knowledge bases, perceptual frameworks and bodies of expertise define and construct the issues and machineries of insolvency in different ways. They also 'locate the solution to the problem in different institutional sites'.[197] If, for example, lawyers play a central role in insolvency processes, proceedings are likely to take place in judicial or quasi-judicial settings in an adversarial fashion.[198] Such processes may place a strong emphasis on fairness but they are likely to be expensive and time-consuming. In contrast, less adversarial procedures conducted by specialist civil servants may be cheaper

---

[192] Ibid., p. 367.   [193] Ibid., p. 369.   [194] See Cork Report, ch. 15.
[195] See Carruthers and Halliday, *Rescuing Business*, pp. 31, 375.
[196] Ibid., pp. 375–6.   [197] Ibid., p. 23.   [198] Ibid., p. 31.

and swifter but are more likely to be tainted by perceptions that political influences, biases or unfairnesses have intruded.

It has been seen above that present arrangements are open to attack on a number of fronts but resort to court officials or civil servants would bring difficulties too. In both cases it would be necessary to use bodies of highly specialised officials and these 'quasi-professionals' might be as prone to exclude outsiders from insolvency processes as any current professionals. Court servants would be reached through judicial processes and dangers of legalism might attach to their use. Civil servants within a specialised unit might well be thought by the public to be susceptible to governmental influence unless their unit or agency was placed at a remove from the minister. Lack of accountability would then be a charge liable to be made. In the case of both sets of public officials, there would be concerns about their lack of business experience and their narrowness of professional background. In the case of current private practitioner IPs, it can be argued, first, that they offer a choice of professional background and, second, that there is value in having IPs with the breadth of training and experience in the private business sector that use of private professionals brings.

In conclusion, then, there seems to be no strong case for replacing private, professional IPs with public officials, of one kind or another, as the main implementers of insolvency procedures. There are, however, good reasons for tightening the mechanisms whereby IPs are regulated, and a number of valuable reforms have been considered above. Not least of these are the proposals to rethink the duties of IPs to the broad array of interests involved in insolvencies and to subject the current IP regulatory regime to more stringently independent oversight. The framework of laws that governs insolvency is of considerable importance but equal attention should be paid to those who shape the application of those laws.

Turnaround professionals

It could be argued that, without the need for any legal changes, another type of actor is, at least partially, replacing the IP as a proponent of insolvency work. The following chapters on corporate rescue will describe how the last decade has seen a shifting in the focal point of corporate rescue work. That period has seen a new emphasis on seeking to effect turnarounds in the fortunes of troubled companies – and doing so at a stage before formal insolvency procedures come into play.[199] This

---

[199] This section draws on Finch, 'Doctoring in the Shadows of Insolvency'.

change of focus has brought a burgeoning group of new actors onto the
scene. These are the individuals and organisations that assist banks and
companies in effecting pre-insolvency turnarounds. They come with a
variety of labels, notably: turnaround professionals, company doctors,
business recovery specialists, interim turnaround executives, risk consultants, solutions providers, independent business reviewers, asset-
based lenders, private equity providers, debt management companies,
credit advisers and insurers, and cash-flow managers.[200]

When, however, more and more work for distressed companies is
carried out in this pre-insolvency or 'twilight' zone,[201] issues are raised
about the growing role that is being played by the turnaround professionals. Does the use of such specialists actually produce processes that
are more rescue-friendly? Are these persons qualified experts who are
properly accountable? Do their interventions raise questions of fairness
between creditors?

The Cork Report cautioned that if those who administer insolvency
systems do not have the confidence and respect, not only of the courts
and of creditors and debtors but also of the general public, then 'complaints will multiply and, if remedial action is not taken, the system will
fall into disrepute and disuse'.[202] These comments were directed at those
who administered formal insolvency procedures but similar concerns
might be voiced about turnaround specialists because these actors, like
IPs, play key roles in rescue processes and, like IPs, may be instrumental
in putting into effect business solutions that impact on the interests of a
host of creditors and other stakeholders.

The efficiency and accountability of the turnaround professional system

Are TPs subject to a control regime that is efficient and that is accountable? In formal terms, it is difficult to argue that the TP regime constitutes an efficient quality control mechanism to the same degree as the

---

[200] See D. MacDonald, 'Turnaround Finance' (2002) *Recovery* (Winter) 17; R. Bingham, 'Poacher Turned Gamekeeper' (2003) *Recovery* (Winter) 27; P. Godfrey, 'The Turnaround Practitioner – Advisor or Director?' (2002) 18 IL&P 3. On the role of credit insurers in turnaround see G. Jones, 'Credit Insurance: A Question of Support' (2004) *Recovery* (Summer) 21.
[201] See D. Milman, 'Strategies for Regulating Managerial Performance in the Twilight Zone' [2004] JBL 493.
[202] Cork Report, para. 732.

IP system (a matter to be returned to in the discussion of expertise below). Could it be contended, however, that the TP system is efficient since TPs' activities contribute to the delivery of lowest-cost rescues? On this point, what is hard to deny is that TPs offer a range of services that are rescue relevant. The market, moreover, has clearly encouraged the development of a group of specialists that offer a wide variety of rescue services. It is, though, difficult to quantify the contribution of TPs to rescue and there are a number of reasons why this is so. First, a number of factors may have an effect on both the incidence of rescue attempts and the success or otherwise of such attempts. Assessing, for instance, the degree to which any particular development – such as the advent of the new cadre of turnaround professional – has impacted on rescue is impossible. Other relevant developments include the Enterprise Act 2002's reforms relating to administrative receivership and administration, the Government's newly invigorated espousal of rescue and the major lenders' revised approaches to rescue.[203] Statistics on overall numbers of corporate liquidations or of rescues, accordingly, would tell us little about the value of the turnaround professional – there are too many possible (and interlinked) drivers of rescue attempts as well as of success or failure. Second, there is an absence of statistical data on the extent to which TPs' interventions produce successful rescues. There is, moreover, likely to be a continuing paucity of such data – and again for good reasons. What constitutes a 'rescue' is hard to define, even when referring to formal, statutory rescue processes.[204] In relation to such processes a rescue can be thought of as a major intervention necessary to avert eventual failure of the company.[205] Characterising a formal rescue as successful raises a host of further issues, notably: for which parties is the rescue a success?[206] Is rescue of the company or rescue of the business what matters? Is the true measure of rescue the protection of employment or creditor value? How much downsizing or reorganisation constitutes failure?

When the focus is on turnaround activities, however, the difficulty of drawing a boundary line around 'rescue' services is yet more extreme. No longer is the focus on major actions that are taken to avert a failure that is

---

[203] See chs. 6–12 below.

[204] See e.g. A. Belcher, *Corporate Rescue* (Sweet & Maxwell, London, 1997) p. 12; and ch. 6 below.

[205] See Belcher, *Corporate Rescue*.

[206] On stakeholders' divergent views on the objectives of rescue see J. Roome, 'The Unwelcome Guest' (2004) *Recovery* (Summer) 30 and see further ch. 7 below.

clearly identifiable and seen to be approaching. Turnaround professionals may assist companies in meeting challenges when those companies are in states ranging from relative health to absolute crisis. The essence of beneficial turnaround activity, moreover, is widely argued to be early intervention – and certainly action at a stage in corporate troubles that is early enough to prevent these from becoming chronic.[207] The most successful 'rescues', accordingly, are likely to be those that are at no time ever labelled as 'rescues' – that is in the nature of preventative activity.

It might be responded that some statistics could be collected on such matters as the number of bank-induced referrals to turnaround specialists and the proportion of these that lead into formal insolvency procedures. Again, however, there would be difficulties in defining what constitutes such a referral. If, for instance, a bank recommended to a debtor company that it sought advice from a risk consultant or a solutions provider, would this be counted as a rescue-relevant referral? It might be suggested that a referral might be categorised as a 'rescue-referral' if it is made when the company is in a state of 'near insolvency' or 'acute crisis' but these terms lack precise meaning and it is to be repeated that much of the preventative work of turnaround professionals is likely to be done before companies reach such desperate straits.

What can be offered as an indication of the contribution of turnaround specialists to rescue is an account of the services that these professionals bring to the rescue party and which conduce to rescue. The list is impressive and includes: conducting independent business reviews (IBRs); carrying out external reviews of managerial performance; advising on financial, operational and managerial restructurings; devising financial plans; arranging the provision of new funds; providing new managerial skills; planning strategic realignments; implementing cash flow management systems and negotiating with customers, suppliers and other stakeholders.[208]

What, it might be posited, is added by using turnaround professionals to provide the above services? Surely these are all functions that have been and could be carried out by companies on the advice of their major creditors? The turnaround professionals, however, would argue, first, that *niche* specialists, in such matters as refinancing, are able to develop

---

[207] See N. Ferguson, 'Early Intervention by STP Independent Executives' (2004) *STP News* (Winter) 14.

[208] See A. Lester, N. Young and C. Hawes, 'Help is at Hand' (2002) *Recovery* (Winter) 18.

a higher level of skill and a more extensive list of contacts than generalists. Second, they would point to the benefits of using professionals that are independent of the major creditors. Such independence may mean that the troubled company's directors are less threatened by turnaround specialists than by creditors' staff and are thus liable to be more co-operative. Turnaround professionals, for their part, are increasingly inclined to work alongside existing managers and to improve the performance of those who are already in place. As the Chief Executive Officer of the Society of Turnaround Professionals (STP – now IFT), Nick Ferguson, has put it: 'There has been a tendency to dispense with the existing management of a troubled company but people now recognise that it is worth trying to keep them, to hold their hand and to mentor them.'[209] On the accountability of TPs, it can be argued that this tends to be modest in the absence of statutory controls and because a high premium is placed on the independence of these specialists. Independence encourages a level of trust, especially in the minds of those less committed creditors whose co-operation may be needed in order to effect a rescue. This allows for more effective negotiations on rescue proposals; it means that business reviews carry an authority that might not be present if they had been carried out by previously involved parties; it allows more objectivity in analyses of managerial capacities and it provides a fresh perspective on the company and its problems. From the point of view of the troubled company's directors, a degree of trust in an independent TP may concentrate the mind wonderfully. It will often be the case that the need for urgent action within the company is only accepted when that necessity is hammered home by an authoritative and independent outsider.

Independence also encourages the development of a cadre of professionals who are specialists in gaining trust and co-operation through effective facilitation. A senior manager of a credit insurer made the point thus:

> The key is how to build trust between stakeholders that allows them to discuss confidently more creative and supportive options that might save

---

[209] N. Ferguson, 'Advice Squad' (2005) *Director* (April) 31. The STP was renamed the Institute for Turnaround (IFT) in June 2008. Another turnaround specialist typified the relationship with existing directors: 'I work with incumbent management rather than threaten their future': see C. Wray, 'A Day in the Life of a Company Doctor' (2002) *Recovery* (September) 51. It is likely that the directors of a troubled company will feel more comfortable with an informal turnaround procedure than a formal rescue procedure which removes them from office.

> some corporate lives … There is also a key role for highly skilled facil-
> itators here. Neither the banks nor credit insurers have the resources to
> spend weeks investigating, planning a strategy and then enforcing that
> strategy. Company doctors and, increasingly, the Big Four accountancy
> firms are becoming interested in this role. The beauty of it is that the
> 'independent' facilitator can engage all the key stakeholders and bridge
> the gap of trust between the banks and insurers.[210]

A further advantage of independent facilitation is that this provides an
often urgently needed boost to information flows within the troubled
company. Establishing such information provision is seen by many as a
central contribution that the TP can make. One highly experienced TP
put it: 'You need great communication skills because usually it is communication that has fallen apart in the company and people aren't telling
anyone anything because they are too scared or too busy.'[211] He added
that, in many troubled companies, the existing directors (or some of
them) often knew what had to be done to effect a turnaround but it
required the input of a TP to allow the necessary messages to strike home
and cause action within the company.

It might be contended, however, that it is easy to overstate the independence of turnaround specialists. In most cases, TPs are hired at the
prompting of the banks[212] and observers might, accordingly, think that
the banks will call the tune in the turnaround. There are, however, factors
that militate against such a bank bias. First, it is the case in the vast
majority of turnarounds that, although the hiring of the TP is at the
instigation of the bank,[213] the client and paymaster is the company itself.
The turnaround specialist, accordingly, is obliged to act in the interests of
the company not the bank.[214] Second, turnaround professionals are
repeat players in relation to corporate difficulties and they have reputational incentives to avoid bank biases. If their reputations for even-
handedness were to diminish this would affect their business prospects
since their success in achieving turnaround will in no small part turn on
the trust they are able to generate amongst stakeholders and on the

---

[210] Jones, 'Credit Insurance', p. 22.
[211] Les Otty, Director of Business Turnaround, BDO Stoy Hayward: interview with author,
8 April 2005.
[212] See e.g. Bingham, 'Poacher Turned Gamekeeper'.
[213] Often, as noted, on the recommendation of a 'catalyst', for example an investigating
accountant appointed by the bank. Author's interview with Les Otty, 8 April 2005.
[214] STP members are, as indicated above, required to give the company advice free from
'external or adverse pressures' which would weaken their independence: STP *Code of
Ethics*, Appendix, para. A.2.

authority with which they can deliver business reviews and proposals for reorganisation, refinancing and so on. To the extent that the clients of turnaround professionals are paying for services that have value by virtue of their independence, the market is valuing their rescue-enhancing rather than bank-serving effects. The market, it seems, is increasingly willing to value such services and rescue-enhancing effects.

Turnaround professionals and fairness

When companies have entered into a statutory insolvency procedure it is clear that the law obliges IPs to act fairly when carrying out functions within these procedures.[215] The duty to act fairly, moreover, has substantive and procedural aspects. The IP who acts as an administrator, for instance, is obliged to pursue his functions 'in the interests of the creditors of the company as a whole'.[216]

Such an administrator would also be obliged to act procedurally fairly. This flows from the administrator's status as an officer of the court (a public official)[217] and because the administrator's substantive duty to

---

[215] As noted above, whether as officers of the court (administrators and liquidators in compulsory liquidations) or as professionals governed by their relevant RPB's code of ethics. What fairness involves in any particular case will be assessed by the courts. (Challenges on the basis of unfairness can be mounted in, for example, the 'new' administration procedure under Insolvency Act Sch. B1, para. 74(1).) On judicial scrutiny of IP activities in the 'new' administration procedure see J. Armour and R. Mokal, 'Reforming the Governance of Corporate Rescue: The Enterprise Act 2002' [2005] LMCLQ 28; R. Mokal and J. Armour, 'The New UK Corporate Rescue Procedure – The Administrator's Duty to Act Rationally' (2004) 1 Int. Corp. Rescue 136; V. Finch, 'Re-invigorating Corporate Rescue' [2003] JBL 527; Finch, 'Control and Co-ordination in Corporate Rescue' and ch. 9 below.

[216] The 'new' administrator owes statutory duties to act in the interests of creditors as a whole and to perform his functions as quickly and efficiently as is reasonably practicable: see Insolvency Act 1986 Sch. B1, paras. 3(2), 4. He must pursue a single hierarchy of objectives set out in para. 3(1) and paying off the secured creditors ranks last in those statutory objectives (in doing so he is under a positive duty not to harm the company's other creditors: para. 3(4)(b)). See ch. 9 below.

[217] See Insolvency Act 1986 Sch. B1, para. 5. As an officer of the court the administrator is bound by the rule in *Ex p. James* (1874) 9 Ch App 609 (obligations to act honourably and fairly). As a public official the administrator must act procedurally fairly and principles of judicial review necessitate the challenged actions of the administrator meeting demands of rationality: see e.g. *Associated Provincial Picture Houses Ltd* v. *Wednesbury Corporation* [1948] 1 KB 223; *Council of Civil Service Unions* v. *Minister for the Civil Service* [1985] AC 314. See further Mokal and Armour, 'New UK Corporate Rescue Procedure'; Finch, 'Control and Co-ordination in Corporate Rescue' and ch. 9 below.

consider the interests of all creditors carries an obligation to act reasonably by recognising the procedural rights of such creditors.[218] Can it be argued that turnaround specialists are, or should be, obliged to act according to similar canons of fairness?[219] A difficulty in making this argument is that a distinction might be sought to be drawn between situations that obtain before and those that are encountered after a company has entered a formal insolvency process. Once the company has entered a statutory insolvency procedure (which may be pre- or post-insolvency)[220] insolvency law is based on the premise that such procedures involve impositions and that those parties who have to make concessions within such procedures must be given process rights in return for these concessions. The CVA procedure, for example, can be used pre-insolvency[221] and involves a variety of procedural protections for creditors (for example, the need for proposals to be approved by specified majorities).[222] Such protections can be seen as a *quid pro quo* for creditors having to submit to proposals that bind them[223] and to a moratorium on enforcing their rights in the 'small company' CVA.[224] In contrast, it might be argued, parties in informal situations – before statutory insolvency procedures come into play – are free to protect

---

[218] As demanded by *Wednesbury*. On the 'new' administration see ch. 9 below.

[219] The STP/IFT *Code of Ethics*, para. 3.1 requires members to act with honesty, fair dealing and truthfulness in all professional appointments and to strive for objectivity in all professional judgements. Objectivity here requires having regard to all considerations relevant to the task in hand and no others. Paragraph 5 of the Code requires the declining of any assignment that would create a conflict of interest. Advice has to be impartial and frank, free from any external or adverse pressures or interests that would weaken the member's professional independence (STP/IFT *Code of Ethics*, Appendix, para. A.2).

[220] A company is insolvent for the purposes of the law if it is unable to pay its debts. Legal consequences only attach to a company, however, on the institution of a formal proceeding, such as winding up or administration: see ch. 4 above.

[221] Unless it is being invoked in conjunction with an administration order made under the Insolvency Act 1986 Sch. B1.

[222] The proposal for a CVA needs to be approved by 75 per cent of creditors voting in person or by proxy by reference to the value of their claims. It also requires the approval of 50 per cent in value of the shareholders present at the shareholders' meeting. If approved the scheme becomes operative and binding upon the company and all of its creditors (save for secured or preferential creditors who have not consented: Insolvency Act 1986 s. 4(3) and (4)). See further ch. 11 below.

[223] As noted above, the Insolvency Act 1986 s. 4(3) and (4) specifies that the CVA proposal cannot affect the rights of secured or preferential creditors without their consent.

[224] See Insolvency Act 1986 s. 1A and Sch. A1 (inserted by the Insolvency Act 2000) and ch. 11 below.

themselves by exercising whatever rights[225] they may possess. There is no need to demand that they act altruistically or recognise any participatory rights of other parties since those parties are not being forced to accept any proposals or settlements.

If the above distinction between pre- and post-formal scenarios is accepted, it can be contended that issues of procedural fairness are not to the fore when, say, a company employs turnaround professionals to devise restructuring plans and applies these in informal processes. It might be responded that, in reality, it is often the case that when a company employs a TP a plan of action will be imposed on less well-resourced creditors and that powerful creditors will negotiate for solutions that are not so much in the best interests of all creditors as they are designed to improve their own positions by increasing their security or equity. (There is evidence, indeed, that during periods of rescue, bank credit tends to contract but unsecured trade credit tends to expand, sometimes dramatically.)[226] From the point of view of an unsecured creditor, it could be pleaded, it matters little whether a bank-orientated strategy impacts on it by means of a formal process such as a CVA or an informal turnaround strategy. Why, therefore, should procedural protections avail in the case of the CVA but not in informal turnaround? One answer, perhaps, is that insolvency law has to draw a line at some point between formal processes, which involve formal, legal protections, and informal processes, which involve contractual and market-driven protections (for example, the unsecured creditor's freedom to refuse to trade or to enforce a debt). It might be argued that what is really at issue here is where the formal/informal line should be drawn. Advocates of greater protection for vulnerable creditors might contend that some informal procedures should be made formal by the imposition of a statutory scheme of processes and protections.[227] This would cover the situation, for instance, in which a floating-charge-holding bank negotiates with the company's turnaround specialists and then presses the company to take steps that do not appear to unsecured creditors to be in their interests (for example, the bank persuades the company both to

---

[225] These may be existing or newly negotiated contractual rights and statutory rights, for example to levy execution for the debt. On informal rescues and reconstructions see ch. 7 below.

[226] See J. Franks and O. Sussman, 'The Cycle of Corporate Distress, Rescue and Dissolution', IFA Working Paper 306 (2000), p. 2: trade credit expansions of up to 80 per cent are noted in cases that end in a formal insolvency procedure.

[227] On arguments for placing the London Approach on a statutory footing see ch. 7 below.

increase the bank's security in return for continued lending and to demand improved credit terms from unsecured creditors). To such advocates of greater protection, it could be replied, first, that the law already offers such unsecured creditors a set of rights that allows them to enforce their debts; second, that if the actions being taken by the company mean that it is likely to be unable to pay its debts, the Insolvency Act 1986 already allows the unsecured creditors to apply for the appointment of, say, an administrator;[228] and third, that to advance the threshold of formal insolvency proceedings further into the activities of non-insolvent companies may create a set of serious uncertainties that would prejudice entrepreneurship. These uncertainties would be considerable, it might be cautioned, because there would be vagueness in the boundary between ordinary healthy commercial activity and activity producing some risks to some creditors which would give rise to extra obligations of fairness.

On behalf of TPs, further arguments might be mounted to suggest that the growth of TP activity positively enhances fairness in most informal turnaround schemes. First, it could be emphasised that the TP generally acts for the company not the bank and that, if he is an IFT member, he is ethically bound to act fairly and to give advice free from outside pressure (from the bank, for example).[229] Second, it could be argued that the work of a specialist TP enhances fairness through improved transparency. The TP carries out a central function – the gaining of creditor agreement to a way forward for the company. In repeatedly performing this function TPs become expert facilitators and mediators. They are the parties who lubricate the machinery of negotiation that is necessary for agreements to be devised. As one turnaround specialist indicated, when talking of a large and successful reorganisation, the first success factor was: 'Communicate directly with all the stakeholders. Many of the banks had no direct contact with the company. We held one to one discussions with each institution to ensure that their issues and concerns were addressed. This was critical to building support for the restructuring.'[230]

The TP, accordingly, can be held out as the person who plays a key role in making turnaround processes open, transparent and intelligible. In doing so, it can be argued, the TP conduces to processes that are more open and fair than would be the case without professional facilitation.

---

[228] See Insolvency Act 1986 Sch. B1, paras. 12 and 22.
[229] See STP/IFT *Code of Ethics*, Appendix, para. A.2.
[230] L. Barlow, 'Turnaround and Restructuring at Stolt Offshore' (2004) *STP News* (Winter) 11.

TPs have an independence from the main creditor bank that allows them to perform the facilitation function in a way that, say, the employee of the bank's 'intensive care' unit would find extremely difficult.

This argument, however, can be pushed too far. It would be an exaggeration to see most informal turnaround processes as inclusive of all creditor voices and interests. Negotiations are often carried out secretly, press coverage is usually avoided and TPs will tend to view negotiations as an exercise in keeping key players on side. Trade or small unsecured creditors are, accordingly, often left out of these processes and dealt with only when they create difficulties on discovering what business solutions are being negotiated. It should also be noted that the modern tendency to finance companies from a variety of credit sources means that TPs often have to conduct negotiations with a large number of banks, venture capitalists, bondholders, distressed debt holders and others. The number of these creditors and the divergence of their attitudes, approaches and expectations[231] makes the TP's task all the more difficult and, in so far as it does, this will make it increasingly unlikely that negotiations will be conducted in a sufficiently inclusive manner to prove receptive to the voices of trade and smaller unsecured creditors.[232]

Expertise

In asking whether the TPs system ensures expertise in the supply of specialists, it has to be acknowledged, first, that turnaround professionals, as a group, display some of the characteristics commonly associated with the self-regulatory professions.[233] The Society of Turnaround Professionals was established in late 2000 and was renamed the Institute for Turnaround (IFT) in June 2008. The STP's stated mission was to be the 'principal source of the highest quality practitioners implementing and advising upon successful turnarounds for the benefit of the national economy and all stakeholders'.[234] The Society saw its creation as 'part of

---

[231] On such divergent expectations see Roome 'Unwelcome Guest' and further ch. 7 below.

[232] The stress that the fragmentation and globalisation of credit imposes on informal processes has been noted in relation to the banks-controlled London Approach where similar considerations apply: see J. Flood, 'The Vultures Fly East: The Creation and Globalisation of the Distressed Debt Market' in D. Nelken and J. Feast (eds.), *Adapting Legal Cultures* (Hart, Oxford, 2001); L. Norley, 'Tooled Up', *The Lawyer*, 10 November 2003 and ch. 7 below.

[233] On professional self-regulation generally see Baldwin and Cave, *Understanding Regulation*, ch. 10; see also p. 199 above.

[234] STP home page (www.stp-uk.org). See now the IFT home page.

the drive towards the rescue culture in the UK' and reported that its advent was encouraged by the UK Government, the clearing banks, other financiers, private equity providers and leading accountancy firms.[235] The STP claimed that, in a very short time, it generated a membership of leading and expert professionals. These did not all possess the same qualifications but all had 'extensive experience of implementing, initiating and advising' on recovery strategies. They comprised the following: independent company chairmen and chief executives (sometimes known as 'company doctors'); other independent company executives with particular skills relevant to turnaround (for example in finance, operations, manufacturing and so on); specialist advisers on turnaround with accountancy or consulting backgrounds; and senior representatives from a variety of stakeholders who specialise in turnaround, including bankers, institutional investors, asset lenders and venture capitalists. As at 2007 there was an STP membership of 188, of whom 122 were full members and 66 were associate members.[236]

The STP's objectives were stated in the kind of terms that are commonly expressed by a self-regulatory body. It aimed to advance the theory and practice of corporate turnaround; to provide high standards of practice and professional conduct; and to provide a forum for involved parties to discuss issues relating to turnaround. The Society also combined representative and regulatory roles – to 'make the case for corporate turnaround to the business community, the UK Government, academia and the media'.[237] As for quality controls, the STP expressed an intention to regulate members within agreed professional standards with the assistance of other professional bodies, where appropriate; and to organise and conduct examinations for members and others in subjects requiring an understanding of the theory and practice of corporate turnaround.

Are STP/IFT controls as rigorous as those that govern insolvency practitioners? It will be remembered that the Cork Report called for eligibility to act as an office holder in a designated insolvency proceeding to be restricted to persons qualified under the 1986 Act.[238] Such qualification was to depend on membership of an approved professional body and the Cork Committee was clear that any acceptable professional body

---

[235] Ibid.   [236] N. Ferguson, 'STP Update' (2007) *Recovery* (Spring) 42.

[237] STP home page.

[238] See Insolvency Act 1986 Pt XIII and the Insolvency Practitioners Regulations 2005 (SI 2005/524) and Insolvency Act 1986 s. 390. See p. 182 above.

would have to meet five conditions.[239] It would have to insist on the observance by members of an ethical code of professional conduct, breach of which would involve professional sanctions; there would have to be a professional obligation to account strictly for moneys belonging to third parties; membership would have to be confined to those who have passed a competitive examination (including a paper on insolvency); there must be an effective disciplinary system with powers to deprive defaulting members of the right to practise; and there must be a system of practising certificates, renewable annually.

Turnaround specialists differ from IPs in so far as they are subject to no mandatory regime of training, experience or qualification. Those who are full members of the IFT are, however, subject to a regime of quality control that is principally governed by a system of accreditation. This demands that a prospective member evidences that he or she has engaged in over 1,200 hours of turnaround in the last five years; presents three case studies that he or she has carried out; provides a referee from the stakeholder community connected to each of these three case studies; produces a professional reference; and submits to an interview with a panel comprising, amongst others, two IFT members and an R3 member. Members and associate members of the IFT are also required to sign up to the Institute's Code of Ethics. This Code is enforced by means of a disciplinary process, which is operated on behalf of the IFT by the Association of Chartered Certified Accountants (ACCA).[240] Breach of the Code may result in suspension or expulsion from the IFT. Membership of the IFT, accordingly, offers a kite-mark of quality to prospective clients, though the latter are perfectly free to engage a turnaround specialist who is not a member of the IFT.[241]

When comparing the regulatory regime for IPs with that governing turnaround professionals it can be concluded that, at the date of writing, there is a good deal of work to be done if turnaround professionals are to be able to claim that their accreditation system offers quality and

---

[239] Cork Report, para. 758.

[240] If a member of the IFT is also a member of an RPB he is subject to the disciplinary process of that RPB; if not he must agree to be governed by ACCA enforcement of the IFT Code.

[241] A number of turnaround specialists offer their services outside the umbrella of IFT membership. The other organisation that offers membership to such specialists is the UK chapter of the Chicago-based organisation, the Turnaround Management Association (TMA). The TMA requires adherence to a Code of Ethics but operates no accreditation system akin to that operated by the IFT.

performance controls to match those that are applicable to IPs or which were demanded by the Cork Committee. The IFT system, for instance, does not involve a compulsory competitive examination including written papers nor does the IFT have the power to deprive defaulting members of the right to practise turnaround – this follows from the non-mandatory nature of the IFT regime.[242] Whether there should be equivalence in the regimes governing turnaround professionals and IPs is, however, an issue for discussion rather than assumption. Much may depend on the tasks that are carried out by TPs, the nature of the clients they serve, the ability of such clients to assess quality of service and the importance of the service to the client.

On the first issue, there is a range of tasks that are carried out by TPs. These include, as already noted: conducting independent business reviews; scrutinising existing management; providing new management skills and recruitment work; negotiating with stakeholders on rescue packages (as well as on the terms of pre-packaged insolvencies to cover the possibilities of failure);[243] designing financial plans for rescue together with the offering of advice and assistance on refinancing; producing rationalisation and restructuring solutions; offering risk management advice; and providing credit insurance and advice.

On refinancing options, a host of specialists offer a variety of services, including: invoice discounting; asset-based lending (on raw materials, finished goods, plant and machinery, commercial property and so on); networking with private investors ('business angels'), factors and other debt financiers.[244]

The above turnaround activities can take place at various points in the progression of a company's affairs. Turnaround work may include the rescue of companies without recourse to formal insolvency procedures and the rescue of businesses following voluntary arrangements. It may involve the 'pre-packaging' of potential administration procedures as underpinnings to informal rescue attempts.[245] Turnaround specialists may also act to facilitate the rescue of companies via formal insolvency procedures.[246]

---

[242] The IFT can, of course, deprive defaulters of the right to offer services as a member of the IFT.

[243] See S. Harris, 'Decision to Pre-pack' (2004) *Recovery* (Winter) 26. On 'pre-packaged' administrations see ch. 10 below.

[244] See Lester, Young and Hawes, 'Help is at Hand'.

[245] See Harris, 'Decision to Pre-pack'. See further ch. 10 below.

[246] See IPA information page (www.ipa.uk.com).

Turning to the nature of the clients served by TPs, are these well-informed, repeat players who are able to assess the expertise of the TP and the quality of the service that they receive, or are they poorly placed and in need of regulatory protections? The major lending banks that trigger most appointments of TPs constitute well-informed, highly expert players that may deploy specialist business care units to liaise with TPs. On any list of consumers in need of regulatory protections they will tend to be placed fairly low down in the order. Most TPs, however, are hired, as noted, by troubled companies rather than their banks and the directors of these companies may not be so capable of looking after their own interests as are the major lenders. Such directors are not always repeat players[247] and, if not, their lack of expertise in coping with financial challenges may be a reason why they are resorting to a TP. When, moreover, a company encounters financial troubles it may be extremely difficult for the directors to shop around for a TP of known high quality or to research this – the situation may be urgent and all management hands may be on the pumps.[248] There may be a strong case for saying that the directors should be able to enjoy confidence in the turnaround services they purchase by employing a TP who is a member of a self-regulatory profession. A separate question is whether that protection should be guaranteed to anyone who employs *any* TP. This will be returned to below.

The ability of the consumer of turnaround services to evaluate the service is, as noted, of relevance here. A distinction can be drawn, here, between search, experience and credence services.[249] The quality of search services can be evaluated in advance of use. (The fish can be seen to be decayed or fresh in the supermarket before purchase.) Experience services can be evaluated after purchase. (The restaurant meal can be evaluated on consumption.) Credence services are difficult to evaluate even after delivery. (The quality of 'disease-preventative' food

---

[247] This may, of course, change if the IFT is successful in seeking to persuade more directors to bring in TPs at the very early stages of corporate troubles. It should also be borne in mind that a proportion of directors may have prior experience of corporate failure: see the data provided by CCN, the credit investigation agency, reported in N. Cohen, 'Dangerous Directors', *Financial Times*, 16 December 1996.

[248] In some cases, it should be noted, the bank that applies pressure to appoint a TP may bring its experience as a repeat player to bear and advise the company's directors on choices of TP. When such advice is given this may ameliorate the poor informational position of the director-consumer.

[249] See P. Nelson, 'Information and Consumer Behaviour' (1970) 78 *Journal of Political Economy* 311.

supplements may never be known because consumers may not be able to identify the causes of their ongoing good health.) The case for regulation becomes stronger when, on a scale from search to credence, the services on offer approach the credence end. At that end of the scale the market will control price and quality quite poorly because of informational difficulties. The case for regulating will also be the more compelling when the importance of obtaining a high quality of service is the greater. This will be so when the difference between good and poor service affects interests and has the more serious consequences (in money, lives, reputations and so on).

With regard to turnaround services, these may be said to occupy a position around the centre of this scale. Once the service is experienced there are some ready indicators of success or failure – notably in the change of corporate fortunes that follows. On the other hand, the causal connection between any change in such fortunes and the TP's actions may not always be easy for the consumer of services to discern. (Did market conditions or other factors produce the change?)[250] It may also be difficult to assess the counterfactual and say what would have happened with an alternative service provider. What can be said with more confidence is that in turnaround the quality of the service delivered is usually of high importance to the client and often to other parties also. A poor TP may fail to rescue the business and extensive economic, employment and wider social costs may ensue.

Such considerations suggest that there is a case for regulatory controls over the quality of TP services – at least if the market will fail to provide such controls. On this point, a concern is that if a significant number of consumers of TP services are non-repeat players and in poor positions to evaluate service quality, the market may be somewhat slow to prevent poorly performing or ill-qualified turnaround advisers from surviving in business by exploiting poorer-placed consumers. A particular danger may be that poorly informed directors may be tempted, under the pressure of time, resources and creditor demands, to select a TP on price with little reference to quality of service. Such directors may, accordingly, be prone to hire non-accredited practitioners of turnaround and to run excessive risks of suffering from poor advice and guidance. This suggests that there is a need, not only to control the quality of TP services, but also to make subjection to the self-regulatory system mandatory. If it is not mandatory then small companies, in particular, may

---

[250] On internal and external causes of corporate failure/distress see ch. 4 above.

suffer from the poor services of 'maverick' turnaround advisers who are not quality controlled.

It might, however, be no easy matter to install a mandatory regime. The problem of boundary definition is acute since, as seen above, TPs provide a wide range of services – from management consultancy for healthy companies right through to rescue advice for companies that are going through formal insolvency processes. In the case of some of these services, it might be hard to justify mandatory regulation since market forces may control matters such as quality of service and price quite acceptably. The boundary problem means, moreover, that a mandatory regime might bring a number of dangers. It might, for instance, prove over-inclusive so that persons offering any advice to a company might be potentially covered by the mandatory rule. Any uncertainties, indeed, on the extent of a mandatory regime might discourage consultants from offering advisory work and this might be counter to the interests of companies generally. These difficulties militate in favour of a non-mandatory approach to self-regulation.[251] It can be pointed out, moreover, that those practitioners who elect not to join the self-regulatory system for TPs may still be regulated by other bodies and by certain statutory regimes. Thus, TPs who are accountants or lawyers will be controlled by the self-regulators of those professions and, if a TP is involved in financial advice, he or she may be covered by the financial services regulatory requirements.

To conclude on the TP regime's assurance of expertise, it can be said that there has been a progression to the point where the foundations of a professional self-regulatory system have been laid. Further work needs to done, though, to match the position obtaining with IPs and boundary issues mean that there are liable to remain difficulties with the provision of turnaround services by persons who are not members of such self-regulatory systems. These are non-trivial difficulties since, as noted, the consequences of poor service provision may be severe.

Conclusions

In this chapter we have seen that there may be a case for reforming the regulatory regime for IPs and that new regulatory challenges have also

---

[251] It is, of course, conceivable that a government might legislate to make the IFT regime mandatory in the wake of a turnaround disaster involving a 'maverick' turnaround adviser. The author is grateful to Les Otty for this point.

arisen with the arrival of TPs on the scene. Regarding IPs there seems, as noted, to be no strong case for replacing private practitioners with public officials as the main implementers of insolvency procedures. There may be a case, though, for tightening the mechanisms used to regulate IPs and a number of potentially valuable reforms have been canvassed above, including proposals to rethink the duties that IPs owe to the array of interests involved in insolvency processes and to subject the current IP regulatory regime to more stringently independent oversight.

The emergence of the turnaround professional, we have seen, raises fresh issues of efficiency, accountability, fairness and expertise. It can be argued, albeit in the absence of cut-and-dried statistics, that turnaround specialists are making a contribution to effective rescue-seeking. The market, at least, seems convinced that the rescue outputs of turnaround specialists are increasingly to be valued. The accountability of TPs appears to be modest but there is a rationale for this in so far as the market appears to value their independence as a factor that facilitates rescue.

As for procedural fairness within turnaround, informal rescue proce-dures do not provide all creditors with the same protections that are provided by statutory insolvency processes. This is not, however, a situation that is necessarily to be deplored. A distinction has to be drawn at some stage between informal and formal procedures and, in any event, the law offers a general set of protections for those who have provided credit to the troubled company. It cannot be guaranteed that turnaround professionals will always consult the whole array of inter-ested parties when carrying out reconstruction negotiations. A number of factors, however, may encourage turnaround professionals generally to favour processes that are accessible, transparent and procedurally fair. One such factor is the incentive that turnaround specialists have to protect their reputations as even-handed and effective negotiators of corporate solutions.

On matters of expertise within the TP regime, it can be said, on the one hand, that these professionals are able to deploy a new set of specialist skills and services in seeking to turn the affairs of troubled companies around. On the other hand, these specialists are not all as comprehen-sively regulated as insolvency practitioners nor are they all subject to the sorts of rigorous quality and entry control regimes that the Cork Committee considered were appropriate for IPs. There are, moreover, serious problems of service boundary definition that would make it difficult to advocate that all turnaround professionals should be subject to a mandatory scheme of regulation.

In summary, there seems no reason for observers of TPs in action to experience fears analogous to those expressed by Cork when that Committee was looking at unlicensed insolvency practitioners. There is, however, more work to be done to devise measures of success for turnaround professionals and to develop the regulation of these specialists. The movement of rescue work further into the pre-insolvency period has shifted a number of familiar debates and raised a host of new challenges. Those challenges will remain to be faced for some time to come.

PART III

The quest for turnaround

6

Rescue

This part of the book assesses the role of rescue procedures in insolvency. We begin by considering what rescue involves, the reasons why rescue may be worth attempting, the different routes to rescue and the UK's new focus on rescue and ever-earlier responses to corporate troubles. The chapter then considers how different countries' rescue regimes can be compared.

What is rescue?

Rescue procedures involve going beyond the normal managerial responses to corporate troubles. They may operate through informal mechanisms as well as formal legal processes. It is useful, therefore, to see rescue as 'a major intervention necessary to avert eventual failure of the company'.[1] This allows the exceptional nature of rescue action to be captured and it takes on board both informal and formal rescue strategies.

Central to the notion of rescue is, accordingly, the idea that drastic remedial action is taken at a time of corporate crisis.[2] The company, at such a point, may be in a state of distress[3] or it may have entered a formal insolvency procedure. Whether or not a rescue can be deemed a success raises a further set of issues. Complete success might be thought to involve a restoration of the company to its former healthy state but in practice this scenario is unlikely. The drastic actions that rescue

---

[1] See A. Belcher, *Corporate Rescue* (Sweet & Maxwell, London, 1997) p. 12; Belcher, 'The Economic Implications of Attempting to Rescue Companies' in H. Rajak (ed.), *Insolvency Law: Theory and Practice* (Sweet & Maxwell, London, 1993). See also D. Brown, *Corporate Rescue: Insolvency Law in Practice* (John Wiley & Sons, Chichester, 1996) ch. 1; M. Hunter, 'The Nature and Functions of a Rescue Culture' [1999] JBL 491; R. Harmer, 'Comparison of Trends in National Law: The Pacific Rim' (1997) 1 *Brooklyn Journal of International Law* 139 at 143–8.

[2] Belcher, *Corporate Rescue*, p. 12; Harmer, 'Comparison of Trends'.

[3] See ch. 4 above, p. 146.

necessarily involves will almost inevitably entail changes in the management, financing, staffing or *modus operandi* of the company and there are likely to be winners and losers in this process. As Belcher observes: 'All rescues can be seen as, in some sense, partial.'[4] This observation also serves to point out that a rescue may be 'successful' from the point of view of some parties (for example, shareholders or employees) but not from the perspective of others (for example, managers or creditors). Assessments of rescues may accordingly have to be qualified in order to reflect these different points of view.

A distinction can also be made between the company and the business. Thus, even where a company is liquidated, successful steps may be taken to retain aspects of the business as operational enterprises, to sustain the employment of groups of workers and to ensure the survival of some economic activity. Similarly, successful results may be obtained where the company is taken over and loses its individual identity accordingly.

The timescales used to judge a rescue may also affect judgements as to its success or failure. Some rescues may produce a short-lived survival of the company or the business and, before success is deemed to have been achieved, it may be necessary to consider whether the rescue efforts have produced sustained results.

As for the end products of rescues, these may be various.[5] The company may be restored to its former state, as noted, but it is more likely to be reorganised (where, for example, managerial reforms are instituted), restructured (where, perhaps, closures of elements of the business are involved), refinanced (as where new capital is injected or debts are rescheduled), downsized (where operations may be cut back, workforces reduced or activities rationalised), subjected to sell-offs (where parts of the business are sold to other firms or even to managers in management buyouts (MBOs)) or taken over (as where the market for corporate control operates with regard to a troubled company and a takeover prompts drastic managerial changes).[6]

---

[4] Belcher, *Corporate Rescue*, p. 23; Harmer, 'Comparison of Trends'.

[5] See Belcher, *Corporate Rescue*, pp. 24–34; Brown, *Corporate Rescue*, pp. 6–8. R3's Ninth Survey of Business Recovery (2001) suggests that nearly one in five businesses survive insolvency and continue in business in one form or another.

[6] On the market for corporate control see J. Franks and C. Mayer, 'Capital Markets and Corporate Control: A Study of France, Germany and the UK' (1990) 10 *Economic Policy* 191–231; C. Bradley, 'Corporate Control: Markets and Rules' (1990) 53 MLR 170; J. Fairburn and J. Kay (eds.), *Introduction to Mergers and Merger Policy* (Oxford University Press, Oxford, 1989).

Why rescue?

Some visions of insolvency processes and laws are highly unsympathetic to the whole notion of corporate rescue.[7] As was seen in chapter 2, the 'creditor wealth maximisation' vision, which sees insolvency as a process of collecting debts for creditors and as a response to the 'common pool' problem, is in tension with the notion that keeping firms in operation (and protecting interests beyond those of creditors) is an independent goal of insolvency law.[8] It may be the case, in some circumstances, that maximising potential returns to creditors will demand some sort of rescue activity but this will not always be the case and a failed rescue may reduce creditors' returns materially.[9] On most occasions, those economic theories that focus on creditor interests will hold that the collective actions of liquidation will reduce transaction costs for individual creditors and make for administratively efficient processes.[10] It is efficient, on such a view, to decline to save 'hopeless' companies and to allow the market to redeploy resources swiftly, and at least cost, to more productive uses.[11]

In chapter 2 it was argued, however, that the creditor wealth maximisation vision was excessively narrow and that, in looking at insolvency processes, attention should be paid to interests beyond those of creditors: to social and distributional goals; to public as well as private interests; and to values such as expertise, fairness and accountability. Whether existing English rescue procedures perform adequately with regard to these factors is best considered when the details of different procedures are examined in the chapters below. At this stage it is worth noting that an

---

[7] If regimes are largely creditor-driven it is likely that prospects for rescue will be less than where regimes are debtor-driven: see Harmer, 'Comparison of Trends', pp. 147–8. On classifying jurisdictions as pro-creditor or pro-debtor regarding, *inter alia*, the general position on insolvency, see P. Wood, *Allen & Overy Global Law Maps: World Financial Law* (3rd edn, Allen & Overy, London, 1997).

[8] See the discussion at pp. 32–7 above; T. H. Jackson, *The Logic and Limits of Bankruptcy Law* (Harvard University Press, Cambridge, Mass., 1986) ch. 9; D. G. Baird, 'The Uneasy Case for Corporate Reorganisations' (1986) 15 *Journal of Legal Studies* 127.

[9] Rescue is likely to increase returns to creditors where there is a good prospect of turning corporate fortunes around (for example, by coping with a short-term dip in the market) or where the company is worth more as a going concern than as assets sold off piecemeal.

[10] See G. Dal Pont and L. Griggs, 'A Principled Justification for Business Rescue Laws: A Comparative Perspective, Part II' (1996) 5 *International Insolvency Review* 47 at 62; G. Lightman, 'Voluntary Administration: The New Wave or the New Waif in Insolvency Law?' (1994) 2 Ins. LJ 59 at 62.

[11] See Lightman, 'Voluntary Administration'; M. White, 'The Corporate Bankruptcy Decision' (1989) 3 *Journal of Economic Perspectives* 129.

approach going beyond creditor wealth maximisation – in short a 'social' as opposed to an 'economic' approach – leaves scope for rescue and justifies rescue activity with reference to a number of objectives and values. In relation to the technically efficient[12] achievement of social and distributional goals, regard can thus be had to the potential of a rescue procedure to achieve a number of results. These may include the preservation of a business that, in the longer term, is worth saving or is worth more as a going concern than if sold piecemeal; the protection of the jobs of a workforce; the avoidance of harms to suppliers, customers and state tax collectors; and the prevention of damage to the general economy or to business confidence in a sector.[13]

For its part, the Cork Committee[14] laid the foundations for a 'rescue culture' and was clear on the legitimacy of considering the broader picture. A good, modern system of insolvency law, said Cork, should provide a means for preserving viable commercial enterprises capable of making a useful contribution to the economic life of the country:

> We believe that a concern for the livelihood and well-being of those dependent upon an enterprise which may well be the lifeblood of a whole town or even a region is a legitimate factor to which a modern law of insolvency must have regard. The chain reaction consequences upon any given failure can potentially be so disastrous to creditors, employees and the community that it must not be overlooked.[15]

---

[12] 'Technically efficient' in the sense that whatever social and distributional goals are set by society, the aim should be to produce these at minimal cost and without waste.

[13] On the social costs of corporate failure see B. G. Carruthers and T. C. Halliday, *Rescuing Business: The Making of Corporate Bankruptcy Law in England and the United States* (Clarendon Press, Oxford, 1998) pp. 69–71; E. Warren, 'Bankruptcy Policy' (1987) 54 U Chic. L Rev. 775 and the reply, D. G. Baird, 'Loss Distribution, Forum Shopping and Bankruptcy: A Reply to Warren' (1987) 54 U Chic. L Rev. 815.

[14] *Report of the Review Committee on Insolvency Law and Practice* (Cmnd 8558, 1982) ('Cork Report').

[15] Cork Report, para. 204. See also paras. 203 and 198(j). When read together these paragraphs indicate that, in the Cork Committee's view, insolvency law should provide mechanisms not only to rescue potentially profitable organisations but also to ensure that a commercial enterprise can survive *even* if there is no immediate prospect of a return to profitability, if it is in the economic interests of the community. See also Hunter, 'Nature and Functions of a Rescue Culture', pp. 497–9; and on the social costs of failure see Carruthers and Halliday, *Rescuing Business*, pp. 69–70.

In the period since the Cork Report, the rescue culture has strengthened and been endorsed by the judiciary as well as bankers and politicians.[16] In *Powdrill* v. *Watson*[17] Lord Browne-Wilkinson stated in the House of Lords:

> The rescue culture, which seeks to preserve viable businesses, was, and is, fundamental to much of the Act of 1986. Its significance in the present case is that, given the importance attached to receivers and administrators being able to continue to run a business, it is unlikely that Parliament would have intended to produce a regime as to employees' rights which renders any attempt at such rescue either extremely hazardous or impossible.[18]

The British Bankers' Association publicly endorsed a rescue culture in its 1997 paper, *Banks and Businesses Working Together*.[19] The Blair governments also sought to encourage a movement towards a more US-style philosophy of enterprise that was less censorious of business failures and more encouraging of rescue. Peter Mandelson, when Trade Secretary in 1998, made a number of speeches that advocated a reassessment of attitudes to business failure and a need to encourage entrepreneurs to take risks.[20] He announced the need to reconsider the position of the Crown as preferential creditor[21] so that hard-pressed companies were not driven into insolvency by demands relating to tax debts. The 1998 White Paper, *Our Competitive Future: Building the Knowledge Driven Economy*,[22] echoed such sentiments and, in 1999, a joint DTI and Treasury initiative was mounted in order to further the rescue culture

---

[16] On the development of the rescue culture see Insolvency Service, *A Review of Company Rescue and Business Reconstruction Mechanisms*, Report by the Review Group (DTI, 2000) ('IS 2000') pp. 12–23.

[17] *Re Paramount Airways Ltd (No. 3) sub nom. Powdrill* v. *Watson* [1995] 2 AC 394, [1995] 2 WLR 312, [1995] 2 All ER 65.

[18] [1995] 2 AC 394 at 442 (quoted in Hunter, 'Nature and Functions of a Rescue Culture', p. 511). For further judicial references to the rescue culture see e.g. *Re Demaglass Holdings Ltd* [2001] 2 BCLC 633 (Neuberger J); *On Demand Information plc (in administrative receivership) and another* v. *Michael Gerson (Finance) plc and another* [2000] 4 All ER 734 (Robert Walker LJ).

[19] British Bankers' Association, *Banks and Business Working Together* (London, 1997) para. 3: 'Banks have long supported a rescue culture and thousands of customers are in business today because of the support of their bank through difficult times.' See now British Bankers' Association, *A Statement of Principles: Banks and Businesses – Working Together When You Borrow* (BBA, London, 2005).

[20] See Hunter, 'Nature and Functions of a Rescue Culture', p. 519.

[21] On the subsequent abolition of the Crown's preferential status see ch. 14 below.

[22] Cm 4176, December 1998, paras. 2.12–2.14.

and examine how it could be made to work more efficiently.[23] More recently, the Enterprise Act 2002 removed the Crown's preferential rights to recover unpaid taxes ahead of other creditors and reduced the role of administrative receivership. It did so following promises from the then Chancellor, Gordon Brown, that steps would be taken to 'reduce the penalties for honest failure and to create a modern and fair commercial system'.[24]

A key issue in any process that purports to be rescue-orientated is whether it provides for intervention at a sufficiently early stage in proceedings and action of a sufficiently speedy nature to allow the above ends to be achieved. In R3's Survey of Business Recovery of 2001, the rescue professionals who responded indicated that in 77 per cent of cases there was, by the time they were appointed, no possible action that could be taken to avert company failure.[25]

The trade-offs between achieving 'social' ends and the costs imposed on various parties have, moreover, to be taken into account.[26] Many rescue activities will involve the forestalling of enforcement actions by certain parties and the use of periods of grace in which realignment efforts are made. During these periods, certain interests will suffer. Creditors, for example, may be prevented from realising their securities. Distributional and social goals may demand that creditors make certain concessions for the purposes of rescue but considerations of both efficiency and fairness impose limits on the sacrifices that can be justi-fied.[27] In assessing such trade-offs, balances have to be drawn between the probabilities of achieving certain desirable ends and the (usually far higher) probabilities of imposing costs on parties who are asked to make sacrifices.[28]

---

[23] This initiative resulted in a September 1999 Consultation Document and a May 2000 Report: Insolvency Service, *A Review of Company Rescue and Business Reconstruction Mechanisms*, Interim Report (DTI, September 1999); IS 2000.

[24] See HM Treasury Press Release, 8 June 2001 and DTI/Insolvency Service, *Productivity and Enterprise: Insolvency – A Second Chance* (Cm 5234, 2001).

[25] R3's Ninth Survey. Business preservation rates were, overall, 18 per cent, with hotel and catering having the highest preservation rate (28 per cent).

[26] On the political consequences of such choices see Carruthers and Halliday, *Rescuing Business*, p. 155.

[27] See Dal Pont and Griggs, 'Principled Justification', p. 47.

[28] Ibid., pp. 61–71 and see the discussion of the policies of (1) redistribution determined by relative ability to bear costs and (2) allocating the costs of business failure to those who stand to benefit most from business success.

A final issue to consider under the heading of technical efficiency is whether a rescue regime is conducive to low cost and effective co-ordination between the different actors that may be involved in working towards a turnaround.[29] A rescue generally involves a number of parties who carry out a variety of roles and tasks and the challenges of co-ordinating roles and actions vary across such tasks. What is clear is that if such involved parties do not work together harmoniously, a considerable amount of unproductive friction will result and this will stand in the way of completing such tasks as collecting the data relevant to the rescue and the taking of timely actions and decisions. These are matters to be given special consideration in chapter 9 when looking at the administration procedure.

To move to another benchmark of chapter 2, attention should also be paid to the propensity of any given rescue procedure to allow business judgements to be taken by experts.[30] (The argument for expert decision-making may, like those for fairness and accountability, be the more important where democratically established goals for rescue are difficult to identify.) Where, for instance, a rescue procedure involves a handover of control from a specialist insider (for example, a director) to a general-ist outsider (for example, an insolvency practitioner), this may involve the expenses of parties coming up to speed with the particular company's financial, operational and market positions but also dangers that judge-ments will be made by persons who are not fully familiar with the relevant market sectors and business circumstances.[31] Experts should also be allowed to *exercise* their expertise. A consideration in judging a rescue regime is, accordingly, whether it gives the expert sufficient information and time to be able to effect a rational, balanced judgement. 'Expert' decisions may amount to little if those taking them are, by force of circumstances, ill-informed and subjected to unduly tight deadlines.[32]

---

[29] See V. Finch, 'Control and Co-ordination in Corporate Rescue' (2005) 25 *Legal Studies* 374; J. Westbrook, 'The Control of Wealth in Bankruptcy' (2004) 82 Texas LR 795.

[30] On the tendency of US rescue processes to place more faith in management than the English system, see Carruthers and Halliday, *Rescuing Business*, pp. 509–10. See also pp. 280, 287–8 below.

[31] See M. Phillips, *The Administration Procedure and Creditors' Voluntary Arrangements* (Centre for Commercial Law Studies, QMW, London, 1996); N. Segal, 'An Overview of Recent Developments and Future Prospects in the UK' in J. Ziegel (ed.), *Current Developments in International and Comparative Corporate Insolvency Law* (Clarendon Press, Oxford, 1994) p. 10.

[32] See Belcher, *Corporate Rescue*, pp. 240–1.

Rescue procedures also stand to be judged according to their fairness. Issues here are whether those processes allow equal weight to be given to the voices of various affected parties; whether the processes are open to self-interested manipulation by certain individuals or groups; and whether those administering the processes are (and can be seen to be) operating even-handedly.

Finally, considerations of accountability are relevant. Acceptable levels of supervision and approval should be instituted so that opportunities for opportunistic behaviour are curtailed and regimes are not only fair but also capable of generating the degree of consent that is necessary for effective rescues to be achieved. This, in turn, demands that supervisory functions are not allocated in a way that itself allows manipulation. The transparency and accessibility of processes must also be sufficient to allow affected parties to apprise themselves of relevant facts and to ensure that such parties' representations are considered. Again, however, the costs of supervision and access have to be borne in mind and the pitfalls of excessively legalistic procedures and undue levels of court supervision should be avoided.[33]

In relation to issues of both fairness and accountability it should be emphasised that different groupings may possess widely divergent interests and incentives when the company meets troubled times.[34] Shareholders and directors will tend to favour ensuring that the company continues to operate for as long as possible. The former are residual claimants in insolvency and have little to lose by trading on. The directors may wish to prolong operations in order to eke out or stabilise their employment.[35] Both shareholders and directors will thus tend to gamble on further business activity since they will enjoy whatever gains result. Corporate creditors, in contrast, will tend to favour ceasing operations sooner rather than later since they will bear the losses that result from any continued trading.[36] Employees, again, will tend to favour continuing trading in the hope of securing their jobs and in the knowledge that further losses will be borne by other parties. Insolvency practitioners, as noted in chapter 5, may possess incentives to encourage companies to

---

[33] See Phillips, *Administration Procedure*, pp. 11–12.

[34] See Carruthers and Halliday, *Rescuing Business*, pp. 48–51.

[35] Directors may not bear the financial risks of continued trading but their inclination to trade on should be constrained by fears of personal liability for wrongful trading, fraudulent trading, breach of duty or of disqualification: see ch. 16 below.

[36] Carruthers and Halliday, *Rescuing Business*, p. 244.

move towards formal insolvency procedures because these are likely to generate fee income. Such acute divergences of interest make it especially important that rescue regimes are not only fair and accountable but seen to be so.

Informal and formal routes to rescue

Troubled companies and their directors, creditors or shareholders are able, as noted, to take informal as well as formal steps in order to effect rescues – most rescues are, indeed, achieved through informal action.[37] Informal actions do not demand any resort to statutory insolvency procedures but are contractually based. They are usually instituted by directors or creditors and they may involve the use of professional help: where, for instance, a 'company doctor' or firm of accountants is appointed (usually on a creditor's insistence) to investigate the company's affairs and to make recommendations. Such informal steps may result in the kinds of remedial action already referred to: changes in management, corporate reorganisations or refinancings, for example. Alternatively, under the 'London Approach', co-ordination of a creditors' agreement in accordance with informal guidelines may be achieved with the Bank of England acting as an honest broker in making efforts to persuade reluctant parties to pursue such informal settlements.[38] Formal arrangements under which rescues may be attempted are provided for in the Insolvency Act 1986[39] and include company voluntary arrangements (CVAs),[40] receiverships and administrative receiverships[41] and administration.[42]

From the company management and shareholders' point of view, a general advantage of informal rescue is that publicity concerning corporate troubles may be minimal, the stigma of formal insolvency may be avoided and the goodwill and reputation of the company preserved. Avoiding the adverse publicity that would often follow the commencement of a formal insolvency proceeding can have a significant impact on the ability of a company to survive and on the realisable value of its

---

[37] See S. Frisby, *Report to the Insolvency Service: Insolvency Outcomes* (Insolvency Service, London, June 2006).

[38] See ch. 7 below. In 1998 the Financial Services Authority took over from the Bank of England as banking regulator.

[39] See also Companies Act 2006 s. 895; chs. 9 and 11 below.

[40] Insolvency Act 1986 ss. 1–7.   [41] Ibid., ss. 28–69, 72A–H.   [42] Ibid., Sch. B1.

assets.[43] The cost of informal procedures is also likely to be lower than where court proceedings are involved.[44] Delays and attendant costs may, furthermore, be reduced where rescues are managed without hostile litigation.[45] Informality also ensures flexibility so that terms can be adjusted and renegotiated in a way that formal procedures (such as approval processes) do not allow. From the point of view of company directors, a further considerable advantage of informality is that this avoids the intervention of an insolvency practitioner in the role of a formal scrutiniser of directorial actions. Where rescues are formal, IPs possess extensive powers to investigate corporate affairs together with a duty to report on the conduct of directors.[46] Such IPs will, moreover, assume control of the company. Informal rescues thus avoid the investigations and changes in power and control that directors may fear.[47] Another incentive for management to see that the company remains outside formal insolvency is that formal insolvency procedures carry with them the stigma of (usually culpable) failure.[48] In terms of external perceptions, particularly in employment markets, it may be 'bad news' for management to be associated with a company which has had recourse to formal insolvency procedures.[49]

From the point of view of many banks and secured lenders, informal rescue may be attractive in ways that can outweigh attendant risks. It not only offers the prospect of repayment in full, if ultimately successful, but

---

[43] See Brown, *Corporate Rescue*, pp. 11–13; N. Segal, 'Rehabilitation and Approaches other than Formal Insolvency Procedures' in R. Cranston (ed.), *Banks and Remedies* (Oxford University Press, Oxford, 1992) p. 133.

[44] But see discussion of the London Approach in ch. 7 below.

[45] 'Formal insolvency not only crystallises parties' rights, but also their attitudes': Brown, *Corporate Rescue*, p. 11.

[46] See e.g. Insolvency Act 1986 ss. 234–7. Once an administrative receiver has been appointed, an administration order made, or the company has gone into liquidation, the relevant IP is under a duty to submit to the Secretary of State a report on the conduct of the directors of the company: Company Directors' Disqualification Act 1986 s. 7(3) and the Insolvent Companies (Reports on Conduct of Directors) No. 2 Rules 1986. This could lead to action being taken for the disqualification of those directors: see ch. 16 below.

[47] Though a cessation of power would, from that point, reduce dangers of subsequent liquidator actions for fraudulent or wrongful trading under the Insolvency Act 1986 ss. 213 and 214: see ch. 16 below.

[48] See Segal, 'Rehabilitation and Approaches', p. 132.

[49] Ibid., where the point is made that we have not yet reached the stage in England (as arguably occurs in the USA) of regarding the reorganisation of companies in difficulty through the use of court procedures as 'being an acceptable, even standard, tool of business management'.

also provides an opportunity to acquire a fresh injection of funds from other sources (such as shareholders or other banks) and allows such well-positioned creditors to extract enhanced or new security, or priority, as the price for supplying further funds to the company. A bank, for instance, may improve its position by taking a floating charge as security and, even if an informal rescue ultimately fails, the bank will often have improved its security position and may then be able to appoint an administrator of its choosing out of court.[50]

A disadvantage of informal rescue, however, is its potential to prejudice the interests of less-well-placed creditors. Informality may be attractive to directors, but, from the point of view of certain creditors, a deficiency of informality may be the absence of investigative powers and the lack of an inquiry into the role of directors in bringing a company to the brink of disaster. A fundamental weakness of informal rescue is, furthermore, that the agreement of all parties whose rights are affected will generally be required if the rescue is to succeed. Informal rescues demand that parties with contractual rights agree to compromise, waive or defer debts, or alter priorities. Dissenting creditors, accordingly, have the power to halt informal rescues by triggering formal insolvency procedures, including liquidation. This renders the informal rescue a fragile device that is dependent on a high degree of co-operation from a range of parties.[51] In contrast, a formal procedure such as administration involves a moratorium on the enforcement of a wide range of creditors' rights and so creates a more sustainable space within which a rescue can be organised.

The new focus on rescue

Since the late 1990s, corporate insolvency law and processes have changed in a way that places a new emphasis on rescue and on early actions to respond to corporate troubles. It can be argued that a fundamental

---

[50] I.e. if holding a 'qualifying floating charge': see Insolvency Act 1986 Sch. B1, para. 14. The administrator may then even be implementing a 'pre-packaged' administration: see further ch. 10 below.

[51] Brown, *Corporate Rescue*, p. 13. In an informal bank rescue, for example, the negotiations between the banks are intensive and, as will be seen in ch. 7 below, negotiation and resolution may become even more difficult if there is a multiplicity of interests to be catered for in the form of hedge funds, distressed debt traders, etc. Even within the grouping of banks different rights and obligations need to be ironed out: 'Some banks may start out as secured, while others start out as unsecured.' Segal, 'Rehabilitation and Approaches', p. 133.

philosophical change has now occurred so that the law, in combination with corporate and creditor practice, has moved from a focus on *ex post* responses to corporate crises to one that increasingly involves influencing the ways that corporate actors manage the risks of insolvency *ex ante*. This movement, it can be said, is consistent with those increasing appetites to audit and to risk manage that are to be observed more generally across public and private sector activities. It can, in addition, be contended that, in parallel with such a philosophical shift, a revision of insolvency roles has taken place so that participants in corporate and insolvency processes have become more encouraged and inclined to see corporate disasters as matters to be anticipated and prevented rather than to be responded to after the event.[52]

The philosophical change

From at least the times of the Cork Report, commentators on insolvency processes have stressed that the furtherance of rescue demands that interventions from outside troubled companies should take place at the earliest opportunity.[53] Now, however, we may be seeing the start of a shift that institutionalises anticipatory approaches to corporate troubles. That shift can be seen in legislation, corporate reporting requirements and bank strategies.

On the legislative front, the Enterprise Act 2002 effected a significant change of stance by introducing a number of reforms that were designed to assist troubled companies and to do so by fostering a rescue culture.[54] As will be detailed in chapter 9 below, it replaced the regime of administrative receivership with provisions that gave pride of place to the new

---

[52] This section builds on V. Finch, 'The Recasting of Insolvency Law' (2005) 68 MLR 713. On the case for considering the roles of different institutions in insolvency law and procedures see J. Westbrook, 'The Globalisation of Insolvency Reform' (1999) NZLR 401, 413. See also ch. 5 above.

[53] See e.g. the Cork Report, ch. 9; Sir Kenneth Cork, *Cork on Cork: Sir Kenneth Cork Takes Stock* (Macmillan, London, 1988) ch. 10.

[54] On the rise of the 'rescue culture' in the UK see Hunter, 'Nature and Functions of a Rescue Culture'; Belcher, *Corporate Rescue*; Carruthers and Halliday, *Rescuing Business*. On the primacy of rescue objectives under the Enterprise Act 2002 see S. Frisby, 'In Search of a Rescue Regime: The Enterprise Act 2002' (2004) 67 MLR 247; and the Secretary of State for Trade and Industry's statement at HC Debates, col. 53, 10 April 2002 (P. Hewitt). On the link between new worldwide concerns with rescue and a growing awareness that global financial waves can distress even fundamentally sound enterprises see Westbrook, 'Globalisation of Insolvency Reform', p. 403.

administration procedure and it also ring-fenced a set portion of funds for the benefit of unsecured creditors.[55]

The Enterprise Act did more, however, than further rescue. It arguably encouraged those involved with potentially troubled companies to think about insolvency risks in advance of the final crisis – to manage such risks *ex ante* rather than *ex post*.[56]

The timescales set up by the Enterprise Act have this effect. The administrator must present proposals to creditors within eight weeks of his appointment and must commence a creditors' meeting within ten weeks of the administration's start.[57] This means that the party that is going to appoint an administrator – which will usually be the bank that holds a qualifying floating charge[58] – will have to be in a position to inform the administrator about the company, its businesses, prospects and risks at the very earliest stages of the administration process. This is not least because the notice appointing an administrator must be accompanied by a statement by the administrator that, *inter alia*, he consents to the appointment and that 'in his opinion the purpose of the administration is reasonably likely to be achieved'.[59] When, accordingly, a bank is faced with a troubled debtor company and approaches a potential administrator, it is likely to be made very clear to the bank that such a statement will not be forthcoming unless the administrator is supplied

---

[55] On the new administration procedure as a rescue procedure see ch. 9 below. See also I. Fletcher, 'UK Corporate Rescue: Recent Developments – Changes to Administrative Receivership, Administration and Company Voluntary Arrangements – the Insolvency Act 2000, the White Paper 2001 and the Enterprise Act 2002' (2004) 5 EBOR 119; V. Finch, 'Re-invigorating Corporate Rescue' [2003] JBL 527; Finch, 'Control and Co-ordination in Corporate Rescue'. But on the same procedure as a route to winding up see A. Keay, 'What Future for Liquidation in the Light of the Enterprise Act Reforms?' [2005] JBL 143; L. Linklater, 'New Style Administration: A Substitute for Liquidation?' (2005) 26 Co. Law. 129. On reforms dealing with administrative receivership and the ring-fenced fund see Insolvency Act 1986 ss. 72A, 72B–72G; Insolvency Act 1986 Sch. B1; Insolvency Act 1986 s. 176A; Insolvency Act 1986 (Prescribed Part) Order 2003 (SI 2003/2097).

[56] On the rise of the pre-packaged administration – the 'pre-pack' as an aspect of the movement towards anticipatory action – see ch. 10 below and V. Finch, 'Pre-packaged Administrations: Bargains in the Shadow of Insolvency or Shadowy Bargains?' [2006] JBL 568.

[57] See the Insolvency Act 1986 Sch. B1, para. 52. Para. 52(1) sets out exceptions from these requirements.

[58] That is per Sch. B1, para. 14. After the Enterprise Act 2002 reforms there are three methods by which a 'new' administrator can be appointed: see Sch. B1, paras. 12, 14–15, 22.

[59] Para. 18.

with all of the information that is needed in order to evaluate the prospects of achieving the purpose of the administration.[60]

For the bank this is no small matter. If it has loaned funds to a number of companies and a proportion of these are liable to encounter some financial difficulties at some time in their corporate lives, it will have an incentive to institute monitoring procedures that, in an ongoing manner, will place it in a position that allows it potentially to instruct an administrator at very short notice. Those monitoring procedures are likely to involve analysing and updating information that is supplied by the debtor company in compliance with lending conditions that require the company to keep the bank appraised of the former's financial position, its prospects and business risks.[61] The bank, moreover, is liable to demand that the debtor company should identify any business risks that are potentially threatening to the company and to state what is being done to manage those risks. The overall effect can be expected to be a driving forward of both a new awareness of insolvency risks and a new rigour in dealing with these before the company's position becomes terminal.

It might be responded that too much is being made of a modest reform here and that the banks monitored their debtors long before the Enterprise Act 2002 came onto the scene.[62] That, however, would be to understate the effect of the Enterprise Act. The imposition of new time-frames for action in that Act means, as indicated, that incentives to monitor are given a new urgency. The Enterprise Act, moreover, did not merely institute new time pressures. Under the former regime of administrative receivership, the bank that loaned funds under the security of a floating charge operated in something of a comfort zone. It knew that if the company entered troubled waters it could enforce its security quickly by appointing an administrative receiver who would act entirely in the interests of the bank so as to realise assets, if necessary, and settle the debt. The 'new' administration procedure, established by the

---

[60] The Enterprise Act 2002 replaced the alternative purposes of the old administration regime under the Insolvency Act 1986 (former) Part II with a hierarchy of objectives: all 'new' administrations (whether instituted by court order or out of court) have the same statutory objectives. See para. 3(1) of Sch. B1, Insolvency Act 1986.

[61] See J. Day and P. Taylor, 'The Role of Debt Contracts in UK Corporate Governance' (1998) 2 *Journal of Management and Governance* 171; G. Triantis, 'Financial Slack Policy and the Law of Secured Transactions' (2000) 29 *Journal of Legal Studies* 35.

[62] On bank monitoring see chs. 7 and 8 below; and J. Armour and S. Frisby, 'Rethinking Receivership' (2001) 21 OJLS 73.

Enterprise Act, replaced administrative receivership as the process for enforcing floating charges.[63] It still placed the banks in a strong position relative to unsecured creditors[64] but it brought changes that the banks would not necessarily have welcomed. First, in contrast with receivership, it provided that administrators should act in the interests of the company's creditors as a whole[65] and, second, it set down inclusive procedures and enforcement provisions that ensured that the interests of creditors as a whole would be taken into account and protected when the administrator took decisions or made judgements about the company's prospects.[66]

For the banks, these changes brought significant new challenges. The bank's interests fell to be protected in the face of inclusive procedures that gave all of the company's creditors a voice. These procedures were, as a result, potentially drawn out in operation and were also capable of leading to legal attacks on a number of fronts.[67] The administrator's statutory objectives were set out in a complex series of contingently phrased subsections that did little to assuage bankers' fears that administrators would be too bogged-down in procedural constraints and

---

[63] The replacement is subject to six exceptions: see Insolvency Act 1986 ss. 72B–G. See further ch. 8 below.

[64] Though see Enterprise Act 2002 s. 252 which inserted a new s. 176A into the Insolvency Act 1986 to ring-fence, for the benefit of unsecured creditors, a prescribed proportion of funds otherwise available for distribution to the holders of floating charges. See also Insolvency Act 1986 (Prescribed Part) Order 2003 (SI 2003/2097). On whether, on the wording of s. 176A, a floating charge holder with an unsecured balance is entitled to participate in the prescribed part see G. McPhie, 'New Legislation' (2004) *Recovery* (Autumn) 24. The Insolvency Service is of the view that the floating charge holder is not so entitled, as is His Honour Judge Purle QC in *Permacell Finesse Ltd (in liquidation)* [2008] BCC 208 and as is Patten J in *Re Airbase (UK) Ltd, Thorniley* v. *Revenue and Customs Commissioner* [2008] BCC 213 (Ch): see A. Walters, 'Statutory Redistribution of Floating Charge Assets: Victory (Again) to Revenue and Customs' (2008) 29 Co. Law. 129.

[65] Insolvency Act 1986 Sch. B1, para. 3(2).

[66] On inclusiveness and challenges to the administrator see Insolvency Act 1986 Sch. B1, paras. 49–58, 74–5.

[67] The administrator is subject to a duty (under Sch. B1, para. 4) to perform his functions as quickly and efficiently as is reasonably practicable. Under para. 74(1) a creditor or member can challenge the administrator by claiming that he is acting or has acted or proposes to act so as to unfairly harm their interests. Para. 74(2) allows the same parties to mount a challenge on the grounds that the administrator is not performing his functions as quickly or as efficiently as is reasonably practicable. Para. 75 allows misfeasance actions to be brought (by, *inter alia*, a creditor) against administrators and the company does not have to be in liquidation for such an action to be commenced.

litigation to be able to protect the banks' interests effectively.[68] These challenges arguably created new needs for the banks to work harder to maximise their potential control of the new administration process and to do so by engaging in anticipatory actions – notably by collecting more, better and earlier information on the company's state of affairs and its prospects. The banks had gained incentives to follow the rugby-playing advice to 'get your retaliation in first'. In this way the insolvency process was shifted in its focal concern – away from debt collecting and towards the management of insolvency risks.

In reply to the above argument it might be contended that the Enterprise Act 2002 may encourage the banks to take steps other than to increase their *ex ante* monitoring of companies. Thus, it might be forecast that, daunted by the uncertainties and complexities of the 2002 Act, the banks may be induced to shift their lending practices away from using floating charge securities and towards more lending via fixed asset security.[69] The result of this, it might be suggested, would be a fragmentation of security as the floating charge loses dominance in favour of a mixture of lending arrangements. The overall effect, it could be contended, would be a diminution in incentives to monitor the activities of the debtor company.[70] This would happen, the argument runs, because it is the concentration of a company's borrowing in a single credit arrangement that makes it worthwhile for the creditor to monitor the company's behaviour – a scenario that was arguably fostered by the floating charge under pre-Enterprise Act arrangements.

Turning to corporate reporting requirements, it can be argued that concerns to monitor companies ahead of troubles have been reinforced by other changes in corporate procedure, notably in reporting requirements through the passing of section 417 of the Companies Act 2006. This section was promulgated in the wake of the short-lived notion of the

---

[68] See the discussions in Frisby, 'In Search of a Rescue Regime'; Finch, 'Re-invigorating Corporate Rescue'; Finch, 'Control and Co-ordination in Corporate Rescue'; British Bankers' Association, *Response to the Report by the Review Group on Company Rescue and Business Reconstruction Mechanisms* (April 2001) and *Response by the BBA to the Insolvency Service White Paper, Insolvency – A Second Chance* (2001).

[69] See ch. 3 above and ch. 9 below; D. Prentice, 'Bargaining in the Shadow of the Enterprise Act 2002' (2004) 5 EBOR 153; J. Armour, 'Should We Redistribute in Insolvency?' in J. Getzler and J. Payne (eds.), *Company Charges: Spectrum and Beyond* (Oxford University Press, Oxford, 2006).

[70] On 'creditor concentration' and its encouragement of monitoring see Armour and Frisby, 'Rethinking Receivership'; Armour 'Should We Redistribute in Insolvency?'. On limitations of the 'concentrated creditor theory' see ch. 8 below.

Operating and Financial Review (OFR)[71] and demands that (unless the company is subject to the small companies' regime) the directors' report includes a 'business review' that informs members and helps them to assess how the directors have performed their duty to promote the success of the company. The review must contain a fair account of the company's business and a description of the principal risks facing it. It must offer an analysis of development and performance but (in requirements going beyond the former provisions of the Companies Act 1985) must, in the case of quoted companies, report on the main trends and factors likely to affect the business's future development and performance.[72] Information about the company's supply chain and arrangements that are essential to the business must be included.[73]

The importance of the new reporting requirements, in insolvency terms, lies in their potential effect in furthering processes in which company directors not only manage serious risks but also disclose to stakeholders how they are managing such risks. This emphasis on managing and controlling risk, the foundations of which were established by the Turnbull Report,[74] goes a significant step further than the Cadbury Code on Corporate Governance of 1992,[75] which established the principle that senior managers are responsible for the maintenance of an internal control system.

It can be anticipated that companies may set out to comply with the new requirements and to identify risks and describe risk management systems in different ways. One group will 'box-tick' and confine itself to

---

[71] In November 2005 the Chancellor, Gordon Brown, announced the repeal of the OFR less than a year after the OFR Regulations had been laid: see the Companies Act 1985 (Operating and Financial Review and Directors' Report etc.) Regulations 2005 (SI 2005/1011). On the background to the OFR see Company Law Review Steering Group (CLRSG), *Modern Company Law for a Competitive Economy: Final Report* (DTI, London, 2001) ch. 5; White Paper, *Modernising Company Law* (Cm 5553, 2002).

[72] Companies Act 2006 s. 417(5).

[73] Ibid. s. 417(5)(c).

[74] See *Internal Control: Guidance for Directors on the Combined Code* (ICAEW, London, 1999).

[75] *Report of the Committee on the Financial Aspects of Corporate Governance* (December 1992). Other guidelines also demand that boards identify risks to the company's value and state how these are managed: see the Association of British Insurers' (ABI) Disclosure Guidelines on Social Responsibility, *Investing in Social Responsibility: Risks and Opportunities* (London, 2001), Appendix 1 (dealing with risks from social, ethical and environmental considerations). See J. Parkinson, 'Disclosure and Corporate Social and Environmental Performance: Competitiveness and Enterprise in a Broader Social Framework', [2003] 3 JCLS 3, 6–11.

'boilerplate' reviews that offer a broad-brush identification of the main risks and uncertainties facing the company and its subsidiaries. A second group will go further and seek to identify the main risks faced and the ways in which these are managed. A third group, however, will take the opportunity to improve its performance by embedding its reporting and risk management systems within the general structure of management and decision-making within the company. Companies in this group will seek to develop best practice methods so that their reports not merely will identify key business risks but will be able to isolate risks that potentially threaten the viability of the business and deal with these alongside other categories of serious and less serious risk. Such companies will describe how the various categories of risk are managed, how risk management systems are organised, evaluated, updated and reported on within management. They will describe how risk management responsibilities are allocated, how information on risks is collected and disseminated and how outsourced risks are dealt with. These section 417 reports will be used by leading companies to persuade stakeholders that the managers of the company are both able to identify any risks that threaten either the business or its achievement of corporate objectives, and are able to manage the full array of risks in a systematic and auditable manner.

The emergence of best-practice reporting is liable to lead, in turn, to a new emphasis on managing insolvency risks in a more open and more preventative manner. This development is likely to be driven ahead as investors and the major lenders to companies – the banks – see the value of best-practice disclosures in informing them about both the risks their debtors are facing and the quality of their debtor companies' managerial responses to such risks.[76] A key point here is that, although the requirement to report on factors likely to affect future business development only applies to quoted companies (of whom many will already produce reports on such lines), this institutionalisation of the requirement may well encourage the banks to demand at least elements of such reporting from a wider range of companies to whom they lend. The banks may thus be increasingly inclined to use their lending power to insist that

---

[76] The *Financial Times* commented that 'it is in companies' interests to produce an insightful statement. There is a lot of investor pressure for this kind of information to be made available. In fact, almost half leading listed companies already produce such information although it may not be grouped under one heading in their annual reports.' (*Financial Times*, Editorial, 26 November 2004.)

companies who borrow from them conform to processes akin to best practice reporting. In doing so, they will not only gain new stocks of information but also sharpen their focus on how insolvency risks are managed. Another step away from debt collecting and towards a preventative philosophy will have been taken.

That step, moreover, is reinforced by the Government's response to the Enron/WorldCom international accounting debacles.[77] This took the form of the Companies (Audit, Investigations and Community Enterprise) Act 2004. This statute encouraged a higher level of pre-insolvency scrutiny of corporate management by introducing a new rigour to directorial disclosures to auditors. Section 9 of the 2004 Act inserted section 234ZA into the Companies Act 1985 to demand that directors state in their directors' report that there is no 'relevant audit information' that they know of and which they know the auditors are unaware of.[78] To such ends, directors must take all the steps that they ought to take as a director in order to become aware of any relevant audit information and to establish that the company's auditors are aware of that information. Directors are to take those steps and make enquiries as required by their duty to exercise reasonable care, skill and diligence as assessed on a combined objective/subjective standard as specified in section 214 of the Insolvency Act 1986.[79] The 2004 Act, moreover, made directors criminally liable if they make a false statement of the above kind – if they knew (or were reckless that) it was false and if they failed to take reasonable steps to prevent the report from being approved.[80] The effect is to enhance auditors' powers of scrutiny and, regarding potential risks to companies, shifts the focus of attention further in advance of the point when such risks have turned into insolvency realities.[81]

---

[77] On reactions to Enron see S. Griffin, 'Corporate Collapse and the Reform of Boardroom Structures – Lessons from America?' [2003] Ins. Law. 214; D. Kershaw, 'Waiting for Enron: The Unstable Equilibrium of Auditor Independence Regulation' (2006) 33 *Journal of Law and Society* 388.

[78] Section 234ZA applied to directors' reports from financial years beginning on or after 1 April 2005. It has been replaced in equivalent terms by s. 418(2) of the Companies Act 2006.

[79] On Insolvency Act 1986 s. 214 see ch. 16 below.

[80] See now the replicated rules in Companies Act 2006 s. 418(5)–(6).

[81] On governmental concerns to increase the transparency and accountability generally in corporate operations see the White Paper, *Company Law Reform* (Cm 6456, March 2005), especially ch. 3.

Increased attention to managerial performance and directorial business risk management has also been encouraged by other changes. Thus, a more intense spotlight has come to rest on directors as the Department of Business Enterprise and Regulatory Reform (BERR) has stepped up its use of disqualification powers. As we will see in chapter 15, a significant reform introduced by the Insolvency Act 2000 was the permitting of disqualification undertakings to be accepted by out-of-court agreement between a director and the Disqualification Unit of the Insolvency Service.[82] The disqualifications involved are identical to those that would be imposed by a court and the streamlined process offered by the 2000 Act has produced a dramatic rise in disqualifications – from a little under 400 in 1995 to 1,200 in 2006–7 (of which 80 per cent were by way of undertakings).[83] It is in more rigorous control of managerial diligence that the increasing scrutiny of pre-insolvency management can principally be seen.

It has also been suggested that the Crown's loss of its preferential status since September 2003[84] may put yet more monitoring pressure on directors. This loss, the argument runs, may make the Crown 'increasingly vigilant in seeking to recoup some of this loss, possibly by funding actions against directors'.[85] In the face of the above kinds of pressure it is to be expected not only that many directors will feel that they are under ever more intense scrutiny but also that they will feel the need to respond to this by making more certain that they can justify the actions and judgements that they have effected.

This series of developments points towards a shift from 'debt collection' to 'risk management' approaches in corporate insolvency law and procedures. Such a shift might be explained by citing new governmental concerns to maximise rescue opportunities.[86] There is, however, another account that links a recasting of corporate insolvency philosophy to

---

[82] See ch. 16 below. See also A. Walters, 'Directors' Disqualification after the Insolvency Act 2000: The New Regime' [2001] Ins. Law. 86; Insolvency Act 2000 s. 6 (introducing a new s. 1A into the Companies Directors' Disqualification Act 1986); Insolvency Act 2000 (Commencement No. 1 and Transitional Provisions) Order 2001 (SI 2001/766) (C27).

[83] Insolvency Service Annual Report 2006–7, p. 15.

[84] See Enterprise Act 2002 s. 251. (Paras. 1, 2, 3–5C, 6 and 7 of the Insolvency Act 1986 Sch. 6 are deleted.) See further ch. 14 below.

[85] See D. Leibowitz, 'Cover Charge', *The Lawyer*, 10 November 2003.

[86] On the Blair Government's espousal of rescue objectives see e.g. *Productivity and Enterprise: Insolvency – A Second Chance* (Cm 5234, July 2001); Secretary of State for Trade and Industry's statement at HC Debates, col. 53, 10 April 2002.

other identifiable and deep-seated movements in the cultures of public and private governance. What is observed in relation to recent insolvency developments is in line with the elements of what has been dubbed the 'audit explosion'.[87] As described by Power, audit is 'an emerging principle of social organisation which may be reaching its most extreme form'.[88] At its heart is the idea that control systems within organisations – be they corporations or government departments – must be auditable and audited. In public and private systems 'there is a commitment to push control further into organisational structures, inscribing it within systems which can then be audited'.[89] Such 'demands and aspirations for accountability and control'[90] are accompanied by a new emphasis on allocating increasing scrutiny powers to outside monitors and developing the role of independent scrutiny as a substitute for professional judgements or trust.[91] Audit becomes a way of reducing risks through the review of control systems. It can be seen in those corporate governance requirements from Cadbury to the Companies Act 2006 that seek to create layers of regulatory systems so as to allow performance at one level to be measured and held accountable at another. It is also exemplified in the new culture of quality assurance – as encountered in the idea of total quality management (TQM). This seeks to make management control systems transparent, accountable and accessible to stakeholder scrutiny and input.[92] Such appetites for the 'layering' of control processes, moreover, are only encouraged by accounting debacles such as Enron and WorldCom which produce political currents in favour of ever more transparency and accountability.

The appetite to audit is echoed in another new drive – towards seeing governmental, regulatory and business challenges in terms of needs to manage risks. Thus, in recent years there have been explosions of initiatives to spread risk management across government, of 'risk-based'

---

[87] See M. Power, *The Audit Explosion* (Demos, London, 1994); Power, *The Audit Society: Rituals of Verification* (Oxford University Press, Oxford, 1997); Power, *The Risk Management of Everything* (Demos, London, 2004).

[88] Power, *Audit Explosion*, p. 47.   [89] Power, *Audit Society*, p. 42.   [90] Ibid., p. 6.

[91] Ibid., pp. 1, 47; Power, *Risk Management of Everything*, pp. 10–11: 'the risk management of everything is characterised by the growth of risk management strategies that displace valuable – but vulnerable – professional judgement in favour of defendable process'.

[92] Stakeholders here may include business partners: see H. Collins, 'Quality Assurance in Subcontracting' in S. Deakin and J. Michie (eds.), *Contracts, Cooperation and Competition* (Oxford University Press, Oxford, 1997), pp. 285–306.

approaches to regulation[93] and of risk-centred strategies for corporate management.[94] In the regulation field, for instance, this development can be seen in regulators' growing inclinations to move away from securing results through externally imposed 'command and control' regimes that target errant corporate behaviour directly and towards ways of pushing regulatory tasks down into the regulated organisations. The new hope lies in using regulatory systems that target enforcement actions according to analyses of the risks presented by regulated companies and which adjust regulatory activities in a way that is 'responsive' to the internal control processes of regulated companies.[95] Some such systems, indeed, may more actively deploy monitoring, review and incentive systems to audit and influence the self-control mechanisms of corporations.[96] Within the environmental field, in particular, the last two decades have seen a mushrooming of schemes that see the auditing of private management systems, rather than external regulation, as the route to optimal results.[97] This is a development that creates a new role for intermediaries:

[93] See J. Black, 'The Emergence of Risk Based Regulation and the New Public Risk Management in the UK' [2005] PL 512, who argues that central government is 'awash' with initiatives to promote risk management; Financial Services Authority, *A New Regulator for the New Millennium* (FSA, London, 2000). On the need to extend risk-based regulation across government see P. Hampton, *Reducing Administrative Burdens: Effective Inspection and Enforcement: Final Report* (HM Treasury, London, March 2005) (the Hampton Review). On governmental willingness to see managerial, operational and regulatory issues as risk issues see e.g. National Audit Office, *Supporting Innovation: Managing Risk in Government Departments* (NAO, London, 2000); Health and Safety Executive, *Reducing Risks, Protecting People* (HSE, London, 2001); Cabinet Office, *Risk: Improving Government's Capacity to Handle Risk and Uncertainty* (Cabinet Office, London, 2002); C. Hood, H. Rothstein and R. Baldwin, *The Government of Risk* (Oxford University Press, Oxford, 2001).

[94] On risk management in the private sector see e.g. Basel Committee on Banking Supervision, *Sound Practices for the Management and Supervision of Operational Risk* (Bank for International Settlements, Basel, 2001); A. Waring and A. Glendon, *Managing Risk* (Thomson, London, 1998); P. Shimell, *The Universe of Risk* (Financial Times/ Prentice Hall, London, 2002); M. McCarthy and T. Flynn, *Risk from the CEO and Board Perspective* (McGraw-Hill, New York, 2004); T. Barton, W. Shenkir, P. Walker *et al.*, *Making Enterprise Risk Management Pay Off* (Financial Times/Prentice Hall, London, 2002); M. Power, *Organised Uncertainty: Designing a World of Risk Management* (Oxford University Press, Oxford, 2007).

[95] See I. Ayres and J. Braithwaite, *Responsive Regulation* (Oxford University Press, New York, 1992). See also N. Gunningham and P. Grabosky, *Smart Regulation* (Oxford University Press, Oxford, 1998).

[96] See e.g. C. Parker, *The Open Corporation: Effective Self-regulation and Democracy* (Cambridge University Press, Cambridge, 2002). For a critique see R. Baldwin, 'The New Punitive Regulation' (2004) 67 MLR 351, 374–83.

[97] Power, *Audit Society*, pp. 62–5.

'consulting markets thrive in the margins of regulatory initiatives. Where central agencies wish to effect management changes in target organizations, management consultants take on the role of mediating regulatory compliance and economic strategy.'[98]

Risk has developed as an organising concept so that, whether governmental, regulatory or business challenges are found in the public or private sectors, they are approached as questions of risk management.[99] The twin appetites for audit and risk management, moreover, combine to create a pervasive thrust towards dealing with problems or meeting opportunities through auditable risk management systems.[100]

The parallels with recent changes in the field of corporate insolvency are manifest. As will be seen in chapter 7, the banks are increasingly concerned to deal with corporate troubles by subjecting companies' management and risk control systems to external scrutiny. They look for measurable quality from management teams. In troubled times they push their 'care' down into management structures and increasingly use independent specialist professionals to evaluate and assist those who underperform and bring the company into danger. The common cultural factor across all these public and private fields is an appetite for, and a faith in the value of, exposing managerial or control systems to measurement, audit and review. The move from debt collection to insolvency risk management is as consistent with that culture as the changes that have recently been seen in public management, regulation or corporate management.

As far as bank strategies are concerned, an additional respect in which insolvency law and practice has moved from a reactive towards an anticipatory philosophy has been in the approaches that the banks have adopted when lending to potentially troubled companies.[101] The banks have long used the conditions of loan agreements to keep in touch with corporate performance and managerial behaviour. They have used

---

[98] Ibid., pp. 64–5; M. Henkel, *Government, Evaluation and Change* (Jessica Kingsley, London, 1991).

[99] See P. Bernstein, *Against the Gods: The Remarkable Story of Risk* (Wiley, New York, 1996); Power, *Risk Management of Everything*; Black, 'Emergence of Risk Based Regulation'; U. Beck, *Risk Society – Towards a New Modernity* (Sage, London, 1992).

[100] See Power, *Risk Management of Everything*, pp. 27–8: 'The private world of organisational internal control systems has been turned inside out, made public, codified and standardised and repackaged as risk management.'

[101] On banks and distressed companies see J. Franks and O. Sussman, 'The Cycle of Corporate Distress, Rescue and Dissolution: A Study of Small and Medium Size UK Companies', IFA Working Paper 306 (2000).

negative covenants in which the borrower agrees not to undertake certain behaviour or change the business in specified ways. They have employed positive covenants to ensure that the borrower supplies the lender with a variety of information on a regular basis and they have used financial covenants (positive as well as negative) to regulate different aspects of financial performance such as gearing, liquidity, profitability or levels of borrowing or working capital.[102] Such conditions have given the major lenders a good deal of power to monitor corporate managers.[103] Since the late 1990s, however, it is arguable that UK banks have adopted a newly organised and proactive approach to their debtor relationships – one that seeks to respond to corporate troubles at a far earlier stage of development than formerly. This approach is manifest in the increasing rigour with which the banks now attend to three things: early warning signals for corporate troubles; the quality of a company's management (most notably its capacity to steer a path through troubles); and the company's performance in managing the business risks it faces.

New attention to early warning signals is founded on the more active monitoring of data. The British Bankers' Association issued a Statement of Principles in 1997 (revised in 2001 and 2005).[104] This document makes it clear that when banks lend to small and medium enterprises, they will normally agree what sort of monitoring information will be required. Included within that information will be a comparison of forecasts and actual results (based on a number of stated performance indicators) as well as details on how the company's bank accounts are

---

[102] See Day and Taylor, 'Role of Debt Contracts'. See further J. Day, P. Ormrod and P. Taylor, 'Implications for Lending Decisions and Debt Contracting of the Adoption of International Financial Reporting Standards' [2004] JIBLR 475; J. Day and P. Taylor, 'Financial Distress in Small Firms: The Role Played by Debt Covenants and Other Monitoring Devices' [2001] Ins. Law. 97; H. DeAngelo, L. DeAngelo and K. Wruck, 'Asset Liquidity, Debt Covenants and Managerial Discretion in Financial Distress: The Collapse of L. A. Grear' (2002) 64 *Journal of Financial Economics* 3; M. Harris and A. Raviv, 'Capital Structure and the Informational Role of Debt' (1990) 45 *Journal of Finance* 321.

[103] On the conditions under which lenders will deal with lending risks through monitoring as opposed to other methods (e.g. increasing security or raising interest rates) see G. Triantis and R. Daniels, 'The Role of Debt in Interactive Corporate Governance' (1995) 83 Calif. L Rev. 1073; S. Franken, 'Creditor and Debtor Oriented Corporate Bankruptcy Regimes Revisited' (2004) 5 EBOR 645; T. H. Jackson and A. T. Kronman, 'Secured Financing and Priorities Among Creditors' (1979) 88 Yale LJ 1143; R. Scott, 'A Relational Theory of Secured Financing' (1986) 86 Colum. L Rev. 901. See also ch. 3 above.

[104] BBA, *Statement of Principles*.

used. The banks now monitor such information on an ongoing basis and use it not only to place the debtor in a risk category[105] but also to provide early warning signs of trouble. There are, indeed, indications that lenders see the provision of early warning signals as by far and away the main purpose of deploying covenants in loan agreements.[106] When difficulties are signalled it will be usual to refer the company to an 'intensive care' unit of the bank – or 'Business Support Team'.[107] At this stage, the bank's involvement becomes more active and may involve the appointment of an accountant to conduct an independent business review (IBR).[108] The bank and the debtor company will then agree a way forward after considering the recommendations that emerge from the IBR. Companies in such circumstances are heavily reliant on the bank's support and, at this stage, managers will have little choice but to accept the turnaround strategies initiated by the bank.[109]

Turning from early warning signals to the control of management, there has been a similar movement towards pre-insolvency action. The approach of Barclays Bank in the post-millennium period exemplifies this change.[110] When a company is first introduced to a Barclays' Business Support Team, that unit will focus increasingly on the quality of the management group and the need to help it to deal with the troubles confronting the company. This will involve, first, a structured approach in assessing the strengths and weaknesses of the company's management and whether it is capable of meeting the challenges faced.[111] If changes

---

[105] See Armour and Frisby, 'Rethinking Receivership', pp. 92–3: 'banks increasingly differentiate the riskiness of their borrowers, and charge accordingly'. The companies will pay a premium rate (a) because they present higher insolvency risks and (b) to pay for the higher level of care that they receive from the bank.

[106] See Day and Taylor, 'Role of Debt Contracts', p. 183.

[107] See L. Otty, 'Banking on the Managers' (2002) *Recovery* (Winter) 12.

[108] Armour and Frisby, 'Rethinking Receivership', p. 92; BBA, *Statement of Principles*, para. 2.3.

[109] See Armour and Frisby, 'Rethinking Receivership', who comment (at p. 93): 'should bank support be withdrawn at this stage, the company would be insolvent in the "cash-flow" sense'. (On cash flow and balance sheet tests and definitions of inability to pay debts see ch. 4 above.)

[110] See Otty, 'Banking on the Managers' (Mr Otty was then Business Support Director at Barclays); J. Dewhirst, 'Turnabout Tourniquet' (2003) *Financial World* 56. The Royal Bank of Scotland set up a Specialised Lending Services Division in 1993 which focuses on restructuring, rescue and intensive care. More than 1,000 companies are in the unit's care at any one time and its head, Derek Sach, claimed that the Division returns around 80 per cent of businesses back to good health: see *Financial Times*, 31 January 2005, p. 24.

[111] Otty, 'Banking on the Managers', p. 12.

are needed in that team, or if 'skills or experience gaps' need to be filled, then additional or replacement personnel will be introduced through specialist suppliers.[112] This may involve bringing on board experts in rescue. As a leading rescue professional commented: 'Introducing the concept of turnaround professionals and helping to find the appropriate individual are becoming an increasingly important part of our solutions tool bag.'[113] Reference to such specialists is facilitated by the emergence of these providers within the marketplace (a matter returned to below) and a significant role is played, in this regard, by organisations such as the Institute for Turnaround, Proturn and EIM Turnaround Practice.[114]

Once again, the effect of this change is, in practice, to focus attention on an earlier stage of corporate troubles than ever before. It is a development driven, not least, by the concern of the large banks to use their monitoring skills to gain market advantage. As Barclays' Chief Executive, Matt Barratt, said of the new attention to managerial performance: 'The ability to make good decisions regarding people represents one of the last reliable sources of competitive advantage.'[115]

Alongside such new attention to early warning signals and to management has come an increasing lender interest in the way that companies are dealing with risks. When Business Support teams become involved with a company's management, or when independent business reviews are carried out, a central task will involve identifying the key business issues and risks that have to be responded to. At such times the capacity of managers to recognise and to meet these challenges comes under review and a spotlight is placed on the risk management capabilities of the team of directors and senior managers in place. Banks and review teams will not, in such processes, confine their attention to assessing the probability of insolvency or of turnaround – they will be looking to see

---

[112] E.g. FD Direct or Proturn Executive in Barclays' case: see ibid.   [113] Ibid., p. 12.

[114] The Society of Turnaround Professionals was established by R3 and was retitled the Institute for Turnaround in 2008: see ch. 5 above and 'Turnaround Talk' (2001) *Recovery* (September). On the work of the turnaround specialist see R. Bingham, 'Poacher Turned Gamekeeper' (2003) *Recovery* (Winter) 27. On turnaround professionals and governance issues see ch. 5 above and V. Finch, 'Doctoring in the Shadows of Insolvency' [2005] JBL 690.

[115] Otty, 'Banking on the Managers'. For a mid-credit crisis view that the banks have learned lessons from past recessions and are now able to spot customers' problems earlier see A. Sakoui, 'The Delicate Task of Restructuring Lehman Begins', *Financial Times*, 27 October 2008.

whether the managers in position can overcome the company's troubles on their own or whether they need active assistance to manage the risks at issue. This, once more, involves a newly proactive approach in dealing with the prospect of corporate insolvency. There may be some evidence, moreover, that a considerable amount of insolvency-related work is now being done at such earlier stages in corporate troubles. Armour and Frisby, for example, reported in 2001 that, in their survey of a number of accountants, banks and lawyers who were regularly involved in receivership, their interviewees stated that only a minority of firms that are the subject of an IBR subsequently enter formal insolvency proceedings.[116]

Reinforcing such a movement towards insolvency risk management has been a developing stakeholder confidence in the ability of specialists to devise and implement rescue strategies. One managing director of a mergers and acquisitions group summarised the market changes over the decade to 2002 in the following terms:

> Turnaround opportunities are increasing because tighter market conditions, high leverage, bad management and over-trading are squeezing poor performers out. In the past, if a company was facing insolvency, it was seen to be prudent to cut one's losses and liquidate what was salvageable to pay off key creditors. Nowadays, investors and businesses have sophisticated mechanisms for quantifying and evaluating risk. So the focus is shifting toward bespoke solutions to what can be temporary strategic problems.[117]

As a culture of rescue and recovery has been developed by lenders and encouraged by the Government,[118] the market has responded by providing the skills that are designed to prevent corporate disaster. Thus, one business underwriting manager has written of recent changes: 'The growing culture of rescue and recovery from a commercial and statutory viewpoint has raised the profile of turnaround finance. There is a cadre of better quality professionals around to assist businesses in turnaround, as well as assisting the lender. Lenders are now more likely to examine the possibilities of rescue and seek alternative solutions.'[119] As noted in

---

[116] Armour and Frisby, 'Rethinking Receivership', p. 94. (The authors do, however, caution about the lack of qualitative data on this issue.) See also the Royal Bank of Scotland's claim to turn around 80 per cent of companies in its intensive care: p. 267 above.

[117] A. Lester (of Aon), (2002) *Recovery* (Winter) 18.

[118] See e.g. *Productivity and Enterprise: Insolvency – A Second Chance* (Cm 5234, July 2001); the Secretary of State for Trade and Industry's statement at HC Debates, col. 53, 10 April 2002; Frisby, 'In Search of a Rescue Regime'.

[119] C. Hawes (GE Commercial Finance), (2002) *Recovery* (Winter) 18.

chapter 5, a burgeoning group of new specialists has come onto the scene. They all have a role in assisting banks or companies to effect turnarounds but come with a variety of labels, notably: turnaround professionals, company doctors, business recovery professionals, risk consultants, solutions providers, debt management companies and cash flow managers.[120] Very often the main lending bank will call in such actors as part of a process in which the troubled company's management capacity is reviewed; a strategy for turnaround is devised; arrangements for reorganising and refinancing are set up; and a programme for implementing necessary changes is put into effect. Banks' incentives to monitor the signs of corporate distress can be expected to grow as they develop confidence in the turnaround capacities of their own staff and of relevant specialists. This, in turn, is likely to produce an increasing bank inclination to intervene in corporate affairs before troubles become potentially terminal.

If such a shift in inclination is typified as a movement from debt collection towards risk management, it might be questioned, first, whether it is possible to quantify this shift – to state how much more work in response to corporate decline is now being done at the informal turnaround as opposed to the formal statutory procedure stage. Second, it might be asked whether the banks are not so much moving towards a focus on risk management as merely relocating their debt collection activities from the formal to the turnaround stage.

On the first issue, a fundamental difficulty in quantifying the amount of work done in the turnaround period is that this will usually be carried out in an undisclosed manner in order to protect the reputation and business prospects of the troubled company.[121] What can be pointed to, however, is the dramatic growth in the amount of turnaround servicing that is now being offered by a growing number of specialists.[122]

---

[120] See D. MacDonald, 'Turnaround Finance' (2002) *Recovery* (Winter) 17. On the role of credit insurers in turnaround see M. Feldwick, 'Engaging Credit Insurers in the Turnaround Process' (2006) *Recovery* (Autumn) 32; G. Jones, 'Credit Insurance: A Question of Support' (2004) *Recovery* (Summer) 21.

[121] See Finch, 'Doctoring in the Shadows'.

[122] See MacDonald, 'Turnaround Finance'; Finch, 'Doctoring in the Shadows'. As for the *relative* proportions of work on corporate troubles that are done through turnarounds and formal procedures, little light, unfortunately, is thrown on the issue by statistics on the ratio between those firms which have undergone turnaround activity (e.g. IBRs) and those of these which subsequently enter formal proceedings. Such statistics leave out of account the number of firms who enter formal procedures without going through any prior turnaround activities.

On the second question, it would be unrealistic to contend that the banks do not, at least at times, act in their own best interests, with the primary aim of debt repayment, whether they are operating at the turn-around or formal procedures stage of corporate decline.[123] As noted above, though, there is increasing evidence that in, say, operating inten-sive care procedures, the banks are routinely prepared to stimulate activities that are designed to enhance the troubled companies' risk management systems and prospects rather than merely to produce early debt repayment. It should be emphasised, moreover, that when banks instigate the intervention of a company doctor in the affairs of a troubled enterprise, that company doctor will, in the vast majority of cases, be employed not by the bank but by the company and will be legally and professionally obliged to act in the interests of the company and not the bank.[124] It is to be expected, moreover, that the earlier that a bank intervenes in the decline of a company's fortunes, the greater will be the bank's incentive to pursue rescue, rather than debt recovery, objectives. This is because the earlier the intervention, the smaller will be the risk of non-repayment to the bank and the greater the prospect of successful turnaround.

All of the above points, however, must be set in the context of the 'new capitalism' (as discussed in chapter 3). In the developing world of credit derivative trading there may be new possibilities of dealing with risks that lead a bank towards exit from its relationship with the troubled company rather than in the direction of doctoring and rescue. In relation to the USA, in particular, it has been argued that, thanks to the explosive growth of credit derivatives, debt holders such as banks and hedge funds will often deal with the risks attached to a troubled company by buying credit or loan default swaps, which trigger payments if the company fails. This brings two noteworthy effects that may prejudice rescue: uncertainty regarding the creditor's position and a 'decoupling' of creditor and company interests that involves incentives to oppose restructuring and rescue. As one practitioner has said of such creditors:

---

[123] On the banks' tendencies to better their own positions during rescue processes see Franks and Sussman, 'Cycle of Corporate Distress'.

[124] If the company doctor is a member of the Institute for Turnaround (IFT) he will be obliged by that Institute's *Code of Ethics* to act for the company in a manner that is impartial and free from any external pressures or interest that would weaken his professional independence (*Code of Ethics*, Appendix, para. A.2).

> Where their interests lie is less predictable, especially if they also hold credit default swaps. Their financial interests may be best served by forcing a default if they are on the right side of a credit default swap position. The problem is compounded by creditors not having to disclose derivatives positions, making it very difficult for companies and regulators to find out their real intentions.[125]

In so far as the derivatives market facilitates dealing with risks by methods that may 'decouple' the creditor from the company, it is to be expected that this may cut against the trend for banks to indulge in doctoring. Similarly it can be said that rescues may not be encouraged by a process of risk spreading that makes interests and incentives ever more complex and opaque. What, however, of the prevalence of such derivatives-based decouplings of creditor and corporate interests? The pioneering commentators in this area suggest that, in the absence of disclosure requirements regarding strategies for risk spreading, 'we simply do not know' the extent to which economic exposures are shed in this way.[126] As for the position in the UK, these are not uncharted issues. In relation to the collapse of the Marconi restructuring talks in 2002, difficulties allegedly arose because some banks had used credit derivatives to lay off risk to the extent that they stood to gain more from Marconi defaulting than from a restructuring.[127] Looking forward past the 2007–8 credit crisis, these are matters to be monitored since the credit derivatives market is global and UK creditors are just as free as their US counterparts to 'decouple' from the company without being subject to any organised provisions calling for disclosure on the extent of that decoupling.

---

[125] See H. Hu and B. Black, 'Equity and Debt Decoupling and Empty Voting 11: Importance and Extensions' (2008) 156 *University of Pennsylvania Law Review* 625. An administrator, Tony Lomas of PWC, appointed to Lehman Brothers International (Europe) stressed in 2008 that, in the wake of Lehman's collapse, funds and other counterparties of Lehman faced having their positions 'frozen for some time' because of the complexities of resolving individual positions and that such complexities were serious impediments to restructuring: see Sakoui, 'Delicate Task of Restructuring Lehman Begins'.

[126] Michael Reilly of the financing and restructuring practice at Bingham McCutchen, reported in F. Guerra, 'Derivatives Boom Raises Risk of Forced Bankruptcy for Companies', *Financial Times*, 28 January 2008. For proposals on the mandatory disclosure of actions that 'decouple' credit holders from economic exposure see Hu and Black, 'Equity and Debt Decoupling'.

[127] See J. Gapper, 'The Winners and Losers of the Restructure', *Financial Times*, 2 November 2004.

Recasting the actors

The philosophical changes outlined earlier are matched by a recasting of the roles fulfilled by the various actors that are commonly concerned with troubled companies.[128] The preceding discussion serves to outline how the major lenders to companies, the banks, have shifted their focus of attention. At the end of the 1980s it was easy for a floating-charge-holding bank to rely on the power to appoint an administrative receiver and to stand at a distance from a troubled company. It knew that it could intervene quickly at the right time and recover its debt. Today the position is different because of legal, procedural and cultural changes. The bank is far more likely to be aware of corporate troubles at an earlier stage than formerly and to intervene by exerting a considerable degree of scrutiny or influence over the company's directors. It will often be concerned to use its voice rather than merely to exit when the company first encounters trouble. It will not be fatalistic about financial difficulties but will use its intensive care teams where possible to prevent troubles from developing to the point where they cannot be turned around. In redefining its role the bank will have constructed a flexible relationship with a healthy company that can slide seamlessly into another form when the company encounters trouble.

As for company directors, a shift towards preventative approaches to insolvency involves a change in role. It is to be expected that as banks move from debt collection to prevention and the monitoring of risk management, directors will be subjected to regimes of scrutiny and assessment that both come into effect at an earlier stage in corporate decline than formerly and involve a greater depth of review. Directors, accordingly, will be held to account more fully as this shift in approach strengthens. Their expertise, as well as their management and risk control systems, will be placed under the microscope. On an optimistic view, it might be argued that company directors stand to gain in such a regime as they will be offered new levels of assistance by banks and independent consultants. They will have moved away from the agonies of the former regime in which the troubled director would be inclined to pursue a lonely and secretive path through troubles – a progress accompanied by the fear that the bank would discover what was going on and call the show to a halt by appointing an administrative receiver. Under the new

[128] On the importance of actors see J. Black, 'Enrolling Actors in Regulatory Processes: The Example of UK Financial Services Regulation' [2003] PL 62; Finch, 'Re-invigorating Corporate Rescue'.

system, the director has to operate in a highly transparent way but when troubles are met, he or she has allies who will step in to help.

Pessimists, however, will be inclined to turn this argument on its head. They will warn that if banks increasingly demand that dangers of insolvency should be dealt with through risk management systems that are auditable, this produces a number of dangers.[129] It may make company directors inward-looking and inclined to see the banks as unwelcome overseers who are to be resisted rather than welcomed as allies. These directors, as a result, may become procedurally defensive and more concerned to create an acceptable record of their behaviour for bank scrutiny than to exercise proper business judgement.[130] Such defensiveness may not merely chill entrepreneurial behaviour but may reduce the flow of useful information to the banks. It may devalue communications between debtors and creditors as these become ritualistic exercises in formal compliance and this may, in turn, render the banks less, not more, able than formerly to spot incipient difficulties or to help companies when they meet troubles. Within companies, information may, as a result, be organised in less and less useful ways because it becomes structured by needs to box-tick, defend and avoid blame rather than to meet business objectives.

Whether the optimists or pessimists are on firmer ground goes beyond the current discussion but much may depend on the skill of the banks in setting up monitoring and assistance regimes that enable them to audit but, at the same time, give directors the freedom and confidence to make and apply business judgements without undue fear or constraint. Much may also turn on the extent to which companies can successfully embed auditable risk management systems within the general processes of wealth creation and governance.

Turning to the role of the insolvency practitioner, one recent change has been a general reorientation of approach. There has developed, as noted in chapter 5, a growing culture of rescue friendliness and with this has come a new emphasis on the IP's role in averting disaster. As one IP described the movement: 'the emphasis has shifted from "pathology" to "preventative medicine"… "managing change" has become a critical new

---

[129] See Power, *Risk Management of Everything*, pp. 43–58.
[130] See C. Hood, 'The Risk Game and the Blame Game' (2002) 37 *Government and Opposition* 15.

discipline'.[131] For IPs, however, the most dramatic change of recent years has been the replacing of administrative receivership with the post-Enterprise Act administration procedure. The post-Enterprise Act administration involves processes that are inclusive and which, with the departure of administrative receivership, oblige the IP to act in the interests of creditors of the company as a whole rather than in pursuit of the bank's interests alone. These developments, when put together, involve a significant recasting of the IP's role. The administrator in the 'new' administration procedure is given the difficult task of devising the best way forward while serving a variety of creditor interests and ensuring that a host of creditors' voices are all respected in decision- and policy-making. A central, and newly acute, challenge will be to effect a balance between acting decisively in order to achieve the best outcome for the company and conducting deliberations in an open and accessible manner so that these are acceptable to all parties. The IP's role has been moved in the direction of mediator as opposed to implementer or technician.

Unsecured creditors are the actors whose role perhaps changes least in the shift towards preventative approaches. That role, nevertheless, does change. For a start, unsecured creditors are given what amounts to a speaking part in the new regimes of corporate insolvency. Their voice has a new power in two respects. First, in the post-Enterprise Act administration process, they have a right to be listened to and the IP has a duty to heed their interests when deciding strategy.[132] Second, their voice is given a potential role in the movement towards more open, transparent and accountable management that is driven by the new intensive care regimes run by the banks. When troubled managers, as never before, have to explain to banks and others how they are dealing with business partners, this stimulates the granting of access and influence to those unsecured creditors who have a continuing commercial relationship with the troubled company. The incentives of such creditors to use their voices may, furthermore, be increased by improvements in their potential returns through insolvency processes – as seen in the ring-fencing (or 'prescribed part') provisions of the Enterprise Act 2002.[133]

---

[131] See L. Hornan, 'The Changing Face of Insolvency Practice' (2005) (March) *International Accountant* 24 at 24.

[132] See paras. 3(2), 49, 51–7. See ch. 9 below.

[133] See Enterprise Act 2002 s. 252 (inserting a new s. 176A into the Insolvency Act 1986). This, as noted, provides that a prescribed part of funds otherwise available for distribution to holders of floating charges shall be retained for the benefit of unsecured creditors. See also Insolvency Act 1986 (Prescribed Part) Order 2003 (SI 2003/2097); ch. 3, pp. 108–10 above.

As for the judges, new concerns to deal with insolvency by preventative means bring some issues newly towards the centre of the stage. An important challenge for the judges is to develop the law in a manner that allows banks and others to assist troubled companies where this is in the general interests of creditors. At the same time, the judges must be concerned to avoid such assistance being used in a self-serving manner so that it prejudices the interests of creditors who are not procedurally involved – as where unsecured creditors' interests may be harmed by banks using intensive care processes to protect themselves at the expense of others (for example by insisting on excessively low-risk strategies when more enterprising behaviour would be more reasonable and would benefit unsecured creditors).

Finally, mention must again be made of the new actors that have become involved in rescues. As noted already, the modern emphasis on prevention and rescue has been accompanied by the advent of new specialists: turnaround professionals, company doctors, risk consultants, solutions providers, independent business reviewers, asset-based lenders, private equity providers and others.[134] These parties offer their services to assist both major lenders and companies when troubles are encountered. Their role is often dual – to scrutinise and monitor on behalf of a major lender and also to assist with the devising and implementation of turnaround solutions. Their growth in number and importance is a measure of the current advancement of concerns to deal with insolvency risks by preventative approaches.

Comparing approaches to rescue

In analysing English rescue procedures it is helpful to consider how other jurisdictions deal with the central challenges of rescue.[135] The purpose of such comparisons is not to argue that English law should follow other countries but to set out key choices with clarity and to show that there may be a wide variety of ways to achieve rescue objectives.[136]

---

[134] See MacDonald, 'Turnaround Finance'; Finch, 'Doctoring in the Shadows'.

[135] For comparative analyses of rescue, see K. Gromek Broc and R. Parry, *Corporate Rescue: An Overview of Recent Developments* (2nd edn, Kluwer, London, 2006); L. S. Sealy, 'Corporate Rescue Procedures: Some Overseas Comparisons' in F. Macmillan (ed.), *Perspectives in Company Law* (Kluwer, London, 1995); IS 2000, Annex A; Brown, *Corporate Rescue*, chs. 24 and 25.

[136] For general discussions of the desirable features of insolvency regimes see the World Bank, *Principles and Guidelines for Effective Insolvency and Creditors' Rights Systems* (World Bank, Washington D.C., 2001) and United Nations Commission on International Trade Law (UNCITRAL), *Legislative Guide on Insolvency Law* (United Nations, New York, 2005);

What then are the important issues to consider in such a comparison? A first must be the priority that an insolvency regime gives to rescue. Is, for instance, insolvency law seen merely as a means of debt collection for creditors or does it place importance on rescue to the extent that creditors' rights are placed on the procedural back burner or even modified? Can the regime be said to be creditor or debtor friendly?[137] Does it, for example, involve a moratorium on the enforcement of creditors' rights and does it allow broad access to the rescue process? A second issue is whether the regime is fault-based. Does it, for instance, treat the directors as responsible for corporate troubles to the extent that they are seen as blameworthy and in need of tight regulation and monitoring?[138] Does it give priority to setting down heavy penalties for directors who misbehave?

A third key consideration relates to the managerial and oversight functions within rescue processes and to whom these are allocated. Regimes may be placed under the control of the courts, the directors, independent professionals or even the market, and they will have quite different characteristics. A court-driven rescue approach, for instance, will tend to be characterised by formality but alternative rescue regimes will rely more heavily on contractual or negotiated forms of dealing.

A fourth issue is whether the rescue process as a whole is focused or diverse. A focused process will rely on a small number of procedures and gateways to rescue whereas the diverse system of rescue may involve a host of different processes and philosophies.

Finally, an important comparative dimension is the financial context within which rescues operate. Rescue opportunities and processes may be heavily influenced by the structures that are available in a jurisdiction for raising corporate finances. Here the informal conventions governing such matters as banking arrangements may be as important as formal statutory structures. A further issue is how the law of a country or its

---

W. McBryde, A. Flessner and S. Kortmann, *Principles of European Insolvency Law* (Kluwer, Deventer, 2003).

[137] On creditor-oriented and debtor-oriented regimes, their comparative efficiency and the governance structures of firms see Franken, 'Creditor and Debtor Oriented Corporate Bankruptcy Regimes'.

[138] Hunter contrasts a 'rescue culture' – marked by a bias in favour of preserving businesses – with old notions 'that the insolvent trader should be regarded as morally defective, and that individuals, partnerships and corporations who or which cannot pay their debts must, as part of the settled scheme of things, be made bankrupt or wound up': Hunter, 'Nature and Functions of a Rescue Culture', p. 499.

bankers makes provision for funding within the rescue context: is, indeed, any special regime available for rescue purposes?

We will see, in the chapters that follow, that present English rescue procedures might be portrayed as giving strong priority to the protection of creditor interests and limited priority to rescue; as quite heavily fault-based and oriented to the control of errant directorial conduct; and as reliant on strong supervision of directors by independent insolvency practitioners and the courts. The English system is also quite diverse in so far as a number of rescue processes and gateways (informal and formal) may have relevance to a troubled company and it is set within a financial system that strongly favours the secured creditor.

The corporate insolvency regime encountered in the USA offers a set of contrasting characteristics and it is worth outlining these, as well as noting the alleged strengths and weaknesses of the US approach.[139] Chapter 11 of the United States Bankruptcy Code (dating from the Bankruptcy Reform Act 1978) is a 'reorganisation' procedure whose policy objective is strongly oriented to the avoidance of the social costs of liquidation and the retention of the corporate operation as a going concern.[140] There is no requirement that the debtor be insolvent or near insolvent in order to apply for Chapter 11 protection: the process is an instrument for debtor relief, not a remedy for creditors.[141] As in England,

---

[139] Chapter 7 of the US Bankruptcy Code is the most common form of bankruptcy. It is a liquidation proceeding in which the debtor's non-exempt assets are sold by the Chapter 7 trustee and the proceeds distributed according to the Code's priorities. It is available for individuals, couples, partnerships and corporations.

[140] For comparison of Chapter 11 with the UK law see G. McCormack, 'Control and Corporate Rescue – An Anglo-American Evaluation' (2007) 56 ICLQ 515; McCormack, 'Super-priority New Financing and Corporate Rescue' [2007] JBL 701; J. Armour, B. Cheffins and D. Skeel, 'Corporate Ownership Structure and the Evolution of Bankruptcy Law' (2002) 55 Vand. L Rev. 1699; R. Broude, 'How the Rescue Culture Came to the United States and the Myths that Surround Chapter 11' (2001) 16 IL&P 194; J. L. Westbrook, 'A Comparison of Bankruptcy Reorganisation in the US with Administration Procedure in the UK' (1990) 6 IL&P 86; G. Moss, 'Chapter 11: An English Lawyer's Critique' (1998) 11 *Insolvency Intelligence* 17; Moss, 'Comparative Bankruptcy Cultures: Rescue or Liquidations? Comparisons of Trends in National Law – England' (1997) 23 *Brooklyn Journal of International Law* 115; R. Connell, 'Chapter 11: The UK Dimension' (1990) 6 IL&P 90; Carruthers and Halliday, *Rescuing Business*, ch. 11; J. Franks and W. Torous, 'Lessons from a Comparison of US and UK Insolvency Codes' in J. S. Bhandari and L. A. Weiss (eds.), *Corporate Bankruptcy: Economic and Legal Perspectives* (Cambridge University Press, Cambridge, 1996).

[141] See generally P. Lewis, 'Corporate Rescue Law in the United States' in Gromek Broc and Parry, *Corporate Rescue*, p. 333.

a central purpose of the process is to preserve the value of the enterprise where this is likely to be greater than the liquidation value. Chapter 11 is, however, to English eyes highly sympathetic to the debtor, almost always started by a voluntary petition by the debtor and marked by the following characteristics.

There is an automatic moratorium or stay on enforcement of claims against the company and its property. This is triggered by the filing of a Chapter 11 petition. Secured creditors and landlords will usually initiate court action to seek to lift the stay but the moratorium will be upheld if the court finds that the debtor has provided the creditor with 'adequate protection' of their property interests. (This usually consists of periodic payments.) The debtor, in turn, must seek court permission to use cash as he is subject to a lien. Such issues, however, are often resolved by the parties by means of an agreement that is approved by the court. There is provision in Chapter 11 for 'cramdown' whereby a plan that is confirmed by the court may be imposed on a class of objecting creditors. (Generally a secured class may be crammed down if it receives the value of its collateral plus interest.) Objecting creditors are shielded by the 'best interest' test under which the court must be satisfied that each objecting creditor will receive, under the plan, as much as they would in liquidation. There is, in addition, a 'feasibility' test under which the court must find that the debtor is reasonably likely to be able to perform the promises it makes in the plan. It is nevertheless the case that in US law prior legal rights may be more dramatically affected than in England in order to effect a reorganisation and a new start for the company. Even unliquidated and unaccrued liabilities, for instance, can be restructured and constrained in Chapter 11.[142] In English administration there is no division of creditors into classes and there is nothing equivalent to the US notion of class cram-down.

An important cultural difference between England and the USA concerns the issue of fault, as Moss has observed:

> In England insolvency, including corporate insolvency, is regarded as a disgrace. The stigma has to some extent worn off but it is nevertheless still there as a reality. In the United States business failure is very often thought of as a misfortune rather than wrongdoing. In England the judicial bias towards creditors reflects a general social attitude which is

---

[142] Westbrook, 'Comparison of Bankruptcy', p. 89. On the effect of the US Bankruptcy Abuse Prevention and Consumer Protection Act 2005 (BAPCPA 2005) see Lewis, 'Corporate Rescue Law in the US'.

inclined to punish risk takers when the risks go wrong and side with
creditors who lose out. The United States is still in spirit a pioneering
country where the taking of risks is thought to be a good thing and
creditors are perceived as being greedy.[143]

This cultural difference is reflected in the allocation of managerial and
control functions. Under Chapter 11, the pre-petition management may
remain in control throughout the proceedings,[144] though in law the
bankruptcy estate vests not in the debtor company but in a separate
conceptual entity: the debtor in possession (DIP).[145] The DIP is akin to a

---

[143] Moss, 'Chapter 11', p. 18; see also Carruthers and Halliday, *Rescuing Business*, p. 246;
Westbrook, 'Comparison of Bankruptcy', p. 143, who argues that in the USA business
failure is more readily seen as 'the inevitable downside of entrepreneurship and risk'.
See also M. Draper, 'Taking a Leaf out of Chapter 11?' (1991) 17 *Law Society Gazette* 28.

[144] The debtor in possession can, however, be a team of corporate salvage experts employed to
reorganise the company or a new management team appointed after the financial troubles
have started. In practice figures suggest that considerably more than half of US managers
lose their jobs within two years of filing for Chapter 11, a stark contrast with the normal
turnover figure of around 6–10 per cent per two years: see Broude, 'How the Rescue Culture
Came to the United States'; K. Ayotte and E. Morrison, 'Creditor Control and Conflict in
Chapter 11' (8 January 2008), Columbia University Center for Law and Economics Studies,
Research Paper Series No. 321 (available at http://ssrn.com/abstract=1081661) – 80 per cent
of CEOs were replaced before or soon after bankruptcy filing (in a sample studied of
privately and publicly held business that filed for Chapter 11 in 2001). Stuart Gilson of
Harvard Business School has also been quoted as stating that around 80 per cent of chief
executives and a high proportion of senior managers lose their jobs in a Chapter 11
restructuring: *Financial Times*, 3 October 2001. See also E. Warren, 'The Untenable Case
for Repeal of Chapter 11' (1992) 102 Yale LJ 437 at 449; L. LoPucki and W. Whitford,
'Corporate Governance in the Bankruptcy Reorganisation of Large, Publicly Held
Companies' (1993) 141 U Pa. L Rev. 669. But see S. Gilson, 'Bankruptcy, Boards, Banks
and Blockholders' (1990) 27 *Journal of Financial Economics* 355; Franks and Torous,
'Lessons from a Comparison', pp. 459–60. On the difficulties of replacing poor managers
in DIP regimes see L. LoPucki, 'The Debtor in Full Control – System Failure Under
Chapter 11 of the Bankruptcy Code (First and Second Installments)' (1983) 57 Am.
Bankruptcy LJ 99 and 247; M. Bradley and M. Rosenzweig, 'The Untenable Case for
Chapter 11' (1992) 101 Yale LJ 1043.

[145] See Brown, *Corporate Rescue*, pp. 753–5. On DIP systems and their merits/demerits see
D. Hahn, 'Concentrated Ownership and Control of Corporate Reorganisations' [2004]
4 JCLS 117; McCormack, 'Control and Corporate Rescue'; R. Nimmer and R. Feinberg,
'Chapter 11 Business Governance: Fiduciary Duties, Business Judgement, Trustees and
Exclusivity' (1989) 6 *Bankruptcy Development Journal* 1; E. Adams, 'Governance in
Chapter 11 Reorganisations: Reducing Costs, Improving Results' (1993) 73 Boston
University LR 581; L. LoPucki and G. Triantis, 'A Systems Approach to Comparing
US and Canadian Reorganization of Financially Distressed Companies' in J. Ziegel (ed),
Current Developments in International and Comparative Corporate Insolvency Law
(Clarendon Press, Oxford, 1994); D. Boshkoff and R. McKinney, 'The Future of
Chapter 11' (1995) 8 *Insolvency Intelligence* 6; Franks and Torous, 'Lessons from a
Comparison'; Broude, 'How the Rescue Culture Came to the United States'.

trustee. An examiner or trustee can be appointed under Chapter 11 if the creditors convince the court that investigation of the directors is necessary[146] but the DIP is in virtually the same position as the trustee except for the latter's powers of investigation and entitlement to compensation.

Before the Enterprise Act 2002, it was the position of the secured creditor that offered the most dramatic contrast between the US and English approaches. In England, as we have seen in chapter 3, there is the concept of a floating security that hovers over the company's assets and crystallises into a fixed security when financial disasters happen. There is no equivalent in the USA and receivership on the pre-2002 English model is unknown there. The security holder in England had a level of control over rescue procedures that a US banker could only dream of. (Westbrook has quipped that 'if an American banker is very, very good, when he dies he will go to the United Kingdom'.)[147] In England the floating security holder was able, when affairs went wrong, to appoint a receiver and manager of the entire business – an 'administrative receiver' – whose task was to obtain the best realisation for the secured creditor that was reasonably practicable. This is unthinkable in the USA. An underpinning English assumption here was that banks would do everything possible to save a company prior to inserting a receiver. In contrast, it has been argued that US businesses regard banks as 'uncertain and fickle business allies at best'.[148] As noted above, all changed with the Enterprise Act 2002, however, when (as will be discussed in chapter 9) the floating charge holder's power to institute receivership was very largely replaced by the new administration procedure and an obligation on the administrator to act in the interests of all of the company's creditors. The 2002 Act thus can be seen as moving English law in the direction of Chapter 11 but, as has been pointed out,[149] it still differs in important respects: administration still hands control to an outsider; there is no method for 'cramming down' secured creditors (i.e. forcing them to accept a reorganisation plan); and there is no provision in

---

[146] Under s. 1104(a) of the Code (as amended by BAPCPA 2005) a court may appoint a Chapter 11 trustee upon showing of cause or if such appointment is in the best interests of the creditors, equity holders and other interests in the estate; and that trustee can also dismiss or convert the Chapter 11 case if the court concludes that to do so is in the best interests of the creditors and the estate. BAPCPA 2005 also adds s. 1104(e) obligating the US Trustee to move for the appointment of a trustee if reasonable grounds exist to suspect fraud by the debtor's board of directors or high-level management.

[147] Westbrook, 'Comparison of Bankruptcy', p. 87.   [148] Ibid., p. 88.

[149] See McCormack, 'Super-priority New Financing', p. 702.

England for attracting new finance in times of trouble by means of statutory super-priority funding arrangements.

The part to be played by a company's shareholders also differs somewhat in the USA and England, and again reflects differing attitudes to corporate distress. In the USA, the shareholders have historically been given a role in rescue proceedings, although this influence may be waning.[150] The inclusion of shareholders has been said to flow from a commitment to the entrepreneurial ethic and, again, a belief that financial troubles often stem from external forces. It produced an emphasis on preserving not merely the business but the troubled company itself. In England, the tendency is to view the prior shareholders as at least in part responsible for the company's troubles (along with their directors) and to have interests that can be treated as having expired once a formal legal insolvency proceeding has started. The products of rescues tend to reflect this divergence of approach. In England most insolvency practitioners tend to look to sell the business but in the USA it can be the case that a rescue produces an agreed composition between the company and its creditors with the former equity owners keeping some ownership.

The parts played by professionals also differ. In English administrations a key individual is the insolvency practitioner. This is the person who, rather than the directors, runs the rescue operation. Rescues under the English system tend to be dominated by a small number of London-based specialist accountants. In the US system, with its DIP regime, bankruptcy tends to be locally operated and to involve lawyers rather than accountants.

The level of court supervision involved in the rescue process is also linked to the above factors. In English administration (before and after the Enterprise Act 2002) the central role of the independent insolvency practitioner means that little court supervision is required. In the USA the power of the DIP and the possibility of cram-down are balanced by

---

[150] Ayotte and Morrison, 'Creditor Control', argue that creditor control is pervasive and that in contrast to the traditional view of Chapter 11, equity holders and managers exercise little or no leverage during the reconstruction process. On secured credit and control rights in Chapter 11 see G. McGlaun, 'Lender Control in Chapter 11: Empirical Evidence' (5 February 2007), available at http://ssrn.com/abstract=961365. For an analysis of those who control Chapter 11 (formally and functionally) see S. Lubben, 'The New and Improved Chapter 11' (30 November 2004), Seton Hall Public Law Research Paper No. 2.

considerable court protections for creditors in the reorganisation. In short, the US regime is closely regulated by the Bankruptcy Court whereas English administration relies more heavily on the administrator's discretion and the agreement of the creditors.

In terms of legal focus, the US rescue system is concentrated on the Chapter 11 reorganisation, whereas in England a number of insolvency processes possess a rescue function: notably schemes of arrangements under sections 895–9 of the Companies Act 2006, company voluntary arrangements under the Insolvency Act 1986, and administrations. As will be seen below, the use of a variety of procedures raises issues of consistency and coherence in the English system.

Finally, note should be taken of the different financial contexts within which the Chapter 11 and English rescue procedures operate. In England it is usual for companies to raise a good portion of their capital by resort to bank loans secured by floating charges. This is consistent with English judicial and legislative policy which encourages financing through secured loans at interest rates that are reduced by giving secured creditors high levels of protection. In the USA, financing is more often achieved through the bond market and the secured creditor 'does not enjoy the general sympathy of the public or the courts'.[151] Where credit is obtained contractually through hire purchase or retention of title arrangements, the English courts tend to approach rights issues with a high respect for the sanctity of contract, whereas US courts look more directly to the need to protect parties collectively in a rescue scenario.

Chapter 11 procedures have been criticised on a number of fronts.[152] A first concern has been the delay and expense involved. Delay is inevitable since Chapter 11 gives debtors 120 days after filing so as to propose a reorganisation plan. This is followed by sixty further days to obtain creditor and shareholder approval. Extensions to such periods have in the past been frequent and it was usual for creditors to be held at bay for one or more years. The Bankruptcy Abuse Prevention and

---

[151] Moss, 'Chapter 11', p. 18.

[152] On Chapter 11 and its weaknesses see e.g. 'Symposium on the Future of Chapter 11', Boston College Law School Working Paper 134 (Boston College, Boston, 2005); LoPucki and Triantis, 'Systems Approach'; Bradley and Rosenzweig, 'Untenable Case for Chapter 11'; Boshkoff and McKinney, 'Future of Chapter 11'; M. Galen with C. Yang, 'A New Page for Chapter 11?' *Business Week*, 25 January 1993, p. 2; Brown, *Corporate Rescue*, pp. 768–72.

Consumer Protection Act (BAPCPA) 2005, however, prohibits extensions of the debtor's exclusive period in which to file a Chapter 11 plan beyond eighteen months after the start of Chapter 11 proceedings (plus two extra months to permit solicitation).[153]

Why do Chapter 11 cases take so long to process?[154] A major reason is that the professionals have few incentives to act quickly. Chapter 11 is based on judicial oversight and lawyers' fees accordingly tend to be very considerable. Under the old Bankruptcy Code, courts linked such fees to creditors' returns, but the present regime allows market rates to be charged for services rendered.[155] The BAPCPA 2005 amendments, however, sought to address some of these issues and bankruptcy judges are now charged to manage the case actively to reduce cost and delay. This includes holding 'status conferences' as are 'necessary to further the expeditious and economical resolution of the case'.[156]

The expenses of litigation tend, furthermore, to be fuelled where the DIP approach leaves managers in control of a company since this may produce a lack of trust between creditors and management: a position that often gives rise to litigation that stands to be paid for out of the estate.

The US judges could place Chapter 11 processes under a tighter rein, but bankruptcy judges are ill-placed to do this because of their workloads. In any event, judges who are in doubt about a Chapter 11 case have tended to opt for the line of least resistance, which was to give the parties more time to think, often granting significant extensions, sometimes of periods of over two years. As for shareholders, their inclination will tend to be to wait rather than liquidate since they have little to lose by this. As for workforces, the indications are that firms tend to have shed half of their workers before a plan is confirmed. These results have prompted some commentators to argue that the millions and millions of dollars

---

[153] For a critique of the BAPCPA 2005 reforms see G. Lee and J. Bannister, 'Taming the Beast' (2005) 21 *Sweet & Maxwell's Company Law Newsletter* 1. See also A. Kornberg, 'The Bankruptcy Abuse Prevention and Consumer Protection Act of 2005 – A Primer on Those Changes Affecting Business Bankruptcies' (2006) 3 *International Corporate Rescue* 33.

[154] Note Justice Small's 'Fast Track Chapter 11': see Boshkoff and McKinney, 'Future of Chapter 11'.

[155] See Galen, 'A New Page for Chapter 11?', p. 3. For a recent and comprehensive empirical study of professional fees in Chapter 11 see S. Lubben, 'ABI Chapter 11 Professional Fee Study' (1 December 2007), Seton Hall Public Law Research Paper No. 1020477, available at http://ssrn.com/abstract=1020477.

[156] 11 USC s. 105(d)(1). See further Lewis, 'Corporate Rescue Law in the US'.

spent on lawyers and accountants might have been better used to repay creditors through swifter liquidations.[157]

The utility of Chapter 11 for small companies has been particularly subjected to question. The National Bankruptcy Review Commission argued in 2000 that for small firms Chapter 11 is too long and costly. This line of argument is supported by statistics that reveal that Chapter 11 produces a far higher success rate for large firms than for small firms.[158]

Lengthy Chapter 11 proceedings give rise to further concerns. One often-voiced comment is that unhealthy distortions of competition can result in some markets. It has thus been argued that when seven US airlines filed for Chapter 11 protection in the 1990s they were able to keep capacity levels artificially high and slash fares to below-cost levels (since their creditors could not enforce). The healthy competitors of these airlines were, as a result, placed under extreme and unfair financial pressures.[159] The effect of long Chapter 11 moratoria has also been said to prevent insolvency law from fulfilling an important function: the weeding out of companies who use resources inefficiently so as to allow the redeployment of those resources for more efficient uses and to leave

---

[157] See Bradley and Rosenzweig, 'Untenable Case for Chapter 11'. On studies confirming a sharp increase (between 1994 and 2002) in the use of Chapter 11 for liquidation but which nevertheless report that 'equity owners still retain an interest going forward in a majority of cases', see J. Westbrook and E. Warren, 'Chapter 11: Conventional Wisdom and Reality' University of Texas Law, Public Law Research Paper No. 125, available at http://ssrn.com/abstract=1009242.

[158] A study by Edith Hotchkiss at Boston College, Massachusetts, examined 200 public companies that emerged from Chapter 11. She found 40 per cent to suffer from operating losses for the next three years and a third of the sample had to restructure their debt a second time, often under court protection: reported in Financial Times, 3 October 2001. Note, however, that amendments were made to small business bankruptcy cases by the BAPCPA 2005, e.g. the small business debtor now has a 180-day exclusivity period (50 per cent longer than the 120-day norm for other Chapter 11 cases): see Lewis, 'Corporate Rescue in the US'.

[159] See C. Daniel, 'Airlines Seek Shelter in a Storm', Financial Times, 19 October 2004; Galen, 'A New Page for Chapter 11?' p. 2. Franks and Torous also note 'serious concern' in the USA that Chapter 11 is used by some firms to secure competitive advantages: see Franks and Torous, 'Lessons from a Comparison', p. 463. Broude, however, cautions that a Chapter 11 filing may fail to produce a competitive advantage because, even when it reduces costs, it affects sales and market positions: 'you'll think twice before buying a laptop made or sold by a company that is in Chapter 11' ('How the Rescue Culture Came to the United States', p. 197). Other commentators have recounted how airlines in Chapter 11 in the early 1990s (for example, Continental, Pan American, Eastern) found that the Chapter 11 stigma discouraged passengers: 'Going Bust for Survival', Financial Times, 3 October 2001.

the field to those firms who are able to act efficiently. Here there is a contrast with the Canadian Companies' Creditors Arrangement Act (CCAA) under which the courts are more likely to terminate reorganisation proceedings at an early stage: for example, on failure to gain a creditors' vote.[160]

The DIP regime gives further grounds for concern. An important worry is that Chapter 11 allows existing managers to trigger the process. This renders Chapter 11 open to abuse as a device employed not for genuine reasons of reorganisation but in order to reap a market advantage or for another purpose. It has been suggested that Chapter 11 is open to use, *inter alia*, to settle tort liabilities or legal judgments; to reduce labour costs; to reject pensions obligations; or to resolve environmental damage liabilities.[161] The absence of an early scrutiny of the reorganisation plans by an independent professional (as in English administration) or a court (as in Canada) means, first, that 'abuses' of Chapter 11 for tactical reasons are not picked up and, second, that proposals that have no real chance of success are allowed to run. The latter scenario means that the early liquidation of non-viable companies is prevented. Where, as in Canada, there is more aggressive court screening of applications for protection, this not only brings more rapid liquidation in hopeless cases but also encourages the firm's managers to produce and disseminate, at an early date, a body of information about the financial condition of a debtor and a reasoned case for the proposal. This points to a further difficulty of DIP. It is the debtor who draws up financial statements in order to file for Chapter 11 and such a debtor may be liable to present a misleading picture of the company's profitability. Chapter 11 procedures

---

[160] See G. Triantis, 'The Interplay between Liquidation and Reorganisation in Bankruptcy: The Role of Screens, Gatekeepers and Guillotines' (1996) 16 *International Review of Law and Economics* 101 at 112. The BAPCPA 2005, as noted above, limited the DIP's ability to obtain potentially unlimited extensions to its initial 120-day exclusive period to file a plan: s. 1121(d) states that the period cannot extend beyond eighteen months from the order for relief. On corporate rescue procedures in Canada see Brown, *Corporate Rescue*, ch. 24; 'CCAA v Chapter 11', Cassels Brock, Business Reorganization Group e-communiqué, vol. 9, no. 5, June 2005. Canadian bankruptcy law has been undergoing reform: the amending Bill-C12 received the Royal Assent on 14 December 2007 and the new laws are predicted to come into force in December 2008.

[161] See Carruthers and Halliday, *Rescuing Business*, p. 266, and K. Delaney, *Strategic Bankruptcy: How Corporations and Creditors Use* Chapter 11 *to their Advantage* (University of California Press, Berkeley, 1989). 'The stark contrast between workers' losses and managers' gains was one reason for changes to Chapter 11 in the bankruptcy reforms [of the BAPCPA 2005]': J. Gapper, 'The Danger of Rewriting Chapter 11', *Financial Times*, 13 October 2005.

can be criticised as not creating, as in Canada, scrutiny processes that will favour the production of early, accurate information. This, in turn, conduces to a lack of trust and to higher litigation costs.

A further worry about Chapter 11 may seem exaggerated. To leave the old managers at the helm of a firm may be 'like leaving an alcoholic in charge of a pub'[162] but corporate troubles do not always stem from mismanagement and, where managers have performed poorly, creditor pressure in the USA will tend to have resulted in the introduction of new managers at an early stage of the reorganisation. The Chapter 11 process, as has been noted, tends to be associated with high managerial turnover and 'is not a safe haven for management'.[163]

In other respects, however, there may be cause for concern about the role of the managers under Chapter 11. Some commentators argue that such managers are poorly disciplined by the Chapter 11 regime.[164] A key objective of Chapter 11 is to solve problems of financial distress but the regime may be so soft on managers that it fails to correct the underlying inefficiencies of which the financial distress was a mere manifestation. If a regime gives strong rights to creditors (as English insolvency law does) those creditors will have an incentive to monitor managers and will be able to punish managerial slackness by demanding changes of underperforming staff. The same creditors will be able to prompt restructuring and asset divestments that enhance efficiency. Managers, in short, will be kept on their toes by the looming presence of the empowered creditor.[165] Chapter 11 may be said to blunt this disciplinary role of creditors by its orientation towards rescue rather than enforcement.

This point can, however, be exaggerated. As already noted, creditors in the USA can bring pressure to bear so as to institute managerial changes, and a number of other factors may give managers an incentive to act efficiently. Firms may operate salary schemes that incentivise efficiency, shareholders may monitor managers, and the market for corporate control, as well as that for managerial talent, may again create healthy

---

[162] Moss, 'Chapter 11', p. 19. For a comparison of the UK's management replacing scheme and the US's DIP approach see McCormack, 'Control and Corporate Rescue'.

[163] Carruthers and Halliday, *Rescuing Business*, p. 265; S. Gilson, 'Management Turnover and Financial Distress' (1989) 25 *Journal of Financial Economics* 241; LoPucki and Whitford, 'Corporate Governance'; Broude, 'How the Rescue Culture Came to the United States'.

[164] See e.g. Triantis, 'Interplay between Liquidation and Reorganisation', p. 104.

[165] Ibid.

incentives.[166] In relation to one worry, though, it is less easy to find reassurance. Chapter 11 may induce even operationally efficient managers to run unjustifiably high business risks. Within Chapter 11 the managers are liable to identify their interests with those of the equity holders and may be likely to indulge in speculative business actions. If these succeed, the benefits will flow to the shareholders but, if they fail, the creditors will bear the losses and the reorganised estate reduces in value. Managers have little to lose from such high-risk activity. In one reported US case the company officials sought to save the business by resorting to the gaming tables of Las Vegas.[167]

From an English perspective, there are perhaps three final reservations about Chapter 11.[168] The first is that the US Code gives the shareholders some role in the rescue process. Moss argues: 'Where in reality there is nothing properly left for shareholders this seems to enable them to use blocking tactics so as to extract value from the situation in which equitably they should receive none.'[169] It should be noted, however, that Chapter 11 is a procedure which is not triggered by insolvency or near insolvency, and it may accordingly be responded that shareholders do have a genuine interest until the point of insolvency arises. A way out of this problem would be to provide that where a Chapter 11 filing does happen to involve a company that is in insolvency or likely to become insolvent, the court should be empowered to reduce the role of the shareholders. A second reservation about Chapter 11 concerns the latter's complex system of classes: a system designed to offer protection to creditors who may suffer from cram-down. The US classes regime makes for a drawn-out process that is legalistic and does not conduce to the quick sale of a going concern: a position that sits oddly with Chapter 11's strong rescue orientation.[170]

---

[166] The BAPCPA 2005 introduced new scrutiny over, and limitations on, the circumstances in which debtors may pay senior managers bonuses (or KERPs – Key Employee Retention Plans) in order to induce them to remain with the company. The hope was to stop managers rewarding themselves excessively for working through Chapter 11 and to link any bonuses closely to the requirements of the company: see Lee and Bannister, 'Taming the Beast', p. 2. On posited unintended consequences of the reforms – 'The law reduces both the carrots given to managers and the sticks they wield without putting much in their place' – see Gapper, 'The Danger of Rewriting Chapter 11'.

[167] *Re Tri-State Paving*, discussed in Boshkoff and McKinney, 'Future of Chapter 11'.

[168] See Moss, 'Chapter 11'.   [169] Ibid., p. 18.

[170] For a view that Chapter 11 has lost its role as a device for the protection of equity, see J. Ayer, 'Goodbye to Chapter 11: The End of Business Bankruptcy as We Know It' (Mimeo, Institute of Advanced Legal Studies, 2001).

A final 'English' worry may relate to the tension in Chapter 11 between rescue of a company and rescue of a business. Preservation of the company may reflect a US concern to encourage investment in entrepreneurial enterprises but in England more emphasis might be placed on saving the business, preserving employment and protecting the wider business community from the fallout of an insolvency. English administrative receivership was (and still is where applicable)[171] well suited to rescuing the business alone and indeed, the post-Enterprise Act 2002 administration procedure prioritises rescuing the business in those circumstances where this will lead to a better result to creditors as a whole than either rescuing the company as a going concern or effecting a winding up.[172] There may, moreover, be good grounds for adopting this position, one of which may be that shareholders are liable to be lower-cost risk bearers than employees or business partners since, *inter alia*, they are liable to be able to spread risks and absorb losses more efficiently than the latter.

A look at the US position should not, however, blind us to the approaches that other jurisdictions adopt, nor should lessons be learned exclusively from the US experience. Other countries have their own special characteristics.[173] The South African system, for instance, relies very heavily on judicial supervision.[174] There is no floating charge in South Africa and no receivership, but the regime of judicial management involves the court appointment of an insolvency practitioner to take control of the business with the object of paying the company's debts and restoring the company to financial success. The process involves the courts throughout, with the master supervising the judicial manager and even calling creditors' meetings. The narrowness and expertise of this

---

[171] See Insolvency Act 1986 ss. 72A, 72B–72G and further ch. 8 below.

[172] See Insolvency Act 1986 Sch. B1, para. 3's 'hierarchy of objectives': M. Phillips and J. Goldring, 'Rescue and Reconstruction' (2002) *Insolvency Intelligence* 76. The effect of these provisions is that the administrator is not obliged to rescue the company at all costs – rescuing the company (as a going concern) gives way to other arrangements (e.g. rescue of the business or part thereof) if these would give a better result to creditors as a whole (see para. 3(3)(b)). On rescuing the business within the company and rescuing a 'balance sheet insolvent company' see further R. Stevens, 'Security after the Enterprise Act' in J. Getzler and J. Payne (eds.), *Company Charges: Spectrum and Beyond* (Oxford University Press, Oxford, 2006) pp. 155–7.

[173] See Sealy, 'Corporate Rescue Procedures'.

[174] On reform developments see further A. Loubser, 'South African Corporate Rescue' in Gromek Broc and Parry, *Corporate Rescue*, pp. 316–17. See also p. 315, where the author reviews the failings of judicial management as 'highlighted in a substantial number of publications'.

process has led most lawyers and businessmen to prefer to use the scheme of arrangement procedure that resembles that set out in the English Companies Act 2006 ss. 895–9.[175]

Many noteworthy features are, of course, shared by different regimes. The French and German systems, for instance, have a single entry point to the insolvency process and the company is then assessed for the most appropriate outcome.[176] This contrasts with the English system in which rescue procedures may be triggered by directors, floating charge holders or creditors according to a number of procedures. In some countries the rescue mechanism is triggered by petition to the court with the company having to be insolvent (as, for example, in Australia)[177] or likely to be insolvent (for example, in Germany and Ireland). In England there is a requirement of likely insolvency for some procedures, but the US Chapter 11 involves no requirement of current or near insolvency at all.[178]

Countries vary on the priority they give to rescue and the balance they effect between creditor and debtor interests. In Japan, for instance, equity and employees are a primary consideration and informal rescues rather than legal bankruptcy procedures are the norm.[179] Banks and trading partners with shares will usually attempt to effect a rescue, and commitments over a number of years are not uncommon. If, however, matters are resolved in court, the legal process looks to give returns to creditors. In Germany there is also a strong emphasis on the informal resolution of

---

[175] See Close Corporations Act 69 of 1984 s. 72: a special composition procedure that is more suitable for small businesses, being straightforward and less costly than judicial management. See Loubser, 'South African Corporate Rescue', p. 315.

[176] IS 2000, p. 39. On German insolvency reforms see E. Ehlers, 'Statutory Corporate Rescue Proceedings in Germany' in Gromek Broc and Parry, *Corporate Rescue*, p. 151. (At the time of writing, a bill to amend the insolvency code had been passed by the German Parliament.) On French insolvency reforms see P. J. Omar, 'Reforms to the Framework of Insolvency Law and Practice in France: 1999–2006' in Gromek Broc and Parry, *Corporate Rescue*, p. 111.

[177] On Australia see A. Keay, 'The Australian Voluntary Administration Regime' (1996) 9 *Insolvency Intelligence* 41; Keay, 'Australian Insolvency Law: The Latest Developments' (1998) 11 *Insolvency Intelligence* 57; P. Lewis, 'Trouble Down Under: Some Thoughts on the Australian–American Corporate Bankruptcy Divide' [2001] Utah L Rev. 189; *Corporate Insolvency Laws: A Stocktake* (Australian Joint Committee on Corporations and Financial Services, 30 June 2004) paras. 5.3–5.41. The Corporations Amendment (Insolvency) Act 2007 implemented a range of changes including amendments (aimed at addressing several technical issues) to the voluntary administration procedures: see Sch. 4 of the 2007 Act, Fine-tuning voluntary administration.

[178] IS 2000, p. 39.

[179] Brown, *Corporate Rescue*, pp. 831–2. See also H. Oda, 'Japan's Case for Reform', *Financial Times*, 6 October 1998.

problems and staying out of court by relying on support from the banks. Creditors in Germany may opt either for a straight liquidation, for a reorganisation or for a restructuring by transfer.[180] Creditors can veto any plans drawn up by the court and firm, but shareholders play no part in the process.

In France the law used to be hard on creditors. In the *redressement judiciaire* process a court-appointed official will help managers to draw up a plan and the law is directed towards the securing of jobs by keeping troubled firms alive. Creditors have no say over which plan the court accepts and the broad body of creditors have one representative (court-appointed) during negotiations. French law thus offers a stark contrast with English law which puts creditors first. The reforms of 2005, however, introduced a new rescue procedure – 'preservation' – where creditors *are* given a say in the approval of the rescue plan through the use of creditors' committees but only, it must be said, regarding businesses above a certain threshold.

It has been noted that as far as running the formal rescue process is concerned, English law places the insolvency practitioner in a prime position, whereas Chapter 11 can give the DIP a central role. Bankers, as floating charge holders, are also given leading insolvency roles in New Zealand,[181] Australia, Ireland and Sweden. The Irish and German regimes place the insolvency practitioner at centre stage, though in the glare of a judicial spotlight, and creditors make the final decision. In France the courts make the key decisions. Voting arrangements also vary markedly across regimes.[182] In English administration a simple majority of creditors (by value of claims) is required but in a company voluntary arrangement or a scheme of arrangement a 75 per cent by value majority is required.[183] In the USA a two-thirds majority of the value and number is required, whereas in Germany it is a simple majority. In Irish examinations the majority has to be numerical, representing also a 75 per cent majority by value of claims represented at the creditors' meeting. In France the court decides the final outcome, and in some countries (for

---

[180] See further Ehlers, 'Statutory Corporate Rescue Proceedings in Germany'.

[181] See D. Brown, 'Corporate Rescue in New Zealand' in Gromek Broc and Parry, *Corporate Rescue*, p. 262: 'Unlike the UK, New Zealand did not adopt the concept of an "administrative receiver" … the Receiverships Act 1993 (NZ) applies to all types of receiver, whether the grantor is personal or corporate, and whether out of court or appointed by the court.'

[182] See Omar, 'Reforms to the Framework of Insolvency Law and Practice in France'; Brown, *Corporate Rescue*, chs. 24 and 25.

[183] A majority in number voting is also required in a CVA.

example, the USA and Ireland) there is a process of cram-down, whereby the court can overturn the creditors' decision.[184]

Moratoria periods again differ. Chapter 11 involves an initial period of 120 days (with a maximum extension to eighteen months)[185] whereas in Australia it is twenty-eight days (extendable to sixty), in Ireland it is sixty-three days (extendable to ninety-three), and in Sweden it is typically a maximum of three months (extendable three-monthly to a year). New Zealand introduced a new business rehabilitation scheme for companies (voluntary administration) similar to the voluntary administration operating in Australia but with some flexibility regarding time periods.[186]

Finally, mention should be made of rescue financing and the provision made for this. In Chapter 11, post-petition financing and supplies can be obtained and priority given to their lender. Super-priority financing is also available in Germany, France, Australia, Sweden and New Zealand, but it is not available in England, although it was proposed by the DTI's Insolvency Service in 1993 and raised again in the business rescue mechanisms consultations in 1999–2000.[187]

To summarise this comparative sketch, other countries display a variety of players, processes and priorities in their insolvency and rescue regimes, but in all regimes certain difficult decisions have to be made on such matters as: Who controls corporate rescue operations? What sort of oversight regimes are appropriate? How should rescue needs be balanced against creditors' rights? Should rescue processes be triggered only on insolvency or near insolvency? Whose voices shall be heard in rescue procedures? Chapters 7–10 below examine how these issues and others are dealt with in England.

Conclusions

In the UK there is a greater stress than ever before on taking early steps to confront corporate troubles and to effect rescues and turnarounds before

---

[184] See IS 2000, Annex A.   [185] 11 USC s. 1121(d).

[186] The NZ Companies Amendment Act 2006 came into effect on 1 November 2007 making amendments to the NZ Companies Act 1993. On voluntary administration see now NZ Companies Act 1993 ss. 239A ff.

[187] DTI/IS, *Company Voluntary Arrangements and Administration Orders: A Consultative Document* (October 1993); IS 2000. On the extended, but ultimately fruitless, discussions on super-priority financing that preceded the Enterprise Act 2002 reforms see McCormack, 'Super-Priority New Financing'. See also ch. 9 below.

there is any need for formal actions. It has been noted, however, that the growth of the credit derivatives market may provide creditors with new options of risk management that cut against the broader trend to pursue rescue options. As for the evaluation of rescue procedures, these are processes that can be assessed in accordance with the measures set out in chapter 2 and, in making such evaluations, interests in addition to those of creditors have to be borne in mind. Rescues involve parties acting with very divergent concerns and interests and rescue processes often demand that important decisions be taken in the most difficult and urgent of circumstances. The procedures that are used in attempts to turn companies around might, accordingly, be expected to be open to serious question when assessments of legitimacy are made. Such assessments demand that the particulars of different rescue arrangements – informal and formal – be dealt with and these are considered in the chapters that follow.

7

Informal rescue

For most troubled companies, entering into formal insolvency procedures is a course of last resort only to be pursued when informal
strategies have been exhausted. Informal procedures, as noted in chapter
6, will often prove more attractive than formal steps and stakeholders will
hope that informality may avoid the negative consequences that are often
the result of commencing an Insolvency Act process.[1] Those consequences may include: the precipitation of contractual breaches across
financing arrangements; liquidations of collateral;[2] rating agency
devaluations; shocks to market confidence; reductions in employee morale; and reputational harms to brands and directors as individuals.
Informal processes are likely to offer more flexibility than statutory
arrangements and they will be more amenable to the early and proactive
involvement of major creditors. They also offer a less confrontational
forum for 'marketplace' negotiations than many a formal procedure.[3]

It is understandable, accordingly, that informal strategies of various
forms are of increasing importance to companies and their advisers.
Different modes of informal action are reviewed in this chapter but,
before looking at particular approaches, it is worth considering the
different parties that may be interested in an informal rescue and the
stages of events that commonly lead up to the selection of an informal
rescue strategy.

---

[1] See J. Armour, 'Should We Redistribute in Insolvency?' in J. Getzler and J. Payne (eds.),
Company Charges: Spectrum and Beyond (Oxford University Press, Oxford, 2006) p. 219;
G. Meeks and J. G. Meeks, 'Self-fulfilling Prophecies of Failure' (Judge Business School
Working Paper, Cambridge, 2004).

[2] On the destructive propensity of asset-based lenders to seek to liquidate collateral when
they hear of a company's difficulties (and the problems of controlling such creditors) see
Armour, 'Should We Redistribute in Insolvency?', p. 219.

[3] On advantages of informality see P. Omar, 'The Convergence of Creditor-Driven and
Formal Insolvency Models' (2005) 2 *International Corporate Rescue* 251; World Bank
Insolvency Initiative, Symposium Paper No. 6, Section 8 'Informal Insolvency Practices'
(World Bank, Washington D.C., 1999); European High Yield Association (EHYA),
Submission on Insolvency Law Reform (EHYA, London, 2007) pp. 3–4.

Who rescues?

When a company encounters problems it has long been the paradigm that informal rescue processes are started when its major creditor, the bank, becomes concerned and starts to take action – either by making enquiries of the directors or by taking a more hands-on approach to overseeing managerial performance. It was noted above, indeed, that the banks have recently taken the 'rescue culture' to heart and many of them have established teams of specialists that are dedicated to the provision of turnaround services to debtor companies.[4] As discussed in chapter 3, however, the last decade has seen radical changes in the credit market and the arrival of new actors with fresh interests in troubled companies.

Three significant changes are to be highlighted. First, alternative lenders of different kinds have burst onto the market to supplement (and often to supplant) the banks. These include the hedge funds,[5] private equity groups, investment banks and distressed debt investors. It is now the case that a troubled company's fate is increasingly dependent on a hedge fund rather than a traditional bank.[6] Second, underperforming companies that seek liquidity can now choose from a huge range of debt financing options including asset-backed lending, subordinated debt products (e.g. mezzanine debt) and debt capital market products (e.g. high-yield bonds). Third, the rate at which debts are sold means that the group of lenders with interests in a rescue may well be fluid during the rescue or restructuring process and that various investors in debt will see their debt in a very different way from traditional bank lenders.[7]

---

[4] See ch. 6 above. See also J. Franks and O. Sussman, 'Financial Distress and Bank Restructuring of Small to Medium Size UK Companies' (2005) 9 *Review of Finance* 65: the average company in the sample spent seven-and-a-half months with the banks' Business Support Units (BSUs) and somewhere between half to three-quarters of these companies emerged from the BSU without going into formal insolvency proceedings (pp. 76–7); Armour, 'Should We Redistribute in Insolvency?' p. 212.

[5] In the USA the hedge funds now dominate trading in US distressed debt: see J. Drummond and C. Batchelor, 'Hedge Funds See Influence Grow', *Financial Times*, 18 November 2005. On UK companies being a growing target for hedge fund activism see Thomson Financial Survey (November 2007), cited in C. Hughes, 'Hedge Funds Home In on UK Targets', *Financial Times*, 5 November 2007.

[6] See L. Verrill, 'ILA President's Column' (2007) *Insolvency Intelligence* 112 (on how 'the market is now dominated by hedge, vulture or "opportunity" funds and private equity houses').

[7] See D. Madoc-Jones and N. Smith, 'Brave New World' (2007) *Recovery* (Summer) 18.

It has been the commodification of credit that has driven changes in the body of rescue-interested actors. Banks have increasingly sold their loans to outside investors, such as hedge funds, and non-bank investors have joined lending syndicates. In the case of riskier European companies, non-banks can now account for up to 80 per cent of the loan finance in private equity deals.[8] The growth of the European bond market in the 1990s introduced a new group of unsecured creditors to large-scale insolvencies and rescues. Unlike the traditional dispersed unsecured creditors, bondholders are now willing and able to participate in rescues of troubled companies.[9] Until recently, corporate bonds were generally held by long-term investors such as pension funds and life assurance companies but now such papers are traded and often used by hedge funds and banks' proprietary trading desks who are exploiting trades that combine bonds and credit derivatives.

Hedge funds and private equity groups[10] have, by such processes, become increasingly important players in the rescue game.[11] Such funds and groups can bring positive qualities to potential rescue scenarios. They tend to be driven by rational profit-directed motives and are able to act quickly (notably to raise funds) in order to institute remedial steps such as restructurings. They tend to be faster moving than the more heavily regulated and more bureaucratic banks. They would also claim to be more flexible in approach, less constrained regarding allowable types of investment and more creative concerning rescues and restructuring than banks.[12] Overall, their proponents would say that they increase general liquidity and improve rescue prospects.[13] The critics of hedge

---

[8] See G. Tett and C. Hughes, 'When Time Runs Out', *Financial Times*, 7 December 2006.

[9] See J. Roome, 'The Unwelcome Guest' (2004) *Recovery* (Summer) 30.

[10] 'Hedge fund' is not a legally defined term but most hedge funds tend to have the following characteristics: they are investment funds in which managers deploy investors' capital; they are subject to little regulation; they may leverage their investments; they invest more freely than regulated mutual funds; and managers share in the fund returns. See T. Hurst, 'Hedge Funds in the 21st Century' (2007) 28 Co. Law. 228. On the likelihood of private equity firms 'with a stomach for risk' making 'a killing' in restructurings and subsequent sales if the debt of companies in distress falls below its fair value see P. Davies, H. Sender and C. Hughes, 'Restructuring Enters a Brave New World', *Financial Times*, 5 February 2008.

[11] Hedge funds are said to represent 35 per cent of the primary leveraged European loan market: see STP, 'Corporate Restructuring in Europe' (STP, London, 2 March 2006).

[12] Tett and Hughes, 'When Time Runs Out'.

[13] See M. Prangley, 'Providing Support to Management in a Highly Leveraged Market' (2007) *Recovery* (Summer) 26. The supplanting of the banks in US rescues has been said to have increased rates of rescue: see Tett and Hughes, 'When Time Runs Out'.

funds would counter that the long-term effects of such funds' highly leveraged and short-term approaches may be uncertain and may include the generation of high levels of systemic risk within financial markets.[14] On the accusation of short-termism, private equity firms would say that they differ from hedge funds in so far as the latter take a short-term, or trader's, view of the company whereas private equity looks for a longer relationship with the company (typically three to seven years before resale).[15] Private equity firms also claim to differ from hedge funds by bringing to the table not only cash but the skills required to restructure the business successfully.[16]

Such developments may be welcomed for bringing liquidity and creativity to the rescue process but the involvement of a host of new parties in rescue processes may have a downside. The buyers and sellers of credit – as discussed above – are joined, within turnarounds, by a number of other types of organisation with various rescue interests and roles. Noteworthy here are credit insurers and turnaround advisory firms. Co-ordinating a rescue when such numbers of organisations are involved may present challenges – especially when the group of interested parties is not constant but is subject to change.[17] In such a fragmented world of competitive credit (and often high leveraging) the power of the lenders to impose traditional banking covenants on deals is weakened as is the ability of key lenders to step in early and insist that the company takes certain steps to deal with its troubles.[18] The challenges of co-ordinating different types of creditors may, furthermore, be compounded because such holders of debt may have very different objectives in mind when looking at the troubled company. They may have different operating methods, values and assumptions and they may operate to different timescales.[19] Thus, a hedge fund with a second-lien loan and a share of equity may have different motives and modes of operating from a bank or holder of bond derivatives. Similarly, banks may be concerned to

---

[14] See Hurst, 'Hedge Funds'.

[15] For a counter-view, arguing that some hedge funds do take the longer view and are managerially active, see R. Tett and B. Jones, 'Hedge Funds – A Fad or Here to Stay?' (2007) *Recovery* (Summer) 22.

[16] See C. Bodie, 'How Private Equity Can Help to Rescue Companies' (2007) *Recovery* (Summer) 28; J. Bickle, 'Private Equity Investors and the Transformation of Troubled Businesses' (2006) *Recovery* (Summer) 28.

[17] See J. Wilman, 'Rescuers Armed with New Ideas', *Financial Times*, 19 March 2007; Prangley, 'Providing Support to Management'.

[18] Prangley, 'Providing Support to Management'.

[19] See EHYA, *Submission on Insolvency Law Reform*.

restructure in a controlled manner so as to leave debts on balance sheets rather than to take equity, whereas bondholders may look to reduce debt levels and maximise creditor recoveries through their equity holdings in businesses with lowered gearings.[20] As Chris Laughton has said of the purchasers of distressed debt: 'Some of them will be prepared to take a medium (or occasionally long) term view ... but many look for a quick gain. For these investors, operational turnaround is much less valuable than their deal gain on balance sheet restructuring.'[21]

Credit trading may also induce the banks to depart markedly from their traditional stances – and in a manner that, again, may reduce rescue options because of divergent interests. As noted in chapter 6, a reported complexity that emerged in the 2002 Marconi rescue effort was that some banks had used credit derivatives to lay off risk so that they could potentially gain more from Marconi defaulting than from agreeing to a restructuring.[22] Hu and Black have said, indeed, that the 'uncoupling' of creditor and company interests may routinely occur when there is trading in credit default swaps (CDSs) and that, as a result of such trading, creditors may possess incentives to vote against a rescue plan.[23] In such situations, derivative trading by some banks but not others may mean not only that the banks have different interests from other groups of creditors but also that not all banks will have consistent interests.[24]

Co-ordination difficulties may also be exacerbated because, as noted in chapter 3, the modern credit derivatives market does not render interests transparent. Various parties (who may be difficult to identify) may hold hugely complex combinations of interests (in, for instance, intricate mixtures of bonds, equity shares and other forms of paper). This may mean that such parties' positions are difficult to assess and that deals and compromises have to be devised by expert intermediaries who may find it difficult to locate all the interested parties and to persuade them that the proposed deal is the

---

[20] Roome, 'Unwelcome Guest'.

[21] C. Laughton, 'Editorial' (2007) *Recovery* (Summer) 2.

[22] See J. Gapper, 'The Winners and Losers of the Restructure', *Financial Times*, 2 November 2004.

[23] See H. Hu and B. Black, 'Equity and Debt Decoupling and Empty Voting 11: Importance and Extensions' (2008) 156 *University of Pennsylvania Law Review* 625; and the discussion in ch. 6 above.

[24] See N. Frome and C. Brown, *Lessons from the Marconi Restructuring* (IFLR, September 2003) p. 19.

best available settlement.[25] It will be seen below that such co-ordination challenges have a dramatic effect on the potential of certain strategies for effecting turnarounds and rescues – such as the London Approach.[26]

The stages of informal rescue

Assessing the prospects

There are seldom clearly identifiable times in corporate life when rescue steps are required. As noted in chapter 4, the financial state of a company can be thought of as a portrait painted by accountants or company directors, a picture that may reflect a variety of 'calculative technologies', disciplinary perspectives and even sets of negotiations.[27] Different actors, moreover, may play key roles in setting up rescues. As suggested, it is traditionally a firm's bank that initiates turnaround steps.[28] In the modern world of complex debt, however, the scenario may be quite different. The earliest signs of trouble may become apparent first to the hedge funds, investment banks and others who are swiftest to notice that a company's high-yield debt has started to trade at below par; or that the rating agencies have downgraded the relevant paper; or that the credit insurers have tightened supply lines.[29] The market may then develop its own momentum as the company's own 'relationship' bank may start to sell its senior debt, the credit market loses confidence, and unfriendly buyers start to purchase controlling positions in the debt structure.

A firm's own directors may also institute actions.[30] They may call in firms of accountants to act as company doctors or specialist corporate

---

[25] See G. Tett, 'GUS Saga Shows the Tide is Turning', *Financial Times*, 15 November 2006, and A. Sakoui, 'The Delicate Task of Restructuring Lehman Begins', *Financial Times*, 27 October 2008.

[26] See pp. 311–14 below.

[27] See P. Miller and M. Power, 'Calculating Corporate Failure' in Y. Dezalay and D. Sugarman (eds.), *Professional Competition and Professional Power: Lawyers, Accountants and the Social Construction of Markets* (Routledge, London, 1995).

[28] R3's Ninth Survey of Business Recovery in the UK reported in 2001 that when insolvency professionals were brought into a firm to carry out turnaround work such a step was instigated by a secured lender in 60 per cent of cases. See also R. Bingham, 'Poacher Turned Gamekeeper' (2003) *Recovery* (Winter) 27 (stating that it is usually the banks that call in interim turnaround executives).

[29] See A. Wollaston, 'The Growing Importance of Debt in European Corporate Transactions' (2005) 18 *Insolvency Intelligence* 145–9.

[30] On the difficulties that directors may encounter in dealing with the credit derivatives market see ibid.

troubleshooters may be consulted. Directors have been said to be responsible for appointing turnaround IPs in a fifth of cases.[31] There are particular dangers to be borne in mind by directors when rescue measures are under consideration. They must look to their potential legal liabilities and must act consistently with their obligations. These are reviewed in chapter 16 but will be noted in outline here.[32]

The first of four main areas of concern is the director's potential liability for wrongful trading under section 214 of the Insolvency Act 1986, which requires directors to monitor the financial position of the company and when they conclude, or should conclude, that there is no reasonable prospect of their company avoiding insolvent liquidation they must take every step which a reasonably diligent person would take to minimise potential loss to the company's creditors. If, after a company has entered insolvent liquidation, a court considers a director has failed to discharge such a duty, it may require the director to make such contributions to the company's assets as it thinks fit.[33] What matters for such purposes is not the actual knowledge of the director but the knowledge that might reasonably be expected of a person carrying out the director's particular functions in the company. In the rescue context, directors must consider the prospects of avoiding insolvent liquidation and, if they are unsure of the position, must take heed of their duties to minimise potential losses to creditors and, when necessary, must cease trading and commence suitable insolvency procedures. A special concern of directors will, accordingly, be whether any agreed arrangement will allow debts to be paid as they fall due and whether projected cash flows and incomes will allow rescheduled loan payments to be met.

Under the Insolvency Act 1986, liability for wrongful trading (under section 214) applies not merely to directors but also to shadow directors, who are defined in section 251 as persons 'in accordance with whose directions or instructions the directors of the company are accustomed

---

[31] R3, Ninth Survey (2001).

[32] See N. Segal, 'Rehabilitation and Approaches other than Formal Insolvency Procedures' in R. Cranston (ed.), *Banks and Remedies* (Oxford University Press, Oxford, 1992) p. 133.

[33] See Insolvency Act 1986 s. 214(1). Such jurisdiction was deemed to be primarily compensatory in *Re Produce Marketing Consortium Ltd* [1989] 5 BCC 569; compare the discussion in ch. 16 below.

to act'.[34] A stakeholder may be treated as a shadow director if they exercise 'real influence' over the board[35] and in the case of *Becker*[36] emphasis was placed on proving that the *de jure* directors followed a consistent pattern of compliance with the instructions of the putative shadow.

When a bank exercises 'intensive care' over a distressed company it accordingly runs risks. It may be deemed a shadow director if, at a time of threatening insolvency, it gives 'directions or instructions' to the client company, as distinct from giving professional advice or merely imposing conditions for making or continuing a loan.[37] There is evidence, however, that some judges may sympathise with the bank's good intentions. Thus, in *Re PFTZM Ltd, Jourdain* v. *Paul*[38] Judge Baker QC stated that a bank was unlikely to be treated as a shadow director, even where it exercised a considerable degree of control over the management of the company, when its actions were motivated by a desire to protect its position. Milman has cautioned, however, that such comments were *obiter dicta* and that 'this is a questionable proposition in that it appears to confuse objective conduct with the subjective motivation behind such actions'.[39]

Nor is the position of the independent consultant to a troubled company one that precludes uncertainty.[40] A professional adviser acting strictly in that capacity is exempt from categorisation as a shadow

---

[34] Based on the definition in the Companies Act 2006 s. 251. Shadow directors will not merely be liable for wrongful trading, they could also be subject to a number of provisions, notably those requiring disclosure or controlling certain types of transaction: see Companies Act 2006 ss. 187(1)–(4), 188(7), 223(1), 230; Insolvency Act 1986 ss. 206 (3), 214(7). (This section builds on V. Finch, 'The Recasting of Insolvency Law' (2005) 68 MLR 713.) See also ch. 16 below.

[35] See *Secretary of State for Trade and Industry* v. *Deverell* [2001] Ch 340, [2000] 2 BCLC 133. See D. Milman, 'A Fresh Light on Shadow Directors' [2000] Ins. Law. 171; J. Payne, 'Casting Light into the Shadows: *Secretary of State for Trade and Industry* v. *Deverell*' (2001) 22 Co. Law. 90; S. Griffin, [2003] 54 NILQ 43. See also *Re Hydrodan (Corby) Ltd* [1994] BCC 161.

[36] *Secretary of State for Trade and Industry* v. *Becker* [2003] 1 BCLC 555. See S. Griffin, 'Evidence Justifying a Person's Capacity as Either a *De Facto* or Shadow Director: *Secretary of State for Trade and Industry* v. *Becker*' [2003] Ins. Law. 127.

[37] See *Re A Company (No. 005009 of 1987), ex p. Copp* [1988] 4 BCC 424.

[38] [1995] BCC 280.

[39] D. Milman, 'Strategies for Regulating Managerial Performance in the Twilight Zone' [2004] JBL 493, 495–6.

[40] See P. Godfrey, 'The Turnaround Practitioner – Advisor or Director?' (2002) 18 IL&P 3.

director[41] but it is clear from *Re Tasbian Ltd (No. 3)*[42] that a company doctor or management consultant may in certain circumstances be deemed a shadow director. In that decision, the Court of Appeal held that there was an arguable case sufficient to go to trial, that an accountant, brought in to advise a troubled company as a consultant and company doctor, was a shadow director, having allegedly gone further than merely acting as a watchdog or adviser.

Such legal questions, nevertheless, do not constitute insuperable impediments to a new focus on preventative measures. The courts have yet to hold a bank to be a shadow director for exercising 'intensive care'. It would be a mistake, moreover, to confuse the timing of, say, a bank's intervention in the management of a company with the intensity and breadth of that intervention. Provided that bank monitoring, scrutiny and advice do not constitute directions or instructions that the directors follow in a consistent pattern, the lenders will not be liable as shadow directors. It is arguable, furthermore, that the courts might well see themselves as having no especially strong reasons for holding banks to account as shadow directors when lenders exercise 'intensive care'.[43] The purpose of the Insolvency Act 1986 section 214 wrongful trading provision is primarily to stop directors from continuing to trade during troubled times so that unjustifiable risks are run at the creditors' expense.[44] There is, accordingly, little cause to hold the major lender to account if the funds at risk were largely their own and if there is evidence that rescue attempts were for the benefit of creditors as a whole. There is a case, perhaps, for holding banks liable under section 214 when there is evidence that the bank's actions as a shadow director prejudiced the interests of other creditors – for example, unsecured creditors.[45] Should

---

[41] Companies Act 2006 s. 251(2); Insolvency Act 1986 s. 251: 'a person is not deemed a shadow director by reason only that the directors act on advice given by him in a professional capacity' (the wording is the same in both sections).

[42] [1992] BCC 358. See O. Drennan (1993) 8 IL&P 176 for comment; and Milman, 'Strategies', p. 496.

[43] On reasons for deeming a party to be a shadow director and the link with mischiefs see *Deverell* where Morritt LJ stated that the definition of a shadow director was to be construed in a normal way to give effect to the parliamentary intention ascertainable from the mischief to be dealt with and the words used: [2000] 2 BCLC 133, 144–5.

[44] See Cork Report, ch. 44; V. Finch, 'Directors' Duties: Insolvency and the Unsecured Creditor' in A. Clarke (ed.), *Current Issues in Insolvency Law* (Stevens, London, 1991).

[45] The bank may, for instance, be found to have brought undue pressure on the directors to cease certain operations where continuing those activities would have improved returns to unsecured creditors without significantly increasing risks to the bank. It is to be expected that the courts would not be quick to hold banks liable as shadow directors

the courts endorse such reasoning, the legal constraints on *ex ante* approaches to insolvency risk management may not prove daunting in most cases since the bank will often be the main creditor and potential liabilities will be relatively small.

It should also be borne in mind that even if it does act as a shadow director, the bank will only be liable for wrongful trading under the Insolvency Act 1986 section 214(2)(b) if it continues to act as a shadow director after it knew, or ought to have concluded, that there was no reasonable prospect that the company would avoid going into insolvent liquidation.[46] Few banks, it is to be expected, will continue to put resources into intensive care after the point when liquidation has become inevitable.

A second area of directors' concern will be their potential liability for fraudulent trading under section 213 of the Insolvency Act 1986. Directors, under this provision, may be liable to make contributions to the company's assets where it appears, in the case of the winding up of the company, that any business has been carried on with intent to defraud creditors or for any fraudulent purpose. Criminal liability may also be involved.[47] Fraudulent trading will thus be engaged in when a director obtains credit for the company when he knows that there is no good reason for thinking that funds will be available for repayment when due or shortly thereafter.[48]

A third area of relevant directorial worry relates to the general fiduciary duty of a director to act bona fide in the interests of the company, a duty that requires consideration of the interests of creditors as well as shareholders.[49] Where rescue arrangements are under discussion,

---

where doing so would chill the provision of rescue funding by creating expectations of liability or uncertainties for banks. There is some evidence that when companies are in 'intensive care' the banks tend to reduce their exposure to the debtors with the effect that, in 25 per cent of failures, the trade creditors would tend to be more exposed: see J. Franks and O. Sussman, 'The Cycle of Corporate Distress, Rescue and Dissolution: A Study of Small and Medium Size UK Companies', IFA Working Paper 306 (2000) pp. 16–19.

[46] On the time at which a party 'knew or ought to have concluded' etc., see *Re Continental Assurance Co. of London plc* [2001] All ER 229, [2001] BPIR 733; *Liquidator of Marini Ltd* v. *Dickenson: sub nom. Marini Ltd, Re* [2004] BCC 172 (Ch). See further ch. 16 below.

[47] Companies Act 2006 s. 993; *R* v. *Grantham* [1984] 2 WLR 815; *Morphitis* v. *Bernasconi* [2003] Ch 552.

[48] *R* v. *Grantham* [1984] 2 WLR 815.

[49] *Liquidators of West Mercia Safety Wear Ltd* v. *Dodd* [1988] 4 BCC 30. See further ch. 16 below; Finch, 'Directors' Duties: Insolvency and the Unsecured Creditor'; Finch, 'Directors' Duties Towards Creditors' (1989) 10 Co. Law. 23; Finch, 'Creditors' Interests and Directors' Obligations' in S. Sheikh and W. Rees (eds.), *Corporate Governance and Corporate Control* (Cavendish, London, 1995). See also Companies Act 2006 s. 172(3).

directors must remember that their fiduciary duty relates to all creditors' interests, not merely those of the dominant creditors who may be those principally engaged in negotiating a rescue.

Finally, directors should consider whether a rescue arrangement may render them liable to disqualification from being a company director. A court must disqualify a director where it is satisfied that he or she was a director or shadow director of a company which has become insolvent and it is satisfied that his or her conduct as a director is such that he or she is unfit to be involved in the management of the company.[50] When companies are in trouble, the real risks on this front tend to arise when directors hold creditors at bay while rescue options are reviewed or repay some debts rather than others for strategic reasons.[51]

The alarm stage

First alarms are often sounded in companies when it is not possible to find the cash to pay immediate bills.[52] The company directors may then raise the issue of rescue steps or a creditor may do this: as where a bank sees that overdraft limits are being exceeded unacceptably and expresses its concerns. A meeting will usually be called at this stage and major creditors will discuss issues with directors. At this point a Governor of the Bank of England has suggested that three things are often evident.[53] The first is that no one, including the company, has a sufficiently complete and robust picture of the company's financial position to make a soundly based decision on its future.[54] Secondly, the amount of debt, including off-balance-sheet items and the number of creditors, is usually larger than anybody supposed and, thirdly, the creditors often find that they have divergent interests.

A further form of alarm may be voiced in the new world of credit derivatives – the directors of a company may start to receive calls and emails from aggressive lenders, with whom they probably have never had any prior contact. Those lenders will have been prompted by their

---

[50] Company Directors' Disqualification Act 1986 s. 6. See V. Finch, 'Disqualifying Directors: Issues of Rights, Privileges and Employment' (1993) Ins. LJ 35; and ch. 16 below.

[51] See Re Sevenoaks Stationers Retail Ltd [1990] BCC 765.

[52] See Segal, 'Rehabilitation and Approaches', p. 147.

[53] Ibid., quoting the Governor's Special Report, 25 October 1990.

[54] On the importance of 'quality information' and 'robust planning' in rescue see J. Dewhirst, 'Turnabout Tourniquet' (2003) Financial World 56.

observations of the credit market to ask the directors a series of difficult questions about the company's cash flows and its ability to make future payments to, and maintain covenants with, the holders of senior debt.[55]

The evaluation stage

When the company's major creditors have become appraised of the company's position there usually follows a period in which urgent attempts are made to identify the nature and extent of a firm's problems and to assess the prospects of turnaround.[56] At this time, deadlines for action vary from case to case but may be very tight and the main pressures on the company are likely to stem from cash flow problems and threats of actions by creditors. Attention will be paid to means of securing a breathing space that will allow the company to regroup and, accordingly, to sources of financing that will cover immediate needs and to gaining the co-operation of creditors. Here it should be emphasised that informal rescues require the unanimous consent of affected creditors[57] and that this may often be difficult to obtain. Where, for example, a good deal of debt is owed to diverse sets of debt holders or to trade creditors who are heterogeneous and not amenable to (or capable of) negotiating rescue agreements, informal solutions will be difficult to achieve.[58] Where, in contrast, debts are owed to small numbers of sophisticated lenders such as banks, the prospects of informal resolutions are brighter. To this end, it is commonly necessary to bring major creditors together and to seek to co-ordinate actions. Where appropriate, the creditors will agree to a period of grace in which existing credit lines are maintained and, if necessary, extra funds are provided for an interim period.

Analysis of the company's state will proceed apace during this period and parties will explore such issues as the reasons for the company's decline, the severity of the problems encountered, the extent of the viable core of the business, the human resources available to the company and the state of relevant markets and positions within these.[59] Financial

---

[55] Wollaston, 'Growing Importance', p. 149.
[56] Ibid., pp. 148–9; C. Campbell and B. Underdown, *Corporate Insolvency in Practice: An Analytical Approach* (Chapman, London, 1991) pp. 62–5.
[57] A. Belcher, *Corporate Rescue* (Sweet & Maxwell, London, 1997) p. 116.
[58] S. C. Gilson, K. John and L. H. P. Lang, 'Troubled Debt Restructurings: An Empirical Study of Private Reorganisation of Firms in Default' (1990) 27 *Journal of Financial Economics* 323.
[59] Campbell and Underdown, *Corporate Insolvency*, p. 62.

reviews of the whole company will be undertaken, including an audit of each of the functions carried out by the company.

Such an evaluation will frequently be carried out by investigating accountants who will usually be nominated by the lead bank. The overall aim is to identify the company's potential for survival and the steps that have to be taken to produce turnaround. Company directors at such a time will not, however, be inactive. They will continue to manage the company's affairs and will usually have been asked to prepare business plans and sets of proposals for dealing with the company's difficulties. The investigating accountants have a role in considering such business plans and both the investigators and creditors will focus on whether the critical ingredients for successful turnaround are to be encountered in the company. These parties will examine whether the managers are sufficiently able, motivated and decisive to effect a rescue, whether there is a core of business that is strong enough to found restoration of corporate fortunes and whether necessary changes can be made within the available timescales.[60]

Towards the end of the evaluation stage, there will occur a review by the rescuing bank or banks.[61] This review will consider the report of the investigating accountants together with the managers' business plan. Discussions with investigators and managers will be conducted and the banks will attempt not only to assess the prospects for company turn-around but also to produce some consistency and co-ordination of approach between the various banks. They will thus come to terms with issues of priorities between creditors in relation to recoveries and also with the banks' collective position. Key issues in relation to the latter are whether additional security should be taken, whether new financial facilities should be provided and whether equity interests should be exchanged for debt.[62]

Agreeing recovery plans

If action at the preceding stages suggests that the prospects of recovery are good, plans for recovery will be devised and agreement on these sought. If the senior creditors are banks, the company will be likely to

---

[60] Ibid., p. 61. See also J. Wilding, 'Instructing Investigating Accountants' (1994) 7 *Insolvency Intelligence* 3.

[61] See A. Lickorish, 'Debt Rescheduling' (1990) 6 IL&P 38, 41.

[62] Ibid.

have agreed with them the terms on which finances will be made available during the support period and on which new securities will be offered. A support agreement will set out relevant provisions. The creditors will also have made settlements between themselves covering, for instance, the sharing of losses and recoveries and the interest rates appropriate.

When recovery objectives and strategies are drawn up by managers and advisers, they must be supported by creditors and also by other key players beyond the company. The assent of a major customer or supplier may, for example, have to be secured if a recovery is to have a prospect of success. Increasingly, in the modern era, it may be necessary to persuade the hedge funds or other holders of credit instruments to agree to a course of action – and the company may rely heavily on the services of a turnaround professional or other restructuring/corporate recovery specialist in seeking to secure such agreements.[63]

A particular response to multi-bank support for companies with liquidity problems was developed in London in the 1970s and became known as the 'London Approach'.[64] The Bank of England identified, at that time, a need to co-ordinate discussions among banks with loans outstanding to firms in difficulty. For broad economic reasons, the Bank wanted to avoid unnecessary receiverships and liquidations and to preserve viable jobs and productive capacity.[65] The principles of the London Approach were established in 1990 and the process has operated entirely informally on the basis of a set of principles providing a framework for bank support.[66] There is, by design, no formal code or

---

[63] See J. Willman, 'Rescuers Armed With New Ideas', *Financial Times*, 19 March 2007. For a case study of turnaround see R. Pugh, 'Turnaround of Dartington Group Limited' (2007) *Recovery* (Autumn) 20. See also ch. 6 above.

[64] See J. Flood, R. Abbey, E. Skordaki and P. Aber, *The Professional Restructuring of Corporate Rescue: Company Voluntary Arrangements and the London Approach*, ACCA Research Report 45 (ACCA, London, 1995); J. Flood, 'Corporate Recovery: The London Approach' (1995) 11 IL&P 82; Belcher, *Corporate Rescue*, pp. 117–22; J. Armour and S. Deakin, 'Norms in Private Insolvency Procedures: The "London Approach" to the Resolution of Financial Distress', ESRC Centre for Business Research, Working Paper Series No. 173, September 2000, reprinted in [2001] 1 JCLS 21; R. Obank, 'European Recovery Practice and Reform: Part I' [2000] Ins. Law. 149, 151–2; P. Brierley and G. Vlieghe, 'Corporate Workouts, the London Approach and Financial Stability' [1999] *Financial Stability Review* 168.

[65] Flood *et al.*, *Professional Restructuring*, p. 27.

[66] See now the guiding principles set out in the British Bankers' Association, 'Description of the London Approach' (Mimeo, 1996).

list of rules[67] and the approach relies on consensus, persuasion and banking collegiality in order to reconcile the interests of different creditors to a company in difficulty.[68] The process involves four phases. First comes a standstill covering all debt owed and all bank lenders must give support at this stage. Second, the bank sends in an investigating accountant (who will not be the company's auditors). Third, the lead bank negotiates with the other banks in order to secure new facilities for the company (which are generally accorded priority) and, finally, where negotiations are successful, a new financing agreement for the company is put into effect and is monitored.

The London Approach has been said to have four main tenets:[69] the banks are supportive and do not rush to appoint receivers; information is shared amongst all parties to the workout; banks and other creditors work in a co-ordinated fashion to reach a collective view on whether and how a company shall be given financial support; and pain is shared on an equal basis. London Approach proposals typically provide that the banks share the benefits of the rescue and the costs of the restructuring process *pro rata* to their outstanding exposure at the time when the banks agree to desist from enforcement actions against the debtor company.

In favour of the London Approach, it can be said to provide an efficient means of rescue that avoids the delays and expense of formal actions. Central to the Approach has been the role of the Bank of England in facilitating the emergence of an agreed course of action by the banks. The Bank has acted as a neutral intermediary and chairman and has used its authority to push discussions through banks' hierarchies. Informal pressures can also be exerted by the Bank of England where the banks are proving difficult. Most lending agreements contain covenants that require the unanimous agreement of creditor banks to the kind of changes of repayment practice that rescues usually demand. This means that one recalcitrant bank can threaten to vote against a rescue proposal and put the company at issue into receivership unless the other

---

[67] The Bank published the approach through a number of papers by Bank officials: see P. Kent, 'The London Approach' (1993) 8 *Journal of International Banking Law* 81–4; Kent, 'The London Approach: Distressed Debt Trading' (1994) *Bank of England Quarterly Bulletin* 110; Kent, 'Corporate Workouts: A UK Perspective' (1997) 6 *International Insolvency Review* 165.

[68] See C. Bird, 'The London Approach' (1996) 12 IL&P 87; R. Floyd, 'Corporate Recovery: The London Approach' (1995) 11 IL&P 82; D. Weston, 'The London Rules and Debt Restructuring' (1992) Sol. Jo. 216.

[69] Belcher, *Corporate Rescue*, p. 118; Kent, 'London Approach: Distressed Debt Trading', p. 110.

banks repay its own loan.[70] Such a stance would prejudice the rescue, but the Bank of England under the London Approach has been able to bring pressure on a rogue bank and encourage it to co-operate. If necessary, the Bank of England has been prepared to talk to a foreign bank's national regulator in order to bring the creditor into line.

A number of factors may lead banks to co-operate in a London Approach rescue.[71] A first consideration has been the threat of Bank of England regulatory sanctions, which may underpin the informal pressure applied by the Bank. This may well have been the case in the 1970s and 1980s but Bank interventions in workouts were reduced from the mid-1980s onwards in favour of the Bank's encouraging the involved parties to organise workouts themselves. The Bank's supervisory role as banking regulator was, moreover, transferred to the Financial Services Authority in June 1998.[72] Other incentives to co-operate do exist, though. Individual banks may fear that if they act obstructively, the banking community will exclude them from further profitable deals or deny them future co-operation. This fear will also reduce 'hold-out' strategies – in which individual banks may attempt to extract better terms by threatening non-cooperation. Co-ordination is also encouraged by the practice whereby a 'lead bank' organises the gathering and distribution of the information relevant to the rescue. This cuts down the information asymmetries that would reduce trust and co-operation levels. It also rules out 'free-riding' in the information collection process, since costs are shared.[73]

The value of the London Approach has, however, been largely confined to very large rescue attempts and extensive borrowings.[74] One reason is that implementation costs have been high – up to £6 million – and the Bank of England has had to be selective in using its good offices.[75]

---

[70] As noted in chs. 8 and 9 above, the Enterprise Act 2002 largely replaced administrative receivership with administration but banks will still be able to appoint administrative receivers if their qualifying floating charge predates the coming into force of the Act (15 September 2003).

[71] See Armour and Deakin, 'Norms in Private Insolvency Procedures'.

[72] Ibid., p. 3. See the Bank of England Act 1998.

[73] See generally R. Haugen and L. Senbet, 'Bankruptcy and Agency Costs' (1988) 23 *Journal of Financial and Quantitative Analysis* 27–38.

[74] Only around 150 London Approach workouts were effected between the late 1980s and the 1990s: see Flood *et al.*, *Professional Restructuring*, p. ii; F. Pointon, 'London Approach: A Look at its Application and its Alternatives' (1994) *Insolvency Bulletin* 5 (March).

[75] Flood *et al.*, *Professional Restructuring*.

The fees of the lawyers and accountants who act in such rescues have been criticised as extremely high and there may be other indirect costs that are not inconsiderable.[76] One variety of indirect costs may arise from the loss of decision-making power that a rescue produces within a firm. With the London Approach, a firm may remain under bank control for up to ten years[77] and the firm's managers may lose the power to take decisions without approval. The market may also respond to rescue measures in a manner that acts to the detriment of the company. In response to these points, however, it is worth bearing in mind that inefficiencies and losses to firms and creditors would be considerably higher if formal processes were to be pursued. What may remain a concern is whether the cost-effectiveness of the London Approach is undermined by the fee levels of lawyers, accountants and other professional consultants. If the market for such services is not highly competitive it is to be expected that the gains of the London Approach will be materially captured not by the companies, shareholders or creditors but by the consulting professions.

A further factor that limits the utility of the London Approach is the lack of any formal moratorium and the need for unanimity of support from relevant creditors. A company that is the subject of such a workout will be exposed to creditors' demands while the terms of the rescue are being negotiated. When a large number of banks are involved in such negotiations the complexities involved may make for extensive periods of discussion and, accordingly, exposure to demands. Whether banks will co-operate with a London Approach rescue will depend on their balancing the costs of negotiation with the prospects of disruption and unproductive outcomes, and high numbers of banks and other creditors will militate against a successful use of the London Approach.

Where large sums are owed to numbers of trade creditors, it is likely to be difficult to obtain informal agreements to a workout. The claims of trade creditors, assuming these creditors are included in deliberations, may also be highly divergent in their characteristics and this may impede negotiations. Trade creditors, moreover, may be less inclined to make

---

[76] See K. Wruck, 'Financial Distress, Reorganisation and Organisational Efficiency' (1990) 27 *Journal of Financial Economics* 419; Belcher, *Corporate Rescue*, p. 121. On the failure of the large London law firms to contain costs in commercial cases see M. Murphy and M. Peel, 'Judge Lambasts Lawyers' Fees in Blackberry Case', *Financial Times*, 18 April 2008.

[77] Flood *et al.*, *Professional Restructuring*, p. ii.

informal arrangements than banks and they may be less well equipped to negotiate such deals.[78]

As for secured creditors, they are likely to see their interests as concurrent with those of unsecured creditors where the troubled company's collateral is small, but, if they are fully secured, their incentive to co-operate may be weak. In some conditions, moreover, a secured creditor may possess an incentive to move towards immediate enforcement – where, for example, delay will reduce the value of the relevant collateral[79] – and here they may prefer insolvency to renegotiation. Where, as in the UK, it is common practice for companies to raise significant sums by secured loans, this imposes limits on negotiated solutions. More optimistically, however, it can be argued that even where banks have secured loans in such circumstances, they may be induced to adopt a co-operative stance because they indulge in 'mutual aid' understandings and anticipate requiring a return favour from other banks in the future, or because they want to protect their reputations.[80]

In cross-border cases, the domestic and international creditors involved may be of very many kinds. They are likely to be geographically dispersed and may have assets spread across a number of jurisdictions. They will have to work together against a background of different attitudes, procedures, expectations, regulatory regimes and laws. Languages, modes of interpretation, conceptual frameworks and insolvency law objectives may also vary.[81] Relationships of trust may also be strained by suspicions that the domestic banks are too favourably disposed towards the domestic debtor (for reasons of longer-term domestic strategy). Co-operation between the banks may, as a result, be low.[82] Such lack of trust may conduce to secrecy and this may impede the flow of accurate, relevant and timely information that is essential to the successful London Approach.[83]

The development of the credit derivatives market and the involvement of a host of new actors in the credit-providing process are changes that

---

[78] See Belcher, *Corporate Rescue*, p. 116.

[79] Armour and Deakin, 'Norms in Private Insolvency Procedures', p. 45 (JCLS version).

[80] Ibid. See also R. Sugden, *The Economics of Rights, Cooperation and Welfare* (Blackwell, Oxford, 1986).

[81] See Obank, 'European Recovery', p. 149.

[82] Ibid. The London Approach has been used as a model in other jurisdictions: see N. Segal, 'Corporate Recovery and Rescue: Mastering the Key Strategies Necessary for Successful Cross Border Workouts – Part I and Part II' (2000) 13 *Insolvency Intelligence* 17, 25.

[83] See Segal, 'Corporate Recovery and Rescue – Part II', p. 28.

place further strains on the London Approach.[84] As financing has becoming more fragmented, creditor co-ordination has become more difficult as banks are increasingly joined, in the pool of parties with debt interests, by hedge funds, private equity groups, bond holders, secondary debt traders, joint venture partners, special creditor and supplier groups and intermediate investors.[85] The London Approach was attuned to the 1980s when banking creditors dominated and institutional shareholders were passive, but with the modern era's dispersion of stakeholder groups, the challenge of steering a rescue operation has changed in degree and kind. As Bird notes:

> Today could not be more different. Bond holders, secondary debt traders, the US private placement market, joint venture partners, special creditor and supplier groups and intermediate investors have all discovered a voice and a willingness to interfere in one way or another ... It pushes the process to the limit and sometimes beyond the sphere of influence of the Bank of England.[86]

The situation nowadays, then, is that the Bank of England has a voice that is joined by others and it has retreated from its central role in influencing renegotiations for a number of reasons: as a matter of policy; through reallocation of regulatory functions;[87] and because, as noted above in chapter 3, large UK companies are resorting less to bank loans and making more use of intermediated debt finance, notably bond issues, to raise funds.[88] The emergence of markets for corporate debt has thus increased the strains on the London Approach[89] not merely because stakeholder groupings are more fragmented, extensive in numbers, hard to track down and difficult to co-ordinate but because the

---

[84] See Bird, 'London Approach'; V. Finch, 'Corporate Rescue in a World of Debt' [2008] JBL 756.

[85] See L. Norley, 'Tooled Up', *The Lawyer*, 10 November 2003; Floyd, 'London Approach'; Bird, 'London Approach'; S. Frisby, *Report to the Insolvency Service: Insolvency Outcomes* (Insolvency Service, London, June 2006).

[86] Bird, 'London Approach', p. 87.

[87] Richard Obank has, however, argued that transfer of banking supervision from the Bank of England to the Financial Services Authority under the Bank of England Act 1998 may not affect the London Approach significantly and 'could actually strengthen the Bank's role in work-outs by boosting its role as an independent mediator': Obank, 'European Recovery', p. 151.

[88] See Armour and Deakin, 'Norms in Private Insolvency Procedures', p. 48 (JCLS version); P. Brierley, 'The Bank of England and the London Approach' (1999) *Recovery* (June) 12.

[89] J. Flood, 'The Vultures Fly East: The Creation and Globalisation of the Distressed Debt Market' in D. Nelken and J. Feast (eds.), *Adapting Legal Cultures* (Hart, Oxford, 2001); Armour and Deakin, 'Norms in Private Insolvency Procedures', pp. 48–51 (JCLS version); Bird, 'London Approach'.

increasing complexity of financial structures produces new levels of opacity concerning the nature and extent of different parties' interests, and, also, new potential for conflicts of interest between junior and senior creditors.[90] The nature and fluidity of the debt market means not only that the costs of communicating with involved parties to a renegotiation are high (because the parties are changing and their interests are often uncertain) but there is an increase in risks of breaches of confidentiality and of unhelpful market responses to these breaches. It might be responded that players in the distressed debt market will tend to co-operate on rescues – for reasons mirroring the banks' incentives – and there is evidence that market associations for distressed debt (as formed in London and New York) may encourage co-operation. Against this view, though, it can be argued, first, that the sheer involvement of a greater number and diversity of players is likely to militate against the rapid, informed and cheap negotiation of rescues, and, second, that, as pointed out above, the different parties in such markets may have very different aims, priorities and approaches when viewing rescue.

The markets in credit products are now global in nature and this further strains the London Approach. Where, as is increasingly the case, companies are bound up with overseas intermediate holding companies or subsidiaries, and where foreign banks, hedge funds and other types of organisation are involved as creditors through the holding of different credit products, the possibilities of gaining informal agreements on reconstruction, investment and short-term cash recovery diminish. Such scenarios tend to reduce the likelihood of repeated interactions between parties with claims against a distressed company. Parties buying bonds or distressed debt or parties operating from abroad

---

[90] See Segal, 'Corporate Recovery and Rescue – Part II', p. 26. Per David Clementi, then Deputy Governor of the Bank of England: 'imbalances in the information available to a company and its creditors, together with possible conflicts of interest between creditors, can lead to serious coordination problems ... Active markets in credit derivatives and secondary loans, whatever their merits in distributing risk, can make it more difficult to identify and organise creditors in order to negotiate any debt workout.' 'News Release, Debt Workouts for Corporates, Banks and Countries: Some Common Themes' (Bank of England, July 2001). On the tensions arising in the GUS demerger negotiations due to the growing involvement of hedge funds see P. Davies and G. Tett, 'GUS in War of Words after Funds and Banks Corner Debt', *Financial Times*, 7 September 2006; 'Bondholders Create Uncertainty for GUS', *Financial Times*, 7 September 2006. On the freezing of restructuring that can be caused by the difficulties of identifying interests see Sakoui, 'Delicate Task of Restructuring Lehman Begins'.

are less likely to have any expectation of repeat business with the banks in question:

> This increases the likelihood that one or more such parties may incorrectly observe the conventions operating in the London Approach workouts and adopt strategies which precipitate insolvency. Simultaneously it reduces the efficiency of the sanctions which the 'club' of London banks can threaten to exert. They are unable to exclude buyers of bonds or distressed debt from participation in future loan syndication.[91]

Should the London Approach be formalised and placed on a statutory footing? This would run counter to its existing philosophy of flexibility and informality, and a regime based on shared values, understandings, moral suasion and favours might be difficult to encapsulate in statutory language. Formalisation would, however, allow steps to be taken that would potentially facilitate the production of agreements between creditors. At present, if a creditor refuses to agree to a proposed arrangement, this may wreck the workout (a difficulty that has led the Bank of England to consider the possibility of replacing unanimity with a qualified majority voting system).[92] Bankers, however, may be reluctant to appear uncooperative to their fellow bankers since they may be seeking cooperation from others in a future rescue. As debt trading becomes even more widespread rescue negotiations may be undermined since some smaller lenders may look to extricate themselves from a situation rather than to work towards solutions.[93] Trading in the distressed market, moreover, remains a challenge to the London Approach since the banks have successfully resisted suggestions that a code of conduct should ban debt trading at 'sensitive' times. The banks are consequently left with their powers of influence and persuasion to deter others from spoiling rescues.[94] A moratorium might, nevertheless, be provided for and the risks of creditors 'defecting' by selling their debt into the

---

[91] Armour and Deakin, 'Norms in Private Insolvency Procedures', pp. 48–9 (JCLS version).

[92] See Belcher, *Corporate Rescue*, p. 119; Kent, 'London Approach: Distressed Debt Trading', p. 115.

[93] See Kent, 'London Approach: Distressed Debt Trading'; Belcher, *Corporate Rescue*, p. 120.

[94] See Flood *et al.*, *Professional Restructuring*, p. 32. Mr Penn Kent, an executive director of the Bank of England, mooted the idea in 1994 of adopting a code of practice requiring buyers of distressed debt to comply with the Bank of England's approach to debt restructuring. The Bank of England dropped this idea, however, after talks with bankers: J. Gapper, 'Bank Seeks Code for Debt Sales', *Financial Times*, 28 January 1994; N. Cohen, 'Debt Trading Reform Rejected in Bank U-Turn', *Financial Times*, 24 March 1994.

secondary distressed debt market might be limited by statutory restrictions on such defection, at least for a stipulated period. As noted above, however, such a ban on debt trading has been opposed by British and foreign banks and legal restrictions of the kind mooted might prove too legalistic to have many supporters. What has proved more acceptable has been the use of a code of practice. In October 2000, INSOL International produced a 'Statement of Principles for a Global Approach to Multi-Creditor Workouts'.[95] This has been described as 'a rare combination of clarity and flexibility'[96] and has been endorsed by bodies such as the World Bank, the Bank of England and the British Bankers' Association. The Statement sets out eight principles[97] which are of relevance to domestic multi-bank situations, and these provide for co-operation on such matters as a 'standstill period' during which creditors should refrain from enforcing claims.

One respect in which such a statement of principles may prove to be of real value is in providing a foundation for the resolution of disputes between creditors. To this end, more use might be made of arbitrators or mediators in the informal rescue process. Such persons would have the task of facilitating negotiations between different stakeholder groups and would seek to secure agreements more rapidly and cost-effectively than is otherwise possible.[98]

As already indicated, the London Approach could be said to lead to some lowering of managerial expertise in so far as supervision arrangements by the bank will detract from decision-making powers. In reply, however, the potential effects on managers of formal alternatives should be compared, and it could be asserted that improvements of expertise are likely to be encountered when managers who have steered the company into financial troubles are led, by negotiations with bankers, to see the error of their ways and to arrive at more financially sound modes of

---

[95] For discussion see Chief Editor, 'International Approach to Workouts' (2001) 17 IL&P 59.

[96] Ibid.

[97] Reproduced verbatim at (2001) 17 IL&P 59, 60. Principle 2 does countenance the disposal of debts to third parties during the standstill period.

[98] A Price Waterhouse survey conducted in 1996 revealed that 53 per cent of respondents favoured the use of such mediators: see J. Kelly, 'Banks Back Plan for Rescuing Big Companies', *Financial Times*, 2 December 1996. The Vice-Chairman of the INSOL Lenders Group has suggested that it would be useful, in international cases, to have an 'honest broker' in each jurisdiction to assist in the application of the INSOL International Principles, a role that could be filled by the appropriate regulator: see (2001) 17 IL&P 59.

conducting business. Another issue relevant to expertise is whether modern banks, subject to severe competitive pressures, have the capacity and will to devote significant resources and senior expertise to the management of a major inter-creditor rescue arrangement.[99] Professional experts can be brought in but these, as noted, tend to be highly priced. If there is, or becomes, a shortage of the kind of banking expertise that is needed to work the London Approach, it is to be expected that the regime will decline in importance.

Moving to issues of accountability and accessibility, the London Approach can be criticised for its secrecy and exclusivity. Not all creditors will have access to negotiations in the London Approach and attempts may be made to conduct operations without, say, trade creditors gaining information on developments. This may be efficient but it would not appeal to excluded creditors on accessibility grounds.

As for those creditors who are involved in negotiations, much depends on the procedures followed by the lead bank. This is the bank that co-ordinates the rescue, appoints the investigators, puts the rescue team together and manages information flows. The London Rules state that the lead bank must have sufficient resources and the necessary expertise to ensure that information is made available to all lenders participating in the rescue on a timely basis. Performance on this front varies, however. In the view of the Bank of England: 'One of the most frequent complaints we receive at the Bank of England is that a lead bank has failed to provide banks with information which they regard as essential for the decisions that they are being asked to make.'[100]

Lead banks, nevertheless, are subject to a number of pressures to release information. They will work closely with the steering committee, which is a body of three or five persons elected by the creditors and which will encourage the dissemination of information. Lead banks also have an incentive to keep the other banks informed and content, for if the latter are not satisfied with their position they may withdraw their co-operation or they may sell their debts in the secondary distressed debt market.

As for fairness, it might be contended that the London Approach workouts operate for the benefit of large lenders and tend to undervalue small, especially unsecured, creditors' interests. Larger creditors might

---

[99] See Bird, 'London Approach', p. 88.
[100] M. Smith, 'The London Approach', conference paper to Wilde Sapte Seminar, 1992, quoted in Flood *et al.*, *Professional Restructuring*, p. 28.

respond that their efforts benefit the broad array of corporate stake-holders and that many small creditors, who do not contribute to the costs of the rescue, are to some extent free-riding on the efforts of the banks. This response might, however, overlook the ability of the banks, in certain instances, to compensate themselves for their efforts by improving their security or equity position in a rescue agreement. There is evidence that during periods of rescue, bank credit tends to contract but unsecured trade credit tends to expand, sometimes dramatically.[101]

In summary, then, the London Approach exemplifies a number of the virtues and vices of informal rescue activity. It tends to be practised in relation to large debtor companies only and gives grounds for concern on a number of fronts. If, however, it is placed alongside the available formal alternative procedures, its virtues appear more prominent.

Implementing the rescue

Once agreement is reached on a strategy for rescue, a number of measures will often be taken in an effort to achieve corporate turn-around.[102] These steps may be put in train by pursuing formal insolvency procedures (as discussed in chapters 8–10 below) or informally, by agreement. The first of these steps may, indeed, have already commenced before any final agreement between creditors is arrived at.

Managerial and organisational reforms

A successful rescue will almost always involve the retention or institution of an appropriate workforce and managerial team. Once the future activities of the company are settled upon, it will be necessary to see that persons with the appropriate skills are employed and that those who will no longer contribute appropriately will part ways with the company. Replacements, recruitments, promotions and staff reductions may all

---

[101] See Franks and Sussman, 'Cycle of Corporate Distress', p. 2: trade credit expansions of up to 80 per cent are noted in cases that end in a formal insolvency procedure.

[102] On turnaround techniques and their use, see Society of Practitioners of Insolvency, Eighth Survey, *Company Insolvency in the United Kingdom* (SPI, London, 1999) pp. 12–14. The survey revealed that turnaround efforts failed (and formal insolvency ensued) in 37 per cent of cases in the manufacturing, wholesale, distribution and construction sectors. R3's Ninth Survey in 2001 revealed that respondent insolvency professionals considered that in 77 per cent of cases there were, by the time they were appointed, no possible actions that might realistically have averted company failure. Nearly one in five businesses did, however, survive insolvency and continued in one form or another.

have to be brought about and attempts made to reduce the attendant disruptions and confusions. Changes at the top of management will often be required in order to move a company in a significant new direction out of crisis and to signal to outsiders and markets that positive remedial steps are being taken. R3's Ninth Survey of Business Recovery (2001) found that insolvency professionals considered that for companies with over £5 million turnover a change of management could have averted company failure in 10 per cent of cases. When the SPI asked its members, in 1998, what actions companies might have taken to avoid falling into 'intensive care' scenarios, a change of management (in 28 per cent of cases) came second only to earlier actions to stem losses.[103] In more than half of SPI-studied cases inadequate management was noted as an obstacle or hindrance to obtaining a non-insolvency solution to corporate difficulties (but such difficulties were rarely so serious as to prevent turnaround).[104] As for methods of company rescue, the R3 Ninth Survey revealed that turnaround practitioners used change of management as a primary tool of rehabilitation in 20 per cent of cases.

On the organisational front, a variety of steps can be taken. The corporate governance structure of the company can be reformed so as to improve checks and balances, but the organisation of operations can also be revised in ways that may improve performance: for example, by decentralising and devolving power so as to create lower-cost modes of supervision, greater senses of responsibility, increases in morale and tighter management. Such decentralisations of operations may also lead to greater flexibility by creating identifiable free-standing parts of a business and, accordingly, greater opportunities to sell off these units as elements in asset reduction strategies.[105]

Asset reductions

A strategy designed to secure profitability is the reduction of corporate activities to a healthy core by cutting away unprofitable products, branches, customers or divisions and disposing of assets that are poorly utilised or are not needed for core profitable business operations.[106] Such

---

[103] SPI Eighth Survey, p. 13. R3's Twelfth Survey (2004) suggested that poor management was responsible in 32 per cent of failure factors cited: see ch. 4 above.

[104] SPI Eighth Survey.

[105] See Campbell and Underdown, *Corporate Insolvency*, p. 67.

[106] Ibid., p. 66. On the use of sell-offs and management buyouts see Belcher, *Corporate Rescue*, pp. 26–31.

reductions may include sales of subsidiaries, equipment or surplus fixed assets, closure of branches or streamlining of stocking arrangements. Asset reductions may, however, involve considerable costs. Beyond the fees payable to lawyers, accountants and other professionals there may be redundancy expenses, prices attached to contract cancellations and other divestment costs.

Cost reductions

An essential element in most rescue packages is a programme of cost reductions.[107] This will involve investigations into current costs and potential savings and will cover not merely raw materials and equipment but also workforce expenditure.

Debt restructuring

Troubled companies are often too highly geared or in possession of a pattern of borrowing that is inefficient. A number of steps can be taken to reorganise corporate debts but successful reorganisation depends on the ability of those managing the company to convince financiers and other interested parties that the appropriate rescue plan has been put into effect, that the prospects of recovery are sound, and that the proposed debt reorganisations offer a better prospect of returns to creditors than would be delivered by resort to formal insolvency procedures.

If the company's main problems relate to cash flows, short-term difficulties or underinvestment, steps can be taken to inject new funds into the company. Creditors in such circumstances will usually demand additional levels of security and may act to improve the overall security of their positions: for example, by using floating charges over the

---

[107] The SPI Eighth Survey indicated that the most common primary turnaround techniques were cost reductions, debt restructurings, raising new equity and negotiating with banks. These steps were followed in (descending) frequency of use by improved financial controls, asset reductions, changes of management, product/market changes, organisational changes and improved marketing (SPI Eighth Survey, p. 13); the R3 Ninth Survey of 2001 indicated that the primary method of rehabilitation used most frequently by turnaround managers was debt restructuring, resorted to in 39 per cent of cases involving such practitioners. Cost reduction, however, was only used as a primary method in just over 11 per cent of cases. The R3 Twelfth Survey of 2004 did not return to this issue.

corporate assets.[108] Co-operation from banks is most likely to be found where large reputable companies encounter such difficulties. Banks fear bad publicity and any association with conspicuous failure or large-scale unemployment. They will, accordingly, tend to be most helpful to large, high-profile and respectable firms with considerable numbers of employees.[109]

Consolidation of funding is a step that can also be taken when banks are helpful. Substantial benefits can be obtained by reorganising a proliferation of funding agreements and bringing these together in a simple financial arrangement. This process may allow a firm to negotiate a reduction in the overall cost of borrowing or a conversion of short- to longer-term credit facilities. Other arrangements, such as sales and lease-backs of property and equipment, may additionally be employed.

Debts can also be rescheduled in order to ease immediate problems. This may be a useful course of action where the company's credit is supplied by a small number of banks and the company's financial problems are short term in nature.[110] Rescheduling does not, however, remove balance sheet deficits or improve gearing ratios. It involves a contract between the debtor company with all or some creditors, and this may alter obligations by deferring payments, harmonising obligations between different creditors or granting security (or additional security) to creditors.

Rescheduling may appeal to banks because, as noted already, such informality avoids the adverse publicity involved in precipitating the liquidation of a company. It may also allow securities to be adjusted and, where a number of banks are involved, rescheduling may prove far less complex and expensive than receivership. Similarly, where creditors in a variety of jurisdictions are involved with a company, it may be quicker and cheaper to respond to difficulties by negotiating new contracts than by resorting to formal proceedings. Problems with rescheduling will tend to arise when many banks are involved but some of them feel uncommitted to the company involved, lack a close relationship to it and feel no loyalty to the enterprise.[111] In these circumstances, the

---

[108] When new security is given to a creditor in a rescue operation it may be questioned whether this constitutes a preference under the Insolvency Act 1986 s. 239; see also Insolvency Act 1986 s. 245. See ch. 13 below.

[109] See Lickorish, 'Debt Rescheduling', pp. 38, 39.

[110] See generally ibid.   [111] Ibid., p. 40.

creditor agreement necessary to make rescheduling work will be difficult
to secure.

Debt/equity conversions

A further mode of informal rescue, and one that can be implemented
through a variety of procedures – following, for instance, a London
Approach process or a hedge fund purchase – is the conversion of debt
to equity.[112] In this procedure, the creditor agrees to exchange a debt for
an equity share in the company and hopes that, at some future date, this
will produce a greater return than would have been obtained in a
liquidation. Recent celebrated cases of such conversions have included
Eurotunnel, which had been overwhelmed by huge debts since it was
floated in 1987.[113] The latest in a long line of restructuring deals was
concluded in 2007 and saw the company taken over by a new holding
company, Groupe Eurotunnel (GE), creditors left in control of about 87
per cent of the shares in GE, and Eurotunnel's debts slashed from £6.2bn
to £2.84bn. Similar debt for equity conversions have been associated with
the names of Saatchi and Saatchi plc (£211 million of debt), Brent Walker
Group plc (£250 million of bank debt), Signet (formerly Ratners
Jewellers, £460 million of debt) and Queens Moat (£200 million of debt).

From a creditor's point of view, a conversion may be attractive because
it offers the prospect of a future return on investment that is potentially
unlimited as the company's fortunes upturn and potentially far more
valuable than the returns available on liquidation. Where banks have
loaned without security – as is often the case with lending to larger
quoted groups that have borrowed from many banks – there is the
prospect of low recovery rates in an insolvency and debt to equity
conversion can be more desirable than resort to formal insolvency
procedures. In contrast, the creditor that is fully or partially secured
has a far weaker incentive to support a troubled company by taking an
equity position. Where the creditors, companies and projects involved
are high profile, a further advantage of the debt to equity conversion is
that it brings public relations returns: the creditor is seen in the public eye

---

[112] See K. Kemp and D. Harris, 'Debt to Equity Conversions: Relieving the Interest Burden'
(1993) PLC 19 (August); Belcher, *Corporate Rescue*, pp. 120–1; DTI, *Encouraging Debt/
Equity Swaps* (1996).

[113] The legacy of construction overrun costs: see A. Osborne, 'Eurotunnel "Saved" as Debts
Cut', *Daily Telegraph*, 26 May 2007; R. Wright, 'Challenge on the Way to Bring Down
Eurotunnel's Debt', *Financial Times*, 28 November 2006.

to be committed to industry and loyal to its customers in their hour of need.

From the company's perspective, a conversion takes away the burden of interest repayment, it eases cash flow and working capital difficulties and it improves the appearance of the balance sheet because managerial workforce efforts will be seen as producing profits rather than as merely servicing interest burdens. The financial profile and gearing of the company will improve as debts and competitive disadvantages are removed. The company will then be better placed to seek new credit lines from creditors, to attract new business and to reassure its current customers. This, in turn, is likely to improve morale within the company and to increase the prospects of turning fortunes around. For directors, particular benefits will occur as the threat of liability for wrongful trading is reduced when debts are taken off the balance sheet in a conversion.

The DTI issued a Consultation Paper in 1996 which stressed the important contribution that debt/equity swaps can make in allowing troubled companies to reorganise their affairs.[114] The DTI favoured encouraging such swaps but thought it inappropriate to require creditors by law to participate in compulsory swaps. Instead, the Department sought to raise the profile of swapping; to make involved parties more aware of the potential benefits of swaps; and to encourage the development of model debt/equity swap schemes that could be adapted to particular circumstances.[115]

Debt to equity conversions do, however, involve a number of difficulties and disadvantages. They can be time-consuming and expensive to negotiate, not least because the consent of the company's existing shareholders, as well as of the main creditors, will usually be required. The former will have to agree to the issue of new shares, and such shareholders may be inclined to hold out in order to improve their positions. Where there are divergences of approach or position on the part of the creditors, it may again be difficult to come to a prompt, agreed restructuring plan. These divergences may arise because exposure levels

---

[114] DTI, *Encouraging Debt/Equity Swaps*.

[115] See, for example, Appendix E – The Economics of Bankruptcy Reform – in the DTI/ Insolvency Service's Consultative Document, *Company Voluntary Arrangements and Administration Orders* (October 1993); P. Aghion, O. Hart and J. Moore, 'Insolvency Reform in the UK: A Revised Proposal', Special Paper No. 65 (LSE Financial Markets Group, January 1995) and in (1995) 11 IL&P 67; A. Campbell, 'The Equity for Debt Proposal: The Way Forward' (1996) 12 IL&P 14. See further ch. 9, pp. 422–6 below.

vary, the banks may be based in different jurisdictions or they may work subject to different regulatory constraints and within their own business cultures.[116] Where foreign banks are involved, it will be necessary to consider, for instance, whether these are subject to regulatory restrictions on the holding of equity.[117]

For creditors, a negative aspect of a conversion is that there will be a loss of priority on a subsequent liquidation in so far as they have become shareholders and as such will be eligible to receive no return until all creditors have been repaid. The financial flexibility of the creditors' operations will also be reduced by conversion since it will be more difficult to realise their investment afterwards: sale of shares after a conversion may prove difficult or unproductive. Ownership of shares may, moreover, involve a culture shock for UK banks who, unlike their German counterparts, are unused to owning material portions of industry. They may be inclined to sell any accumulated shares once the market becomes liquid but such liquidity may be a long time coming.

For these reasons, there may be alternatives to either formal insolvency proceedings or debt to equity conversions that may be more attractive to creditors and debtors. Debt rescheduling may be appropriate where the number of bank creditors is small and the company's financial problems can be overcome by changing the progressive interest or principal repayments. What rescheduling will not do is remove balance sheet deficits or improve gearing ratios.

Another alternative is to convert debt to limited recourse or subordinate debt. In such a process, the creditors agree either that their debts will be converted from a general corporate obligation into claims secured against specific assets or that they will rank for repayment behind other debts (but ahead of equity). This will give some protection to directors with regard to wrongful trading liabilities but, again, it will not remove balance sheet deficits or gearing problems.[118]

In summary, debt to equity conversions can provide an effective and efficient means of allowing troubled companies to continue operations and of avoiding formal insolvency procedures. The main effectiveness and efficiency concerns relate to the time and money that has to be

---

[116] See further Kemp and Harris, 'Debt to Equity Conversions', pp. 22–3.
[117] Ibid., p. 25. The US Bank Holding Company Act 1956 with few exceptions generally prohibits US banks from acquiring equity securities.
[118] Kemp and Harris, 'Debt to Equity Conversions', p. 22.

expended in achieving the agreements of involved parties. Here much depends on the numbers and types of creditors involved.

The worry, in terms of expertise and the scope for exercising it, is that banks may not always be attuned to the assessment of equity risks. Some may be better placed than others. The Royal Bank of Scotland set up a unit called Specialised Lending Services in the early 1990s in order to help companies by taking equity share stakes. Banks, moreover, are able to buy in expertise from accountants and other consultants in order to make equity assessments. Whether banks can operate sufficiently astutely to make equity-holding activities profitable is another issue. The National Westminster Bank was forced in 1991 to acknowledge the failure of its Growth Options equity stakeholding venture, and has since conceded that it had not been able to make money out of small equity shareholdings.[119]

The accessibility and accountability of conversion processes tend to be high in relation to major creditors since their consent will be required for those processes to work. Similarly, the requirement of shareholder approval for new share issues will ensure that those stakeholders gain a voice in the rescue process. Minor creditors may not be offered easy access in a debt to equity conversion but their interests will not usually be affected detrimentally, and they may well benefit from the reductions of debt that follow a conversion and from the reductions in the length of the potential queue for insolvency payments that will follow a conversion that changes the status of certain creditors to shareholders. For these reasons, it is also difficult to criticise conversions on the grounds that they involve unfairness to any affected parties. A company's shareholders may suffer when a conversion takes place: Eurotunnel shareholders were diluted to 13 per cent in the 2007 restructuring deal. Such shareholders, however, take risks openly and they suffer less in a conversion than they would in a liquidation.

Conclusions

Since the mid-1990s, a new emphasis has been placed on informal responses to corporate troubles and on the taking of remedial actions at the pre-insolvency stage. Sometimes these responses centre on the

[119] See C. Batchelor, 'From Lender to Investor', *Financial Times*, 23 March 1993.

monitoring of corporate performance, sometimes they focus on restructuring. New actors have come onto the scene to challenge both the former dominance of the banks and the approaches to corporate troubles that tend to be adopted by the banks. Whatever the approach to rescue – be it one that focuses on turnaround of the existing company or on restructuring the business – resort to informal action offers a number of potential gains. It avoids the constraints of formal insolvency procedures and it offers companies new opportunities to enjoy business success. Assessing the efficiency of informal rescue procedures, individually or as a group, is, however, fraught with a number of difficulties. Informal rescue ranges from crisis management and turnaround to the use of consultancy services to improve management. It is, accordingly, almost impossible to separate out rescue activity from routine negotiations with creditors and other business partners. The lack of any formal gateway rules out such identification. Nor will information on much turnaround work be readily available: publicity, after all, will often be highly counterproductive. What can be looked to is the success rate of forms of rescue work that involve certain parties. Thus, the figures of R3 reveal that in a small sample of cases where IPs were appointed, the ratio of turnaround projects that succeeded or were still in progress to turnaround projects that failed and resulted in a formal insolvency was 62:50.[120]

Informal action can be swifter and cheaper than formal procedures but this is not always the case and it can also be more partial and less well informed. We have seen that informality does give grounds for concern on some fronts. The expenses of informal actions may be high. The expertise being applied at key points in informal processes may not always be appropriate. The accessibility and accountability of some procedures may be low (secrecy may be treated as a virtue in some informal rescues) and whether all affected parties are dealt with fairly can be a matter of fortune.

The philosophy of rescuing companies, it should be emphasised, is very different in orientation from many aspects of formal insolvent liquidation procedures. It is less strictly guided by statutory rules and its main focus is not the maximisation of returns for the various creditors in strict order of priority. It looks towards ongoing commercial viability and involves the application of skills relevant to marketing, manufacturing, product development and general management as well as the legal

---

[120] R3's Ninth Survey.

issues. Those practising rescue have accordingly to exercise judgement and adopt a different stance from the insolvency practitioner engaged in liquidation who is content simply to collect assets for distribution. Experience, competence and powers of staff motivation are all called for in the ideal rescue professional. It is in the arena of rescue that insolvency moves furthest from the mechanical application of rules for the benefit of creditors.

8

Receivers and their role

A first legally structured insolvency procedure with some potential for rescue to be considered here is receivership.[1] It follows from the earlier chapters that an appraisal of receivership should go further than offering an outline of powers and duties and should analyse the role and conception of receivership as it operates. This chapter, accordingly, will look at receivership as a process as well as an institution. The laws, procedures and actors involved in receivership will be examined and the benchmarks of efficiency, expertise, accountability and fairness will be employed in asking whether receivership plays an acceptable role in insolvency as a whole. The part played by receivers in rescues will be a focus here, but attention will also be paid to ongoing corporate operations and the impact of receivership on these.

At this stage it might be objected that administrative receivership has largely been abolished and so does not need to be examined here – that the Enterprise Act 2002 took away the floating charge holder's right to appoint an administrative receiver and, in doing so, largely replaced receivership with administration. It is true that the 2002 Act restricted the use of administrative receivership but receivership is not dead yet. Creditors with 'qualifying' floating charges[2] that were created

---

[1] Receivership is generally regarded as a method by which a secured creditor can enforce his security rather than a true collective insolvency proceeding: see, *inter alia*, R. M. Goode, *Principles of Corporate Insolvency Law* (3rd edn, Sweet & Maxwell, London, 2005) pp. 247–8; B. M. Hannigan, *Company Law* (Lexis Nexis/Butterworths, London, 2003) p. 727; Insolvency Service, *A Review of Company Rescue and Business Reconstruction Mechanisms*, Interim Report (DTI, September 1999) p. 9. On some consequences of this approach see F. Dahan, 'The European Convention on Insolvency Proceedings and the Administrative Receiver: A Missed Opportunity?' (1996) 17 Co. Law. 181. See also the distinction between insolvency proceedings and other proceedings such as receivership adopted by the Transfer of Undertakings (Protection of Employment) Regulations 2006 (SI 2006/246): discussed in ch. 17 below.

[2] See Insolvency Act 1986 Sch. B1, para. 14.

before the 2002 Act,[3] or those with charges which, though created after that date, fall within one of the specified exceptions[4] may still appoint administrative receivers. 'Ordinary' receivers, moreover, can still be appointed by the courts and debenture holders. It is, accordingly, necessary to consider the operation of receivership and the reasons for its curtailment. This discussion is best commenced by outlining the development of receivership, the procedures that are adopted in receivership and the duties and obligations that form the legal framework for receivership.

The development of receivership

Receivership is a long-established method by which secured creditors can enforce their security.[5] There have traditionally been two types of receiver in English law: the receiver appointed by the court and the receiver appointed by a debenture holder under the terms of the debenture deed.[6] The 'administrative receiver' was an institution introduced by

---

[3] Numerous banks rushed to take out floating charges before the 2002 Act came into effect on 15 September 2003 and ended the qualifying floating charge holder's right to veto administration and curtailed the right of such floating charge holders to appoint an administrative receiver. Armour, Hsu and Walters point out, however, that, numerically, the new administration procedure has largely replaced receivership and report that their interviewees explained this by referring to the banks' desires to distance themselves from the negative publicity associated with receivership: see J. Armour, A. Hsu and A. Walters, *Report for the Insolvency Service: The Impact of the Enterprise Act 2002 on Realisations and Costs in Corporate Rescue Proceedings* (Insolvency Service, London, December 2006); Armour, Hsu and Walters, 'The Costs and Benefits of Secured Creditor Control in Bankruptcy: Evidence from the UK', University of Cambridge Centre for Business Research Working Paper No. 332 (Cambridge, September 2006). Between 2000–1 and 2005–6 the number of receiverships fell from 1,639 to 565 whereas administrations grew in number from 775 to 2,661: see Insolvency Service, *Enterprise Act 2002 – Corporate Insolvency Provisions: Evaluation Report* (Insolvency Service, London, 2008) p. 17.

[4] See Enterprise Act 2002 s. 250 which inserts a new s. 72A into the Insolvency Act 1986 listing the exceptions.

[5] See also A. Keay and P. Walton, *Insolvency Law: Corporate and Personal* (2nd edn, Jordans, Bristol, 2008) ch. 6. See *Re Maskelyne British Typewriter Ltd* [1898] 1 Ch 133. On aspects of administrative receivership still left to private contract see L. Clarke and H. Rajak, '*Mann v. Secretary of State for Employment*' (2000) 63 MLR 895 at 899.

[6] I.e. all-assets receivers appointed by the court and receivers of only part of the company's property. See further S. Fennell, 'Court-appointed Receiverships: A Missed Opportunity?' (1998) 14 IL&P 208. Although the appointment of court-appointed receivers is rare, the procedure can be used to good effect to gain control of assets held overseas 'when all other avenues look doomed to fail': see D. Wood, 'Can a Court Appointed Receiver Secure Assets Held Overseas?' (2008) *Recovery* (Spring) 30.

the Insolvency Act 1986 and is covered by a distinct statutory regime. The receiver is thus a person appointed to take possession of property that is the subject of a charge and he or she is authorised to deal with it primarily for the benefit of the holder of the charge. The court has an inherent jurisdiction to appoint a receiver in order to take care of property until the rights of the interested parties can be determined. This jurisdiction includes, in the case of a business, the power to appoint a manager so that courts can appoint a receiver/manager even in the absence of any express power in the relevant debenture. After the Law of Property Act 1925[7] all mortgages by deed contain an implied power to appoint a receiver.

The modern term 'administrative receiver' refers to the individual who, under the Insolvency Act 1986, is the receiver and manager of the whole (or substantially the whole) of a company's property, appointed by the holders of a debenture secured by a charge which was, as created, a floating charge.[8] In the pre-Enterprise Act 2002 scenario, this individual was typically appointed by the secured creditor under the terms of the relevant floating charge at a time of crisis in the debtor firm's affairs.[9] They have to be a qualified insolvency practitioner within the meaning of Part XIII of the Insolvency Act 1986.[10]

---

[7] On the advantages of LPA receivers see L. Verrill, 'The Use of LPA Receiverships' (2007) 20 *Insolvency Intelligence* 160 (noting the virtues of speed, lender control, no court process, no statutory filings, no IP requirement, no capital gains tax, no business rates, no fee scrutiny and no dealing with creditors). See also R. Connell, 'Enterprising Receivers' (2003) *Recovery* (Spring) 20: 'it is likely that, as an alternative to administration, the fixed charge receivership will continue to have most appeal in cases of single asset or special purpose companies'.

[8] Insolvency Act 1986 s. 29(2).

[9] Frisby's study suggests that, from 2001 to 2004, the clearing banks continued to be the main users of administrative receivership but a fifth of all receivership appointments were made by independent firms engaged in factoring and/or invoice discounting: see S. Frisby, *Report to the Insolvency Service: Insolvency Outcomes* (Insolvency Service, London, June 2006) (hereafter 'Insolvency Outcomes, 2006'). Franks and Sussman report that, in spite of dispersed security of lending, and with the main bank supplying only around 40 per cent of all debt and trade creditors supplying most of the remainder, 'the liquidation rights are almost entirely concentrated in the hands of the main banks': see J. Franks and O. Sussman, 'Financial Distress and Bank Restructuring of Small to Medium Size UK Companies' (2005) 9 *Review of Finance* 65–96.

[10] It is an offence under the Insolvency Act 1986 ss. 388, 389 for a person to act as an IP without being properly qualified under the Insolvency Act 1986 s. 390. The IP must be a member of a recognised professional body or obtain authorisation to act under the Insolvency Act 1986 s. 393. See ch. 5 above.

This chapter focuses on administrative receivership, the roots of which are to be found in the Cork Report[11] and the Insolvency Act 1986. The Cork Committee (Cork) saw the aims of insolvency law in terms of the dozen objectives set out in paragraph 198 of the Cork Report and discussed in chapter 2 above. Cork stressed that the public interest should be protected by corporate insolvency processes because groups in society beyond the insolvent company and creditors were affected by an insolvency. Cork also emphasised that means should be provided for preserving 'viable commercial enterprises capable of making a useful contribution to the economic life of the country'. After the enactment of the Insolvency Act 1986, four different formal insolvency procedures were available to play a part in corporate rescues and reorganisations. These were: (1) administrative receivership; (2) administration under Part II of the Insolvency Act 1986; (3) company voluntary arrangements under Part I of the Insolvency Act 1986; and (4) creditor schemes of arrangement under the Companies Act 1985 (now the Companies Act 2006). These procedures establish regimes for the management of the affairs of a business and they are binding on the managers of the business as well as on the creditors. In this sense they are 'formal' procedures to be distinguished from the informal methods that can be adopted in response to corporate troubles. It should be emphasised that companies in financial difficulties do not have to resort to formal procedures. As was noted in chapter 7, if the involved parties (directors, shareholders and creditors) can come to (and sustain) an agreement on the steps to be taken to effect a rescue then informal processes are likely to offer a far speedier and cheaper way of reversing corporate fortunes than resort to formality. Research suggests that there is 'an elaborate rescue process outside formal procedures' with about 75 per cent of firms emerging from rescue and avoiding formal insolvency procedures altogether by either turning around their fortunes or repaying their debts.[12]

When the Cork Committee looked at receivership, a receiver might be put in place by the traditional methods of appointment by the court or under the powers contained in an instrument such as a mortgage

---

[11] *Report of the Review Committee on Insolvency Law and Practice* (Cmnd 8558, 1982) ('Cork Report').

[12] See J. Franks and O. Sussman, 'The Cycle of Corporate Distress, Rescue and Dissolution: A Study of Small and Medium Size UK Companies', IFA Working Paper 306 (2000) p. 2. It has been argued that if most rescues are informal, changes in the formal structures may make little difference to the incidence of corporate rescues: see Armour, Hsu and Walters, *Report for the Insolvency Service*.

debenture. Despite receiving numerous suggestions for the reform of receivership and numbers of complaints concerning the institution,[13] Cork remained unpersuaded that radical legal changes were called for,[14] advocating instead that receivership should be strengthened – an exhortation which resulted in the creation of 'administrative receivership' to which we now turn.[15]

Processes, powers and duties: the Insolvency Act 1986 onwards

The Insolvency Act 1986 established the 'pre-Enterprise Act' version of administrative receivership. The position after 1986 and before the Enterprise Act 2002 came into effect was that the administrative receiver (hereafter 'receiver') could be appointed by a creditor of a company who had taken security over the whole or substantially the whole of a company's property by a package of security interests that must include a floating charge.[16] This meant that a floating charge holder was entitled to appoint a receiver even if a series of fixed charges and preferential debts had priority over the floating charge. All that was necessary was that the floating charge covered a substantial part of the company's property.[17] Such a creditor would normally be present in the case of most troubled companies since it is usual practice for UK companies to rely to a considerable extent on finance from banks and for the latter to take out security packages that will render them eligible to appoint a receiver to protect their loan.

It is common for debentures to set out lists of the situations entitling the debenture holder to appoint a receiver. Typical events include: failures to meet demands to pay principal or interest;[18] the presentation of a

---

[13] On which see pp. 346–7, 350–1, 356–60 below.

[14] On Cork's 'exaggerated representation of the virtues of receivership' see G. McCormack, 'Receiverships and the Rescue Culture' [2000] 2 CFILR 229, 236. On the efficiencies generated by receiverships, however, see J. Armour and S. Frisby, 'Rethinking Receivership' (2001) 21 OJLS 73.

[15] For cases when receivership could not be used, Cork recommended the creation of a new rescue procedure – administration: see ch. 9 below.

[16] Insolvency Act 1986 s. 29(2). On the phrase 'substantially the whole' see Goode, *Principles of Corporate Insolvency Law*, p. 253.

[17] Note that where the security is composed of fixed and floating charges the AR's appointment is effected under the floating charge: see *Meadrealm Ltd* v. *Transcontinental Golf Construction Ltd* (1991, unreported).

[18] On the 'reasonable opportunity' to pay test see D. Milman and C. Durrant, *Corporate Insolvency: Law and Practice* (3rd edn, Sweet & Maxwell, London, 1999) p. 56 and *Bank of Baroda* v. *Panessar* [1986] BCLC 497 ('adequate time' test preferred to 'reasonable opportunity').

winding-up petition or the passing of a resolution to liquidate the company voluntarily;[19] the presentation of a petition for administration or the initiation of a CVA; the levying of distress or execution against the company; failure to meet any obligations, or to abide by any restrictions that are set out in the debenture;[20] ceasing to trade; placing the assets in jeopardy; or being unable to pay debts. Frequently a bank would appoint a receiver suddenly and against the wishes of the directors.[21]

A debenture holder who was able to appoint a receiver was also in a position to block the effective operation of other insolvency procedures. The party entitled to appoint a receiver had to be given notice of a petition for administration and could then put in the receiver – a course of action that would lead to the dismissal of the petition for administration.[22] Similarly in the case of a CVA, the creditors' meeting called to consider this may not approve a proposal affecting the enforcement rights of a secured creditor without the latter's approval.[23] Nor may a liquidator take possession of assets under the control of a previously appointed receiver.[24]

Appointment of a receiver does not bring the company's trading to a halt since company contracts will generally continue to be enforceable by and against it; its assets remain in its ownership and its directors remain in office.[25] Legal control of the company, however, passes to the receiver even though factual control may seem, to an outsider, not to have changed. This legal control means that the receiver is entitled to direct the company as to the conduct of the firm's management.[26] The

---

[19] If the court has appointed a liquidator its leave is required before a receiver can be appointed, but such leave will normally be forthcoming: Insolvency Act 1986 s. 130(2); *Henry Pound and Sons Ltd* v. *Hutchins* (1889) 42 Ch D 402.

[20] An example would be a grant by the company of a new security interest in contravention of the terms of the debenture.

[21] See Milman and Durrant, *Corporate Insolvency*, p. 54, who noted also that the directors could occasionally welcome the appointment of a receiver who took the difficult decisions (and was blamed by employees for these). Receivers could also have a 'better chance of persuading creditors to be patient than the directors who have been promising a cheque for months'.

[22] Insolvency Act 1986 s. 9(2)(a); s. 9(3). Administrative receivers can still be appointed, even after the reforms of the Enterprise Act 2002, although such appointment is much restricted: see further p. 360 below.

[23] Insolvency Act 1986, s. 4(3).

[24] See Armour and Frisby, 'Rethinking Receivership', p. 76; *Re Crigglestone Coal Co.* [1906] 1 Ch 523.

[25] See L. Doyle, 'The Residual Status of Directors in Receivership' (1996) 17 Co. Law. 131.

[26] *Re Joshua Shaw & Sons Ltd* [1989] BCLC 362. Directors' powers of management are suspended as regards assets comprised in the security and the general conduct of the business: see further Goode, *Principles of Corporate Insolvency Law*, pp. 273–4.

contracts of employment of employees are generally unaffected by the appointment of a receiver out of court, but termination of contracts will be involved if certain events take place, such as sale of the business.[27]

The powers of the receiver will be stipulated in the relevant debenture and in any subsequent orders.[28] A series of implied powers is also set out in Schedule 1 of the Insolvency Act 1986.[29] Receivers are thus equipped to take a series of actions for the enforcement of the debenture holder's rights: to manage the company's business;[30] to borrow using the company's assets as security;[31] and to take possession of the company's assets.[32] They may also institute legal proceedings,[33] go to arbitration or settle disputes,[34] and prove for debts owed to the company by insolvent debtors.[35] Cheques can be issued and documents executed in the company's name[36] and necessary payments made.[37] Once the assets are collected the receiver possesses power to sell these in order to create funds for repaying the debenture holder; subsidiary companies can be established and portions of the business transmitted to these as ongoing operations or for sale.[38]

A receiver may apply to the court for directions in relation to the performance of his or her functions and the court may give directions or make an order declaring the rights of persons (before the court or otherwise) as it thinks fit.[39] Receivers can thus apply to the court for directions in order to resolve disputes about entitlement to the secured property.[40] Receivers, furthermore, can dispose of property subject to a

---

[27] Or if the receiver arranges for new inconsistent employment contracts and if the continued employment of an employee is incompatible with a receiver taking over the running of the company: see Milman and Durrant, *Corporate Insolvency*, pp. 61–4.

[28] The receiver has powers *in rem* (relating to the company's assets comprised in the security) and rights *in personam* (or agency powers) relating to everything else.

[29] See Insolvency Act 1986 s. 42 which provides that the powers conferred on an administrative receiver by the appointing debentures shall be deemed to include the list of powers set out in Sch. 1 to the 1986 Act and these deemed powers operate 'except in so far as they are inconsistent with any of the provisions of those debentures'. The list of powers includes, *inter alia*, the power to carry on the business of the company, to sell or otherwise dispose of the property of the company by public auction or private contract and to raise and borrow money and grant security over the property of the company.

[30] Insolvency Act 1986 Sch. 1, para. 14.

[31] Ibid., para. 3. [32] Ibid., para. 1. [33] Ibid. [34] Ibid., paras. 6 and 18.

[35] Ibid., para. 20. [36] Ibid., paras. 10 and 8. [37] Ibid., para. 13.

[38] Ibid., paras. 15 and 16. [39] Insolvency Act 1986 s. 35.

[40] See, for example, *Re Ellis, Son & Vidler Ltd* [1994] BCC 532.

third-party's security (which ranks in priority to the rights of the receiver's appointee) on an order of the court.[41]

Receivers, however, possess powers not merely to act for the debenture holder, but to act for the company. These follow from the execution of the debenture.[42] Receivers are thus placed in a strange position: they have two principals but are not subject to the control of either of them. They cannot be instructed or sacked by the company's board[43] and, as Fox LJ said in *Gomba Holdings*:[44]

> The relationship set up by the debenture and the appointment of a receiver is tripartite and involves the mortgagor, receiver and debenture holder. The receiver becomes the mortgagor's agent whether the mortgagor likes it or not. The mortgagor has to pay the receiver's fees as a matter of contract. The mortgagor cannot dismiss the receiver and cannot instruct him in the course of his receivership.

The debenture holder, in return, is largely protected from responsibility for the acts and omissions of the receiver.[45]

In summary, it has been said of the receiver: 'He can best be described as an independent contractor whose primary responsibility is to protect the interests of his appointor, but who also owes a duty to his deemed principal, the company, to refrain from conduct which needlessly damages its business or goodwill, and a separate duty, by statute, to observe the priority given to preferential creditors over claims secured by a floating charge.'[46]

When receivers agree contracts, employment or otherwise, they act as agents of the company but they may incur personal liabilities (except in so far as the contract provides otherwise). An important issue here concerns the circumstances under which the receiver will be deemed to

---

[41] Insolvency Act 1986 s. 43. Note that this would not cover property subject to a ROT clause: see s. 43(7).

[42] See further Goode, *Principles of Corporate Insolvency Law*, pp. 276–82.

[43] ARs can only be removed by an order of the court: Insolvency Act 1986 s. 45(1).

[44] *Gomba Holdings UK Ltd and Others* v. *Homan and Bird* [1986] 1 WLR 1301.

[45] See Insolvency Act 1986 s. 44(1)(a).

[46] Goode, *Principles of Corporate Insolvency Law*, p. 262. For a critique of the receiver as deemed agent see J. S. Ziegel, 'The Privately Appointed Receiver and the Enforcement of Security Interests: Anomaly or Superior Solution?' in Ziegel (ed.), *Current Developments in International and Comparative Corporate Insolvency Law* (Clarendon Press, Oxford, 1994). Ziegel (p. 459) asks: 'Why not reverse the statutory presumption and declare the receiver to be the secured party's agent or, alternatively, an independent functionary?'

have adopted an employment contract for which he or she will be personally liable. The Insolvency Act 1986 governed such issues through section 44(1)(b), which made the receiver personally liable on contracts adopted by him in carrying out these functions. Receivers have a statutory indemnity covering such liabilities[47] but until the mid-1990s receivers sought to avoid such liabilities by issuing a standardised letter informing each employee that the office holder was not adopting, and would not adopt, their contract of employment. The company, the letter went, would continue to be their employer for the time being (this became known as a *Specialised Mouldings* letter).[48] The validity of *Specialised Mouldings* letters was, however, put to the test in the *Paramount* case.[49] Lord Browne-Wilkinson, in the House of Lords, was forced to the view that such letters did not exclude adoption once the fourteen-day period of grace[50] ran out and that contracts of employment were inevitably adopted if a receiver (or administrator) caused the employment to continue beyond the fourteen days. *Paramount* thus left receivers in an awkward position since it may be difficult to form a professional judgement on the feasibility of rescue within such a short time.[51]

The deficiencies of the law in this area were partially addressed before the House of Lords decided *Paramount*, when the Insolvency Act 1994 was passed. This applied only to employment contracts adopted on or after 15 March 1994 (and thus left *Paramount* to address contracts adopted between the commencement of the Insolvency Act 1986

---

[47] Insolvency Act 1986 s. 44(1)(c). See also I. F. Fletcher, *The Law of Insolvency* (3rd edn, Sweet & Maxwell, London, 2002), p. 371 and, on employment contracts, see Milman and Durrant, *Corporate Insolvency*, p. 67; *Re Paramount Airways Ltd (No. 3)*, reported as *Powdrill* v. *Watson* [1995] 2 WLR 312, [1995] BCC 319, [1995] 2 All ER 65 ('*Paramount*'); Insolvency Act 1994 amendments. See further P. L. Davies, 'Employee Claims in Insolvency: Corporate Rescue and Preferential Claims' (1994) 23 Ins. LJ 141; I. F. Fletcher, 'Adoption of Contracts of Employment by Receivers and Administrators: The *Paramount* Case' [1995] JBL 596.

[48] See unreported ruling of Harman J in *Re Specialised Mouldings* (13 February 1987).

[49] *Paramount*: the case that laid the foundation for this issue was *Nicol* v. *Cutts* [1985] 1 BCC 99.

[50] Provided for in the Insolvency Act 1986 s. 44(2) which states that an AR is not taken to have adopted a contract of employment by reason of anything done or omitted within fourteen days of his/her appointment.

[51] See Fletcher, 'Adoption of Contracts', p. 602; P. Mudd, 'The Insolvency Act 1994: *Paramount* Cured?' (1994) 10 IL&P 38; Mudd, '*Paramount*: The House of Lords Decision – Is There Still Hope of Avoiding Some of Those Claims?' (1995) 11 IL&P 78.

(January 1987) and 15 March 1994). Under sections 44 (2A–D) of the Insolvency Act 1986 (as amended by the Insolvency Act 1994), where a contract of employment is adopted, a receiver will only become liable personally for 'qualifying liabilities', which are defined (for example, to include liabilities to pay wages or salary or pension contributions incurred when the receiver is in office) and which accrue and relate to services rendered only after the date when the contract was adopted. This means that where services are rendered partly before and partly after adoption of contracts, only such a sum as reflects services rendered after adoption will qualify under sections 44 (2A–D) and will be accorded the enhanced protection that flows from the receiver's personal liability.[52] With regard to payments referable to periods pre-adoption or before the receiver's appointment, employees will thus stand as unsecured creditors with claims against the company alone.

Turning to the duties of the receiver, the primary obligation is to act *bona fide* to realise the assets of the company in the interests of the debenture holder.[53] The receiver's powers of management have been said to be ancillary to that duty.[54] There is, as indicated, no duty to obey the firm or generally to provide the company with details and information concerning the conduct of the company's affairs.[55] At one time, however, the courts assumed that receivers owed a duty of care in tort to the company and subsequent encumbrancers and guarantors of the company's debt. The duty was to use care to obtain the best possible price when selling company property.[56] In the *Downsview Nominees* case[57] the

---

[52] In administration such employees would have 'super-priority' by virtue of the Insolvency Act 1986 s. 19(4) and (5) which gives such payments priority over any charges. In receivership there is personal liability of the receiver, who is entitled to indemnity out of the company's assets: s. 44(1)(c). On the case for a 'uniform approach which transcends the differences between the various forms of insolvency proceedings' see H. Anderson, 'Insolvent Insolvencies' (2001) 17 IL&P 87.

[53] *Re B. Johnson & Co. (Builders) Ltd* [1955] Ch 634, 661–2; *Downsview Nominees Ltd* v. *First City Corporation* [1993] AC 295.

[54] *Gomba Holdings UK Ltd and Others* v. *Homan and Bird* [1986] 1 WLR 1301 at 1304–5 (Hoffmann J); [1986] 3 All ER 94.

[55] Ibid.

[56] Per Lord Denning MR in *Standard Chartered Bank Ltd* v. *Walker* [1982] 1 WLR 1410; *Cuckmere Brick Co. Ltd* v. *Mutual Finance Ltd* [1971] Ch 949; *American Express* v. *Hurley* [1986] BCLC 52. For analysis and criticism see L. Bentley, 'Mortgagee's Duties on Sale: No Place for Tort?' (1990) 54 *Conveyancer and Property Lawyer* 431. See also H. Rajak, 'Can a Receiver be Negligent?' in B. Rider (ed.), *The Corporate Dimension: An Exploration of Developing Areas of Company and Commercial Law* (Jordans, Bristol, 1998) p. 129; *Parker-Tweedale* v. *Dunbar Bank plc* [1991] Ch 12 at 18 (Nourse LJ).

[57] *Downsview Nominees Ltd* v. *First City Corporation* [1993] AC 295.

Privy Council held that a receiver only owed equitable duties to non-appointing debenture holders and to the company to act in good faith. Specific equitable duties were owed to these parties to do such things as keep premises in repair and avoid waste. The Privy Council accepted that a receiver was subject to a specific equitable duty to take reasonable care to obtain a proper price for assets sold, but it denied the existence of a general duty of care in tort to subsequent encumbrances or the company with regard to dealing in the secured assets.[58] The Court of Appeal, however, in *Medforth* v. *Blake*,[59] reasserted that the duties of receivers are equitable rather than tortious but stated that a receiver owed a duty, if managing the mortgaged property, to do so with due diligence, which amounted to an equitable duty of care. In that case, Medforth, the owner–manager of a pig farm, owed sums to the Midland Bank that became unacceptable to the lender. The loan terms provided for the appointment of a receiver and a receiver was appointed with power to run the business. The business was run by the receiver for four years before new terms were agreed between Medforth and the bank. During that period, the receiver had not negotiated with the relevant pre-existing pig feed suppliers in order to obtain the 10 to 15 per cent discounts that Medforth had received and which Medforth had repeatedly advised the receiver to ask for. Around £200,000 of discounts had not been obtained during the receivership. The issue was whether the receiver owed Medforth a duty of care that had been breached or whether there had been a breach of good faith.

Sir Richard Scott VC delivered the sole judgment of the Court of Appeal and stated: 'The proposition that in managing and carrying on the mortgaged business the receiver owed the mortgagor no duty other than of good faith offends in my opinion commercial sense ... If [the

---

[58] See further Rajak, 'Can a Receiver be Negligent?', pp. 140–3; A. Berg, 'Duties of a Mortgagee and a Receiver' [1993] JBL 213; R. Nolan, '*Downsview Nominees Ltd* v. *First City Corporation Ltd* – Good News for Receivers – In General' (1994) 15 Co. Law. 28; A. Hogan, 'Receivers Revisited' (1996) 17 Co. Law. 226; L. Doyle, 'The Receiver's Duties on a Sale of Charged Assets' (1997) 10 *Insolvency Intelligence* 9. See also *Huish* v. *Ellis* [1995] BCC 462; C. Pugh, 'Duties of Care Owed to Mortgagors and Guarantors: The Hidden Liability' (1995) 11 IL&P 143.

[59] [2000] Ch 86, [1999] 3 All ER 97. See S. Bulman and L. Fitzsimons, 'To Run or Not to Run ... (the Borrower's Business)' [1999] Ins. Law. 306; S. Frisby, 'Making a Silk Purse out of a Pig's Ear: *Medforth* v. *Blake and Others*' (2000) 63 MLR 413; McCormack, 'Receivership and the Rescue Culture'; L. S. Sealy, 'Mortgagees and Receivers: A Duty of Care Resurrected and Extended' [2000] CLJ 31; L. Ife, 'Liability of Receivers and Banks in Selling and Managing Mortgaged Property' (2000) 13 *Insolvency Intelligence* 61.

receiver] does decide to carry on the business why should he not be expected to do so with reasonable competence?'[60] It was argued for the receiver in *Medforth* that the cases of *Re B. Johnson & Co. (Builders) Ltd*[61] and *Downsview*[62] established that receivers owed no duty to exercise skill and care and that to go beyond the duty to perform with good faith would undermine receivership by doing away with the judicially sanctioned advantages that receivership as an institution offered.[63] Scott VC's response was that the authorities cited gave non-exhaustive lists of the obligations of receivers and that, since, on strong authority, receivers had to take reasonable steps to obtain proper prices on asset sales, it would be anomalous not to impose a corresponding duty in relation to the management of those assets. Scott VC went on to state that principle and authority supported the following seven propositions:

1. A receiver managing mortgaged property owes duties to the mortgagor and anyone else with an interest in the equity of redemption.
2. The duties include, but are not necessarily confined to, a duty of good faith.
3. The extent and scope of any duty additional to that of good faith will depend upon the facts and circumstances of the particular case.
4. In exercising his powers of management the primary duty of the receiver is to try and bring about a situation in which interest on the secured debt can be paid and the debt itself repaid.
5. Subject to that primary duty, the receiver owes a duty to manage the property with due diligence.
6. Due diligence does not oblige the receiver to carry on a business on the mortgaged premises previously carried on by the mortgagor.
7. If the receiver does carry on a business on the mortgaged premises, due diligence requires reasonable steps to be taken in order to try and do so profitably.[64]

Whether the imposition of *Medforth* duties of competence on receivers will enhance the institution of receivership or detract from it will be considered below. Taking the issue of financial competence further, though, another case has considered the receiver's duty to maximise value before the sale of secured assets. In *Silven Properties*,[65] the Court

---

[60] [1999] 3 All ER 97 at 103.   [61] [1955] Ch 634.   [62] [1993] AC 295.

[63] See Frisby, 'Making a Silk Purse', p. 415; McCormack, 'Receivership and the Rescue Culture', pp. 238–40.

[64] [1993] 3 All ER 97 at 111 G–J.

[65] *Silven Properties and Another v. The Royal Bank of Scotland plc* [2003] BCC 1002.

of Appeal stated that the obligations of a receiver did not extend to postponing the exercise of a power of sale until after the decision of a planning application where the outcome might have been to increase the market value of a mortgaged property. Nor was the receiver, as agent of the mortgagee, obliged to invest time or money in steps designed to increase the value of the mortgaged property. The limit of the receiver's duty was to take reasonable care to obtain a price that reflected the added value offered by the potential granting of the planning application. The primary duty of the receiver was to secure repayment of the secured debt and the primary obligation was to the bank. In short, the duties of the receiver were the same as those of a mortgagee[66] and there was no duty to delay by taking steps to increase the value of the property or by otherwise improving it.[67]

In addition to the mixture of common law duties owed by a receiver is the set of statutory obligations imposed by the Insolvency Act 1986. Notable among these is the obligation of a receiver appointed to enforce a floating charge[68] to ensure that the regime of statutory preferential claims is correctly applied and to retain for the benefit of the general creditors the prescribed part of the net property subject to a floating charge.[69] Provisions on disclosure of information include duties to furnish annual accounts to the company's registry, the company, the appointor and the creditors' committee;[70] a duty to prepare a report within three months of receiving a statement of affairs from the company officers;[71] and an obligation to summon a meeting for unsecured

---

[66] Thus a receiver cannot remain passive if that would damage the interests of the mortgagee or mortgagor – he must preserve the value of property over which he is appointed. In *Bell* v. *Long and Others* [2008] EWHC 1273 (Ch) Patten J confirmed that the receivers were entitled to choose the time of sale even if it turned out to be disadvantageous to the mortgagor who could have recovered more had the properties been sold later. The receiver is not a trustee of his power of sale for the mortgagor.

[67] See *Silven Properties and Another v. The Royal Bank of Scotland plc* [2003] BCC 1002: Lightman J (co-opted into the Court of Appeal) went on to list the 'peculiar', but 'significant', incidents of the receiver's agency (at 1012 G–H). See further G. Stewart, 'Legal Update' (2003) *Recovery* (Winter) 6.

[68] But not a fixed charge: *Re G. L. Saunders Ltd* [1986] 1 WLR 215.

[69] Insolvency Act 1986 s. 40; *IRC* v. *Goldblatt* [1972] Ch 498; *Woods* v. *Winskill* [1913] 2 Ch 303; Insolvency Act 1986 s. 176A(2). It is the receiver who is obliged to see that preferential claims are settled when receivership and liquidation coincide: *Re Pearl Maintenance Services Ltd* [1995] 1 BCLC 449.

[70] Insolvency Rules 1986 r. 3.32. [71] Insolvency Act 1986 ss. 47 and 48.

creditors to consider this report.[72] As for the enforcement of the receiver's duties, the statutory obligations are usually underpinned by criminal sanctions of fines and the common law duties can be backed up by enforcement actions taken in the ordinary courts. It is now clear that the company can bring a direct action against its receiver.[73]

Finally, as far as termination of the receivership is concerned, this may result from the receiver's death,[74] removal by court order,[75] or ceasing to be a qualified IP.[76] The usual process, however, involves the completion of duties, notably realisation of all valuable assets and the making of all possible distributions to interested parties in the order of priority fixed by the law. Notification is then given to the company and the creditors' committee and any surplus funds are passed to the company. Resignations of receivers require at least seven days' notice of intention to be given to the appointor company, any liquidator and the creditors' committee.[77] The receiver will also have to vacate office if an administrator is appointed by the court.[78] Removal of the receiver by the appointor is, after the Insolvency Act 1986 s. 45(1), only possible following a successful application to the court. The purpose of this reform was to make the receiver independent of the appointing debenture holder.[79]

Efficiency and creditor considerations

In some regards the administrative receiver may be thought to be particularly well placed to secure the rescue of an ailing company. As noted, the receiver is not necessarily required to go to court in order to act and there is no need to secure the agreement of directors, shareholders or creditors before actions to protect the debenture holders' interests are taken. The company's assets can be disposed of free from security interests (apart from those of the appointor) if the court gives leave.[80] Receivers owe obligations to report to other creditors but have no duties

---

[72] Ibid., s. 48(2); Insolvency Rules 1986 rr. 3.9–3.15; see Milman and Durrant, *Corporate Insolvency*, p. 73.

[73] *Watts* v. *Midland Bank plc* [1986] BCLC 15.

[74] The replacing includes giving notice under Insolvency Rule 3.34.

[75] Insolvency Act 1986 s. 45(1).   [76] Ibid., ss. 45(2), 389, 390.

[77] Insolvency Rules 1986 r. 3.33.   [78] Insolvency Act 1986 ss. 45(2), 11(1)(b).

[79] Milman and Durrant, *Corporate Insolvency*, p. 76.   [80] Insolvency Act 1986 s. 43.

to accede to their wishes or even to listen to their views.[81] After appointment they act in a highly independent fashion and, as noted, the debenture holder can only remove them from office by securing an order of the court.[82]

It could be contended, however, that the independent and swiftly responsive model of receivership may now have been prejudiced by the *Medforth v. Blake*[83] imposition of a duty of care on receivers.[84] In *Medforth* it was argued on behalf of the receivers that imposing a duty of due diligence would undermine receivership. In response, though, it has been noted:

> Scott VC was unimpressed by that submission and justifiably so. The advantages of receivership to the modern day financial institutions go far beyond the avoidance of wilful default liability. Statute has [conferred] an array of powers on administrative receivers, all of which will accrue to the benefit of the appointor, so much that escaping liability as mortgagee in possession will be little more than an afterthought to the contemporary debenture holder.[85]

Receivership as an institution may have had powerful institutional supporters[86] but *Medforth* could give rise to legal uncertainties that are liable to produce defensive attitudes on the part of receivers and which could decrease the efficiency of receivership as an institution. As already noted, Scott VC's judgment left some doubt as to the scope of the equitable duty owed by the receiver.[87] In suggesting that this might 'depend on the facts and circumstances of the particular case'[88] Scott

---

[81] See E. Ferran, 'The Duties of an Administrative Receiver to Unsecured Creditors' (1988) 9 Co. Law. 58. Ferran suggested that the disclosure requirements could benefit unsecured creditors in an indirect way, namely by providing them with ammunition with which to persuade a liquidator that an action should be brought against the administrative receiver.

[82] Insolvency Act 1986 s. 45.   [83] [1999] 3 All ER 97.

[84] For a review of the discussion see Frisby, 'Making a Silk Purse', pp. 420–2; Sealy, 'Mortgagees and Receivers'.

[85] Frisby, 'Making a Silk Purse', p. 420.

[86] See B. G. Carruthers and T. C. Halliday, *Rescuing Business: The Making of Corporate Bankruptcy Law in England and the United States* (Clarendon Press, Oxford, 1998) pp. 134–6, 197–205, 286.

[87] For criticism of the *Medforth* reasoning on the equitable duty see Sealy, 'Mortgagees and Receivers'.

[88] [1999] 3 All ER 97 at 111: a point taken by Nicholas Warren QC in *Hadjipanayi v. Yeldon et al.* [2001] BPIR 487 at 492–5, when, in reviewing the duties of a mortgagee-appointed receiver, he deemed it arguable (but no more) that receivers may owe a duty to co-operate with the mortgagor in selling the mortgaged property with its attendant business as a going concern.

VC missed the opportunity to lay down a guiding rule. The facts in *Medforth* indicated a very high level of negligence in so far as the warnings concerning the pig feed discount were repeatedly not acted upon. The receiver's behaviour could be construed as close to a breach of good faith and this leaves open a series of questions about receiver failure, notably whether the *Medforth* type of behaviour would have involved a breach of duty in the absence of the warnings that were given. A number of receivers will, as a result of such uncertainty, be exposed to litigation and, until the law is clarified, the institution of receivership will involve higher transaction costs than would be the case with a more legally definite rule.

Such a process of legal clarification may indeed take some time because Scott VC's judgment in *Medforth* contained what has been dubbed some 'fancy footwork'[89] in escaping the constraints of previous case law, in 'applying an equitable label to a common law concept'[90] and by declining to arrive at the just result by reasoning in terms of wilful default and good faith. As one critic of the decision wrote: '*Medforth* is an attempt wholly to outmanoeuvre the *Downsview* analysis by rewriting the obligations in equity of the receiver by creating an equitable duty of care which can hardly be distinguished in practice from the common law tortious duty of care so comprehensively forsworn in *Downsview*.'[91] Whatever the doctrinal rights and wrongs here, the potential for litigation on these points should not be written off. That is the danger for receivers and for all parties who see legal certainty as serving their interests.

There is a response to such concerns, however, that may offer some reassurance to the parties just mentioned. It can be argued, first, that *Medforth* does not add significantly to uncertainties for the receiver

---

[89] McCormack, 'Receiverships and the Rescue Culture', p. 240.

[90] See J. Anderson, 'Receivers' Duties to Mortgagors. Court of Appeal Makes a Pig's Ear of It' (1999) 37 *CCH Company Law Newsletter* 6. On the content of the equitable duty to take care, its history and its existence in other equitable relationships see R. Gregory, 'Receiver's Duty of Care Considered' (1992) *CCH Company Law Newsletter* 9.

[91] Anderson, 'Receivers' Duties to Mortgagors', p. 7. But see *Medforth* v. *Blake* at [2000] Ch 102 E: Scott VC remonstrated 'I do not, for my part, think it matters one jot whether the duty is expressed as a common law duty or a duty in equity. The result is the same.' Lightman and Moss point out that the 'issue may well be of some significance given the limited application of the Unfair Contracts Terms Act 1977, which only applies to common law duties of care': see Sir G. Lightman and G. Moss, *The Law of Administrators and Receivers of Companies* (4th edn, Thomson/Sweet & Maxwell, London, 2007) p. 279.

because the long-established obligation to secure a reasonable price[92] is liable to overlap significantly with a *Medforth* obligation of competence: many instances of lack of competence will mean there is a failure to secure a reasonable price. They might also constitute instances of wilful default per *Downsview*.[93] Second, it can be added that receivers who are wary of *Medforth* should not find it beyond their capabilities to protect themselves from legal attack by establishing proper procedures that reflect the minimal levels of competence of a reasonable business person.[94]

A second concern about *Medforth* might be the belief (consistent with the judgment in *Downsview*)[95] that imposing an equitable duty of care on receivers will compromise the receiver's primary obligation to act in the interests of the debenture holder. This worry is perhaps readily responded to by stating that a duty to exercise skill and care should not impinge on such a primary obligation or place other interests on a par with those of the debenture holder in the considerations of the receiver: the requirement is merely that 'decisions be competently taken'.[96] (As noted above, the *Silven Properties* decision, moreover, reaffirmed the primacy of the obligation to the mortgagee.)[97] As the Insolvency Service has commented: 'Some respondents asserted that the effect of [*Medforth*] was to remind receivers of their wider duties and that, accordingly, this diluted the force of the criticisms that receivership was not a collective procedure. This is arguably an overstatement of the *Medforth* decision.'[98] *Medforth* does not change the balance of power so much as demand an absence of behaviour lacking in care. This response

---

[92] See also *Silven Properties and Another* v. *The Royal Bank of Scotland plc* [2003] BCC 1002.

[93] See also A. Walters, 'Round Up: Corporate Finance and Receivership' (1999) 20 Co. Law. 324, who argues, at p. 329, that: 'Given the possible damage that an incompetent receiver could do to the equity of redemption, it is perhaps not surprising to see the Court of Appeal applying a modern form of equitable duty analogous in some respects to the old-fashioned concept of "wilful default" by a mortgagee in possession.' Walters thus equates *Medforth* v. *Blake* [1999] 3 All ER 97 with *Knight* v. *Lawrence* [1991] BCC 411.

[94] See V. Swain, 'Taking Care of Business' (1999) *Insolvency Bulletin* 9.

[95] See Frisby, 'Making a Silk Purse', p. 420.

[96] Ibid. Frisby argues that what is being targeted is careless behaviour rather than a deliberate course of conduct that will benefit the mortgagee to the detriment of the mortgagor. Thus *Medforth* does not overturn the balance of power between the mortgagee and mortgagor (when properly analysed and applied): pp. 420–1.

[97] *Silven Properties and Another* v. *The Royal Bank of Scotland plc* [2003] BCC 1002.

[98] Insolvency Service, *A Review of Company Rescue and Business Reconstruction Mechanisms*, Report by the Review Group (DTI, 2000), p. 52 ('IS 2000').

also provides an answer to a further concern about *Medforth* – represented by Lord Templeman's view in *Downsview* – that liability in negligence would lead receivers to sell assets 'as speedily as possible'.[99] If there is a clear duty to the appointor, an obligation to act competently should have, at worst, a neutral effect on speed of disposition, and in many cases it will favour a less precipitate, more deliberate, style of decision-making. Whether receivers' duties to creditors should be broadened is a matter to be returned to below in considering issues of fairness.

Note should now be taken of a number of difficulties that constitute limitations on the collectivity of receivership. Receivership involves no moratorium on the enforcement of claims against the company. This means that a receiver is powerless to stop other creditors from acting to enforce their claim and, in doing so, throwing a spanner in the works of the rescue plan. Nor is there any power in the receiver's hands to stop the company from entering into liquidation. Liquidation will not stop receivers from acting. They will continue in office, exercising powers in the interests of their appointor (acting as agent for the appointor, no longer for the company). But the chances of a successful rescue will be reduced by the advent of liquidation. Once that stage is reached there is no prospect of corporate survival, although the receiver may succeed in selling off some part of the business as a going concern.

Nor, as we have seen, is the receiver always obliged to attempt to rescue the business. The receiver is only obliged to pursue the rescue option if this course is in the interests of the appointing debenture holder. If the interest of the appointor is best served by a simple realisation of the assets, the administrative receiver is obliged not to attempt to rescue unless the full approval of the appointor is forthcoming. There are reasons for thinking, moreover, that receivers will tend to play safe and to favour simple realisations rather than rescues when in doubt. Receivers are private professionals not public officials and are dependent for their livelihood and appointment on a relatively small group of financial institutions, such as banks, taking floating charges. Although administrative receivers cannot be removed from office once appointed, except by order of the court, they would jeopardise future appointments if they disregarded their appointor's wishes.[100]

---

[99] [1993] AC 295 at 316.
[100] A. Clarke, 'Corporate Rescues and Reorganisations in English Law after the Insolvency Act 1986' (Mimeo, University College, London, 1993) p. 7.

The statistics of the nineties indicated that receivership resulted in rescue in fewer instances than other formal procedures: the DTI's 1993 Consultative Document on Company Voluntary Arrangements reported that in 1993, 50 per cent of administrative receiverships terminated with a break-up sale of the company's assets, but that 67 per cent of all administrations and 75 per cent of all CVAs achieved a complete or partial survival of the enterprise.[101] When, indeed, the Royal Bank of Scotland (RBS) adopted a rescue culture, it immediately cut the number of receivers appointed.[102] This is perhaps because, as has been pointed out, receivership can only be effectively used for rescue purposes if the company has a dominant creditor (perhaps a bank or consortium of banks); if that creditor is willing actively to support rescue; and if other parties refrain from spoiling actions. If such conditions exist, moreover, it may well be possible to forgo receivership and mount a rescue by means of informal agreements.

When the Insolvency Service consulted on rescue mechanisms for its 2000 Review[103] it encountered very different appraisals of receivership. Most of its respondents were favourably disposed towards the institution of receivership, a situation that was not surprising given that most responses came from law firms and trade associations.[104] These respondents stressed that administrative receivership was an integral part of the rescue culture in the UK that contributed to rescue and corporate survival. They emphasised the ability of receivers to take rapid and effective actions to prevent deterioration in the viability of businesses (particularly where fraud was evident or suspected); the sizeable number of businesses that go into receivership and then are sold as going concerns; and the relatively low costs of initiating the procedure (as seen by creditors and practitioners). The 'larger professional service firms' considered that the banks took a responsible attitude towards receivership and only appointed receivers as a last resort. They conceded, however,

---

[101] R3's Ninth Survey of Business Recovery in the UK (2001) indicated business preservation rates associated with appointments as follows: receiverships 59 per cent; administrators 79 per cent (up from 41 per cent in a small sample); CVAs 74 per cent. Receiverships were found in the SPI's Eighth Survey, *Company Insolvency in the United Kingdom* (SPI, London, 1999), to save 31 per cent of jobs compared to 37 per cent for CVAs and 40 per cent for administrators (1997–8).

[102] In 1992 the RBS appointed 418 receivers (11 per cent of the national total); in 1996 it appointed 48 (5 per cent of the national total): see M. Hunter, 'The Nature and Functions of a Rescue Culture' [1999] JBL 491 at 508, n. 66.

[103] IS 2000, p. 53.   [104] Ibid., pp. 15, 48.

that non-bank floating charge holders were 'more likely to act precipitately as they tended to be less focused on preserving a long term relationship with the debtor'. Research conducted by Franks and Sussman and
discussed by the IS[105] gives some support to the 'last resort' account. The
IS noted the key research finding that: 'It seems clear that banks rarely
petition for the liquidation of a company and that, in recent years, they
have tended to see administrative receivership as a last resort for a
troubled company. Where an administrative receiver is appointed,
going concern sales (of the whole of the business or of some part of it)
are achieved in about 44 per cent of cases.'[106] More recent empirical
research has suggested that the displacement of receivers with administrators in the post-Enterprise Act 2002 regime has resulted in very little
increase in the number of corporate rescues and no significant difference
in outcomes between new style administrations and receiverships under
the old law – both in terms of going-concern sales versus break-up sales
and in terms of returns for creditors.[107]

Many business people consulted by the Insolvency Service were,
however, concerned about the power of the floating charge holder:

> They were very sceptical about the banks' contentions that receivers
> would only ever be appointed as a last resort and tended to be wary of
> their banks in times of difficulty. Some business people told us of personal
> experiences where the banks appeared to have acted very unreasonably.
> Many considered that banks were only adopting a more relationship
> driven style at the larger end of the market and that the banks did not
> have the same interest in the SME end of the market – with the result that
> in times of trouble, the banks would be looking to exit the relationship as
> quickly as possible, via receivership if necessary.[108]

Respondents who voiced reservations about the effectiveness of administrative receivership as a rescue device emphasised three points.[109] The
first was that: 'It can lead to unnecessary business failures and undermines the rescue culture, particularly when the relationship between the

---

[105] Ibid., pp. 16–19; Franks and Sussman, 'Cycle of Corporate Distress'.
[106] IS 2000, p. 17.
[107] See Armour, Hsu and Walters, *Report for the Insolvency Service* (2006); A. Katz and
M. Mumford, *Report to the Insolvency Service: Study of Administration Cases*
(Insolvency Service, London, December 2006); Frisby, *Insolvency Outcomes* (2006) –
who notes 'a startling similarity between the performance of receiverships and administrations regarding frequency of outcomes'.
[108] IS 2000, p. 17. See also Carruthers and Halliday, *Rescuing Business*, p. 286.
[109] IS 2000, p. 15. Points relating to the consistency of administrative receivership with
international and EU requirements have been left out of account here.

floating charge holder and the business breaks down; the floating charge holder may then decide to withdraw support from the business and appoint an administrative receiver when an alternative lender might have elected to continue such support.[110] The second was that: 'Because the purpose of the receivership is primarily to ensure repayment of the amount due to the secured creditor, there is no (or there is insufficient) incentive to maximise the value of the debtor company's estate.'[111] The third point was that the growth of asset-backed lending, factoring and invoice discounting as modes of corporate financing, together with a growing diversity of parties able to appoint administrative receivers, has made it more difficult to ensure that the appointment of an administrative receiver is effectively treated as a measure of last resort by lenders. Such diversity, in turn, makes it more difficult to rely on self-regulatory measures by creditors, such as the British Bankers' Association's Statement of Principles.[112]

The pessimistic view of receivership, however, has to be contrasted with what has been called the 'concentrated creditor governance' theory of receivership.[113] This theory urges that the law on receivership can generate significant and worthwhile efficiencies. Two propositions lie at the heart of this argument: first, that debt finance can act as a mechanism of corporate governance, especially in small and medium-sized enterprises (SMEs) where other governance mechanisms such as hostile takeovers are less important; and second, that concentrating a firm's

---

[110] See DTI/Insolvency Service, *Productivity and Enterprise: Insolvency – A Second Chance* (Cm 5234, 2001). Franks and Sussman ('Financial Distress and Bank Restructuring') argue that a bank's typical response to distress is to attempt a rescue, while reducing credit, but suggest that evidence of banks' tendencies to liquidate prematurely is 'mixed'.

[111] On the tendency of receivership to lead to premature closures and 'inefficient liquidations' of good firms, see DTI/Insolvency Service, *Insolvency – A Second Chance*. On returns to secured creditors, Frisby's research for the Insolvency Service suggests that in pre-Enterprise Act receiverships, secured creditors recovered on average 29.3 per cent on debts owed, compared to 34.6 per cent for post-Enterprise Act administrations and 13.4 per cent for pre-Enterprise Act administrations: see S. Frisby, *Interim Report to the Insolvency Service on Returns to Creditors from Pre- and Post-Enterprise Act Insolvency Procedures* (Insolvency Service, London, July 2007) (hereafter '*Returns to Creditors, 2007*').

[112] See British Bankers' Association (BBA), *A Statement of Principles: Banks and Businesses – Working Together When You Borrow* (BBA, London, 2005). See further D. Milman and D. Mond, *Security and Corporate Rescue* (Hodgsons, Manchester, 1999).

[113] See Armour and Frisby, 'Rethinking Receivership'.

debt finance in the hands of a relatively small number of creditors can reduce total monitoring and decision-making costs. The suggestion here is that giving control over enforcement to a 'concentrated creditor' allows that creditor to utilise the information it has gathered during the course of its deliberations on whether or not to continue to support the debtor, and that this both enhances the disciplining effect of credit and allows for quicker and cheaper enforcement than would take place with the collective insolvency procedure in which an outsider appointee takes over the firm. Consistent with this suggestion are studies published in 2006 suggesting that the direct costs of pre-Enterprise Act 2002 receivership cases are lower than those of post-Enterprise Act administrations.[114] They also indicate that the average net recoveries to creditors in receiverships are no lower than in the new administrations.[115]

The arguments for creditor concentration emphasise that a number of problems are faced in creditor collective actions. First, there is the issue of information. It will cost creditors money to gain information on whether to enforce the debt or renegotiate it, but the benefit of such information will be only a fraction of the total value at stake and so individual creditors will be notionally under-informed. They may, moreover, seek to free-ride on the monitoring of others and, overall, there will be collective underinvestment in monitoring. 'Hold out' problems may also affect collective action since collective renegotiation or decisions to sell the firm as a going concern may demand that all creditors agree the course of action. Individual creditors will thus have incentives to hold out against such agreements until their co-operation is bought. If such problems are severe, a race to enforce debts may result as collectivity breaks down.[116]

The suggested solution to such problems is not to follow Jackson and argue for state-imposed collectivism: this, say Armour and Frisby, will reduce enforcement costs but it will do 'nothing to ameliorate collective

---

[114] Armour, Hsu and Walters, *Report for the Insolvency Service*, p. iv (who suggest that concentration allows repeat-playing banks to negotiate down the fees of IPs more effectively in a receivership than is possible for dispersed unsecured creditors in an administration).

[115] Ibid., p. v. But see Frisby's argument that administration as a procedure is likely to produce better outcomes *for all creditors* than receivership: Frisby, *Returns to Creditors*, 2007, p. 34.

[116] Armour and Frisby, 'Rethinking Receivership', p. 84; S. Levmore, 'Monitors and Freeriders in Commercial and Corporate Settings' (1982) 92 Yale LJ 49 at 53–4; T. H. Jackson, 'Bankruptcy, Non-Bankruptcy Entitlements and the Creditors' Bargain' (1982) 92 Yale LJ 857 at 859–68.

action problems associated with information gathering beforehand'.[117] A more comprehensive solution, in their view, is for the debtor to have one main creditor who will act as a whistle blower. This will produce savings because creditor concentration means that the main creditor has appropriate incentives to monitor the debtor for default and, also, can renegotiate swiftly and efficiently since there is only one significant creditor. It is argued that enforcement in this manner is better informed and quicker than if carried out by a state official. It is a low-cost strategy for the creditor bank and so this increases the effectiveness of debt as a disciplinary mechanism for underperforming managers. Receivership thus is a vehicle for facilitating the efficient disposal of assets by a concentrated creditor.

Empirical research was said to support the case for the creditor concentration approach. Professionals involved in receivership thought that, in the majority of cases, receivers were appointed by a bank that was the debtor firm's principal lender. Statistics also indicated that receivership appointments were largely confined to SMEs with annual turnovers of less than £5 million and that the majority of appointments were made by banks.[118] As for monitoring, there was evidence that clearing banks typically lend to SMEs through local business relationship managers, but that some routine monitoring of debtors is conducted and that risk evaluations are carried out. If performance dropped below a certain point, the debtor's file would be transferred to a central 'intensive care' division of the bank and into the hands of specialist staff acting with the primary objective of turning corporate affairs around. Scrutiny by the bank would then become more intensive and, if the firm's fortunes did not change, the bank might appoint an accountant to carry out an independent business review. The function of that review would be to build a bridge between the bank and the troubled company's management in order to find a solution – which might or might not be a receivership. The whole process, in terms of creditor concentration theory, amounts to an information-gathering exercise initiated by the concentrated creditor that generates benefits for other creditors in terms of improved quality decision-making.

The creditor concentration theory is, however, subject to a number of objections. Leaving aside issues of fairness to non-appointing creditors, and focusing on economic efficiency considerations, the first problem is

---

[117] Armour and Frisby, 'Rethinking Receivership', p. 85.
[118] Ibid., p. 92; SPI Eighth Survey, p. 11.

that concentration may produce inefficient and distorted decisions concerning the continuation of the business as a going concern. Proponents of concentration concede that (consistently with their legal obligations) receivers generally see their role as being to maximise recoveries for the main creditor (hereafter 'the bank'). The danger, as summarised by one commentator, is:

> The receivership system may lead to an equilibrium in which the company is prematurely and inefficiently liquidated. The problem stems from the feature of this system which allows creditors to act in individualistic self-interest. They have the right to recover the value of their claim without considering the overall value of the pool of assets upon which they draw. This may force the company to liquidate its assets even though on efficiency grounds it should continue business.[119]

Proponents of the creditor concentration theory, however, might respond that there is little evidence that banks tend to act in a precipitate fashion. Franks and Sussman have concluded from a study of 542 financially distressed small and medium-sized companies that there are no clear indications of such a tendency.[120]

A second defence of receivership might lie in the argument that banks will be unwilling to close marginal businesses since indirect costs will be involved where the closed firm's customers, suppliers and employees are also bank customers and stand to be adversely affected by closures. It could be added that banks will not act precipitately for reputational reasons, since closing SMEs will not sit well alongside advertising campaigns stressing the banks' caring and listening characteristics.[121] This defence, however, has limited mileage. On the bank's decision to institute a receivership, it may well be the case that some banks, in buoyant financial conditions, will act in an understanding manner, but it would be rash to design insolvency regimes by presupposing continuing general goodwill in banks. Such goodwill may be sketchily distributed and short lived in hard times when insolvencies will multiply. The incentive will be for banks to put receivers into post with an eye to their own selfish

---

[119] D. Webb, 'An Economic Evaluation of Insolvency Processes in the UK: Does the 1986 Insolvency Act Satisfy the Creditors' Bargain?' (1991) *Oxford Economic Papers* 144.

[120] Franks and Sussman, 'Financial Distress and Bank Restructuring', pp. 91–2.

[121] British Bankers' Association, *Banks and Business Working Together* (London, 1997) sets out a number of principles for dealing with SMEs, stating, *inter alia*, 'Banks have long supported a rescue culture and thousands of customers are in business today because of the support of their bank through difficult times': discussed in Hunter, 'Nature and Functions of a Rescue Culture'.

interests. Some would argue, moreover, that the general UK trend is for banks to operate in an increasingly hard-nosed manner and to move away from 'gentlemen's club' altruistic stances.[122] Once the receiver is appointed, moreover, the bank is not running operations and the receiver has a legal obligation and, as seen above, an inclination to act in the bank's interests rather than broader interests.

Empirical research, however, suggests that if receivership is compared to post-Enterprise Act administration procedure, concentrated and dispersed creditor governance regimes may prove functionally equivalent. This is because, although gross realisations may have increased with post-Enterprise Act administration's collective regime, those increases have tended to be eaten up by the increased process costs associated with the collective regime.[123]

The creditor concentration theory is also open to contest on its assumptions concerning the monitoring of corporate managers. A key assumption is that banks will possess strong incentives through concentration to monitor managerial performance. This will produce benefits to the general body of creditors. There are, however, reasons for thinking that this will not always be the case. In so far as credit is not 100 per cent concentrated in the secured loan from the bank, the bank will under-monitor since its incentive to oversee will relate to the extent of its secured loan and not the total sum owed to creditors and at risk through managerial activities. It is, moreover, the case that where the secured creditor is not first in the queue to be paid (e.g. where there are fixed charges and preferential creditors) any incentive to monitor will be reduced. Thus, if the prospect of recovery of the sum owed stands to be reduced to 25 per cent by the existence of prior

---

[122] W. Hutton, *The State We're In* (Vintage, London, 1996); Carruthers and Halliday, *Rescuing Business*, pp. 197–205. But see the argument that banks are now tending to favour administration rather than receivership (even when they have powers to appoint receivers) because of reputational concerns: Armour, Hsu and Walters, *Report for the Insolvency Service*.

[123] See Armour, Hsu and Walters, *Report for the Insolvency Service*. Frisby's study gives gross returns for pre-EA receiverships as 29.3 per cent for secured creditors and 1.9 per cent for unsecured creditors, and, for post-EA administrations, 34.6 per cent for secured creditors and 2.8 per cent for unsecured creditors: see Frisby, *Returns to Creditors*, 2007, p. 5. Note, however, Frisby's caution (p. 4) on drawing such comparisons and her pointing to a series of complicating variables – including the abolition of the Crown's preferential status by the EA 2002 which might be expected to have increased the body of unsecured creditors and, at the same time, swelled the mass of funds available for secured creditors.

claims, the inducement to monitor will be a quarter of the efficient incentive.

Attention must, in addition, be paid to the purposes to which such monitoring is put. It would be rash to assume that monitoring relates to the general health and well-being of the enterprise rather than the prospect of repayment of the loan.[124] The more modest the loan is in relation to overall corporate turnover, the more likely it is that the bank will take its eye off overall business health. It may even be the case that a generally poorly performing company would, on receivership, be able to meet the sum owing to the bank on the floating charge.[125]

The monitoring of management, moreover, can be seen as merely one of a number of ways in which a creditor can deal with the risks of lending. Taking increased security offers an alternative way of managing developing risks as do the processes of spreading risks and of adjusting interest rates and associated charges for credit. From the point of view of a creditor, the objective in lending will be to manage risks in the most efficient manner: that is, the one that allows the bank best to compete in the marketplace and best to maximise returns for its own shareholders. Such an objective is likely to be met by the bank adopting a mixture of strategies: perhaps combining some taking of security, some monitoring and some adjustment of interest rates. The problem for the creditor concentration theory is that, even if concentration is assumed, it cannot be taken for granted that the bank's incentive will be to monitor managerial practice with an eye either to ongoing corporate health or to instituting receivership at the appropriate time. Many banks will often find it cheaper to deal with risks by increasing security and by increasing charge rates.

Nor should the virtues of monitoring be accepted unquestioningly in setting these up as a justification for any unfairness in underprotecting the interests of certain classes of creditor. The notion that monitoring protects creditors assumes that there is a linkage between this and improvements in the management of the firm. It may well be the case that underperforming managers fail to deliver the goods in many instances because of irrationalities, lack of ability, failures of strategy

---

[124] See V. Finch, 'Company Directors: Who Cares About Skill and Care?' (1992) 55 MLR 179 at 189–95.

[125] Webb, 'Economic Evaluation', p. 145. On variations in the propensity to monitor at different stages of corporate distress see J. Armour, 'Should We Redistribute in Insolvency?' in J. Getzler and J. Payne (eds.), *Company Charges: Spectrum and Beyond* (Oxford University Press, Oxford, 2006) p. 208.

and deficiencies of understanding. It takes a considerable leap of faith to believe that such poor performers will be highly responsive to the messages received from monitoring banks. If a typical unsecured creditor was to be offered the choice of a larger share of the insolvency estate or better monitoring of management he or she might well opt for the former. The point can also be made that even if creditor concentration is present, the bank may only possess partial control over the firm since finance may have been raised by quasi-security devices such as hire purchase or retention of title arrangements. The claims of such finance suppliers will take precedence over the floating charge and the bank will have reduced *de facto* control over the firm's assets.

A final difficulty concerns creditor concentration itself and how this is to be ensured. If levels of concentration are left to the market, it may or may not be (or remain) the case that the typical SME has only one main (bank) secured creditor. There is considerable evidence, as discussed in chapter 3, that credit arrangements are increasingly fragmenting for a number of reasons.[126] It would, accordingly, be risky to design a regime of insolvency law on the continuing assumption of concentration. If, on the other hand, insolvency law is set up to offer firms an incentive to resort to only one main secured creditor, this would not be consistent with the provision of the flexible financing opportunities that firms need in order to respond efficiently to market changes. There may also be problems of 'reverse agency costs' in so far as the main creditor bank may chill the firm's investment decisions – leading to valuable opportunities being forgone in favour of lower-risk alternatives.[127]

Expertise

The Insolvency Act 1986, as noted, provides that all receivers must be qualified insolvency practitioners within the meaning of Part XIII of the Act. The Act, in turn, responded to Cork's view that persons performing as IPs must possess some minimal professional qualifications and be subjected to control.[128] General issues relating to the expertise of IPs have been discussed in chapter 5 and will not be rehearsed here, save to note that some commentators have questioned whether the training and

---

[126] See Frisby, *Insolvency Outcomes*.
[127] See G. Triantis and R. Daniels, 'The Role of Debt in Interactive Corporate Governance' (1995) 83 Calif. L Rev. 1073 at 1090–1103.
[128] Cork Report, para. 756.

approach of IPs gives them a sufficient grounding in managerial skills and provides them with a proper orientation towards rescue rather than mere debt collection. Within the context of receivership it can be argued that there are particular institutional factors that militate unduly against rescue options, notably the ongoing relationship that most receivers have with the major lending banks and the primary legal obligations of receivers to act to protect the bank's interests. Receivers, even if managerially trained, would find themselves ill-positioned to put such skills into good effect for the purposes of rescue. They may be proved to be highly expert at protecting the bank's interests but this may constitute a narrower expertise than the overall public interest demands. Receivers, moreover, act with one hand tied behind their backs even if disposed to exercise their skills in favour of rescue. Receivership is not a collectivist approach proper and, accordingly, other parties cannot be bound in a manner that prevents interference with the receiver's proposed route out of corporate troubles.

As far as particular or sectoral skills are concerned, problems may arise when receivers are appointed at an early stage of corporate troubles. If those troubles are mainly to do with financial management then the IPs acting as receivers may be able to assist the company by rationalising affairs. If, however, attention to corporate problems demands detailed knowledge of a particular industry, market or mode of organising the business, there may be a danger that the receiver is far less well equipped to effect a rescue or appropriate sale of assets than managers who are familiar with the scene. Receivers will accordingly have to rely heavily on management.

As was seen above, receivers are, at law, obliged to perform their functions with certain levels of skill. It is clear from the judgment of Scott VC in *Medforth* v. *Blake*[129] that a receiver, if managing the business, owes the mortgagor more than a duty to exercise good faith. Reasonable competence must also be displayed and an equitable duty of care is owed. As noted also, *Medforth* was adopting a policy line consistent with prior case law that demanded that a receiver must take reasonable steps to obtain a proper price from the sale of assets.

Accountability and fairness

The receiver operates at a low level of accountability. The appointing debenture holder, as noted, has no power to direct the receiver and the

---

[129] [1999] 3 All ER 97.

receiver owes the troubled company neither a duty of obedience nor a duty to provide information in relation to the management and conduct of its affairs.[130] On selling assets, however, there is, as we have seen, legal accountability through the obligation to take reasonable steps to obtain a proper price and, during management, again, a duty of care is owed to the debtor company – though subject to a fiduciary duty to act in the interests of the debenture holder.[131]

Just as the troubled company has little input into the receiver's decision-making, so the array of junior creditors is distanced from such processes. Cork responded to complaints on this front with proposals designed to create 'a relationship of accountability' between the receiver and the unsecured creditor.[132] It has been suggested, however, that the resultant legislative steps did little to ensure meaningful participation rights: the requirement that there be a creditors' committee, for instance, is designed to assist the receiver in discharging his functions but it contains no power to direct the receiver in relation to the carrying out of these functions.[133] This contrasts with the stronger powers possessed by liquidation committees[134] and meetings of creditors in administration.[135] In any event, the Insolvency Service noted that 'very few such committees are appointed' and concluded that the framework for administrative receivership does not 'provide a basis for accountability or properly aligned incentives in relation to the bulk of cases'.[136]

Turning to fairness, it can be argued that receivership operates in a manner that is procedurally and substantively unfair to non-appointing creditors and others. In substance it is a private procedure that allows enforcement of the appointor's security rights to the potential detriment of other creditors, employees, the company and a range of stakeholders including suppliers and customers. Procedurally it is unfair because the interests of these parties may be affected by the receiver's actions but

---

[130] *Gomba Holdings UK and Others* v. *Homan and Bird* [1986] 3 All ER 94.

[131] Armour and Frisby, 'Rethinking Receivership', p. 77.

[132] Cork Report, para. 481. See Insolvency Act 1986 s. 48(2) and Insolvency Rules 1986 rr. 3.9–3.15 on the calling of a meeting of the creditors. See further Armour and Frisby, 'Rethinking Receivership', p. 79.

[133] See Armour and Frisby, 'Rethinking Receivership'; Ferran, 'Duties of an Administrative Receiver'.

[134] Armour and Frisby, 'Rethinking Receivership'; I. Grier and R. E. Floyd, *Voluntary Liquidation and Receivership* (3rd edn, Longman, London, 1991) p. 184.

[135] Insolvency Act 1986 Sch. B1, paras. 51–3. On administration see ch. 9 below.

[136] DTI/Insolvency Service, *Insolvency – A Second Chance*, p. 9.

there is no appropriate regime of access and input into decision-making for such potentially prejudiced parties. Indeed, in a climate of concern with corporate governance issues and stakeholder interests,[137] the system of receivership could be said to raise serious governance considerations in that it allows a number of companies to be handed over and dealt with by one interested party with little or no concern for other claimants.[138]

It is clear, moreover, that there was particular concern about such unfairness in the lead up to the Enterprise Act 2002. The Insolvency Service noted in 2000 that a number of the respondents to its consultation were worried that the floating charge and administrative receivership placed too much power in the hands of one creditor and caused unfairness in so far as there was no incentive for the floating charge holder to consider the interests of any other party; the floating charge holder could take decisions having a significant impact on returns to other creditors without there being any requirement for their consent; the administrative receiver owed a duty of care to the floating charge holder and not to creditors in general; and, unlike in other procedures, the cost of administrative receivership would fall on unsecured and preferential creditors if there were surplus funds over and above those needed to discharge the secured creditor's debt.[139] On the last point, research by Franks and Sussman for the IS[140] noted that the costs of receivership are significant and tend to be borne by the bank 'only in the minority of cases in which they recover less than 100 per cent', and that when the bank is paid in full 'the junior creditors are effectively paying the cost of realising the bank's security'. As for the quantum of such costs, the White Paper of 2001 noted that 'unsecured creditors have no right to challenge the level of costs in a receivership, even though they have an identifiable financial interest where there are sufficient funds to pay the secured creditor in full'.[141] That said, however, the more recent evidence

---

[137] See, for example, the Company Law Review Steering Group's Consultation Documents: *Modern Company Law for a Competitive Economy: The Strategic Framework*, URN 99/654 (February 1999) and *Developing the Framework*, URN 00/656 (March 2000).

[138] Milman and Mond, *Security and Corporate Rescue*, p. 48.

[139] See IS 2000, p. 15. See also Davies, 'Employee Claims in Insolvency', p. 150: 'The promotion of rescues as distinct from the promotion of banks' interests in rescues, requires the decision as to the best way of realising the company's assets to be taken in the general interests of the company's creditors and not by the agent of one particular type of creditor.'

[140] IS 2000, pp. 16–19.   [141] DTI/Insolvency Service, *Insolvency – A Second Chance*, p. 9.

suggests that the costs of receivership tend to be lower than those of the 'new' administration to the extent that this compensates for any lower levels of recovery for creditors.[142]

Floating charge holders might argue that receivership is fair because they have paid for their right to appoint a receiver in so far as they have lowered interest rates in reflection of the easy enforcement and risk control that such a right gives them. The banks, furthermore, may suggest that they charge very low margins on secured loans while trade creditors' gross profit margins may be anything up to 50 per cent, 'so the latter's losses will be offset by the higher profits they made when the company was trading profitably and paying its debts'.[143] It may be responded, however, that many unsecured creditors are simply in no position to negotiate security arrangements, that typically they lack the bank's knowledge of the company's financial position, that markets often do not allow high profit margins, that the institution of receivership offers a ready means for the better placed banks to exploit their positions, and that the interest rates charged by the floating charge holders are excessively profitable because risks are loaded onto unsecured creditors.

The concerns of trade and expense creditors are reinforced by the work of Franks and Sussman which has found that bank rescues often lead to a rise in debts due to such creditors while the indebtedness to the bank decreases. Their 2000 research for the IS suggested that, during bank intensive care periods, the debt owed to the bank tends to contract (by averages, for the three banks involved in the study, of 34 per cent, 19 per cent and 45 per cent respectively where the 'rescue' is successful and the company returns to the branch, and by averages of 15 per cent and 8 per cent for Banks 1 and 2 where the company moves to a debt recovery unit) whilst trade credit expands modestly.[144] Later figures, published in 2005, indicate that bank lending in periods of intensive bank support tends to contract by between 30.8 and 43.3 per cent while trade credit tends to grow by between 11.1 and 32.6 per cent.[145]

---

[142] See Frisby, *Insolvency Outcomes*; Armour, Hsu and Walters, *Report for the Insolvency Service*. Frisby argues that unsecured creditors are not prejudiced by the receiver's prioritisation of his appointor's welfare in the majority of cases: see Frisby, *Returns to Creditors*, 2007, p. 30.

[143] IS 2000, p. 18.

[144] IS 2000, p. 17. 'If formal insolvency ensues the bank will recover anything between 60–80 per cent of its indebtedness whilst trade creditors will recover nothing': ibid.

[145] Franks and Sussman, 'Financial Distress and Bank Restructuring', p. 85.

Society as a whole may also complain about the unfairness of receivership since this is a regime that does not aim to maximise overall social benefit: its purpose is merely to secure a return to the debenture holder. This would be an empty complaint if it could be argued with conviction that receivership brings overall benefits to society because, for example, debenture holder monitoring is generally effective in protecting interests across the range of corporate creditors and stakeholders. As we have seen, however, it is difficult to make out the case that such benefits are achieved. The Insolvency Service made the point in 2000 that a number of problems bedevil consumers of different insolvency regimes, notably the difficulty of assessing the impact of different insolvency procedures while making allowance for other factors such as the selection that takes place before a company enters a particular procedure and the stage in corporate decline at which resort is made to a procedure.[146]

Revising receivership

As far back as the Cork Committee's deliberations, the institution of receivership was the focus of complaints: 'mainly from or on behalf of ordinary unsecured creditors who are highly critical of the apparent lack of concern for their interest when the receiver has been appointed'.[147] Cork noted such, and other, concerns[148] but was unconvinced of the need for radical reform.[149] The Committee took the view that it would be wrong to make the receiver specifically accountable to anyone, even the debenture holder, if that would involve a requirement to take instructions.[150] The receiver, said Cork, owes fiduciary duties to the debenture holder and duties to the charge holder and company to exercise reasonable care to obtain proper prices for property and to preserve the goodwill of the business. Statutory obligations were also owed to preferential creditors. Cork's overall view was that incidences of damage to third parties in receivership were few in number and it would be 'wrong and

---

[146] IS 2000, p. 18. For studies comparing the performance of different regimes see Armour, Hsu and Walters, *Report for the Insolvency Service*; Frisby, *Insolvency Outcomes*; Franks and Sussman, 'Financial Distress and Bank Restructuring'.

[147] Cork Report, para. 436.   [148] Ibid., paras. 437–9.

[149] For a personal account of the benefits of receivership see K. Cork, *Cork on Cork: Sir Kenneth Cork Takes Stock* (Macmillan, London, 1988). On Cork's 'exaggerated representation of the virtues of receivership' see McCormack, 'Receiverships and the Rescue Culture', p. 236.

[150] Cork Report, para. 444.

unhelpful' to treat receivers as merely the nominees of appointors.[151] Cork cautioned that if receivers had to have regard to a statutory list of matters and interests, 'the effectiveness of the floating charge would be seriously weakened'[152] since creditors would be driven to early enforcement of fixed securities, to greater use of hybrid forms of security (e.g. fixed charges on future book debts)[153] and to direct enforcement of the security without the appointment of a receiver. None of these steps, the Committee urged, would advance the conduct of trade generally or the interests of unsecured creditors. Such a list of matters and interests to be considered might also increase opportunities for 'expensive and delaying litigation' without benefit to unsecured creditors.

As to the idea that statute law should make receivers accountable to all the creditors, secured and unsecured, Cork responded that this again would drive prospective lenders away from floating charges into other alternatives.[154] If such difficulties were anticipated and receivers were bound to have regard to priorities *inter se* when looking to protected interests, this again would lead to unhelpful legal challenges, delays and expenses. Cork, accordingly, was unwilling to introduce any fundamental reform of the law to change receivers' accountability and summarised:

> It is an undoubted virtue in the eyes of those who appoint them, that receivers can act economically, swiftly and with little danger of successful challenge before the event. A statutory provision of the kind now under consideration offers potential detriment to the holders of floating charges without, it seems to us, any real advantage to anyone else.[155]

In the new millennium, however, matters were viewed differently and a consensus had developed that administrative receivership was questionable as a way to maximise economic value and was also inconsistent with those notions of collectivism that ought to operate when a company entered insolvency. In 2001 the Blair Government announced that, on grounds of both efficiency and equity, the time had come 'to make changes which tip the balance firmly in favour of collective insolvency proceedings – proceedings in which all creditors participate, under

---

[151] Ibid., para. 446.   [152] Ibid., para. 447.   [153] Ibid., para. 449.

[154] For arguments that the Enterprise Act 2002 has produced such a shift towards more complex and fragmented forms of credit see Armour, 'Should We Redistribute in Insolvency?'; Armour, Hsu and Walters, *Report for the Insolvency Service*, p. iii; Frisby, *Insolvency Outcomes*.

[155] Cork Report, para. 451.

which a duty is owed to all creditors and in which all creditors may look to an office holder for an account of his dealings with a company's assets'.[156] The lack of fit between the collective approaches of international law and administrative receivership was also noted[157] and the Government stated that it believed 'that administrative receivership should cease to be a major insolvency procedure'.[158]

The Insolvency Service had proposed restricting the use of receivership and developing a more effective and flexible administration procedure and the Enterprise Act 2002 (EA) made the necessary changes. That Act made administration, rather than administrative receivership, the governmentally preferred procedure for attempting to rescue troubled companies. The EA prohibits (subject to stated exceptions) the use of administrative receivership by the holders of floating charges.[159] Instead, the EA provides for the general enforcement of floating charges to be carried out through use of the administration process – a process in which the administrator differs from the traditional receiver in so far as he is charged to pursue his functions 'in the interests of the company's creditors as a whole'.[160] The exceptions to the prohibition are not, however, trivial. Secured creditors holding charges created before 15 September 2003 retain, as noted, the right to appoint an administrative receiver and, in addition, a large range of specialist financing arrangements allow the possibility of administrative receivership.[161]

---

[156] DTI/Insolvency Service, *Insolvency – A Second Chance*, ch. 2, para. 2.3. On collectivisation improving the prospects of UK creditors in international insolvencies, see Editorial, 'A Radical New Look for Insolvency Law' (2002) 23 Co. Law. 1.

[157] The European Insolvency Regulation came into force on 31 May 2002 to provide for automatic recognition by all EU Member States of EU compliant collective proceedings: Council Regulation (EC) No. 1346/2000 (29 May 2000) on Insolvency Proceedings [2000] OJ L 160/1. Receivership was viewed by negotiators as non-compliant: see Armour, Hsu and Walters, *Report for the Insolvency Service*, p. 6.

[158] DTI/Insolvency Service, *Insolvency – A Second Chance*, p. 10. See also R3 Ninth Survey which noted the declining use of receivership over the years surveyed. Receivership accounted for 6.6 per cent of all insolvency proceedings in the Ninth Survey, 8.8 per cent in the Eighth (SPI) Survey and 14.4 per cent in the Seventh (SPI) Survey.

[159] Insolvency Act 1986, s. 72A.

[160] Ibid., Sch. B1, para. 3(2).

[161] These are itemised in ss. 72B–72G of Insolvency Act 1986, as supplemented by the Insolvency Act 1986 (Amendment) (Administrative Receivership and Capital Markets) Order 2003 (SI 2003/1468) and the Insolvency Act 1986 (Amendment) (Administrative Receivership and Urban Regeneration etc.) Order 2003 (SI 2003/1832). The six exceptions relate to capital market arrangements, public/private partnerships, utilities projects, project finance, certain financial market contracts and registered social landlords/housing authorities. The aim of these exceptions, however, is arguably to deliver the same outcome as was sought to be

The wisdom of moving away from receivership perhaps remains to be seen as the performance of the administration procedure becomes assessable over time. Cork's fears perhaps hang in the air: that weakening floating charge holders' powers and widening obligations to creditors will cause increased delays and expenses and will drive lenders to the early enforcement of fixed securities, to greater use of hybrid forms of securities and to direct enforcement of their security.[162]

Conclusions

Receivership has proved to be a contentious process and one that has largely given way to the post-Enterprise Act 2002 administration procedure.[163] This is not to say that the positions of the banks and other traditional floating charge holders have been entirely weakened. Under the 2002 Act the holders of 'qualifying' floating charges are 'fast tracked' into administration in so far as they can apply out of court for an administration order[164] without the need for a Rule 2.2 report.[165] The

achieved through the Enterprise Act changes. Thus 'the purpose of appointing an administrative receiver in capital market arrangements, public–private partnership projects, utility projects and financed project companies is to ensure the continuation of the income stream, protecting the provision of the public service or completion of the project. This results in the company continuing to trade and thereby the interests of the secured creditors and the ordinary unsecured creditors are catered for in a mutually beneficial way': S. Leinster, 'Policy Aims of the Enterprise Act' (2003) *Recovery* (Autumn) 27 at 28. See also *Feetum and Others* v. *Levy and Others* [2005] BCC 484 regarding an (unsuccessful) attempt to uphold the appointment of an administrative receiver under the 'project exception' of s. 72E of the Insolvency Act 1986 as amended: see further G. Stewart, 'Legal Update' (2005) *Recovery* (Summer) 6, p. 7.

[162] Cork Report, paras. 449–50. It has been argued that the Enterprise Act 2002's new scheme and virtual abolition of receivership effectively heralds the demise of the floating charge: see R. Mokal, 'The Floating Charge – An Elegy' in S. Worthington (ed.), *Commercial Law and Commercial Practice* (Hart, Oxford, 2003). For a contrary view arguing, *inter alia*, that the floating charge still facilitates 'concentrated creditor control even without receivership' see Armour, 'Should We Redistribute in Insolvency?', p. 215.

[163] In 2006 there were 'barely' 500 cases of receivership recorded: see D. Milman, 'Corporate Insolvency Law: An End of Term Report' (2007) *Sweet & Maxwell's Company Law Newsletter* (August).

[164] See Insolvency Act 1986 Sch. B1, paras. 14–21.

[165] See Insolvency Rules 1986 r. 2.2. Under the 'old' administration procedures an application to the court for administration was invariably accompanied by an independent report from the proposed administrator: r. 2.2. These reports were not mandatory but tended to be viewed as carrying considerable weight: see *Re Newport County Association Football Club Ltd* [1987] BCC 635. See also Practice Note (Administration Order Applications: Independent Reports) [1994] 1 WLR 160 which attempted to cut the length and application (and thus the costs) of these reports.

banks, which routinely use floating charge security, have, moreover, been offered a sweetener for giving up receivership in so far as the 2002 Act abolishes the Crown's status as preferential creditor.[166] Banks may, nevertheless, be expected to object that the effect of the Enterprise Act 2002 changes is to force them to secure their investments increasingly on fixed assets, which will raise the cost of capital and reduce the flexibility of financing arrangements.

Receivership, it should be emphasised, is a process that can still operate for some time because of exemptions and pre-2003 floating charges.[167] It is nevertheless viewable now as something of an anachronism and out of tune with modern, and international, endorsements of collectivism. Receivership was criticisable on a number of fronts, notably on grounds of fairness and accountability, but whether its replacement with administration will produce the efficiency losses that Cork associated with dispersed creditor obligations will, as noted, remain to be seen. It is, indeed, to the virtues and vices of the new administration procedure that we now turn.

---

[166] Enterprise Act 2002 s. 251. On preferential creditors see ch. 14 below.

[167] For evidence of continuing judicial support for the institution of receivership see *Brampton Manor (Leisure)* v. *McLean Ltd* [2007] BCC 640; *OBG Ltd* v. *Allan* [2007] 2 WLR 920; Milman, 'An End of Term Report', p. 2.

9

Administration

The Cork Committee, as we have seen, placed emphasis on the value of insolvency processes that provide ways of rescuing troubled companies, as well as help realise corporate assets.[1] Its recommendations led to the procedures governing administration orders and company voluntary arrangements (CVAs) that are set out in the Insolvency Act 1986. This chapter examines the administration regime, as now revised by the Enterprise Act 2002, considers how this regime tends to satisfy the values set out in chapter 2 and reviews the philosophy underpinning modern administration.

The rise of administration

The roots of administration can be seen in the Cork Committee's belief that corporate rescue could often be furthered by allowing an independent expert to take over the management of a distressed company. Cork noted that one particular advantage flowed from the floating charge holder's power to appoint a receiver and manager over a company's undertaking: receivers were given extensive powers to manage and, in some cases, had been able to restore troubled companies to profitability and return them to their former owners. In others, the receivers had been able to dispose of all or part of the business as a going concern and, in either case, the preservation of the profitable parts of the enterprise had

---

[1] *Report of the Review Committee on Insolvency Law and Practice* (Cmnd 8558, 1982) ('Cork Report') ch. 9. On the rescue culture see e.g. M. Hunter, 'The Nature and Functions of a Rescue Culture' [1999] JBL 491; B. G. Carruthers and T. C. Halliday, *Rescuing Business: The Making of Corporate Bankruptcy Law in England and the United States* (Clarendon Press, Oxford, 1998); Insolvency Service, *A Review of Company Rescue and Business Reconstruction Mechanisms*, Interim Report (DTI, 1999) ('IS 1999') p. 4; Insolvency Service, *A Review of Company Rescue and Business Reconstruction Mechanisms*, Report by the Review Group (DTI, 2000) ('IS 2000') pp. 12–13. See also ch. 6 above.

been 'of advantage to the employees, the commercial community and the general public'.[2]

In the absence of a floating charge there was, however, no possibility of such an appointment and the choice lay between an informal moratorium and a formal scheme of arrangement under the Companies Act 1948. Neither procedure was, however, wholly satisfactory. Formal schemes of arrangement were expensive and time-consuming and informal procedures were not binding on non-assenting creditors and were difficult to sustain in practice. When neither course of action was possible, the directors had no option but to cease trading and the results were bleak: 'We are satisfied that in a significant number of cases, companies have been forced into liquidation and potentially viable businesses capable of being rescued have been closed down, for want of a floating charge under which a receiver and manager could have been appointed.'[3]

Cork, accordingly, proposed the institution of the administrator who would be appointed in order to consider: reorganisations with a view to restoring profitability or maintaining employment; ascertaining the chances of restoring a company of dubious solvency to profitability; developing proposals for realising assets for creditors and stockholders; and carrying on business when this would be in the public interest but where it was unlikely that the business could be continued under the existing management.[4]

Three key notions underpinned Cork's vision of the administrator: that rescue opportunities should be taken sufficiently early in corporate troubles to stand a chance of success; that companies should be given a breathing space from the pressure of claims; and that consideration should be given to the interests, not merely of creditors and shareholders, but of the widest group of parties potentially affected by the insolvency. As Sir Kenneth Cork wrote in his autobiography:[5]

> We saw that if a company was to be saved, action should be initiated a long time *before* the time when a bank normally appointed a receiver ... [Companies] needed a period when the dogs were called off and they were able to recover a degree of equilibrium. They needed, in other words, a moratorium for which existing law made no provision ... The appointment of an administrator, we suggested, would not constitute an 'act of

[2] Cork Report, para. 495.   [3] Ibid., para. 496.   [4] Ibid., para. 498.
[5] Sir Kenneth Cork, *Cork on Cork: Sir Kenneth Cork Takes Stock* (Macmillan, London, 1988) p. 195.

insolvency'. None of the things would happen which happened when a company became officially insolvent. For an administrator should be brought in *before* a company was declared insolvent, where for instance, the directors were obviously incompetent or dishonest and the ordinary processes could not remove them, or where in the national interest the government should take a hand ... He would have all the powers and more of a receiver, and he would have to realise the assets for the general good ... He would be responsible to *all parties* who were interested in the particular debtor company.

From the Insolvency Act 1986 to the Enterprise Act 2002

The Insolvency Act 1986 provided a mechanism for appointing an administrator by applying for an order of the court that directed that the affairs, business and property of the company should be managed by the administrator.[6] The effect of presenting a petition for an administration order was that a moratorium was triggered and a stop imposed on the enforcement of most types of claim, secured and unsecured, against the company. The company could not be wound up and the leave of the court was required for such actions as enforcing a security against the company, repossessing goods in the company's possession under a hire purchase agreement, or the commencement or continuation of any other legal proceedings or levying distress against the company or its property.[7] Protection also extended to property owned by the company but in the possession of third parties such as lessees.[8] Before the Enterprise Act 2002, such a moratorium did not, however, stop a debenture holder from appointing an administrative receiver, nor did the presentation of a petition stop the directors from calling a meeting of members to consider voluntary liquidation or stop a creditor from presenting a winding-up petition.[9] Managerial powers were unaffected by the petition[10] and the company could create secured interests.[11]

[6] Insolvency Act 1986 s. 8(2).   [7] Ibid., s. 10(1). See further pp. 375–8 below.

[8] *Re Atlantic Computer Systems plc (No. 1)* [1992] Ch 505, [1992] 2 WLR 367, [1990] BCC 859.

[9] Entry into liquidation was not permitted, however, until the petition was heard: Insolvency Act 1986 s. 10(1)(a).

[10] Though the court on hearing the petition could make an interim order appointing an interim manager: see D. McKenzie Skene and Y. Enoch, 'Petitions for Administration Orders – Where there is a Need for Interim Measures: A Comparative Study of the Approach of the Courts in Scotland and England' [2000] JBL 103; Insolvency Act 1986 s. 9(4).

[11] *Bristol Airport plc v. Powdrill* [1990] Ch 744, 768.

The pre-Enterprise Act position was that when an administration order was made, any winding-up petition had to be dismissed.[12] An administrative receiver had to vacate office,[13] and during the operation of the administration order there was a stronger freeze on the enforcements of right against the company than operated on presentation of the petition. After the order was made, an administrative receiver could not be appointed and no winding-up petition might be presented without the consent of the administrator or the leave of the court.[14] Powers of the company and its officers were not exercisable without the administrator's consent and this effectively divested the directors of their powers.[15] The directors, moreover, were given obligations to co-operate with the administrator.[16]

Administration did not provide for a permanent restructuring of creditors' interests or for a distribution to unsecured creditors.[17] The process operated as a temporary freeze during which proposals for a permanent solution to the company's problems could be devised. These solutions then had to be put into effect through the institution of another insolvency regime such as a CVA or liquidation or a compromise arrangement (under the then s. 425 of the Companies Act 1985), to operate either during the currency of the administration order or after it had been brought to an end.[18]

The powers of administrators resembled those of administrative receivers. Similar managerial functions were carried out with commensurate powers, in both cases exercised as agents of the company.[19] The administrator possessed the additional power to remove and appoint directors and to call any meeting of the members or creditors of the company.[20]

The evidence suggests that, before the enactment of the Enterprise Act 2002, administration had been 'less efficacious' as a rescue device than

---

[12] Insolvency Act 1986 s. 11.   [13] Ibid.   [14] Ibid., s. 11(3)(d).   [15] Ibid., s. 14(4).

[16] Ibid., s. 235. Breach of this duty renders the directors liable to disqualification: see CDDA 1986 s. 9, Sch. 1, Part II, para. 10(g).

[17] Contrast with the US Chapter 11 procedure: see ch. 6 above.

[18] See H. Rajak, 'The Challenges of Commercial Reorganisation in Insolvency: Empirical Evidence from England' in J. Ziegel (ed.), *Current Developments in International and Comparative Corporate Insolvency Law* (Clarendon Press, Oxford, 1994).

[19] Insolvency Act 1986 s. 14(5). Unlike a normal agent the administrator was not subject to control and direction by the company, his principal: section 14(4). Section 14 aimed to ensure that an administrator normally incurred no personal liability on any contract or other obligation he could enter into on the company's behalf.

[20] Insolvency Act 1986 s. 14, Sch. 1.

expected.[21] The insolvency regime, as envisaged by Cork, was thought to offer company directors a set of incentives to opt for administration in times of trouble. It provided them, in the first instance, with protection from disqualification and wrongful trading actions: punitive prospects that Cork hoped would lead directors to seek outside help at early stages of trouble.[22] Administration also offered directors some continuing role in the management of the business and the chance of persuading creditors, within the protection of the moratorium, to accept something less than full-blown insolvency. They would, furthermore, be able to nominate a friendly Insolvency Practitioner (IP) who would sympathise with their positions. Such incentives, thought Cork, would produce effective rescue mechanisms. The Committee's view was that if insolvency practitioners could become involved with companies at an early stage of their decline they stood a good chance of saving the business and 'four out of five never needed to have become insolvent'.[23] Not only that, but lack of legal rescue provisions at such an early stage had led, according to Cork, to a series of evils. It had encouraged directors to keep trading, delayed the introduction of expert reviews and given rogue creditors incentives to break ranks on informal moratorium debt collection, all of which factors militated against successful corporate rescues.[24]

The DTI's 1993 consultative document revealed that from 1990 to 1993 there were 88,000 corporate insolvencies in England. Of these, 21,500 had entered receivership, over 40,000 had gone into creditors' voluntary liquidation, and over 26,000 into compulsory liquidation. Only 296 CVAs and 447 administration orders were encountered.[25] By the time the DTI Insolvency Service published the 1999 figures for corporate proceedings under the Insolvency Act 1986, the ratio of administration appointments to liquidations (voluntary and

---

[21] R. Goode, *Principles of Corporate Insolvency Law* (3rd edn, Sweet & Maxwell, London, 2005) p. 317.

[22] Carruthers and Halliday, *Rescuing Business*, p. 289.

[23] Quoted in ibid., p. 286. In R3's Ninth Survey of Business Recovery in the UK (2001) rescue professional respondents indicated their belief that in 77 per cent of cases by the time they were appointed there were no possible actions that could realistically have averted company failure. In younger companies (under one year) in 90 per cent of cases there was thought to be no such rescue action possible.

[24] Carruthers and Halliday, *Rescuing Business*, p. 286.

[25] Rajak, 'Challenges of Commercial Reorganisation', p. 202 reported that in 1990 there were 211 administrations compared to 15,051 liquidations and 4,318 receiverships.

compulsory) was 440:14,280 (with 1,618 administrative receiverships).[26] The business preservation rate in administrations in 1998–9 was given by R3 (formerly the SPI) in 2001 as 79 per cent[27] and the job preservation rate was put at 40 per cent by the SPI in its Eighth Survey.[28]

Why then did administration not operate as the popular rescue option that Cork had hoped to establish? It is possible to identify a number of factors that weakened the effectiveness of administration as a rescue device and tended to discourage its use.[29] First, administration was a procedure that could be blocked by a floating charge holder who chose to appoint an administrative receiver as a means of protecting his or her own interest. If, indeed, a petition for administration did not contain what amounted to the consent of any person entitled to appoint an AR, the petition would be dismissed. Administration, accordingly, was a process that could only be used if the firm had no creditor with a floating charge (a rare occurrence given the proliferation of secured lending in standard British financing arrangements and banking practice)[30] or if the floating charge holder was happy to see the company's troubles dealt with by administration rather than administrative receivership. In some circumstances the latter situation might have obtained and some considerations might have led the floating charge holder to accept administration as preferable to the insertion of a receiver.[31] Factors favouring this approach included the attractiveness of the moratorium which might have been seen to outweigh the disadvantages of administration: for example, where protection was needed against suppliers of goods who had retained title[32] or where a large firm had a complex structure and considerable time and effort had to be put in before a way forward was arrived at.[33] Administration might also have been attractive if: criticisms from creditors would have been directed towards the administrator

---

[26] IS 2000, p. 14; as the Insolvency Service's 1999 Review points out, such figures do not give the whole picture of insolvency because they do not take on board all the companies that are struck off the register but do not enter any formal process.

[27] R3 Ninth Survey: up from 41 per cent in the SPI's Eighth Survey of *Company Insolvency in the United Kingdom* (SPI, London, 1999) on a small sample.

[28] SPI Eighth Survey (1999): the figure had dropped from 65 per cent in the Seventh Survey.

[29] See DTI/Insolvency Service, *Company Voluntary Arrangements and Administration Orders: A Consultative Document* (October 1993) ('DTI 1993') ch. 5.

[30] IS 2000, p. 12, para. 36.

[31] See Rajak, 'Challenges of Commercial Reorganisation', p. 206.

[32] Ibid., p. 206: ROT holders were blocked by the wide definition of hire purchase agreements in the Insolvency Act 1986 s. 10(4).

[33] DTI 1993, p. 30.

rather than the debenture holder or their receiver; the size of the sum due did not justify the appointment of a receiver; the debenture holder thought that his or her charge was vulnerable; or the debenture holder had been given the right to nominate the administrator. Additional considerations favouring administration rather than administrative receivership may have been that a court-appointed insolvency officer might have been better placed than a receiver to recover assets from foreign jurisdictions[34] and an administrator, but not an AR, could apply to have suspect pre-insolvency transactions set aside.[35]

Surveys, nevertheless, suggested that in 60 per cent of cases where administration orders were made, the floating charge holder would appoint a receiver.[36] In most cases of corporate decline the floating charge holder would have been very aware that administrative receivers acted in the interests of the appointing floating charge holder, whereas administrators acted for all creditors. It is unlikely, accordingly, that the floating charge holder would, in normal cases, have allowed administrations to run unhindered. Floating charge holders, moreover, lost control if they allowed administration to occur rather than put in a receiver. Once the administrator was appointed, even fixed-charge security holders could not enforce without leave and the general creditors enjoyed the income generated by the property subject to such charges. Floating charge holders faced with an administration also stood to see a diminution of the value of the assets covered by the floating charge, since their debt would have been satisfied after the expenses and remuneration of the administrator had been met, as well as after there had been payment of all debts and liabilities (including certain taxes) that had been incurred by the administrator as a result of contracts he or she had entered into. Administration also brought temporal uncertainty to the floating charge holder since the administrator had no power to make distributions and considerable time might elapse before payments were made on debts.

The procedural costs of administration were also very considerable.[37] This was largely due to the high level of judicial supervision involved in

---

[34] Rajak, 'Challenges of Commercial Reorganisation', p. 206.

[35] Ibid. See Insolvency Act 1986 ss. 238, 239, 244.

[36] See M. Homan, *A Survey of Administration Under the 1986 Insolvency Act* (Institute of Chartered Accountants, London, 1989); Rajak, 'Challenges of Commercial Reorganisation', p. 205. See further H. Anderson, 'Receivers Compared with Administrators' (1996) 12 IL&P 54.

[37] DTI 1993, p. 29.

administration. The court was involved in appointing the administrator and would usually be involved when the administrator was given power to interfere with private rights.[38] Nor was the judicial role confined to checking to see that the administrator had acted in good faith and *intra vires*: the court would often have to examine the issue in depth and make its own judgement. Such a process would frequently involve the use of expert evidence, and decision-making, as a result, would be slow as well as costly. The expenses of obtaining the administration order itself could be very considerable. Figures as high as £20,000 were cited as minimum starting costs, with the money having to be provided in advance in order to secure the services of the necessary IPs.[39] The Rule 2.2 (of the Insolvency Rules) report, which became in practice a prerequisite[40] to the making of an order, was almost always written by an accountant and often involved the practitioner's solicitors. This tended to increase the obligations of the IP, the company and the court and so raised costs considerably and placed applications beyond the reach of smaller firms.[41] Banks who instigated formal insolvency procedures may, moreover, have possessed undesirably low incentives to control the costs of these procedures (about half of which comprise fees to IPs). This is because such costs would be borne disproportionately by unsecured creditors in a regime that distributed assets by priority.[42] Administration, accordingly, was too expensive a process to be used for the rescue of small or even medium-sized businesses.

A further reason for the low uptake of administration was the administrator's lack of any obligation to consult creditors before taking

---

[38] See Insolvency Act 1986 s. 15, but note s. 15(1), (3) and (4) where the court's consent is not needed.

[39] DTI 1993, p. 29. But see C. Morris and M. Kirschner, 'Cross-border Rescues and Asset Recovery: Problems and Solutions' (1994) 10 IL&P 42–3, suggesting that in smaller cases the expense could be only £1,500–£2,000. See also n. 131 below.

[40] The DTI's 1993 Consultative Document described the report as 'almost mandatory', DTI 1993, p. 29. These reports were not, in fact, mandatory but tended to be viewed as carrying considerable weight: see *Re Newport County Association Football Club* [1987] BCC 635. See also Practice Note (Administration Order Applications: Independent Reports) [1994] 1 WLR 160, which attempted to cut the length and application (and thus the costs) of these reports.

[41] See Justice, *Insolvency Law: An Agenda for Reform* (Justice, London, 1994) pp. 37–8; D. Brown, *Corporate Rescue: Insolvency Law in Practice* (John Wiley & Sons, Chichester, 1996) p. 656.

[42] See J. Franks and O. Sussman, 'The Cycle of Corporate Distress, Rescue and Dissolution: A Study of Small and Medium Size UK Companies', IFA Working Paper 306 (2000).

action.[43] This meant that he or she could sell the company's property before holding a creditors' meeting. Such a lack of involvement could make creditors reluctant to instigate or (in the case of floating charge holders) accede to administration. When the administration process was employed it achieved rescue in about 40 per cent of cases and liquidation occurred in around 50 per cent of instances.[44]

Yet another reason for the inefficiency of administration as a rescue device – and a factor tending to reduce the incidence of resort to administration[45] – was that administration orders could only be applied for at the latest stages of corporate decline, when chances of rescue had severely diminished. As noted, the court, under section 8(1)(a) of the Insolvency Act 1986, had to be satisfied that the company 'is or is likely to become unable to pay its debts' within the meaning of the Insolvency Act 1986 s. 123. This requirement of near-insolvency was starkly at odds with the Cork vision, which demanded that an administrator should be appointed at an earlier stage in corporate decline. This was, as noted, a point of great disappointment to Sir Kenneth Cork, who commented on the Government's Insolvency Act 1986 approach:

> They said [an administrator] could only be appointed when a company was insolvent or was in the process of becoming insolvent which missed the whole point ... To them insolvency was insolvency; for them it was essential that a company went broke before anyone took action. Behind it lay the absurd theory that shareholders could always remove incompetent directors.[46]

Sir Kenneth's view of section 8(1)(a) was perhaps more pessimistic than it needed to be. It was open to the court to operate administration as a pre-insolvency rather than an insolvency procedure. There was no case law, however, that offered guidance on the restrictiveness with which 'likely to become unable to pay its debts' (section 8(1)(a)) would be interpreted. Some commentators suggested that the subsection did not require insolvency to be likely in the immediate future but only 'fairly soon'.[47] If administration had been seen in a pre-insolvency sense by the

---

[43] DTI 1993, p. 30.

[44] H. Rajak, 'Administration of Insolvent Companies in England 1987–1990: An Empirical Survey' (quoted in R. Goode, *Principles of Corporate Insolvency Law* (2nd edn, Sweet & Maxwell, London, 1997) p. 322).

[45] For a review see DTI 1993, ch. 5.   [46] Cork, *Cork on Cork*, p. 197.

[47] Goode, *Principles of Corporate Insolvency Law* (2nd edn), p. 286. Note that Edington plc went into administration on the grounds of 'prospective insolvency': see D. Milman and C. Durrant, *Corporate Insolvency: Law and Practice* (3rd edn, Sweet & Maxwell, London, 1999) p. 39.

courts then it might have served rescue purposes if used for such objectives as: protecting the company from creditors during a period of cash flow difficulties; overcoming short-term problems more serious than cash flow difficulties but which could be survived by using CVAs or schemes of arrangements to reschedule debts; or reorganising the firm and selling unsustainable parts of the business so as to leave the company with the profitable parts under the protection of the moratorium.[48] There might, however, have been difficulties in convincing courts to endorse administration at early stages in decline. This was a procedure that involved curtailment of the rights of at least some of the creditors of the company and it might have proved difficult to persuade the court that such interference was merited unless insolvency was imminent.

A judicial willingness to grant administration orders on a pre-insolvency basis would not, however, have ensured that parties would come forward with applications. There may have been numerous reasons why such early applications tended to be few in number. Company directors often lack knowledge of the applicable insolvency procedures. They may, in addition, possess poor internal accounting and information systems and may not know that the business is approaching insolvency. They may, furthermore, be unwilling to put the company into an insolvency procedure which they see as ceding control of the business to an outside accountant.[49] The administrator had power to remove and appoint directors, and directors will tend to opt for courses of action that leave them with an assured role in the company's immediate future. Other suggested reasons for directorial slowness to resort to administration in times of trouble were put to the DTI in its 1999–2000 consultations and included: mistrust of IPs; unrealistic optimism; fear of failure; fear of the bank withdrawing support; and concern over the cost of advice.[50] Directorial fears for their own reputations and future job prospects must also have constituted a reason for inaction.

Nor have the courts always decided cases in a manner that enhances the effectiveness of administration as a rescue device. In the case of *Powdrill* v. *Watson*,[51] for instance, the Court of Appeal held that administrators who kept employees in post after the administration came into effect (and after the fourteen-day period of grace provided for in section

---

[48] See M. Phillips, *The Administration Procedure and Creditors' Voluntary Arrangements* (Centre for Commercial Law Studies, QMW, London, 1996) p. 21.
[49] I.e. as an IP: DTI 1993, p. 30.   [50] IS 2000, pp. 54–5.   [51] [1994] 2 BCLC 118.

19(5) of the Insolvency Act 1986)[52] had adopted the relevant employment contracts. The administrators were, accordingly, liable to pay not only the wages, pension contributions and holiday pay referable to the post-administration order period, but were also obliged to pay liabilities under the adopted employment contracts out of the company assets in priority to most creditors. The effect, critics noted,[53] was to force administrators (and administrative receivers) to dismiss employees within the fourteen-day period. This contrasted with the established practice of retaining employees but making it clear to them that their contracts were not being adopted.[54]

The Court of Appeal's decision in *Powdrill* prompted a strong adverse reaction from the insolvency profession and others. Following energetic lobbying of the President of the Board of Trade, legislation designed to redress the effects of *Powdrill* was rushed through Parliament and became the Insolvency Act 1994. This Act had the effect on administrations of introducing a new subsection, 19(6), to the Insolvency Act 1986, to provide that sums payable in respect of liabilities incurred while the administrator was in office under contracts of employment that had been adopted by him or by any predecessor were to be paid out of the assets covered by a floating charge created as such and were to have the same priority as sums covered by section 19(5) – namely sums owed under contracts entered into by the administrator or a predecessor – but only to the extent that they constituted 'qualifying liabilities' as defined in the new subsections 19(7)–(9) of the Insolvency Act.[55] The effects of the 1994 Act were, however, limited. It applied only to contracts of employment entered into on, or after, 15 March 1994, and this left

---

[52] On the 'inadequacy' of the fourteen-day period for administrators see R. Agnello, 'Administration Expenses' (2000) *Recovery* (March) 24–5; *Re Douai School Ltd*, reported as *Re a Company (No. 005174 of 1999)* [2000] BCC 698.

[53] See I. F. Fletcher, 'Adoption of Contracts of Employment by Receivers and Administrators: The *Paramount* Case' [1995] JBL 596–604.

[54] Brown, *Corporate Rescue*, p. 660; *Re Specialised Mouldings Ltd* (unreported) 13 February 1987 (Harman J).

[55] A qualifying liability per s. 19(7)–(9) was one to pay a sum by way of wages or salary or contributions to an occupational pension, which was in respect of services rendered wholly or partially after the adoption of the contract but disregarding payment for services rendered before the adoption of the contract. This included wages or salary payable in respect of holiday, absence through sickness or other good cause. Sums payable in lieu of holiday were deemed wages or salary in respect of services rendered in the period by reference to which the holiday entitlement arose (Insolvency Act 1986 s. 19(9) and (10); Insolvency Act 1994 s. 1(6)). See *In re FJL Realisations Ltd* [2001] ICR 424 (also reported as *Inland Revenue Commissioners* v. *Lawrence* [2001] BCC 663) in

considerable potential for post-*Powdrill* claims; it did not affect the concept of 'adoption' or the issue of contracting out (though it did take away the most undesirable consequences of the 1986 provisions as interpreted in *Powdrill*). It left a number of questions open – such as when liabilities are incurred and whether it is possible to dismiss and re-employ workers in a manner not amounting to a sham[56] – and it was unclear on the consequences of voluntary payments by administrators.

When the House of Lords decided consolidated appeals on the meaning of 'adopt' within sections 19 and 44 of the Insolvency Act 1986, the liabilities under employment contracts of both administrators and administrative receivers were at issue.[57] Focusing here on administration, their Lordships were concerned with the rights of parties affected by the 1,200 or so administrations commencing between 29 December 1986 (the commencement date of the Insolvency Act 1986) and 15 March 1994 (the commencement date of the Insolvency Act 1994). The House of Lords decided unanimously that the contracts of employment in question had been adopted by the administrators. This ruling was greeted with 'shock and disappointment'[58] by the insolvency and banking community. It meant that cases involving adoption of employment contracts by administrators after 15 March 1994 would be dealt with under the Insolvency Act 1994 but that cases on adoption between 1986 and 1994 would be dealt with on the basis set out by the House of Lords in *Powdrill*. Further complications were to follow when the Enterprise Act 2002 replaced section 19 of the Insolvency Act with paragraph 99 of the new Schedule B1 and, in doing so, introduced new levels of confusion in defining administrators' liabilities regarding 'wages and salary'. These complications, and the general rescue implications of transferring employee contracts and protecting employees' acquired rights in the

---

which the Court of Appeal held that, as the administrator's liability under contracts of employment was to pay the employee the full salary *including* the statutory amounts in respect of PAYE and national insurance contributions, it was not possible for the administrator to split the contractual liability in two. Accordingly, the sums deducted to the Inland Revenue were a liability of 'any sums payable in respect of debts or liabilities incurred' for the purposes of s. 19(5) and (6) and as such enjoyed special priority over any charges arising under s. 19(4) of the Insolvency Act 1986. See now Sch. B1, para. 99 (introduced by the Enterprise Act 2002) and ch. 17 below.

[56] See Brown, *Corporate Rescue*, p. 481.

[57] *Powdrill* v. *Watson* (also known as *Re Paramount Airways Ltd No. 3*) [1995] 2 WLR 312, [1995] 2 All ER 65 (House of Lords).

[58] Brown, *Corporate Rescue*, p. 489.

insolvency context, will, however, be considered below in outlining the post-Enterprise Act administration regime and, in chapter 17, when discussing the positions of employees at times of corporate distress.

The role of the judiciary was always important in relation to the moratorium accompanying administration.[59] The effectiveness of the moratorium stood to be reduced by the court's exercise of a ready discretion to allow enforcement actions against the company during the moratorium, or if the courts interpreted the coverage of the moratorium restrictively.

On issues of scope and coverage, the indications are that all relevant actions and claims against the company were seen as within the moratorium's area of protection.[60] Sir Nicholas Browne-Wilkinson VC emphasised in *Bristol Airport plc v. Powdrill*[61] that it was the essence of administration that businesses would be carried on by administrators who had acquired the right 'to use the property of the company free from interference by creditors and others'. The courts, however, were not content to allow the administrator to judge whether to allow a creditor to enforce a claim or to balance the interests of a single creditor against those of the company and its creditors as a whole. The judiciary, accordingly, rejected the view that they should desist from interfering with the administrator's decision if the claimant failed to show that something in the administrator's conduct merited adverse criticism.[62] Dangers of excessive litigation expense and court involvement were met by the courts making it clear, first, that they expected administrators themselves to consent to the enforcement of claims where there would be no attendant adverse effect on the conduct of the administration and, second, that administrators who unjustifiably refused consent would be penalised in costs.[63] As to the criteria that were to govern decisions whether or not to permit enforcement of a particular claim, the courts tended to balance the interests of the petitioning creditor against those of

---

[59] See D. Milman, 'The Administration Order Regime and the Courts' in H. Rajak (ed.), *Insolvency Law: Theory and Practice* (Sweet & Maxwell, London, 1993); Milman, 'Firming Up Moratoria' [2001] 3 *Palmer's In Company* 1; Milman, 'The Courts and the Administration Regime: Supporting Legislative Policy' [2001] Ins. Law. 208.

[60] *Bristol Airport plc v. Powdrill* [1990] Ch 744; *Exchange Travel Agency Ltd v. Triton Property Trust plc* [1991] BCC 341; *Re Atlantic Computer Systems plc* [1990] BCC 859; *London Flight Centre (Stansted) Ltd v. Osprey Aviation Ltd* [2002] BPIR 1115.

[61] [1990] Ch 744.   [62] *Re Meesan Investments Ltd* [1988] 4 BCC 788.

[63] *Re Atlantic Computer Systems plc* [1990] BCC 859.

other corporate creditors.[64] They avoided taking into account the wider public, employee or trade-dependent interests that might be affected by the potential rescue of the business. Nicolls LJ stated in *Re Atlantic Computer Systems plc*:[65]

> In carrying out the balancing exercise, great importance or weight is normally to be given to ... proprietary interests ... [T]he administration procedure is not to be used to prejudice those who were secured creditors when the administration order was made in lieu of a winding up order ... The underlying principle here is that an administration for the benefit of unsecured creditors should not be conducted at the expense of those who have proprietary rights which they are seeking to exercise, save to the extent that this may be unavoidable and even then this will usually be acceptable only to a strictly limited extent.

In *Re Olympia & York Canary Wharf Ltd*,[66] moreover, Millett J was of the opinion that, to the extent that the moratorium represents an interference with private rights, it should go no further than is required to support the ability of the administrator to carry out his functions.[67] Such an approach might have been of value to the court in imposing limits on the interests that have to be taken into account when deciding enforcement issues, but it was hardly consistent with Cork's vision of administration as a process that takes on board the broad array of interests affected by the potential insolvency.

As for the statutory extent of the moratorium, section 11(3) of the Insolvency Act 1986 provided that on the making of an administration order: 'No other steps may be taken to enforce any security over the company's property, or to repossess goods in the company's possession under any hire purchase agreement, except with the consent of the administrator or the leave of the court and subject (where the court gives leave) to such terms as the court may impose'; and 'no other proceedings and no execution or other legal process may be commenced or continued, and no distress may be levied, against the company or its property except with the consent of the administrator or the leave of the court and subject (where the court gives leave) to such terms as aforesaid'.

---

[64] Ibid., at 879 (Nicolls LJ). On *Re Atlantic Computer Systems* see further M. G. Bridge, 'Company Administrators and Secured Creditors' (1991) 107 LQR 394; Bridge, 'Form, Substance and Innovation in Personal Property Security Law' [1992] JBL 1 at 18–21.

[65] [1990] BCC 859 at 880. [66] [1993] BCLC 453.

[67] Ibid., at 456. See G. Lightman and G. Moss, *The Law of Administrators and Receivers of Companies* (4th edn, Thomson/Sweet & Maxwell, London, 2007) p. 581.

What constituted 'a security' for such purposes was defined in section 248(b)(i) as 'any mortgage, charge, lien or other security'. This reference to 'other security' both gave the court considerable discretion to determine whether certain enforcement actions were ruled out by section 11(3) and created some uncertainty. In *Bristol Airport v. Powdrill* the court took a wide view of the moratorium and the airport was prevented by section 11 from asserting a statutory lien for unpaid airport charges with respect to an aircraft leased by a third party to the company. In *Re Atlantic Computer Systems plc* items of computer equipment were leased or let under hire purchase agreements to a company which sublet them to third parties. The company went into administration and the Court of Appeal ruled that the owners of the equipment were not entitled during the administration period to receive from the administrators, as expenses of the administration,[68] the payments due under the head leases and hire purchase agreement. The equipment was held to be within the possession of the company for section 11(3) purposes and so leave was required to take steps to terminate the head agreements, repossess the equipment and enforce any security in relation to it – though leave would be granted in the circumstances.[69]

A particular concern was whether the landlord of the company in administration could exercise a right of peaceable re-entry to the corporate premises or whether this was ruled out as 'enforcement of security' under section 11(3).[70] The importance of this point to a troubled company is difficult to exaggerate: the protection offered by the moratorium would have assisted rescue efforts very little if the company had been liable to lose access to its work premises. Peaceable re-entry, moreover, was a procedure allowing a landlord to forfeit a lease without having to obtain a court order and could be instigated on non-payment of rent or breaches of covenant by the tenant. All the landlord normally had to do

---

[68] The Court of Appeal refused to invoke an 'expenses of the administration' principle (similar to liquidation: see ch. 13 below) because administration was a novel regime and solutions to problems it posed were not to be found in settled areas of insolvency law. See further Bridge, 'Company Administrators', p. 395.

[69] See Bridge, 'Company Administrators'.

[70] See P. McCartney, 'Insolvency Procedures and a Landlord's Right of Peaceable Re-entry' (2000) 13 *Insolvency Intelligence* 73; P. Shaw, 'Administrators: Peaceable Re-entry by a Landlord Revisited' [1999] Ins. Law. 254; J. Byrne and L. Doyle, 'Can a Landlord Forfeit a Lease by Peaceable Re-entry?' [1999] Ins. Law. 167. On the power of a landlord to distrain for unpaid rent by taking goods and, in a receivership, bypassing other unsecured creditors, see P. Walton, 'The Landlord, his Distress, the Insolvent Tenant and the Stranger' (2000) 16 IL&P 47.

in practice was to change the locks and exclude the tenant from the premises.

Over the years preceding the Enterprise Act 2002 it had become clear that the courts were unlikely to extend the protection of the section 11 moratorium so as to stop peaceable re-entry. The case of *Exchange Travel Agency* v. *Triton plc*[71] had suggested that peaceable re-entry would be covered by the moratorium as it involved enforcement of the security interest. But matters changed with *Razzaq* v. *Pala*,[72] a decision which put forward a more recent and dominant view that the moratorium would not cover peaceable re-entry. The DTI review group was of the view in 2000 that the law should be changed to bring landlords within the ambit of the statutory moratorium.[73] This change was effected in the Insolvency Act 2000 and the same position then obtained in relation to moratoria in administration and within the CVA procedure set out in the Insolvency Act 2000.[74]

Turning to the issues of information and expertise, a criticism of the pre-Enterprise Act administration procedure was that expert judgements tended to be too narrowly channelled through the Rule 2.2 report, which both increased costs and detracted from other means of informing judgements such as consulting a wide range of parties affected by the insolvency. Rule 2.2 reports, on this view, tended to become excessively elaborate and expensive without always adding a great deal to decision-making. A simpler, cheaper, more accessible regime, the criticism ran, would be likely to improve rescue decisions as well as make them more acceptable to a wide range of affected parties.[75]

As for the accountability and fairness of pre-Enterprise Act administration, a first problem was that the administrator was not obliged or entitled to consider the public interest or the interests of all parties materially affected by the potential insolvency. This meant that

---

[71] [1991] BCC 341.

[72] [1997] 1 WLR 1336 (dealing with security interests per s. 383(2) of the Insolvency Act 1986); *Razzaq* dealt with bankruptcy but it was likely that the courts would take the same view in relation to corporate insolvency: see *Ezekiel* v. *Orakpo* [1976] 3 All ER 659; *Clarence Coffey* v. *Corchester Finance* (unreported) 3 November 1998; *Re Lomax Leisure Ltd* [1999] EGCS 61; *Christopher Moran Holdings Ltd* v. *Bairstow* [1999] All ER 673.

[73] IS 2000, p. 37.

[74] See M. McIntosh, 'Insolvency Act 2000: Landlords' Right of Peaceable Re-entry' (2001) 17 IL&P 48. See Insolvency Act 2000 s. 9 – peaceable re-entry covered by the administration moratorium; Sch. A1, para. 12 – peaceable re-entry covered by the 'small company' CVA moratorium: see ch. 11 below.

[75] See Phillips, *Administration Procedure*, p. 5.

customers, suppliers and employees of the company – all of whom might have considerable stakes in its future – had no voice in administration if they did not constitute creditors of the firm. The company's unsecured creditors had a voice through the creditors' meeting and approval mechanism in determining the course of action taken by the administrator, but such creditors voted according to the value of their debts and not according to the extent of their dependence on the company's fortunes. An employee, accordingly, would only have a vote that reflected any money owed to him or her and account was not taken of their future role within the company. When, moreover, the court scrutinised, at various points, the administrator's actions, it would look to the financial interests of creditors and members rather than broader concerns.[76] Such an approach, again, was at odds with the Cork Committee's argument that the court should appoint an administrator, *inter alia*, to restore profitability or maintain employment; or to carry on a business 'where this is in the public interest'.[77] Sir Kenneth Cork himself spoke of his committee's intention that an administrator would have a role to play '[w]here, in the national interest, the government should take a hand – as happened in the case of Rolls Royce'.[78]

Shareholders as members of the company could apply to the court under section 27 of the Insolvency Act 1986 if they had a complaint that the administrator's proposal, if implemented, would prejudice some part of them or them generally. Such shareholders, however, were not involved in approval of the administrator's proposals, which under section 24 was a function given to the creditors alone. On this point it might be argued that there was some consistency with Cork's suggestion that society's interest lies not in the preservation or rehabilitation of a company as such but in the commercial enterprise.[79] Such an argument, however, can be taken too far: even if it is accepted that society's interest lies in the enterprise and not the company, this does not in itself mean that the interest of shareholders should be ignored by granting shareholders no procedural rights. If there is a prospect of rescue can shareholders be said wholly to have given over their interests in the company to the creditors? Shareholders clearly did have an interest in the administrator's actions. There was, indeed, no basis for stating that

---

[76] See, for example, Insolvency Act 1986 s. 27(1)(a).   [77] Cork Report, para. 498.
[78] Cork, *Cork on Cork*, p. 195.   [79] Cork Report, para. 193.

Parliament established administration in pursuit of the survival of the enterprise and that the company's survival was not a legitimate objective in view. Section 8(3)(a) of the 1986 Act stated explicitly that an administration order could be made for the purpose, *inter alia*, of 'the survival of the company and the whole or any part of its undertaking as a going concern'. It seems, accordingly, hard to deny the legitimacy of shareholder interest in administration.

To summarise the discussion thus far, administration (between the Insolvency Act 1986 and the Enterprise Act 2002) was a procedure that was oriented towards rescue as well as asset realisation but it underperformed in a number of respects when assessed on efficiency, expertise, accountability and fairness counts. Whether the 2002 reforms corrected such underperformance and whether administration has been reformulated in an improved guise are matters to which we now turn.

The Enterprise Act reforms and the new administration

By 2000, the Insolvency Service Review Group had come firmly to the view that reform of administration was necessary – principally to remove its vulnerability to the actions of floating charge holders: 'Our firmest recommendation is that the law should be changed to remove the right enjoyed by the holder of the floating charge to veto the making of an administration order, thus bringing the position in administration in line with that proposed for the moratorium in a CVA.'[80] By July 2001, the Government had endorsed this proposal in its White Paper on *Productivity and Enterprise*[81] and legislative steps followed when the Enterprise Act was passed in 2002. This Act came into force on 15 September 2003 and substituted the original Part II of the 1986 Act with a new Part II, the provisions of which are set out in a new Schedule B1 to the 1986 Act.[82] The effect was to make administration

---

[80] IS 2000, p. 21.

[81] White Paper, *Productivity and Enterprise: Insolvency – A Second Chance* (Cm 5234, July 2001) para. 2.15.

[82] Hereafter references to Sch. B1 will be referred to as 'para. ...'. Note, however, that the 'old' administration procedure survives in relation to a number of categories of public utility company and to building societies: EA 2002 s. 249. It also survives where an administration order petition was presented to the court before 15 September 2003 (SI 2003/2039, art. 3(2)).

rather than administrative receivership the governmentally preferred procedure for attempting to rescue troubled companies.[83] The new law prohibits (subject to stated exceptions) the use of administrative receivership by the holder of a qualifying floating charge (QFC).[84] Instead, the EA provides for the general enforcement of floating charges to be carried out through use of the administration process. The EA streamlines administration by introducing an out-of-court appointment procedure[85] and by abolishing the need for the administrator's Rule 2.2 report.[86] After the EA 2002 there are, accordingly, three methods by which an administrator can be appointed: *by the court* on the application of the company, its directors, one or more of the company's creditors or a combination of these parties;[87] *out of court* on the application of the holder of a qualifying floating charge;[88] and *out of court* on the

---

[83] For HM Treasury proposals for a special insolvency regime for UK banks (made in the wake of the Northern Rock crisis) see: HM Treasury, *Banking Reform – Protecting Depositors: A Discussion Paper* (HM Treasury, London, 2007). See now the Banking (Special Provisions) Act 2008 (to be replaced: see Banking (No. 2) Bill (HL, 4 December 2008).

[84] Insolvency Act 1986 s. 72A. The general prohibition applicable to holders of 'qualifying floating charges' is subject to six exceptions relating to capital markets: see ss. 72B–72G of the IA 1986 and ch. 8 above. Transactions that predate the implementation of the EA 2002 will still allow holders of qualifying floating charges both to appoint administrative receivers and to block the appointment of an administrator.

[85] I.e. on the application of the holder of a qualifying floating charge (IA 1986 Sch. B1, paras. 14–21) and on the application of a company or a company's directors (IA 1986 Sch. B1, paras. 22–34).

[86] See p. 370 above. Under the 'old' administration procedures an application to the court for administration was invariably accompanied by an independent report from the proposed administrator: Insolvency Rule 2.2. Note, however, that even though there is no longer a requirement to prepare a Rule 2.2 report, IPs are still under an obligation to make a statement that it is reasonably likely that 'the purpose of the administration' will be achieved (Sch. B1, paras. 18(3), 29(3), r. 2.33(2)(m), as applicable). See r. 2.33 for the list of matters the administrator is required to include regarding his proposals for the administration, some of which could be said to be 'unrealistic': H. Sims and N. Briggs, 'Enterprise Act 2002 – Corporate Wrinkles' (2004) 17 *Insolvency Intelligence* 49 at 50.

[87] IA 1986 Sch. B1, paras. 11–13. If the directors, company or secured creditor want to ensure that the administrator's appointment will have extraterritorial effect under the EC Regulation on Insolvency Proceedings 2000 (1346/2000), they should use the court-application route: see G. Moss, 'On the Edge of Non-Recognition? Appointment of Administrators under the Enterprise Act and the EC Regulation' (2004) 17 *Insolvency Intelligence* 13.

[88] IA 1986 Sch. B1, paras. 14–21.

application of a company or a company's directors.[89] The court may only make an order (under paragraph 11) if it is satisfied that the company is or is likely to become unable to pay its debts (paragraph 11(a)) but this requirement does *not* apply in the case of applications to court *or* out-of-court applications by holders of qualifying floating charges.[90] Inability, or likely inability, to pay debts *is* a prerequisite for out-of-court appointments by the company or by directors (under paragraph 22).[91]

The EA lays down the objectives to be pursued and the purpose of administration in paragraph 3 of the new Schedule B1 of the Insolvency Act 1986.[92] Paragraph 3(1) states that the administrator of a company must perform his functions with the objective of (a) rescuing the company as a going concern, or (b) achieving a better result for the company's creditors as a whole than would be likely if the company were wound up (without first going into administration) or (c) realising property in order to make a distribution to one or more secured or preferential creditors. The first stated objective is to rescue the company as a going concern.[93] The administrator must act to pursue objective (a) unless he thinks either that it is not reasonably practicable to achieve that objective or that the objective set out in (b) would achieve a better result for the company's creditors as a whole.[94] The

---

[89] Ibid., paras. 22–34. Note that with regard to FSA-authorised companies the FSA's written consent is needed. On IPs' responsibilities under the Financial Services and Markets Act (FSMA) 2000 see further C. Rafferty and O. Gayle, 'Financial Services and Markets Act 2000: Considerations for the IP' (2007) *Recovery* (Summer) 35.

[90] IA 1986 Sch. B1, paras. 35(1)(a); 35(2)(a).

[91] See para. 27(2)(a) involving a statutory declaration as to the company's inability to pay debts.

[92] I.e. EA 2002 s. 248 'substitutes' the four statutory purposes for which an 'old' administration order could be obtained under the IA 1986 s. 8(3) with paragraph 3 of Sch. B1. The decision of *DKLL Solicitors* v. *HMRC* [2007] BCC 908 shows that the purpose of the administration is a self-standing test rather than a function of the wish of creditors, even if they control the voting at the creditors' meeting at which the administrator's proposals might come to be considered: see S. Frisby, 'Judicial Sanction of Insolvency Pre-Packs? *DKLL Solicitors* v. *HMRC* Considered' (2008) 27 *Company Law Newsletter* 1; S. Frieze, 'Round-up of Some Recent Cases on Administration' (2008) 21 *Insolvency Intelligence* 14.

[93] The Explanatory Notes to the Enterprise Act 2002 (ch. 40) refer to the 'company and as much of its business as possible' (para. 647). Rescuing the company as a going concern may also involve the creditors agreeing to a CVA or Scheme of Arrangement: see S. Elboz, 'Exiting Administration – Railtrack and the Future' (2002) IL&P 187, 189; R. Pedley, 'The Enterprise Bill' (2002) IL&P 123; M. Phillips and J. Goldring, 'Rescue and Reconstruction' (2002) *Insolvency Intelligence* 76 at 76.

[94] The administrator, in the absence of some special relationship, owes no general common law duty of care to (individual) unsecured creditors regarding the conduct of the administration: see *Kyrris* v. *Oldham* [2004] BCC 111, [2004] 1 BCLC 305. See further pp. 444–6 below.

objective set out in (c) is only to be pursued if he thinks that it is not reasonably practicable to achieve either (a) or (b) and the administrator does not unnecessarily harm the interests of the creditors of the company as a whole. Subject to the provisions governing the pursuit of (c), the administrator is to pursue his functions 'in the interests of the company's creditors as a whole' (paragraph 3(2)). The effect of the above is that the administrator is not obliged to rescue the company at all costs.[95] The tension between protecting the company and protecting the business is managed by paragraph 3(3) and notably by 3(3)(b), which stipulates that rescuing the company gives way to arrangements that would give a better result for the creditors as a whole. This gives primacy to saving the *business* where this gives the better result for creditors.[96]

The administrator acts as the company's agent and has an impressive range of powers to assist him in doing 'anything necessary or expedient for the management of the affairs, business and property of the company'.[97] These powers are listed in Schedule 1 and in paragraphs 61–3 and 70–3 of Schedule B1 of the Insolvency Act 1986 and the administrator must use these statutory powers to aid his management of the company in accordance with any proposals which have been approved by a meeting of creditors or in accordance with any directions given by the court.[98] As an officer of the court, the administrator is under a duty to act in good faith, with independence, impartiality and loyalty, and not to

[95] Compare with 'the hierarchy of objectives' found in para. 3 of Sch. B1 of the Enterprise Bill under which it 'was clear that administration was first and foremost about rescuing the corporate entity': see Phillips and Goldring, 'Rescue and Reconstruction', p. 76.

[96] As noted above, the Explanatory Notes to the Enterprise Act 2002 state that 'rescuing the company as a going concern' is intended to mean 'the company and as much of its business as possible' (para. 647). Rescuing the company alone/simply allowing the survival of the corporate shell will thus not satisfy this objective: see further Phillips and Goldring, 'Rescue and Reconstruction'; S. Frisby, 'In Search of a Rescue Regime: The Enterprise Act 2002' (2004) 67 MLR 247, 262–3.

[97] See Sch. B1, para. 69; para. 59(1).

[98] See Sch. B1, para. 68. Administrators are under no obligation to dispose of assets in a particular manner but there is a duty to maximise realisations. Assets should therefore be the subject of a professional independent valuation and the prudent administrator would seek the views of the creditors' committee, if there is one, where practicable to do so. See *Coyne and Hardy* v. *DRC Distribution Ltd and Foster* [2008] BCC 612 where the Court of Appeal, *inter alia*, comprehensively analysed the actions of the administrators and set out guidelines as to what is expected of office holders when undertaking their work. According to Rimmer LJ, the administrators' conduct 'had the potential for disaster written all over it; and disaster is what happened. As the judge said, they "did not act expeditiously and with the robustness of purpose that one would have hoped for and which [one] is entitled to expect".'

act dishonourably or unfairly.[99] Also, as discussed below,[100] the administrator must act rationally and thus, in exercising a discretion or discharging a duty, must act in the way that a reasonable administrator would act.[101]

The EA may shift English law in the direction of US Chapter 11 but it does not go the whole way. Administration involves handing control of the company to an outsider – the insolvency practitioner (IP) – and is thus not a debtor in possession ('DIP') system. Furthermore, unlike the US position, secured creditors cannot be 'crammed down' and compelled to accept a reorganisation plan against their wishes.[102] Nor does the EA provide a US-style mechanism for financing companies in financial difficulties – a matter to be returned to below. As for timings, the EA limits the duration of the administration to twelve months.[103]

An important aspect of administration is that there is a moratorium, which frees the company temporarily from harassment by creditors.[104] The moratorium available under the 'new' administration[105] is established in much the same form as found in the earlier provisions of the IA 1986[106] and the pre-EA case law is thus relevant to the construction of the new provisions.[107] In the post-EA administration process there are two types of moratoria – a moratorium for the period the company is in administration[108] and an interim moratorium pending

[99] *Ex parte James* (1874) 9 Ch App 609: see D. Milman, 'The Administration Order Procedure' (2002) 17 *Company Law Newsletter* 1 at 3. It is as yet unclear whether the administrator is to be deemed a 'public authority' for the purposes of the Human Rights Act 1998 s. 6: see further Lightman and Moss, *Law of Administrators*, pp. 236–41.

[100] See pp. 446–51 below. The administrator is both a statutory office holder and an agent of the company owing fiduciary obligations to it: see further Lightman and Moss, *Law of Administrators*, pp. 246–59.

[101] See *Re Edennote Ltd* [1996] 2 BCLC 389, 394–5 combined with *Edge* v. *Pensions Ombudsman* [2000] Ch 602, 627–31: cited in Lightman and Moss, *Law of Administrators*, p. 246 at note 94. On regulating the administrator's conduct and rendering him liable see Sch. B1, paras. 74 and 75; *Re Charnley Davies Ltd* [1990] BCC 605 (regarding the scope of IA 1986 ss. 27 and 212 – the similar provisions relating to the 'old' administration) and discussions at pp. 444–51 below.

[102] See G. McCormack, 'Super-priority New Financing and Corporate Rescue' [2007] JBL 701; ch. 6 above.

[103] Subject to agreed extensions: see para. 76.

[104] See A. Keay and P. Walton, *Insolvency Law: Corporate and Personal* (2nd edn, Jordans, Bristol, 2008) p. 106.

[105] Sch. B1, paras. 42 and 43.

[106] IA 1986 ss. 10 and 11.

[107] See Lightman and Moss, *Law of Administrators*, p. 581. See also pp. 376–8 above.

[108] Para. 43.

the disposal of an administration order application or the coming into effect of an out-of-court appointment of an administrator.[109]

The interim moratorium becomes effective, if applying to court for administration, as soon as the application is made. When a floating charge holder applies under paragraph 14, the moratorium takes effect from the date a copy of the notice of intention is filed at the court, as that is when the company or directors are seeking to appoint. The provisions of paragraphs 42 and 43 of Schedule B1 generally apply during the period of the interim moratorium.[110]

When an administrator has been appointed there is a general moratorium on the enforcement of remedies without the consent of the administrator or the permission of the court.[111] As noted previously, the moratorium is procedural in nature, suspending the power to enforce rights but not destroying such rights. The company cannot then be wound up[112] and the consent of the administrator or the leave of the court is required for such actions as enforcing a security against the company, repossessing goods in the company's possession under a hire purchase agreement, exercising a right of forfeiture by re-entry,[113] or the commencement or continuation of any other legal proceedings or levying distress against the company or its property.[114] Protection also extends to property owned by the company but in the possession of third parties such as lessees.[115] An administrative receiver cannot be appointed when the company is in administration and an administrative receiver already in office must vacate.[116]

Financial collateral arrangements

At this point consideration must be given to the insolvency effects of the Financial Collateral Regulations 2003[117] and their implementation of the

---

[109] Para. 44.

[110] Except that winding-up petitions on public interest grounds under IA 1986 s. 124A or Financial Services and Markets Act 2000 s. 367 are not prevented: see further V. Finch, 'Public Interest Liquidation: PIL or Placebo?' [2002] Ins. Law. 157 and ch. 13 below. The appointment of administrators by qualifying floating charge holders (QFCs) (under para. 14) is similarly not prevented under the interim moratorium, nor is the appointment of administrative receivers.

[111] Paras. 42, 43 – applicable whether the administration is out of court or via a court order.

[112] Para. 42(2)(3).

[113] See *Metro Nominees (Wandsworth) (No. 1)* v. *Rayment* [2008] BCC 40.

[114] Para. 43.

[115] *Re Atlantic Computer Systems plc (No. 1)* [1992] Ch 505, [1992] 2 WLR 367, [1990] BCC 859.

[116] Paras. 43(6A), 41(1).

[117] Financial Collateral Arrangements (No. 2) Regulations 2003 (SI 2003/3226).

EU Directive on Financial Collateral Arrangements.[118] The purpose of the Directive was to enhance the effective use of financial collateral across the EU and its implementation involves streamlining arrangements for creating collateral and providing for easier realisation of collateral through enforcement.[119] For insolvency lawyers, the significance of the 2003 Regulations lies in their neutralising certain insolvency provisions so as to benefit particular lenders. The Regulations go beyond the Directive and apply to all banks and companies taking financial collateral. Such collateral includes cash and financial instruments (government securities, shares, bonds and other financial instruments such as units in collective investment schemes).[120] Collected book debts and other sums credited to bank accounts will be covered but not uncollected book debts or other types of collateral, such as commercial property, plant and machinery. The Regulations apply to security interests such as mortgages and fixed charges and to floating charges provided that the collateral is 'in the possession or control of the collateral taker'.[121]

In the case of such collateral, Regulation 8 disapplies various insolvency provisions relating to administration and winding-up, notably: the Schedule B1 paragraph 43(2) veto on enforcing a security when the company is in administration without the consent of the administrator or the court's permission; the Schedule B1 paragraph 44 interim moratorium on enforcing a security that operates as soon as an application for administration is made; the Schedule B1 paragraph 41(2) rule that any receiver shall vacate office if required to do so by the administrator; and the Schedule B1 paragraphs 70–1 power of the administrator to dispose of property subject to certain types of charge.[122] The effect of the Regulations is to assure lenders of easy enforcement in the case of insolvency. Such provisions, however, can be seen as reducing the availability of company cash deposits to fund administrations and to

---

[118] Directive on Financial Collateral Arrangements 2002/47/EC.

[119] See S. Lawson, 'New Financial Collateral Regulations' (2004) *Recovery* (Autumn) 22; A. Sharp, 'The Collateral Directive – A New Way of Thinking About Security' (2004) 17 *Insolvency Intelligence* 145.

[120] Lawson, 'New Financial Collateral Regulations'.

[121] 'Given the current debate on floating charges, this can only safely apply to floating charges that have crystallised.' See Lawson, 'New Financial Collateral Regulations', p. 22 and J. Benjamin, *Financial Law* (Oxford University Press, Oxford, 2007) pp. 476–8.

[122] The 2003 Regulations also disapply the automatic avoidance provisions of the Insolvency Act 1986 s. 245 (floating charges), s. 127 (property dispositions) and s. 88 (share transfers after a winding-up resolution): see Sharp, 'Collateral Directive', pp. 147–8.

fly in the face of the Enterprise Act's conception of administration as a rescue mechanism.[123]

Preferential creditors, the prescribed part and the banks

Other important provisions of the Enterprise Act 2002 concern priorities and the protection of vulnerable creditors. The Crown's status as preferential creditor was abolished by section 251 of the EA.[124] It is estimated that this will result in some £70 million per annum flowing to other creditors.[125] The EA also introduced 'ring-fencing' of a prescribed proportion of the company's net floating charge proceeds. These proceeds are to be made available to the company's unsecured creditors and only surpluses of funds following such use will be available for distribution to the floating charge holders.[126] The 'prescribed part' of funds for ring-fencing is stipulated by Statutory Instrument.[127]

---

[123] See the comments of practitioners: Sharp, 'Collateral Directive'; Lawson, 'New Financial Collateral Regulations': 'Secured lenders will have increased leverage over cash assets which may otherwise be used to fund the administration ... [They] may be able to avoid the new prescribed part provisions altogether either by taking certain floating charge assets for themselves or relying on the Regulations to disapply the prescribed part provisions once the charge has crystallised.'

[124] Paras. 1, 2, 3–5C, 6, 7 of the IA 1986 Sch. 6 are deleted. Preferential debts that remain are: unpaid contributions for occupational pensions; four months of unpaid employee wages and holiday entitlements; and unpaid levies in respect of coal and steel production. See further ch. 14 below.

[125] See IS, *Regulatory Impact Assessment for Insolvency Provisions in the Enterprise Act 2002* (IS, London, 2002) (hereafter 'EA 2002 RIA') para. 5.29 – this is based on the Crown recovering £90 million per annum preferentially in all insolvencies and the estimate that this would drop to some £20 million per annum when the Crown became unsecured.

[126] See IA 1986 s. 176A. This is an echo of the Cork Report's proposal for a 10 per cent fund: Report of the Review Committee, paras. 1538–49. On the 'prescribed part' see further ch. 3 above and ch. 13 below. Whether, on the wording of s. 176A, a floating charge with an unsecured balance is entitled to participate in the prescribed part funds has been a matter of debate. The Insolvency Service is of the view that the floating charge holder is not entitled to participate in any distribution, a view upheld by His Honour Judge Purle QC in *Permacell Finesse Ltd (in liquidation)* [2008] BCC 208: noted D. Offord, 'Case Digest' (2008) 21 *Insolvency Intelligence* 30. See also *Re Airbase (UK) Ltd, Thorniley v. Revenue and Customs Commissioner* [2008] BCC 213: noted A. Walters, 'Statutory Redistribution of Floating Charge Assets: Victory (Again) to Revenue and Customs' (2008) 29 Co. Law. 129; see also ch. 15 below. For a contrary view see G. McPhie, 'New Legislation' (2004) *Recovery* (Autumn) 24.

[127] See Insolvency Act 1986 (Prescribed Part) Order 2003, SI 2003/2097 – 50 per cent of net property where that net property is less than £10,000; above £10,000, then 50 per cent of the first £10,000 in value and 20 per cent of the excess, up to an overall limit of £600,000. See also ch. 3 above.

For the banks, as holders of post-EA (or 'qualifying') floating charges, the EA produces a significant alteration in substantive rights. Whereas a receiver owes a duty to look only to the interests of the floating charge holder, the administrator has a duty to act in the interests of the creditors as a whole and in pursuance of the 'tiered' objectives set out now in Schedule B1, paragraph 3(1)(a), (b) and (c). Under paragraph 3(3) of Schedule B1 the administrator, as noted, is only to realise property to distribute to one or more secured or preferential creditors if (a) he thinks that it is not reasonably practicable to achieve either of the objectives in 3(1)(a) or (b) (i.e. rescuing the company as a going concern or achieving a better result for creditors as a whole than would be likely in a winding up) *and* (b) he does not unnecessarily harm the interests of the creditors of the company as a whole. The reforms do not change priorities in an insolvency but may have a substantive effect on the floating charge holder. This is because a floating charge holder who appoints an administrator rather than an administrative receiver is dealing with a regime in which the administrator has to take into account interests other than the floating charge holder's and in which rescuing the company has a degree of primacy in relation to satisfying the secured creditors' interests.

Lobbying by powerful lenders in the period leading up to the EA produced a set of impressive procedural rights for the banks.[128] The British Bankers' Association (BBA) argued forcefully during 2001 that administrative receivership had been a very successful 'engine for reconstruction and enterprise in the UK'.[129] Receivership, said the BBA, had allowed secured creditors to 'appoint somebody who is able to act quickly and manage the restructuring process in a way which has saved businesses and jobs in a cost effective manner'.[130] The thrust of this argument was that any new administration procedure that was to be rescue-friendly had to be streamlined and fast. The Enterprise Act 2002 moved towards such streamlining by removing the need for a Rule 2.2 report and limiting the number of circumstances requiring a court

---

[128] A remarkable dilution of the Government's original intentions achieved by the banks' 'tremendous power in the lobby': see J. Willcock, 'How the Banks Won the Battle for the Enterprise Bill' (2002) *Recovery* (June) 24, 26 (quote attributed to D. Mond of Hodgsons).

[129] BBA, *Response by the BBA to the Insolvency Service White Paper, Insolvency – A Second Chance* (October 2001) (hereafter 'BBA, *Response to White Paper*').

[130] Ibid., p. 3; on receivership as a rescue procedure, see ch. 8 above.

procedure.[131] Now a lender (bank) files a notice of appointment declaring that: they are the holders of a qualifying floating charge in respect of a company's property; the charge is enforceable; and the appointment is in accordance with Schedule B1 to the Insolvency Act 1986.[132] For the secured lender, appointing an administrator will differ little from the current process for appointing a receiver. Banks are able to use the streamlined appointment procedure in all cases, not merely situations of urgency, and they are able to determine who should be appointed to the post of administrator.[133] This gives the banks the power to insert their chosen administrator with speed and without regard to the other creditors or the courts. As has been observed: 'Even if the company or its directors choose an administrator, effectively the holder of the floating charge can choose an alternative administrator.'[134] The overall effect, then, is that floating charge holder concerns have largely been sought to be met in the Enterprise Act – to the extent that one group of practitioners has argued: 'It may be better to describe the reforms as a "transmutation" or "merger" of administrative receivership and administration

---

[131] The Association of Business Recovery Professionals (R3) estimated a standard r. 2.2 report to be between £4,000 and £8,000 (based on £1 million turnover, £500,000 book value of assets expected to realise £200,000): see EA 2002 RIA, para. 5.27.

[132] If there is a prior qualifying charge (per Sch. B1, para. 14(2)) to that held by the lender (the bank), then the bank may not appoint an administrator unless it has given at least two business days' written notice to the prior charge holder (enabling the prior qualified floating charge holder to consider appointing an administrator itself): see Sch. B1, para. 15.

[133] See Sch. B1, paras. 14(1), 18(3). On how the court resolves competing proposals regarding the identity of the administrators where there is no QFC see R. Tett and F. Paterson 'World Class Administrators' (2005) Recovery (Summer) 24; Re World Class [2005] 2 BCLC 1. See also The Oracle (North West) Ltd v. Pinnacle Services (UK) Ltd [2008] EWHC 1920 – where significant creditors have a clear preference for one administrator over another and the secured creditor and other creditors are neutral, the court should decide in favour of the wishes of those creditors, particularly given that administration is intended for their benefit.

[134] See M. Stevenson, 'The Enterprise Bill 2002 – A Move Towards a Rescue Culture?' (2002) 18 IL&P 155, 157. Mond argues: 'I don't like the fact the bank can appoint an administrator of its own choice without reference to the court. That is very, very dangerous. It feels like a back door way of receivership' (quoted in Willcock, 'How the Banks Won the Battle', p. 26). See also p. 428 below on the effect this may have to incentivise administrators to keep the banks happy. If an administration application is made by a party other than the floating charge holder (e.g. by a company or directors) and the floating charge holder applies to have its chosen administrator appointed instead, the court shall allow this unless it thinks it right to refuse 'because of the particular circumstances of the case' (Sch. B1, para. 36(2)).

procedures rather than as being the end of the administrative receivership procedure.'[135]

Exiting from administration

A number of routes out of administration are possible.[136] An administrator
will automatically vacate office one year from the date the administration
commenced, unless this term has been extended by the court (for such
period as the court deems necessary) or extended with the consent of the
creditors for up to six months.[137] Furthermore, the new-style administration
can be converted to a Creditors' Voluntary Liquidation (CVL) by filing
documents at Companies House if the administrator thinks that there will
be a distribution to unsecured creditors.[138] This process obviates the needs
for advertising the office holder's appointment or for holding a creditors'
meeting. In the alternative, the administrator can now make a distribution
to the company's creditors, generally the secured and preferential creditors,[139] and can then move to put the company into CVL under Schedule
B1, paragraph 83, as noted above.

---

[135] S. Davies, *Insolvency and the Enterprise Act 2002* (Jordans, Bristol, 2003) pp. 40–1; 'the
new deal is merely "son of receivership"': see Willcock, 'How the Banks Won the Battle'.
R3 commented on the White Paper proposals, *Insolvency – A Second Chance*, that the
status quo was being upheld and that banks would have the same real powers in case of
administration as they did with receivership: *Financial Times*, 1 August 2001.

[136] See G. Todd, 'Administration Post-Enterprise Act – What Are the Options for Exits?'
(2006) 19 *Insolvency Intelligence* 17.

[137] Sch. B1, paras. 76–9. This automatic termination of administration after twelve months
is a feature introduced by the EA 2002 reforms and evidences the clear aim of the
legislature to make administration a short-lived, transitory process to be dealt with
'quickly and efficiently': see also para. 4. For a pragmatic interpretation of the exit routes
available under para. 79 see *Re TM Kingdom Ltd* [2007] BCC 480 (Norris J).

[138] Sch. B1, para. 83. Preconditions are laid down in para. 83(1) and (2), namely that
provision must have been made to ensure that all secured creditors will be paid off and,
after that, there must be something remaining available for the unsecured creditors. The
procedure is available for court-appointed or out-of-court-appointed administrators
and with the former it is not necessary to seek a court order: see *Re Ballast plc (in
administration) and Others* [2005] BCC 96. See *Re GHE Realisations (formerly
Gatehouse Estates Ltd)* [2006] BCC 139 regarding exit modes in paras. 83 and 84.

[139] Sch. B1, para. 65. If a distribution is sought to any other type of creditor the court's
permission must be obtained. The Financial Markets Law Committee has raised concerns that these new rules to make distributions to unsecured creditors (which include
set-off provisions – Insolvency Rules 1986 r. 2.85 – and administration expenses – IA
1986 Sch. B1, para. 99 and IR 1986 r. 2.67) could give rise to potential legal uncertainties

Alternatively the administrator can institute a process to dissolve the company. Such a direct move into dissolution is possible where the administrator thinks that there is no property left which might permit a distribution to creditors.[140] The administrator will achieve this result by sending a notice to the registrar of companies and, at the end of three months, the company will be dissolved automatically.

Where an administrator has been appointed out of court and there has been a rescue and a return of the company to the directors, the administrator may end the process of administration by giving notice that the purpose of the administration has been achieved.[141]

A court order may also end the administration.[142] This may happen when the administrator applies for such an order (for instance when he feels the objective cannot be achieved, or that the company should not have entered administration or if a creditors' meeting so directs him to apply). If the administrator has been appointed by the court then he may apply to the court to end the administration if he thinks the purpose has been achieved. When the administrator reports to the court that there is a stalemate regarding the administrator's proposals, the court may also end the administration.[143] A creditor may apply for an order to end the administration on the basis that there has been an 'improper motive' behind the appointment,[144] and where a creditor or member wishes to challenge the conduct of the administrator on grounds of unfairness or harm to the interests of the applicant, the court can provide for the administrator's appointment to cease to have effect.[145] Finally, the Secretary of State may apply to the court to have the company

---

which could, in turn, discourage counterparties from dealing with companies in administration, thereby harming any rescue attempt: see FMLC discussion paper, 'Administration – Set-off and Expenses' (Issue 108, 17 January 2008), available on the FMLC website (www.fmlc.org). (On set-off see ch. 14 below.) The administrator can also make payments other than through para. 65 'if he thinks it likely to assist achievement of the purpose of administration' (para. 66). This could allow the administrator to pay off arrears owed to a creditor who made such a payment a condition of making further essential supplies, e.g. fuel or raw materials: see L. S. Sealy and D. Milman, *Annotated Guide to the Insolvency Legislation 2007/2008* (10th edn, Thomson/Sweet & Maxwell, London, 2007) p. 550.

[140] Sch. B1, para. 84. See *Re GHE Realisations Ltd* [2006] BCC 139, which indicated that an administrator was only required to think *at that time* that there was no further property to distribute (and prior distributions were immaterial). This decision departed, in this regard, from *obiter* comments in *Re Ballast plc* [2005] BCC 96.

[141] Sch. B1, para. 80.   [142] Ibid., para. 79.   [143] Ibid., para. 55.

[144] Ibid., para. 81.   [145] Ibid., para. 74(4)(d).

wound up on grounds of public interest during the course of an administration.[146]

Evaluating administration

The introduction of a new administration procedure raises a host of questions concerning its value as a rescue process and its cost-effectiveness, as well as its amenability to the exercise of expertise, its accountability and its fairness. It is now time to turn to these matters and, *inter alia*, to consider the findings of the valuable research that the Insolvency Service has undertaken or commissioned regarding different aspects of these matters.[147]

Administration and rescue: efficiency issues

Use, cost-effectiveness and returns to creditors

An aim of the EA was to promote the use of administration rather than receivership[148] and this objective has been achieved. The number of annual administrations rose from 649 in 2002–3 to 2,661 in 2005–6 at a time when total numbers of corporate insolvencies dropped slightly (from 17,810 to 16,907) and this represented a rise in administration as the procedure employed in instances of insolvency from 3.6 per cent to 15.7 per cent.[149] Receiverships, in the same period, fell from 1,310 to 565.[150] One reason for the popularity of the new procedure may have been the new streamlined out-of-court route of entry into

---

[146] Ibid., para. 82(1)(a).

[147] See, notably, Insolvency Service, *Enterprise Act 2002 – Corporate Insolvency Provisions: Evaluation Report* (Insolvency Service, London, 2008) ('*Insolvency Service Evaluation, 2008*'); S. Frisby, *Interim Report to the Insolvency Service on Returns to Creditors from Pre- and Post-Enterprise Act Insolvency Procedures* (Insolvency Service, London, 2007) ('Frisby, *Returns to Creditors, 2007*'); J. Armour, A. Hsu and A. Walters, *Report for the Insolvency Service: The Impact of the Enterprise Act 2002 on Realisations and Costs in Corporate Rescue Proceedings* (Insolvency Service, London, 2006) ('Armour, Hsu and Walters, 2006'); S. Frisby, *Report to the Insolvency Service: Insolvency Outcomes* (Insolvency Service, London, 2006) ('Frisby, *Report, 2006*'); A. Katz and M. Mumford, *Report to the Insolvency Service: Study of Administration Cases* (Insolvency Service, London, 2006) ('Katz and Mumford, 2006').

[148] The EA was not retrospective and holders of qualifying floating charges (QFCs) created before 15 September 2003 can still appoint administrative receivers.

[149] And to 17.2 per cent in the first quarter of 2007: *Insolvency Service Evaluation, 2008*, p. 23.

[150] Ibid., p. 11. These figures are consistent with the findings of Katz and Mumford, 2006.

administration. This proved immediately attractive, especially in relation to smaller enterprises,[151] so that, in 2003–4, 65.5 per cent of entries into administration were by this route compared to 29.8 per cent by court order.[152] The EA also sought to speed up administrations by introducing a time limit of one year, creating defined exit routes[153] and demanding that administrators complete their functions as quickly and efficiently as is reasonably practicable.[154] Again, the objective seems to have been achieved, with average durations of administration dropping from 438 days for pre-EA cases to 348 for post-EA cases.[155]

On whether the new procedure conduces to rescue, the Insolvency Service's conclusion is that the overall outcomes of administrations, in terms of corporate and business rescue, appear to be largely unchanged from those associated with administrative receivership and there appear to be proportionately fewer 'rescues' than under the previous adminis-tration regime – though more in absolute numbers.[156]

As for the costs of administration, direct entry expenses may have been lowered but the overall average costs of the more collective pro-cesses of administration appear to be higher than for administrative receivership.[157]

The realisations in post-EA administrations have been found to be significantly higher than in pre-EA receivership cases – especially in instances where the corporate assets were worth more than the secured creditor was owed.[158] This supports the view that the duty of the admin-istrator to act in the interests of all the creditors is impacting on total realisations.[159] The beneficial effects of such increases may, however, be enjoyed more by professionals than by creditors. Armour, Hsu and Walters found that the direct costs of administrations (primarily IP

---

[151] See N. Hood, 'How the Enterprise Act is Helping to Preserve Businesses' (2005) *Recovery* (Spring) 14 at 15: 'the advisors of most cash-strapped SMEs shied away from going to court to get protection'.

[152] Frisby, *Report*, 2006. The instituting actions in 70.6 per cent of these cases were taken by directors, 10.6 per cent were taken by the company and 18.1 per cent by a charge holder.

[153] See Sch. B1, paras. 79, 80, 81, 82.   [154] Sch. B1, para. 4.

[155] Frisby, *Report*, 2006; *Insolvency Service Evaluation*, 2008, p. 55.

[156] *Insolvency Service Evaluation*, 2008, p. 5 – though noting evidence of 'liquidation substitution' whereby administration is used in circumstances that formerly involved resort to liquidation (p. 6). This is consistent with Armour, Hsu and Walters, 2006. See further pp. 396–7 below.

[157] *Insolvency Service Evaluation*, 2008, Section 3.9.

[158] Armour, Hsu and Walters, 2006.   [159] Ibid.

and legal fees) were significantly higher in post-EA administrations than in pre-EA receiverships and that this generally occurred when the senior charge holders were over-secured (and, it seems, lacking incentives to monitor professional costs).[160] Such were these costs that the impact of increased recoveries in administrations had been negated by increased costs and fees so that there had been no resultant increase in returns to creditors.[161] Frisby has issued updated research suggesting that returns to secured and preferential creditors have improved in post-EA administrations but 'unsecured creditors do not yet appear to be benefiting from the Act'.[162] Her figures show that, comparing post-EA administrations with pre-EA receiverships, average returns to secured creditors rose from 29.3 per cent to 34.6 per cent and unsecured creditors rose from 1.9 per cent to 2.8 per cent. Unsecured creditors' returns from pre- and post-EA administrations, however, fell from 6.7 per cent to 2.8 per cent.[163]

The Insolvency Service responded to issues of process costs in late 2007 by issuing a consultation paper setting out proposals for streamlining insolvency procedures.[164] Of the eight proposals involved, two may have a bearing on administration processes: first, to modernise and make more flexible the means of communication and the exchange of information between office holders and creditors[165] and, second, to remove the

---

[160] Ibid.

[161] Ibid. Katz and Mumford, 2006, state at p. 49: 'there appears at this stage to be no strong grounds for either celebrating or regretting the substitution of administration for administrative receivership'.

[162] Frisby, *Returns to Creditors*, 2007.

[163] Ibid., noted in the *Insolvency Service Evaluation*, 2008, p. 155. Frisby suggests that this drop may be due to 'receivership substitution' (use of administration in circumstances formerly using receivership), 'liquidation substitution' and the rise of pre-packaged administrations – where the price for a business is discounted.

[164] Insolvency Service, *A Consultation Document on Changes to the Insolvency Act 1986 and the Company Directors Disqualification Act 1986 to be made by a Legislative Reform Order for the Modernisation and Streamlining of Insolvency Procedures* (IS, London, 2007). See further ch. 13 below.

[165] By, for example: introducing a provision requiring creditors to 'opt in' if they wish to receive information issued by the insolvency office holder during the conduct of the proceedings; updating insolvency legislation to make it explicit that communication can be effected electronically where the legislation requires it to be 'in writing'; enabling insolvency office holders to provide information by sending a link to a website on which information is posted; and providing a legislative framework that will allow insolvency office holders to hold meetings which are required to be held as part of their conduct of insolvency cases through media other than meetings held at a physical venue. It is noteworthy here that, in *Re Sporting Options plc* [2005] BCC 88, the administrators were not allowed to serve notice of appointment and proposals to creditors by email: see further 'Administrators: Electronic Communication with Creditors' (2006) 19

requirement for any document in insolvency proceedings to be sworn by affidavit and to replace it with a less burdensome requirement. It remains to be seen whether, post-consultation, the above steps will be introduced in a form that significantly reduces the costs of administration.

Will administration continue as a popular insolvency process or will its expense and complexity prompt a revival of other procedures such as the Law of Property Act 1925 (LPA) receivership (which allows holders of charges over particular assets to appoint receivers)?[166] For a large lender, administration involves not merely intricate procedural burdens (including notification requirements and the pressure imposed by a year's deadline for completion) but also a duty on the administrator to act in the interests of creditors as a whole.[167] There are, however, advantages of using the qualifying floating charge (QFC) and administrator route, and these include: a right to receive five days' notice of any directors' or company's application to court for an administration order or out-of-court appointment; a right to at least two days' notice of an intended appointment of an administrator by a junior holder of a QFC; and a right to apply for the appointment of their own nominee that will prevail over the nominating rights of non-QFC holders (for example, the company, its directors or its creditors). The administrator route also allows the QFC holder to apply for the appointment of an administrator when a winding-up order has been made and to benefit from the administrator's significant legal powers as well as the statutory moratorium.

If resort is made to fixed security and the LPA route, the lender will be aware that, if an LPA receiver is appointed, they can be required to vacate office by a subsequently appointed administrator – and, on such appointment, the lender will not be able to act further to enforce their security

---

Insolvency Intelligence 15. The present terms of reference to the Insolvency Rules Committee include a direction to review and, if thought appropriate, recommend the modernisation of the Insolvency Rules to allow for the greater use of electronic disclosure. The Insolvency Service is undertaking a general restructuring of the Insolvency Rules 1986 and substantive changes are being made. The final implementation of the consolidation of insolvency secondary legislation and the restructuring of the Rules has been subject to delay and, at the time of writing, is expected on 1 October 2009. See G. Davis, 'The Role of the Insolvency Rules Committee' (2007) 20 *Insolvency Intelligence* 65; P. Bailey, 'The Insolvency (Amendment) Rules 2005 – Yet More Changes for Insolvency Folk' (2006) 19 *Insolvency Intelligence* 24.

[166] See L. Verrill, 'The Use of LPA Receiverships' (2007) 20 *Insolvency Intelligence* 160; R. Connell, 'Enterprising Receivers' (2003) *Recovery* (Spring) 20; ch. 8 above.

[167] On the confusions arising from the terms of the new administration see S. Gale, 'Insolvency Law Post Enterprise Act: Does It Do What It Says on the Tin?' (2007) *Recovery* (Autumn) 34.

without the consent of the administrator or the consent of the court. A receiver will lack the investigative powers of an administrator and will not have the protection of the moratorium against forfeiture, execution or legal proceedings. The LPA receiver, moreover, will become personally liable regarding contracts entered into (subject to the right of indemnity). A fixed, rather than floating, charge is needed to trigger the LPA route and this may involve difficulties, notably the risk that the charge may be deemed floating[168] and the commercial reality that using a fixed charge may impede the company's commercial responsiveness.

An attractive aspect of administration has been said to be its potential as a substitute for liquidation.[169] When a company is put into administration and then into liquidation, the once customary creditors' meeting is bypassed. This is because companies can now appoint an administrator without the need for a court order and then, instead of creditors appointing a liquidator, the company makes the appointment. In liquidation, the identity of the office bearer rests primarily with the general body of creditors but, in administration, the company can make the appointment and unsecured creditors will have little input into selection of the office holder. This difference in control is likely to be to the advantage of directors and IPs rather than unsecured creditors.[170] On the incidence of 'liquidation substitution', research by Katz and Mumford, published in 2006,[171] found that in 14 per cent of post-EA

---

[168] See the discussion of *Spectrum Plus* at pp. 411–15 below.

[169] See L. Linklater, 'New Style Administration: A Substitute for Liquidation?' (2005) 26 Co. Law. 129; A. Keay, 'What Future for Liquidation in Light of the Enterprise Act Reforms?' [2005] JBL 143. The Lords' decision in *Buchler* v. *Talbot* [2004] 2 AC 298 held that, in contrast with administration, the expenses of liquidation were not recoverable from property subject to a floating charge. This ensured the popularity of administration until the Companies Act 2006 s. 1282 reversed *Buchler* and inserted a new s. 176ZA into the Insolvency Act 1986, providing that if the company's assets available to meet the claims of unsecured creditors are not sufficient to meet the expenses of winding up, those expenses have priority to and are to be paid out of any property subject to a floating charge created by the company.

[170] In *El-Ajou* v. *Dollar Land (Manhattan) Ltd* [2007] BCC 953, however, it was stated that, in the absence of economic advantage through using the administration procedure, the court favoured liquidation over administration due to the visible independence of the liquidators from those concerned with the company. In *Re Lafayette Electronics Europe Ltd* [2007] BCC 890 the court, in deciding to appoint joint administrators as joint provisional liquidators, was influenced by the fact that the administrators were effectively in office, were up to speed with the affairs of the company and did not need paying for reading into the company's plight. The Insolvency Service has warned practitioners of its expectation that liquidation will be the usual exit route where rescue is not possible.

[171] Katz and Mumford, 2006, p. 5.

administrations (and 3 per cent by value) administration had been the procedure selected solely to provide a convenient method of sale of a business or package of assets when this result appeared to have been equally achievable in liquidation. The 'disenfranchising' of unsecured creditors in administration will be returned to below in considering accountability within the administration process.

Responsiveness

Turning from banks' incentives to use administration to the need for rescue actions to be taken decisively and rapidly, there may be concerns that the move from administrative receivership to the new administration may reduce the ability of key players to behave in this manner. As noted above, the British Bankers' Association (BBA) has for some time argued that receivership operated as an effective way of saving businesses (not necessarily companies) because receivers, acting for the banks, could operate very dynamically.[172] The BBA's fear about the new administration is that it will involve more parties, delays and uncertainties and will accordingly make rescues more difficult than under receivership. 'Concentrated creditor' theory[173] holds that a multiplicity of creditors increases negotiating frictions whereas the concentration of the old receivership system reduced these. Similarly it can be contended that the inclusiveness of the post-EA regime, and the enfranchising of parties other than floating charge holders, increases negotiation costs relative to receivership[174] and reduces the chances of rapid and effective responses to corporate troubles. It is further arguable that, in the past, the existence of receivership, and its potential use, served a useful purpose in concentrating the minds of all the classes of creditor involved with the potential rescue of a troubled company – that it was this prospect that gave urgent life to many a general agreement on reorganisation and rescue.[175] In contrast, the post-EA regime involves no such draconian fall-back position and in other ways it also increases the incentives of the broader band of creditors to contest strategies and actions – for instance by ring-fencing provisions to increase the prospects of unsecured creditors.

---

[172] See BBA, *Response to White Paper* and BBA, *Response to the Report by the Review Group on Company Rescue and Business Reconstruction Mechanisms* (April 2001) ('BBA, *Rescue*'). On the various advantages of creditor concentration see J. Armour and S. Frisby, 'Rethinking Receivership' (2001) 21 OJLS 73 at 84.

[173] See Armour and Frisby, 'Rethinking Receivership'.

[174] See the discussion at pp. 429–35 below.

[175] See Armour and Frisby, 'Rethinking Receivership'.

This could be said to be a statutory trading-off of efficient rescue in favour of more fairness to unsecured creditors.

As a counterbalance to such fears, however, it can be pointed out that in many recovery scenarios there is little point in making rescue-related decisions quickly (for example to seek to ensure that requisite funds are available) if the conditions that underpin continued trading are not sustained – and one thing that the EA does do is to increase the incentives to support rescue of those business partners who are unsecured creditors. Those incentives will be encouraged not merely by the administrator's duty to consider their interests (as compared to the receiver's duty to act in the interests of the floating charge holder) but also by the abolition of Crown preference and the ring-fencing provisions set out in sections 251 and 252 of EA 2002.[176] Both of these reforms increase the anticipated returns to unsecured creditors in a potential liquidation. This, in turn, may reduce the risks faced by unsecured creditors in supporting the rescue – though it will not always do so on a dramatic scale.[177]

Decisive action in pursuit of rescue demands that administrators act to further their statutory rescue objectives in a purposive way. They have, as noted, a statutory duty to perform their functions 'as quickly and efficiently as is reasonably practicable'[178] but, as far as rescue is concerned, the administrator's statutory objectives, as established by Schedule B1, paragraph 3(1), do not even give absolute priority to rescue. The administrator must act with the aim of rescuing the company as a going concern[179] unless he thinks that it is either not 'reasonably practicable'

---

[176] See Insolvency Act 1986 s. 176A.

[177] See H. Rajak, 'The Enterprise Act and Insolvency Law Reform' (2003) Co. Law. 3. Under the 'ring-fencing' or 'prescribed part' provisions the quantum of the 'prescribed part' of funds reserved for unsecured creditors out of property otherwise available for distribution to the holders of a floating charge is established by Statutory Instrument: see Insolvency Act 1986 (Prescribed Part) Order 2003 SI 2003/2097 (see p. 387 above). Without such a 'ring-fencing' measure the consequence of the abolition of the major part of the Crown's preferential status as a creditor would be a windfall for the charge holder. John Armour argues that unsecured creditors may in fact be worse off in that they will receive only a trivially small increase in their expected payout on insolvency through the prescribed part while facing the risk that, if fragmented capital structures make it more difficult for banks to orchestrate workouts, the probability of default may increase: 'Should We Redistribute in Insolvency?' in J. Getzler and J. Payne (eds.), *Company Charges: Spectrum and Beyond* (Oxford University Press, Oxford, 2006) p. 223. See also ch. 3 above.

[178] Insolvency Act 1986 Sch. B1, para. 4.   [179] Under Sch. B1, para. 3(1)(a).

to achieve it or that other actions will produce a better result than winding up for the creditors and that this would be a better result for the creditors as a whole than seeking to rescue the company.[180] Only if he thinks that neither of these objectives can reasonably practicably be achieved can property be realised in order to make a distribution to one or more secured or preferential creditors.[181] As has been pointed out above, the terms of the EA mean that it is arguable that an administrator is obliged to pursue a going concern sale where he thinks this will serve creditors better than efforts made to rescue the company – even where it might be possible to rescue the company.[182] Primacy is accordingly given to maximising overall returns to creditors, rather than to rescue *per se*.

The courts have made it clear that they are inclined to encourage the development of administration as a streamlined and cost-effective regime. In the cases of *Re Transbus International Ltd*[183] and *Re Ballast plc*[184] the courts indicated that para. 68(1) – which provided that the administrator shall manage the company's affairs in accordance with the proposals approved by the creditors' meeting and any directions given by the court – meant neither that the administrator had to await the creditors' meeting before acting, nor that he or she could not act without court directions. The two cases suggest, additionally, that the courts are keen to defer to the administrator's commercial judgement and to allow a considerable margin to such judgements.[185] Such judicial approaches are designed to allow the administrator to act in decisive ways without fear of delays or second-guessing from the judicial oversight process.

Decisiveness is also called for on the part of company directors. Ever since the Cork Report commentators have urged that the purposes of rescue and the maximising of returns to creditors will be served best where the directors of troubled companies do not delay unduly in calling in rescue professionals.[186] It is, after all, the directors of a company who,

---

[180] Under Sch. B1, para. 3(3). For consideration of the likelihood of achievement of this purpose and potential abuse of the administration process see *Re British American (Holdings) plc* [2005] BCC 110, [2005] 2 BCLC 234; *Doltable Ltd* v. *Lexi Holdings* [2006] BCC 918.

[181] Under Sch. B1, para. 3(4).

[182] See p. 383 above; Frisby, 'In Search of a Rescue Regime', p. 262.

[183] [2004] 1 WLR 2654, [2004] BCC 401.   [184] [2005] 1 WLR 1928, [2005] BCC 96.

[185] See A. Walters, 'Corporate Restructuring under Sch. B1 of the Insolvency Act 1986' (2005) 26 Co. Law. 97.

[186] See e.g. Cork Report, ch. 10 and generally D. Milman, 'Strategies for Regulating Managerial Performance in the Twilight Zone' [2004] JBL 493.

in the main, must be relied upon to trigger rescue-oriented proceedings. These are the parties who have the requisite hands-on knowledge of a company's immediate state of affairs rather than the creditors or shareholders. What the EA 2002 does do to expedite rescues is to move from the old regime – in which an administrator could only be appointed by an order of the court on a petition by the company or its directors or creditors[187] – to the new process, which allows a company to enter administration out of court on application by the company, its directors or the holder of a qualifying floating charge.[188]

Statutory procedures are one thing, incentives to resort to these another, and, from the directors' point of view, the nature of the regime being entered may, as noted, be highly material. A difficulty with an insolvency practitioner or practitioner in possession (PIP) regime is that it demands that the directors give up control of the company and so offers directors only limited encouragement to seek early help. For a start, the practitioner in possession, the administrator, is likely to be a person of the bank's choice rather than their own. If the company or its directors wish to appoint an administrator out of court they must give the holder of a qualifying floating charge five days' notice[189] and that holder may then appoint their own administrator in the interim period.[190] The qualifying floating charge holder's appointment prevails – as would also be the case where the application to court procedure is followed. The danger is that if the company's managers anticipate that any formal procedure will involve their giving up the reins of office they will tend to delay commencement of entry into such a procedure beyond the point when the situation calls for external help and involvement. During such a troubled period, moreover, the company directors are likely to take unjustifiably large business risks in the hope, not merely of rescuing the company from its troubles, but of clinging onto their offices. Further dangers are that the directors will dissipate the going concern value of the company's assets and, in doing so, will prejudice any rescue operations and force the company into liquidation. Such delays will

---

[187] (Pre-15 September 2003) Insolvency Act 1986 s. 9(1).

[188] See paras. 22 and 14. As noted above, however, the company's inability (or likely inability) to pay its debts is a prerequisite for court appointments of administrators at the behest of the company, its directors or its (non-QFC) creditors (para. 11) and for out-of-court appointments by the company or by directors under paragraph 22 (see para. 27(2)(a)). On valid appointment of administrators out of court see *Fliptex Ltd* v. *Hogg* [2004] BCC 870.

[189] Para. 26.   [190] Para. 14.

accordingly be likely to diminish the value of the assets available for distribution to creditors.[191]

The disincentives to seek help that flow from PIP might be sought to be countered by legal liabilities for directors who wrongfully trade[192] or by disqualification provisions.[193] The effectiveness and desirability of such responses to problems of overtrading have, however, been questioned[194] on the grounds of their limited deterrent value and because the imposition of such liabilities may chill healthy entrepreneurship. Here debtor in possession (DIP) systems offer a contrast in so far as they leave the directors in charge of the company and this removes at least one disincentive to seeking help. As Hahn argues: 'Given the shortcomings of the stick, handing management a carrot may prove more effective. To accomplish this ... some "tax" needs to be paid to those decision makers. Leaving management in control of the debtor corporation while the reorganisation is pending is precisely that tax.'[195]

The danger of DIP, however, is that this may distort the choice of procedure entered into.[196] In a DIP system, managers who opt for liquidation face immediate replacement by an appointed trustee in liquidation. If they opt for reorganisation they may remain in office. They will, accordingly, tend to file for reorganisation[197] even in circumstances where liquidation would be judged the better course of action for the creditors and the corporation as a whole. Such an inclination will be encouraged where, as will often be the case, the managers expect that they will be able to use their control in reorganisation proceedings to obtain value for themselves in the reorganised corporation[198] or they

[191] D. Hahn, 'Concentrated Ownership and Control of Corporate Reorganisations' (2004) 4 JCLS 117; J. Day and P. Taylor, 'The Role of Debt Contracts in UK Corporate Governance' (1998) 2 *Journal of Management and Governance* 171.

[192] Insolvency Act 1986 s. 214. See ch. 16 below.

[193] Company Directors' Disqualification Act 1986. See ch. 16 below.

[194] See M. White, 'The Cost of Corporate Bankruptcy: A US–European Comparison' in J. Bhandari and L. Weiss (eds.), *Corporate Bankruptcy: Economic and Legal Perspectives* (Cambridge University Press, Cambridge, 1996); Milman, 'Strategies', pp. 498–9.

[195] See Hahn, 'Concentrated Ownership', p. 141.

[196] See e.g. D. Bogart, 'Unexpected Gifts of Chapter 11: The Breach of a Director's Duty of Loyalty Following Plan Confirmation and the Postconfirmation Jurisdiction of Bankruptcy Courts' (1998) 72 Am. Bankr. LJ 303.

[197] P. Aghion, O. Hart and J. Moore, 'The Economics of Bankruptcy Reform' (1992) 8 *Journal of Law, Economics and Organisation* 523; Hahn, 'Concentrated Ownership'.

[198] See M. Bradley and M. Rosenzweig, 'The Untenable Case for Chapter 11' (1992) 101 Yale LJ 1043. On DIP financiers filling the 'governance vacuum' in Chapter 11 see D. Skeel, 'The Past, Present and Future of Debtor-in-Possession Financing' (2004) 25 Cardozo LR 101.

may anticipate being able to use their period of control in order to serve their ongoing career opportunities. Such a bias in favour of reorganisation means that managers will not consider choices of insolvency proceedings in undistorted ways and they will not make judgements in a detached, expert manner with an eye to efficient rescue.

The advantage of PIP is that it involves a lower risk of bias or delay in decisions to liquidate since control under all the procedural options will move from directors to independent professionals.[199]

To return to PIP as established in the new administration: if a problem is that the new process fails to encourage directors to seek help, can the banks be relied upon to institute rescue processes in a timely fashion? The answer to this question turns on the impact of the EA reforms on banks' rights, incentives and attitudes. Here one relevant consideration, as already indicated, is the array of legal uncertainties that the EA reforms may involve. This is a statute that provides a complex set of objectives and which may make the administrator's actions seem highly vulnerable to challenge.[200] It also involves uncertainties with respect to the administrator's allocation of realisations to fixed and floating charges for the purpose of identifying the funds covered by ring-fencing under the Insolvency Act 1986 section 176A.

Such uncertainties may sow the seeds of doubt about rescue in the minds of the banks. The banks may expect procedural and legal costs to be high in post-EA rescues and this may lead them to avoid lending with floating charge security and to move, as noted, towards greater use of secured, asset-based financing and more personal security. The effect of the post-EA regime may, as a result, be the production of a fragmentation of security that will not prove rescue-enhancing. As Prentice has pointed out, the Act does not affect the right of banks to characterise charges as they see fit, to insert the terms and conditions that they consider appropriate and to control the timing of any enforcement action.[201] The banks,

---

[199] Hahn, 'Concentrated Ownership'.

[200] See Sch. B1, para. 3(1). The reality may be that the judges prove reluctant to interfere with the judgements of administrators (at least where aims are phrased subjectively): see notes 361–5 below and accompanying text. There is, as yet, a 'conspicuous' absence of case law where administrators have been sued for breach of duty: see Keay and Walton, *Insolvency Law*, p. 116. The authors comment, however, that this is likely to change as administration begins to take over from administrative receivership 'as the most common non-terminal corporate insolvency procedure' and actions under para. 75 for breach of equitable or common law duties become more frequent.

[201] See D. Prentice, 'Bargaining in the Shadow of the Enterprise Act 2002' (2004) 5 EBOR 153 at 156.

when lending in the shadow of the EA 2002 reforms, will be free to determine the property that is subject to the charge and the type of charge securing the debt. If they are induced by the uncertainties of the EA regime to be selective about the company's assets that are subject to a charge this will affect the collectivity and coverage of post-EA rescue processes. An advantage of the former regime was that an administrative receiver managed the whole of the corporate property and that the banks were induced to opt for charges that were as comprehensive as possible.[202] This may not be the case with the post-EA processes and fragmentation of the secured assets may ensue. A bank may, accordingly, take a fixed charge over certain corporate assets that are sheltered via the creation of a special purpose vehicle (SPV) that is a subsidiary of the parent company.[203] The overall effect will detract from efficient rescue in so far as the administrator is likely to face more serious problems of asset co-ordination than was the case for administrative receivers. Rapid, decisive, rescue-orientated action will be the more difficult in the face of such fragmentation.[204]

The inclination of the banks to lend by means of secured asset-based financing may, moreover, be strengthened by the EA's ring-fencing, for the benefit of unsecured creditors, a prescribed part of the funds otherwise available to floating charge holders.[205] Even when banks do lend under floating charge security they will tend to ask for higher rates of interest in reflection of the post-EA uncertainties that, from their point of view, compare badly with the attractions of the old administrative receivership system. The need to demand such raised rates may, in turn, produce a shift towards raising company financing through other routes such as factoring, discounting, leasing or hire purchase arrangements.[206]

There are implications here for the role of the banks in acting to institute rescue proceedings at the optimal time. Proponents of the

---

[202] Ibid.

[203] Ibid., p. 7. A fixed charge can be taken over the parent company's shares in the SPV. See also Insolvency Act 1986 Sch. B1, paras. 70 and 71, but, as Prentice notes, these provisions need the appointment of an administrator and, in the case of a fixed charge, a court order. See also ch. 3 above.

[204] See also ch. 7 above. On the comparative efficiency of debtor-oriented (as opposed to creditor-oriented) insolvency regimes where debt is not concentrated, see S. Franken, 'Creditor and Debtor Oriented Corporate Bankruptcy Regimes Revisited' (2004) 5 EBOR 645.

[205] Insolvency Act 1986 s. 176A; see pp. 387, 398 above.

[206] See Davies, *Insolvency and the Enterprise Act 2002*, p. 50.

'concentrated creditor' theory stress the benefits of concentration in encouraging the efficient monitoring of corporate affairs and the summoning of help at the right time during troubles.[207] The uncertainties of the EA reforms may, however, diminish creditor concentration as resort is made to wider ranges of financing and this may mean that the banks are less committed to the role of judging the best point for precipitating changes in a company's management.

A worrying effect of such changes, from the perspective of rescue, is that as banks become more uncertain about their role in rescue proceedings and if they have doubts about the potential of rescue processes to serve banks' interests quickly and efficiently, they may be increasingly inclined to be impatient with troubled companies and to take direct enforcement action at an earlier stage in corporate decline than was the case before the EA. This opens up the prospect of potentially precipitate bank action which would detract from efficient rescue. Other aspects of post-EA administration – such as the vulnerability of inclusive procedures to delaying tactics by reluctant directors[208] – may also produce limited bank patience with post-EA procedures

Super-priority funding

A further aspect of timely rescue is the availability of funds for the purposes of recovery. On this front, a problem with the EA is that it did not provide for a regime of 'super-priority' funding[209] for administration. For banks, accordingly, the new arrangements are less conducive to rescue funding than was receivership, which gave them a power of veto over administration.[210] Such a power, in practice, allowed the banks to use the threat of appointing receivers to negotiate administration strategies that were designed to protect against dissipations of their security during the period of the administration. The banks' power in such respects has been weakened by the EA reforms and this may reduce incentives to fund rescue attempts.

---

[207] See Armour and Frisby, 'Rethinking Receivership'; J. Franks and O. Sussman, 'Financial Distress and Bank Restructuring of Small to Medium Size UK Companies' (2005) 9 *Review of Finance* 65, suggest that there is evidence that bank domination may make banks 'lazy' in monitoring receivers' costs but not with regard to the replacement of management. On limitations of the concentrated creditor theory, see ch. 8 above.

[208] See BBA, *Response to White Paper*.

[209] This was proposed in the House of Lords but the Government rejected the proposal: see HL Debates, 21 October 2002. See further pp. 408–9 below.

[210] See IA 1986 s. 9(3).

Companies involved in any potential rehabilitation process face the central problem that funds must be obtained in order to allow a turn-around to be effected:[211]

> Continued trading is essential for some form of going concern to emerge at the end of the process and for a company to continue trading through an insolvency procedure, it will routinely require access to some form of external finance. Unless that finance is available, the rescue will fail, the assets will have to be sold piecemeal and the company will be forced into liquidation.[212]

When a company enters a formal insolvency process, the difficulties of obtaining financing may increase considerably. At such times creditors will view lending to the company on an unsecured or undersecured basis as a very risky activity in which repayment depends on the success of the proposed rescue. Few lenders, as a result, may come forward under these conditions.

A super-priority regime seeks to address these difficulties by providing that the suppliers of funds during a moratorium are to be given priority over all existing creditors.[213] This concept is found in the US Chapter 11 provisions and, in 1993, the DTI invited comments on its suitability in the UK. Such super-priority, the DTI said, might be financed either from cash flow or (in England and Wales) by a lien over specific uncharged assets. Such funds would have to be used only in the ordinary course of business (e.g. to pay employees during the moratorium) and any extra-ordinary items would have to be authorised by the lender. One advantage of super-priority, suggested the DTI, was that where funds were provided by the main secured lender on such a basis, there would be reassurance to the lender that their security was not being dissipated during the

---

[211] R3's Ninth Survey of 2001 indicated that in one in five cases of failed companies with in excess of £5m turnover, the main factor preventing a positive outcome was lack of funding.

[212] IS 2000, p. 33. In 1999 the Insolvency Service cited the SPI's Eighth Survey, indicating that lack of security for extra funding was cited in 51 per cent of cases as a barrier to turnaround and lack of appropriate finance in 43 per cent of cases.

[213] On super-priority financing generally see McCormack, 'Super-priority New Financing' (looking at the UK, USA and Canada); D. Milman and D. Mond, *Security and Corporate Rescue* (Hodgsons, Manchester, 1999). The INSOL International *Statement of Principles for a Global Approach to Multi-Creditor Workouts* (October 2000) is endorsed by the Bank of England. Principle 8 states that where additional funding is provided in a standstill period, the repayment of this should 'so far as practicable, be accorded priority status'.

moratorium. It had to be faced, however, that, should the company fail, the super-priority funding would operate at the expense of other creditors.

The idea of super-priority has, however, been subject to ebbs and flows of favour at the DTI.[214] In 1995 the DTI looked at CVA procedures and rejected super-priority on the grounds that the comfort of super-priority might militate against a lender's giving proper consideration to the viability of a business. As for the earlier suggestion that super-priority loans might be repaid earlier from cash flow, or secured by a lien over specific uncharged assets, the DTI was concerned that a company contemplating a CVA would not have sufficient cash flows or uncharged assets during a moratorium. Given such worries, the DTI proposed that nominees should be required to consider the availability of funding as part of the initial assessment of the CVA's prospects of success. If the assessment was favourable, said the DTI, there was no substantial reason why funders would not support the company. In 1999, the Insolvency Service was more favourably disposed and announced that its Review of Company Rescue and Business Reconstruction Mechanisms would reconsider super-priority. Note was taken of London Business School research by Maria Carapeto which showed that of 326 firms that had filed for Chapter 11 protection in the USA, some 135 had raised super-priority (or 'debtor in possession') financing which had comprised around 19 per cent of the total debt of the company. About half of the new finance was advanced by pre-petition lenders and high levels of such lending were associated with positive effects on recovery rates.[215]

In 2000 the Insolvency Service Review Group Report noted that for most CVAs additional funding tended to be provided by owners/directors or by existing lenders, often with the benefit of existing or increased security and/or personal guarantees. New secured finance was available only to the extent that existing secured creditors agreed to this or if the company had uncharged assets or charged assets with surplus value that

---

[214] The DTI became the Department for Business, Enterprise and Regulatory Reform (BERR) on 28 June 2007.

[215] The IS 1999 makes no reference, however, to the interest rates in Chapter 11 lending. These rates are frequently at a premium. As Gregory notes, 'Some argue that the total volume of Chapter 11 financing (19 per cent of total company debt) is more of a comment on the cost of Chapter 11 procedures than a reflection of the commercial needs of the company … Statistical comparisons here are actually misleading because like is not being compared with like': R. Gregory, *Review of Company Rescue and Business Reconstruction Mechanisms: Rescue Culture or Avoidance Culture?* (CCH, Bicester, December 1999) p. 21. On Chapter 11 procedures see ch. 6 above.

could be offered as security. The prevalence of the floating charge meant, however, that uncharged assets were rare in corporate insolvencies

The Review Group had considered in detail the options for post-petition funding under Chapter 11 of the US Bankruptcy Code[216] but did not think it appropriate to attempt to replicate Chapter 11 in the different business cultural and economic environment of the UK. The basic principles underlying US practice were nevertheless deemed relevant. These principles were summarised[217] as holding that:

- Making additional finance available to a business in distress could be 'value enhancing' for the business, provided that it was part of a properly considered plan for financial recovery.
- If it was value enhancing for the business in the short, medium or long term, it would also be value enhancing for creditors or it would at least not worsen their position.
- The partiality of their outlook might prevent individual creditors from seeing this potential for value creation or giving it the same value as one would in relation to the business as a whole.
- The specialist insolvency judges and courts could take a broader view and they have the power to grant security to new finance during Chapter 11 even if this displaces the security held by an existing creditor: but displacement must not diminish the expected return to that creditor. The principle is that additional finance should only be provided where it is genuinely value enhancing for all.
- There is no automatic approval for post-petition financing but practice has evolved so that in the early stages of Chapter 11 some form of such financing 'necessary to avoid immediate and irreparable harm to the company's estate' is usually approved without difficulty.

The Review Group floated the idea that the law might allow the authorities supervising an insolvency procedure to have regard to similar considerations to those in the USA when assessing proposals for super-priority finance. In practice this approach would allow super-priority financing to be approved by the courts (or a subordinate tribunal) if several criteria were met. The principal criteria suggested[218] were:

- The super-priority finance could reasonably be expected to enhance the value of the enterprise as a whole and, thus, returns to all creditors.

---

[216] IS 2000, pp. 33–5.   [217] Ibid., pp. 33–4.   [218] Ibid., p. 35.

- The position of each individual creditor would be protected and their expected return would be at least the same as if the finance were not provided.
- The courts would need to be given significant discretion and the criteria to be satisfied before super-priority finance was granted would need to be demanding. Practice would no doubt evolve over time regarding the operation of such provisions.
- Secured creditors would need to be given appropriate influence over the selection or confirmation of the insolvency practitioner.[219]

In such a regime there is an attempt to ensure that a proper judgement is made about the prospects of viability.[220] Concerns that super-priority funders will not assess viability on a proper basis are addressed by making the court or tribunal the arbiter on such matters. It is essential, accordingly, that a properly resourced and skilled system of courts or tribunals be established and that these incorporate appropriate insolvency expertise.[221] It might be objected that such judgements will not be located in a commercial or market context but, in response, the Insolvency Service's suggestion is that an option might be to have 'a system of expert tribunals with a strong commercial flavour dealing with cases on a day to day basis and to focus on the role of the higher courts as resolving disputes as to the application of the law and reviewing the procedures followed by the expert tribunal'.[222]

Despite the Insolvency Service considering that there was a case for such an approach to super-priority funding in 2000, the Government declined, two years later, to accept an amendment to the Enterprise Bill that would have created a statutory framework for super-priority financing during administration and which its proponent suggested was essential if administration was to operate as an effective rescue tool.[223] The Government took the view that the decision to lend in times of trouble was best left to the commercial judgement of the market and that it would be wrong to offer a guaranteed return to a super-priority investor whether or not the rescue proposals had satisfied

---

[219] Ibid., p. 35.
[220] On the US position see e.g. M. White, 'Does Chapter 11 Save Economically Inefficient Firms?' (1994) 72 Wash. ULQ 1319.
[221] A point made in IS 2000, p. 35, para. 137.   [222] Ibid.
[223] Lord Hunt, HL Debates, 29 July 2002, discussed in McCormack, 'Super-priority New Financing', p. 713; Davies, *Insolvency and the Enterprise Act 2002*, pp. 20–6.

the market.[224] Such views were taken against a background of confidence that the market would meet the financing requirements of troubled companies on appropriate terms. Here consideration was given to the growth of asset financing, factoring and discounting and the increasing orientation of these financing systems towards rescue.[225]

A potential route to super-priority funding is, however, provided by the Insolvency Act 1986 section 19(5) and Schedule B1, paragraph 99.[226] These provisions cover debts incurred under contracts entered into by the administrator, in the carrying out of his functions.[227] Such debts are given a priority ranking above that of the administrator's statutory charge for his own remuneration and expenses (which, in turn, rank above a floating charge in priority of payment from the corporate estate).[228] McCormack has argued that the words of paragraph 99 'seem sufficiently broad to encompass liabilities under loan contracts entered into by the administrator on behalf of the company'.[229] The High Court has also considered the matter. In *Bibby Trade Finance Ltd v. McKay*[230] a financier had provided funds to administrators in order

---

[224] For a comment on the 'regrettable' failure to provide for super-priority funding see A. McKnight, 'The Reform of Corporate Insolvency Law in Great Britain – the Enterprise Bill 2002' (2002) 17 JIBL 324 at 333.

[225] See McCormack, 'Super-priority New Financing', p. 713.

[226] Ibid. See also the discussion concerning IA 1986 s. 19 at pp. 373–5 above.

[227] Contracts entered into before the administration will not enjoy the priority of those entered into by the administrator in carrying out his functions: see *Freakley* v. *Centre Reinsurance International Co.* [2006] BCC 971.

[228] See Sch. B1, para. 99(3), which provides for payment of a 'former administrator's remuneration and expenses' out of assets in the custody or control of the administrator in priority to any charge which, as created, was a floating charge. Para. 99(4)–(6) gives 'super-priority' to debts or liabilities arising out of contracts entered into by the administrators and (regarding 'qualifying liabilities') to debts and liabilities under adopted employment contracts. In *Re Trident Fashions plc* [2006] All ER 140 the Court of Appeal accepted that an expense payable pursuant to rule 2.67 (introduced by the Insolvency (Amendment) Rules 2005 (SI 2005/527)) was actionable by the expense creditor against administrators who had drawn remuneration in priority to such an expense. See further Lightman and Moss, *Law of Administrators*, pp. 134–45; and p. 417 below.

[229] See McCormack, 'Super-priority New Financing', pp. 727–8.

[230] [2006] All ER 266. See A. Bacon, 'Administration Costs: Some Welcome News' (2007) 20 *Insolvency Intelligence* 1. In *Freakley* v *Centre Reinsurance International Co.* [2006] BCC 971 the House of Lords stated that the power to decide what expenditure was necessary for the purposes of the administration, and which should therefore receive priority, rested with the administrator (subject to the supervision of the court). Lord Hoffmann indicated that it would be unusual for the courts to interfere with the business judgement of the administrator on such matters.

to allow the completion of a single profitable order. On completion of the order the administrators deducted the advances prior to accounting for the proceeds – on the basis that the liabilities from the administrators to the financier were expenses of the administration. The directors of the company (who had guaranteed the company's indebtedness to the financier) challenged these deductions, arguing that the sums paid to the financier by the administrators were paid on behalf of the company and should reduce their liabilities to the financier. The court rejected the directors' contentions, saying that their proposed course would give them a windfall at the expense of unsecured creditors. What was accepted, though, was that the administrators' liability to the financier was a legitimate administration expense.[231]

The significance of the *Bibby* case lies in its demonstrating that the English courts are capable of authorising super-priority funding without there being any need for new legislation.[232] If *Bibby* is followed, this may herald the arrival of a system in which new funds can be raised as an administration expense under super-priority arrangements. It remains to be seen whether, in the future, the courts will further develop such a regime so as to require that administrators seek the consent of different creditors to such arrangements.

Rethinking charges on book debts

In continuing the discussion of funding arrangements as the underpinnings of effective rescue procedures, it is necessary to deal with the issue of book debts. Book debts are sums outstanding and owed to the troubled company and, during a rescue procedure, book debts are often the only funds that are available for the purposes of financing continuing operations through the rescue period. Between 1978 and 2005 many lenders

---

[231] In the case of *Re Huddersfield Fine Worsteds Ltd* [2005] 4 All ER 886 the Court of Appeal stated that protective awards under the Trade Unions Labour Relations (Consolidation) Act 1992 and payments in lieu of notice did not enjoy super-priority since they did not fall within Sch. B1, para. 99(5) and (6). A similar decision regarding claims for wrongful dismissal subsequent to the adoption of a contract of employment by the administrator was made in *Re Leeds United Association Football Club Ltd (in administration)* [2008] BCC 11. See pp. 415–16 and ch. 17 below.

[232] As Bacon observes, the decision shows 'a continued commitment by the courts to the rescue culture and a realistic attitude to striving to ensure that professionals involved in corporate recovery are dealt with even-handedly': 'Administration Costs', p. 4. See, however, D. Fletcher, 'Time for a DIP?' (2007) *Recovery* (Summer) 30, who cautions (at p. 30) that it cannot be assumed that the courts will follow the *Bibby* judgment in cases where the *primary* issue is whether DIP funding can be classed as an administration expense. (In *Bibby* the judgment focused on interpretation of the wording contained in a Tomlin Order.)

sought to secure their loans by way of fixed charges over the borrowing company's book debts.[233] The decision of the House of Lords in the *Spectrum Plus*[234] case, however, changed matters. *Spectrum Plus* over-ruled the decision in *Siebe Gorman*[235] and held that the company charges over present and future book debts that were modelled on the form used in *Siebe Gorman* were floating in spite of their being designated on their face as fixed. In *Spectrum Plus*[236] there was a charge describing itself as fixed; a covenant by the company to pay into its account with the bank all

[233] If a bank is deemed to possess a floating charge over the book debt proceeds, it will rank behind preferential creditors; if the charge is deemed fixed, the charge holder will precede the preferential creditors in the queue for repayment – the distinction between fixed and floating charges is thus of practical importance.

[234] *Spectrum Plus Ltd* v. *National Westminster Bank plc* [2005] 3 WLR 58; [2005] BCC 694: the reasoning in *Brumark (Agnew* v. *Commissioner of Inland Revenue, Re Brumark Investments Ltd)* [2001] 2 AC 710, [2001] All ER 21, was approved and *Re New Bullas Trading Ltd* [1994] BCC 36 was said to be wrongly decided. On the *Brumark* decisions (NZCA and Privy Council) see M. Armstrong, '"Return to First Principles" in New Zealand: Charges Over Book Debts are Fixed – But the Future's Not!' [2000] Ins. Law. 102; R. Gregory and P. Walton, 'Book Debt Charges: Following *Yorkshire Woolcombers* Are We Sheep Gone Astray?' [2000] Ins. Law. 157; Gregory and Walton, 'Book Debt Charges: The Saga Goes On' (1999) 115 LQR 14; F. Oditah, 'Fixed Charges over Book Debts after *Brumark*' (2001) 14 *Insolvency Intelligence* 49; A. Berg, '*Brumark Investments Ltd* and the "Innominate Charge"' [2001] JBL 532; F. Coulson and S. Hill, '*Brumark*: The End of Banking as We Know It?' (2001) *Recovery* (September) 16. On *Re New Bullas* see R. M. Goode, 'Charges over Book Debts: A Missed Opportunity' (1994) 110 LQR 592; M. G. Bridge, 'Fixed Charges and Freedom of Contract' (1994) 110 LQR 340; I. Narey and P. Rubenstein, 'Separation of Book Debts and their Proceeds' [1994] CLJ 225; S. Griffin, 'The Effect of a Charge over Book Debts: The Indivisible and Divisible Nature of the Charge' [1995] 46 NILQ 163.

[235] *Siebe Gorman & Co. Ltd* v. *Barclays Bank Ltd* [1979] 2 Lloyd's Reports 142. After *Siebe* a fixed charge could cover future assets in a manner that, until the decision, had been considered the exclusive domain of the floating charge. According to *Siebe*, the creditor had to be able to prevent withdrawals from the account into which the proceeds of the book debts were paid but the cash flow implications of this position were not fully explored. In the wake of *Siebe* an extensive case law had sought to delineate the conditions under which fixed charges could be held over book debts and their proceeds and judges and commentators struggled to make clear the basis for designating book debt charges as fixed or floating: see, for example, *Re Brightlife Ltd* [1987] Ch 200; *Re Keenan Bros. Ltd* [1986] BCLC 242; *Re New Bullas Trading Ltd* [1993] BCC 251. For discussion see E. Ferran, *Company Law and Corporate Finance* (Oxford University Press, Oxford, 1999) pp. 518–33; Armstrong, '"Return to First Principles"'; Gregory and Walton, 'Book Debt Charges: Following *Yorkshire Woolcombers*'; Gregory and Walton, 'Book Debt Charges: The Saga Goes On'. The Cork Report had urged statutory reversal of *Siebe* in 1982: paras. 1585–6.

[236] On *Spectrum Plus* and its significance see J. Getzler and J. Payne (eds.), *Company Charges: Spectrum and Beyond* (Oxford University Press, Oxford, 2006); D. Capper, '*Spectrum Plus* in the House of Lords' [2006] 6 JCLS 447; A. Berg, 'The Cuckoo in the

moneys that it might receive in respect of the charged book debts; an agreement not to sell, factor, charge or assign the charged debts without the bank's written permission; and an undertaking, if called upon by the bank, to assign the charged book debts to the bank. The House of Lords had to decide whether the charge was a floating charge per section 175(2)(b) of the IA 1986 and ruled that the unrestricted right to draw on the account into which Spectrum was obliged to pay the proceeds of the book debts was inconsistent with there being a fixed charge over those debts. The debenture left the company free to use the proceeds of the book debts in the ordinary course of its business and that was the essence of a floating charge.[237]

What their lordships did not do was offer a clear set of details on the nature and degree of control that a chargee must possess over the charged assets in order for the charge to be categorised as a fixed charge. The hanging question is how, in the absence of practical guidance from the judges, it is now possible to create a fixed charge over book debts by setting up an arrangement in which the proceeds of book debts are not made available for use in the course of business – for example by providing that all such proceeds are to be paid into a 'blocked' account.[238] The Lords did, however, take the view that what is of relevance in deciding whether a charge is fixed or floating is the substance and reality of the situation rather than the form of the transaction. Berg suggests that: 'This is unsurprising since whether the chargee has control over the charged assets is a question of commercial reality not legal technicalities.'[239] A residual problem is that there are considerable costs to certainty in commercial transactions if matters are decided with reference to the substance of the particular transactional

Nest of Corporate Insolvency' [2006] JBL 22; D. Henderson, 'Problems in the Law of Property after *Spectrum Plus*' [2006] ICCLR 30; R. Gregory, '*Spectrum Plus* – Common Law Makes Takeover Bid for Equity' (2005) 13 *Sweet & Maxwell's Company Law Newsletter* 1.

[237] *Spectrum Plus*, paras. 112, 138–40. The immediate practical result of the *Spectrum* decision was that IPs were able to distribute the book debt proceeds in an estimated 550 or more insolvency cases which had been held up in the system as a result of uncertainty following the earlier decision in *Brumark* [2001] All ER 21. HM Revenue and Customs and the Insolvency Service issued a joint statement in 2005 explaining their expectations regarding such distribution of book debt proceeds post-*Spectrum*.

[238] As Marshall notes, it will be interesting to see whether the *Spectrum* decision adds anything to the debate, post-*Brumark*, regarding particular collection account arrangements in structured finance, project finance and securitisation transactions: J. Marshall, '*Spectrum Plus*: A Wasted Opportunity?' (2005) *Recovery* (Summer) 30.

[239] Berg, 'Cuckoo in the Nest', p. 32.

arrangement.[240] On this matter, the Lords agreed with Lord Millett's statement, in *Brumark*,[241] that it was not enough to provide for blocking in the debenture if it was not in fact operated as a blocked account.

A more recent trend in English cases had, however, moved away from *Siebe Gorman* before *Spectrum Plus* was decided.[242] The decision in *Re Atlantic Computer Systems plc*[243] concerned a clause dealing with the assignment of leases. This provided for the assignee to have the benefit of all rentals and moneys under certain subleases but no provision was made concerning the application of the individual rent payments made under these subleases. The Court of Appeal ruled that there might have been an intention for Atlantic Computer Systems to be free to use the rent instalments until the assignee intervened, but this did not mean that the charge was floating rather than fixed. Nicholls LJ distinguished, however, between a charge on existing income-producing property (such as a lease) and a charge on present and future property (for example, a typical charge on present and future book debts).[244] The decision has thus been criticised as an old-fashioned approach inconsistent with the modern view that what distinguishes fixed and floating charges is not the nature of the asset but the location of the power to manage and control its use.[245] In the wake of *Spectrum Plus*, it can be argued that *Atlantic Computers* is no longer good law and that the arrangement in *Atlantic Computers* would now be likely to be viewed as one involving a floating charge as per *Spectrum Plus*.[246] This view is reinforced by the first application of *Spectrum Plus* principles to assets other than book debts. In *Re Beam Tube Products* in 2006[247] a

---

[240] See Capper, '*Spectrum Plus* in the House of Lords', p. 458 (speaking of 'a dangerously schizophrenic approach to the categorisation of security interests').

[241] *Re Brumark Investments Ltd, Agnew v. Commissioner of Inland Revenue* [2001] 3 WLR 454; [2002] BCC 259.

[242] On such developments see Ferran, *Company Law and Corporate Finance*, pp. 524–9; D. Milman, 'Company Charges: Recent Developments' [2000] 7 *Palmer's In Company* 1; A. Walters, 'Round Up: Corporate Insolvency' (2000) 21 Co. Law. 262 at 262–5.

[243] [1992] Ch 505, [1992] 2 WLR 367, [1990] BCC 859.

[244] Ferran, *Company Law and Corporate Finance*, p. 525.

[245] Ibid., pp. 525–6. See also Bridge, 'Company Administrators', pp. 396–7; *Re Atlantic Medical Ltd* [1992] BCC 653; *Re CCG International Enterprises Ltd* [1993] BCC 580.

[246] See Henderson, 'Problems in the Law after *Spectrum Plus*', p. 31. For further analysis of the status of *Atlantic Computer Systems* ([1990] BCC 859) post-*Spectrum* see Berg, 'Cuckoo in the Nest'; S. Worthington, 'Floating Charges: Use and Abuse of Doctrinal Analysis' in Getzler and Payne, *Company Charges*, p. 25; N. Frome and K. Gibbons, '*Spectrum* – An End to the Conflict or the Signal for a New Campaign?' in Getzler and Payne, ibid.

[247] [2006] BCC 615.

debenture created purported fixed charges over (*inter alia*) all plant and machinery and all book and other debts and a floating charge over all assets not covered by fixed charges. With regard to the charge over the plant and machinery, the company was left free to deal with many of these items in the ordinary course of business. The court, accordingly, held that, in spite of the description of the charge as fixed, it was floating in nature. It, moreover, took an 'all or nothing' approach in saying that the fixed or floating nature of the charge related to all of the assets that it covered and that it could not be treated as fixed regarding some assets and floating regarding others.[248]

What is likely to be the effect of *Spectrum Plus?* In combination with the EA 2002 reforms, the effect on bank lenders is likely to be significant. The EA 2002 renders the floating charge less attractive since it removes the right of the holder to appoint a receiver and it reserves a prescribed part of funds for the benefit of unsecured creditors.[249] *Spectrum*, in addition, reduces the availability of the fixed charge.[250] It seems unlikely, therefore, that banks will react to *Spectrum* by taking floating charges to secure receivables financing or by imposing day-to-day controls over customers' accounts so as to render charges 'fixed' within the terms of *Spectrum*.[251] Reducing the availability of fixed charges over book debts may have the effect of increasing the fragmentation of credit as

---

[248] See R3, *Technical Bulletin*, Issue 76, October 2006, para. 76.1. With regard to the charge over book debts, the court in *Beam* noted that recent authority had held that where the security documentation envisages a fixed charge over those debts and a floating charge over the proceeds of those debts, the fixed charge will be treated as a floating charge: consequently the present charge over the book and other debts was a floating one.

[249] A fund in which floating charge holders cannot participate for any shortfall: see *Permacell Finesse Ltd (in liquidation)* [2008] BCC 208 and further Offord, 'Case Digest'. See also *Re Airbase (UK) Ltd, Thorniley* v. *Revenue and Customs Commissioner* [2008] BCC 213 (Ch) and further Walters, 'Statutory Redistribution of Floating Charge Assets'.

[250] The *Spectrum* judgment does not rule out a lender's being able to take a fixed charge over book debts. Their Lordships agreed that it was conceptually possible and gave examples of ways in which this could be achieved: by assigning the book debts to the security holder; by preventing all dealings with the debts other than their collection and requiring the proceeds to be paid to the chargee in reduction of the chargor's debts; by preventing all dealings with the debts other than their collection and requiring the proceeds to be paid into an account with a third party over which the chargee takes a fixed charge; and by preventing all dealings with the debts other than their collection and requiring the proceeds to be paid into a blocked account with the chargee bank.

[251] See Armour, 'Should We Redistribute in Insolvency?'. As Armour notes, the effect of the decision is to make it far more difficult for banks to take fixed security over receivables without 'micro-managing the debtor company's dealings' in those assets – a process which would be 'likely to be uneconomic for banks' (pp. 202, 203).

companies look to an increasingly wide variety of lenders and methods of raising money – and, notably, to asset-based finance arrangements such as invoice discounting or factoring.[252] In terms of rescue, the fear (as noted in chapters 3 and 6) is that such arrangements do not lend themselves to turnarounds because creditor co-ordination costs and difficulties are increased and more obstacles are placed in the way of a successful rescue.[253] Alternatively, lenders may take charges that are not QFCs but are fixed charges over certain of the company's assets. The holder of such a charge is then placed to appoint a receiver should the need arise. Similarly, complex arrangements can be devised whereby lending is carried out through numbers of subsidiaries, each of which has a fixed charge over part of the company's property but none of which has security over the whole or substantially the whole.[254] The EA 2002, by encouraging these strategies, however, may be said not to further rescue objectives since it incentivises the selling off of parts of the company and may lead to piecemeal disintegration of the business.

Administrators' expenses and rescue

The successful pursuit of a rescue requires that the administrator decides that it is appropriate to continue trading so as to produce a better return for creditors than would be likely in an immediate liquidation.[255] This decision may turn in no little part, however, on how the law deals with debts owed to employees by virtue of employment legislation[256] and on how priority is attached to the expenses of the administration.[257]

The Insolvency Act 1986 Schedule B1 paragraph 99(4) and (5) provides that where the administrator adopts employees' contracts, the

---

[252] On techniques for lenders to avoid the controls of the EA 2002 see R. Stevens, 'Security after the Enterprise Act' in Getzler and Payne, *Company Charges*, at pp. 166–7.

[253] See IS 1999. Lack of 'creditor consensus' may thus be an increasing problem: see Armstrong, '"Return to First Principles"', p. 110. Armstrong argues, however, that he has seen 'no empirical evidence to prove that increasing fragmentation of the small companies finance market frustrates rescue': p. 111.

[254] See Stevens, 'Security After the Enterprise Act'.

[255] IA 1986 Sch. B1, para. 3(1).

[256] See pp. 372–5 above. For further discussion of employees in insolvency see ch. 17 below.

[257] See also A. Walters, 'The Impact of Employee Liabilities on the Administrator's Decision to Continue Trading' (2005) 26 Co. Law. 321; H. Lyons and M. Roberts, 'Administration Expenses – "Friday Afternoon Drafting" and the Rescue Culture' (2005) 16 *Sweet & Maxwell's Company Law Newsletter* 1.

wages and salaries involved have 'super-priority' and are payable in advance of not merely the claims of floating charge holders and preferential creditors but also the expenses of the administration and even the administrator's own remuneration.[258] The rescue issue is, however, that if 'wages and salary' is interpreted broadly, this places the administrator in a very difficult position. The broad interpretation reduces the prospects of turnaround considerably by reducing the assets available to fund a rescue and, in order to limit such liabilities, the administrator may have to lay-off the very staff that are needed for realistic prospects of continued trading.[259] The courts have considered these matters and sought to further rescue objectives. In *Re Allders Department Stores Ltd*[260] the court held that redundancy or unfair dismissals payments were not 'wages and salary' enjoying priority under paragraph 99 since they arose from statute, not the contract of employment. Similarly in *Re Huddersfield Fine Worsteds Ltd*[261] it was held that protective payments under the Trade Union Labour Relations (Consolidation) Act 1992 were not payable in priority to administration expenses.

[258] Administration expenses, as noted, are payable ahead of floating charge holders: IA 1986 Sch. B1, para. 99(3)(b). See the House of Lords' decision in *Freakley v. Centre Reinsurance International Co.* [2006] BCC 971 – handling expenses incurred by insurers (who under the policy were entitled to handle insurance claims of the company in administration) did not have priority over administration expenses under the then s. 19(5) of the Insolvency Act 1986. Note that after the Enterprise Act 2002 there are new rules governing the fixing of the administrator's remuneration. Insolvency Rule 2.106 provides for the fixing of the administrator's remuneration on a percentage or time-spent basis by the creditors' committee, by a meeting of creditors or by the court: see further Sims and Briggs, 'Enterprise Act 2002 – Corporate Wrinkles', p. 52. Note also that after the Enterprise Act 2002 removed Crown preference the Treasury changed the rules so that when a company goes into administration, its existing accounting period comes to an end and a new one starts. Consequently any corporation tax chargeable on the profits earned in the administration becomes an expense of the administration as opposed to an unsecured claim: see generally B. Walsh and S. Martins, 'Tax in Enterprise Act Administrations: Some Practical Issues' (2008) 21 *Insolvency Intelligence* 103.

[259] See Walters, 'Impact of Employee Liabilities', p. 321 and the judgment of Neuberger LJ in *Re Huddersfield Fine Worsteds Ltd* [2005] 4 All ER 886, [2005] BCC 915. See further ch. 17 below.

[260] [2005] 2 All ER 122, [2005] BCC 289.

[261] [2005] 4 All ER 886, [2005] BCC 915. See similarly *Leeds United AFC Ltd* [2008] BCC 11: damages for wrongful dismissal would not be covered by para. 99 and would not be payable ahead of the other expenses of the administration. Pumfrey J further deemed that liabilities for wrongful dismissal would not count as necessary disbursements for the purpose of r. 2.67(1)(f) of the Insolvency Rules 1986 so as to rank in priority to the ordinary creditors.

Less conducive to rescue, however, is the effect of the new version of rule 2.67 that is set out in the Insolvency (Amendment) Rules 2005.[262] In the *Exeter City (Trident)* case[263] it was held that non-domestic rates were necessary disbursements within rule 2.67(1)(f) and paragraph 99(3). This ruling followed the liquidation expenses rule set out by the House of Lords in *Toshoku*[264] but *Exeter City (Trident)* is not rescue friendly since, by giving priority to non-domestic rates for the period of the administration, funds available for continued trading are reduced. Gabriel Moss QC has dubbed *Exeter City (Trident)* 'a potential disaster' and commented: 'This could make an administration insolvent from day one if there are a large number of leasehold retail premises incurring new liabilities for rates.'[265] David Richards J said in *Exeter City (Trident)* that his conclusion was arrived at in spite of the overall policy of promoting a rescue culture and stood in the face of evidence that the effect of the decision would be detrimental to successful administrations. He suggested that the legislators had subordinated the policy of rescue to the desire to give priority to the payment of rates.[266]

Some relief from the effects of *Exeter City (Trident)* was offered in 2008 when the Department for Communities and Local Government promulgated new regulations to exempt companies in administration from liability for unoccupied property rates.[267] This followed lobbying from R3 who argued that, in view of *Exeter City (Trident)*, companies in administration should have the same exemption from empty property rates as companies in liquidation. This reform, accordingly, renders empty property rates neutral regarding decisions about whether to enter administration or liquidation.

---

[262] SI 2005/527. On tensions between this rule and the statutory provisions of Sch. B1, para. 99 see G. Moss, 'Rescue Culture Speared by *Trident*' (2007) 20 *Insolvency Intelligence* 72.

[263] *Exeter City Council v. Bairstow and Others, Re Trident Fashions plc* [2007] BCC 236. See J. Bannister, 'Legal Update' (2007) *Recovery* (Summer) 11; R. Heis, 'Technical Update' (2007) *Recovery* (Autumn) 14; L. C. Ho, 'Sealing Administration Expenses, Puncturing Rescue Culture?', available at http://ssrn.com/abstract=981795, (2007) 23 IL&P.

[264] In *Re Toshoku Finance UK plc* [2002] UKHL 6; [2002] 1 WLR 671.

[265] See Moss, 'Rescue Culture Speared by *Trident*', p. 75.

[266] *Exeter City Council v. Bairstow and Others, Re Trident Fashions plc* [2007] BCC 236, para. 8.

[267] See Non-domestic Rating (Unoccupied Property) (England) Regulations 2008 (SI 2008/386), effective from 1 April 2008. The new rules apply to companies already in administration on 1 April 2008 but do not apply retrospectively: see T. Bugg, 'Legislative Changes Afoot' (2008) *Recovery* (Spring) 10.

The case for cram-down and supervised restructuring

At this point it is relevant to consider an argument that the new administration procedure is, in reality, old hat: that it addresses an outdated set of challenges; that it does not provide the rescue procedure that modern restructurings really require; and that there is a need to move to a regime of cram-down and court supervision. This argument has been put forward strongly by the European High Yield Association (EHYA), an association representing participants in the European high yield bond markets.[268] The EHYA contends that, against a background of huge growth in the leveraged lending market, most restructurings occur outside formal procedures[269] and administrations will have only limited use in coming years because use of a formal procedure is seen as reflecting corporate failure; the ability of suppliers and customers to abandon contracts frustrates purposes and destroys value; and funding difficulties often impair trading through the proceedings. The EHYA suggests, furthermore, that the out-of-court debt restructuring processes that can now be used will face increasing challenges due to the growing complexities of capital structures, the dispersion of debt and the multiplicity of parties generally involved with troubled companies:[270]

> Stakeholders approach each restructuring with their own agenda and strategy, often looking for positions of control and influence to gain leverage, not always seeking common ground and consensus. The absence of a predictable, supervised restructuring process creates a considerable layer of uncertainty, increases costs and can alter the economics of a deal.[271]

What is needed, the EHYA argues, is a court-supervised restructuring process that includes a stay on enforcement actions, including a ban on the exercise of contract termination provisions by suppliers and customers (as found in the USA and France); judicial resolution of valuation disputes; and a system of cram-down to prevent those without an

---

[268] See EHYA, *Submission on Insolvency Law Reform* (EHYA, London, 2007), discussed by R. Heis, 'Technical Update' (2007) *Recovery* (Autumn) 15. In February 2008 the EHYA reported that its extensive consultations with industry had produced 'nearly unanimous' support for its proposals: see the revised *EHYA Submission on Insolvency Law Reform* (EHYA, London, 2008) and P. J. Davies, 'Treasury Urged to Reform Insolvency Laws', *Financial Times*, 26 February 2008.

[269] The EHYA acknowledged that the informality of such actions means that statistics on numbers of restructurings are not available.

[270] On such tensions in informal rescues and reconstructions see ch. 7 above.

[271] EHYA, *Submission on Insolvency Law Reform* (2007), p. 3.

economic interest (the 'out of the money' parties) from frustrating the proceedings. The effect would, *inter alia*, be that when a company is in administration, the power of customers and suppliers[272] would be curbed and there would be no vetoing of a restructuring plan by those shareholders and creditors who no longer have economic interests in the company (because available company funds do not allow them a return). The EHYA's stated intention is to streamline the claims of 'financial stakeholders' (i.e. 'structural investor debt' and shareholder claims) as opposed to 'trade' creditors 'whose claims arise out of the day to day operations of the business'.[273] There is no advocacy of a cram-down applicable to trade creditors.

Excluding the 'out of the money' parties from the restructuring process is a contentious point but one on which the EHYA takes a firm line: 'As a policy matter, we do not consider that creditors or shareholders with no economic interest in the enterprise (on a proper valuation basis) should be in a position where their "veto" forces full insolvency proceedings.'[274] The *quid pro quo* for removing the veto of the 'out of the money' parties is the proposed system of judicial supervision.

In support of the proposal, it can be said that the 1986 Insolvency Act, as amended, already allows the administrator to avoid calling a creditors' meeting if there is no prospect of a return to unsecured creditors.[275] The administrator, moreover, has a general duty to act in the interests of all creditors of the company. As for shareholders, it can be said that the dispersion of equity which the 'new capitalism' involves[276] means that, for practical purposes, many holders of equity interests will be unable to participate in a restructuring to rescue-essential, tight timescales in any

---

[272] Note that the Insolvency Act 1986 s. 233 already prohibits utility suppliers (for gas, electricity, water and communication services) from cutting off connections unless, for example, arrears are paid. The supplier may require the administrator (or 'office holder') to undertake personal responsibility for payment for any new supply but may not make the provision of a new supply conditional on receiving payment or security for the old.

[273] EHYA, *Submission on Insolvency Law Reform (2007)*, Appendix 1, p. 6.

[274] Ibid., p. 5. No weakening of protections for employees is envisioned by the EHYA: see p. 6.

[275] Under Sch. B1, para. 52(1)(b) the administrator is not obliged to call an initial creditors' meeting (under para. 51(1)) if he thinks that the company lacks the property to make a distribution to unsecured creditors other than the prescribed part under IA 1986 s. 176A(2)(a). Creditors holding over 10 per cent of total debts can, nevertheless, call for a creditors' meeting under Sch. B1, para. 52(2)(a).

[276] See ch. 3 above, pp. 133–40.

event. If, moreover, their holdings have no economic value, the EHYA argument that they have no economic interest carries some weight.

The difficulties with the proposals, however, are not trivial.[277] The EHYA anticipates that the suggested court-supervised restructurings would be effected by either a scheme of arrangement or a Company Voluntary Arrangement (CVA) procedure and would involve a court-appointed 'monitor' to prevent improper use of the stay and reporting back to the court. Some observers, however, fear that resort to a court-run procedure would see the UK rescue regime descend into bitter litigation and delays: '[B]y pushing so much of the UK's insolvency and restructuring process into the courts these proposals could lead us into the mire of expensive litigation that US companies are now so keen to escape. Insolvencies will change from being relatively quick and pragmatic into huge set piece multi-party litigation of the kind that exists in the US.'[278]

A central worry about the EHYA proposals is that the cram-down rules would turn on drawing a distinction between 'in the money' and 'out of the money' parties. This distinction might well raise difficult issues and precipitate the complex and economically technical litigation that would undermine the speedy route to rescue that the EHYA desires. In a world of highly structured, complex debt – in which creditors increasingly hold bundles of debts of quite different kinds – it might prove more and more difficult to identify the parties that are 'out of the money' and much might depend on debatable assumptions and contentious modes of calculation. All of this could fuel litigation.

---

[277] See V. Finch, 'Corporate Rescue in a World of Debt' [2008] 8 JBL 756, 773–6. See also the concerns expressed by the Insolvency Service in concluding that there was not sufficient evidence to show that the UK needed the EHYA proposed procedure (IS letter to the Managing Director, EHYA, 8 May 2008, reproduced on IS website: www. insolvency.gov.uk). The IS expressed particular concerns about: retaining managers in place when there might have been mismanagement or fraud; dangers that shareholder challenges and 'legal wrangles' would delay restructurings; the likelihood that, where potential overridings of rights were anticipated, this would distort commercial arrangements; the possibility that the EHYA regime would stimulate a move towards more use of fixed charges and/or higher interest rates, with possible shorter call periods – all of which could deter investment in UK enterprises. A further IS worry was that an automatic stay outside insolvency would give an unfair advantage to a company in temporary difficulty compared to its competitors. The IS suggested that the proposed EHYA regime did not offer much that was unavailable under administration.

[278] Per P. Flood of City law firm Reynolds Porter Chamberlain, quoted in N. Neveling, 'Hedge Funds Push for Radical Insolvency Review', *Accountancy Age*, 10 May 2008.

As for shareholders, it could be argued that they would often be inclined to contest both their being condemned to the ranks of the 'out of the money' and the company's grounds for going to court because it (in the EHYA phrase) 'believes there is a real prospect of it becoming unable to pay its financial debts'. The EHYA put forward its reforms as a way to cut down on the uncertainties associated with the current judicial position on shareholder approvals[279] but many may fear that, given the issues involved in judicial supervision, significant uncertainties may be generated within their own proposed regime.

The EHYA's critics, moreover, may fear that the proposed scheme will operate as a procedure that allows the hedge funds and other economically powerful operators to secure court approval for essentially pre-packaged deals and approaches to valuation[280] that favour their own interests and make it difficult for less well-positioned, less well-resourced and less fleet-footed creditors to challenge the settlements put to the court. The critics might contrast the proposed regime with the post-Enterprise Act administration procedure and its emphasis on the administrator's duty to act in the interests of all creditors. The big difference, they might say, would be that less powerful creditors will find it far more difficult to secure protection of their own interests in a court-driven procedure than in one that relies on the administrator to produce a set of proposals that reflects the interests of all of the company's creditors.[281]

As for the proposal to apply a stay so as to prevent customers and suppliers from enforcing contractual terminations triggered by insolvency, the likely objection is that this element of the EHYA system involves shifting risks to unsecured creditors by removing their ability to adjust their positions in the light of the company's troubles – that more risk is being loaded onto those parties who are least able to evaluate or handle that risk and most vulnerable to financial shocks. There may be concerns that this is not only unfair but that it undermines the

---

[279] See the cases of *Marconi*, *British Energy* and *My Travel* as discussed in EHYA, *Submission on Insolvency Law Reform* (2007), p. 5.

[280] In the EHYA scheme, the company would submit its own valuation evidence with the draft scheme documents to support any proposed cram-down, debt to equity swap or other division of the value of the company.

[281] In administration procedure it is the administrator, not the court, who will exclude the 'out of the money' parties within the terms of Sch. B1, para. 52(1)(b) – by not calling a creditors' meeting where he believes that funds will not allow a distribution to unsecured creditors.

value of contracts and may impede the general efficiency of business operations by making suppliers and customers less confident in dealing with possibly troubled companies.[282] In the EHYA world, it could be cautioned, customers and suppliers will face higher business costs since they will feel the need to expend more resources than at present on checking the viability of companies that they enter into business relationships with.

Equity conversions

A more radical and 'market' approach to the design of a cost-effective rescue regime is the proposal put forward by Aghion, Hart and Moore.[283] In the suggested procedure, the administrator would convert the company into an all-equity firm and allocate rights to this equity among the former claim holders in exchange for their former claims. Senior creditors would be given equity, junior creditors and former shareholders would be given options to buy equity; the IP would invite bids for all or part of the 'new' firm. Non-cash bids might include proposals to reorganise the firm as a going concern and to take on new debts. These two tasks would be completed within a specified time, say within three months, and then junior creditors and former shareholders would decide whether to exercise their options. Following this stage, the new shareholders would vote on which bid to select and the firm would exit from insolvency. Junior creditors would thus be required to buy out senior creditors before they receive anything.

Aghion, Hart and Moore aim to offer a regime that is quick, cheap and leaves minimal discretion in the hands of the judiciary and experts. Their main goal is the Jacksonian one of maximising the total value of the proceeds (measured in money terms) that are received by existing claimants. The main perceived evils countered are, first, the danger that senior creditors will vote for liquidation when this serves their interests

---

[282] See the concerns expressed by the Insolvency Service in concluding that there was not 'sufficient evidence to show that the UK needs [the EHYA] procedure': IS letter of 8 May 2008 to the Managing Director of the EHYA (reproduced on the IS website, www.insolvency.gov.uk). The IS expressed particular concerns which have been noted above: see p. 420, n. 277. In the autumn of 2008 discussions between the IS and the EHYA were still ongoing, however.

[283] P. Aghion, O. Hart and J. Moore, 'A Proposal for Bankruptcy Reform in the UK' (1993) 9 IL&P 103, summarised in DTI 1993, Appendix E.

but is not in the general interest of affected parties and, second, the tendency of the administrator when exercising discretion to be involved in inefficient and time-consuming bargaining in an attempt both to secure agreement on taking a firm forward and to decide how to distribute the resulting cash or securities.[284]

The regime's proponents point to a number of its supposed strengths.[285] First, conversion to equity gives the main creditor ('the bank') a stake in the recovery of its debt (assumed to be secured by a floating charge) but also an interest in equity value increases beyond that point. This reduces the bank's incentive to enforce its debt prematurely when it is probable that waiting would increase returns or rescue prospects. The bank also has an incentive to sell the company for as much as possible, rather than for merely enough to satisfy its security. Second, the banks in general may end up holding equity more often than at present and this may have a desirable effect on their propensity to appraise and monitor corporate debtor performance. Third, the system overcomes the fast-increasing problems that administrators face in attempting to negotiate resolutions of problems when different creditor groups have divergent interests. Fourth, the regime avoids the voting distortions that present administration arrangements may produce when junior creditors are placed in a position where they can, without justification, block plans and extract more money than they are allowed under priority. Finally, the system reduces the need for a moratorium because it allows the companies with good prospects to be saved within either administration or receivership.

A number of objections to the scheme and a number of potential difficulties can, however, be identified.[286] In the first instance, some confusion surrounds the issue of entitlement to instigate the equity conversion, with critics noting that a single unsecured creditor might be able to trigger the process irrespective of the amount owed and questioning whether a small unsecured creditor would have the right to

---

[284] The Enterprise Act's removal of the floating charge holder's right to appoint an administrative receiver to some extent reduces dangers of precipitate and self-interested actions by floating charge holders but the administrator's duty to act in the interest of all creditors does not remove the *practical* power of the large creditor: see pp. 428–9 below.

[285] See P. Aghion, O. Hart and J. Moore, 'Insolvency Reform in the UK: A Revised Proposal', Special Paper No. 65 (LSE Financial Markets Group, January 1995) and in (1995) 11 IL&P 67.

[286] For criticism see Brown, *Corporate Rescue*, pp. 680–4.

displace an administrative receiver or an administrator appointed by the court.[287]

It can also be objected that if the procedure is not made compulsory it will add little to present procedures. In many schemes of arrangement, formal and informal, there is an element of debt/equity conversion and shareholders or junior creditors can always 'buy out' senior creditors: for example, by managerial buyouts of the business.[288] The position of the unsecured creditor in the scheme also gives ground for concern. Such creditors will only retain the right to claim outstanding debts if they exercise options to buy shares in the company by a specified date. All the equity in the scheme is, after all, given to the holder of the floating charge and unsecured creditors have to purchase their equity. This has been called a 'fundamental injustice' as it requires a group of creditors who have lost money to put up further funds to keep their debt alive.[289] Junior creditors may also be placed in a difficult position if they find it difficult to sell their options and, if these lapse, the effect will be to leave the senior creditors with all the equity.[290] The conversion proposal can indeed be seen as allowing floating charge holders to exploit their superior resourcing, information and bargaining positions in a manner that worsens the predicament of unsecured creditors. This is liable to be the case since the very factors that lead to the granting of unsecured loans will produce poor positioning to effect purchases of equity options, notably: informal modes of business operation; lack of familiarity with legal structuring in commercial relations; modest levels of staffing operations; and modes of business operation involving large numbers of small, fast-moving transactions and players. Of all creditors, the unsecured creditors are least likely to be able to put their hands on cash at short notice in order to purchase equity shares. As a result of their poor positioning, unsecured creditors will tend to be worse off within an equity conversion scheme than under many alternative arrangements. As is to be expected with proposals based on economic efficiency-seeking, there is a neglect of

---

[287] See A. Campbell, 'The Equity for Debt Proposal: The Way Forward' (1996) 12 IL&P 14 at 15.

[288] Brown, Corporate Rescue, p. 680, who concedes that Aghion, Hart and Moore acknowledge this point in 'Insolvency Reform in the UK', at p. 70. On schemes of arrangement see ch 12 below.

[289] J. Francis, Technical Secretary of the Society of Practitioners in Insolvency, 'Insolvency Law Reform: The Aghion, Hart and Moore Proposals' (1995) (Winter) Insolvency Practitioner, p. 10, quoted in Campbell, 'Equity for Debt Proposal', p. 15.

[290] Brown, Corporate Rescue, p. 680.

distributional justice issues and an inbuilt bias in favour of giving more to those who already have. Those who already have tend, after all, to be the parties who are best placed to make use of the opportunities on the table.

The deadlines involved in the conversion proposal only exacerbate the position of the unsecured creditor. Tight time limits are involved and options have to be exercised before the IP's plan is placed before the shareholders' meeting. As has been commented: 'At this stage it is unlikely that such creditors would have sufficient information to make an informed decision about the survival prospects of the company and exercising options could amount to throwing good money after bad.'[291] From the point of view of the strongest players – the banks with the floating charges – the position is, in contrast, rosy. The conversion process allows the bank to commence formal proceedings, trigger the conversion procedure and force the unsecured creditors to buy them out or else give up all their claims.[292]

As for the hope that an equity conversion scheme will keep transaction costs, and particularly legal costs, low, this may not be achievable in practice. There is the potential for much litigation and the need for a good deal of court supervision within the scheme in relation to issues of asset valuation, protections against abuse, control of the process and bias; the acceptability of the decisions of the IP; whether 'urgency procedures' can be used to meet deadlines; and the discretion exercised by the IPs. Administrators, in particular, may be placed in a difficult position if they are seeking bids for the company and, at the same time, assisting junior creditors to dispose of their options. As one commentator has cautioned: 'Widespread adoption of this procedure will generate new forms of potential duties and liabilities as administrators.'[293] The difficulty, in short, is that without legal oversight and controls, the very considerable discretions exercisable by IPs are open to abuse and liable to prompt many disputes in court. If, on the other hand, a high level of court supervision is involved, the scheme loses one of its heralded virtues. On the question of asset valuation, there are particular difficulties. The scheme's proponents suggest that disputes can be avoided by incorporating (in relation to fixed charges at least) 'forced sale' valuations by professional firms. Here there is a huge potential for fee paying, expense, litigation and delay. It is by no means the case, moreover, that

---

[291] Campbell, 'Equity for Debt Proposal', p. 15.
[292] Francis, 'Insolvency Law Reform', p. 4.   [293] Brown, *Corporate Rescue*, p. 680.

a company's assets and liabilities can be ascertained quickly and easily.[294] Such calculations may be lengthy, fraught and highly contentious. Nor can such uncertainties be dealt with easily by Aghion, Hart and Moore's suggestion that disputes can be set aside and dealt with once the company has come out of insolvency. The existence of a body of contested claims will constitute, apart from anything else, a cloud of uncertainty that will hang over unsecured creditors' decisions on whether to exercise options and, as has been pointed out, such creditors may 'invest money to keep claims alive only to discover later that their equity holding is worth far less than they had calculated because of the existence of deferred claims'.[295] In sum, the equity conversion scheme has as its major probable effect the improvement of the position of banks at the expense of unsecured creditors. Nor is the deterioration of the unsecured creditors' position unconnected with the public interest in general. Commercial life depends to a large extent on the efficient giving of unsecured credit. In so far as unsecured creditors face large risks due to uncertain processes they will tend to resort to quasi-security devices and withdrawals of credit (demanding payment on the spot). Such a tendency will hinder rather than lubricate the wheels of commerce.

Expertise

Can the new administration procedure be said to constitute a regime that allows expert judgements to be brought to bear on turnaround? A first issue on these fronts is whether the procedure conduces to the generation and use of the information that is needed to make expert and well-founded judgements.[296] From the administrator's point of view, the need for information is urgent. He must present proposals to creditors within eight weeks of his appointment.[297] He must also commence a creditors' meeting within ten weeks of the administration's start.[298]

---

[294] Campbell, 'Equity for Debt Proposal', p. 16; Francis, 'Insolvency Law Reform', p. 9.

[295] Campbell, 'Equity for Debt Proposal', p. 17.

[296] This section builds on V. Finch, 'Control and Co-ordination in Corporate Rescue' (2005) 25 *Legal Studies* 374.

[297] Para. 49(5)(b).

[298] Para. 51(2). (Unless the administrator thinks (a) creditors will be paid in full; (b) there is insufficient property to make a distribution to unsecured creditors; or (c) the company cannot be rescued as a going concern or a better result for the company's creditors as a whole than would be likely on a winding up cannot be achieved: para. 52(1).)

Administrators will have considerable knowledge of the laws and processes relevant to rescue but they are unlikely to have detailed understandings of the company and its operations. On such matters, the
existing management constitutes the major reservoir of relevant information and the administrator will need to use the resources that are
represented by existing directors and employees.[299]

Co-ordination between directors and the IP is essential if information
is to flow and, at this point, it is useful to consider the various factors that
are likely to affect the degree to which the participants in administration
will co-ordinate on the generation and use of information. A first issue is
commitment to the rescue enterprise and the incentives of different
actors to co-operate in the pursuit of rescue. This is likely to be affected,
in turn, by perceptions of personal, corporate or other gains but also by
perceptions of, and confidence concerning, other actors' incentives.
Where interests are seen as divergent, this will undermine co-operation
but so will uncertainty about motives and the alignment of interests.
Directors, moreover, may possess personal incentives to control the flow
of information into the rescue process. Directors who want to prolong
their employment at a company – for example while they seek new job
opportunities – will be disinclined to precipitate action by the administrator by laying all their informational cards on the table. Instead they
may seek to preserve uncertainty about the company's position and
future prospects so that the decision-maker is induced to delay taking
decisions.[300]

It is arguable that the EA 2002 reforms will increase directorial incentives to stay on during the rescue process because the directors will
recognise that IPs have rescue, and the interests of all creditors, in
mind, rather than a predisposition simply to act rapidly to realise returns
for the floating charge holder – as in the 'old' system of administrative
receivership. Directors here may be conscious of the IP's Schedule B1,

---

[299] See Phillips and Goldring, 'Rescue and Reconstruction', pp. 75, 78.

[300] See D. Baird and E. Morrison, 'Bankruptcy Decision Making' (2001) *Journal of Law,
Economics and Organization* 356, 369. It may be, of course, that if directors are
considering appointing an administrator, they might also consider, and discuss with
an IP, whether the IP would consent to their continued management of aspects of the
business under Sch. B1, para. 64. (The administrator may leave some functions in the
directors' hands but, in doing so, cannot absolve himself from his own responsibilities.)
The appointment of an administrator has the effect of making the directors' powers
exercisable only with the administrator's consent in so far as they might 'interfere with
the exercise of the administrator's powers' (para. 64(2)(a)) and the administrator has
the power to appoint or remove directors under para. 61.

paragraph 3(1)(a) primary obligation to rescue the company as a going concern. Against such arguments, however, it might be contended that the process established by the EA may prove unpalatable to directors and that the EA's emphasis on recognising the voices and interests of all creditors 'may result in battle-weary key management figures who resign'.[301] It is also the case that in many instances of corporate distress the incumbent directors are ousted as a result of pressure from banks or shareholders and so they are removed from the scene and do not constitute providers of ongoing information.[302]

It might also be contended that directors will often be highly uncertain about the motivations of the administrator in the post-EA regime. Directors may think that the main incentive for an administrator will, in reality, be to keep the banks happy rather than to pursue rescue. Such perceptions will be encouraged on reflecting that IPs are repeat players in insolvency work, that they will depend on banks for most of their current and future business, and that the banks' powers to appoint administrators of choice[303] will lead to ongoing relationships between IPs and the banks. As has been commented, moreover, administrators will rely on the provision of funds when negotiating rescue and the secured lenders, the banks, will be the usual providers of funds. These banks will be very concerned that the administrator's proposals meet their approval: 'there is no legislation that can address the economic facts of life: he who pays the piper will call the tune'.[304] As discussed above, the EA did not

---

[301] See M. Jervis, 'A Tough Act To Follow' (2003) *Recovery* (Summer) 13.

[302] In Gilson's study of US firms only 46 per cent of incumbent directors were in place when the firms emerged from bankruptcy or settled privately with creditors two years later and in 8 per cent of cases the whole board was replaced: see S. Gilson, 'Bankruptcy, Boards, Banks and Blockholders' (1990) 27 *Journal of Financial Economics* 355. It may well be, of course, that in DIP regimes a higher turnover of directors is to be expected than in PIP regimes since the banks will be more concerned about directorial quality in regimes that leave directors in power rather than give control to a professional. On reasons for directorial departure in US firms see S. Gilson, 'Management Turnover and Financial Distress' (1989) 25 *Journal of Financial Economics* 241, 271–81 (suggesting that bank-lenders frequently institute managerial changes). For a discussion of poor performance as a driver of board change see J. Warner, R. Watts, K. Wruck *et al.*, 'Stock Prices and Top Management Changes' (1988) *Journal of Financial Economics* 461. See also ch. 6 above.

[303] Holders of qualifying floating charges (QFCs) can appoint administrators out of court. If other eligible parties intend to make such appointments they must give notice to qualifying floating charge holders (QFCHs) (para. 26(2)) which allows QFCHs to appoint their own choice of administrator: see further Davies, *Insolvency and the Enterprise Act 2002*, pp. 164–5.

[304] See C. Swain, 'A Move Towards a Stakeholder Society' (2003) IL&P 5, 7–8.

introduce super-priority funding for any rescue initiative and, in the absence of super-priority, banks advancing rescue funds are liable to prove extremely highly motivated to negotiate the rescue plans that protect their own interests. If directors are conscious of such potential biases, they may be restrained in their commitments to assist the administrator.

A second factor that may affect co-ordination on the generation and use of information is the size and urgency of the challenge faced. This will be greater where participants in a potential rescue are large in number, divergent in character, outlook and interest and are widely dispersed. Further co-ordination difficulties arise when business challenges have to be responded to according to tight schedules.

A third, and related, issue is communication. In order to derive assurance about other actors' intentions, each participant in a rescue operation will have to trust disclosures made about those intentions and will also have to understand these. Here there may be a set of communications difficulties that flow from the various systems within which the different actors attribute meanings to communications. Directors, banks and administrators, for instance, see the world differently from each other and are engaged in very different endeavours. Some directors, for instance, may see rescues in terms of protecting employment whereas banks may tend to see protection of corporate assets as a priority and administrators will focus strongly on their statutory objective to protect the interests of creditors as a whole. These actors possess different value frameworks and, accordingly, it is to be expected that frictions and distortions will infect communications.[305] This means that insolvency regimes that involve multi-party systems of collecting information, devising strategies or implementing those strategies run serious risks that confusions, delays and uncertainties will arise during these processes – that is the downside of the inclusive processes set up by the EA 2002.[306] Such communication difficulties, moreover, will affect not

---

[305] On the 'fundamentally different views' that banks and bondholders have regarding rescue – and the frictions that this can create within negotiations – see J. Roome, 'The Unwelcome Guest' (2004) Recovery (Summer) 30; and ch. 7 above. See generally N. Luhmann, Social Systems (Stanford University Press, Stanford, 1984); Luhmann, 'Law as a Social System' (1989) 83 Northwestern Univ. LR 136; G. Teubner, Law as an Autopoietic System (Blackwell, Oxford, 1993); G. Teubner and A. Febbrajo (eds.), State, Law and Economy as Autopoietic Systems (Giuffre, Milan, 1992).

[306] For a discussion of the problems of dual decision-making (where authority in insolvency is shared) see Hahn, 'Concentrated Ownership', pp. 152–4.

merely the propensities of different parties to commit to co-operation but also their *ability* to co-operate where they share a desire to co-operate – even the best-motivated choir sounds poor if its members read their song sheets in different ways.

Other factors may aggravate communication difficulties, notably increases in numbers of participants and differences of outlook and character. Here the EA creates potential gains as well as difficulties. It calls on the administrator to pursue his/her functions 'in the interest of the company's creditors as a whole'.[307] It gives the banks considerable procedural rights,[308] obliges the administrator to disclose proposals,[309] and gives any creditor or member of the company a power to challenge the administrator's conduct.[310] Such provisions seek to implement the White Paper vision of a more inclusive insolvency regime.[311] On the one hand, this expands inputs and access into the regime and might be said to encourage the flow of information into the rescue process from a variety of sources. On the other, it might be cautioned that such multiple inputting is likely to lead to confusions and contests as different perspectives underpin the pursuit of various interests. The overall effect may be to reduce co-operation and free flows of information. Such a situation may be exacerbated by legal provisions, such as those in paragraph 3 of Schedule B1, which create a complex hierarchy of objectives in laying down the administrator's obligations to serve a wide variety of creditors' interests.[312]

Will the dominant banks operate as ready suppliers of rescue-relevant information to administrators?[313] It is arguable that the EA institutionalises the position of the floating charge holding bank as the primary source of information to the administrator about the company's affairs and prospects. This is because all three routes into administration demand that the administrator makes a statement of the objectives intended to be pursued and formulates proposals within eight weeks of

---

[307] Para. 3(2).
[308] See V. Finch, 'Re-invigorating Corporate Rescue' [2003] JBL 527, 534–5.
[309] A statement of the proposals has to be sent to creditors within eight weeks of appointment of the administrator (IA 1986 Sch. B1, para. 49(5) and (6)) and an initial creditors' meeting to consider them convened within ten weeks (para. 51(2)(b)).
[310] See para. 74.   [311] See Insolvency Service, *Insolvency – A Second Chance*.
[312] See Frisby, 'In Search of a Rescue Regime'.
[313] On the governance role of banks at times of corporate distress see Gilson, 'Bankruptcy, Boards, Banks and Blockholders'; Franken, 'Creditor and Debtor Oriented Corporate Bankruptcy Regimes'.

his or her appointment. The effect of these requirements will be that prospective administrators will have to be in possession of detailed information on nearly all aspects of the company and its business before they agree to act. They are likely, accordingly, to make it clear to the banks that they expect to be provided with such data on being approached and, thus advised, institutional lenders will routinely carry out independent business reviews whenever any of their debtor companies seems to be nearing financial difficulties. The banks will facilitate such reviews by making their loans conditional on the debtor company agreeing to supply information on request and to co-operate with any business review processes instituted by the bank.[314] The banks are likely to possess a stock of valuable financial and operational information about many of their debtors[315] but their inclination to use this for rescue purposes cannot be taken for granted. Here again the central issue is whether post-EA administration will operate as a reconstituted form of receivership or a genuinely rescue-orientated process.[316] If banks use their strong positions with an eye to turning administration into receivership and the pursuit of bank rather than general creditor interests, it is to be expected that they will be little concerned to feed rescue-relevant information into the administration process.[317] Administration, however, is *not* receivership and the interests of all creditors have to be taken into account.[318] Where it is clear from the administrator's proposals that rescue is being considered, the banks may well be concerned to inject

---

[314] See Phillips and Goldring, 'Rescue and Reconstruction', pp. 75, 76; Frisby, 'In Search of a Rescue Regime', p. 261.

[315] See e.g. D. Citron, 'The Incidence of Accounting-Based Covenants in UK Public Debt Contracts: An Empirical Analysis' (1995) 25 *Accounting and Business Research* 139; Day and Taylor, 'Role of Debt Contracts'; H. DeAngelo, L. DeAngelo and K. Wruck, 'Asset Liquidity, Debt Covenants and Managerial Discretion in Financial Distress: The Collapse of L. A. Grear' (2002) 64 *Journal of Financial Economics* 3; R. Mokal and J. Armour, 'The New UK Corporate Rescue Procedure – The Administrator's Duty to Act Rationally' (2004) 1 Int. Corp. Rescue 136; M. Harris and A. Raviv, 'Capital Structure and the Informational Role of Debt' (1990) 45 *Journal of Finance* 321.

[316] See e.g. Willcock, 'How the Banks Won the Battle'; but *cf.* Lord McIntosh of Haringey, HL Debates, 21 October 2002: col. 1101. The banks may even use the process as a route to winding up: see pp. 396–7 above and generally Keay, 'What Future for Liquidation?'; Linklater, 'New Style Administration'; Insolvency Act 1986 Sch. B1, para. 83. Where banks are engaged in such use of the procedure they will seldom be inclined to supply rescue-relevant information.

[317] On whether events post-EA will be driven by ideas, interests or legally allocated rights see Finch, 'Re-invigorating Corporate Rescue'.

[318] See para. 3(2).

information into the administration process – even if this is done in an effort to demonstrate the non-viability of a rescue option. The banks' commitment to inform should not, however, be exaggerated. Banks may consider that post-EA they are not so strongly positioned as formerly to influence the IP's actions and this may make them reserved participants in the rescue process. They may be happy to stay with entrenched and modest ways of monitoring their investments. They may, indeed, protect their investments by resorting to asset-based fixed securities rather than relying on gaining and deploying information.[319] The EA, moreover, in 'abolishing' administrative receivership and curtailing the bank's ability to deploy a rapid, self-interested enforcement tool may have reduced both the bank's ability and its inclination to insist on very extensive ongoing supplies of information from the debtor company.[320]

As for unsecured creditors, these are parties who might be expected to possess useful information about a company in some circumstances – for example when they are established trading partners of the enterprise. The hoped-for effect of the EA reforms was to encourage informational input (and corporate monitoring) by unsecured creditors since it promises them more receptivity for their views than was the case with receivership.[321] Instances where unsecured creditors will be well informed about companies, well placed to participate in rescue processes and highly committed to such participation (for example, through extent of interest) may, however, be few and far between.[322] Frisby's research, moreover, suggests that there is 'a lack of participation in the insolvency process by unsecured creditors' with creditors' meetings generally being very poorly attended.[323]

Thus far the discussion has focused on information flows to the administrator but attention should also be paid to the information

---

[319] See pp. 403, 414–15 and ch. 3 above; D. Prentice, 'Bargaining in the Shadow of the Enterprise Act 2002' (2004) 5 EBOR 153; Armour, 'Should We Redistribute in Insolvency?'.

[320] See Armour and Frisby, 'Rethinking Receivership', pp. 87–8 and on 'active' reasons for taking security see R. Scott, 'A Relational Theory of Secured Financing' (1986) 86 Colum. L Rev. 901.

[321] See the administrator's duty to consider the interests of creditors as a whole: para. 3(2). On the reception of creditors' input in receivership see ch. 8 above; E. Ferran, 'The Duties of an Administrative Receiver to Unsecured Creditors' (1988) 9 Co. Law. 58.

[322] Average returns to unsecured creditors may be so low post-administration that this may not conduce to high commitment: an R3 Survey of July 2004 revealed that unsecured creditors, on average, gained returns from 'old' administrations of 6.3 pence in the pound (5.4 pence from administrative receiverships).

[323] *Insolvency Service Evaluation*, 2008, p. 115.

flows that involve other participants in rescue processes. The courts, for instance, have a role to play in the post-EA regime – one that may prove highly significant given the terms of the EA. It has been contended that if receivers were to owe duties to a wide range of parties, the judges would be liable to face considerable informational difficulties:

> the information available to them about the specific facts of the decision is almost always likely to be less than that available to the decision-maker in question. Furthermore their decision must be made with hindsight. Actions which at the time of taking were known to be risky but justifiable in terms of expected benefits, can be seen [to be] unjustifiable with hindsight when a 'bad' outcome has materialised ... [they] are likely to give receivers incentives to behave in too risk-averse a fashion, thus reducing the expected returns to all parties.[324]

The same points can be made about judicial scrutiny of the administrator's actions in the post-EA regime. Overall, then, does the post-EA system contribute as well as might be desired to the supply and use of the information needed for expert judgements? The answer is that it leaves a large number of issues up in the air. The banks, for instance, may feel the need to secure good information flows from debtors in order to be able to brief administrators well and early but they may have doubts about their abilities to insist on this information and the use that the administrator will make of it. What, perhaps, can be said at this stage is that information use is unlikely to be enhanced by uncertainties within the system – for example, regarding the rigour with which the courts will oversee the administrator's duty to serve all creditors' interests.

Good information flows are essential to the application of expertise but attention should also be paid to the sources of expertise. On this point, it should be borne in mind that a given corporate rescue may involve a number of areas of specialisation or expertise. A distinction has already been drawn between expertise in insolvency procedures (the expected province of the IP) and expertise in business affairs. The latter expertise can, in turn, be disaggregated into expertise regarding such matters as: reorganisation strategies; finances; operations; marketing; product development and human resources. On such disaggregation it can be seen that across such areas there will be variations in the balance of expertise between the administrator, the directors of the troubled company and the major creditors (the banks). Within the post-EA regime expertise in reorganisation strategies and finances

---

[324] Armour and Frisby, 'Rethinking Receivership', p. 100.

may be offered by the IP and the banks, who may not need to rely a great deal on the input of directors regarding such matters. On human resource or operational issues, however, it is likely that the existing directors possess far greater firm-specific knowledge than the IP or the banks. Herein lies a potential problem with the post-EA regime. It relies on inclusive procedures and it attributes competences generally. It gives final authority to the IP on all rescue-relevant issues rather than allocating competences (or sharing these) according to anticipated areas of expertise.

The inclusive processes established by the EA produce a further danger: that expertise may be stifled. On this point it may be useful to distinguish between three different scenarios for exercising expertise: single authority; multiple authority; and inclusive. In single authority systems there is a single dominant decision maker – as in pre-EA receivership. This allows a judgement to be made with one voice – as where one coach picks the team. In multiple authority decision or policy-making, responsibility is shared and a process of exchanging views is encouraged. This brings the gains of discussion but the dangers of potential deadlock. With inclusive decision-making, as in the post-EA regime, there may be a single formal authority who makes policies or decisions, but the dominance of that actor is reduced by arrangements for consultation, negotiation and discussion. This produces potential gains in openness and accountability and it may improve fairness but, like multiple authority, it brings dangers – of confusion, delay, compromise and deadlock.[325] These problems may detract from both the application of expertise and the efficient formulation of strategies for rescue. As indicated in the previous section, it involves negotiations between parties who differ not merely in interests but in cultural frameworks and ways of conceptualising the purposes of rescue. It is to be expected that communications between such parties will be delayed and distorted as a result of such differences.

A further danger inherent in the post-EA administration process is that the price paid for inclusiveness may be too high in that expert judgements and strategies are over-constrained and over-contested. Timescales, as noted, may also be relevant and here there are tensions. Tight scheduling is desirable in so far as it protects against indecision and tardiness on the

---

[325] See e.g. O. Brupbacher, 'Functional Analysis of Corporate Rescue Procedures: A Proposal from an Anglo-Swiss Perspective' [2005] 5 JCLS 105; Frisby, 'In Search of a Rescue Regime'.

part of the administrator.[326] If, however, proposals have to be presented to creditors within eight weeks of appointment[327] – even in the case of complex corporate scenarios – this may militate in favour of those strategies that are the least contentious rather than the most expert – that are sub-optimal because they are devised at speed and with an eye to minimising contest from any of the creditors with powers to take legal issue. In practice this may mean that the banks will exert strong pressure on investment decisions in an attempt to ensure that strategies carrying very low risks to bank interests are the ones that are chosen.[328] These may not always be the strategies that are most conducive to rescue (or the most fair to creditors other than the bank) and they are likely to be implemented by administrators of the bank's choosing.[329] A further danger is that in the newly inclusive post-EA regime, parties other than the floating charge holding banks – such as unsecured creditors – will contest the pro-bank policies and if agreement cannot be reached within statutory timescales, they will resort to court challenge. The result may be a loss not only of expertise in choices of strategy but also of efficiency in that rescue-necessary schedules cannot be adhered to. As already indicated, the EA sets up objectives for administrators that offer numerous pegs upon which disgruntled creditors may hang lawsuits and this legal setting creates further difficulty for those administrators who would make judgements and strategies on best appraisal of their merits.

The post-EA system is not trouble free on the above fronts but it might be argued that it deserves approval for other characteristics that conduce to the expert and efficient making of high-quality rescue judgements. It might be said, for instance, that in times of corporate difficulty there is a case for taking the strategic function away from existing managers and for practitioner in possession (PIP) rather than debtor in possession (DIP) arrangements. The strength of this case turns a good deal on the model of the company director that underpins the analysis. English insolvency law has traditionally been built on the assumption that

---

[326] The administrator, as noted, has a duty to perform his functions as quickly and efficiently as is reasonably practicable (para. 4) which creditors or members can enforce by means of an application to court under para. 74(2).

[327] Para. 49(5).

[328] See Armour and Frisby, 'Rethinking Receivership'; G. Triantis and R. Daniels, 'The Role of Debt in Interactive Corporate Governance' (1995) 83 Calif. L Rev 1073.

[329] As noted above, qualifying floating charge holders (QFCHs) can appoint administrators out of court; other parties who intend to make such appointments have to give notice (para. 26(1)) to QFCHs which then allows QFCHs to appoint their own choice of administrator.

where a company becomes insolvent this is usually due to a failure of management and that the last people to delegate judgements to, or to leave in control, are those who are responsible for the company's plight in the first place.[330] Numerous analyses of the causes of corporate failure put poor management at the top of the list of factors inducing decline.[331] This may not always be the case, however, and external pressures may sometimes place a company in acute difficulty in spite of faultless management.[332] The English model of the director of the troubled company, moreover, contrasts with that implicit in the US regime, which is more inclined both to trust the skill and judgement of the existing managers and to treat corporate difficulties as problems that merit attention rather than blame.[333]

One response to the English view of the (often failing) corporate manager is, of course, to take steps to improve directorial skills. It could be argued that business people ought to be required to possess some sort of elementary qualification before they are allowed to act as company directors. Such qualifications would indicate that the individual has a basic understanding of company law and finance as well as the legal obligations going with directorship.[334] (They might also certify that the person possessed a basic knowledge of insolvency procedures and obligations.) The IS noted that a number of business people opposed a requirement to hold qualifications on the ground that this could operate as a brake on enterprise.[335] The directors consulted, however, said that they would be willing to undertake some sort of instruction provided that it was not expensive or time consuming and, overall, there was moderate support for the idea.[336] Mandatory basic training for directors could,

---

[330] See discussion in ch. 6 above. Sir Kenneth Cork has written that insolvency provides an occasion for a change 'from incompetent hands to people who not only have the wherewithal but also hopefully the competence, the imagination and the energy to save the business': *Cork on Cork*, pp. 202–3. On the UK insolvency system's development as a 'manager-displacing' regime see J. Armour, B. Cheffins and D. Skeel, 'Corporate Ownership Structure and the Evolution of Bankruptcy Law: Lessons from the United Kingdom' (2002) 55 Vand. L Rev. 1699, 1734–50.

[331] See ch. 4 above; R3, Twelfth Survey, *Corporate Insolvency in the UK* (2004).

[332] See ch. 4 above.

[333] See ch. 6 above; G. Moss, 'Chapter 11: An English Lawyer's Critique' (1998) 11 *Insolvency Intelligence* 17, 18; J. L. Westbrook, 'A Comparison of Bankruptcy Reorganisation in the US with Administration Procedure in the UK' (1990) 6 IL&P 86.

[334] See V. Finch, 'Company Directors: Who Cares About Skill and Care?' (1992) 55 MLR 179 at 210.

[335] IS 2000, para. 58.   [336] Ibid.

furthermore, be advocated on the grounds that the Companies Act 2006 spells out directors' duties[337] and creates new insolvency regimes but that such provisions will only have limited effect if steps are not taken to bring those duties and regimes to the attention of directors. Some firms and directors will voluntarily acquaint themselves with such legal matters but these more responsible firms and directors are less likely to breach legal obligations or to meet financial troubles than more maverick operators. It is the latter who are disproportionately in need of training and higher standards. As for placing a brake on enterprise, it can be responded that ill-informed and irresponsible directorial behaviour may itself hinder enterprise. A world in which traders act defensively because of fears about their solvency or financial responsibilities is not a dynamic, responsive, low-transaction-cost world. It might be conceded that directors of firms with a level of turnover below a certain figure should be exempted from the qualification requirement – this concession may be justifiable in order to encourage new business – but above that level the qualification could be mandatory. Those who object to the expense and difficulty of testing thousands of directors may be reminded, first, that each year huge numbers of would-be drivers of vehicles are tested in theory as well as in practice, and, second, that the actions of ill-informed directors may wreck businesses and lives, and, third, that a minimum competence may be a reasonable *quid pro quo* for the privilege of limited liability.[338]

Knowledge of directorial obligations and of insolvency procedures does not in itself ensure that directors will input more effectively into rescue processes or be inclined to seek help at an earlier stage of corporate decline than occurs now. What is needed, according to some commentators, is a cultural change in attitudes to insolvency. This change can be encouraged on a number of fronts. First, the notion that seeking help evidences managerial failure can be countered by public rejection of the condemnatory approach to insolvency. The speeches of Peter Mandelson when Trade Secretary exemplified such a rejection.[339] Second, as indicated already, directors, where possible, can be involved

---

[337] See Companies Act 2006, Part 10 and, for example, ss. 171–7.

[338] See ch. 16 below.

[339] See the extract in Hunter, 'Nature and Functions of a Rescue Culture', p. 519; *The Times*, 14 October 1998; White Paper, *Our Competitive Future: Building the Knowledge Driven Economy* (Cm 4176, December 1998), section entitled 'Fear of Failure', paras. 212–14, which Hunter argues evidences the endorsement of this approach by Peter Mandelson's successor, Stephen Byers. See also White Paper on *Enterprise, Skill and Innovation*

in rescue operations (under supervision arrangements) rather than excluded on the basis that they are inevitably culpable incompetents. Third, investors and large creditors can move to assure directors that taking early steps to secure help involves, in itself, no greater blot on the *curriculum vitae* than a decision to hire management consultants. Finally, such changes might be reinforced by tougher attitudes to those who indulge in wrongful and reckless trading, with greater use of the CDDA 1986 and stronger penalties imposed on errant directors.[340] Such measures may go some way towards encouraging the view that failure to seek help is a more serious matter than being at the helm of a company that encounters difficulties.

Note should also be taken of the potential role of unsecured creditors in providing special expertise to rescue processes. Many unsecured creditors will know little of their business partners' activities but some will have a detailed knowledge of the troubled company's affairs – perhaps because of an established trading relationship in a specialised marketplace. What the collectivity of the EA processes and the duty to all creditors offers to such creditors is the chance to voice an opinion on rescue options. The unsecured creditor, accordingly, has an opportunity to attempt to persuade the administrator that there is a solution to corporate problems that allows rescue and a better than winding-up return to creditors.[341] This contrasts with the prior position in receivership where the receiver had no obligation to listen to such voices and in which speedy action on behalf of the floating charge holder tended to be accorded precedence over sustained consideration of various creditors' views.[342]

So will the new administration process as set up by the EA produce more expert rescue judgements more efficiently than other systems such as DIP? Much will depend on the particular company and particular management team involved in a given corporate decline. The virtue of

---

(2001), ch. 5, paras. 5.9–5.15: 'An entrepreneurial economy needs to support responsible risk taking. Insolvency law must be updated so that it strikes the right balance. It must deal proportionately with financial failure, whilst assuring creditors that it is handled efficiently and effectively' (para. 5.10).

[340] See IS 2000, para. 59. See also A. Hicks, *Disqualification of Directors: No Hiding Place for the Unfit?* ACCA Research Report No. 59 (London, 1998). See ch. 16 below.

[341] As per para. 3(1)(a) or (b). The EA does, however, allow creditors' meetings to be bypassed in certain circumstances: see Sch. B1, para. 52. On the 'capture' of creditors' meetings generally see S. Wheeler, 'Empty Rhetoric and Empty Promises: The Creditors' Meeting' (1994) 21 *Journal of Law and Society* 350.

[342] See Ferran, 'Duties of an Administrative Receiver'.

the PIP system is that greater or lesser roles can be given to directors according to assessments of their powers of judgement and expertise that are carried out by an independent generalist familiar with insolvency situations.

Fairness and accountability

If expert judgements concerning responses to corporate distress are to merit approval, they have to be made fairly and accountably. Here the post-EA regime might be expected to score high marks as it places an independent officer of the court in control.[343] It also sets up open procedures that are designed to allow reasonable input to creditors[344] and which hold administrators to account through creditors' meetings[345] as well as through the imposition of a series of legal duties.[346] Such creditors' meetings allow unsecured creditors to hold administrators to account in a way that was not possible in administrative receivership. It should be noted, however, that accountability to the creditors' meeting is avoided where the administrator acts without reference to such a meeting in accordance with the terms of Schedule B1, paragraph 52(1)[347] or acts in advance of such a meeting – subject to any court directions given under paragraph 68(2) of Schedule B1. In the former instances (which would occur when the administrator thinks, for example, that there are insufficient funds for a distribution to unsecured creditors) there would be no requirement of court approval and aggrieved creditors would only be able to hold that administrator to account by commencing proceedings in court.[348] Some practitioners have, as noted, voiced particular

---

[343] The administrator, as noted, is an officer of the court and thus subject to the ethical requirements of the rule in *Ex parte James* (1874) 9 Ch App 609: see D. Milman, 'The Administration Order Procedure' (2002) 17 *Company Law Newsletter* 1, 3.

[344] See Hahn, 'Concentrated Ownership'.

[345] See Insolvency Act 1986 Sch. B1, paras. 51–7.

[346] See J. Armour and R. Mokal, 'Reforming the Governance of Corporate Rescue: The Enterprise Act 2002' [2005] LMCLQ 28. On accountability in the new administration process see further Brupbacher, 'Functional Analysis', pp. 126–38.

[347] Under which, as noted, an administrator is not obliged to call a creditors' meeting if he thinks that creditors can be paid in full; there is insufficient property for a distribution to unsecured creditors; or that it will not be possible to rescue the company as a going concern or achieve a better result for the company's creditors as a whole than would be likely if the company were wound up.

[348] Sch. B1, para. 74 governs challenges to the administrator's conduct of the company by creditors or members. Para. 75 allows misfeasance actions against administrators by, *inter alia*, a creditor and the company does not have to be in liquidation for such an action to be commenced.

worries about the process in which a company can be put into administration out of court and then be converted into a creditors' voluntary
liquidation.[349] As one expressed the concern: 'Companies are put into
administration for no other reason than to take advantage of the opportunity to put them into liquidation later without holding a creditors'
meeting.'[350] In such scenarios another worry is that only a liquidator has
a complete set of powers for dealing with wrongful and fraudulent
trading and that use of the administration route may inhibit investigation of directorial actions because the directors may appoint an administrator out of court to realise and distribute assets and exit
administration – all without the need to hold a meeting of creditors.[351]

In the modern distressed debt market, moreover, it can be argued that
there are numbers of actors who are not so much interested in rescue as a
fast return. As John Verrill, former president of R3, has stated:

> The modus operandi of the new-style entrants into the distressed debt
> market is that they fund the administrator and provide the stock.
> Normally under the old regime the administrator would have to show
> the court that he had the financial backing or funding to achieve the
> purpose for which he was seeking the order ... Now if a floating charge
> holder wants to appoint an administrator, he can do so without the old
> checks and balances and no independent verification by the court. A
> company can now buy the debenture off a creditor who would otherwise
> be whistling for the money and then say to the administrator: 'Do you
> want the job or not?'[352]

A system of practitioner in possession, as found in administration,
could, however, be supported as avoiding the danger of unfairness or bias
that comes from shareholder manipulation and which has been said to be

---

[349] A mechanism for converting new-style administration to a CVL is found in Sch. B1,
para. 83. Alternatively, in less complex cases, the IP may wish to take advantage of the
ability to pay all creditors whilst the company is in 'new' administration rather than
moving to liquidation: see further Todd, 'Administration Post-Enterprise Act'. See
pp. 396–7 above.

[350] Nick Hood of Begbies Traynor, quoted in *Accountancy Age*, 18 December 2003, p. 11.
See also Linklater, 'New Style Administration'. See pp. 396–7 above.

[351] At which meeting creditors would have had the opportunity to question the directors on
the company's demise. Administrators are entitled, however, to institute proceedings to
have transactions at undervalue and preferences adjusted: IA 1986 ss. 238–9. The
administration–liquidation route could, moreover, reduce costs and time and allow
directors to have more input during the process: see further Keay, 'What Future for
Liquidation?', pp. 152–5.

[352] Quoted in J. Robins, 'The Enterprise Act Has Failed to Earn Respect' (2005) *Finance
Week* (25 May).

associated with DIP regimes – the risk that, where ownership is concentrated, shareholders will tend to encourage the management to engage in risky projects during troubled times since they are gambling with creditors' money.[353] Here there is a trade-off to be considered. A DIP regime might be expected to place rescue in the hands of directors – who are the parties with best knowledge of the business and its prospects – but it brings dangers of shareholder manipulation. A PIP system would be expected to involve lower levels of business-specific knowledge but greater resistance to such shareholder pressure.

In deciding whether DIP or PIP brings the preferable trade-off a number of considerations may be relevant. A first is the severity of the risks of bias through potential shareholder manipulation. On this point Hahn argues that concentration of ownership conduces to such manipulation but that, in the UK, the shareholding of listed corporations tends to be widely dispersed.[354] If risks of manipulation tend to be low, this militates, according to Hahn, in favour of DIP rather than PIP as the fairer regime. Such an analysis, however, focuses on the relationship between manager-directors and shareholders and may understate the dangers of manipulation by other interests. In the case of many troubled UK companies there will be a degree of creditor concentration and creditor power (as where the company is in debt to a bank that holds a floating charge). This, as already indicated, may lead the bank to press those in charge of the company to develop and apply strategies that principally protect bank interests. On this count, it is arguable that, although administrator-IPs may not be immune to such pressures (a point made above), they are likely to be more resistant than the company's directors, who will not only be predisposed to keeping their major creditors happy,[355] but may well be conditioned by their troubled experiences to give way to bank pressure.

Even within PIP, however, it should be emphasised that the importance of eleventh-hour funding in rescue operations may enhance the banks' already strong positions to manipulate. In times of corporate distress it is common for the banks to supply rescue funds under terms

---

[353] Ibid.; Scott, 'Relational Theory', p. 909.

[354] Hahn, 'Concentrated Ownership', p. 134. It should be emphasised, of course, that Hahn's argument relates to listed corporations. Private companies would not offer the same dispersion of shareholding and, accordingly, risks of shareholder manipulation would be higher, and the attractions of DIP lower.

[355] Directors' tendency to align their decision-making to the bank's interests is likely to be the greater if the directors have also given the bank personal guarantees.

that give them very considerable powers to influence strategy.[356] Covenants in restructured lending agreements will frequently impose restrictions on such matters as: operating activities (e.g. maximum out-lays on administration); new investments (e.g. on levels and kinds of investment); dispositions of assets; payouts to shareholders; and financial activities (e.g. levels of borrowing; levels of working capital).[357] When banks supply new rescue funds they may increase their equity share in the corporation and accordingly may exercise considerable power as shareholders as well as creditors. They may also negotiate representation on the board which allows them, for example, to put turnaround specialists in place and gives *de facto*, if not formal, influence over the strategy formulation process.[358] The effect of such bank power is that, within the post-EA regime, the administrator is supposed to advert to the interests of creditors as a whole (a contrast with receivership) but, in doing so, will have to co-ordinate closely with the bank. There are dangers of both friction and manipulation (and hence of unfairness to some creditors) in such arrangements.

Turning to accountability through judicial oversight, this can be assessed by considering the courts' role in shaping the administration regime. That shaping may involve the judges in influencing interactions between a variety of different actors by, for example, adjusting incentives to resort to law and detailing areas of expertise within which certain actors' judgements will be deferred to. In order to explore the potential judicial role it is necessary, first, to outline the main ways in which the EA 2002 reforms allow the judges to impact on the new administration process and, second, to indicate how the judiciary might make best use of their potential impact in accordance with a co-ordination perspective that focuses on key rescue tasks.

The EA revises the involvement of the judiciary in the process of administration in a number of ways.[359] In some respects, judicial super-vision is weakened – as over the appointment process, where Schedule

[356] See e.g. J. Day and P. Taylor, 'Financial Distress in Small Firms: The Role Played by Debt Covenants and Other Monitoring Devices' [2001] Ins. Law. 97.

[357] See e.g. Gilson, 'Bankruptcy, Boards, Banks and Blockholders', p. 367.

[358] Ibid., pp. 380–5. See also D. Baird and R. Rasmussen, 'The End of Bankruptcy' (2003) 55 Stanford L Rev. 751, 784–5. On the role of turnaround specialists in insolvency see V. Finch, 'Doctoring in the Shadows of Insolvency' [2005] JBL 690 and ch. 5 above.

[359] On the role of the judiciary in relation to the 'new' administration see also Armour and Mokal, 'Reforming the Governance of Corporate Rescue'; Finch, 'Re-invigorating Rescue' and 'Control and Co-ordination in Corporate Rescue'.

B1, paragraphs 14 and 22 involve a dramatic shift to out-of-court activity. Holders of qualifying floating charges as well as the company and its directors are able to appoint an administrator without going to court by filing a notice of appointment accompanied by a statement from the identified administrator that he consents to the appointment and that, in his opinion, the purpose of the administration is reasonably likely to be achieved.[360] The route to appointment of an administrator via court order is retained by paragraph 10 of Schedule B1 which requires an administration application to court by either the company, its directors or one or more creditors.[361]

On some issues, however, the courts are given new areas of judgement by the EA. Paragraph 13(1)(e) of Schedule B1 now empowers the court to treat an application for administration as a winding-up petition, carrying associated winding-up powers. The court is thus given a wide discretion to make the order it thinks most appropriate and it is likely to treat the application as a winding-up petition if the company is revealed to be hopelessly insolvent and the interests of creditors as a whole require an immediate investigation of its affairs by a liquidator and if this consideration outweighs any likely advantage to be achieved by realisation of assets in administration.[362]

Another area in which there is at least the potential for considerable judicial input is in reviewing the exercise of the administrator's powers as deployed in pursuit of the Schedule B1 paragraph 3 objectives. As noted above, a central issue here is whether the administrator should act to rescue the company as a going concern (paragraph 3(1)(a)); to achieve a better result than on winding up for creditors as a whole (paragraph 3(1)(b)); or to realise property in order to make a distribution to one or more secured or preferential creditors (paragraph 3(1)(c)). Selecting between these objectives is governed by paragraph 3(3), which is phrased in subjective terms and, to repeat, states that the administrator *must* act to rescue the company as a going concern unless he *thinks* either that this

---

[360] The company or its directors will also need to declare that the company is or is likely to become unable to pay its debts as a precondition to the appointment of an administrator. This contrasts with the holder of the qualifying floating charge who is not required to demonstrate this inability or likely inability: see pp. 381–2 above. On inability to pay debts and definitions of insolvency see ch. 4 above.

[361] The company has to be or be likely to become unable to pay its debts and the court must be satisfied that the administration order is reasonably likely to achieve the purpose of administration: Sch. B1, para. 11(b).

[362] The court may also make an interim order to restrict the exercise of directorial powers or to make these subject to supervision by an IP or the court (paras. 13(3)(a) and (b)).

course is not reasonably practicable or that a better result for creditors as a whole can be achieved by pursuing the second of the listed objectives.[363] Paragraph 3(2) overlays a general duty on the administrator to perform his functions in the interests of the company's creditors as a whole.[364] The administrator, moreover, is subject to a duty, under paragraph 4, to perform his functions as quickly and efficiently as is reasonably practicable. Under paragraph 74(1) a creditor or member can challenge the administrator by claiming that he is acting or has acted or proposes to act so as to harm their interests unfairly. Paragraph 74(2) allows the same parties to mount a challenge on the grounds that the administrator is not performing his functions as quickly or as efficiently as is reasonably practicable.[365]

Do these provisions offer the judges an opportunity to render administrators accountable through the exercise of energetic supervision? It would appear that the subjective phrasing of paragraph 3(3) (which was inserted late in the passage of the Enterprise Bill through Parliament) evidences a Government intention that administrators' business judgements should not be interfered with lightly by the courts and not without evidence of irrationality.[366] Both Lord Hoffmann and Sir Gavin Lightman have stated extrajudicially that such subjective phrasing

---

[363] On the use of 'thinks' see M. Simmons, 'Some Reflections on Administrations, Crown Preference and Ring Fenced Sums in the Enterprise Act' [2004] JBL 423, 426–8.

[364] For arguments that this means that administrators should act to maximise 'total expected net recoveries' see Armour and Mokal, 'Reforming the Governance of Corporate Rescue', pp. 46–7.

[365] As has been noted, misfeasance actions (by, *inter alia*, a creditor) can be brought against administrators (or purported administrators) under para. 75 and the company does not have to be in liquidation for such an action to be commenced. On administrators owing no general common law duty of care in relation to their conduct of the administration to unsecured creditors see *Kyrris* v. *Oldham* [2004] BCC 111 (CA) and on duties of care to the company see *Re Charnley Davies Ltd (No. 2)* [1990] BCLC 760 where Millett J noted that the distinction between 'misconduct' and 'unfairly prejudicial management' does not lie in the particular acts or omissions of which the complaint is made but in the nature of the complaint and the remedy necessary to meet it: p. 783. As noted above, there is, to date, a 'conspicuous' absence of case law where administrators have been sued for breach of duty: see Keay and Walton, *Insolvency Law*, p. 118. This situation is unlikely to pertain as administration takes over from administrative receivership and actions under para. 75 for breach of equitable or common law duties become more frequent.

[366] See Simmons, 'Some Reflections', pp. 427–8; Mokal and Armour, 'New UK Corporate Rescue Procedure', p. 138; HL Debates, 21 October 2002, vol. 391, col. 1101 (on the Government's expectation that the courts will review the rationality of the administrator's decision).

makes it virtually impossible for a court to interfere with the administrators' commercial judgements provided that they are made in good faith,[367] and, as noted above, the cases of *Re Transbus International Ltd*[368] and *Re Ballast plc*[369] support the view that the courts are content to defer to the judgements of administrators.

It should be noted, however, that the paragraph 3(2) duty to act in the interests of the company's creditors as a whole is not similarly phrased in subjective terms – the obligation is to act objectively in pursuit of such interests, not in a manner that the administrator *thinks* is in the interests of creditors as a whole. The resultant tension between the subjectivity of paragraph 3(3) and the objectivity of paragraph 3(2) may open the way for judicial intervention. Thus a party challenging an administrator's decision to act in pursuit of a better than winding-up result for creditors (under paragraph 3(1)(b)) rather than a going-concern rescue (paragraph 3(1)(a)) not only would be able to contest the administrator's subjective estimation of what was reasonably practicable or in the interests of creditors as a whole but would be able to take issue on the grounds that the course chosen was not in fact in the interests of creditors as a whole.[370] There is a similar combination of subjective and objective elements in paragraph 3(4) which empowers the administrator to realise property for distribution to secured or preferential creditors (paragraph 3(1)(c)) if he *thinks* it is not reasonably practicable to achieve either of the paragraph 3(1)(a) or 3(1)(b) objectives *and* 'he does not unnecessarily harm the interests of the creditors of the company as a whole' (paragraph 3(4)(b)).[371] These provisions are liable to come into play when an administrator might have a choice of ways to realise assets, one of which involves a quick break-up sale, payment of the floating charge

[367] See Swain, 'Move Towards a Stakeholder Society'; Editorial (2002) IL&P 121–2. See also Insolvency Service Guide, para. 4.1.6 and DTI Explanatory Notes, para. 648 which suggest that the court will only interfere if bad faith can be established or the decision was one that no reasonable administrator would have taken. On the facilitative attitude of the courts see Walters, 'Corporate Restructuring under Sch. B1'.

[368] [2004] 1 WLR 2654, [2004] BCC 401.   [369] [2005] 1 WLR 1928, [2005] BCC 96.

[370] Mokal and Armour, 'New UK Corporate Rescue Procedure', p 137.

[371] See Simmons, 'Some Reflections'; Simmons, 'Enterprise Act and Plain English' (2004) 17 *Insolvency Intelligence* 76 (considering the use of the words 'thinks' and 'harm' in the statutory provisions). See also *Unidare plc* v. *Cohen* [2006] 2 WLR 974 and Lewison J's reasoning (at p. 991) on the administrator's 'thinking' apropos Sch. B1, para. 83, discussed by Lightman and Moss, *Law of Administrators*, pp. 251–2; L. C. Ho, 'Connected Persons and Administrators' Duty to Think: *Unidare* v. *Cohen*' [2005] JIBLR 606.

holder's debt and a low return to unsecured creditors, and the other of which involves greater delay, more considered marketing and a higher return to unsecured creditors after the debt secured by the floating charge has been paid.

The status of the administrator as an officer of the court[372] means that, in addition to being expected to act fairly and honourably, the courts may potentially treat administrators' activities as reviewable on the usual public law grounds of illegality, irrationality and procedural impropriety.[373] As an alternative to judicial review on public law grounds, it has been argued that 'the courts will draw on the case law providing substance to the rationality test in the context of other fiduciary relationships'.[374]

Even, accordingly, where the subjective phrasing of paragraph 3(3) is used, the administrator may be open to attack on 'irrationality' grounds where he fails to take a relevant consideration into account in making a decision or takes into account an irrelevant consideration. The potential role for the courts is, accordingly, to rule on whether, in considering different possible courses of action (for example, to aim for rescue as a going concern or to achieve a better than winding-up outcome; or to realise property and distribute to secured or preferential creditors), the administrator has taken relevant factors into account, has avoided reference to irrelevant factors and has avoided taking actions that are so unreasonable that no reasonable administrator would take them.[375] For an administrator subject to such potential review, this means that care should be taken to make it clear on the record that all creditors' interests

---

[372] Sch. B1, para. 5; *Ex parte James* (1874) 9 Ch App 609; D. Milman, 'A Question of Honour' [2000] Ins. Law. 247.

[373] See Lord Diplock in *Council of Civil Service Unions* v. *Minister for the Civil Service* [1985] AC 374, 411–14. On the status of a decision- or policy-maker as 'public' for the purposes of judicial review see e.g. *R* v. *Panel on Takeovers and Mergers ex parte Datafin plc* [1987] QB 815; M. Beloff, 'Judicial Review – 2001: A Prophetic Odyssey' (1995) 58 MLR 143.

[374] See Mokal and Armour, 'New UK Corporate Rescue Procedure', pp. 137–8. The duty to act rationally has its roots in the law governing fiduciaries and can be seen as analogous to the public law concept of reasonableness: see Lightman and Moss, *Law of Administrators*, p. 246. Here the tests applied to trustees, according to the rule in *Re Hasting-Bass* [1975] Ch 25, are similar to those applied to public bodies according to *Associated Provincial Picture Houses Ltd* v. *Wednesbury Corporation* [1948] 1 KB 223. On the rule in *Hasting-Bass* see *Stannard* v. *Fisons Pensions Trust Ltd* [1992] IRLR 27 (trustees were bound to give properly informed consideration to the value of a trust fund in calculating the just and equitable level of funds required to be transferred).

[375] *Associated Provincial Picture Houses Ltd* v. *Wednesbury Corporation* [1948] 1 KB 223.

have been taken into account in assessing the array of possible actions on the basis of the information that is reasonably to be expected to be assessed. This will be central to the administrators showing that they have acted in accordance with their duty and have identified the relevant considerations and used all proper care and diligence in obtaining advice.[376] The administrator, moreover, is obliged[377] (when making a statement setting out proposals for achieving the purposes of administration) to *explain* why he thinks the objective mentioned in paragraph 3(1)(a) or 3(1)(b) cannot be achieved. Administrators, accordingly, should be prepared to disclose their proposals and reasons for action.[378]

The above considerations suggest that the judges, if inclined, could boost the accountability of administrators by exercising intensive review over administrators' activities. Whether they will be so inclined is a moot point. On one view, the judges are likely to prove reluctant to engage in interventions that amount to second-guessing the commercial judgements of administrators[379] or, when thinking in public law terms, to do other than defer to the judgements of those actors to whom Parliament has entrusted specialised functions.[380]

In support of this view, it might be argued that the judges have shown themselves to be slow to second-guess directors on issues involved in wrongful trading (which involves objective and subjective elements)[381] and that consistency should produce a similar judicial reluctance regarding administrators. There are, however, a number of differences to bear in mind between the parties and roles involved in the comparison. Administrators are quasi-public officials. Directors inhabit the realms of private law. The consequences of intervention are also different. Reviewing an administrator's action under paragraph 74 is most likely to result in the court making an order to regulate the administrator's

---

[376] Lightman J in *Re Barr's Settlement Trusts* [2003] Ch 409; G. Lightman – see Editorial (2002) IL&P 121, 122.

[377] Para. 49(2)(b).

[378] I.e. at creditors' meetings, if under a duty to call them (see para. 52(1) and (2)).

[379] See Swain, 'Move Towards a Stakeholder Society'; Editorial, (2002) IL&P 121.

[380] See *R* v. *Independent Television Commission, ex parte TSW Broadcasting Ltd* [1996] EMLR 291 (the House of Lords stated that courts would be most reluctant to second-guess regulatory bodies on substantive issues) but *cf. Mercury Communications Ltd* v. *Director General of Telecommunications* [1996] 1 All ER 575 (HL) – criticised in A. McHarg, 'Regulation as a Private Law Function' [1995] PL 539. On judicial reluctance to second-guess decisions on budgetary allocation see *R* v. *Cambridge Health Authority ex parte B* [1995] 2 All ER 129, 137.

[381] See Insolvency Act 1986 s. 214(4)(a) and (b); see also ch. 16 below.

exercise of his functions or to vary procedures adopted. This can be seen as less dramatic than making a finding of wrongful trading which may involve a director in substantial personal liability and arguably a degree of stigma.[382] For both these reasons, it might be contended that the courts will be more inclined to interfere with administrators' actions under paragraph 74 challenges than they would be to second-guess directorial behaviour for the purposes of wrongful trading.

If, however, it is assumed, for the moment, that the courts will exert a degree of control over administrators, how might they best use that control to serve the interests of rescue? One way to do this would be to exercise their powers so as to enhance expertly and efficiently co-ordinated actions between the various actors involved in a rescue process – while, of course, protecting the legal interests of those actors and holding the ring fairly between them. When seeking to enhance such co-ordination, furthermore, the judges might have in mind the need for key rescue decisions and actions to be based on good information, to incorporate sound judgements and to be implemented in a timely fashion.

On the generation of a good information base, the judicial role is likely to come into play when the administrator's duty to garner and consider information from different parties is placed at issue. That administrator will be obliged, *inter alia*, to take all relevant considerations into account when devising a policy or making a decision.[383] The stance of the pro-rescue judiciary might be to insist that administrators make all reasonable attempts to secure inputs from all of those actors who are well placed to contribute information relevant to the pursuit of the administrator's statutory objectives. The administrator, accordingly, would be obliged to consult with, and take into account, the representations of such parties as directors, banks, unsecured creditors and any others who can provide relevant information. Such a judicial stance might demand of administrators that they do more than provide an *opportunity* for various actors to participate in the administration process – it might call for administrators actively to take all reasonable steps to seek out relevant information and to consider this.

It has, however, been stressed above that inclusive processes involve considerable dangers of inefficiency and losses of expertise through stultification, delay and confusion. Bearing this in mind, the judges

---

[382] See ch. 16 below.

[383] See e.g. *Associated Provincial Picture Houses* v. *Wednesbury Corporation* [1948] 1 KB 223; *Council of Civil Service Unions* v. *Minister for the Civil Service* [1985] AC 374.

might make it clear in their decisions that administrators only have to seek out information and process it in so far as this is reasonable within the practical constraints of time and resourcing that they are faced with.[384] In subjecting administrators to reasonableness-testing, accordingly, the judges should take the view that challenges to administrators' decisions will only be successful where they have been shown clearly to have gone beyond the bounds of reasonableness (for example by refusing to receive inputs from parties where patently relevant information is involved). The general stance of the judiciary should be to ensure accountability and fairness through protecting the procedural rights of the various parties but, above all else, to further efficiency and expertise by shielding administrators from legal delays and second-guessing and to do so sufficiently to allow them to pursue their statutory objectives expeditiously. If this is not done the danger is that the administration process will prove generally too slow-moving and indecisive ever to serve the interests of rescue. The stance described may demand that the judges show a degree of deference to the administrators' judgements on such matters as whether the need for action means that they should not carry out further investigations and consultations.

On the encouragement of sound judgements, this will, to a degree, be served by judicial actions to encourage expertise by ensuring that relevant information is considered and irrelevant matters are not taken into account. Closely related to the exclusion of irrelevancies is, moreover, protection against unfairness through bias and here it might be suggested that the judiciary should be ready to counter a number of predictable risks.

A first such risk is, as noted above, that banks holding qualifying floating charges and acting as potential suppliers of rescue funds will use their legal and financial muscle to induce administrators to act in their favour rather than in the interests of the body of creditors as a whole.[385] Manipulation of this kind may occur through open negotiations between bank and administrator but a second risk may be that such influence, or 'capture', may occur in less visible ways – as where administrators adopt strategies that are excessively low risk and do so for fear of offending powerful actors, such as banks, who might contest their actions.

---

[384] See the references to reasonableness in the para. 4 duty to perform functions as quickly and efficiently as is reasonably practicable.

[385] That is on 'he who pays the piper calls the tune' principles: see Swain, 'Move Towards a Stakeholder Society'.

The judiciary, however, may face a difficult task in exercising review so as to control the above kinds of manipulation or bias. It is one thing to ensure that administrators adopt the fair and correct procedures, and consider the relevant matters and exclude irrelevant factors, it is another to assess whether the substantive strategies or actions effected by administrators are calculated, or likely, to involve a favouring of a certain creditor or class of creditors. It is true that the paragraph 3(2) duty to act in the interests of the company's creditors is, as noted, objectively phrased, but ruling against an administrator under this paragraph demands, first, that the court is prepared to make a judgement on business risks and, second, that the court is willing to substitute its own judgement for that of the administrator.

What, then, would a rescue-friendly judicial stance look like when faced with this dilemma – whether to pursue fairness by protecting weaker creditor interests or to promote efficiency by leaving administrators free enough in their judgements to be able to act expeditiously? The analysis here suggests that the role of the judge should be to exercise their review powers so as to maximise the extent to which administrators are induced to serve the interests of all creditors, and to do so by counterbalancing those risks of bias that are likely within the post-EA regime. That regime places an IP in power and so the dangers of shareholder manipulation that are encountered in DIP systems are, as noted above, replaced by risks of bank manipulation. The aim of the judiciary, accordingly, can be envisaged as ensuring that the administrator performs on a level playing field – and they can do so by offering a counter-balance to the administrator's natural inclination to err in favour of the banks. That counter-balance can be seen in the shape of the prospect of judicial interference where a bias is sufficiently grave to take the administrator out of his 'protected' area of judgement and to constitute a patent breach of paragraph 3(2).

Turning to the judges' role in ensuring that actions and decisions are taken in a timely fashion, a first contribution, as indicated, is judicial action to ensure that the administrator's ability to act quickly is not prejudiced by excessive legal attack and second-guessing. A second judicial task is to do what can be done to ensure that directors do not delay the instigation of insolvency processes unduly. It was noted above that disincentives to delay, through wrongful trading or disqualification provisions,[386] may be of dubious value and, accordingly, the courts might

---

[386] See IA 1986 s. 214; CDDA 1986; see also ch. 16 below.

do all that they can to reassure directors that entering administration under a PIP regime will not necessarily rule out their inputting into decisions about the future of the company or business. This can be done, as suggested above, by ensuring that administrators gather and consider all information relevant to the company's future when making decisions and strategies or taking actions.

Conclusions

The Enterprise Act 2002 succeeded in placing administration at the heart of efforts to deal with companies in distress. There is work to be done, however, to make this process the finished product with regard to cost-effectiveness, accountability, fairness and conduciveness to the exercise of informed and expert judgements. There is scope, for instance, for further procedural streamlining in order to lower costs.

Current arrangements and approaches leave a number of questions to be resolved. It remains to be seen whether the judgements of administrators will be enhanced by the inclusiveness of the administration process or whether that inclusiveness will operate within tight scheduling so as to stifle expertise. Further residual issues are whether lenders will retreat from the use of administration and increasingly secure loans in ways that revive other procedures such as the LPA receivership; whether the use of administration as a substitute for liquidation needs to be controlled further; and whether the EA reforms will lead to a fragmentation of credit arrangements that makes rescues excessively difficult.

On this last issue, a central question is whether a point will be arrived at when it is necessary, as suggested by the EHYA, to restrict the rights of certain parties in a more radical fashion so as to render administration more responsive to corporate crises. A related question is whether there is, or will soon come, a need for a new approach to super-priority funding in order to incentivise the supply of rescue funds appropriately.

Co-ordination between administrators, directors and others will remain an issue within administration and attention may have to be paid to the propensity of the regime to encourage directors both to seek appropriate and timely help from outsiders and to assist the administrators in carrying out the latter's functions. Whether the complexities of the paragraph 3 statement of administrators' objectives will unduly inhibit co-operation and information supplies is a matter for continued monitoring and much may depend here on the way that the courts oversee the administrator's duty to pursue those objectives and to serve the interests of all creditors.

As for the judges, the indications are that they are sympathetic to the development of administration as a streamlined tool of rescue. They have sown the seeds for a version of super-priority lending and have shown that they are inclined to defer to the business judgements of administrators. In other respects, though, the implications of the judges' decisions are less certain. The *Spectrum Plus* case left issues hanging concerning the control that is necessary if charges over book debts are to be deemed fixed rather than floating. It also remains to be seen whether *Spectrum Plus* (together with the prescribed part provisions of the EA 2002) will increase the fragmentation of credit to a degree that significantly impedes rescue. A further worry may be whether giving priority to non-domestic rates during the administration – as in *Exeter City/ Trident* – will prove a 'disaster' for rescue in spite of recent legislative responses. The judges, as well as the variety of other actors involved with administration, will have to rise to a number of challenges if administration is to realise its full potential as a rescue and reorganisation process.

10

Pre-packaged administrations

In chapter 6 it was argued that, over recent years, responses to corporate troubles have increasingly tended to be made before any final crisis precipitates formal action. One form of anticipatory action is the pre-packaged administration. This is a device that has been encountered on the UK insolvency scene since the mid-1980s but which has grown in use more recently. It is a device that some commentators herald as a freshly effective mechanism for furthering rescue objectives and others see as a means by which powerful players can bypass carefully constructed statutory protections.[1]

The 'pre-pack' is a process in which a troubled company and its creditors conclude an agreement in advance of statutory administration procedures.[2] This has the effect of establishing a deal in advance of the appointment of an administrator and it allows statutory procedures to be implemented at maximum speed. The danger most commonly pointed to is that such speedy implementations of *faits accomplis* will tend to ride roughshod over the procedural and substantive interests of less powerful creditors.

This chapter looks at the development of the pre-pack, identifies the issues raised by this device, and considers how insolvency law might respond to the burgeoning popularity of such agreements. A particular

---

[1] See e.g. S. Harris, 'The Decision to Pre-pack' (2004) *Recovery* (Winter) 26; M. Ellis, 'The Thin Line in the Sand' (2006) *Recovery* (Spring) 3; J. Moulton, 'The Uncomfortable Edge of Propriety – Pre-packs or Just Stitch-ups?' (2005) *Recovery* (Autumn) 2; S. Frisby, *A Preliminary Analysis of Pre-packaged Administrations: Report to R3 – The Association of Business Recovery Professionals* (R3, London, August 2007) ('Frisby, *R3 Analysis*'); L. Qi, 'The Rise of Pre-packaged Corporate Rescue on Both Sides of the Atlantic' (2007) 20 *Insolvency Intelligence* 129; P. Walton, 'Pre-packaged Administrations – Trick or Treat?' (2006) 19 *Insolvency Intelligence* 113; V. Finch, 'Pre-packaged Administrations: Bargains in the Shadow of Insolvency or Shadowy Bargains?' [2006] JBL 568 (upon which this chapter builds).

[2] Pre-packs have historically been used in relation to receiverships but are increasingly employed in conjunction with administrations. This chapter focuses on administration-related pre-packs.

concern will be whether the advent of the pre-pack calls for a rethinking of current approaches to the protection of those interests that are affected by corporate troubles.

The rise of the pre-pack

In the United States, pre-packaged bankruptcy filings first emerged in the mid-1980s and rapidly grew in popularity in the early 1990s, so that by 1993 over 20 per cent of all public bankruptcies were pre-packaged.[3] A common arrangement involves a troubled company seeking to trade debt for equity in order to shed the burdens of onerous interest payments. In order to make a pre-pack work the debtor will require the agreement to an arrangement of a significant majority of creditors (often around 90 per cent). The company then makes a Chapter 11 filing. The advantage gained is that, in a pre-pack plan, negotiations, distributions of disclosure statements and voting all take place before the bankruptcy case is filed in court.[4] The debtor typically files not only a petition but also a plan and a disclosure statement. Such *ex ante* approval from creditors often allows the court to hold a single hearing to determine the adequacy of pre-petition disclosure and whether the plan should be confirmed. As a result, the company will frequently emerge from statutory proceedings quickly (sometimes in thirty to thirty-five days rather than years, as is common in conventional Chapter 11 proceedings).[5]

---

[3] See *Managing Credit, Receivables and Collections*, (2003) March issue, p. 1. In 1995 a quarter of all Chapter 11 cases of public corporations involved a pre-pack: see V. Vilaplana, 'A Pre-pack Bankruptcy Primer' (1998) 44 *The Practical Lawyer* 33. The pre-pack has been said to be the single most important development in US corporate bankruptcy practice in recent years, so that it has now become routine and the strategy of choice for corporations with complicated financial structures: see D. A. Skeel, *Debt's Dominion* (Princeton University Press, Princeton, 2001), quoted in P. Cranston (Eversheds LLP), 'Pre-packaged Business Disposals: White Knight or Thief in the Night?', presentation to ILA Annual Conference, Bath, 18 March 2006.

[4] See Vilaplana, 'Pre-pack Bankruptcy Primer'; M. Plevin, R. Ebert and L. Epley, 'Pre-packaged Asbestos Bankruptcies: A Flawed Solution' (2002) 44 South Texas L Rev. 883, 888.

[5] The US Bankruptcy Code Chapter 11 is a reorganisation procedure whose policy objective is strongly oriented to the avoidance of the social costs of liquidation and the retention of the corporate operation as a going concern. On Chapter 11 generally see ch. 6 above; R. Broude, 'How the Rescue Culture Came to the United States and the Myths that Surround Chapter 11' (2001) 16 IL&P 194. Note, however, that the Bankruptcy Abuse Prevention and Consumer Protection Act 2005 (BAPCPA) has tightened up timescales regarding Chapter 11 plans: see revised s. 1121(d) of the Bankruptcy Code (capping the debtor's exclusive right to file a plan at eighteen months and the exclusive

Adverse and lengthy negotiations with creditors are often avoided and professional fees are far less than would be the case without the pre-pack. In many instances, argue advocates of pre-packs, employees' jobs will be protected and trade creditors will be paid in full. Pre-packs, moreover, can be agreed long before financial difficulties are encountered. This means that the company has the resources to continue operating in an effective manner.

In the UK, pre-packaging will typically involve a pre-agreed restructuring deal and the appointment of an office holder – either an administrator or an administrative receiver.[6] This individual will then execute the restructuring transaction on behalf of the troubled company.[7] A corporate restructuring director at Ernst & Young LLP has summarised the appeal of the pre-pack: 'In a pre-pack the restructuring process is condensed and offers the secured creditors a high level of control and certainty, making it a very attractive alternative to any protracted formal insolvency process.'[8]

The pre-pack has grown in popularity in the UK in parallel with the growth in 'live side' or 'pre-insolvency' approaches to corporate troubles.[9] It has come to serve an important role in contingency and recovery planning as 'the divide between informal and formal [insolvency] continues to blur'.[10] The process has accelerated in use, most

right to solicit acceptances to the plan at twenty months). On BAPCPA see further A. Kornberg, 'The Bankruptcy Abuse Prevention and Consumer Protection Act of 2005 – A Primer on Those Changes Affecting Business Bankruptcies' (2006) 3 *International Corporate Rescue* 33.

[6] See e.g. Harris, 'Decision to Pre-pack'. The Enterprise Act 2002 reforms prohibit (subject to stated exceptions) the use of administrative receivership by the holders of qualifying floating charges: see now ss. 72B–72G of the Insolvency Act 1986. Transactions that predate the implementation of EA 2002 still allow holders of qualifying floating charges both to appoint administrative receivers and to block the appointment of an administrator: see ch. 8 above.

[7] The pre-pack may be instituted and driven by a variety of parties: senior debt providers; Insolvency Practitioners (IPs) and advisers to distressed companies; specialist funds; bargain hunters; MBO teams; or groups/companies themselves: see Cranston, 'Pre-packaged Business Disposals'.

[8] Harris, 'Decision to Pre-pack', p. 27.

[9] See chs. 6 and 7 above. Katz and Mumford found that in 2004, a pre-pack was involved in 44 per cent of cases in which rescue was an objective of proposals for an administration: see A. Katz and M. Mumford, *Report to the Insolvency Service: Study of Administration Cases* (Insolvency Service, London, 2006). Orbis, the council house cleaner listed on AIM, is an example of a recent pre-packaged administration: see P. Davies, H. Sender and C. Hughes, 'Management Rescue Orbis in "Pre-pack" Sale', *Financial Times*, 5 February 2008.

[10] Harris, 'Decision to Pre-pack', p. 26.

notably in relation to post-Enterprise Act administrations.[11] It was estimated in 2006–7 that at least a third and perhaps half of all going concern sales during an administration involved a pre-pack.[12]

Advantages and concerns

Efficiency

As indicated above, the proponents of pre-packs would point to a number of advantages produced by the device.[13] As far as efficiency is concerned, pre-packs are said to be rescue-efficient in so far as they offer low-cost and speedy routes to recovery, they often involve repaying trade creditors in full, they keep legal and other professional costs low[14] and they allow firms to implement recovery plans before they lose the funding that allows turnarounds to be executed. It might also be claimed that pre-packs are associated with better records of job preservation than business sales without pre-packs.[15] The pre-pack offers support to incumbent management and provides a way to retain key employees who might leave the company if not confident that a sale can be agreed in the short to medium term – a step that is often essential if value is to be maximised.[16] A pre-pack may prove particularly useful if the

[11] S Frisby, 'Unpacking Pre-packs: The Story So Far' (2007) *Recovery* (Autumn) 25.

[12] See S. Davies QC, 'Pre-pack – He Who Pays the Piper Calls the Tune' (2006) *Recovery* (Summer) 16 at 17. Frisby, *R3 Analysis* (p. 15), suggests a figure of 35.5 per cent, but Frisby quotes estimates elicited in interview at from 50 per cent to 80 per cent.

[13] See e.g. Vilaplana, 'Pre-pack Bankruptcy Primer', pp. 34–5.

[14] Vilaplana cites an example in which Anglo Energy filed twice for Chapter 11 protection. The cost with a pre-pack was $1 million, without $12 million: see ibid., p. 34. See also Walton, 'Trick or Treat?'; J. Ayer, M. Bernstein and J. Friedland, 'Chapter 11 – "101": Out of Court Workouts, Pre-packs and Pre-arranged Cases: A Primer' (2005) 24 *American Bankruptcy Institute Journal* (April).

[15] The Frisby *R3 Analysis* suggests that business sales involve 100 per cent transfers of staff in 65 per cent of all cases but that pre-packs save all staff in 92 per cent of cases. Whether this superior performance is due to the process used or because pre-packs tend to be used where prospects of rescue are brightest is a separate issue. It can be argued that there are not the opportunities for opportunistic lay-offs of workers in a pre-pack that exist in a straight administration (which will give more scope for dismissals that will not be deemed legally unfair): see Frisby, *R3 Analysis*, p. 72. The relative success of the pre-pack in preserving jobs in the short term may, however, have to be set against the higher subsequent failure rates of pre-packs as compared to business sales (39 per cent failure compared to 35 per cent).

[16] Cranston, 'Pre-packaged Business Disposals'; D. Flynn, 'Pre-pack Administrations – A Regulatory Perspective' (2006) *Recovery* (Summer) 3; Frisby, *R3 Analysis* notes (p. 32) that staff retention figured strongly in reasons for using a pre-pack. Other cited reasons included: protecting book debt collections; ensuring continuity of insurance cover or a contract; and preserving goodwill.

volume of creditors makes negotiations impractical or if a significant minority of these are liable to hold the majority to ransom in the hope of extracting an improved return for themselves. The High Court has, moreover, upheld a pre-packed sale of a solicitors' business entering administration, in the face of opposition from the major creditor, on the grounds that the pre-packaged sale minimised disruption to clients and was the best way to protect jobs.[17]

It has also been argued that pre-packs usefully help to counter the holdout problems associated with the growth of 'vulture funds'.[18] Holders of such funds are prone to engage in holdouts in the hope of a better deal since they purchased their claims at a deep discount. A pre-pack in the USA allows such holdouts to be defeated since US law provides that a plan of reorganisation will bind dissidents so long as two-thirds in amount and more than half in number of those voting have approved the plan.[19]

The speed of the pre-pack process may be particularly valuable in sectors or businesses where a protracted, public restructuring would dramatically affect corporate value – as, for instance, in a regulated sector (where possibilities of retaining licences, franchises and other valued positions may be affected) or where a business is built on human rather than physical assets (where there are dangers that the best staff will be lost to competitors), or where a brand or portfolio would be damaged by adverse publicity or public uncertainty.[20] The pre-pack offers the prospect of a seamless transition to turnaround that minimises disruption and reduces the risks of declines in markets, reputations, assets or business partner relationships.[21] It has also been suggested that the

---

[17] *DKLL Solicitors* v. *HM Revenue & Customs* [2007] BCC 908.

[18] Vilaplana, 'Pre-pack Bankruptcy Primer'. On 'vulture funds' and the stress that the fragmentation and globalisation of credit imposes on informal processes such as the bank-controlled 'London Approach' see ch. 7 above; J. Flood, 'The Vultures Fly East: The Creation and Globalisation of the Distressed Debt Market' in D. Nelken and J. Feast (eds.), *Adapting Legal Cultures* (Hart, Oxford, 2001) p. 257.

[19] See US Bankruptcy Code s. 1126: in the USA pre-packs are voted on, while in the UK the pre-pack involves no formal voting arrangement.

[20] Harris, 'Decision to Pre-pack', p. 27; Davies, 'Pre-pack – He Who Pays the Piper Calls the Tune', p. 16. The very announcement of insolvency proceedings usually provokes a precipitous decline in goodwill: see G. Meeks and J. G. Meeks, 'A Gouldian View of Corporate Failure in the Process of Economic Natural Selection' (Mimeo, Centre for Business Research, University of Cambridge, 2002).

[21] Cranston, 'Pre-packaged Business Disposals'. On survival rates a comparison of administration business sales and administration pre-packs reveals that the latter are slightly more likely to fail – but it is said to be difficult to draw a certain conclusion that survival rates differ significantly: see Frisby, *R3 Analysis*, pp. 76–7.

Enterprise Act 2002 significantly encouraged the use of pre-packs by introducing the streamlined system of out-of-court routes into administration and simpler means of exiting administration.[22] Martin Ellis, a partner at Grant Thornton, has argued that five reasons underpin the steady growth in popularity of pre-packs:[23]

- The increased incidence of consignment stocks and valid reservations of ownership claims.
- The impact of TUPE[24] and the risk that a sale may not ultimately be achievable.
- Demands for ransom payments by monopoly suppliers.
- Increased professional costs.
- The inherent risks of trading.

Sceptics, however, may worry that pre-packs will not always deliver the above goods and may prove less cost-effective than proponents would suggest. A concern that has been voiced in the USA[25] relates to cost-effectiveness and is that, from the debtor's point of view, the pre-pack may involve considerable legal risks. A bankruptcy court, for instance, may find a disclosure statement inadequate. If this happens, the statement will have to be amended or redistributed. The debtor will then have to re-solicit acceptances and this may produce lengthy delays in confirmation.[26] An opportunity to vote will have to be offered or else such claimants may be well placed to mount a legal challenge to the pre-pack. In either case, delays, uncertainties and additional expenses will be generated. Where objectors delay or derail the proposed plan, the anticipated benefits of the pre-pack are liable to be lost.[27]

Such worries are reinforced by evidence from other sources. In LoPucki and Doherty's study of 1991–6 reorganisations in, *inter alia*, Delaware and New York (covering ninety-eight reorganisations), the

---

[22] See Flynn, 'Pre-pack Administrations'. See also ch. 9 above.

[23] Ellis, 'Thin Line in the Sand'.

[24] See the Transfer of Undertakings (Protection of Employment) Regulations 2006 (SI 2006/246); J. McMullen, 'An Analysis of the Transfer of Undertakings (Protection of Employment) Regulations 2006' (2006) 35 *Industrial Law Journal* 113; see further ch. 17 below.

[25] See Plevin, Ebert and Epley, 'Pre-packaged Asbestos Bankruptcies', pp. 888–9.

[26] Ibid.; and see *In re City of Colorado Springs* 177 BR 684, 691 (Bankr. D. Colo. 1995).

[27] See Plevin, Ebert and Epley, 'Pre-packaged Asbestos Bankruptcies', who cite the instance of two asbestos industry pre-packs that failed to include the insurers whose policy proceeds were to fund the trust under the plan. The resulting litigation deprived the debtors of the benefits of the pre-pack (p. 889).

authors found that debtors who reorganised by way of pre-packs had lower post-bankruptcy earnings than those who reorganised without pre-packs.[28] By this measure, they suggested, 'pre-packaged organisations are more likely to fail than non pre-packaged organisations'.[29] The speed of pre-packs could also be exaggerated, argued LoPucki and Doherty. The evidence suggested that pre-packs were, at an average of 21.6 months, only 25 per cent shorter than traditional Chapter 11 cases (at 28.5 months).[30] Speed, moreover, inversely correlated with success in the LoPucki and Doherty study, which concluded: 'Faster reorganisations are significantly more likely to fail than slower ones.'[31]

As to the reasons for the higher failure rates of speedy or pre-packaged bankruptcies, LoPucki and Doherty admit that they can only guess – but they do surmise that this may be because such processes can stand in the way of parties coming to grips with the challenges that corporate troubles present:

> We speculate that at the core of this market failure is the parties' desire to appear to reorganise without in fact doing so. Effective reorganisation is unpleasant. Managers must at least acknowledge their past failures and perhaps also resign their positions. Creditors must accept substantial reductions in the amounts owed to them. The interests of shareholders must be finally and permanently extinguished ... But no party wants the firm to actually face up to its problems.[32]

Fairness and expertise

If the pre-pack procedure is compared to a normal Chapter 11 filing, it is more likely in a pre-pack that there will have been a failure to solicit relevant parties and to provide a voting opportunity to all persons asserting claims.[33] If there is an absence of such a chance of voting, this

---

[28] L. LoPucki and J. Doherty, 'Why are Delaware and New York Bankruptcy Reorganisations Failing?' (2002) 55 Vand. L Rev. 1933, 1972.

[29] Ibid.; Vilaplana, 'Pre-pack Bankruptcy Primer', p. 41, argues that pre-packs 'are not useful for companies that have fundamental problems such as major contractual disputes, asbestos problems or pension fund issues'. The usual pre-pack involves a basically healthy company that is over-leveraged.

[30] See E. Tashjian, R. Lease, J. McConnel et al., 'Pre-packs: An Empirical Analysis' (1996) 40 Journal of Financial Economics 135, 142.

[31] LoPucki and Doherty, 'Why are Delaware and New York Bankruptcy Reorganisations Failing?', p. 1976.

[32] Ibid., p. 2002.

[33] All persons whose claims are 'impaired' by the plan are entitled to vote on it: see Plevin, Ebert and Epley, 'Pre-packaged Asbestos Bankruptcies', p. 889.

raises concerns not only about the costs and uncertainties associated with potential challenges but also regarding procedural and substantive fairness. Plevin, Ebert and Epley, a trio of Washington, D.C. practitioners in bankruptcy, have written that the pre-pack bankruptcy is seen by many troubled companies as a panacea in the asbestos litigation world, but: 'Such bankruptcies have drawn rigorous objections by persons claiming that pre-packaged asbestos bankruptcies, as currently practiced, violate the Bankruptcy Code and Rules, improperly treat some claimants more favourably than others, and disregard the contractual rights of the insurers expected to fund the payment under the plan ...'[34]

In the UK also there have been similar worries about pre-packs.[35] One practitioner has argued that the rapid growth of pre-packs has given rise to 'unpleasant practices' in which directors and shareholders of troubled companies are offered ways to shed their creditors and buy back their businesses at very modest cost.[36] The danger, according to this argument, is one of unfairness in so far as administrators, banks and directors have strong incentives that may not serve all creditors well:

> The organising administrator has a clear conflict of interest as typically he wants to get the appointment and the management can influence that – such a pre-pack is a good idea for practice development for him and for advising lawyers.[37] It may suit a bank as it can allow it to participate in the equity going forward in a controlled way or provide it with an assured return potentially at the expense of other creditors. Administrators generally like helping banks.[38]

Stephen Davies QC has raised issues of expertise alongside that of fairness in arguing that a small number of 'professional bad apples' who operate via pre-packs facilitate phoenix trading: 'not withstanding the considerable antipathy of both the profession and the courts towards phoenix operations, insolvency sales to unscrupulous

---

[34] Ibid., p. 923.   [35] See Frisby, *R3 Analysis*, pp. 8–9.

[36] Moulton, 'Uncomfortable Edge of Propriety'. The typical pre-pack in the UK is said to involve an MBO: see Cranston, 'Pre-packaged Business Disposals'; A. Sakoui and S. O'Connor, 'Clampdown on use of Pre-Pack Rules', *Financial Times*, 31 December 2008.

[37] On fears of lack of objectivity on the part of those organising pre-packs see Davies, 'Pre-pack – He Who Pays the Piper Calls the Tune', p. 16; Moulton, 'Uncomfortable Edge of Propriety'.

[38] Davies, 'Pre-pack – He Who Pays the Piper Calls the Tune'.

management still occur and the pre-pack is the jemmy in the burglar's jacket'.[39]

As for the incidence of Newco being owned and controlled by the same people as Oldco, Frisby's 2007 study suggests that administration pre-packs involve a slightly higher proportion of sales to connected parties (59 per cent) than is the case with all business sales (52 per cent). The trend also seems to be towards more connected sales after the Enterprise Act. The figures for sales to connected parties in pre- and post-Enterprise Act administration pre-packs are 53 per cent and 62 per cent respectively.[40] These compare with a figure of 51 per cent in post-Enterprise Act administration business sales.[41] The post-transfer survival rates of businesses transferred to connected parties appear also to be lower than is the case in transfers to unconnected parties. The respective rates, in the case of sales, are 58 per cent to 71.9 per cent and, in the case of pre-packs, 51.4 per cent to 71.5 per cent.[42]

Critics who are concerned about the fairness of pre-packs are liable also to argue that, with such arrangements, the market will rarely have been properly tested,[43] some interested parties may not have been made

---

[39] Ibid., p. 17. See Insolvency Act 1986 s. 216: this section is aimed at countering the 'phoenix syndrome' – a term used to describe an abuse of the privilege of limited liability whereby a company would be put into receivership or voluntary liquidation at a time when it owed large sums to its unsecured creditors. The receiver (frequently appointed by a controlling shareholder who had himself taken a floating charge over the whole of the company's undertaking) would sell the entire business as a going concern at a knock-down price to a new company incorporated by the former directors of the defunct company. Thus, what was essentially the same company would rise phoenix-like from the ashes of the old and the business would be carried on by the same people in disregard of the claims of the first company's creditors, who effectively subsidised the 'birth' of the new company debt-free: see L. S. Sealy and D. Milman, *Annotated Guide to the Insolvency Legislation* (10th edn, Thomson/Sweet & Maxwell, London, 2007) vol. I. See ch. 16 below.

[40] Frisby, *R3 Analysis*, pp. 42–5.

[41] Frisby suggests that the movement towards sales to connected parties via pre-packs may be due to Enterprise Act changes in entry into administration and that director-led entry may be a driver: ibid.; see also ch. 9 above.

[42] Frisby, *R3 Analysis*, p. 79.

[43] On failure to market as a central worry see Flynn, 'Pre-pack Administrations', p. 3. Frisby's *R3 Analysis* (p. 49) states that in only 7.9 per cent of pre-packs was the company marketed, in comparison with a figure of 55.6 per cent for business sales without pre-packs. She argues (p. 38) that if the business has not been exposed to market forces 'the complete lack of control rights and an inadequate provision of information on the part of the practitioner to unsecured creditors effectively disables them from calling upon the practitioner to demonstrate that he has paid due regard to the statutory scheme for protecting their interests'.

aware of the sale[44] and the business may have been undersold.[45] Further objections are that certain creditors may have been left out of consultation processes so that they feel 'frustrated and impotent' when informed about events,[46] and the advisers may have been too aligned with certain interests – which may be those of well-placed creditors or involved managers.

What may make the position worse regarding fairness is that in the period before a pre-pack the directors may seek to build up stock at the expense of trade creditors – perhaps in anticipation of purchasing the business at an advantageous price from the administrator.[47] Often, it is alleged, the 'victims' of pre-packs are the general creditors who see assets sold at undervalue but have difficulty in proving this. Such victims, moreover, face a difficult choice: do they sue the company (with its empty pockets), the directors (who may have concealed their transactions) or the administrator (who is a well-informed repeat player)?[48]

As for fairness and substantive returns to creditors, the figures available indicate that returns to *all creditors*[49] are no less in pre-pack

---

[44] See Davies, 'Pre-pack – He Who Pays the Piper Calls the Tune'; S. Mason, 'Pre-packs from the Valuer's Perspective' (2006) *Recovery* (Summer) 19: Mason notes the role, in pre-packs, of specialist independent valuers of property, equipment and stock.

[45] See G. Rustling, 'Pre-packaged Sales via Insolvency Processes', *Barclays Bank Protocol* (Barclays, London, 10 November 2005), arguing that last-minute approaches to support a pre-pack are 'unlikely to demonstrate that best commercial value of a business is being achieved'.

[46] See Davies, 'Pre-pack – He Who Pays the Piper Calls the Tune', p. 16. On disenfranchisement being an issue that is not confined to pre-packs see Frisby, *R3 Analysis*, p. 35, who argues that considerations of speed and business continuity lead to considerable disenfranchisement in non-pre-pack business sales in administration. In *T&D Industries plc* [2000] 1 WLR 646, [2000] BCC 956 it was held (pre-Enterprise Act 2002) that an administrator had the power to sell the assets of a company prior to obtaining creditor approval – though the court stressed the importance of placing the proposals before creditors as soon as reasonably possible. See also *Re Transbus International Ltd* [2004] BCC 401 which also recognised that sometimes substantial actions have to be taken in administration without prior creditor approval: see S. Frisby, 'Judicial Sanction of Insolvency Pre-packs? *DKLL Solicitors* v. *HMRC* Considered' (2008) 27 *Company Law Newsletter* 1.

[47] See Flynn, 'Pre-pack Administrations', p. 3.

[48] Moulton, 'Uncomfortable Edge of Propriety', p. 3. On IPs and repeat player control of processes see e.g. S. Wheeler, 'Capital Fractionalised: The Role of Insolvency Practitioners in Asset Distribution' in M. Cain and C. B. Harrington (eds.), *Lawyers in a Post Modern World: Translation and Transgression* (Open University Press, Buckingham, 1994).

[49] Frisby, *R3 Analysis*, p. 50, puts pre-pack administration returns to all creditors at 22.7 per cent on average compared to 22.8 per cent for business sales without pre-packs.

administration cases than in administration business sales without pre-packs, but that average returns to secured creditors are considerably higher in administration pre-packs than in administration business sales (59.1 per cent to 27.5 per cent) and that unsecured creditors do twice as badly in administration pre-packs as in administration business sales (2 per cent to 4 per cent).[50] In post-Enterprise Act administration pre-packs the average return for unsecured creditors was only an eleventh of the return from post-Enterprise Act administration business sales.[51] Such results, it seems, support the contention that administration pre-packs favour secured creditors at the expense of unsecured creditors.[52]

Accountability and transparency

On the transparency of pre-packs, Frisby's 2007 study considered whether practitioners' reports on pre-packs disclosed sufficient information to creditors to allow them to determine whether their interests had been adequately protected.[53] The quality of such reports varied greatly but their most common omission was the identity of the purchaser. Most gave details of the consideration but the overall informative value was rated, disturbingly, as 'haphazard', with significant gaps in a number of cases such as 'to provoke suspicion and mistrust among creditors and unsecured creditors in particular'.[54] That said, Frisby found that disclosures in non-pre-pack business sales were no better and concluded that disclosure deficiencies were not an exclusively pre-pack problem.[55]

Statutory insolvency procedures offer a number of procedural and substantive protections for the creditors in a troubled company.[56] Focusing on the post-Enterprise Act 2002 administration procedure, it was seen in chapter 9 that administrators must perform their functions in the interests of the company's creditors as a whole and as quickly and efficiently as is reasonably practical. Administrators are officers of the court, they must act as agents of the company, and they have to operate within a framework of detailed rules on such matters as appointments,

---

[50] Ibid., pp. 53–64.   [51] Ibid., p. 66.
[52] The conclusion drawn by Sandra Frisby, ibid., p. 65.
[53] Ibid.   [54] Ibid., p. 31.   [55] Ibid., p. 32.
[56] See A. Lockerbie and P. Godfrey, 'Pre-packaged Administration – The Legal Framework' (2006) Recovery (Summer) 21.

statements of purposes and proposals, notifications and notices, moratoria, creditors' meetings, and reports to the court and to creditors.

The use of pre-packs does not do away with the need for such statutory procedures. The pre-pack does, however, create at least the risk that the administration procedure will be reduced to a formal or presentational process rather than one offering real protections. This, the critics of pre-packs would argue, is liable to happen, first, when the pre-pack closes the effective options for the company and establishes a single way forward without reference to the full array of creditors. Second, it may happen when the administrator fails to act in a manner that is consistent with his obligations to act in the interests of the company's creditors as a whole. This failure, it may be contended, is liable to occur when administrators are excessively inclined to treat the pre-pack deal as a *fait accompli* or are too heavily influenced by the banks.[57] Walton argues, for example, that if a deal to sell a company's business has been made in a pre-pack without leave of the court, and prior to a creditors' meeting, it is difficult to see how the administrator who proceeds with their mind very much on the sale can be said to be complying with the statutory duty to consider rescue.[58]

Given that pre-packs are not prohibited by law[59] it is clear that the pre-pack raises new questions about the role of the administrator and the place of regulatory or other controls in ensuring that there is accountability within procedures based on pre-packaging arrangements. A key focus for attention here is whether such changes demand a corresponding movement away from legal control and towards more managerial or professional approaches. How such control systems might govern pre-packs so as to increase efficiency, accountability, fairness and expertise is accordingly a matter for our consideration, and managerial and professional ethics and regulatory strategies will be looked at.[60]

---

[57] See Moulton, 'Uncomfortable Edge of Propriety'. On challenging administrators' conduct see IA 1986 Sch. B1, paras. 74 and 75 and ch. 9 above. On administrators' duties (under the old regime) see *Re Charnley Davies Ltd* [1990] BCC 605.

[58] See Walton, 'Trick or Treat?', p. 116: 'ironically, in this type of administration, the secured creditor may control the whole process ... more than in the old-style administrative receivership'.

[59] See *Re T&D Industries plc* [2000] 1 WLR 646, [2000] BCC 956; Lockerbie and Godfrey, 'Pre-packaged Administration'.

[60] On the division of control strategies into state, quasi-regulatory and corporate/managerial types see N. Gunningham and P. Grabosky, *Smart Regulation* (Oxford University Press, Oxford, 1998).

Controlling the pre-pack

The 'managerial' solution: a matter of expertise

One strand of thought sees the pre-pack as giving rise to a set of challenges that can at least partially be seen in managerial terms.[61] Thus, it might be said that potential difficulties of holdouts and legal challenges can be dealt with by taking active steps to negotiate pre-packs in a manner that persuades potentially dissatisfied parties to accept that their interests could not be better protected. The key to success lies in expertise: in astute management of the proposed arrangement and the involved parties. This might entail the concluding of deals in which equity stakes are given in return for co-operation. As has been argued:

> The risks of nuisance reaction around valuation and value break can be reduced, if necessary, by offering 'out of the money' stakeholders a minority participation in the restructured entity. But there are often technical hurdles here, particularly given the limitations on the extent of cram down in the UK ... In the end, the ability to approach and effect a pre-pack confidently turns on the quality of the steps and debate that occur during the live side process.[62]

Ellis has argued that: 'What we need is [for] responsible IPs to be bold, to have the courage of their convictions and to state publicly and transparently why the business was sold through a pre-pack without advertising or market testing.'[63] In order to encourage such transparency, Ellis has advocated not regulation but a simple requirement for IPs to explain publicly how the return to creditors was optimised.

Such explanations will deal with the reasons why particular approaches were taken on such matters as marketing the proposed arrangement. What is clear is that a considerable amount of judgement is involved in, for example, balancing the need to market a sale properly and the need to limit disclosure in order to prevent losses of reputations, business positions and consumer confidence. As one experienced practitioner has stated: 'Open marketing is about identifying the market and making it aware of the opportunities – it is not about exposing the proposal to the whole world.'[64] In the well-managed pre-pack the IP

---

[61] See Harris, 'Decision to Pre-pack', p. 27; Ellis, 'Thin Line in the Sand'.
[62] Harris, 'Decision to Pre-pack', p. 27.   [63] Ellis, 'Thin Line in the Sand'.
[64] Cranston, 'Pre-packaged Business Disposals'.

will be able to explain why a particular level of market exposure effected a reasonable balance between such factors.

The market, moreover, may demand that IPs operate to certain standards in setting up pre-pack proposals. Barclays Bank, for instance, produced a protocol on pre-packs in 2005. This set down the issues that the bank expected to be addressed in letters of recommendation where a pre-pack was being proposed. Such issues included: details of the value being obtained and the marketing activities that have been undertaken and by whom; any third-party valuations; the identities of purchasers and their funding mechanisms; outcome statements comparing expectations from a traditional insolvency with those from the pre-pack (to include the position for the bank, other stakeholders and unsecured creditors); the risks to trading the business or to maintaining asset values; and whether it will be possible to trade the business profitably. The effect of such protocols will be to flesh out what market participants expect of a well-managed pre-pack and to develop common understandings regarding the information disclosures involved in well-managed pre-packs. It can be argued that reputational considerations will induce IPs to negotiate pre-packs in a manner that accords with such expectations and understandings.[65]

Astute management of the pre-pack may prove helpful in ensuring that enough creditors approve of the deal on the table. It may, accordingly, reduce problems of holdouts and legal challenges. This may, in turn, involve the conducting of rigorous consultations and (on the Ellis model) a degree of *ex post facto* transparency. It would be rash, however, to equate astute management of the pre-pack with the conducting of procedures that are fair across the board to all creditor interests. 'Managing' the deal efficiently may, in the eyes of sceptics, involve good public relations and leadership rather than efforts to protect vulnerable interests and wholehearted attempts to identify the solution that is the fairest to all of the company's creditors.

The professional ethics solution: expertise and fairness combined

A variation on the above approach to protecting creditor interests is to rely on the expertise of the administrator but to emphasise the need for that expertise to be informed by a system of professional ethics. Such an approach accepts the highly discretionary nature of the administrator's

---

[65] Ibid.

task and puts a high premium on arriving at the 'right' judgement. As one practitioner has put it: 'A pre-pack must "feel right" and IPs must be careful. It is not just about getting an agent's valuation – you need to carefully assess all the options available and balance the interests of secured creditors with other stakeholders. This can often come down to experience and a gut feeling of what is right.'[66]

A director in corporate restructuring from a 'Big Four' firm has similarly emphasised the issue of ethical judgement: 'For office holders, lenders and other stakeholders there are equally important ethical and reputational matters to assess. Fundamentally, the decision to pre-pack – to adjust the rights of stakeholders against their will or without reference to them – must "feel right" in all circumstances and must be conducted with a sense of fair play.'[67]

For IPs the relevant code of ethics is the BERR 'Guidance to Professional Conduct and Ethics for Persons Authorised by the Secretary of State as Insolvency Practitioners'. This has relevance on such matters as the duty to 'strive for objectivity in all professional judgements' and relates to such questions as whether an IP who has been involved in negotiating a pre-pack has a 'material professional relationship' (with, for example, the company's directors) that prejudices their objectivity.[68] What is clear is that the pre-pack process raises highly acute issues regarding objectivity and conflicts of interest. As Walton argues: 'Insolvency Practitioners who operate pre-packs have seemingly insuperable conflict of [interest] duty problems.'[69]

The regulatory answer

Commentators who are concerned about the above modes of controlling pre-packs are liable to assert that regulation of the administrator (and the pre-pack process) is needed if the more vulnerable creditor interests are to be protected. Thus Jon Moulton, the managing partner of Alchemy Partners, has argued: 'This whole area of pre-packs needs regulation

---

[66] J. Godefroy, 'A Mixed Bag' (2005) MCR/Upside (Winter) 11.
[67] Harris, 'Decision to Pre-pack', p. 27.
[68] In this situation, argues Walton: 'The administrator's objectivity would appear to be impaired by a potential and actual conflict of duties.' See Walton, 'Trick or Treat?', p. 117 and *passim* for a discussion of conflicts of interest and duty in pre-packs.
[69] Ibid., p. 120.

(I generally despise regulation!) or the image of the profession will suffer deservedly from the very dubious actions of a few BMW owners.'[70]

Moulton has suggested that pre-packs might be controlled from beyond the profession by requiring them to be blessed by a judge before they are implemented. At the least, he argues, practitioners who use them extensively should be scrutinised closely by their professional bodies. The head of regulation at the Insolvency Service has also expressed some concerns.[71] Mike Chapman has argued that regulators need to be alert to the advent of pre-packs and should adapt their monitoring procedures so that action can be taken on the abuses that organising administrators may be party to before taking up appointments as office holders.[72] Similarly it has been contended by insolvency consultants Wilson Pitts that scrutiny of pre-packs is a matter of professional regulation so that: 'It is the responsibility of the insolvency profession's authorising bodies to root out early sales where creditors are dissatisfied as to how those sales have been conducted whilst supporting well orientated pre-pack sales which can be shown to be in the general interest of all creditors.'[73] R3 has now issued guidance on pre-packs but some commentators have argued for rigorous complaints mechanisms to control 'the professional bad apples'.[74]

A further possibility is to extend statutory controls so that these cover the solicitation of approvals for pre-packs.[75] In the USA, it is to be noted, a network of legal rules governs such solicitations in the period

---

[70] Moulton, 'Uncomfortable Edge of Propriety', p. 3 – whose example of an unethical organiser of pre-packs has him driving a 'very nice BMW'.

[71] M. Chapman, 'The Insolvency Service's View of Regulation' (2005) *Recovery* (Winter) 24. In 2008 the Chief Executive of the Insolvency Service, Stephen Speed, emphasised that IPs need to think 'very carefully in the pre-administration stage about the relationship they have with the company and how transparent what they are doing is to the creditors': see (2008) *Recovery* (Autumn) 59.

[72] See also Flynn, 'Pre-pack Administrations', who discusses the Statement of Insolvency Practice (SIP) 13 obligations on IPs not to assist clients in conduct that will 'undermine public confidence in insolvency procedures or assist directors in any conduct which amounts to misfeasance' (see SIP 13 paras. 4.1.1–2).

[73] Wilson Pitts, 'Pre-packs: Fast Track or Fast Buck', *Insolvency News*, www.wilson-pitts.co.uk/news.

[74] In January 2009 the R3's *Statement of Insolvency Practice 16 – Pre-Packaged Sales in Administrations* took effect. This guidance note was approved by the RPBs and covers disclosures and processes relevant to pre-packs. See also Davies, 'Pre-pack – He Who Pays the Piper Calls the Tune'; Flynn, 'Pre-pack Administrations'.

[75] Walton, 'Trick or Treat?', p. 120 argues that some provision for creditors to vote (perhaps by post) on a pre-pack deal prior to appointment of the administrator 'may be the answer'.

before the commencement of a Chapter 11 case.[76] Thus, the Bankruptcy
Code, section 1126(b) states that a party is deemed to have accepted or
rejected a plan in the pre-Chapter 11 period if the relevant solicitation was
in compliance with the applicable non-bankruptcy rule or regulation, or, if
there is no such relevant rule or regulation, the solicitation followed disclosure
of 'adequate information' as defined in section 1125 of the Code. In addition,
rules 3017 and 3018 of the Federal Rules of Bankruptcy Procedure require,
inter alia, that plans and disclosure statements be distributed to all affected
creditors and equity interest holders; that plans be sent to beneficial owners of
securities; and that solicitation periods be reasonable. Securities laws in the
USA will, moreover, treat pre-pack solicitations as 'sales' of securities and
liable to regulation unless the nature of the steps being taken comes within an
exemption as set out in the terms of the Bankruptcy Code or the securities laws
(e.g. on the grounds that the offering is not 'public'). Where the Bankruptcy
Code applies to a pre-pack, dissatisfied parties may file objections within the
time limits indicated in the bankruptcy court's 'scheduling order'.[77] In the UK
Stephen Davies QC has argued that it should be mandatory for advisers to file
a statement at court (or possibly with the Registrar of Companies) giving
details of the pre-pack, including: the date of first instruction; the reasons for
the pre-pack; the period of marketing; all valuations received; the terms of sale;
and the total fees by the adviser's firm and the source of those fees.[78] Desmond
Flynn, Agency chief executive of the Insolvency Service, has furthermore
suggested that it might be provided that administrators should only be
allowed to take expenses incurred prior to formal appointment once these
have been expressly authorised by the creditors within the administration
proceedings. This proposal is designed to ensure not only transparency
but also more effective creditor scrutiny of the administrator's actions.[79]

---

[76] See Vilaplana, 'Pre-pack Bankruptcy Primer', pp. 35–42. The BAPCPA 2005 amends s.
1125 of the Bankruptcy Code to the effect that, notwithstanding the prohibition on post-
(bankruptcy filing) petition solicitation of pre-packaged plan votes in the absence of a
court-approved disclosure statement, votes may be solicited if the pre- and post-petition
solicitation complies with applicable non-bankruptcy law (i.e. securities laws): see
Kornberg, 'Bankruptcy Abuse Prevention and Consumer Protection Act', p. 35.
[77] Kornberg, 'Bankruptcy Abuse Prevention and Consumer Protection Act', p. 35.
[78] Davies, 'Pre-pack – He Who Pays the Piper Calls the Tune', p. 18.
[79] Flynn, 'Pre-pack Administrations', p. 3. In 2007 the IS carried out a consultation exercise
on draft amendments to the Insolvency Rules 1986 which would allow pre-pack administrators to claim the costs of their pre-appointment work as an administration expense
subject to the approval of the creditors of the company: see further P. Walton, 'Pre-
appointment Administration Fees – Papering Over the Crack in Pre-packs?' (2008) 21
Insolvency Intelligence 72.

Evaluating control strategies

A first point in evaluating systems for controlling pre-packs is to identify the potential mischief at issue. Critics of pre-packs would raise questions of fairness and accountability and argue that the key mischief the device presents is the undermining of those protections for creditors that are offered by (increasingly collective) statutory procedures. What, then, is the protection that administration procedures offer to creditors? If such protections, themselves, amount to little, then the pre-pack arguably involves no significant loss of protection.

As indicated above, the post-EA 2002 administration procedure offers a number of statutory consultation rights – notably by establishing creditors' meetings and requirements that proposals be approved by these meetings. In substantive terms the administrator must act in the interests of all creditors of the company.[80] These rules are underpinned by the requirement that the administrator must be an insolvency practitioner (IP) and by the existence of a regime of professional regulation for IPs.[81]

Do these requirements offer effective protections for creditors? Are accountability and fairness ensured? As noted in chapter 9, critics of the new administration procedure might caution that under paragraph 52 of Schedule B1 of the Insolvency Act 1986, no initial creditors' meeting needs to be called if the administrator thinks either that the company cannot be rescued as a going concern or that administration cannot achieve a better result for the company's creditors as a whole than will be likely on a winding up without first being in administration. Cynics might argue that an administrator who is excessively inclined to keep the banks happy will, accordingly, be well placed to produce proposals for a quick sell off in pursuance of bank interests without going through the creditors' meeting. As noted above, the legal phrasing of paragraph 3 of Schedule B1 gives administrators a considerable breadth of discretion that makes their judgements extremely difficult to challenge and judicial oversight of the administration process may be the weaker because of the potential for out-of-court appointments of administrators without the need for a Rule 2.2 Report.

In spite of these concerns about administration procedure, critics of pre-packs might argue that matters are worse in a pre-pack. Under

---

[80] Insolvency Act 1986 Sch. B1, para. 3(2).   [81] See ch. 5 above.

normal Schedule B1 procedures, administrators will take a disinterested view of options in the light of their obligation to act in the interests of all creditors. This position might be contrasted by the critics with that found in pre-packs, in which administrators may be involved in pre-negotiations, they may be committed to a course of action before entering administration, and they may have an incentive to push proposals through statutory procedures as quickly as possible. In reply, the advocates of pre-packs might respond that the post-EA 2002 administration procedure itself demands that a good deal of work has to be done before the administrator is appointed. When, for instance, there is a direct appointment of an administrator under paragraph 14 of Schedule B1, the qualifying floating charge holder must, as noted, file a notice of appointment with the court, together with other documents, including a statement by the administrator that he is, *inter alia*, of the opinion that the purpose of administration is reasonably likely to be achieved.[82] In practice this will mean that when a major creditor, for example a bank, seeks to appoint an IP as administrator, the bank will have to brief that person on the proposed turnaround package. This will inevitably involve a certain degree of pre-packaging. Proponents of pre-packs would thus argue that there is a continuum of scenarios ranging from appointments of administrators that involve very little homework to those involving much more considerable research and negotiation. A pre-pack, they would say, is merely a highly developed arrangement that does all the work that an administrator would want to have been carried out before he or she agrees to take up a position.

Such arguments, however, may go too far. The most serious concerns about pre-packs may arise not because a good deal of homework and research has been carried out in advance of court applications but because agreements on the company's way forward have been concluded informally in advance of the statutory process – and that such agreements foreclose alternative courses of action in a manner that may prejudice less powerful creditors. The danger is that when powerful creditors agree to a pre-pack such an agreement creates a momentum that is difficult for the administrator to upset. The proposals on the table will constitute something close to a *fait accompli* in so far as many administrators, when surveying possible options for the company, will have a strong bias towards the pre-pack. This may arise because all non-pre-pack options are likely to carry the prospect of greater uncertainties

[82] IA 1986 Sch. B1, para. 18(3)(a) and (b). See ch. 9 above.

and more protracted negotiations. Unlike the pre-pack, they involve the opening of new cans of worms. If this is the case, the pre-pack commits the administrator to a course of action that is agreed outside statutory procedures and it is extremely difficult for less powerful creditors to scrutinise the pre-pack and to renegotiate terms. The administrator's duty to act in the interest of all creditors has been bypassed and it is no answer to this to say that the IP can take an unbiased view of the pre-pack to assess whether it serves all interests fairly – the IP will have to compare the pre-pack proposals with other realistic options but the latter will have been weakened by the development of the pre-pack. The playing field is already tilted in favour of the pre-packaged agreement.

If such concerns point to a need to control pre-packs, what potential is offered by managerial or professional ethics or regulatory strategies? The problem with managerial strategies is that the *cost-effective* management of a pre-packaged rescue is not necessarily the same thing as the *fair* management of the rescue. As noted above, the lowest-cost way to manage turnaround may involve a narrow focusing of consultations on major creditors and the construction of a deal that is offered to other stakeholders on what may be close to a take it or leave it basis. This may differ quite markedly from a procedure in which an administrator holds the ring to see that proposals are developed on the basis of inputs from all relevant creditors. Such dangers of unfairness militate in favour of tempering 'pure' managerial approaches with provisions on transparency as suggested by Katz and Mumford – who say that where a sale completes a pre-packed agreement, creditors should be provided with such documentation as would allow them to understand the rationale for the sale.[83] Other disclosure proposals have not been slow to emerge. Desmond Flynn has made proposals regarding creditor approval of pre-pack expenses;[84] Stephen Davies QC[85] has argued for the filing in court of a pre-pack statement and Martin Ellis has suggested that IPs should, in law, have to make public an explanation of why and how the return to

---

[83] Katz and Mumford, *Study of Administration Cases*. As noted above, a new SIP on pre-packs was promulgated in January 2009. The SIP is concerned with transparency, not commerciality, and seeks to set out minimum levels of information to be provided to creditors so that they are properly informed and can form a view as to whether the pre-pack was in their interests. See also R. Heis, 'Pre-packs – A New SIP' (2008) *Recovery* (Spring) 14.

[84] Flynn, 'Pre-pack Administrations'.

[85] Davies, 'Pre-pack – He Who Pays the Piper Calls the Tune'.

creditors was optimised.[86] Even when such transparency requirements are in operation, however, it may be protested that explaining why the *fait accompli* was the best available option for the IP does not remove the inevitable bias towards the pre-pack solution.

Using professional ethics to control pre-packs offers, on its face, considerable potential for encouraging fairness. The notion here is that professional IPs only construct pre-packs in a manner that satisfies reasonable expectations of fairness across all creditors. These expectations would be established within the framework of ethics promulgated by systems of selection, training and guidance within the profession.

The problems with this solution may be, firstly, those of adverse selection and incentives. A danger here is that the major creditors, the banks, would possess considerable incentives to use IPs with low ethical sensitivities and 'more practical' approaches to the pursuit of bank-friendly turnaround proposals. The market, accordingly, might punish ethical practitioners and reward those of a more 'practical' disposition. From this viewpoint there is little reassurance in the contention that reputational concerns will lead IPs to operate even-handedly and openly – the market may reward IPs with reputations for amenability to bank rather than broad creditor interests. A further difficulty with the 'professional ethics' solution is that many stakeholders, and the public more generally, may be disinclined to place trust in the ethical judgements of professionals. This is a general problem with self-regulatory systems[87] but it is all the more acute a difficulty in circumstances where the relevant professionals have clear incentives to favour the interests of powerful players – as, for instance, when the IPs who act as administrators are seen to be dependent on the goodwill of the banks in developing their practices.[88] An additional problem may be that

---

[86] Ellis, 'Thin Line in the Sand'. Lockerbie and Godfrey, 'Pre-packaged Administration' (p. 22) suggest that the factors that an administrator may cite as justifying use of a pre-pack may include: preservation of business relationships; protection of assets; retention of employees; funding requirements; and regulatory factors such as the retention of essential licences.

[87] See generally M. Moran, *The British Regulatory State* (Oxford University Press, Oxford, 2003) ch. 4.

[88] On bank power Davies has written: 'the power of the clearing banks in the market is such that there is barely a major firm of accountants or solicitors prepared publicly to criticise their conduct or practice, no matter how professionally objectionable'. On incentives and interests of 'actors' in administration see ch. 9 above; V. Finch, 'Re-invigorating Corporate Rescue' [2003] JBL 527.

pre-packs may not always be set up by IPs – they may be negotiated in-house by the major creditors or they may be set up by independent, non-professional, unregulated specialists (Moulton's 'men in BMWs'). Such a pre-pack organiser may operate free from the constraints of any system of professional ethics whatsoever. The real worry is that if such an 'ethically free' person constructs a pre-pack that is self-fulfilling (in the sense that it is *de facto* not feasible to re-open the agreement within realistic timeframes) no amount of ethical shepherding of the deal on the part of the administrating IP will rectify the situation.

Such arguments point to the possible case for regulating pre-packs. On this front a number of strategies may be considered: professional regulation, external oversight mechanisms and legislative reforms.

A system of professional regulation of pre-packs might be furthered by tightening the monitoring regimes relating to pre-packs.[89] The Insolvency Practices Council argued in 2006 that the IS and recognised professional bodies should require IPs acting as administrators to: report promptly to creditors when they have executed a pre-packaged sale; explain any decision not to advertise the business on the open market; bear in mind potential conflicts of interest where they have advised the managers of the relevant company on a pre-pack; and disclose potential conflicts of interest to creditors. To this end, R3 issued an SIP on pre-packs to cover such matters.[90] It might, however, be required that when IPs process a pre-pack through an administration, they file a report to their professional body for scrutiny. A complaints processing regime could also be established so that dissatisfied creditors' views might be taken on board. Such a system of control, of course, would not solve the problem of 'mavericks' and the difficulties that might arise from pre-packs that are arranged by parties other than qualified IPs. This is a matter to be returned to below.

What of the role of external oversight mechanisms? Some commentators, as noted, have argued that judges should perhaps bless pre-packs before they are implemented.[91] Such judicial oversight would correspond to the scrutiny that is involved when the pre-pack proposals are

---

[89] See Flynn, 'Pre-pack Administrations'. On the monitoring and regulation of IPs see ch. 5 above.

[90] IPC, *Annual Report 2006* (IPC, London, 2006), noted in C. Laughton, 'Editorial' (2007) *Recovery* (Summer) 2. R3, *Statement of Insolvency Practice 16* (2009).

[91] See Moulton, 'Uncomfortable Edge of Propriety', p. 3.

implemented by means of an application to court for an administration order. It is to be noted, however, that paragraphs 14 and 22 of Schedule B1 of the Insolvency Act 1986 allow qualifying floating charge holders, the company or directors to commence administrations without the need for a court order. It could, accordingly, be argued that, having gone this far to create out-of-court routes into administration, Parliament might be reluctant to institute a judicial approvals mechanism in relation to pre-packs. Such an approvals process would undermine the speed and flexibility of the process[92] and, moreover, would be difficult to set up in a way falling short of abolishing the paragraphs 14 and 22 routes into administration. It might be provided in law that the entry into administration would have to be by court order whenever there is a pre-pack but this would present two real problems. First, it would be necessary to define the precise circumstances, understandings or agreements that constitute a 'pre-pack' (which would create much work for lawyers and a good deal of uncertainty). Second, parties wishing to avail themselves of the out-of-court route into administration might find it relatively easy to circumvent any stipulations regarding the judicial approval of pre-packs by keeping their negotiations at a sufficient level of informality to escape the definition of pre-pack – at least until the point at which they have appointed an administrator.

Nor can it be expected that any system of judicial oversight (whether involving pre-packs or not) will involve a significant judicial willingness to interfere with the judgements of administrators. As noted above, the courts have shown themselves to be reluctant to second-guess commercial decisions that are made in difficult corporate circumstances even when the administration process is sought to be instituted by court order.[93] In *DKLL Solicitors* v. *HM Revenue & Customs*[94] a firm was insolvent (to the tune of about £2.4 million) and owed HMRC £1.7 million. Two of the equity partners of DKLL made an administration application to the court with a view to effecting a pre-pack sale for £400,000. HMRC opposed the application, arguing that it would have opposed the sale (because the price was too low) had it been given the opportunity to do so at a creditors' meeting. Acting judge Andrew

---

[92] See Flynn, 'Pre-pack Administrations'.

[93] See IA 1986 Sch. B1, paras. 11–13. It is arguable that the judicial oversight role is restricted by Parliament's allocation of extensive discretion to the administrator.

[94] *DKLL Solicitors* v. *HM Revenue & Customs* [2007] BCC 908; see Frisby, 'Judicial Sanction of Insolvency Pre-packs?'. See also *Re Structures and Computers Ltd* [1988] BCC 348.

Simmonds QC, however, granted the administration order, holding that the court had a discretion to grant such an order even where the majority creditor opposed it. (The legality of a pre-pack *per se* was treated as uncontentious.) He stated that in applications for the granting of an administration order the court would 'give weight to the expertise and experience of impartial insolvency practitioners'.[95] This statement indicates that a 'business judgement' approach may be forthcoming from the judges when they are faced with future pre-packaged administrations.[96] Ellis has, furthermore, cast doubt on the capacity of the judiciary to deliver rigorous and fair oversight: 'Judges aren't in a position to make commercial decisions, and, even if they were, who would represent the interests of the divergent stakeholders? Where would they source their information?'[97]

Would legislative reform usefully control pre-packs? A first proposal might be to restrict the negotiation of pre-packs to IPs in order to increase the impact of professional and ethical systems of control and deal with the maverick problem. There may be issues of borderline to be dealt with here. How, for instance, might one stop a bank or another stakeholder from using their good offices to construct turnaround agreements? One way to do this would be to ensure that all pre-packs that underpin applications to court for administration orders are scrutinised or audited by IPs and certified as fair to all creditors. Such a procedure would address the 'borderline' and 'maverick' issues and would involve oversight not by the judiciary but by professionals specialising in the conduct of such negotiations and capable of making judgements about the feasibility, fairness and reasonableness of business proposals. A system of monitoring by the IPs' professional body might be combined with such a legislative change. Further legislative reforms might, if necessary, be introduced to place the IPs' pre-pack auditing function on a statutory basis. A statutory provision might, accordingly, impose an obligation on the IP to ensure, before approving a pre-pack, that the

---

[95] *DKLL Solicitors* v. *HM Revenue & Customs* [2007] BCC 908 at 913, para. 10.

[96] In the USA the so-called 'business judgement rule' is a principle that makes company directors and officers immune from liability to the company for loss incurred in corporate transactions that were within their authority and power to make when sufficient evidence demonstrates the transactions were made in good faith and with reasonable skill and prudence: see further D. Branson, 'The Rule that isn't a Rule – The Business Judgment Rule' (2002) 36 Valparaiso Univ. LR 631; V. Finch, 'Company Directors: Who Cares About Skill and Care?' (1992) 55 MLR 179, 202.

[97] Ellis, 'Thin Line in the Sand'. See also Flynn, 'Pre-pack Administrations' and Davies, 'Pre-pack – He Who Pays the Piper Calls the Tune', p. 18.

procedural and substantive interests of all creditors have been reasonably dealt with. This could involve (as Ellis and Davies have both urged) a requirement that the IP is required to explain publicly why the proposed outcome is fair to all creditors.

A step further would be involved if the US regime were to be used as a model so that solicitations of agreements to pre-pack were to be governed by statutory requirements designed to ensure that any information is adequate or timescales involved are reasonable and that proposals are distributed to substantially all affected creditors and equity interest holders.

Such provisions would arguably offer a response to the feared mischiefs involved in pre-packs but there may be a downside involved in extending statutory regulation into the currently pre-formal area of commercial life. First, this would be likely to increase the complexity of turnaround procedures as well as the cost. Second, this might undermine the advantages of pre-packs and reduce their value as ways of effecting turnarounds before reputations and market positions are lost. If those running the pre-pack process were to have to operate procedures that would give them confidence of compliance with the law, this would involve very considerable risks to continuity of trading, business relationships and rescue objectives. Third, such an extended system of control might prove only partially successful in providing control over pre-formal deal-making. The effect might be to produce not only a series of new legal uncertainties (as parties contest such issues as whether a discussion constitutes a solicitation) but also more resort to 'pre-solicitation' deals of a highly secretive nature. Critics would caution that such 'over-regulation' is liable to lead to less transparency in turnaround negotiations, not more, and to less efficiency in rescue.

Conclusions

If pre-packs are a significant problem, it does seem possible to devise responses. Why, though, should yet more regulation be introduced into business life? Are levels of potential prejudice to creditors great enough to justify new monitoring systems and rules? To recap: the case for action rests on the prejudice to unsecured creditor interests caused by the use of pre-packs and the difficulties that vulnerable creditors have in challenging unsatisfactory pre-packs through the procedures established by the Insolvency Act 1986. Where pre-packs are used cynically it may well be the case that it is extremely difficult to mount challenges: first, because the informational hurdles are high; second, because the administrator's discretion is wide and difficult to challenge; and third, because pre-packs have a self-fulfilling effect in so far as, once agreed, they genuinely do make other rescue options less feasible.

The issue of pre-packs points again to the need for insolvency lawyers to come to grips with the issue of displacement and the propensity of corporate control systems to shift across from traditional insolvency processes and scenarios and into the pre-insolvency stages of governance. A clear message is that statutory processes such as the post-EA administration procedure can never be seen as complete or lasting solutions. Negotiations will always be conducted in the new shadows of the latest legislative procedures. The constant challenge may be to assess how statutory regimes sit alongside informal negotiations so that fresh light can be cast into the developing shadows.

Company arrangements

This chapter looks at the statutory arrangements that companies may voluntarily enter into so as to deal with troubles or adapt to changes in market conditions. The two main procedures for effecting voluntary arrangements either within or outside administration or liquidation are schemes of arrangement under section 895 of the Companies Act 2006 and Company Voluntary Arrangements (CVAs), as provided for in Part I and Schedule A1 of the Insolvency Act 1986.

Before looking at these two methods, it should be emphasised that informal arrangements made contractually can, as noted in chapter 7, provide very useful ways of attempting rescues before there is need to resort to the formalities of section 895 or CVA provisions. Informal steps, moreover, may be taken confidentially and, in the international context, may provide a useful way of negotiating between different insolvency systems.[1] Such contractual steps, however, possess a number of weaknesses. They are only binding on contracting parties and cannot tie dissenting parties to an agreement. They offer no form of moratorium to shield the company from its creditors and, even if approved by meetings of creditors and members, offer no protection from the enforcement of claims. Informal procedures may also lend themselves to domination by large secured creditors in a way unmatched by CVAs and section 895 processes.

Schemes of arrangement under the Companies Act 2006 sections 895–901

The roots of the scheme of arrangement lie in Victorian legislation[2] but, as set out in the Companies Act 2006, the process allows a 'compromise or arrangement' to be agreed between a company and 'its creditors, or any

---

[1] See ch. 7 above; D. Brown, *Corporate Rescue: Insolvency Law in Practice* (J. Wiley & Sons, Chichester, 1996) p. 647.

[2] Joint Stock Companies Act 1870.

class of them'.[3] An arrangement here may include a reorganisation of share capital by the consolidation of shares of different classes or by the division of shares into different classes.[4] Such schemes are commonly used to effect compromises and moratoria with creditors and schemes with policy holder creditors of insurance companies have also been common.[5] They are also used in takeover and merger transactions and in reorganisations of rights allocated to classes of shares or debt, often where the articles or instruments constituting the capital are inadequate.[6]

The relevant procedure for a scheme involves an initial approach to the court by the company or any creditor, member, liquidator or administrator of the company, or else the summoning (with court approval) of meetings of the company's members and creditors.[7] On such approval being obtained, the scheme must be approved by the court, which will consider

---

[3] Companies Act 2006 Part 26, ss. 895–901 restate ss. 425–7 of CA 1985 with effect from 6 April 2008. CA 2006 s. 895 also applies as between the company and the members or any class of them. On the meaning of 'creditor' as any person who has a pecuniary claim against the company, whether present or contingent, see *Re T & N Ltd and Others* [2006] 3 All ER 697 (on which see further J. Bannister and N. Hamilton, 'Future Claims, Present Redress? Schemes, CVAs and Liquidations after *T & N*' (2006) *Recovery* (Summer) 36 and G. Stewart, 'Legal Update – The Challenge of the *T & N* Case' (2006) *Recovery* (Spring) 7); *Re Midland Coal, Coke and Iron Co.* [1895] 1 Ch 267, approved by *Re Cancol Ltd* [1996] 1 BCLC 100. On the predecessor s. 425 schemes see generally A. Wilkinson, A. Cohen and R. Sutherland, 'Creditors' Schemes of Arrangement and Company Voluntary Arrangements' in H. Rajak (ed.), *Insolvency Law: Theory and Practice* (Sweet & Maxwell, London, 1993); D. Milman, 'Schemes of Arrangement: Their Continuing Role' [2001] Ins. Law. 145.

[4] Companies Act 2006 s. 895(2). A proposal under s. 895 has to involve an 'arrangement' or 'reconstruction': see further *Re My Travel Group plc* [2005] 1 WLR 2365, [2005] BCC 457 (where Mann J agreed with subordinate bondholders that the scheme as initially proposed was not a 'reconstruction' for the purposes of the statute because only 4 per cent in value of the shares in the new company were held by the shareholders in the old company, with the bulk of the new company's shares going to the old company creditors. Mann J also indicated, however, that the subordinated bondholders had 'no economic interest' in the company. This recital was set aside on appeal: *Re My Travel Group plc* [2005] 2 BCLC 123.) See N. Segal, 'Schemes of Arrangement and Junior Creditors – Does the US Approach to Valuations Provide the Answer?' (2007) 20 *Insolvency Intelligence* 49; *Re T & N Ltd and Others* [2006] 3 All ER 697 – per David Richards J – a mere expropriation of rights does not qualify as an arrangement; D. Milman, 'Arrangements and Reconstructions: Recent Developments in UK Company Law' (2006) 21/22 *Sweet & Maxwell's Company Law Newsletter* 1.

[5] See CLRSG, *Modern Company Law for a Competitive Economy: Completing the Structure* (November 2000) p. 206. A scheme of arrangement can also be put in place after the principal terms of an informal restructuring have been agreed, thus binding dissentient creditors: see further the discussion on informal rescue in ch. 7 above.

[6] Ibid.

[7] The Notes to Part 26 of the Companies Act 2006 state that one of the (two) changes of substance in the 2006 provisions is that 'S. 899(2) makes clear that the persons who may apply

issues of procedural fairness, hear objections from dissenters and decide whether the scheme is 'fair and reasonable'[8] and would have been supported by any intelligent and reasonable bystander.[9] The court will, *inter alia*, consider whether each common interest group (for which there must be a separate meeting) is fairly constituted and whether the class's decision to approve the scheme was one that could reasonably have been made.[10]

One advantageous feature of the scheme of arrangement is that, if the arrangement is approved, it may modify the rights of shareholders and creditors and may do so without their consent. It is binding on all affected parties,[11] not just those who, in accordance with the rules, were entitled to vote at the meeting approving the arrangement (as with a CVA under the Insolvency Act 1986 sections 1–7). Schemes, moreover, may be tailored to corporate needs. They are very flexible and there are no statutory prescribed contents for such schemes.[12] They can be used in conjunction with liquidation (in order to reach a particular compromise

---

for a court order sanctioning a compromise or arrangement are the same as those who may apply to the court for an order for a meeting (under s. 896(2))' (para. 1166). The other substantive change is that 'S. 901 requires a company to deliver to the registrar a court order that alters the company's constitution. It also requires that every copy of the company's articles subsequently issued must be accompanied by a copy of the order unless the effect of the order has been incorporated into the articles by amendment' (para. 1167).

[8] *Re Anglo-Continental Supply Co. Ltd* [1922] 2 Ch 723, 726; *Re Dorman Long* [1934] 1 Ch 635; *Re NFU Development Trust Ltd* [1972] 1 WLR 1548; *Re RAC Motoring Services Ltd* [2000] 1 BCLC 307. See also Practice Direction: Schemes of Arrangements with Creditors [2002] BCC 355, [2002] 1 WLR 1345.

[9] See *Re Abbey National plc* [2005] 2 BCLC 15. On the issue of whether junior creditors have any residual economic interest in the debtor and the courts' ability to deal with this issue when deciding whether the scheme is reasonable see Segal, 'Schemes of Arrangement and Junior Creditors'; *My Travel Group plc* [2005] 1 WLR 2365 (Mann J); *My Travel Group plc* [2005] 2 BCLC 123 (CA).

[10] The court must be satisfied that the scheme does not operate unfairly between groups and will ask whether an intelligent and honest member of the class could reasonably have approved the proposal: see *Re Linton Park plc* [2008] BCC 17; *RAC Motoring Services Ltd* [2000] 1 BCLC 307; D. Milman, 'Schemes of Arrangement' [2001] 6 *Palmer's In Company* 1.

[11] A majority in number representing three-quarters in value of the creditors, or class of creditors, or members, or class of members, is binding on all creditors, or the class of creditors, or the members, or class of members, where the arrangement is sanctioned by the court: Companies Act 2006 s. 899(1). The court has complete discretion, when approving a scheme, to make consequential directions. This may be useful where the proposal put to the court differs from the proposal considered by the shareholders: *Re Allied Domecq plc* [2000] BCC 582.

[12] Schemes must, however, be within the corporate powers of the company – *Re Ocean Steam Navigation Co. Ltd* [1939] Ch 41 – and must comply with the Companies Act requirements on reductions of capital or issues of redeemable shares – *Re St James Court Estate Ltd* [1944] Ch 6.

with creditors) or as an alternative to liquidation or as one of the
purposes for which administration can be entered into.[13] Section 895
schemes can also be embarked upon with regard to solvent companies.[14]
Securities may be removed or rights to enforce securities may be curtailed and creditors' payment rights can be modified if the majority
of secured creditors agree. (The court's powers under the Companies
Act 2006 section 900 are more extensive here than in relation to administration orders.)

A second advantage, of relevance to rescue scenarios, is that schemes
may be formulated and approved without any requirement that there be an
impending insolvency. Early attention to corporate difficulties and timely
responses to problems may, accordingly, be instituted. (This may be a
considerable advantage over some of the entry routes into the 'new'
administration.)[15] A third favourable factor is that schemes of arrangement
are in essence agreements between companies and their creditors and,
accordingly, there is no need to involve an insolvency practitioner in
formulating or in implementing the scheme. This allows the existing
directors to stay in control of the company and the process does not
deter them from taking remedial action by holding out the real prospect
of a ceding of control to an outside IP. Schemes, moreover, can be applied
to companies not registered in the UK, and, if the company has assets in the
UK, the scheme can prevent enforcement against these. This overcomes
jurisdictional problems.[16] A final attraction of the scheme of arrangement
is that it can be used to reorganise corporate groups: debt can be exchanged
for equity and schemes can provide for the transfer of shares or assets
between companies or even the amalgamation of a number of companies.[17]

---

[13] See e.g. the broadly defined purposes of para. 3 in Sch. B1 of IA 1986; see ch. 9 above.

[14] See, *inter alia*, *Re British Aviation Insurance Co. Ltd* [2006] BCC 14; *Re Abbey National plc* [2005] 2 BCLC 15.

[15] See, for example, IA 1986 Sch. B1, paras. 11(a), 27(2) – an appointment of an administrator by the court (unless on the application of a QFCH), or out of court by the
company or its directors, can only be made if the company is insolvent or nearly so: see
ch. 9 above.

[16] Milman notes that the English courts have adopted 'an open-door policy' consistent with
the 'general policy of the English courts to expand our corporate law jurisdiction
wherever possible': see the discussions of *Drax Holdings Ltd* [2004] BCC 334; *Re
Home Insurance Co.* [2006] BCC 164; *Re DAP Holding NV* [2006] BCC 48 and *Re
Sovereign Marine & General Insurance Co. Ltd* [2006] BCC 774 in 'Arrangements and
Reconstructions', p. 2.

[17] Note, however, that the Third and Sixth Company Law Directives of the EC – the
Companies (Mergers and Divisions) Regulation 1987 (SI 1987/1991); EEC Council
Directive 78/855, OJ 1978/295/36 and EEC Council Directive 82/891, OJ 1982/378/

In spite of such advantageous characteristics, schemes of arrangement have been used on relatively few occasions. This infrequency of resort is understandable once the disadvantages of the scheme of arrangement are considered. A major constraint on use has been that such schemes have been so rigorously protective of minority interests that, in practice, schemes have not been approved unless they have happened to satisfy the interests of all parties affected by them. This protective stance is seen in the complexity of the approval arrangements. It is necessary to ensure that separate meetings are held for each different class of member or creditor affected by the proposed scheme. It is often difficult, however, to know what constitutes a class for these purposes, and the court will not offer guidance on such matters at the application stage.[18] Different types of shareholding clearly produce different classes, and preferential, secured and unsecured creditors will also be separately grouped. Other interest groups within these classes may also, however, have to be organised into different classes, and if such classes are not established properly from the start, the whole scheme will be nullified.[19] There have, however, been recent signs of a less protective stance by the judiciary – a change of approach that has prompted some concern. When the Company Law Review Steering Group (CLRSG) looked at these issues, it considered that, in an important case, the Court of Appeal had not given sufficient protection to minority creditors and members. The decision in *Re Hawk Insurance Co. Ltd*[20] was seen as worrying in so far as a scheme of arrangement under (the then) section 425 was approved where a single meeting of all the creditors had been held,

47 – are implemented by Part 27 of the Companies Act 2006, and s. 903 provides that, in the case of mergers or divisions within the scope of Part 27, ss. 895–901 are to have effect subject to the provision of Part 27: see *Boyle and Birds' Company Law* (6th edn, Jordans, Bristol, 2007) p. 826.

[18] The CLRSG favoured the idea that the court should have discretion to decide class issues at the application stage: see CLRSG, *Modern Company Law for a Competitive Economy: Final Report* (July 2001) para. 13.8.

[19] A petition for approval of a scheme will be nullified: Practice Note [1934] WN 142.

[20] [2001] EWCA Civ 241. Chadwick LJ stated that: 'those whose rights are sufficiently similar to the rights of others that they can properly consult together should be required to do so, lest by ordering separate meetings the court gives a veto to a minority group. The safeguard against majority oppression … is that the court is not bound by the decision of the meeting'; see further R3, 'Legal Update' (2001) *Recovery* (September) 8. See also CLRSG, *Completing the Structure*, p. 215. The *Report of the Review Committee on Insolvency Law and Practice* (Cmnd 8558, 1982) ('Cork Report') noted the difficulties of class definition (paras. 405–18), and CVA procedures avoid separations of classes in favour of remedial procedures for those who consider they have been unfairly prejudiced: see Insolvency Act 1986 s. 6.

notwithstanding that the creditors appeared to have had different rights. The courts have taken varying approaches to class definition[21] and the CLRSG looked favourably on legislating to define classes so as to restore the pre-*Hawk Insurance* position and state that the only persons entitled to attend and vote at a (then) section 425 meeting would be 'persons whose rights are not so dissimilar as to make it impossible for them to consult together with a view to acting in their common interest'.[22] The CLRSG also suggested that the courts should be able to sanction a scheme even if classes had been wrongly constituted or, in appropriate circumstances, where separate meetings had not been held.[23] Neither of these suggestions found their way into the Companies Act 2006 but recent cases suggest that the judges are adopting constructive approaches both to procedural issues[24] and to the sanctioning of schemes.[25]

On top of complications relating to definitions of classes, there are elaborate provisions relating to schemes of arrangement that are designed to ensure that all members and creditors will be notified of

---

[21] On approaches to the definition of a class see, *inter alia*, the '*tour de force* judgement that will become a benchmark for the future' (Milman, 'Arrangements and Reconstructions', p. 3) – *Re British Aviation Insurance Co. Ltd* [2006] BCC 14. See also *Re BTR plc* [1999] 2 BCLC 675: 'those persons whose rights are not so dissimilar as to make it impossible for them to consult together with a view to acting in their common interest'; *Re Sovereign Marine & General Insurance Co. Ltd* [2006] BCC 774 (on which see T. McMahon, J. Wardrop and A. Wood, 'Solvent and Insolvent Schemes of Arrangement …WFUM: The Story So Far' (2006) 19 *Sweet & Maxwell's Company Law Newsletter* 1: 'This highly detailed judgement demonstrates the careful and balanced view that the court will take when reviewing proposed schemes and will have a huge impact on the structuring of solvent schemes in the future'). See also *Re Telewest Communications plc (No. 1)* [2004] BCC 342 (the rights of sterling and dollar bondholders were not identical but they were sufficiently similar to be treated as a single class); *Re Osiris Insurance Ltd* [1999] 1 BCLC 182 (Neuberger J indicated that a single class might contain members whose interests were not exactly the same).

[22] CLRSG, *Final Report*, 2001, para. 13.8; see also *Re BTR plc* [1999] 2 BCLC 675; *Re Sovereign Marine & General Insurance Co. Ltd* [2006] BCC 774.

[23] CLRSG, *Final Report*, 2001, paras. 13.7, 13.8.

[24] See for example *Re Abbey National plc* [2005] 2 BCLC 15, cited in Milman, 'Arrangements and Reconstructions', p. 4. Such pragmatism, however, does not go so far as to endorse a class 'meeting' as valid when attended by a single person where there was no evidence that there was only one person in that particular class: *Re Altitude Scaffolding Ltd* [2006] BCC 904.

[25] See *In re Cape plc* [2006] EWHC 1316, [2007] Bus LR 109 where David Richards J confirmed that three different types of asbestos claimant could be combined in a single class and that arrangements containing provision for future amendment could be sanctioned by the court, albeit in exceptional cases. On *In re Cape* see further J. Townsend, 'Schemes of Arrangement and Asbestos Litigation: *In re Cape plc*' (2007) 70 MLR 837.

the meetings and fully informed of the issues. A very extensive explanatory statement must be sent out with notices of meetings, and this
statement will be both scrutinised in its terms and subjected to a power
of approval by the court.[26] The court is thus involved in the procedure in
at least two stages, first, on convening the necessary meetings of creditors
and members and, second, on the petition to sanction the scheme as
approved by the appropriate majorities of the meetings. On a petition for
approval, moreover, a substantial review of information has to be provided to the court on such matters as the capital, business and financial
history of the company, the terms of the scheme and the effects of the
scheme on each relevant class of creditor or contributory. Dealings with
the court on these matters involve substantial formality, routine and
complexity as well as numerous attendances at court or chambers.
Variations in schemes are also overseen by the court. When a scheme
is approved by the court it must be filed at the Companies Registry[27] and
it cannot then be varied without court approval. In such circumstances
the court will demand that further class meetings are held in order to
approve the variation.

A further posited disadvantage of the scheme of arrangement is that,
as noted, it involves no moratorium. In the period between the initial
formulation of a scheme and its becoming effective by court order, each
individual creditor is thus able to exercise all the rights and remedies that
he or she possesses against the company debtor. Cork estimated that,
because of the complex procedure involved, this period of high vulnerability was unlikely to be less than eight weeks.[28] In this period the
troubled company cannot prevent winding up or the random seizure of
assets by individual creditors, and this will make it extremely difficult to
launch even the simplest scheme.[29] In 2000 the Insolvency Service
recommended that it should liaise with the CLRSG to give full consideration to proposals for a moratorium in schemes of arrangement,
one to resemble the CVA moratorium then proposed (and later

---

[26] See Companies Act 2006 ss. 897–8. The statement must state all relevant facts:
Re Dorman Long [1934] 1 Ch 635; *Re Jessel Trust Ltd* [1985] BCLC 119.

[27] Note that the Companies Act 2006 s. 901 now requires a company to deliver to the
registrar a court order that alters the company's constitution. It also requires that every
copy of the company's articles subsequently issued must be accompanied by a copy of the
order unless the effect of the order has been incorporated into the articles by
amendment.

[28] Cork Report, para. 406 (discussing the Companies Act 1948 s. 206 scheme, the statutory
predecessor of s. 425 of the Companies Act 1985).

[29] Ibid., para. 408.

implemented),[30] and in its Final Report the CLRSG recommended further DTI consideration of the issue. The 2006 legislative restating of the rules on schemes, however, provided no addition of a moratorium.[31] Schemes may, accordingly, have to be coupled with administration orders if any protection is to be secured.

It should, finally, be noted that the prominent role of the company's existing management in a scheme of arrangement may bring some advantages (for example, the mentioned lack of disincentives to respond to troubles) but there may be concurrent disadvantages. Schemes of arrangement depend substantially on the management of the company to take new initiatives, often defensively. These qualities may often be lacking in companies, particularly troubled companies. As Cork noted:

> It is, however, often the case that, where a company has become insolvent, the management has lost interest, or lost its grip, and there is a vacuum. All too often a scheme of arrangement with creditors would be of advantage to all concerned, but there is no one with the authority within the company, the means of information, and the energy to push the scheme through.[32]

In recent years the scheme of arrangement has revived in popularity[33] – a revival due, in no little part, to the constructive attitude taken by the courts, whose concern to facilitate the implementation of schemes has been exemplified in an approach to assessing junior creditors' 'real economic interests' with reference to the sums that such parties would receive in the alternative to the scheme (notably by enforcing their bonds within a winding up).[34]

---

[30] Insolvency Service, *A Review of Company Rescue and Business Reconstruction Mechanisms*, Report by the Review Group (DTI, 2000) ('IS 2000') para. 43; CLRSG, *Final Report*, 2001, para. 13.11.

[31] It has been argued, however, that the lack of a moratorium provision combined with a simplified scheme of arrangement procedure could actually facilitate the restructuring of companies in providing a cheaper and more cost-effective process: see J. Tribe, 'Company Voluntary Arrangements and Rescue: A New Hope and a Tudor Orthodoxy' (Mimeo, Kingston University, 2008).

[32] Cork Report, para. 417.

[33] In the Takeover Panel's consultation paper, *Schemes of Arrangement* (Takeover Panel, London, June 2007) the Code Committee noted that schemes of arrangement have been used increasingly in recent years to effect takeover transactions regulated by the Takeover Code. (The aim of the consultation paper's proposals is to codify the application of the Code to such schemes.) See further 'Takeover Panel Consults on Schemes of Arrangement' (2007) 12 *Sweet & Maxwell's Company Law Newsletter* 8.

[34] As in *Re My Travel Group plc* [2005] 1 WLR 2365: see Segal, 'Schemes of Arrangement and Junior Creditors', p. 51; and p. 481 above.

As for ways forward, the CLRSG's Final Report of 2001 advocated that the requirement that a majority *in number* of those who cast the votes needed to agree a scheme be dispensed with so that a threshold of 75 per cent in value alone would apply.[35] Regarding the latter point, the CLRSG had argued that in many modern listed companies shareholders consisted to such a great extent of nominees that the decision of the true owners 'bears little or no relation to whether or not a majority in number is attained'.[36] No other meetings of members of a company, the Committee pointed out, required a majority other than by reference to value or voting powers.

Looking more broadly at reforms to section 895 procedures, there is a strong case for contending that the procedures for schemes of arrangement should be modelled along the lines of those relating to CVAs so that the class meeting regime as presently set up should be replaced with a statutory framework of meetings in combination with remedial powers to challenge the process by parties who are able to demonstrate that they have suffered prejudice – as per the Insolvency Act 1986 section 6 provisions on CVAs. Improvements in the transparency of the CVA process (as discussed below) could also be applied to schemes of arrangement.

Adopting this revised procedure for schemes of arrangement would offer a cheaper and quicker route to affirmation than mechanisms involving the court in routine approvals and decision-making on the procedural requirements of individual corporate circumstances. Cork, indeed, doubted whether 'painstaking perusal of documents by court officials with little or no experience of commerce or finance provides any real protection for creditors or contributories'.[37] There would be efficiency gains without material losses in fairness or accountability. As for the requirement of a numerical as well as a 75 per cent by value majority, the argument in favour of the existing rule is that this serves to limit the ability of creditors with large claims to impose their wills on their smaller creditor brethren. A further consideration is that if the schemes of arrangement process is streamlined so as to involve lower levels of court scrutiny

---

[35] CLRSG, *Final Report*, 2001, para. 13.10. See also C. Maunder, 'Bondholder Schemes of Arrangement: Playing the Numbers Game' (2003) 16 *Insolvency Intelligence* 73 at 76, for argument that removing the majority in number requirement would make schemes (now used as the tool of choice for many major restructurings involving bond issues) more 'flexible and attractive as well as saving significant amounts of costs for the debtor company and its creditors without necessarily putting at risk the rights of minority creditors'.

[36] CLRSG, *Completing the Structure*, p. 216.   [37] Cork Report, para. 419.

and if it continues to differ from the CVA by its non-reliance on the independent IP, there is a case for retaining small creditor protections in excess of those applicable to CVA procedures. Small creditors, after all, might rightly complain about their exposed positions if very large creditors were able to agree arrangements with managers under conditions of low scrutiny and little independent oversight and small creditors could only rely on *ex post facto* challenges in court: challenges that might well have to be mounted by parties who are ill-resourced, ill-informed and generally very poorly placed to protect their positions.

Is there a case for retaining the scheme of arrangement process when resort might be made to other procedures such as CVAs and administrations? This is a matter to be returned to once the CVA device has been discussed.

Company Voluntary Arrangements

The CVA, like administration, owes its origins to the Cork Committee. Cork considered that the law it reviewed was deficient in failing to provide that a company, like an individual, could enter into a binding arrangement with its creditors by a simple procedure that would allow it to organise its debts.[38] Under the then law, the company would have to obtain the separate consent of every creditor or else use the slow and cumbersome scheme of arrangement process.[39] The Insolvency Act 1986 sections 1–7 set out a simpler scheme based on the Cork recommendations, and these provisions were hailed as the arrival of a new 'rescue culture' in English insolvency procedures.[40] The Insolvency Act 1986 provides that the directors of a company can take the initiative in setting up a voluntary arrangement, though the first steps can be taken by the liquidator or the administrator if the company is being wound up or is in administration. It is not necessary for the company to be 'insolvent' or 'unable to pay its debts' for the procedure to be used. The directors may nominate an IP to act in relation to the CVA and may make a proposal for consideration by a meeting of the company's members and creditors. It is common for the

---

[38] Ibid., paras. 400–3.

[39] See the then Companies Act 1985 ss. 425–7 (formerly Companies Act 1948 ss. 206–8), a scheme of compromise or arrangement; Companies Act 1985 s. 582 (formerly Companies Act 1948 s. 287), a scheme of liquidation and reconstruction; or Companies Act 1985 s. 601 (formerly Companies Act 1948 s. 306), a 'binding arrangement'.

[40] M. Phillips, *The Administration Procedure and Creditors' Voluntary Arrangements* (Centre for Commercial Law Studies, QMW, London, 1996) p. 7.

directors to produce the proposal with the assistance of a licensed IP. The person nominated to act in a CVA as a trustee or supervisor must, within twenty-eight days[41] of notice of the proposal for a CVA, report to the court, stating whether, in his opinion, meetings of the company and creditors should be summoned to consider the proposal.[42] The proposal needs to be approved by 75 per cent of creditors voting in person or by proxy by reference to the value of their claims. It also requires the approval of 50 per cent in value of the members/shareholders present at a shareholders' meeting.[43] If approved,[44] the scheme becomes operative and binding upon the company and all of its creditors who were entitled to vote at the meeting or would have been so entitled if they had had notice of it.[45] The scheme even binds those creditors who did not approve the proposal. The scheme is administered by a supervisor, usually the person who was the nominee,[46] who must be a qualified IP, and a CVA operates under the aegis of the court but without the need for court involvement[47] unless there is a disagreement requiring judicial resolution.[48]

---

[41] Or longer if the court allows: Insolvency Act 1986 s. 2(2).

[42] Where the nominee is not the liquidator or administrator he must also state in his report whether, in his opinion, the proposed CVA has 'a reasonable prospect of being approved and implemented': Insolvency Act 1986 s. 2(2).

[43] Value being determined by the number of votes conferred on each of them by the company's articles of association: Insolvency Rules 1986, r. 1.20(1).

[44] Where there is a conflict between a creditors' meeting decision to approve a proposal and a shareholders' meeting decision, the creditors' meeting decision prevails, subject to the shareholders' right to challenge by application to the court: Insolvency Act 1986 s. 4A(2), (3), (4).

[45] Insolvency Act 1986 s. 5. The CVA thus binds even unknown creditors and creditors not receiving notice of the meeting because it was sent to the wrong address. A person entitled to vote at the meeting (whether or not with notice) can apply to court (under s. 6(2)) on the grounds that the CVA unfairly prejudices the interests of a creditor, member or contributory of the company or that there has been some irregularity at the meeting: see *Re Trident Fashions* [2004] 2 BCLC 35. On the position of creditors not bound by the CVA see *Re TBL Realisations Ltd, Oakley-Smith v. Greenberg* [2004] BCC 81, [2005] 2 BCLC 74; L. C. Ho and R. Mokal, 'Interplay of CVA, Administration and Liquidation: Part 1' (2004) 25 Co. Law. 3; cf. R. M. Goode, *Principles of Corporate Insolvency Law* (3rd edn, Sweet & Maxwell, London, 2005) pp. 401–3.

[46] Insolvency Act 1986 s. 7(2).

[47] See the Insolvency Act 2000 Sch. 2, para. 3 for amendments to the circumstances in which the court may replace a nominee (i.e. for failure to submit a report, death or where impracticable or inappropriate for nominee to continue to act).

[48] See Insolvency Act 1986 s. 7; *Re Pinson Wholesale Ltd* [2008] BCC 112 – on a s. 7 application by joint CVA supervisors, the court was willing to imply a term into the statutory contract effected by the CVA so as to provide for fair remuneration for the joint supervisors who had successfully claimed £70,000 from a former office holder in relation to the company.

What a CVA does not do within the terms of section 4 of the Insolvency Act 1986 is affect, without agreement, the rights of secured creditors of the company to enforce their securities: meetings shall not approve any proposals or modifications that interfere with such enforcement rights except with the concurrence of the creditor concerned.[49] Similarly, company or creditors' meetings cannot approve proposals or modifications providing for the paying of preferential debts other than in priority to non-preferential debts or other than equally with other preferential debts.[50]

Nor did the Insolvency Act 1986 provide for a general moratorium and a period of protection during which the company can draw up and consider an arrangement.[51] A moratorium could only be achieved under the Act by combining a proposal for a CVA with an application to the court for the appointment of an administrator.[52] This would constitute a complex and expensive procedure. The introduction of a CVA moratorium for small companies, as will be seen below, was the major change effected by the Insolvency Act 2000.

The gestation period for this development was, however, considerable. In 1993 the DTI concluded that, on balance, an immediate moratorium would be useful in allowing discussions to take place between the company, major creditors and secured lenders.[53] It would also allow the company to carry on trading without facing such threats as landlord distraints or winding-up petitions or repossessions of goods under hire purchase or leasing contracts. This was to take effect on the filing in court by the directors of an intention to set up a CVA together with a consent to act by the nominee, but only if the moratorium was additional to the existing CVA procedure and involved an appropriate level of

---

[49] Insolvency Act 1986 s. 4(3).

[50] The Insolvency Act 1986 Part I contains provisions obliging preferential creditors to accept a decision made by a majority of them even if passed in a separate class meeting. This contrasts with the Companies Act 2006 s. 895.

[51] This contrasts with the 'interim order' available in the case of insolvent individuals under the Insolvency Act 1986 ss. 252–4.

[52] See now Insolvency Act 1986 Sch. B1; ch. 9 above.

[53] DTI/Insolvency Service, *Company Voluntary Arrangements and Administration Orders: A Consultative Document* (October 1993) (DTI 1993) p. 11. On landlords' right to peaceable re-entry see ch. 9 above. The arguments ranged against the moratorium, however, were that it is a device open to abuse by directors of companies that have no chance of turnaround and that it tends simply to prolong agonies, dissipate more assets and make realisations less efficient.

supervision.[54] The 1993 proposals went to consultation and the DTI reported two years later that a 'broad consensus' had favoured a short moratorium for rescue purposes. A proposed new CVA procedure was presented and aimed 'to make company rescue simpler, cheaper and more accessible, particularly for the smaller company'.[55]

The small companies' moratorium

In February 2000, the Insolvency Bill was introduced into Parliament. It received royal assent on 30 November 2000 and its moratorium provisions came into effect on 1 January 2003.[56] The 2000 Act amends the Insolvency Act 1986 by inserting a new section 1A and a new Schedule A1 (which provides for the 'small companies' moratorium). Consistently with the DTI's proposals, this legislative change allows the directors of an 'eligible' company to obtain a moratorium when proposing a CVA under Part I of the Insolvency Act 1986.[57] A company is eligible under the IA 1986 Schedule A1, paragraph 3(2) if, in the year before filing for a moratorium or the prior financial year, it has satisfied two or more of the requirements for constituting a small company under section 382(3) of the Companies Act 2006. This means that moratoria will only be available to companies with at least two of the following requirements: a turnover of not over £6.5 million per annum; fewer than fifty employees; and a balance sheet total which does not exceed £3.26 million.[58] These are very small companies indeed. It can be argued that if moratoria are useful to small companies they should be of benefit to all companies.[59] The Insolvency Act 2000 leaves open the possibility of extending the moratorium to larger companies by providing that the Secretary of

---

[54] So that companies which would be adversely affected by a stay on creditors' rights could take the more private and informal actions already available and that the existing CVA procedure would remain in place as an exit route for administration (DTI 1993, p. 12).

[55] Ibid.

[56] For comment see A. Smith and M. Neill, 'The Insolvency Act 2000' (2001) 17 IL&P 84.

[57] Insolvency Act 1986 s. 1A(1).

[58] Certain companies are not eligible for moratoria under Sch. A1, para. 2(2). These include, inter alia, insurance companies, companies authorised to engage in banking business, companies which are parties to market contracts and any company whose property is subject to a market charge or collateral security charge: see further Insolvency Act 1986 Sch. A1, paras. 2–4.

[59] See J. Alexander, 'CVAs: The New Legislation' (1999) Insolvency Bulletin 5 at 8. As Fletcher notes, the main reason for tying the availability of the moratorium to the size of the company 'appears to have been the desire to channel all rescue proceedings involving

State may promulgate regulations to modify the terms of eligibility for a moratorium.[60] One reason why eligibility might be extended arises from the vulnerability of the current rules to abuse. As the Law Society pointed out in its comments on the Insolvency Bill 2000,[61] a company might have an incentive to arrange its affairs so that it meets the requirements for being a small company in order to gain the protection of a moratorium for a CVA.

A company may not file for a moratorium if an administration order is in force; it is being wound up; an administrative receiver has been appointed; a CVA has effect; there is a provisional liquidator; or in the prior twelve months a moratorium has been in force, or a CVA has ended prematurely and a section 5(3)(a) order has been made, or an administrator has held office.[62] Before a moratorium is obtained, the directors will submit to the nominee the proposed terms of the CVA and a statement of company affairs. The nominee will then indicate to the directors, in a statement, his opinion on whether the CVA has a reasonable prospect of approval and implementation; whether the company is likely to have sufficient funds to carry on its business; and whether meetings of the company and creditors should be summoned to consider the proposed CVA. Filing for a moratorium is carried out by the directors and involves submission to the court of a statement of proposals and of company affairs. The court also receives, *inter alia*, a nominee statement. The moratorium commences on filing the appropriate documents and lasts until the day on which the meetings of the company and its creditors are first held.[63]

The effects of the moratorium are to offer protection against petitions for winding up or administration orders, meetings of the company,

---

larger companies through the new, streamlined administration procedure': I. F. Fletcher, 'UK Corporate Rescue: Recent Developments – Changes to Administrative Receivership, Administration and Company Voluntary Arrangements – the Insovency Act 2000, the White Paper 2001 and the Enterprise Act 2002' (2004) 5 EBOR 119 at 131.

[60] In commenting on the Trade and Industry Committee Report on the draft Insolvency Bill, the Government said that 'the results of experience to date should be a significant factor in any decision to extend eligibility for a moratorium': see Trade and Industry Committee, Fourth Special Report, *Government Observations on the First and Second Reports from the Trade and Industry Committee* (session 1999–2000) HC 237.

[61] Law Society Company Law Committee, *Comments on the Insolvency Bill*, March 2000, No. 396, p. 4.

[62] Insolvency Act 1986 Sch. A1, para. 4(1).

[63] Ibid., para. 8. The time limit for the holding of the first meetings is twenty-eight days from the day on which the moratorium comes into force, unless an extension is granted under Sch. A1, para. 32.

winding-up resolutions, appointments of receivers and other steps 'to enforce any security over the company's property or to repossess goods in the company's possession under any hire purchase agreement except with the leave of the court'.[64] No other proceeding or execution or legal process or distress can be commenced, continued or levied against the company except by court leave, nor can a landlord forfeit the lease of a company's premises by means of peaceable re-entry.[65]

Security granted during the moratorium is only enforceable if, at the time of granting, there were reasonable grounds for believing that it would benefit the company.[66] The company is not allowed to obtain credit of over £250 during a moratorium from a person who has not been informed that the moratorium is in force.[67] Disposals of company property and payments of debts and liabilities existing prior to the moratorium are only permissible if there are reasonable grounds for believing that such actions will benefit the company or there was approval by a meeting of the company and its creditors (or the nominee in absence of such 'moratorium committees').[68] Property of the company subject to security or held in possession under hire purchase agreement can be disposed of with court leave or consent of the security holder/owner of the goods.[69] In the case of dispositions of property subject to a security which, as created, was a floating charge, the security holder's priority will not change regarding property representing the property disposed of.[70]

Where court leave is given as described, this is to be notified by the directors to the Registrar of Companies within fourteen days or liability to a fine results.[71] During the moratorium the nominee is obliged to monitor the company's affairs for the purposes of forming an opinion on whether the proposed CVA has a reasonable prospect of approval and implementation and whether the company is likely to have sufficient funds during the remainder of the moratorium to allow it to carry on its business.[72] The nominee must withdraw his or her consent to act if he or she forms the opinion that such reasonable prospects of funds are no longer likely, if he or she becomes aware that the company was not, at the

---

[64] Ibid., para. 12(1).
[65] Ibid., para. 12(1). On peaceable re-entry see P. McCartney, 'Insolvency Procedures and a Landlord's Right of Peaceable Re-entry' (2000) 13 *Insolvency Intelligence* 73 and ch. 9 above.
[66] Insolvency Act 1986 Sch. A1, para. 14.   [67] Ibid., para. 17.
[68] Ibid., paras. 18, 19, 29 and 35.   [69] Ibid., para. 20.   [70] Ibid., para. 20(4).
[71] Ibid., para. 20(8) and (9).   [72] Ibid., para. 24(1).

date of filing, eligible for a moratorium or if the directors fail to comply with their duty to supply the nominee with information needed to form an opinion on the above matters.[73] On withdrawal of nominee consent, the moratorium ends.

As for challenges to the nominee's actions, any creditor, director or member of the company or other person affected by a moratorium may apply to the court if dissatisfied with an act or omission or decision of the nominee during the moratorium.[74] The court is then empowered to confirm, reverse or modify any nominee decision, give him directions or make such other order as it thinks fit. The acts of directors within the moratorium can be challenged similarly.

The meetings of the company and creditors are to be called by the nominee when he or she thinks fit and these meetings shall decide whether to approve the proposed CVA with or without modifications.[75] Such modification shall not, however, affect the enforcement rights of secured creditors without consent or the priorities or *pari passu* payment of preferential debts.[76] A person entitled to vote at either meeting or the nominee has a right to challenge the CVA in court on the grounds that it unfairly prejudices the interests of the creditor member or contributory of the company; or that there has been a material irregularity in relation to or at either meeting.[77]

Once an approved CVA has taken effect, the person formerly known as the nominee becomes the supervisor of the CVA[78] and any of the company's creditors or other persons dissatisfied by any act, omission or decision of the supervisor may challenge this in court.[79]

Achieving a successful rescue may also require that the directors are able to effect advantageous transactions with third parties. Here, however, the terms of the Insolvency Act 2000 create unhelpful uncertainties. Such third parties will be reluctant to deal with the directors if they are not certain that they will be protected from a subsequent failure of the moratorium or a non-approval of the voluntary arrangement. Schedule A1, paragraph 12(2) of the Insolvency Act 1986 now suspends section 127 of the Insolvency Act 1986 (which prohibits property dispositions

---

[73] Ibid., para. 25(2).   [74] Ibid., para. 26.   [75] Ibid., paras. 29–31.

[76] Ibid., para. 31(4) and (5).   [77] Ibid., para. 38.

[78] Ibid., para. 39. The Insolvency Act 2000 s. 4(4) amended the Insolvency Act 1986 s. 389: to act as a supervisor or nominee of a CVA the individual in question must be an IP or a person authorised to act as a supervisor etc. by a body recognised by the Secretary of State for that purpose: see IA 1986 s. 389A.

[79] Insolvency Act 1986 Sch. A1, para. 39(3).

after the commencement of a winding up unless the court has otherwise authorised).[80] It does so where a petition for winding up has been presented before the beginning of the moratorium. The effect is that section 127 will not operate to render void any dispositions of property, transfers of shares or alterations in status of the members of the company during the moratorium. Such dispositions are then governed by the moratorium provisions. Uncertainties arise because there may not be a petition for winding up pending at the date of the start of the moratorium. The Law Society has argued that there should be an express provision confirming that 'the criteria for disposals, payments, charges and other permitted transactions during the moratorium regime fully supplant the criteria for escaping all the "normal" invalidating provisions of the Insolvency Act 1986 and third parties acting in good faith are protected in being party to such transactions'.[81] If that is not the case, said the Society, there should be provisions allowing directors to seek court confirmation that any transactions are valid and proper. A danger is that if such worries are not countered, companies may be encouraged to petition for a winding up immediately before filing for a moratorium in order to protect transactions within the moratorium from being attacked as preferences or transactions at undervalue under the Insolvency Act 1986 sections 238 and 239.

The CVA as an efficient rescue mechanism

If a CVA is to lead to rescue rather than liquidation it needs to achieve a number of results.[82] First, the business needs to generate cash profits that are sufficient to pay off past debts and deal with ongoing liabilities. Second, the credit control procedures of the company must be effective enough to avoid such an accumulation of bad debts as is likely to prejudice the recovery. Third, there will need to be a corporate strategy, implementable through the CVA proposal, that will lead to financial survival by taking all necessary steps, such as disposals of non-core activities or assets where appropriate. In order to achieve these results,

---

[80] On the Insolvency Act 1986 s. 127 see e.g. G. Stewart, 'Section 127 and Change of Position Defences' (2003) *Recovery* (Autumn) 6; and further ch. 13 below.

[81] Law Society Company Law Committee, *Comments*, p. 6.

[82] See, for example, Alexander, 'CVAs: The New Legislation'. For an empirical study of CVAs see G. Cook, N. Pandit, D. Milman and A. Griffiths, *Small Business Rescue: A Multi-Method Empirical Study of Company Voluntary Arrangements* (ICAEW, London, 2003).

a further requirement is likely to be directorial commitment and motivation. Enterprising directors will often possess incentives to leave a troubled company for greener corporate pastures, especially if they have no equity interest or do not require the business to succeed in order to protect their income. A CVA, accordingly, may need to create incentives for good directors to see the rescue through.

A number of difficulties will face the proponents of a CVA. In the first place this is a 'debtor in possession' system that leaves in control the directors who have led the company into difficulty. The prospects of continuing poor management are, accordingly, real.[83] Suppliers will often be reluctant to continue normal trading with the company and they, as well as main creditors, will have to be persuaded to support the CVA. Creditors may often suspect that those putting forward CVA proposals are using the CVA as a device that will allow the management to set up a phoenix operation in order to effect a transfer of the business and its assets and leave creditors empty handed. Directors' motives for seeking a CVA may similarly be called into question because the institution of a CVA will rule out charges of wrongful trading on a subsequent liquidation.[84]

The uptake of CVAs has been disappointingly low since 1986. In 1999–2000 there were 526 CVAs (and appointments) compared to 427 administrations and 1,665 receiverships. In 2005–6, two years after the introduction of the CVA moratorium, there were only 540 CVAs compared to 2,661 administrations and 565 receiverships.[85] In a series of reports[86] the DTI reviewed the reasons why CVAs have not proved

[83] Cook et al., Small Business Rescue, report that continued poor management was a frequently cited problem.

[84] Note, however, that the Insolvency Act 2000 imposed new 'whistleblowing' obligations on the nominee/supervisor: see now Insolvency Act 1986 s. 7A. The 2000 Act also sought to prevent abuse of the CVA mechanism 'by installing a degree of integrity reinforced by the criminal law': see now IA 1986 s. 6A (see L. S. Sealy and D. Milman, *Annotated Guide to the Insolvency Legislation 2007–08* (Thomson/Sweet & Maxwell, London, 2007) p. 35).

[85] Numbers of CVAs were, moreover, considerably down on the previous two years: see Insolvency Service, *Enterprise Act 2002 – Corporate Insolvency Provisions: Evaluation Report* (Insolvency Service, London, 2008) p. 17. Potential use of CVAs has, however, been extended to National Health Service Trusts: see National Health Service Act 2006 s. 53; 'In view of the difficulties currently encountered in this sector one suspects that this provision will not be underused in the years to come': D. Milman, 'Corporate Insolvency Law: An End of Term Report' (2007) 214/5 *Sweet & Maxwell's Company Law Newsletter* 1 at 2.

[86] DTI 1993; DTI/IS, *Revised Proposals for a New CVA Procedure* (April 1995) ('DTI 1995'); Insolvency Service, *A Review of Company Rescue and Business Reconstruction Mechanisms*, Interim Report (DTI, September 1999) ('IS 1999'); IS 2000.

popular and the IS played a central role in developing the reform proposals that were implemented with the Insolvency Act 2000.

Many of the reasons for the non-use of CVAs overlap with the reasons for the low resort to pre-Enterprise Act 2002 administration orders that were considered in chapter 9. Cost has been a material factor. Research has suggested that for very small companies the CVA may be too expensive a procedure to exploit[87] and that there is often a preference for making a clean break and using liquidation to save some of the business rather than the company.[88] In one survey, only 8 per cent of companies undergoing CVA processes had turnover of less than £100,000 in the last financial year.[89] The DTI's 1993 Consultative Document included in its list of 'barriers to the use of CVA provisions': the secured creditor's right to appoint a receiver; the directors' lack of knowledge and IP's lack of experience of the provisions; fear by directors of provisions connected with the Insolvency Act 1986 and supervised by IPs; and rescues being attempted too late. To these reasons, a study for the ICAEW has added the suggestion that IPs have been deterred from using CVAs by the perceived risk, lack of effective control and uncertainty involved in the process and the difficulty of trying to forecast cash flows up to five years ahead. The same study noted that IPs may worry about their committing to turnarounds that depend on improved management, and to engaging in considerable amounts of work only for the rescue to founder.[90]

The DTI argued in 1993 that some of the above disincentives and barriers could nevertheless be reduced in effect. The lack of knowledge of directors could be countered by awareness campaigns and education, and directors' fears of insolvency processes might be responded to by placing rescue provisions in companies' statutes rather than in insolvency legislation, or by relabelling IPs as 'rescue consultants'. The lateness of rescue efforts could be remedied by improving directors' use of financial information and by raising the consciousness of auditors and non-insolvency advisers to make them more aware of, and more likely to recommend, rescue processes.[91]

Other barriers to use were, however, particularly severe in relation to CVAs. A major problem was lack of finance to fund corporate operations during CVAs. Banks tended to act cautiously in consideration of their own

---

[87] See D. Milman and F. Chittenden, *Corporate Rescue: CVAs and the Challenge of Small Companies*, ACCA Research Report 44 (ACCA, London, 1995).
[88] Cook *et al.*, *Small Business Rescue.*   [89] Ibid.   [90] Ibid.   [91] DTI 1993, p. 20.

shareholders' interests and in fear of 'throwing good money after bad'.[92] The DTI opinion was that a foremost weakness of the CVA was the absence of a moratorium. As indicated above, however, the use of the CVA has not increased materially since the moratorium came into effect in 2003 and this may suggest that the other disincentives to use that are cited above may have proved more powerful than the DTI supposed in 1993.

Have the Insolvency Act 2000 changes produced an efficient rescue regime? R3's Ninth Survey of Business Recovery, published in 2001, indicated that where CVAs are used, there is a 74 per cent preservation rate.[93] As for returns to creditors, the R3 Twelfth Survey of Business Recovery (2004) indicated that CVAs returned just under 50 pence in the pound to creditors overall compared to around 30 pence for administrative receiverships, compulsory liquidations and administrations. For unsecured creditors, the CVA proved much more rewarding, with CVAs averaging returns of 17 pence in the pound compared to 5.4 pence for administrative receiverships and compulsory liquidations and 6.3 pence for administrations.[94]

It remains to be seen whether the rescue potential of the CVA will develop in coming years. In the past, general concerns have been voiced in relation to the role that preferential creditors have played in CVA processes, the nominee's scrutiny role, rescue funding, corporate relations with landlords or utility suppliers and those who lease the tools of the trade to the company. It should be emphasised, moreover, that the CVA moratorium, as now set up, only applies to very small companies and here some particular problems may arise. Nominees, after the Insolvency Act 2000 amendments, have to be prepared to state in writing at the outset that the CVA has a reasonable prospect of being approved and implemented and also that the company is likely to have sufficient funds available during the moratorium to enable it to carry on business.[95] In order to place themselves in a position to make such a statement responsibly, nominees may have to engage in extensive consultations with

---

[92] Ibid., p. 15. On distributing moneys held by CVA supervisors once the company goes into liquidation and whether liquidation terminates the CVA, see the guidelines laid down by Peter Gibson LJ in *Re NT Gallagher & Son Ltd* [2002] BCLC 133 at 150.

[93] The SPI Eighth Survey (covering 1997–8) indicated that where CVAs were used, 37 per cent of jobs were saved (receiverships saved 31 per cent, administrations 40 per cent and company voluntary liquidations 11 per cent). The SPI was renamed R3, the Association of Business Recovery Professionals, in January 2000.

[94] R3 Twelfth Survey, *Company Insolvency in the United Kingdom* (R3, London, 2004).

[95] See Insolvency Act 1986 Sch. A1, para. 6(2).

proposed funders as well as major suppliers and other trading partners. Assurances from such parties will have to be sought and trading projections analysed. The overall effect, it has been suggested, may be that the amount of work involved, and the attendant expenses, will prevent the moratorium CVA procedure from performing as a cost-effective device for smaller companies.[96] The CVA, moreover, may be further reduced in its attractiveness because the moratorium does not protect the company during the period in which proposals are being developed and a nominee may fear that consulting with creditors before a moratorium comes into effect may trigger their taking precipitate action against the company.

Crown creditors and CVAs

In the consultations that the IS held in its 1999 Review Group discussion paper on rescue and reconstruction mechanisms the 'most heartfelt' response on CVAs concerned 'the uncommercial attitude of the revenue departments (Inland Revenue and Customs and Excise (HMRC)) to proposals for CVAs'. At that time the Crown enjoyed preferential status for such debts and IS consultees complained that the revenue departments' insistence on 100 per cent payment, and the time taken to consider proposals, frustrated many CVA proposals that unsecured creditors would otherwise approve. Respondents consistently criticised the apparent unwillingness of these departments to deal with CVA proposals on their merits or to take a longer-term view of the prospects of a company's survival. The Review Group recommended that the Inland Revenue (IR) and Customs and Excise should work to develop a more commercial approach to CVAs so that proposals *were* judged on their merits and, where appropriate, less than 100 pence in the pound should be settled on if it was judged that a CVA would offer superior returns.[97]

In order to produce a more consistent and responsive approach to CVA proposals, the Review Group recommended that the two revenue departments should investigate integrating their work on CVAs, look at the staffing implications of a more responsive approach and consider the need to bring in private sector skills to bear on decisions relating to CVAs and their commercial viability. They should also, said the Review Group, explore with the Insolvency Service how to take a more proactive role in

---

[96] See Smith and Neill, 'Insolvency Act 2000', p. 85. R3 also made this argument: see R3, 'The Moratorium Provisions for the Company Voluntary Arrangement Procedure in the Insolvency Bill 2000' (2000) 16 IL&P 77.

[97] IS 2000, p. 24.

warning directors of the possible consequences of continuing to trade during insolvency and of the possible need for professional advice.

In accordance with these suggestions, the IR and the Customs and Excise set up a Voluntary Arrangements Service (VAS) in Worthing which has been running since 2 April 2001. It is managed by the IR on behalf of HM Revenue and Customs.[98] The stated aims of the VAS are 'to help its customers, to work collaboratively with the private sector and other government departments and to make a full contribution to business rescue by supporting viable businesses through periods of temporary financial difficulty'.[99] To this end, the VAS publishes criteria by which it will judge the acceptability of proposals put to it by troubled companies.[100]

The Enterprise Act 2002 abolished the Crown's right to be paid as a preferential creditor.[101] Has this development enhanced or detracted from the CVA as a rescue process? In the lead up to the 2002 Act there was a general acceptance that abolition of the Crown's preferential status would produce more successful CVAs[102] but, in 2003, the President of R3 reported a number of R3 members' concerns that, in the light of abolition, the VAS had changed its policy on voting for voluntary arrangements. In response to communications on this matter, the VAS 'emphatically confirmed that there is absolutely no effort being made by them to increase the amount of return from voluntary arrangements'.[103] The VAS emphasised that it supported proposals that were workable and designed to increase returns for creditors, including the Crown, without detracting from the company's survival prospects.[104]

---

[98] See D. Ellis, 'Inland Revenue and Business Rescue' (2001) *Recovery* (September) 18–19.

[99] Ibid., p. 18.

[100] On HMRC standard modifications that it likes to see in CVAs and HMRC expectations on the duration of CVAs see G. Krasner, 'Duration of CVAs' (2006) *Recovery* (Winter) 3.

[101] Enterprise Act 2002 s. 251.

[102] In 1999 the Review Group reported the broad view that this would be the effect of abolition since: 'the larger the dividend that can be proposed to unsecured creditors, and as importantly, the earlier it can be paid to them, the more likely they are to support proposals which would allow the survival of the company': see IS 2000, pp. 25–6. The Review Group added that it would be important that the benefits of abolition should accrue to unsecured creditors and not to the holders of floating charges – hence the Enterprise Act 2002's creation of the ring-fenced fund or 'prescribed part' under which a percentage in value of assets subject to a floating charge has to be given over to form a fund available to unsecured creditors: see now IA 1986 s. 176A; and ch. 3 above.

[103] See J. Verrill, 'President's Column' (2003) *Recovery* (Winter) 36–7.   [104] See ibid.

The nominee's scrutiny role

An advantage of CVA procedures since the Insolvency Act 2000 is that moratorium protection from creditors can be achieved without the need to incur the trouble and expense of a court action.[105] The IP who acts as nominee accordingly fulfils an important role in assessing prospects of success and filtering out non-viable proposals. This is a reason for insisting that the nominee be a fully qualified IP, or a person authorised to act as a nominee or supervisor by a body recognised by the Secretary of State.[106] The role is, however, a difficult one since nominees rely heavily on information supplied to them by the directors and they will not have the power or time to conduct thorough investigations.[107] One commentator described the predicament: 'If too much reliance is placed on the nominee as a filter it will inevitably lead to escalation in cost as nominees seek to protect their own position by "due diligence", or become conservative in recommending a CVA as viable; the result is that the proposed cheap and speedy procedure aimed at smaller companies will become prohibitively expensive and slow.'[108]

The Insolvency Act 2000 demands that when the nominee submits to the directors a statement[109] which indicates an opinion on, *inter alia*, whether the CVA has a reasonable prospect of approval and implementation, the nominee is 'entitled to rely on the information submitted to him' by the directors in their CVA proposal 'unless he has reason to doubt its accuracy'.[110] The Law Society cautioned that there was a 'clear danger' in the nominee simply relying on the information supplied by directors.[111] Concern has also been raised that for a nominee to be able to give the statement referred to above, he will need to be involved 'in the day to day management of the business and to have carried out a

---

[105] Of course, after the reforms of the Enterprise Act 2002 it is now also possible to put a company into administration (and gain the protection of a moratorium) without going to court: see ch. 9 above.

[106] Insolvency Act 1986 s. 4(2).

[107] It is noteworthy also that the chairman of a creditors' meeting will be allowed by the court to value claims on the basis of the evidence produced by the creditor or debtor and has no duty to investigate independently: see *Re Newlands (Seaford) Educational Trust* [2007] BCC 195. (Chair supported in valuing landlords' claim – for in excess of £1 million – at £1 in accordance with Rule 1.17(3) of the Insolvency Rules 1986, since representations did not allow the ascertaining of the claim's appropriate value.)

[108] Brown, *Corporate Rescue*, pp. 663–4.

[109] See now Insolvency Act 1986 Sch. A1, para. 6(2).

[110] Insolvency Act 1986 Sch. A1, para. 6(3).

[111] Law Society Company Law Committee, *Comments*, p. 5.

significant investigation'.[112] This could prove expensive. Concern was also expressed that the nominee will have significant responsibilities without authority in that he has no control over the assets which he would have if he were a provisional liquidator or other office holder, nor does he control the actions of the directors during the period of the moratorium.[113]

A further worry that was expressed by the Law Society perhaps evidenced a low opinion of the professional standards of IPs. The Society said: 'We are also concerned that companies will be encouraged to shop around amongst those authorised to act as nominees until they can locate one prepared to provide an appropriate statement in order to secure a moratorium. This concern was shared by the Select Committee.'[114] The Society added that such loopholes created the potential for a voluntary arrangement to go badly wrong, bringing the whole process into disrepute amongst creditors.[115]

In defence of the Insolvency Act 2000 regime, it could, however, be argued that nominee scrutiny, even if erring on the defensive side, is liable to be quicker and cheaper than resort to court and that the twenty-eight-day limit of the moratorium should restrict some of the dangers of abuse that are associated with the longer terms of the United States Chapter 11 moratorium.[116]

Rescue funding

A fundamental challenge for troubled companies is that of securing new funds in order to finance continuing activities while a CVA is being negotiated and in order to provide for the longer-term survival of corporate operations.[117] The availability of longer-term financing will crucially affect the success or failure of the CVA since creditors are unlikely to agree to the company's proposals without the prospect of secure funding.[118] The SPI survey for 1997–8 suggested that in 43 per cent of cases the biggest barrier to turnaround was lack of appropriate finance[119] and R3's 1998–9 survey indicated that in one in five cases of

---

[112] Alexander, 'CVAs: The New Legislation', pp. 8–9.   [113] Ibid.

[114] Law Society Company Law Committee, *Comments*, pp. 4–5.

[115] Ibid., p. 5.   [116] See ch. 6 above.

[117] The adequacy of an adequate funding stream for the period until approval can be secured is a legal as well as practical requirement: see IA 1986 Sch. A1, para. 6(2)(b). On rescue and funding more generally see chs. 6 and 9 above.

[118] DTI 1993, p. 5. On the importance of funding see IS 2000, pp. 33–5.

[119] IS 1999, p. 12.

companies with a turnover of over £5 million 'the main factor preventing a more positive outcome was the inability to secure funding'.[120]

In many cases it is the company's own bank that has to be persuaded that there is a viable future for the company and generally the IPs guiding the CVA will attempt to secure the bank's approval for proposals before other creditors are approached. Other sources of funds are also available. The BERR, for instance, sponsors a Small Firms Loan Guarantee scheme which provides a guarantee covering 75 per cent of loans of up to £250,000 with terms of up to ten years. Other financing options include new equity funding and the provision of funds by the firm's managers.

Short-term funding will generally be sought, as noted, through negotiation with the company's main lender (usually the bank); through negotiating limited credit periods with major suppliers; or by sale of assets. Negotiating supplier credit periods is, however, a fraught process for directors because such trading or credit may expose them to liabilities for fraudulent or wrongful trading[121] and it may involve further dissipation of the assets charged to creditors. Many such steps will in practice have to be carried out with the approval of secured lenders because the spending of money or selling of assets will reduce the security cover of such lenders.

A further option for enhancing funding during a moratorium might be offered by provision for super-priority. The issues surrounding such potential changes have been discussed in chapter 9 and will not be rehearsed here.

Landlords, lessors of tools and utilities suppliers

The rights of peaceable re-entry by landlords have been discussed in chapter 9 and that debate will not be repeated here.[122] As for those who lease tools to the company and utilities suppliers, the Insolvency Act 1986 Schedule A1 provisions on the moratorium state that during the

---

[120] R3, Ninth Survey of Business Recovery in the UK. See also statement by R3, 'R3 Calls for Government to Commit to Action on Business Rescue' (2001), that the 'most intractable problem in business rescue today is the provision of post-rescue finance'. R3's Twelfth Survey of Corporate Insolvency in the UK reported (p. 26) that loss of finance was the major cited factor in the failure of companies surveyed.

[121] Insolvency Act 1986 ss. 213 and 214; see further ch. 16 below.

[122] On the ability of creditors to use a CVA to force landlords to give up their rights in return for rights under a CVA – and landlords as creditors who do not fall within the class of creditors who are not bound by a CVA – see *Thomas* v. *Ken Thomas Ltd* [2006] EWCA Civ 1504 and P. Godfrey, 'Legal Update' (2007) *Recovery* (Spring) 9–11. See also the discussion of landlords, unfair prejudice and the *Powerhouse* case at pp. 509–12 below.

moratorium no steps may be taken 'to repossess goods in the company's possession under any hire purchase agreement except with the leave of the court. No other proceeding and no execution or other legal process may be commenced or continued and no distress may be levied against the company or its property except with the leave of the court.'[123] This provision is based on Insolvency Act 1986 Schedule B1, paragraphs 43(3) and 43(6) dealing with the post-Enterprise Act administration order moratorium which, together with case law, makes it clear that the moratorium on enforcement applies to goods supplied on hire purchase or similar agreements (which include conditional sale agreements, chattel leasing agreements and retention of title agreements).[124]

Utility supplies to troubled companies are protected at present by section 233 of the Insolvency Act 1986 which governs the situations in which an administration order is made, an administrative receiver or provisional liquidator is appointed, a CVA is approved by meetings of the company and of creditors, or the company goes into liquidation. In these circumstances, where the office holder (administrator, administrative receiver and so on) requests that gas, electricity, water or telecommunications supplies be continued, the supplier may make it a condition of supply that the office holder personally guarantees payment of supplies, but that supplier shall not make it a condition of supply (or effectively make it a condition of supply) that any outstanding charges be paid. In the case of a CVA moratorium it would be appropriate to make such a provision effective at the time at which the CVA moratorium comes into force (when relevant documents are filed or lodged with the court).[125]

Expertise

The IP's expertise in, and orientation to, rescue has already been discussed[126] but consideration should be given to the CVA procedure and whether this is conducive to the making of informed and expert judgements on corporate rescues. Research into the operation of CVA procedures in the 1990s suggests that the expertise of IPs in operating CVA

---

[123] Insolvency Act 1986 Sch. A1, para. 12(1)(g) and (h).
[124] Hire purchase agreements and conditional sale agreements are defined in the Consumer Credit Act 1974 s. 189(1) (see Insolvency Act 1986 s. 436); and chattel leasing agreements and ROT agreements are defined in the Insolvency Act 1986 s. 251.
[125] Insolvency Act 1986 Sch. A1, paras. 7 and 8.   [126] See ch. 5 above.

procedures may vary enormously. Flood and his colleagues suggested in 1995 that knowledge about CVA processes was very highly concentrated within the body of IPs: 'three individuals' names arose time and time again'. These were the key players and other IPs tended to have very modest experience or knowledge concerning CVA procedures.[127] The rise of the rescue culture can be expected, however, to have significantly developed the orientation and experiences of IPs regarding the rescue potential of the CVA.[128]

If attention is focused, however, on the CVA process as a whole and its ability to deliver expert decisions, it should be remembered that this is not a procedure in which an IP lays down a judgement from on high. A CVA tends to involve an extended process of negotiation between the IP, the directors, the banks and other creditors. With this point in mind, a key issue is whether this is a negotiating process that is able to take on board the relevant information and produce sound decisions on rescue. One difficulty here may have stemmed, pre-rescue culture, from the widespread ignorance of professional lawyers, bankers and accountants concerning CVAs. A second problem may centre on the need to generate trust within CVA procedures. An important role of the IP is to develop such trust between different groups of creditors and the company direc-tors. Without mutual confidence, even the best-informed, most astute commercial judgements will come to nothing. Of central importance here is faith in the competence of the management team and its ability to turn fortunes around.[129] It follows that the expertise built into the CVA procedure will depend to a great extent on the skill not merely of the IP but also of the company's directors. Nor can the part to be played by the major creditors be ignored: these are the parties who have to be con-vinced that a CVA will succeed. The major creditors have to possess the expertise in rescues that allows them to distinguish between good and less convincing CVA proposals.

Above all else then, the CVA demands a co-ordination of expertise. It is a procedure that might be thought to conduce to such co-ordination since the CVA provides a forum for discussion of the rescue scheme's strengths and weaknesses. The quality of that discussion may, however,

---

[127] J. Flood, R. Abbey, E. Skordaki and P. Aber, *The Professional Restructuring of Corporate Rescue: Company Voluntary Arrangements and the London Approach*, ACCA Research Report 45 (ACCA, London, 1995) pp. 17–18.

[128] On the reorientation of the IP within the developing rescue culture see ch. 5 above.

[129] See Flood *et al.*, *Professional Restructuring*, p. 19.

be sub-optimal for a number of reasons. First, there may be conflict of interest between creditors of different classes who bear different levels of risk and who, accordingly, see proposed solutions in different lights. These conflicts may produce disagreements and conversations at cross-purposes. Second, the company's directors may not see solutions in the same light as other involved parties because they have different perspectives or interests. They may, for instance, be reluctant to accede to the IP's and creditors' wishes to install new directors because the directors' estimations of their own value to the company may be higher than those of the IPs and creditors. Third, such differences of interest may reduce levels of trust below optimal levels and this may affect information flows: when, for instance, directors conceal facts from the IP because they fear some adverse reaction such as replacement. Finally, the standard of participation in the negotiation may be low because the key players are not fully trained in CVA procedures or are not fully in touch with the company's state of affairs.

What can be done to improve expertise? If the CVA is seen as a broad-based negotiation it follows that it is not enough to improve the knowledge of IPs concerning CVAs. Other involved actors have to be brought up to speed also. Steps designed to improve performance here might involve training all company directors in basic insolvency procedures and the provision of similar training for bankers and other major creditors. Within the banking industry attention might also be given to the provision of a continuing expertise in insolvency at the appropriate organisational level. Over and above such sectoral training it may be appropriate to develop interdisciplinary skills so that accountants, bankers and lawyers can work on rescues together. As Flood *et al.* comment: 'It is worth reflecting that professional relationships across jurisdictional boundaries are crucial to the satisfactory resolution of something like the CVA.'[130]

Accountability and fairness

Information and transparency are vital prerequisites of accountability within CVAs. CVAs, as noted, only come into effect (under the Insolvency Act 1986 section 5) when proposals have been approved by both the meeting of the company and the meeting of the creditors. Creditors who are considering the proposal put forward after discussions

---

[130] Ibid., p. 23.

between the IP and the directors need to be given information on such matters as: the assets and valuations; projections of income on future contracts; cost savings and ongoing expenses; whether suppliers and customers will remain loyal; potential repossessions/forced sales; whether third-party funds are available; the commitment of the directors; and potential claims against the company.[131] The IP is obliged to take reasonable steps to be satisfied that assets and liabilities are not materially different from the position outlined in the proposal; that the proposal will be implemented as represented and that there is no 'already manifest yet unavoidable unfairness' in admitting, rejecting or valuing voting claims.[132] Here much depends on the skill of the IP and his/her commitment to giving a full picture to the company and creditors. Guidelines on best practice are made available to IPs by the Association of Business Recovery Professionals (R3). There are, moreover, incentives to inform: as has been pointed out, the IP's role in a CVA demands that central importance be given to the creation of trust among affected parties.[133] As for judicial scrutiny, there are indications that the courts will be inclined to defer to the professional judgements of IPs. In *SISU Capital Fund Ltd* v. *Tucker* Warren J dismissed a challenge from bondholders, stating that there was no unfair prejudice arising from the terms of the CVA that affected their position as creditors. Furthermore, the court was not in a position to judge whether proposals put forward as part of the CVA could be improved upon – this was a matter for the professional judgement of the IPs.[134]

The process of holding the IP to account demands not merely that information be made available but that this can be used. For a creditor this will mean that the creditors' meeting has to be attended or a proxy be used. (Under the Insolvency Rules 1986 (Rule 1.17(1)) every creditor 'who was given notice of the creditors' meeting' is entitled to vote at the meeting.) There is no procedure, though, for advertising for creditors of whom the company may not be aware at the time of summoning the

---

[131] See R. Gregory, *Review of Company Rescue and Business Reconstruction Mechanisms: Rescue Culture or Avoidance Culture?* (CCH, Bicester, December 1999) p. 15.

[132] Ibid., pp. 15–16; *Greystoke* v. *Hamilton-Smith* [1997] BPIR 24, 28. It is a criminal offence for a past or present officer of a company to make 'any false representation' or commit any other fraud to obtain creditors' or members' approval: Insolvency Rules 1986 (SI 1986/1925) r. 1.30. An 'officer' here includes a shadow director (r. 130(2)). See also Insolvency Act 1986 Sch. A1, paras. 41 and 42; IA 1986 ss. 6A and 7A.

[133] See Flood *et al.*, *Professional Restructuring*, pp. 5, 20–2.

[134] *SISU Capital Fund Ltd* v. *Tucker* [2006] BCC 463. Warren J did, however, give guidance on how to structure proposals to avoid complaints of unfair prejudice under IA 1986 s. 6.

meeting. (The DTI had advocated a requirement to advertise the moratorium in the *Gazette* and a newspaper in its 1995 paper.)[135] Under the Insolvency Act 2000 amendments, however, advertising is called for when the moratorium comes into force.[136] A CVA approved by a creditors' meeting, nevertheless, binds all parties who are entitled to vote at the meeting (whether or not they were present or represented) or who would have been so entitled had they been given notice.

As for the interests of unknown creditors in a CVA, these are dealt with in Schedule A1, paragraph 38 of the Insolvency Act 1986, which gives parties who have not been given notice of the creditors' meeting a power to apply to the court to challenge a decision of the meeting on the grounds of unfair prejudice or material irregularity. They are given twenty-eight days from the date of their awareness that the meeting has taken place to make such an application to challenge. The court, if satisfied of the basis of such a challenge, can revoke or suspend the decision but can also direct the summoning of further meetings to consider revised CVA proposals. This provision substitutes for the DTI's 1995 proposal that a further meeting of creditors should be convened where the effect of unknown claims would be to reduce the payment to creditors by 10 per cent or more. It is arguable that an advertising requirement would be fair to 'unknown' creditors likely to be bound by the CVA and it would enhance overall transparency and conduce to effective creditor communications.

Holding the directors to account may be as important in a CVA as the appropriate accountability of IPs. During a moratorium the directors will continue to manage the affairs of the company and secured creditors may fear that secured assets may be dissipated, with the possible result that if the CVA is not approved there will be little left over to satisfy the security.[137] Some respondents to the DTI's 1993 proposals (notably IPs and lenders) expressed concern at the low level of monitoring involved in the CVA moratorium, but the 1995 revised proposals suggested that levels of supervision by the IP nominee would 'very much depend on the company's circumstances'.[138] The level of supervision should be settled before the nominee agrees to act, said the DTI, and it might include the nominee having full access to the company's records and premises. Variations in supervision levels were called for because the level of supervision appropriate for a company with a large number of

---

[135] DTI 1995, p. 22.   [136] Insolvency Act 1986 Sch. A1, para. 10.
[137] Brown, *Corporate Rescue*, p. 666.   [138] DTI 1995, p. 16.

retail outlets operating on a cash basis would differ from that called for in relation to an operation relying on one director serving two or three customers. What there should be, said the Department, was a statutory level of supervision comprising scrutiny of weekly management accounts by the nominee. Further control of directorial activities during the moratorium would be provided for by a series of provisions.[139] First, criminal sanctions and civil penalties would apply to directors who, for example, concealed, removed or destroyed assets and/or records; second, directors would only be able to dispose of assets (other than in the ordinary course of business) with the approval of the nominee and either the court or the creditors' committee; and third, there would be general provisions for creditors and shareholders to apply to the court for relief. The Insolvency Act 2000 amendments duly made provision for such criminal sanctions,[140] asset dispositions[141] and applications for relief.[142]

The philosophy underlying such control provisions was that directors who were left in control of the troubled company should be strongly aware of their obligations: 'the supervision and regulation of directors' activities and the existence of penalties for non-compliance are thought necessary to provide a very clear signal that abuse of the moratorium period will not be tolerated. It should also allay concerns that creditors may have about management being left in charge of the company during the moratorium period.'[143]

The fairness of the approval process has been debated with regard to three main issues: the unfair prejudice rule; whether the approval majority for creditors' meetings is set at the right level; and whether shareholders should, through the company meeting, have a power to approve the CVA at all.

Unfair prejudice

Under section 6 of the Insolvency Act 1986 any creditor who was entitled to vote at the creditors' meeting may apply to court to challenge the CVA on grounds of unfair prejudice or material irregularity. In relation to the former ground, a notable difference between the CVA and the Companies Act 2006 scheme of arrangement creates considerable scope for allegations of unfairness. In the scheme of arrangement, as discussed above, account is taken of the divergences of interest between different creditor groups. Each class must approve with a majority in number representing three-quarters

---

[139] See ibid., p. 17. [140] See now Insolvency Act 1986 Sch. A1, paras. 41–2.
[141] Ibid., para. 18. [142] Ibid., para. 38. [143] DTI 1995, p. 17.

in value of the creditors for a scheme of arrangement to be approved. This is not the case in a CVA where all creditors vote together and, provided that the threshold of three-quarters in value in favour is reached, the CVA is approved. Such an arrangement can lead certain creditor groups to pursue their own interests in a contentious manner and the courts have looked at the issues in a number of cases.[144] In the *Wimbledon Football Club* case,[145] Lightman J stated that unequal or differential treatment of creditors in the same class did not constitute unfairness *per se* but might require an explanation; that, in looking at the unfairness issue, the surrounding circumstances should be considered, including alternatives to the arrangement at issue (taking in both liquidation and the possibility of a fairer scheme);[146] and that differential treatment might be required to ensure fairness or the continuation of the business. Where, however, a group of creditors uses its votes to deprive a creditor or group of their rights against third parties while preserving its own rights, the courts are likely to find that unfair prejudice is suffered. This was so in *Re a Debtor (No. 101 of 1999)*[147] and in the important *Powerhouse* decision.[148]

Powerhouse concerned the possibility that a troubled company might be able to 'cram-down' landlords by obtaining approval for a CVA in which those landlords surrender their proprietorial rights. In that case, a struggling electrical retailer (PRG Powerhouse Ltd) wanted to rid itself of thirty-five unprofitable leases (on underperforming stores) in pursuit of turnaround. The CVA demanded, *inter alia*, a release by the landlords but also a release by the parent company of Powerhouse from the lease guarantees that it had given. The CVA was approved in February 2006 at a meeting to which *all* creditors were invited –whether or not the CVA directly affected

---

[144] See Godfrey, 'Legal Update'; Segal, 'Schemes of Arrangement and Junior Creditors', p. 55. See pp. 513–14 below.

[145] *IRC* v. *Wimbledon Football Club Limited* [2005] 1 BCLC 66; see also *SISU Capital Fund Ltd* v. *Tucker* [2006] BCC 463.

[146] [2005] 1 BCLC 66 at para. 18. In *Re Greenhaven Motors Ltd* [1999] 1 BCLC 635, however, Chadwick LJ stated that the court's role was not to speculate on whether the proposed arrangements were the best available: the onus was on the disaffected creditors to show that some option presenting less prejudice to unsecured creditors was available to the company.

[147] [2001] BCLC 54 (creditors used their votes to force the Revenue to receive a reduced amount for its debt while retaining their own rights in full and this was held to be unfairly prejudicial).

[148] *Prudential Assurance Co. Ltd* v. *PRG Powerhouse Ltd* [2007] BCC 500. See the discussion in M. Chalkiadis, '*Powerhouse*: Has the Power Really Gone?' (2007) 21 *Company Law Newsletter* 1; L. Verrill and P. Elliot, 'Reflections on the *Powerhouse* Case' (2007) *Recovery* (Autumn) 28.

them. Some of the unwanted landlords sought a declaration that the CVA was ineffective and/or invalid in so far as it purported to affect their rights against the parent company guarantors. (Posing the question: had the guarantees provided by PRG been released or ought they to be treated as released as a result of the CVA?) In the alternative they sought the revocation of the CVA approval under section 6 of the Insolvency Act 1986 on the grounds that it was unfairly prejudicial to them and/or the meeting was materially irregular since all creditors were allowed to vote on the CVA.

Etherton J found that the CVA was indeed unfairly prejudicial to the claimants. He did not rule that the CVA was invalid because it purported to affect claims against parties other than Powerhouse (i.e. the guarantors). The proposals for the CVA had contained a number of alternative mechanisms to effect the release of third-party guarantees enjoyed by various landlords. The judge decided that, on the particular wording of this CVA, the release of the guarantees was enforceable.[149] The claimants did, however, win on the 'unfair prejudice' point. The landlord creditors had been asked to give up not only their rights against Powerhouse but also against the guaranteeing parent company. The effect would be to move them from being better off than other creditors (because of their guarantees) to being deprived of claims and guarantees. Key points were that: the CVA gave the landlords no extra benefit for the value of the guarantees – all landlords, including those without the benefit of the guarantees, were treated in the same way; all other categories of creditor unaffected by the CVA were to be paid in full; and a winding-up would have allowed the guaranteed landlords the benefit of the guarantees. Had the landlord creditors voted as one class of creditors, they would not have approved the CVA. The effect of the single vote for all creditors was to swamp the interests of the landlord creditors and this constituted unfair prejudice.[150] On the particular facts of this case, the landlords succeeded but none of the grounds which proved successful present insuperable

---

[149] In other words a CVA can propose that a guarantee be treated as being released. Etherton J stated 'it follows in my judgment there is nothing to preclude Powerhouse enforcing clause 3.14 against the guaranteed landlords including the claimants ... on the true construction of the CVA and of the guarantees the claimants are obliged to Powerhouse to treat the guarantees as having been released': see further Verrill and Elliot, 'Reflections on the *Powerhouse* Case', p. 29.

[150] On 'unfairness' Etherton J referred to the review by Warren J in *SISU Capital Fund Ltd v. Tucker* [2006] BCC 463. There is no single or universal test but the cases showed that a comparative analysis should be conducted under which all the circumstances were considered, including the alternatives to what was proposed and the practical consequences if the CVA went ahead.

obstacles to stressed companies wishing to cram-down unwanted land-lords in future.[151]

The approval majority for creditors' meetings

The creditors' approval majority is set out in Rule 1.19 of the Insolvency Rules 1986 and demands, as noted, that, to be effective, approvals must be given by a three-quarters majority in value of the creditors present in person or by proxy and voting on the resolution. This rule contrasts with the position for creditors of companies in administration, a simple majority by value of whom is required in order to agree restructuring proposals. The 75 per cent rule, said the DTI, was designed to encourage companies only to enter a moratorium if a successful rescue is likely and to provide an effective bar to unsound proposals being accepted.[152] The requirement was also said to recognise that the decision of the meeting would affect the return to all creditors. In 1999 the IS suggested that a way to promote more use of CVAs would be to change the voting provisions so as to reduce the threshold for acceptance by creditors.[153] Post-consultation, however, the IS doubted whether such a reform would be advisable. It was moved by the argument that lowering the threshold would not necessarily have any significant effect on acceptance levels; and that concerns would be aroused by binding creditors against their will by a simple majority.[154]

The shareholders' power to approve the CVA

The argument that shareholders should not participate in the CVA approvals process through the company meeting can be represented thus: 'The present rules require there to be a meeting of shareholders. This gives them a veto over any CVA. Given that they have no economic interest in the insolvent company, that is unjustifiable.'[155] This criticism of shareholder voting contrasts with the approach put forward by the DTI in 1995.[156] The Department argued that shareholders were not usually deprived of their shares when a CVA was proposed and that they should, therefore, have a right to receive information about the CVA and vote on it with or without modifications. The DTI considered,

---

[151] See Chalkiadis, '*Powerhouse*', p. 4: 'All that is needed is some more detailed thought and some careful drafting.' Thus landlords are likely, *inter alia*, to revisit the security of leases being granted and to seek to strengthen that security for the future: see further Verrill and Elliot, 'Reflections on the *Powerhouse* Case', p. 29.
[152] DTI 1995, p. 15.   [153] IS 1999, p. 11.   [154] IS 2000, p. 36.
[155] Phillips, *Administration Procedure*, p. 24.   [156] DTI 1995, p. 16.

however, that the decisions of shareholders should not prevail over those of the creditors unless they could show to the court that they were being unfairly prejudiced. The reasoning here was that shareholders should not have any say in whether a CVA was accepted if they did not have a demonstrable financial interest at the time. The proposal was thus akin to the situation in a liquidation: 'If the company is insolvent the shareholders are in no worse position than if the company were to go into insolvent liquidation rather than enter into a CVA. If, however, the company is saved, their shares may begin to reflect real worth.'[157] The proposal to allow the shareholders to go to court on grounds of unfair prejudice was designed to allow shareholders' positions to be taken into account when there was an interest that was being unfairly affected.

The DTI view is preferable to the 'no economic interest' approach in so far as it is difficult to deny the actual and potential interest of a shareholder in the CVA.[158] This is a procedure that does not necessarily commence with the company's insolvency: the directors can propose a CVA prior to insolvency (when shareholders still possess valid interests). What the insolvency legislation does is to provide that a decision to approve a CVA is effective if taken by both the creditors' and company meetings or the creditors' meeting on its own.[159] Where a CVA is approved, it has effect as if made by the company at the creditors' meeting but where a decision of the creditors' meeting differs from one taken by the company meeting, a member of the company can apply to the court which may either order the decision of the company rather than the creditors to have effect or make such order as the court thinks fit.[160] A person entitled to vote at either a creditors' or a company meeting has, as noted, power to challenge a decision in court on the grounds of unfair prejudice or that there has been a material irregularity at either meeting.[161] If the court is satisfied on the 'unfair prejudice' or 'material irregularity' grounds, it is given powers of revocation, suspension or direction.[162] Provisions, accordingly, give primacy to the creditors' meeting but do

---

[157] Ibid., p. 16.

[158] On the economic interests of junior creditors in a s. 895 CA 2006 scheme of arrangement see pp. 480–1 above and Mann J in *Re My Travel Group plc* [2005] 1 WLR 2365. (The Court of Appeal in *Re My Travel Group plc* [2005] 2 BCLC 123 deemed that Mann J had not, in fact, needed to determine the economic interest issue because the only issue was whether the meetings of creditors with whom My Travel intended to make an arrangement had been properly constituted, which they had been.)

[159] Insolvency Act 1986 Sch. A1, para. 36(2).

[160] Ibid., para. 36. See also IA 1986 s. 5 regarding non-moratorium CVAs.

[161] Insolvency Act 1986 Sch. A1, para. 38.   [162] Ibid.

allow creditors with interests that are liable to be prejudiced by a CVA to challenge the approval of the CVA or the process followed in such approval.

It might be questioned whether there is any purpose in providing for a members' meeting when the CVA can be approved by the creditors' meeting on its own.[163] Such a meeting does, however, provide shareholders with a forum and a route to information and discussion that would otherwise be lacking. Such a meeting, moreover, might, in some situations, alert shareholders to issues of potential prejudice of which they were unaware. It can be supported on that basis.

Conclusions

CVA procedures have been enhanced by the moratorium[164] but, in concluding this discussion, it is worth emphasising that legal provisions on CVAs can only go so far in effecting corporate rescues. The CVA does offer a reasonably accountable and fair mechanism for rescue but residual concerns must relate to the degree of co-ordination between directors and IP supervisors that any particular CVA will involve; the absence of provisions advertising proposed CVAs; whether a regime for super-priority funding is necessary for effective rescue; and whether training for directors is a prerequisite for effective rescue.

If seen in broader terms, the CVA procedure can be said to be based on a 'forum' approach to insolvency: one that operates on the basis that rescues can be negotiated into existence. This approach assumes that creditors will produce mutually acceptable solutions if all possibilities can be discussed openly and at low cost. This notion is open to criticism by those who see conflicts of interest as looming large in insolvency. From this perspective, it might be argued that the CVA is unlikely ever to offer the most popular or effective route to rescue because in most areas of corporate trouble the creditors tend to have such divergent interests and powers that rescue options are most likely to be arrived at by degrees of imposition rather than negotiation.

Drawing such a contrast suggests that a way to improve rescue prospects through CVAs may be to institute changes that will reduce the divergences of interest (or perceived divergences of interest) between different creditor groupings. How, though, can this be done consistently

---

[163] Phillips, *Administration Procedure*, p. 24.
[164] Introduced by the Insolvency Act 2000.

with allowing financing options to remain flexible? One route forward may be to revise the legal rules so that oppositions of interest are less starkly drawn. This can be done, for example, by offering more information to unsecured creditors or by opting for courses of action that favour unsecured creditors where this involves no cost to the charge holder. Another route would be to institute changes not through legal adjustments of interest but by measures designed to change the cultures, values and assumptions of involved parties: to encourage banks, for example, to identify their own long-term interests more closely with those of the body of unsecured creditors and employees.

Arguing from a further perspective, it might be contended that what really affects prospects of rescue is not so much the legal process involved, or the arrays of interests encountered, but the levels of business skill that are involved. Reforms reflecting this point of view could focus on continuing steps designed to enhance the skill levels of nominees and supervisors as well as those of directors. Improvements here might be secured through increased attention to training and the qualifications necessary for adopting any of the normal named roles. The measures might be constituted on a mandatory or a voluntary basis.

At this point we should return to a question posed earlier in relation to section 895 schemes of arrangement: is there a case for retaining these when resort can be made to CVAs or administration? The Company Law Review Steering Group suggested, as noted, that there would be strong support for a process allowing company managers to impose reorganisation proposals on a minority[165] and it is arguable that there are circumstances in which internally generated reforms may produce rescues more efficiently, expertly, accountably and fairly than procedures involving external practitioners. A streamlined version of the existing schemes of arrangement procedure may have a place in modern company law. Where the troubled company happens to be managed by directors who are able to initiate turnarounds and where these directors are able to see the need for such steps before prospects of rescue have become minimal, the scheme of arrangement has a valuable role. Again this raises the issues of directorial training and incentives within the insolvency process.

Finally, it should be noted that schemes of arrangement and CVAs are both procedures that operate with distinct visions of the insolvency process in mind – ones that make numerous assumptions about the

---

[165] CLRSG, *Completing the Structure*, p. 205.

actors that should be involved, the procedural and substantive rights the parties should have and the ways in which prospects of rescue are best secured. The visions of insolvency seen within these processes may not be the same as the visions implied in other processes such as receiverships or administrations and it may be asked whether consistency between these visions (or even a single agreed vision) should be aimed for. This is an issue to be returned to in the next chapter.

12

Rethinking rescue

These are interesting times for corporate rescue. On the one hand, a new emphasis on rescue has developed over the last decade or so and turnaround has emerged as a main priority in dealing with troubled companies. The 'rescue culture' has been evident in legislation and in endorsements by the UK Government and also the judiciary.[1] The banks have instituted new intensive care regimes and a new group of turnaround specialists has come onto the scene to assist in the process of dealing with corporate troubles at an ever-earlier stage in their development. In parallel, increasing attention is being paid to the management of risks to corporate welfare. On the other hand, the advent of 'the new capitalism' and the commodification of credit have produced a fragmentation of interests in troubled companies and a new set of pressures that favour exiting from relationships with distressed firms rather than doctoring such companies. This fragmentation has imposed new strains on the 'London Approach' and has given rise to new difficulties in securing agreements to informal turnaround proposals.

Against this background, considerable changes have been made to insolvency procedures. The phasing out of administrative receivership has been accompanied by a rebirth of administration and the CVA procedure has been enhanced with a moratorium for small companies. The Crown's status as preferential creditor has been removed and the 'prescribed part' has been introduced in order to provide greater economic protection for unsecured creditors. Holders of floating charges have not only largely lost the right to appoint administrative receivers but have been made to bear the cost of giving unsecured creditors the benefit of the prescribed part. As for fixed charge holders, membership of this club has been restricted after *Spectrum Plus*[2] and the courts' new inclination to treat charges over book debts as

---

[1] See e.g. Neuberger LJ in *Thomas v. Ken Thomas Ltd* [2006] EWCA Civ 1504; Neuberger J in *Re Farnborough-Aircraft.com Ltd* [2002] 2 BCLC 641; Lord Browne-Wilkinson in *Powdrill v. Watson* [1995] 2 AC 394.

[2] *Re Spectrum Plus Ltd* [2005] 2 AC 680.

floating rather than fixed. The arrival of the 'pre-packaged' administration has led to new levels of concern regarding the undermining of statutory procedures and the substitution of closed agreements for traditionally more transparent processes.

Rescue procedures, it should furthermore be pointed out, operate as packages. If, accordingly, we ask whether the procedures that have been discussed in the last five chapters are appropriate or capable of improvement, we should consider not merely the individual processes involved but the broad package of procedures on offer. If that package is assessed, this raises the issue of coherence and whether the different procedures hang together in sympathy or undercut each other. It may be argued that it is beneficial to provide companies with a number of different routes to rescue, but that contention will only hold if those routes are in harmony. If some modes of rescue undermine others, the effect of variety may not be benign choice but inefficiency and confusion.

An overall assessment of rescue procedures must also bear in mind that different procedures may be applied to different stages of corporate troubles. Some routes into the post-Enterprise Act administration, for instance, demand that the company is, or is likely to be, unable to pay its debts.[3] Other routes do not,[4] nor is the CVA procedure tied to insolvency or near insolvency. The importance of this point is that at different stages of corporate difficulty, the aspirations and objectives of parties may vary. At a very early stage of corporate trouble it will be natural for directors and other parties to focus on rescue and the machinery for achieving this. On the brink of insolvency, the law and the involved parties may be concerned with how the remaining assets can be most efficiently distributed to creditors. These differences of emphasis are also likely to be reflected in the extent to which different parties' rights stand to be adjusted so as to encourage rescue. When rescue is the chief end it will be appropriate to facilitate this objective by adjusting creditors' rights (for example, by prohibiting enforcement of these). When distribution is the main objective, the emphasis will more properly be on the effective enforcement of creditors' rights.

A difficult situation arises when shareholder interests in a company are diminishing in a period just before insolvency. What is special about insolvency – and rescue more particularly – is that the nature of the game

---

[3] See IA 1986 Sch. B1 para. 11(a); para. 22 with para. 27(2).
[4] Ibid., paras. 14 and 35: administration applications by holders of qualifying floating charges.

and even the list of players will vary as the company progresses through difficulties towards insolvency or turnaround. This can be seen in the position of a shareholder of a company. When a healthy company is operating, the directors may be perceived as working to further the shareholders' interests.[5] In an insolvency the position has changed. The company cannot pay its debts and the directors are now operating not with the company/shareholders' assets but with those of the creditors.[6] The interests of the creditors, at this stage, fall to be looked to as primary objects of directorial endeavour and procedural fairness to creditor interests becomes a first priority.

The difficulty for a designer of rescue procedures is that a procedure may operate across corporate life, from the situation in which the company is essentially healthy but needs to reorganise or adjust operations, right through to the company's entry into insolvency. The procedure may thus have to protect rights that are shifting in relationship to each other and it will have to operate fairly when what is procedurally and substantively fair will change in accordance with the shifts in rights that occur as the company nears insolvency.

How then should a *system* of rescue procedures be designed?[7] Do present rescue procedures match up to such a design? First, there should be clarity concerning the objectives in sight – the ends that are to be achieved efficiently. This means that a rescue system must be precise about the relative weights to be given to rescue and asset distribution. Nor should it be forgotten that the same insolvency laws that serve rescues may also need to accommodate the purposes of healthy operating

---

[5] On views of shareholders as the owners of the company or as the residual claimants of its assets see, for example, H. Butler, 'The Contractual Theory of the Corporation' (1989) 11 Geo. Mason UL Rev. 99; R. Sappideen, 'Ownership of the Large Corporation: Why Clothe the Emperor?' (1996–7) 7 King's College LJ 27. On different characterisations of the nature of a shareholder's interest see E. Ferran, *Company Law and Corporate Finance* (Oxford University Press, Oxford, 1999) pp. 131–3. On the status of groups other than shareholders as 'residual claimants' see Sappideen, 'Ownership'; G. Kelly and J. Parkinson, 'The Conceptual Foundations of the Company' [1998] 2 CfiLR 174. (The formulation of s. 172 of the Companies Act 2006 makes it clear that – in the context of a director's duty to promote the success of the company – the company means the shareholders and gives effect to a principle of 'enlightened shareholder value'. For a discussion of arguments relating to the 'stakeholder analysis' of companies see T. Beauchamp and N. Bowie (eds.), *Ethical Theory and Business* (5th edn, Prentice Hall, Upper Saddle River, N.J., 1997) ch 2.)

[6] See *West Mercia Safetywear Ltd* v. *Dodd* [1988] 4 BCC 30, [1988] BCLC 250, per Dillon LJ. See also ch. 16 below.

[7] For a general guide to such design see United Nations Commission on International Trade Law (UNCITRAL), *Legislative Guide on Insolvency Law* (UN, New York, 2005).

companies. It would not, for instance, make sense to create efficient rescue procedures if the processes interfered unduly with, or imposed excessive costs on, healthy companies (for instance, because the rescue procedures can be abused for non-rescue reasons, as some fear may be the case with Chapter 11 in the USA). There is, accordingly, a balance to be set between rescue and operational concerns.

It may well be that at different stages of corporate life and decline, the optimal balances of different objectives will change. Rescue processes can cope with such difficulties but it is undesirable for different rescue procedures to target priorities divergently when operating at the same stage in corporate troubles. Here we saw the problems with the system of floating charges and the tension between pre-Enterprise Act administrative receivership and administration. The administration regime incorporated a moratorium and gave protection from creditors, and in doing so it effected a particular balance between ongoing corporate concerns (for example, to obtain financing when healthy), the interests of creditors and the wider interests to be served by rescue. The floating charge and administrative receivership system undermined administration (not to say schemes of arrangement and CVAs) and did so by setting out to achieve different ends (notably protection of the floating charge holder's interest) at the same time as schemes of arrangement and CVAs looked to broader rescue interests. Insolvency law spoke with two voices and provided one procedure that undermined another. The route to a clearer design of insolvency/rescue regime is to decide on the appropriate balance of interests and to set up a procedure that pursues those interests consistently with that balancing. This argument favours a movement towards a 'single gateway' rescue regime where possible – and indeed the Enterprise Act 2002 moved in this direction by restricting the use of administrative receivership in favour of the enhanced administration process.

A second prerequisite of clear rescue design is the identification of those values to be pursued in a rescue. Again these need to be targeted with consistency. This book, as indicated in chapter 2, argues that emphasis should be given to efficiency, expertise, fairness and accountability throughout the various stages of rescue. Efficiency, it has just been noted, demands clarity concerning objectives, and one recurring message of the last five chapters has been that efficiency in rescue may require that directors are able to resort to a rescue procedure *before* the chances of turnaround have become hopeless. Here the addition by the Insolvency Act 2000 of a small companies' moratorium to the CVA procedure may be helpful, but questions can be asked about the continued requirement that when directors or the company seek entry to administration the company must be, or be likely to become, unable to pay its debts.[8]

Turning to the issue of expertise, if we consider the allocations of managerial and oversight functions in English rescue procedures – and do so with a view to the trust impliedly being placed in different experts – we see quite different assumptions being made. Many informal rescue procedures, including the London Approach, rely on a process of negotiation between the companies, directors, the bank(s) and other creditors. If formal processes are examined, we see that schemes of arrangement place faith in the expertise of the directors, subject to court oversight, and there is no need to resort to an independent IP to formulate or implement the scheme. The directors remain in control and a great deal of faith is placed in their initiative and ability to take corrective steps to avert disaster. The CVA, in contrast, places control in the hands of an external expert. The company's directors, as noted, may propose a CVA but this must provide for a nominee to supervise the CVA's implementation and the nominee must be qualified to act as an IP in relation to the company.[9] This faith in the expertise of the independent IP may sometimes be well placed (increasingly so as IP experience with CVAs grows) but any expert judgement may have to survive an extended negotiation procedure, involving the IP, the directors, the banks and other creditors. This negotiation, moreover, may be conducted in a context of only limited trust. At the end of the day, then, expertise has to flow from a process of co-ordination with the IP at the helm.

In administration, the expertise of the IP is again central in both setting up the process and implementing it, but, given the role of the company's directors in instituting 70 per cent of non-court-order entries into administration,[10] the skill of those directors in seeing the need to institute an administration is also important. As noted, the company has to be near to, or actually, insolvent for directors or the company to trigger administration and the window of rescue opportunity is, accordingly, very narrow. This gives more prominence to the galvanising role of the company directors. The law here trusts the directors' expertise too little

---

[8] See IA 1986 Sch. B1, paras. 11(a), 12(1)(a) and (b), 22 with 27(2)(a).

[9] Note that with the 'small company' CVA, established by the Insolvency Act 2000, nominees do not specifically have to be IPs: see ch. 11 above.

[10] Insolvency Service, *Enterprise Act 2002 – Corporate Insolvency Provisions: Evaluation Report* (IS, London, 2008) p. 25. The *IS Report* indicates that around 65 per cent of administrations are non-court-order and 30 per cent are by court order (5 per cent are route uncertain).

to allow the debtor to stay in possession, but sets up a procedure whose rescue prospects depend crucially on the same directors.

To summarise, in looking for the expertise that will generate successful rescues, insolvency law operates with a scattergun approach rather than a considered analysis of informational position, training, disinterestedness, specialist knowledge of the market, ability to judge financing options or commitment to implementation for rescue purposes. The formal procedures relevant to rescue again speak with inconsistent voices: schemes of arrangements are marked by high trust in directors; CVAs look to independent experts and negotiated or group expertise; and administrations look to independent experts that rely on directorial triggers. To repeat, a system of insolvency law that is thought through should operate on assumptions concerning expertise that are consistent rather than vacillating. These assumptions, moreover, could be based on analyses of the kind of factors noted above, along with the host of others that together underpin the exercise of independent judgement. All of these discrepancies are compounded by the growth of processes such as the pre-packaged administration that do much of the 'traditional' work of rescue procedures through informal mechanisms and which are largely unregulated, unstructured and varying in approach.

A discussion of accountability within rescue procedures proceeds on similar lines. Schemes of arrangement involve no oversight of directors by IPs but control by meetings of creditors and members together with judicial oversight. CVAs require that IPs structure directors' proposals and the latter also have to be approved by creditors and members. The skill of the IP is crucial to the flow of information and accountability to creditors and members in a CVA. An array of criminal sanctions and civil liabilities also serves to hold directors to account in cases of concealment, removal or distribution of assets and/or records. General court scrutiny is also made possible by provisions allowing creditors and shareholders to apply for relief. In administration, court involvement has been reduced by the Enterprise Act 2002 reforms and accountability to shareholders is absent in so far as the members are not involved in approval of the administrator's proposals (which are approved by the creditors alone).[11] The accountability found within 'pre-packs' contrasts more dramatically with the above descriptions and constitutes a potential undermining of statutory requirements of openness and access.

---

[11] Shareholders can, however, apply to the court under the Insolvency Act 1986 Sch. B1, para. 74 if they have a complaint that the proposals will unfairly harm their interests.

Looking at accountability in different insolvency procedures, we again see not only varying rules but also divergent philosophies. Schemes of arrangement build on the notion that directors can be left largely free from monitoring by IPs but CVAs and administrations imply that there is considerable value in specialist control over the directors' behaviour, proposals and informational roles. In administrations there is no need for shareholders' approval. This contrast with schemes of arrangement procedures may be defended by some on the grounds that administration necessarily occurs when the company is close to insolvency but it is perhaps jumping the gun to argue that shareholders should drop out of the approval process completely when insolvency is a likelihood, rather than a given.

Finally, the issue of fairness falls to be considered. Considerable emphasis is placed on fairness to minority interests in schemes of arrangement. Meetings of creditors and shareholders have to approve proposals and, as noted in chapter 11, it is the court's protective stance on this front that produces a complex process with elaborate provisions on notice. In relation to CVAs one means of ensuring fair treatment of creditors is through the approvals mechanism and the requirement of 75 per cent in value approvals. As noted, though, this rule contrasts with not only the class-based system of schemes of arrangement but also the simple majority required in administration. CVAs, moreover, have to be approved by shareholder meetings whereas administrations do not. As argued above, the exclusion of shareholders from votes on administrations may be difficult to justify, at least in the pre-insolvency situations that Schedule B1 of the Insolvency Act 1986 covers. It can also be contended that administrations do not fairly take on board the interests of parties beyond creditors, notably employees. The primary purpose of making an administration order under Schedule B1 paragraph 3 of the Insolvency Act 1986 is rescuing the company as a going concern but the employee stakeholders whose livelihoods are at stake are offered no formal input into the decision-making process governing administration. Where a 'pre-pack' administration is used, the particular danger is that less powerful creditor interests may be railroaded to an outcome and have very little say in the route taken or the nature of that outcome.

In summarising on fairness, we see that the law relating to the various insolvency procedures operates with divergent assumptions on the rights of parties involved in insolvency. As a result, the models of fairness implicit in the processes discussed are inconsistent. The law does have to confront the difficult problem of changing balances between the interests of certain classes. This is apparent in the position of the share-holder in, say, the administration procedure since the shareholder's interest can be said to be considerable pre-insolvency but diminishing as full insolvency looms. An organised approach to insolvency law would decide which parties have which rights at which stages of insolvency and set the rules accordingly and consistently across the procedures.

To conclude on rescue procedures, the individual procedures possess strengths and weaknesses as outlined, but, as an overall system, they may be said to constitute a disjointed package. There are a number of poten-tial explanations for this state of affairs. Many such explanations are historical and political. Long-established deference to security interest holders as major property owners created a resistance to organised rescue strategies and sets of laws that might be seen as interfering with such property rights.[12] Cork's recommendations were cherry picked and post-Cork law reforms in this area were for many years piecemeal efforts that failed to take on the broader strategic issues. The Enterprise Act 2002 reforms have been welcomed in many quarters as moving towards a more generally collective regime – though, as seen above, that regime still has to face residual challenges.

The argument presented in this book is that insolvency law can and should take on board the shifting nature of rights and relationships in troubled corporate affairs. Other things being equal, however, it should offer a range of insolvency processes that caters for the values of effi-ciency, expertise, accountability and fairness and does so on the basis of assumptions that are consistent across different procedures. At present, formal and informal rescue processes offer a range of routes to turn-around but that variety creates a potential for tensions and conflicts.

Finally, we should return to the issues raised at the start of this chapter and consider whether current procedures address an outdated set of challenges and fail to provide the rescue procedures that modern restruc-turings and credit market conditions really require. In chapter 9 we saw that this argument has been presented forcefully by the European High Yield Association (EHYA)[13] which has contended that current

---

[12] See A. Clarke, 'Security Interests as Property: Relocating Security Interests within the Property Framework' in J. W. Harris (ed.), *Property Problems from Genes to Pension Funds* (Kluwer, London, 1997).

[13] See EHYA, *Submission on Insolvency Law Reform* (EHYA, London, 2007), discussed in R. Heis, 'Technical Bulletin' (2007) *Recovery* (Autumn) 15. On EHYA proposals as modestly revised (EHYA, *Submission on Insolvency Law Reform*, 2008) see P. J. Davies, 'Treasury Urged to Reform Insolvency Laws', *Financial Times*, 26 February 2008.

restructuring processes are ill-suited to the growing complexities of capital structures, the dispersion of debt and the multiplicity of parties generally involved with troubled companies. The EHYA's case for a court-supervised restructuring process deserves to be looked at on its merits – for present purposes, however, it is the making of such a case that raises an important point. It is one thing to decide what is wanted from a corporate insolvency regime and to attempt to design a system accordingly. It is another to ensure that a rescue regime that is good for today's companies and markets will adjust appropriately to tomorrow's conditions. The need for monitoring and appraisal is constant and the ongoing challenge is to produce approaches to corporate rescue that both satisfy current concerns and are also responsive to needs for change.

PART IV

Gathering and distributing the assets

13

Gathering the assets: the role of liquidation

Liquidation is the end of the road for the troubled company. It involves its winding up and the gathering in of the assets for subsequent distribution to creditors. On the commencement of liquidation the principle of collectivity takes effect[1] and this is reflected in a moratorium on hostile actions and the restraining of uncompleted executions.[2] Liquidation, nevertheless, raises issues of efficiency, expertise, accountability and fairness as much as processes involving prospects of rescue. This chapter explores those issues as well as the conceptual underpinnings of liquidation. Liquidations are encountered in three main forms: voluntary, compulsory and public interest, and to set the scene, it is necessary to review the varieties of liquidation and the legal framework that supports the liquidation process.

The voluntary liquidation process

A voluntary liquidation of a solvent company is termed 'a members' voluntary winding up' and, where an insolvent company is involved, this is then known as 'a creditors' voluntary winding up'. This distinction flows from the Insolvency Act 1986 sections 89 and 90 which provide that if the directors have made a statutory declaration of solvency under section 89, a members' voluntary liquidation[3] occurs, but that the liquidation is a creditors' voluntary liquidation in the absence of such a declaration.

Both types of voluntary liquidation are, however, triggered by the actions of the company's members. These members can initiate a

---

[1] For discussion see ch. 2 above and ch. 14 below.
[2] See Insolvency Act 1986 ss. 126–8, 130(2), 183. See e.g. *Re Modern Jet Support Ltd* [2005] BPIR 1382; and, on the court's unfettered discretion to lift the s. 130(2) stay, *New Cap Reinsurance Corp. Ltd* v. *HIH Casualty and General Insurance Ltd* [2002] BPIR 809 at 819 (Jonathan Parker LJ).
[3] See J. Tribe, 'Members' Voluntary Liquidations: A Declaration of Under Use' (2005) 26 Co. Law. 132.

winding up by passing a special resolution in favour of a voluntary liquidation.[4] Resolutions must be advertised in the *Gazette* within fourteen days of passing (on penalty of a fine where the officers of a company are in default).[5]

Creditor involvement in a creditors' voluntary winding up is provided for in the rule that a company must call a creditors' meeting within fourteen days of the meeting at which the resolution for voluntary liquidation is to be proposed.[6] Such creditors, moreover, must be given at least seven days' warning and a notice of the meeting has to be placed in the *Gazette* and two local newspapers. This advertisement must give the name of the IP who is qualified to act as the company's voluntary liquidator and it must also indicate the place where a list of creditors can be found.

A main source of information to creditors is the Statement of Affairs that the Insolvency Act 1986 section 99 requires the company directors to lay before the creditors' meeting. The directors, moreover, must nominate one of their number to run the creditors' meeting.[7] The creditors at that meeting are able to nominate a liquidator. The members

---

[4] Insolvency Act 1986 s. 84(1)(b). The Companies Act 2006 (Commencement No. 3, Consequential Amendments, Transitional Provisions and Savings) Order 2007, SI 2007/2194, introduced changes to the rules relating to company meetings and resolutions, some of which affected the resolutions which need to be taken to put a company into liquidation. Thus, for example, from 1 October 2007, the Insolvency Act 1986 s. 84(1)(c) provision was repealed (this provided that the company could be wound up voluntarily if it resolved by extraordinary resolution that it 'cannot by reason of its liabilities continue its business and that it is advisable to wind up').

[5] Insolvency Act 1986 s. 85(2).

[6] Ibid., s. 98; Insolvency Rules 1986 rr. 4.51(as amended), 4.53, 4.62. Under the Companies Act 2006 s. 307 the period of notice required for a meeting of a private company at which a special resolution is to be proposed was reduced from twenty-one days to fourteen days (although the company's articles may specify a longer period: s. 307(3)). In relation to private company winding-up resolutions the articles can also prevail regarding the majority needed for a meeting to be held on short notice – set at 90 per cent of voting rights per s. 307(5) CA 2006. See also *Re Centrebind Ltd* [1967] 1 WLR 377 which held that failure to comply with the specified meetings procedures did not invalidate proceedings but, now, the Insolvency Act 1986 s. 166 prevents a liquidator, as a general rule, from exercising any section 156 powers (e.g. of property disposal) until the creditors' meeting required by section 98 has been held. Section 166(5) of the Insolvency Act 1986 gives the court powers to make directions where there has been a failure to comply with sections 98 and 99: on the exercise of these see R. Tateossian, 'The Scope of Section 166(5) Insolvency Act 1986: An Analysis' (2001) *Finance and Credit Law* 4.

[7] Failure of the nominated director to attend the meeting will not necessarily invalidate proceedings: see *Re Salcombe Hotel Development Co. Ltd* [1991] BCLC 44, [1989] 5 BCC 807.

of the company may also nominate a liquidator at their meeting but if members and creditors choose divergently, the nominee of the creditors will be appointed.[8] Where the company is not content with a creditors' choice, a challenge may be made in court within seven days.[9] As for the powers of the company's directors, these are limited by section 114 of the Insolvency Act 1986 which covers the period prior to the appointment of a liquidator and only allows directorial powers to be exercised with the sanction of the court or in order to secure compliance with section 98 provisions on the creditors' meeting or section 99 on the directors' statement of affairs.

The person chosen to act as a liquidator in a creditors' voluntary winding up must be a qualified IP.[10] IPs, moreover, often have a strong influence on choice of liquidator. As Milman and Durrant indicate:

> IPs commonly offer a service to their commercial clients of attending on their behalf at creditors' meetings of their insolvent debtors and reporting on the proceedings free of charge. Professionals in the field, usually representatives of the larger accountancy firms, are well known to each other, and commonly discussions take place before the meeting to find out which of them commands the most voting power, now measured by value of the debt under Rule 4.63(1). By arrangement, some of the professionals attend the creditors' meeting, and frequently one of them proposes the appointment of one of the others, either as liquidator, in place of the members' nominee, or, more commonly nowadays, as joint liquidator.[11]

Joint liquidators may be appointed by such a process and the court has power to appoint a further liquidator to join a sole liquidator.[12] On appointment, any liquidator has fourteen days in which to advertise his appointment in the *Gazette* and to notify the Companies Register.[13]

In a creditors' voluntary liquidation, creditors play a central control function. They are placed in a fiduciary position regarding the company

---

[8] Insolvency Act 1986 s. 100(2).
[9] Ibid., s. 100(3); Insolvency Rules 1986 r. 4.102.
[10] Insolvency Rules 1986 r. 4.100.
[11] D. Milman and C. Durrant, *Corporate Insolvency: Law and Practice* (3rd edn, Sweet & Maxwell, London, 1999) p. 80.
[12] *Re Sunlight Incandescent Ltd* [1906] 2 Ch 728.
[13] In furtherance of the EC Directive 2003/58/EC the Companies (Registrar, Language and Trading Disclosures) Order 2006 requires that the statement that a company is in liquidation must be included not only on all its stationery but also on its website (amending IA 1986 s. 188(1)(a)).

and its assets and act in the main through the Liquidation Committee.[14] This body has a maximum membership of five creditors and five contributories. Creditors, moreover, possess the preponderance of power since they can veto all or any of the contributories (under section 101(3) of the Insolvency Act 1986). The quorum for such a committee is two members, and any member may be removed by the creditors at large. It has a right to information as the liquidator is advised to report all relevant matters to it. Members may require meetings to be called but generally meetings are instituted at the discretion of the liquidator.

Creditors may apply to the court for directions;[15] they have powers to remove liquidators[16] or apply to the court for removal of a voluntary liquidator; and they may ask the court to have the company compulsorily wound up under the Insolvency Act 1986 section 116.[17]

As for court supervision of voluntary liquidations, this is light and it is not a day-to-day activity. The court may, nevertheless, become involved where there is a request to remove a liquidator or where a liquidator, contributory or creditor applies to it to determine a question arising in the winding up or to use the powers it might employ in a winding up by the court to enforce calls or other matters.[18]

When voluntary liquidation is entered into, the general powers of the directors, as noted, cannot be exercised,[19] but a series of powers is given to the liquidator under section 165 and Schedule 4 of the Insolvency Act 1986. The liquidator, with the sanction of the Liquidation Committee or the court,[20] may pay any class of creditors in full; make compromises or arrangements with creditors or alleged creditors; compromise calls, debts, potential debts, claims and any question relating to the assets or the winding up of the company. Security, moreover, may be taken in the course of discharging these claims.

The sanction of the Liquidation Committee is not required in relation to the exercise of a number of other powers, including: the bringing or

---

[14] See Insolvency Act 1986 s. 101. On the functions, membership and procedural rules relating to Liquidation Committees see also IR 1986 rr. 4.151 ff.

[15] Insolvency Act 1986 s. 112.   [16] Ibid., s. 171(2).

[17] See *Re Lowestoft Traffic Services Co. Ltd* [1986] 2 BCC 98.

[18] Insolvency Act 1986 s. 112. Confirmation of the winding-up procedure through the court is possible throughout the EU under Council Regulation (EC) No. 1346/2000 (implemented by Insolvency Act 1986 (Amendment) (No. 2) Regulations 2002) and foreign companies with centres of main interests in the UK can be wound up voluntarily (in addition to compulsorily under the Insolvency Act 1986 s. 221(4)); *Re TXU Europe German Finance BV* [2005] BPIR 209, [2005] BCC 90.

[19] IA 1986 s. 103.   [20] Obtainable in advance or by ratification.

defending of actions or legal proceedings on behalf of the company;[21] carrying on the business of the company as is necessary for a beneficial winding up; selling or transferring any of the company's property; executing deeds for the company and using its seal; proving in the insolvency of any contributory; dealing in bills of exchange; borrowing against the security of a company's assets; taking out letters of administration to the estate of a deceased contributory; appointing an agent to perform business; and doing all such other things as may be necessary for the winding up of a company's affairs and distribution of its assets.

These powers described are general and implied. A number of statutory powers sit alongside these, however. All types of liquidator may disclaim onerous property under the Insolvency Act 1986 sections 178–82. This may be done without court leave[22] and notwithstanding the liquidator taking possession of the property, attempting to sell it or exercising rights of ownership in it.[23] Onerous property here includes unprofitable contracts or other property that is not saleable or readily saleable or such that may create a liability to pay money or perform an onerous act.[24] The effect of disclaiming is to terminate the rights and liabilities of the company with regard to the property disclaimed, but rights and liabilities of other parties are not affected.[25] In exercising this power the liquidator's hand may be forced by interested parties who may require the liquidator to decide whether there is an intention to

---

[21] The onus appears to be on an objector to establish that an action was not beneficial to the winding up: see *Hire Purchase Co.* v. *Richans* [1887] 20 QBD 387.

[22] A notice of disclaimer 'in the prescribed form' has to be filed in court under Insolvency Rules 1986 r. 4.187 and Form 4.53.

[23] Insolvency Act 1986 s. 178(2).

[24] Ibid., s. 178(3). Per Chadwick LJ in *Re SSSL Realisations (2002) Ltd, Manning* v. *AIG Europe Ltd* [2006] Ch 610, [2006] BCC 233 – 'a contract is not an "unprofitable contract" … merely because it is financially disadvantageous or merely because the company could have made or could make a better bargain. The critical feature is that performance of the future obligations will prejudice the liquidator's obligation to realize the company's property and pay a dividend to creditors within a reasonable time' (at para. 42).

[25] *Hindcastle Ltd* v. *Barbara Attenborough Associates* [1996] 2 WLR 262. On disclaimers and waste management licences see *Official Receiver of Celtic Extraction and Bluestone Chemicals* v. *Environment Agency* [2000] BCC 487, [1999] 4 All ER 684 (waste management licences held by the Court of Appeal to be disclaimable); J. Armour, 'Who Pays When Polluters Go Bust?' (2000) 116 LQR 200. See also *Environment Agency* v. *Hillridge Ltd* [2004] 2 BCLC 358. See *Re SSSL Realisations (2002) Ltd* [2006] Ch 610, [2006] BCC 233 (see note 24 above) where the Court of Appeal examined and explained the terms 'property' and 'onerous contract'; *Re Park Air Services (Christopher Moran Holdings Ltd* v. *Bairstow and Ruddock)* [1999] BCC 135, [2000] AC 172 where the House of Lords gave guidance on calculating compensation for a landlord where a liquidator disclaims a lease.

disclaim, and the liquidator has twenty-eight days to give notice of disclaiming or then forfeit the right to disclaim. If, moreover, persons suffer a loss as a result of the liquidator's disclaiming, they can prove as creditors in the winding up.

As will be discussed further below, the statutory powers of liquidators allow them to set aside prior transactions at undervalue or transactions which amount to preferences. Liquidators, moreover, may obtain orders for the examination of company affairs in order to secure information[26] and may apply for an order that directors or former directors make a contribution to the assets.[27] If the liquidator wishes to obtain court guidance on questions relating to a winding up, an application can be made under section 112 of the Insolvency Act 1986 and the court may also be asked to appoint a special manager.[28] When a liquidator is appointed he or she is not personally bound by pre-liquidation contracts enforceable against the company, except where he or she has actually adopted them.[29] Such contracts, however, retain their force with regard to the company unless they are disclaimed by the liquidator. Contracts entered into by liquidators for the purposes of effecting a winding up do not bind them personally since they act in this regard as agents of the company.[30]

As for the duties of the liquidator, the first of these is to realise the company's assets effectively and to apply the company's property 'in satisfaction of the company's liabilities *pari passu*'[31] so that there is a distribution 'among the members according to their rights and interests in the company'. There is a duty to contact known creditors and meet their claims as well as an obligation to consider all known debts before distributing assets.[32] Where dividends are to be paid, liquidators must give notice of their intention to declare a dividend[33] and must provide for debts relating to claims undetermined at that time and the claims of creditors who may not have had time to establish their proofs because of the distance of their place of residence.[34] When a dividend is declared,

---

[26] Insolvency Act 1986 s. 236.   [27] Ibid., s. 214. See ch. 16 below.

[28] Insolvency Act 1986 s. 177.   [29] *Re S. Davies & Co. Ltd* [1945] Ch 402.

[30] But see *Plant (Engineers) Sales Ltd* v. *Davis* (1969) 113 Sol Jo 484 regarding contracts under seal.

[31] Insolvency Act 1986 s. 107. For discussion of the *pari passu* principle see chs. 14 and 15 below.

[32] See *Re Armstrong Whitworth Securities Ltd* [1947] Ch 673; *Argylls Ltd* v. *Coxeter* [1913] 29 TLR 355.

[33] Insolvency Rules 1986 r. 4.180(2).   [34] Ibid., r. 4.182.

however, creditors who have not proved cannot disturb the dividends. Dividends must be paid by the liquidator when this is possible and proper accounts, minutes of meetings and records must be kept.[35] The liquidator is in a fiduciary position in relation to the company and must not derive personal profit from his role: this rules out employing him to do legal work flowing from the winding up.[36]

Liquidators can be removed by the court[37] or the creditors and may only resign by reasons of ill-health, retirement from insolvency practice, conflict of interests or changes in personal circumstances that make it impossible for them to continue to act. Where a resignation is to be effective, a creditors' meeting must be called and asked to accept this. In the absence of such an acceptance, the liquidator may apply to the court. A creditors' voluntary winding up terminates normally with the realisation of all available assets and their distribution to claimants in order of priority. After this is done, the liquidator must call final meetings of members and creditors[38] to which accounts of realisations and distributions must be submitted. These accounts must, in turn, be sent to the Companies Registry within a week of the meeting. The Registrar will then record the liquidator's account and return under the Insolvency Act 1986 section 201 and the company is deemed dissolved three months from registration of a return.[39] After this date the company does not exist and can neither be sued nor initiate court proceedings.

---

[35] Insolvency Regulations 1994 (SI 1994/2507).

[36] See Milman and Durrant, *Corporate Insolvency*, p. 91; *Re Gertzenstein Ltd* [1997] 1 Ch 115; r. 4.149 of the Insolvency Rules 1986 allows the court to set aside dealings between the liquidator and his associates which involve company assets. For a detailed discussion of the liquidators' general duties see B. McPherson, *The Law of Company Liquidation* (5th edn, Lawbook Co., Australia, 2007) paras. 8.30 ff.

[37] In *AMP Enterprises Ltd* v. *Hoffman* (*The Times*, 13 August 2002) Neuberger J (regarding a section 108(2) application for replacement) emphasised the dangers of encouraging applications by disgruntled creditors, the importance of maintaining standards of independence and the bearing in mind of any costs and delay involved in replacement. In *Re Buildlead Ltd (in liquidation) (No. 2)* [2005] BCC 138 liquidators undertaking a creditors' voluntary winding up were removed under s. 108(2) because they had lost the confidence of key creditors due to the over-zealous approach to investigating a possible preference claim. The loss of confidence was key – there was no need to show any breaches of duty on the liquidators' part: see further D. Milman, 'Winding Up of Companies: Reflections on Recent Jurisprudence' (2006) 4 *Sweet & Maxwell's Company Law Newsletter* 1, 4.

[38] Insolvency Act 1986 s. 106.   [39] Ibid., s. 106.

Compulsory liquidation

Compulsory liquidation or winding up by the court generally involves actions initiated against the company's wishes, in contrast to members' or creditors' voluntary windings up. Proceedings are commenced by a petition that may be presented by any creditor (including contingent or prospective creditors),[40] the company, the directors (with all directors joining the petition acting as a board following unanimous or majority resolution), a contributory or the clerk of a magistrates' court in enforcement of a fine.[41] Receivers and administrators are also able to present petitions: in the case of the former, to aid realisation of the assets and, in the case of the latter, after a distribution.[42] In the case of creditors whose claims are disputed by the company, the court will exercise a discretion and will tend not to accede to the petition where the company disputes the claim on substantial grounds and in good faith.[43] The creditor whose claim is genuinely disputed is thus poorly placed to assert that the company has 'neglected to pay' the debt. Where, moreover, the debtor company has an enforceable cross claim against the petitioner –

---

[40] Ibid., s. 124(1). Where a voluntary winding up has been commenced and the majority of creditors wish it to continue, a petitioning creditor has to show some good reason for there to be a compulsory winding up: see *Re Ziceram Ltd* [2000] BCC 1048.

[41] Insolvency Act 1986 s. 124(1).

[42] See Insolvency Act 1986, Sch. B1, paras. 65, 66, 83, 84; and pp. 390–2 above.

[43] *Re London and Paris Banking Corporation* (1875) LR 19 Eq 444; *Brinds Ltd* v. *Offshore Oil* [1986] 2 BCC 98. See further *Favermead Ltd* v. *FPD Savills Ltd* [2005] BPIR 715, where a disputed debt was present, and *Abbey National plc* v. *JSF Financial and Currency Exchange Co. Ltd* [2005] BPIR 1256, where the dispute was not deemed to be 'real, genuine and substantial'; see also *dicta* of Pumfrey J in *Re Ringinfo Ltd* [2002] 1 BCLC 210 at 220. See generally A. Keay, 'Disputing Debts Relied on by Petitioning Creditors Seeking Winding Up Orders' (2000) 22 Co. Law. 40. Keay argues (p. 46): 'To qualify as a substantial dispute a dispute must be real and not fanciful, but it does not matter that the company bears malice towards the petitioner … But, where at least £750 is indisputably owed to the petitioner, after taking into account the disputed part of the debt, courts may decline to dismiss the petition.' See also *Hammonds (a firm)* v. *Pro-Fit USA Ltd* [2007] EWHC 1998 – a case which highlights the difference between winding up and administration, e.g. in showing the difference between the treatment of disputed debts under the two procedures. In the winding-up context the court's practice is that petitions based on a disputed debt will normally be dismissed. According to Warren J, this practice does not apply to administration – a procedure designed to revive and rescue a company rather than to end the company's life. In administration the court has a discretion at large, unconstrained by practice, as to whether or not to make an order on the particular facts of the case. Thus, where there may be a dispute regarding a creditor's claim raised by the company, the creditor may be well advised to consider applying for an administration order: see further T. Smith, (2007) *Recovery* (Winter) 12.

for a sum exceeding the claim – the court may dismiss or stay a winding-up petition.[44]

The primary grounds for a winding-up petition are that 'the company is unable to pay its debts'.[45] The Insolvency Act 1986 deems this inability to occur: (a) if a creditor who is owed over £750 has served the company with a written demand for payment (in prescribed form at the company's registered office) and the company has 'for three weeks neglected to pay the sum or to secure or compound for it to the reasonable satisfaction of the creditor';[46] or (b) if, in England and Wales, execution or other process issued on a judgment, decree or order of the court in favour of a creditor of the company is returned unsatisfied in whole or in part;[47] or (c) if it is proved to the satisfaction of the court that the company is unable to pay its debts as they fall due;[48] or (d) if it is proved that the value of the company's assets is less than the amount of its liability, taking into account its contingent and prospective liabilities.[49] Petitions based on the above grounds will also commonly refer to the grounds set out in the Insolvency Act 1986 section 122(1)(g) that 'the court is of the opinion that it is just and equitable that the company should be wound up'.[50]

Procedurally, a winding-up petition has to be served on the company and other parties as well as advertised according to the Insolvency Rules.[51] Service at the company's registered office is demanded and advertising must take place at least seven days after service and at least seven days before the hearing. The period between presentation of a winding-up petition and its hearing is a difficult one for the company and the petitioner. The company will often want to continue trading and petitioners may fear that the directors will dissipate assets and devalue their claims. In anticipation of these potential problems, the law provides

---

[44] See *Re Bayoil SA* [1999] 1 WLR 147, though the court may decide to deal with a cross-claim in the litigation: see *Re Richbell Information Systems Inc.* v. *Atlantic General Investments Trust Ltd* [1999] BCC 871.

[45] Insolvency Act 1986 s. 122(1)(f). See further ch. 4 above.

[46] Insolvency Act 1986 s. 123(1)(a).   [47] Ibid., s. 123(1)(b).

[48] Ibid., s. 123(1)(e).   [49] Ibid., s. 123(2).

[50] See *Ebrahimi* v. *Westbourne Galleries Ltd* [1973] AC 360; *Re J. E. Cade & Son Ltd* [1991] BCC 360. Section 122(1) also provides that a company may be wound up if: the company has by special resolution resolved that it be wound up by the court; it, being a public company, has not been issued with a share capital requirement certificate within a year of registration; it is an 'old company'; it does not commence or operate business for a whole year; or the number of its members is reduced to below two.

[51] Insolvency Rules 1986 rr. 4.8–4.10.

that where a petitioner can show that there is a serious risk that the directors will dissipate the company's assets and prejudice their claim, the court can appoint a provisional or interim liquidator to oversee the assets until the petition is heard.[52] This person may be a private IP but usually the Official Receiver will be appointed.

Protection for claimants is also offered by the rules on avoidance of transactions and the retrospectivity of the rule governing the start of a winding up. When a winding-up order is made, the winding up is deemed to commence at the time of presenting the petition.[53] Section 127 of the Insolvency Act 1986 covers dispositions of company property after this time and provides that any such dispositions and transfers of shares or alterations in the status of the company's members shall be void unless the court otherwise orders.[54]

More general shielding of the company is offered by sections 126 and 128 of the Insolvency Act 1986, which provide that, during winding up, a company creditor or contributory may apply to the court for a stay of legal proceedings against the company and that, again during a winding up, any attachment, sequestration, distress or execution in force against a company is void.

---

[52] Insolvency Act 1986 s. 135. The Public Interest Unit of the Insolvency Service, also known as the PIU, deals with provisional liquidations. The court can appoint a provisional liquidator to take control of the company at any time after a petition to wind up a company has been presented. The provisional liquidator can either be the Official Receiver or a licensed insolvency practitioner. The usual function of a provisional liquidator is to protect the company's assets and records until the court makes a ruling on the winding-up petition. In cases dealt with in the PIU, this will usually, but not always, mean that the company will be made to cease trading.

[53] Ibid., s. 129(2).

[54] See *Bank of Ireland* v. *Hollicourt (Contracts) Ltd* [2001] 2 WLR 290, [2001] 1 All ER 289, [2001] 1 BCLC 233 (CA). (Where a bank which is merely acting as an agent of a troubled company honours a cheque drawn on co-account unaware of a petition's presentation, the liquidator can recover from the payee only. The bank was not liable under section 127 to make restitution to the company of amounts paid to the company's creditors out of its account following presentation of a winding-up petition.) See C. Pugh, '*Hollicourt* to Reduce Banks' Exposure under Section 127' (2001) 17 IL&P 53; H. Mistry, '*Hollicourt*: Bringing the Authorities Out of Disarray' (2001) 22 Co. Law. 278; A. McGee and G. Scanlon, 'Section 127 IA 1986: Practical Problems in its Application' (2004) 25 Co. Law. 102. See also *Re Tain Construction* [2003] All ER 91, [2004] BCC 11 – change of position defences to a claim under s. 127 should be available. The deputy judge in *Re Tain* noted potential tensions between such restitutionary defences and the *pari passu* doctrine (both of which were based on 'an overarching concept of fairness'): see further G. Stewart, 'Section 127 and Change of Position Defences' (2003) *Recovery* (Autumn) 6 at 7; cf. L. C. Ho, '*Pari Passu* Distribution and Post-petition Disposition: A Rationalisation of *Re Tain Construction*' (21 November 2005, SSRN). See also ch. 14 below. The courts also have sought to bring clarity by offering procedural guidance on section 127 validation orders: see Practice Note: Validation Orders [2007] BCC 91.

As for the discretion of the court to grant a winding-up order, this will normally be exercised in favour of the petitioner if there is no opposition.[55] The court may, however, refuse an order under section 125 of the Insolvency Act 1986 if it is opposed by the majority of creditors. In deciding this issue, the court will look to the numbers of opposing creditors, to the value of the debts owed, and to the quality of those creditors.[56] On this last point, the court will give less weight to the claims of creditors who are connected with the company (for example, as directors or shareholders)[57] or who are fully secured[58] (and so have a limited interest in the liquidation). The court, moreover, will resist the use of liquidation to serve the petitioners' ulterior motive rather than general creditor benefit.[59]

As soon as a winding-up order is made, the Official Receiver automatically assumes the role of the liquidator until another liquidator is appointed.[60] After this time no legal actions may be taken against the company without the leave of the court and, subject to any conditions imposed by the court, the winding-up order ends the powers of the directors, passes control of the company's assets to the Official Receiver and operates as notice discharging the employees (except where the business continues for the purposes of beneficial winding up, the liquidator indicates a wish that employment should continue and the employees agree to continuation).[61] A winding-up order does not, in itself, however, repudiate other types of contract and the company is not deprived of the legal title to its assets.[62]

The liquidator is an officer of the court and has powers (and is obliged) to take into his custody or control all the property of the company.[63] Under section 144 of the Insolvency Act 1986 this includes all the

---

[55] Conversion to compulsory liquidation may be supported by the court, particularly where there is a deemed need for investigation into the directors' conduct.

[56] See, for example, *Re Holiday Stamps Ltd* (1985) 82 LSG 2817; *Re Flooks of Bristol (Builders) Ltd* [1982] Com LR 53.

[57] *Re Vuma Ltd* [1960] 1 WLR 1283.

[58] *Re Flooks of Bristol (Builders) Ltd* [1982] Com LR 53.

[59] Milman and Durrant, *Corporate Insolvency*, pp. 107–8; *Re Greenwood* [1900] 2 QB 306; *Re A Company (No. 0013925 of 1991), ex parte Roussel* [1992] BCLC 562; *Re Leigh Estates Ltd* [1994] BCC 292.

[60] Insolvency Act 1986 s. 136(1) and (2). As in voluntary liquidation the powers of the directors cease.

[61] See *Re Oriental Bank Corporation (Macdowell's Case)* (1886) 32 Ch D 36.

[62] *Ayerst v. C and K Construction Ltd* [1976] AC 167.

[63] On the implications of status as an officer of the court see e.g. C. Villiers, 'Employees as Creditors: A Challenge for Justice in Insolvency Law' (1999) 20 Co. Law. 222.

property to which the company appears entitled. He or she may call on officers and employees of the company to provide statements of affairs[64] and, as in a voluntary liquidation, there is a power to disclaim onerous property and contracts. There is, in addition, a discretion to call meetings of creditors and contributors, though these parties may compel the calling of a meeting if they have the support of one tenth in value of their body.[65]

Turning to controls over the liquidator in a compulsory winding up, he or she will be answerable to the Liquidation Committee of a company's creditors set up under section 141 of the Insolvency Act 1986. The liquidator may, with the sanction of the court or the Liquidation Committee, exercise any of the powers set out in Parts 1 and 2 of Schedule 4 of the Insolvency Act 1986 (payment of debts, compromise of claims etc., institution and defence of proceedings, carrying on of business of the company) and, as in a voluntary liquidation, the liquidator may carry out, without the need for court approval, the set of powers contained in Part 3 of Schedule 4. In compulsory liquidations, however, liquidators will be subject to control to a greater degree than in voluntary liquidations. They will, for example, require the sanction of the court or committee to initiate or defend legal proceedings in their name or in the name of the company, or to carry on the business of the company.[66] Court review of liquidator activities is provided for by section 168(5) of the Insolvency Act 1986 which allows any person aggrieved by a liquidator's act or decision to apply to the court, whereupon the court may confirm, reverse or modify the act/decision and make orders as it thinks fit.

The key function of the liquidator is to 'secure that the assets of the company are got in, realised and distributed to the company's creditors and, if there is a surplus, to the persons entitled to it'.[67] Failure to fulfil that function may result in penalties for the liquidator, which may

---

[64] Insolvency Act 1986 s. 131; Insolvency Rules 1986 rr. 4.32–4.38.

[65] Insolvency Act 1986 s. 168. A creditor who wishes to vote and who requires dividends is required to submit (lodge) a formal claim – a proof of debt – to the liquidator: IR 1986 rr. 4.73, 11.6(1). On proof of debt see, for example, *Wight* v. *Eckhardt Marine GMbH* [2004] 1 AC 147, [2003] 3 WLR 414; I. Fletcher, 'Right to Participate in a Distribution' (2004) 17 *Insolvency Intelligence* 91; *Day* v. *Haine and Secretary of State* [2007] EWHC 2691 (protective awards granted to employees after a company had gone into liquidation were held not be provable debts as they had been made after the date of liquidation (decision reversed on appeal – [2008] EWCA Civ 626)).

[66] Ratification is, however, possible for uncontentious actions: see r. 4.184(2).

[67] Insolvency Act 1986 s. 143(1).

involve misfeasance actions,[68] deprivations of costs[69] and actions for negligence.[70] Duties that must be discharged include keeping proper accounts and lodging, with the Insolvency Service's account at the Bank of England, any funds realised. The accounts of the liquidator will be audited by the Secretary of State and there is an obligation to file accounts and returns under section 170 of the Insolvency Act 1986. It is, moreover, the duty of the liquidator to keep minutes of meetings and administrative records, to act independently and to avoid conflicts of interest.

The end of a compulsory liquidation occurs when the liquidator has realised all the potential assets of the company and distributed all available funds. The liquidator will then report to the final meeting of creditors which may release him. If the liquidator is not so released he or she may apply to the Secretary of State.[71] The liquidator must report the outcome of the final meeting to the court and the Companies Registry and, when three months have elapsed, the company will automatically dissolve.[72]

Public interest liquidation

The BERR and the Financial Services Authority (FSA) have powers to petition the court to wind up a company on 'just and equitable' grounds.[73] These powers, typically, would be used to stop enterprises trading where they engage in practices that defraud customers and swindle the vulnerable – where, for example, worthless insurance policies or non-existent products are sold to the public or dubious financial schemes are marketed.[74] They are powers that bypass the requirement

---

[68] Ibid., s. 212. See *Re Centralcrest Engineering Ltd* [2000] BCC 727; *Whitehouse* v. *Wilson* [2007] BPIR 230.

[69] *Re Silver Valley Mines* (1882) 21 Ch D 381.

[70] *IRC* v. *Hoogstraten* [1985] QB 1077.   [71] Insolvency Rules 1986 r. 4.121.

[72] An expedited process for dissolving a company is available in Insolvency Act 1986 s. 202 where the company's realisable assets will not cover the cost of the liquidation and where full investigation of the company's affairs is not required. Here the OR may apply to the Registrar of Companies for an early dissolution order, though twenty-eight days' notice of the intention to apply has to be given to the company's creditors and contributories and administrative receiver (if there is one).

[73] In 2006–7 the Insolvency Service of BERR secured 95 winding-up orders following 174 investigations: Insolvency Service, *Annual Report* 2006–7.

[74] For discussion see Report of the Review Committee on Insolvency Law and Practice (Cmnd 8558, 1982) ('Cork Report'), paras. 1745–51, noting the particular problem of 'pyramid selling', which involves purchasers of products being induced (usually by commissions) to sell to others and to recruit these persons in turn as sales operatives:

that creditors must be owed in excess of £750 if they are to petition the court for a winding up and are especially useful where it comes to light that a company is defrauding large numbers of creditors of relatively small sums of money: as where 40,000 football World Cup tickets were sold by a company but no tickets were supplied.[75]

The Secretary of State for BERR has powers under section 124A of the Insolvency Act 1986 to present a petition to the court to wind up a company. This may be done where it appears to the Secretary of State that it is 'expedient in the public interest that a company should be wound up'.[76] The basis for the Secretary of State's conviction on this front must be a report or information obtained under Part XIV of the Companies Act 1985; a report made by inspectors under sections 167, 168, 169 or 284 of the Financial Services and Markets Act 2000 (FSMA 2000); any information or documents obtained under sections 165, 171, 172, 173 or 175 of FSMA 2000;[77] information obtained under section 2 of the Criminal Justice Act 1987;[78] or information obtained under section 83 of the Companies Act 1989. The court, in turn, is empowered to wind the company up 'if the court thinks it just and

---

see, for example, *Re Secure and Provide plc* [1992] BCC 405, 406; *Re Drivertime Recruitment Ltd* [2005] 1 BCLC 411. For an example of a pyramid-selling winding up see *Re Alpha Club (UK) Ltd*, Judgment, 23 April 2002 (noted: (2002) 8 *Sweet & Maxwell's Company Law Newsletter* 7). See also V. Finch, 'Public Interest Liquidation: PIL or Placebo?' (2002) Ins. Law. 157; C. Campbell, 'Protection by Elimination: Winding Up of Companies on Public Interest Grounds' (2001) 17 IL&P 129; A. Keay, 'Public Interest Petitions' (1999) 20 Co. Law. 296; D. Milman, 'Winding Up in the Public Interest' (1999) 3 *Palmer's In Company* 1–2; Cork Report, paras. 1745–51.

[75] See Campbell, 'Protection by Elimination', p. 131.

[76] The Secretary of State thus acts not to protect his or her own interests but in the interests of the public: see Keay, 'Public Interest Petitions', p. 297; *Re Lubin Rosen and Associates Ltd* [1975] 1 WLR 122 at 129. On defining the public interest as the interest of 'the public at large' see Megarry J in *Re Lubin Rosen* at 129 and see also Nicholls LJ in *Re Walter L. Jacob & Co. Ltd* [1989] 5 BCC 244 at 256.

[77] See Insolvency Act 1986 s. 124A(b), as amended by the Financial Services and Markets Act 2000 (Consequential Amendments and Repeals) Order 2001 s. 305. Section 305 further details that where the company is an open-ended investment company (within the meaning of FSMA 2000), regulations made as a result of section 262(2)(k) of FSMA 2000 are relevant for the Secretary of State's decision.

[78] The Serious Fraud Office (SFO) has a specific remit to investigate serious or complex fraud and to prepare reports that may be used as a basis for winding-up petitions. Information and evidence collected by the SFO (under section 2 of the Criminal Justice Act 1987) may be passed to the CIB for the purposes of a winding-up petition under s. 124(a) of the Insolvency Act 1986: see Campbell, 'Protection by Elimination', p. 131.

equitable'. Indeed, the court may make any order it thinks fit, including an interim order.[79]

As for the Financial Services Authority (FSA), this body possesses powers to petition for a winding up under FSMA 2000. Section 367(1) of FSMA 2000 provides that the FSA may ask the court to compulsorily wind up any company or partnership which is or has been an authorised person[80] or an appointed representative[81] or is carrying on or has carried on a regulated activity without authorisation in contravention of the general prohibition on this in FSMA 2000. On such a petition, the court may wind up the body if it is unable to pay its debts[82] or if the court 'is of the opinion that it is just and equitable that it should be wound up'.[83] The Secretary of State has some of the same powers that the FSA possesses under FSMA 2000, but not the FSA's insolvency powers.

The philosophies underpinning PIL do, however, vary both between petitioning institutions and across the processes of securing and enforcing a PIL. To start with the BERR, this Department acts through the Companies Investigation Branch (CIB) (which is located within the Insolvency Service, an executive agency of BERR). The ruling objective of the CIB is to protect the public from the activities of unscrupulous or otherwise errant companies and their directors or employees. The purpose here is not necessarily to trigger the liquidation of a company that is insolvent. The company does not have to be shown to be insolvent in order to petition the court.[84] Nor, indeed, is the major purpose of the CIB to put the company out of business – it is to put an end to a practice or way of conducting business that is harmful to the public, though not necessarily illegal.[85]

---

[79] The court may, as an alternative to winding up, extract an undertaking from the company or its directors: see *Bell Davies Trading Ltd* v. *Secretary of State for Trade and Industry* [2005] BCC 564 and (on the court's general discretion) *Re Supporting Link Ltd* [2004] BCC 764.

[80] Per s. 31(2) FSMA 2000 (a person within Part IV FSMA 2000 permitted to carry on one or more regulated activities, a firm qualifying for authorisation under Schedule 3 or 4 or a person otherwise authorised under FSMA 2000).

[81] Per s. 39(2) FSMA 2000 (a party contracted by an authorised person to engage in business of a prescribed description).

[82] FSMA 2000, s. 367(3)(a).   [83] Ibid., s. 367(3)(b).

[84] On why it might be in the public interest to wind up a solvent company see *Re A Company (No 007923 of 1994)* [1995] BCC 634, 637; Keay, 'Public Interest Petitions', p. 300.

[85] *Re SHV Senator Hanseatische Verwaltungs Gesellschaft mbH* [1997] BCC 112, 119 (Millett LJ).

The FSA's position might be contrasted as being more explicitly 'regulatory'. When the FSA petitions the court, it does so in relation to regulated parties and activities and it does not petition in pursuit of 'the public interest' as stated in those terms. The Secretary of State has, as noted, to make a section 124A petition on the basis of evidence derived from specified reports or sources of information. The FSA, in contrast, has neither the obligation to refer to such designated bodies of evidence nor the duty to apply the 'expedient in the public interest'[86] test in deciding whether to apply for a winding up. Under FSMA 2000 the court may look to whether the body is insolvent or whether it is just and equitable to wind it up[87] but the FSA petitions in pursuit of its statutory objectives, namely of maintaining confidence in the financial system, promoting public understanding of the financial system, securing the appropriate degree of protection for consumers and reducing financial crime.[88] The FSA thus proceeds with a more particular focus than the CIB, which may act in order to uphold principles of commercial morality quite generally, but which is not concerned to sustain the health of a particular sector or to retain confidence in a particular market.

Differences in the legal powers of the FSA and CIB create potential differences of approach. The FSA has a wider range of specific statutory powers than the CIB. These allow it to stop an objectionable commercial practice by an individual or company within the financial services sector. These powers may thus rule out the need to apply for PIL in many instances. If, for instance, the FSA is concerned about the trading behaviour of an individual or company which is an authorised person, it can use its administrative powers and does not need to seek court approval before it acts. For instance, it may exercise its 'own initiative' power to vary an authorised person's permission to carry on regulated activity – as set out in Part IV of FSMA 2000. Under section 53(2)(a) of this Act the FSA may exercise this power so that a variation is of immediate effect and the Authority is likely to act urgently where this is necessary to protect consumer interests, where financial crime is involved, where the person or company has submitted misleading information to the FSA, or there is concern about the company's ability to continue to meet its conditions of carrying out business.[89] Where, similarly, there are worries about the practices of persons (whether authorised or not), section 380 FSMA 2000 allows the FSA (and, to a more limited extent, the Secretary of State) to

---

[86] See Insolvency Act 1986 s. 124A(1).   [87] FSMA 2000 s. 367(3)(a) and (b).
[88] Ibid., ss. 2–6.   [89] See *FSA Enforcement Handbook* (FSA Online).

apply to court for an injunction to restrain a contravention of a relevant regulatory requirement. Section 381 also allows the FSA (but not the Secretary of State) to apply to the court to injunct a person to restrain a market abuse. In addition to section 380 or 381 restraining injunctions, the FSA (and, in some cases, the Secretary of State) may ask the court to restrain a person from disposing of or dealing with assets. Restraining injunctions may be sought in a precautionary manner – where the FSA has evidence that there is a reasonable likelihood that a person will contravene a requirement of the 2000 Act – and these and asset freezing orders may be obtained from the court on an interim basis. Nor should it be forgotten that conduct that might be the subject of an injunction application may also be an offence or a regulatory breach for which the FSA has prosecutorial or disciplinary powers under the 2000 Act.

To return to CIB-instituted petitions to wind up in the public interest, philosophical differences are also encountered at different stages in the process from application to enforcement. The CIB's central concern may be to protect the public from the actions of an individual or firm, but it cannot be assumed that the courts will take an identical or purely protective view when considering if it is 'just and equitable' to wind up. It is clear from decided cases that the courts will not accept the Secretary of State's arguments unquestioningly, but will consider and test these in the same manner as the submissions of other parties.[90] The courts, moreover, will not look in a narrow fashion at the interests of the public but will balance the interests of all parties involved – the company, the members, creditors and investing members of the public.[91] There is, in addition, some evidence that certain judges may temper their instincts to protect the public by demanding evidence of some culpability on the part of the company or its directors. Courts generally stress that ordering the winding up of an active company is a very serious step[92] and, in declining a winding up in *Re Secure and Provide plc*,[93] Hoffmann J seemed to lay particular stress on the issue of blameworthiness. In that case, the

---

[90] See Campbell, 'Protection by Elimination', p. 132; Keay, 'Public Interest Petitions', p. 298; *Re Secure and Provide plc* [1992] BCC 405; *Re Walter L. Jacob & Co. Ltd* [1989] 5 BCC 244, 251–2.

[91] *Re SHV Senator Hanseatische Verwaltungs Gesellschaft mbH* [1997] BCC 112, [1997] 1 WLR 515; *Re Market Wizard Systems (UK) Ltd* [1998] 2 BCLC 282.

[92] *Re Walter L. Jacob & Co. Ltd* [1989] 5 BCC 244, 252; *Re Golden Chemical Products Ltd* [1976] 1 Ch 300, 310–11.

[93] [1992] BCC 405. See also *Secretary of State for Trade and Industry* v. *Travel Time (UK) Ltd* [2000] BCC 792.

commercial practice at issue was that of using pyramid selling schemes to market insurance packages. The Secretary of State's petition alleged fraud on the part of the company but Hoffmann J refused the petition. He accepted that some of the statements used in the sales literature were either exaggerated or wrong but he also believed the evidence of the scheme's designer who claimed that he had acted in good faith and had not intended to deceive. His Lordship thought that winding up was not justified as it would have been a 'grossly disproportionate response' to the errors involved.[94]

Hoffmann J's approach here might be interpreted as inconsistent with a strict public protection rationale – which would seek to shield the public from potentially harmful conduct whether the behaviour involved was deliberate or not. It might be countered that in *Re Secure and Provide plc* the court was really taking exception to the quality of the evidence that the DTI had amassed against the company.[95] In another case, however, *Secretary of State for Trade and Industry* v. *Travel Time (UK) Ltd*,[96] the court was again concerned with whether the public had been *deliberately* defrauded or misled and suggested that where a petition was presented it was desirable, though not essential, that there be evidence of some intentional or dishonest deceit of the public.

Such judicial reasoning leaves certain questions hanging, notably whether issues of culpability are relevant because the courts are reluctant to take the serious step of winding up without there being some blame-worthiness to merit this, or whether the courts are interested in delibera-tion and blameworthiness because the courts are concerned to protect the public by upholding standards of commercial morality – which, in turn, calls for evidence on the degree of culpability that a particular practice involves. Consistent with the latter approach is the judgment of Nicholls LJ in *Re Walter L. Jacob & Co. Ltd*.[97] A key issue in that case was whether the petition for winding up should be refused because the company had ceased trading in securities immediately before the presentation of the petition and therefore no longer presented a threat to the investing public. His Lordship was unpersuaded by this line of

---

[94] See also *Re A Company (No. 007923 of 1994)* [1995] BCC 634 and *Re A Company (No. 007924 of 1994)* [1996] 15 Lit. 201–3 – petitions refused, giving credit to the fact that the directors involved had all honestly believed that they were acting lawfully.

[95] See Campbell, 'Protection by Elimination', p. 132, who notes that such 'antipathy to the DTI's poorly researched argument presented *ex parte*' was further manifested by the court allocating the provisional liquidator's costs against the Secretary of State.

[96] [2000] BCC 792.   [97] [1989] 5 BCC 244.

argument, stating that it would 'offend ordinary notions of what is just and equitable that, by ceasing to trade on becoming aware that the net is closing around it, a company which has misconducted itself on the securities market can thereby enable itself to remain in being despite its previous history'.[98] Nicholls LJ granted the petition, stating that the public interest required that individuals or companies who deal in securities should maintain at least the generally accepted minimum standards of commercial behaviour and that those who, for whatever reason, fall below those standards should have their activities stopped.[99] He emphasised that his judgment sent a message to the financial services community: 'of spelling out ... that the court will not hesitate to wind up companies whose standards of dealing with the investing public are unacceptable'.[100]

When awarding costs, the courts, it seems, will be prepared to advert to issues of culpability and to take even retribution into account. Directors whose defences to petitions cause unnecessary losses to other parties are plainly liable to be penalised by the courts.[101] Where a petition to wind up is sought, it is common for a provisional liquidator to be appointed and the Insolvency Service has considerable experience in fulfilling this role. Again, however, the approach of the Insolvency Service (IS) may not be identical to that of the CIB. An official of the IS made the point at interview: 'The purpose, from the CIB's point of view, of appointing Official Receivers as provisional liquidators is to close the business down and we can't do that because, as a provisional liquidator, we are acting as an officer of the court not as a liquidator and we are as answerable to the company as we are to the petitioner.'[102]

There is thus a divergence here between the approaches of the IS and its sub-department: 'The CIB want to stop the company trading, stop the wrongdoing, but we [the IS] have to be sure that it isn't a viable concern – our job is to protect the estate, only that – to collect and protect the assets pending the determination of the court. There is a certain tension there

---

[98] Ibid. at 257H.   [99] Ibid. at 256E.   [100] Ibid. at 258A.

[101] *Secretary of State for Trade and Industry v. Aurum Marketing Ltd* [1999] 2 BCLC 498; *Re North West Holdings plc; Secretary of State for Trade and Industry v. Backhouse* [2002] BCC 441 – the Court of Appeal ordered that the owner-controller of two companies (B) should pay the costs of the section 124A liquidation because B had not given any serious consideration as to what was in the interests of the companies and their creditors apropos defending the petition. Per Aldous LJ the costs had been expended for B's individual interests and it was therefore just that B paid the Secretary of State's costs even though B was not a party to the proceedings.

[102] Interview, Insolvency Service, 15 March 2002.

and we have been working on this [aspect] for three years now and it has been pretty tense throughout that time.'[103]

Such tensions and differences of approach as are described above raise questions about the philosophical consistency of the PIL process and these differences, in turn, may impinge on the potential of the PIL regime to protect the public against the actions of errant directors. This is a matter to be returned to in chapter 16 below.

The concept of liquidation

When the Cork Committee reviewed the state of insolvency procedures in 1982 it was concerned that liquidation, like other ways of dealing with insolvency, was based on a myth: that creditors would control processes. The principle underlying insolvency law, from at least Victorian times to the 1980s, was said to be that: 'Since the estate is being administered primarily for the benefit of the creditors, they are the persons best calculated to look after their own interests.'[104] In accordance with this notion, the Companies Act 1948 section 246 obliged the liquidator to have regard to any directions given by the creditors in general meeting or by the committee of inspection and, in exercising certain powers, the liquidator required express authority from the committee of inspection.

It was suggested to the (receptive) Cork Committee that the system of creditor control was illusory because of apathy and indifference on the part of the creditors. Three reasons were given for the weakness of creditor oversight: first, the general belief that most liquidators were efficient, reliable and experienced; second, the propensity of business creditors to allow for occasional bad debts in fixing prices and to write these off so as to reduce taxable profits, a propensity producing a lack of real interest in insolvency processes; and, third, an acceptance that in most cases of insolvency the general body of creditors was likely to receive only a small dividend. Such factors produced a situation, said Cork, in which creditors were reluctant to attend meetings or serve on committees and where there was an indifference towards the supervision of insolvency processes.[105]

---

[103] Ibid.   [104] Cork Report, para. 912.

[105] A new body aiming to encourage activism on the part of creditors was established in 2004 when the Insolvency Creditors Association was set up, its spokesman stating that it planned to turn matters around so that creditor involvement became the norm rather than the exception: see (2004) *Recovery* (Summer) 6.

Cork made a number of recommendations that were designed to encourage ordinary creditors to play an active role in insolvency proceedings.[106] A broader solution was, however, to involve a rethinking of the insolvency procedures '[t]o move away from the concept of creditor control toward one based on creditor participation'. This shift, in turn, would be achieved by requiring liquidators (like receivers and administrators) to give more information to creditors generally and to reduce the duties placed upon creditors.

In terms of the benchmarks employed throughout this book, what Cork proposed was a change in emphasis so that liquidation could be seen less as a matter of accountability and control (by creditors) and more as an issue of expert (professional) management by the IP: though in combination with higher levels of transparency and more modest (but more realistic) levels of creditor supervision. Whether liquidation operates in a manner that is supportable by reference to the chapter 2 benchmarks is the next concern.

Efficiency

Central to liquidators acting efficiently is the effective protection of the entitlements of creditors in the gathering together of the insolvency estate. In such endeavours, liquidators are assisted by the Insolvency Act 1986 which seeks to avoid a number of transactions that might defeat creditors, notably actions involving: dispositions after presentation of the winding-up petition;[107] late executed floating charges;[108] transactions at undervalue;[109] preferences;[110] and transactions defrauding creditors.[111]

Such provisions, if enforced, allow creditors' entitlements to be restored and, furthermore, in the case of wrongful trading, provide for

---

[106] For example, Cork's proposals to increase the share in the distribution available for the general body of creditors by reducing preferential debt and conferring a stake in receiver realisation. See now the 'prescribed part' provisions in IA 1986 s. 176A(2): see ch. 3 above and chs. 14 and 15 below.

[107] Insolvency Act 1986 s. 127.   [108] Ibid., s. 245.   [109] Ibid., s. 238.   [110] Ibid., s. 239.

[111] Ibid., s. 423. Other provisions, such as Insolvency Act 1986 s. 244 (extortionate credit transactions) and Companies Act 2006 ss. 860, 874 (non-registration of charges), also seek to prevent transactional avoidance. See generally D. Milman and R. Parry, *A Study of the Operation of Transactional Avoidance Mechanisms in Corporate Insolvency Practice*, Insolvency Lawyers' Association Research Report (1997); R. Parry and D. Milman, 'Transaction Avoidance Provision in Corporate Insolvency: An Empirical Study' (1998) 14 IL&P 280.

compensatory payments to be made by directors.[112] Efficient application of these laws may also deter the directors of troubled companies from taking actions that prejudice legitimate creditor interests.[113] Such efficient enforcement action by liquidators is only possible if there is access to the funding that is necessary to pursue cases against errant directors.[114] This section of the chapter accordingly focuses on the funding of liquidator actions but also considers whether liquidators are well placed to amass the information that is necessary for the effective deploying of legal challenges. Whether liquidation and the rules on the avoidance of transactions operate substantively fairly as between different creditors (or between creditors and others) is left to the next section, but overlaps are inevitable and fairness clearly demands that there be efficient enforcement.

The background to funding and its importance to liquidators is that liquidators will often view litigation from a position of reluctance to pursue some actions (for example, avoidable transactions) where there are economically powerful defending parties (for example, banks) or where lucrative professional relationships (with, say, banks) are liable to be soured. As Parry and Milman note: 'It should not be forgotten that the receivership and investigation work, which banks put the way of IPs, will be a far more lucrative source of income than transaction avoidance.'[115] Liquidators, moreover, have to protect the insolvency estate by entering a game in which their own funding problems could routinely be exploited by defenders as a tactic designed to kill the case.[116] As for those funding problems, a number will be faced by liquidators.[117] The difficult reality a liquidator encounters is that actions will have to be taken when a company is insolvent and necessarily short of funds, a position not aided by the non-eligibility for legal aid of a company in administration or liquidation.[118] The Cork Committee commented that the task facing the liquidator was 'too difficult' and led to a paucity of challenges to

---

[112] See Insolvency Act 1986 s. 214; see further ch. 16 below.

[113] See R. Parry, 'Funding Litigation in Insolvency' [1998] 2 CfiLR 121.

[114] See further ch. 16 below.   [115] Parry and Milman, 'Transaction Avoidance', p. 282.

[116] Ibid. On the difficulties of office holders where the costs and expenses of insolvency proceedings exceed the assets in the estate see H. Anderson, 'Insolvent Insolvencies' (2001) 17 IL&P 87. For an instance in which a director was ordered to pay the costs of a successful winding-up petition in the public interest as he induced the company to defend the petition to serve his ulterior interests, see *Secretary of State for Trade and Industry* v. *Backhouse* [2002] BCC 441.

[117] See Milman and Parry, *Study*, ch. 2.   [118] Access to Justice Act 1999 s. 4.

illegitimate payments,[119] and, to date, a series of problems confronts the liquidator.

In some circumstances there may be sufficient liquid funds in the pool of realised assets to fund litigation. If the liquidator wishes to litigate to protect creditor interests, he will need the approval of the creditors' Liquidation Committee to bring an action in the company's name[120] and, following the Enterprise Act reforms,[121] will require the sanction of the creditors[122] if seeking to bring clawback proceedings.[123] Such creditor sanctioning cannot, however, be taken for granted and the liquidator cannot assume that the unsecured creditors will be prepared to use the funds made available to them by virtue of the 'prescribed part' rules as a fighting fund.[124] In the case of an unsuccessful action brought by the liquidators in their name personally, they may claim indemnification in respect of costs borne, but a significant issue here is the place in the order of priorities that such claims will occupy.

Before the Companies Act 2006 amendment it had become clear that the general costs and expenses of the liquidator could not be paid out of floating charge realisations. The 2004 House of Lords decision in *Leyland DAF Ltd; Buchler* v. *Talbot*[125] made this plain in overruling *Re Barleycorn*.[126] Their Lordships' position was that a distinction was to be drawn between the proceeds of the free assets, which belong to the company and are administered by the liquidator in a winding up, and the proceeds of assets subject to a floating charge, which belong to the charge holder. Each of these funds was to be treated as bearing its own costs but

---

[119] Cork Report, para. 1257.

[120] See Insolvency Act 1986 Part II, Sch. 4, para. 4.

[121] See EA 2002 s. 253, which inserts para. 3A into Part 1 of Sch. 4 of the IA 1986.

[122] In compulsory liquidation the court's sanction is required.

[123] I.e. proceedings under ss. 213, 214, 238, 239, 242, 243 or 423 of the Insolvency Act 1986. See Lord McIntosh, Third Reading of Enterprise Bill, House of Lords, 21 October 2002, col. 1123: 'it is a commercial decision for the creditor to choose between, say, a five pence in the pound dividend payable now or whether to allow the liquidator to pursue a claim which may result in a fifty pence in the pound dividend at a later stage'. See also S. Davies, *Insolvency and the Enterprise Act 2002* (Jordans, Bristol, 2003).

[124] See Davies, *Insolvency and the Enterprise Act 2002*, p. 301.

[125] *Re Leyland DAF Ltd; Buchler* v. *Talbot* [2004] 2 AC 298. For discussion see J. Armour and A. Walters, 'Funding Liquidation: A Functional View' (2006) 122 *Law Quarterly Review* 295 at 323–5; A. Walters, 'Floating Charges and Liquidation Expenses' (2006) 27 Co. Law. 193; R. Mokal, 'Liquidation Expenses and Floating Charges – The Separate Funds Fallacy' [2004] LMCLQ 387.

[126] [1970] Ch 465. See G. McCormack, 'Swelling Corporate Assets: Changing what is on the Menu' [2006] 6 JCLS 39.

not those of the other.[127] An advantage of this position was that it stopped general creditors from funding actions from floating charge assets with a view to generating recoveries that would belong exclusively to them and not the floating charge holder.[128] The line taken in *Leyland DAF* affirmed that winding-up proceedings were for the benefit of unsecured creditors – and to be funded by such creditors from the 'free' assets.[129]

The decision in *Leyland DAF* did, however, reduce the likely size of the asset pool available for paying liquidation expenses and thus increased IPs' prospects of not being paid their costs and expenses for winding up a company[130] – which, in turn, might be expected to have reduced liquidators' inclinations to pursue office-holder actions.[131] Critics argued, moreover, that it was a nonsense to have different expenses regimes for liquidations and administrations.[132] A product of that difference was that *Leyland DAF* gave IPs an incentive to conduct *de facto* liquidations through the Schedule B1 administration procedure since the expenses of that procedure have statutory priority over the floating charge.[133] *Leyland DAF* can, accordingly, be seen as underplaying the public interest role of liquidation proceedings and the value of such proceedings in reinforcing commercial morality – notably through the institution of investigations and the reporting requirements that may result in the prosecution of company officers.[134] It can also be said to have allowed

---

[127] [2004] 2 AC 298, Lord Millett at para. 62.

[128] See McCormack, 'Swelling Corporate Assets', p. 63

[129] Armour and Walters, 'Funding Liquidation', pp. 322–3.

[130] See G. Moss, 'Liquidators Stung for Costs and Expenses' (2004) 17 *Insolvency Intelligence* 78.

[131] 'In the light of the *Leyland DAF* ruling, no IP will spend time investigating and incur personal risk in situations where his or her own fees and expenses are in doubt': see R. Welby, 'Antecedent Recoveries and Litigation Funding – A Practical Perspective' (2006) *Recovery* (Winter) 32. Walters, in 'Floating Charges and Liquidation Expenses', points out that such considerations led the Association of Business Recovery Professionals (R3) to press the Government to reverse the *Leyland DAF* position. McCormack posits, however, that the *Leyland DAF* decision could lead to a 'richer source of funding available to pursue recovery proceedings; namely, an all-assets floating charge holder': 'Swelling Corporate Assets', p. 65.

[132] M. Rollins, 'Technical Update' (2006) *Recovery* (Summer) 11, 12.

[133] Administrators' expenses and remuneration are paid in priority to a floating charge: see Insolvency Act 1986 Sch. B1, para. 99(3) and ch. 9 above. For an argument that the incentive to use administration might inadvertently prove rescue-enhancing see L. Hiestand and C. Pilkington, 'The Impact of *Leyland DAF*' (2005) *Recovery* (Spring) 18.

[134] See further ch. 16 below. For judicial endorsement of the public interest role of liquidations see *Re Pantmaenog Timber Co. Ltd* [2004] 1 AC 158.

secured creditors to free ride on the public interested actions that are funded out of assets belonging to unsecured creditors.[135]

Leyland DAF has, however, been reversed by section 1282 of the Companies Act 2006 which provides for the insertion of a new section 176ZA into the Insolvency Act 1986. This insertion was effected by Statutory Instrument in April 2008 and provides that the expenses of winding up 'have priority over any claims to property comprised in or subject to any floating charge created by the company and shall be paid out of any such property accordingly' and that this applies so far as the assets of the company available for payment of general creditors are insufficient to meet them.[136] Any sums constituting the 'prescribed part' made available to meet unsecured claims under section 176A(2)(a) of the 1986 Act will not be included within the pool of assets which are to be applied to meet liquidation expenses ahead of distributions to the general creditors.[137]

The granting of 'super-priority' to liquidation expenses places emphasis on the categorisation of expenditure as an expense of the liquidation.[138] Reference here must be made to Rule 4.218 as amended.[139] This rule makes it clear that the liquidator's remuneration is such an expense, as are liabilities incurred before the liquidation in respect of property retained by the liquidator for the benefit of the estate (such as rent or hire purchase charges). Rule 4.218 includes as expenses 'any necessary disbursements by the liquidator in the course of his administration' and the

---

[135] See R. Mokal, 'What Liquidation Does for Secured Creditors and What It Does for You' (2008) 71 MLR 699.

[136] See the Insolvency (Amendment) Rules 2008 (SI 2008/737) which came into effect on 6 April 2008. The amended Rules provide specifically that the assets available for the payment of the general creditors include the proceeds of any legal action which the liquidator has power to bring. Only property that is covered by a fixed charge thus escapes the claims of liquidation expenses. See I. Fletcher, 'Companies Act 2006: Reversal of *Leyland DAF* Ruling' (2007) 20 *Insolvency Intelligence* 30.

[137] See section 176ZA(2)(a). For arguments that the reversal of *Leyland DAF* will cause secured lenders to demand additional collateralisation – and that this will detract from the City of London as a centre for project finance and securitisation transactions – see Financial Markets Law Committee, *Issue 120 – Section 868 of the Company Law Revision Bill: Statutory Reversal of* Leyland DAF (FMLC, London, March 2006).

[138] See generally *Boyle and Birds' Company Law* (6th edn, Jordans, Bristol, 2007) pp. 938–40.

[139] Said by Lord Hoffmann in *Re Toshoku Finance (UK) plc, Kahn* v. *Commissioners of Inland Revenue* [2002] 1 WLR 671 (paras. 15–17 and 38–9) to contain a complete list of what counts as a liquidation expense – and subject neither to implied qualification nor court discretion.

House of Lords held, in *Toshoku Finance*,[140] that this includes liability to corporation tax.[141]

Originally, the costs incurred by the liquidator in unsuccessfully seeking to recover assets were not treated as expenses of the liquidation. In *Re M. C. Bacon Ltd (No. 2)*[142] Millett J ruled that the costs of unsuccessful preference and wrongful trading actions could not rank, for priority purposes, as taken for the purpose of preserving, realising or getting in the assets within Rule 4.218(1) of the Insolvency Rules 1986,[143] nor could they be regarded as expenses of the winding up for the purposes of section 115 of the Insolvency Act 1986. The Court of Appeal in *Re Floor Fourteen Ltd*[144] reasserted[145] the restrictive approach taken in *Re M. C. Bacon*[146] and deemed that the expenses incurred by a liquidator in pursuing claims under section 214 and section 239 of the Insolvency Act 1986 were indeed not 'expenses of the liquidation'.[147]

Matters have since changed, however. Rule 23 of the Insolvency (Amendment) (No. 2) Rules 2002[148] amended Rule 4.218(1)(a) of the Insolvency Rules 1986 to provide that costs properly chargeable in

---

[140] *Re Toshoku Finance (UK) plc, Kahn* v. *Commissioners of Inland Revenue* [2002] 1 WLR 671, [2002] BCC 110. See further H. Lyons and M. Birch, 'Insolvency Expenses' (2005) 18 *Insolvency Intelligence* 150; G. Stewart, 'Heresy in the House of Lords' (2002) *Recovery* (September) 6; A. Walters, 'Liquidation Expenses – Ruling in *Re Toshoku Finance (UK) plc* Considered' (2002) 4 *Sweet & Maxwell's Company Law Newsletter* 1.

[141] On statutory liabilities to pay redundancy and unfair dismissal payments as non-'necessary disbursements' and expenses of the administration see *Allders Department Stores Ltd (in administration)* [2005] 2 All ER 122, [2005] BCC 289; ch. 17 below.

[142] [1990] 3 WLR 646.   [143] See also *Re Yagerphone* [1935] Ch 392.

[144] *Re Floor Fourteen Ltd, Lewis* v. *Commissioners of Inland Revenue* [2001] 3 All ER 499, [2001] 2 BCLC 392: Peter Gibson LJ accepted that *Re R. S. & M. Engineering Co. Ltd, Mond* v. *Hammond Suddards* [2000] Ch 40, [1999] 3 WLR 697, which expressly approved *Re M. C. Bacon (No. 2)*, was binding on the court.

[145] In *Katz* v. *McNally* [1997] BCC 784 the Court of Appeal had gone some way in countering the reasoning of Millett J in *Re M. C. Bacon (No. 2)* and in assuring office holders that litigation expenses could be met from the company's assets.

[146] [1990] 3 WLR 646.

[147] For comment and criticism of *Re Floor Fourteen* see A. Walters, '*Re Floor Fourteen Ltd* in the Court of Appeal' (2001) 22 *Co. Law.* 215; T. Pope and M. Woollard, 'Part 2 – Lewis' (2001) 14 *Insolvency Intelligence* 20; G. Stewart, 'Liquidation Expenses – Litigation' (2001) *Recovery* (July) 8 – who argues, *inter alia*, 'it surely cannot be right that the recoupment by a liquidator of his costs of preference and wrongful trading actions depends solely upon whether or not he succeeds. The test must be whether it was reasonable and prudent for him to bring the action in the first place ... it is excessive and contrary to the principles of office-holder responsibility to make it necessary for the liquidator to get prior court clearance for incurring costs (presuming that there is a judicial basis for the court intervening which the Court of Appeal in *Lewis* found difficult to identify).'

[148] SI 2002/2712 which came into force on 1 January 2003.

relation to any legal proceedings which the Official Receiver or liquidator has power to bring, whether in his own name or that of the company, are payable as a first priority out of the assets.[149] While this amendment endeavoured to assist liquidators by ameliorating the difficulties caused by the Court of Appeal decision in *Re Floor Fourteen*[150] and allowing them to recover such costs out of the company's assets, the reality is, of course, that those assets may be limited. The amended rule, moreover, did not appear to cover the costs of solicitors and others doing work in relation to the investigation of preferences, transactions at undervalue or wrongful trading: the amendment refers simply to costs relating to 'the conduct of any legal proceedings'.[151] This omission appeared to sit at odds with the views expressed by the House of Lords in *Re Pantmaenog Timber Co. Ltd*[152] concerning the importance of investigation and emphasising that such investigation was part of the duty of an office holder.[153] In 2008, however, the Insolvency (Amendment) Rules (SI 2008/737) were promulgated, which, as noted above, stemmed from the power under the Companies Act 2006 section 1282 insertion of section 176ZA into the Insolvency Act 1986. These Rules amend the Insolvency Rules 1986 by replacing r. 4.218(1)(a) with new r. 4.218(1), (2) and (3)(a) and by inserting new rr. 4.218A–4.218E. The amendments relate to liquidation expenses and in particular provide expressly for the expenses of liquidation to be payable also out of the proceeds of any legal proceedings which the liquidator has power to bring in his own name, or in the name of the company, and also for the recovery of expenses and costs relating not only to the conduct but also to the *preparation* of any such legal proceedings.[154]

---

[149] Thus Rule 4.128 now deems the costs of such proceedings to be expenses of the liquidation.

[150] [2001] 3 All ER 499, [2001] 2 BCLC 392.

[151] The omission of pure investigation work did not seem to accord with the view of Anthony Mann QC in *Re Demaglass Ltd, Lewis* v. *Dempster* [2002] All ER 155. See A. Walters, 'Recovering Costs of Litigation as a Liquidation Expense' (2003) 24 Co. Law. 84; G. Stewart, 'Liquidation Expenses – Provisional Liquidators' Remuneration' (2002) *Recovery* (Winter) 6.

[152] [2004] 1 AC 158. See p. 552 above.

[153] See speeches of Lords Millett and Hope in *Re Pantmaenog*.

[154] The right of recourse to floating charge assets is restricted with respect to litigation expenses. If the costs of the proceedings to be instituted, continued or defended are likely to exceed £5,000 and the liquidator thinks that recourse to the floating charge assets will be needed to meet those costs, then the approval or authorisation of the creditor(s) whose financial interest is most likely to be affected by the payment of such costs must be obtained. (The liquidator has a right to apply to the court for approval in specified circumstances, e.g. urgency: see rr. 4.218B and 4218E.)

One method for securing financing may be for liquidators to obtain funds from individual creditors so that their interests can be protected. Such creditors, however, may be slow to provide cash for a number of reasons.[155] First, they may be wary of the lengthy legal processes involved, the uncertainties of any positive result and the potential wrecking tactics of defendants. Small creditors may prefer to cut their losses and large creditors may be happier to absorb the loss rather than become involved in funding a process whose outcome is uncertain. Second, creditors may be wary of the motives of the liquidator and may fear that actions are taken not so much to protect creditors as to increase professional fees or to enforce commercial morality. If creditors believe that public interest concerns are driving the liquidator's strategy, they may be highly unenthusiastic about subsidising protection of these. Third, creditors may fear that if they fund an action that fails, the court might make a costs order against them under the Supreme Court Act 1981 section 51.[156] Fourth, creditors who are asked to fund an action cannot be offered, in return, a higher proportion of the proceeds of an action than is to be distributed to other creditors: the *pari passu* principle will apply. (Here there is a contrast with the position in Australia where the court can order distributions of recoveries that reward funding creditors.)[157]

A further potential method of financing litigation is for the liquidator to agree with an outside funder that the latter will be assigned the claim for an agreed sum or will finance the action in return for a share in the fruits of the litigation.[158] The case of *Re Oasis Merchandising Services*

---

[155] See Editorial, (1998) 14 IL&P 3; Milman and Parry, *Study*, pp. 18–20; D. Milman, 'Litigation: Funding and Procedural Difficulties' (1997) *Amicus Curiae* 27. For notes of caution regarding sales of causes of action by liquidators see Sir G. Lightman, 'Recent Developments in Insolvency Law – A Judicial View' (2005) 19 *Sweet & Maxwell's Company Law Newsletter* 1–2; *Hopkins v. TL Dallas Group Ltd* [2005] 1 BCLC 543 (paras. 105–6).

[156] See Milman, 'Litigation'; D. Milman, 'Security for Costs: Principles and Pragmatism in Corporate Litigation' in B. Rider (ed.), *The Realm of Company Law* (Kluwer, London, 1998); *Eastglen Ltd v. Grafton* [1996] BCC 900: refusal of third-party costs against a funding creditor where genuine interest and good faith shown.

[157] See Corporations Law s. 464, cited in Milman, 'Litigation', p. 27; *Re Glenisla Investments Ltd* (1996) 18 ACSR 84; *Bell Group v. Westpac Banking Corp.* (1996) 22 ACSR 337.

[158] On the development in 'litigation funding' in the UK (the growing practice of inviting third parties, such as banks or hedge funds, to put up funds to allow a legal claim to be pursued) see N. Tait, 'Lawyers Test Litigation Funding Waters', *Financial Times*, 5 January 2007: noting pioneering developments in Australia and the arrival of 'for profit' litigation-funding companies (who receive fees equivalent to about 30 per cent of

Ltd^{159} involved such selling of the fruits of an action. In that Court of Appeal decision, attention was paid to *Grovewood*,[160] which had considered that a sale of the fruits of an action was not a 'sale' for the purposes of the Insolvency Act 1986 Schedule 4, paragraph 6 and so was not exempt from the rules on champerty.[161] *Oasis* was more favourably disposed than *Grovewood* to allow such sales and the Court of Appeal noted that there was much to be said for allowing liquidators to sell the fruits of actions, provided that the purchasers were not given the right to influence the liquidator's conduct of the proceedings.[162] More negative, however, was the *Oasis* attitude to the disposal of rights of action that are personal to the liquidator (as are many transactional avoidance rights). In *Oasis*, the Court of Appeal rejected an arrangement whereby the liquidator assigned the potential proceeds of an Insolvency

net settlements plus costs). On a setback to the business of financing lawsuits for profit and the 'throwing out' of the multi-million dollar negligence claim against a City accountancy firm Moore Stephens see M. Murphy, 'Third-party Lawsuit Funding Hit as Case Thrown Out', *Financial Times*, 19 June 2008.

[159] [1997] BCC 282; [1997] 2 WLR 764. For discussion see A. Walters, 'Staying Proceedings on Grounds of Champerty' [2000] Ins. Law. 16; Walters, 'Enforcing Wrongful Trading: Substantive Problems and Practical Disincentives' in B. Rider (ed.), *The Corporate Dimension* (Jordans, Bristol, 1998) pp. 153–9; Walters, 'Anonymous Funders and Abuse of Process' (1998) 114 LQR 207; Walters, '*Re Oasis Merchandising Services Ltd* in the Court of Appeal' (1997) 18 Co. Law. 214; Walters, 'A Modern Doctrine of Champerty?' (1996) 112 LQR 560; Walters, 'Foreshortening the Shadow: Maintenance, Champerty and the Funding of Litigation in Corporate Insolvency' (1996) 17 Co. Law. 165; K. Houston, 'Agreement to Share Fruits of Wrongful Trading Claim Void' (1997) 18 Co. Law. 297.

[160] *Grovewood Holdings* v. *James Capel & Co.* [1995] BCC 760; but see *ANC Ltd* v. *Clark Goldring and Page Ltd* [2001] BCC 479 (Robert Walker LJ at p. 485) and *Farmer* v. *Moseley Holdings Ltd* [2002] BPIR 473 (Neuberger J at p. 470), indicating that liquidators should have the power to assign fruits of action without infringing rules on champerty.

[161] The rule on champerty prohibits the selling of a cause of action or its fruits to a party with no legitimate interest in the proceedings. As a general rule such sales are not champertous in insolvency if it is within the office holder's power (under Insolvency Act 1986 Sch. 4, para. 6 – the 'insolvency exception') to sell or dispose of the assets of the company: see Parry, 'Funding Litigation in Insolvency', p. 123. See Walters, 'Modern Doctrine of Champerty?'; P. Winterborne, 'The Second Hand Cause of Action Market' (2001) 14 *Insolvency Intelligence* 65 (who notes, at p. 66, the conflicting public policy considerations operating in assignment of causes of action cases, namely (1) that causes of action should not be traded and that persons without a legitimate interest in litigation should not become involved, and (2) that office holders should not be prevented from pursuing legitimate causes of action (and recovering valuable funds for creditors) due to lack of funding).

[162] [1997] 2 WLR 764, 777H; *ANC Ltd* v. *Clark Goldring and Page Ltd* [2001] BCC 479. See Milman and Parry, *Study*, p. 21.

Act 1986 section 214 wrongful trading action in return for litigation finance provided by a commercial body. The court, moreover, held that an assignment was not possible because the fruits of the wrongful trading action were not 'property' subject to the liquidator's power of sale under Schedule 4, paragraph 4 of the Insolvency Act 1986. An important distinction was drawn between assets that are the property of a company (including rights of action open to the company *prior* to winding up) and assets arising only after liquidation and recoverable only by the liquidator. The latter were not to be regarded as the 'company's property' under Schedule 4, paragraph 6.[163] Particular court objection was also taken in *Oasis* to the reservation by the funder of certain powers of control over the litigation. The Court of Appeal noted that the wrongful trading provisions possessed a penal aspect[164] and considered that acts of such a nature should remain within the control of the office holder (an official acting under court direction).

Objections to the restrictiveness of *Oasis* can, however, be taken.[165] It might be argued, first, that allowing the funding of liquidator actions through the assignment of proceeds would do more potential good (in assisting creditor protection and deterring errant directorial behaviour) than it would cause harm in undermining the administration of justice (by giving a commercially uninvolved party an interest in the case or allowing 'trafficking' in cases).[166] The dangers involved in such funding arrangements can, moreover, be reduced by restrictions on the degree of control over the litigation process that can be conceded to a funder[167] – perhaps limiting this to such matters as choice of lawyer or a voice in settlement negotiations – for, as has been pointed out, commercial realities demand that funders be given some influence.[168]

A second objection is that the *Oasis* approach gives too little attention to the merits of a case when it deems a stay of proceedings to be the appropriate judicial response to the funding of liquidation litigation by

---

[163] For discussion of the finding that office holder recoveries are not 'company property' see Armour and Walters, 'Funding Liquidation', pp. 323–5; L. C. Ho, 'Whose Claim Is It? A Critical Assessment of the *Re Oasis Merchandising Services* Orthodox' (2007) 23 IL&P 70.

[164] See discussion in ch. 16 below.

[165] See Walters, 'Staying Proceedings', 'Enforcing Wrongful Trading'; Armour and Walters, 'Funding Liquidation'.

[166] Walters, 'Staying Proceedings', p. 20; Milman and Parry, *Study*, p. 40.

[167] See the judgment of Peter Gibson LJ at [1997] 2 WLR 764 at 777; *Giles* v. *Thompson* [1994] 1 AC 142 (some funder interference acceptable).

[168] Walters, 'Staying Proceedings', p. 22.

the assignment of proceeds. Where the case is strong and there is good evidence of malpractice to the detriment of creditor interests, it is arguable that the courts should take this factor into account in deciding whether to allow an action to proceed.[169]

A further difficulty with *Oasis* is that it draws a distinction between the Insolvency Act 1986 section 212 misfeasance action (which the law treats as corporate property able to be assigned) and section 214 wrongful trading action (which cannot). Apart from the conceptual difficulties involved in treating proceeds of wrongful trading actions as non-assignable,[170] this produces perverse incentives to 'overload' misfeasance and bring actions under section 212 or to test the limits of directors' duties at common law when claims may fall squarely within section 214. One commentator has dubbed this 'absurd'.[171]

Finally, it can be argued that *Leyland DAF*[172] impliedly overruled *Oasis* by holding that debenture holders' and unsecured creditors' assets form two separate funds. The import of this is that it would be strange to hold that office-holder recoveries were not available to pay the expenses of the liquidation (because they were not 'assets of the company') when those expenses had been incurred for the exclusive benefit of the unsecured creditors – especially since such recoveries are a fund available for the unsecured creditors.[173]

Conditional fee arrangements (CFAs) offer another potential means of funding liquidator actions.[174] Under such agreements, the liquidator will pay no lawyers' fees in an unsuccessful action but will be charged a 'success fee' or 'uplift' by the legal firm if the desired outcome is

---

[169] Ibid., p. 23. See *Abraham v. Thompson* [1997] 4 All ER 362; *Stocznia Gdanska SA v. Latvian Shipping Co. (No. 2)* [1999] 3 All ER 822 (proceedings only to be stayed if, on the particular facts, the likelihood of abuse is sufficient to deny access to justice).

[170] Armour and Walters have said: 'if office holder recoveries were not "assets of the company" in liquidation, then how were they to be administered, given that the statute directs the liquidator to distribute only "assets of the company"?': 'Funding Liquidation', p. 323.

[171] Walters, 'Enforcing Wrongful Trading', p. 158.

[172] *Re Leyland DAF Ltd; Buchler v. Talbot* [2004] 2 AC 298.

[173] Armour and Walters, 'Funding Liquidation', p. 323. Arguably this point holds in spite of the effect of the Companies Act 2006 s. 1282 in overruling *Leyland DAF* regarding the payment of liquidation expenses out of floating charge holders' returns.

[174] Permitted by the Conditional Fee Agreement Order 1995 (SI 1995/1674), Conditional Fee Agreement Regulations 1995 (SI 1995/1675). See generally W. Christopher, 'Conditional Fee Arrangements' (2006) *Recovery* (Autumn) 38.

achieved.[175] Proceedings by liquidators relating to companies being wound up are 'specified proceedings' to which conditional fee arrangements can be applied.[176] Lawyers' costs are usually the largest element of the sums that liquidators require in order to pursue those assets that a debtor may have hidden away. The liquidator's ability to retain lawyers on a conditional fee basis is designed to facilitate actions since the risk of legal fees is transferred to the liquidator's own lawyer and the risk of having to pay the other side's costs in an unsuccessful case can be covered by insurance. The main attractions of such arrangements for clients are said to be that it removes the burden of funding the matter on an ongoing basis – since solicitor's costs do not have to be paid as the case progresses – and such a strength of client position can increase the chances of securing an early settlement. Even if the case is lost, the client will not have to pay the solicitor's basic charges or the success fee.[177]

The introduction of conditional fee arrangements has been found, however, not to have made a huge impact in the insolvency sector.[178] This may be because informal arrangements of a similar nature are already being used by solicitors and liquidators and because restrictions have limited the enthusiasm of practitioners. It has, for instance, been suggested that solicitors did not warm to the upper limit of 25 per cent that is imposed on their demanded recoveries.[179] A further difficulty has arisen because conditional fees do not adequately deal with adverse costs, which, under the Insolvency Lawyers' Association Model Conditional Fee Agreement, have to be borne by the liquidator or the estate as client. Many IPs will, accordingly, give serious consideration, before pursuing an action, to the personal financial risks involved.[180] Insurance for adverse costs is possible, as noted, and recent years have seen a growth in the availability of legal costs insurance. The London market in such insurance has been said to have been boosted by the Government's decision to widen the use of no-win no-fee agreements: solicitors' firms that take on such conditional fee work will very often insist that their

---

[175] Note that conditional fees are not like contingency fees employed in the USA. The US style agreements often provide for a client to pay the lawyer a percentage of the damages if the client wins. An English lawyer is still restricted from agreeing with a client to be paid a percentage of the recoveries from an action. See further LCD Consultation Paper, *Access to Justice with Conditional Fees*, March 1998.

[176] Conditional Fee Agreements Order 1995 (SI 1995/1674).

[177] Christopher, 'Conditional Fee Arrangements', p. 38.

[178] Milman and Parry, *Study*, p. 21.   [179] Ibid.

[180] For advice that they should do so see Welby, 'Antecedent Recoveries and Litigation Funding', p. 35.

clients take out insurance to cover opponents' costs in the event of a lost case. Liquidators, nevertheless, may see such insurance as not entirely problem free.[181] In order to obtain cover, a counsel's opinion will often be required and this may be costly. Liquidators have to find the premiums out of the available company funds and premiums have risen sharply in recent years. The conditions that insurers impose on such cover (for example, demanding the use of lawyers on the insurance company's panel) may also restrict the liquidator's enthusiasm for such arrangements.[182] There is, moreover, evidence that solicitors' firms will tend to demand a very strong case indeed before proceeding on a conditional fee basis.

The above analysis suggests that efficient liquidator action to protect the interests of creditors is likely to be impeded by funding difficulties. What can be done to ease these difficulties? A first step would be to amend the law as stated in the Insolvency Act 1986 so as to allow liquidators to assign shares in the fruits of an action, provided that they do not cede control of such claims.[183] As Milman and Parry conclude: 'A much wider range of parties [should be allowed] to undertake transactional avoidance litigation. Commercial organisations, which are increasingly prominent in the area of litigation finance, should be permitted to purchase and prosecute actions to avoid dubious transactions and the courts should be prepared to reconsider their traditional hostility to such "trafficking".'[184]

---

[181] See Welby, 'Antecedent Recoveries and Litigation Funding', p. 35: 'such policies can have traps for the unwary'.

[182] See BDO Stoy Hayward Survey, reported in (1999) 12 *Insolvency Intelligence* 48, revealing that 75 per cent of those questioned considered that such restrictive clauses in insurance agreements were a deterrent to taking out cover.

[183] Milman and Parry, *Study*, p. 39. Winterborne suggests that the claims that office holders can bring (under ss. 339, 340, 214, 238 or 239 of the Insolvency Act 1986) cannot be assigned because this would be to delegate a statutory power. Where, in contrast, a claim is one that the company could have brought, the cause, as noted, is an asset that can be sold by the office holder for the benefit of creditors with the terms of Sch. 4, para. 6: Winterborne, 'Second Hand Cause of Action Market', p. 67. See also *ANC Ltd* v. *Clark Goldring and Page Ltd* [2001] BPIR 568.

[184] Milman and Parry, *Study*, pp. 39–40. The practice of 'litigation funding' (inviting third parties such as banks or hedge funds to put up funds to allow a legal claim to be pursued) is still in its infancy in the UK but may be given fresh impetus as IPs grow more proactive in pursuing claims and as 'access to justice' issues loom large as the UK Government has sought to cap or reduce legal aid: see Tait, 'Lawyers Test Litigation Funding Waters'.

State funding of 'public interest' litigation to prevent avoidance has also been put forward as a response to funding difficulties,[185] and the Harmer Report[186] on insolvency law reform in Australia recommended this for the corporate insolvency arena. This funding might be organised around a levy on directors or companies and reimbursement of the fund could be provided for in the case of successful liquidator actions.[187] Indeed, Katz and Mumford have suggested that the Insolvency Service explore the system of aid that is made available by the New Zealand Insolvency Service, which provides funding for cases which it believes are winnable (recovering funds out of the proceeds of the action).[188] This is not, however, a problem-free area and processes would have to be established so as to avoid the taking of speculative cases or cases that lack real merit and are pursued for tactical reasons.

A further way of funding avoidance litigation would be to make use of the profits of the Insolvency Services Account (ISA) (which imposes a levy on compulsory liquidation funds paid into and out of the account).[189] The profits of the ISA have been used to investigate the past conduct of parties (including directors) for the purposes *inter alia* of bringing prosecutions or disqualification proceedings. It has been argued[190] that the deterrent effects of disqualification are undramatic and that:

> The funds in the ISA could be better employed in subsidising ... the costs of investigating and bringing financial claims against directors, shadow directors and recipients of the benefits of voidable transactions. Financial claims against them ... would be a far more effective deterrent and public protection and, what is more, would bring more tangible benefits to the creditors.[191]

---

[185] Milman and Parry, *Study*.

[186] Australian Law Reform Commission, *General Insolvency Inquiry*, Report No. 45 (Canberra, 1988) 26.

[187] Ibid. See also Editorial, (1998) 14 IL&P 185–6.

[188] A. Katz and M. Mumford, *Making Creditor Protection Effective* (Centre for Business Performance, ICAEW, 2008 Draft) Part 5. The authors note that when it comes to creditor protection and office holder fees, the insolvency office holder has an unusual role, and one that may well involve conflict. 'On the one hand he is charged with protecting creditors' interests, but on the other hand his own commercial interests and the right to charge fees may be detrimental to creditors' interests. There is a subtle balance to be struck.'

[189] Since 1 April 2004 moneys from voluntary liquidations need only to be paid voluntarily into the ISA and all deposits earn interest at a competitive rate: see ch. 5 above.

[190] Editorial, (1998) 14 IL&P 185–6.   [191] Ibid., p. 186.

A further move in the direction of Australian law might also be desirable. In that country the court has the power to approve an arrangement in which a creditor who has indemnified the liquidator against the costs of proceedings can be allocated a higher share of the proceeds recovered: one that reflects the degree of risk assumed by the creditor.[192] In the UK the court might be given the power to approve such arrangements between liquidators and funders as seem appropriate and fair to all affected creditors under the court's inherent jurisdiction.

Funding is not the only difficulty that liquidators face in attempting to combat transaction avoidance. The substantive rules of insolvency law can also be criticised as giving secured creditors, normally banks, excessive levels of protection.[193] The law on the avoidance of preferences, for instance, is set out in section 239 of the Insolvency Act 1986 and is designed to protect *pari passu* distribution by stopping an insolvent company from favouring one creditor at the expense of others. Section 239 modified the law, in a manner prompted by Cork,[194] so as to allow a liquidator to succeed in a challenge by establishing that one contributing influence behind the transaction was the desire to prefer.[195] In the case of *M. C. Bacon Ltd*,[196] however, Millett J held that a defence exists if it can be shown that the directors entered a transaction not in order to prefer but with a view to securing financing in order to keep the business going. This focus on subjective motivation increases the liquidator's problems of proof, though, in the case of beneficiaries to the transaction who are connected persons, there is onus reversal so that such a person has to show that the transaction is not influenced by a desire by the company to prefer.[197] An objective or 'effects' test in the law of preferences would eradicate the problems brought to the fore by *Re M. C. Bacon Ltd* and would correspond to the approach taken in other jurisdictions such as Australia and the USA.[198] As Milman notes, this removal of the 'desire' test could be balanced by an opportunity to defend the transaction if it was *bona fide* in the ordinary course of business and for the benefit of the company.[199] An

---

[192] See *Re Glenisla Investments Ltd* (1996) 18 ACSR 84.

[193] Milman and Parry, *Study*, p. 36. [194] Cork Report, paras. 1241–88.

[195] See Insolvency Act 1986 s. 239(5). [196] [1990] BCLC 324.

[197] *Re Exchange Travel Holdings* [1996] 2 BCLC 524; discussed by R. Parry [1997] Ins. Law. 11–13.

[198] See Milman and Parry, *Study*, p. 36; S. Quo, 'Insolvency Law: A Comparative Analysis of the Preference Tests in the UK and Australia' (2007) 28 Co. Law. 355.

[199] D. Milman, 'Revitalising the Assets of an Insolvent Company – Where Are We Now?' (2002) 2 *Sweet & Maxwell's Company Law Newsletter* 1 at 4: 'This trade off would of course require a reversal of the burden of proof in such cases.'

alternative step of assistance to liquidators would be the institution of a statutory presumption of preference where there is a grant of security so that the court should set this aside unless the debenture holder is able to give good reason for sustaining it. Liquidators would also benefit by abolition of the requirement (in sections 238, 239 and 245 of the Insolvency Act 1986) that the liquidator should show that the company was unable to pay its debts within the meaning of section 123 of the Insolvency Act 1986. The incompleteness of company financial records and problems of valuation may make proof of insolvency at the relevant time very difficult for the liquidator, who would be assisted by abolition of this requirement in favour of establishing that the company subsequently became insolvent within the specified time period.[200] Milman and Parry have argued that in dealing with transactions at undervalue the law should recognise (contra Millett J in *Re M. C. Bacon Ltd*) that creating a security does devalue a company's assets so that in looking to section 238 of the Insolvency Act 1986 (transactions at undervalue) a devaluation effected in this way is only acceptable if the recipient of the transaction can show that a corresponding economic benefit has accrued to the company.[201] The *obiter* comments of Arden LJ in *Hill* v. *Spread Trustee Company Limited*[202] seem consistent with such an approach.

Turning now to information, there is little utility in providing for a properly funded liquidation system if liquidators are ill-informed concerning the extent and whereabouts of the insolvent company's assets or concerning relevant directors' dealings. The liquidator's powers, as already outlined, do, however, contain extensive powers to gather information, and section 235 of the Insolvency Act 1986 provides that officers, employers, administrators or administrative receivers of the company (past and present) have a duty to provide the liquidator with such information as may reasonably be required.[203] The liquidator may also ask the court to exercise its powers under section 236 of the Insolvency

---

[200] Milman and Parry, *Study*, p. 38.

[201] Ibid., p. 36. See also A. Clarke, 'Security Interests as Property: Relocating Security Interests within the Property Framework' in J. W. Harris (ed.), *Property Problems from Genes to Pension Funds* (Kluwer, London, 1997) pp. 119–20.

[202] [2006] BCC 646. See further p. 576 below.

[203] See, for example, *Daltel Europe Ltd (in liquidation)* v. *Makki* [2005] 1 BCLC 594 – courts may be prepared to grant orders for private examination and discovery of documents under section 236 despite the fact that the officer in question was subject to proceedings brought by the liquidator. Section 235 complements the powers to have persons examined either publicly (IA 1986 s. 133) or privately (IA 1986 s. 236) before the court. Note also that company officers are required to be proactive, and not merely

Act 1986 to call before it for examination any officer of the company, any person known or suspected of having in their possession any property of the company or any person supposed to be indebted to the company; or any person whom the court thinks capable of giving information concerning the business dealings, property, etc. of the company. Account books, papers or records may also be demanded by the court and powers of seizure and arrest are provided for in section 236(5).

The court has a broad discretion to conduct examinations in order to further a winding up and the liquidator will have some influence on the exercise of that discretion. The view of an office holder that an examination is required is normally given 'a good deal of weight'[204] but the power to examine is not designed to offer liquidators special advantages in ordinary litigation and should not be operated oppressively.[205] Its purpose has been described as allowing the office holder 'to get sufficient information to reconstitute the state of knowledge a company should possess'.[206] The House of Lords has held that an order could properly be made to extend to all documents and information which office holders reasonably require to carry out their functions.[207]

---

reactive, under Insolvency Act 1986 ss. 206–11: see *Re McCredie, The Times*, 5 October 1999, per Henry LJ. (The Insolvency Act 1986 s. 208(1), for example, makes it a criminal offence to fail 'fully and truly to discover to the liquidator all the company's property' and to fail to deliver up company property under the director's custody and control. The same applies to books and papers.) The court has the power to order the production of books, papers or records which relate to the company even if they are not the company's property and the company itself could not have obtained them: *Re Training Partners Ltd* [2002] 1 BCLC 655.

[204] *Joint Liquidators of Sasea Finance Ltd* v. *KPMG* [1998] BCC 216, 220; cf. *Re XL Communications Group plc* [2005] EWHC 2413. See further C. Campbell, 'Investigations by Insolvency Practitioners – Powers and Restraints: Part I' (2000) 16 IL&P 182.

[205] *Re Embassy Art Products Ltd* [1987] 3 BCC 292.

[206] Browne-Wilkinson VC in *Re Cloverbay Ltd* [1991] Ch 90, 102; [1990] BCC 415, 419–20.

[207] *Bristol and Commonwealth Holdings plc (Joint Administrators)* v. *Spicer and Oppenheim (Re British and Commonwealth Holdings plc No. 2)* [1993] AC 426. On the potential impact of the Human Rights Act 1998 here, see W. Trower, 'Bringing Human Rights Home to the Insolvency Practitioner' (2000) 13 *Insolvency Intelligence* 52. See also Insolvency Act 2000 s. 11, which amended Insolvency Act 1986 s. 219 to make the section compatible with the European Convention on Human Rights. (Section 219 had allowed answers obtained under powers of compulsion, derived from the Companies Act 1985, to be used as evidence against that person. In *Saunders* v. *UK* [1997] BCC 872 the ECHR decided that for the prosecution to use answers given pursuant to a power of compulsion in subsequent criminal proceedings infringed Mr Saunders' rights under Article 6 of the Convention. *Saunders* was followed in *Kansal* v. *UK* [2004] BPIR 740.)

Turning to the issue of transaction costs, it can be said that a liquidation regime is only efficient in the technical sense if it operates with minimal transaction costs. If, accordingly, there is a good case for streamlining the process, this may point to underachievement on efficiency. Whether there is such a case was an issue raised by the Insolvency Service in September 2007 when it published a consultation document on streamlining insolvency procedures.[208] This document proposed to change the relevant items of primary legislation by means of a Legislative Reform Order[209] in order to effect the following steps:

1. To provide more flexibility in the means of communication, and the exchange of information, between insolvency office holders and creditors (and others) by: instituting 'opt-in' arrangements for creditors who wish to receive information or participate in proceedings; allowing notifications to be by electronic communication (where required to be 'in writing'); and allowing meetings to be held through media rather than physically.
2. To remove the need for liquidators and trustees in bankruptcy to obtain sanction for certain actions.
3. To allow discretionary advertising of the appointment of a voluntary liquidator.
4. To remove the requirement that liquidators summon annual meetings of members and/or creditors to account for their acts and dealings.
5. To remove the requirement for any document in insolvency proceedings to be sworn by affidavit and replace it with a requirement for verification by a statement of truth.
6. To end the need for an insolvency practitioner, acting as liquidator, to submit a report to the Secretary of State on the conduct of the

---

[208] *A Consultation Document on Changes to the Insolvency Act 1986 and the Company Directors' Disqualification Act 1986 to be made by a Legislative Reform Order for the Modernisation and Streamlining of Insolvency Procedures* (Insolvency Service, London, 2007). In February 2008 the IS announced that the consolidation of insolvency secondary legislation and the restructuring of the Insolvency Rules 1986 (originally announced in 2005) had been further delayed and, at the time of writing, the date for completion is 1 October 2009.

[209] Made under section 1 of the Legislative and Regulatory Reform Act 2006. The IS recognised that the changes to secondary legislation (see above) will require amendments to primary legislation. Thus an opportunity is presented to attempt to modernise, streamline and make easier for users some processes in the insolvency legislation – thereby hopefully increasing returns to creditors.

directors of a company if he has already submitted such a report as administrator of the same company.

7. To remove the requirement that the Insolvency Services Account be held with the Bank of England.

8. To remove the court power to order that a person owing moneys to a company in liquidation pay those moneys into an account, in the liquidator's name, at the Bank of England.

At the time of writing, the Insolvency Service is yet to act on the above proposals but it does appear likely that modernising and streamlining the communications systems that operate within liquidation will ensure a lowering of overall transaction costs. The consultation process will no doubt prove useful in seeking to ensure that such efficiencies are not secured at the cost of diminutions in accessibility, transparency and accountability.

Expertise

A liquidator must be a qualified IP[210] and the general characteristics of IPs have been discussed in chapter 5 above. The issue of particular concern here is whether the winding-up process, as presently set up, is consistent with the exercise of an appropriate level of expertise. In asking this question, it is not necessary to assess the potential of the liquidator as an agent of possible rescue. His or her role is more focused than that of, say, an administrator and centres on gathering in the assets and distributing them. It is in the gathering process that there is a particularly strong role for expertise. At this stage of operations, the liquidator has both to defend the body of corporate assets and seek to increase it. The former task is evident in liquidator dealings with those who claim that property in the possession of a company does not form part of the estate: because, for instance, it is asserted that the owner has retained title. Socio-legal studies of practice reveal, in this area, a high level of IP expertise and dominance.[211] Claimant suppliers to companies are often out of their depth and IPs tend to be in possession of the goods, to know the supply needs and to be both legally competent and familiar with the legal game being played. They are sophisticated repeat players who will

---

[210] Insolvency Act 1986 s. 388.

[211] See S. Wheeler, 'Capital Fractionalised: The Role of Insolvency Practitioners in Asset Distribution' in M. Cain and C. B. Harrington (eds.), *Lawyers in a Post Modern World: Translation and Transgression* (Open University Press, Buckingham, 1994).

use devices such as delay and bluff to protect the assets of the estate.[212] Liquidators, moreover, have an incentive to deploy their expertise to the full: their fees have to be paid out of the assets that are realised and the less that is removed from the company by, say, successful uses of the retention of title device the more remains for fee-paying purposes. Questions may arise as to the fairness of such arrangements but lack of liquidator expertise is not the primary issue.

The challenge to the expertise of the liquidator is perhaps more severe when he or she attempts not to retain assets but to secure these, for example, by using the avoidance powers given to liquidators to challenge transactions that prejudice creditors. What is clear from the empirical research, however, is that the self-policing of insolvency professionals can operate in a manner that upholds ethical or professional standards, as where IPs use their powers in order to remove from office at the creditors' meeting a liquidator of whose conduct they did not approve.[213]

Running counter to such expert upholding of standards, however, is the tendency of IPs to use their professional expertise at creditors' meetings not to further transparency in liquidation processes but to engage in self-serving activities of a collective or individual nature. Wheeler argues that the creditors' meeting is often used by IPs as a public forum to parade their standards of practice; to compete for the work involved in the liquidation (by 'stealing' the liquidation from the provisional liquidator through use of rhetoric to gain creditor support); and to sideline creditors and exclude trade creditors from a process amounting to an 'exclusionary discourse'.[214] Such an account, of course, emphasises the danger of evaluating insolvency processes by using a benchmark of expertise without reference to objectives: liquidation may be a process that lends itself to certain misdirections of expertise.

Accountability

In both voluntary and compulsory liquidations the liquidator is obliged to convene a meeting of creditors to consider his removal from office if he is requested to do so by more than 25 per cent in value of the creditors, and if he fails to do so the creditors may apply to the court to order such a

---

[212] Ibid., p. 90. See also ch. 3 above and ch. 15 below.

[213] S. Wheeler, 'Empty Rhetoric and Empty Promises: The Creditors' Meeting' (1994) 21 *Journal of Law and Society* 350, 360.

[214] Ibid., pp. 367–9.

meeting.[215] At such a meeting, a simple majority of those present and voting may remove the liquidator.[216]

Such may be the formal position but, on the ground, the accountability of a liquidator – particularly to the creditors' meeting – may operate quite differently. Legal accountability may be described as 'empty rhetoric'.[217] As was seen in the last section, IP expertise and repeat playing may produce dominance over the creditors' meeting rather than accountability so that such meetings are seen by IPs and liquidators not so much as holdings to account as opportunities for pursuing or defending business.

Does the Human Rights Act 1998 (HRA) introduce the prospect of greater legal accountability for liquidators?[218] The HRA applies to the decision-making procedures of all public bodies and it is unlawful under section 6 for a public authority to act in a way that is incompatible with a Convention right. A liquidator is liable to be considered as a public authority under section 6(3) as he or she undertakes a public function, for the benefit of society as a whole. (An administrator of a company is also likely to be seen as a 'public authority'.)[219]

The European Court of Human Rights (ECHR) has held that Article 6 of the Human Rights Convention is satisfied where there is a proper right of appeal to a court and the determining of rights is properly reviewable by the court after a fair hearing.[220] In the case of liquidator activities relating to a company being wound up by the court, the Insolvency Act 1986 provides for court control in sections 167(3) and 168(5). The courts, however, have indicated that they will only interfere with a liquidator's decision on grounds of reasonableness[221] and that they would think carefully before replacing an

---

[215] Insolvency Rules 1986 rr. 4.114-CVL and 4.115.   [216] IA 1986 ss. 171, 172.

[217] Wheeler, 'Empty Rhetoric and Empty Promises'.

[218] See generally M. Simmons and T. Smith, 'The Human Rights Act 1998: The Practical Impact on Insolvency' (2000) 16 IL&P 167; C. Gearty, 'Insolvency … and Human Rights?' [2000] Ins. Law 68; W. Trower, 'Human Rights: Article 6 – The Reality and the Myth' [2001] Ins. Law. 48; Trower, 'Bringing Human Rights Home'; N. Pike, 'The Human Rights Act 1998 and its Impact on Insolvency Practitioners' [2001] Ins. Law. 25.

[219] The position is less clear in relation to administrative receivers, supervisors of voluntary arrangements and office holders when not undertaking 'public functions': see Simmons and Smith, 'Human Rights Act 1998', p. 170.

[220] See I. F. Fletcher, 'Juggling with Norms: The Conflict between Collective and Individual Rights under Insolvency Law' in R. Cranston (ed.), Making Commercial Law (Clarendon Press, Oxford, 1997) pp. 411–14.

[221] See Re Edennote Ltd, Tottenham Hotspur plc v. Ryman [1996] BCC 718; Leon v. York-O-Matic Ltd [1966] 1 WLR 1450; Mitchell v. Buckingham International plc [1998] 2 BCLC 369.

honest and independent liquidator just because he had fallen short of the ideal in one or two respects.[222] It has been questioned, however, whether this approach meets Article 6 requirements.[223] Suggested areas where liquidators may face HRA attack have included: preventing trading by presenting a winding-up petition;[224] exercising investigative powers;[225] and using confidential statements.[226] The potential impact of the HRA should not, however, be exaggerated since the concept of 'justifiable interference' will shield the decisions of many office holders, as will the usual array of informational, evidential and resource restraints that limit challenges through court action.

If Wheeler's portrait of the creditors' meeting rings true and there is less to creditor scrutiny than meets the eye, what is to be done? Here it could be argued that the answer is not to increase levels of judicial oversight: that would do little for the less well-informed and less well-positioned creditors and might do much to increase costs and delays. The appropriate response may be for the IP profession to police its professional standards more rigorously so that greater attention is paid to informing creditors and listening to them rather than holding them at a distance by conducting an arcane 'players' dialogue'.

Fairness

Avoidance of transactions

Fairness in liquidation demands that the general body of creditors be protected from dispositions of the company's assets in the period leading up to liquidation which confer improper advantages on certain creditors or other parties. It demands that the collective nature of the insolvency process be protected.[227] The law on the avoidance of transactions,

---

[222] See *AMP Enterprises Ltd* v. *Hoffman* (*The Times*, 13 August 2002). For an instance of the court's ordering the removal of a liquidator in the absence of evidence of misconduct – but on grounds that it was unlikely that the liquidator would pursue the directors with sufficient rigour – see the Court of Appeal in *Re Keypack Homecare Ltd* [1987] BCLC 409.

[223] See Simmons and Smith, 'Human Rights Act 1998', p. 170.

[224] Insolvency Act 1986 s. 127.

[225] Ibid., ss. 235–6; see *Re Esal Commodities Ltd* [1988] PCC 443 at 457–8.

[226] Insolvency Act 1986 s. 236. See Simmons and Smith, 'Human Rights Act 1998', p. 170.

[227] For an example of a court preferring a petition to wind up rather than one for an administration order because the former brought the independence and objectivity of the Official Receiver and more collective control over choice of any liquidator in succession see *El-Ajou* v. *Dollar Land (Manhattan) Ltd* [2007] BCC 953.

accordingly, seeks to protect collectivity and the principle of *pari passu* distribution and to deal with the unjust enrichment of a particular party at the expense of the general body of creditors.[228] This section of the chapter discusses the major avoidance provisions that are found in the Insolvency Act 1986, namely: preferences (sections 239–41); transactions at undervalue and transactions defrauding creditors (sections 238, 240–1, 423); and avoidance of floating charges (section 245).

Preferences

A preference occurs when a creditor – to the detriment of other creditors – receives more from a company before it goes into liquidation than he or she would have obtained in a formal distribution in liquidation. The broad aim of preference law is to ensure the fair treatment of creditors in a liquidation, but it can also be claimed that preference laws increase the assets available for distribution to creditors by protecting the collective nature of the liquidation process.[229] Preference laws may thus be thought to discourage the piecemeal dismembering of the estate in the lead up to liquidation and thus to maximise its value. As Prentice points out, however,[230] preference law claws back transactions only where there is a desire to prefer and this means that the law will only deter such dismembering if the parties involved are aware of the impending insolvency of the company.[231]

---

[228] See generally McCormack, 'Swelling Corporate Assets'; Quo, 'Insolvency Law'; M. Hemsworth, 'Voidable Preference: Desire and Effect' (2000) 16 IL&P 54; A. Keay, 'The Recovery of Voidable Preferences: Aspects of Restoration' [2000] 1 CFILR 1; Keay, 'Preferences in Liquidation Law: A Time for Change' [1998] 2 CfiLR 198; Keay, 'The Avoidance of Pre-Liquidation Transactions: Anglo-Australian Comparison' [1998] JBL 515; D. Prentice, 'Some Observations on the Law Relating to Preferences' in R. Cranston (ed.), *Making Commercial Law* (Clarendon Press, Oxford, 1997); L. Verrill, 'Attacking Antecedent Transactions' [1993] 12 JIBL 485.

[229] On the advantages of collectivity see the discussion in ch. 2 above; T. H. Jackson, *The Logic and Limits of Bankruptcy Law* (Harvard University Press, Cambridge, Mass., 1986) pp. 16–17. On different bases for the preference provisions see McCormack, 'Swelling Corporate Assets', who suggests three possibilities: ensuring fairness between creditors; preventing premature collapse of the company; and protecting the collective nature of liquidation proceedings. A fourth potential ground might be 'preserving commercial morality and the prevention of fraud': see Lord Mansfield in *Alderson* v. *Temple* (1768) 98 ER 1277, 1279, discussed in McCormack 'Swelling Corporate Assets', p. 44.

[230] Prentice, 'Some Observations', p. 443.

[231] Directors may, however, fear that if they grant a preference they may be vulnerable to a disqualification order under the Company Directors' Disqualification Act 1986 Sch. 1, Part 2, para. 8 which makes preferences relevant in assessing unfitness to take part in the management of the company: see ch. 16 below.

Under the terms of the Insolvency Act 1986 sections 239–41, a liquidator can successfully challenge a transaction as a preference by showing
that: the transaction was entered into within six months of insolvency,[232]
or within two years if the defendant is a person 'connected with a
company';[233] the recipient is a creditor, surety or guarantor of any of
the company's debts; the company does anything which places the
recipient in a position that, in the event of the liquidation, will be better
than the position he would have been in had the thing not been done; the
company was influenced in deciding to enter into the impugned transaction by a desire to make a preference; and at the time of, or as a result of,
the preference the company was unable to pay its debts and was insolvent
within the meaning of the Insolvency Act 1986 section 123.

A controversial aspect of the law here is its subjective basis, as seen in
the need for the liquidator to show that the company was 'influenced' by
a 'desire' to prefer. On this point, Cork examined the case for objectivity
but concluded that proof of intention to prefer should be retained in the
law and that 'genuine pressure by a creditor should continue to afford a
defence'.[234] The law, said Cork, should be reluctant to allow the recovery
of payments made to discharge lawful debts due and Cork considered
that recovery was only justifiable if the payment was 'really improper'. As
critics have suggested, however,[235] this misses the point since it may well
be thought to be improper to subvert *pari passu* by preferring one
creditor to another in the lead up to insolvency. What is clear is that
the liquidator's task in protecting both the estate and the principle of
equal distribution is made harder by the need to show the influence of a
desire to prefer. On how dominant the section 235(5) desire to prefer
must be, the case of *Re M. C. Bacon Ltd*[236] casts some light. Millett J, in an
influential judgment, stated that it was not necessary to adduce direct
evidence of the desire – which could be inferred from the circumstances
of the case – but the desire must have influenced the decision or the
transaction being attacked by the liquidator. It was not necessary to show
that the desire was the only or the decisive factor behind the preference: it

---

[232] The onset of insolvency is defined in the Insolvency Act 1986 s. 240(3) as the date of the
commencement of the winding up (at the time of presentation of the petition for
winding up per s. 129(2) or the passing of the resolution for winding up in a voluntary
winding up per s. 86). Administrators can also challenge preferences: s. 239(1) and (2).
[233] Insolvency Act 1986 s. 240(1)(a).   [234] Cork Report, para. 1256.
[235] Prentice, 'Some Observations'; Keay, 'Preferences in Liquidation Law'.
[236] [1990] BCLC 324.

might only be one of the influencing factors. In the case of preferences to persons connected with the company, there is some assistance for the liquidator in section 239(6) of the Insolvency Act 1986 which creates a (rebuttable) presumption of a section 239(5) desire to prefer.[237]

The use of a subjective test here has been dubbed 'unrealistic and unreasonable'.[238] It is always difficult for a court to ascertain subjective motive[239] and especially problematic in the case of a corporate body with no easily identifiable mind.[240] The courts have proved reluctant to make inferences concerning the mind of the debtor company[241] and, in many cases, troubled companies make payments to creditors not in order to execute a preference but in order to ease creditor pressure or to ensure continuity of business activity.[242] If, accordingly, the creditor is not a 'connected' person, the liquidator faces an uphill task in establishing the desire to prefer as well as the company's insolvency.[243]

A further difficulty for the liquidator is that a payment to a creditor may be made when a company is acting in a disorganised fashion. In this confusion it may be especially difficult to show the influence of a desire to prefer and it can be argued that fairness – through protection of *pari passu* distribution – is as deserving of protection from transfers that are unthinking as from those that are designed to prefer.[244] The argument for a subjective approach is weak if couched simply in terms of Cork's desire to see companies pay 'lawful debts properly due'.[245] Cork also argued that the diligent creditor 'might in principle be allowed to retain

---

[237] See e.g. *Re Cityspan Ltd; Brown (Liquidator of Cityspan Ltd)* v. *Clark* [2008] BCC 60 where the liquidator's claim was successful and the director was ordered to pay a sum to the liquidator, with interest at base rate plus 1 per cent; *Weisgard* v. *Pilkington* [1995] BCC 1108 where directors failed to rebut the presumption of a desire to prefer. In *Re 38 Building Ltd* [1999] BCC 260 the family beneficiaries of a trust executed by a troubled family company were held not to be preferred connected persons since the trustees of the fund were collectively to be treated as creditors for the purposes of s. 239.

[238] Keay, 'Preferences in Liquidation Law'.

[239] As recognised by the Cork Report at para. 1253.

[240] See Keay, 'Preferences in Liquidation Law', pp. 206–7; and more generally J. Coffee, '"No Soul to Damn: No Body to Kick": An Unscandalized Inquiry into the Problem of Corporate Punishment' (1981) 79 Mich. L Rev. 386.

[241] *Re Beacon Leisure Ltd* [1991] BCC 213; *Re Fairway Magazines Ltd* [1992] BCC 924; but see *Re Agriplant Services Ltd* [1997] BCC 842.

[242] Keay, 'Preferences in Liquidation Law', p. 207.

[243] See K. Offer, 'Influential Desire and Dominant Intention' (1990) 3 *Insolvency Intelligence* 42.

[244] On the centrality of protecting *pari passu* in preference law, see the Privy Council in *Lewis* v. *Hyde* [1997] BCC 976, 979. On *pari passu* see ch. 14 below.

[245] Cork Report, para. 1256(a).

the fruits of his diligence'[246] but this contention has limited force in the period leading to a liquidation: if accepted it gives the green light to a creditors' race to collect. It encourages precipitous actions and it undermines the collective approach to liquidation with all its advantages of efficiency and fairness.

Cork also favoured adherence to the established legal rule that transfers made under pressure from creditors could be defended as there was no free intention to prefer in such circumstances.[247] Again, however, the position is difficult to sustain as it undermines collectivity by rewarding those who indulge in a race to collect. The position invites creditors to apply pressure (again precipitately) and it favours more powerful creditors who are given an incentive to collude with companies to give the appearance of pressure.[248]

What, though, of the argument that an objective 'effects-based' approach to preferences is undesirable as it would make creditors nervous of having any dealings with the troubled company; that it would chill commercial activity in a generally undesirable way? In response, it can be said that financing for companies is not likely to be less forthcoming (or less continuing) under an effects rule than under a subjective rule that positively encourages them to demand repayment of their loan at the first sniff of trouble. Should the contrary prove to be the case, a 'creditor's defence' rule could be introduced to protect transactions that are made in good faith as part of the ordinary course of business (a defence seen in some jurisdictions[249] that adopt effects-based preference rules). This kind of rule should, however, not be endorsed without good cause since it makes the liquidator's task of protecting *pari passu* distribution more difficult and, again, favours the powerful creditor.

---

[246] Ibid., para. 1256(b).

[247] Ibid., para. 1256. See *Alderson* v. *Temple* (1768) 6 Burr. 2235; 98 ER 1277; *Scott* v. *Thomas* (1834) 6 C&P 661; *Re Liebert* (1873) 8 Ch App 283; *Smith* v. *Pilgrim* (1876) 2 Ch D 127; *Re FLE Holdings* [1967] 1 WLR 140 (where it was indicated by the court that if the company mistakenly believed it had to pay because of the pressure its intention was not to grant a preference but to save itself).

[248] Keay, 'Preferences in Liquidation Law', pp. 211–12; I. F. Fletcher, 'Voidable Transactions in Bankruptcy Law: British Law Perspectives' in J. Ziegel (ed.), *Current Developments in International and Comparative Corporate Insolvency Law* (Clarendon Press, Oxford, 1994) pp. 307, 309.

[249] See New Zealand Companies Act 1955 s. 266(2); *Countrywide Banking Corporation Ltd* v. *Dean* [1998] BCC 105 (PC) (payment not in course of business but part of disposition of business).

To conclude on preferences, it cannot be claimed that the current law with its subjective test operates in a manner that comes near to maximising creditor fairness. The present subjective approach and its weak protection of *pari passu* has the effect of adding further to the unfair burden that unsecured creditors bear: they, after all, are the parties that depend on strong application of the *pari passu* principle.[250] An objective approach has been seen to lead to more frequent and more successful liquidator actions to set aside unfair preferences and, overall, would increase fairness.[251]

Transactions at undervalue and transactions defrauding creditors

Under section 238(4) of the Insolvency Act 1986, a transaction at undervalue is entered into by a company if, at a relevant time,[252] it makes a gift to a person or enters into a transaction on terms giving the company no consideration or enters a transaction for a consideration whose value in money or money's worth is significantly lower than the value of the consideration provided by the company.[253] In *Brewin Dolphin*, Lord Scott suggested that, in considering the issue of undervalue, the value of an asset being offered for sale is *prima facie* 'not less than the amount

---

[250] See further chs. 14 and 15 below.

[251] Keay, 'Preferences in Liquidation Law', p. 215.

[252] Within two years (connected person) or six months (unconnected person) of insolvency: the rule on the relevant time is the same as for a preference and is contained in the Insolvency Act 1986 s. 240.

[253] Dealings with different parties may be treated collectively in assessing the transaction as a whole and the consideration given: *Phillips* v. *Brewin Dolphin Bell Lawrie Ltd* [2001] 1 WLR 143. See K. Dawson, 'Transaction Avoidance: *Phillips* v. *Brewin Dolphin* Considered' (2001) 72 *CCH Company Law Newsletter* 1; G. Moss, 'Avoidance of Transactions – No Cherry Picking' (2001) 14 *Insolvency Intelligence*; R. Parry, 'Case Commentary' [2001] Ins. Law. 58; B. Hackett, 'What Constitutes a Transaction at an Undervalue?' (2001) 17 IL&P 139; D. Milman, Editorial, 'Swelling the Assets' [2001] Ins. Law. 85; R. Mokal, 'Consideration, Characterisation, Evaluation: Transactions at Undervalue after *Phillips* v. *Brewin Dolphin*' [2001] JCLS 359. In *Brewin Dolphin* shares in a company with a business worth £1.25 million had been sold for £1 but the purchasers' parent company had simultaneously promised to pay four years' worth of computer lease payment to the vendor, which happened to total £1.25 million. The House of Lords concluded that there was so much uncertainty as to whether the payments would be made that no value at all should be given to the sub-lease and the agreement to make payments under it and consequently there had been a transaction at undervalue. In so holding Lord Scott looked beyond the artificial division of the agreements that the participants made and at the wider picture and adopted a flexible interpretation of 'consideration' based upon a commercial reality test.

that a reasonably well-informed purchaser is prepared, in arms length negotiations, to pay for it'.[254] As for the nature of the consideration that may be traded at undervalue, the prevailing view had long been that the grant of security could not amount to a transaction at undervalue because the grant of security did not *per se* reduce the value of the debtor's assets.[255] It has now, however, been suggested in the Court of Appeal that the grant of a security can amount to a transaction at undervalue[256] and that where there is no consideration given for a charge, that charge is capable of being struck down under section 423.[257]

In contrast with the law on preferences (section 239), the liquidator's power to challenge transactions at undervalue under section 238 does not depend on establishing any particular intention or motive on the part of the company, but the 'in good faith and for the purpose of carrying on its business' defence[258] favours parties seeking to sustain a transaction. If, however, the liquidator succeeds in a section 238 challenge, the court must make such an order as it thinks fit for restoring the position to what

---

[254] *Phillips* v. *Brewin Dolphin Bell Lawrie Ltd* [2001] 1 WLR 143, para. 30. For a discussion of valuation of consideration in the context of transactions at undervalue see G. Peters, 'Undervalues and the Value of Creditor and Debtor Covenants: A Comparative Analysis' (2008) 21 *Insolvency Intelligence* 81.

[255] The logic of Millett J in the case of *Re M. C. Bacon Ltd* [1990] BCC 78 at 91–2.

[256] Notably where the equity of redemption retained is less than the value of the assets prior to the granting of the charge – which will not always be the case: see R. Stubbs, 'Section 423 of the Insolvency Act in Practice' (2008) 21 *Insolvency Intelligence* 17, 21.

[257] See *Hill* v. *Spread Trustee Co. Ltd* [2007] 1 WLR 2404, [2006] BCC 646; although it was not necessary for the Court of Appeal to express a final view on these points, Arden LJ stated that: 'Obviously there was no change in the physical assets of the debtor when the security was given but there seemed to be no reason why the value of the right to have recourse to the security and to take priority over other creditors, which the debtor created by granting the security, should be left out of account.' The judgment of Millett J in *M. C. Bacon Ltd* [1990] BCC 78 was doubted and Arden LJ suggested (arguably building on the 'commercial reality' approach of *Brewin Dolphin* [2001] 1 WLR 143 and citing comments by Lords Hoffmann and Millett in *Buchler* v. *Talbot* [2004] 2 AC 298, paras. 29, 51) that granting a security may constitute a disposition in favour of the lender and could be a transaction at undervalue (para. 138); see also Stubbs, 'Section 423 of the Insolvency Act'. It is arguable, following the decision in *Hill* v. *Spread Trustee Co. Ltd*, that the possibility of challenging charges under ss. 238 and 423 is again a live issue amongst insolvency and restructuring professionals: see A. Cohen, 'Legal Update' (2006) *Recovery* (Winter) 8, 10. For a case in line with *M. C. Bacon Ltd* see *Re Mistral Finance Ltd* [2001] BCC 27.

[258] Insolvency Act 1986 s. 238(5)(a). See D. Shah, 'Undervalue Transactions and Preferences: The "Good Faith" Defence' (2007) 20 *Insolvency Intelligence* 76. On the relationship between preferences and transactions at undervalue see *Re Sonatacus Ltd* [2007] BCC 186.

it would have been had the company not entered the transaction.[259] This will have the effect of placing the recovered assets back in the pool and making them available for the benefit of creditors generally.[260]

As a device for ensuring the fair treatment of creditors in liquidation, this action is limited by the 'in good faith and for the purpose of carrying on its business' defence. Liquidators, for instance, might find it difficult to challenge golden handshakes; or *ex gratia* payments to retiring directors, dividend payments or grants of security for existing unsecured loans.[261] In the case of the latter, in particular, there is, again, considerable opportunity for powerful creditors such as banks to benefit, to the eventual cost of the body of smaller unsecured trade creditors.[262]

A precondition for bringing an action under section 238 regarding a transaction at undervalue is that the company must have been unable to pay its debts at the time or have become unable to do so because of the transaction. Excluded from coverage, however, are transactions entered into by the company in good faith for business purposes where there were reasonable grounds for believing the transaction would benefit the company.[263] In the case of potentially questionable transactions with directors, (the then) section 320 of the Companies Act 1985 sought to provide some control by requiring general meeting approval for transactions with directors or persons connected with them during times when the company is trading. This section, however, offered little protection where directors controlled the general meeting. The CLRSG argued that if a transfer of assets to a phoenix company[264] had taken place, an effective remedy for a liquidator, one compensating creditors, would be

---

[259] Insolvency Act 1986 s. 238(3). See *Lord (liquidator of Rosshill Properties Ltd)* v. *Sinai Securities* [2004] BCC 986, [2005] 1 BCLC 295 – the court would not necessarily be deterred from making an order under section 238(3) by the fact that the applicant secured creditor could not be put back into the position he was in immediately prior to the compromise. It was at least arguable that the court's primary, and possibly only, concern under section 238(3) was the restoration of the company's position.

[260] On transactions at undervalue and possible infringement of Article 1 of the First Protocol of the Human Rights Act 1998 see J. Ulph and T. Allen, 'Transactions at Undervalue, Purchasers and the Impact of the Human Rights Act 1998' [2004] JBL 1.

[261] Note that administrators can also use s. 238: see s. 238(1).

[262] See *Re M. C. Bacon Ltd* [1990] BCC 78.

[263] Insolvency Act 1986 s. 238(5)(a); *Re Inns of Court Hotel Co.* (1868) LR 6 Eq 82. The burden of proof in establishing these defences rests on the party seeking to avoid the application of section 238: see *Re Barton Manufacturing Co. Ltd* [1998] BCC 827.

[264] The term 'phoenix' company was used to describe the practice of putting a company into voluntary liquidation (or receivership) at a time when it owed large sums to its unsecured creditors; the liquidator (or receiver) would frequently be appointed by a

to enforce remedies under section 320.[265] The CLRSG accordingly recommended that section 320 should be amended to state that where, at the time of a section 320(1)(a) transaction, the company was insolvent (or became insolvent because of the transaction and went into insolvent liquidation within twelve months of the approval) and the second party to the transaction was a connected person or a director, the resolution would not be valid for section 320 purposes if it would not have been passed without the votes of the director (and/or connected persons) unless the transaction in question was supported by an independent valuation.[266] The corresponding sections in the new Companies Act 2006, however, contain no such provision – sections 190–6 are in substance the same as their predecessors although arguably set out in a more accessible format.

Transactions at undervalue are also dealt with under the heading of 'Transactions defrauding creditors' in section 423 of the Insolvency Act 1986.[267] This remedy has its roots in the bankruptcy laws of the sixteenth century and operates with the same definition of a transaction at undervalue as is used in section 238. Section 423 actions, however, differ from those under section 238 in so far as they incorporate no time limits for the transactions challenged.[268] Liquidators do not have to show that the

---

controlling shareholder (who might have also taken a floating charge over the company's undertaking); and the liquidator (or receiver) would sell the entire business at a knockdown price to a new company incorporated by the former controllers of the defunct company. Consequently what was essentially the same business would be carried out by the same people under the same or a similar name in disregard of the claims of the creditors of the first company – the second, new company rising 'phoenix-like' from the ashes of the old. Section 216 of the Insolvency Act 1986 is aimed at countering the 'phoenix' syndrome: see further ch. 16 below.

[265] CLRSG, *Modern Company Law for a Competitive Economy: Final Report* (July 2001) pp. 327–30. The CLRSG recommended amending the Insolvency Act 1986 s. 216 so that the court would not ordinarily grant leave under section 216 if there was a material transfer of assets (within twelve months prior to liquidation) to a new company in which a director of the first company was also interested, unless there was compliance with the (amended) section 320.

[266] Such a revised rule would offer the same Companies Act 1985 s. 322 remedies as would obtain in the absence of approval, including the right of the company to set the transaction aside and to sue the director to account for his profits or to indemnify the company against its losses.

[267] See S. Elwes, 'Transactions Defrauding Creditors' (2001) 17 IL&P 10; Stubbs, 'Section 423 of the Insolvency Act'.

[268] The Insolvency Act 1986 s. 423 arguably cannot be used to extend the time zone for contesting preferences: see *Re Lloyd's Furniture Palace Ltd, Evans* v. *Lloyd's Furniture Palace Ltd* [1925] Ch 853. See also *Law Society* v. *Southall* [2001] EWCA Civ 2001

company was insolvent at the time of the transaction but they do have to establish that the company had entered into the deal with an intention[269] to put the assets beyond the reach of, or otherwise prejudice, a person[270] who is making or who may make a claim against the company.[271] A further difference between sections 238 and 423 of the Insolvency Act 1986 powers is that, in the case of the former, the court shall make an order to restore the position prior to the transaction, but under section 423 the court is empowered to make a similar order or to protect the interests of persons who are victims of the transaction: a power that will allow the court to order property to be handed over or reimbursement to be made to a particular prejudiced party.[272]

(courts reluctant to re-open transactions going back many years); *Hill* v. *Spread Trustee Co. Ltd* [2007] 1 WLR 2404, [2006] BCC 646 – according to the Court of Appeal there was no inherent objection to the notion that there could be separate limitation periods for different applicants under section 423. See further C. Brougham QC, 'Limitation Periods and Section 423 Explained: *MC Bacon* Questioned' (2006) 19 *Insolvency Intelligence* 135.

[269] In *Hill* v. *Spread Trustee Co. Ltd* the Court of Appeal stated that section 423(3) requires a person entering into a transaction to have a particular purpose – it was not enough that the transaction has a particular result. In *Inland Revenue Commissioner* v. *Hashmi* [2002] 2 BCLC 489 (Court of Appeal) it was said (by Arden LJ) that a purpose must be a real, substantial purpose in contrast with what might be a consequence; or that, per Laws LJ, the applicant must establish the debtor's 'substantial motivation' by one of the section 423(3) aims when entering the transaction; or that a 'substantial purpose' of the transaction was to permit the debtor to escape his or her liabilities (Brown LJ).

[270] This may be a single creditor, and it has been said to be immaterial that creditors as a whole are not prejudiced: see *National Westminster Bank plc* v. *Jones* [2002] 1 BCLC 55; I. Dawson, '*National Westminster Bank plc* v. *Jones*' [2002] Ins. Law. 61. See also *Hill* v. *Spread Trustee Co. Ltd* [2007] 1 WLR 2404, [2006] BCC 646 – there was no reason why a person could not cease to be the person within s. 423(3) but become a victim for the purposes of s. 423(5) before the court made its order so as to be a person whose interests may be protected by such an order. Section 423 was sufficiently flexible to allow this.

[271] See *Arbuthnot Leasing International Ltd* v. *Havelet Leasing (No. 2)* [1991] 1 All ER 591. The requirement of prejudice in s. 423(3)(b) will not be satisfied where a party transfers an asset that is so encumbered that it lacks value or if, prior to the transaction, the company has no asset of value: see *Pinewood Joinery* v. *Starelm Properties Ltd* [1994] 2 BCLC 412, [1994] BCC 569. The intention to place assets out of reach of creditors does not have to be the *sole* purpose of the debtor: see *Chohan* v. *Saggar & Another* [1992] BCC 306, 321; *Spa Leasing Ltd* v. *Lovett and Others* [1995] BCC 502; Elwes, 'Transactions Defrauding Creditors'.

[272] A victim for such purposes is a person capable of suffering prejudice, which may include a creditor or litigant: see *Re Ayala Holdings* [1993] BCLC 256; *Pinewood Joinery* v. *Starelm Properties Ltd* [1994] 2 BCLC 412, [1994] BCC 569. See also *Hill* v. *Spread Trustee Co. Ltd* [2007] 1 WLR 2404, [2006] BCC 646.

Avoidance of floating charges

A liquidator may seek to increase the fund available for unsecured creditors by challenging the practice of lenders obtaining new floating charges during a company's troubled times in order to better their position in an anticipated insolvency distribution. To this end, the liquidator can resort to section 245 of the Insolvency Act 1986 which is designed to invalidate floating charges that are executed close to insolvency and which secure post-indebtedness without providing new assets or benefits to the company. Section 245 provides for challenge where the charge has been made with a connected person within two years ending with the onset of insolvency; or with any other person within twelve months of that date. A charge will not be invalidated under this section to the extent that the assets have been increased by the sum of the value of fresh money, goods or services supplied to the company at the same time as[273] or after the charge; any discharges or reductions of any debt of the company (again at the same time or after the creation of the charge); and such interest as is payable on the above consideration. Such fresh sums must have been passed to the company and it is not enough if those are forwarded by the lender to the company's bank to reduce an overdraft that the third party has guaranteed. This is because the money paid to the bank has not become freely available to the company and so is not paid to it within the meaning of section 245.[274]

This is an area of statute law that has proved difficult for liquidators to put to good effect. Section 245 covers floating, but not fixed, charges, and it does not have purchase where the company has paid off the debenture holder secured by the floating charge.[275] If the floating charge is in favour of an unconnected person, the liquidator will have to prove that the company was then unable to pay its debts per section 123 of the Insolvency Act 1986 or was, as a result of the transaction, unable to pay its debts as they fell due.[276] The effect of the loan under which the

---

[273] On the 'same time as' see *Re Shoe Lace Ltd (sub nom. Power v. Sharp Investments Ltd)* [1994] 1 BCLC 111 where Sir Christopher Slade stated (at p. 123) that, in order to come within the terms of s. 245(2)(a), moneys paid before the execution of the debenture would have to be paid at a 'minimal' interval so that payment and execution could be regarded as 'contemporaneous'.

[274] See *Re Fairway Magazines Ltd* [1993] 1 BCLC 643.

[275] The effect of a successful challenge is to invalidate the floating charge but the debt is not extinguished.

[276] See the definition in *Re Patrick and Lyon Ltd* [1933] Ch 786. Additional tests of inability to pay debts (e.g. the balance sheet test) also operate here: see ch. 4 above.

floating charge was created has to be taken into account and the liquidator may have a complex and difficult case to make out: section 245(4)
places the onus on the liquidator as challenger of the charge to show that
the company was insolvent. Overall, then, section 245 is designed to
increase fairness in the insolvency process but its effect is limited by the
noted difficulties experienced by the liquidator. Where, however, an
action might constitute a preference or a late floating charge (as where
a floating charge is granted to a previously unsecured creditor just prior
to liquidation) the liquidator might prefer a section 245 challenge rather
than a preference avoidance action under section 239. A floating charge
would be invalidated automatically if covered by section 245 and there is
no need to show that the grantor was influenced by a desire to prefer. In
the case of non-connected persons, moreover, the vulnerability period
under section 239 is six months but, under section 245, it is twelve
months. Finally, section 245 challenges are possible when the transaction
occurs during solvency whereas, for section 239, the 'insolvency' requirement is absolute.[277]

Fairness to group creditors

In asking whether liquidation processes operate fairly, it is necessary to
consider the special position of creditors of groups of companies. What
constitutes a group is not formally defined in English law[278] but it is a
concept understood commercially as a family of related companies or
businesses in which one company (the parent or holding company)
maintains effective control over the others through shareholding and
managerial controls.[279] Issues of fairness arise if it is asked whether the

---

[277] See McCormack, 'Swelling Corporate Assets', p. 53.

[278] The Companies Act 2006 refrained from addressing the issue of liability within corporate groups: see pp. 592–3 below. Parent and subsidiary companies and undertakings
are respectively dealt with in the Companies Act 2006 ss. 1159 and 1162. See also the
Companies Act 2006 s. 399 for requirements for consolidated group accounts. On the
definition of the corporate group for accounting purposes see *Boyle and Birds' Company
Law*, pp. 500–4. See also C. Napier and C. Noke, 'Premium and Pre-acquisition Profits:
The Legal and Accounting Professions and Business Combinations' (1991) 54 MLR 810.

[279] On groups generally see T. Hadden, 'The Regulation of Corporate Groups in Australia'
(1992) UNSW LJ 61; Lord Wedderburn, 'Multinationals and the Antiquities of
Company Law' (1984) 47 MLR 87; C. Schmitthoff and F. Wooldridge (eds.), *Groups
of Companies* (Sweet & Maxwell, London, 1991); J. McCahery, S. Picciotto and C. Scott
(eds.), *Corporate Control and Accountability* (Oxford University Press, Oxford, 1993)
chs. 16–20; R. Grantham, 'Liability of Parent Companies for the Actions of the
Directors of their Subsidiaries' (1997) 18 Co. Law. 138; S. Wheeler and G. Wilson,
Directors' Liabilities in the Context of Corporate Groups (Insolvency Lawyers'
Association, Oxfordshire, 1998); D. Milman, 'Groups of Companies: The Path towards

law imposes risks on creditors (of parent companies or subsidiaries) that are inequitable. This question is the first concern here. A second issue – whether any unfairnesses the law imposes in the group context are justifiable as efficient – is one which will be returned to. Unfairness in this discussion will be treated as being involved where risks are imposed on parties who are significantly less well placed than others to evaluate risks; to adjust their terms of business to reflect such evaluations; or to bear the consequences of economic harms that result from such risk bearing.[280]

Here we are dealing with no small issue. The corporate group has developed during the last century to become an almost uniform form of business and one that routinely crosses national and regulatory boundaries.[281] Most businesses of any size or substance now conduct their operations through subsidiaries that are owned by a parent company. The essential problem, however, is that there is a disjuncture between the law's vision of the limited liability company and the reality of commercial life. The law does not hold parent companies liable for subsidiaries because it treats companies as juristic persons with separate corporate personality.[282] The reality is that groups operate as economically and managerially cohesive operations, often with high levels of unity. They move resources around and operate as organically whole institutions.

For managers and shareholders of the parent company there are a number of reasons for operating via the group mechanism.[283] It has been

Discrete Regulation' in D. Milman (ed.), *Regulating Enterprise* (Hart, Oxford, 1999); R. Austin, 'Corporate Groups' in R. Grantham and C. Rickett (eds.), *Corporate Personality in the Twentieth Century* (Hart, Oxford, 1998); J. Dine, *The Governance of Corporate Groups* (Cambridge University Press, Cambridge, 2000).

[280] See the discussion of non-adjusting creditors at pp. 607–14 below.

[281] On the development of the group see J. Wilson, *British Business History 1720–1994* (Manchester University Press, Manchester, 1995); T. Hadden, 'Inside Corporate Groups' (1984) 12 *International Journal of Sociology of Law* 271.

[282] *Salomon* v. *A. Salomon & Co. Ltd* [1897] AC 22. See also the reaffirmation of the separation of parent and subsidiary obligations in *Adams* v. *Cape Industries* [1990] 2 WLR 657 (CA). If a subsidiary acts as an agent for the parent company the latter will incur liability on ordinary agency principles: see *Canada Rice Mills Ltd* v. *R* [1939] 3 All ER 991; E. Ferran, *Company Law and Corporate Finance* (Oxford University Press, Oxford, 1999) p. 35. On a parent company liability through guarantees or in tort see Ferran, *Company Law and Corporate Finance*, pp. 35–7; P. Muchlinski, 'Holding Multinationals to Account' (2002) 23 Co. Law. 168.

[283] See, for example, Austin, 'Corporate Groups'; T. Eisenberg, 'Corporate Groups' in M. Gillooly (ed.), *The Law Relating to Corporate Groups* (Butterworths, Sydney, 1993); CLRSG, *Modern Company Law for a Competitive Economy: Completing the Structure* (DTI, November 2000) ch. 10.

suggested that a primary reason is to distribute risks in a manner that serves the group as a whole.[284] The group device, however, also provides a degree of managerial autonomy for buying, selling or operating certain business activities; it allows geographically dispersed businesses to be managed separately; it caters for compliance with local laws (where, for example, a country demands a home-based corporate presence); it can allow tax advantages to be achieved; it may usefully limit the influence of anti-trust laws or a regulator (by removing parent companies from the regulator's domain); it allows legal liabilities of various kinds to be shifted and limited in ways that protect the parent company; it provides a means of keeping labour costs down;[285] and it allows for investments, profits and losses to be distributed in ways that maximise benefits to the group.[286]

In spite of the prevalence of the group, insolvency law very largely fails to take on board the interdependency of many companies.[287] The law is still focused almost exclusively on the individual company; there is no legally developed doctrine of group enterprise or notion of 'group interest'; there are no clear rules on the liability of the parent company for the firms within its group; and there is virtually no legal control over the complexity of the group's structure.[288] The creditors of companies within a group can only assert claims against their particular debtor company, not the group. The potential for unfair treatment stems from the ability of a parent company's directors to manipulate the rules governing limited liability companies to the group's or parent company's advantage. A typical large group may involve more than a hundred subsidiaries or subsidiaries of subsidiaries and some of the latter may be placed as far as five removes from the main board of directors.[289] These extended organisations are tied together by arrangements of ownership, contract, management and economic interdependence yet the

---

[284] See CLRSG, *Completing the Structure*, p. 177.

[285] See H. Collins, 'Ascription of Legal Responsibility to Groups and Complex Patterns of Economic Integration' (1990) 53 MLR 731.

[286] See T. Hadden, 'Insolvency and the Group: Problems of Integrated Financing' in R. M. Goode (ed.), *Group Trading and the Lending Banker* (Chartered Institute of Bankers, London, 1988).

[287] The legislature failed to take the opportunity to address or resolve the issue under the Companies Act 2006. See further pp. 592–3 below.

[288] See T. Hadden, 'Regulating Corporate Groups: International Perspectives' in McCahery, Picciotto and Scott, *Corporate Control*.

[289] Collins, 'Ascription of Legal Responsibility', p. 733; Hadden, *The Control of Corporate Groups* (Institute of Advanced Legal Studies, London, 1983) p. 9.

companies involved are regarded by the law as so many independent units.

This difference between commercial reality and legal framework can result in unfair allocations of risk to creditors for a number of reasons. The creditors of a subsidiary face at least the following difficulties.[290] They may face enormous costs in calculating the risks they are bearing, because the parent company enjoys freedom to move resources and risks around the group in a manner that favours the group rather than the subsidiary.[291] Corporate decisions will be made with a view to maximising overall returns rather than ensuring the health of any subsidiary and it may be extremely difficult to assess the financial or risk position of a subsidiary at any one time. Creditors of subsidiaries within a group may be misled about the ownership of assets that are available to pay their debts; transactions within groups may not be conducted at arm's length; assets may be transferred, or loans given, at non-market rates; and guarantees and dividends may be given without reference to the interests of the companies affected.[292] A firm may be made excessively dependent on other group firms for funds, business or both, and one firm may be used clandestinely within the group as a dumping ground for losses, liabilities and risks. A further problem for a subsidiary creditor is that amidst the above complexities it may be difficult to find out such basic matters as which companies are members of the group and which inter-company dependencies are intra-group.[293] Nor can creditors of subsidiaries take comfort in the rules governing directors' duties. The tradition of the law dictates that directors owe duties to their own company, not to the subsidiaries that their decisions may affect.[294] The directors of a

---

[290] See J. Landers, 'A Unified Approach to Parent, Subsidiary and Affiliate Questions in Bankruptcy' (1975) 42 U Chic. L Rev. 589 (see reply by R. Posner, 'The Rights of Creditors of Affiliated Corporations' (1976) 43 U Chic. L Rev. 499; and reply by Landers, 'Another Word on Parents, Subsidiaries and Affiliates in Bankruptcy' (1976) 43 U Chic. L Rev. 527).

[291] 'Firms enjoy considerable freedom both in law and practice to determine the limits of their boundaries': see Collins, 'Ascription of Legal Responsibility', pp. 736–8, on 'the capital boundary problem'.

[292] See Cork Report, para. 1926. On the 'implied statutory duty' (under the Insolvency Act 1986 s. 238) of a lending bank to consider, in seeking the security of a corporate guarantee, the interests of the surety's creditors, see D. Spahos, 'Lenders, Borrowing Groups of Companies and Corporate Guarantees: An Insolvency Perspective' [2001] JCLS 333.

[293] See Milman, 'Groups of Companies', pp. 222–3.

[294] *Lindgreen v. L & P Estates Ltd* [1968] 1 Ch 572; *Charterbridge Corp. Ltd v. Lloyds Bank* [1970] 1 Ch 62.

parent company, moreover, may use cross-holdings to entrench themselves in control of the group, yet they may have very small commitments of capital themselves.

The above considerations may make creditors of a subsidiary nervous.[295] Other consequences of the law may move them towards indignation. The Cork Report noted a scenario in which a wholly owned subsidiary is mismanaged and abused for the benefit of a parent company but in which loans from the parent company are employed. When the subsidiary goes into liquidation its creditors find that the parent company submits a proof in respect of its loan and a substantial proportion of the funds realised by the liquidator go to the parent company and (where the loan is secured) do so before the unsecured creditors of the subsidiary are repaid.[296]

Cork saw such a legal position as 'undoubtedly defective'[297] and one commentator has noted widespread criticism of the process by which 'the liberal creation of undercapitalised subsidiaries [creates] a second level of limited liability protection for businesses wishing to insulate themselves from enterprise liabilities'.[298] Realigning the law so as to deal with the problems posed by groups has, however, not proved easy. The difficulties can be outlined by considering the main proposals that have been canvassed to date. These can be grouped into three broad responses: subordinating debts owed to companies within the group to the claims of non-group creditors; consolidating group debts; and tightening directors' obligations and liabilities.

---

[295] If a subsidiary becomes insolvent the parent and other subsidiaries may still prosper 'to the joy of the shareholders without any liability for the debts of the insolvent subsidiary': see *Re Southard* [1979] 1 WLR 1198 (CA), per Templeman LJ.

[296] The rules on transactional avoidance may come into play: see Insolvency Act 1986 ss. 239 and 245; *Re Shoe Lace Ltd (sub nom. Power v. Sharp Investments)* [1994] 1 BCLC 111; Milman, 'Groups of Companies', p. 225. Proof of debt between group members was allowed in *Re Polly Peck International plc (No. 3)* [1996] 1 BCLC 428. On instances where the parent company may not deny liability see Milman, 'Groups of Companies', pp. 226–8.

[297] Cork Report, para. 1934; the words 'seriously inadequate' are used of the law at para. 1950. See also paras. 1924 and 1928 for reflections of views that the position was 'offensive to ordinary canons of commercial morality' and that it was 'absurd and unreal to allow the commercial realities to be disregarded'.

[298] See Milman, 'Groups of Companies' p. 225, and for judicial concern see Staughton LJ in *Atlas Maritime Co. v. Avalon Maritime Ltd (No. 1)* [1991] 4 All ER 769 at 779. On the capacity of groups to avoid the legal regulation of business transfers and TUPE (on TUPE see ch. 17 below) see *Michael Peters Ltd v. Farnfield & Michael Peters Group plc* [1995] IRLR 190.

Subordination was a route advocated in limited form by Cork.[299] Several parties who gave evidence to the Cork Committee argued that all debts owed by a company in liquidation to other companies in the same group should be deferred to the claims of external creditors. Cork, however, drew a distinction between debts arising from ordinary trading activities between group companies and debts 'which in substance represent long term working capital and which arise from finance provided by the parent company'.[300] In making this distinction, Cork drew on the US courts' equitable jurisdiction to subordinate, as preserved by statute,[301] under which the courts examined the conduct of parties and tended to look for fraud, mismanagement, wrongful conduct or under-capitalisation where finance was by the controlling shareholder.[302] Cork suggested that it would not be equitable to subordinate in the case of ordinary trading debts but it would be fair to do so in the case of liabilities, secured or unsecured, which are owed to connected persons or companies and which represent all or part of the long-term capital of the company.[303]

One problem with Cork's approach (which has not been implemented) is that the distinction upon which it builds constitutes an invitation to lengthy and expensive litigation.[304] A further issue, however, relates to the broad exemption of ordinary trading debts. In a group there are, as noted, real dangers that transactions at other than market value will be entered into for manipulative reasons (for example, to load risks onto a subsidiary whose creditors are ill-placed to respond to such a risk shift). There seems no reason why such transactions should

---

[299] Cork Report, paras. 1958–65.   [300] Ibid., para. 1960.

[301] 11 USC s. 510(C) 1978, giving statutory recognition to the 'Deep Rock' doctrine (the name being taken from a subsidiary company featuring in *Taylor* v. *Standard Gas and Electric Co.* (1939) 306 US 307) where the claims (as a creditor) of a controller of a company can be subordinated to the claims of the other creditors: see Landers, 'Unified Approach', pp. 597–606.

[302] See Milman, 'Groups of Companies', p. 230; R. Schulte, 'Corporate Groups and the Equitable Subordination of Claims on Insolvency' (1997) 18 Co. Law. 2; *Taylor* v. *Standard Gas and Electric Co.*

[303] Cork recommended that where such liabilities were secured by fixed or floating charges that security should be invalid as against the liquidator, administrator or any creditor to the company until all claims to which it had been deferred were met: Cork Report, para. 1963.

[304] See Milman, 'Groups of Companies', p. 229. Cork's rejection of subordination for 'ordinary trading activity' claims was not argued out: the Committee merely reported hostility in the United States Congressional hearings and the fact that it was 'not persuaded' on its own account.

escape subordination because they are encountered in an ordinary trading context. If the objective is fairness to creditors of subsidiaries, debts to group companies relating to such transactions should be subordinated.

A second major response to unfair risk shifting is to consolidate (to lift the veil on the group)[305] to deal with the commercial realities and to order a pooling of the assets of related companies in liquidation so as to improve the dividend prospects for creditors. There are a number of ways to implement such an approach. In Germany the legislation of 1965 (*Konzernrecht*) dealt with the issue in a formalistic way by seeking to lay down the parameters of formal legal relations between the companies in a group.[306] The drawback of such a strategy is that it produces a somewhat rigid legal framework that may unduly restrict enterprise, prove unresponsive to change and yet not remove the need for judicial intervention. An alternative method relies more explicitly on the use of judicial discretion. In New Zealand, legislation passed in 1980 empowered the courts to order one company in a group to *contribute* towards the assets of a fellow group company in the event

---

[305] On the English courts' approach to lifting the veil in the group context see *Adams* v. *Cape Industries* [1990] 2 WLR 657; discussed by S. Griffin in (1991) 12 Co. Law. 16. See also *Boyle and Birds' Company Law*, pp. 76–80; Schulte, 'Corporate Groups'. The European Court of Justice shows more inclination to treat a group of companies as a single economic entity: see *Istituto Chemioterapico Italiano SpA* v. *EC Commission*, Case 6, 7/73 [1974] ECR 223; *SAR Schotte GmbH* v. *Parfums Rothschild SARL*, 218/86 [1992] BCLC 235. In the USA the flexible concept of equitable subordination has been adopted and piercing the veil of incorporation is also resorted to. On piercing the veil in the United States context, see Landers, 'Unified Approach', who would pierce the veil whenever the parent company has failed to endow the subsidiary with sufficient resources to make it economically viable or failed to observe the legal formalities for creating a separate corporation.

[306] See Milman, 'Groups of Companies', p. 231; E. Hintz, 'German Law on Cash Pooling in the Insolvency Context' (2007) Int. LR 78; J. Rinze, 'Konzernrecht: Law on Groups of Companies in Germany' (1993) 14 Co. Law. 143; K. Hopt, 'Legal Elements and Policy Decisions in Regulating Groups of Companies' in Schmitthoff and Wooldridge, *Groups of Companies*; D. Sugarman and G. Teubner (eds.), *Regulating Corporate Groups in Europe* (Nomos, Baden-Baden, 1990). In the European Draft Ninth Directive (Commission Document III/1639/84-EN) an approach modelled on the German group regime was promoted but this measure received a hostile reception and has not been implemented. On the possibility of future European initiatives regarding regulation of corporate groups see K. Hopt, 'Legal Issues and Questions of Policy in the Comparative Regulation of Groups' [1996] *I Gruppi di Società* 45. On the German courts' developing jurisprudence concerning the '*de facto* group liability' of private companies see M. Shillig, 'The Development of a New Concept of Creditor Protection for German GmbHs' (2006) 27 Co. Law. 348.

of the latter's insolvency.[307] Such orders are to be granted when the court considers this just and equitable, and attention will be paid to the role of the parent company, especially its part in the subsidiary's collapse.[308] In the case of collapses of the group as a whole, the New Zealand law grants judges an analogous discretion to *pool* the assets and liabilities of the group.[309] Here the New Zealand courts must have regard to the extent to which the related company took part in the management of any of the other companies; the conduct of any of the companies towards the creditors of any of the other companies; the extent to which the businesses have been combined; the extent to which the causes of the liquidation of any of the companies are attributable to the actions of any of the other companies; and such other matters as the court thinks fit.[310] A similar approach has been adopted in Ireland[311] and, in Australia, pooling was advocated by the Harmer Committee and the Corporations and Securities Advisory Committee.[312] In the latter jurisdiction, the Corporations Amendment

---

[307] Companies Amendment Act 1980 (New Zealand); see now Companies Act 1993 s. 271(1)(a); see further Austin, 'Corporate Groups', pp. 84–6.

[308] See *Rea* v. *Barker* (1988) 4 NZCLC 6, 312; *Rea* v. *Chix* (1986) 3 NZCLC 98, 852; *Bullen* v. *Tourcorp Developments Ltd* (1988) 4 NZCLC 64, 661.

[309] See Companies Act 1993 s. 271(1)(b); *Re Dalhoff and King Holdings Ltd* [1991] 2 NZLR 296; *Re Pacific Syndicates (NZ) Ltd* (1989) 4 NZCLC 64, 757; Milman, 'Groups of Companies', p. 230; Austin, 'Corporate Groups', pp. 83–6.

[310] Companies Act 1993 (New Zealand) s. 272(1).

[311] Companies Act (Ireland) 1990 s. 140 (contributions) and s. 141 (pooling). In France statutory provisions address the parent–subsidiary relationship on a number of points but also rely on judicial discretion: see Milman, 'Groups of Companies', p. 231.

[312] Australian Law Reform Commission, *General Insolvency Inquiry*, Report No. 45, para. 857: discussed in Austin, 'Corporate Groups', p. 86; Corporations and Securities Advisory Committee, *Corporate Groups: Final Report* (May 2000) at para. 6.97 and recommendations 22 and 23 (proposing that liquidators should be allowed to pool the assets of two or more companies in liquidation with the prior approval of all the unsecured creditors of those companies and that courts should be permitted to make pooling orders in the liquidation of two or more companies). See also J. Harris, 'Pooling Options for Insolvent Corporate Groups' (2005) 26 Co. Law. 125 (arguing the need for legislative provision for liquidators to pool in appropriate circumstances (see now the Corporations Amendment (Insolvency) Act 2007)); Harris, 'Corporate Group Insolvencies: Charting the Past, Present and Future of "Pooling" Arrangements' (2007) 15 Ins. LJ 78; J. Dickfos, C. Aderson and D. Morrison, 'The Insolvency Implications for Corporate Groups in Australia – Recent Events' (2007) 16 Int. Ins. Rev. 103. In Australia, prior to the 2007 legislation, the Federal Court had suggested that a voluntary administrator has the power to propose (without court approval) a pooling arrangement as part of a deed of company arrangement (*Mentha* v. *GE Capital Ltd* (1997) 154 ALR 565; *Re CAN 004 987 866 Pty Ltd* [2003] FCA 849) and the Australian

(Insolvency) Act 2007 introduced legislative amendments to provide
that the courts may, by order, determine (on 'just and equitable'
criteria)[313] that a group is a 'pooled group'.[314] The effect of such an
order is that unsecured creditors are able to claim against any or all of
the companies in the pooled group – who are rendered jointly and
severally liable for the unsecured debts owed by each member.[315] The
court's power here requires that each company in the group is being
wound up and the pooling order applies to debts or claims that are
present or future, certain or contingent, and whether ascertained or
sounding only in damages.[316]

In the USA, the court may order consolidation (known as 'substantive
consolidation')[317] under the auspices of its general equitable powers and

courts allowed pooling on the basis that where it is impracticable to keep the assets and
liabilities of different companies in a group separate they may be consolidated if
consolidation is for the benefit of creditors generally: see *Dean-Willcocks* v. *Soluble
Solutions Hydroponics Pty Ltd* (1997) 13 ACLC 833, 839; *Re Ansett Australia Ltd* (2006)
151 FCR 41: discussed by J. Harris, 'Seeking Court Approval for Pooling Arrangements:
Lessons from the *Ansett* Case' (2006) 24 C&SLJ 443.

[313] See Corporations Amendment (Insolvency) Act 2007 Sch. 1, s. 579E(12)(a)–(f): for
example, the court *must* have regard to the extent to which a company in the group,
officers or employees of a company in a group was/were involved in the management of
any other companies in the group; the conduct of a company in the group or officers or
employees of a company in the group towards the creditors of any of the other
companies in the group; the extent to which the circumstances that gave rise to the
winding up of any companies in the group are directly/indirectly attributable to the
acts/omissions of any of the other companies in the group or the officers or employees
of any of the other companies in the group; the extent to which the activities and
business of the companies in the group have been intermingled; the extent to which
creditors of the companies in the group may be advantaged or disadvantaged by the
making of the order; and any other relevant matters.

[314] Section 579E(1).

[315] Section 579E(2) and (3). For discussion see Harris, 'Corporate Group Insolvencies',
pp. 91–2. The court must not make a pooling order if it is satisfied that such an order
would disadvantage an eligible unsecured creditor materially and that creditor has not
consented to the order: s. 579E(10)(a); or if the company in the group is being wound up
under a members' voluntary winding up and the court is satisfied that a member (not
being a company in the group) would be materially disadvantaged and has not consented to the making of the order: s. 579E(10)(b).

[316] Section 579E(3). Note that provision is also made for a voluntary pooling 'determination' by administrators and liquidators: see Corporations Amendment (Insolvency) Act
2007 Sch. 1, Part 4, ss. 571–2. See further M. Hughes, 'Pooling, Part 1' (2007) *Australian
Insolvency Journal* (January–March) 12.

[317] As opposed to procedural consolidation where the bankruptcy proceedings of different
entities are consolidated for procedural purposes only, having no effect on creditors'
substantive rights. On US 'substantive consolidation' see further A. Borrowdale,
'Commentary on Austin' in Grantham and Rickett, *Corporate Personality*, pp. 91–2.

will do so where the companies' affairs are inextricably linked or the
creditors can be shown to have dealt with the debtor companies as a
single economic unit. In such consolidations the group assets and liabilities are dealt with as a single unit as part of a pooling arrangement.[318]

A further route to consolidation, parent company contributions and
an acknowledgement of commercial realities, lies through holding the
parent liable for debts of the subsidiary where there is insolvent or
wrongful trading. Section 588V of the Australian Corporations Law
2001, as amended, for instance, renders a parent company liable for a
subsidiary's debt when the latter has carried on trading while insolvent or
likely to become insolvent and the parent or any of the parent's directors
was aware or should have been aware of such trading.[319] The strength of
this approach is that it does not rely on a finding that the parent company
is a shadow director of the subsidiary but imposes a positive duty on the
parent to safeguard the interests of the subsidiaries' unsecured creditors.
The weakness is that it relies on finding a relationship of parent to
subsidiary and legal definitions of this relationship may both fail to
capture instances of *de facto* control and be vulnerable to circumvention
through manipulation of shareholdings.[320]

In English law, liability for wrongful trading under section 214 of the
Insolvency Act 1986 also applies to shadow directors,[321] who are defined
(in section 251) as persons 'in accordance with whose directions or
instructions the directors of the company are accustomed to act'.[322]
The concept of a shadow director can encompass a parent company

---

[318] For an account of the informal pooling arrangements in the BCCI group liquidations
see C. Grierson, 'Issues in Concurrent Insolvency Jurisdiction: English Perspectives' in
Ziegel, *Current Developments*. On US consolidation see further C. Frost, 'Operational
Form, Misappropriation Risk and the Substantive Consolidation of Corporate Groups'
(1993) 44 Hastings LJ 449; C. Grierson, 'Shareholder Liability, Consolidation and
Pooling' in E. Leonard and C. Besant (eds.), *Current Issues in Cross-Border Insolvency
and Reorganisations* (Graham and Trotman, London, 1994). Note can also be made of
the possibility of consolidated legal insolvency procedures apropos groups of companies spread within the EU under the Council Regulation (EC) No. 1346/2000: see
I. Fletcher, *Insolvency in Private International Law* (2nd edn, Oxford University
Press, Oxford, 2005) ch. 7.

[319] See I. Ramsay, 'Allocating Liability in Corporate Groups: An Australian Perspective'
(1999) 13 Connecticut JIL 329.

[320] Ibid. One suggestion for limiting such vulnerability to evasion is to resort to definitions
of subsidiarity that are founded in economic substance rather than legal classification.

[321] On shadow directors see ch. 16 below.

[322] The concept was borrowed from the Companies Act 1985 s. 741. See now Companies
Act 2006 s. 251.

and this paves the way for liability for wrongful trading and contributing to the insolvent company's assets by order of the court (under section 214(1)). Such use of the shadow direction concept does not make parent companies generally liable for the debts of subsidiaries but it may cover situations of wrongful trading and it looks to the realities of economic control rather than the formalities of ownership.[323]

The courts have dealt with the matter of parent companies as shadow directors. In *Hydrodan*[324] it was made clear that the issue was whether the directors of a subsidiary exercise their own independent discretion and judgement and that, to prove shadow directorship, it had to be shown that the board of the subsidiary did not exercise this discretion and judgement but acted in accordance with the directions of the parent company. A broadening of approach can be discerned in *Deverell*[325] where, in the Court of Appeal, Morritt LJ suggested *inter alia* that the fact that the board of directors may be characterised as subservient clearly indicates the existence of a shadow directorship.[326] *Deverell* thus opens the door to the liability of a parent company to a subservient subsidiary's creditors, but there are limitations to this remedy. As noted, it only applies where wrongful trading is established and, second, it looks to instances in which the parent board dominates the subsidiary board as a matter of governance. Whether it will cover situations where the companies are commercially linked but are formally and managerially independent is far less certain.[327]

It is noteworthy that Cork declined to recommend that a holding company be liable for an insolvent subsidiary company's debts.[328] Some of the Committee favoured the radical view (that the parent company should always be liable) and other members of the Committee favoured the New Zealand discretionary approach. Cork, however, drew back from making a recommendation because of anticipated effects on entrepreneurship, difficulties of apportioning liability, potential impacts on long-term existing creditors and other ramifications

---

[323] See Collins, 'Ascription of Legal Responsibility', p. 741, who argues that the concept opens the possibility of offering a powerful response to the 'capital boundary problem'.

[324] *Re Hydrodan (Corby) Ltd* [1994] BCC 161.

[325] *Secretary of State for Trade and Industry v. Deverell* [2000] 2 WLR 907, [2000] BCC 1057.

[326] [2000] 2 WLR 907 at 919–20.

[327] See Collins, 'Ascription of Legal Responsibility', p. 742. See also J. Payne, 'Casting Light into the Shadows: *Secretary of State for Trade and Industry v. Deverell*' (2001) 22 Co. Law. 90; D. Milman, 'A Fresh Light on Shadow Directors' [2000] Ins. Law. 171.

[328] See the discussion in Ferran, *Company Law and Corporate Finance*, pp. 39–40.

outside insolvency: notably that the directors of a parent company would have to have regard for not only the interests of that company but also the interests of other group companies. Such matters were so important, said Cork, that a wide review covering company and insolvency law issues was needed.[329] The response to the point concerning a widening of directors' duties, of course, may be that the directors of parent companies now possess such extensive powers to influence subsidiaries by methods of such extremely low transparency that such a broadening of directors' obligations could be healthy.

A further method of making holding company assets available to creditors in subsidiaries is the proposal discussed by the CLRSG in 2000.[330] In the mooted 'elective regime' the parent company would guarantee the liabilities of the subsidiary and would satisfy certain publicity requirements. The subsidiary, in return, would be exempted from Companies Act requirements relating to annual accounts and audit. By 2001, however, the CLRSG had been convinced by consultees that there was no solid case for 'the elective regime'.[331] Concerns were expressed to the CLRSG about the regime's low potential to reduce burdens on groups significantly.[332] Further worries were that the proposed regime would offer little help to the creditors of subsidiaries since parents could 'ring-fence' valuable assets in subsidiaries kept out of the elective regime; and that the requirement that electing subsidiaries must be 'wholly owned' provided a way of evading the bite of the parental guarantee.[333] It could, additionally, be objected that the regime could be abandoned by parental rescinding and that it did not pool the assets of the group for the benefit of the claimants, but only the assets of the parent, which may not amount to much if the parent is not asset-rich (perhaps because it had removed assets offshore).[334] The proposal would, moreover, involve an unacceptable loss of publicly available information at the individual company

---

[329] Cork Report, paras. 1951–2.   [330] See CLRSG, *Completing the Structure*, ch. 10.
[331] CLRSG, *Final Report*, 2001, pp. 179–80.
[332] The requirements of HMRC would still have to be satisfied and this diminishes the reductions of costs that the elective regime offers: see A. Boyle, 'The Company Law Review and Group Reform' (2002) 23 Co. Law. 35. Assessment of risk would also still be necessary despite a guarantee of liabilities since there are residual risks of the parent company. For creditors of subsidiaries analysing parent company risks may be complex and time-consuming.
[333] See Boyle, 'Company Law Review', p. 36.
[334] See Muchlinski, 'Holding Multinationals to Account'.

level and would distance the creditors of a subsidiary from the information that they need in order to assess risks.

A third canvassed response[335] to the difficulties faced by group creditors is to develop the concept of duties of dominant shareholders. Thus it has been suggested that a dominant shareholder (the parent company) should owe fiduciary duties (of loyalty and fairness) to its subsidiary and other subordinated companies and that the dominant parent should have the burden of proving that transactions with the dominated company are fair, unless those transactions have been authorised by 'disinterested' shareholders.[336]

All the above suggestions are designed to reduce the unfairnesses that stem from the facility with which the directors of a parent company can shift risks to the creditors of a subsidiary. The broad objections to this 'family' of proposals are that they would interfere unwarrantably with directors' managerial freedoms, would violate the separate entity principle, would stifle enterprise and would create uncertainty – that it is better to tolerate present unfairnesses than to escalate overall costs very substantially in pursuit of fairness.[337] This seems, however, no answer to the case for subordinating parent company debts to other debts. That case is based on the unfairness of allowing companies who control subsidiaries to prove for debts alongside other creditors of the subsidiary. The strategic and informational advantages enjoyed by the parent company are adequate compensation for subordination. As far as consolidation is concerned, the least legally uncertain proposal is the radical one – that a parent company should automatically be responsible for the liabilities of a subsidiary. It might be argued, however, that practical uncertainties would raise capital costs unduly. Objectors would contend that a

---

[335] One posited as building on *US Principles of Corporate Governance*, American Law Institute, Draft No. 5 (1986).

[336] See A. Tunc, 'The Fiduciary Duties of a Dominant Shareholder' in Schmitthoff and Wooldridge, *Groups of Companies*. See also M. Lower, 'Good Faith and the Partly Owned Subsidiary' [2000] JBL 232. On the 'unfair prejudice' remedy under the (then) s. 459 of the Companies Act 1985 (now Companies Act 2006 s. 994) (which allows (minority) shareholders to petition the court for relief when the company's affairs are being conducted in a manner that unfairly prejudices their interests) and the treating of conduct within the subsidiary as within the affairs of the parent company for s. 459 purposes, see *Gross* v. *Rackind* [2004] EWCA Civ 815 and R. Goddard and H. Hirt, 'Section 459 and Corporate Groups' [2005] JBL 247.

[337] See, for example, the Law Council of Australia objections discussed by Austin, 'Corporate Groups', p. 86 and by J. O'Donovan, 'Group Therapies for Group Insolvencies' in Gillooly, *Law Relating to Corporate Groups*.

welcome effect of limited liability is that the suppliers of credit know the risks they face, they know that these risks are limited and so are induced to lend on reasonable rates. Shareholders and creditors benefit by the certainties generated.[338] If parent groups are liable for subsidiaries, it could be said, such benefits of limited liability are undermined because it is difficult to assess risks across groups.

This argument can, however, be overstated. The shareholders of the parent company will still be shielded from personal liability by the limited liability that they enjoy.[339] It is true that inefficiencies are caused by the uncertainties that flow from the complexities of risk assessments within groups. These do have to be paid for, but non-liability of the parent company for its subsidiaries creates perhaps greater overall uncertainties through incentives to produce poor information flows to lenders to the group.[340] Those lenders will charge rates that reflect uncertainties. Directors of parent companies that are not liable for subsidiaries will perhaps not be too worried: they will consider the balance between the higher capital costs they face across the group (due to the nervousness of lenders to group subsidiaries) and their ability to offload risks onto the creditors of subsidiaries, notably trade creditors. The banks lending to the parent company may not be very concerned either because they will have confidence that insolvency risks are being shifted away from the parent company to the subsidiary and its creditors. Such powerful decision-makers are likely, accordingly, to favour a regime that is highly uncertain and high cost, provided that other parties (the unsecured creditors of subsidiaries) are bearing those costs. Those other parties, however, would be unlikely to welcome such a system.

The advantage of making the parent company liable is that its managers may be induced to take risks responsibly and the parties bearing the risks will be those that are best informed and best able to control the flow of finances. Where the parent is not liable, its managers will be prone to engage in excessive risk taking because they can shift risks to subsidiaries.[341] Indeed, without the liability of the parent, the managers of a subsidiary may also take excessive risks because they may be confident of relocation to another company within the group that has benefited from

---

[338] See Posner, 'Rights of Creditors', pp. 501–3.

[339] See Ferran, *Company Law and Corporate Finance*, p. 32.

[340] See Landers, 'Another Word on Parents', p. 539: 'the present system effectively rewards owners who can hide from public view'.

[341] See P. Blumberg, *The Multinational Challenge to Corporation Law: The Search for a New Corporate Personality* (Oxford University Press, New York, 1993) p. 134.

the excessive risk bearing of the first subsidiary.[342] The creditors and the directors of the parent company will be more efficient risk bearers than the creditors of subsidiaries because the former have far better levels of information. Posner objects to the parent company liability approach on the grounds that lenders to the parent company will have to investigate the creditworthiness of the group's subsidiaries[343] but (given their access to group information) it is easier and cheaper for them to do this than for the subsidiary's trade creditors to review the whole group's financial risks. General levels of uncertainty, moreover, are likely to be lower where the parent company is liable because the broad incentives favour openness and transparency rather than manipulation and secrecy. Apart from anything else, parent company liability would reduce the tendency to construct massively complex group corporate structures for non-productive reasons (for example, to avoid regulatory obligations or to create 'dump' subsidiaries).[344] The answer to Posner, in short, is not that a parent company is losing its limited liability advantages but that it is retaining these and losing its facility to shift risks unfairly – losing the subsidy to entrepreneurship that is now being paid for by the creditors of insolvent subsidiary companies.

The case for parent company liability, accordingly, seems strong but, as has been seen above, such a radical reform is politically unlikely.[345] A discretionary regime is more likely to be introduced but it is more vulnerable to attacks for uncertainty. Lenders to companies within the group are liable to charge rates that reflect the difficulties of assessing when and whether the courts will impose liability on the parent company. One proposed solution to this problem is to exempt the parent company from such potential liability where subsidiaries are specified: 'provided that those subsidiaries are financially managed in a manner which segregates their assets and liabilities from the assets and liabilities of the rest of the group and that the segregation is documented in a manner that would permit a liquidator to trace the assets affected by

---

[342] F. H. Easterbrook and D. R. Fischel, *The Economic Structure of Corporate Law* (Harvard University Press, Cambridge, Mass., 1991) pp. 56–7.

[343] Posner, 'Rights of Creditors', p. 517.

[344] See further Hadden, 'Regulating Corporate Groups'.

[345] See Milman, 'Groups of Companies', p. 231, and pp. 592–3 above. In December 2006, however, UNCITRAL (Working Group V) commenced consideration of the treatment of corporate groups in insolvency. At the time of writing, this work is still under way: see UNCITRAL Annotated Provisional Agenda for the 34th Session of Working Group V (Insolvency Law) March 2008.

it'.[346] It is difficult, however, to see how such preservation of the separate entity could be managed within the commercial interrelationships and complexities of a group's structure and how, if attempted, it could be achieved without such restrictiveness as would negate the advantages of group membership.

The discretionary route, it seems, has to face up to the likelihood that it will involve time-consuming and expensive litigation in circumstances where finances are highly constrained. As commentators have observed, this may explain the poor success rate of such mechanisms and even steps to reverse the onus of proof (so that parent companies are presumed liable for subsidiaries' debts unless they show that they have operated at arm's length) will not avoid considerable costs.[347] If the creditors of group subsidiaries are to be protected, yet costs kept to a reasonable level, it may be necessary to be bold and to opt for a regime of consolidation.

Conclusions

The above account outlines a number of respects in which the process of liquidation is open to criticism and improvement on the efficiency, expertise, accountability and fairness fronts. A further issue concerns the conceptual underpinnings of liquidation. These should be examined to see if there is value in approaching liquidation in terms that differ from the model implicit in current English insolvency law. Cork espoused a shift from a 'creditor control' to a 'creditor participation' model of insolvency proceedings but there are other directions from which to approach liquidation. One such direction involves seeing liquidation as other than a process that centres precisely on a set of formal legal rules. This is perhaps against the inclination of lawyers who devote much attention to extensive sets of statutory provisions, but it is already clear from the above account that liquidation can be portrayed in a number of non-rule-centric ways: as an institutional contest involving such different parties as expert insolvency practitioners, banks and other major creditors, directors, shareholders, unsecured trade creditors, the courts and the BERR – participants with very different aims, interests, incentives, levels of information, expertise and access to the insolvency process. Liquidation, moreover, can be seen as a reflection of long-

---

[346] See Austin, 'Corporate Groups', p. 87.   [347] Milman, 'Groups of Companies', p. 231.

established conventions of deference to powerful institutions. On this view, an observer might explain much of the liquidation process in terms of the exalted positions that English insolvency law has long given to powerful secured creditors.[348] Linked to this vision are notions that modern English liquidation is driven in shape and operation by those who possess information and skill. It is, on this view, the preserve of the repeat players, as exemplified by the manner in which IPs dominate creditors' meetings.

Different portraits of liquidation can also be placed in opposition to each other. On the one hand, it can be seen as a process in which professionals act in a detached way so as to ensure that creditors are dealt with fairly and the public interest is served by monitoring the behaviour of directors *ex post facto*. On the other, liquidation can be seen in strictly private interest terms, with IPs, creditors, directors and others all pursuing their own interests in a highly focused manner.

Alternative visions of liquidation can also be generated by moving one's disciplinary viewpoint away from law. Economists would be liable to espouse a private interest approach but sociologists and anthropologists, for instance, would emphasise the social and cultural contexts within which liquidation takes place and the extent to which liquidation is driven by group-based ideas, understandings and traditions. Psychologists might be expected to place more emphasis on the attitude of the individual and might focus on the approaches that individual IPs tend to adopt because of their background and training.

What, though, do these different ways of seeing liquidation tell us about issues of design, reform and evaluation? A key message is that achieving better performance on the efficiency, expertise, accountability and fairness fronts will not come simply through changes in the legal rules. The world is not that rule-centred and other approaches have to be embraced.[349] Training, for example, is a strategy with considerable potential. The liquidation process may be improved through refinements in the training of IPs (in, for example, consultative techniques) or in directorial training (to cover ongoing company contexts and insolvency or near insolvency situations and rescue processes, as well as information-gathering techniques).[350] Institutional roles, moreover, might be reconceived so that, for instance,

---

[348] See ch. 3 above and ch. 15 below.

[349] On the extent to which behaviour is rule-governed see, for example, Mary Douglas' discussion of 'grid' and 'group' relations in M. Douglas, *In the Active Voice* (Routledge, London, 1982).

[350] See V. Finch, 'Company Directors: Who Cares About Skill and Care?' (1992) 55 MLR 179.

the part played by the courts in scrutinising processes is reformulated. One way in which this could be done is to replace resort to court with other processes, such as the use of administrative powers.[351] Liquidators, on this model, could be empowered to adopt a designated administrative power to 'call in' property that has been transferred out of the estate in a suspect manner. Such a regime could make resort to court[352] a secondary matter rather than a primary process in relating to the relevant set of issues.[353]

Finally, a fresh look might be taken at the overall objectives of the liquidation process – a review that might bear in mind the balance between ends such as efficiency and fairness. Consistency between this area of insolvency law and others is a matter to be adverted to here. It would be muddled thinking to give efficiency primacy of place in relation to one insolvency process but (without reason) to give greater emphasis to, say, fairness or accountability in another. There may, of course, be reasons for differences of emphasis but coherence and clarity demand that we should be clear about these. One such reason may be that liquidation, unlike other insolvency processes, can be seen in non-rescue terms and as relating to a narrower set of interests than, say, administration. To conclude, there is, as noted, much to be done to refine insolvency law as it affects liquidation but insolvency law and processes must be seen in the round and we should be aware of the improvements that can be gained by looking beyond the narrowly legal and towards adjustments in cultures, traditions, incentives, expectations, institutions, training and roles.

---

[351] On mediation and alternative dispute resolution see M. Humphries, E. Pavlopoulos and P. Winterborne, 'Insolvency, Mediation and ADR' (1999) *Insolvency Bulletin* 7.

[352] See Insolvency Act 1986 s. 208 (misconduct in the course of winding up), s. 234 (getting in the company's property), s. 235 (duty to co-operate with the office holder), s. 236 (inquiry into company's dealings, etc.).

[353] It should be remembered, as noted above (pp. 569–70), that human rights issues may arise. Under the Human Rights Act 1998 and Article 6 of the Convention there is a right to an independent and impartial tribunal. If an office holder determines the rights of a person, there may be a lack of independence where the office holder is an administrative receiver: see generally Simmons and Smith, 'Human Rights Act 1998'; Trower, 'Human Rights'.

The *pari passu* principle

The *pari passu* principle is often said to constitute a fundamental rule of corporate insolvency law.[1] It holds that, in a winding up, unsecured creditors shall share rateably in those assets of the insolvent company that are available for residual distribution. In what might be called the 'strong' version of *pari passu*, 'rateably' means that unsecured creditors, as a whole, are paid *pro rata* to the extent of their pre-insolvency claims. This contrasts with the 'weak' version of *pari passu* in which such creditors share rateably within the particular ranking that they are given on insolvency by the law – a system of ranking that draws distinctions between different classes of unsecured creditors (e.g. preferred employees and ordinary unsecured creditors).[2]

This chapter and the one following consider whether the *pari passu* principle (hereafter discussed and referred to in its strong version unless otherwise stated) operates in an efficient and fair manner and whether there is a case for approaching post-insolvency distribution in a different way. Issues of accountability and expertise will not be addressed since

---

[1] See R. Goode, *Principles of Corporate Insolvency Law* (3rd edn, Sweet & Maxwell, London, 2005) p. 175; D. Milman, 'Priority Rights on Corporate Insolvency' in A. Clarke (ed.), *Current Issues in Insolvency Law* (Stevens & Sons, London, 1991) p. 51; *Report of the Review Committee on Insolvency Law and Practice* (Cmnd 8558, 1982) ('Cork Report') para. 1220. The *pari passu* principle is now contained in the Insolvency Act 1986 s. 107 (voluntary winding up) and the Insolvency Rules 1986 r. 4.181(1) (compulsory winding up). For argument that *pari passu* should not be treated as a fundamental rule see R. Mokal, 'Priority as Pathology: The *Pari Passu* Myth' [2001] CLJ 581.

[2] The strong and weak senses of *pari passu* referred to here correspond to what have been called the 'orthodox' and the 'multi-layered' understandings of the term: see L. C. Ho, 'Goode's Swan Song to Corporate Insolvency Law' (2006) 17 EBLR 1727 – suggesting that in the *orthodox* understanding all creditors of a particular pre-insolvency form (unsecured creditors as a group) share equally. In the *multi-layered* understanding, as encountered in the UNCITRAL *Legislative Guide on Insolvency Law* (United Nations, 2005), creditors that are similarly ranked by insolvency law share equally within their given rank. See R. Mokal, *Corporate Insolvency Law: Theory and Application* (Oxford University Press, Oxford, 2005). See also ch. 15 below.

pari passu is a substantive rule governing the distribution of goods and little is to be gained by asking whether a principle is, in itself, accountable or expert. Whether insolvency principles are administered accountably and expertly are matters dealt with in other chapters.

As noted in chapter 13, creditors are free, prior to winding up, to pursue whatever enforcement measures are open to them: for example, repossession of goods or judgment execution. Indeed, the race goes to the swiftest. Liquidation puts an end to the race as the liquidator is responsible for the orderly realisation of assets for the benefit of all unsecured creditors and for distributing the net proceeds *pari passu*.[3] The *pari passu* principle, however, can only apply to unencumbered assets of the insolvent company that are available for distribution. If a company holds property as a bailee or trustee, that property is not part of the common pool for distribution. Similarly, goods possessed by the company under a contract of sale that reserves title to the seller until completion of payment do not form part of the pool. Where, moreover, the company has given security rights over property, this property is available for distribution only to the extent that its value exceeds the sum of the secured indebtedness.[4]

Corporate insolvency law is faced here with two important challenges: how to stipulate which assets will be available for distribution and whether exceptions should be made to the *pari passu* rule when distributing those available assets. This chapter focuses on the latter issue and chapter 15 considers the construction of the insolvent company's estate for distribution.

At this point, the discussion of insolvency law rationales that was contained in chapter 2 should be recalled. Different visions of corporate insolvency law will produce different approaches to the distribution and

---

[3] Steps taken to protect the residual estate from leakage can thus be seen as underpinning the *pari passu* distribution of that estate – the view taken in *Re Tain Construction* [2003] 1 WLR 2791, [2004] BCC 11, a judicial view described as 'highly unfortunate and misguided', an 'irredeemable mistake' and a 'total misunderstanding' by Look Chan Ho ('*Pari Passu* Distribution and Post-petition Disposition: A Rationalisation of *Re Tain Construction*' (21 November 2005, SSRN)), who prefers to see preservation of the estate as sustaining the order of priority of distribution. In defence of the court it can be argued that, whatever exceptions to *pari passu* are allowed (e.g. preferential status), to allow degradation of the residual estate would be to allow bypassing of the *pari passu* mode of distribution applicable to that estate.

[4] On the limits to *pari passu* see F. Oditah, 'Assets and the Treatment of Claims in Insolvency' (1992) 108 LQR 459 at 468–76; Mokal, 'Priority as Pathology', pp. 585–90; pp. 667–9 below.

construction of the insolvency estate. If corporate insolvency law is seen as centrally concerned to maximise the assets available for distribution to creditors,[5] creditors' rights in a liquidation will be treated as governed by prior non-insolvency entitlements. What has been bargained for in advance will dictate priorities in a subsequent liquidation. If, on the other hand, insolvency law is seen as having a redistributional role – one that allows prior private bargains to be adjusted in the public interest or in pursuit of democratically established policies – creditors' rights in a liquidation will be influenced by a range of factors other than rights established outside insolvency and departures from the strong version of *pari passu* will be more readily contemplated.[6]

As indicated in chapter 2, the approach taken in this book rejects the narrow 'creditor wealth maximising' vision of corporate insolvency law and sees insolvency law as properly concerned with redistributional and public interest aspects as well as with respect for private bargains and property. This implies, first, that exceptions to *pari passu* may be entertained on their public interest merits and, second, that in constructing the estate of the insolvent company that is available for distribution, it may be legitimate to restrict the extent to which private bargaining will be allowed to circumvent the principles of collectivity and *pari passu* distribution.

Before considering whether certain exceptions to *pari passu* can be justified on efficiency or on fairness grounds, the rationale for *pari passu* should be noted. In terms of efficiency, the case for *pari passu* is that within a mandatory, collective regime it conduces to an orderly means of dealing with unsecured creditor claims.

Legal costs and delays are said to be kept low by a simple *pari passu* rule because, in the absence of any legislative direction to differentiate

---

[5] See T. H. Jackson, *The Logic and Limits of Bankruptcy Law* (Harvard University Press, Cambridge, Mass., 1986); D. G. Baird and T. Jackson, 'Corporate Reorganisations and the Treatment of Diverse Ownership Interests: A Comment on Adequate Protection of Secured Creditors in Bankruptcy' (1984) 51 U Chic. L Rev. 97; D. G. Baird, 'Loss Distribution, Forum Shopping and Bankruptcy: A Reply to Warren' (1987) 54 U Chic. L Rev. 815. Arguably the *pari passu* principle, *stricto sensu*, with collectivity mimics the notional 'creditors' bargain' posited by Jackson. See also the discussion in S. S. Cantlie, 'Preferred Priority in Bankruptcy' in J. Ziegel (ed.), *Current Developments in International and Comparative Corporate Insolvency Law* (Clarendon Press, Oxford, 1994).

[6] See, for example, E. Warren, 'Bankruptcy Policy' (1987) 54 U Chic. L Rev. 775; Warren, 'Bankruptcy Policymaking in an Imperfect World' (1993) 92 Mich. L Rev. 336.

between unsecured creditor claims, it avoids the need for courts to make difficult choices, as would be involved were they to adopt other possible principles: for example, distribution according to need or inability to sustain losses.[7] In terms of the efficiency of the 'creditors' bargain' and 'creditor wealth maximisation' theories, compulsory, collective proceedings are held out as reducing strategic costs and increasing the aggregate pool of assets.[8] The collectivity of dealings with unsecured creditors as a class is enhanced by the *pari passu* principle which is efficient in so far as it avoids the costs of dealing with claims on their individual merits.[9]

Fairness in the procedural and substantive senses may also be said to be protected by the *pari passu* principle in that it prevents an intra-class race to enforce claims that is destined to be won by the strongest and swiftest and it also involves equality of treatment between unsecured creditors.[10] Where, of course, the law creates exceptions to *pari passu*, questions arise regarding the fairness of those exceptional treatments.

Exceptions to *pari passu*

Liquidation expenses and post-liquidation creditors

Liquidation expenses and the claims of post-liquidation creditors will, for convenience, be dealt with here but, more strictly speaking, they can be said to fall outside the *pari passu* rule rather than constitute true exceptions. This is because the strong version of *pari passu* adverts to the

---

[7] See Milman, 'Priority Rights', p. 59.

[8] See Jackson, *Logic and Limits of Bankruptcy Law*, ch. 1; see also ch. 2 above.

[9] Mokal argues ('Priority as Pathology', p. 593) that it is collectivity not *pari passu* that avoids value-destroying races to collect; that *pari passu* is not necessary for efficiency. Value, however, is lost by processes that give rise to the high costs of dealing with claims individually. *Pari passu* reduces such costs within the class of unsecured creditors and accordingly may be justified on efficiency (as well as fairness) grounds. There is, in short, more to securing efficiency than stopping the race to collect and having creditors form an orderly queue. The claims of parties in the queue have to be dealt with efficiently. It can be conceded, however, that the claims of unsecured creditors could be dealt with collectively and at low cost without reference to *pari passu*, for example by paying debts according to date of loan. On the acceptability of alternatives to *pari passu* see ch. 15 below.

[10] On justice in insolvency see J. Finnis, *Natural Law and Natural Rights* (Clarendon Press, Oxford, 1980) p. 190; see also ch. 15 below.

pre-liquidation position of unsecured creditors and so has no application to unsecured creditors whose claims arise post-liquidation.[11] Liquidation expenses are paid out of the company's assets ahead of all other claims on the estate and are settled in full before even preferential debts.[12] In order to effect the most beneficial winding up of a company the liquidator may have to sustain a period of continued trading for a given time. This may benefit all creditors. During this period, funds may be required in order to keep employees in post and to achieve continuity in the supply of materials. If creditors were asked to supply funds during this post-liquidation period they would be unlikely to oblige if the debts involved were to enjoy no priority over those of pre-liquidation creditors. Such super-priority can, however, be achieved by treating the liquidator's transactions with such creditors as expenses of the liquidation so that post-liquidation creditors do not have to prove for a dividend in competition with other creditors.[13] Expenses of the liquidation (including post-liquidation creditors' claims) are thus paid first, followed by the claims of preferential creditors,[14] and only the remaining pool of assets[15] becomes available for distribution to the general body of unsecured creditors. While it is clear that new transactions by the liquidator constitute post-liquidation claims, difficulties may arise in relation to obligations under existing contracts or leases. The relevant test is whether the liquidator

[11] See Ho, 'Goode's Swan Song'; *Re HIH Casualty and General Insurance* [2005] EWHC 2125 (Ch) at para. 40.

[12] Secured creditors will be entitled to be paid out of the proceeds of their security ahead of all other claims, but if the security is by way of a floating charge, liquidation expenses and debts that are preferential debts must be paid first. See Insolvency Act 1986 ss. 115, 107; Companies Act 2006 s. 1282 (but note s. 1282(3)); Insolvency Rules 1986 r. 4.180(1). See Insolvency Act 1986 ss. 115, 156, 175(2)(a); Insolvency Rules 1986 r. 4.218 regarding liquidators' costs and expenses. For further discussion of liquidation expenses see *Re Leyland DAF, Buchler v. Talbot* [2004] 2 AC 298, *Re Toshoku Finance (UK) plc* [2002] 1 WLR 671, *Re M. C. Bacon Ltd (No. 2)* [1991] Ch 127, *Re Floor Fourteen Ltd, Lewis v. IRC* [2001] 3 All ER 499, Enterprise Act 2002 s. 253 and IR r. 4.218(1)(a); and ch. 13 above.

[13] Rule 12.2 of the Insolvency Rules 1986 lists items to be regarded as expenses of the winding up and r. 4.218, as amended, gives the order of priority for payment of expenses of the winding up – subject, however, to the courts' powers under the Insolvency Act 1986 s. 156. On paying corporation tax (on interest receivable after the start of a winding up) as a necessary disbursement and an expense of the winding up see *Re Toshoku Finance (UK) plc* [2002] 1 WLR 671, [2002] BCC 110 (HL); H. Lyons and M. Birch, 'Insolvency Expenses' (2005) 18 *Insolvency Intelligence* 150; D. Milman, 'Post Liquidation Tax as a Winding Up Expense' [2000] Ins. Law. 169.

[14] See Insolvency Act 1986 s. 175(2)(a) and (b).

[15] Which will have been depleted, of course, by payment to any floating charge holders.

had adopted the transaction and taken it over for the purposes of the winding up.[16]

Before the Insolvency Act 1986, this treatment of post-liquidation debts placed utility companies in a strong position relative to other trade suppliers. The large providers of gas, electricity, water and telecommunications services could use their dominant market positions to compel the payment of debts on accounts incurred before the commencement of a winding up. They would do this by threatening to cut off a supply unless arrears were paid in full or payment was personally guaranteed by the liquidator or receiver.[17] Where the supply was essential to preserve the company's assets, payment was difficult to avoid and the effect was to pay the utility debt in priority even to the statutory preferential creditors.[18] Following strong criticism of this process in the Cork Report,[19] section 233 (as amended) of the Insolvency Act 1986 prohibited resort to this practice. The supplier may now require the office holder to undertake personal responsibility for payment of any new supply but may not make the availability of a new supply conditional on receiving payment or security for the old supply.

Preferential debts

The Cork Committee noted that *pari passu* distribution of uncharged assets was in practice seldom, if ever, attained because, in the overwhelming majority of cases, the existence of preferential debts frustrated such distribution.[20] Preferential debts are unsecured debts which, by force of statute, fall to be paid in a winding up in priority to all other unsecured debts (and to claims for principal and interest secured by a

---

[16] See *ABC Coupler and Engineering Co. Ltd (No. 3)* [1970] 1 All ER 656; *Re Downer Enterprises Ltd* [1974] 2 All ER 1074; *Re Oak Pits Colliery Co.* (1882) 21 Ch D 322; *Re National Arms and Ammunition Co.* (1885) 28 Ch D 474; and *Re Atlantic Computer Systems plc* [1992] Ch 505 (for a review of the earlier authorities). More or less automatically included now (subject to the discretion of the court) are continuing rent or hire purchase charges in respect of land or goods in the possession of the company which the liquidator continues to use for the purposes of the liquidation: see *Boyle and Birds' Company Law* (6th edn, Jordans, Bristol, 2007) pp. 938–9.

[17] On the powerful positions of suppliers of strategic raw materials see *Leyland DAF Ltd* v. *Automotive Products plc* [1993] BCC 389.

[18] The legality of this practice was upheld in *Wellworth Cash & Carry (North Shields Ltd)* v. *North Eastern Electricity Board* [1986] 2 BCC 99, 265.

[19] Cork Report, ch. 33, esp. para. 1462.

[20] Ibid., p. 317. Preferential debts were introduced in the Preferential Payments in Bankruptcy Act 1897.

floating charge)[21] but which abate rateably as amongst themselves. Preferential debts are listed in Schedule 6 of the Insolvency Act 1986[22] and, *before* the enactment of the Enterprise Act 2002, included: inland revenue debts;[23] certain Customs and Excise debts;[24] social security contributions for the twelve months prior to the relevant date;[25] contributions to occupational pension schemes;[26] certain employee benefits;[27] and levies on coal and steel production.[28] Assessed taxes such as income tax and corporation tax were not given preferential status in Schedule 6 of the Insolvency Act 1986 since the government yielded to Cork's arguments that there was no case for priority in such instances.[29]

---

[21] Preferential creditors rank in priority not only above unsecured creditors, but also above debenture holders with assets covered by floating, not fixed, charges: see Insolvency Act 1986 s. 175(2)(b). See also Insolvency Act 1986 s. 251 which defines 'floating charge' so as to include a charge, which, though originally floating, has since become fixed. Thus, any charge which was originally a floating charge but has become a fixed charge (e.g. by crystallisation or by a notice of conversion) before the 'relevant date' defined by s. 387 will be subordinated to the preferential debts under s. 175(2)(b), thus depriving such decisions as *Re Woodroffes Ltd* [1986] Ch 366, *Re Brightlife Ltd* [1987] Ch 200 and *Re Griffin Hotel Co. Ltd* [1941] Ch 129 of force. On priority of preferential debts over charged assets see *HM Commissioners for Revenue & Customs* v. *Royal Bank of Scotland plc* [2008] BCC 135; *Re Oval 1742 Ltd (in liquidation): Customs and Excise Commissioners* v. *Royal Bank of Scotland* [2007] BCC 567 (discussing CA 1985 s. 196 (now CA 2006 s. 754) and the relationship with IA 1986 s. 40).

[22] See also Insolvency Act 1986 ss. 386, 387; IA 1986 s. 175 (winding up), s. 40 (receivership: see *Re H & K Medway Ltd* [1997] BCC 853).

[23] PAYE income tax deductions due from payments made in the twelve months prior to the relevant date (Sch. 6 paras. 1 and 2 – the deductions relate to s. 203 of the Income and Corporation Taxes Act 1988): see generally Keay and Walton, *Insolvency Law*, pp. 466–71. The decision in *Re Toshoku Finance (UK) plc* [2002] BCC 110 (HL), as noted above, makes it clear that corporation tax liabilities arising after the start of a winding up are properly to be treated as expenses of the winding up and are therefore to be paid in advance of preferential debts: see Milman, 'Post Liquidation Tax'.

[24] Unpaid VAT for six months prior to the relevant date and unpaid car tax; certain betting and gaming duties as well as lottery duty that became due in the twelve months prior to the relevant date (Sch. 6, paras. 4, 5 and 5B); insurance premium tax, landfill tax, beer duty and air passenger duty referable to the six months prior to the relevant date (Sch. 6, paras. 3A, 3B, 5A, 5C).

[25] Sch. 6, paras. 6 and 7.   [26] Sch. 6, para. 8.

[27] Remuneration for up to four months prior to the relevant date subject to the stipulated maximum sum (Sch. 6, para. 9); accrued holiday pay (Sch. 6, para. 10); and any sum loaned and used for the specific purpose of paying employees' remuneration (Sch. 6, para. 11).

[28] Sch. 6, para. 15A.

[29] See Cork Report, paras. 1409–50. Different considerations were said, however, to apply to taxes such as PAYE or national insurance, VAT and car tax since the Crown's claim in such cases was for money collected by the debtor from other parties and the debtor could properly be viewed as a tax collector rather than a tax payer. Unless such debts were

The coming into effect of section 251 of the Enterprise Act 2002, however, abolished the Crown's status as preferential creditor.[30] As a result, the preferential debts remaining are: four months of unpaid employee wages (up to a prescribed maximum limit per employee of £800) and accrued holiday entitlements;[31] unpaid contributions to state and occupational pension schemes;[32] and unpaid levies on coal and steel production.[33] Abolition of the Crown preference created a potential

given priority the moneys collected would swell the insolvent's estate to the benefit of private creditors rather than the state. For the case against Crown priority see A. Keay and P. Walton, 'The Preferential Debts' Regime in Liquidation Law: In the Public Interest?' [1999] 3 CfiLR 84; DTI/Insolvency Service White Paper, *Productivity and Enterprise: Insolvency – A Second Chance* (Cm 5234, 2001) ('White Paper, 2001') para. 2.19.

[30] On the case for directing the benefits of abolishing the Crown preference towards unsecured creditors see Insolvency Service, *A Review of Company Rescue and Business Reconstruction Mechanisms, Report by the Review Group* (DTI, 2000) ('IS 2000') p. 26. Prior to the Enterprise Act 2002 reform the Crown recovered some £60–90 million of preferential debt in insolvencies each year: see Insolvency Service, *A Review of Company Rescue and Business Reconstruction Mechanisms, Interim Report* (DTI, September 1999) ('IS 1999') para. 8(b). Other countries (e.g. Germany, Austria, Canada and Australia) were ahead of the UK in either abolishing or severely restricting revenue authorities' priority.

[31] Insolvency Act 1986 s. 386, Category 5, Sch. 6. Employees have defined preferential status but can also draw on the National Insurance Fund: for discussion of employee protections see pp. 608–9, 612–14 and ch. 17 below. The Crown's right of subrogation to employees' preferential debts paid from the National Insurance Fund remains: Employment Rights Act 1996 s. 18; Pension Schemes Act 1993 s. 127(3).

[32] See D. Pollard and I. Carruthers, 'Pensions as a Preferential Debt' (2004) 17 *Insolvency Intelligence* 65; and further ch. 17 below.

[33] In the case of insolvencies of insurance companies, the EU Insurers' Reorganisation and Winding-Up Directive was transposed into UK law by the Insurers (Reorganisation and Winding Up) Regulations 2004 (SI 2004/353, effective 18 February 2004). Regulation 21 applies in the case of a winding up of a long-term insurer, a general insurer or a composite insurer and provides that the debts of the insurer must be paid in the following order of priority: preferential debts; insurance debts; then all other debts. ('Insurance debt' here means a debt to which a UK insurer is, or may become, liable, pursuant to a contract of insurance, to a policy holder or to any person who has a direct right of action against that insurer, and includes any premium paid in connection with a contract of insurance (whether or not that contract was concluded) which the insurer is liable to refund.) Preferential debts are to rank equally among themselves and must be paid in full, unless the assets are insufficient to meet them, in which case they abate in equal proportions. Insurance debts are to rank equally among themselves and must be paid in full, unless the assets available after the payment of preferential debts are insufficient to meet them, in which case they abate in equal proportions. So far as the assets of the insurer available for the payment of unsecured creditors are insufficient to meet the preferential debts, those debts (and only those debts) have priority over the claims of holders of debentures secured by, or holders of, any floating charge created by the insurer, and must be paid accordingly out of any property comprised in or subject to

windfall for the holders of floating charges and, to adjust for this, the Enterprise Act section 252 inserted a new section 176A into the 1986 Act to ring-fence, for the benefit of unsecured creditors, a prescribed part of the company's net property that, otherwise, would be available to satisfy the claims of holders of debentures secured by floating charges. The quantum of the prescribed part is thus intended to compensate broadly for the benefit to floating charge holders of no longer being subordinated to Crown claims for unpaid taxes[34] and holders of floating charges are not entitled to participate with unsecured creditors in the prescribed part fund as regards any unsecured shortfalls in their security positions except in so far as the fund exceeds the amount needed to satisfy 'unsecured debts'.[35] According to Patten J in *Re Airbase (UK) Ltd*,[36] sense could only be made of section 176A(2)(b) if 'unsecured debts' excluded the unsecured balance of the secured creditor's claim and the *pari passu* rule was 'modified' by the provision to 'differentiate between unsecured creditors with no form of security and the unsecured claims of secured creditors'.

Can preferential debts be justified in economic efficiency terms?[37] A general argument relating to unsecured creditors asserts that if parties constitute involuntary, non-adjusting creditors, their debtors will not bear the full costs of defaulting and so will not take optimal care to avoid default. The debtor will thus take excessive risks with, say, the credit offered by employees and there will be an inefficient allocation of resources in society. Employees who are paid in arrears have little option but to provide credit to their employing company for the period between wage payments.[38]

---

that charge. Section 176A of the Insolvency Act 1986 has effect with regard to an insurer so that insurance debts must be paid out of the prescribed part in priority to all other unsecured debts.

[34] The relevant percentages/quantum to be paid is fixed by the Insolvency Act 1986 (Prescribed Part) Order 2003 (SI 2003/2097): see further ch. 3 above, pp. 108–10.

[35] IA 1986 s. 176A(2)(b). See also *Re Permacell Finesse Ltd (in liquidation)* [2008] BCC 208, discussed in D. Offord, 'Case Digest' (2008) 21 *Insolvency Intelligence* 30; *Re Airbase (UK) Ltd, Thorniley* v. *Revenue and Customs Commissioner* [2008] BCC 213, discussed in A. Walters, 'Statutory Redistribution of Floating Charge Assets: Victory (Again) to Revenue and Customs' (2008) 29 Co. Law. 129.

[36] *Re Airbase (UK) Ltd, Thorniley* v. *Revenue and Customs Commissioner* [2008] BCC 213. Similarly the holder of a fixed charge facing a shortfall would not be able to participate in the prescribed part: see Walters, 'Statutory Redistribution of Floating Charge Assets'.

[37] See generally Cantlie, 'Preferred Priority in Bankruptcy'; V. Finch, 'Is Pari Passu Passé?' [2000] Ins. Law. 194, 206.

[38] See Cantlie, 'Preferred Priority in Bankruptcy', pp. 422–3.

As for the ability to adjust credit terms, this is crucially important. If employees could adjust the terms on which they provide credit so as to take account of default risks, the economic inefficiencies noted would not arise (the risk-related component of the credit arrangement would induce the appropriate level of credit provision and care taken). Employees are ill-positioned to adjust their credit rates to take account of default risks.[39] When they negotiate employment contracts with a firm there will be little discussion of insolvency risks, the employee is liable to lack the information or expertise necessary to calculate the extent of such risks and, even if employees could make the appropriate calculations, they might well be unable to negotiate wages that incorporate a risk element because they face severe competition in the market for jobs and because others in that market may be unable or disinclined to hold out for such risk elements in their wages. Arguments about the general inefficiencies of unsecured credit do not, however, explain why employees should be more sympathetically treated than other ordinary (e.g. trade) creditors. The latter, as was noted in chapter 3, may also be poorly placed to adjust their terms to cope with default risks.

All unsecured creditors now enjoy the protection offered by the prescribed part and, as argued in chapter 3, this would to some extent limit these inefficiencies in credit supply that stem from non-adjustment of rates. In deciding whether, over and above this, it is desirable in economic efficiency terms to give employees protection beyond that enjoyed by trade creditors, it is necessary to consider the possible basis for favouring some non-adjusting creditors rather than others.

A key factor here concerns the costs of risk bearing. Where given levels of risk are allocated in a manner that gives rise to inefficiency because the decision-maker relieved of risk is liable to behave with sub-optimal care, it is relevant to consider variations in the costs of bearing undue risks. It may, in turn, be desirable to give most protection to those who will incur the greatest costs in bearing the risks at issue.[40]

The ability to spread risks increases a party's capacity to withstand the consequences of default.[41] Trade creditors will have a certain capacity to spread risks but small suppliers may be very hard hit by defaults. The costs of default in their cases may be high, with employees losing jobs or

---

[39] See generally B. Gleig, 'Unpaid Wages in Bankruptcy' (1987) 21 UBC L Rev. 61–83. On employees, see C. Villiers, 'Employees as Creditors: A Challenge for Justice in Insolvency Law' (1999) 20 Co. Law. 222; ch. 17 below.
[40] See Cantlie, 'Preferred Priority in Bankruptcy', p. 430.   [41] Ibid., pp. 433–44.

even businesses folding. Employees, as noted, are seldom able to spread default risks and so will suffer considerable hardship: for example, where lack of moneys owed prevents them from generating or gaining further employment. Not only are employees poor self-insurers against debtor default (their lack of diversification prevents effective self-insuring) but they will also be unlikely to find insurance markets in which they can contract to spread risks.[42] What makes shifting risks to employees especially undesirable is that the costs of such a risk shift are liable to be higher than when insolvency risks are placed elsewhere. On this reasoning, tort creditors do not merit especially high levels of protection in insolvency because they are less likely than employees to be highly vulnerable to instances of default and, accordingly, they will not usually be extremely high-cost risk bearers. They will routinely have other sources of income, funds and products and risks will be spread by such diversification.

It has been proposed that other creditors (including secured creditors) should be deferred to tort claimants in insolvency[43] but a further consideration here is the special effect that deferment to tort creditors may have on major lenders. Banks, for instance, might be deterred from advancing funds on the basis of secured loans where they face risks of giving way to potentially huge tort claims. As argued in chapter 3,[44] other ways of protecting involuntary tort creditors – such as compulsory tort liability insurance for companies – might prove more consistent with efficient corporate financing.

The issue of vulnerability to risks may also militate against placing pre-paying consumer creditors in a better position than ordinary unsecured creditors. Ogus and Rowley have contended[45] that there are material reasons for giving consumer pre-payers special protection – reasons based on economic efficiency. Their argument, in brief, is that few problems arise in the general provision of credit when there is voluntary choosing of investments, full information and equal bargaining power. In so far as such conditions are lacking in a trading relationship there may be a case for protecting the ill-placed party and, in so far

---

[42] Ibid., p. 437.

[43] For discussion see D. Leebron, 'Limited Liability, Tort Victims and Creditors' (1991) 91 Colum. L Rev. 1565 at 1643–50; H. Hansman and R. Krackman, 'Towards Unlimited Shareholder Liability for Corporate Torts' (1991) 100 Yale LJ 1879; V. Finch, 'Security, Insolvency and Risk: Who Pays the Price?' (1999) 62 MLR 633 at 657.

[44] See pp. 110–12 above.

[45] A. Ogus and C. Rowley, *Prepayments and Insolvency* (OFT Occasional Paper, 1984).

as one group of creditors is liable to be more poorly placed than another, a relatively superior level of protection is appropriate. Consumer pre-payers, Ogus and Rowley state, may be eligible for such superior protection because they tend to be 'distanced from the company in a way that the trade creditor typically is not and may well regard the cost of negotiating over the risk of insolvency as excessive in relation to the amount at stake'.[46]

Consumer pre-payers may also be geographically dispersed (for example, in mail order contracting) which weakens their position, and they will rarely have easy access to such information on the trader as will allow them to assess insolvency risks. (The Office of Fair Trading has reported that it 'does not regard it as feasible' that consumers be expected to check on the financial standing of traders.)[47] Finally, many consumer creditors may fail to see themselves as creditors of the company at all, especially where they are led by the trading company to believe that the period of prepayment is short.

Whether consumer creditors are placed in positions materially worse than those occupied by small trade creditors is, however, open to argument. For its part, the Cork Committee decided against special treatment for consumers, saying of consumer and trade creditors: 'There is no essential difference. Each gives credit and if the credit is misplaced, each should bear the loss rateably.'[48] What is more strongly arguable is that consumer creditors tend to be lower-cost risk bearers than employees because their risks are more widely spread (across products). This argument suggests that if preferential treatment should be given, employees, not consumer creditors, should be favoured.[49]

A second factor that may influence the case for protecting an unsecured creditor is his or her ability to prevent default and the taking of inefficiently low levels of care. If a party is able to intervene and forestall disaster, we may, on fairness grounds, be less inclined to protect them from default risks by giving them priority than we would in the case of someone who has no power to intervene.[50] On this front, trade creditors

---

[46] Ibid., p. 12.   [47] Ibid., para. 5.11.   [48] Cork Report, para. 1052.

[49] In the survey reported by A. Keay and P. Walton, 'Preferential Debts: An Empirical Study' [1999] Ins. Law. 112, 60 per cent of IP respondents said that they would not introduce a new preference category for prepayment consumer creditors.

[50] See Keay and Walton, 'Preferential Debts Regime in Liquidation Law', p. 96; *Report of the Study Committee on Bankruptcy and Insolvency Legislation* (Canada, 1970), para. 3.2.076–7; M. Shanker, 'The Worthier Creditors (and a Cheer for the King)' (1975–6) 1 Canadian Bus. LJ 341.

in a regular supply relationship with a debtor may occasionally be able to impose conditions on supply and may adjust terms or decline to supply further items. Small suppliers to a large number of customers are, however, unlikely to be in this position and, in the case of all trade creditors, market conditions and competitive pressures may rule out the institution of preventative measures. Employees may decline to supply further labour if worried about their employer's solvency but, in a market where alternative employment is unavailable, this may be difficult. If the employee occupies a managerial position in the employing company there may, however, be opportunities to influence decision-making so as to limit default dangers, but such opportunities and influence may be very limited in many cases. Tort creditors, in contrast, will rarely, if ever, be able to take steps to influence default rates, or levels of care, and consumer creditors will occupy a similar position. The above points indicate that in terms of ability to prevent default, there is no particularly strong case for sustaining exceptions to the *pari passu* principle.

Do considerations of fairness suggest that certain non-adjusting creditors should be preferred to others in insolvency? Here we come to the issue that for Cork was central:

> Since the existence of any preferential debts militates against the principle of *pari passu* distribution and operates to the detriment of ordinary unsecured creditors, we have adopted the approach that no debt should be accorded priority unless this can be justified by reference to principles of fairness and equity which would be likely to command general public acceptance.[51]

Thus it might be argued that if creditors cannot tailor their credit terms it is wrong to burden those creditors with risks that they are in no position to recognise, calculate, adjust terms to, or protect themselves against.[52] This contention, however, found little resonance with consultees of the Insolvency Service Review Groups 1999–2000. Many unsecured creditors cannot adjust and the rationale offers no justification for giving priority to one category of unsecured creditors over another. Fairness considerations point in the direction of general protections for

---

[51] Cork Report, para. 1398. It is arguable that the system of preferential debts causes considerable discontent in the ranks of unsecured creditors. A survey reported by Keay and Walton, 'Preferential Debts: An Empirical Study', revealed that 68 per cent of respondent IPs thought that there was unsecured creditor discontent.

[52] Cantlie, 'Preferred Priority in Bankruptcy', p. 419. See IS 1999, p. 15.

unsecured creditors – as offered by the prescribed part provisions – but not towards more particular safeguards.

Does fairness demand priority for employee creditors?[53] Most employees are likely to be poorly placed to assess the financial standing of their employers, or to insist on employment terms that protect them against insolvency risks. Cork, however, rejected the case for employee creditor priority on the grounds that it would give 'an excessive degree of indemnity to higher paid employees, including directors and senior management, at the expense of ordinary creditors who in many cases may be more deserving of sympathy'.[54] Employees are protected by the Employment Protection Acts,[55] said Cork, and there was no need for overlapping insolvency law protections. At present the Employment Rights Act 1996 (ERA) offers employees of an insolvent company more extensive protection than the Insolvency Act 1986. The 1986 Act gives preferential priority to unpaid wages and accrued holiday pay owed and provides for payment by the Secretary of State for up to eight weeks of pay arrears during the statutory minimum period,[56] up to six weeks' holiday pay and a basic award for unfair dismissal.[57] The Secretary of State makes such payments out of the National Insurance Fund and then stands in the shoes of the employee in attempting to recover such funds from the liquidator. Less than a quarter of the money paid out of the ERA scheme can be claimed by the Crown as preferential.[58]

---

[53] See Cantlie, 'Preferred Priority in Bankruptcy'; Keay and Walton, 'Preferential Debts Regime in Liquidation Law'; Gleig, 'Unpaid Wages in Bankruptcy'; C. Symes, 'The Protection of Wages When Insolvency Strikes' (1997) 5 Ins. LJ 196; D. Zalman, 'The Unpaid Employee as Creditor' (1980) 6 Dalhouse LJ 148; Villiers, 'Employees as Creditors'.

[54] Cork Report, para. 1430.

[55] See now the Employment Rights Act 1996 (ERA 1996). On employees more generally see ch. 17 below.

[56] I.e. up to eight weeks at up to £330 per week: ERA 1996 s. 186(1)(a); Employment Rights (Increase of Limits) Order 2007 (SI 2007/3570), from 1 February 2008.

[57] ERA 1996 ss. 182, 186, 167. Up to six weeks' holiday pay with a limit of £330 per week, accrued during the twelve months before insolvency. The maximum compensatory award for unfair dismissal is £63,000 (as at 1 February 2008). The NIF also guarantees payments of statutory notice pay (up to a maximum of £330 per week); unpaid contributions to an occupational or personal pension scheme; the basic award for unfair dismissal; up to eight weeks at a maximum of £330 per week of a protective award; and statutory redundancy pay.

[58] See Keay and Walton, 'Preferential Debts Regime in Liquidation Law', p. 100, who note that on 31 March 1996 £762 million was owed by insolvent employers to the Fund, of which only £177 million (23 per cent) ranked as preferential. The Crown's right of subrogation to employees' preferential debts paid from the National Insurance Fund remains (after the changes of the Enterprise Act 2002): Employment Rights Act 1996 s. 18; Pension Schemes Act 1993 s. 127(3).

Current law, accordingly, gives employees limited priority in relation to unpaid wages and the ERA gives further protection. The effect of limited priority in such a regime is to allow the National Insurance Fund to recover a proportion of sums paid out to employees. To abolish employees' preferential status under the 1986 Act would consequently impose a loss not on employees but on the National Insurance Fund. It would, in doing so, make available considerable sums for other unsecured creditors. This may be no bad thing in economic efficiency terms since the Crown is likely to be a lower-cost risk bearer than the other unsecured creditors referred to, but it may be objected that it is unfair for taxpayers to foot part of the bill for an insolvency when they have enjoyed no direct involvement with the company.[59] What the body of taxpayers has enjoyed, it could be riposted, is the prospect of gaining tax revenue from the potentially successful company. Having been happy to accept tax from a viable company and, in this sense, having shared in profits, such taxpayers, it could be said, are in no position to complain if they stand to bear some of the costs of failure. The Cork Committee,[60] for its part, favoured the Canadian approach in which the state's subrogated rights are not preferential. Cork noted Canadian thinking – that leaving a greater body of funds for unsecured creditors would be useful in encouraging them to play a more active part in the administration of the insolvent company's estate – but the Committee stressed that the case for meeting employees' debts was rooted in social policy considerations.[61]

In such discussions the further question arises as to the appropriateness of treating all employees who are owed wages in like terms. It is possible to distinguish some employee groups from others on the issue of fairness. Directors, for instance, might be thought to be less worthy of protection from the risks of unpaid wages than other employee creditors on the grounds that they can be taken to be better informed about risks; they are better able to monitor the activities of the company; they share *ex officio* some responsibility for the company's insolvency; and they are better able to gain compensation for insolvency risks than other

---

[59] The Cork Report, para. 1433, favoured replacing insolvency law priority with statutory employment protection. As the Crown's general preferential rights are now surrendered and the resulting fund is ring-fenced (subject to a prescribed part), then calls for abolition of employees' preferential status may have more force: see, for example, D. Milman, 'Insolvency Reform' [2001] Ins. Law. 153; Mokal, 'Priority as Pathology', pp. 616–20.

[60] Cork Report, para. 1434.   [61] Ibid., para. 1435.

employees and creditors.[62] This reasoning might be thought to justify excluding company directors from the group of those creditors able to benefit from the prescribed part; giving no priority to such directors' claims to unpaid wages; and rendering directors ineligible for benefits from the National Insurance Fund in relation to unpaid wages. Directors' claims would, on such reasoning, be subordinated/deferred to those of other creditors. Such steps might, however, be considered to be too draconian and to exaggerate the extent to which company directors are able to self-inform concerning their company's insolvency risks, to influence financial risk-taking or to exit from excessively risky situations.[63]

Set-off

A well-established principle of insolvency law is that where there are mutual debts existing between a creditor and a company in liquidation, the smaller debt is to be set against the larger debt and only the balance is to be paid to the creditor out of the insolvency estate.[64] Thus, if company A has supplied materials to now insolvent company B and is owed £10,000 for these but company A also owes company B £6,000 for equipment supplied by company B to company A, the principle of set-off means that £6,000 of the £10,000 debt is extinguished. There is no defence or counterclaim to an action involved here. Company B does not have to go to court to establish a counterclaim, it merely uses the debt to pay off part of the debt to company A. The effect of this, as will be returned to below, is that where company A has provided the £10,000 credit without security, it is placed in a better position than insolvent

---

[62] See generally K. Van Wezel Stone, 'Policing Employment Contracts Within the Nexus-of-Contracts Firm' (1993) 43 U Toronto LJ 353.

[63] On Cork's approach to discouraging irresponsibility to creditors on the part of directors see Cork Report, ch. 43; and ch. 16 below. See also White Paper, *A Revised Framework for Insolvency Law* (Cmnd 9175, 1984) which emphasised that all directors should ensure they have full awareness of their company's financial position; D. Milman, 'Insolvency Act 1986' (1987) 8 Co. Law. 61.

[64] See generally Cork Report, ch. 30; R. Derham, *Set-off* (3rd edn, Clarendon Press, Oxford, 2003); Derham, 'Some Aspects of Mutual Credit and Mutual Dealings' (1992) 108 LQR 99; A. McKnight, *The Law of International Finance* (Oxford University Press, Oxford, 2008) pp. 855–60; D. Capper, 'Contracting Out of Insolvency Set-off: Irish Possibilities' [2000] Ins. Law. 248. On varieties of set-off see P. Ridgway, 'Corporation Tax in Insolvency: Part 3 – Equitable Set-off and Crown Debts' (2000) 13 *Insolvency Intelligence* 9.

company B's other unsecured creditors with regard to the £6,000 debt which is effectively paid back to company A before other unsecured debts are looked to.

Insolvency set-off applies within the terms of amended Rule 4.90 of the Insolvency Rules 1986 which applies where, before liquidation,[65] there have been 'mutual credit, mutual debts or other mutual dealings between the company and any creditor of the company proving or claiming to prove for a debt in liquidation'.[66] If there have been such mutual dealings then 'account shall be taken ... and the sums due from one party shall be set-off against the sums due from the other'.[67] Mutuality is essential: sums due from the company to another party will not be included in the set-off.[68] Mutuality demands that the two parties each have a debt owed

---

[65] Note that after the Enterprise Act 2002 reforms, administrators can be given permission by the court to make a distribution (see Insolvency Act 1986 Sch. B1, para. 65(2)). Administrators, so authorised by the court, can now give notice (per IR r. 2.95) that they intend to make a distribution and the rules of set-off will apply: IR r. 2.85 (as amended by the Insolvency (Amendment) Rules 2005 (SI 2005/527)). The Financial Markets Law Committee (an independent body sponsored by the Bank of England) has argued, however, that there is a need to clarify the Insolvency Rules since counterparties may be discouraged from dealing with a company in administration because of legal uncertainties regarding set-off in administration – notably concerning which set-off rules will apply to the counterparty and whether any liabilities incurred by the insolvent company post-administration will be available for set-off: see FMLC, *Administration Set-off and Expenses* (Bank of England, London, November 2007). See further R. Heis, 'Technical Update: Set-off in Administrations' (2008) *Recovery* (Autumn) 12.

[66] The availability of set-off generally is governed by the following conditions: (1) there must be debts, credits or dealings between the company and the person seeking to assert the set-off and (2) these debts, credits or dealings must be mutual. Mutual debts are liquidated amounts owing from each of the parties to the other. Mutual credits are credits which will eventually result in money claims, e.g. where one party, who is indebted to the other, supplies the other party with property on the basis that the property is to be resold and the proceeds handed over. Mutual dealings are arrangements in which the parties extend credit to each other in respect of individual sums with the express or implied intention that at some point the individual sums will be brought into account and set off against each other: see *Boyle and Birds' Company Law*, p. 931. On the arising of a right of set-off see e.g. *Rother Iron Works* v. *Canterbury Precision Engineers Ltd* [1974] QB 1 but compare *Business Computers Ltd* v. *Anglo-African Leasing Ltd* [1977] 1 WLR 578. On the considerable scope of 'Crown set-off' and the operation of set-off in relation to contingent debts see *Secretary of State for Trade and Industry* v. *Frid* [2004] 2 AC 506, [2004] BPIR 841; I. Fletcher, 'Crown Set-off and Contingent Liabilities' (2005) 18 *Insolvency Intelligence* 6.

[67] Insolvency Rules 1986 r. 4.90(2).

[68] Ibid., r. 4.90(3). See *Smith (Administrator of Coslett (Contractors) Ltd)* v. *Bridgend CBC (Re Coslett (Contractors) Ltd (in administration))* [2001] BCC 740 (HL): conversion of a company's property was not a mutual dealing between the Council and the company (Lord Hoffmann at p. 748); *Smith* v. *Blake* [1996] AC 243.

by and to the other but the claims involved need not be connected or of the same type. They may be in contract, tort or restitution, of statutory or other legal origin. Both claims, however, must be monetary in nature.[69] If one debt is proprietary in nature then no set-off is allowed.

A case focusing on the mutuality condition for set-off was *Morris v. Agrichemicals*.[70] In that instance the bank, BCCI, had loaned money to A but had taken a deposit from B, a majority shareholder in the borrower company. The issue for the court was whether the bank was required to apply the rules of insolvency set-off and use the deposits from B to reduce the debts owed to the bank by the borrower company. The House of Lords held that the depositors could not insist on set-off because there was no mutuality: the borrowers owed the bank the sums of the loans but the bank owed the depositors the amount of the deposits. This was the case because the borrower and depositor were legally separate entities, though they were not separate economically. The decision in *Morris* thus contrasted with that of *MS Fashions*[71] where the facts were generally similar but with a key difference: the depositors had not only pledged their deposits for the loans but they had guaranteed the obligation of the borrower and had thus established mutuality of claims for the purposes of mandatory set-off.[72]

The set-off rule applies to all companies in liquidation, be this compulsory or voluntary, where the English courts have jurisdiction to wind up. It does not apply to companies subject to the appointment of an administrative receiver or companies in voluntary arrangements

---

[69] On the requirements of mutuality see *Smith* v. *Blake* [1996] AC 243; *Morris* v. *Agrichemicals Ltd (Morris* v. *Rayners Enterprises Inc.) (BCCI No. 8)* [1997] BCC 965 at 973–4 (*'Morris* v. *Agrichemicals'*).

[70] [1997] 3 WLR 909; [1997] BCC 968. The House of Lords in *Morris* also considered whether a bank can take an effective charge over its own customer's credit balance (answering in the affirmative) or whether this amounted to a contractual set-off and not a true security at all: see further R. Calnan, 'Fashioning the Law to Suit the Practicalities of Life' (1998) 114 LQR 174; R. M. Goode, 'Charge-Backs and Legal Fictions' (1998) 114 LQR 178; G. McCormack, 'Charge-Backs and Commercial Certainty in the House of Lords *(Re BCCI (No. 8))*' [1998] CfiLR 111; R. Mokal, 'Resolving the *MS Fashions* "Paradox"' [1999] CfiLR 106; C. Rotherham, 'Charges Over Customers' Deposit Accounts' [1998] CLJ 260; M. Evans, 'Decision of the Court of Appeal in *Morris* v. *Agrichemicals Ltd*: A Flawed Asset' (1996) 17 Co. Law. 102; G. McCormack, 'Security Interests in Deposit Accounts: The Anglo-American Perspective' [2002] Ins. Law. 7.

[71] *MS Fashions* v. *Bank of Credit and Commerce International SA (No. 2)* [1993] BCC 70; Mokal, 'Resolving the *MS Fashions* "Paradox"'.

[72] As the depositors owed an obligation to the bank under the guarantee and the bank owed the depositors an obligation in respect of the deposit.

with creditors. The credits and debits involved must have arisen before the company 'goes into liquidation': that is, before the time of the winding-up order or the passing of the resolution to wind up the company.[73] Rule 4.90, as amended in 2005, makes it clear, however, that actual, contingent and future debts owed both *by* and *to* the company are to be taken into account for the purposes of set-off (formerly only contingent and future debts owed *by* the company were taken into account).[74]

When a debtor company goes into insolvency, the statutory rules set out in Rule 4.90 of the Insolvency Rules 1986 are mandatory[75] and displace all other forms of set-off not exercised prior to the winding up.[76] The courts have, however, had to come to grips with various attempts to exclude the mandatory application of insolvency set-off. Thus, in *Rolls Razor* v. *Cox*[77] the court held that a washing-machine salesman was entitled to set-off £106 of sale proceeds against the £406 of retained commission that the now insolvent company owed him. The set-off that was involved, said the court, could not be excluded by the contractual agreement between the parties which had purported to rule it out.[78]

---

[73] Note that this is not the same definition of the 'commencement of winding up' that is used elsewhere in the Insolvency Act 1986, which refers, for other purposes, to the time the petition was presented or the resolution is passed.

[74] In the case of *Secretary of State for Trade and Industry* v. *Frid* [2004] 2 AC 506, [2004] BPIR 841, the House of Lords ruled that a contingent debt to the company could be included in set-off and that it was not necessary for the debt to have been due and payable before the insolvency date – it was sufficient that there should have been an obligation from contract or statute by which a monetary debt would become payable on the occurrence of some future event or events (Lord Hoffmann, at para. 9). See Fletcher, 'Crown Set-off and Contingent Liabilities'.

[75] On the mandatory nature of statutory set-off see *National Westminster Bank Ltd* v. *Halesowen Presswork and Assemblies Ltd* [1972] AC 785; *Morris* v. *Agrichemicals*.

[76] See Goode, *Principles of Corporate Insolvency Law*, pp. 214–16, where the five types of set-off are listed as: (1) independent set-off; (2) transaction set-off; (3) current account set-off; (4) contractual set-off; and (5) insolvency set-off.

[77] [1967] 1 QB 552.

[78] For criticism of this decision see Goode, *Principles of Corporate Insolvency Law*, pp. 235–7. See also *National Westminster Bank Ltd* v. *Halesowen Presswork and Assemblies Ltd* [1972] AC 785 where the House of Lords held that a person for whom a right exists cannot waive that right so as to exclude the statutory rules of set-off: see discussion at pp. 619–21 below. In *British Eagle International Airlines Ltd* v. *Compagnie Nationale Air France* [1975] 1 WLR 758, [1975] 2 All ER 390 ('*British Eagle*') debts were cleared through a clearing house with seventy-six IATA member airlines. The court held that the liquidator of British Eagle had a legitimate claim for the net sum owed by Air France to British Eagle (after sums owed by the latter to the former had been set-off

Why should insolvency set-off be mandatory? Should contracting out of insolvency set-off be resisted on efficiency or fairness grounds? As one commentator has asked: 'What is so special about insolvency set-off which makes contracting out of it totally impossible whereas contracting out of the *pari passu* rule is to be possible provided the contracting out operates to the detriment rather than the benefit of the creditor which is a contracting party?'[79]

The Cork Committee noted the efficiency benefits of allowing contracting out of set-off.[80] When the law allowed contracting out,[81] a company in financial difficulties, attempting to reorganise its affairs, found it useful to open a new account with the bankers to whom it was indebted. This account would be maintained in credit and the bank would agree that in a subsequent liquidation it would not set-off any credit balance on the account against existing indebtedness. This meant that the funds in the new account would be handed over intact to the liquidator and the bank would not become preferred to other creditors through the funds in the new account. For its part, the company would be able to run the business on a cash basis for the general benefit of all creditors. After contracting out was legally prevented, such a company might open a new account with a new bank but not, if properly advised, its former bank.[82] Cork deemed this need for new banking arrangements to be an 'unnecessary and undesirable complication'.[83] The Committee

---

under the statutory rules). To allow pre-insolvency clearing arrangements to continue post-liquidation would offend the *pari passu* principle as sums due from Air France to British Eagle would, on clearing, be used to satisfy the debts of clearing house member creditors to the 'determent' of non-members. See further M. Bridge, 'Clearing Houses and Insolvency' (2008) 2 *Law and Financial Markets Review* 418; Oditah, 'Assets', p. 466; Mokal, 'Priority as Pathology', pp. 598–601. On the 'football creditor rule' and a decision indicating that the *British Eagle* approach is not offended when the claims of certain (but not all) unsecured creditors are paid off, not out of club assets, but by a purchaser of the club, see *Commissioners of the Inland Revenue* v. *Wimbledon Football Club* [2004] BCC 638.

[79] See E. Ferran, 'Subordinated Debt Agreements' (1993) *CCH Company Law Newsletter* (28 June 1993) 8, 9; Ferran, *Company Law and Corporate Finance*, pp. 552–4; Capper, 'Contracting Out of Insolvency Set-off'. On contracting out of *pari passu* to the detriment of the contracting creditor see *Re Maxwell Communications Corp. (No. 2)* [1994] 1 BCLC 1, [1993] BCC 369, [1994] 1 All ER 737 (*'Maxwell Communications'*) and discussion below.

[80] See Cork Report, paras. 1341–62.

[81] That is, until the decision in *National Westminster Bank Ltd* v. *Halesowen Pressworks and Assemblies Ltd* [1972] AC 785.

[82] See V. Selvam, 'Revisiting the Justifications for Insolvency Set-off' (2004) 25 Co. Law. 343.

[83] Cork Report, para. 1341.

urged that contracting out should be allowed. There was no sound reason of policy for the prohibition and there were good commercial reasons for ending it.

In *Maxwell Communications Corporation (No. 2)*[84] Vinelott J urged, in contrast, that the mandatory nature of insolvency set-off could be justified in efficiency terms because this was a procedure from which the company and the body of creditors could benefit. The creditor could settle at least part of his debt without having to prove for it and the troubled company would be relieved of the need to engage in potentially expensive proceedings in order to recover the debt due to it. Complications such as determination of whether a dividend was owing in the liquidation to a creditor who had waived set-off in circumstances where proceedings against him were still afoot could also be avoided with a mandatory rule. In the *Halesowen* case,[85] also, Lord Simon stressed that set-off was part of the procedure whereby insolvent estates are administered in a proper and orderly way. It was not a private right which those who benefited from it were free to waive; it was a matter in which the commercial community generally had an interest and accordingly this was a right that could not be contracted out of. Counter to such views it might be contended that allowing set-off may create uncertainty in commercial transactions because lenders and business partners will find it difficult to assess the financial status of a borrower, supplier or purchaser since there may exist rights of set-off that will diminish any insolvency estate and these rights will often be 'invisible'.

In spite of such concerns about the uncertainties caused by set-off, a strong efficiency case for allowing set-off has, nevertheless, been said to be rooted in commercial reality and its overall effect in the lowering of business costs. As one commentator has argued:

> A reduction of exposure by $300 trillion per annum in foreign exchange markets and $50 trillion in swap markets is simply too difficult to ignore. This reduction in exposure has manifold benefits: capital adequacy costs are correspondingly reduced and so is systemic risk. This cost reduction frees capital which benefits the economy at large ... the risk reducing effect makes insolvency set-off truly unassailable.[86]

Will mandatory set-off, however, lead to disadvantages for companies in need of turnaround? Mandatory set-off can introduce difficulties for a troubled company, as Cork was aware, because it makes it harder for the

---

[84] [1993] BCC 369, [1994] 1 BCLC 1, [1994] 1 All ER 737.   [85] [1972] AC 785.
[86] Selvam, 'Revisiting the Justifications for Insolvency Set-off', p. 344.

company to refinance its operations by arranging additional credit facilities. This will happen where existing creditors will not agree to the refinancing deal if it involves a new creditor being given preference through set-off.[87] Implementation of the Cork recommendation to allow contracting out of set-off would give greater financing flexibility in such scenarios.

Is mandatory set-off fair? In *Forster* v. *Wilson*[88] the aim of insolvency set-off was said to be to do 'substantial justice' between the parties.[89] This implies that if creditor A owes troubled company B £1,500, yet A is owed £2,000 by B, it is just that the £1,500 debt is allowed to be set-off. The effect, however, is to repay to A £1,500 of his debt as a matter of preference over other creditors of B (who, when deciding to lend, may have seen the debt in the company (B's) account as an asset). Allowing set-off worsens the position of other creditors who are not engaged in a mutual debt relationship with the company and who may have difficulty in discovering the existence of 'an unpublished security'.[90] The effect of set-off is to remove from the insolvency estate the asset that is the debt due from the creditor to the company.[91] An alternative would be for A to pay the £1,500 debt to B and then prove for the £2,000 in Company B's insolvency, taking a percentage dividend on the sum owed alongside other unsecured creditors. To an independent observer this alternative arrangement might seem fairer than set-off because set-off 'rewards', with priority, those solvent creditors who happen also to have borrowed

---

[87] Ibid., p. 343. Mandatory set-off is likely, of course, to make creditors more willing to lend to the troubled company if they also owe debts to the company that are sufficiently large to allow them to set-off their own debts against debts owed to them by the company (see Lord Hoffmann in *Smith* v. *Blake* [1996] AC 243). When they reach the point at which their loans exceed their debts to the company this incentive disappears since any set-off will apply only to a sum equal to their debt to the company and, beyond that point, they will recover only *pro rata* as an unsecured creditor.

[88] (1843) 12 M&W 191 at 203–4. See Oditah, 'Assets', p. 467.

[89] The 'substantial justice' purpose attributed to Parke B in *Forster* v. *Wilson* has been quoted with approval several times: see, for example, *Stein* v. *Blake* [1996] 1 AC 243 at 251E; *Gye* v. *McIntyre* [1991] 171 CLRT 609 at 618. In *National Westminster Bank Ltd* v. *Halesowen Pressworks and Assemblies Ltd* [1972] AC 785 Viscount Dilhorne stated that set-off prevented the 'unfairness' of the creditor having to pay off a debt to the company and then prove for a dividend.

[90] Selvam, 'Revisiting the Justifications for Insolvency Set-off', p. 343.

[91] Of course, the principal limiting requirement is that of mutuality. Insolvency set-off is usually said to guard against injustice to the solvent party, i.e. against the solvent party's having to pay in full knowing it will in turn merely get a few pence in the pound.

from an insolvent company.[92] In short, then, a regime of mandatory set-off involves a trading of efficiency gains and fairness losses.

Subordination

It is clear from the above that the *pari passu* principle is not one that can be bypassed to one's advantage by simple contractual agreements with no proprietary effect.[93] It is also clear that statutory exceptions to *pari passu* are encountered: the Insolvency Rules make set-off mandatory and, again, there is no contracting out of set-off within current corporate insolvency law. On the matter of contractual subordination,[94] however, it is possible to make an effective agreement that one's own debt will rank *behind* the other unsecured debts of a company. The ground-breaking decision here was *Re Maxwell Communications Corporation plc (No. 2)*.[95] The question before the court was whether the holders of convertible subordinated bonds might effectively contract not to be repaid until after the general unsecured creditors had been satisfied in full. Vinelott J did not see why bondholders, who had entered into an investment arrangement fully aware of the subordination of their claims, should be elevated to the level of the rest of the creditors at the time of insolvency. The bondholders had freely contracted with relevant knowledge and the court saw no reason to re-open the contractual bargain. Contracting out of the *pari passu* principle was thus allowed on the basis that a

---

[92] See discussion in B. G. Carruthers and T. C. Halliday, *Rescuing Business: The Making of Corporate Bankruptcy Law in England and the United States* (Clarendon Press, Oxford, 1998) pp. 181–6.

[93] See *British Eagle* [1975] 2 All ER 390; *MMI* v. *LSE* [2001] 4 All ER 223 and Neuberger J's ten propositions, concerning 'deprivation provisions' and the *British Eagle* principle; G. Stewart, 'The British Eagle has Landed' (2001) *Recovery* (December) 7–8; ch. 15 below. On whether direct payment clauses in construction contracts offend the *pari passu* principle see e.g. D. Capper, 'Direct Payment Clauses and the *Pari Passu* Principle' [1998] CfiLR 54; G. McCormack, *Proprietary Claims and Insolvency* (Sweet & Maxwell, London, 1997) pp. 17–25.

[94] On contractual subordination see generally B. Johnston, 'Contractual Debt Subordination and Legislative Reform' [1991] JBL 225; F. Oditah, *Legal Aspects of Receivables Financing* (Sweet & Maxwell, London, 1991); R. Nolan, 'Less Equal than Others: *Maxwell* and Subordinated Unsecured Obligations' [1995] JBL 484; Ferran, *Company Law and Corporate Finance*, pp. 549–61; Ferran, 'Recent Developments in Unsecured Debt Subordination' in B. Rider (ed.), *The Realm of Company Law* (Kluwer, London, 1998). On trust subordination and contingent-debt subordination see Ferran, *Company Law and Corporate Finance*, pp. 561–4; K. Thomas and C. Ryan, 'Section 459, Public Policy and Freedom of Contract' (2001) 22 Co. Law. 199, 200–1.

[95] [1994] 1 All ER 737, [1994] 1 BCLC 1.

creditor would be permitted to waive a debt in full (or in part) and that this might be agreed in advance of, or after, a liquidation. After all, noted Vinelott J, a creditor could waive a right to prove in liquidation and could agree to postpone his debt after winding up had commenced. Other creditors, indeed, might have given credit on the understanding that another creditor's subordination agreement would be effective. Vinelott J also noted that contractual subordination was effective in other leading common law and civil law jurisdictions[96] and he considered that, given that such agreements were recognised as effective, to strike them down would be a triumph of form over substance[97]

What may be difficult to deny is the value of subordinated borrowing as a form of corporate finance. Subordination may be useful in a number of circumstances,[98] notably: to allow shareholders or directors to inject funds into a company where existing creditors will not allow further unsubordinated borrowings; to allow parent companies to enhance the credit of a subsidiary that is issuing securities (so that an appropriate rating for the securities will be obtained); to allow companies to appeal to investors who seek high incomes in return for higher risk bearing; and to allow a bank to issue funds for treatment as capital for capital adequacy purposes.

Why, however, allow contracting out of *pari passu* on subordination but not on set-off or more generally? The key consideration is fairness. On this matter the courts have consistently taken the view that an

---

[96] For example, Australia and New Zealand: see Ferran, 'Recent Developments', pp. 206–9 for a discussion of provisions and case law.

[97] See also *SSSL Realisations (2002) Limited (in liquidation) and Save Group plc (in liquidation)* [2004] EWHC Ch 1760: see G. Stewart, 'Legal Update' (2004) *Recovery* (Winter) 6. Lloyd J decided that where a parent company had covenanted not to prove in a subsidiary's liquidation until the claims of a senior creditor had been met in full, the *British Eagle* principle did not prevent contractual subordination even though the parent company was in liquidation and its creditors stood to suffer from the subordination. The judge stated that the *pari passu* principle had to be considered separately in relation to the insolvencies of the parent and of the subsidiary and that the parent's creditors were bound by the consequences of the parent's agreement to subordinate its claims to those of the senior creditor in the liquidation of the subsidiary. (Other arguments relating to the subordination arrangements – e.g. that they resulted in the parent company creating a (registrable) charge (over book debts) or that the parent's liquidator might be entitled to disclaim them as 'onerous property' under IA 1986 s. 178(3)(a) – were also not upheld by Lloyd J. The judge's s. 178 ruling, *inter alia*, was upheld by the Court of Appeal: see *Squires (Liquidators of SSSL Realisations (2002) Ltd) v. AIG Europe (UK) Ltd* [2006] BCC 233.)

[98] See Ferran, 'Recent Developments', p. 201.

agreement that purports to improve the position of a creditor who would normally be subject to the *pari passu* rule will not, for reasons of public policy, be effective when the debtor company is in liquidation.[99] Subordination, as mentioned above, however, has been seen, notably by Vinelott J in the *Maxwell Communications* case, as worsening only the position of the contracting party and, accordingly, as a manoeuvre involving no unfairness to other creditors.[100] This would be the case if such contracts could not be terminated or adjusted in the periods leading up to insolvency.

It is possible, however, to think of circumstances in which, under current conditions, unfairness could be occasioned by use of a subordination agreement. If bank A agrees to advance funds to company B in difficult times and agrees to subordinate its debt to those of creditors C, D and E, creditors C, D and E may be inclined to increase their lending to company B in the knowledge that A's advance is subordinated to their own claims.[101] If, at a later date, A renegotiates the terms of its loan to B and ends the subordination, lenders C, D and E may have been led to make loans available in unfair conditions. If, in the alternative, the debtor company seeks to make payments to the allegedly subordinated creditor, the unsubordinated unsecured creditors are poorly positioned to protect their own interests as they are not parties to the subordination agreement and the doctrine of privity of contract will rule out enforcement against the company.[102] Nor do arguments that contractual subordinations constitute waivers of statutory rights give the unsubordinated creditors any rights of enforcement or allow them to prevent variations in the terms of the subordination agreement.[103] The potential to subordinate at

---

[99] See *British Eagle* [1975] 2 All ER 390.

[100] For Commonwealth judgments consistent with the line of Vinelott J in *Maxwell Communications* see *Horne* v. *Chester & Fein Property Development Pty Ltd and Others* (1986–7) 11 ACSR 485; *Ex parte de Villiers, Re Carbon Developments (Pty) Ltd (in liquidation)* [1993] 1 SA 493.

[101] On reliance on subordination by third-party creditors see Nolan, 'Less Equal than Others', p. 495, who argues that there is little that third-party creditors can do to protect themselves against variations in subordination terms. The advent of liquidation should, however, prevent variations after the start of the winding up: see Ferran, 'Recent Developments', p. 214.

[102] See Nolan, 'Less Equal than Others', p. 495; *Dunlop Pneumatic Tyre Co. Ltd* v. *Selfridge & Co. Ltd* [1915] AC 847 at 853.

[103] See Nolan, 'Less Equal than Others', pp. 496–7, who also reviews arguments that unsubordinated creditors might be able to secure damages from a liquidator who distributes in breach of valid contracts of subordination and arguments that restitution could be sought from subordinated creditors who have received funds contrary to the terms of the subordination agreement: see *Ministry of Health* v. *Simpson* [1951] AC 251.

will creates uncertainties in the lending regime, it makes the task of liquidation more complex and this, in itself, will increase costs. Where lenders C, D and E gain the relevant information on subordination (or non-subordination) by A, they are likely to increase their interest rates to reflect any uncertainties in the system. Moving beyond a simple subordination agreement – in which a creditor agrees to rank behind all other creditors of a particular debtor – that creditor may wish to agree to rank behind some, but not all, of the other creditors.[104] A group of creditors, indeed, may seek to agree a ranking order amongst themselves, so that, for example, A, B and C agree to rank behind all other general creditors but to rank between themselves, A first, B second and C last. The central issue here is whether the *British Eagle* ruling is offended by such arrangements and parties are seeking to opt out of *pari passu* to their own advantage. Where a creditor agrees to subordinate to some, but not all, other creditors, it is arguable that the *pari passu* principle is not breached because the subordinator gains no advantage over parties who are not involved in the subordination agreement. Where, as in the example of A, B and C above, a ranking order is agreed, third-party creditor interests are not prejudiced but A will gain a priority advantage over B and C. This is a consensual agreement, however, that has been treated in Commonwealth case law as not infringing the public policy of the *pari passu* rule.[105]

Deferred claims

Claims may be deferred by statute, that is placed in priority *below* the claims of other creditors.[106] Thus section 215(4) of the Insolvency Act 1986 provides that 'where a court makes a declaration under [sections

---

[104] See Ferran, *Company Law and Corporate Finance*, pp. 554–6.

[105] See *Horne* v. *Chester & Fein Property Development Pty Ltd and Others* (1986–7) 11 ACSR 485, discussed in Ferran, *Company Law and Corporate Finance*, p. 555. See also *US Trust Corporation* v. *Australia and New Zealand Banking Group* (1995) 17 ACSR 697.

[106] See Finch, 'Is *Pari Passu* Passé?', p. 199. See generally Goode, *Principles of Corporate Insolvency Law*, pp. 198–200. Goode notes the development in the USA of the doctrine of equitable subordination but suggests that in England the terms of the Insolvency Act 1986 give the courts the powers they need. On the doctrine of equitable subordination and inter-company loans see ch. 13 above. See also Justice, *Insolvency Law: An Agenda for Reform* (Justice, London, 1994) p. 25. For a discussion of an adjustable priority rule involving the deferral of secured claims to the unsecured claims of non-adjusting parties see ch. 15.

213 or 214 of the Insolvency Act 1986] in relation to a person who is a creditor of the company, it may direct the whole or any part of any debt owed by the company to that person and any interest thereon shall rank in priority after all other debts owed by the company and after interest on those debts'. Similarly the Insolvency Act 1986 defers sums due to members of the company by way of dividends, profits or otherwise. Such claims are ranked below those of all other creditors.[107] It is clear, however, from the case of *Soden*[108] that the relevant section (section 74(2)(f)) subordinates to the rights of unsecured creditors only sums due to a member 'in his character as member'. This covers sums due under the (then) section 14 (Companies Act 1985) statutory contract which draws a contract out of the terms of the company's memorandum and articles and other obligations imposed by the Companies Act.[109] Sums due to a member independently of that (now) section 33 (Companies Act 2006) membership contract are excluded as, for example, are sums due as court awards in an action for misrepresentation, as in the *Soden* decision itself. Such sums owed would not be deferred but would rank *pari passu* with unsecured creditors. The broader importance of the *Soden* decision is the approach it lays down concerning the ranking of claims of members whose financial relationship with their company goes beyond simply share ownership. Issues of set-off are also affected since *Soden* holds that sums arising out of the statutory membership contract will provide no set-off from, say, non-fully-paid-up shares, but other independent claims outside the statutory contract may be set-off against the obligation of contribution.

Conclusions: rethinking exceptions to *pari passu*

The following chapter considers whether *pari passu*, in its strong sense, is so frequently bypassed and flawed in shape and application that it is appropriate to look to alternative approaches to distribution. Here, however, it is necessary to consider whether the current exceptions to *pari passu* are in need of reform. Thus far the case for abolishing Crown preferences has been accepted and it has been indicated that there may be reasons for revising the rules on set-off.

---

[107] Insolvency Act 1986 s. 74(2)(f).
[108] *Soden v. British & Commonwealth Holdings plc (in administration)* [1997] BCC 952.
[109] See now Companies Act 2006 s. 33: on which see *Boyle and Birds' Company Law*, pp. 145–52.

Are there, however, other classes of unsecured creditor that are in need of greater or lesser protection than at present? In the case of one group put forward for greater priority – that of consumer creditors – we have seen difficulties with the argument for favourable treatment. The problem with this proposal is that it is difficult to distinguish 'consumer' from 'trade' creditors since there will be similarity between many of the contractual and practical arrangements entered into by such parties. Many trade creditors, moreover, may not have been repeat players in their dealings with the insolvent company yet many consumer creditors may have sustained a continuing relationship. We have seen that, compared with employees, the case for protecting the consumer creditor may be weak since the consumer is likely to enjoy a greater freedom to contract or decline to contract with the company; is more able to exit from the relationship in favour of forming a connection with another company; is more likely to spread risks by relying on more than one company to supply its required consumer goods; and is accordingly a lower-cost risk bearer than the typical employee.

A further proposal is designed to protect those creditors who have acted in a manner that benefits their fellow creditors. Prentice has argued that where creditor A takes action through the courts to enforce a debt but that action is overtaken by a winding-up order,[110] the court should have a discretion to award creditor A the costs of the litigation but not the benefit of any judgment.[111] Awarding such costs to such creditors would give priority to those costs and would compensate creditor A for the expenses of an action that is likely to benefit other creditors by signalling to them that the debtor company's viability may be at issue. The court's discretion, the argument runs, could be used to keep the floodgates closed on precipitate actions to enforce debts and this would discourage enforcement races. The award of such court costs would also prevent debtor companies from prevaricating when asked to settle accounts while using the threat of a voluntary winding up to discourage creditors from pressing their claims: the threat would be empty if the creditor would be liable to recover costs. This might, in turn, prevent unnecessary liquidations. Finally, the principle of *pari passu* would be respected by limiting the effective priority being given to the costs of the action only.

A difficulty with the proposal is that, as we have seen in chapter 3, signalling is a flawed process. When creditor A seeks to enforce a debt

---

[110] Thereby staying the enforcement of all actions: see further ch. 13 above.

[111] See D. Prentice, 'The Effect of Insolvency on Pre-liquidation Transactions' in B. Pettet (ed.), *Company Law in Change* (Stevens & Sons, London, 1987).

against company B in court, this may be the product of A's lack of information and panicky state of mind rather than any process of rational evaluation of B's viability. There may, moreover, be reasons for A's seeking to enforce a debt at a particular time that are entirely unrelated to B's viability: the state of A's own financial affairs (or internal corporate politics) may be the driving factor behind the legal action. It could be responded that the envisaged judicial discretion regarding costs might be employed in a manner that rewards only actions offering good signalling to other creditors but this is to presuppose unrealistic levels of information in the hands of the judiciary. The extent of a discretion to award costs, rather than a right to costs, might be said also to undermine any incentives that creditors might have to bring actions and send signals to other creditors. The state of the present law does allow creditors other than creditor A to nullify the benefits of any judgment obtained by A: the other creditors can simply await A's judgment and then present a winding-up petition. It could be argued, however, that creditor A did have the option of presenting a winding-up petition him- or herself and that accordingly he/she has no basis for complaint. This argument holds except that the courts will not allow a creditor to use a winding-up procedure to collect small debts.[112] Overall, the case for the proposed discretion to award litigation costs to A seems not to be made out. It is based on assumptions about signalling that are difficult to sustain and it would create, at least to a degree, an incentive to litigate that is liable to render the overall costs of winding up a company higher than would otherwise be the case.

To conclude, it should be emphasised that, in considering exceptions to *pari passu*, it is the *relative* cases for preferring the different types of creditor that are at issue. In the above discussion, the group for whom the strongest case for a protected status can be sustained is that of company employees and the criteria relevant to an assessment of that case included: ability to gain and use information concerning default risks; ability to adjust terms to take on board such risks; capacity to exit from excessively risk-laden arrangements; vulnerability to risks; and status as a low- or high-cost bearer of risks. Employees are protected in employment protection legislation but it is questionable whether the Crown should still enjoy the statutory preferential status of employees' debts through subrogation now that the Crown's own preferential status has been abolished.

---

[112] I.e. under £750: see Insolvency Act 1986 s. 123(1)(a), though creditors may combine their debts to qualify: *Re Leyton & Walthamstow Cycle Co.* [1901] WN 275; see ch. 13 above.

15

Bypassing *pari passu*

The main potential bases for supporting *pari passu* as a principle of corporate insolvency law are that it provides an efficient and a fair ground rule for allocating the residual insolvency estate. As was seen in the last chapter, however, exceptions to *pari passu* produce a principle that is unduly complex and uncertain. This chapter considers the extent to which *pari passu* can be bypassed[1] and a central issue will be whether bypassing is so easily and frequently practised that the value of *pari passu* is undermined. Here, therefore, we return to the second of the two key problems that corporate insolvency law faces in this area: how a company's insolvent estate is to be constructed.

As a preliminary point, it should be emphasised that the law does not readily countenance contracting out of collective arrangements for dealing with the insolvency estate. It was noted in chapter 14 that parties may be allowed by the courts to enter into contracts in a manner that worsens their status in the distribution of an insolvent company's estate.[2] What the courts will not do is allow creditors to 'contract with [their] debtor [to] enjoy some advantage in a bankruptcy or winding up which is denied to other creditors'.[3] The House of Lords made it clear in the *British Eagle*

---

[1] The word 'bypassed' here refers to arrangements that the law allows and which have the effect of preventing assets from being included in the company's (residual) estate that is available for distribution to unsecured creditors. For a discussion of the circumstances in which the UK courts will allow assets held in the UK to be remitted to another jurisdiction for distribution with results that may diverge from those flowing from UK approaches to *pari passu*, see *HIH Insurance (McGrath v. Riddell)* [2008] 1 WLR 852, [2008] BCC 349.

[2] Cf. *National Westminster Bank Ltd v. Halesowen Presswork and Assemblies Ltd* [1972] AC 785 where an agreement (altering a creditor's priority position) was struck down despite the fact that it would have increased insolvency value to the remaining creditors.

[3] Vinelott J in *Re Maxwell Communications Corporation plc (No. 2)* [1994] 1 All ER 737 at 750.

case[4] that this would be contrary to public policy whether or not the contractual provision was expressed to take effect only on insolvency.[5] Effect would not be given to a contractual arrangement that attempted to avoid collectivity by purporting to allow certain creditors to opt out of *pari passu* distribution of the residual estate to their advantage.[6] British Eagle[7] was a member of an International Air Transport Association (IATA) clearing house scheme in which moneys due from airlines to each other would be netted out each month. When British Eagle went into liquidation it owed money to a number of airlines but it had a claim against Air France, which the liquidator sought to recover. Air France

---

[4] *British Eagle International Airlines Ltd* v. *Compagnie Nationale Air France* [1975] 1 WLR 758, [1975] 2 All ER 390 (*'British Eagle'*). See also *Re Rafidain Bank* [1992] BCLC 301; D. Milman and C. Durrant, *Corporate Insolvency: Law and Practice* (3rd edn, Sweet & Maxwell, London, 1999) ch. 8; D. Capper, 'Direct Payment Clauses and the *Pari Passu* Principle' [1998] CfiLR 54. On the *British Eagle* principle's application, in Australia, not only to liquidations but universally to bankruptcy regimes, including administrations and company arrangements, see the Victorian Court of Appeal in *Ansett Australia Holdings Ltd* v. *International Air Transport Association* [2006] VSCA 242, 10 November 2006.

[5] See also *Carreras Rothmans Ltd* v. *Freeman Mathews Treasure Ltd* [1985] 1 Ch 207 at 226; M. Simmons, 'Avoiding the *Pari Passu* Rule' (1996) 9 *Insolvency Intelligence* 9. On the principle against divestiture (or deprivation principle), providing that an agreement to divest a person or company of an asset in the event of bankruptcy or liquidation is void for public policy (and its making no difference that no formal insolvency proceedings had begun), see *Fraser* v. *Oystertec plc* [2004] BCC 233; L. C. Ho, 'The Principle against Divestiture in Insolvency Revisited: *Fraser* v. *Oystertec*' (21 November 2005) SSRN; and for criticism of this approach: R. Henry, 'The Impurity at the Heart of the *Oystertec* Decision Considered' (2004) *Company Law Newsletter* 1; A. Henderson, '*Fraser* v. *Oystertec* and the Principle Against Divestiture in Insolvency: An Unprincipled Departure' (2004) 25 Co. Law. 313. It may be the case that if the insolvent estate is deprived of property as a result of an arrangement that was not designed to escape insolvency rules, the courts may allow that deprivation as an exception to the *British Eagle* principle: see Neuberger J in *MMI* v. *LSE* [2001] 4 All ER 223; G. Stewart, 'The British Eagle has Landed' (2001) *Recovery* (December) 7-8. (A company was liquidated and the London Stock Exchange (LSE), in accordance with the LSE articles, deprived the company of its shares on the Exchange. Neuberger J noted that there was no coherent set of rules to enable one to assess where a 'deprivation' provision fell foul of the *British Eagle* principle but he extracted ten propositions derived from case law. On the facts of the case before him Neuberger J concluded that the deprivation provision fell within an exception to the general *British Eagle* principle and the liquidator could not sustain his claim.) On third party purchases as distinct from contracting out, see *Commissioners of Inland Revenue* v. *Wimbledon Football Club* [2004] BCC 638.

[6] Contracts that prevent property from entering the estate – i.e. contracts with proprietary effect such as retention of title clauses – will be recognised, as will be seen. For decisions focusing on the intent, rather than the effect, of a contract see *Ex parte Mackay* (1873) LR 8 Ch App 643; F. Oditah, 'Assets and the Treatment of Claims in Insolvency' (1992) 108 LQR 459 at 466.

[7] See [1975] 2 All ER 390.

argued that British Eagle's liquidator was bound by the contractual regime of the clearing house scheme and could only collect the sum due after netting out the claims of those creditors who were creditors of British Eagle. The liquidator successfully contended that such a process would breach the *pari passu* principle because it would remove from British Eagle's estate the sum due from Air France – a sum that, otherwise, would be available to the body of British Eagle's general creditors. In accepting this contention, a bare majority of the House of Lords accepted crucially that British Eagle's claim against Air France was a direct one, with IATA acting simply as a collecting agent, rather than a mere element in British Eagle's net balance with the principal IATA.[8]

Creditors may not be able to contract out of the *pari passu* principle to their advantage but they can take a series of other steps that will bypass *pari passu*. In taking these steps they are taking advantage of the fact that it is only the assets in which the company has a beneficial interest that are available to creditors. Property held, for instance, on trust by the company will not enter the estate and where the company has granted security over property the asset enters the estate only to the extent of the equity of redemption (the difference between the value of the asset and the sum of the secured indebtedness). Here, as Goode notes, the distinction between property rights and personal rights is vitally important for insolvency purposes: the holder of a property right can enforce it ahead of the general body of creditors, whereas the holder of a personal right can only prove for a dividend in competition with other creditors.[9]

As will be seen below, there may be a strong case for the law allowing holders of property rights to enforce these ahead of creditors' rights in the insolvency estate. As we will also see, however, the ability to make assets available to a company while avoiding entry of those assets into the corporate estate leads to a deterioration in the position of the ordinary unsecured creditor. 'Every new property right, every added security

---

[8] The absence of mutuality precluded set-off of third-party claims. If the House of Lords had treated IATA as a principal then set-off would have been applicable: see R. M. Goode, *Principles of Corporate Insolvency Law* (3rd edn, Sweet & Maxwell, London, 2005) p. 223. For criticisms of *British Eagle* see Oditah, 'Assets', p. 466; R. Mokal, 'Priority as Pathology: The *Pari Passu* Myth' [2001] CLJ 581 at 598–601. For a discussion of amendments made to the IATA clearing house scheme in the wake of *British Eagle* and of the Australian High Court's decision in *International Air Transport Association* v. *Ansett Holdings* [2008] HCA 3 see M. Bridge, 'Clearing Houses and Insolvency' (2008) *Law and Financial Markets Review* 418.

[9] R. M. Goode, *Commercial Law in the Next Millennium* (Sweet & Maxwell, London, 1998) p. 62.

interest, every proprietary restitutionary remedy, every equity has eroded his or her stake in the insolvency process.'[10]

It is time to consider in detail the devices that can be used to avoid entry into the residual estate and thereby to bypass *pari passu* distribution.

Security

If creditors take security over loans they will *take* and *keep* property rights for themselves by way of such security. The property subject to the secured claim thus belongs to the secured claimant to the value of the claim and accordingly it does not enter the insolvency estate and become available for distribution.[11] Such arrangements may involve fixed or floating charges. As was noted in chapter 3, the institution of security can be supported on broad efficiency grounds, though elements of inefficiency are involved in so far as risks may be loaded excessively upon unsecured creditors. The earlier discussion of attendant issues will not be rehearsed here but the further question of whether security taking involves unfairness should be addressed at this point.[12]

To give priority to secured creditors and to allow the bypassing of *pari passu* can be argued to lead to no unfairness to unsecured creditors. This contention rests on three main arguments: that the security has been freely bargained or contracted for; that it does not deprive the company of value; and that relevant parties are given due notice of security arrangements and so cannot, with justice, complain.[13]

The essence of the 'bargain' justification is as follows.[14] When a debtor company grants a security interest to a creditor this will increase the risks faced by the other creditors because it reduces their expected value in an insolvency. Other creditors will, however, be aware of this risk and will

---

[10] Goode, *Principles of Corporate Insolvency Law*, p. 58.

[11] Statute may, however, make certain debts (e.g. preferential ones) payable from the estate in priority to rights to property that is not part of the estate (e.g. that forming the subject of a floating charge). On floating charges see also ch. 3 above.

[12] This discussion draws on V. Finch, 'Security, Insolvency and Risk: Who Pays the Price?' (1999) 62 MLR 633 at 660–7.

[13] See J. Hudson, 'The Case Against Secured Lending' (1995) 15 *International Review of Law and Economics* 47 at 55; R. M. Goode, 'Is the Law Too Favourable to Secured Creditors?' (1983–4) 8 Canadian Bus. LJ 53.

[14] See T. H. Jackson and A. T. Kronman, 'Secured Financing and Priorities Among Creditors' (1979) 88 Yale LJ 1143 at 1147–8; F. Buckley, 'The Bankruptcy Priority Puzzle' (1986) 72 Va. L Rev. 1393; *Salomon v. A. Salomon & Co. Ltd* [1897] AC 22 at 52: 'Every creditor is entitled to get and to hold the best security the law allows him to take', per Lord Macnaghten.

adjust loan rates accordingly or seek their own security or quasi-security. Voluntary contracting parties, accordingly, are treated fairly because they are free to contract at the rates and on the terms they consider appropriate.

The first objection to the 'bargain' argument is that those who enter into arrangements for credit in the commercial world do not always do so from equal negotiating positions.[15] Inequalities, indeed, can be quite striking. Small trade creditors, for reasons discussed in chapter 3, may often be in no position to gain the information that would make them equal bargainers with those seeking security. They may lack the resources, expertise and time to evaluate risks accurately and the nature of their products and business arrangements may not allow for the appropriate adjustments of business terms.

Competitive conditions in the market may also undermine the small trade creditor's ability to renegotiate interest rates when new securities are offered. (Contractual terms reflecting such conditions may also rule out such rate adjustments.) If equality of bargaining power was evenly spread between different types of creditor, one would expect a random distribution of security taking across all types of creditor but, in fact, the vast majority of security arrangements involve banks, finance houses or building societies, not firms in commercial business.[16] Small trade creditors suffer not only from information asymmetries in relation to banks but also from a lack of economies of scale. Banks, who repeat play (with regard to small as well as large loans), operate with large volumes of lending and offer longer terms of credit than trade creditors. They tend to make extensive use of security, to have specialist advisers and to have lower set-up and monitoring costs.[17] These factors all increase their bargaining power in relation to other creditors.

A second objection to the 'bargain' rationale is that a number of creditors are truly involuntary. They cannot take account of security arrangements because they did not choose to become creditors at all.[18]

---

[15] See B. G. Carruthers and T. C. Halliday, *Rescuing Business: The Making of Corporate Bankruptcy Law in England and the United States* (Clarendon Press, Oxford, 1998) p. 171; L. LoPucki, 'The Unsecured Creditor's Bargain' (1994) 80 Va. L Rev. 1887 at 1896–8; M. G. Bridge, 'The *Quistclose* Trust in a World of Secured Transactions' (1992) 12 OJLS 333 at 341; Justice, *Insolvency Law: An Agenda for Reform* (Justice, London, 1994) p. 6 on dissatisfaction with the imbalance of power between the large, secured creditors and the trade and other unsecured creditors.

[16] See Hudson, 'Case Against Secured Lending', p. 55.   [17] Ibid., p. 56.

[18] See LoPucki, 'Unsecured Creditor's Bargain', pp. 1896–7.

In this position, particularly, are tort victims. When parties agree security arrangements, they expropriate value that otherwise would rest, at least partly, with the body of involuntary creditors.

There are few reasons, furthermore, for treating freedom of contract as sacrosanct. The law has a long history of laying down the kinds of security that can be agreed to (all of which stipulations curtail the contractual freedoms of parties) and Parliament has clearly recognised that the right of a creditor to take security needs to be constrained if a fair balance is to be drawn between the interests of all creditors.[19]

A final concern is that the 'bargain' argument might have impetus where all affected parties are included in the bargaining process but it has little persuasive power when a bargain between a creditor and debtor imposes costs on others: 'freedom of contract arguments have force only with respect to arrangements that do not create direct externalities ... [W]hen the contract directly impinges on the rights of third parties, there is no prima facie presumption of freedom of contract.'[20] Arrangements that allow debtors to increase the insolvency share of one party, and which come at the expense of other parties, involve externalities. Priority seeking is, after all, central to security taking.[21]

The 'value' argument offers a response to the last point. It asserts that when a creditor takes security for new value[22] this does not prejudice third-party unsecured creditors because the secured creditor is not withdrawing from the company more than he or she paid in.[23] A particular difficulty, however, is that after-acquired property clauses may draw assets into the original security

---

[19] See *Report of the Review Committee on Insolvency Law and Practice* (Cmnd 8558, 1982) ('Cork Report') pp. 335–6. Freedom of contract is ignored, for example, when avoiding pre-insolvency transactions: Insolvency Act 1986 ss. 238–41, 245; preferential creditors are given priority even though they have not 'bargained' for it: Insolvency Act 1986 ss. 40, 175, 386, 387 and Sch. 6, paras. 8–11, 15A: see chs. 13 and 14 above.

[20] L. Bebchuk and J. Fried, 'The Uneasy Case for the Priority of Secured Claims in Bankruptcy' (1996) 105 Yale LJ 857 at 933; cf. A. Schwartz, 'Taking the Analysis of Security Seriously' (1994) 80 Va. L Rev. 2073 at 2082.

[21] See Cork Report, ch. 35. Indeed, some US commentators describe the grant of security as the issue of insolvency rights: see A. Schwartz, 'Security Interests and Bankruptcy Priorities: A Review of Current Theories' (1981) 10 *Journal of Legal Studies* 1; Buckley, 'Bankruptcy Priority Puzzle', who argues (at p. 1406) that unsecured creditors should not demand insolvency distribution rights for which they have not paid. See also Bridge, 'Quistclose Trust', pp. 340–1.

[22] I.e. contemporaneous or subsequent value: see further Goode, 'Is the Law Too Favourable to Secured Creditors?', pp. 60–3.

[23] See ibid. This assumes the terms of the loan are not unreasonable and thus do not require adjustment or setting aside.

arrangement.[24] As each new asset is acquired by the debtor, more and more security builds up without the injection of fresh value by the original secured creditor. That creditor enjoys the windfall benefit of diminishing risks of default and the existing interest rate proves increasingly advantageous to them. New assets do not enter the pool for the potential benefit of unsecured creditors but create such windfalls. The floating charge has thus long been criticised as a device that unfairly allows a charge upon all future property[25] and Cork suggested that: 'The matter for wonder is that such a device should ever have been invented by a Court of Equity.'[26]

The 'notice' argument urges that security is justified when other creditors are duly apprised of the situation.[27] These creditors, it is contended, can be in no position to complain about secured loans when they have been supplied with adequate information. This justification, however, fails to give due consideration to the position of involuntary creditors or to those voluntary creditors who cannot reasonably be expected to adjust their terms to the granting of security. Particular problems, moreover, arise with the floating charge. As Cork noted, the requirement that such charges be registered does little to assuage the feelings of grievance generated by such charges since the register gives very inadequate information to the trade creditor.[28] Where

---

[24] See *Holroyd* v. *Marshall* [1862] 10 HL Cas 191; I. Davis, 'The Trade Creditor and the Quest for Security' in H. Rajak (ed.), *Insolvency Law: Theory and Practice* (Sweet & Maxwell, London, 1993); M. G. Bridge, 'Form, Substance and Innovation in Personal Property Security Law' [1992] JBL 1.

[25] See Buckley J in *Re London Pressed Hinge Co. Ltd* [1905] 1 Ch 576 at 583; Cork Report, para. 107.

[26] See Cork Report, para. 107.

[27] See Goode, 'Is the Law Too Favourable to Secured Creditors?', p. 63.

[28] Cork Report, para. 109. In 2005 the Law Commission produced proposals for a new regime of electronic registering of company charges. The Government decided not to implement the Commission's proposals – which would have allowed the checking of details to be carried out online and, following registration, would have made information available instantly. All charges, unless exempted, would have been covered and the regime would have applied to sales of receivables. Registration would not have been compulsory and there would have been no time limit for registering but, if the company had become insolvent before a charge had been registered, the charge would have been ineffective against the administrator or liquidator. It would also have been ineffective unless the filing preceded the 'onset of insolvency'. Until it had been registered, further-more, a charge would have lost its priority to a subsequent charge since priority would have depended on the date of filing. For the proposals see Law Commission, *Company Security Interests* (Law Com. No. 296, August 2005); Law Commission Draft Company Security Regulations 2006; and generally G. McCormack, 'The Law Commission and Company Security Interests – A Climbdown' (2005) 18 *Company Law Newsletter* 1; 'The Law Commission Consultative Report on Company Security Interests: An Irreverent Riposte' (2005) 68(2) MLR 286; M. Bridge, 'The Law Commission's Proposals for the

floating charges secure bank overdrafts[29] the amount outstanding on the latter may fluctuate daily. It is, accordingly, impossible to tell from the register how much the floating charges secure. Even the latest company balance sheet offers little further assistance on this front since it is usually out of date by some months and will be unlikely to disclose contingent liabilities such as guarantees of the overdrafts of associated companies, which may also be secured by the floating charge. The twenty-one-day time limit as a condition of validity has, indeed, been dubbed 'inappropriate', since the proper sanction for failure to make a timely filing is subordination to a subsequent interest before the filing and (in the case of eve of insolvency filing) voidability as a preference.[30]

Registration and notice requirements in English law are further weakened by their non-applicability to retention of title under a conditional sale or hire purchase agreement. Where unsecured creditors are not informed about such quasi-security devices, they are unaware of the additional risks they face and the force of the notice argument is again spent.[31]

To summarise: the bargain, value and notice arguments are used in asserting the fairness of bypassing *pari passu* by excluding secured property from the insolvency estate. There are, however, material problems concerning the inequalities, competitive conditions and third-party effects of secured credit bargains, not to say their relevance to involuntary creditors. The value argument is undermined by such provisions as relate to after-acquired property and the notice contention is unconvincing in relation to involuntary creditors or to those who cannot adjust, suffer from poor information or are affected by a quasi-security device.

If abolishing security would be inadvisable on efficiency grounds, as was discussed above in chapter 3, what could be done to make the balance between secured and unsecured creditors fairer? Looking, first, to the problems of unequal bargaining, the 10 per cent fund was proposed by Cork[32] with reference to floating charges and was advocated on fairness grounds, as a response to the 'real injustice'[33] that floating charges were

---

Reform of Corporate Security Interests' in J. Getzler and J. Payne (eds.), *Company Charges: Spectrum and Beyond* (Oxford University Press, Oxford, 2006) p. 267.

[29] Most companies grant floating charges to their bankers to secure 'all sums due or to become due' on their current overdrafts.

[30] Goode, 'Is the Law Too Favourable to Secured Creditors?', p. 64. On preferences see Insolvency Act 1986 s. 239 and ch. 13 above. On the registration of charges see Companies Act 2006 Part 25, ss. 860 and 874 of which render charges void for non-registration.

[31] See ch. 3 above and pp. 642–8 below on ROT clauses.

[32] See Cork Report, paras. 1523–49.   [33] Ibid., para. 1527.

capable of producing. A similar simple redress, in the form of the 'prescribed part' provisions, was effected by the Enterprise Act 2002 changes.[34] As with the Cork proposal, however, the prescribed part rules do not bring assets subject to fixed charges within their remit. Fixed charges, however, may draw within their scope after-acquired assets of the originally specified class. Where the sum of assets covered by the fixed charge grows in value there is a transfer of insolvency wealth from non-adjusting unsecured creditors and an issue of fairness arises. Adjustment in relation to such charges is, however, potentially easier than with floating charges because a view of the registration documents will reveal a specification of assets that offers unsecured creditors some guidance as to the types of asset movement which may affect their potential insolvency claims.

In relation to fixed charges, unsecured creditors' problems of adjustment are likely to be less severe than with floating charges for another reason: relevant asset movements are liable to be fewer in the case of fixed charges because the debtor has to obtain the fixed charge holder's permission for asset substitution.[35] With floating charges, of course, the debtor is free to deal with the charged assets on their own account and without reference to the chargee. These points suggest that the need for a 'prescribed part' fund is perhaps less pressing in relation to fixed charges than it was with respect to floating charges. The prescribed part or ring-fenced fund is no complete answer[36] but it does have the merit of reducing the possibility that unsecured creditors will be faced with empty coffers.

One of the major advantages of the floating charge was the ability it gave to all-assets debenture holders to appoint an administrative receiver. It has been noted above in chapter 8 that, prior to the reforms of the Enterprise Act 2002, secured creditors were free to enforce their security interests in a manner that prejudiced the interests of other creditors. In England, the pre-*Medforth*[37] freedom of the debenture holder and the receiver to act purely selfishly was criticised,[38] as was the ability of the

---

[34] See Insolvency Act 1986 s. 176A; Insolvency Act 1986 (Prescribed Part) Order 2003 (SI 2003/2097); and ch. 3 above.

[35] Where debtors anticipate the need for routine asset substitution they are very likely to agree to the grant of a floating charge.

[36] See ch. 3 above, pp. 108–9; J. Armour, 'Should We Redistribute in Insolvency?' in Getzler and Payne, *Company Charges*, pp. 223–4.

[37] *Medforth* v. *Blake* [1999] 3 All ER 97. See ch. 8 above.

[38] See *Palk* v. *Mortgage Services Funding plc* [1993] Ch 330 (Sir Donald Nicholls VC); R. M. Goode, 'Proprietary Rights and Unsecured Creditors' in B. Rider (ed.), *The Realm of Company Law* (Kluwer, London, 1998), pp. 192–3.

debenture holder to throw a spanner in the process leading to the making of an 'old' administration order by appointing an administrative receiver. In 2002 the Enterprise Act sought to address such inequalities of enforcement and abolished administrative receivership outside exempted categories and replaced it with a new administration regime for the benefit of all creditors.[39]

A more radical approach to balancing creditor interests is to repackage the floating charge and place it within a new, statutory, regime to cover all security and quasi-security interests along North American lines. This potential development has been discussed, *inter alia*, by the Company Law Review Steering Group and the Law Commission[40] and has been referred to above. Such a repackaging of the floating charge[41] not only would allow a wholesale review of a confused mass of law but would

---

[39] See chs. 8 and 9 above. 'Ordinary' receivers are still appointable, however, and, even post-*Medforth* v. *Blake* [1999] 3 All ER 97, a receiver's primary duty is to the debenture holder. *Medforth* itself still has its limitations: it cannot be said with certainty, for instance, that the receiver has to take such actions as will benefit creditors generally provided that the appointing debenture holder's interests are not prejudiced. Nor can we be confident that any obligation to continue the business in the general interest of creditors will be read into *Medforth*. *Medforth* may in coming years be treated as demanding no more than the receiver's managing a business with due diligence *where* it is decided to continue operating that business. (But see *AIB Finance Ltd* v. *Alsop and Another* [1998] BCC 780 and *Hadjipanayi* v. *Yeldon et al.* [2001] BPIR 487 at 494–5.)

[40] On the case for abolition of the floating charge see *Report of the Committee on Consumer Credit* (Cmnd 4596, 1971) ('Crowther Report') para. 5.5.6. The Diamond Report, *A Review of Security Interests in Property* (DTI, HMSO, London, 1989), suggested that a new register of security interests was all that was needed (paras. 11.6.2, 16.8) though Diamond recommended that negative pledge clauses should be registered (para. 16.10). In 2000 the Company Law Review Steering Group published a consultation document on the subject of registering company charges (*Modern Company Law for a Competitive Economy: Registration of Company Charges* (URN 00/1213) (October 2000)). It invited views, *inter alia*, on the merits of going over to the North American approach of a 'notice filing' system under which priority is determined by the date of filing. The CLRSG *Final Report* of 2001 (ch. 12) advocated the introduction of a notice-filing system. See also Law Commission, Consultation Paper No. 164, *Registration of Security Interests: Company Charges and Property other than Land* (July 2002); Law Commission, *Company Security Interests: A Consultative Report* (Law Com. No. 176, September 2004); Law Commission, *Company Security Interests* (Law Com. No. 296, August 2005). The Law Commission's initial proposals were wide ranging and adopted a functional approach to security along the lines of UCC Article 9 and recommended by the Crowther and Diamond Reports. See also ch. 3 above.

[41] The new form of security interest, even if described as 'floating', would be a fixed security interest and the floating charge would have disappeared as a distinct security device: see *Company Security Interests: A Consultative Report*; R. M. Goode, 'The Case for Abolition of the Floating Charge' in Getzler and Payne, *Company Charges*, p. 17.

provide an opportunity to state that the interests of unsecured creditors should not give way to those of secured creditors where this would be unfair in the substantive or the procedural senses.[42] With the Law Commission's final report of 2005, however, there came a hesitancy regarding potential impacts on insolvency law which led to an abandonment of the recommendation to remove the fixed/floating charge distinction and the opportunity for such wholesale reform was again missed.[43]

Changes might also be made so as to reinforce the 'value' justification for security, which holds that security is fair when it does not dilute the interests of others. One such reform would be to outlaw secured lending on existing corporate assets (while allowing it on new assets). As noted in chapter 3, however, such a severe restriction on the raising of finance might lead many companies into difficulty. A less draconian step would be to echo Article 9 of the US Uniform Commercial Code,[44] again, and provide that priority would be given to 'purchase money security interests' (PMSIs)[45] as against earlier creditors with perfected securities.[46]

---

[42] Policy decisions would have to be made concerning the position of preferential creditors (who now rank before floating, and after fixed, charge holders in priority). On Diamond's position see Diamond Report, p. 85.

[43] The entire programme of company security reform had to be geared to the timing of the introduction of what is now the Companies Act 2006 and 'there was simply no time to go working over the insolvency effects of abolition of the floating charge'. The outcome of the Law Commission's report (and their subsequent Draft 2006 Regulations) amounts to 'conceptual confusion' since floating charges, instead of being subordinate to subsequent fixed charges, have priority according to the time of filing, 'thus obliterating the primary distinction between fixed and floating charges': Goode, 'Case for Abolition of the Floating Charge', p. 20.

[44] See Bridge, 'Form, Substance and Innovation', p. 14; Jackson and Kronman, 'Secured Financing', p. 1171; Diamond Report, paras. 11.7.5–11.7.7.

[45] On English judicial efforts in this direction see *Abbey National Building Society* v. *Cann* [1991] 1 AC 56; *Re Connolly Bros. Ltd (No. 2)* [1912] 2 Ch 25. See further J. Jeremie, 'Gone in an Instant: The Death of "*Scintilla Temporis*" and the Growth of Purchase Money Security Interests in Real Property Law' [1994] JBL 363; J. de Lacy, 'The Purchase Money Security Interest: A Company Charge Conundrum' [1991] LMCLQ 531; de Lacy, 'Retention of Title, Company Charges and the *Scintilla Temporis* Doctrine' [1994] Conv. 242; H. Bennett and C. Davis, 'Fixtures, Purchase Money Security Interests and Dispositions of Interests in Land' (1994) 110 LQR 448; A. Schwartz, 'A Theory of Loan Priorities' (1989) 18 *Journal of Legal Studies* 209. (Note also the proposals of the DTI/IS, *Company Voluntary Arrangements and Administration Orders: A Consultative Document* (October 1993) and the Insolvency Service's *Reviews of Company Rescue and Business Reconstruction Mechanisms* (1999) and (2000) for statutory super-priority for providers of *capital* during a rescue/reconstruction procedure giving these lenders priority over all existing *lenders*.) See further ch. 9 above.

[46] I.e. those who had registered their interests or given possession of the asset to the debtor.

The PMSI is a security interest that favours a creditor who advances sums to fund the acquisition of a particular asset when those sums are in fact so used. Such an interest prevails over all others in a priority conflict.[47] Recognising PMSIs would mean that where a financier provides new assets to the company, the assets would not be drawn into the scope of the floating charge covering after-acquired property. This would reduce the unfairness involved in the floating charge holder gaining the windfall benefit of security in after-acquired assets and doing so at the expense of the later creditor. The PMSI holder can also point to the new value added to the company and the lack of any attendant prejudice to other creditors' security interests. This is because purchase money loans contemplate payments that correspond to the new asset's depreciation and so repossession normally satisfies the PMSI creditor. The cushion of free assets that protects earlier lenders against default is accordingly unaffected.[48]

The Law Commission's consultative report of 2004 in fact recommended recognition of PMSIs[49] but their final report of 2005 noted simply that the priority rules on PMSIs were included in the Consultative Report on the assumption that title retention devices were to be covered, and, given the fact that the initial stages of reform would not include such devices, PMSI rules would also be excluded.[50]

A further way to reinforce the value justification for security is to strengthen preference rules. These rules are designed to prevent insolvent companies from preferring one creditor to another within a specific period leading to a winding up.[51] At present, these rules are subjectively phrased in looking to whether the company desired to confer a preference in giving a security. A strengthening of the law would involve a move in the direction of the Australian and US regimes and the adoption of an objective

---

[47] For a definition of the PMSI see Article 9:107 UCC. On procedural requirements to obtain 'perfection' see Article 9:312(3). On the operation of simple ROT clauses as PMSIs see Diamond Report, pp. 88–9.

[48] See Davies, 'Trade Creditor and the Quest for Security', pp. 57–8.

[49] *Company Security Interests: A Consultative Report* (Law Com. No. 176, September 2004) – the PMSI would outrank an earlier general creditor whose security interest extended to the latter property.

[50] See *Company Security Interests* (Law Com. No. 296, August 2005) paras. 1.29 and 3.146; McCormack, 'Law Commission and Company Security Interests', p. 3. On title retention see pp. 641–8 below.

[51] See Goode, 'Proprietary Rights and Unsecured Creditors'. On preferences generally see, *inter alia*, D. Milman and R. Parry, *A Study of the Operation of Transactional Avoidance Mechanisms in Corporate Insolvency Practice*, ILA Research Report (1997); A. Keay, 'Preferences in Liquidation Law: A Time for Change' [1998] 2 CfiLR 198. See also ch. 13 above.

approach.[52] The issue would then be whether the *effect* of granting the security was to improve the position of one creditor at the expense of others, and the company's desires would drop out of account.[53]

Turning to the issue of notice, unfairness can be reduced by improving information flows to unsecured creditors. As noted, proposals have been made that secured creditors might have to go beyond mere registration and take reasonable steps to inform unsecured creditors of their intentions if they are to place the latter in a subordinate position.[54] Again, however, it should be emphasised that such requirements may increase costs and the supply of information and notice is only of value to certain unsecured creditors. It is of little assistance to involuntary creditors or to those who are unable to adjust for the variety of reasons already discussed.[55]

To summarise, then, it can be said that bypassing *pari passu* by excluding secured property from the insolvent company's estate is difficult to justify in fairness terms with reference to arguments based on bargaining and freedom of contract, supply of value and sufficiency of notice: at least this is so given the present state of English law. Inequalities of bargaining positions, information asymmetries, impositions of externalities and enforcement biases undermine the free bargaining rationale. After-acquired property clauses and weak preference rules detract from claims to the supply of new value, and inadequacies of registration processes and inabilities to adjust place question marks against assertions that notice is adequate.

Steps can be taken to reduce unfairness on most of the above fronts and in some cases the same reforms would also improve overall efficiency. Certain reforms have moved in this direction – as with the Insolvency Act 1986

---

[52] On these regimes see Keay, 'Preferences in Liquidation Law'; M. Shanker, 'The American Bankruptcy Preference Law: Perceptions of the Past, the Transition to the Present, and Ideas for the Future' in J. Ziegel (ed.), *Current Developments in International and Comparative Corporate Insolvency Law* (Clarendon Press, Oxford, 1994).

[53] See Keay, 'Preferences in Liquidation Law'; Goode, 'Proprietary Rights and Unsecured Creditors', p. 187: defences such as good faith or change of position would still, however, be relevant. An objective approach to preferences is likely to facilitate the prevention of unfair grantings of security on past rather than new value; cf. *Re M. C. Bacon Ltd* [1990] BCC 78. See further ch. 13 above.

[54] See LoPucki, 'Unsecured Creditor's Bargain', p. 1948; S. Block-Lieb, 'The Unsecured Creditor's Bargain: A Reply' (1994) 80 Va. L Rev. 1989. Article 9 filing of a security agreement will not, in itself, ensure that detailed information flows to other creditors since a filing notice may give bare outlines only: it is the right to call for particulars of the security agreement that yields valuable information. See Bridge, 'Form, Substance and Innovation', p. 15; Diamond Report, p. 94.

[55] See pp. 607–14 above.

section 176A 'prescribed part' fund for unsecured creditors. Other steps remain possibilities, such as a compulsory tort liability insurance mechanism designed to reduce the unfairness involved in subsidies from involuntary non-adjusting, unsecured tort creditors.

Retention of title and quasi-security

In chapter 3 it was noted that many companies raise finance and arrange the use of assets by using sale arrangements in a manner that substitutes for security. 'Quasi-security' devices such as retentions of title, hire purchase and leasing agreements, factoring and sale and lease-back contracts are used in order to supply credit but avoid the scope of *pari passu* by keeping the assets at issue out of the corporate insolvency estate. The efficiency considerations attending the use of such devices were considered in chapter 3[56] and concerns noted on a number of fronts: that quasi-security devices may produce inefficient transfers of insolvency wealth away from unsecured creditors; that quasi-security undermines the efficiencies associated with security because it increases the uncertainties associated with lending; that poor information on the use of quasi-security devices and legal unknowns produce unnecessary uncertainties; and that quasi-security devices do not, in reality, deliver real protections for creditors who resort to them.

Before questions of fairness are addressed, it is as well to make clear the nature of the legal limitations that affect quasi-security devices. Rather than deal with all varieties of quasi-security, one example of the genre – the retention of title (ROT) clause – will be focused on here. To commence, the terms upon which title to goods can be retained by a creditor should be outlined.[57]

---

[56] See pp. 125–33 above.

[57] See generally S. Wheeler, *Reservation of Title Clauses* (Oxford University Press, Oxford, 1991); Wheeler, *Reservation of Title Clauses: Impact and Implications* (Clarendon Press, Oxford, 1992); I. Davies, *Effective Retention of Title* (Fourmat, London, 1991); G. McCormack, *Reservation of Title* (2nd edn, Sweet & Maxwell, London, 1995); G. Moffat, *Trusts Law: Text and Materials* (4th edn, Cambridge University Press, Cambridge, 2005) ch. 15; Sir G. Lightman and G. Moss, *The Law of Administrators and Receivers of Companies* (4th edn, Thomson/Sweet & Maxwell, London, 2007) ch. 17. On the importance and enforcement of ROT clauses see S. Wheeler, 'Capital Fractionalised: The Role of Insolvency Practitioners in Asset Distribution' in M. Cain and C. B. Harrington (eds.), *Lawyers in a Post Modern World: Translation and Transgression* (Open University Press, Buckingham, 1994). On the interaction of unjust enrichment, restitutionary techniques and retention of title see G. McMeel, 'Retention of Title: The Interface of Contract, Unjust Enrichment and Insolvency' in F. Rose (ed.), *Restitution and Insolvency* (Lloyd's of London Press, London, 2000).

A simple ROT clause will involve a provision in a contract of sale that stipulates that property in the goods being sold will not pass from seller to buyer until the purchase price has been paid in full.[58] Such a clause will not require registration as a security interest in order to be effective.[59]

In more complex arrangements, sellers may attempt to reserve title not merely in the original goods (for example, raw materials) but also in the proceeds of sale of such goods or in products manufactured from such goods or in the proceeds of sale of such products.[60] In the *Romalpa* case[61] the Court of Appeal held that when a seller S supplies goods to buyer B under a ROT clause and authorises B to sell the goods on condition that B accounts for the proceeds of sale, S may, on B's insolvency, rely on the fiduciary relationship established[62] and have an equitable right to trace those proceeds and prevent them from falling into the insolvent estate of B. (A key issue is whether the relationship created between the parties is fiduciary rather than merely that of debtor to creditor.) By such use of a ROT clause, S is given a right *in rem* in the

---

[58] See Sale of Goods Act 1979 s. 19(1) (the statutory basis for ROT clauses). If a seller attempts to reserve merely equitable, as opposed to legal, title to the goods this will be treated as a charge void for non-registration: see *Re Bond Worth Ltd* [1979] 3 All ER 919. On the EC Late Payment Directive and Member States' obligations to recognise contractually agreed-upon ROT clauses see G. McCormack, 'Retention of Title and the EC Late Payment Directive' [2001] 1 JCLS 501.

[59] See *Aluminium Industrie Vaassen BV* v. *Romalpa Aluminium Ltd* [1976] 1 WLR 676; *Armour* v. *Thyssen Edelstahlwerke AG* [1990] 3 WLR 810, [1991] 2 AC 339. In its initial deliberations on these issues, the Law Commission had strongly favoured the registration of title retention devices but it changed its view in its final report (Law Commission, *Company Security Interests* (Law Com. No. 296, August 2005) para. 1.66) and did not recommend registration as a condition of effectiveness. The Commission decided to give such matters further consideration in a wider context going beyond company security interests: see McCormack, 'Law Commission and Company Security Interests', p. 3.

[60] The danger with a complex ROT clause is that it will be found by the courts to create a registrable charge and will be void if not registered under the Companies Act 2006 s. 860: see, for example, *E. Pfeiffer WW GmbH* v. *Arbuthnot Factors Ltd* [1988] 1 WLR 150, [1987] BCLC 522; *Carroll Group Distributors Ltd* v. *Bourke Ltd* [1990] ILRM 285; *Compaq Computers Ltd* v. *Abercorn Group Ltd* [1992] BCC 484.

[61] *Aluminium Industrie Vaassen BV* v. *Romalpa Aluminium Ltd* [1976] 1 WLR 676.

[62] For criticisms of this point see J. Ulph, 'Equitable Proprietary Rights in Insolvency: The Ebbing Tide?' [1996] JBL 482 at 498; R. Bradgate, 'Reservation of Title Ten Years On' (1987) Conv. 434 at 440; J. de Lacy, '*Romalpa* Theory and Practice under Retention of Title in the Sale of Goods' (1995) 24 *Anglo-American Law Review* 327 at 337.

proceeds and does not have to compete with the creditors for a share in B's insolvency estate.[63]

In the *Romalpa* instance, the aluminium foil had not been processed or mixed with other goods. When, however, materials are supplied subject to a ROT clause and there is such a processing or mixing, an issue is whether the seller can rely on the ROT clause to trace into the product that results from processing or mixing. A distinction is to be drawn between cases of mixing goods and instances in which the goods have been processed so as to lose their identity.[64] In the *Borden*[65] decision, resin was supplied for use in the manufacture of chipboard and the Court of Appeal held that if S sells goods to a manufacturer knowing that the goods will be subject to the manufacturing process before being sold, there is no fiduciary relationship between S and B and S cannot rely on a simple ROT clause to ensure tracing: a right over the finished product will have to be provided for by express contractual stipulation.[66] *Borden* thus leaves open difficult issues concerning the point at which the seller's goods lose their identity and become a new product.[67] Where the sold goods have been mixed with other goods and are identifiable readily and can be separated easily then the seller can retain them.[68] Where, moreover, the goods have been mixed with similar goods then, even if

---

[63] If a buyer has become insolvent then the seller can achieve 'debt recovery' via his ability to assert a right *in rem*. If, on the other hand, the proprietary remedy available to the seller is confined to operating by way of a security charge, then, as noted above, ROT sellers invariably lose out upon the buyer's insolvency due to their failure to register the security charge as per the Companies Act 2006 s. 860.

[64] See M. Phillips, 'Retention of Title and Mixing – Exploding the Myth' (2007) 20 *Insolvency Intelligence* 81.

[65] *Borden (UK) Ltd* v. *Scottish Timber Products Ltd* [1981] Ch 25. See also *Re Bond Worth Ltd* [1980] Ch 228; *Re Peachdart* [1984] Ch 131.

[66] For an example see a High Court of Australia case involving the sale of steel and claimed entitlement to products manufactured with the steel: *Associated Alloys Pty Ltd* v. *ACN 001 452 106 Pty Ltd* [2001] HCA 25, [2000] 202 CLR 588 – discussed in K. Stock, 'Australian Developments in the Law of Retention of Title' (2002) 15 *Insolvency Intelligence* 1; J. de Lacy, 'Corporate Insolvency and Retention of Title Clauses: Developments in Australia' [2001] Ins. Law. 64. (In *Associated Alloys* the majority of the High Court distinguished the English cases and held that a ROT clause could be drafted allowing the seller to trace proceeds of sub-sale by way of trust: see further Lightman and Moss, *Law of Administrators*, p 475.)

[67] For discussion see J. de Lacy, 'Processed Goods and Retention of Title Clauses' [1997] 10 *Palmer's In Company*; Ulph, 'Equitable Proprietary Rights in Insolvency'; A. Hicks, 'When Goods Sold Become a New Species' [1993] JBL 485; P. Birks, 'Mixing and Tracing' (1992) 45(2) *Current Legal Problems* 69.

[68] *Hendy Lennox (Industrial Engines) Ltd* v. *Grahame Puttick Ltd* [1984] 1 WLR 485. See Phillips, 'Retention of Title and Mixing – Exploding the Myth'.

separation is not possible, title may be retained where it is possible to decide the retaining party's contribution to the total stock of the goods. In *CKE Engineering*,[69] Judge Norris QC ruled that where, by agreement, a zinc ingot had been mixed and melted with other zinc, there was no difficulty in two companies agreeing that the contents of the melting tank should be treated as owned in proportion to their contributions and in giving effect to a ROT clause with respect to an agreed proportion of the mixed goods.[70] Case law post-*Borden* suggests that when attempts are made to draft ROT clauses so as to retain title in new products or proceeds thereof, the courts will construe these as intending to vest legal ownership of the manufactured product in the hands of the buyer subject only to a registrable charge in favour of the seller.[71] It may, however, be possible for the seller and buyer to agree which of them is to become the owner of any manufactured product: this was the suggestion of Goff and Oliver LJJ in *Re Clough Mill Ltd*.[72]

From a creditor's point of view, a particularly useful version of the ROT clause is the 'all-monies' provision which retains title in the seller's hands until all debts owed to the seller on any grounds are fully paid. (It has been suggested that about half of all ROT clauses are of the 'all-monies' kind.)[73] In an insolvency a benefit of such a clause is that it is not necessary to identify which items in a stock of supplied goods have been paid for: with an 'all-monies' clause all of the stock remains the seller's property. It is arguable that such reference to obligations unconnected with the immediate sale should be viewed as involving a charge, but in the *Armour*[74] case the House of Lords did not regard such a clause as creating a right of security and unanimously held that all-monies clauses are 'legitimate retention of title'.[75]

---

[69] *Re CKE Engineering Ltd (in administration)* [2007] BCC 975.

[70] See also *Spence* v. *Union Marine Insurance Co. Ltd* (1867–8) LR 3 CP 427; *Sandeman and Sons* v. *Tyzak & Branfoot Steamship Co. Ltd* [1913] AC 680; *Glencore International AG* v. *Metro Trading International Inc. (No. 2)* [2001] 1 Lloyd's Rep 284.

[71] *Re Peachdart* [1984] Ch 131.

[72] [1985] 1 WLR 111, 115, 124. See also *Re CKE Engineering Ltd (in administration)* [2007] BCC 975. See further de Lacy, 'Corporate Insolvency and Retention of Title Clauses', pp. 70–5.

[73] See A. Hicks, 'Retention of Title: Latest Developments' [1992] JBL 398 at 400; J. Spencer, 'The Commercial Realities of Reservation of Title Clauses' [1989] JBL 220 at 227: in Spencer's survey 59 per cent of materials suppliers (of various sizes) said that they used ROT clauses.

[74] *Armour* v. *Thyssen Edelstahlwerke AG* [1990] 3 All ER 481, [1990] 3 WLR 810.

[75] See Hicks, 'Retention of Title', p. 403 and also the discussion therein on part-payment.

The value of an all-monies clause is particularly high when the value of the goods sold is rising. If, for example, paintings are supplied by A to a gallery B under an all-monies arrangement, retained ownership of these will operate in effect as security for the debt the purchaser owes in relation to the purchase price for the paintings but also for other debts (for example, relating to furnishings supplied by A to B under other contracts). Keeping an asset of escalating value out of the insolvency estate has the effect of advancing in priority a series of formerly unsecured debts beyond the immediate transaction. It places that asset out of the reach of floating charge holders[76] and ordinary unsecured creditors.[77]

Do ROT clauses offer a means of bypassing *pari passu* that creates unfairness? A first key consideration here is that, as noted, ROT clauses do not have to be registered.[78] Unsecured creditors may, accordingly, be unfairly misled concerning the insolvency risks they are running when they supply goods on credit to a company.[79] Trade suppliers, for instance, may see an array of assets in their debtor's possession but these assets may belong to other parties and there is no register that can be resorted to so as to reveal this information. The existence, never mind the nature and extent, of the ROT clauses will remain invisible.[80] Not only is the *pari passu* principle bypassed but so are the disclosure protections attending the use of security devices.

Matters are made yet worse for the unsecured creditors referred to because corporate accounts will routinely treat goods supplied under ROT arrangements as purchases by the debtor company. Goods which are not the property of the company concerned thus commonly appear as assets in the balance sheet and it is rare for auditors' notes on accounts to

---

[76] But see judges' comments re the hypocrisy of banks complaining of ROTs when they have the floating charge: *Re Clough Mill Ltd* [1985] 1 WLR 111.

[77] The Cork Report, para. 1645, recommended that ROTs should be restricted to the price outstanding on the goods involved in the transaction and that securing the payment of moneys beyond this should be achieved by the creditor using a fixed or floating charge.

[78] The CLRSG recommended in 2001 that a notice-filing system be introduced for company charges. Complex retention of title clauses would be registrable but not simple ROTs: see CLRSG, *Final Report*, para. 12.60. See also the Law Commission, Consultation Paper No. 164, *Registration of Security Interests: Company Charges and Property other than Land* (July 2002); Law Commission, *Company Security Interests: A Consultative Report* (Law Com. No. 176, September 2004); Law Commission, *Company Security Interests* (Law Com. No. 296, August 2005). See p. 648 below.

[79] See Cork Report, paras. 1631–65.

[80] See A. Belcher and W. Beglan, 'Jumping the Queue' [1997] JBL 1, 16–17.

mention retentions of title.[81] As has been commented about ROTs: 'they remain invisible until they become important'.[82]

When the Cork Committee took evidence on ROTs, a 'cry for certainty' was made by 'consultee after consultee'.[83] The complaint was that claims involving ROTs were often confused and that, without clarity, the prospect of expensive litigation overshadowed commercial life. Cork's response was to accept that such complexities could not be avoided and could be negotiated around.[84] It could be contended, however, that all unnecessary legal uncertainties compound the informational unfairness that ROTs can occasion.

A second basis for seeing ROTs as conducing to unfairness is that such devices are not equally available to all creditors. The costs of using ROTs may be relatively low for many suppliers because standardised contracts can be employed but, as noted in chapter 3, the suppliers of certain goods, such as fuels, paint, food and fodder, are unable to use ROTs at all because such materials disappear on consumption and leave the creditor with an unsecured claim.[85] The effect is to load insolvency risks unduly onto the shoulders of those suppliers who happen to deal in goods that are consumed in the short term. A similar point can be made in relation to those suppliers who are repeat players and those who are engaged in a series of 'one-off' transactions. The latter may find it far more difficult to impose ROT clauses on their debtors.

A third cause of unfairness may arise from the use of ROTs to secure debts beyond the immediate transaction. As already noted, this is a particularly acute problem where the asset involved is of escalating value. That growth in value, combined with an all-monies (or all-liabilities) clause, will not be a windfall that becomes available to the body of unsecured creditors but will serve to prioritise certain unsecured debts (those owed to the asset supplier) and will ultimately[86] leave other unsecured creditors looking at a smaller insolvency estate than they anticipated.

Such unfairnesses as are noted may be compounded by inequalities of bargaining power. Powerful creditors will be able to impose ROT clauses

---

[81] C. Williams, 'Retention of Title: Some Recent Developments' (1991) 12 Co. Law. 54.

[82] Belcher and Beglan, 'Jumping the Queue', p. 17.

[83] Cork Report, para. 1627.   [84] Ibid., paras. 1628–9.

[85] Contrast the situation and approach taken regarding processed goods in the Antipodes: see *Re Weddel (NZ) Ltd* [1996] 5 NZBLC 104; *Associated Alloys Pty Ltd* v. *ACN 001 452 106 Pty Ltd* [2001] HCA 25, [2000] 202 CLR 588; de Lacy, 'Processed Goods and Retention of Title Clauses' and 'Corporate Insolvency and Retention of Title Clauses'.

[86] Of course the floating charge holder is the first to 'suffer'.

on debtors but those with less market power (or subject to more competitive circumstances) may be unable to retain title.[87] The ROT is accordingly a device that may prove unfair in so far as it shifts insolvency risks to those who are the newest and weakest players in the market.

There is an argument, however, that use of ROT clauses can be conducive to fairness. The Cork Committee did not advocate the outlawing of ROT clauses in insolvency, noting that this would usually benefit floating charge holders, not unsecured creditors, and stating:

> suppliers have opted for reservation of title clauses precisely because they seek to avoid the unfairness which results when they supply goods on credit, a floating charge crystallises and a receiver then takes the goods and realises them for the benefit of the debenture-holder leaving the supplier with nothing. It seems to us that suppliers are entitled, in such circumstances, to take steps to protect themselves and that it would be wrong to deny them the protection they seek.[88]

Cork was disposed not to curtail contractual freedoms more than necessary[89] but was faced with its respondents' 'wide unanimity' of view that ROTs should be subjected to disclosure. The Committee recommended that a disclosure requirement along the lines of Article 9 of the US Uniform Commercial Code should be adapted to English needs so that there should be disclosure of names of suppliers imposing ROTs; descriptions of the types or classes of goods covered by the ROT; and the maximum amount that at any one time could be secured by the ROT.[90] Consumer goods, as covered by the Sale of Goods Act 1979 (covering goods ordinarily bought for private use or consumption), would, on Cork's recommendations, not be covered by a disclosure requirement. Cork did not take a view on how far tracing should be allowed to extend but, as noted, did consider that a duly registered ROT should be limited to the price outstanding on the goods immediately contracted for and should not take the all-monies or all-liabilities form.

---

[87] See *Leyland DAF Ltd* v. *Automotive Products plc* [1993] BCC 389 which demonstrates the potential for a ROT clause to *contribute* to a supplier's bargaining power, i.e. where continued supplies are vital to a receiver's attempts to keep a company running (noted in Belcher and Beglan, 'Jumping the Queue', pp. 18–19).

[88] See Cork Report, paras. 1633–4; G. Elias, *Explaining Constructive Trusts* (Clarendon Press, Oxford, 1990) p. 135: 'It is only fair that suppliers of goods to businessmen should be able to stipulate for ROTs in respect of the goods which they supply. It would be unprincipled to give the power to take property rights by way of security to the lending institutions and nobody else.'

[89] Cork Report, para. 1637. [90] Ibid., para. 1638.

As noted, the Law Commission has put the matter of ROT registration aside for further consideration.[91] Were the Cork recommendations to be implemented, however, they would go some way to meet criticisms based on the unavailability of information concerning ROTs and the unfairness of extending ROTs beyond the immediate transaction.[92] In France and Italy, like the USA, ROTs require registration to be effective but the EC Regulation on Insolvency Proceedings 2000, while making express provision for ROT claims (Article 7), does not require registration.[93]

Trusts

Parties involved in commercial relations with a company may, for reasons discussed above, find it difficult to take security or retain title so as to protect themselves against a potential insolvency. The consumer, for example, who pays in advance for goods may be ill-placed to resort to such measures. Another kind of refuge may, however, be available by reference to equitable doctrines which separate property held on trust from property forming part of the insolvent company's estate.[94] As the Cork

---

[91] *Company Security Interests* (Law Com. No. 296, August 2005) para. 1.66; see p. 645 and ch. 3 above. Reference can, however, be made to the added weight of the reports of the Diamond and Crowther Committees which both advocated a new register of 'security interests' that would have included retentions of title to secure the payment of money. On ROT registration generally see S. Wheeler, 'The Insolvency Act 1986 and ROTs' [1987] JBL 180.

[92] The Company Law Review Steering Group's 2000 Consultation Document (*Registration of Company Charges*) put forward proposals for defining those retention of title clauses that are deemed registrable but, as noted, the CLRSG's *Final Report* (ch. 12) would have treated complex, but not simple, ROTs as registrable in its proposed notice-filing system. For discussions leading up to the suggested new notice-filing system for registrable charges set out in the Law Commission's Draft Company Security Regulations 2006 (which, as indicated, contra to many proposals, did not in the end extend to ROTs) see Law Commission, Consultation Paper No. 164, *Registration of Security Interests: Company Charges and Property other than Land* (July 2002); Law Commission, *Company Security Interests* (Law Com. No. 296, August 2005); and generally McCormack, 'Law Commission and Company Security Interests'; McCormack, 'Rewriting the English Law of Personal Property Securities and Article 9 of the US Uniform Commercial Code' (2003) 24 Co. Law. 69.

[93] Per Article 4(2)(m): 'The law of the State of opening of proceedings shall determine the conditions for the opening of those proceedings, their conduct and their closure. It shall determine in particular: ... (m) the rules relating to the voidness, voidability or unenforceability of legal acts detrimental to all other creditors.' See Lightman and Moss, *Law of Administrators*, p. 478.

[94] On trusts and insolvency see generally Moffat, *Trusts Law*, ch. 15; R. Stevens, 'Insolvency' in W. Swadling (ed.), *The Quistclose Trust: Critical Essays* (Hart Publishing, Oxford, 2004) p. 153; A. Belcher, *Corporate Rescue* (Sweet & Maxwell, London, 1997) ch. 9; H. Anderson, 'The Treatment of Trust Assets in English Insolvency Law' in E. McKendrick (ed.), *Commercial*

Committee stressed, property held by an insolvent company on trust for others has never passed to the liquidator representing the general body of the company's creditors because the liquidator takes on the 'free assets' of the insolvent company.[95] Proprietary interests in favour of third parties prevail against the general body of creditors unless, of course, they are invalidated under any particular statutory provisions (e.g. those relating to the avoidance of floating charges or non-registration of charges). If a lender is placed in the position of a beneficiary of a trust imposed on the company, that lender has a claim *in rem* against the money at issue in priority to all others claiming against the company's assets.[96] As with retention of title, it is thus possible to avoid *pari passu* distribution by keeping property out of the body of assets available for settling the company's debts.

This section of the chapter outlines the conditions under which the law will recognise trusts in the corporate insolvency context. It then considers efficiency issues arising from the use of trusts and finally looks to questions of fairness. (Questions of accountability and expertise were dealt with in chapter 13 when assessing liquidation processes in which the principle of *pari passu* distribution is applied to the residual estate.)

The recognition of trusts

For a trust relationship to be recognised, the courts must find there to exist both an equitable proprietary interest in the property in question and a fiduciary relationship.[97] Circumstances satisfying these conditions may involve three distinct types of trust: express, resulting and constructive.[98] For an express trust to be established there are 'three certainties' to be shown to be present:[99] of intention, subject matter and objects. On the first point, intention will not necessarily involve writing (unless land is

---

Aspects of Trusts and Fiduciary Obligations (Clarendon Press, Oxford, 1992); Cork Report, ch. 22; A. Oakley, 'Proprietary Claims and their Priority in Insolvency' [1995] CLJ 377.

[95] See Cork Report, para. 1042.

[96] See Milman and Durrant, *Corporate Insolvency*, p. 161.

[97] See Oakley, 'Proprietary Claims', pp. 381–3; *Agip (Africa)* v. *Jackson* [1989] 3 WLR 1367 at 1386; *Re Diplock* [1948] Ch 465.

[98] See S. Worthington, *Proprietary Interests in Commercial Transactions* (Clarendon Press, Oxford, 1996) pp. 44–5, who argues that some judges and commentators describe a single express trust while others require two trusts: a primary express trust linked with a secondary trust which operates if the primary trust fails, the secondary trust being variously described as an express trust, a resulting trust or even a constructive trust.

[99] See Milman and Durrant, *Corporate Insolvency*, p. 166; M. Ellis and L. Verrill, 'Twilight Trusts' (2007) 20 *Insolvency Intelligence* 151 at 152–3; P. Sidle, 'Whose Money is it Anyway?' (2005) *Recovery* (Autumn) 24.

involved)[100] and the key issue is whether in substance a sufficient intention has been manifested.[101] As for subject matter, it must be possible to
identify the property that is covered by the trust: a special difficulty where
money is involved and where trust claims are liable to succeed only if the
money at issue is retained in a separate bank account.[102] Certainty of
objects requires clarity concerning the purposes of the trust relationship.
If, for instance, there is an intended trust relationship but it is unclear
when funds are to be distributed in a particular way, the trust will fail and
money held by a company will, on an insolvency, enter the insolvency
estate. This was the position in *Re Challoner Club Ltd (in liquidation)*[103]
where members of a company (an incorporated club) donated funds to
the troubled company which attempted to create a trust over those funds.
The trust terms were too uncertain to identify when the money was to
return to the members and consequently the trust failed.

Resulting trusts are based on the presumed intentions of the settlor
and are generally held to arise where a party purchases property in the
name of another[104] or transfers property into the name of another.[105]
Constructive trusts[106] are trusts imposed independently of the intentions
of the parties and can be seen as devices used by the courts in pursuit of
justice. Cases have suggested that claims to constructive trusts are difficult to establish and in practical insolvency contexts the constructive
trust may be of limited importance.[107] Recent *dicta*, however, in *Re*

---

[100] See *Re Kayford Ltd* [1975] 1 All ER 604 at 607. As Milman and Durrant (*Corporate Insolvency*, p. 166) note: 'a trust can arise even though the transaction is not framed in terms of a trust; the crucial factor, as always, is the substantive operation of the arrangement'. See, for example, *Re English & American Insurance Co.* [1994] 1 BCLC 649 and *Re Fleet Disposal Services Ltd* [1995] 1 BCLC 345 but compare *Swiss Bank Corp.* v. *Lloyds Bank Ltd* [1981] 2 WLR 893. The lack of certainty of intention was critical in *Re Multi Guarantee Co. Ltd* [1987] BCLC 257.

[101] See *Re Kayford Ltd* [1975] 1 All ER 604.

[102] See also *Re London Wine Shippers Ltd* [1986] PCC 121; *Re Ellis, Son & Vidler Ltd* [1994] BCC 532; *Export Credits Guarantee Dept.* v. *Turner* 1981 SLT 286. See further Ulph, 'Equitable Proprietary Rights in Insolvency', pp. 489–93.

[103] *The Times*, 4 November 1997.

[104] See Oakley, 'Proprietary Claims', p. 386; *Dyer* v. *Dyer* (1788) 2 Cox Eq 92.

[105] *Vandervell* v. *Inland Revenue Commissioners* [1967] 2 AC 291. See also the discussion of 'presumed' and 'automatic' trusts by Megarry J in *Vandervell*.

[106] See *Re Goldthorpe Exchange Ltd* [1995] 1 AC 74 (PC).

[107] Regarding remedial constructive trusts see *Re Polly Peck International (No. 4)*, *The Times*, 18 May 1998, per Mummery LJ: 'The insolvency road was blocked off to the remedial constructive trusts, at least when judge-driven in a vehicle of discretion ... to a trust lawyer and, even more so to an insolvency lawyer, the prospect of a court

Farepak Food and Gifts Ltd[108] indicate a judicial willingness to recognise the possibility of institutional constructive trusts arising in the context of corporate insolvency.[109]

In relation to corporate insolvency, trusts are of particular importance in two contexts which are worthy of more detailed attention. These are where funds are advanced for particular purposes and where consumers make payments for goods or services in advance.

Advances for particular purposes

During the nineteenth century the suppliers of funds for speculative enterprises commonly protected their investments by advancing moneys not to companies directly but to trustees.[110] The latter would then release funds as required and if the company involved became insolvent any funds left in the hands of the trustees would be recoverable by the investors.[111] Such a procedure offered protection but it did involve the inconvenience of using intermediaries.

Whether funds advanced directly to the company for a specific purpose might be held on trust was the issue considered by the House of Lords in *Barclays Bank Ltd* v. *Quistclose Investments Ltd*.[112] In that case,

---

imposing such a trust was inconceivable.' See further G. Stewart, 'No Remedial Trust in Insolvency' (1998) (August) *Insolvency Practitioner* 8; Worthington, *Proprietary Interests*, p. 50. See generally C. Rickett, 'Of Constructive Trusts and Insolvency' in F. Rose (ed.), *Restitution and Insolvency* (Lloyd's of London Press, London, 2000); D. Wright, 'The Remedial Constructive Trust and Insolvency' in Rose, *Restitution and Insolvency*.

[108] [2008] BCC 22.

[109] Mann J in *Re Farepak Food and Gifts Ltd (in administration)* [2008] BCC 22, paras. 37–44, admitted that remedial constructive trusts are not recognised by English law but felt that there was a strong argument that moneys paid to Farepak after it ceased trading (and at a time when it had indicated that payments should not be received) were held by it as constructive trustee (i.e. per an institutional constructive trust). On the facts, however, it could not be established that all the moneys in relation to which the court was asked to make a decision fell within that line of argument. Mann J 'very much regretted coming to this decision' but considered 'the material does not exist which makes it sufficiently clear for present purposes that the sums which are said to come within the constructive trust do in fact do so'.

[110] See Milman and Durrant, *Corporate Insolvency*, p. 161.

[111] *National Bolivian Navigation Co.* v. *Wilson* (1880) 5 App Cas 176.

[112] [1970] AC 567, [1968] 3 All ER 651. See further W. Swadling (ed.), *The Quistclose Trust: Critical Essays* (Hart Publishing, Oxford, 2004); A. McKnight, *The Law of International Finance* (Oxford University Press, Oxford, 2008) pp. 860–4; L. Ho and P. Smart, 'Re-interpreting the *Quistclose* Trust: A Critique of Chambers' Analysis' (2001) 21 OJLS 267.

Rolls Razor Ltd was in difficulties but declared a dividend on its shares and Quistclose loaned the company £209,719 solely for the purpose of paying the dividend. The sum was paid into a separate account with Barclays Bank, with whom Rolls Razor were currently overdrawn. Barclays were aware of the payment by Quistclose. Rolls Razor then went into liquidation before the dividend was paid and Barclays claimed to be entitled to set off the money from Quistclose against the overdraft. The House of Lords decided unanimously, however, that the money had been received by the company and held on a primary trust for payment of the dividend and that, the primary trust having failed, that money was held on a secondary trust for Quistclose. Since Barclays had been given notice of the trust disposition, its own claim failed.

The *Quistclose* type of arrangement is now commonly used and its effect is to give the lender protection in relation to sums not yet expended on the specific purpose.[113] Such an arrangement differs from a secured loan in that it does not have to be registered and there is no public notice given of the transaction.

Central to Lord Wilberforce's analysis in *Quistclose* was the 'two trust' approach – involving the primary trust for the initial purpose and the secondary trust for the lender that commences with the failure of the purpose. The 'two trust' approach was, however, criticised in the House of Lords in the *Twinsectra* case of 2002.[114] Lord Millett urged that such an approach created 'formidable difficulties' where the trust was for an abstract purpose, since the beneficial interest could not be invested in an abstract purpose (as opposed to, say, a benefiting individual). His own approach was to state that the property was vested in the donor on a resulting trust, with the borrower holding the money as a trustee for the lender and having either a power or a duty to apply the money for the stated purpose. *Twinsectra* was applied in the *Margaretta* decision in 2005[115] but, whether the 'two trust' or the *Twinsectra* approach is adopted, it is clear that, if there is a *Quistclose* trust and the purpose

---

[113] For recognition of a purpose trust in the context of payments made to administrators to facilitate the discharge of liabilities owed to third parties by the company in administration see *Re Niagara Mechanical Services International Ltd (in administration)* [2001] BCC 393, described (2000) *Recovery* (August) 7, [2001] 80 *CCH Company Law Newsletter* 6.

[114] *Twinsectra v. Yardley* [2002] 2 AC 164.   [115] *Margaretta Ltd* [2005] All ER 262.

fails (e.g. because the borrower becomes insolvent) the funds will not form part of the borrower's estate but will revert to the lender.[116]

In order for a *Quistclose* trust to arise, there must be an obligation to put the money aside for the special purpose. In the highly publicised *Farepak*[117] case, the company had operated a Christmas savings scheme involving the collection of money from large numbers of small savers by thousands of agents and the forwarding of such funds to the company in advance payment for Christmas hampers and vouchers. After the company had entered administration on 13 October 2006, the administrators accepted that most of the money collected had disappeared and could not be returned to the customers – who stood, in their thousands, to recover only around five pence in the pound.[118] In the three days prior to the start of the administration, however, the directors had sought to ring-fence moneys received during that short period by creating a deed of trust over funds received into the company's bank account. Mann J, however, rejected the argument that the company held the customers' money under a *Quistclose* trust. The collecting agents were agents of the company, not of the customers, and so the money passed to the company when it was given to the agents and not when it was placed in the company's bank account. Nor was there any requirement that the agents

---

[116] See Sidle, 'Whose Money is it Anyway?'. Diversity of opinion thus centres on the location of the beneficial interest in the money before the failure of the purpose for which the funds were advanced. Leading views are that there is a trust of the money for the lender with a power to use the money to pay the beneficiary (Lord Millett in *Twinsectra*) or there is an entitlement in the borrower to use the money beneficially subject to the lender's proprietary right to prevent misuse of the money (R. Chambers, *Resulting Trusts* (Oxford University Press, Oxford, 1997) ch. 3; see also R. Chambers, 'Restrictions on the Use of Money' in Swadling, *Quistclose Trust,* p. 77). For a discussion of these and other approaches see Stevens, 'Insolvency'; Ho and Smart, 'Re-interpreting the *Quistclose* Trust'; Moffat, *Trusts Law,* ch. 15; A. Tettenborn, 'Resulting Trusts and Insolvency' in Rose, *Restitution and Insolvency.*

[117] *Re Farepak Food and Gifts Ltd (in administration)* [2008] BCC 22 (Ch). Around 150,000 British families lost an estimated £40 million in the collapse of Farepak: see Editorial, 'Farepak and the Ghost of Christmas Present', *Financial Times,* 17 November 2006.

[118] In October 2007 Gordon Brown pledged 'to ensure justice' for the victims of Farepak: *Financial Times,* 18 October 2007. Victims received just £8m from a government-backed charity fund: 'Un-Farepak', *Financial Times,* 20 November 2007. Earlier in 2007, following the Treasury's (Pomeroy) *Review of Christmas Savings Schemes* (Treasury, March 2007) the Government announced that it had secured industry agreement to a scheme of ring-fenced accounts for customers' money. By May 2008, an investigation by BERR's Companies Investigation Branch had been completed and the CIB was taking advice on possible legal action against the Farepak directors. See J. Pickard, 'Regulator Completes Farepak Collapse Probe', *Financial Times,* 13 May 2008.

should hold the money on trust or that the money be put aside pending transmutation from collected money to goods or vouchers.[119] The relationship between Farepak and its customers was, thus, a contractual one and there was no *Quistclose* trust.[120]

Consumer prepayments

When consumers make payments in advance to companies for goods or services – for example, by sending money to mail order firms – they run considerable risks. If the company becomes insolvent before the goods or services are supplied (as in *Farepak*) the consumers have no remedies except as unsecured creditors, a position in which they are unlikely to receive even a substantial portion of their money back. The Cork Report[121] noted that a good deal of public and media concern attended this state of the law and in 1984 an Office of Fair Trading (OFT) survey suggested that there were at least 15 million prepayments per year, that 2 per cent of these involved a loss of money and that total losses exceeded £18 million.[122]

Such difficulties have been responded to in a variety of ways. A number of trade associations have established voluntary compensation schemes[123] and certain statutes deal with prepayments in particular sectors. The Estate Agents Act 1979 section 13 thus requires a client's

---

[119] Mann J stated that a failure to keep the received money separate from other money was not fatal to a *Quistclose*-type resulting trust but that what was crucial in the Farepak situation was the lack of any suggestion that the money had to be put on one side by Farepak pending transmutation from credited money to goods or vouchers. If there were a *Quistclose* trust then that obligation would have been inherent in it.

[120] Nor was Mann J prepared to hold that money received after the company had ceased trading was held on constructive trust: see p. 651 above. He was sympathetic to this possibility, following *Neste Oy* v. *Barclays Bank* [1983] 2 Lloyds Rep 658, but the limited evidence available did not provide a sufficient basis for such a decision.

[121] Cork Report, paras. 1048–9.

[122] OFT, *The Protection of Consumer Prepayments: A Discussion Paper* (1984) ('OFT'). See also Moffat, *Trusts Law*, ch. 15.

[123] Moffat, *Trusts Law*, p. 765, notes those of the Newspaper Proprietors Association, the Mail Order Protection Scheme and the Direct Marketing Association. See also T. Sears, 'Turbulence in the Travel Trade' (2008) *Recovery* (Spring) 28, describing the operation of protection schemes run by tour operators and travel agencies (e.g. the ABTA bonding arrangement, the ATOL Bonding Protection Scheme, the IATA travel agents' agency for IATA member airlines). 'The practical result of this protection for passengers will be that they will not form the bulk of unsecured creditors in a travel insolvency; but rather the bulk will be trade creditors and those who provide the bonding protection for the organisations referred to above' (at p. 28).

money to be held in trust in a separate bank account.[124] General legislation also plays a part here in so far as the Sale of Goods (Amendment) Act 1995 provides that pre-paying buyers of part of a bulk will obtain undivided proprietary rights in the bulk.[125] This amending legislation went some way in helping with problems of identifying the subject of the trust (though the bulk of goods may itself present difficulties of identification) but such legislative responses have not solved all the problems and uncertainties left by judicial decisions in this area.

Customer interests may, however, be protected where it is decided that funds are held in trust for their benefit. A key decision on such trusts is *Re Kayford*.[126] This case concerned a company (K) that ran a mail order business. K had loaned its main supplier considerable sums of money but the supplier entered financial difficulties. This, in turn, threatened K's solvency. K was advised by an accountant to open a separate 'Customers' Trust Deposit Account', to pay into it any money received from customers for the purchase of goods which had not yet been delivered and to withdraw money only on delivery of the goods. K accepted the device but, in the first instance, paid money into a dormant deposit account in the company's name, only at a later stage altering the name of the account. After K had entered involuntary liquidation Megarry J found sufficient evidence of an intention to create a trust. This was contained in the discussions of K's managing director, the accountant and the bank manager. Megarry J found that the three certainties of a trust were established and commented:

> No doubt the general rule is that if you send money to a company for goods which are not delivered you are merely a creditor of the company unless a trust has been created. The sender may create a trust by using appropriate words when he sends the money ... or the company may do it by taking suitable steps on or before receiving the money. If either is done the obligations in respect of the money are transformed from contract to property, from debt to trust.[127]

Megarry J suggested, further, that it was entirely 'proper and honourable' for a company to use such a trust account as soon as there were doubts about the firm's ability to fulfil its obligations. He, indeed, welcomed the taking of such steps.

---

[124] See OFT, paras. 3.1–3.13; G. Howells and S. Weatherill, *Consumer Protection Law* (Dartmouth, Aldershot, 1995).

[125] See Ulph, 'Equitable Proprietary Rights in Insolvency'.

[126] [1975] 1 All ER 604, [1975] 1 WLR 279.   [127] [1975] 1 WLR 279 at 282.

There was, however, no trust of customer deposits in *Holiday Promotions (Europe) Ltd*[128] where the court held that the payment of customer deposits created a purely contractual relationship of debtor and creditor. In *Holiday Promotions*, deposits were not segregated in a separate account but were mixed with company money and, importantly, the company was free to use the deposits for its general purposes. There was nothing in the terms of any contract, nor in the general circumstances, to indicate any intention or agreement that the funds should not form part of the general assets available to creditors.

It would now appear, though, that initial payment into the company's general account is not necessarily fatal to the existence of a trust. In the *Tiny Computers* case,[129] a trust was expressly and successfully set up for sums forthcoming from customers. These sums constituted deposits and, in anticipation of insolvency, were deposited with the company's bank with instructions that the bank should hold the funds on trust for customers in a customer trust account. The complication was that the deposits were paid into the company's general account from which transfers were periodically made into the customer trust account. The court stated, however, that there was no difficulty regarding certainty of intention or subject matter and that there was certainty of objects since (though difficult) it was possible to determine the relative interests of the depositing customers by referring to the customer lists held by the company.[130] Where, moreover, there is an intention to establish a trust for listed beneficiaries and there is a shortfall in the trust account, it has been held that beneficiaries' entitlements should be assessed with reference to the sums owed to them in the trust period rather than by looking at the quantum of funds that had actually been placed in trust for them. Thus in *Sendo International Ltd*[131] a schedule set out the debts owed to each beneficiary and it was stated that there was a clear intention to release sums equal to the scheduled debts from the security that would otherwise cover those funds. It was the scheduled amounts, accordingly, that were said to define each creditor's interest.

---

[128] [1996] 2 BCLC 618.

[129] *OT Computers Ltd (in administration)* v. *First National Tricity Finance* [2003] EWHC 1010.

[130] A parallel trust for suppliers failed since its object ('payments due to urgent suppliers') was uncertain in the absence of any listing of such suppliers and because the term 'urgent' was too vague to define any class of beneficiary.

[131] *Sendo International Ltd (in administration)* [2007] BCC 491.

Efficiency

Do trust devices offer an efficient way for parties to protect themselves when advancing funds or making prepayments? What is clear is that trusts are often set up to ring-fence moneys received in the twilight period prior to an anticipated insolvency since this serves to protect customers and suppliers and it also suggests to the outside world that business is being carried on as usual. This is particularly useful in sustaining a position while a pre-pack or other turnaround strategy is being brought into effect.[132] 'Twilight trusts' can thus be seen as useful in allowing the directors to continue trading in the hope of attracting investors and maximising returns to creditors. The counter view is that such trusts are often used to protect the directors from liabilities for wrongful trading and that the time-consuming and expensive process of setting up such 'fireproofing' trusts tends to distract the management of the company away from the needs of a business in crisis.[133] A significant difficulty in using such trusts is that they often have to be set up rapidly and they are, in legal terms, notoriously fragile.[134]

In relation to express trusts and resulting trusts, as encountered in *Quistclose*, there are also issues of uncertainty. As commentators have pointed out,[135] the precise nature of the equitable right to see that the loan is applied 'for the primary designated purpose' is unclear and it is not always apparent when the primary purpose is fulfilled, the 'trust' spent and the equitable right extinguished. Moffat also notes: 'Similar uncertainty surrounds the status of the particular class of creditors for whose benefit the primary trust in *Quistclose* was created, i.e. the shareholders post-declaration of a dividend. Are they beneficiaries under a private express trust with associated rights of enforcement? If not, are we presented with an example of a "purpose trust" infringing the beneficiary principle?'[136]

Questions also arise as to the characterisation of the assets to be placed in trust. This area of uncertainty is encountered in the *Carreras*

---

[132] See D. Redstone, 'Customer Deposits (in the Twilight Zone)' (2008) *Recovery* (Spring) 17; M. Ellis and L. Verrill, 'Twilight Trusts' (2007) 20 *Insolvency Intelligence* 151; Sidle, 'Whose Money is it Anyway?' On pre-packs see ch. 10 above.

[133] See Ellis and Verrill, 'Twilight Trusts', who question (p. 115) whether it is right for directors to pursue self-protection rather than safeguarding business value.

[134] Redstone, 'Customer Deposits (in the Twilight Zone)'.

[135] Ibid.; J. Heydon, W. Gummow and R. Austin, *Cases and Materials on Equity and Trusts* (4th edn, Butterworths, Sydney, 1993) p. 476; Swadling, *Quistclose Trust*.

[136] Moffat, *Trusts Law*, p. 775.

Rothmans[137] case. Rothmans owed an advertising agency money for services and renegotiated an agreement so that the sums involved were paid by the agency into a special account for the purpose of paying these expenses. The agency went into liquidation and Rothmans contested their claim to the funds with the liquidator. The case was decided on *Quistclose* lines and the funds were said never to have belonged to the agency and to be repayable to Rothmans. Such an approach is, however, questionable since the agency had effectively made an existing asset (the Rothmans' debt) available exclusively to one class of creditor, and this should probably now be seen as a preference or contrary to the principle established in *British Eagle*.[138]

Quistclose, it should also be noted, involved an attempted corporate rescue, and the extent to which *Quistclose* principles are liable to be extended by the courts to cover more routine advances of corporate finance is a further area of uncertainty.[139] The courts may well act consistently with the advice of commentators and be less inclined to recognise trusts where rescues are not involved and where the language used does not evidence the intention to establish a trust in rigorous terms.[140] Here, again, the philosophical underpinnings of *Quistclose* are unclear and further cases raise the questions whether the *Quistclose* trust is to be seen as an express trust or a constructive trust and whether it is to be viewed in pure trusts law terms or remedially.[141]

Such uncertainties reduce the present value of the *Quistclose* type of trust as an effective and efficient means of protecting investors but there is no necessary reason why the courts or the legislature could not bring new clarity into this area of the law. If it is asked whether such trusts hold out the promise of effective and efficient protection in routine cases of lending, other considerations have to be taken into account. First, a creditor may demand that a debtor company should place the funds at issue into a special account to be used for a specific purpose but the company may resist such a request for a number of reasons. Administrative costs will be

---

[137] *Carreras Rothmans Ltd* v. *Freeman Mathews Treasure Ltd* [1985] 1 Ch 207, [1984] 3 WLR 1016.

[138] On preferences see Insolvency Act 1986 ss. 239, 240 and ch. 13 above; *British Eagle International Airlines Ltd* v. *Compagnie Nationale Air France* [1975] 1 WLR 758, [1975] 2 All ER 390 and ch. 14 above.

[139] See Belcher and Beglan, 'Jumping the Queue', p. 7; Moffat, *Trusts Law*, ch. 15.

[140] See Bridge, '*Quistclose* Trust'.

[141] See Belcher and Beglan, 'Jumping the Queue', p. 8; C. Rickett, 'Different Views on the Scope of the *Quistclose* Analysis: English and Antipodean Insights' (1991) 107 LQR 608; Moffat, *Trusts Law*, ch. 15; Chambers, 'Restrictions on the Use of Money'.

incurred by the company and these may be seen as excessive and unnecessary. Other creditors may insist on similar separate accounts and there may be fears of a deluge of such requests that, overall, would impose tight and inconvenient restraints on the uses to which money can be put. The company, moreover, may consider that it is not possible to designate specific purposes for its borrowings without giving up the flexibility of financing that it needs to compete in the marketplace. In the face of such company resistance to the use of a *Quistclose* trust, the small supplier of funds or the infrequent/one-off supplier may be ill-positioned to insist on the arrangement and may be ill-equipped to calculate the advantages, disadvantages and ways of arranging such a trust.

Turning to consumer prepayments and the *Kayford* type of trust, this also possesses limitations.[142] In the first instance, it requires that the consumer, on forwarding money, should use appropriate words to manifest the intention to establish a trust, or the company supplying the goods must itself take actions demonstrating such an intention.[143] Most consumers will not be aware of the possibilities offered by *Kayford* trusts and are unlikely to use the required forms of words when making purchases. They may not occupy bargaining positions that allow them to insist on such arrangements and the trading companies themselves will have weak incentives to establish *Kayford* trusts. A second difficulty arises from the need to identify the funds at issue. The law provides rules to trace assets in mixed accounts but these rules are complex and do not allow involved parties to predict legal effects clearly. Legal uncertainties also infect the process of establishing a *Kayford* type of trust. Thus, the courts may refuse to recognise such trusts where they are deemed to infringe the *pari passu* principle of residual insolvency distribution and when such infringements will be declared is a matter of some uncertainty.[144]

Pursuing the issue of efficiency prompts the question whether it is desirable to offer consumer pre-payers the protections of *Kayford* trusts and to place them ahead of other unsecured creditors in whose body they would take their place in the absence of a trust. Practical considerations may undermine the efficiency case for consumer protections through

---

[142] See W. Goodhart and G. Jones, 'The Infiltration of Equitable Doctrine into English Commercial Law' (1980) 43 MLR 489; Moffat, *Trusts Law*, pp. 768–70; A. Ogus and C. Rowley, *Prepayments and Insolvency* (OFT Occasional Paper, 1984).

[143] See Ogus and Rowley, *Prepayments and Insolvency*, p. 6.

[144] See Cork Report, para. 1068; *British Eagle International Airlines Ltd* v. *Compagnie Nationale Air France* [1975] 2 All ER 390.

trusts so that, even if the case for consumer protection was accepted, it could be argued that trusts do not provide the best route to such protection. The OFT recognised in 1984 that administrative costs for firms might be high if separate accounts and trusts were routinely employed.[145] These costs would have a disproportionate effect on small new companies. Public policing of such practices might prove expensive since firms would possess incentives to transfer funds from special to general accounts before contracts were fulfilled. Prepayments also provide, in many cases, an 'essential part of the trader's working capital'.[146] Ogus and Rowley suggest that in general terms there is no efficiency presumption that such financing is better provided by commercial rather than customer creditors (though they qualify this comment by stating that if poorly informed consumers falsely maintain uneconomic market operations, there may be efficiency losses to society). A danger that can be pointed to with more confidence, however, is that if superior protections were given to consumer creditors, the effect would be to increase the incentives of other parties to take security and to leave fewer assets available for unsecured creditors. A further danger is that funds to replace those currently provided by prepayment might be hard to come by. Ogus and Rowley caution: 'Given capital market imperfections, it is by no means clear that alternative finance would be available, save at loaded rates of interest, even where the trader was essentially solvent, especially in the case of new enterprise.'[147] The risk is that gains for consumers would be achieved at the price of significant increases in legal and administrative costs.

Other means of consumer protection have been suggested.[148] In rejecting preferred status for consumer creditors and compulsory trust accounts, the Cork Committee relied on more general measures to discourage irresponsible corporate behaviour or limit its effects. These came in the form of tighter disqualification rules for errant directors and the introduction of the wrongful trading concept together with the proposed 10 per cent fund which would be available for consumer as well as other unsecured creditors. Ogus and Rowley pointed out that a number of protective arrangements had already been introduced (most

---

[145] Ogus and Rowley, *Prepayments and Insolvency*, paras. 6.9–6.24.

[146] Cork Report, para. 1050.

[147] Ogus and Rowley, *Prepayments and Insolvency*, p. 28; cf. P. Richardson, 'Consumer Protection and the Trust' [1985] JBL 456.

[148] See the Customer Prepayment (Protection) Bill 1982: C. M. Schmitthoff, 'A Consumers' Prepayment (Protection) Bill?' [1984] JBL 105. See also the Insolvency Act 1986 s. 176A – the 'prescribed part' or 'ring-fenced' fund.

following negotiations with the OFT) so as to protect consumers in relation to certain types of transaction. Thus, certain statutes such as the Estate Agents Act 1979 demand that clients' money must be held in trust in a separate account.[149] Some trade associations, moreover, had voluntarily established compensation schemes to reimburse disappointed consumers: these, as noted above, were encountered, for instance, in the newspaper, periodical, travel agency, vehicle building and glazing installation sectors. As for further responses to the predicament of consumer pre-payers, these commentators backed Cork on wrongful trading controls as a way forward, and viewed as promising the institution of steps to educate traders on the causes of collapse (where possible involving the banks and expert creditors); the wider dissemination of corporate accounting information; 'the linking of bank guarantees to the obtaining of secured creditor status – thereby inducing self-interested monitoring of trading company performance'; and the encouraging of voluntary trust funds and insurance bonds. There was, they added, no clearly established public interest case for the compulsory introduction of any of the above solutions.

Before leaving the question of efficiency in relation to trusts, the special case for 'rescue fund trusts' should be considered.[150] The argument for regularising arrangements whereby finances are supplied to a troubled company for the purposes of assisting in its survival is that it may be in the economic interest of the community to encourage the supply of funds (by consumers, bankers or traders) in circumstances that facilitate rescues and increase corporate survival rates.[151] This type of arrangement could operate on a regularised *Quistclose* basis when a purchaser of goods offers prepayment expressly on the basis that this funding is to assist in a rescue and is given for a specific purpose to be held on trust. Recognition of the trust would thus keep the fund out of the insolvency estate and encourage rescue funding by traders as well as banks.

The possible problem with the trust-based regime, as described, is that it may be open to the same criticisms as were made of the statutory super-priority (SSP) as proposed by the DTI/Insolvency Service in 1993,

---

[149] Section 13.

[150] On the general issues attending 'twilight' trusts that are established at times of corporate stress and are 'becoming an integral part of the rescue culture' see Ellis and Verrill, 'Twilight Trusts'; Redstone, 'Customer Deposits (in the Twilight Zone)'; and p. 657 above.

[151] See R. Austin, 'Commerce and Equity: Fiduciary Duty and Constructive Trust' (1986) 6 OJLS 444 at 455.

dropped in 1995 after consultation[152] and mooted again in 1999.[153] SSP would give providers of funding during a moratorium a statutory super-priority over all existing creditors. (Such lenders would be *at the head* of the queue for the insolvency estate, not placed *outside* the queue as would be the case in a trust-based system.) The proposal was dropped in 1995 on the grounds that it might militate against the proper consideration of the viability of the business by a lender: it would lead to inefficiently large incentives to lend and to unjustifiable financing.[154] In such a scenario, the supposed danger is that the highly protected investor encourages the company to continue trading beyond the point where this is justified and this results in greater damage to existing creditors than would otherwise be the case.

Such reasoning, however, is open to question. In a *Quistclose* type of arrangement where the lender to the troubled company places funds on trust and is well informed, there is no excessive incentive to invest because the investor is not free-riding on the security of other parties but is able to calculate the relevant investment risks and to agree a price or interest rate accordingly. The use of a separate trust account, in this regard, keeps the affairs of the new finance supplier separate from those of the creditors of the company. (It is, of course, the requirements of specific purpose and separate accounting that, as noted, restrict the potential role of the *Quistclose* trust as a general form of flexible corporate financing.) Inefficiencies might arise where such new trust-based finance suppliers are ill-informed (a position likely where consumer prepayments are involved) or where the company's creditors have no information on the trust-based funding. More generally, indeed, it can be argued that recognition of the *Quistclose*-type of trust contributes to a lack of transparency since this is a device that 'by its very nature will misrepresent to the world, and in particular to prospective creditors, the true financial state of a company'[155] (an argument to be returned to below in looking at questions of fairness). From the point of view of a company's existing creditors, there is a balance to be considered in

---

[152] DTI Consultative Documents: *Company Voluntary Arrangements and Administration Orders* (1993), *Revised Proposals for a New Company Voluntary Arrangement Procedure* (1995).

[153] See Insolvency Service, *A Review of Company Rescue and Business Reconstruction Mechanisms* (1999). See ch. 9 above.

[154] DTI, *Revised Proposals*, para. 2.2.

[155] See J. Penner, *The Law of Trusts* (5th edn, Oxford University Press, Oxford, 2006) ch. 9, pp. 242 ff.

assessing the desirability of encouraging 'rescue fund trusts'. On the one hand, there are dangers that their positions will be worsened by ill-informed funders allowing the company to descend into greater troubles than would otherwise be the case; on the other hand, it is to their advantage if prospects of corporate decline can be reduced by encouraging injections of rescue funds. This emphasises that any problems in this area stem from deficiencies in information supplies and use rather than from resort to *Quistclose*-type trusts.

Fairness

Do trusts of the *Quistclose* type operate consistently with the fair treatment of corporate creditors? It can be argued that in *Quistclose* no creditors were misled into making further loans by the existence of a separate dividend account and the bank was aware of the agreement between the parties. This will not always be the case, however.[156] *Quistclose*-type arrangements are not subject to the registration and disclosure requirements associated with security and one effect, indeed purpose, of a *Quistclose*-type transaction 'may be to create an impression of commercial solidity so as to enable the borrower to continue trading and avoid insolvency, with the consequence that fresh liabilities to creditors will probably be incurred'.[157] Actual and potential creditors of a company may, thus, be deceived in so far as they are led to see the potential insolvency estate as larger than it really is: the property held on an undisclosed trust will lie at the heart of the 'deception'. Similarly with a *Kayford* trust, the firm's general creditors may observe a high level of economic activity and stocking but may not realise that a proportion of this is funded out of consumer prepayments and the involved moneys and assets will at no time enter the insolvency estate. When, moreover, an existing asset (a debt in *Carreras Rothmans*) is placed in trust for a particular creditor or class of creditor, there is, as has been noted above, a transaction approaching a preference or a breach of *British Eagle* principles.[158] In *Kayford* the company chose unilaterally to protect a particular set of (new) customers by means of a new trust arrangement. Megarry J decided that this did not constitute a fraudulent preference because the case involved 'the question not of preferring creditors but of preventing those who pay money from becoming creditors, by making them the beneficiaries under a

---

[156] Moffat, *Trusts Law*, p. 594.   [157] Ibid.   [158] See p. 658 above.

trust'.[159] As Goodhart and Jones have argued,[160] however, it is difficult to accept that the customers in *Kayford* were never creditors since that would demand acceptance that the money received from the customers was subject to a trust the moment it was received. The facts were, however, that the customers forwarded money without any binding undertaking from Kayford to pay it into a trust account. It would clearly be a preference for a company to take money from general funds and pay this into a trust account for the benefit of certain creditors but it is difficult to see how the arrangement adopted in *Kayford* differed materially from such a process.[161] In summary, then, it is arguable that a *Kayford* arrangement is likely to infringe *British Eagle* principles and to involve unfairness for that reason.[162]

Are trust arrangements equally available to all suppliers of corporate funds? Here the problem in relation to the *Kayford* trust is that it is the voluntary action of the receiving company that establishes the trust and, accordingly, that company may act in a selective or discriminatory manner beyond the control of any particular fund supplier. With a *Quistclose* trust instituted by the fund provider, disparities of information collection and handling will create a bias in favour of better-resourced funders and repeat players will be advantaged as compared to one-off providers. Overall, as with many other modes of bypassing *pari passu*, the effect of such trust mechanisms will be to disadvantage the poorly resourced, ill-informed, one-off trade creditor who will, at the end of the day, constitute an unsecured creditor surveying a shrunken insolvency estate.

Such a situation could be avoided, as already noted, by instituting statutory reforms to oblige suppliers to hold consumer prepayments in separate accounts and on trust.[163] Leaving aside efficiency issues and the problem of removing working capital from the company, can a case be made out for such a course of action on grounds of fairness? Treating consumer creditors preferentially (as compared to unsecured trade creditors) might be argued for on the basis of their special vulnerability.[164] Consumer creditors, it could be said, tend to be less wealthy than other creditors; are less likely and able to spread risks through diversification or

---

[159] [1975] 1 WLR 279 at 281.
[160] Goodhart and Jones, 'Infiltration of Equitable Doctrine', p. 496.   [161] Ibid., p. 497.
[162] See the comments of Templeman LJ in *Borden (UK) Ltd* v. *Scottish Timber Products Ltd* [1979] 3 WLR 672.
[163] See p. 659 above and Cork Report, para. 1053, for rejection of this proposal.
[164] See Ogus and Rowley, *Prepayments and Insolvency*, paras. 5.39, 5.11.

self-insurance; and are not fully voluntary creditors because they are poorly informed concerning insolvency risks, are ill-placed to negotiate terms with traders and, indeed, may not see themselves as credit suppliers.

The Cork Committee was unmoved by these arguments, though it did not respond to them in detail and merely urged that consumer creditors extend credit like traders and said that between the two groups, there is 'no essential difference'. The problem for the proponents of consumer protection lies in any contention that consumers are in a worse position than all unsecured trade creditors. The small unsecured trade creditor who is not in a continuing relationship with a debtor company may (as indicated in chapter 14) be very poorly positioned to evaluate risks, may not consider himself as a credit supplier and, arguably, may be more vulnerable than the average consumer in cases of default. The consumer may be deprived, on default, of a luxury consumer item; the small trade creditor may lose out on the payment that allows his business to continue. The consumer may suffer a personal loss; the small trader's loss may affect a host of employees very significantly. Any rationale for preferential treatment that is based on a vulnerability assessment might have to include numbers of unsecured trade creditors as well as consumers. Given these considerations, the case in fairness for special treatment of consumers as a general class seems not to be made out.

To conclude on the use of trust devices, there may be a case for encouraging the use of trust-based protections for parties who supply funds in rescue scenarios. Any potential prejudice to the general body of corporate creditors may then be compensated for by attendant increases in the company's prospects of survival. In relation to non-rescue situations, the justification for trust devices seems highly questionable on efficiency and fairness grounds. Widespread use of trust arrangements is likely to lead to inflexible regimes of financing that are not efficient and consistent with dynamism in the marketplace. Unfairness is also likely to result because of informational and resourcing disparities, with the end result of worsening the positions of unsecured creditors. Legal uncertainties further compound these problems. The way forward on trust may, as Goodhart and Jones suggest,[165] be to treat fund suppliers as *de facto* creditors and to seek to ameliorate the position of unsecured creditors more generally rather than to create yet another protected group.

---

[165] Goodhart and Jones, 'Infiltration of Equitable Doctrine', p. 512.

Alternatives to *pari passu*

In moving to consider possible alternatives to *pari passu* it is useful to focus, again, on what a regime for distributing an estate post-insolvency should achieve. The contention in this book is that insolvency laws and processes should be designed to produce acceptable combinations of efficiency, expertise, fairness and accountability characteristics.[166] This implies that the devices and processes that make up the regime for distribution should offer players in the marketplace a range of low-cost modes of protection against insolvency risks but that they should also avoid allocating risks in ways that produce unfairness or inefficiency and should satisfy principles of accountability and transparency in seeking to ensure that both fairness and efficiency concerns are satisfied.

The means for delivering the above desiderata may, accordingly, be to offer a range of devices (for example, security, retentions of title, trusts) but to set those devices up so that they are legally certain as well as identifiable and employable at minimal cost. The protections offered by insolvency law should also be designed to protect vulnerable parties who would bear insolvency risks inefficiently or unfairly if left unprotected.

How are the vulnerable to be identified?[167] It can be repeated, first, that parties will *not* be vulnerable if they can (at reasonable cost) secure preferential positions in distributions or if they can (again at reasonable cost) adjust terms and loan rates to reflect risks borne. The Crown is able to position its tax levels in a manner that anticipates default rates – and this is a consideration that endorses the Enterprise Act 2002's abolition of the Crown's preferential status. Employees, in contrast, exemplify parties who are ill-positioned to adjust their credit rates to take account of default risks.[168] Some traders may be unable to adjust rates because the time scales they work to are too short, the costs of information collection are too high or relevant data may be unavailable. Accepted commercial procedures within a trade may, moreover, make accurate risk assessment non-feasible.

Another sign of vulnerability – one also noted in chapter 14 – is a low capacity to absorb losses. The ability to spread risks increases a party's capacity to withstand the consequences of default.[169] The Crown, again,

---

[166] See ch. 2 above.

[167] This section builds on V. Finch, 'Is *Pari Passu* Passé?' [2000] Ins. Law. 194 at 206–10.

[168] See generally B. Gleig, 'Unpaid Wages in Bankruptcy' (1987) 21 UBC L Rev. 61–83. But see p. 609 above.

[169] S. S. Cantlie, 'Preferred Priority in Bankruptcy' in Ziegel, *Current Developments*, pp. 433–44.

is well placed and can spread default risks across taxpayers who, in turn, are likely to be able to cope with marginal increases in tax rates without suffering catastrophic consequences. Resilient traders tend to be those whose businesses are not totally dependent on the viability of one particular debtor[170] and who are involved in the supply of goods or services to a large number of customers. If one of their customers becomes insolvent they are less exposed to disaster than those trade creditors who deal with only one main customer. Most trade creditors are relatively protected in this respect, as are many tort victims. Employees, on the other hand, are seldom able to spread default risks and so are highly vulnerable.[171] Tort creditors and consumer creditors, as has been seen, will tend to be lower-cost risk bearers than employees since they will usually have other sources of income, funds and products, and risks will be spread by such diversification.

Bearing in mind such issues of fairness to the vulnerable and efficiency, it is almost time to consider particular alternatives to *pari passu* but before doing so we should map out the limitations of the role that *pari passu* plays in the insolvency process.[172]

The first such limitation is in the breadth of that role. It can be argued that by the time the *pari passu* principle comes into play many of the difficult insolvency law questions have been posed and answered.[173] There is force in this point. The role of *pari passu* is defined and limited by the shape of exceptions and bypassing arrangements that insolvency law allows. As has been indicated, those exceptions and bypassing devices raise, in themselves, numerous issues of efficiency and fairness (not to mention expertise and accountability). To allow the use of such devices is not merely to reduce the role of *pari passu*, it introduces principles and priorities to override *pari passu*. When teachers say 'The sweets will be distributed equally to all children in the class' we see a single, clear principle of fairness. When they say 'All red-haired children's appetites will, however, be satisfied first and then equal distribution will take place', the fairness of *Animal Farm* comes to mind.

Limitations of scope do not in themselves, however, constitute reasons for abandoning *pari passu*. Questions arise as to the acceptability of the overriding principles that qualify *pari passu* but it could still be argued

---

[170] Ibid.   [171] Ibid.

[172] For arguments that *pari passu* is less important than it is generally held out to be, see F. Oditah, 'Assets and the Treatment of Claims in Insolvency' (1992) 108 LQR 459 at 468–76; Mokal, 'Priority as Pathology'; L. C. Ho, 'Goode's Swan Song to Corporate Insolvency Law' (2006) 17 EBLR 1727; see also ch. 14 above.

[173] See Mokal, 'Priority as Pathology', esp. pp. 587–8.

that *pari passu* is the most appropriate method of redistributing residual assets and that other principles would, even in relation to the residual assets, produce significantly different (perhaps less acceptable) results for residual claimants.

If, however, the role of *pari passu* is seen in terms of ensuring that unsecured creditors are dealt with in an efficient and fair way, it should be noted that there are approaches to this issue that go beyond asking how the residual assets should be distributed and that these can be seen as further limitations on the importance of *pari passu*. Five such approaches can be noted. These look to protect unsecured creditors through:

- rethinking how the estate is constructed (for example, by considering priorities and deferrals);[174]
- procedural protections (for example, improving transparency and disclosure through insolvency regimes);
- substantive protections (for example, augmenting the residual estate with the section 176A prescribed part fund or directors' contribution through personal liability);
- reducing insolvency risks (for example, through training of directors, corporate governance improvements, educating traders in reasons for corporate collapse, encouraging banks and secured creditors to monitor);
- spreading insolvency risks: either across groups of companies;[175] or through compensation schemes;[176] or through insurance mechanisms.[177]

If these alternatives are borne in mind it can be concluded that the role of *pari passu* is modest, given that issues concerning *pari passu* are linked to, and surrounded by, a host of not inconsiderable questions. This does not, however, mean that *pari passu* is of insignificant importance.

A second limitation of *pari passu*'s role is that it is not wholly clear. The principle can be said to be weak because it operates in a confused manner due to the multiplicity of potential exceptions and bypassing arrangements encountered in law and practice. The above discussion

---

[174] A class of creditor that might be dealt with specifically by statute is the company director: see ch. 14 above, pp. 613–14.

[175] On insolvency issues raised by corporate groups see ch. 13 above.

[176] As in the travel industry via ABTA: see p. 654 above.

[177] On insurance limitations and availability see S. Shavell, 'On Liability and Insurance' (1982) 13 *Bell Journal of Economics* 120; V. Finch, 'Personal Accountability and Corporate Control: The Role of Directors' and Officers' Liability Insurance' (1994) 57 MLR 880 at 887–92.

suggests that there is scope for clarifying the rules governing exceptions and bypasses. Such clarification might be expected to reduce the costs incurred by parties seeking to protect themselves from insolvency risks but distributional consequences may flow: ordinary creditors who are still ill-placed to secure protections may be faced with a yet smaller residual estate as other parties take greater advantage of newly facilitated protections.

A number of questions are raised. A first issue is whether particular exceptions and bypasses are justifiable in themselves. This chapter and the last have explored a number of issues that arise on that front. A further matter, however, is whether, as a collectivity, the array of exceptions and bypasses involves too great a degree of confusion and too large a mass of uncertainty to offer efficiency and fairness. Viewed collectively, the question is whether a simpler, more rational and legally certain array of devices might be devised. If it is accepted that well-resourced, well-informed creditors will take any steps they think rational to protect themselves against the risks of insolvency, the challenge is to allow them to do this at lowest cost consistent with the fair treatment of other unsecured creditors: to achieve an acceptable balance of efficiency-serving and distributionally fair ends. At present, it could be argued, the worst of two worlds is achieved: the well-resourced expend too much money and time on protection and the poorly-resourced are left with too small a fund to draw from. Such reasoning suggests that a statutory clarification of the law relating to exceptions and bypasses would have much to offer provided that this reduced legal uncertainties and the costs of achieving protections while, at the same time, it provided adequate protections for those who cannot reasonably be expected to negotiate themselves into protected positions.

The final question for consideration in this chapter is whether the residual ordinary creditors who are left with a collectively 'fair' fund should be allocated shares in it *pari passu* or by other principles of distribution. To return to the children in our Orwellian classroom, distribution to the pupils might be governed by a principle of evenness but alternatives could be argued for. Larger shares could, for instance, be given to well-behaved children; to those who lodge confectionery claims first; to those who shout loudest; to those who need sugar most; to those who fared badly in prior distributions; or to those who would create most trouble if not favoured.

Let us now turn to consider the main alternatives to *pari passu* distribution of the residual estate.

Debts ranked chronologically

A first alternative to *pari passu* is to provide that debts be repaid from the residual estate with reference to the date of accrual on a first-come-first-served basis. Those with debts established at the earliest dates would, accordingly, be paid first. Such a regime might involve recording and disclosure mechanisms that would allow each creditor to assess the position before entrenching funds.

Such a regime would not, in itself, address the problems of exceptions and bypassing noted above and there might be efficiency costs. As a company entered troubled economic waters it would become progressively more difficult to raise funds since prospective creditors would know that, arriving 'late', they would rank low in the distributional order. The effect would be an increasing resort to security, quasi-security and trust devices, and transaction costs would accordingly rise. The newly strong incentive to avoid the estate would, in turn, create increased uncertainty for other prospective unsecured creditors because assessing their lending risks would demand ever more complex and time-consuming analyses of the estate-avoiding measures that have been used in relation to the company. This would involve not only inefficiency but unfairness to the most poorly placed unsecured creditors since the latter would be in no position to evaluate their loan risks.

Debts ranked ethically

It would be possible to pay unsecured creditors according to their, or society's, needs, so that repayments would be organised on an ethical basis: say, in order to maximise the sum of human happiness.[178]

Such a utilitarian approach would be vulnerable to the standard criticisms of utilitarianism: how is happiness to be calculated and measured? Whose happiness counts? Does happiness achieved by unethical, even monstrous, means count?[179] Even if the tenets of utilitarianism were

---

[178] On ethics and insolvency generally see J. Kilpi, *The Ethics of Bankruptcy* (Routledge, London, 1998). For a utilitarian strategy see P. Shuchman, 'An Attempt at a "Philosophy of Bankruptcy"' (1973) 21 UCLA L Rev. 403.

[179] On the limits of utilitarianism see e.g. A. Sen and B. Williams (eds.), *Utilitarianism and Beyond* (Cambridge University Press, Cambridge, 1982). On utilitarianism and legal and ethical efficiency issues see R. Posner, 'Utilitarianism, Economics and Legal Theory' (1979) 8 *Journal of Legal Studies* 103; R. M. Dworkin, 'Is Wealth a Value?' (1980) 9 *Journal of Legal Studies* 191; Dworkin, *A Matter of Principle* (Clarendon Press, Oxford, 1986) ch. 13; V. Finch, 'The Measures of Insolvency Law' (1997) 17 OJLS 227 at 239–40; ch. 2 above.

accepted, however, applying such an approach to insolvency would be difficult. There would be high levels of creditor uncertainty since predicting positions in the repayment queue would be nearly impossible (how does one unsecured creditor assess the likely advent of another unsecured creditor who is more worthy or needing of payment?). This would produce huge inefficiencies unless simpler, more predictable, more collectivist distributional rules were employed.[180]

Ethical approaches to repayment, however, raise general issues of collectivity. If the individual position or worth of a creditor is taken into account in distributing the residual estate then that individual position – whether it is assessed according to utilitarian principles or corrective justice[181] or other ethical principles – will be difficult to assess in advance and inefficiencies and unfairnesses would be caused by the inability of creditors to assess present and future risks. This is not to say that certain *classes* of creditor (for example, consumers, employees or other non-adjusting groups) might not merit special protections on ethical grounds. Reference to such classes in principles of estate distribution would be possible without the uncertainties involved in individual assessments and we see this approach already in the statutory treatment of preferential creditors. Questions arise, however, concerning the definition of such classes; the relative claims of different classes; the wide divergence of claims to deserve protection within the class membership; and the need to translate such ethical approaches into democratically endorsed policy form.

Debts ranked on size

It might be argued that small creditors should be paid at a higher rate of return than those ordinary unsecured creditors who have loaned larger sums to troubled firms. (David Milman has suggested a £750 threshold below which such special treatment should be applicable.)[182] The basis

---

[180] On rule utilitarianism and artificial virtues see D. Hume, *A Treatise of Human Nature*, L. Selby-Bigge and P. Nidditch (eds.) (Oxford University Press, Oxford, 1978); Shuchman, 'An Attempt', pp. 460–5.

[181] See Ogus and Rowley, *Prepayments and Insolvency*, p. 15; R. Epstein, 'A Theory of Strict Liability' (1973) 2 *Journal of Legal Studies* 151; Schwartz, 'Security Interests and Bankruptcy Priorities'. See also Kilpi, *Ethics of Bankruptcy*.

[182] See D. Milman, 'Priority Rights on Corporate Insolvency' in A. Clarke (ed.), *Current Issues in Insolvency Law* (Stevens & Sons, London, 1991) p. 78.

for doing so would be that small creditors are more vulnerable and deserve high levels of protection.

The problem with such a proposal is that it is difficult to correlate the size of the loan with the vulnerability of the creditor. Small lenders, for instance, may be better and more energetic risk spreaders than medium or large lenders: their businesses may involve large numbers of small loans rather than fewer loans of greater size. Small lenders may be able to adjust their loan rates quite effectively because the market may offer a range of deals and attendant risks. Small creditors may be more risk resilient and lower-cost risk bearers than some larger creditors: where, for example, the former's financial eggs are not all in one basket, they can absorb an insolvency loss fairly easily and there are no substantial ripple effects flowing from the loss. Nor can it be assumed that small creditors are necessarily less well informed, expert or strongly positioned to negotiate than larger creditors. This may depend on the particular market or organisational set-up involved, the relevant regulatory regime or even the state of the economy.

Debts paid on policy grounds

If policy grounds underpin the placing of some creditors ahead of the residual estate this is not so much an alternative way of residual estate distribution as an alternative construction of the estate as a whole. A genuine alternative to *pari passu* in relation to the residual estate would involve paying different ordinary creditors at different rates. One mooted candidate for special treatment is the consumer creditor. It has been argued that this class of unsecured creditor might be entitled to a higher rate of return as compared to trade creditors because the latter 'should be more aware of the risks involved in extending credit to the company' and because 'bad debt insurance is increasingly available to trade creditors'.[183] Consumer creditors, moreover, are said to suffer disproportionately on the debtor's insolvency.[184]

It might be countered that the mooted special treatment would make life more difficult for IPs, would increase transaction costs and should be opposed on that basis. Such efficiency costs might be worth paying, however, if more than compensated for by attendant improvements in fairness. On these points, however, reference can be made to the last

---

[183] Ibid.   [184] Ibid., p. 78.

chapter's discussion of preference for consumer creditors and, to recap, it could be said that many trade creditors are far more harshly affected by corporate insolvencies than the average consumer creditor: their livelihood may depend on payment, and some trade creditors may be less able to evaluate risks, adjust terms or insure against bad debts than some consumers. On such questions of creditor vulnerability much turns, again, on such matters as the type of transaction involved, the pattern of risk spreading, the mode of payment, the market traditions, the levels of competition in the sector, the quality of information on suppliers that is available and the rate of turnover of business in the sector. If one is really concerned with fairness, it could be said, attention should be paid not to consumers as a class but to protections for individual creditors who are ill-positioned to evaluate risks or sustain economic shocks. Here, though, proponents of change are in a difficult position. It is difficult to make a general class claim, and to take on board individual circumstances introduces the uncertainties and inefficiencies noted above in relation to ethical approaches.

Conclusions

Any discussion of *pari passu* has to bear in mind the link between issues of residual estate distribution and issues of estate construction as a whole. The import of the above discussion is that if fairness and efficiency are sought in the distribution of the residual estate, the case for a generally collective approach is a strong one. To take on board individual positions, vulnerabilities or ethical merits produces too great an accumulation of uncertainties and transaction costs to provide either fair or efficient processes.

It has also been argued above, however, that concerns for the fair and efficient treatment of creditors may be served by looking beyond questions of residue distribution. A blinkered focus on *pari passu* should, accordingly, be avoided. Not only is it relevant to look to questions of estate construction more generally but attention should also be paid to protections for 'vulnerable' risk bearers in the form of procedural requirements (of information provision and disclosure); to substantive protections of a general nature (such as a 'prescribed part' fund for ordinary unsecured creditors); to ways of reducing overall risks of insolvency (for example, by improvements in managerial standards and training); and to modes of lowering risks to the vulnerable by spreading insolvency risks. This spreading can be achieved, for instance, by extending risks across corporate groups; by establishing compensation regimes and by relying on (or instituting and requiring) insurance provision.

Pari passu plays a role in insolvency proceedings but this role is limited by the context described above. Improvements in the legal regime are possible, however. Exceptions and bypasses could be clarified and steps could be designed to limit the extent to which poorly placed creditors bear undue risks because of their inability to adjust terms in the light of assessable risks. One general improvement could be the infusion of greater transparency and more readily available information into insolvency processes (for example, by disclosure rules on ROT clauses). There seems no strong case, however, for major new allocations of preferential status.[185] As for the contention that *pari passu* is not the best way to distribute the residual estate, those alternatives to *pari passu* that are based on assessments of the individual position or the merit of the creditor would be objectionable, as noted, on grounds of uncertainty, inefficiency and unfairness. Those based on new approaches to the definition of classes face problems of heterogeneity in class membership and of demonstrating why classes selected for new special rates of repayment have claims that are generally stronger than competing classes.

---

[185] A minor new allocation might be claimants seeking restitution of unjust enrichments: see V. Finch and S. Worthington, 'The *Pari Passu* Principle and Ranking Restitutionary Claims' in Rose, *Restitution and Insolvency*.

PART V

The impact of corporate insolvency

.

16

Directors in troubled times

The rules and processes that make up insolvency law operate as a set of incentives and constraints that influence how company directors behave at times of both good and bad corporate fortune. This chapter considers how those incentives and constraints operate and examines the assumptions and philosophies that underpin the role of the company director in insolvency law. The analysis offered here continues the approach set out in chapter 2 and asks whether current insolvency law deals with directors in a manner that renders directors appropriately accountable, makes the best use of directorial expertise, fosters efficiently produced outcomes and is consistent with the fair treatment of directors and parties affected by directorial behaviour. For the purposes of clarity of exposition, the issue of account-ability will be considered first, since this involves a mapping out of the broad array of influences and constraints that insolvency law applies to directors – a mapping exercise that should provide a useful background to the discussions of expertise, efficiency and fairness that follow.

Accountability

Directorial accountability can operate through a variety of devices – which will be considered below – but the purposes to be served by such devices may also vary. Insolvency law, for instance, might set out to punish an errant director; to protect creditors at risk from directorial actions; or to compensate parties who have suffered losses at the hands of directors. Insolvency law, together with company law, may also seek to achieve a number of other ends such as raising standards of business conduct and entrepreneurship.

A search for the purposes underlying current corporate insolvency law controls over directors can begin with the Cork Report.[1] Cork emphasised that the function of insolvency law was not merely to distribute the

---

[1] *Report of the Review Committee on Insolvency Law and Practice* (Cmnd 8558, 1982) ('Cork Report').

insolvency estate to creditors. Other objectives were to encourage debt recovery (and persuade debtors to pay or propose settlements of debts) and, through investigations and disciplinary actions, to meet 'the demands of commercial morality'.[2] Central here, then, was the notion that insolvency law and investigative processes would uncover assets concealed from creditors, ascertain the validity of creditors' claims, and expose the circumstances surrounding the debtor's failure. Anything less, said Cork, would be unacceptable in a trading community and would lead to 'a lowering of business standards and an erosion of confidence in our insolvency law'.[3] This was a matter not merely of punishing the errant, said Cork, but of exposing affairs to creditors and encouraging public scrutiny.[4] Society had an interest in insolvency processes and attention, accordingly, needed to be paid to whether or not fault or blame attached to the conduct of the insolvent party, whether punishment was merited, whether the party should be restricted so as to prevent repetition of errant conduct and whether responsibility for the insolvency was attributable to someone other than the director.[5] Cork, thus, emphasised the need for insolvency law to promote the 'highest standards of business probity and competence' and noted, in particular, the disquiet that was widespread in the commercial and practitioner communities concerning the lenient manner in which the law dealt with the directors of insolvent companies, which was often compared unfavourably with the law's stricter approach to the individual bankrupt.[6] Cork accepted that a fresh approach was justified, not least to deal with the dishonesty and malpractices of 'fly by night' operators and the losses imposed on ordinary unsophisticated creditors. That fresh approach was to be implemented through Cork's proposals *inter alia* for a new concept of wrongful trading liability and broader powers for court disqualification of delinquent directors (with automatic exposure to personal liability for certain debts). These were proposals infused with rationales ranging from punishment to restitution;

---

[2] Cork Report, para. 235; see B. G. Carruthers and T. C. Halliday, *Rescuing Business: The Making of Corporate Bankruptcy Law in England and the United States* (Clarendon Press, Oxford, 1998) pp. 266–83.

[3] Cork Report, para. 238.   [4] Ibid., para. 239.   [5] Ibid., para. 1735.

[6] See further W. R. Cornish and G. de N. Clark, *Law and Society in England 1750–1950* (Sweet & Maxwell, London, 1989) ch. 3, part 2. On attitudes to bankrupts and proposals for reform see Insolvency Service, *Bankruptcy: A Fresh Start* (2000); DTI/IS White Paper, *Productivity and Enterprise: Insolvency – A Second Chance* (Cm 5234, July 2001). The Enterprise Act 2002 subsequently effected substantial reforms to the Insolvency Act 1986's bankruptcy regime: see e.g. D. Milman, *Personal Insolvency Law, Regulation and Policy* (Ashgate, Aldershot, 2005).

prevention to retribution.[7] It should not be forgotten, however, that Cork saw proposals that were designed to impose stricter controls on directors as merely one aspect of a package of reforms that, amongst other things, aimed to facilitate rescues and to limit the losses that might result from directorial deficiencies or other misfortunes.

The statutory legacy of Cork will be dealt with below but it is worth noting, first, that recent years have seen a shift in emphasis away from Cork's concerns both to redress the law's lenient treatment of directors and to do something about 'phoenix company' problems.[8] The Blair Government was marked by a stress on the virtues of entrepreneurship and risk taking as necessary components of wealth creation and the White Paper on Enterprise, Skill and Innovation of 2001[9] encapsulated this approach with its aims to 'help create an ambitious business culture' and proposals including 'significantly relaxing insolvency rules so that honest businesses and individuals who go bankrupt have a better chance of starting again quicker while cracking down on the fraudulent and irresponsible'.[10]

As for cracking down on 'rogue' directors, Companies House, in 1997, created a new website listing directors subject to disqualification orders.[11] In 1998 a 'hotline' was set up to allow the public to report rogue directors to the Insolvency Service (IS) and, in 2006–7, the IS took 328 calls, of which 26 resulted in reports to the prosecution authority.[12] In 2000, the Minister for Competition and Consumer Affairs, Dr Kim Howells,

---

[7] See Carruthers and Halliday, *Rescuing Business*, pp. 274–7.

[8] The 'phoenix' syndrome occurs when the activities of a failed company are continued by those responsible, using the vehicle of a new company, or where a director engages in serial corporate failure, leaving creditors stranded with those failures, and moves on to a new company while concealing past failures from the public. See S. Frith, 'Acting as a Director of a Phoenix Company' (2003) 16 *Insolvency Intelligence* 37; T. Carter, 'The Phoenix Syndrome – The Personal Liability of Directors' (2006) 19 *Insolvency Intelligence* 38.

[9] DTI, *Opportunity for All in a World of Change – A White Paper on Enterprise, Skill and Innovation* (DTI, February 2001).

[10] See ch. 6 above; DTI White Paper, *Our Competitive Future: Building the Knowledge Driven Economy* (Cm 4176, December 1998) paras. 2.12–2.14; Insolvency Service, *A Review of Company Rescue and Business Reconstruction Mechanisms*, Interim Report (1999); *A Review of Company Rescue and Business Reconstruction Mechanisms*, Report by the Review Group (2000). On the European Commission's approach to insolvency as part of its strategy for promoting entrepreneurship and 'desirable risk taking' see European Commission, *Communication from the Commission to the Council and the European Parliament: Progress Report on the Risk Capital Action Plan*, COM (November 2003).

[11] See www.companieshouse.gov.uk. On disqualification of directors see pp. 717–38, 750–3 below.

[12] Insolvency Service, *Annual Report and Accounts* 2006–7 (HC 752, London, 2007) p. 20. The figure for reports to prosecutors in 2005–6 was 135. Reports can be made online via

announced the setting up by the IS of a specialist team to investigate directors who asset-strip companies which then become insolvent. The Forensic Insolvency Recovery Service (FIRS) was established as a team of private sector and Insolvency Service partners comprising lawyers, insolvency practitioners and enquiry agents. The team was given powers to take legal actions to recover assets from unfit directors where there had been suspected misappropriation, misfeasance or negligence.[13] Dr Howells urged, in April 2001, that there should be 'no hiding place' for unscrupulous directors. Of further interest to creditors and IPs, who will often be concerned to trace assets which may have been moved illegally, is the Assets Recovery Agency (ARA), which was set up in 2003 as a non-prosecuting authority to carry out operational functions including the recovery of assets under the Proceeds of Crime Act 2002.[14] It is also noteworthy that the 'credit crisis' of 2007–8, together with growing worries about fraudulent dealings and transfers, produced a new focus on the directorial management of assets near insolvency and the increasing propensity of major lenders and office holders to resort to the services of newly skilled consultants specialising in forensic accountancy.[15]

What, then, are the mechanisms that insolvency law establishes for holding directors to account and controlling their behaviour? If the rules on disqualification are left out of consideration – for discussion later under the heading of expertise – accountability mechanisms can best be reviewed by focusing first on the array of rules that provide for directors' liability and the associated issues of enforcement. Mention should then be made of the processes that are designed to control the activities of directors by providing that a company may be wound up in the public interest.

---

enforcement.hotline@insolvency.gsi.gov.uk. The Companies Act 2006 contains provisions increasing the powers to investigate companies: see e.g. CA 2006 Part 32, ss. 1035–9; *Boyle and Birds' Company Law* (6th edn, Jordans, Bristol, 2007) pp. 531–4 and 719–30.

[13] See D. Milman, 'Controlling Managerial Abuse: Current State of Play' [2000] Ins. Law. 193; DTI Press Notice P/2000/510.

[14] See A. Leong, 'The Assets Recovery Agency' (2007) 28 Co. Law. 379; D. Ingram, 'The Proceeds of Crime and Insolvency' (2007) *Recovery* (Winter) 22; D. Lawler, 'The Money Detectives' (2007) *Recovery* (Winter) 24. On the wide-ranging powers of the court to assist IPs seeking to trace and secure assets see L. Katz, 'Asset Tracing: Getting Evidence and Injunctive Relief' (2007) *Recovery* (Winter) 18.

[15] See J. Willcock, 'Credit Panic Stokes Forensic Boom' (2007) *Recovery* (Winter) 17; F. O'Connell, J. Outen and A. Stephens, 'Forensic Recovery: A Blend of Insolvency and Forensics' (2007) *Recovery* (Winter) 20.

Common law duties

A starting point in examining directors' liability is the set of common law duties that a director owes to a company. In general, a director cannot be made liable in insolvency for the obligations of his or her company.[16] It has long been established, however, that a director owes a fiduciary duty to act bona fide in the best interests of the company[17] and, in an insolvency, this duty may come into play. A liquidator, for instance, may mount a claim against the director personally where the director's negligent conduct has diminished the insolvency estate.[18]

A second set of issues surrounds the set of duties that directors owe to company creditors. These are usually underpinned by the arguments that, as a company approaches insolvency,[19] the commercial risks involved fall increasingly on the company's creditors rather than shareholders; that not all creditors will be well placed to protect themselves (by, for example, taking security, demanding guarantees, spreading risks, or costing such risks into their loan agreements); and that the directors of the company may, in the absence of legal controls, both breach the canons of commercial morality and take unreasonable, unfair and inefficient risks with the creditors' money.[20]

---

[16] *Salomon* v. *A. Salomon & Co. Ltd* [1897] AC 22. See generally A. Keay, *Company Directors' Responsibilities to Creditors* (Routledge-Cavendish, London, 2007).

[17] See *Re Smith and Fawcett Ltd* [1942] Ch 304. On the degree of care owed see Romer J in *Re City Equitable Fire Insurance Co.* [1925] Ch 407; *Dorchester Finance Co. Ltd* v. *Stebbing* [1989] BCLC 498; V. Finch, 'Company Directors: Who Cares About Skill and Care?' (1992) 55 MLR 179. See the statutory encapsulation of this duty in the Companies Act 2006 s. 172 and see pp. 694–6 below.

[18] See *Re D'Jan of London Ltd* [1993] BCC 646. But see *Swan* v. *Sandhu* [2005] EWHC 2743 and *Extrasure Travel Insurances Ltd* v. *Scattergood* [2003] 1 BCLC 598 on the confining of fiduciary duties to matters of honesty and loyalty, not competence. Thus 'mere' incompetence does not constitute a breach of fiduciary duty despite the tendency of courts to characterise the duty of care owed by directors of a failing company to its creditors in fiduciary terms: see *Re Pantone 485 Ltd* [2002] 1 BCLC 266.

[19] See generally D. Milman, 'Strategies for Regulating Managerial Performance in the Twilight Zone' [2004] JBL 493.

[20] On rationales for directors' duties to creditors (and arguments for distributional justice concerns to be considered as well as efficiency justifications) see generally A. Keay, 'A Theoretical Analysis of the Director's Duty to Consider Creditor Interests: The Progressive School's Approach' (2004) JCLS 307; Keay, 'Directors' Duties to Creditors: Contractarian Concerns Relating to Efficiency and Over-Protection of Creditors' (2003) 66 MLR 665; Keay, 'The Duty of Directors to Take Account of Creditors' Interests' [2002] JBL 379. See also P. Davies, 'Directors' Creditor-regarding Duties in Respect of Trading Decisions Taken in the Vicinity of Insolvency' (2006) 7 EBOLR 301.

As for the nature and content of the duties, the Companies Act 2006, as will be discussed below, codifies the common law's provision of directors' duties in a statutory statement but in a manner that leaves the decisions of the courts of relevance with regard to duties to creditors. This is because the 2006 Act (section 170(4)) stipulates that its codified terms are to be applied in a like manner to the common law and equitable principles that predated the Act. Section 172(3) of the 2006 Act, moreover, states that the directors' general duties to promote the success of the company (under section 172) have effect 'subject to any enactment or rule of law requiring directors, in certain circumstances, to consider or act in the interests of creditors of the company'.

The courts, however, have taken divergent views on the nature, as well as the content, of the duty owed by directors to creditors. On one approach it is seen as an aspect of the traditional fiduciary duty of directors to act bona fide in the interests of the company,[21] on another, it is viewed as an independent, positive duty owed directly to creditors and founded either on ordinary principles of directors' duty of care or on tortious principles.[22]

In favour of the idea that duties to creditors flow from the traditional fiduciary duty to act in the best interests of the company, there are a number of English court decisions that build on a series of Commonwealth cases. Notable among the latter is *Walker* v. *Wimborne*[23] in which the Australian High Court spoke of 'directors of a company in discharging their duty to the company [having to] take account of the interest of its shareholders and its creditors' (Mason J). Similarly, in *Nicholson* v. *Permakraft*[24] Cooke J, sitting in the New Zealand Court of Appeal, concluded *obiter* that directors' duties to the company 'may require them to consider *inter alia* the interests of

---

[21] See *Re Smith and Fawcett Ltd* [1942] Ch 304.

[22] This account draws on V. Finch, 'Creditors' Interests and Directors' Obligations' in S. Sheikh and W. Rees (eds.), *Corporate Governance and Corporate Control* (Cavendish, London, 1995) and Finch, 'Directors' Duties: Insolvency and the Unsecured Creditor' in A. Clarke (ed.), *Current Issues in Insolvency Law* (Stevens, London, 1991) p. 87. On directors' duties to creditors see also R. Grantham, 'The Judicial Extension of Directors' Duties to Creditors' [1991] JBL 1; D. Prentice, 'Creditors' Interest and Directors' Duties' (1990) 10 OJLS 265; L.S. Sealy, 'Directors' "Wider" Responsibilities: Problems, Conceptual, Practical and Procedural' (1987) 13 Monash LR 164; J.S. Ziegel, 'Creditors as Corporate Stakeholders' (1993) 43 U Toronto LJ 511.

[23] [1976] 50 ALJR 446 at 449. Noted: R. Baxt (1976) 50 ALJ 591.

[24] [1985] 1 NZLR 242.

creditors'.[25] During the 1980s the English courts echoed this approach. In *Lonrho* v. *Shell Petroleum*[26] Diplock LJ indicated that the 'best interests of the company' might not be exclusively those of shareholders 'but may include those of creditors'. Buckley LJ in *Re Horsley and Weight Ltd*[27] referred to the 'loose' terminology of 'directors owing an indirect duty to creditors not to permit any unlawful reduction of capital to occur' and stated that it was more accurate to say that directors 'owe a duty to the company in this respect'. In both the Court of Appeal and the House of Lords decisions in *Brady* v. *Brady*[28] it was indicated (by Nourse LJ and Lord Oliver) that directors needed to consider creditors' interests if they were to act in the interests of the company.[29]

Contrasting with this approach are dicta suggesting that there is a direct and specific duty that is owed to creditors. Thus, in *Winkworth* v. *Edward Baron Developments Co. Ltd*[30] Lord Templeman stated: 'A duty is owed by the directors of the company and to the creditors of the company to ensure that the affairs of the company are properly administered and that its property is not dissipated or exploited for the benefit of directors themselves to the prejudice of creditors.'[31] His Lordship's distinction between the company and the creditors here implied the notion of a specific duty to the latter.[32]

---

[25] Ibid., at 249. Noted: [1985] JBL 413. See also *Kinsela* v. *Russell Kinsela Pty Ltd* (1986) 4 ACLC 215, noted: Baxt (1986) 14 ABLR 320. See also the Supreme Court of Canada in *Peoples Department Stores* v. *Wise* [2004] SCC 68; A. Keay, 'Directors' Duties – Do Recent Canadian Developments Require a Rethink in the UK on the Issue of the Directors' Duties to Consider Creditors' Interests?' (2005) 18 *Insolvency Intelligence* 65.

[26] [1980] 1 WLR 627 at 634.   [27] [1982] 3 All ER 1045 at 1055–6.

[28] [1989] 3 BCC 535 (CA), [1988] 2 All ER 617 (HL).

[29] For an attack on the view that fiduciary duties should shift to creditors when the company is in financial distress see J. Lipson, 'Directors' Duties to Creditors: Power Imbalance and the Financially Distressed Corporation' (2003) 50 UCLA L Rev. 1189 (arguing for adverting to power imbalances expressed as disparities of volition, cognition and exit when considering who should benefit from directors' duties). For opposition to the shift towards duties owed to creditors at any stage before a formal filing see H. Hu and J. Westbrook, 'Abolition of the Corporate Duty to Creditors' (2007) 107 *Columbia Law Review* 1321.

[30] [1987] 1 All ER 114.   [31] Ibid., at 118.

[32] See also *Hooker Investments Pty Ltd* v. *Email Ltd* (1986) 10 ACLR 443. If a direct duty to creditors were to be recognised routinely by the courts (which, as noted below, seems unlikely) then the question as to the nature of that duty would arise. Is the duty, for example, to be seen as an extension of the directors' traditional duty of care or is it to be seen as one grounded in tortious principles? See further Finch, 'Creditors' Interests and Directors' Obligations'.

The most recent indications are, however, that the courts are unwilling to recognise a duty owed directly to creditors and, indeed, academic opinion now seems to accept that the duty is an indirect one.[33] In the *Yukong* case[34] Toulson J considered *West Mercia*[35] and stated that where a director acted in breach of his duty to the company by causing assets of the company to be transferred in disregard of the interests of its creditor or creditors, he was answerable through the scheme Parliament had provided in the Insolvency Act 1986 section 212 (misfeasance or breach of fiduciary or other duty) but 'he does not owe a direct fiduciary duty towards an individual creditor nor is an individual creditor entitled to sue for breach of the fiduciary duty owed by the director to the company'.[36]

To view duties to creditors as part of the traditional duty to act *bona fide* in the company's interests is, however, not without problems. Are creditors' interests to be considered independently or merely in so far as they are relevant to the company's interests? Are creditors' interests to be part of a package of claims (i.e. including those of shareholders and employees), in which case how will directors proceed if these constituent company interests conflict?[37] Is, moreover, directorial consideration of

---

[33] See *Colin Gwyer & Associates Ltd* v. *London Wharf (Limehouse) Ltd* [2003] 2 BCLC 153; *Yukong Lines Ltd of Korea* v. *Rendsburg Investments Corporation* [1998] BCC 870; *Kuwait Asia Bank EC* v. *National Mutual Life Nominees Ltd* [1991] 1 AC 187; *Spies* v. *The Queen* (2000) 201 CLR 603, (2000) 173 ALR 529; *Re New World Alliance Pty Ltd*, Fed. No. 332/94, 26 May 1994. See also Prentice, 'Creditors' Interest', p. 275; L. S. Sealy, 'Personal Liability of Directors and Officers for Debts of Insolvent Corporations: A Jurisdictional Perspective (England)' in J. Ziegel (ed.), *Current Developments in International and Comparative Corporate Insolvency Law* (Clarendon Press, Oxford, 1994) p. 486; A. Keay, 'Another Way of Skinning a Cat' (2004) 17 *Insolvency Intelligence* 1 at 3; D. McKenzie Skene, 'The Directors' Duty to the Creditors of a Financially Distressed Company: A Perspective from Across the Pond' (2007) *Journal of Business and Technology Law* 499.

[34] *Yukong Lines Ltd of Korea* v. *Rendsburg Investments Corporation* [1998] BCC 870; see also T. Ogowewo, 'A Perfect Case for the Application of Section 423 of the Insolvency Act 1986: *Yukong Lines of Korea* v. *Rendsburg Investments Corp. of Liberia (No. 2)*' [1999] Ins. Law. 106.

[35] *West Mercia Safetywear Ltd* v. *Dodd* [1988] 4 BCC 30. In *West Mercia* it was noted that shareholders are replaced by creditors on insolvency as residual claimants, thus implying that the company's interests are now represented by the creditors' interests.

[36] *Yukong Lines Ltd of Korea* v. *Rendsburg Investments Corporation* [1998] BCC 870 at 884. As Toulson J indicated, enforcement of the duty can be effected through s. 212 of the Insolvency Act 1986 – a summary remedy which applies if, in the course of winding up, it appears that an officer of the company (s. 212(1)(a)) has been guilty of any misfeasance or *breach of any fiduciary duty* or other duty in relation to the company: see further below.

[37] See V. Finch, 'Directors' Duties Towards Creditors' (1989) 10 Co. Law. 23.

creditors' interests to be assessed subjectively or objectively? Subjectivity may be consistent with principle[38] but would pose problems of account-ability[39] and an objective approach could draw the judges into assess-ment of directors' business decisions.[40] The judges have yet to resolve these questions, but, as noted above, the weight of argument does currently favour treating the duty to creditors as part of the duty to act in the interests of the company.[41]

The beneficiaries of the duty

Judges have tended to speak of creditors as a homogeneous group but have failed to state clearly whether directors owe a duty to creditors generally, to individual creditors, or to a class of creditors.[42] Attempts have been made to distinguish the interests of existing creditors from those of future creditors but, even in this endeavour, inconsistent approaches are to be encountered. Thus, in *Nicholson* v. *Permakraft*[43] Cooke J indicated that future creditors might normally be expected to 'take the company as it is' and guard their own interests, whereas in

---

[38] See *Re Smith and Fawcett* [1942] Ch 304: the duty is to act *bona fide* in what the director considers, not what the court considers, is in the company's interests (per Lord Greene). See also *Regentcrest plc (in liquidation)* v. *Cohen* [2001] BCC 494, where Jonathan Parker J, in dismissing a claim brought by liquidators against a director for breach of his fiduciary duty to act *bona fide* in the best interest of the company, stated the duty was to be judged on a subjective basis: if the director 'honestly believed that he was acting in the best interests of the company' he was not in breach.

[39] How could creditors ever be secure in the knowledge that consideration of their interests was ever more than lip service? See Sealy, 'Directors' "Wider" Responsibilities'.

[40] See *Carlen* v. *Drury* [1812] 1 Ves & B 154. But see dicta of Temple LJ in *Re Horsley and Weight Ltd* [1982] 3 All ER 1045: 'the directors ought to have known the facts', at 1056; Cooke J in *Nicholson* v. *Permakraft* [1985] 1 NZLR 242 at 250 also favoured an objective approach.

[41] See e.g. *Yukong Lines Ltd of Korea* v. *Rendsburg Investments Corporation* [1998] BCC 870. As noted above, enforcement of the duty can thus be effected through s. 212 of the Insolvency Act 1986 – a summary remedy which applies if, in the course of winding up, it appears that an officer of the company has been guilty of any misfeasance or *breach of any fiduciary duty* or other duty in relation to the company. As for the proceeds of actions for breaches of duties to creditors, a weakness of the law here is that these will not go primarily to the unsecured creditors (who are the parties most in need of protection) but, since the company will be in liquidation, such proceeds will be caught by any security interests the company has granted: see Davies, 'Directors' Creditor-regarding Duties'.

[42] For an argument that approaches to directors' duties to creditors fail sufficiently to take account of the divergent positions of creditors, see Lipson, 'Directors' Duties to Creditors'.

[43] [1985] 1 NZLR 242.

Winkworth v. *Edward Baron*[44] Lord Templeman urged that 'duties were owed to creditors present and future to keep its property inviolate and available for the payment of debts'.

As for existing creditors, these may possess highly conflicting interests: the unsecured trade creditor is in a quite different position from the bank with a floating charge over the company's property. The courts have yet to offer clear guidance to the director who has to choose between such competing interests[45] and an undifferentiated approach may reduce the force of such a duty quite considerably: 'Where duties are owed to persons with potentially opposed interests, the duty bifurcates and fragments so that it amounts ultimately to no more than a vague obligation to be fair ... If the law does this it abandons all effective control over the decision maker.'[46]

In *Re Pantone 485 Ltd*[47] it was stated that 'the creditors' meant the creditors as a whole, i.e. the general creditors. Consequently, if directors acted consistently with the interests of the general creditors but inconsistently with the interest of a creditor or a section of creditors with special rights in a winding up then the directors would not be in breach of their duty.[48] Distinguishing between classes of creditor seems necessary, however, if nothing else, for the purposes of rendering duties potentially effective. If unsecured creditors are to be protected, the judges will have to construe the duty as owed to them either individually or as a specific class and the latter approach would seem more consistent with the notion of bankruptcy as a collective procedure concerned with *pari passu* distribution according to pre-bankruptcy entitlements.[49]

---

[44] [1987] 1 All ER 114; see also *Kinsela* v. *Russell Kinsela Pty Ltd* (1986) 4 ACLC 215 at 221 (future creditors); *Jeffree* v. *National Companies & Securities Commission* (1989) 7 ACLC 556 at 561 (contingent creditors).

[45] For example, directors may have to choose between using remaining assets to pay off preferential creditors or continuing trading in the hope of benefiting unsecured creditors. (Of course, choosing to trade on for the benefit of unsecured creditors rather than immediately paying preferential debts is not necessarily improper: see *Re CU Fittings Ltd* [1989] 5 BCC 210 (a disqualification case, noted in V. Finch, 'Disqualification of Directors: A Plea for Competence' (1990) 53 MLR 385).)

[46] Sealy, 'Directors' "Wider" Responsibilities', p. 175.   [47] [2002] 1 BCLC 266.

[48] Ibid., 286–7 (Richard Field QC). McKenzie Skene notes that this still leaves questions unanswered, e.g. what is meant by 'general creditors' and 'creditors with special rights in a winding up': see 'Directors' Duty to the Creditors of a Financially Distressed Company'.

[49] To give unsecured creditors a class action would guide directors rather than leave them to attempt to be fair 'to all creditors' and would not seem prejudicial to secured creditors who would be able to realise their security or appoint a receiver to act on their behalf. Furthermore such an approach could align with the view that directors owe their duty to the company's residual owners, who stand to lose the most in corporate insolvency, the unsecured creditors.

A further issue that the courts have yet to resolve concerns the exclusivity of the attention that directors should give to creditor interests when those interests fall to be considered.[50] In the case of *Whalley* v. *Doney*[51] Park J said that, at the pre-insolvency stage of financial difficulties, the duties owed to the company extended to encompass the interests of the creditors as a whole as well as those of a shareholder.[52] It is noteworthy here that *Whalley* talks of creditor interests joining those of the shareholder. Some authorities, however, come close to making creditor interests an exclusive focus – at least at the stage when insolvency is questionable or imminent. Thus, in *Brady* v. *Brady*,[53] Nourse LJ, in the Court of Appeal, indicated that after the advent of insolvency (or doubtful insolvency) the interests of the company 'are in reality the interests of existing creditors alone'.[54] This implies that the directors have a duty to pursue the advantage of creditors, an approach consistent with the comments of Street CJ in *Kinsela*[55] to the effect that in an insolvent company it is the creditors' and not the shareholders' assets that are under the management of the directors.[56] More recently, in the *Colin Gwyer* case,[57] it was emphasised that, where the company was on the verge of insolvency, the interests of the creditors must be considered *paramount*.[58]

A contrasting approach allows directors to act post-insolvency in the interests of the company as a whole, provided that actions do not prejudice creditors. Thus, in *Re Welfab Engineers Ltd*,[59] Hoffmann J considered the position where a company was insolvent but had not been placed in the hands of a receiver. He stated that although the directors were not, at such a stage, entitled to act in a manner leaving the creditors in a worse position than on a liquidation, they had not failed in their duty to the company when they had borne in mind the effect on employees of different courses of action.[60]

---

[50] See generally R. Grantham, 'Directors' Duties and Insolvent Companies' (1991) 65 MLR 576.

[51] [2004] BPIR 75.

[52] See also *Re Cityspan Ltd* [2008] BCC 60; D. Hopkins, 'A Company's Interests – A Question of Balance' (2004) 17 *Insolvency Intelligence* 103.

[53] [1989] 3 BCC 535.

[54] Ibid., p. 552. This appears unaffected by the House of Lords' decision in *Brady* and indeed is impliedly accepted by Lord Oliver: see [1988] 2 All ER 617 at 632.

[55] (1986) 4 ACLC 215.   [56] Ibid., p. 730.

[57] *Colin Gwyer & Associates Ltd* v. *London Wharf (Limehouse) Ltd* [2003] 2 BCLC 153.

[58] See also *Re Pantone 485 Ltd* [2002] 1 BCLC 266.   [59] [1990] BCC 600.

[60] See Grantham, 'Directors' Duties and Insolvent Companies', p. 578: 'the importance of *Welfab* lies in Hoffmann J's affirmation that, while they should not be exploited, so long

A way to resolve such tensions is to read dicta in *Brady* and *Kinsela* as being concerned with the reorientation of focus from shareholder to creditor interests that occurs around the point of insolvency rather than being concerned to address the issue of exclusivity of interest. The judges could endorse *Welfab* and stress that creditor interests fall to be considered on insolvency (or doubtful insolvency) but that such interests do not have to be the exclusive concerns of directors. Just as directors are entitled to look beyond shareholder interests before insolvency[61] they should be given a degree of flexibility in relation to the interests of the creditors, who, on insolvency, have stepped into the shoes of the shareholders.

When does the duty arise?

Even if it is accepted that the duty to creditors flows from the traditional duty to act in the company's interests, the courts have been tentative in stating when creditors' interests fall to be considered by directors as part of those company interests. Three positions on the issue can be distinguished:

(a) When a company becomes insolvent the interests of creditors are company interests.
(b) Creditors' interests transform into company interests as the company approaches insolvency or when insolvency is threatened.
(c) The interests of the company include those of creditors and directors should bear in mind creditors' interests at all times.

The judges have hovered, sometimes uneasily, between these three positions. In support of position (a) is the *West Mercia*[62] decision of the Court of Appeal in which a director effected a fraudulent preference and was found to be guilty of a breach of duty (the director had, for his own purposes, made a transfer between accounts in disregard of the interests of the general creditors of the insolvent company). *West Mercia* indicated that where a company is insolvent, a director's duty to act in the best interests of the company includes a duty to protect the interests of the company's creditors. Dillon LJ noted with approval Street CJ's statement in the Australian case of *Kinsela* v. *Russell Kinsela Property Ltd*:[63]

> as creditors leave the company in the directors' hands, the company will not be run primarily for their benefit'. See also the discussion of the Companies Act 2006 s. 172(1) duties below, where the 'have regard to' provisions could make it difficult to establish the exact beneficiaries of the duty.

[61] See Sealy 'Directors' "Wider" Responsibilities'; Companies Act 2006 s. 172(1).
[62] [1988] 4 BCC 30.   [63] (1986) 4 ACLC 215 at 401.

> In a solvent company the proprietary interests of the shareholders entitle them as a general body to be regarded as the company when questions of the duty of directors arise ... But where a company is insolvent the interests of creditors intrude. They become prospectively entitled, through the mechanism of liquidation, to displace the power of the shareholders and directors to deal with the company's assets.

Whether insolvency is a precondition of creditor interests being subsumed within company interests is, however, a matter not beyond doubt. A number of cases extend the principle to incipient insolvency or even threatened insolvency. Thus the Court of Appeal in *Re Horsley and Weight Ltd*[64] stated that insolvency, or near insolvency, was a precondition, and a similar stance appeared to be taken by the New Zealand Court of Appeal in *Nicholson v. Permakraft*.[65] In *Nicholson* the company was solvent at the relevant time but Cooke J considered situations in which directors should consider creditors' interests. These included circumstances of insolvency or near insolvency or doubtful insolvency or if the 'contemplated payment or other course of action could jeopardise its solvency'. Such reasoning may accord to some extent with position (b) and the idea that creditor interests fall to be considered in so far as insolvency looms. This is echoed in, for example, Nourse LJ's dicta in *Brady* v. *Brady*[66] where His Lordship considered the meaning of 'given in good faith in the interest of the company' in section 153 of the Companies Act 1985[67] and stated that where the company is insolvent or even doubtfully solvent, the interests of the company are in reality the interests of the existing creditors alone. In *Whalley* v. *Doney*[68] Park J urged that a company did not have to be insolvent for a director to have breached his duties to the company by being motivated only by the interests of shareholders and employees. In *Whalley* there was a pre-liquidation sale to an entity in which the principal shareholder and director was a participant and the liquidator argued that the price represented an undervaluation. The judge found for the liquidator on a misfeasance claim and said that the company might have a good claim

---

[64] [1982] 3 All ER 1045.

[65] [1985] 1 NZLR 242. See also *Grove* v. *Flavel* (1986) 4 ACLC 654, where the court rejected the argument that there was a general duty owed by directors to protect creditors' interests irrespective of the company's financial position.

[66] See [1989] 3 BCC 535 at 552.

[67] Nourse LJ assumed that the words in the (then) Companies Act 1985 s. 153(1)(b) had the same meaning in that context as when considering directors' fiduciary duties.

[68] [2004] BPIR 75. See also *Re Cityspan Ltd* [2008] BCC 60.

against a director when the company 'whether technically insolvent or not, is in financial difficulties to the extent that its creditors are at risk'.[69]

Certain cases go further, however, and adopt a stance close to position (c) by suggesting that insolvency *per se* is no precondition to consideration of creditors' interests. In the High Court of Australia in *Walker* v. *Wimborne*[70] Mason J indicated that creditors' interests should be considered even before insolvency because 'those interests may be prejudiced by the movement of funds between companies in the event that the companies become insolvent'. Thus, creditors' interests could always be relevant given the theoretical possibility of future insolvency.[71] *Nicholson* v. *Permakraft*[72] is not far short of this position in referring to circumstances in which a contemplated payment or other course of action might jeopardise solvency. There are dicta, moreover, in two House of Lords decisions in which duties to creditors are mooted and the issue of insolvency is not even referred to.[73]

The courts have thus adopted a variety of positions on directors' duties to creditors[74] but, post-*Gwyer*[75] and *Whalley*,[76] there does seem to be a shift by the English judiciary towards position (b) above. The *West Mercia* and *Gwyer* cases, however, did not address the issue of whether the directors' state of appreciation of the company's solvency was to be judged objectively or subjectively.[77]

---

[69] See Hopkins, 'A Company's Interests – A Question of Balance'. See also *Colin Gwyer & Associates Ltd* v. *London Wharf (Limehouse) Ltd* [2003] 2 BCLC 153, [2003] BCC 885, where the deputy judge expressed the principle as follows: 'where a company is insolvent or of doubtful solvency or on the verge of insolvency and it is the creditors' money that is at risk, the directors, when carrying out their duty to the company, must consider the interests of the creditors as paramount and take those into account when exercising their discretion'.

[70] (1976) 137 CLR 1, (1978) 3 ACLR 529. See also *Facia Footwear Ltd (in administration)* v. *Hinchliffe* [1998] 1 BCLC 218; *Galladin Pty Ltd* v. *Aimnorth Pty Ltd* (1993) 11 ACSR 23; *Wright* v. *Frisnia* (1983) 1 ACLC 716.

[71] See Barrett (1977) 40 MLR 229.   [72] [1985] 1 NZLR 242.

[73] In *Lonrho* v. *Shell Petroleum* [1980] 1 WLR 627, Lord Diplock, when speaking of the best interests of the company not necessarily being those of shareholders alone but possibly including those of creditors, made no mention of solvency or insolvency. Neither did Lord Templeman in *Winkworth* v. *Edward Baron Developments Co. Ltd* [1986] 1 WLR 1512, when he was speaking of the duty apparently directly owed to creditors.

[74] Per Giles JA in *Linton* v. *Telnet Pty Ltd* (1999) 30 ACSR 465 at 473: there is significant difficulty in deciding when directors should have regard to creditors' interests and it depends on the particular facts.

[75] [2003] 2 BCLC 153, [2003] BCC 885.   [76] [2004] BPIR 75.

[77] In *Whalley* v. *Doney*, ibid., Park J seems, indeed, to adhere to both assessments: 'whether IM Ltd was technically insolvent before the transaction or not (and in my view it was anyway) it was *on any view* in a dangerous financial position, and *Mr Doney knew it*' (emphasis added).

On the 'prospect of insolvency' issue, the Cork Committee[78] acknowledged that although insolvency arises at the moment when debts have not been met as they fall due, 'the moment is often difficult to pinpoint precisely'. It is often extremely hard to identify when the value of a business starts to fall below the level needed to pay creditors in full. Even on valuations, there are divergent approaches. Thus, the distressed sale value of assets will be very low but the 'enterprise valuation' will be high (though very subjective) and there will be numbers of potential valuations between these extremes.[79] The English courts, nevertheless, would not be without guidance in seeking to devise a legal test. Cooke J in *Nicholson* suggested that, although balance sheet solvency and the ability to pay capital dividends were important in assessing any actions taken, nevertheless:

> as a matter of business ethics it is proper for directors to consider also whether what they will do will prejudice the company's practical ability to discharge promptly debts owed to current and likely continuing trade creditors ... because if the company's financial position is precarious the futures of such suppliers may be so linked with those of the company as to bring them within the reasonable scope of the directors' duty.[80]

An alternative approach to definition might be derived from the statutory criteria of the Insolvency Act 1986: for example, the definition of inability to pay debts found in section 123(2) which, *inter alia*, adopts the liabilities test and the strict balance sheet approach of total assets exceeding total liabilities, 'taking into account contingent and prospective liabilities'. Section 123(1)(e), on the other hand, provides a cash flow test by which a company is deemed unable to pay its debts 'if it is proved to the satisfaction of the court that the company is unable to pay its debts as they fall due'.[81]

As for the test to be applied regarding the director's state of appreciation of the company's solvency, different approaches, again, might be taken. Templeman LJ took an objective approach in *Horsley and Weight* in stating that if expenditure threatens the existence of the company 'the directors ought to have known the facts'.[82] In contrast, it can be argued that the subjective approach is appropriate in all cases involving the

---

[78] Cork Report, para. 205.
[79] See K. Baird, 'Legal Update – The Companies Act 2006' (2007) *Recovery* (Autumn) 9; A. Katz and M. Mumford, *Making Creditor Protection Effective* (Centre for Business Performance, ICAEW, 2008 (Draft)) part 5.
[80] [1985] 1 NZLR 242, 249. [81] See ch. 4 above. [82] [1982] 3 All ER 1045 at 1056.

general fiduciary duty of directors to act in good faith in the interest of the company. Thus Jonathan Parker J has stated that this duty is satisfied where the director does what he honestly believes to be in the company's best interest.[83]

One reason for moving to greater objectivity, however, is the argument that creditors' interests warrant greater protection than can be offered by a subjective test. After all, it can be contended, if creditors' interests only enter the scene when solvency is at issue and if creditors are disadvantaged vis-à-vis shareholders in so far as they are likely to have less information as to the company's solvency, then a director's appreciation of whether a transaction will prejudice the creditors further should be measured against an objective benchmark. Such reasoning favours the approach adopted in the wrongful trading provisions of the Insolvency Act 1986 section 214.[84] According to this approach, directors should be expected to exhibit the same degree of appreciation of their company's viability as would reasonably be expected of a diligent person exercising their functions in the company. A standard of performance is demanded, accordingly, which is consistent with the idea of a minimum level of competence.[85] Directors, on this view, would be bound to give good faith consideration to creditors' interests from the moment they know *or ought to have concluded* that the company's solvency is at the very least doubtful.

To summarise, then, the judges have yet to state consistently when the duty arises or what state of mind or knowledge renders the director potentially liable. Directors seeking guidance on the former issue have

---

[83] *Regentcrest plc (in liquidation)* v. *Cohen* [2001] BCC 494. See also *Extrasure Travel Insurances Ltd* v. *Scattergood* [2003] 1 BCLC 598 and D. Milman, 'Company Directors – Their Duties and Liabilities Revisited' (2004) *Sweet & Maxwell's Company Law Newsletter* 1.

[84] See Insolvency Act 1986 s. 214(4)(a). On s. 214, however, and problems of inconsistency of judicial approach, see pp. 698–703 below.

[85] For discussion of the influence of the 'statutory lead' of Insolvency Act 1986 s. 214 on the general duty of skill and care, see Finch, 'Company Directors', pp. 202–4; D. Arsalidou, 'The Impact of Section 214(4) of the Insolvency Act 1986 on Directors' Duties' (2000) 21 Co. Law. 19; Law Commission and Scottish Law Commission, *Company Directors: Regulating Conflicts of Interest and Formulating a Statement of Duties* (Law Commission Report No. 261, Scottish Law Commission Report No. 173, 1999) paras. 15.3–15.5 and 15.9–15.10; CLRSG, *Modern Company Law for a Competitive Economy: Developing the Framework* (March 2000) ch. 3; *Modern Company Law for a Competitive Economy: Completing the Structure* (November 2000) ch. 13; and the resultant statutory statement of the director's duty to exercise reasonable care, skill and diligence in the Companies Act 2006 s. 174 – which adopts the criteria set out in the Insolvency Act 1986 s. 214(4).

to rely on a confusion of dicta and statutory tests. Judges may inevitably have to exercise discretion in assessing the point of doubtful solvency in particular contexts but more coherent structuring of that discretion is necessary if directors and creditors are to know where they stand.

An Institute of Directors survey of members was published in 1999[86] and revealed that there was widespread uncertainty in UK boardrooms over directors' obligations to consider the interests of different groups of stakeholders when considering corporate actions. Three-quarters of respondents thought that directors' duties were difficult to understand; over half thought that they had to account to creditors and employees;[87] a quarter thought the same of customers and suppliers, and 87 per cent believed that the law needed to be clarified if directors were to understand their obligations.

In 2001, the Company Law Review Steering Group considered the case for a statutory statement of directors' duties to creditors in a situation where the company is insolvent or threatened by insolvency.[88] The CLRSG's consultations led it close to the view that such a statement was needed.[89] As for the director's obligations at the pre-insolvency stage of corporate decline, the CLRSG draft stated that what is reasonable must be decided in good faith, giving more or less weight to the need to reduce risk as the risk is more or less severe.[90] In deciding how to promote the success of the company for the benefit of its members as a whole the director must take account, in good faith, of all the material factors that it is practicable in the circumstances for him to identify (which includes the need to achieve outcomes that are fair between members).

When the Companies Act 2006 codified directors' duties, it did not adopt such a risk-based approach, however, and there are reasons why this kind of formulation might be resisted. Such an approach could produce dangers that directors will act excessively cautiously, fail to take reasonable risks and flee from companies at the first signs of trouble.[91] What the 2006 Act did do was set down a statutory statement

---

[86] News Digest, (1999) 20 Co. Law. 302.   [87] On employees, see ch. 17 below.

[88] See CLRSG, *Modern Company Law for a Competitive Economy: Final Report* (July 2001) pp. 42–5.

[89] The initial draft statement had not advocated such a statement of a special duty to creditors: see CLRSG, *Developing the Framework*, paras. 3.72–3.73.

[90] CLRSG, *Final Report*, 2001, p. 347.

[91] The CLRSG was aware of these issues: see ibid., p. 44. For the progression of policy towards the Companies Act 2006 see the White Papers *Modernising Company Law* (Cm 5553, 2002) and *Company Law Reform* (Cm 6456, 2005).

of directorial duties but leave directors' duties to creditors to be governed by an uneasy combination of statute and common law.

Statutory duties and liabilities

General duties

The Companies Act 2006 offered the first statutory formulation of directors' duties and these are set out in sections 170–7.[92] (These duties are separate from the company directors' disqualification legislation.) Section 170 states that the statutory provisions replace the duties of directors at common law and equity but section 170(4) provides that the general duties shall be interpreted and applied in the same way as common law rules or equitable principles and that: 'regard shall be had to the corresponding common law rules and equitable principles in interpreting those general duties'.[93] The specific duties are: to act within powers (section 171); to promote the success of the company (section 172); to exercise independent judgement (section 173); to exercise reasonable care, skill and diligence (section 174);[94] to avoid conflicts of interest (section 175); to desist from accepting benefits from third parties (section 176); and to declare personal interests in proposed transactions or arrangements (section 177).[95]

---

[92] Ss. 171–4 came into effect on 1 October 2007 and ss. 175–7 came into effect on 1 October 2008. See further S. Griffin, 'The Regulation of Directors Under the Companies Act 2006' (2008) 224 *Sweet & Maxwell's Company Law Newsletter* 1; L. Sealy, 'The Statutory Statement of Directors' Duties: The Devil in the Detail' (2008) 228 *Sweet & Maxwell's Company Law Newsletter* 1.

[93] See D. Milman, 'Directors and the Transition to the New Regime' (2007) 8 *Sweet & Maxwell's Company Law Newsletter* 1. What constitutes 'interpreting' is a difficult point – especially when the terms of s. 172(1) are subjective but the case law imports objective tests, as in *Charterbridge Corp. Ltd* v. *Lloyds Bank Ltd* [1970] 1 Ch 62: see A. Keay, 'Section 172(1) of the Companies Act 2006' (2007) 28 Co. Law. 106.

[94] As noted above, the s. 174 duty is akin to that of s. 214 of the Insolvency Act in its objective expectation of the reasonably diligent person possessing the general skill and experience of a person carrying out the functions of the company director in that company, and is consistent with the common law: see *Re D'Jan of London Ltd* [1993] BCC 646.

[95] A statutory derivative action under s. 260 of the Companies Act 2006 allows a member of the company to proceed against a director for a breach of duty or trust or an act or omission involving negligence or default: see G. Pendell, 'Derivative Claims: A Practical Guide' (2007) 20 *Sweet & Maxwell's Company Law Newsletter* 1. See also A. Keay, 'Can Derivative Proceedings be Commenced when a Company is in Liquidation?' (2008) 21 *Insolvency Intelligence* 49.

For insolvency lawyers, section 172 is of special interest.[96] It applies a highly subjective standard in demanding that directors act in the way they consider, in good faith, will be most likely to promote the success of the company for the benefit of the members as a whole. They must, in doing so, have regard to (*inter alia*): the interests of employees; the need to foster the company's business relationships with suppliers, customers and others; and the impact of the company's operations on the community and the environment (section 172(1)). (It may be presumed that 'suppliers, customers and others' in section 172(1)(c) includes creditors.) Regard must, furthermore, be had to the need to act fairly as between members of the company. With respect to creditors, section 172(3), as noted above, states that the section 172 duty has effect 'subject to any enactment or rule of law requiring directors, in certain circumstances, to consider or act in the interests of creditors of the company'.[97] The legal effect, accordingly, is that common law duties are not negated and directors will continue to have an overriding duty to consider or act in the interests of creditors if the company is insolvent or on the verge of insolvency.[98] The Act thus appears to accept the 'common law principle of husbandry adopted by the Court of Appeal in *West Mercia Safetywear*'.[99] What the 2006 Act does not do is provide clarity on when the section 172 duty (to have regard to the list of considerations listed therein) gives way to the established duties to consider or act in the interests of the creditors. As noted, it is often extremely difficult, in practice, to identify the point at which the value of a business falls below the level needed to pay the creditors in full – and the law is not user-friendly in setting out the directors' obligations at a given time. On the one hand, judicial decisions create a 'zone of uncertainty' in which creditor interests have to be taken into account as the company approaches insolvency and, on the other, the troubled director will be attuned to his or her obligation to observe the section 172 duties.[100] For

---

[96] See Keay, 'Section 172(1) of the Companies Act 2006'.

[97] The Explanatory Notes to the 2006 Act (para. 332) indicate that s. 172(3) will 'leave the law to develop in this area'.

[98] The other sections of the 2006 Act do not contain a similar provision and so all other duties would appear to apply regardless of the company's solvency.

[99] Milman, 'Directors and the Transition to the New Regime'.

[100] See Baird, 'Legal Update', p. 11: 'The problem being that, if a company is not in the "zone of uncertainty", it becomes much easier for a director to say that he must "have regard to" things that are contained in s. 172 … Lawyers will have a great deal more to do to make it clear that the "have regard to" matters … must not be allowed to distract directors from doing the right thing when the company's solvency is in question.'

the courts and legal observers, a residual question is whether the section 172 duties will impact on current approaches to the reorientation of duties as companies approach insolvency.

Fraudulent trading

Turning to statutory provisions creating personal liability, directors may be liable to compensate creditors where they have been party to fraudulent trading by the company. Section 213 of the Insolvency Act 1986 provides:

(1) If in the course of the winding up of the company it appears that any business of the company has been carried on with intent to defraud creditors of the company, or creditors of any other person, or for any fraudulent purpose, the following has effect.

(2) The court, on the application of the liquidator, may declare that any persons who were knowingly parties to the carrying on of the business in the manner above mentioned are liable to make such contributions (if any) to the company assets as the court thinks proper.

The purpose of this provision is to compensate rather than to punish. Thus it has been said that there must be a connection between the losses caused by the fraudulent trading and the quantum of compensation and that the court has no power under section 213 to impose a punitive element in the compensation order made.[101] The section has a long history and, indeed, was introduced particularly to protect unsecured creditors from the abuse of 'filling up' floating charges.[102] Now, however, it is recognised[103] that the aim of fraudulent trading provisions – to discourage directors from carrying on business at the expense of creditors – is severely restricted by the requirement of dishonest intent[104] and

---

[101] *Morphitis* v. *Bernasconi* [2003] Ch 552, [2003] BCC 540 (a contrast with cases under the prior legislation: see e.g. *Re Cyona Distributors Ltd* [1967] Ch 889). In *Morphitis* it was stated that the provision catering for punishment was (the then) s. 458 of the Companies Act 1985 which made fraudulent trading a criminal offence. On the nexus between losses and compensation amounts *Morphitis* has been followed by *Morris* v. *Bank of India* [2005] BCC 739.

[102] A process whereby directors lent money secured by floating charges to their asset-less companies, bought stock on credit which became subject to the floating charges, then appointed receivers who sold off the stock to satisfy the directors' charges, leaving the creditors 'whistling'. Now, however, the company would have to be kept afloat for two years to avoid the operation of the Insolvency Act 1986 s. 245: see ch. 13 above.

[103] See Cork Report, p. 398.

[104] In the subjective sense: 'actual dishonesty ... real moral blame' per Maugham J in *Re Patrick and Lyon Ltd* [1933] Ch 786 at 790. Maugham J noted that the provision was 'by

the courts' insistence on strict standards of pleading and proof.[105] Such an approach may be understandable for criminal liability under section 993 of the Companies Act 2006, but its imposition on the civil liability provided for in section 213 of the 1986 Act has led to the latter section's virtual obsolescence. This obsolescence is now even more apparent with the advent of section 214, the 'wrongful trading'[106] provision. What is more, the Court of Appeal appears to have adopted a concept of intention for the purposes of section 213 that is even harder to demonstrate than would be the case in the criminal law. In criminal law it is established by the House of Lords that a person 'intends' the consequences of an action that are foreseen as virtually certain – and that whether those consequences were desired or were the main motive for the action is irrelevant.[107] In the Court of Appeal case of *Morphitis* v. *Bernasconi*,[108] however, Chadwick LJ did not treat the phrase 'with intent to defraud' as a composite whole, finding that fraud alone is not sufficient to ground liability and defining the word 'intent' in isolation. Thus, according to Chadwick LJ, there had been no 'intent to defraud' since the aim or objective underlying the company's (TMC (1)) trading was to protect the directors from liability under section 216 of the Insolvency Act rather than to defraud creditors or in particular the landlord. It would, however, have been equally possible to recognise that the purpose behind the scheme was to enable TMC (1) to divest itself of onerous leasehold premises while simultaneously protecting the TMC brand or, alternatively, as an attempt to minimise rent payments while forestalling the

---

no means easy to construe'. See also *Re William Leach Brothers Ltd* [1932] 2 Ch 71; *Re L. Todd (Swanscombe) Ltd* [1990] BCC 127; *R v. Miles* (1992) Crim L Rev 657; *Re Bank of Credit and Commerce International SA (No. 14)* [2003] EWHC 1868 (CA). Liability will extend, however, to all parties who knowingly participate in the company's fraudulent trading (which covers not only parties with actual knowledge but also those who were deliberately blind or recklessly indifferent to the fraudulent nature of the transaction): see *Morris* v. *Bank of India* [2005] BCC 739 and I. McDonald and D. Shah, 'Fraudulent Trading' (2005) *Recovery* (Winter) 18.

[105] Ian Fletcher has noted the degree of uncertainty 'whether civil or criminal proceedings for fraudulent trading will prove to be successful in any given case': *The Law of Insolvency* (3rd edn, Sweet & Maxwell, London, 2002) p. 706.

[106] Section 214, according to the marginal note, is concerned with 'wrongful trading', but it is notable that the word 'trading' is not used in the text of the Act: see further L. S. Sealy and D. Milman, *Annotated Guide to the Insolvency Legislation* (10th edn, Thomson/ Sweet & Maxwell, London, 2007) vol. I, p. 233.

[107] See e.g. *R v. Woollin* [1998] 3 WLR 382 at 389.

[108] [2003] Ch 552, [2003] 2 BCLC 53 (which concerned application of (the fraudulent trading) s. 213 of the Insolvency Act 1986).

issue of a writ.[109] Whether the ruling in *Morphitis* v. *Bernasconi* will survive scrutiny should the House of Lords consider this matter in the future may be doubtful since, as one commentator has said: 'the test of oblique intention … in *Morphitis* is wholly out of step with contemporary thinking on the issue in criminal law cases proper'.[110]

As for the criminal offence of fraudulent trading, this was formerly set out in section 458 of the Companies Act 1985 and is now provided for in section 993 of the Companies Act 2006. This has been called 'a valuable weapon in countering crime'.[111] Problems of under-deterrence, however, prompted the CLRSG to propose, in 2001, that the penalty for the offence should be raised to a level comparable with that for deception under the Theft Act. In due course, the Fraud Act 2006 section 10 increased the maximum penalty under section 993 of the Companies Act 2006 to ten years on indictment and section 9 of the Fraud Act 2006 provided for a similar offence to apply to sole traders who would otherwise be beyond the scope of section 993.

Wrongful trading

Section 214 of the Insolvency Act 1986 owes its birthright to the Cork Committee,[112] and, as stated previously, was the White Paper's great hope for the unsecured creditor.[113] In terms of increasing directors' duties to unsecured creditors, section 214 provides that where a company is in liquidation, a liquidator can apply to the court to have a person who is or has been a director declared personally liable to make such contribution to the company's assets as the court thinks proper. The liquidator must establish that, at some time before the commencement of the winding up of the company, that person knew or ought to have concluded that there was no reasonable prospect that the company would avoid going into insolvent liquidation and that the respondent was either a director or a shadow director[114] of the company at that time. Here it is noteworthy that

---

[109] A. Savarimuthu, '*Morphitis* in the Court of Appeal' (2005) 26 Co. Law. 245 at 248.
[110] Ibid.
[111] See CLRSG, *Final Report*, 2001, para. 15.7. The CLRSG recommended that the offence should be extended to companies incorporated overseas and trading in the UK and to individuals and partnerships. For an equivalent to the Companies Act 2006 s. 993 that is of relevance to sole traders, see the Fraud Act 2006 s. 4.
[112] Cork Report, ch. 44.
[113] Academics and practitioners also saw s. 214 as a potentially valuable tool: see Prentice, 'Creditors' Interest'; F. Oditah, 'Wrongful Trading' [1990] LMCLQ 205.
[114] That is, a person in accordance with whose instructions the directors of the company are accustomed to act. On shadow directors see Insolvency Act 1986 s. 251; Company Directors' Disqualification Act 1986 s. 22(5); Companies Act 2006 s. 251(2); pp. 720–1 below.

a point may arise, during a cumulation of failures to produce funds, when directors must realise that insolvency is unavoidable.[115] Thus, in *Rubin* v. *Gunner and Another*,[116] the court found directors to be liable for wrongfully trading after the date at which they ought to have concluded that promised funds would not be forthcoming from an investor who had given numerous assurances but had repeatedly failed to produce the moneys needed to avoid insolvent liquidation. From the said date, said the court, the directors should have concluded that there was no reasonable prospect of the company avoiding going into insolvent liquidation.

A defence is, however, available if the respondent director shows that, having reached the state of knowledge referred to, he took *every step* with a view to minimising potential loss to the company's creditors that he ought to have taken (section 214(3)).[117] Here there is a movement away from the subjective test of skill and care applied to directors in the common law cases such as *Re City Equitable Fire Insurance Co.*[118] Under section 214, a director is judged not only by the knowledge, skill and experience that he actually has (section 214(4)(b)) but also by the 'general knowledge, skill and experience that may reasonably be expected of a person carrying out the same functions' (section 214(4)(a)). A director can, therefore, under this limb be judged by standards of the 'reasonable director' even though he may be well below those standards himself.[119]

---

[115] See also Katz and Mumford, *Making Creditor Protection Effective*, part 5, who, in discussing what form of evidence is needed to establish that 'a director knew or ought to have concluded …', state that 'the key evidence includes cash flow forecasts, prepared at intervals, that reflect the perceived seriousness of the company's financial situation'.

[116] [2004] BCC 684, [2004] 2 BCLC 110. In *Re Hawkes Hill Publishing Co. Ltd* (2007) 151 SJLB 743 Lewison J stressed that the use of hindsight was not always fair in judging whether a director had reasonable grounds to believe the company would not survive.

[117] For suggestions on steps and strategies which directors could adopt (including, *inter alia*, taking appropriate outside professional advice, holding weekly board meetings, keeping major creditors and all directors in the loop and recording all recommendations for remedial action made by the directors) see C. Swain, 'Light at the End of the Tunnel – Operating in the Twilight Zone' (2006) 19 *Insolvency Intelligence* 33, 35.

[118] [1925] Ch 407.

[119] This sets a minimum standard and, in deciding whether this minimum has been obtained, regard can be had to the particular company and its business: see *Re Produce Marketing Consortium* [1989] 5 BCC 569 per Knox J at 594. For a further discussion of this case see Prentice, 'Creditors' Interest'; L. S. Sealy [1989] CLJ 375. See also Park J in *Re Continental Assurance Co. of London plc* [2001] BPIR 733 for a judicial analysis of the nature of individual directors' potential liabilities, quantum and issues of several liability versus joint and several liability under s. 214; see further A. Walters, 'Wrongful Trading: Two Recent Cases' [2001] Ins. Law. 211.

The wrongful trading section has, however, proved to be a disappointment in terms of numbers of reported cases.[120] The reason may be that it is often seen as easier to make out a case of misfeasance, preference or transaction at undervalue than to chart the difficult waters of wrongful trading.[121] Central to those difficulties is often the liquidator's challenge in identifying the 'relevant date or time' when the director should have been aware that there was no reasonable prospect that the company would avoid going into insolvent liquidation. Establishing this time will often be problematic, especially if the company's records are incomplete.[122] Also, as Keay has commented, the courts have been reluctant to second-guess directors' commercial decisions. They usually recognise that directors have to make tough decisions, often in difficult circumstances, and 'have generally come down on the side of the directors'.[123]

Problems in the funding of wrongful trading actions clearly have not helped to develop wrongful trading as a strong force for directorial accountability and these have been discussed above.[124] Judicial

---

[120] But in terms of s. 214's influence on directorial standards of care this has been far reaching: see Re D'Jan [1993] BCC 646; Companies Act 2006 s. 174.

[121] The courts require compelling evidence to be convinced of wrongful trading and often prefer to impose liability through other mechanisms. As Milman notes: 'This is because wrongful trading rarely occurs in a vacuum but usually in a context of other managerial shortcomings which are easier to prove through legal action.' D. Milman, 'Improper Trading: Can it be Effectively Regulated?' (2004) 4 *Sweet & Maxwell's Company Law Newsletter* 3. A cited example of a wrongful trading action that failed to impress the court was *Liquidator of Marini Ltd* v. *Dickenson* [2004] BCC 172 in which the claim foundered because there was no evidence of an increase in the net deficiency of the company during the relevant period of alleged wrongful trading (an application of *Re Continental Assurance plc* [2001] All ER 229, where Park J had stated that there had to be more than a 'mere "but for" nexus ... to connect the wrongfulness of the director's conduct with the company's losses'): see Milman, 'Improper Trading'; N. Spence, 'Personal Liability for Wrongful Trading' (2004) 17 *Insolvency Intelligence* 11.

[122] The liquidator, in seeking to maximise assets for the general creditors, may, understandably, be tempted to select the time period which would provide the possibility of the highest attainable contribution. On the courts' approaches as to whether the liquidator's exact selection of time is sacrosanct or whether there can be some latitude see A. Keay, 'Wrongful Trading and the Point of Liability' (2006) 19 *Insolvency Intelligence* 132. See also *Rubin* v. *Gunner and Another* [2004] BCC 686, [2004] 2 BCLC 110, where the liquidator appeared to rely on several dates during the course of the litigation and trial and where a specific time was then settled upon by the court itself.

[123] A. Keay, 'Wrongful Trading and the Liability of Company Directors' (2005) 25 *Legal Studies* 432, 439–40 (citing *Re Continental Assurance plc* [2001] All ER 229).

[124] See ch. 13 above. The Insolvency (Amendment) Rules 2008 (SI 2008/737) amend the Insolvency Rules 1986 by replacing r. 4.218(a) with a new r. 4.218(1), (2) and (3)(a) and by inserting new rr. 4.218A–4.218E. (The amendments, *inter alia*, provide expressly for

approaches to section 214 have, furthermore, not added to the efficacy of the provision. This is an area where there has been an unhelpful confusion about the role and purpose of the law. Cork had envisaged that civil liability for wrongful trading would effect a balance between encouraging the growth of enterprises and discouraging 'downright irresponsibility'.[125] This balancing, as involved in section 214, has allowed different judges to adopt different approaches to wrongful trading and a degree of uncertainty has resulted. In *Re Produce Marketing Consortium Ltd*[126] Knox J treated the section 214 jurisdiction as 'primarily compensatory rather than penal'.[127] It is clear, however, from other cases such as *Re Sherborne Associates Ltd*,[128] that the wrongful trading provisions are being seen by some judges not so much as a civil remedy to raise standards among directors and to compensate creditors, but as a way to punish directors whose actions are seen as immoral. Such a punitive conception may also sit more comfortably with a 'pro-enterprise'/'pro-rescue' stance rather than a 'pro-creditor' position.[129] In *Sherborne*, the actions were dismissed and the judge was sympathetic to the honest, hard-working, well-respected businessmen who acted as directors in times of difficulty.[130] Even on a finding of liability under section 214,

the expenses of liquidation to be payable out of the proceeds of any legal proceedings which the liquidator has power to bring and also for the recovery of expenses and costs relating not only to the conduct but also to the preparation of any such legal proceedings.)

[125] Cork Report, para. 1805.   [126] [1989] 5 BCC 569.

[127] Ibid., at 597. On the public law function of s. 214 in prescribing standards of directorial behaviour see Robert Walker J in *Re Oasis Merchandising Services Ltd* [1995] BCC 911 at 918.

[128] [1995] BCC 40. See P. Godfrey and S. Nield, 'The Wrongful Trading Provisions: All Bark and No Bite?' (1995) 11 IL&P 139.

[129] Terms used by A. Walters, 'Enforcing Wrongful Trading: Substantive Problems and Practical Disincentives' in B. Rider (ed.), *The Corporate Dimension: An Exploration of Developing Areas of Company and Commercial Law* (Jordans, Bristol, 1998) p. 149. It can similarly be argued that there is a tension between compensatory and standard-raising rationales: see S. Shulte, 'Enforcing Wrongful Trading as a Standard of Conduct for Directors and a Remedy for Creditors: The Special Case for Corporate Insolvency' (1999) 20 Co. Law. 80.

[130] Note, however, that the principal director had died by the time of the hearing and consequently the court may have been anxious not to judge with hindsight someone who was unable to defend himself: see I. F. Fletcher, 'Wrongful Trading: "Reasonable Prospect" of Insolvency' (1995) 8 *Insolvency Intelligence* 14. The dangers of acting on hindsight (noted in *Re Sherborne* itself), and of assuming that what has happened was always bound to happen and was apparent, were noted in *Re Brian D. Pierson (Contractors) Ltd* [1999] BCC 26 when Hazel Williamson QC, in the Chancery Division, declined to be 'wise with hindsight' and gave respect to the directors'

the court may exercise its discretion under section 214(1) when deciding the appropriate amount of compensation to be paid by a director and may take account of the degree of culpability exhibited by the director.[131] The court can, therefore, note whether the director's conduct resulted from a failure to appreciate rather than from a deliberate course of wrongdoing; whether or not there were heeded or unheeded warnings from the auditors;[132] and whether there was any misappropriation of assets by the directors for their own benefit.[133] In *Re Purpoint Ltd*,[134] however, Vinelott J did not look kindly on directors who failed to monitor their company's financial affairs and in *Re DKG Contractors Ltd*[135] there was a similar approach to directors who failed to abide by the basic requirements of company law. In *Re Continental Assurance of London plc*[136] it was emphasised, moreover, that it was directors who had 'closed their eyes to the reality of the company's position ... had been irresponsible and had not made any genuine attempt to grapple with the company's real position' who had something to fear apropos liability under section 214.

Thus, in exercising their discretions to order directorial contributions, the courts may, as noted, vary their responses according to their espousal of different approaches to section 214, be these compensatory (as in *Re Produce Marketing*)[137] or inclined to advert to issues of culpability (as discernible, for example, in such cases as *Re Sherborne, Re Purpoint, Re DKG Contractors* and *Re Continental Assurance*).[138] The bite of the wrongful trading provisions is, therefore, diminished not merely by the legal uncertainties that liquidators face on seeing widely varying judicial rulings, but also by the propensity of the judiciary to look to culpability (rather than pure compensation) as a factor of relevance in deciding both

---

judgement as to the company's prospects. Nevertheless, on the facts, she was satisfied that the directors ought to have concluded that there was no reasonable prospect of avoiding insolvent liquidation and they were liable under s. 214. In *Re Continental Assurance Co. of London plc* [2001] BPIR 733, [2001] All ER 229, however, a sympathetic view of directors appears to have been taken again when Park J rejected a wrongful trading action, noting that the directors had not acted unreasonably in difficult circumstances when they sought expert advice and, reasonably, traded on.

[131] See M. Simmons, 'Wrongful Trading' (2001) 14 *Insolvency Intelligence* 12.

[132] *Re Brian D. Pierson (Contractors) Ltd* [1999] BCC 26.

[133] *Re Produce Marketing Consortium Ltd (No. 2)* [1989] BCLC 520, [1989] 5 BCC 569.

[134] [1991] BCLC 491.   [135] [1990] BCC 903.

[136] [2001] All ER 229.   [137] [1989] 5 BCC 569.

[138] [1995] BCC 40; [1991] BCLC 491; [1990] BCC 903. In *Re Continental Assurance Co. of London plc* [2001] BPIR 733, [2001] All ER 229, Park J seemed much influenced by the directors' 'wholly responsible, conscientious attitudes'.

whether to declare a liability to contribute and subsequent issues of quantum.[139]

'Phoenix' provisions

Personal liability for directors also arises in relation to sections 216 and 217 of the Insolvency Act 1986, the provisions designed to deal with the 'phoenix syndrome'. These sections prohibit a director of a company that has entered insolvent liquidation from being involved, for the next five years, in the management of a company using the same name as the insolvent company or a name so similar as to suggest an association with it.[140] The prohibition covers using any name by which the old company was known[141] and even a name that has not been used for trading but has been used internally as a promotional shorthand name.[142] The rule also applies to any director who has left a company within twelve months of liquidation. Breach of the rule involves civil or criminal liability and the major effect is to make the person concerned personally liable to contribute towards the debts of the 'new' company.[143] An individual may seek the court's leave to act as the director of a similarly named company, however, and there is evidence that the courts will be well disposed to grant such leave where the applicant was not to blame for the failure of the initial company.[144] An advantage of sections 216 and 217 to the creditor is that these provisions allow an individual to bring an action to

---

[139] For further discussion of the wrongful trading provisions in the context of efficiency see pp. 741–3, 746–9 below.

[140] *Archer Structures Ltd* v. *Griffiths* [2004] BCC 156. See M. Tempest, 'Re-use of Company Names' (2006) *Recovery* (Summer) 25; T. Mayer, 'Personal Liability for Trading in a Prohibited Name' (2006) 27 Co. Law. 14; Carter, 'Phoenix Syndrome'; Frith, 'Acting as a Director of a Phoenix Company'. On exceptions to the ss. 216 and 217 rules (outlined in the Insolvency Rules 1986 (SI 1986/1925) (amended in 2007: see below), particularly rr. 4.227–4.230) see *ESS Production Ltd* v. *Sully* [2005] BCC 435; *Commissioners for HM Revenue & Customs* v. *Walsh* [2006] BCC 431. In *Churchill* v. *First Independent Factors and Finance Ltd* [2007] BCC 45 the Court of Appeal adopted a literal and inconvenient interpretation of (the then) r. 4.228 and precluded its usage for notice of business transfers to successor companies unless the director in question had taken up appointment *after* the notice was given. The *Churchill* case led to a revision of the Insolvency Rules: see Insolvency (Amendment) Rules 2007 (SI 2007/1974) effective from 6 August 2007.

[141] *Commissioners of Inland Revenue* v. *Nash* [2003] BPIR 1138.

[142] *ESS Production Ltd* v. *Sully* [2005] BCC 435.

[143] On the operation of s. 217 see *Thorne* v. *Silverleaf* [1994] 1 BCLC 637; *Commissioners of Inland Revenue* v. *Nash* [2003] BPIR 1138; *First Independent Factors and Finance Ltd* v. *Mountford* [2008] EWHC 835 (Ch).

[144] See *Penrose* v. *Official Receiver* [1996] 1 BCLC 389; *Re Lightning Electrical Contractors Ltd* [1996] 2 BCLC 302; Rule 4.227 Insolvency Rules 1986; *Churchill* v. *First*

recover a specific debt. This is a material difference to actions for wrongful trading (Insolvency Act 1986 section 214) or to transactions at undervalue (Insolvency Act 1986 section 238) which can only be brought by the liquidator and whose proceeds enter the creditor pool for general distribution.[145]

Transactions at undervalue, preferences and transactions defrauding creditors

Further areas of directorial liability relate to transactions at undervalue and preferences and transactions defrauding creditors under sections 238, 239 and 423 of the Insolvency Act 1986. These provisions and their enforcement have, however, been discussed in chapter 13 and will not be dealt with here.

Enforcement

The above discussion sets out the main rules governing the potential liability of directors in cases of corporate insolvency. Matters of enforcement need, however, to be considered if the real accountability of directors is to be assessed. In relation to the common law duties that directors owe to creditors, there are considerable enforcement difficulties. The judges have tended to see directors' duties to creditors in exhortatory terms and so have failed to grasp the enforcement nettle. If creditors' interests derive from general duties owed to the company then breaches should properly be dealt with by the company as contemplated in *Nicholson*[146] and *Walker* v. *Wimborne*.[147] The problem, however, is

---

Independent Factors and Finance Ltd [2007] BCC 45 (CA) and subsequently amended Rule 4.228. See further I. Clarke, 'Re-use of Company Names: Applications to Court by a Director for Leave to Act' (2007) *Recovery* (Spring) 32 and the discussion of the 'phoenix' problem by the CLRSG, *Final Report*, 2001, paras. 15.55–15.77. The Review Group, *inter alia*, distinguishes between 'good phoenix' situations (i.e. where 'honest individuals may, through misfortune or naïve good faith, find that they can no longer trade out of their difficulties ... and the only way to continue an otherwise viable business ... may be for them to do so in a new vehicle using the assets and trading style of the original company') and 'bad phoenix' situations (i.e. where individuals 'seek to abuse the system or deliberately evade their responsibilities').

[145] See Carter, 'Phoenix Syndrome'. This recovery mechanism has been used extensively over the past years, particularly by HM Revenue and Customs: see e.g. *HMRC* v. *Benton-Diggins* [2006] BCC 769, where deputy judge Michael Crystal QC applied the test as to whether there was a real probability of the public associating the two companies.

[146] [1985] 1 NZLR 242.

[147] [1976] 50 ALJR 446, (1976) 137 CLR 1, (1978) 3 ACLR 529.

that enforcement of the duty is likely to be difficult before the company goes into administration, receivership or liquidation since creditors cannot rely on the existing board or the shareholders to complain about the ill-treatment of creditors' interests. On liquidation, the possibility arises of a misfeasance action under section 212 of the Insolvency Act 1986, which allows proceedings where a director has been guilty of 'any misfeasance or breach of any fiduciary or other duty in relation to the company'.[148] Duties to creditors may thus arise at the stage of doubtful solvency but creditors *per se* are given a right of action only on winding up.

Such enforcement would, of course, offer little assistance to unsecured creditors since any recovered funds will go to company assets and will come within the scope of any floating charge.[149] The 'prescribed part' provisions found in the Insolvency Act 1986 section 176A thus seek to ensure that a certain percentage of the net realisations of property subject to any floating charge will be set aside and made available to the unsecured creditors on the company's insolvency.[150]

Are creditors, however, in a good position to enforce duties against directors? As has been argued elsewhere,[151] effective enforcement demands an ability to acquire and use information; expertise or understanding of the relevant activity; a commitment to act; and an ability to bring pressure or sanctions to bear on the party to be controlled.

On the first issue, creditors may have not inconsiderable access to information. The disclosure rules operating throughout company

---

[148] The Insolvency Act 1986 extended the ambit of misfeasance to 'include breach of any duty including the duty of care': per Hoffmann LJ in *Re D'Jan of London Ltd* [1994] 1 BCLC 561 at 562. On misfeasance see further *Re Eurocruit Europe Ltd* [2007] BCC 916 (claims under s. 212 do not have a limitation period distinct from that applicable to the underlying claim); *Whitehouse* v. *Wilson* [2007] BPIR 230 (clarifies liquidators' responsibilities to the various stakeholders apropos offers to settle misfeasance claims); *Mullarkey* v. *Broad* [2008] 1 BCLC 638 (the onus of proof in misfeasance rests on the claimant); *Walker* v. *Walker and Another* [2005] All ER 277 (liquidator ordered to pay the director's costs as the action was commercially worthless from the start in that the director had limited assets); *Re Brian D. Pierson (Contractors) Ltd* [1999] BCC 26; *Re Westlowe Storage & Distribution Ltd* [2000] BCC 851; *Re Continental Assurance Co. of London plc* [2001] BPIR 733; F. Oditah, 'Misfeasance Proceedings against Company Directors' [1992] LMCLQ 207.

[149] See *Re Anglo-Austrian Printing and Publishing Co.* [1895] Ch 152 (damages received from directors for misfeasance are available to the charge holder).

[150] See the Insolvency Act 1986 (Prescribed Part) Order 2003 (SI 2003/2097) and chs. 3 and 13 above.

[151] Finch, 'Company Directors'.

legislation generally reflect the principle that these operate for creditors' as well as shareholders' benefit. Creditors, like shareholders, can obtain information on the financial state of the company at the Company Registry in the form of copies of certain classes of resolution, annual accounts and directors' and auditors' reports. Copies of these documents have, moreover, to be sent to 'all debenture holders'. When a company enters or nears insolvency, further sources of information arise. Administrators must be furnished with information from the company's directors to enable the preparation of a notice of the administrator's appointment and, on the commencement of the procedure, the administrator must provide a statement of affairs to creditors.[152] Where voluntary arrangements are made in order to conclude an agreement with creditors, the directors' proposal and statement of the company's affairs will become available to creditors,[153] and when liquidators act they will provide creditors' meetings with a body of information. Data concerning directorial behaviour may also flow from the creation of contractual rights to information.[154] The terms of debentures may provide for the supply of information and financial data and detailed figures, for example, may be requested on a periodic basis by financial creditors.

As with shareholders, informal sources of information may assist creditors, and major financial creditors will often use their influence to obtain a steady flow of information from senior managers. Major creditors may also obtain representation on the company's board and subsequently will gain access to new sources of information. Trade creditors will be less likely to use such sources but if a continuing trading relationship has been formed, they may acquire information informally.

Can more be done to inform creditors? One potential response to the 'phoenix syndrome' has been put forward by the Federation of Small Businesses (FSB), which has argued that the BERR should designate certain individuals as 'provisional directors' where they have been at the helm of several failed companies. Such directors would then be required to disclose their track records so that trade creditors, for instance, would

---

[152] See Insolvency Act 1986 Sch. B1, para. 47.

[153] Insolvency Act 1986 s. 2(2) and (3); Insolvency Act 2000 Sch. A1, para. 30; Insolvency Rules 1986 rr. 1.3(1) and (2), 1.5(1) and (2), 1.12(3); Insolvency Act 1986 s. 3(2) and (3).

[154] See J. Day and P. Taylor, 'The Role of Debt Contracts in UK Corporate Governance' (1998) 2 *Journal of Management and Governance* 171; C. Smith and J. Warner, 'On Financial Contracting: An Analysis of Bond Covenants' (1979) 7 *Journal of Financial Economics* 117.

be aware of these. Monthly financial returns for the companies of such directors might also be demanded so that creditor monitoring of financial health could be facilitated. The FSB argument here is that such steps offer smaller creditors lower-cost information sources and help them to assess risks. There seems an arguable case for such requirements also on grounds of fairness to unsecured creditors.

Even when creditors possess information, however, they may have problems in using it to good effect. The value of information deriving from insolvency-related regimes may be questioned. Creditors may well gain much information only at a very late stage in corporate troubles and this tardiness will often rule out actions designed to forestall directorial failures or negligence. Creditor expertise, indeed, may vary considerably. Financial creditors might be expected to be expert in assessing risks and managerial performance, but trade creditors may possess expertise in a particular business sector only and may be less able to evaluate directorial performance beyond those areas.

Will creditors be committed to enforcing directorial duties? They may be where they foresee any threat to their prospects of repayment but, in general, creditors are not disposed to review the actions of managers. Factors that might, nevertheless, affect the propensity to enforce might be the size of the investment, the nature of any security, the type of business and the levels of directorial discretion that are usual in the sector. For small trade creditors, such factors may well not come into play unless the debtor is a major purchaser of the creditor's product. Such creditors will tend to look for supply elsewhere rather than to continue a relationship in the hope of recovering from directors on the basis of a breach of duty.

What incentive, indeed, is there for creditors to seek to recover from directors? Secured creditors will focus on realising their security and only if such realisation fails to meet the sum outstanding will such creditors have anything to gain from the contributions of directors. In the case of creditors secured with floating charges, incentives may similarly operate only to cover shortfalls (directorial contributions will form part of the company's assets). Ordinary unsecured trade creditors will possess questionable incentives to pursue errant directors since they will be paid after floating charge holders.[155]

---

[155] Though some incentive may be provided by the 'prescribed part' of funds made available to unsecured creditors which would otherwise have been paid to holders of floating charges: see Insolvency Act 1986 s. 176A. If creditors consent the liquidator could use these moneys as a fighting fund to bring actions: see further ch. 13 above.

After a liquidation has been initiated by qualifying creditors, actions may be brought by creditors against directors under a number of heads: for example, misfeasance actions for breaches of fiduciary or other duties in relation to the company. Such duties, however, are, as noted already, owed to the company and contributions obtained from directors, as a result, will go to the company assets for the benefit of all creditors. Individual creditors may be discouraged from bringing such actions, moreover, because the liquidator may proceed similarly on behalf of all creditors and will have investigative powers that individual creditors do not possess.[156] As for liquidators' actions, we have seen in chapter 13 that creditors may have to indemnify costs where it is anticipated that there may be insufficient assets to support litigation. Section 176ZA of the Insolvency Act 1986 and the amended Insolvency Rules have now, however, provided that litigation expenses are expenses of the winding up[157] – a negation of the Court of Appeal's decision in *Re Floor Fourteen*.[158]

The common law duty offers little to the unsecured creditor since it is owed to the general body of creditors rather than unsecured creditors individually or as a class. A duty owed directly to individual creditors seems, as already noted, to have been denied by *Yukong*[159] and would conflict with insolvency's collectivist principles, might lead to a multiplicity of suits, and could lead individual creditors to place improper pressure on directors to settle their particular claims.[160] As has been argued elsewhere, the alternative may be to place directors under a duty to unsecured creditors as a class.[161] Such a class action could

---

[156] Insolvency Act 1986 ss. 131–4, 235.

[157] See ch. 13 above; Companies Act 2006 s. 1282(1) and the Insolvency (Amendment) Rules 2008 (SI 2008/737) amending the Insolvency Rules 1986 by replacing r. 4.218(1) (a) with new r. 4.218(1), (2) and (3)(a) and by inserting new rr. 4.218A–4.218E. (Expenses of liquidation can also be payable out of proceeds of litigation brought by the liquidator; and expenses and costs relating to the conduct and preparation of any such legal proceedings can be recovered.)

[158] [2001] 3 All ER 499, [2001] 2 BCLC 392 (adhering to the approach in *M. C. Bacon (No. 2)* [1991] Ch 127). See ch. 13 above.

[159] *Yukong Lines Ltd of Korea* v. *Rendsburg Investments Corporation* [1998] BCC 870, [1998] 1 WLR 294; see p. 684 above.

[160] See further Finch, 'Directors' Duties: Insolvency and the Unsecured Creditor' and 'Creditors' Interests and Directors' Obligations'; D. Prentice, 'Directors, Creditors and Shareholders' in E. McKendrick (ed.), *Commercial Aspects of Trusts and Fiduciary Obligations* (Clarendon Press, Oxford, 1992) pp. 74–5.

[161] See Finch, 'Directors' Duties: Insolvency and the Unsecured Creditor'. See generally R. Mulheron, *The Class Action in Common Law Systems* (Hart, Oxford, 2005).

exceptionally allow unsecured creditors collectively to seek injunctions where necessary to prevent directors from acting in a manner jeopardising the company's solvency or to ensure the consideration of unsecured creditors' interests in circumstances of marginal solvency.[162]

The position of creditors generally might be strengthened by another reform: one to allow creditors to take action in the company's name in enforcement of directorial duties. The Companies Act 2006 sections 260–4 provided a statutory derivative action for members but not for creditors.[163] Are there, nevertheless, good reasons for a creditors' counterpart?[164] One reason advanced for the inclusion of creditors has been that, in some circumstances, creditors might be in receipt of better relevant information than is available to 'other outsiders'.[165] The opportunity of using creditors as monitors of corporate management seems, however, a less convincing argument than the need to protect creditor interests. If, as was indicated in *Whalley*[166] and *Gwyer*,[167] creditor interests become company interests not merely post-insolvency but also when insolvency threatens, then it may be appropriate to allow creditors to act before the liquidator comes onto the scene (so as to protect their interests) by injuncting any directorial actions that are likely to prejudice solvency severely.[168]

Enforcement of the statutory controls over such matters as fraudulent or wrongful trading, transactions at undervalue and preferences depends on action, not by a creditor, but by an office holder of the company. As was made clear in chapter 13, however, liquidators have traditionally faced severe funding problems in resorting to law in order to enforce

---

[162] For their part, directors might have few grounds to fear that unsecured creditors would interfere in the workings of the company. Such creditors would have to demonstrate to a court reasonable cause to anticipate that insolvency would result from the action in question and this would be an onerous burden to discharge.

[163] See Pendell, 'Derivative Claims'; Keay, 'Can Derivative Proceedings be Commenced when a Company is in Liquidation?'.

[164] See Australian Companies and Securities Law Review Committee, *Enforcement of the Duties of Directors and Officers of a Company by Means of a Statutory Derivative Action* (Report No. 12, 1990) ('CSLRC').

[165] CSLRC, p. 50. [166] *Whalley v. Doney* [2004] BPIR 75.

[167] *Colin Gwyer & Associates Ltd v. London Wharf (Limehouse) Ltd* [2003] BCC 885.

[168] Section 1234 of the Australian Corporations Law of 1991 enabled the courts to grant injunctive relief to 'any person' affected by contraventions of the Corporations Law. The Australian Corporations Law 2001 (Part 2F.1A) provided for a derivative action on the part of current and former members and officers of a company but not creditors: see I. Ramsay and B. Saunders, 'Litigation by Shareholders and Directors: An Empirical Study of the Statutory Derivative Action' [2006] 2 JCLS 397.

directors' duties. Although such practical difficulties have to some extent been ameliorated by legislative reform,[169] problems of funding allocation[170] and legal uncertainty still remain, particularly in the case of wrongful trading, and to date we have seen an accountability regime of seemingly low impact.[171]

Public interest liquidation

As indicated above, one further way to hold directors to account – and to protect the public from errant directors – is to prevent ongoing trading through compulsory liquidation of the company on public interest grounds. This procedure is, in the main, carried out by the Companies Investigation Branch (CIB) of the Insolvency Service.[172] As noted in chapter 13, a key value of public interest liquidation (PIL) is that it allows the public authorities to seek a winding up in order to protect consumers and the public from the activities of errant directors – and to do so where no individual member of the public has an economic interest that would

---

[169] See the Insolvency (Amendment) Rules 2008 (SI 2008/737); ch. 13 above.

[170] The IP has an unusual role and one that may well involve conflict. As Katz and Mumford (*Making Creditor Protection Effective*, part 5) note: 'On the one hand he is charged with protecting creditors' interests, but on the other hand his own commercial interests and the right to charge fees may be detrimental to creditors' interests. There is a subtle balance to be struck ... Putting to one side concerns as to whether office holders always put creditors' interests ahead of their own, the law has not always been accommodating to office holders who may very properly wish to incur costs to bring recovery actions that have a good prospect of increasing the funds available to creditors. We suggest that the Insolvency Service explore the system of aid made available by the New Zealand Insolvency Service, which provides funding for cases which it believes are winnable (recovering the funds out of the proceeds of the action).' See also ch. 13 above.

[171] Lack of visible enforcement of the wrongful trading provisions may give an excessively negative view of their impact, however, since insolvency practitioners may use the threat of proceedings to concentrate directors' minds, extract sums from directors in order to settle claims and force quick settlements: see Walters, 'Enforcing Wrongful Trading', p. 159; C. Williams and A. McGee, *A Company Director's Liability for Wrongful Trading*, ACCA Research Report 30 (London, 1992) p. 16.

[172] The FSA also has the power to apply for a 'just and equitable' winding up. The FSA has only infrequently proceeded with an application for a just and equitable winding up. When deciding whether to petition for such a winding up, the FSA will consider, amongst other things, whether the needs of consumers and the public interest require the body to cease to operate and whether consumer needs and the public interest can be met by using the FSA's other powers: see FSA, *Enforcement Handbook*, online. Some types of breach that are of relevance to the FSA may be covered by other authorities such as professional bodies or overseers or other regulators such as the Director General of Fair Trading or the Serious Fraud Office (SFO).

justify this.[173] It does not require that any illegal activity is involved[174] and, accordingly, it does not demand that the criminal burden of proof is satisfied through the amassing of a highly elaborate body of evidence. Nor, indeed, does it have to be established that the errant company is insolvent.

As a device for controlling an individual director, however, PIL may constitute a blunt instrument because it does not target mischiefs or mischief-makers precisely. The misbehaviour at issue may be just one activity being carried out by a healthy company that conducts a range of otherwise reputable trading practices and PIL may destroy 'any good that may co-exist within the company alongside the bad'.[175] In some cases, indeed, the reluctance of the court to grant petitions for PILs may be due to such perceived bluntness – and Hoffmann J's comments about 'grossly disproportionate responses' in *Re Secure and Provide plc*[176] may reflect this perception. PIL may, indeed, be deployed bluntly because it has to play a role that other controls might well fulfil. In some circumstances the disqualification of a director may be called for but, as will be discussed below, disqualification may have developed into a tool that is ill-attuned to the protection of the public. As one senior official of the CIB put it:

> PIL is the only vehicle we have got to stop a company from conducting business we think is wrong. Disqualification was meant to be quick. We saw the 1986 Insolvency Act as meaning the Secretary of State takes a view of the person who should be disqualified. The court's role is only to determine how long to make the order. There was no concept that you would go and get these massive trials. The idea was you went in and the bloke was disqualified, so you would do it in days ... The courts just messed it up.[177]

---

[173] Under the Insolvency Act 1986 s. 123(1)(a) a creditor's interest has to exceed £750 before a petition to wind up can be made (SI 1984/1199, para. 2).

[174] *Re SHV Senator Hanseatische mbH* [1997] BCC 112, 119; cf. *Secretary of State for Trade and Industry* v. *Travel Time (UK) Ltd* [2000] BCC 792. In cases where illegal activities *are* involved, the criminal law can be used and offences under, say, the Theft Act 1968 such as obtaining property by deception can be prosecuted. The FSA also possesses a variety of options, including some powers that it can exercise without having to seek court approval. The FSA can vary permissions to engage in regulated activities; cancel such permission; withdraw approvals; seek injunctions; issue prohibition orders; apply for restitution orders; apply disciplinary measures; petition for administration orders against companies and partnerships and bankruptcy orders against individuals; and prosecute for criminal offences (FSMA 2000 s. 56).

[175] DTI, *Company Investigations: Powers for the 21st Century* (2001).

[176] [1992] BCC 405, 414.   [177] Interview, CIB, 10 April 2002.

It might be argued, however, that the undertakings regime inserted into the Company Directors' Disqualification Act 1986 (CDDA) by the Insolvency Act 2000[178] may have allowed the disqualification system to be redeployed along more responsive lines. The effect of the undertaking system, as will be noted below, is to rule out the need for the Secretary of State to seek a disqualification order from the court. It is seen by senior CIB staff as a device that is potentially useful in some circumstances and has been used in a small number of cases to date. It should be borne in mind, however, that in relation to section 8(2)(A) undertakings, just as in relation to disqualification orders under section 8(1), the Secretary of State will have to form an opinion that it is expedient in the public interest that a disqualification should be made before applying to court for such an order. The feeling of CIB officials seems to be that in relatively clear cases, the undertaking system may offer public protection, but in complex scenarios or where directors are making large profits from gullible parties, unscrupulous individuals are liable to delay giving undertakings for three or so years while they continue to plunder the market.[179]

A system of more precise targeting would be possible. Within the financial services regime, the FSA (and to a lesser extent BERR) can target specific practices, individuals or firms and the (then) DTI suggested in its 2001 Discussion Paper on Company Investigations that it also should possess a power to seek a targeted restraint order from the courts.[180] The proposal was that the Secretary of State should be able to seek an order restraining the company from engaging in a specified business activity or carrying on all or part of its business in a specified way.[181] On controlling particular directors, the DTI argued that, for a restraining order to be effective, it would need to bind directors and the Department put forward for discussion the idea that the Secretary of State should be able to seek an order removing a person from office as the director of a particular company as part of a restraining order.[182] Such a power, it was mooted, would be less severe than disqualification and might be appropriate where the conduct did not merit such a serious course of action as general disqualification.[183]

---

[178] Insolvency Act 2000 s. 6: see pp. 718–19, 732–3, 751–3 below.

[179] Interview, CIB, 10 April 2002.   [180] DTI, *Company Investigations*, paras. 120–35.

[181] Ibid., para. 120. The DTI conceded that it would be unwilling to use such a power to enter into a 'regulatory' relationship with a firm (para. 129).

[182] Directors and company officers responsible for breaches of restraining orders would also be personally liable for relevant debts of a company: ibid., para. 129.

[183] Ibid., para. 126.

A restraining order in the above terms would not, however, be efficacious where the errant company director engaged in 'phoenix' manoeuvres[184] and moved on from the restrained company only to replicate the undesirable practice by operating through a new corporate vehicle. In order to deal with this problem, the DTI consulted on whether restraining orders should be able to 'follow' the director in such circumstances.[185] Such an order would be used to restrict the activities of a director who had been required to give up office under a restraining order. It would deal with objectionable conduct by the director whether acting as a director in a new company or as a sole proprietor.

The Department, moreover, also invited suggestions on whether an *interim* restraining order should be available where it becomes clear, early on in an investigation, that a practice should be restrained but the investigation still has time to run until completion. This is a power that is less draconian than applying for the immediate appointment of a provisional liquidator and thus brings advantages. Appointing a provisional liquidator might be useful in bringing the powers of the directors to an end and reducing the risk that corporate assets will be dissipated, but it effectively terminates the company's usual trading and is such a serious step that the court is likely to demand substantial evidence of misconduct.[186] This, in turn, will require that a good deal of time is spent amassing such evidence and preparing a case. In contrast, an interim restraining order allows the company or director to carry on trading subject to abandoning the harmful practice. The court is being asked to take a relatively modest and specific step and the burden of establishing the case for such an order will be far less onerous (and far less time-consuming) for the CIB. The order possesses similar advantages over a petition for a director's disqualification order. As for the circumstances in which such an order might be sought, the DTI gave the following example: 'A multinational conglomerate is operating a lottery as a promotional exercise without complying with the necessary legislation. In such an instance the Department would not wish to wind up the entire company but merely prevent it from continuing an illegal practice. A restraining order would be more appropriate.'[187]

---

[184] See pp. 703–4 above.   [185] DTI, *Company Investigations*, para. 127.

[186] See C. Campbell, 'Protection by Elimination: Winding Up of Companies on Public Interest Grounds' (2001) 17 IL&P 129 at 131.

[187] DTI, *Company Investigations*, para. 15(a).

Can it be said that the PIL process effectively protects the public from the actions of unscrupulous directors? Statistically it is difficult to contend that PIL leads the way among devices designed to protect the public from directorial misdemeanours – only a modest number of companies each year are wound up following PIL petition.[188] It could be argued, however, that until the phoenix problem is adequately dealt with, errant directors are only effectively restrained by the PIL mechanism. It might, nevertheless, be responded that the PIL procedure is insufficiently preventative and only allows corporate operations to be ended when large numbers of creditors have been harmed. As the law presently stands, the CIB has to amass a good deal of information before petitioning the court. The burden of proof in a PIL case may only have to be discharged to the civil, not the criminal, standard but establishing a case, even on a balance of probabilities, may demand that a lengthy and detailed investigation of corporate activities is carried to a conclusion. Here again, the issue of co-ordination across the PIL process is raised. If a petition is to be triggered by a CIB investigation of a company's affairs, that investigation may aim to discover a host of issues that go beyond the terms of a PIL petition. These matters will usually be concluded and a report made before action on a PIL is taken. During this research and investigation period, large numbers of the public may be forwarding funds to the company at issue. As noted already, the DTI raised the possibility of its being able to apply for an interim order to restrain a company engaging in a specific activity.[189] Without such a power it was conceded by the DTI that an excessive time may pass during the completion of investigations and the obtaining of the appointment of a provisional liquidator on a winding-up order against the company.[190]

A particular difficulty with PIL is that the CIB, the courts and the Insolvency Service may diverge in their approaches to this as a control device. These divergencies not merely make for philosophical confusion but have the potential to impair the efficiency of the PIL process – as where, for example, the courts place weight on a need to establish corporate culpability before an order is granted but the CIB operates on a different basis – that of public protection rather than blame attribution. To some extent the CIB's difficulties may, on occasion, flow from its

---

[188] In 2006–7 the combined number of winding-up orders and disqualification orders obtained by CIB was 116: see Insolvency Service, *Annual Report and Accounts 2006–7*, HC 752 (Stationery Office, London, 2007).
[189] DTI, *Company Investigations*, para. 131.   [190] Ibid.

using PIL where a more narrowly targeted procedure would distinguish more clearly between unacceptable and acceptable directorial or corporate behaviour and would allow the former to be eradicated without threatening the latter.

PIL does not, in its present form, operate as a highly effective measure for protecting the public from errant directors – it is too confused in conception and too cumbersome in operation. This is not a complaint that can be placed readily at the door of the judges. The courts have resisted the CIB's petitions on occasion but have tended to do so for reasons that are supportable – because using a winding up to control a specific problem is too ill-focused and extreme a course of action.

As for the deterrent value of PIL and its influence in controlling directors' business practices and standards of behaviour, it has been pointed out that the PIL procedure has a very low public profile and most companies and their controllers will be unaware of the Secretary of State's powers until they are brought into effect.[191] Here there is considerable scope for promotional work either through BERR public information or through requirements that company direction should involve a level of basic training in the fundamentals of corporate law and governance.[192]

Recent developments and proposals do, however, offer a way forward for PIL. The proposed restraining order and interim restraining order system would allow the CIB to provide a more rapid response to unacceptable trading than is possible with PIL. It would also allow unacceptable directorial or corporate behaviour to be dealt with in a more closely targeted manner than PIL allows. When applied to directors, the restraining order would allow the 'phoenix' operation to be constrained and, with the interim restraining order, it would prove a more readily deployable response to mischief than is provided by the directors' disqualification procedure which, even with the undertaking process introduced by the Insolvency Act 2000, can prove excessively broad and draconian. As for the need for the CIB to apply to the court for a restraining order (as proposed by the (then) DTI) it could be contended that controls analogous to the FSA's 'own initiative' powers should be

---

[191] A. Keay, 'Public Interest Petitions' (1999) 20 Co. Law. 296 at 301. On directors' low awareness of sanctions generally see R. Williams, 'Disqualifying Directors: A Remedy Worse than the Disease?' [2007] 7 JCLS 213.

[192] For a discussion of which, see, *inter alia*, Law Commission and Scottish Law Commission, *Company Directors* (1999); CLRSG, *Final Report*, 2001, paras. 3.9, 6.18; Finch, 'Company Directors'; and pp. 738–9 below.

aimed for – that the CIB ought to have the power to prohibit a certain commercial practice without having to go to court for approval.[193] To this argument it might be objected that it is one thing to give the FSA such a power in relation to a specific sector but a far more serious step to allow the CIB to do this in any sector. Such an objection, however, misses the point that such a power will relate to a specific practice (even, potentially, a specific individual) and so would be limited in scope. The CIB would, moreover, be accountable through the Secretary of State to Parliament for its actions.

Further thought might also be given, first, to ways in which CIB operations can be more closely co-ordinated (informationally and in policy terms) with those of other enforcement agencies and, second, to the triggers for PIL petitions. If the protection of consumers is a major (albeit not exclusive) concern of the CIB then further consideration could be given to the possibility of allowing the National Consumer Council or other consumer representative bodies to play a greater role in triggering PIL petitions, perhaps by developing closer links with the CIB.

To summarise, the PIL process does have potential as a means of controlling directors but it can be seen as coming to a crossroads in its development. It has evolved over the years into a procedural jack-of-all-trades, one that is sometimes awkwardly deployed but which is useful in so far as it can be instituted where objectionable behaviour is difficult to counter with other strategies. What it is not yet is an optimally effective legal device that is co-ordinated into a network of linked controls. The above discussion suggests that PIL is a device that should be retained but that the mooted steps that are designed to give it a secure role within the framework of insolvency law could be pursued with some urgency.

Expertise

Does insolvency law encourage directorial behaviour that is expert, honest and free from incompetence? Here the focus will rest on the rules on disqualification before note is made of alternative means of influencing directorial expertise. In so doing it is necessary to consider both the rationales that the judges espouse in disqualifying directors and

---

[193] See also the above discussion concerning a potential power for the Secretary of State to accept undertakings in lieu of petitioning for a restraining order.

whether the rules are enforced in a manner that actually encourages expert, honest and competent company direction.

The director of an insolvent company may be found unfit to run a limited liability company and be disqualified by the courts under section 6 of the Company Directors' Disqualification Act 1986 (CDDA).[194] The Secretary of State[195] or Official Receiver[196] may apply to the court for such a disqualification and, on a finding of unfitness, the court must disqualify the director from being concerned in the management of a company for a minimum of two years.[197] It is the use of mandatory disqualification that sets section 6 apart from the other provisions of the CDDA which involve judicial discretion to disqualify and may be used, for example, where there is misconduct in relation to the company (involving, perhaps, conviction of an indictable offence in relation to the company,[198] persistently breaching companies legislation on documents and returns,[199] or participation in frauds or fraudulent trading[200]); where there is a finding of unfitness following the Secretary of State's application on an inspector's report or departmental investigation;[201] or where there is a wrongful trading,[202] company direction by an

---

[194] See CDDA 1986 s. 6(2) for a definition of 'insolvent'. For the background to s. 6 and to the importance of disqualification in insolvency law's investigative role, see Cork Report, paras. 235–40, 1813–18; see also I. F. Fletcher, 'Genesis of Modern Insolvency Law: An Odyssey of Law Reform' [1989] JBL 365. On disqualification generally see A. Walters and M. Davis-White, *Directors' Disqualification and Bankruptcy Restrictions* (Thomson/Sweet & Maxwell, London, 2005).

[195] Per CDDA 1986 s. 7(3) it is the duty of liquidators, official receivers, administrators or administrative receivers to report cases of suspected 'unfitness' to the Secretary of State.

[196] At the Secretary of State's discretion, CDDA 1986 s. 7(1). In *Official Receiver* v. *Wadge Rapps & Hunt* [2003] UKHL 49 the House of Lords stated that the Official Receiver could legitimately use the investigative powers conferred by s. 236 of the Insolvency Act 1986 to gather information to pass to the Secretary of State for the purpose of disqualification proceedings – and this could be viewed as incidental to the functions of winding up, even where there were no assets worth recovering.

[197] CDDA 1986 s. 6(4). Mandatory disqualification for a minimum period reflected the Cork Committee's concern for the tightening up of the previous discretionary jurisdiction of Companies Act 1985 s. 300.

[198] CDDA 1986 s. 2. [199] Ibid., ss. 3 and 5.

[200] Ibid., s. 4; Companies Act 2006 s. 993; Insolvency Act 1986 s. 10. [201] CDDA 1986 s. 8.

[202] Ibid., s. 10. On allowing the company to trade when insolvent even where this does not amount to wrongful trading see C. Bradley, 'Enterprise and Entrepreneurship' (2001) 1 *Journal of Corporate Law Studies* 53 at 66; *Secretary of State for Trade and Industry* v. *Imo Synthetic Technology Ltd* [1993] BCC 549; *Re Bath Glass* [1988] 4 BCC 130.

undischarged bankrupt[203] or failure to pay under a County Court administration order.[204]

A change that was designed to allow the disqualification system to be redeployed along more responsive lines is the undertakings regime that was introduced into the CDDA by the Insolvency Act 2000. Sections 1 (A), 7(2)(A) and 8(2)(A) of CDDA 1986 now allow the Secretary of State to accept a disqualification undertaking where it appears to the Secretary of State that there is satisfaction of the conditions for disqualifying a person as an unfit director of an insolvent company (CDDA sections 6 and 7) or where it similarly appears that a director is a person unfit to be concerned in the management of a company (section 8).[205] It must appear to the Secretary of State that it is in the public interest to accept such an undertaking. The undertaking may be for up to fifteen years and will state *inter alia* that the person will not be a director of a company or in any way directly or indirectly concerned in the promotion, formation or management of a company without leave of the court. The effect of the undertaking system is to rule out the need for the Secretary of State to seek a disqualification order from the court. The aim of the new procedure is to reduce enforcement costs; make regulation more responsive (by reducing the period during which proceedings are pending and directors are still empowered to act); save court resources; and reduce the uncertainties involved in lengthy disqualification processes.[206] It should be borne in

---

[203] CDDA 1986 s. 11.

[204] Ibid., s. 12. The CDDA is thus aimed at catching a plethora of directorial wrongdoing: for example, paying some creditors but not others (see *Re Carecraft Construction Co. Ltd* [1993] 4 All ER 499, 511; *Re New Generation Engineers* [1993] BCLC 435; *Official Receiver* v. *Barnes* (*Re Structural Concrete Ltd*) [2001] BCC 478 (regarding non-payment of Crown debts)) and paying the director's own debts (see *Secretary of State* v. *Imo Synthetic Technology Ltd* [1993] BCC 549).

[205] S. 8(1) of the CDDA 1986 is amended by the Financial Services and Markets Act 2000 (Consequential Amendments and Repeals) Order 2001, s. 39 to read: 'S. 8(1) If it appears to the Secretary of State from investigative material that it is expedient in the public interest that a disqualification order be made against a person who is, or has been, a director or shadow director of a company, he may apply to the court for such an order; s. 8(1A) "Investigative material" means (a) a report made by inspectors under s. 437 of the Companies Act 1985, ss. 167, 168, 169 or 284 of FSMA 2000, regulations made as a result of s. 262(2)(k) of FSMA and (b) information or documents obtained under ss. 447 or 448 of the Companies Act 1985, s. 2 of the Criminal Justice Act 1987, s. 83 of the Companies Act 1989 or ss. 165, 171, 172, 173 or 175 of FSMA 2000.'

[206] Commenting on the new powers, Kim Howells, Consumer Affairs Minister, said: 'Ensuring that the business community and consumers are protected from the activities of rogue directors at the earliest opportunity is vital. The new power to

mind, however, that in relation to section 8(2)(A) undertakings, just as in relation to disqualification orders under section 8(1), the Secretary of State will have to form an opinion that disqualification is expedient in the public interest. His decision will have to be based on 'investigative material' – which is defined in section 8(1)(A) (as amended)[207] as (a) reports made by inspectors under s. 437 of the Companies Act 1985, sections 167, 168, 169 or 284 of the Financial Services and Markets Act 2000 (FSMA), or regulations made as a result of section 262(2)(k) of FSMA and (b) information or documents obtained under sections 447 or 448 of the Companies Act 1985, section 2 of the Criminal Justice Act 1987, section 83 of the Companies Act 1989 or sections 165, 171, 172, 173 or 175 of FSMA.[208]

Other reforms of the disqualification system followed a NAO Report of 1993 which criticised the Insolvency Service's enforcement endeavours.[209] There followed a considerable increase in the volume of disqualification proceedings.[210] In 1998 the IS set up a twenty-four-hour disqualification hotline[211] to enable members of the public to report possible contraventions of prohibitions on direction and, in 2000, the Government announced the setting up of a specialist team to investigate

disqualify administratively will save time in the courts.' See Comment, '"Fast Track" Disqualification is Under Way' (2001) 22 Co. Law. 213 at 214. On the tension between the public interest in 'quickie' disqualifications and the public interest in the promotion of good corporate governance see A. Walters, 'Bare Undertakings in Directors' Disqualification Proceedings: The Insolvency Act 2000, Blackspur and Beyond' (2001) 22 Co. Law. 290; see also pp. 732–3, 751–3 below.

[207] See the Financial Services and Markets Act 2000 (Consequential Amendments and Repeals) Order 2001.

[208] Part XIV of the Companies Act 1985 (as amended by the Companies Act 1989) remains in force subject to certain new provisions in the Companies Act 2006 inserted into Part XIV by Part 32 of the CA 2006. Thus no attempt has been made to consolidate the legislation on company investigations by the Secretary of State.

[209] NAO, Company Director Disqualification (October 1993, HC 907). The Enterprise Act 2002 s. 204 introduced a new statutory regime (into the CDDA 1986, ss. 9A–9E) which allows the Office of Fair Trading and other specified regulators to apply to court to disqualify a director of a company where that company has committed a relevant breach of competition law. Discussion of this goes beyond the scope of this chapter: for details see Walters and Davis-White, Directors' Disqualification and Bankruptcy Restrictions, ch. 6.

[210] See A. Walters, 'Directors' Disqualification after the Insolvency Act 2000: The New Regime' [2001] Ins. Law. 86. In 2006–7, 1,200 disqualification orders/undertakings were secured against directors (80 per cent by undertaking) as compared to 1,173 in 2005–6: Insolvency Service, Annual Report and Accounts 2006–7 (HC 752, London, 2007) p. 15.

[211] See p. 679 above; in 2006–7 the hotline received 328 calls which resulted in 26 reports to the prosecuting authority (compared to 135 in 2005–6): Insolvency Service, Annual Report and Accounts 2006–7.

directors who asset-strip companies. The Forensic Insolvency Recovery Service (FIRS) was given the power to take legal action to recover money from fraudulent and negligent directors of failed companies.[212]

The Court of Appeal has also played a role in extending the scope of disqualification. Section 22 of the CDDA extends liability for disqualification on the grounds of unfitness to shadow directors, defined by section 22(5) of the CDDA as persons 'in accordance with whose directions or instructions the directors of a company are accustomed to act (but that person is not deemed a shadow director by reason only that the directors act on directions given by him in a professional capacity)'.[213] In *Secretary of State for Trade and Industry* v. *Deverell*[214] the concept of the shadow director in CDDA section 22 was at issue and the court widened the category of persons who may be regarded as such directors and so may be covered *inter alia* by the rules on directors' liability and disqualification. Morritt LJ was concerned 'to identify those with real influence in the corporate affairs of the company'. He stated that the intention of Parliament was to protect the public and that 'all that is required is that what is said by the shadow to the board is not by way of professional advice but is usually followed over a wide enough area and for long enough'. Subservience by the board was not required, a capacity for some degree of independent judgement did not rule out shadow direction, and the influence of the shadow director need not extend to the whole field of the company's activities.[215] The shadow director, moreover, did not

---

[212] See p. 680 above; Milman, 'Controlling Managerial Abuse: Current State of Play'. See also Willcock, 'Credit Panic Stokes Forensic Boom'; O'Connell, Outen and Stephens, 'Forensic Recovery'.

[213] See G. Morse, 'Shadow Directors and *De Facto* Directors in the Context of Proceedings for Disqualification on the Grounds of Unfitness and Wrongful Trading' in Rider, *Corporate Dimension*; S. Griffin, 'The Characteristics and Identification of a *De Facto* Director' [2000] 1 CFILR 126; G. Bhattacharyya, 'Shadow Directors and Wrongful Trading Revisited' (1995) 15 Co. Law. 313. A person whose directions or instructions are customarily acted upon by a governing majority of the board can be a shadow director but that majority must act as a consequence of the directions/instructions and the shadow status does not follow where actions are retrospectively linked to directions: see *Ultraframe UK Ltd* v. *Fielding* [2005] EWHC 1638.

[214] [2000] 2 WLR 907.

[215] See also *Secretary of State for Trade and Industry* v. *Becker* [2002] All ER 280, [2003] 1 BCLC 555, which applied *Deverell* but suggested that 'accustomed' meant that directions had to be given during periods encompassing the general course of the company's history as opposed to a particular episode or incident. See further S. Griffin, 'Evidence Justifying a Person's Capacity as Either a *De Facto* or Shadow Director: *Secretary of State for Trade and Industry* v. *Becker*' [2003] Ins. Law. 127.

need to wield influence as part of the internal management structure of the company. Whether a communication amounted to 'directions or instructions', moreover, was to be objectively assessed.[216] After *Deverell*, it has been argued that the characteristics of a shadow director appear to be identifiable with those of a *de facto* director[217] but some commentators have emphasised that 'the concept of shadow directorship has different defining characteristics and serves fundamentally different purposes to the concepts of *de jure* or *de facto* directorship'.[218]

In *Re Kaytech*[219] the court took, as in *Deverell*, a practical approach to determining whether a person is a *de facto* director and amenable to the directors' liability and disqualification rules: all relevant internal and external factors were to be taken into account and the issue was to be determined as a question of fact and not by applying one single test.[220]

In applying the disqualification provisions, different judicial philosophies or rationales can be discerned.[221] What might be called a 'rights' approach sees directing a company incorporated with limited liability as a valuable asset or right worthy of protection in the exercise of commercial ventures. This model reflects the 'business enterprise' perspective on company law, which sees the director as a taker of business risks, subject to a company law that respects and enables his or her freedom to manage rather than rendering managerial decisions liable to judicial second-guessing.[222] An alternative standpoint sees incorporation with limited

---

[216] See J. Payne, 'Casting Light into the Shadows: *Secretary of State for Trade and Industry* v. *Deverell*' (2001) 22 Co. Law. 90; D. Milman, 'A Fresh Light on Shadow Directors' [2000] Ins. Law. 171. For an earlier restrictive view see *Re PFTZM Ltd* [1995] BCC 280.

[217] See Griffin, 'Evidence Justifying a Person's Capacity'. In *Secretary of State for Trade and Industry* v. *Hollier and Others* [2007] BCC 11, however, Etherton J said that a *de facto* director had to participate in directing the affairs of the company – he did not have to have day-to-day control and might only act in relation to part of its activities but he had to be part of the company's governing structure: on which see also *Secretary of State for Trade and Industry* v. *Tjolle* [1998] BCC 282 at 290. On *de facto* directors see *Re Kaytech* [1999] 2 BCLC 351; *Secretary of State for Trade and Industry* v. *Jones* [1999] BCC 366; *Re Red Label Fashions Ltd* [1999] BCC 308; *Secretary of State for Trade and Industry* v. *Hollier* [2007] BCC 11; *Statek Corp.* v. *Alford* [2008] BCC 266; J. de Lacy, 'The Concept of a Company Director' [2006] JBL 267.

[218] See C. Noonan and S. Watson, 'The Nature of Shadow Directorship' [2006] JBL 763.

[219] [1999] 2 BCLC 351; compare with *Re Hydrodan (Corby) Ltd* [1994] BCC 161: see N. Campbell, '*Re Hydrodan (Corby) Ltd*' [1994] JBL 609.

[220] See Payne, 'Casting Light'.

[221] This discussion builds on V. Finch, 'Disqualifying Directors: Issues of Rights, Privileges and Employment' (1993) Ins. LJ 35. See also Finch, 'Plea for Competence'.

[222] See, for example, L. S. Sealy, *Company Law and Commercial Reality* (Sweet & Maxwell, London, 1984) p. 46.

liability as a privilege, a facility to be used in the public interest. This view could be said to reflect the social responsibility perspective on company law which looks not merely at the interests of investors, managers, directors and creditors but to the 'legitimate needs, too, of the public interest, of the consumer, of the employee'.[223]

The respective logics of the rights and privileges approaches may be represented as two packages, each comprising a distinct set of tenets. The rights approach implies, in its pure form, the following: that interference with the right to direct a limited liability company is only merited where culpability is present; that culpability is relevant in assessing the period of disqualification on, *inter alia*, retributive principles; that the process of disqualification is accordingly best seen as a penal one; that withdrawal of the right to direct not only deprives the person concerned of an asset but involves stigma; that the onus is on the 'prosecution' to justify disqualification; and that unfitness should be proved beyond reasonable doubt in satisfaction of the criminal burden of proof. Furthermore, the *mens rea* required should be intention, recklessness or, at least, gross negligence.

In contrast, the privilege approach sees procedures as not being penal and, accordingly, unfitness may be proved on a balance of probabilities according to the usual civil standard. The privilege approach is consistent with the notion that disqualification is most appropriately justified by the need to protect the public rather than to punish the director.[224] Since disqualification is seen as non-penal, withdrawal of the privilege of direction is not viewed as stigmatic and the period of withdrawal is seen as assessable on protective principles. Nor are employment prospects held to be dashed on a disqualification since business may be carried out by other methods (for example, in partnership or as a sole trader) rather than by the exercise of the privilege of incorporating a limited liability company. Culpability is, therefore, not required in order

---

[223] K.W. Wedderburn, *Company Law Reform* (Fabian Society, London, 1965) p. 10; Wedderburn, 'The Social Responsibility of Companies' (1985) 15 Mel. ULR 4.

[224] See *Re Lo-Line Electric Motors Ltd* [1988] 4 BCC 415; *Re Westmid Packaging Services Ltd, Secretary of State for Trade and Industry v. Griffiths* [1998] 2 All ER 124, [1998] BCC 836; *R v. Evans* [2000] BCC 901; *Re Westminster Property Management Ltd, Official Receiver v. Stern* [2001] BCC 121. On disqualification undertakings under the Insolvency Act 2000 being seen as protective rather than punitive see *Re Blackspur Group plc (No. 2)* [1998] 1 WLR 422; *Re Migration Services International Ltd* [2000] BCC 1095; *Re Cubelock Ltd* [2001] BCC 523; pp. 726, 728–9 below. On treating disqualification in ordinary civil terms rather than as a quasi-criminal process see A. Walters, 'Directors' Disqualification' (2000) 21 Co. Law. 90 at 91.

to justify disqualification: 'mere' incompetence will suffice – as in the *Swan* case where a non-executive director was disqualified for three years on the grounds, not that he knew of certain financial irregularities but because his behaviour on finding out about the irregularities fell below the level of competence to be expected of a director in his position.[225] From a privilege perspective, it also follows that public interest considerations may prevail over issues of culpability. Thus, in *Hennelly's Utilities*[226] the court allowed a disqualified director to act as a director of a company on accepting evidence that this would allow business expansion. The court took the view that the public's interest in protecting employment prevailed over its interest in being protected from an errant director.

Were the judiciary to follow the logic of either of the above approaches in a consistent manner, decisions on section 6 CDDA would possess a coherence that they now lack. As things stand, some decisions can be placed firmly within the rights approach, some reflect the privilege viewpoint, and some have a foot in both camps.

The rights approach is marked, as noted, by an emphasis on culpability and an eye to retributive notions of justice.[227] Thus, judges have distinguished between the fitness of directors of the same company on the basis

---

[225] See *Secretary of State for Trade and Industry v. Swan (No. 2)* [2005] All ER 102; [2005] BCC 596; and J. Lowry, 'The Whistleblower and the Non-Executive Director' [2006] 6 JCLS 249; C. Howell, '*Secretary of State v. Swan and North*' [2005] JBL 640. For an example of a failure to take advice (on VAT liability after insolvency) not being seen as such incompetence as would justify disqualification see *Secretary of State for Trade and Industry v. Walker* [2003] 1 BCLC 363.

[226] *Re Hennelly's Utilities Ltd* [2005] BCC 452. Conditions were imposed which were capable of being policed and the court took account of the fact that there was a real risk to the future profitability of the company with knock-on effects for employment prospects in the workforce. In *Re Uno plc (Secretary of State for Trade and Industry v. Gill)* [2006] BCC 725 Blackburne J was clearly influenced by the fact that several hundred employees' jobs were at risk when he found no unfitness regarding directors who had taken a 'balanced commercial decision to continue trading' and used customers' advance deposits as working capital after receiving legal, accounting and insolvency advice. In *Secretary of State for Trade and Industry v. Blackwood* [2005] BCC 366 the Court of Session (in dismissing the Secretary of State's appeal) indicated underlying sympathy for the directors of a distressed business who had traded on an insolvent business but had done so to protect employees' jobs rather than to benefit themselves.

[227] See *R v. Young* [1990] BCC 549, where the court declared that a disqualification order was 'unquestionably a punishment' and ruled that it was inappropriate to link such an order with a conditional discharge. On the retributive tradition see, for example, R. Nozick, *Philosophical Explanations* (Clarendon Press, Oxford, 1981). For arguments favouring conceptualisation of the possible purposes of the disqualification regime in terms of retribution and protection see C. Riley, [2000] CFILR 372 at 373–4.

of their culpability. In *Re Cladrose*[228] a director lacking accounting qualifications escaped disqualification following a complete failure to produce audited accounts and to file annual returns. His colleague, a qualified accountant, was, however, disqualified because of his 'unwarrantable' conduct in his failing vis-à-vis the accounts and returns. The latter's qualifications, it was stressed, rendered his omissions 'far more blameworthy' than those of his co-director.[229]

Not only does the rights approach stress culpability, it, as indicated, treats interfering with company direction as stigmatic and involving a serious interference with substantive, rather than merely procedural, rights. Thus in *Re ECM (Europe) Electronics*[230] Mervyn Davies J found no 'blameworthiness' sufficient to justify 'stigmatising' the director and in *Re Crestjoy Products Ltd*[231] Harman J stressed the 'substantial interference with the freedom of the individual' involved in section 6 disqualifications. This emphasis has been echoed in other decisions. Thus in *R v. Holmes*[232] Tucker J said of the disqualification of a director: 'It deprived him of a businessman's best asset, that is recognition in the eyes of the public that he is fit to act as a director of a limited company.'[233]

The mandatory nature of disqualification involved under section 6 of the 1986 Act has encouraged such a rights view on the part of some judges. Thus Harman J stated in *Re Crestjoy Products Ltd*[234] that the statutory predecessor of section 6, section 300 of the Companies Act 1985, had given the judges a discretion on whether to disqualify following a finding of unfitness – a discretion exercisable in the public interest. He contrasted this with the position under section 6 CDDA which implied the appropriateness of a more penal approach: 'disqualification under the former disqualification provision was not penal ... [I]t seems to me, however, that when I am faced with a mandatory two year

---

[228] [1990] BCC 11.

[229] See further Finch, 'Plea for Competence'. In *Secretary of State for Trade and Industry* v. *Bairstow and Others (No. 2)* [2004] EWHC 1730 a director was disqualified for six years under CDDA s. 8. While not guilty of dishonesty, the director had been grossly negligent in his duties because, although not an accountant, he was 'very experienced as a director' and consequently, on the information available to him, he should have noticed that the accounts were misleading.

[230] [1991] BCC 268.   [231] [1990] BCC 23 at 26.   [232] [1991] BCC 394.

[233] Ibid., p. 396. See also *Re ECM (Europe) Electronics Ltd* [1991] BCC 268 at 275.

[234] [1990] BCC 23. See also Mummery J in *Re Cedac Ltd* [1990] BCC 555 at 558–9. But cf. Court of Appeal in *Re Cedac* [1991] BCC 148.

disqualification if facts are proved, the matter becomes more nearly penal.'[235] When Hoffmann J decided *Re Swift* in 1992[236] he felt able to comment in unequivocal terms: 'these being penal proceedings Mr Ettings must, I think, be given the benefit of the doubt'[237] while in 1995, in *Secretary of State* v. *Gray*,[238] Hoffmann LJ (now in the Court of Appeal) was again clearly influenced by the mandatory nature of section 6, indicating that the purpose of making the section mandatory was to ensure that everyone whose conduct fell below the appropriate standard was disqualified for at least two years whether 'the individual court thought this was in the public interest or not'.[239]

That the judges often adopt a penal approach is further evidenced by instances in which factors bearing on culpability rather than public protection are deemed relevant in assessing the appropriate period of disqualification. In *Re Sevenoaks Stationers*[240] Dillon LJ accepted as a mitigating factor the director's personal monetary losses and lack of personal gain.[241] In *Re Churchill Hotel (Plymouth) Ltd*[242] Peter Gibson J decided not to disqualify, noting *inter alia* that the director had apologised for his defaults and 'expressed regret' for the failure of the companies.[243] Similarly in *Re Swift*[244] Hoffmann J noted that the director had 'already suffered considerable misfortune' and had gained nothing financially out of his failure of duty as a director. Consequently he was disqualified for just a year longer than the minimum period. All of these matters relate more readily to culpability and questions of retribution

---

[235] [1990] BCC 23 at 26. See also *Re Cedac Ltd* [1990] BCC 555; *Secretary of State for Trade and Industry* v. *Langridge* [1991] Ch 402 at 412: 'While a disqualification order is not of itself penal, it is clearly restrictive of the liberty of the person against whom it is made, and its contravention can have penal consequences', per Balcombe LJ.

[236] *Re Swift 736 Ltd* [1992] BCC 93.   [237] Ibid., p. 95.   [238] [1995] 1 BCLC 276.

[239] See also *Re Living Images Ltd* [1996] 1 BCLC 348, where Laddie J spoke of 'moral turpitude' and the need for 'cogent evidence'.

[240] [1990] BCC 765, [1991] Ch 164. Note that in *Re Sevenoaks* three levels of unfitness to be a director were related to different lengths of the disqualification period. In *Re Polly Peck International plc (No. 2)* [1994] 1 BCLC 574 it was stated that, since the minimum period of disqualification was two years, an order should not be made if the defendant's misconduct was not serious enough to merit such a term of disqualification.

[241] [1990] BCC 765 at 780. See also *Re Pamstock* [1994] 1 BCLC 716; *Re CEM Connections Ltd* [2000] BCC 917; cf. *Re Firedart* [1994] 2 BCLC 340, where Arden J refused to accept, as a matter of mitigation, the fact that the director had personally guaranteed the company's overdraft and had provided security over his own property to the bank.

[242] [1988] BCC 112.   [243] Ibid., p. 122.   [244] [1992] BCC 93 at 97.

than to issues of public protection.[245] In *Re Chartmore*[246] Harman J imposed the minimum disqualification period on a director who had *inter alia* failed to keep proper accounts, traded on the back of creditors and exhibited a 'total lack of attention to proper duties'. The basis of this leniency was that the director was 'still only about 30', and, in his Lordship's words, was 'really very young' and 'pretty young' respectively when the two relevant companies went down.[247] This indicated, said Harman J, 'conduct at the bottom end of the scale of blameworthiness'. Either Harman J possessed a highly optimistic view of maturation as a public protection, or, as formerly in *Crestjoy*,[248] he was assessing conduct on punitive principles.

Some cases take an approach that is penal in so far as culpability is seen as justifying disqualification in circumstances where there is no remaining need for public protection. Thus in *Re D. J. Matthews (Joinery Design) Ltd*[249] the errant director's counsel argued that his client had evidenced unfitness in directing two previous companies but had 'learned his lessons', was now managing a third company successfully and that, accordingly, the public no longer needed protection from the director's acting irresponsibly. Peter Gibson J was, however, less inclined to gloss over the past culpability, saying: 'Just as there is joy in heaven over a sinner that repenteth, so this court ought to be glad that a director, who has been grossly in dereliction of his duties, now wishes to follow the path of righteousness. But I must take into account the misconduct that has occurred in the past.'[250]

---

[245] For a case in which culpability and protection are linked see *Re Barings plc, Secretary of State for Trade and Industry* v. *Baker* [1998] BCC 583 at 590, in which Sir Richard Scott VC urged that evidence of a director's 'general conduct in discharge of the office of director goes to the question of the extent to which the public needs protection'.

[246] [1990] BCLC 673.

[247] In *Re Melcast (Wolverhampton) Ltd* [1991] BCLC 288 the age of the director was again considered to be a mitigating factor in imposing a more lenient disqualification period. The director was aged sixty-eight and his conduct was deemed by Harman J to warrant a ten-year disqualification period. The director was nevertheless disqualified for seven years because the judge considered that by the age of seventy-five it was unlikely that the director would ever again be concerned in the management of a company. In *Re Moorgate Metals Ltd* [1995] 1 BCLC 503 at 520, in contrast, Warner J considered that the age of the director (seventy) should not be considered as a mitigating factor.

[248] [1990] BCC 23.   [249] [1988] 4 BCC 513.

[250] Ibid., p. 518. See also *Re Samuel Sherman plc* [1991] BCC 699 at 712 concerning a public company and CDDA 1986 s. 8; *Re Blackspur Group plc (No. 2)* [1998] 1 WLR 422, [1998] BCC 11: disqualification intended to have a real deterrent effect on others. See also *Re City Truck Group Ltd (No. 2); Secretary of State for Trade and Industry* v. *Gee* [2008] BCC 76, where Mann J stressed the culpability of a director in failing to find out and note that fraudulent activities were going on.

Turning to the privilege approach, the purpose of disqualification for unfitness has been said to be the protection of the public 'against those who use limited liability to abuse the privileges of limited liability and to ... "rip off" the public'.[251] This offers a view of limited liability as a privilege accorded upon terms and susceptible to withdrawal for the public good rather than because of any need for retribution.[252] The approach is consistent with the notion that disqualification may protect the public in three ways: by keeping unfit directors 'off the road'; by deterring unfit directors from repeating their misconduct; and by encouraging other directors to act properly so as to raise standards of corporate governance.[253] A director may, on such a view, be disqualified for 'mere' incompetence. Thus in *Re Bath Glass*[254] Peter Gibson J indicated that for a finding of unfitness: 'the court must be satisfied that the director has been guilty of serious failure ... whether deliberately or through incompetence to perform those duties of a director which are attendant on the privilege of trading through companies with limited liability'. Consistent with such a concern for both deliberate shortcomings and incompetence has been a judicial movement away from language focusing on turpitude[255] and towards

---

[251] Harman J in *Re Douglas Construction Services Ltd* [1988] BCLC 397 at 402. See also *Re Cladrose Ltd* [1990] BCC 11 at 18; *Secretary of State for Trade and Industry v. Gray* [1995] Ch 241; *Re Westmid Packaging Services Ltd, Secretary of State for Trade and Industry v. Griffiths* [1998] 2 All ER 124, [1998] BCC 836 (CA); *R v. Evans* [2000] BCC 901; *Re Westminster Property Management Ltd, Official Receiver v. Stern* [2001] BCC 121.

[252] *Re Rolus Properties* [1988] 4 BCC 446 at 449 (Harman J).

[253] See Walters, 'Directors' Disqualification', p. 91. For an argument that there is little evidence of disqualification being used to encourage the broader objectives of protecting customers and standards of directorial behaviour (as opposed to suppressing wealth-reducing opportunism) see Williams, 'Disqualifying Directors: A Remedy Worse than the Disease?', p. 221, but, in favour of the 'broader objectives' view, see Walters and Davis-White, *Directors' Disqualification and Bankruptcy Restrictions*, pp. 32–6, 50; *Re Swift 736 Ltd* [1993] BCC 312 at 315 (CA); *Secretary of State for Trade and Industry v. McTighe* [1997] BCC 224; *Re Atlantic Computers Ltd*, 15 June 1998, Ch D (unrep.); *Re Barings plc (No. 5)* [1999] 1 BCLC 433; *Re Continental Assurance* [1996] BCC 888; *Re Landhurst Leasing plc* [1999] 1 BCLC 286; *Re Westmid Packaging Services Ltd* [1998] 2 All ER 124; *Re Blackspur Group plc (No. 2)* [1998] 1 WLR 422.

[254] [1988] 4 BCC 130 at 133.

[255] For examples of the language of turpitude see *Re Dawson Print Group Ltd* [1988] 4 BCC 322 ('breach of standards of commercial morality'); *Re CU Fittings Ltd* [1989] 5 BCC 210 ('commercial impropriety' needed); *Re Cedac Ltd* [1990] BCC 555 (Mummery J: 'a lack of commercial probity' or 'commercially culpable manner'); *Re Park House Properties Ltd* [1997] 2 BCLC 530 (Neuberger J: 'attributable to ignorance born of a culpable failure to make enquiries or, where enquiries were made, of culpable failure to consider or appreciate the results of those enquiries').

examining if regard has been paid to 'proper standards'[256] of 'probity and competence'.[257]

The privilege approach thus justifies actions against two very different kinds of errant director, 'the person who is simply exploiting limited liability in a cynical way with a disregard for proper responsibility' or alternatively the director who is exploiting it 'because he is so stupid and ignorant that he is quite incapable of appreciating what has happened and thereby causes large losses by in a sense incompetence'.[258] In both of these cases it has been indicated that there is a need to 'protect the public' from further abuse of the privilege of limited liability.[259]

The privilege approach does not imply that disqualification is a penal process – rather it is a public policy decision that pays heed to the *procedural* rights of directors. Thus, in *Re Lo-Line*[260] disqualification was portrayed in the following terms:

> The primary purpose ... is not to punish the individual but to protect the public against the future conduct of companies by persons whose past records as directors of insolvent companies have shown them to be a danger to creditors and others. Therefore, the power is not fundamentally penal. But ... disqualification does involve a substantial interference with the freedom of the individual. It follows that the rights of the individual must be fully protected.[261]

---

[256] See Harman J in *Re Keypack Homecare Ltd (No. 2)* [1990] BCC 117; Peter Gibson J in *Re Churchill Hotel (Plymouth) Ltd* [1988] BCC 112 at 117.

[257] *Re Landhurst Leasing* [1999] 1 BCLC 286 at 344. The standard may vary according to the nature and size of the company and the role which the defendant played in its affairs: *Re Continental Assurance Co. of London plc (sub nom. Secretary of State for Trade and Industry v. Burrows)* [1996] BCC 888, [1997] BCLC 48; *Re Barings plc* [1998] BCC 583 at 586; *Re Barings plc (No. 5)* [1999] 1 BCLC 433; *Re Kaytech International plc* [1999] BCC 390; *Official Receiver v. Vass* [1999] BCC 516.

[258] Harman J in *Re Douglas Construction Services Ltd* [1988] BCLC 397 at 402. In *Baker v. Secretary of State for Trade and Industry* [2001] BCC 273 the Court of Appeal upheld the trial judge's disqualification order covering a director who had failed to heed clear warning signals, 'hoped for the best' and showed 'incompetence to a high degree'.

[259] *Re Douglas Construction Services Ltd*, at 402. In *Re Westminster Property Management Ltd, Official Receiver v. Stern* [2001] 1 All ER 633, [2001] BCC 121, the Court of Appeal held that the imposition of disqualification (whose primary purpose was deemed not penal but to protect the public against those whose past record as a director has shown them to be a danger to creditors and others) was compatible with, as a justified derogation from, Article 43 (freedom of establishment) and Article 49 (freedom to provide services) of the European Community Treaty.

[260] *Re Lo-Line Electric Motors Ltd* [1988] 4 BCC 415.

[261] Ibid., p. 419. Browne-Wilkinson VC stated in *Re Lo-Line* (p. 486) that in the normal case an ordinary commercial misjudgement would not justify disqualification – rather the conduct must display a lack of commercial probity or constitute an extreme case of gross negligence or total incompetence.

From the privilege perspective, it matters little whether disqualification affects a director's personal employment prospects adversely: the public interest is the dominant consideration. The courts, nevertheless, have tended, when applying the privilege approach, to stress that loss of the facility of limited liability does not end all employment prospects. In *Re Southbourne Sheet Metal Co. Ltd* [262] Harman J stated that the disqualification jurisdiction was 'of a somewhat hybrid character'. It was not a prosecution neither was it an ordinary civil proceeding:

> it is not a penal proceeding. It is not intended to punish the director. It is a proceeding where the DTI or the Official Receiver ... is proceeding with a view to protecting the public by removing from a man the privilege of trading under the cover of limited liability. It does not stop a man's freedom to trade, either as a sole trader or in a partnership, upon ... 'his own bottom', where he is liable down to his last collar stud. [263]

The errant director might well take a more serious view of disqualification and its effects, particularly when, in the aftermath, he or she seeks credit under the cloud of such an order. Harman J has, nevertheless, repeatedly stressed that it is always open to any disqualified person to carry on trading in business, on their own account or as a partner. [264]

The *strength* of the procedural protections offered to a director may also depend on the courts' conception of the disqualification process as non-penal or penal. Thus a notice requirement is more likely to be seen as directory rather than mandatory when a court stresses public protection rather than private interest. [265] Balcombe LJ in *Re Tasbian Ltd (No. 3)* [266] put the unanimous Court of Appeal view in stating that it would not be right to preclude trial of a disqualification issue 'merely' because the Official Receiver had supported an *ex parte* application with inaccurate facts. His Lordship stressed: 'this is public interest litigation'. [267]

---

[262] [1991] BCC 732.   [263] Ibid., p. 734.

[264] See also *Re Chartmore Ltd* [1990] BCLC 673 at 675; *Re Probe Data Systems Ltd (No. 3)* [1991] BCC 428 at 434 (see Court of Appeal at [1992] BCC 110). For an example of plans to continue trading by accepting personal liability after disqualification, see *Re D. J. Matthews (Joinery Design) Ltd* [1988] 4 BCC 513 at 518.

[265] Contrast the majority and minority judgments in *Re Cedac Ltd* [1990] BCC 555, [1991] BCC 148 (Court of Appeal), concerning application of CDDA 1986 s. 16(1).

[266] [1992] BCC 358.

[267] Ibid., p. 366. For those concerned with employment issues more generally, an attractive feature of the privilege approach, with its focus on the public interest, may be its attention to the wider employment implications of disqualification. Under the former s. 300 of the Companies Act 1985 the judicial discretion to disqualify or not on a finding of unfitness was,

Is there a discernible judicial trend favouring either the rights or the privilege approach? It seems not. Decisions offer examples, as noted, of both approaches, with, for example, *ECM Europe*[268] and *Southbourne*[269] offering quite different perspectives. Individual judges have also been seen to adopt elements of both the rights and privilege standpoints. Thus Harman J has been noted under the rights heading in *Crestjoy*[270] and *Chartmore*[271] and as paying heed to privilege-based factors in *Southbourne*.[272] Even within individual judgments the language associated with the two approaches intermixes. Thus Dillon LJ's judgment in *Re Sevenoaks*[273] stresses both the public protection rationale of disqualification and the absence of personal gain on the director's part. A similar confusion is encountered in *Re Keypack*[274] and in *Griffiths*[275] where disqualification was based on ostensibly protective principles but where the period of disqualification for the 'offence' was approached by assessments of culpability.[276]

on numerous occasions, exercised so as to avoid undue consequences for clients or employees of the director's other companies. Thus in *Re Majestic Sound Recording Studios Ltd* [1988] 4 BCC 519 and in *Re Lo-Line Electric Motors Ltd* [1988] 4 BCC 415 (see also *Re Artic Engineering Ltd (No. 2)* [1986] BCLC 253) directors were allowed to continue in office but subject in each case to supervisory arrangements. The mandatory nature of disqualification under CDDA 1986 s. 6 might be expected to rule out such courses of action and demand that concessions be made only at the stage of establishing unfitness. That some flexibility of judicial approach remains possible has, however, been made clear in *Re Chartmore Ltd* [1990] BCLC 673, in which Harman J granted leave to waive disqualification in respect of a particular company for a one-year trial period subject to conditions. It may be the case, therefore, that by resort to CDDA 1986 ss. 1(1) and 17 – the bases for the waiver in *Chartmore* – continued attention can be given to the employment effects of disqualification. On leave to act under CDDA 1986 s. 17 see further Walters and Davis-White, *Directors' Disqualification and Bankruptcy Restrictions*, chs. 12 and 15; T. Clench, 'Applications for Permission to Act under Section 17 of the Company Directors Disqualification Act 1986' (2008) 21 *Insolvency Intelligence* 113; *Secretary of State for Trade and Industry* v. *Baker* [1999] 1 All ER 1017; *Secretary of State for Trade and Industry* v. *Rosenfeld* [1999] BCC 413; *Re TLL Realisations Ltd, Secretary of State for Trade and Industry* v. *Collins* [2000] BCC 998.

[268] *Re ECM (Europe) Electronics Ltd* [1991] BCC 268, [1992] BCLC 814.
[269] *Re Southbourne Sheet Metal Co. Ltd* [1991] BCC 732.
[270] *Re Crestjoy Products Ltd* [1990] BCC 23, [1990] BCLC 677.
[271] *Re Chartmore Ltd* [1990] BCLC 673.   [272] [1991] BCC 732.
[273] *Re Sevenoaks Stationers (Retail) Ltd* [1990] BCC 765, [1991] Ch 164.
[274] *Re Keypack Homecare Ltd* [1987] BCLC 409; *(No. 2)* [1990] BCC 117.
[275] *Secretary of State for Trade and Industry* v. *Griffiths, Re Westmid Packaging Services Ltd (No. 3)* [1998] BCC 836, the Court of Appeal stating that while protection of the public is the primary purpose of disqualification, in truth the exercise engaged in when making a disqualification order is little different from any sentencing exercise.
[276] See also *Re Manlon Trading Ltd, Official Receiver* v. *Haroon Abdul Aziz* [1995] 1 All ER 988, per Evans-Lombe J: 'The legislature must have envisaged that it was in the public

Both policy considerations and conceptual coherence favour adopting a single approach to disqualification: one based on the notion of privilege/public protection rather than rights/penalty. Looking to wrongful trading and fraudulent trading under the Insolvency Act 1986, we have seen above that these contain a compensatory dimension.[277] In parallel with such an approach, there seems no good case for adopting an exclusively penal viewpoint in relation to unfitness where the director's behaviour does not fall foul of explicitly criminal provisions.[278]

It has been argued that a combined approach may be necessary since 'disqualification periods are, and can often only be, decided on the basis of a penal principle not a solely protective one'.[279] It has also been suggested that public opinion demands a punitive response to 'dishonest and fraudulent directors'.[280] If, however, a privilege approach is adopted this does not mean that a director's misconduct or moral turpitude is irrelevant. Rather (as indicated in *Lo-Line*)[281] it means that disqualification may, where appropriate, be used to protect the public against the potential misbehaviour of a person who has manifested an undesirable attitude to the privilege of limited liability. The 'dishonest and fraudulent director' is thus likely to be dealt with sufficiently severely to assuage public opinion. Central to the privilege approach is, however, a rejection of using disqualification per section 6 merely for the purposes of punishment in the retributive sense.

A privilege standpoint emphasises that incompetence may provide a basis for disqualification.[282] (Incompetence, after all, is, when combined with mismanagement, the major cause of corporate insolvency.)[283] Being

---

interest that a businessman whose past conduct had justified disqualification should, after an appropriate period in which the public was to be protected and during which it must be presumed he became aware of the consequences of his past failings, have restored to him the right to manage businesses with the protection of limited liability', at p. 1003.

[277] See *Re Produce Marketing Consortium Ltd* [1989] 5 BCC 569 at 597 and *Morphitis* v. *Bernasconi* [2003] Ch 552, [2003] 2 BCLC 53. See discussion at pp. 696–703 above.

[278] For example, CDDA 1986 ss. 2, 4, 5. See also CDDA 1986 s. 10 re disqualification for fraudulent trading and wrongful trading. See *R* v. *Holmes* [1991] BCC 394 regarding the 'difficulty' in reconciling a compensation order, per Insolvency Act 1986 s. 213, and a disqualification order.

[279] S. Wheeler (1990) IL&P 174 at 175.

[280] See Newbegin, 'Disqualifying Directors', *The Lawyer*, 24 September 1991.

[281] [1988] 4 BCC 415 at 419.   [282] *Re Bath Glass Ltd* [1988] 4 BCC 130 at 133.

[283] See ch. 4 above; J. Argenti, *Corporate Collapse: The Causes and Symptoms* (McGraw-Hill, London, 1976); C. Campbell and B. Underdown, *Corporate Insolvency in Practice: An Analytical Approach* (Chapman, London, 1991) ch. 2.

non-penal, the burden of proof should, according to such a view, be on balance of probabilities, as indicated in *Re Southbourne*.[284] A privilege approach does not, however, imply that a director's interests are to be ignored. The errant director does not, on such a view, have a substantive right to retain the facility of limited liability but does possess procedural rights. These exist in the CDDA[285] and offer some protection against potential prejudice in spite of the courts' increased inclination, on adopting a privilege approach, to treat them as directory rather than mandatory.[286]

A case such as *Re Chartmore*[287] suggests that the courts are capable of giving section 6 a degree of flexibility. Recent cases do not, however, show that a consistent or coherent approach to section 6 disqualifications has been arrived at. The privilege rationale offers a route to such coherence. More importantly it emphasises that, in removing the facility of limited liability, public protection is paramount.[288]

So much for the rationales underpinning the use of disqualification. The second issue for consideration is whether the disqualification rules actually make a difference to expertise, honesty and competence on the ground. On this point, a number of commentators have argued that the impact of the rules has been small.[289] A thousand or so disqualifications a year has been said to 'make little impact on the legions of the unfit'.[290] There are around 3 million directors with millions more who could buy a company off the shelf and so current levels of disqualification may have a

---

[284] *Re Southbourne Sheet Metal Co. Ltd* [1991] BCC 732 at 734.

[285] See CDDA 1986 ss. 7 and 16; see also S. Wheeler (1991) IL&P 141.

[286] See, for example, *Re Cedac Ltd* [1991] BCC 148 (CA), re CDDA 1986 s. 16(1). See *Re Probe Data Systems Ltd (No. 3)* [1992] BCC 110 and *Re Tasbian Ltd (No. 3)* [1992] BCC 358: Court of Appeal judgments re CDDA 1986 s. 7(2) applications.

[287] [1990] BCLC 673.

[288] Whether the judges are prepared to accept this approach is, of course, an issue: see 'The Fourth Annual Leonard Sainer Lecture – The Rt Hon. Lord Hoffmann' (1997) 18 Co. Law. 194. See further p. 735 below.

[289] See, for example, Williams, 'Disqualifying Directors: A Remedy Worse than the Disease?'; S. Griffin, 'Accelerating Disqualification under s. 10 of the Company Directors' Disqualification Act' [2002] Ins. Law. 32; A. Hicks, 'Director Disqualification: Can It Deliver?' [2001] JBL 433; Hicks, *Disqualification of Directors: No Hiding Place for the Unfit?* ACCA Research Report No. 59 (London, 1998); A. Walters, 'Directors' Duties: The Impact of the Directors' Disqualification Act 1986' (2000) 21 Co. Law. 110; Walters, 'New Regime'.

[290] Comment (1999) 20 Co. Law. 97. *The Times*, 4 June 1998, described disqualification as a 'limp lettuce leaf'. As indicated above, 1,200 disqualification orders were obtained in 2006–7 (80 per cent by undertaking) compared to 1,173 in 2005–6: see Insolvency Service, *Annual Report and Accounts* 2006–7 (HC 752, London, 2007) p. 15.

small impact and a small deterrent effect. There are, moreover, risks in the plea-bargaining approach involved in the undertakings regime – notably that periods of disqualification will be reduced overall and that the deterrent and control effects of disqualification will be weakened. From the directors' point of view, there are dangers that the new regime creates incentives to accept disqualification early in negotiations (to avoid escalating costs)[291] and that they will be economically distanced from a just hearing of their case.[292]

A further concern regarding the undertakings procedure is that the low profile of this process might reduce the potential of disqualification to discourage unfit behaviour through the publicising of disqualification cases. There is no scope, after all, for undertakings to be publicised by entry into the register of disqualification orders maintained by the Secretary of State under CDDA section 18(2). Parties are not required by the law to agree a statement of unfit conduct and the Secretary of State has the power to accept a bare undertaking which provides no description of the conduct found to be unfit. The Secretary of State can in practice, however, demand an admission of unfit conduct for recording in a schedule to the undertaking.[293] On this point, moreover, some assurance can be taken from *Re Blackspur Group plc (No. 3), Secretary of State for Trade and Industry v. Eastaway.*[294] That case involved a director who had offered a disqualification undertaking but was unwilling to agree to the annexing of a schedule of unfit conduct. (He feared the anticipated stigma and the effect on his accountancy career.) The Secretary of State insisted on the schedule of admissions and the Court of Appeal stated that it was open to the Secretary of State to form the view that it was not in the public interest to accept a bare undertaking without admissions.[295] This reinforced the rationale of disqualification as a means of both protecting the public and setting proper standards through making the factual bases of disqualification transparent. It paved the way for the Secretary of State to make it publicly clear what kind of conduct would be treated as rendering a director unfit.

---

[291] See Walters, 'New Regime', p. 93; Practice Direction: Directors' Disqualification Proceedings [1996] 1 All ER 445, para. 28.1.

[292] See further pp. 751–2 below.

[293] See A. Walters, 'Bare Undertakings in Directors' Disqualification Proceedings' (2001) 22 Co. Law. 290.

[294] [2002] 2 BCLC 263.

[295] See A. Walters, 'Bare Undertakings in Disqualification Proceedings' (2002) 23 Co. Law. 123.

Two National Audit Office (NAO) Reports (of 1993 and 1999)[296] respectively criticised the efficacy of the Insolvency Service's administration of the CDDA and cautioned that disqualification was perceived as having only a marginal effect on improving the behaviour of directors generally. A survey, reported in 2001, also revealed that insolvency practitioners were sceptical concerning the effectiveness of disqualification which was 'not influential ... not well placed and ... difficult to enforce'.[297] More recently, Williams has argued[298] that, on 2005–6 figures, the direct financial benefit of the regime to creditors had been £14.52 million – which had been achieved at a cost to the public purse of £30 million. Insolvencies directly prevented by the regime[299] were put at an estimated 85 in number in 2005–6 compared to 15,351 insolvencies occurring during that year. As for the effect of the regime in (indirectly) deterring undesirable conduct, Williams suggested that around two-thirds of directors are likely to be unaware of the regime or what 'unfit' conduct is and that 'empirical evidence does not, therefore, suggest that disqualification successfully deters unfit conduct'.[300]

One explanation for the low incidence of disqualification orders may be that the officials who are involved in implementation are no more consistent about the aims and objectives of disqualification than the judiciary. Wheeler, for instance, argues that the disqualification process involves a 'unique mix of public regulation, public interest and private funding'.[301] She stresses that lack of resources and inefficiencies in the enforcing agency are not sufficient explanations of low numbers of disqualifications and that much can be explained by the inconsistencies of approach that are found amongst IPs and between IPs and the enforcing agency. Her portrait is of an implementation breakdown born out of philosophical differences. In selecting cases for disqualification, she argues, many actions fail to proceed because a large number of conduct reports contain 'moral frames and end goals which do not accord with

---

[296] NAO, *Company Director Disqualification* (October 1993, HC 907), *Company Director Disqualification: A Follow-up Report* (May 1999, HC 424). See S. Wheeler, 'Directors' Disqualification: Insolvency Practitioners and the Decision-making Process' (1995) 15 *Legal Studies* 283.

[297] See Hicks, 'Can It Deliver?', p. 437.

[298] Williams, 'Disqualifying Directors: A Remedy Worse than the Disease?', pp. 228–32.

[299] I.e. through disqualifications preventing further insolvencies involving the same directors.

[300] Williams, 'Disqualifying Directors: A Remedy Worse than the Disease?', p. 234.

[301] Wheeler, 'Directors' Disqualification', p. 286.

the goals and resulting construction of the public interest used by the Disqualification Unit'.[302]

In the 1996 Sainer lecture[303] Lord Hoffmann argued that disqualification had done little to raise standards of skill and care and that disqualification for incompetence was extremely rare, with the courts tending to emphasise conduct which breaches standards of accepted commercial morality. 'It is said that incompetent directors ought to be put off the road for a while like incompetent drivers, simply for the protection of the public. But the courts have never completely accepted this philosophy.'[304]

Sympathy with a 'rights' approach to direction may thus make judges reluctant to disqualify in a manner that produces a dramatic impact on standards. Lord Hoffmann noted that the courts were often mindful of the serious impact of disqualification on an individual. More practical factors, however, reduce the protective effect of disqualification for unfitness.[305] The law requires no prior qualification for becoming a company director,[306] limited liability companies can be incorporated at minimal cost and it is not easy to fix an *ex post facto* standard of competence for disqualification.[307] The disqualification process, moreover, only comes into play in cases where the incompetence (or 'unfitness') at issue is followed by insolvency (which may be a matter of happenstance). Routine investigations and the making of unfit conduct reports by the Official Receiver, administrators[308] or liquidators only follow entry into formal insolvency proceedings.[309] The conduct of

---

[302] Ibid., p. 304.

[303] Note, 'Hoffmann Plays Down Law's Contribution to the Efficiency of Corporate Management' (1997) 18 Co. Law. 56; Lord Hoffmann, 'Sainer Lecture'.

[304] Note (1997) 18 Co. Law. 56. For an argument that there is a 'growing judicial intolerance of honest or uninformed incompetence' see E. Ferran, *Company Law and Corporate Finance* (Oxford University Press, Oxford, 1999) p. 234.

[305] See Hicks, 'Can It Deliver?', pp. 439–40 and *Disqualification of Directors*, pp. 68–9.

[306] Lord Hoffmann made the point that it was difficult to find an *ex post facto* standard of competence for disqualification because the law does not require any qualification to become a director: Lord Hoffmann, 'Sainer Lecture' at p. 197.

[307] Sch. 1 of the CDDA 1986 gives a definition of improper conduct but offers the well-intentioned director little guidance on standards of best practice to creditors.

[308] Administrators, like other office holders, have a duty to bring potential unfit conduct to the attention of the Secretary of State under CDDA s. 7(3). The wording of CDDA s. 7(3)(c) was introduced by the Enterprise Act 2002 s. 248 and Sch. 17, para. 42 to reflect the fact that administration is no longer an exclusively court-based procedure. (Administrative receivers are also under a duty to report but since the Enterprise Act 2002 their appointment has been much reduced: see ch. 8 above.)

[309] On investigative powers of office holders see C. Campbell, 'Investigations by Insolvency Practitioners – Powers and Restraints: Part I' (2000) 16 IL&P 182.

directors of companies that are merely struck off the register and dissolved is not investigated and, in 2003–4, for instance, 154,300 companies were struck off the register and dissolved but only 15,700 were subject to formal insolvency proceedings.[310] Even when formal insolvency proceedings are involved, the IP or Official Receiver has to find sufficient evidence of unfit conduct to prompt reporting to the Secretary of State and the latter has to decide to proceed further.[311]

Many incompetent directors, moreover, may escape disqualification due to good fortune or the skill of other parties. Another factor reducing the effectiveness of disqualification is the period of time needed to collect evidence for a formal hearing: this may be so considerable as to lead to a number of disqualifications being dropped because they are out of time.[312] The majority of periods of disqualification, furthermore, tend to be relatively short (in 2006–7 around 700 disqualifications were from one to five years, around 400 from six to ten years and about 100 from eleven to fifteen years)[313] and the enforcement of orders is difficult. In the case of self-employed directors, these individuals may avoid the impact of disqualification by setting up in their own name. It is, indeed, arguable that disqualification is a sanction that is most effective when applied to professional, employed executives but one that in practice is used more widely in relation to the self-employed individual with regard to whom it has less impact.[314] A further consideration reducing the

---

[310] See DTI, *Companies in 2003–4* (HMSO, London, 2004) table C1; cited in Williams, 'Disqualifying Directors: A Remedy Worse than the Disease?', p. 234; Hicks, 'Can It Deliver?', pp. 443–5.

[311] The indications are that the Secretary of State will proceed in less than a third of cases of unfitness reports: Williams, 'Disqualifying Directors: A Remedy Worse than the Disease?', p. 235.

[312] See CDDA 1986 s. 7: the application for disqualification must be made within two years from the date the company 'became insolvent', but the court may, exceptionally, give leave to make a later application (s. 7(2)); *Re Probe Data Systems Ltd (No. 3)* [1992] BCC 110 at 111: Scott LJ's factors to be taken into account when considering whether to grant leave.

[313] See Insolvency Service, *Annual Report and Accounts 2006–7*, p. 16. Of course with most of the minor cases being disposed of via undertakings a significant number of the *reported* cases now feature unfitness at the 'upper end of the spectrum': see e.g. *Re Vintage Hallmark plc* [2008] BCC 150 (fifteen-year ban imposed on directors of a public company); *Re City Truck Group (No. 2)*; *Secretary of State for Trade and Industry* v. *Gee* [2008] BCC 76 (twelve-year ban on two directors); *Kappler* v. *Secretary of State for Trade and Industry* [2006] BCC 845 (eleven-year ban): see D. Milman 'Current Judicial Perspectives on the Managerial Role' (2008) 237 *Sweet & Maxwell's Company Law Newsletter* 1, 3–4.

[314] See Hicks, 'Can It Deliver?', p. 446.

protective impact of the disqualification regime is that disqualification does not remove ill-gotten gains.

If disqualification were to be relied upon significantly to boost the expertise of directors, then steps would have to be taken to overcome its inherent weaknesses. Enforcement costs and periods could be reduced further by establishing a specialist tribunal;[315] sanctions could be made more severe and also more flexible; more rigorous policing could be directed at those who breach disqualification orders; more information could be given to directors and the public on disqualifications[316] and a greater emphasis placed on protecting the public.[317] More radically, there could be a rethinking of the conditions under which directorial conduct is the subject of reporting so that the current dependency on formal insolvency processes would be reduced and investigations could be instigated following such events as complaints or examples of errant behaviour that do not lead to insolvency.[318] Another suggestion is that more use could be made of the court's power to disqualify under section 10 of the CDDA 1986 following a finding of liability for fraudulent or wrongful trading under section 213 or 214 of the Insolvency Act – a course of action that could be facilitated by removing some of the procedural barriers that restrict the application of section 214.[319]

It should not be forgotten that other approaches to improving directorial expertise can be considered. The criminal law has a role to play in limiting the worst forms of directorial misbehaviour and directors may be held to account by such mechanisms as fraudulent trading,[320] which, as noted, the CLRSG considered a valuable weapon in countering crime.[321] Laws providing for the personal liability of directors (for example, for wrongful trading) might also be said to encourage directorial expertise and standards. The use of criminal laws, however, demands that high standards of proof be satisfied and it has been pointed out that the criminal offences established in the Companies Acts are hugely

---

[315] As advocated by Hicks, ibid.

[316] This might involve the issue of guidance to directors on their duties and responsibilities together with the expected standards of behaviour: see ibid., pp. 449–51.

[317] See ibid.; Finch, 'Disqualifying Directors'.

[318] Though this offers no easy route to a solution: see the discussion in Williams, 'Disqualifying Directors: A Remedy Worse than the Disease?', pp. 239–41. On BERR investigations under the Companies Acts see Boyle and Birds' Company Law, pp. 531–4 and 719–30.

[319] See Griffin, 'Accelerating Disqualification under s. 10 of the Company Directors' Disqualification Act'.

[320] Companies Act 2006 s. 993.   [321] CLRSG, Final Report, 2001, para. 15.7.

underenforced.[322] Hicks has, nevertheless, argued that evidential problems in the current law might be overcome and that 'New, strict liability offences and civil penalties which preclude the misuse of corporate property to the detriment of creditors could be highly effective, being easier to prove than the broad and uncertain test of unfitness.'[323]

A potential route to raising standards lies through increasing directors' awareness of their obligations in times of trouble. What is clear is the extent of work that has to be done. A 2001 survey of directors of companies with an average of over 700 employees and £167 million annual turnover revealed that they were 'fundamentally ignorant' about their duties and liabilities on insolvency.[324] Two-thirds of finance, legal and managing directors were unaware that their personal liability might be higher if they had above-average expertise and experience. The same proportion did not know that their company could continue to trade if it was insolvent provided that it had a reasonable prospect of avoiding liquidation.

The issue of information for directors has been considered by the Law Commission and the Scottish Law Commission[325] as well as by the CLRSG.[326] The CLRSG wanted 'greater clarity on what is expected of directors' and to make the law more accessible as well as to bring the law into line with modern business practice. It wanted 'clear, accessible and authoritative guidance for directors on which they may safely rely, on the basis that it will bind the courts and thus be consistently applied'.[327] As noted already, however, the Companies Act 2006 statutory statement of directors' duties provides no detailed blueprint regarding the duties of directors in the vicinity of insolvency and the courts must still be relied upon to give flesh to the rules.[328] It may, moreover, be the case that it will

---

[322] See Hicks, 'Can It Deliver?', p. 454.

[323] See Hicks, *Disqualification of Directors*, p. v, who suggests that disqualifying courts might be empowered to make compensation orders and that the IS might provide resources for pursuing wrongful trading and other compensation claims.

[324] Survey by Taylor, Joynson and Garrett, *Legal Director* magazine, reported in *Financial Times*, 1 November 2001.

[325] Law Commission and Scottish Law Commission, *Company Directors*, 1998.

[326] CLRSG, *Final Report*, 2001, pp. 42–5. See also CLRSG, *Developing the Framework*, paras. 3.12–3.85; CLRSG, *Completing the Structure*, ch. 3.

[327] CLRSG, *Final Report*, 2001, para. 3.9.

[328] On questioning whether the judges are equipped to review directors' actions near insolvency, or to assess business risks, see T. Telfer, 'Risk and Insolvent Trading' in R. Grantham and C. Rickett (eds.), *Corporate Personality in the Twentieth Century* (Hart, Oxford, 1998) pp. 138–9; G. Varollo and J. Fukelstein, 'Fiduciary Obligations of

be the brightest, best and most competent directors that make themselves aware of their duties, rather than the less able and less competent. The effect may be to polish the standards of directors who already perform well rather than to raise the standards of those who cause greatest losses to creditors. It can be pointed out, moreover, that knowledge of one's duties is not the same as knowing how to turn around a company's fortunes in times of trouble. It is only one of many expectations that we may have of directors in troubled times.[329] More rigorous standards, of course, might prompt directors to behave more responsibly but it can be argued that such steps have to be combined with new training initiatives to have real effects.[330]

Other proposals on raising directorial expertise relate to company direction in general, rather than to performance in the specific context of insolvency, and space does not allow a full review here.[331] Steps such as professionalisation and training[332] and the monitoring and regulation of directorial behaviour may, however, encourage higher standards of performance across the spectrum of corporate fortunes.[333] The market,

Directors of the Financially Troubled Company' (1982) 48 *Business Lawyer* 239; D. Wishart, *Company Law in Context* (Oxford University Press, Auckland, 1994).

[329] See L. Hitchens, 'Directorships: How Many Is Too Many?' [2000] CFILR 359.

[330] It can also be questioned whether directors are driven by the prospects of personal sanctions. There is survey evidence that only around a third of directors cite such sanctions as an important driver of their conduct: see R. Baldwin, 'The New Punitive Regulation' (2004) 67 MLR 351.

[331] See Finch, 'Company Directors'.

[332] Ibid. The Institute of Directors (IOD) introduced the concept of a 'chartered director' in 1999. To achieve this status directors must have experience as a director, must pass an examination and must subscribe to the IOD's Code of Professional Conduct: see further R. Esen, 'Chartered Directors' Qualification: Professionalism on UK Boards' (2000) 21 Co. Law. 289. The IOD has also developed a Diploma in Company Direction and promoted a range of measures designed to improve directorial competence. Degrees in company direction are now available at various academic institutions. It is, however, questionable whether this burgeoning demand is not raising the standards of the most able and competent rather than the performance of those individuals most likely to underperform. On the issuing of guidance for directors and the need to deal with functions as well as duties, see Hitchens, 'Directorships', pp. 367–8. The CLRSG rejected the notion that company directors should be required to have formal qualifications or age limits (see CLRSG, *Final Report*, 2001, para. 3.49). The Companies Act 2006 provides for no formal directorial qualifications but s. 157 specifies a minimum age of sixteen for a person to be appointed as a director.

[333] The Combined Code recommends that on first appointment to be a director of a listed company directors should be given training on their role, but directors of listed companies are only a small minority of directors: see Hitchens, 'Directorships', p. 366; C. Riley, 'The Company Director's Duty of Care and Skill: The Case for an Onerous but Subjective Standard' (1999) 62 MLR 697.

indeed, may supply incentives that may raise directors' standards. Thus, banks may consider the training and track records of directors when assessing loan risks and may require personal guarantees in the case of less impressive directors. A straw poll at an INSOL conference, moreover, revealed that a 'sizeable majority' of delegates favoured a compulsory competence test that directors would sit (along 'driving test' lines) before being allowed to act as directors.[334] Informational solutions are also being increasingly advocated. It has been suggested that the Government could prepare directors' 'information packs' to advise new directors on their functions and obligations[335] and, in practice, bodies such as R3 are taking information solutions forward with business 'survival guides' for directors.[336]

Such approaches can, however, offer no guarantees that directorial expertise will save companies in a given situation: enterprise necessarily involves risks. What *insolvency* procedures should not do is discourage directors from seeking help or prevent directors from applying their skills in times of corporate troubles: for instance, by creating excessive incentives to depart from troubled companies or by excluding directors too fully from, or at too early a stage in, rescue or insolvency processes.

Efficiency

Do insolvency laws and processes induce directors, efficiently and economically efficiently, to balance the protection of creditor interests with needs to pursue rescue options and encourage enterprise?[337] It has been pointed out above that certain insolvency processes (e.g. administration) can be criticised as offering directors too weak a set of incentives to apply their expertise to rescue or creditor protection objectives in times of trouble. That discussion will not be repeated, nor is there the space here to discuss how the law generally conduces to directorial skill and care.[338] What can be done is to focus on the position of the director during corporate troubles and those controls and incentives that operate at such

---

[334] See Editorial, (2001) 17 IL&P 121.
[335] Ibid. The suggestion is to fund such packs by a modest levy on companies each time a notice of appointment or change of directors is filed with the Registrar of Companies.
[336] See R3 (formerly SPI), *Ostrich's Guide to Business Survival* (R3, London, 2002).
[337] This, it will be seen, is not a Jacksonian test of whether the law conduces to maximising the pool of assets available to all the company's creditors. On the reasons for rejecting this test see ch. 2 above.
[338] On which see Finch, 'Company Directors'; Riley, 'Company Director's Duty of Care and Skill'.

times. As a preliminary issue, then, the efficiency implications of imposing incentives and disincentives on directors, rather than corporations, should be noted. A first reason for targeting directors is that the total costs of sanctioning directors may be lower than the costs involved in controlling corporations so as to achieve the same reductions in wrongdoing.[339] Personal liability, moreover, is less liable to impose costs on a firm that will either increase the likelihood of insolvency or worsen the position of creditors in an insolvency. Making directors liable may also provide an efficient way to raise standards of management as it assists investigators by providing them with levers with which to bargain with managers for information concerning other corporate failings.[340]

Looking at economic efficiency, an advantage of holding directors liable is that this may leave risk evaluation and risk spreading to those individuals who are the best acquirers of information concerning corporate risks, levels of capitalisation, internal control systems and insurance. It thus permits managers to select the optimal strategies for dealing with risks.[341] Finally, of course, personal liability improves the prospects of compensation by bringing the pocket of the wrongdoer within range of the victim, and where that pocket is deep, it may produce compensation for wrongdoing that is unavailable from the insolvent company.[342]

A number of further points can be gleaned by examining a particular rule in more detail. Here it is worth looking at the wrongful trading provision and asking whether insolvency processes leave directors prone to undesirable diversion from the economically efficient and balanced pursuit of rescue or creditor protection objectives and whether the costs of ensuring that directors pursue such ends, rather than personal interests, are excessive.[343]

---

[339] See R. H. Kraakman, 'Corporate Liability Strategies and the Cost of Legal Controls' (1984) 93 Yale LJ 857; V. Finch, 'Personal Accountability and Corporate Control: The Role of Directors' and Officers' Liability Insurance' (1994) 57 MLR 880 at 881–7.

[340] As noted above, however, it may be easy to exaggerate the degree to which directors are aware of, or are driven by, prospects of personal liabilities: see Baldwin, 'New Punitive Regulation'; Williams, 'Disqualifying Directors: A Remedy Worse than the Disease?'.

[341] See Kraakman, 'Corporate Liability Strategies', p. 874.

[342] On legal and non-legal strategies to control the agency problem, see H. Hansmann and R. Kraakman, 'Agency Problems and Legal Strategies' in R. Kraakman et al., The Anatomy of Corporate Law: A Comparative and Functional Approach (Oxford University Press, Oxford, 2006) pp. 21 ff.

[343] The wrongful trading section, Insolvency Act 1986 s. 214, it should be noted, does not attack the incompetence or mismanagement that may have brought a company to the verge of insolvency. It covers the taking of proper steps to protect creditors beyond the point when the company's failure seems inevitable.

A central issue here, as has been pointed out,[344] is one of agency costs.[345] These costs relate to three main areas of potential directorial economic inefficiency. First, the managers of a troubled firm may expend assets in a desperate gamble to trade out of trouble and save their jobs. They will, in doing so, take inefficiently large risks because the risk bearers are in the first instance the shareholders (to be followed increasingly by the creditors as the firm declines).[346] A second danger is that managers will act in ways that prejudice the interests of creditors who were granted loans at early stages of corporate life: by, for example, taking out later secured loans that involve draconian terms and are not justified by the chances of potential recovery. Third, directors may, in times of trouble, act in a manner biased towards their shareholders[347] and they may be able to do so because their information is superior to that possessed by creditors.

It has been argued that shareholders and creditors would be likely to agree to an open-ended section 214 type of directorial duty as a way of dealing with such problems.[348] They are likely to do so, the argument runs, because the economically efficient mode of applying the right incentives is for creditors to be allowed to decide on the efficient balance between, on the one hand, spending on control or monitoring activity, and, on the other, adjusting loan terms to take on board the risks of adverse actions by directors. Shareholders are likely to be content both that the company will pay the loan rates that are set in this manner and for directors to look to creditor interests as insolvency looms, because such a creditor-centred regime is cheaper overall than one in which shareholders and creditors seek, *ex ante*, to anticipate and agree all the steps that managers should take

---

[344] See R. Mokal, 'An Agency Cost Analysis of the Wrongful Trading Provisions: Redistribution, Perverse Incentives and the Creditors' Bargain' [2000] 59 CLJ 335.

[345] The costs a principal incurs in ensuring that an agent acts in his, rather than the agent's, own interests: see generally M. C. Jensen and W. H. Meckling, 'Theory of the Firm: Managerial Behaviour, Agency Costs and Ownership Structure' (1976) 3 *Journal of Financial Economics* 305.

[346] On the 'perverse' incentive for an insolvent company to continue to trade see Telfer, 'Risk and Insolvent Trading'; Prentice, 'Creditors' Interest'. On excessive risk aversion see pp. 744–5 below.

[347] Directors may tend to ally with shareholders because the latter hold equity, have voting rights and hold the power to appoint them. In the face of insolvency this may result in excessive distribution and undue and over-investment: see S. C. Myers, 'Determinants of Corporate Borrowing' (1977) 5 *Journal of Financial Economics* 147.

[348] See Mokal, 'An Agency Cost Analysis', p. 349; cf. B. Cheffins, *Company Law: Theory, Structure and Operation* (Clarendon Press, Oxford, 1997) pp. 541–2.

in troubled times.[349] The company, after all, will pay interest rates that are reduced in reflection of the creditor orientation that comes with insolvency.

It may, however, be the case that, in certain circumstances, there are ways of reducing agency costs that are more economically efficient than a section 214 type of duty. In assessing these alternatives, it has to be borne in mind that, as noted, section 214 may be formulated and enforced in a manner that renders it a control device of low impact, low control effect, low deterrence and poor compensation. Under-deterrence may, indeed, occur because the wrongful actions of directors may produce losses to creditors that vastly exceed any sums liable to be forfeited by directors.[350] The pessimistic view of personal liability rules generally is that they tend to be difficult to enforce because of organisational secrecy, the numbers of responsible parties involved and the evidential problems that are associated with attempts to isolate culprits and prove cases. In many cases, relevant knowledge (e.g. about the nature of the corporate decline) may, rightly or wrongly, be scattered across the management or firm and not held by one individual.[351] Personal liability rules, moreover, may discourage the conscientious from acting as directors while failing to provide effective deterrence for, or remedies against, cavalier directors.[352]

As for the argument that personal liability rules will encourage intra-company monitoring of potential wrongdoing, the effects of such rules on non-executive directors may be undesirable.[353] Executive directors tend to dominate corporate boards and possess considerable advantages over outsiders vis-à-vis their time, resources, quality of information and access to board policy-making procedures.[354] The outsider faces severe obstacles in

---

[349] Mokal, 'An Agency Cost Analysis'.

[350] See S. Shavell, 'Liability for Harm Versus Regulation of Safety' (1984) 13 *Journal of Legal Studies* 357; S. Polinsky and S. Shavell, 'Should Employees be Subject to Fines and Imprisonment Given the Existence of Corporate Liability?' (1993) 13 *International Review of Law and Economics* 239.

[351] See generally C. D. Stone, 'The Place of Enterprise Liability in the Control of Corporate Conduct' (1980) 90 Yale LJ 1.

[352] See J. Freedman, 'Limited Liability: Large Company Theory and Small Firms' (2000) 63 MLR 317, who notes (at p. 344) that if the 'device' of making directors personally liable is to be relied upon, 'it may be important for a clear and reasonably consistent body of case law to be built up in order to provide guidance and for principles drawn from this case law to be communicated to business owners prior to incorporation. Such reliance, however, presupposes a highly rational system of deterrence in which directors show a high level of understanding of detailed legal information.'

[353] See Finch, 'Personal Accountability and Corporate Control', pp. 885–6.

[354] See Finch, 'Company Directors', pp. 197–200; V. Brudney, 'The Independent Director: Heavenly City or Potemkin Village?' (1982) 95 Harv. L Rev. 597.

monitoring board activity and the prospect of being held personally liable for failing in such monitoring functions may prove an excessive deterrent to non-executive direction, notably when the economic benefits of non-executive direction are seen to be dwarfed by potential liabilities for damages. Companies may, in spite of such relevant factors, persuade non-executive directors to serve on their boards but the prospect of personal liability may result in such directors demanding high-risk premiums; perhaps excessive investment by the company in monitoring for offences; and the avoidance of conduct that is potentially profitable but gives rise to legal uncertainties.[355] Alternatively, companies, when selecting outside directors, may seek to avoid such problems by choosing directors who are either non-risk averse or uncritical of risk taking. An incentive to select on such a basis would run counter to notions of outside directors constituting checks on corporate folly.

The imposition of personal liability can have further cost and economic efficiency implications. Thus, the costs of compensating managerial risk bearers may be greater than the costs of deterrence by means of enterprise liability since directors bear risks of an undiversified kind. Unlike shareholders who can spread risks across a portfolio, the directors' eggs are in the one corporate basket.[356] It is preferable, say the Chicago school,[357] to punish the corporation. This will create incentives for internal corrective action[358] and the firm is better positioned than the state to deter misconduct by its employees and to do so efficiently.[359]

Another danger of personal liability is that those who *are* prepared to operate as company directors will become excessively risk averse, so much so that they are unwilling to take commercially justifiable risks for fear of triggering personal liability. Either such risks may be left untaken (an economically inefficient result)[360] or those properly responsible may evade

---

[355] See Kraakman, 'Corporate Liability Strategies', p. 892.

[356] Ibid., pp. 865, 887; D. Mayers and C. Smith, 'On the Corporate Demand for Insurance' (1982) 55 *Journal of Business* 281 at 283.

[357] See R. Posner, *Economic Analysis of Law* (6th edn, Aspen Law and Business, New York, 2002).

[358] Incentives perhaps dependent on the firm itself facing high levels of punishment and probability of detection: see Stone, 'Place of Enterprise Liability', p. 30.

[359] Where, however, the firm itself is unlikely to suffer sanctions, it may even endorse directorial wrongdoing: see J. Coffee, '"No Soul to Damn: No Body to Kick": An Unscandalized Inquiry into the Problem of Corporate Punishment' (1981) 79 Mich. L Rev. 386 at 408.

[360] See R. Rosh, 'New York's Response to the "D & O" Insurance Crisis' (1989) 54 Brooklyn LR 1305 at 1317. On economic theory behind risk aversion see, *inter alia*, Jensen and Meckling, 'Theory of the Firm'; Stone, 'Place of Enterprise Liability', pp. 34–5; Telfer, 'Risk and Insolvent Trading', pp. 135–7.

their responsibilities. Risk avoidance can be achieved most readily by delegating legally awkward tasks to subordinates,[361] closing companies down too early[362] or by shifting risks to outside consultants.[363] Economic inefficiencies may result in so far as managers shy away from decisions, fail to trade or assume responsibilities, desist from establishing effective lines of control and delegate decisions to parties less well positioned to decide relevant issues. Even where the right levels of risks are taken by directors, it may be the case that statutory regulation causes directors to spend an inordinate amount of time on compliance issues and that this may impose ongoing costs on the company that outweigh the value of any protections that ensue. In 1962 the Jenkins Report raised this issue, asking whether further statutory regulation would 'to any significant extent hamper or impede the company in the efficient conduct of its legitimate business'.[364]

Nor may directors find reassurance in judicial responses. Heavy reliance on personal liability places a good deal of faith in the courts as arbiters of the business decisions of directors. As has been seen above, however, the judges have left the wrongful trading law in an uncertain state that (if enforced) would be likely to chill efficient directorial risk taking. This uncertainty might make directors 'likely to shy away from taking the sort of bold resolute decisions that are required to maximise profits'.[365]

[361] Kraakman, 'Corporate Liability Strategies', p. 860.

[362] See T. Cooke and A. Hicks, 'Wrongful Trading: Predicting Insolvency' [1993] JBL 338.

[363] R. Daniels and S. Hutton, 'The Capricious Cushion: The Implications of the Directors' and Officers' Insurance Liability Crisis in Canadian Corporate Governance' (1993) Canadian Bus. LJ 182 at 187; R. H. Kraakman, 'Gatekeepers: The Anatomy of a Third Party Enforcement Strategy' (1986) *Journal of Law, Economics and Organization* 53 at 55–7. Relying on advice will not always protect a director from, for example, disqualification: see *Official Receiver* v. *Ireland, Re Bradcrown Ltd* [2002] BCC 428.

[364] *Report of the Company Law Committee* (Cmnd 1749, 1962) p. 3; Telfer, 'Risk and Insolvent Trading', p. 134; D. Wishart, 'Models and Theories of Directors' Duties to Creditors' (1991) 14 NZULR 323; J. Mannolini, 'Creditors' Interests in the Corporate Contract' (1996) 6 *Australian Journal of Corporate Law* 1; M. Byrne, 'An Economic Analysis of Directors' Duties in Favour of Creditors' (1994) 4 *Australian Journal of Corporate Law* 275; M. Moffat, 'Directors' Dilemma: An Economic Evaluation of Directors' Liability for Environmental Damages and Unpaid Wages' (1996) 54 U Toronto Fac. LR 293 at 306.

[365] Cheffins, *Company Law*, p. 541. See also Cooke and Hicks, 'Wrongful Trading'; Grantham, 'Judicial Extension'. On the 'liability chill' see R. Daniels, 'Must Boards Go Overboard? An Economic Analysis of the Effects of Burgeoning Statutory Liability on the Role of Directors in Corporate Governance' in J. Ziegel (ed.), *Current Developments in International and Comparative Corporate Insolvency Law* (Clarendon Press, Oxford, 1994); F. H. Easterbrook and D. R. Fischel, *The Economic Structure of Corporate Law* (Harvard University Press, Cambridge, Mass., 1991); Telfer, 'Risk and Insolvent Trading'.

It may be the case, however, that the disciplines of the labour market will reinforce the wrongful trading and other insolvency provisions, so as to give directors incentives to behave properly during times of decline. The optimistic argument here is that a director's value in the market will be influenced by his reputation for behaving reasonably: 'He has an incentive to signal to the market that he is capable of effectively doing all that any reasonably competent manager would do to abate the damage done to the company's creditors.'[366] In response to such optimism, however, it can be said that even if a director was governed by the labour market, this would not necessarily demand that an appropriate balancing of creditor and shareholder interests was ensured by the director. Such a market might look to issues of basic competence, but a 'balanced' approach to different interests would only be valued by a market that itself reflected such interests. A labour market dominated by shareholder concerns would reward directors who favoured members' rather than creditors' interests.

As for the power of the labour market, this, like the market for corporate control, may encounter severe informational problems in assessing directorial behaviour, especially during periods of corporate difficulty when affairs move fast, data may not be collected efficiently, there is confusion and blame-shifting as 'tracks are covered'. For all these reasons it is difficult to see the labour markets as making up for the deficiencies of personal liability rules in encouraging efficient company direction.

Economically efficient rules for influencing directorial behaviour must incentivise the taking of remedial actions at the right stage of a company's troubles. In focusing on the wrongful trading rules it is, accordingly, relevant to ask whether these trigger the duty to have regard to creditor interests at the right stage in corporate decline. To recap, the objective of the provision can be seen as giving directors proper incentives to avoid taking unreasonable risks with creditors' funds at the point in corporate decline at which duties to shareholders and shareholders' (now diminished) equity interests no longer operate effectively to prevent excessive risk taking by the directors.[367] Here it is worth emphasising again that insolvency is a precondition for liquidators enforcing section 214 duties but the duty to regard creditor interests arises at an

---

[366] Mokal, 'An Agency Cost Analysis', pp. 351–2; R. Daniels, 'Must Boards Go Overboard?' (1994–5) 24 Canadian Bus. LJ 229 at 241.

[367] Davies, 'Directors' Creditor-regarding Duties'.

earlier stage – when the director realises or ought to realise that there is no reasonable prospect of avoiding insolvent liquidation.[368] It is at that point that the directors must take reasonable steps to minimise potential losses to creditors. The precondition of insolvency will be returned to below but, focusing on the arising of the duty to regard creditor interests, could the formulation above be improved upon so as better to balance creditor protections with desires to encourage entrepreneurship and rescue? The CLRSG gave this matter much deliberation and, as noted above, canvassed the potential rule that directors should be required: 'where they know or ought to recognise that there is a substantial probability of an insolvent liquidation, to take such steps as they believe, in their good faith judgement, appropriate to reduce the risk, without undue caution and thus continuing also to have in mind the interests of members'.[369] The Government, however, rejected this version as inconsistent with the promotion of a rescue culture and it is also likely that the courts would have been reluctant to have interfered with the judgements of directors on the basis of such a test.[370] Three conclusions can, perhaps, be drawn from the CLRSG's discussion: first, that it may be extremely difficult to produce a formulation of a rule that better encapsulates the relevant policy objective than section 214; second, that reliance on the judges to assess the particular circumstances of directors' decisions to continue trading may be unavoidable; and, third, that any problems now encountered with section 214 (at least regarding the point at which the duty arises) may flow, in the main, from how it has been applied in different courts rather than its essential formulation.

A further aspect of an economically efficient insolvency law is that it should render creditors well placed to police directors' behaviour in times of trouble.[371] It is certainly the case that creditors possess significant power that is capable of being exercised at such times. Secured creditors can apply real pressure merely by threatening to exercise their legal rights upon default or even prospective default of debenture terms. Such creditor stances would impinge on directors' reputations and prompt reappraisals of company plans and top management. Unsecured trade creditors are unlikely to exert the same broad influence

---

[368] See the discussion in Davies, ibid., who argues that the English courts operate on the basis of a cash flow test of incipient insolvency, as in *Re Purpoint* [1991] BCLC 491.

[369] CLRSG, *Final Report*, 2001, para. 3.17.

[370] Davies, 'Directors' Creditor-regarding Duties', p. 318.

[371] On the creditors' ability to monitor directors and their role in controlling general directorial competence see Finch, 'Company Directors', pp. 189–95.

as financial creditors but, where a company fails to pay its debts, trade creditors may apply pressure by threatening to disclose this fact to other suppliers, the market and the public. As the company moves from financial difficulty to financial crisis, creditor power increases further. The company's prospects of survival almost wholly depend on creditor co-operation. Financial creditors may be able and inclined to demand broad changes as conditions of assistance.

Threats cease and legal steps are initiated when rescue is deemed inappropriate.[372] At this stage, creditors may replace the directors with a liquidator. At this time, actions potentially covering negligence may be brought against directors personally. Such actions, as we have seen, may be brought under a number of heads. First, like a shareholder, any creditor may bring a misfeasance action against past or present company officers for a breach of fiduciary or other duty in relation to the company.[373] This action, however, demands a certain altruism on the petitioning creditor's behalf. Such duties are owed to the company: thus, any contributions or compensation received from negligent directors will enter into the company's assets and, as such, will be available to all creditors generally. These actions are, in addition, made less attractive because a misfeasance action can also be brought by the liquidator as the representative of the general creditors. Thus, liquidators, on behalf of creditors, can collect and evaluate the evidence for taking action against former directors, aided by investigative powers unavailable to individual creditors.[374] Action by liquidators, however, is not always to be assumed even if the evidence of directorial negligence exists. Wheeler has noted the pragmatism of liquidators:

> An important concern is with the location and realisation of saleable assets, from which their fees will be paid ... A fruitless but well-intentioned search for assets is unlikely to be a cost-effective use of time. An action of misfeasance, for example, becomes a reality only after a balancing exercise of factors such as cost, time involved, and the financial situation of the directors from which the recovery is sought.[375]

---

[372] On corporate rescues see J. R. Lingard, *Corporate Rescues and Insolvencies* (2nd edn, Butterworths, London, 1989); 'Britain Needs a "Rescue Culture" Now', Cork Gully Discussion Paper No. 1 (London, June 1991).

[373] Insolvency Act 1986 s. 212(1), (3).

[374] See Insolvency Act 1986 ss. 131–4. See also ch. 13 above.

[375] S. Wheeler, 'Disqualification of Directors: A Broader View' in H. Rajak (ed.), *Insolvency Law: Theory and Practice* (Sweet & Maxwell, London, 1993) p. 193. See also Katz and Mumford, *Making Creditor Protection Effective*, part 5.

In the case of wrongful trading actions, we must return to the insolvency preconditions for enforcement. A central limitation of section 214
is that wrongful trading actions have to be instigated by liquidators after
insolvent liquidation. This means that if directors breach their section
214 duty but the company is not liquidated, they will escape liability. In
addition, if there is a dissolution of the company without a formal
insolvency procedure (perhaps because the funds are lacking to support
a formal procedure) the section 214 process is bypassed. Finally, if the
insolvent company enters administration – the post-Enterprise Act preferred way of handling troubled companies – and the administrator
effects a rescue, the directors who breached their section 214 duty will
again escape liability.[376] These factors all suggest that section 214 will
greatly under-incentivise directors to have regard for the interests of
creditors at times of corporate trouble. Those incentives might be
increased by allowing individual creditors to bring section 214 actions
where a company has been dissolved and no liquidator has been
appointed – and by incentivising such creditors by allowing them to
receive, as a first call, a portion of the directors' contributions.[377] Such a
reform, however, possesses the limitations that the directors' pockets
have to be deep enough to encourage such actions and the creditors have
to possess the time, resources and commitment to pursue such courses,
as well as the information needed to evaluate the potential returns.

There are, thus, general dangers that enforcement difficulties in relation to such actions as wrongful trading and misfeasance may lead to
under-deterrence. Under-deterrence may also occur because errant
directors' pockets may not be sufficiently deep to induce creditors to
incur the expenses of enforcing their rights.[378] Some lenders can resort to
third-party security to make up for such deficiency. They may, accordingly, seek charges from shareholder-managers of closely held firms to
cover personal property, even homes.[379] Such actions may, however,
only be feasible for powerful banks that are dealing with smaller companies in circumstances where third parties hold considerable assets.

In concluding, then, it can be said that the present law falls short
in conducing to economically efficient company direction in times of

---

[376] See Davies, 'Directors' Creditor-regarding Duties'.
[377] See ibid.; Griffin, 'Accelerating Disqualification under s. 10 of the Company Directors'
Disqualification Act'.
[378] See A. Hicks, 'Advising on Wrongful Trading: Part 1' (1993) 14 Co. Law. 16.
[379] See Mokal, 'An Agency Cost Analysis', p. 359.

corporate trouble. A number of key difficulties can be identified. Enforcement problems may render actions such as wrongful trading suits a blunted and inefficient tool. Similarly, when liquidators or creditors face high costs in gaining relevant information about company affairs, inefficiency results. Such high costs may result from an excessive reliance on the use of outside professionals in insolvency processes and sets of incentives (or uncertainties) that lead directors to depart too early from the company scene. Legal uncertainties, as seen in the wrongful trading law, create inefficiencies both by chilling desirable risk taking by directors and by reducing the ability of shareholders and creditors to assess and manage risks at lowest cost. If it is asked whether the current statutory scheme would have been arrived at by allowing participants to negotiate,[380] one thing is clear. Participants in such a discussion would have wanted a regime in which directors, creditors and shareholders could assess and allocate risks in as clear a fashion as possible. That is the precondition for maximising returns. From both technical and economic efficiency perspectives what matters is certainty, what is undesirable is the chill wind of unknown risks.[381] From this point of view the current formulation of the law on directors' duties fails to deliver.

Finally, the broad limitations of individual liability rules have to be returned to. The deterrence of sub-optimal behaviour requires not merely that legal rules are rigorously applied but that sanctions involve a correspondence between the assets that a director puts at risk and the potential losses that directorial actions may place on creditors or shareholders. This condition is rarely satisfied and, accordingly, responses such as improved directorial training, intra-company controls and accountability regimes have to be looked to.

Fairness

Directors might complain that, in a number of respects, they are treated unfairly by the laws and processes discussed above. Disqualification under the CDDA may have very serious implications for individuals but, as has been seen above, the courts have failed to offer clear guidance on the position of the director. Some judges have applied a 'rights' approach to company direction. Others have seen direction of a

---

[380] See Telfer, 'Risk and Insolvent Trading', pp. 146–7; Cheffins, *Company Law*, pp. 540–4.
[381] See generally P. Halpern, M. Trebilcock and M. Turnbull, 'An Economic Analysis of Limited Liability in Corporation Law' (1980) 30 U Toronto LJ 117.

company incorporated with limited liability as a privilege. If the judiciary were to follow the logic of either of the above approaches in a consistent manner, directors might not be in a position to complain that it is unfair to subject them to a law that is incoherent and inconsistently applied. A single consistent judicial trend, however, is yet to emerge and decisions, as noted, often contain elements of both 'rights' and 'privileges' approaches.[382]

Before the Insolvency Act 2000, company directors might have complained that the disqualification process was so slow as to constitute an unfair regime. The Insolvency Service's 2000 Report on Company Rescue and Business Reconstruction Mechanisms[383] noted that:

> There were strong arguments made that for many honest directors of failed companies, the length of time which it currently takes the Secretary of State ... to bring on disqualification proceedings (or to reach a decision that proceedings will not be brought) acts as a considerable inhibition on any attempts they may wish to make to go back into business.[384]

The Review Group recommended that steps be taken to speed up the disqualification process and the Insolvency Act 2000 section 6 offered a response by developing the 'fast-track' procedure. As already noted, this procedure empowers the Secretary of State to accept consensual undertakings equivalent to disqualification orders without a full court hearing.[385] Another potential complaint of unfairness, however, emerges with this process. The Institute of Directors, among others, has complained that a plea-bargaining culture may develop in which directors will be placed under undue economic pressure to accept disqualification rather than have their day in court.[386] One commentator has argued that the new procedure 'will do little to dissuade the rogue with deep pockets. The real danger is that directors with limited resources and no desire for

---

[382] See p. 730 above and, for example, *Secretary of State for Trade and Industry* v. *Griffiths, Re Westmid Packaging Services Ltd (No. 3)* [1998] BCC 836; *Re Keypack Homecare Ltd (No. 2)* [1990] BCC 117.

[383] *Report by the Review Group* (DTI, 2000). [384] Ibid., para. 104.

[385] The Secretary of State may, however, require a statement of grounds for the undertaking: see *Re Blackspur Group plc (No. 3)* [2002] 2 BCLC 263.

[386] See Walters, 'New Regime', pp. 92–3. See also M. Simmons and T. Smith, 'The Human Rights Act 1998: The Practical Impact on Insolvency' (2000) 16 IL&P 167 for suggestions (at p. 172) that it is a breach of Article 6 for the individual to face 'such proceedings without proper legal representation' and that if directors are unable to 'contest the proceedings effectively due to financial considerations' this too could amount to a breach of Article 6.

litigation against the Secretary of State will be persuaded to agree a disqualification undertaking with little or no professional advice.'[387]

Moving away from disqualification to the other personal liabilities of directors, the latter may again complain of unfairness on the grounds that uncertainty infuses a host of liability provisions. In relation to wrongful trading, for instance, it has been suggested that the key finding – whether the director knew, or ought to have concluded, that there was 'no reasonable prospect' of avoiding insolvent liquidation – poses a question that is 'inherently elusive'.[388] A director can 'only speculate whether injecting more capital, cajoling other directors to take corrective action, tightening up accounting procedures, pursuing plans to achieve a turnaround, consulting an insolvency practitioner, or putting the company into liquidation will be sufficient'.[389]

Such complaints of unfairness and demands for legal certainty are given added weight when it is remembered that, in times of corporate trouble, directors will very often be compelled to make decisions within short deadlines and under extreme pressure. The director's difficulties are only added to by uncertainties in determining when a company is insolvent and which approach to accounting data should be used in making this calculation.[390] English directors are not protected by a 'business judgement rule' as encountered in the USA and some commentators have questioned whether judges are qualified to strike the right balance in judging the performance of directors.[391] A director has a duty to consider creditors' interests at some stage in a company's decline but whether this duty only operates when the company is insolvent or of 'doubtful solvency' rather than at some point earlier remains uncertain. The Companies Act 2006 left the judges to formulate the content of the

---

[387] R. Tateossian, 'The Future of Directors' Disqualification' (2000) *Insolvency Bulletin* 6 at 7. An editorial in the *Financial Times* (16 November 1999) suggested that prior to the Insolvency Act 2000 directors were faced with a Hobson's choice: 'either accept the ban, and be barred from business for at least two years; or run the risk of a long, extremely expensive court battle to try to clear your name'. Sir Richard Scott, the Vice Chancellor, argued to the Chancery Bar Association in 1999 that a solution might be to allocate costs under the 'just and reasonable' test of criminal cases, rather than the 'loser pays all' civil litigation formula: see (2000) 21 Co. Law. 90.

[388] D. Prentice, 'Corporate Personality, Limited Liability and the Protection of Creditors' in R. Grantham and C. Rickett (eds.), *Corporate Personality in the Twentieth Century* (Hart, Oxford, 1998) p. 119.

[389] Cheffins, *Company Law*, pp. 542–3, quoted by Telfer, 'Risk and Insolvent Trading', pp. 139–40.

[390] See Katz and Mumford, *Making Creditor Protection Effective*, part 5; ch. 4 above.

[391] See Cheffins, *Company Law*, p. 543.

directors' duties to creditors and, as indicated, the judiciary will enjoy a wide scope for judgement in shaping those duties as they are considered in relation to particular circumstances. The way forward here may be to hope, not that a blueprint set of rules is placed in statutory form, but that clear impediments are removed from enforcement processes and that the courts will use their judgement to produce rules and applications of these that are increasingly commercially operable and consistent.

Conclusions

The current regime of insolvency laws and processes fails to deal with company directors in a convincing manner. The sections above have identified deficiencies on the accountability, expertise, efficiency and fairness fronts. In many ways, the root cause of insolvency law's failure is one that has been alluded to already. Present insolvency law is not underpinned by a conception of the company director, or the company director's insolvency role, that is explicable in relation to a sustained set of values or principles. Instead, we see an institutional inconsistency in which company directors are sometimes seen as competent and trustworthy individuals with private rights to direct limited liability companies that are worthy of strong protection. On other occasions, directors are seen as fortunate individuals who exercise the privilege of directing limited liability companies and who should not be too surprised if, in the public interest, they lose that right in order to protect the public or to raise standards of direction as a matter of policy.

Recent governmental policy has sought to promote enterprise and competitiveness, and to control directors' activities through a body of law that is as simple and accessible as possible.[392] To this end the Companies Act 2006 statutory statement of directors' duties has been developed but no guidance has been offered in that statement regarding the point at which a particular director should start to treat creditors rather than shareholders as the risk bearers whose interests are to be taken into account. The judges have to be relied upon to put flesh on such rules. What should be avoided are unexplained divergences of philosophy. Directors cannot rightfully complain if the judges produce laws that are complex; they can complain if the laws are philosophically confused.

---

[392] CLRSG, *Final Report*, 2001, p. vii.

Employees in distress

The insolvency of a company may prove traumatic for employees, especially those who have invested years of effort and skill in the enterprise. A range of outcomes for employees may be triggered by insolvency, and the law, in some respects, seeks to minimise the negative consequences of insolvency for employees. Insolvency law, however, has other interests to look to, notably those of creditors and possibly those of shareholders and the state. Issues of fairness come to the fore, as do considerations of rescue and the design of rules that allow efficient transfers of enterprises.

This chapter begins by outlining how the law treats employees in an insolvency. It then moves to a now familiar set of issues by asking four questions. Do insolvency laws relating to employees lead to efficient rescue processes and corporate operations? Do these laws make best use of employee expertise? Are employees given an appropriate voice within the schemes of accountability that operate in insolvency? Does the law allocate rights to employees that are fair? A further, more general issue is then discussed: whether insolvency law's conception of the employee evidences a coherent and appropriate philosophy.

A preliminary issue, however, has to be dealt with: the scope of the term 'employee' for the purpose of insolvency protections. A starting point here is that, in order to claim priority as an employee, a person must be employed under a contract of service with the company rather than, say, operate as an independent contractor.[1] The courts, moreover, will consider a number of factors in assessing whether a person is an employee or not, factors that include: whether the person is under the control of another or an integral part of another organisation; whether they are in business on their own account; and the economic reality of the relationship with the

---

[1] A. Keay and P. Walton, *Insolvency Law: Corporate and Personal* (2nd edn, Jordans, Bristol, 2008) p. 469; K. Wardman, 'Directors and Employee Status: An Examination of Relevant Company Law and Employment Law Principles' (2003) 24 Co. Law. 139; *Re CW & AL Hughes Ltd* [1966] 1 WLR 1369.

alleged employer.[2] As for the status of a director, it appears that a non-executive director who acts on his own account cannot be a company employee[3] but that an executive director may be. In the *Bottrill* case,[4] it was said that where a director held a controlling interest in the company, this did not rule out his being an employee but was merely one factor to be taken into account. Directors who were controlling owners have been held not to be employees in certain instances[5] but, in the *Nesbitt* decision of the Employment Appeal Tribunal,[6] a husband and wife with written employment contracts, salaries, a 99 per cent shareholding and a history of managing the company were held to be employees. The Tribunal stated that a majority shareholding and directorship did not affect a person's status as an employee unless the company was a 'mere simulacrum'.[7] Further guidance from the Employment Appeal Tribunal came in *Clark v. Clark Construction Initiatives Ltd*[8] when the Tribunal pointed to three sets of circumstances in which it might be legitimate not to give effect to an allegedly binding contract of employment: where the company was a sham; where the contract was entered into for an ulterior reason (e.g. to secure a statutory payment); and where the parties did not in fact conduct their relationship according to the terms of the contract. *Clark* also listed factors that might be considered in deciding whether to give effect to a contract of employment and emphasised: that the onus rested on the party seeking to deny the contract; that a controlling shareholding, or role as founder of, lender to, or guarantor of the company, did not rule out a contract of employment; and that a history of acting in accordance with the contract was a strong indicator of its validity. Factors that militated against attributing the status of employee included: not acting in accordance with the alleged employment contract and a failure to reduce the terms of the contract to writing.

---

[2] *Ivey* v. *Secretary of State for Employment* [1997] BCC 145, 146. Other relevant factors mentioned in *Ivey* are whether there is mutuality of obligation between the person and the alleged employer and the respective bargaining powers of the person and the alleged employer. (In *Montgomery* v. *Johnson Underwood Ltd* (*The Times*, 9 March 2001) the Court of Appeal indicated that an employee must be under the control of the employer.)

[3] Keay and Walton, *Insolvency Law*, p. 470.

[4] *Secretary of State for Employment* v. *Bottrill* [1999] BCC 177.

[5] *Brooks* v. *Secretary of State for Employment* [1999] BCC 232.

[6] *PG Nesbitt & AE Nesbitt* v. *Secretary of State for Trade and Industry* (UKEAT/0091/07/DA), [2007] IRLR 847.

[7] See also *Lee* v. *Lee's Air Farming Ltd* [1961] AC 12 PC (NZ).

[8] [2008] IRLR 364. See R. Parr, 'A Lifeline for the Controlling Shareholder Director?' (2008) 21 *Insolvency Intelligence* 108.

Protections under the law

At common law, employees are merely unsecured creditors of a company but a company's directors may be entitled to consider employee interests when dealing with corporate troubles. Thus, in *Re Welfab Engineers Ltd*[9] the directors of a troubled company sold it on terms that they hoped were conducive to the business's survival as a going concern and the court held that, in doing so, it was lawful for the directors to take such employment considerations into account.[10]

The Insolvency Act 1986 provisions on preferential debts are also of some assistance to employees.[11] In chapter 14 it was noted that these provisions give preferential priority to unpaid wages and accrued holiday pay owed.[12] The effect is that such payments are payable out of the available assets of the company in advance of unsecured claims and claims secured by floating charges but after relevant insolvency expenses and other secured claims. In addition, however, two pensions debts are treated as preferential.[13] Unpaid employee contributions are preferential to the extent of sums deducted from pay by the employer in the last four months but not yet paid to the pension scheme. There is no ceiling limit set on the amount that can be preferential under this heading. In the case of unpaid employer contributions, the preferential status is limited, firstly, to amounts owing in the last twelve months to a contracted-out occupational pension scheme[14] and, secondly, to the amount of the national insurance rebate applicable. The preferential amount is thus restricted to a percentage of relevant earnings.[15]

---

[9] [1990] BCC 600.

[10] See also the Court of Appeal decision in *Re Saul D Harrison & Sons plc* [1994] BCC 475.

[11] Insolvency Act 1986 s. 386 and Sch. 6.

[12] Insolvency Act 1986 Sch. 6, Category 5 (limited, in the case of pay arrears, to payments due regarding the four months before the relevant date (up to a maximum of £800) under Sch. 6 para. 9(b)); Insolvency Proceedings (Monetary Limits) Order 1986 (SI 1986/1996).

[13] Insolvency Act 1986 Sch. 6, Category 4. See D. Pollard and I. Carruthers, 'Pensions as a Preferential Debt' (2004) 17 *Insolvency Intelligence* 65.

[14] The preferential status thus does not attach to sums owing to personal pensions or non-contracted-out schemes.

[15] Pollard and Carruthers ('Pensions as a Preferential Debt') thus calculate that, on 2003–4 figures, the maximum preferential amount *per* employee would be £1,240 – if the employee had earned over the upper earnings limit of £30,940.

A second, and often more productive, source of statutory protection flows from employment law and the social security system.[16] Employees of a company which has entered insolvency proceedings are entitled to claim against the state National Insurance Fund on the terms set out in the Employment Rights Act 1996 ss. 166–70 and 182–90. These provisions enable employees to claim in respect of unpaid arrears of wages (for up to eight weeks at up to £330 per week),[17] notice pay, holiday pay, the basic award for unfair dismissal compensation, any statutory redundancy pay and any award made by an industrial tribunal for failure to consult with representatives of the workforce. The effect is that if the Secretary of State/National Insurance Fund makes any payments to employees the National Insurance Fund is then subrogated, by statute, to the rights of the employees against the insolvent employer (including their rights as preferential creditors).[18]

From the employee's point of view, the advantages of the National Insurance Fund route are that National Insurance Fund entitlements are guaranteed as opposed to preferred.[19] Employees are thus certain to be paid such entitlements in full (up to the statutory limit) even if the insolvent employer has no funds. They are also spared the delays involved in allowing insolvency processes to run their full course in meeting their preferential claims and they avoid the danger that the claims of fixed charge security creditors will exhaust the insolvency estate before the preferential claims come to be dealt with.[20]

---

[16] See, for example, L. Clarke and H. Rajak, '*Mann* v. *Secretary of State for Employment*' (2000) 63 MLR 895; H. Collins, K. Ewing and A. McColgan, *Labour Law Text and Materials* (2nd edn, Hart, Oxford, 2005) ch. 10.

[17] Employment Rights Act 1996 s. 186(1)(a); Employment Rights (Increase of Limits) Order 2007 (SI 2007/3570), increasing, *inter alia*, the maximum compensatory award for unfair dismissal to £63,000 and the maximum amount of a week's pay (for calculating the basic or additional award for unfair dismissal or redundancy payment) to £330.

[18] The law here implements EC Directive 80/987/EEC on the approximation of the laws relating to the protection of employees in the event of the insolvency of their employer. For an example of such a claim see *McMeechan* v. *Secretary of State for Employment* [1997] ICR 549 (CA). On the European aspects (and when a company is in insolvency) see *Mann* v. *Secretary of State for Employment* [1999] IRLR 566 (discussed by Clarke and Rajak, '*Mann* v. *Secretary of State*'); Collins *et al.*, *Labour Law*, pp. 1028–33; *Everson and Barrass* v. *Secretary of State for Trade and Industry and Bell Lines Ltd (in liquidation)* [2000] IRLR 202 (ECJ).

[19] Claimants on the National Insurance Fund do, however, have to establish their redundancy claims before a tribunal: see R. Morgan, 'Insolvency and the Rights of Employees' [1989] *Legal Action* 21.

[20] See Clarke and Rajak, '*Mann* v. *Secretary of State*', p. 89, who also noted the danger that increasingly wide drafting of fixed charges tended to reduce the value of statutory preferential status; see further ch. 9 above.

Employees are also protected by a series of laws that conduce to the continuation of their paid employment. When the employer company becomes insolvent, prospects of payment diminish. If the company remains the employer during rescue attempts, the employees' claims for wages are protected by the priority rules already noted. Where, however, an administrator becomes their employer, in relation to adopted contracts, sums due regarding 'wages or salary' are payable ahead of the claims of secured creditors and even ahead of the administrator's own remuneration and expenses.[21] The administrator will be indemnified by the secured creditor and the effect is to give retained workers 'super-priority' for their wages. Under the Insolvency Act 1986, Schedule B1, paragraph 99(5) no account is taken of actions taken in the first fourteen days of the administration when assessing whether the administrator has adopted a contract. This provision gives fourteen days of grace in which an administrator can decide whether and how to effect a rescue. Adopting employee contracts preserves employment and makes the administrator the guarantor of the wages but the 'super-priority' rule also means that the administrator risks his expenses.

What the phrase 'wages or salary' covers for the purposes of paragraph 99(5) has been considered by the courts. In *Re Allders Department Stores Ltd*,[22] Lawrence Collins J stated that, when contracts of employment were terminated after adoption, redundancy and unfair dismissal payments were not 'wages or salary' under paragraph 99.[23] This was not the view taken at first instance in *Huddersfield Fine Worsteds*[24] but the Court of Appeal, in the same case,[25] ruled that, in spite of the changes to the wording of section 19 of the Insolvency Act as it was transformed into

---

[21] I.e. secured creditors holding floating charges: Insolvency Act 1986 Sch. B1, para. 99(3)(b) and 99(4)(b). Para. 99(6) states that 'wages or salary' includes sums due regarding holiday pay (or in lieu of holiday pay), illness or good cause absence, periods that would be treated as earnings under a social security enactment, and contributions to occupational pension schemes. For a discussion of employee claims and the respective legal liabilities of companies and insolvency practitioners see D. Pollard, 'Personal Liability of an Insolvency Practitioner for Employee Claims', Parts 1 and 2 (2007) 10 *Insolvency Intelligence* 145, (2008) 11 *Insolvency Intelligence* 7.

[22] [2005] 2 All ER 122, [2005] BCC 289.

[23] See H. Lyons and M. Roberts 'Administration Expenses – Friday Afternoon Drafting and the Rescue Culture' (2005) 16 *Sweet & Maxwell's Company Law Newsletter* 1; G. Stewart, 'Legal Update' (2005) *Recovery* (Summer) 6.

[24] *Krasner (Administrator of Globe Worsted Co. and Huddersfield Fine Worsteds Ltd) v. McMath* [2005] BCC 896.

[25] The joined case: *Re Huddersfield Fine Worsteds Ltd, Re Ferrotech Ltd and Re Granville Technology Group Ltd* [2005] BCC 915.

paragraph 99 of Schedule B1,[26] there was no significant change of priorities regarding employment liabilities and that protective awards under section 189 of the Trade Union Labour Relations (Consolidation) Act 1992 were not payable in priority to the expenses of the administration.[27] Such awards were not sums covered by the term 'wages or salary' per paragraph 99(6).[28] It was clear that, in taking this view, the Court of Appeal was mindful that a construction of the statute that rendered the adoption of employment contracts more expensive would undermine the rescue culture by tending to lead the administrator to dismiss workers during the first fourteen days of the administration rather than to keep them on and seek to implement a strategy of continued trading.[29]

---

[26] Notably, introducing (in para. 99(6)(d)) the reference to liabilities 'treated as earnings under an enactment about social security'. For a critique of the revised (and confused) wording resulting from the transposition of s. 19 to paragraph 99 see Neuberger LJ in *Re Huddersfield Fine Worsteds* and Lyons and Roberts, 'Administration Expenses – Friday Afternoon Drafting and the Rescue Culture'.

[27] In *Day v. Haine* [2007] EWHC 2691 (Ch) the High Court stated that employees who become entitled to a protective award *after* the onset of liquidation cannot claim against their employer or liquidator. Their only remedy is against the Secretary of State for BERR under the Employment Rights Act 1996: see R. Nicolle, 'Employee Rights in a Restructuring' (2008) *Recovery* (Spring) 37.

[28] The respondents failed on another front also. The court stated that there were two conditions for super-priority: the sum had not only to be 'wages or salary', it had also to be a 'liability arising under a contract of employment'. A protective award under the employment protection legislation at issue did not, according to the court, arise from a contract of employment.

[29] Echoing the approach of Lord Browne-Wilkinson in *Powdrill v. Watson* [1995] BCC 319, 330; [1995] 2 AC 394, 443–4, who spoke of not impeding the rescue of viable businesses through 'imponderable liabilities to employees': see Lyons and Roberts, 'Administration Expenses – Friday Afternoon Drafting and the Rescue Culture'. See also A. Walters, 'The Impact of Employee Liabilities on the Administrator's Decision to Continue Trading' (2005) 26 Co. Law. 321: 'It is plausible to suggest that the decisions in *Allders* and *Huddersfield* are entirely in tune with the spirit of the insolvency legislation'; cf. R. Parr and N. Bennett, 'The Rescue Culture v. Collective Employment Rights' (2005) 18 *Insolvency Intelligence* 156: 'A victory for common sense? Well, yes, if you are a supporter of the rescue culture. But there will be those who support the European approach to the enhancement of collective employment rights who wouldn't agree. They will see [the Court of Appeal *Huddersfield*] decision as giving administrators the green light to ride roughshod over the rights of employees of an insolvent company. (In *Powdrill v. Watson* the Court of Appeal had given 'super-priority' not only to wages payable for the period for which notice of termination of employment should have been given, but also for holiday pay for the period before the appointment of the administrator. The Insolvency Act 1994 quickly amended s. 19 (the predecessor to para. 99) to limit administrators' liabilities to wages or salary or occupational pension payments in respect of services rendered wholly or partly after the adoption of the contract (s. 19(6)–(8)) (holiday and sick pay were deemed wages or salary for such purposes).) See also ch. 9 above.

Another set of laws covers the situation in which there is a sale of the company or part of the business: a sale that might be made as part of a rescue operation or the realisation of assets by the liquidator, administrator or receiver. Employees in such scenarios may be faced with new owners who wish to vary terms of employment, close down some units or downsize by dismissing a portion of the workforce. General employment laws cover workforce reductions and variations of contract and will not be discussed here.[30] Mention must, however, be made of the Transfer of Undertakings (Protection of Employment) Regulations 1981 (hereafter 'old TUPE') which implemented the European Acquired Rights Directive 77/187[31] and the Transfer of Undertakings (Protection of Employment) Regulations 2006 (hereafter 'TUPE') which replaced and revoked the old TUPE Regulations and came into force on 6 April 2006.[32]

The original Acquired Rights Directive of 1977 was designed to preserve the contractual rights of employees on a transfer of their employing business[33] and, as a result, the old TUPE regulations were introduced by a 'reluctant' government.[34] They affected transfers in insolvency and non-insolvency situations. Before the introduction of old TUPE, a

---

[30] See generally Collins *et al.*, *Labour Law*.

[31] Transfer of Undertakings (Protection of Employment) Regulations 1981 (SI 1981/1794). On 'old' TUPE see, for example, R. Eldridge, 'TUPE Operates to Damage Rescue Culture' (2001) *Recovery* (September) 21; S. Frisby, 'TUPE or not TUPE? Employee Protection, Corporate Rescue and "One Unholy Mess"' [2000] 3 CFILR 249; J. Armour and S. Deakin, 'Insolvency, Employment Protection and Corporate Restructuring: The Effects of TUPE' (ESRC Centre for Business Research, Cambridge, Working Paper No. 204, June 2001); H. Collins, 'Transfer of Undertakings and Insolvency' (1989) 18 Ins. LJ 144; P. L. Davies, 'Acquired Rights, Creditors' Rights, Freedom of Contract and Industrial Democracy' (1989) 9 *Yearbook of European Law* 21.

[32] The new TUPE Regulations (SI 2006/246) are intended to give effect to Directive 23/ 2001, which amends the original Acquired Rights Directive (77/187/EEC). See generally M. Sargeant, 'TUPE – The Final Round' [2006] JBL 549; D. Pollard, 'TUPE and Insolvency, I and II' (2006) 19(6) *Insolvency Intelligence* 81 and (2006) 19(7) *Insolvency Intelligence* 102; and on the history of TUPE see R. Henry, 'Application of the Proposed TUPE Regulations to Insolvency Proceedings' (2005) 22 *Sweet & Maxwell's Company Law Newsletter* 1.

[33] On the definition of a 'transfer', the construction of 'identity', the effect of amending Directive 98/50/EC and contracting out, see Case C-172/99, *Oy Liikenne Ab* v. *Pekka Liskjarvi and Pentti Juntunen* [2001] IRLR 171 (ECJ) and P. L. Davies, 'Transfers: The UK Will Have to Make Up its Own Mind' (2001) 30 Ins. LJ 231. See also V. Shrubsall, 'Competitive Tendering, Out-sourcing and the Acquired Rights Directive' (1998) 61 MLR 85.

[34] See David Waddington MP, Under-Secretary of State for Employment, HC Debates, vol. 14, col. 680.

business transfer terminated all employment contracts under the common law[35] and employees of insolvent companies that were involved in a transfer were able to rely only on their preferential claims or their access to the National Insurance Fund. The purchaser of a going concern sale of an insolvent business was, accordingly, not liable for the acquired rights of its employees. Following old TUPE, matters were different. Under Regulation 5 of old TUPE (now TUPE Regulation 4) a transfer of an undertaking passed contracts of employment over to the transferee and previously employed persons became employees of the transferee under the same terms and conditions as were set out in their initial contracts.[36] Unsatisfied liabilities of the transferor also passed to the transferee.

The TUPE Regulations of 2006 keep in place the rights and obligations of old TUPE but some revised wordings are used (in efforts to clarify the law and in reflection of post-1981 case law) and some changes are effected by TUPE 2006 – notably to widen the scope of the Regulations to cover cases where services are outsourced, insourced or assigned by a client to a new contractor.[37] A stated purpose of the new regulations is to provide some relief from the transfer of liabilities in a formal insolvency so that some liabilities will be met by the National Insurance Fund instead of passing to the transferee.[38] New provisions thus make it easier for insolvent businesses to be transferred to new employers and new rules set down the ability of employers and employees to agree to vary contracts of employment where a relevant transfer occurs.[39] A new duty is also imposed on the old transferor to supply information about the transferring employees to the new transferee employer.[40] Fresh provisions also set down the circumstances in which it is unfair for

---

[35] *Nokes* v. *Doncaster Amalgamated Collieries* [1940] AC 1014.

[36] Under Regulation 7 of old TUPE and Regulation 10 of TUPE, an employee's right to participate in an occupational pension scheme does not carry over to the transferee under Regulations 5 and 6 of old TUPE or Regulations 4 and 5 of TUPE. See generally D. Pollard, 'Pensions and TUPE' (2005) 34 *Industrial Law Journal* 127 and the discussion below on the protections for employees offered by the Pensions Act 2004.

[37] See TUPE Regulation 3.

[38] See TUPE Regulation 8 and below. The effect is that the state subsidises transfers in potential rescue situations: see R. Dhindsa, 'The Draft TUPE Regulations and Insolvency' (2006) 19 *Insolvency Intelligence* 8; Sargeant, 'TUPE – The Final Round'.

[39] See TUPE Regulation 9. A person's contract of employment will not transfer if the individual informs the transferor or the transferee that he or she objects to being so transferred: see TUPE Regulation 4(7); *Hay* v. *George Hanson* [1996] IRLR 427; *New ISG Ltd* v. *Vernon and Others* [2007] EWHC Ch 2665; J. McMullen, 'The "Right" to Object to Transfer of Employment under TUPE' [2008] 37 Ins. LJ 169.

[40] See TUPE Regulations 11 and 12.

employers to dismiss employees for reasons connected with a relevant transfer.

TUPE has, however, been roundly criticised as being badly drafted and 'bringing confusion to new heights'.[41] A core difficulty concerns the definitions of different kinds of insolvency proceedings – upon which much depends. Transfers that are effected in the context of a formal insolvency are governed by two sets of provisions depending on the type of insolvency procedure involved.[42] Regulation 8(1)–(6) deals with insolvency proceedings 'opened in relation to the transferor not with a view to the liquidation of the assets of the transferor and which are under the supervision of an insolvency practitioner'.[43] In these 'relevant insolvency proceedings' certain of the transferor's debts to employees will not pass over to the transferee but will be satisfied out of the National Insurance Fund. Thus, regarding employees who pass over to the transferee, and notwithstanding the non-termination of their employment, the National Insurance Fund will meet payments due under the insolvency provisions of the Employment Rights Act 1996.[44] In the case of employees who have been dismissed by reason of the transfer – and therefore dismissed unfairly – the debts that the National Insurance Fund will meet are those payable as statutory redundancy pay by the Secretary of State under the insolvency and redundancy provisions of the Employment Rights Act 1996.[45]

In the case of proceedings that (in the terms of TUPE Regulation 8(7)) have been 'instituted with a view to the liquidation of the assets of the transferor and are under the supervision of an insolvency practitioner' Regulations 4 and 7 do not apply and there is, accordingly, no automatic

---

[41] See Lord Hunt of Wirral in House of Lords Debates, 3 May 2006 (8 p.m.); S. Bewick, 'TUPE 2006 – A Missed Opportunity' (2006) 3 *International Corporate Rescue* 228; M. Rollins, 'Technical Update' (2006) *Recovery* (Summer) 11.

[42] See TUPE Regulation 8.

[43] The Employment Appeal Tribunal has ruled, in *Secretary of State for Trade and Industry v. Slater* [2008] BCC 70 that, for Regulation 8(6) or 8(7) to apply, the transfer must take place after the date on which the insolvency proceedings have commenced (which was to be identified with reference to the statutory provisions governing the start of the particular process) and, also, when those proceedings have come under the supervision of an insolvency practitioner – which, in the case at issue, was not until he was appointed liquidator.

[44] That is (according to the Guidance of the Redundancy Payments Directorate): arrears of pay, holiday pay, sums due for failures to give statutory minimum periods of notice, and basic awards for unfair dismissal, subject to statutory limits under the Employment Rights Act 1996 s. 182.

[45] These provisions give effect to Article 5(2) of Directive 23/2001.

passing of rights and obligations under employment contracts to the transferee. Nor are dismissals made by reason of the transfer automatically deemed to be unfair.

Regulation 9 of TUPE enlarges the scope for the transferor and/or transferee varying the terms of employment contracts before or after the transfer takes place. Thus, variations can be allowed where the sole or principal reason is the transfer itself or a reason that is connected with it which is not an economic, technical or organisational reason and is designed to safeguard employment opportunities by ensuring the survival of the whole or part of the undertaking.[46] Such variations must be agreed with representatives of the employees.

As for dismissals of employees because of the relevant transfer, TUPE Regulation 7 takes the place of Regulation 8(1) of old TUPE and states that employees will be deemed to have been unfairly dismissed if the sole or principal reason for dismissal is the transfer, or a reason connected with it that is not an 'economic, technical or organisational' (ETO) reason entailing changes in the workforce of the transferor or transferee 'before or after the relevant transfer'.[47]

The insolvency implications of old TUPE depended a great deal on the courts. One central issue was whether the purchaser of an insolvent business could avoid inheriting employee liabilities if the IP, acting as agent of the transferor company, effected dismissals prior to the transfer. Matters here turned on the construction of the phrase 'employed immediately before the transfer' in old TUPE Regulation 5(3) (a phrase repeated in TUPE Regulation 4(3)). An opportunity to avoid employee-related obligations was provided by the *Spence* case[48] where the Court of Appeal held that an employee dismissed three hours in advance of a transfer was not employed 'immediately before' that event. The House of Lords, however, took a different view in *Litster*[49]

---

[46] Regulation 9 responds to the inflexibility of the old TUPE Regulations: in *Wilson* v. *St Helens Borough Council* [1999] 2 AC 52 the House of Lords held that if employees were transferred on a relevant transfer under (old) TUPE, their terms and conditions could not be varied lawfully for a reason connected with the transfer, regardless of their consent or the period of time between the transfer and the variations of terms. See further Dhindsa, 'Draft TUPE Regulations and Insolvency'.

[47] TUPE Regulation 7(2).

[48] *Secretary of State for Employment* v. *Spence* [1986] ICR 651. But see *Bork International A/S* v. *Foreningen 101/87* [1988] ECR 3057, [1990] 3 CMLR 701 (ECJ rules that if a worker is dismissed before transfer at the behest of the transferee, and in breach of Article 4(1), the worker is regarded as being employed at the time of transfer).

[49] *Litster* v. *Forth Dry Docks and Engineering Co. Ltd* [1990] 1 AC 546. See also *Re Maxwell Fleet Facilities Management Ltd (No. 2)* [2000] 2 All ER 860.

where there was an hour's gap between dismissal and transfer. Their Lordships focused on the purpose of the Acquired Rights Directive – which they said was to ensure the protection of the acquired rights of employees – and accordingly read old TUPE Regulation 5(3) in the light of old TUPE Regulation 8(1). The effect was to add to the words 'employed immediately before the transfer' the phrase 'or would have been so employed if he had not been unfairly dismissed in circumstances described in Regulation 8(1)'.[50] The new TUPE Regulation 4(3) follows *Litster* (only dropping the word 'unfairly' and renumbering the referenced regulation) by using the phrase 'or would have been so employed if he had not been dismissed in circumstances described in Regulation 7(1)'.

A further complication flows from Regulation 7(2) of TUPE, which (like old TUPE Regulation 8(2)) offers the employer a defence. The dismissal will not be unfair if, as already noted, there was an 'economic, technical or organisational reason' for it (the ETO defence).[51] The courts have held, regarding old TUPE Regulation 8(2), that improving the price of a sale will not constitute such a reason and have tended to look for a justification connected with the prospects of operating the business as a going concern.[52] The courts have thus developed case law relevant to TUPE Regulations 4 and 7[53] but, from the IP's point of view, a concern is

[50]   See Frisby, 'TUPE or not TUPE?', p. 256; Lord Oliver in *Litster* [1990] 1 AC 546 at 563A–B. Cases subsequent to *Litster*, such as *Re Maxwell Fleet Facilities Management Ltd (No. 2)* [2000] 2 All ER 860, also indicated that where a hive-down had taken place in an effort to avoid the transfer of employment liabilities, the courts would treat the device unsympathetically and apply the *Litster* approach. The courts would thus ensure that where dismissals were made prior to the eventual transfer of the hive-down vehicle, the employment liabilities would pass through to the ultimate transferee. (In a hive-down it is usual to transfer the viable parts of the business to a subsidiary of the insolvent company and to seek to sell that subsidiary as a 'clean commercial package': see Davies, 'Acquired Rights', pp. 32–3.)

[51]   See, for example, Eldridge, 'TUPE Operates to Damage Rescue Culture', p. 20.

[52]   See Pollard, 'TUPE and Insolvency, II'; *Whitehouse v. Charles A. Blatchford & Sons Ltd* [2000] ICR 542 (CA); *Wheeler v. Patel and J. Goulding Group of Companies* [1987] ICR 631 (EAT); *Gateway Hotels Ltd v. Stewart* [1988] IRLR 281 (EAT). See also *Dynamex Friction Ltd and Ferotec Realty Ltd v. Amicus and Others* [2008] EWCA Civ 381, where the Court of Appeal held that dismissals of staff made by an administrator because of lack of funds were made for a genuine economic reason, and not a reason connected with a transfer, notwithstanding that the business was subsequently sold to companies controlled by the former director. On the approach of the ECJ see *Abels v. Administrative Board of the Bedrijfsvereniging voor de Metaal-Industrie en de Electrotechnische Industrie* (Case C-135/83) [1987] 2 CMLR 406; *Jules Dethier Equipment SA v. Dassy* (Case C-319/94) [1998] ICR 541.

[53]   See, for example, Frisby, 'TUPE or not TUPE?'; Pollard, 'TUPE and Insolvency, I and II'; Collins *et al.*, *Labour Law*.

that this is bedevilled by uncertainties on a number of points: for instance, regarding the ETO defence and the connection between a dismissal and the transfer.[54] Such a practitioner would, in an ideal world, be able to calculate the reliability of any TUPE-avoiding measures and his or her exposure to potential employee claims. The DTI/BERR, moreover, has not decided to determine precisely the extent to which TUPE will apply to different insolvency procedures and this means that insolvency practitioners have to rely on uncertain developments in case law. It should also be stressed that whether TUPE will apply to a process will be an important factor in selecting which procedure to follow and will impact considerably on the practitioner's ability to attract a purchaser of the troubled company or business. On present evidence, that practitioner is faced with a legal state of affairs that is uncertain and far from ideal.[55]

Turning to TUPE and the position of pension rights following a transfer, Regulation 10 stipulates that rights and obligations relating to occupational pensions schemes do not carry forward to transferees. The Pensions Act 2004 sections 257 and 258, however, introduced new pension protections with respect to transfers of employment that come within the terms of TUPE.[56] Regarding transfers after 6 April 2006 to which TUPE applies, transferees are required to offer transferred employees a minimal level of pension provision if they had, immediately before the transfer, enjoyed access to an occupational pension scheme with an employer contribution element. The transferee may choose whether to offer a defined benefit scheme of a defined standard or a money purchase scheme to which the employer contributes at a specified rate.[57] Immediately before the transfer the transferring employee must be either an active member of the scheme; eligible to be such a member; or potentially such a member if employed by the transferor for a longer period. The 2004 Act protections, however, only apply to future benefit accruals – they do not protect benefits that relate to service before the

---

[54] Frisby, 'TUPE or not TUPE?', p. 259, for instance, asserts: 'Both insolvency practitioners and transferees will never be entirely certain whether "financial constraints" dismissals will be adjudged to be unconnected to a transfer.'

[55] See, for example, Pollard, 'TUPE and Insolvency, I and II'; M. Sargeant, 'Business Transfers and Corporate Insolvencies: The Effect of TUPE' (1998) 14 IL&P 8; Eldridge, 'TUPE Operates to Damage Rescue Culture', p. 20.

[56] See D. Pollard, 'Pensions and TUPE'; S. Bewick, 'Pensions – A Roadmap for Users' (2006) *Recovery* (Winter) 16.

[57] See Transfer of Employment (Pension Protection) Regulations 2005 (SI 2005/649) for stipulations regarding the minimal standards of schemes.

transfer, the rights and obligations regarding which remain with the transferor. What the 2004 Act does involve, for prospective purchasers of troubled companies, is the prospect of having to bear a minimum level of future pension obligations and the need to investigate, before purchasing, the transferor's pension schemes, the contribution levels of employees and the relevant waiting periods. Obligations to match the contributions of the employee up to a maximum of 6 per cent of the employee's salary will have to be factored into financial plans.[58]

For employees, the Pensions Act 2004 brought not merely the above TUPE-related protections but also those offered by the Pensions Regulator and the Pension Protection Fund (PPF). The latter fund became operational on 6 April 2005 and provides compensation to employees who are members of eligible defined benefit schemes if the employer becomes insolvent and the scheme is underfunded.[59] To be covered by the PPF the scheme must be an eligible one and must not have commenced winding up before 6 April 2005; the employer must be insolvent, its scheme funded below the PPF level of benefits, and the IP must have issued a scheme failure notice stating that a scheme rescue is not possible. In the alternative, the trustees of the fund must have applied to the Board of the PPF to assume responsibility for the scheme because it appears that the employer is unlikely to continue as a going concern; or the Pensions Regulator must have notified the Board that the employer is unlikely to continue as a going concern.

The Pensions Regulator became operational on 6 April 2005 also and is responsible, *inter alia*, for protecting pension benefits, reducing the risk of claims on the PPF and promoting the good administration of pension schemes.[60] The powers of the Pensions Regulator include measures designed to reduce the 'moral hazard' whereby employers may seek to avoid their pension obligations at the expense of the PPF. Thus, the Pensions Regulator is able to require employers to make contributions or

---

[58] See Pollard, 'Pensions and TUPE', p. 139.

[59] See Pensions Act 2004 Part 2; R3, Technical Bulletin, No. 70, May 2006. Prior to 6 April 2005 employees' pensions were protected by the Government's Financial Assistance Scheme. On the merits and otherwise of the PPF and discussion of other options see B. Shaw, 'Occupational Persions Trusts' (2008) *Recovery* (Autumn) 40.

[60] Since 30 December 2005 it has been the case that each scheme has to meet a statutory funding objective – as detailed in the relevant regulations (the Occupational Pension Schemes (Scheme Funding) Regulations 2005 (SI 2005/3377)). The Regulator also issued a code of practice, 'Funding Defined Benefits', in December 2005.

give financial support to a scheme[61] and to issue financial support directions that are designed to prevent employers avoiding pension debts by using group structures.[62]

Insolvency practitioners are obliged to give various notifications in order to assist in the operations of the Pensions Regulator and the PPF. The IP must, thus, notify the Board of the PPF, the Regulator and the trustees of the relevant pension scheme of his appointment and his ceasing to act.[63] Under section 120 of the Pensions Act 2004, the IP must notify the same parties when an 'insolvency event' occurs in relation to an employer who operates an occupational pension scheme.[64] After such an event, the IP must also inform these parties about the status of the scheme – including his view on whether a rescue of the scheme is possible. For such purposes, an 'insolvency event' means, in essence, the commencement of any insolvency process other than a members' voluntary liquidation.[65] The IP who acts within his duties is not, however, subject to the Pensions Regulator's power to require contributions or financial support.

Efficiency

In assessing whether the law's treatment of employees leads to efficiency in insolvency processes, it is necessary to keep the efficiency question

---

[61] S. 38 of the Pensions Act 2004 empowers the Pensions Regulator to issue a contribution notice requiring a person to make good a shortfall under a scheme – and for such purposes a person made liable may be an employer or a person connected with, or an associate of, the employer. The circumstances allowing the use of this power include those where the Regulator is of the opinion that the person was party to an act (or deliberate failure to act) the main purpose of which was to prevent the recovery of a debt which might become due from the employer in relation to the scheme. On 15 April 2008 the Government announced that it would strengthen this power by, *inter alia*, removing the need for the Regulator to prove intent to avoid properly funding the scheme, taking away the employer's 'good faith' defence and allowing reference to the resources of the group of companies in judging whether a financial support direction should be made (see R3 Members' News, 17 April 2008).

[62] Occupational Pension Schemes (Scheme Funding) Regulations 2005, Regulation 6.

[63] See s. 22 of the Pensions Act 1995 (as modified by the Pensions Act 2004).

[64] The notice must be given within fourteen days of the event or the date when the IP becomes aware of the scheme. The notice will trigger an 'assessment period' during which the Board of the PPF will determine whether the PPF will cover the scheme. On the low number of s. 120 notices and the growing problem of 'orphan pension sehemes' see D. Toms, 'Pensions: Another Ticking Time Bomb for Insolvency Practitioners' (2008) *Recovery* (Spring) 36.

[65] See Pension Protection Fund (Entry Rules) Regulations 2005 (SI 2005/590) and Pension Protection Fund (Entry Rules) Amendment Regulations 2005 (SI 2005/2153).

separate from the issue of fairness or distributional justice. Central fairness questions (to be returned to below) are whether employees' acquired employment rights should be recognised and, if so, whether creditors, the state or other parties should bear the associated costs. Key efficiency questions are whether the law conduces to low-cost rescues or realisations (and distributions) of the insolvent company's assets and whether the law creates economically inefficient distortions in the allocation of resources. In answering these questions it is necessary to bear in mind the broad array of employees' protections outlined above, though this discussion will focus centrally on the TUPE regulations.

A first point to make is that the changes made with the TUPE Regulations 2006 can be seen as rescue friendly in so far as they leave the social security system to pick up a portion of the debts that the transferring company owes to employees. Such a state funding of some transfer costs will, however, not be an option under Regulation 8(6) when there is a mere liquidation of assets of the transferor, and this consideration may incline creditors and insolvency practitioners towards rescue. Where the social security system does take on some of the transferor's liabilities, this can be expected to make the transferred business more valuable and attractive to a purchaser and, again, to encourage creditors and administrators to look more favourably on rescue options than they would otherwise do. The costs of effecting rescue may, moreover, be lowered overall if it is assumed that a clear legal undertaking to pay certain debts out of the National Insurance Fund will involve lower transaction costs than would be incurred by leaving the parties to contest liabilities of this kind.

It can be said, secondly, that employee protections may in some circumstances conduce to the efficient negotiation of insolvency solutions. As indicated, the system of employee 'super-priority', the rules on contract adoption, the set of employment protections and, in particular, the TUPE regulations, will sometimes operate to encourage key employees to stay with a troubled company and to help it out of its troubles. This may prove more efficient than a position in which employees rush for the door and companies that might have been turned around and rescued are liquidated. As commentators have argued: 'The first step to assist a corporate rescue is to induce the retained workforce to continue to work. Employees will be reluctant to help, however, unless they receive a better assurance that they will receive their wages than a promise from an insolvent company.'[66]

---

[66] Collins *et al.*, *Labour Law*, p. 1034.

Protections for employees may also help to shore up morale. It has been noted that office holders tend to fear that employees who feel that a business is doomed will have a propensity to withdraw co-operation or will be likely 'to develop mysterious illnesses' or simply be liable not to apply very much effort once they know that they are certain to be made redundant.[67] Similarly, some protective rules, notably those on employee consultation, may encourage the successful pursuit of solutions. As Armour and Deakin have commented: 'On the positive side, TUPE provides a basis on which a designated representative of the employee – either the recognised trade union or unions in the enterprise concerned, or the default representatives provided for by statute – has the power to enter into negotiations with the employer over the terms on which the restructuring may take place.'[68]

Contrary to this optimistic view, however, are ranged a number of objections. In response to the argument that TUPE encourages rescue by shielding the transferee from liabilities, it can be cautioned that the reforms under discussion are modest and that much more could have been done to encourage rescue.[69] TUPE provides that basic awards for unfair dismissal are paid out of the National Insurance Fund but compensatory awards for unfair dismissal (which will often dwarf other liabilities) will still pass over to the transferee – a situation that may deter the potential purchasers of troubled companies who are likely to fear not merely the quantum of such compensatory awards but their indeterminacy.[70]

Uncertainties in the law may be another concern because they tend to raise transaction costs, produce solutions inefficiently and render rescues more difficult. Present TUPE regulations, as indicated above, are uncertain in so far as it is difficult for a transferor or a transferee to judge whether redundancies made pre- or post-transfer in order to reduce a

---

[67] Armour and Deakin, 'Insolvency, Employment Protection and Corporate Restructuring', p. 37.

[68] Ibid., p. 46. See also the arguments for employees' participation in M. Armstrong and A. Cerfontaine, 'The Rhetoric of Inclusion? Corporate Governance in Insolvency Law' [2000] Ins. Law. 38.

[69] See Bewick, 'TUPE 2006 – A Missed Opportunity'.

[70] Ibid., where it is suggested that in a typical case (of average earnings and ten years of service) the quantum of liabilities that do not transfer under TUPE is likely to be exceeded tenfold by that of transferring liabilities. Collins notes the role of Regulations 11 and 12 in seeking to control the uncertainties confronting potential purchasers through mandating the notification by the transferor to the transferee of information regarding potential liabilities to employees: Collins et al., Labour Law, para. 10.44.

wage bill will produce costs to transferees following the application of Regulations 4 and 7.[71] Special difficulty, as indicated, attends the definitions of different kinds of insolvency proceedings – which are crucial in deciding whether transfers of rights occur. The source of the difficulty with TUPE on this point is that the definitions of procedures used are derived from the imprecise language of the Directive and it is not certain which UK procedures are referred to – or even whether reference should be made to the type of procedure involved or the outcome of the given procedure that is anticipated in a particular context.[72] Not only that, but the BERR Guidance Note on TUPE does not take the same view on these points as the 2006 DTI Redundancy Payments Directorate's Guidance.[73]

A second issue is whether (leaving uncertainties aside) shifting acquired rights costs onto the purchasers of insolvent companies does indeed obstruct rescues and thereby impede efficiency. Here much depends on the particular circumstances.[74] In cases where there is no prospect of rescue, acquired rights have no effect. In instances where there is a clear case for a going concern sale, acquired rights are likely not to affect the rescue although purchasers will discount the price paid in reflection of their expected liabilities to employees (a solution principally raising issues of fairness rather than efficiency). In some cases, however, the transfer of acquired rights will mean that an office holder will raise more through a break-up sale than by selling as a going concern to a buyer who will make an offer that is acquired rights discounted. Armour

---

[71] On the predecessor regulations 5 and 8 see G. Morris, 'Transferring Liability for Employee Claims' [2000] JBL 188; Frisby, 'TUPE or not TUPE?', pp. 265–6, where an interviewee is quoted as calling TUPE 'one unholy mess'; Sargeant, 'Business Transfers and Corporate Insolvencies'; Armour and Deakin, 'Insolvency, Employment Protection and Corporate Restructuring', p. 38.

[72] See Rollins, 'Technical Update'; M. Sargeant, 'More Flexibility for Insolvent Transfers: The Amended Acquired Rights Directive' (1999) 15 IL&P 6. (For example, even administration can be embarked upon with a view to liquidation of some, or all, of the assets of the company: see ch. 9 above.)

[73] See R3, Technical Bulletin, No. 77, November 2006. The view of the DTI Redundancy Payments Directorate (Guidance of 8 June 2006) is that Regulations 4 and 7 will not apply to compulsory liquidations and creditors' voluntary liquidations but (contrary to the statement contained in the BERR Guidance of March 2007) will apply to members' voluntary liquidations (since these are not insolvency proceedings). In administrations, administrative receiverships and voluntary arrangements, the NIF will meet payments owed to transferring employees under the insolvency provisions of the Employment Rights Act.

[74] See Armour and Deakin, 'Insolvency, Employment Protection and Corporate Restructuring', pp. 25–39.

and Deakin thus quote as 'largely representative' the following comment from a party experienced in the conduct of administrations and administrative receiverships: 'The Acquired Rights Directive I think is bad news for employees because it makes businesses harder to sell and therefore jobs harder to rescue ... [A]t the margin I'm sure there are cases where the businesses didn't sell because of the burdens that the purchaser would have had to take on.'[75]

The 2006 reforms of TUPE were designed to make transfers more attractive to purchasers but, as noted, liabilities for unfair dismissal compensatory payments continue to pass to transferees and this may mute the rescue-enhancing effects of the 2006 regulations. Whether the process of protecting acquired rights actually impedes rescue rather than merely reduces sale price may, again, depend on a number of considerations, such as the number of employees involved, the length of their service and the quality and timing of information possessed by the potential purchaser.[76]

A further issue alluded to above is whether the overall effect of TUPE is economically inefficient when the National Insurance Fund pays out for redundancies in circumstances where continuing employment for some of the workforce would have lowered net costs.[77] On this point, the DTI consultation of 2001 argued that the benefits of rescue-enhancement were 'expected to outweigh the relatively modest additional "deadweight" costs' in insolvency payments from the National Insurance Fund.[78] A danger, however, is that, since employees, under TUPE, will not be able to recover unfair dismissal compensation from the National Insurance Fund and will carry this forward to the transferee, this may induce IPs to engage routinely in pre-transfer dismissals.[79] On this last point, however, something may turn on the information possessed by the IP. If the quality of information is high, it might be hoped that the IP would assess the need to dismiss or retain on the (acceptable) basis of the employee's value to the

---

[75] Ibid., p. 31. The European Court of Justice considered this issue in the case of *Abels* v. *Administrative Board of the Bedrijfsvereniging voor de Metaal-Industrie en de Electrotechnische Industrie* (Case-135/83) [1987] 2 CMLR 406.

[76] Frisby, 'TUPE or not TUPE?', p. 265.

[77] Ibid, p. 264.

[78] DTI, *TUPE: Government Proposals for Reform: Public Consultation Document* (DTI, 2001, URN 01/1133), para. 30. (Some costs would be offset by savings in benefit payments to employees who lost their jobs on liquidation.)

[79] A concern expressed by Frisby, 'TUPE or not TUPE?', p. 268. Cost to the state would, however, be limited in the DTI's proposed regime as the National Insurance Fund only pays up to statutory limits.

ongoing business. On grounds of certainty there may be a case for this version of state-funded acquired rights rather than one in which proof of an 'objective' case for dismissal is a precondition of the National Insurance Fund's paying for acquired rights costs rather than the transferee.[80] A more pessimistic view of the IPs' motivation might, however, suggest a tendency to take advantage of 'tactical' dismissals: which might involve, for example, the shedding of senior staff and replacing them with more junior personnel possessing fewer acquired rights.

Expertise

The law would contribute to the best use of employee expertise at times of trouble if it induced loyalty on the part of those employees whose expertise is necessary to ensure an efficient sale or rescue. As the law stands, however, the employees of a troubled company are confronted by all of the uncertainties described above and they will tend to be far less well equipped than transferors, IPs or transferees to assess their levels of job security or the financial risks they would run if they decided to stay with the company. From the narrow perspective of employee expertise, therefore, the case for measures to increase certainty can be made with special force. Here, again, therefore, there may be an argument for the state to bear acquired rights costs. Such a set up would, as noted, allow IPs and other involved parties to assess whether there is a case for dismissal on legitimate economic grounds. There is liable to be far greater consistency between that process of reasoning and the employee's deliberations on his or her value to the firm than between the latter deliberations and an employee's assessment of the security that he or she is likely to derive from the statutory and case law on acquired rights.

Accountability

Are employees given an appropriate voice within the schemes of accountability that operate in insolvency procedures? Insolvency law, together with employment law, protects that voice in a number of respects.[81] First, the law on unfair dismissal requires a 'reasonable'

---

[80] Frisby, 'TUPE or not TUPE?', p. 269, suggests that uncertainties involved in distinguishing 'objective', or justifiable, dismissals from others can be reduced by introducing a rebuttable presumption that a dismissal is not justifiable.

[81] See Collins *et al.*, *Labour Law*, pp. 1059–69.

employer to engage in consultation with an individual employee prior to dismissal and, where the employee is represented by an independent union recognised by the employer, that reasonable employer will also give as much warning as possible to the union and consult the union as to the best way to achieve the desired result with minimum hardship to employees.[82] The law on unfair dismissal thus can collectivise worker participation in decisions about economic dismissals, but this depends on there being a relevant union and an employee may not enjoy such rights if the tribunal is satisfied that the outcome would not have differed had consultation been conducted.[83] A second protection derives from the Trade Union and Labour Relations (Consolidation) Act 1992 ss. 188–98 which provide that if an employer proposes to dismiss twenty or more workers at one establishment for economic reasons, he or she must consult in good time with representatives of the workforce[84] with a view to agreeing ways of avoiding or reducing dismissals or mitigating the consequences of dismissal. Failure to comply with this requirement may result in a tribunal making a protective award[85] to the dismissed employee.

A third source of employee process rights covering the sale of a business is TUPE. The TUPE Regulations 2006 oblige the employer (transferor and transferee) to inform affected employees' representatives in advance about a transfer and its implications.[86] The employer must consult and consider representations from a recognised trade union or (in the absence of a union) other workforce representatives with a view to seeking their agreement on intended measures affecting employees. Failure to observe these requirements to inform and consult may mean that the employer has to pay 'appropriate' compensation to affected employees.[87] TUPE Regulation 5 also states that collective agreements shall be preserved in effect across a company transfer where those

---

[82] *Williams* v. *Compair Maxam* [1982] ICR 156 (EAT).

[83] Where an employer fails to act in a reasonable manner procedurally and this does not affect the outcome, the unfairly dismissed employee will often, at the discretion of the tribunal, receive no compensation in excess of the redundancy payment (*Polkey* v. *A. E. Dayton Services Ltd* [1988] ICR 142 (HL)). This development 'subverts the procedural protections dramatically, because the employer can usually argue extremely plausibly that workforce reductions were inevitable': Collins *et al.*, *Labour Law*, p. 1063.

[84] Who may be the recognised trade union or (in the absence of one) elected representatives. For an example of an award for failure to consult on redundancies as required by s. 188 see *Hutchins* v. *Permacell Finesse Ltd* (UKEAT/0350/07/CEA).

[85] Consisting of wages for the period during which proper consultation should have taken place.

[86] TUPE Regulation 13.   [87] TUPE Regulation 15.

agreements are made by or on behalf of the transferor and a trade union recognised by the transferor in respect of an employee whose contract of employment is preserved by TUPE. Trade union recognition is similarly preserved by Regulation 6.

Overall, the effect of these provisions is to give employees a voice – but, perhaps, only a modest one – in insolvency.[88] As has been stated: 'The notion that the workforce should routinely participate in managerial decisions that might affect their livelihoods seems like a distant peak on the horizon of British industrial relations ... The culture of British management seems to be one of preferring to keep strategic decisions confidential and to regard business reorganisations as part of the managerial prerogative.'[89]

Employee rights, then, hardly impinge on the governance of insolvency processes[90] but they may have some effects. The TUPE obligations of consultation are backed up by potentially punitive provisions and this creates an incentive for managers to collectivise negotiations in troubled times. This may lower the cost of planning and implementing new strategies,[91] which may bring a number of further advantages.[92] It may facilitate planning reorganisations. It may increase employee loyalty, by offering reassurance, and help avoid the destructive effects of industrial action. A further gain from listening to the worker voice may be that expertise and knowledge within the workforce may be tapped, so that more efficient or fairer ways of realising reorganisational objectives may be arrived at. The co-operation of the workforce may also result in financial assistance: where, for example, employees make wage concessions in an effort to make a turnaround work. Finally, there may be social gains from consultation. If employees are given advance notice of reorganisations, they may find new jobs, retrain, retire or take other steps that will lower the overall impact of an insolvency on society.

Such advantages suggest that (assuming transaction costs can be kept modest) there is a case in efficiency terms for strengthening the voice of

---

[88] See B. Cheffins, *Company Law: Theory, Structure and Operation* (Clarendon Press, Oxford, 1997) p. 574; Armstrong and Cerfontaine, 'Rhetoric of Inclusion?', p. 40.

[89] Collins *et al.*, *Labour Law*, p. 1066.

[90] See Armour and Deakin, 'Insolvency, Employment Protection and Corporate Restructuring', p. 17.

[91] Collectivising negotiations may lower costs in so far as employers can deal with the unions or worker representatives rather than engage in protracted individual negotiations.

[92] See Collins *et al.*, *Labour Law*, p. 1060.

employees within insolvency processes and reorganisation procedures. With reference to fairness also it can be argued that it is socially just to increase the voice of those parties who have committed their efforts and working lives to the enterprise.[93] It is, indeed, to issues of fairness that we should now turn.

Fairness

Is insolvency law's application of employee rights fair? In answering this question we may ask whether the acquired rights of employees should be recognised and, if they are to be recognised, who should bear the cost of compensating the employees of insolvent companies. (In this discussion we might note that the issues are similar whether the transfer is made via a liquidator, a receiver or an administrator.)[94] On the recognition issue, responses may vary according to different ways of conceptualising the employee. One vision of the employee sees him or her as merely another unsecured creditor. As was seen in chapter 14, however, there is a case, even within such a vision, for giving employees rights that are superior or preferential to those of other unsecured creditors. It would be unfair, for instance, not to recognise that employees are especially high-cost risk bearers who tend to enjoy modest levels of information and have very limited abilities to adjust rates or negotiate terms so as to reflect risks.[95] Such protections as are offered by the Insolvency Act 1986 section 175's preferential treatment for employees' accrued wages and the 'super-priority' given to employees' wage and payment claims in administration under the Insolvency Act 1986 Schedule B1, paragraph 99, are, for the time being, on this view, justified.

Another approach, however, might treat the employee not as some species of unsecured creditor but as a stakeholder who has an entitlement to rights and protections that derives from his or her contribution to the assets of the company.[96] That contribution, it could be argued, is

[93] See C. Villiers, 'Employees as Creditors: A Challenge for Justice in Insolvency Law' (1999) 20 Co. Law. 222

[94] See Davies, 'Acquired Rights'.

[95] See S. S. Cantlie, 'Preferred Priority in Bankruptcy' in J. Ziegel (ed.), Current Developments in International and Comparative Corporate Insolvency Law (Clarendon Press, Oxford, 1994).

[96] See Armstrong and Cerfontaine, 'Rhetoric of Inclusion?'; G. Bastin and P. Townsend, 'Should We Make the Redundancy Scheme Redundant?' (1996) 17 Co. Law. 252; J. Pound, 'The Rise of the Political Model of Corporate Governance and Corporate Control' (1993) 68 NYU L Rev. 1003.

different in kind from that of an individual who supplies finance or goods to the company. Labour and working commitment, on this view, are factors that create superior moral claims based on desert and contribution as well as need.[97] A similar argument can be made in implied contractual terms. Employees, it could be said, are engaged with the company on the basis of implicit expectations of careers, continuing prospects and pensions and these expectations should be recognised by insolvency law.[98]

A comparative perspective on these issues can be achieved by looking across the Channel. In France, a series of reforms followed the election of Mitterand's socialist government in 1981. These promulgated a strong participatory model of the employee.[99] This model fully recognised the employee as a 'participant' in the company, in good times as well as bad. Indeed, the more a company experienced difficulties, the more the employee representative institutions enjoyed a voice and powers of action. Employees possessed rights not only to be informed and consulted but to influence decision-making. The judges, moreover, endorsed this vision so that employee representatives in France have been treated as an organ comparable to the board of directors or the general meeting.[100] In 1985 the legislature made employees' interests part of the 'interests of the company', and employee representative institutions were entitled to intervene very extensively as participants in insolvency procedures.[101]

---

[97] See Villiers, 'Employees as Creditors', p. 229; D. R. Korobkin, 'Rehabilitating Values: A Jurisprudence of Bankruptcy' (1991) 91 Colum. L Rev. 717; Korobkin, 'Contractarianism and the Normative Foundations of Bankruptcy Law' (1993) 71 Texas L Rev. 541; Korobkin, 'The Role of Normative Theory in Bankruptcy Debates' (1996–7) 82 Iowa L Rev. 75; M. Walzer, *Spheres of Justice* (Basil Blackwell, Oxford, 1995); J. Finnis, *Natural Law and Natural Rights* (Clarendon Press, Oxford, 1980); P. Shuchman, 'An Attempt at a "Philosophy of Bankruptcy"' (1973) 21 UCLA L Rev. 403; A. Gewirth, *The Community of Rights* (University of Chicago Press, Chicago, 1996).

[98] See K. Van Wezel Stone, 'Labour Markets, Employment Contracts and Corporate Change' in J. McCahery, S. Picciotto and C. Scott (eds.), *Corporate Control and Accountability* (Clarendon Press, Oxford, 1993); M. O'Connor, 'Restructuring the Corporation's Nexus of Contracts: Recognizing a Fiduciary Duty to Protect Displaced Workers' (1991) 69 North Car. L Rev. 1189.

[99] See Armstrong and Cerfontaine, 'Rhetoric of Inclusion?'.   [100] Ibid., p. 42.

[101] Law 85–98 of January 1985, Article 10. See now Law 2005–845 of 26 July 2005 on the preservation of enterprises and P. J. Omar, 'French Insolvency Law and the 2005 Reforms' (2005) 16 *International Company and Commercial Law Review* 490; Omar, 'The Position of Employees in French Insolvency Law' (1996) 7 *International Company and Commercial Law Review* 394. When a petition for insolvency is considered by the

Employee participation is firmly entrenched in France but it has not proved a panacea for troubled companies since insolvency tends to be a small company problem and to occur where employee representation is non-existent.[102] It may be the case that further steps are required to assist SMEs but proponents of the French system urge the strong ethical basis of the participatory model, as 'social justice has an imperative quite independent of efficiency rationales'.[103]

If it is accepted that employees have acquired rights that should be recognised in an insolvency, who should pay? When such acquired rights are passed onto transferees who discount the prices that they pay for troubled firms, the costs of acquired rights are, as noted, liable in practice to be borne by the secured creditors of the insolvent company.[104] These creditors are the parties who stand to take the lion's share of the residual estate and they will be the first to suffer from a strict transfer of acquired rights. If, on the other hand, rights do not transfer, the state and taxpayer (through the National Insurance Fund) will compensate those employees who lose their jobs (though payments are subject, in practice, to limitations). In discussing efficiency we saw that (if low levels of 'tactical' dismissals can be assumed) there may be a case for state funding of acquired rights protections on the grounds that this will reduce uncertainty. Is such a solution fair to the taxpayer though?

A risk-based analysis might raise difficult questions here. It is arguable that the state is an involuntary creditor who may find it easy to spread risks but who is very ill-placed to monitor and influence risk taking and who will not reap the benefits of risk taking. It could be argued that it would be unfair to burden taxpayers for these reasons and that it would be more equitable to burden creditors with employee-related costs. Creditors, especially the banks, are, after all, not only efficient risk spreaders but they are parties who advance loans voluntarily, can adjust

---

court the court is obliged to hear the representations of the employees' representatives: see Omar, 'Position of Employees'; but see *French Republic* v. *Klempka (administrator of ISA Daisytek SAS)* [2006] BCC 841 reversing the decision of the Court of Appeal of Versailles which had accepted the argument that proceedings issues in the UK were against French public policy as they failed to protect the rights employee representatives would have had (to a hearing) under French law.

[102] Armstrong and Cerfontaine, 'Rhetoric of Inclusion?', p. 44.

[103] Ibid. It should be noted, though, that a shift towards strengthening the position of creditors has taken place in France: see Law 94–475 of 10 June 1994 and Omar, 'French Insolvency Law and the 2005 Reforms'.

[104] And by unsecured creditors if assets are sufficient to satisfy secured creditors' claims and leave a fund.

their terms to perceived risks, are well informed and stand to benefit (at least through interest mechanisms and sales of ancillary bank services) from the profits made by the enterprise. There are, however, some reasons why the state can be said to enjoy the benefits of risk taking and should be prepared on grounds of fairness to fund acquired rights. Entrepreneurial risk taking will be encouraged by such funding and this will conduce to wealth creation which in turn will benefit the state in many ways.[105] It would allow rescues and redistributions to occur in a lower friction manner than would be possible under a regime demanding that creditors should bear such costs. This may prove fair to taxpayers in so far as there is a return to the state for its efforts: the lower friction regime of enterprise would be likely to produce, overall, greater wealth for the state.

On both efficiency and fairness fronts, it seems there is a case for state funding of acquired rights in two situations.[106] First, if the anticipated incidence of abuse through 'tactical' dismissals is reasonably small – and outweighed by gains in net wealth creation – it would be sensible to fund *all* insolvency-related dismissals from state sources. If, however, the likelihood of such abuse is high, it will be necessary to distinguish, at lowest cost, between objectively necessary dismissals (which would be state funded) and unjustifiable or 'tactical' dismissals (which would not be paid for by the National Insurance Fund). Guidance on these choices can best be derived from research into the severity of risks that state funding might be abused and into the potential of new laws and processes (such as reversals of proof)[107] to reduce the uncertainties and transaction costs that flow from efforts to separate economically necessary from unjustifiable dismissals.

Conclusions

Employees are in some ways the lost souls of insolvency law. Their working contributions are the lifeblood of companies, yet the law does remarkably little to involve them in insolvency procedures. This is

---

[105] Amongst other things there would, as noted above, be savings on National Insurance Fund benefit payments where rescues are effected.

[106] On the (attractive) case for socialising employee claims, see Davies, 'Acquired Rights', p. 53.

[107] See Frisby's suggestion (noted above) of lowering costs by applying a rebuttable presumption that a dismissal is not objectively necessary where dismissal and re-engagement occurs pre- and post-transfer: Frisby, 'TUPE or not TUPE?', p. 269.

because the law has failed to develop on the basis of a coherent and appropriate conception of the employee. On the one hand, insolvency law sometimes sees the employee as a creditor who merits a certain amount of protection. On the other, he or she is occasionally treated in a manner consistent with the rhetoric of stakeholding. Policies on employees, moreover, are driven, in relation to some issues, by considerations of economic efficiency yet on others they are shaped by reference to ethical and social justice arguments. The way to resolve such difficulties is, first, to develop a solid informational and research base so that the implications of dealing with employees in different ways can be calculated rather than guessed at. Some of the works referred to in this chapter offer evidence that the foundations of such research are now being laid. Much more work needs to be done, however, before reliable judgements can be made on issues such as the role of employee loyalty within rescues; the quality of information that tends to be available to potential parties to rescue; or the role played by employee representatives in designing and achieving turnarounds. Second, there needs to be greater clarity not merely about the objectives of insolvency law as a whole, but about the conception, nature and extent of employees' rights in the corporation. Finally, and building on these developments, there needs to be a greater openness (even political honesty) regarding the trade-offs of risks, values and interests that are involved in insolvency law.[108] This means that tensions between the interests of shareholders, creditors, employees, the state and other stakeholders have to be confronted rather than hidden away.

---

[108] See, for example, Armstrong and Cerfontaine, 'Rhetoric of Inclusion?', p. 45 and the authors' attack on (the then) DTI approaches as 'tinkering'.

18

Conclusion

In some ways corporate insolvency law has come a long way since the Cork Report.[1] Numerous statutes, court decisions and administrative reforms have sought to develop the law so as to remedy deficiencies and secure newly appreciated needs. In the new millennium, the UK Government has shown a renewed desire to attune insolvency laws to the requirements of enterprise while, at the same time, avoiding abuses and injustices. In other ways, however, corporate insolvency law can be seen, to date, as an area marked by missed opportunities and modest achievements. It has, first, failed to develop as an organised, consistent and purposeful body of rules and processes. This has been a legal sector in which Cork's prescriptions were cherry-picked and where, subsequently, particular issues have been dealt with piecemeal by both legislators and judges. Corporate insolvency law has, secondly, been developed without close co-ordination with relevant legal sectors and processes. It has not been linked sufficiently tightly with company law – in spite of its relevance to the ongoing needs of healthy companies – nor has it been tied in with an analysis of the arrangements for providing finances for companies that are found in the UK. As was made clear in chapter 3, corporate insolvency law is faced with a pattern of corporate funding that is dictated very largely by the legal frameworks that govern the provision of credit, notably those relating to security and quasi-security. To design insolvency law without looking at those arrangements is to cut the cloth without measuring the client.

A third deficiency is that this has been an area of law that has developed without a consistent guiding philosophy. As was stressed in chapter 12, different procedures have been developed on the basis of inconsistent assumptions not only about the values and objectives that are properly to be pursued, but also about the potential and roles of the different actors that are involved in insolvency processes. Directors and

---

[1] *Report of the Review Committee on Insolvency Law and Practice* (Cmnd 8558, 1982).

employees are central figures in corporate insolvency law and processes, but the law is based on notions of directorial roles and employee rights that are multiple, inconsistent and competing. This has led to a host of confusions, uncertainties, inefficiencies, unfairnesses and misplaced accountabilities. The broad end-product has been a system of corporate insolvency law that has offered, for much of the period since Cork, not so much a choice of processes that pull together harmoniously as an ill-organised array of procedures that, in many respects, have undermined each other.

There may be signs, though, that matters have improved in recent years. The Enterprise Act 2002, for instance, went some way to harmonise processes when it ended the potential for deploying receivership so as to ride roughshod over other corporate insolvency mechanisms such as administration and company voluntary arrangements. UK insolvency law has, moreover, embraced the rescue culture as a framing objective of insolvency law and it has espoused a generally collectivist approach to insolvency processes with the establishing of the post-Enterprise Act administration procedure.

The challenges facing insolvency lawyers and practitioners are, however, as acute now as they have ever been and a host of rapid changes has altered the nature of insolvency practice. As noted in the Introduction, much more 'insolvency work' is now being carried out prior to the institution of any formal insolvency process and the growing use of devices such as the 'pre-packaged' administration demand that we pay increasing attention to the quality of informal procedures for dealing with corporate troubles. New and acute questions have arisen concerning the efficiency, accountability and fairness of those procedures and actors that are encountered in the 'twilight zone' of insolvency. A related concern may be the level of expertise that is brought to bear by the new corporate distress specialists who operate in the shadows of insolvency.

The development of the 'new capitalism' has also imposed new strains on the world of insolvency. As sources of credit have become more disparate, and as the ever more complex packaging of debt has lowered the transparency of lending, it has become increasingly difficult to rely on the old assumptions that have traditionally underpinned insolvency processes. Thus, it can no longer be assumed that a dominant bank lender will be present to monitor and organise a company's attempts to turn its affairs around. Similarly, the 'London Approach' to rescue has been taken to breaking point by the difficulties of securing essential undertakings across ever larger numbers of lenders with increasingly divergent natures and interests. In such a world of change, the unavoidable danger is that the rules of insolvency law – even if they are coherent and satisfactory – will not be able to exert real control in those areas of activity where the real decisions are being made. Nor can it be assumed that such a danger will be less acute after the credit crisis has passed. The credit crisis of 2007–8 and aftermath may stimulate the taking of steps to increase the transparency of credit-related transactions. There may be new regulatory reforms that are designed to render the credit markets more stable, but such responses are unlikely to reduce the number and variety of parties who provide financing in the 'new capitalism'.

To return to insolvency law's need to mesh with other legal domains, consistency of philosophy means not only that insolvency law has to be characterised by purpose and direction but that company and employment laws need to be both internally coherent and consistent with insolvency law. The chapter 16 and 17 discussions of directors and employees give an indication of the dangers and challenges being confronted here. To give a simple example, it is of little value to design insolvency laws that are rescue friendly if laws on employment protection offer strong disincentives to the corporate transfers that are necessary to keep businesses alive.

The returns from philosophical consistency are, moreover, important. At various points throughout this book it has been argued that legal uncertainties produce high costs, inefficiencies and unfairnesses. It might be responded, though, that laws can never be certain, that judges have to apply rules to differing circumstances, and that judges need to adjust criteria, standards and rules to cope with changes in such matters as business practices and ways of setting up commercial relationships. There is, however, an important distinction to be drawn between the unavoidable uncertainties that flow from the factors just noted and the unnecessary uncertainties that arise because inconsistent philosophies are vying with each other in driving legal developments. If, for example, punitive approaches to company direction are sustained in competition with public protection philosophies (or if rescue-oriented and creditor protection responses are set against each other) a great deal of uncertainty will unnecessarily arise if there is no set of overarching principles that indicates which of the competing approaches will prevail in which circumstances, or what balance between the approaches is appropriate.

It is philosophical consistency – within and across the areas of insolvency, company and employment law – that offers such guiding principles. This, it should be emphasised, does not mean that a single substantive blueprint has to be laid down – in a changing world such blueprints rapidly pass their sell-by dates. What is required is an approach that confronts competitions between values and objectives and explains how these can be understood and argued out. It is the ability to explain – and so to understand and predict – that reduces uncertainties.

This book has set out to respond to these questions of philosophical deficiency. It has done so, first, by making out the case for an 'explicit values' approach to the design and evaluation of corporate insolvency processes. This is an approach that is applicable to all corporate insolvency procedures and encourages the development of mechanisms that are consistent in so far as they link to a common philosophy and to a limited number of identifiable values. Second, this book has set out to examine not merely the formal rules of corporate insolvency law but also the procedures, actors and institutions that give substance to the law as an aspect of corporate life and decline. The law, after all, does not achieve a great deal if formal rules are harmonious but confusions and inconsistencies of approach pervade the processes and institutional structures that are needed to implement these rules. Attending to procedures, actors and institutions means that difficult questions have to be tackled concerning not merely the substantive and procedural rights of individuals, groups and firms but also the capacities and incentives of these parties to deliver the appropriate levels of managerial skill and commitment to rescue or winding-up processes. The return from coming to grips with these issues is that corporate insolvency law can be assessed and redesigned with an eye to operational matters and not merely to the formal rules.

A third way of responding to the current problems that are encountered in the law has been to examine whether the assumptions that underpin existing laws, procedures and institutions need to be challenged so that new ways of conceiving rules, processes and actors are necessary if an explicit values approach is best to be served.

The chapters above have presented arguments in favour of a number of changes that seem likely to lead to gains in efficiency, expertise, accountability or fairness without unduly negative side-effects. On the financing of corporate organisations, current arrangements involve significant dangers that transfers of insolvency wealth will be effected from unsecured to secured creditors and to parties who are well equipped to make use of quasi-security devices. Such transfers, where they occur, may prejudice healthy companies' needs as well as the interests, in insolvencies, of certain creditor classes (notably the unsecured trade creditors). Procedures could and should be adopted to allow unsecured creditors to inform themselves more easily about the risks they are running when they provide credit. This is not a complete answer for all unsecured creditors but it is a step that will help reduce inefficiencies and unfairness with regard to certain parties.

As for the system of priorities that insolvency law establishes, this is rendered uncertain and confused by the capacity of 'creditors' to employ quasi-security devices such as retention of title clauses. Steps could be taken to reduce such confusions and, in turn, to lower general transaction costs. Thus, for example, a more rigorous approach to the registration of retentions of title would increase transparency and reduce the costs of borrowing by lowering the levels of financial uncertainty that creditors face when providing funds.

Turning to the major actors in corporate insolvency processes – the IPs – it has been argued above that there is no strong case for reforms to replace IPs with court officials or civil servants. There may be good grounds, however, for tightening the mechanisms used to regulate IPs, for rethinking the breadth of the duties that IPs owe in insolvency procedures and for subjecting IP regulation to more rigorously independent oversight. Where, moreover, much insolvency work is being undertaken informally by non-IPs there is a need to monitor, on an ongoing basis, the activities of turnaround specialists and those other parties who impact on corporate troubles. The hanging question is whether it makes sense for the law to control IPs tightly and yet leave unregulated a series of practitioners who engage in work of a similar nature and impact.

Current governmental endorsements of a rescue orientation in corporate insolvency procedures are to be welcomed but the discussion of rescue in chapters 6 to 12 revealed considerable scope for improvements in present arrangements. First, there is a need for harmonisation so that different rescue procedures do not undermine each other – so that, for instance, the use of 'pre-packs' does not allow the sidestepping of those procedural protections and balances that are established by the law governing post-Enterprise Act administrations. Efficiency in rescues may also be served by giving directors greater incentives and capacities to resort to rescue procedures before the company's chances for turnaround have evaporated. Thought should be given, for instance, to ending the requirement, in the Insolvency Act 1986 Schedule B1, paragraph 11(a) that a court must be satisfied that a company is, or is likely to become, unable to pay its debts before it can make an administration order. Consistent assumptions ought also to be made across rescue procedures concerning the roles of different actors such as directors or IPs. Such assumptions, moreover, should be based not on traditions of deference or unexplored notions of culpability but on a considered analysis of factors such as informational position; training; incentives; specialist knowledge of the relevant market; ability to assess financial options; and commitment to rescue.

Accountability within rescue procedures should, again, be ensured in reflection of a philosophy that is consistent across procedures. To this end, the use of pre-packs, again, may prompt the observer to ask whether such processes allow vulnerable creditors properly to hold decision-makers to account and to bring an appropriate voice to bear on proceedings. There may also be a case for reconsidering whether shareholders should be excluded from the approval process in Schedule B1 administrations when insolvency is merely likely. Such an exclusion may not be fairness-enhancing and it may, similarly, be argued that fairness demands that the interests of employee stakeholders should be reflected in greater access to, or recognition in, the decision-making processes governing administration.

As far as the substantive principles governing post-insolvency contributions are concerned, it is collectivity and the *pari passu* principle that have long occupied centre stage as regards residual assets. *Pari passu* has, however, been subjected to a variety of exceptions and bypassing arrangements. The Crown preference has been abolished but the case for revising the rules on set-off is one not to be dismissed. It is difficult to support proposals for giving consumer creditors increased priority – largely because it is so difficult to distinguish 'consumer' from 'trade' creditor vulnerability – but employees can, for the moment, be identified as the creditor group most deserving of special treatment because of their status as non-adjusting, high-cost risk bearers. On replacing the *pari passu* principle with another approach to distribution of the residual assets, it has been argued that alternatives that involve assessing the individual position or merits of the creditor would give rise to much uncertainty and would involve both inefficiencies and unfairnesses. New approaches to the definition of creditor classes face severe difficulties in dealing with heterogeneities within the memberships of such redefined classes and there would be problems in showing why such newly favoured classes would have claims that are stronger than those of competing classes.

It has been emphasised in chapter 15 that *pari passu* only comes into operation once the relevant, residual, insolvency estate has been constructed. Values such as efficiency and fairness have, accordingly, to be pursued in constructing the estate more generally and in establishing protections for 'vulnerable' risk bearers in the form of: procedural requirements (of information provision and disclosure); substantive protections (such as setting the 'prescribed part' at the appropriate level); ways of reducing overall risks of insolvency (for example, by improving directorial standards and training); and ways of spreading insolvency risks and, thereby, lowering risks borne by vulnerable parties.

The position of employees needs to be clarified not merely for the sake of employed persons but so that parties buying and selling companies can do so without excessive costs. A way forward, in the corporate transfer area, may lie through building on the TUPE 2006 Regulations by increasing further the state funding of employees' acquired rights costs in corporate transfers post-insolvency. The law should also move towards a conception of the employee that recognises his or her participatory rights and contributions to the company. The relationship between this conception of the employee and the dictates of economic efficiency should be set out clearly in the law and such a relationship sustained in a consistent manner by the judiciary. As an underpinning to such developments in the law, more research should be undertaken (and state funded) on such matters as the potential role of the employee in rescues. Only against a reliable background of research can legislators, policy-makers, judges or others make informed judgements on implications for employees, other creditors or the variety of affected parties when they are shaping corporate insolvency processes or deciding issues.

As a final conclusion, a return should be made to the nature of the corporate insolvency law philosophy that is being argued for here. The 'explicit values' approach, it should be emphasised, is one that seeks to embrace both the public and private dimensions of corporate insolvency law. It is always difficult to reconcile public interests with those of private contractors, especially where private contractors vary sharply in their economic power, information levels, expertise and so on. A way to effect a 'least-worst' reconciliation, and to argue out the merits of this, is, however, to identify the values that are sought to be furthered within corporate insolvency processes. This, in the first instance, helps us to identify the ways in which different rules, processes and institutional arrangements affect various parties in divergent ways. Greater transparency is thus given to decisions about trade-offs. We can be clearer, for instance, on how much a new statutory requirement might affect small trade creditors compared to large secured bank lenders. Such an approach also helps us to identify more easily the contradictory effects and assumptions that are associated with different processes and arrangements.

If corporate insolvency law is to move forward as a coherent, consistent and purposeful set of rules and processes, it is necessary to rethink a number of its elements in the light of such transparency. Some of those elements have been identified here and one route towards greater clarity of design and evaluation has, I hope, been mapped out in this book.

BIBLIOGRAPHY

Adams, E., 'Governance in Chapter 11 Reorganisations: Reducing Costs, Improving Results' (1993) 73 Boston Univ. LR 581

Adler, B., 'Financial and Political Theories of American Corporate Bankruptcy' (1993) 45 Stanford L Rev. 311

'A World Without Debt' (1994) 72 Wash. ULQ 811

Aggarwal, G., 'Securitisation – An Overview' (2006) 3 *International Corporate Rescue* 285

Aghion, P., O. Hart and J. Moore, 'The Economics of Bankruptcy Reform' (1992) 8 *Journal of Law, Economics and Organisation* 523

'A Proposal for Bankruptcy Reform in the UK', Discussion Paper No. 167 (LSE Financial Markets Group, 1993), also published in (1993) 9 IL&P 103

'Insolvency Reform in the UK: A Revised Proposal', Special Paper No. 65 (LSE Financial Markets Group, January 1995) and in (1995) 11 IL&P 67

Agnello, R., 'Administration Expenses' (2000) *Recovery* (March) 24

Altman, E. I., 'Financial Ratios, Discriminant Analysis and the Prediction of Corporate Failure' (1968) 23 *Journal of Finance* 589

Corporate Bankruptcy in America (D. C. Heath, London, 1971)

Anderson, H., 'Insolvency Practitioners: Professional Independence and Conflict of Interest' in A. Clarke (ed.), *Current Issues in Insolvency Law* (Stevens, London, 1991)

'The Treatment of Trust Assets in English Insolvency Law' in E. McKendrick (ed.), *Commercial Aspects of Trusts and Fiduciary Obligations* (Clarendon Press, Oxford, 1992)

'Receivers Compared with Administrators' (1996) 12 IL&P 54

'Insolvent Insolvencies' (2001) 17 IL&P 87

Anderson, J., 'Receivers' Duties to Mortgagors. Court of Appeal Makes a Pig's Ear of It' (1999) 37 *CCH Company Law Newsletter* 6

Argenti, J., *Corporate Collapse: The Causes and Symptoms* (McGraw-Hill, London, 1976)

Armour, J., 'Share Capital and Creditor Protection: Efficient Rules for a Modern Company Law' (2000) 63 MLR 355

'Who Pays When Polluters Go Bust?' (2000) 116 LQR 200

'Should We Redistribute in Insolvency?' in J. Getzler and J. Payne (eds.), *Company Charges: Spectrum and Beyond* (Oxford University Press, Oxford, 2006)

Armour, J., B. Cheffins and D. Skeel, 'Corporate Ownership Structure and the Evolution of Bankruptcy Law: Lessons from the United Kingdom' (2002) 55 Vand. L Rev. 1699

Armour, J. and S. Deakin, 'Norms in Private Insolvency Procedures: The "London Approach" to the Resolution of Financial Distress' (ESRC Centre for Business Research, Cambridge, Working Paper Series No. 173, September 2000, reprinted in [2001] 1 JCLS 21)

'Insolvency, Employment Protection and Corporate Restructuring: The Effects of TUPE', ESRC Centre for Business Research, Cambridge, Working Paper Series No. 204, June 2001

Armour, J. and S. Frisby, 'Rethinking Receivership' (2001) 21 OJLS 73

Armour, J., A. Hsu and A. Walters, *Report for the Insolvency Service: The Impact of the Enterprise Act 2002 on Realisations and Costs in Corporate Rescue Proceedings* (Insolvency Service, London, December 2006)

'The Costs and Benefits of Secured Creditor Control in Bankruptcy: Evidence from the UK', University of Cambridge Centre for Business Research Working Paper No. 332 (Cambridge, September 2006)

Armour, J. and R. Mokal, 'Reforming the Governance of Corporate Rescue: The Enterprise Act 2002' [2005] LMCLQ 28

Armour, J. and A. Walters, 'Funding Liquidation: A Functional View' (2006) 122 LQR 295

Armstrong, M., '"Return to First Principles" in New Zealand: Charges Over Book Debts are Fixed – But the Future's Not!' [2000] Ins. Law. 102

Armstrong, M. and A. Cerfontaine, 'The Rhetoric of Inclusion? Corporate Governance in Insolvency Law' [2000] Ins. Law. 38

Arnold, G., *The Handbook of Corporate Finance* (Pearson Education, London, 2005)

Arora, A., 'The Human Rights Act 1998: Some Implications for Commercial Law and Practice' (2001) 3 *Finance and Credit Law* 1

Arsalidou, D., 'The Impact of Section 214(4) of the Insolvency Act 1986 on Directors' Duties' (2000) 21 Co. Law. 19

Association of British Insurers, *Investing in Social Responsibility: Risks and Opportunities* (London, 2001)

Austin, R., 'Commerce and Equity: Fiduciary Duty and Constructive Trust' (1986) 6 OJLS 444

'Corporate Groups' in R. Grantham and C. Rickett (eds.), *Corporate Personality in the Twentieth Century* (Hart, Oxford, 1998)

Australian Joint Committee on Corporations and Financial Services, *Corporate Insolvency Laws: A Stocktake* (30 June 2004)

Australian Law Reform Commission, *General Insolvency Inquiry*, Report No. 45 (Canberra, 1988)

Ayer, J., 'Goodbye to Chapter 11: The End of Business Bankruptcy as We Know It' (Mimeo, Institute of Advanced Legal Studies, 2001)

Ayer, J., M. Bernstein and J. Friedland, 'Chapter 11 – "101": Out of Court
    Workouts, Pre-packs and Pre-arranged Cases: A Primer' (2005) 24
    American Bankruptcy Institute Journal (April)
Ayers, I. and J. Braithwaite, *Responsive Regulation* (Oxford University Press, New
    York, 1992)
Bacon, A., 'Administration Costs: Some Welcome News' (2007) 20 *Insolvency
    Intelligence* 1
Bailey, P., 'The Insolvency (Amendment) Rules 2005 – Yet More Changes for
    Insolvency Folk' (2006) 19 *Insolvency Intelligence* 24
Baird, D. G., 'The Uneasy Case for Corporate Reorganisations' (1986) 15 *Journal
    of Legal Studies* 127
    'Loss Distribution, Forum Shopping and Bankruptcy: A Reply to Warren'
    (1987) 54 U Chic. L Rev. 815
    'Bankruptcy's Uncontested Axioms' (1998) 108 Yale LJ 573
Baird, D. G. and T. Jackson, 'Corporate Reorganisations and the Treatment of
    Diverse Ownership Interests: A Comment on Adequate Protection of
    Secured Creditors in Bankruptcy' (1984) 51 U Chic. L Rev. 97
    Cases, Problems and Materials on Security Interests in Personal Property
    (Foundation Press, Mineola, N.Y., 1987)
Baird, D. and E. Morrison, 'Bankruptcy Decision Making' (2001) *Journal of Law,
    Economics and Organization* 356
Baird, D. and R. Rasmussen, 'The End of Bankruptcy' (2003) 55 Stanford L
    Rev. 751
Baird, K. and P. Sidle, 'Cash Flow Insolvency' (2008) 21 *Insolvency Intelligence* 40
Baister, S., 'Remuneration, the Insolvency Practitioner and the Courts' (2006)
    IL&P 50
Bakan, J., *The Corporation: The Pathological Pursuit of Profit and Power*
    (Constable, London, 2004)
Baldwin, R., 'Health and Safety at Work: Consensus and Self-regulation' in R. Baldwin
    and C. McCrudden (eds.), *Regulation and Public Law* (Weidenfeld & Nicolson,
    London, 1987)
    'The Next Steps: Ministerial Responsibility and Government by Agency' (1988)
    51 MLR 622
    Rules and Government (Oxford University Press, Oxford, 1995)
    Understanding Regulation (Oxford University Press, Oxford, 1999)
    'The New Punitive Regulation' (2004) 67 MLR 351
Baldwin, R. and M. Cave, *Understanding Regulation* (Oxford University Press,
    Oxford, 1999)
Baldwin, R., M. Cave and K. Malleson, 'Regulating Legal Services – Time for the
    Big Bang?' (2004) 67 MLR 787
Baldwin, R. and C. McCrudden (eds.), *Regulation and Public Law* (Weidenfeld &
    Nicolson, London, 1987)

Bank of England, Occasional Paper, *Company Reorganisation: A Comparison of Practice in the US and the UK* (Bank of England, 1983)

Finance for Small Firms, Fifth Report (Bank of England, 1998)

Finance for Small Firms, Sixth Report (Bank of England, 1999)

Finance for Small Firms, Eighth Report (Bank of England, March 2001)

Finance for Small Firms, Eleventh Report (Bank of England, April 2004)

Financial Stability Review (Bank of England, 2005)

Financial Stability Review (Bank of England, 2007)

Shocks to the UK Financial System (Bank of England, 2007)

Financial Stability Report – Issue 24 (Bank of England, 2008)

News Release, *Financial Stability Report: Rebuilding Confidence in the Financial System* (28 October 2008)

Bank of England and HM Treasury, *Financial Stability and Depositor Protection: Further Consultation* (Cm 7436) (July 2008)

Bannister, J. and N. Hamilton, 'Future Claims, Present Redress? Schemes, CVAs and Liquidations after *T & N*' (2006) *Recovery* (Summer) 36

Barclay, M. and C. Smith, 'The Priority Structure of Corporate Liabilities' (1995) 50 *Journal of Finance* 899

Bardach, E. and R. A. Kagan, *Going by the Book: The Problem of Regulatory Unreasonableness* (Temple University Press, Philadelphia, 1982)

Barnes, R., 'The Efficiency Justification for Secured Transactions: Foxes with Soxes and Other Fanciful Stuff' (1993) 42 Kans. L Rev. 13

Barton, T., W. Shenkir, P. Walker *et al.*, *Making Enterprise Risk Management Pay Off* (Financial Times/Prentice Hall, London, 2002)

Basel Committee on Banking Supervision, *Sound Practices for the Management and Supervision of Operational Risk* (Bank for International Settlements, Basel, 2001)

Bastin, G. and P. Townsend, 'Should We Make the Redundancy Scheme Redundant?' (1996) 17 Co. Law. 252

BDO Stoy Hayward Survey, reported in (1999) 12 *Insolvency Intelligence* 48

Beale, H., M. Bridge, L. Gullifer and E. Lomnicka, *The Law of Personal Property Security* (Oxford University Press, Oxford, 2007)

Beauchamp, T. and N. Bowie (eds.), *Ethical Theory and Business* (5th edn, Prentice Hall, Upper Saddle River, N.J., 1997)

Bebchuk, L. 'A New Approach to Corporate Reorganisations' (1988) 101 Harv. L Rev. 775

Bebchuk, L. and J. Fried, 'The Uneasy Case for the Priority of Secured Claims in Bankruptcy' (1996) 105 Yale LJ 857

Beck, U., *Risk Society – Towards a New Modernity* (Sage, London, 1992)

Beetham, D., *The Legitimation of Power* (Macmillan, London, 1991)

Belcher, A., 'The Economic Implications of Attempting to Rescue Companies' in H. Rajak (ed.), *Insolvency Law: Theory and Practice* (Sweet & Maxwell, London, 1993)

Corporate Rescue (Sweet & Maxwell, London, 1997)

Belcher, A. and W. Beglan, 'Jumping the Queue' [1997] JBL 1

Beloff, M., 'Judicial Review – 2001: A Prophetic Odyssey' (1995) 58 MLR 143

Benjamin, J., *Financial Law* (Oxford University Press, Oxford, 2007)

Bennett, H. and C. Davis, 'Fixtures, Purchase Money Security Interests and Dispositions of Interests in Land' (1994) 110 LQR 448

Bentley, L., 'Mortgagee's Duties on Sale: No Place for Tort?' (1990) 54 *Conveyancer and Property Lawyer* 431

Berg, A., 'Duties of a Mortgagee and a Receiver' [1993] JBL 213
  '*Brumark Investments Ltd* and the "Innominate Charge"' [2001] JBL 532
  'The Cuckoo in the Nest of Corporate Insolvency' [2006] JBL 22

Bernstein, P., *Against the Gods: The Remarkable Story of Risk* (Wiley, New York, 1996)

Better Regulation Task Force, *Regulation – Less is More* (Cabinet Office, London, 2005)

Bewick, S., 'TUPE 2006 – A Missed Opportunity' (2006) 3 *International Corporate Rescue* 228
  'Pensions – A Roadmap for Users' (2006) *Recovery* (Winter) 16

Bhandari, J. S. and L. A. Weiss (eds.), *Corporate Bankruptcy: Economic and Legal Perspectives* (Cambridge University Press, Cambridge, 1996)

Bhattacharyya, G., 'Shadow Directors and Wrongful Trading Revisited' (1995) 15 Co. Law. 313

Bickle, J., 'Private Equity Investors and the Transformation of Troubled Businesses' (2006) *Recovery* (Summer) 28

Bingham, R., 'Poacher Turned Gamekeeper' (2003) *Recovery* (Winter) 27

Bird, C., 'The London Approach' (1996) 12 IL&P 87

Birks, P., 'Mixing and Tracing' (1992) 45(2) *Current Legal Problems* 69

Black, F., 'Bank Funds in an Efficient Market' (1975) *Journal of Financial Economics* 323

Black, J., 'Constitutionalising Self-Regulation' (1996) 59 MLR 24
  Rules and Regulators (Clarendon Press, Oxford, 1997)
  'Decentring Regulation' (2001) 54 *Current Legal Problems* 103
  'Enrolling Actors in Regulatory Processes: The Example of UK Financial Services Regulation' [2003] PL 62
  'The Emergence of Risk Based Regulation and the New Public Risk Management in the UK' [2005] PL 512

Blackstone, W., *Commentaries on the Laws of England* (8th edn, Clarendon Press, Oxford, printed for W. Strahan, T. Cadell and D. Prince, 1778 (facsimile of 1st edn, 1765–9))

Block-Lieb, S., 'The Unsecured Creditor's Bargain: A Reply' (1994) 80 Va. L Rev. 1989

Bloom, N., *Inherited Family Firms and Management Practices* (Centre for Economic Performance, LSE, London, 2006)

Blumberg, P., *The Multinational Challenge to Corporation Law: The Search for a New Corporate Personality* (Oxford University Press, New York, 1993)

Bodie, C., 'How Private Equity Can Help to Rescue Companies' (2007) *Recovery* (Summer) 28

Bogart, D., 'Unexpected Gifts of Chapter 11: The Breach of a Director's Duty of Loyalty Following Plan Confirmation and the Postconfirmation Jurisdiction of Bankruptcy Courts' (1998) 72 *American Bankruptcy Law Journal* 303

Borrowdale, A., 'Commentary on Austin' in R. Grantham and C. Rickett (eds.), *Corporate Personality in the Twentieth Century* (Hart, Oxford, 1998)

Boshkoff, D. and R. McKinney, 'The Future of Chapter 11' (1995) 8 *Insolvency Intelligence* 6

Bowers, W., 'Whither What Hits the Fan? Murphy's Law, Bankruptcy Theory and the Elementary Economics of Loss Distribution' (1991) 26 Ga. L Rev. 27

'Rehabilitation, Redistribution or Dissipation: The Evidence of Choosing Among Bankruptcy Hypotheses' (1994) 72 Wash. ULQ 955

Boyle, A., 'The Company Law Review and Group Reform' (2002) 23 Co. Law. 35

Boyle, J., J. Birds, B. Clark *et al.*, *Boyle and Birds' Company Law* (6th edn, Jordans, Bristol, 2007)

Bradgate, R., 'Reservation of Title Ten Years On' (1987) Conv. 434

Bradley, C., 'Corporate Control: Markets and Rules' (1990) 53 MLR 170

'Enterprise and Entrepreneurship' (2001) 1 *Journal of Corporate Law Studies* 53

Bradley, M. and M. Rosenzweig, 'The Untenable Case for Chapter 11' (1992) 101 Yale LJ 1043

Branson, D., 'The Rule that isn't a Rule – The Business Judgment Rule' (2002) 36 Valparaiso Univ. LR 631

Bratton, W. W., 'The "Nexus of Contracts Corporation": A Critical Appraisal' (1989) 74 Cornell L Rev. 408

Breyer, S., *Regulation and Its Reform* (Harvard University Press, Cambridge, Mass., 1982)

Briault, C., *The Rationale of a Single National Financial Services Regulator* (FSA Occasional Paper, Series 2, London, May 1999)

Revisiting the Rationale for a Single National Financial Services Regulator (FSA Occasional Paper, Series 2, London, February 2002)

Bridge, M. G., 'Company Administrators and Secured Creditors' (1991) 107 LQR 394

'Form, Substance and Innovation in Personal Property Security Law' [1992] JBL 1

'The *Quistclose* Trust in a World of Secured Transactions' (1992) 12 OJLS 333

'Fixed Charges and Freedom of Contract' (1994) 110 LQR 340

'How Far Is Article 9 Exportable? The English Experience' (1996) 27 Canadian Bus. LJ 196

'The Law Commission's Proposals for the Reform of Corporate Security Interests' in J. Getzler and J. Payne (eds.), *Company Charges: Spectrum and Beyond* (Oxford University Press, Oxford, 2006) p. 267

Brierley, P., 'The Bank of England and the London Approach' (1999) *Recovery* (June) 12

Brierley, P. and G. Vlieghe, 'Corporate Workouts, the London Approach and Financial Stability' [1999] *Financial Stability Review* 168

British Bankers' Association (BBA), *Description of the London Approach* (Mimeo, 1996)

    Banks and Business Working Together (London, 1997)

    Response by the BBA to the Insolvency Service White Paper, Insolvency – A Second Chance (2001)

    Response to the Report by the Review Group on Company Rescue and Business Reconstruction Mechanisms (April 2001)

    A Statement of Principles: Banks and Businesses – Working Together When You Borrow (2005)

British Chamber of Commerce, *Small Firm Survey No. 24: Finance* (July 1997)

British Venture Capital Association (BVCA) *Annual Report 2006* (London, May 2006)

Broude, R., 'How the Rescue Culture Came to the United States and the Myths that Surround Chapter 11' (2001) 16 IL&P 194

Brougham, C., 'Limitation Periods and Section 423 Explained: *MC Bacon* Questioned' (2006) 19 *Insolvency Intelligence* 135

Brown, D., *Corporate Rescue: Insolvency Law in Practice* (John Wiley & Sons, Chichester, 1996)

    'Corporate Rescue in New Zealand' in K. Gromek Broc and R. Parry (eds.), *Corporate Rescue: An Overview of Recent Developments* (2nd edn, Kluwer, London, 2006) p. 262

Brudney, V., 'The Independent Director: Heavenly City or Potemkin Village?' (1982) 95 Harv. L Rev. 597

Brupbacher, O., 'Functional Analysis of Corporate Rescue Procedures: A Proposal from an Anglo-Swiss Perspective' [2005] 5 JCLS 105

Buckley, F., 'The Bankruptcy Priority Puzzle' (1986) 72 Va. L Rev. 1393

Bugg, T., 'Cheyne Finance' (2008) *Recovery* (Spring) 10

Bulman, S. and L. Fitzsimons, 'To Run or Not to Run ... (the Borrower's Business)' [1999] Ins. Law. 306

Butler, H., 'The Contractual Theory of the Corporation' (1989) 11 Geo. Mason UL Rev. 99

Byrne, J. and L. Doyle, 'Can a Landlord Forfeit a Lease by Peaceable Re-entry?' [1999] Ins. Law. 167

Byrne, M., 'An Economic Analysis of Directors' Duties in Favour of Creditors' (1994) 4 *Australian Journal of Corporate Law* 275

Byrne, T., 'Credit Management and Cash Flow in Businesses' (2007) *Recovery* (Spring) 38

Cabinet Office, *The Citizens' Charter: Five Years On* (London, 1996)

Risk: Improving Government's Capacity to Handle Risk and Uncertainty (London, 2002)

Calabresi, G. and A. Melamed, 'Property Rules, Liability Rules and Inalienability: One View of the Cathedral' (1972) 85 Harv. L Rev. 1089

Calnan, R., 'Fashioning the Law to Suit the Practicalities of Life' (1998) 114 LQR 174

Campbell, A., 'The Equity for Debt Proposal: The Way Forward' (1996) 12 IL&P 14

Campbell, C., 'Investigations by Insolvency Practitioners – Powers and Restraints: Part I' (2000) 16 IL&P 182

'Protection by Elimination: Winding Up of Companies on Public Interest Grounds' (2001) 17 IL&P 129

Campbell, C. and B. Underdown, *Corporate Insolvency in Practice: An Analytical Approach* (Chapman, London, 1991)

Campbell, N., '*Re Hydrodan (Corby) Ltd*' [1994] JBL 609

Cane, P. (ed.), *Atiyah's Accidents, Compensation and the Law* (7th edn, Cambridge University Press, Cambridge, 2006)

Cantlie, S. S., 'Preferred Priority in Bankruptcy' in J. Ziegel (ed.), *Current Developments in International and Comparative Corporate Insolvency Law* (Clarendon Press, Oxford, 1994)

Capper, D., 'Direct Payment Clauses and the *Pari Passu* Principle' [1998] CfiLR 54

'Contracting Out of Insolvency Set-off: Irish Possibilities' [2000] Ins. Law. 248

'*Spectrum Plus* in the House of Lords' [2006] 6 JCLS 447

Carlson, D. G., 'Philosophy in Bankruptcy (Book Review)' (1987) 85 Mich. L Rev. 1341

Carruthers, B. G. and T. C. Halliday, *Rescuing Business: The Making of Corporate Bankruptcy Law in England and the United States* (Clarendon Press, Oxford, 1998)

Carter, T., 'The Phoenix Syndrome – The Personal Liability of Directors' (2006) 19 *Insolvency Intelligence* 38

CBI, *Cutting Through the Red Tape: The Impact of Employment Legislation* (November 2000)

Chalkiadis, M., '*Powerhouse*: Has the Power Really Gone?' (2007) 21 *Company Law Newsletter* 1

Chambers, R., *Resulting Trusts* (Oxford University Press, Oxford, 1997)

'Restrictions on the Use of Money' in W. Swadling (ed.), *The Quistclose Trust: Critical Essays* (Hart Publishing, Oxford, 2004) p. 77

Chapman, M., 'The Insolvency Service's View of Regulation' (2005) *Recovery* (Winter) 24

Cheffins, B., *Company Law: Theory, Structure and Operation* (Clarendon Press, Oxford, 1997)

Christopher, W., 'Conditional Fee Arrangements' (2006) *Recovery* (Autumn) 38

Citron, D., 'The Incidence of Accounting-Based Covenants in UK Public Debt Contracts: An Empirical Analysis' (1995) 25 *Accounting and Business Research* 139

Clarke, A., 'Corporate Rescues and Reorganisations in English Law after the Insolvency Act 1986' (Mimeo, University College, London, 1993)

'Security Interests as Property: Relocating Security Interests within the Property Framework' in J. W. Harris (ed.), *Property Problems from Genes to Pension Funds* (Kluwer, London, 1997)

Clarke, F., G. Dean and K. Oliver, *Corporate Collapse: Accounting, Regulatory and Ethical Failure* (rev. edn, Cambridge University Press, Cambridge, 2003)

Clarke, I., 'Re-use of Company Names: Applications to Court by a Director for Leave to Act' (2007) *Recovery* (Spring) 32

Clarke, L. and H. Rajak, '*Mann* v. *Secretary of State for Employment*' (2000) 63 MLR 895

Clementi, D., *Review of the Regulatory Framework for Legal Services in England and Wales* (DCA, London, December 2004)

Clench, T., 'Applications for Permission to Act under Section 17 of the Company Directors Disqualification Act 1986' (2008) 21 *Insolvency Intelligence* 113

CLRSG, *Modern Company Law for a Competitive Economy: The Strategic Framework*, URN 99/654 (February 1999)

Modern Company Law for a Competitive Economy: Developing the Framework, URN 00/1656 (March 2000)

Consultation Document, *Modern Company Law for a Competitive Economy: Registration of Company Charges* (October 2000)

Consultation Document, *Modern Company Law for a Competitive Economy: Completing the Structure* (November 2000)

Modern Company Law for a Competitive Economy: Final Report (July 2001)

Coase, R., 'The Problem of Social Cost' (1960) 3 J Law and Econ. 1

Coffee, J., '"No Soul to Damn: No Body to Kick": An Unscandalized Inquiry into the Problem of Corporate Punishment' (1981) 79 Mich. L Rev. 386

Cohen, J., 'History of Imprisonment for Debt and its Relation to the Development of Discharge in Bankruptcy' (1982) 3 *Journal of Legal History* 153

Collins, H., 'Transfer of Undertakings and Insolvency' (1989) 18 Ins. LJ 144

'Ascription of Legal Responsibility to Groups and Complex Patterns of Economic Integration' (1990) 53 MLR 731

'Quality Assurance in Subcontracting' in S. Dealin and J. Michie (eds.), *Contracts, Cooperation and Competition* (Oxford University Press, Oxford, 1997) p. 285

Collins, H., K. Ewing and A. McColgan, *Labour Law: Text and Materials* (2nd edn, Hart, Oxford, 2005)

Companies and Securities Law Review Committee, *Enforcement of the Duties of Directors and Officers of a Company by Means of a Statutory Derivative Action* (Report No. 12, 1990)

Connell, R., 'Chapter 11: The UK Dimension' (1990) 6 IL&P 90

'Enterprising Receivers' (2003) *Recovery* (Spring) 20

Cook, G., N. Pandit, D. Milman, and A. Griffiths, *Small Business Rescue: A Multi-Method Empirical Study of Company Voluntary Arrangements* (ICAEW, London, 2003)

Cooke, T. and A. Hicks, 'Wrongful Trading: Predicting Insolvency' [1993] JBL 338

Cork Advisory Committee, Cmnd 6602 (1976). Interim report to the Minister, published in July 1980 as *Bankruptcy: Interim Report of the Insolvency Law Review Committee* (Cmnd 7968, 1980)

Cork, K., *Cork on Cork: Sir Kenneth Cork Takes Stock* (Macmillan, London, 1988)

Cornish, W. R. and G. de N. Clark, *Law and Society in England 1750–1950* (Sweet & Maxwell, London, 1989)

Corporations and Securities Advisory Committee, *Corporate Groups: Final Report* (May 2000)

Cosh, A. and A. Hughes, *British Enterprise in Transition* (ESRC Centre for Business Research, Cambridge, 2000)

British Enterprise: Thriving or Surviving? (ESRC Centre for Business Research, Cambridge, 2007)

Coulson, F. and S. Hill, '*Brumark*: The End of Banking as We Know It?' (2001) *Recovery* (September) 16

Countryman, V., 'The Concept of a Voidable Preference in Bankruptcy' (1985) 38 Vand. L Rev. 713

Cousins, J., A. Mitchell, P. Sikka, C. Cooper and P. Arnold, *Insolvency Abuse: Regulating the Insolvency Service* (Association for Accounting and Business Affairs, 2000)

Craig, P. P., 'The Monopolies and Mergers Commission, Competition and Administrative Rationality' in R. Baldwin and C. McCrudden (eds.), *Regulation and Public Law* (Weidenfeld & Nicolson, London, 1987)

Public Law and Democracy in the United Kingdom and the United States of America (Clarendon Press, Oxford, 1990)

Cranston, R., *Principles of Banking Law* (2nd edn, Oxford University Press, Oxford, 2002)

Cressy, R., *Why Do Most Firms Die Young?* (Kluwer, Netherlands, 2005)

Crompton, *Practice Common-placed: Or, the Rules and Cases of the Practice in the Courts of King's Bench and Common Pleas*, vol. LXVII (3rd edn, 1786)

Cruickshank, D., *Competition in UK Banking: A Report to the Chancellor of the Exchequer* (HMSO, London, 2000)

Cuming, R., 'Canadian Bankruptcy Law: A Secured Creditor's Haven' in J. Ziegel (ed.), *Current Developments in International and Comparative Corporate Insolvency Law* (Clarendon Press, Oxford, 1994)

'The Internationalization of Secured Financing Law: The Spreading Influence of the Concepts UCC, Article 9 and its Progeny' in R. Cranston (ed.), *Making Commercial Law: Essays in Honour of Roy Goode* (Clarendon Press, Oxford, 1997)

Dahan, F., 'The European Convention on Insolvency Proceedings and the Administrative Receiver: A Missed Opportunity?' (1996) 17 Co. Law. 181

Dal Pont, G. and L. Griggs, 'A Principled Justification for Business Rescue Laws: A Comparative Perspective, Part II' (1996) 5 *International Insolvency Review* 47

Daley, C. and C. Dalton, 'Bankruptcy and Corporate Governance: The Impact of Board Composition and Structure' (1994) 37 *Academy of Management Journal* 1603

Daniels, N. (ed.), *Reading Rawls: Critical Studies on Rawls' 'A Theory of Justice'* (Stanford University Press, Stanford, 1989)

Daniels, R., 'Must Boards Go Overboard? An Economic Analysis of the Effects of Burgeoning Statutory Liability on the Role of Directors in Corporate Governance' in J. Ziegel (ed.), *Current Developments in International and Comparative Corporate Insolvency Law* (Clarendon Press, Oxford, 1994)

'Must Boards Go Overboard?' (1994–5) 24 Canadian Bus. LJ 229

Daniels, R. and S. Hutton, 'The Capricious Cushion: The Implications of the Directors' and Officers' Insurance Liability Crisis in Canadian Corporate Governance' (1993) Canadian Bus. LJ 182

Davies, I., *Effective Retention of Title* (Fourmat, London, 1991)

'The Trade Creditor and the Quest for Security' in H. Rajak (ed.), *Insolvency Law: Theory and Practice* (Sweet & Maxwell, London, 1993)

Davies, P. L., 'Acquired Rights, Creditors' Rights, Freedom of Contract and Industrial Democracy' (1989) 9 *Yearbook of European Law* 21

'Employee Claims in Insolvency: Corporate Rescue and Preferential Claims' (1994) 23 Ins. LJ 141

'Legal Capital in Private Companies in Great Britain' (1998) 8 *Die Aktien Gesellschaft* 346

'Transfers: The UK Will Have to Make Up its Own Mind' (2001) 30 Ins. LJ 231

'Directors' Creditor-regarding Duties in Respect of Trading Decisions Taken in the Vicinity of Insolvency' (2006) 7 EBOR 301

Gower and Davies' Principles of Modern Company Law (8th edn, Thomson/ Sweet & Maxwell, London, 2008)

Davies QC, S., *Insolvency and the Enterprise Act 2002* (Jordans, Bristol, 2003)

'Pre-pack – He Who Pays the Piper Calls the Tune' (2006) *Recovery* (Summer) 16

Davis, G., 'The Role of the Insolvency Rules Committee' (2007) 20 *Insolvency Intelligence* 65

Dawson, I., 'The Administrator, Morality and the Court' [1996] JBL 437

'*National Westminster Bank plc* v. *Jones*' [2002] Ins. Law. 61

Dawson, K., 'Cross Border Insolvency: The EC Regulation and the UNCITRAL Model Law' in K. Gromek Broc and R. Parry (eds.), *Corporate Rescue: An Overview of Recent Developments* (2nd edn, Kluwer Law, London, 2006)

Day, J., P. Ormrod and P. Taylor, 'Implications for Lending Decisions and Debt Contracting of the Adoption of International Financial Reporting Standards' [2004] JIBLR 475

Day, J. and P. Taylor, 'The Role of Debt Contracts in UK Corporate Governance' (1998) 2 *Journal of Management and Governance* 171

'Financial Distress in Small Firms: The Role Played by Debt Covenants and Other Monitoring Devices' [2001] Ins. Law. 97

DeAngelo, H., L. DeAngelo and K. Wruck, 'Asset Liquidity, Debt Covenants and Managerial Discretion in Financial Distress: The Collapse of L. A. Grear' (2002) 64 *Journal of Financial Economics* 3

de Lacy, J., 'The Purchase Money Security Interest: A Company Charge Conundrum' [1991] LMCLQ 531

'Retention of Title, Company Charges and the *Scintilla Temporis* Doctrine' [1994] Conv. 242

'*Romalpa* Theory and Practice under Retention of Title in the Sale of Goods' (1995) 24 *Anglo-American Law Review* 327

'Processed Goods and Retention of Title Clauses' [1997] 10 *Palmer's In Company*

'Corporate Insolvency and Retention of Title Clauses: Developments in Australia' [2001] Ins. Law. 64

'The Concept of a Company Director' [2006] JBL 267

Deakin, S. and A. Hughes, 'Economics and Company Law Reform: A Fruitful Analysis?' (1999) 20 Co. Law. 212

'Economic Efficiency and the Proceduralisation of Company Law' [1999] CfiLR 169

Derham, R., 'Some Aspects of Mutual Credit and Mutual Dealings' (1992) 108 LQR 99

Set-off (3rd edn, Clarendon Press, Oxford, 2003)

Devlin, P., *The Enforcement of Morals* (Oxford University Press, London, 1965)

Dewhirst, J., 'Turnabout Tourniquet' (2003) *Financial World* 56

Dhindsa, R., 'The Draft TUPE Regulations and Insolvency' (2006) 19 *Insolvency Intelligence* 8

Diamond, A. L., *A Review of Security Interests in Property* (Diamond Report) (DTI, HMSO, London, 1989)

Dickfos, J., C. Aderson and D. Morrison, 'The Insolvency Implications for Corporate Groups in Australia – Recent Events' (2007) 16 Int. Ins. Rev. 103

Dine, J., *The Governance of Corporate Groups* (Cambridge University Press, Cambridge, 2000)

Douglas, M., *In the Active Voice* (Routledge, London, 1982)

Doyle, L., 'The Residual Status of Directors in Receivership' (1996) 17 Co. Law. 131

'The Receiver's Duties on a Sale of Charged Assets' (1997) 10 *Insolvency Intelligence* 9

Draper, M., 'Taking a Leaf out of Chapter 11?' (1991) 17 *Law Society Gazette* 28

Drewry, G., 'Forward from FMI: The Next Steps' [1988] PL 505

    'Next Steps: The Pace Falters' [1990] PL 322

DTI, *Encouraging Debt/Equity Swaps* (1996)

    Consultation Paper, *Improving the Payment Culture* (July 1997)

    Company Investigations: Powers for the 21st Century (2001)

    Opportunity for All in a World of Change – A White Paper on Enterprise, Skill and Innovation (February 2001)

    TUPE: Government Proposals for Reform: Public Consultation Document (URN 01/1133) (2001)

DTI/Insolvency Service, *Company Voluntary Arrangements and Administration Orders: A Consultative Document* (October 1993)

    Revised Proposals for a New Company Voluntary Arrangement Procedure (April 1995)

    A Review of Company Rescue and Business Reconstruction Mechanisms (1999)

    A Review of Company Rescue and Business Reconstruction Mechanisms: Report by the Review Group (2000)

    Productivity and Enterprise: Insolvency – A Second Chance (Cm 5234, July 2001)

Duggan, A., 'Contractarianism and the Law of Corporate Insolvency' (2005) 42 Canadian Bus. LJ 463

Dunscombe, J., 'Bankruptcy: A Study in Comparative Legislation' (1893) 2 *Columbia University Studies in Political Science* 17

Dworkin, R. M., *Taking Rights Seriously* (Duckworths, London, 1977)

    'Is Wealth a Value?' (1980) 9 *Journal of Legal Studies* 191

    A Matter of Principle (Clarendon Press, Oxford, 1986)

Dyson, K. and S. Wilks, 'The Character and Economic Content of Industrial Crisis' in Dyson and Wilks (eds.), *Industrial Crisis: A Comparative Study of the State and Industry* (Blackwell, Oxford, 1985)

Easterbrook, F. H. and D. R. Fischel, 'Voting in Corporate Law' (1983) 26 *Journal of Law and Economics* 395

    'The Corporate Contract' (1989) 89 Colum. L Rev. 1416

    The Economic Structure of Corporate Law (Harvard University Press, Cambridge, Mass., 1991)

Ehlers, E., 'Statutory Corporate Rescue Proceedings in Germany' in K. Gromek Broc and R. Parry (eds.), *Corporate Rescue: An Overview of Recent Developments* (2nd edn, Kluwer, London, 2006) p. 151

EHYA, *Submission on Insolvency Law Reform* (EHYA, London, 2007 and 2008)

Eisenberg, T., 'Corporate Groups' in M. Gillooly (ed.), *The Law Relating to Corporate Groups* (Butterworths, Sydney, 1993)

Elboz, S., 'Exiting Administration – Railtrack and the Future' (2002) IL&P 187

Eldridge, R., 'TUPE Operates to Damage Rescue Culture' (2001) *Recovery* (September) 21

Elias, G., *Explaining Constructive Trusts* (Clarendon Press, Oxford, 1990)

Ellis, D., 'Inland Revenue and Business Rescue' (2001) *Recovery* (September) 18

Ellis, M., 'The Thin Line in the Sand' (2006) *Recovery* (Spring) 3

Ellis, M. and L. Verrill, 'Twilight Trusts' (2007) 20 *Insolvency Intelligence* 151

Elwes, S., 'Transactions Defrauding Creditors' (2001) 17 IL&P 10

Epstein, R., 'A Theory of Strict Liability' (1973) 2 *Journal of Legal Studies* 151

Esen, R., 'Chartered Directors' Qualification: Professionalism on UK Boards' (2000) 21 Co. Law. 289

European Commission, *Communication from the Commission to the Council and the European Parliament: Progress Report on the Risk Capital Action Plan*, COM (November 2003)

Evans, M., 'Decision of the Court of Appeal in *Morris* v. *Agrichemicals Ltd*: A Flawed Asset' (1996) 17 Co. Law. 102

Fairburn J. and J. Kay (eds.), *Introduction to Mergers and Merger Policy* (Oxford University Press, Oxford, 1989)

Fama, E. F., 'Agency Problems and the Theory of the Firm' (1980) 88(1) *Journal of Political Economy* 288

Farrar, J. H., 'Company Insolvency and the Cork Recommendations' (1983) 4 Co. Law. 20

Farrar's Company Law (4th edn, Butterworths, London, 1998)

Federation of Small Businesses Report, *Barriers to Survival and Growth in UK Small Firms* (London, 2000)

Feldwick, M., 'Engaging Credit Insurers in the Turnaround Process' (2006) *Recovery* (Autumn) 32

Fennell, S., 'Court-appointed Receiverships: A Missed Opportunity?' (1998) 14 IL&P 208

Fennell, S. and S. Dingles, 'Working with Companies in Financial Difficulties – Will You Be Paid?' (2006) 19 *Insolvency Intelligence* 49

Ferguson, N., 'Advice Squad' (2005) *Director* (April) 31

Ferran, E., 'The Duties of an Administrative Receiver to Unsecured Creditors' (1988) 9 Co. Law. 58

'Subordinated Debt Agreements' (1993) *CCH Company Law Newsletter* (28 June 1993)

'Recent Developments in Unsecured Debt Subordination' in B. Rider (ed.), *The Realm of Company Law* (Kluwer, London, 1998)

Company Law and Corporate Finance (Oxford University Press, Oxford, 1999)

'Regulation of Private Equity-Backed Leveraged Buy-out Activity in Europe', ECGI Working Paper 84/2007

Ferris, J., 'Report of Mr Justice Ferris' Working Party on *The Remuneration of Office Holders and Certain Related Matters*' (London, 1998)

'Insolvency Remuneration: Translating Adjectives into Action' [1999] Ins. Law. 48

Financial Markets Law Committee, *Issue 120 – Section 868 of the Company Law Revision Bill: Statutory Reversal of* Leyland DAF (FMLC, London, March 2006)

Financial Services Authority, *A New Regulator for the New Millennium* (FSA, London, 2000)

'Hedge Funds: A Discussion of Risk and Regulatory Engagement' (FSA Discussion Paper 05/4, London, June 2005)

Finch, V., 'Directors' Duties Towards Creditors' (1989) 10 Co. Law. 23

'Disqualification of Directors: A Plea for Competence' (1990) 53 MLR 385

'Directors' Duties: Insolvency and the Unsecured Creditor' in A. Clarke (ed.), *Current Issues in Insolvency Law* (Stevens, London, 1991) p. 87

'Board Performance and Cadbury on Corporate Governance' [1992] JBL 581

'Company Directors: Who Cares About Skill and Care?' (1992) 55 MLR 179

'Disqualifying Directors: Issues of Rights, Privileges and Employment' (1993) Ins. LJ 35

'Corporate Governance and Cadbury: Self-regulation and Alternatives' [1994] JBL 51

'Personal Accountability and Corporate Control: The Role of Directors' and Officers' Liability Insurance' (1994) 57 MLR 880

'Creditors' Interests and Directors' Obligations' in S. Sheikh and W. Rees (eds.), *Corporate Governance and Corporate Control* (Cavendish, London, 1995)

'The Measures of Insolvency Law' (1997) 17 OJLS 227

'Insolvency Practitioners: Regulation and Reform' [1998] JBL 334

'Controlling the Insolvency Professionals' [1999] Ins. Law. 228

'Security, Insolvency and Risk: Who Pays the Price?' (1999) 62 MLR 633

'Is *Pari Passu* Passé?' [2000] Ins. Law. 194

'Public Interest Liquidation: PIL or Placebo?' [2002] Ins. Law. 157

'Re-invigorating Corporate Rescue' [2003] JBL 527

'Control and Co-ordination in Corporate Rescue' (2005) 25 *Legal Studies* 374

'Doctoring in the Shadows of Insolvency' [2005] JBL 690

'Late Payment of Debt: Re-thinking the Response' (2005) 18 *Insolvency Intelligence* 38

'The Recasting of Insolvency Law' (2005) 68 MLR 713

'Regulating Insolvency Practitioners: Rationalisation on the Agenda' (2005) 18 *Insolvency Intelligence* 17

'Pre-packaged Administrations: Bargains in the Shadow of Insolvency or Shadowy Bargains?' [2006] JBL 568

'Corporate Rescue in a World of Debt' [2008] JBL 756

Finch, V. and S. Worthington, 'The *Pari Passu* Principle and Ranking Restitutionary Claims' in F. Rose (ed.), *Restitution and Insolvency* (Lloyd's of London Press, London, 2000)

Finnis, J., *Natural Law and Natural Rights* (Clarendon Press, Oxford, 1980)

Fish, S., *Doing What Comes Naturally: Change, Rhetoric and the Practice of Theory in Literary and Legal Studies* (Clarendon Press, Oxford, 1989)

Flaschen, E. and T. DeSieno, 'The Development of Insolvency Law as Part of the Transition from a Centrally Planned to a Market Economy' (1992) 26 *International Lawyer* 667

Flessner, A., 'Philosophies of Business Bankruptcy Law: An International Overview' in J. S. Ziegel (ed.), *Current Developments in International and Comparative Corporate Insolvency Law* (Clarendon Press, Oxford, 1994)

Fletcher, D., 'Time for a DIP?' (2007) *Recovery* (Summer) 30

Fletcher, I. F., 'Genesis of Modern Insolvency Law: An Odyssey of Law Reform' [1989] JBL 365

'Voidable Transactions in Bankruptcy Law: British Law Perspectives' in J. Ziegel (ed.), *Current Developments in International and Comparative Corporate Insolvency Law* (Clarendon Press, Oxford, 1994)

'Adoption of Contracts of Employment by Receivers and Administrators: The *Paramount* Case' [1995] JBL 596

'Wrongful Trading: "Reasonable Prospect" of Insolvency' (1995) 8 *Insolvency Intelligence* 14

'Juggling with Norms: The Conflict between Collective and Individual Rights under Insolvency Law' in R. Cranston (ed.), *Making Commercial Law* (Clarendon Press, Oxford, 1997)

The Law of Insolvency (3rd edn, Sweet & Maxwell, London, 2002)

'The Quest for a Global Insolvency Law: A Challenge for Our Time' in M. Freeman (ed.), 55 *Current Legal Problems* (Oxford University Press, Oxford, 2002)

'Right to Participate in a Distribution' (2004) 17 *Insolvency Intelligence* 91

'UK Corporate Rescue: Recent Developments – Changes to Administrative Receivership, Administration and Company Voluntary Arrangements – the Insolvency Act 2000, the White Paper 2001 and the Enterprise Act 2002' (2004) 5 EBOR 119

'Crown Set-off and Contingent Liabilities' (2005) 18 *Insolvency Intelligence* 6

Insolvency in Private International Law: National and International Approaches (2nd edn, Oxford University Press, Oxford, 2005)

'Reflections on the EC Regulation on Insolvency Proceedings – Parts 1 and 2' (2005) 18 *Insolvency Intelligence* 49 and 68

'"Better Late than Never": The UNCITRAL Model Law Enters into Force in GB' (2006) 19 *Insolvency Intelligence* 86

'Companies Act 2006: Reversal of *Leyland DAF* Ruling' (2007) 20 *Insolvency Intelligence* 30

Flood, J., 'Corporate Recovery: The London Approach' (1995) 11 IL&P 82

'The Vultures Fly East: The Creation and Globalisation of the Distressed Debt Market' in D. Nelken and J. Feast (eds.), *Adapting Legal Cultures* (Hart, Oxford, 2001) p. 257

'Rating, Dating and the Informal Regulation and the Formal Ordering of Financial Transactions' in M. B. Likosky (ed.), *Privatising Development* (Martinus Nijhoff, Netherlands, 2005) p. 147

Flood, J., R. Abbey, E. Skordaki and P. Aber, *The Professional Restructuring of Corporate Rescue: Company Voluntary Arrangements and the London Approach*, ACCA Research Report 45 (ACCA, London, 1995)

Flood, J. and E. Skordaki, *Insolvency Practitioners and Big Corporate Insolvencies*, ACCA Research Report 43 (ACCA, London, 1995)

Floyd, R., 'Corporate Recovery: The London Approach' (1995) 11 IL&P 82

Flynn, D., 'Pre-pack Administrations – A Regulatory Perspective' (2006) *Recovery* (Summer) 3

FMLC, *Administration Set-off and Expenses* (Bank of England, London, November 2007)

'Administration – Set-off and Expenses' (discussion paper, Issue 108, 17 January 2008), available on FMLC website: www.fmlc.org

Foster, C., *Financial Statement Analysis* (2nd edn, Prentice-Hall, Englewood Cliffs, N.J., 1986)

Francis, J., 'Insolvency Law Reform: The Aghion, Hart and Moore Proposals' (1995) (Winter) *Insolvency Practitioner* 10

Franken, S., 'Creditor and Debtor Oriented Corporate Bankruptcy Regimes Revisited' (2004) 5 EBOR 645

Franks, J. and C. Mayer, 'Capital Markets and Corporate Control: A Study of France, Germany and the UK' (1990) 10 *Economic Policy* 191

Franks, J. and O. Sussman, 'The Cycle of Corporate Distress, Rescue and Dissolution: A Study of Small and Medium Size UK Companies', IFA Working Paper 306 (2000)

'Financial Distress and Bank Restructuring of Small to Medium Size UK Companies' (2005) 9 *Review of Finance* 65

'The Economics of English Insolvency: Recent Developments' in J. Getzler and J. Payne (eds.), *Company Charges: Spectrum and Beyond* (Oxford University Press, Oxford, 2006)

Franks, J. and W. Torous, 'Lessons from a Comparison of US and UK Insolvency Codes' in J. S. Bhandari and L. A. Weiss (eds.), *Corporate Bankruptcy: Economic and Legal Perspectives* (Cambridge University Press, Cambridge, 1996)

Fraser, S., *Finance for Small and Medium Enterprises* (Warwick University Centre for Small and Medium Enterprises, 2004)

Freedman, J., 'Accountants and Corporate Governance: Filling a Legal Vacuum?' (1993) *Political Quarterly* 285

'Limited Liability: Large Company Theory and Small Firms' (2000) 63 MLR 317

Freedman, J. and M. Godwin, 'Incorporating the Micro Business: Perceptions and Misperceptions' in A. Hughes and D. Storey (eds.), *Finance and the Small Firm* (Routledge, London, 1994)

Frieze, S., 'Round-up of Some Recent Cases on Administration' (2008) 21 *Insolvency Intelligence* 14

Frisby, S., 'Making a Silk Purse out of a Pig's Ear: *Medforth* v. *Blake and Others*' (2000) 63 MLR 413

'TUPE or not TUPE? Employee Protection, Corporate Rescue and "One Unholy Mess"' [2000] 3 CFILR 249

'In Search of a Rescue Regime: The Enterprise Act 2002' (2004) 67 MLR 247

Report to the Insolvency Service: Insolvency Outcomes (Insolvency Service, London, 26 June 2006)

Interim Report to the Insolvency Service on Returns to Creditors from Pre- and Post-Enterprise Act Insolvency Procedures (Insolvency Service, London, 2007)

A Preliminary Analysis of Pre-packaged Administrations: Report to R3 – The Association of Business Recovery Professionals (R3, London, August 2007)

'Unpacking Pre-packs: The Story So Far' (2007) *Recovery* (Autumn) 25

Frith, S., 'Acting as a Director of a Phoenix Company' (2003) 16 *Insolvency Intelligence* 37

Frome, N. and C. Brown, *Lessons from the Marconi Restructuring* (IFLR, September 2003)

Frome, N. and K. Gibbons, '*Spectrum* – An End to the Conflict or the Signal for a New Campaign?' in J. Getzler and J. Payne (eds.), *Company Charges: Spectrum and Beyond* (Oxford University Press, Oxford, 2006)

Frost, C., 'Operational Form, Misappropriation Risk and the Substantive Consolidation of Corporate Groups' (1993) 44 Hastings LJ 449

Frug, G. E., 'The Ideology of Bureaucracy in American Law' (1984) 97 Harv. L Rev. 1277

Fuller, G., *Corporate Borrowing: Law and Practice* (Jordans, Bristol, 2006)

Gaffney, M., 'Small Firms Really Can Be Helped' (1983) *Management Accounting* (February)

Gale, S., 'Insolvency Law Post Enterprise Act: Does It Do What It Says on the Tin?' (2007) *Recovery* (Autumn) 34

Galen, M. with C. Yang, 'A New Page for Chapter 11?' *Business Week*, 25 January 1993

Galligan, D. J., *Discretionary Powers: A Legal Study of Official Discretion* (Clarendon Press, Oxford, 1986)

Gearty, C., 'Insolvency … and Human Rights?' [2000] Ins. Law. 68

Gee, L., *How Effective are Voluntary Arrangements?* (Levy Gee, London, 1994)

Getzler, J. and J. Payne (eds.), *Company Charges: Spectrum and Beyond* (Oxford University Press, Oxford, 2006)

Geva, E., 'National Policy Objectives from an EU Perspective: UK Corporate Rescue and the European Insolvency Regulation' (2007) 8 EBOR 605

Gewirth, A., *The Community of Rights* (University of Chicago Press, Chicago, 1996)

Gilson, S., 'Management Turnover and Financial Distress' (1989) 25 *Journal of Financial Economics* 241

'Bankruptcy, Boards, Banks and Blockholders' (1990) 27 *Journal of Financial Economics* 355

Gilson, S. C., K. John and L. H. P. Lang, 'Troubled Debt Restructurings: An Empirical Study of Private Reorganisation of Firms in Default' (1990) 27 *Journal of Financial Economics* 323

Gilson, S. and M. Vetsuypens, 'Creditor Control in Financially Distressed Firms: Empirical Evidence' (1994) 72 Wash. ULQ 1005

Gleig, B., 'Unpaid Wages in Bankruptcy' (1987) 21 UBC L Rev. 61

Goddard, R. and H. Hirt, 'Section 459 and Corporate Groups' [2005] JBL 247

Godfrey, P., 'The Turnaround Practitioner – Advisor or Director?' (2002) 18 IL&P 3

Godfrey, P. and S. Nield, 'The Wrongful Trading Provisions: All Bark and No Bite?' (1995) 11 IL&P 139

Goetz, C. J. and R. E. Scott, 'Liquidated Damages, Penalties and the Just Compensation Principle: Some Notes on an Enforcement Model and a Theory of Efficient Breach' (1977) 77(4) Colum. L Rev. 554

'Principles of Relational Contracts' (1981) 67 Va. L Rev. 1089

Goode, R. M., 'Is the Law Too Favourable to Secured Creditors?' (1983–4) 8 Canadian Bus. LJ 53

'Surety and On-Demand Performance Bonds' [1988] JBL 87

'Charges over Book Debts: A Missed Opportunity' (1994) 110 LQR 592

'The Exodus of the Floating Charge' in D. Feldman and F. Meisel (eds.), *Corporate and Commercial Law: Modern Developments* (Lloyd's of London Press, London, 1996)

'Charge-Backs and Legal Fictions' (1998) 114 LQR 178

Commercial Law in the Next Millennium (Sweet & Maxwell, London, 1998)

'Proprietary Rights and Unsecured Creditors' in B. Rider (ed.), *The Realm of Company Law* (Kluwer, London, 1998)

Legal Problems of Credit and Security (3rd edn, Sweet & Maxwell, London, 2003)

Commercial Law (3rd edn, Penguin Books, London, 2004)

Principles of Corporate Insolvency Law (3rd edn, Sweet & Maxwell, London, 2005)

'The Case for Abolition of the Floating Charge' in J. Getzler and J. Payne (eds.), *Company Charges: Spectrum and Beyond* (Oxford University Press, Oxford, 2006)

Goode, R. M. and L. Gower, 'Is Article 9 of the Uniform Commercial Code Exportable? An English Reaction' in J. Ziegel and W. Foster (eds.), *Aspects of Comparative Commercial Law* (Oceana, Montreal, 1969)

Goodhart, W. and G. Jones, 'The Infiltration of Equitable Doctrine into English Commercial Law' (1980) 43 MLR 489

Graham, C., 'Self-regulation' in G. Richardson and H. Genn (eds.), *Administrative Law and Government Action* (Clarendon Press, Oxford, 1994)

Grantham, R., 'Directors' Duties and Insolvent Companies' (1991) 65 MLR 576
'The Judicial Extension of Directors' Duties to Creditors' [1991] JBL 1
'Liability of Parent Companies for the Actions of the Directors of their Subsidiaries' (1997) 18 Co. Law. 138
'Refloating a Floating Charge' [1997] CfiLR 53

Green, R. and E. Talmor, 'Asset Substitution and the Agency Costs of Debt Financing' (1986) 10 *Journal of Banking Law* 391

Green Paper, *Bankruptcy: A Consultative Document* (Cmnd 7967, 1980)

Gregory, R., *Review of Company Rescue and Business Reconstruction Mechanisms: Rescue Culture or Avoidance Culture?* (CCH, Bicester, December 1999)

Gregory, R. and P. Walton, 'Book Debt Charges: The Saga Goes On' (1999) 115 LQR 14
'Book Debt Charges: Following *Yorkshire Woolcombers* – Are We Sheep Gone Astray?' [2000] Ins. Law. 157

Grier, I. and R. E. Floyd, *Voluntary Liquidation and Receivership* (3rd edn, Longman, London, 1991)

Grierson, C., 'Issues in Concurrent Insolvency Jurisdiction: English Perspectives' in J. S. Ziegel (ed.), *Current Developments in International and Comparative Corporate Insolvency Law* (Clarendon Press, Oxford, 1994)
'Shareholder Liability, Consolidation and Pooling' in E. Leonard and C. Besant (eds.), *Current Issues in Cross-Border Insolvency and Reorganisations* (Graham and Trotman, London, 1994)

Griffin, S., 'The Effect of a Charge over Book Debts: The Indivisible and Divisible Nature of the Charge' [1995] 46 NILQ 163
'The Characteristics and Identification of a *De Facto* Director' [2000] 1 CFILR 126
'Accelerating Disqualification under s. 10 of the Company Directors' Disqualification Act' [2002] Ins. Law. 32
'Corporate Collapse and the Reform of Boardroom Structures – Lessons from America?' [2003] Ins. Law. 214
'Evidence Justifying a Person's Capacity as Either a *De Facto* or Shadow Director: *Secretary of State for Trade and Industry* v. *Becker*' [2003] Ins. Law. 127

Gromek Broc, K. and R. Parry, *Corporate Rescue: An Overview of Recent Developments* (2nd edn, Kluwer, London, 2006)

Gross, K., 'Taking Community Interests into Account in Bankruptcy: An Essay' (1994) 72 Wash. ULQ 1031
Failure and Forgiveness: Rebalancing the Bankruptcy System (Yale University Press, New Haven, 1997)

Gunningham, N. and P. Grabosky, *Smart Regulation* (Oxford University Press, Oxford, 1998)

Hackett, B., 'What Constitutes a Transaction at an Undervalue?' (2001) 17 IL&P 139

Hadden, T., 'Inside Corporate Groups' (1984) 12 *International Journal of Sociology of Law* 271

'Insolvency and the Group: Problems of Integrated Financing' in R. M. Goode (ed.), *Group Trading and the Lending Banker* (Chartered Institute of Bankers, London, 1988)

'The Regulation of Corporate Groups in Australia' (1992) UNSW LJ 61

'Regulating Corporate Groups: International Perspectives' in J. McCahery, S. Picciotto and C. Scott (eds.), *Corporate Control and Accountability* (Oxford University Press, Oxford, 1993)

Hahn, D., 'Concentrated Ownership and Control of Corporate Reorganisations' [2004] 4 JCLS 117

Halpern, P., M. Trebilcock and M. Turnbull, 'An Economic Analysis of Limited Liability in Corporation Law' (1980) 30 U Toronto LJ 117

Hamilton, R., B. Halcroft, K. Pond and Z. Liew, 'Back from the Dead: Survival Potential in Administrative Receiverships' (1997) 13 IL&P 78

Hampton, P., *Reducing Administrative Burdens* (HM Treasury, London, 2005)

Hannigan, B. M., *Company Law* (Lexis Nexis/Butterworths, London, 2003)

Hansman, H. and R. Krackman, 'Towards Unlimited Shareholder Liability for Corporate Torts' (1991) 100 Yale LJ 1879

Hare, D. and D. Milman, 'Corporate Insolvency: The Cork Committee Proposals I' (1983) 127 Sol. Jo. 230

Harlow, C. and R. Rawlings, *Law and Administration* (2nd edn, Butterworths, London, 1997)

Harmer, R., 'Comparison of Trends in National Law: The Pacific Rim' (1997) 1 *Brooklyn Journal of International Law* 139

Harris, J., 'Pooling Options for Insolvent Corporate Groups' (2005) 26 Co. Law. 125

'Seeking Court Approval for Pooling Arrangements: Lessons from the *Ansett* Case' (2006) 24 C&SLJ 443

'International Regulation of Hedge Funds: Can the Will Find a Way?' (2007) 28 Co. Law. 277

'Corporate Group Insolvencies: Charting the Past, Present and Future of "Pooling" Arrangements' (2007) 15 Ins. LJ 78

Harris, M. and A. Raviv, 'Capital Structure and the Informational Role of Debt' (1990) 45 *Journal of Finance* 321

Harris, S., 'The Decision to Pre-pack' (2004) *Recovery* (Winter) 26

Harris, S. and C. Mooney, 'A Property Based Theory of Security Interests: Taking Debtors' Choices Seriously' (1994) 80 Va. L Rev. 2021

Hart, H. L. A., *Law, Liberty and Morality* (Oxford University Press, Oxford, 1963)

Haugen, R. and L. Senbet, 'Bankruptcy and Agency Costs' (1988) 23 *Journal of Financial and Quantitative Analysis* 27

Health and Safety Executive, *Reducing Risks, Protecting People* (HSE, London, 2001)

Heidt, K. R., 'The Automatic Stay in Environmental Bankruptcies' (1993) 67 *American Bankruptcy Law Journal* 69

Heis, R., 'Pre-packs – A New SIP' (2008) *Recovery* (Spring) 14

'Technical Update: Set-off in Administrations' (2008) *Recovery* (Autumn) 12

Hemsworth, M., 'Voidable Preference: Desire and Effect' (2000) 16 IL&P 54

Henderson, A., '*Fraser v. Oystertec* and the Principle Against Divestiture in Insolvency: An Unprincipled Departure' (2004) 25 Co. Law. 313

Henderson, D., 'Problems in the Law of Property after *Spectrum Plus*' [2006] ICCLR 30

Henkel, M., *Government, Evaluation and Change* (Jessica Kingsley, London, 1991)

Hewitt, A., 'Asset Finance' (2003) 43 *Bank of England Quarterly Bulletin* 207

Heydon, J., W. Gummow and R. Austin, *Cases and Materials on Equity and Trusts* (4th edn, Butterworths, Sydney, 1993)

Hicks, A., 'Retention of Title: Latest Developments' [1992] JBL 398

'Advising on Wrongful Trading: Part 1' (1993) 14 Co. Law. 16

'When Goods Sold Become a New Species' [1993] JBL 485

Disqualification of Directors: No Hiding Place for the Unfit? ACCA Research Report No. 59 (ACCA, London, 1998)

'Director Disqualification: Can It Deliver?' [2001] JBL 433

Hiestand, L. and C. Pilkington, 'The Impact of *Leyland DAF*' (2005) *Recovery* (Spring) 18

Hill, C., 'Is Secured Debt Efficient?' (2002) 80 Texas L Rev. 1117

Hill, S., 'Company Voluntary Arrangements' (1990) 6 IL&P 47

Hintz, E., 'German Law on Cash Pooling in the Insolvency Context' (2007) Int. LR 78

Hitchens, L., 'Directorships: How Many Is Too Many?' [2000] CFILR 359

HM Treasury, *Banking Reform – Protecting Depositors: A Discussion Paper* (2007)

HM Treasury and Small Business Service, *Bridging the Finance Gap* (London, 2003)

Ho, L. C. '*Pari Passu* Distribution and Post-petition Disposition: A Rationalisation of *Re Tain Construction*' (21 November 2005, SSRN)

'Connected Persons and Administrators' Duty to Think: *Unidare v. Cohen*' [2005] JIBLR 606

'Goode's Swan Song to Corporate Insolvency Law' (2006) 17 EBLR 1727

'Whose Claim Is It? A Critical Assessment of the *Re Oasis Merchandising Services* Orthodox' (2007) 23 IL&P 70

Ho, L. C. and R. Mokal, 'Interplay of CVA, Administration and Liquidation: Part 1' (2004) 25 Co. Law. 3

Ho, L. and P. Smart, 'Re-interpreting the *Quistclose* Trust: A Critique of Chambers' Analysis' (2001) 21 OJLS 267

Hoffmann, Lord, 'The Fourth Annual Leonard Sainer Lecture – The Rt Hon. Lord Hoffmann' (1997) 18 Co. Law. 194

Hogan, A., 'Receivers Revisited' (1996) 17 Co. Law. 226

Holderness, C., 'Liability Insurers as Corporate Monitors' (1990) 10 *International Review of Law and Economics* 115

Homan, M., *A Survey of Administration Under the 1986 Insolvency Act* (Institute of Chartered Accountants, London, 1989)

Hood, C., 'The Risk Game and the Blame Game' (2002) 37 *Government and Opposition* 15

Hood, C., H. Rothstein and R. Baldwin, *The Government of Risk* (Oxford University Press, Oxford, 2001)

Hood, N., 'How the Enterprise Act is Helping to Preserve Businesses' (2005) *Recovery* (Spring) 14

Hopkins, D., 'A Company's Interests – A Question of Balance' (2004) 17 *Insolvency Intelligence* 103

Hopt, K., 'Legal Elements and Policy Decisions in Regulating Groups of Companies' in C. Schmitthoff and F. Wooldridge (eds.), *Groups of Companies* (Sweet & Maxwell, London, 1991)

  'Legal Issues and Questions of Policy in the Comparative Regulation of Groups' [1996] I *Gruppi di Società* 45

Horn, J., D. Lovallo and S. Viguerie, 'Learning to Let Go: Making Better Exit Decisions' (2006) 2 *McKinsey Quarterly* 64

Hornan, L., 'The Changing Face of Insolvency Practice' (2005) (March) *International Accountant* 24

Houston, K., 'Agreement to Share Fruits of Wrongful Trading Claim Void' (1997) 18 Co. Law. 297

Howell, C., '*Secretary of State* v. *Swan and North*' [2005] JBL 640

Howells, G. and S. Weatherill, *Consumer Protection Law* (Dartmouth, Aldershot, 1995)

Hu, H. and B. Black, 'Equity and Debt Decoupling and Empty Voting 11: Importance and Extensions' (2008) 156 U Pa. L Rev. 625

Hu, H. and J. Westbrook, 'Abolition of the Corporate Duty to Creditors' (2007) 107 Colum. L Rev. 1321

Huberman, G., D. Mayers and C. Smith, 'Optimal Insurance Policy Indemnity Schedules' (1983) 14 *Bell Journal of Economics* 415

Hudson, J., 'Characteristics of Liquidated Companies' (Mimeo, University of Bath, 1982)

  'The Case Against Secured Lending' (1995) 15 *International Review of Law and Economics* 47

Hughes, M., 'Pooling, Part 1' (2007) *Australian Insolvency Journal* (January–March) 12

Hume, D., *A Treatise of Human Nature*, L. Selby-Bigge and P. Nidditch (eds.) (Oxford University Press, Oxford, 1978)

Humphries, M., E. Pavlopoulos and P. Winterborne, 'Insolvency, Mediation and ADR' (1999) *Insolvency Bulletin* 7

Hunter, M., 'The Nature and Functions of a Rescue Culture' [1999] JBL 491

Hurst, T., 'Hedge Funds in the 21st Century' (2007) 28 Co. Law. 228

Hutton, W., *The State We're In* (Vintage, London, 1996)

ICAEW, Statement, *Guidance for Auditors on the Implications of Goods Sold Subject to Reservation of Title* (1977)

Guide to Professional Ethics, Statement on Insolvency Practice (September 1998)

Internal Control: Guidance for Directors on the Combined Code (London, 1999)

Memorandum TECH 13/99, *A Review of Company Rescue and Business Reconstruction Mechanisms* (1999)

Ife, L., 'Liability of Receivers and Banks in Selling and Managing Mortgaged Property' (2000) 13 *Insolvency Intelligence* 61

Ingram, D., 'The Proceeds of Crime and Insolvency' (2007) *Recovery* (Winter) 22

Insolvency Regulation Working Party, *Insolvency Practitioner Regulation – Ten Years On* (DTI, 1998)

A Review of Insolvency Practitioner Regulation (DTI, 1999)

Insolvency Service, *Framework Document 1990* (DTI, 1990)

Company Voluntary Arrangements and Administration Orders: A Consultative Document (1993)

Revised Proposals for a New Company Voluntary Arrangement Procedure (1995)

A Review of Company Rescue and Business Reconstruction Mechanisms, Interim Report (DTI, September 1999)

Bankruptcy: A Fresh Start (2000)

A Review of Company Rescue and Business Reconstruction Mechanisms, Report by the Review Group (DTI, 2000)

Regulatory Impact Assessment for Insolvency Provisions in the Enterprise Act 2002 (2002)

A Consultation Document on Changes to the Insolvency Act 1986 and the Company Directors' Disqualification Act 1986 to be made by a Legislative Reform Order for the Modernisation and Streamlining of Insolvency Procedures (London, 2007)

Enterprise Act 2002 – Corporate Insolvency Provisions: Evaluation Report (London, 2008)

Institute of Directors, *Sign of the Times* (1998)

IOSCO Technical Committee, *Report on the Subprime Crisis – Final Report* (May 2008)

Jackson, D., 'Foreign Maritime Liens in English Courts: Principle and Policy' [1981] 3 LMCLQ 335

Jackson, T. H., 'Bankruptcy, Non-bankruptcy Entitlements and the Creditors' Bargain' (1982) 92 Yale LJ 857

The Logic and Limits of Bankruptcy Law (Harvard University Press, Cambridge, Mass., 1986)

Jackson, T. H. and A. T. Kronman, 'Secured Financing and Priorities Among Creditors' (1979) 88 Yale LJ 1143

Jackson, T. H. and R. Scott, 'On the Nature of Bankruptcy: An Essay on Bankruptcy Sharing and the Creditors' Bargain' (1989) 75 Va. L Rev. 155

James, R., Private Ombudsmen and Public Law (Ashgate, Dartmouth, 1997)

Jensen, M. C. and W. H. Meckling, 'Theory of the Firm: Managerial Behaviour, Agency Costs and Ownership Structure' (1976) 3 Journal of Financial Economics 305

Jeremie, J., 'Gone in an Instant: The Death of "Scintilla Temporis" and the Growth of Purchase Money Security Interests in Real Property Law' [1994] JBL 363

Johnston, B., 'Contractual Debt Subordination and Legislative Reform' [1991] JBL 225

Jones, G., 'Credit Insurance: A Question of Support' (2004) Recovery (Summer) 21
'RPBs and Conflict' (2007) Recovery (Spring) 3

Jones, W. J., 'The Foundations of English Bankruptcy: Statutes and Commissions in the Early Modern Period' (1979) 69(3) Transactions of American Philosophical Society 69

Justice, Bankruptcy (Justice, London, 1975)
Insolvency Law: An Agenda for Reform (Justice, London, 1994)

Katz, A. and M. Mumford, Report to the Insolvency Service: Study of Administration Cases (Insolvency Service, London, December 2006)
Making Creditor Protection Effective (Centre for Business Performance, ICAEW, 2008) (Draft)

Katz, L., 'Asset Tracing: Getting Evidence and Injunctive Relief' (2007) Recovery (Winter) 18

Keay, A., 'The Australian Voluntary Administration Regime' (1996) 9 Insolvency Intelligence 41
'Australian Insolvency Law: The Latest Developments' (1998) 11 Insolvency Intelligence 57
'The Avoidance of Pre-Liquidation Transactions: Anglo-Australian Comparison' [1998] JBL 515
'Preferences in Liquidation Law: A Time for Change' [1998] 2 CfiLR 198
'Public Interest Petitions' (1999) 20 Co. Law. 296
'Disputing Debts Relied on by Petitioning Creditors Seeking Winding Up Orders' (2000) 22 Co. Law. 40
'The Recovery of Voidable Preferences: Aspects of Restoration' [2000] 1 CFILR 1
'The Duty of Directors to Take Account of Creditors' Interests' [2002] JBL 379

'Directors' Duties to Creditors: Contractarian Concerns Relating to Efficiency and Over-Protection of Creditors' (2003) 66 MLR 665

'Another Way of Skinning a Cat' (2004) 17 *Insolvency Intelligence* 1

'A Theoretical Analysis of the Director's Duty to Consider Creditor Interests: The Progressive School's Approach' [2004] JCLS 307

'Directors' Duties – Do Recent Canadian Developments Require a Rethink in the UK on the Issue of the Directors' Duties to Consider Creditors' Interests?' (2005) 18 *Insolvency Intelligence* 65

'What Future for Liquidation in Light of the Enterprise Act Reforms?' [2005] JBL 143

'Wrongful Trading and the Liability of Company Directors' (2005) 25 *Legal Studies* 432

'Wrongful Trading and the Point of Liability' (2006) 19 *Insolvency Intelligence* 132

Company Directors' Responsibilities to Creditors (Routledge-Cavendish, London, 2007)

'Section 172(1) of the Companies Act 2006' (2007) 28 Co. Law. 106

'Can Derivative Proceedings be Commenced when a Company is in Liquidation?' (2008) 21 *Insolvency Intelligence* 49

Keay, A. and P. Walton, 'Preferential Debts: An Empirical Study' [1999] Ins. Law. 112

'The Preferential Debts' Regime in Liquidation Law: In the Public Interest?' [1999] 3 CfiLR 84

Insolvency Law: Corporate and Personal (2nd edn, Jordans, Bristol, 2003)

Kelly, G. and J. Parkinson, 'The Conceptual Foundations of the Company' [1998] 2 CfiLR 174

Kemp, K. and D. Harris, 'Debt to Equity Conversions: Relieving the Interest Burden' (1993) PLC 19 (August)

Kent, P., 'The London Approach' (1993) 8 *Journal of International Banking Law* 81

'The London Approach: Distressed Debt Trading' (1994) *Bank of England Quarterly Bulletin* 110

'Corporate Workouts: A UK Perspective' (1997) 6 *International Insolvency Review* 165

Kershaw, D., 'Waiting for Enron: The Unstable Equilibrium of Auditor Independence Regulation' (2006) 33 *Journal of Law and Society* 388

Kilpi, J., *The Ethics of Bankruptcy* (Routledge, London, 1998)

Klein, B., 'Vertical Integration, Appropriable Rents and the Competitive Contracting Process' (1978) 21 *Journal of Law and Economics* 297

Knippenberg, S., 'The Unsecured Creditor's Bargain: An Essay in Reply, Reprisal or Support' (1994) 80 Va. L Rev. 1967

Kornberg, A., 'The Bankruptcy Abuse Prevention and Consumer Protection Act of 2005 – A Primer on Those Changes Affecting Business Bankruptcies' (2006) 3 *International Corporate Rescue* 33

Korobkin, D. R., 'Rehabilitating Values: A Jurisprudence of Bankruptcy' (1991) 91
　　Colum. L Rev. 717
　　'Contractarianism and the Normative Foundations of Bankruptcy Law' (1993)
　　71 Texas L Rev. 541
　　'The Role of Normative Theory in Bankruptcy Debates' (1996–7) 82 Iowa L
　　Rev. 75
Kothari, V., *Credit Derivatives and Synthetic Securitisation* (Vinod Kothari, India,
　　2002)
Kraakman, R. H., 'Corporate Liability Strategies and the Cost of Legal Controls'
　　(1984) 93 Yale LJ 857
　　'Gatekeepers: The Anatomy of a Third Party Enforcement Strategy' (1986)
　　Journal of Law, Economics and Organization 53
Kraakman, R. *et al.*, *The Anatomy of Corporate Law: A Comparative and
　　Functional Approach* (Oxford University Press, Oxford, 2006)
Krasner, G., 'Duration of CVAs' (2006) *Recovery* (Winter) 3
Kripke, H., 'Law and Economics: Measuring the Economic Efficiency of
　　Commercial Law in a Vacuum of Fact' (1985) 133 U Pa. L Rev. 929
Kronman, A. 'Wealth Maximisation as a Normative Principle' (1980) 9 *Journal of
　　Legal Studies* 227
Landers, J., 'A Unified Approach to Parent, Subsidiary and Affiliate Questions in
　　Bankruptcy' (1975) 42 U Chic. L Rev. 589
　　'Another Word on Parents, Subsidiaries and Affiliates in Bankruptcy' (1976) 43
　　U Chic. L Rev. 527
Laughton, C., 'Review of European Corporate Insolvency Regimes Part 1' (2004)
　　Recovery (Autumn) 16; 'Part 2' (2005) *Recovery* (Summer) 20
Lavargna, C. S., 'Government-sponsored Enterprises are "Too Big to Fail":
　　Balancing Public and Private Interests' (1993) 44(5) Hastings LJ 991
Law Commission, *Registration of Security Interests: Company Charges and
　　Property other than Land* (Law Com. Consultation Paper No. 164, 2002)
　　Company Security Interests (Law Com. Consultative Report No. 176, 2004)
　　Final Report on *Company Security Interests* (Law Com. No. 296, Cm 6654,
　　2005)
Law Commission and Scottish Law Commission, *Company Directors: Regulating
　　Conflicts of Interests and Formulating a Statement of Duties*, LCCP 153,
　　SLCDP 105 (TSO, London, 1998) part III
　　*Company Directors: Regulating Conflicts of Interest and Formulating a
　　Statement of Duties* (Law Commission Report No. 261, Scottish Law
　　Commission Report No. 173, 1999)
Law Society Company Law Committee, *Comments on the Insolvency Bill*, March
　　2000, No. 396
Lawler, D., 'The Money Detectives' (2007) *Recovery* (Winter) 24
Lawson, S., 'New Financial Collateral Regulations' (2004) *Recovery* (Autumn) 22

Leebron, D., 'Limited Liability, Tort Victims and Creditors' (1991) 91 Colum. L Rev. 1565

Leibowitz, D., 'Cover Charge', *The Lawyer*, 10 November 2003

Leinster, S., 'Policy Aims of the Enterprise Act' (2003) *Recovery* (Autumn) 27

Leong, A., 'The Assets Recovery Agency' (2007) 28 Co. Law. 379

Lester, A., N. Young and C. Hawes, 'Help is at Hand' (2002) *Recovery* (Winter) 18

Lester, V. M., *Victorian Insolvency* (Oxford University Press, Oxford, 1996)

Levmore, S., 'Monitors and Freeriders in Commercial and Corporate Settings' (1982) 92 Yale LJ 49

Lewis, N., 'The Citizens' Charter and Next Steps: A New Way of Governing?' (1993) *Political Quarterly* 316

Lewis, P., 'Trouble Down Under: Some Thoughts on the Australian–American Corporate Bankruptcy Divide' [2001] Utah L Rev. 189

'Corporate Rescue Law in the United States' in K. Gromek Broc and R. Parry, *Corporate Rescue: An Overview of Recent Developments* (2nd edn, Kluwer, London, 2006) p. 333

Lickorish, A., 'Debt Rescheduling' (1990) 6 IL&P 38

Lightman, G., 'Voluntary Administration: The New Wave or the New Waif in Insolvency Law?' (1994) 2 Ins. LJ 59

'The Challenges Ahead' [1996] JBL 113

'Office Holders: Evidence, Security and Independence' [1997] CfiLR 145

'Office Holders' Charges: Cost, Control and Transparency' (1998) 11 *Insolvency Intelligence* 1

Lightman, Sir G., and Moss, G., *The Law of Administrators and Receivers of Companies* (4th edn, Thomson/Sweet & Maxwell, London, 2007)

Lingard, J. R., *Corporate Rescues and Insolvencies* (2nd edn, Butterworths, London, 1989)

Linklater, L., 'New Style Administration: A Substitute for Liquidation?' (2005) 26 Co. Law. 129

Lipson, J., 'Directors' Duties to Creditors: Power Imbalance and the Financially Distressed Corporation' (2003) 50 UCLA L Rev. 1189

Lockerbie, A. and P. Godfrey, 'Pre-packaged Administration – The Legal Framework' (2006) *Recovery* (Summer) 21

LoPucki, L., 'The Debtor in Full Control – System Failure Under Chapter 11 of the Bankruptcy Code (First and Second Installments)' (1983) 57 *American Bankruptcy Law Journal* 99 and 247

'Reorganisation Realities, Methodological Realities, and the Paradigm Dominance Game' (1994) 72 Wash. ULQ 1307

'The Unsecured Creditor's Bargain' (1994) 80 Va. L Rev. 1887

LoPucki, L. and J. Doherty, 'Why are Delaware and New York Bankruptcy Reorganisations Failing?' (2002) 55 Vand. L Rev. 1933

LoPucki, L. and G. Triantis, 'A Systems Approach to Comparing US and Canadian Reorganization of Financially Distressed Companies' in J. Ziegel (ed.),

Current Developments in International and Comparative Corporate Insolvency Law (Clarendon Press, Oxford, 1994)

LoPucki, L. and W. Whitford, 'Corporate Governance in the Bankruptcy Reorganisation of Large, Publicly Held Companies' (1993) 141 U Pa. L Rev. 669

Loubser, A., 'South African Corporate Rescue' in K. Gromek Broc and R. Parry, *Corporate Rescue: An Overview of Recent Developments* (2nd edn, Kluwer, London, 2006)

Loughlin, M., *Public Law and Political Theory* (Clarendon Press, Oxford, 1992)

Lower, M., 'Good Faith and the Partly Owned Subsidiary' [2000] JBL 232

Lowry, J., 'The Whistleblower and the Non-Executive Director' [2006] 6 JCLS 249

Lubben, S., 'The New and Improved Chapter 11' (30 November 2004), Seton Hall Public Law Research Paper No. 2

Luhmann, N., *Social Systems* (Stanford University Press, Stanford, 1984)
  'Law as a Social System' (1989) 83 Northwestern Univ. LR 136

Lupica, L. R., 'Asset Securitization: The Unsecured Creditor's Perspective' (1998) 76 Texas L Rev. 595

Lyons, H. and M. Birch, 'Insolvency Expenses' (2005) 18 *Insolvency Intelligence* 150

MacDonald, D., 'Turnaround Finance' (2002) *Recovery* (Winter) 17

MacNeil, J., 'Economic Analysis of Contractual Relations' in P. Burrows and C. Veljanovski (eds.), *The Economic Approach to Law* (Butterworths, London, 1981)

Madoc-Jones, D. and N. Smith, 'Brave New World' (2007) *Recovery* (Summer) 18

Mannolini, J., 'Creditors' Interests in the Corporate Contract' (1996) 6 *Australian Journal of Corporate Law* 1

Manolopoulos, L., 'Note – A Congressional Choice: The Question of Environmental Priority in Bankrupt Estates' (1990) 9 *UCLA Journal of Environmental Law and Policy* 73

Marshall, J., '*Spectrum Plus*: A Wasted Opportunity?' (2005) *Recovery* (Summer) 30

Mason, C. and R. Harrison, 'Public Policy and the Development of the Informal Venture Capital Market' in K. Cowling (ed.), *Industrial Policy in Europe: Theoretical Perspectives and Practical Proposals* (Routledge, London, 1999)

Mason, S., 'Pre-packs from the Valuer's Perspective' (2006) *Recovery* (Summer) 19

Maunder, C., 'Bondholder Schemes of Arrangement: Playing the Numbers Game' (2003) 16 *Insolvency Intelligence* 73

Mayer, T., 'Personal Liability for Trading in a Prohibited Name' (2006) 27 Co. Law. 14

Mayers, D. and C. Smith, 'On the Corporate Demand for Insurance' (1982) 55 *Journal of Business* 281

Mayson, S. W., D. French and C. L. Ryan, *Mayson, French and Ryan on Company Law* (24th edn, Oxford University Press, Oxford, 2007)

McBryde, W., A. Flessner and S. Kortmann, *Principles of European Insolvency Law* (Kluwer, Deventer, 2003)

McCahery, J., S. Picciotto and C. Scott (eds.), *Corporate Control and Accountability* (Oxford University Press, Oxford, 1993)

McCarthy, M. and T. Flynn, *Risk from the CEO and Board Perspective* (McGraw-Hill, New York, 2004)

McCartney, P., 'Insolvency Procedures and a Landlord's Right of Peaceable Re-entry' (2000) 13 *Insolvency Intelligence* 73

McCormack, G., *Reservation of Title* (2nd edn, Sweet & Maxwell, London, 1995)

Proprietary Claims and Insolvency (Sweet & Maxwell, London, 1997)

'Charge-Backs and Commercial Certainty in the House of Lords (*Re BCCI (No. 8)*)' [1998] CfiLR 111

'Receiverships and the Rescue Culture' [2000] 2 CFILR 229

'Retention of Title and the EC Late Payment Directive' [2001] 1 JCLS 501

'Personal Property Security Law Reform in England and Canada' [2002] JBL 113

'Security Interests in Deposit Accounts: The Anglo-American Perspective' [2002] Ins. Law. 7

'Rewriting the English Law of Personal Property Securities and Article 9 of the US Uniform Commercial Code' (2003) 24 Co. Law. 69

'The Law Commission Consultative Report on Company Security Interests: An Irreverent Riposte' (2005) 68(2) MLR 286

'Swelling Corporate Assets: Changing what is on the Menu' [2006] 6 JCLS 39

'Control and Corporate Rescue – An Anglo–American Evaluation' (2007) 56 ICLQ 515

'Super-priority New Financing and Corporate Rescue' [2007] JBL 701

McDonald, I. and D. Shah, 'Fraudulent Trading' (2005) *Recovery* (Winter) 18

McGee, A. and G. Scanlon, 'Section 127 IA 1986: Practical Problems in its Application' (2004) 25 Co. Law. 102

McHarg, A., 'Regulation as a Private Law Function' [1995] PL 539

McIntosh, M., 'Insolvency Act 2000: Landlords' Right of Peaceable Re-entry' (2001) 17 IL&P 48

McKenzie Skene, D., 'The Directors' Duty to the Creditors of a Financially Distressed Company: A Perspective from Across the Pond' (2007) *Journal of Business and Technology Law* 499

McKenzie Skene, D. and Y. Enoch, 'Petitions for Administration Orders – Where there is a Need for Interim Measures: A Comparative Study of the Approach of the Courts in Scotland and England' [2000] JBL 103

McKnight, A., 'The Reform of Corporate Insolvency Law in Great Britain – The Enterprise Bill 2002' (2002) 17 JIBL 324

The Law of International Finance (Oxford University Press, Oxford, 2008)

McMeel, G., 'Retention of Title: The Interface of Contract, Unjust Enrichment and Insolvency' in F. Rose (ed.), *Restitution and Insolvency* (Lloyd's of London Press, London, 2000)

McMullen, J., 'An Analysis of the Transfer of Undertakings (Protection of Employment) Regulations 2006' (2006) 35 *Industrial Law Journal* 113

'The "Right" to Object to Transfer of Employment under TUPE' [2008] 37 Ins. LJ 169

McPherson, B., *The Law of Company Liquidation* (5th edn, Lawbook Co., Australia, 2007)

McVea, H., 'Hedge Funds and the New Regulatory Agenda' (2007) 7 *Legal Studies* 709

Meeks, G. and J. G. Meeks, 'A Gouldian View of Corporate Failure in the Process of Economic Natural Selection' (Mimeo, Centre for Business Research, University of Cambridge, 2002)

'Self-fulfilling Prophecies of Failure' (Judge Business School Working Paper, Cambridge, 2004)

Meuwissen, R., G. Mertens and L. Bollen, *Classification and Analysis of Major European Business Failures* (Accounting, Auditing and Information Management Research Centre and RSM Erasmus University, Maastricht/ Rotterdam, October 2005)

Miller, M., 'Wealth Transfers in Bankruptcy: Some Illustrative Examples' (1977) 41 *Law and Contemporary Problems* 39

Miller, P. and M. Power, 'Calculating Corporate Failure' in Y. Dezalay and D. Sugarman (eds.), *Professional Competition and Professional Power: Lawyers, Accountants and the Social Construction of Markets* (Routledge, London, 1995)

Milman, D., 'Insolvency Act 1986' (1987) 8 Co. Law. 61

'Priority Rights on Corporate Insolvency' in A. Clarke (ed.), *Current Issues in Insolvency Law* (Stevens & Sons, London, 1991)

'The Administration Order Regime and the Courts' in H. Rajak (ed.), *Insolvency Law: Theory and Practice* (Sweet & Maxwell, London, 1993)

'Litigation: Funding and Procedural Difficulties' (1997) *Amicus Curiae* 27

'Security for Costs: Principles and Pragmatism in Corporate Litigation' in B. Rider (ed.), *The Realm of Company Law* (Kluwer, London, 1998)

'Groups of Companies: The Path towards Discrete Regulation' in D. Milman (ed.), *Regulating Enterprise* (Hart, Oxford, 1999)

'Controlling Managerial Abuse: Current State of Play' [2000] Ins. Law. 193

'A Fresh Light on Shadow Directors' [2000] Ins. Law. 171

'Post Liquidation Tax as a Winding Up Expense' [2000] Ins. Law. 169

'A Question of Honour' [2000] Ins. Law. 247

'Remuneration: Researching the Fourth R' (2000) *Recovery* (August) 18

'Company Charges: A Return to Harsh Reality' [2001] Ins. Law. 135

'Company Law Review: Company Charges' [2001] Ins. Law. 180

'The Courts and the Administration Regime: Supporting Legislative Policy' [2001] Ins. Law. 208

'Schemes of Arrangement: Their Continuing Role' [2001] Ins. Law. 145

'Strategies for Regulating Managerial Performance in the Twilight Zone' [2004] JBL 493

Personal Insolvency Law, Regulation and Policy (Ashgate Publishing, Aldershot, 2005)

Milman, D. and F. Chittenden, *Corporate Rescue: CVAs and the Challenge of Small Companies*, ACCA Research Report 44 (ACCA, London, 1995)

Milman, D. and C. Durrant, *Corporate Insolvency: Law and Practice* (3rd edn, Sweet & Maxwell, London, 1999)

Milman, D. and D. Mond, *Security and Corporate Rescue* (Hodgsons, Manchester, 1999)

Milman, D. and R. Parry, *A Study of the Operation of Transactional Avoidance Mechanisms in Corporate Insolvency Practice*, Insolvency Lawyers' Association Research Report (1997)

Mistry, H., '*Hollicourt*: Bringing the Authorities Out of Disarray' (2001) 22 Co. Law. 278

Moffat, G., *Trusts Law: Text and Materials* (4th edn, Cambridge University Press, Cambridge, 2005)

Moffat, M., 'Directors' Dilemma: An Economic Evaluation of Directors' Liability for Environmental Damages and Unpaid Wages' (1996) 54 U Toronto Fac. LR 293

Mokal, R., 'Resolving the *MS Fashions* "Paradox"' [1999] CfiLR 106

'An Agency Cost Analysis of the Wrongful Trading Provisions: Redistribution, Perverse Incentives and the Creditors' Bargain' [2000] 59 CLJ 335

'The Authentic Consent Model: Contractarianism, Creditors' Bargain and Corporate Liquidation' (2001) 21 *Legal Studies* 400

'Consideration, Characterisation, Evaluation: Transactions at Undervalue after *Phillips* v. *Brewin Dolphin*' [2001] JCLS 359

'Priority as Pathology: The *Pari Passu* Myth' [2001] CLJ 581

'The Floating Charge – An Elegy' in S. Worthington (ed.), *Commercial Law and Commercial Practice* (Hart, Oxford, 2003)

'Liquidation Expenses and Floating Charges – The Separate Funds Fallacy' [2004] LMCLQ 387

Corporate Insolvency Law: Theory and Application (Oxford University Press, Oxford, 2005)

'What Liquidation Does for Secured Creditors and What It Does for You' (2008) 71 MLR 699

Mokal, R. and J. Armour, 'The New UK Corporate Rescue Procedure – The Administrator's Duty to Act Rationally' (2004) 1 *International Corporate Rescue* 136

Moran, M., *The British Regulatory State* (Oxford University Press, Oxford, 2003)

Morgan, R., 'Insolvency and the Rights of Employees' [1989] *Legal Action* 21

Morris, C. and M. Kirschner, 'Cross-border Rescues and Asset Recovery: Problems and Solutions' (1994) 10 IL&P 42

Morris, G., 'Transferring Liability for Employee Claims' [2000] JBL 188

Morris, R., *Early Warning Indicators of Corporate Failure* (Ashgate/ICCA, London, 1997)

Morse, G., 'Shadow Directors and *De Facto* Directors in the Context of Proceedings for Disqualification on the Grounds of Unfitness and Wrongful Trading' in B. Rider (ed.), *The Corporate Dimension: An Exploration of Developing Areas of Company and Commercial Law* (Jordans, Bristol, 1998)

Moss, G., 'Comparative Bankruptcy Cultures: Rescue or Liquidations? Comparisons of Trends in National Law – England' (1997) 23 *Brooklyn Journal of International Law* 115

   'Chapter 11: An English Lawyer's Critique' (1998) 11 Insolvency Intelligence 17

   'Avoidance of Transactions – No Cherry Picking' (2001) 14 *Insolvency Intelligence*

   'Independent Assessor Helps To Set "Independent" Fees' (2003) 16 *Insolvency Intelligence* 61

   'On the Edge of Non-Recognition? Appointment of Administrators under the Enterprise Act and the EC Regulation' (2004) 17 *Insolvency Intelligence* 13

   'Liquidators Stung for Costs and Expenses' (2004) 17 *Insolvency Intelligence* 78

   'Rescue Culture Speared by *Trident*' (2007) 20 *Insolvency Intelligence* 72

Moss, G. and C. Paulus, 'The European Insolvency Regulation – The Case for Urgent Reform' (2006) 19 *Insolvency Intelligence* 1

Moulton, J., 'The Uncomfortable Edge of Propriety – Pre-packs or Just Stitch-ups?' (2005) *Recovery* (Spring) 2

Muchlinski, P., 'Holding Multinationals to Account' (2002) 23 Co. Law. 168

Mudd, P., 'The Insolvency Act 1994: *Paramount* Cured?' (1994) 10 IL&P 38

   '*Paramount*: The House of Lords Decision – Is There Still Hope of Avoiding Some of Those Claims?' (1995) 11 IL&P 78

Mujih, E., 'Legitimising Charge-Backs' [2001] Ins. Law. 3

Mulheron, R., *The Class Action in Common Law Systems* (Hart, Oxford, 2005)

Mulligan, M. and J. Tribe, 'The Remuneration of Office Holders in Corporate Insolvency – Liquidators, Administrators and Administrative Receivers: Part 1' (2003) 3 Ins. Law. 101

Myers, S., 'Determinants of Corporate Borrowing' (1977) 5 *Journal of Financial Economics* 147

NAO, *Company Director Disqualification* (October 1993, HC 907)

   Supporting Innovation: Managing Risk in Government Departments (NAO, London, 2000)

   Supporting Small Business (HC 962 Session 2005–6, London, May 2006)

Napier, C. and C. Noke, 'Premium and Pre-acquisition Profits: The Legal and Accounting Professions and Business Combinations' (1991) 54 MLR 810

'Accounting and Law: An Historical Overview of an Uneasy Relationship' in M. Bromwich and A. G. Hopwood (eds.), *Accounting and the Law* (Institute of Chartered Accountants in England and Wales, London, 1992)

Narey, I. and P. Rubenstein, 'Separation of Book Debts and their Proceeds' [1994] CLJ 225

Nelson, P., 'Information and Consumer Behaviour' (1970) 78 *Journal of Political Economy* 311

Newbegin, 'Disqualifying Directors', *The Lawyer*, 24 September 1991

Nicolle, R., 'Employee Rights in a Restructuring' (2008) *Recovery* (Spring) 37

Nimmer, R. and R. Feinberg, 'Chapter 11 Business Governance: Fiduciary Duties, Business Judgement, Trustees and Exclusivity' (1989) 6 *Bankruptcy Development Journal* 1

Nolan, R., '*Downsview Nominees Ltd* v. *First City Corporation Ltd* – Good News for Receivers – In General' (1994) 15 Co. Law. 28

'Less Equal than Others: *Maxwell* and Subordinated Unsecured Obligations' [1995] JBL 484

Noonan, C. and S. Watson, 'The Nature of Shadow Directorship' [2006] JBL 763

Norley, L., 'Tooled Up', *The Lawyer*, 10 November 2003

Nozick, R., *Anarchy, State and Utopia* (Blackwell, Oxford, 1974)

Philosophical Explanations (Clarendon Press, Oxford, 1981)

Oakley, A., 'Proprietary Claims and their Priority in Insolvency' [1995] CLJ 377

Obank, R., 'European Recovery Practice and Reform: Part I' [2000] Ins. Law. 149

O'Connell, F., J. Outen, and A. Stephens, 'Forensic Recovery: A Blend of Insolvency and Forensics' (2007) *Recovery* (Winter) 20

O'Connor, M., 'Restructuring the Corporation's Nexus of Contracts: Recognizing a Fiduciary Duty to Protect Displaced Workers' (1991) 69 North Car. L Rev. 1189

Oditah, F., 'Wrongful Trading' [1990] LMCLQ 205

Legal Aspects of Receivables Financing (Sweet & Maxwell, London, 1991)

'Assets and the Treatment of Claims in Insolvency' (1992) 108 LQR 459

'Misfeasance Proceedings against Company Directors' [1992] LMCLQ 207

'Fixed Charges over Book Debts after *Brumark*' (2001) 14 *Insolvency Intelligence* 49

Oditah, F. and A. Zacaroli, 'Chattel Leases and Insolvency' [1997] CfiLR 29

O'Donovan, J., 'Group Therapies for Group Insolvencies' in M. Gillooly (ed.), *The Law Relating to Corporate Groups* (Butterworths, Sydney, 1993)

Offer, K., 'Influential Desire and Dominant Intention' (1990) 3 *Insolvency Intelligence* 42

Office of Fair Trading, *The Protection of Consumer Prepayments: A Discussion Paper* (1984)

Ogowewo, T., 'A Perfect Case for the Application of Section 423 of the Insolvency Act 1986: *Yukong Line of Korea* v. *Rendsburg Investments Corp. of Liberia (No. 2)*' [1999] Ins. Law. 106

Ogus, A. I., *Regulation: Legal Form and Economic Theory* (Oxford University Press, Oxford, 1994)

Ogus, A. and C. Rowley, *Prepayments and Insolvency* (OFT Occasional Paper, 1984)

Ogus, A. and C. Veljanovski, *Readings in the Economics of Law and Regulation* (Oxford University Press, Oxford, 1984)

Omar, P. J., 'The Position of Employees in French Insolvency Law' (1996) 7 *International Company and Commercial Law Review* 394

European Insolvency Law (Ashgate Publishing, Aldershot, 2004)

'The Convergence of Creditor-Driven and Formal Insolvency Models' (2005) 2 *International Corporate Rescue* 251

'French Insolvency Law and the 2005 Reforms' (2005) 16 *International Company and Commercial Law Review* 490

'Reforms to the Framework of Insolvency Law and Practice in France: 1999–2006' in K. Gromek Broc and R. Parry, *Corporate Rescue: An Overview of Recent Developments* (2nd edn, Kluwer, London, 2006) p. 111

Omar, P. (ed.), *International Insolvency Law: Themes and Perspectives* (Ashgate Publishing, Aldershot, 2008)

Otty, L., 'Banking on the Managers' (2002) *Recovery* (Winter) 12

Painter, C., 'Note: Tort Creditor Priority in the Secured Credit System: Asbestos Times, the Worst of Times' (1984) 36 Stanford L Rev. 1045

Parker, C., *The Open Corporation: Effective Self-Regulation and Democracy* (Cambridge University Press, Cambridge, 2002)

Parkinson, J. E., *Corporate Power and Responsibility: Issues in the Theory of Company Law* (Clarendon Press, Oxford, 1993)

'The Contractual Theory of the Company and the Protection of Non-Shareholder Interests' in D. Feldman and F. Meisel (eds.), *Corporate and Commercial Law: Modern Developments* (Lloyd's of London Press, London, 1996)

'Disclosure and Corporate Social and Environmental Performance: Competitiveness and Enterprise in a Broader Social Framework' [2003] 3 JCLS 3

Parr, C., 'Due Diligence: Seek and You Shall Find' (2008) *Recovery* (Spring) 42

Parr, R. and N. Bennett, 'The Rescue Culture v. Collective Employment Rights' (2005) 18 *Insolvency Intelligence* 156

Parry, R., 'Funding Litigation in Insolvency' [1998] 2 CfiLR 121

Parry, R. and D. Milman, 'Transaction Avoidance Provision in Corporate Insolvency: An Empirical Study' (1998) 14 IL&P 280

Partnoy, F. and D. Skeel, 'The Promises and Perils of Credit Derivatives' (U Pa. Law School Working Paper 125, 2006)

Pateman, C., *Participation and Democratic Theory* (Cambridge University Press, London, 1970)

Payne, J., 'Casting Light into the Shadows: *Secretary of State for Trade and Industry v. Deverell*' (2001) 22 Co. Law. 90

Pedley, R., 'The Enterprise Bill' (2002) IL&P 123

Penner, J., *The Law of Trusts* (5th edn, Oxford University Press, Oxford, 2006)

Penner, M., 'Hedge Funds: Risk Management and Valuation "Red Flags"' (2007) *Recovery* (Winter) 30

Pesse, J. and D. Wood, 'Issues in Assessing MDA Models of Corporate Failure: A Research Note' (1992) 24 *British Accounting Review* 33

Peters, G., 'Undervalues and the Value of Creditor and Debtor Covenants: A Comparative Analysis' (2008) 21 *Insolvency Intelligence* 81

Peterson, M. and R. Rajan, 'The Benefits of Lending Relationships: Evidence from Small Business Data' (1994) 49 *Journal of Finance* 3

Pettet, B., 'Limited Liability: A Principle for the 21st Century?' in M. Freeman and R. Halson (eds.) (1995) 48 *Current Legal Problems* 125

Pettit, G., 'A Level Playing Field?' (2007) *Recovery* (Autumn) 3

Phillips, M., *The Administration Procedure and Creditors' Voluntary Arrangements* (Centre for Commercial Law Studies, QMW, London, 1996)
'Retention of Title and Mixing – Exploding the Myth' (2007) 20 *Insolvency Intelligence* 81

Phillips, M. and J. Goldring, 'Rescue and Reconstruction' (2002) *Insolvency Intelligence* 76

Pike, N., 'The Human Rights Act 1998 and its Impact on Insolvency Practitioners' [2001] Ins. Law. 25

Platt, H. D., *Why Companies Fail: Strategies for Detecting, Avoiding, and Profiting from Bankruptcy* (Lexington Books, Lexington, Mass., 1985)

Plevin, M., R. Ebert, and L. Epley, 'Pre-packaged Asbestos Bankruptcies: A Flawed Solution' (2002) 44 South Texas L Rev. 883

Pointon, F., 'London Approach: A Look at its Application and its Alternatives' (1994) *Insolvency Bulletin* 5 (March)

Polinsky, S. and S. Shavell, 'Should Employees be Subject to Fines and Imprisonment Given the Existence of Corporate Liability?' (1993) 13 *International Review of Law and Economics* 239

Pollard, D., 'Pensions and TUPE' (2005) 34 *Industrial Law Journal* 127
'TUPE and Insolvency, I and II' (2006) 19(6) *Insolvency Intelligence* 81 and (2006) 19(7) *Insolvency Intelligence* 102
'Personal Liability of an Insolvency Practitioner for Employee Claims, Parts 1 and 2' (2007) 10 *Insolvency Intelligence* 145, (2008) 11 *Insolvency Intelligence* 7

Pollard, D. and I. Carruthers, 'Pensions as a Preferential Debt' (2004) 17
  Insolvency Intelligence 65
Pope, T. and M. Woollard, 'The Balance of Power in the Expenses Regime: Part 1 –
  Leyland DAF' (2001) 14 *Insolvency Intelligence* 9
  'Part 2 – *Lewis*' (2001) 14 *Insolvency Intelligence* 20
Posner, R., 'The Rights of Creditors of Affiliated Corporations' (1976) 43 U Chic. L
  Rev. 499
  'Utilitarianism, Economics and Legal Theory' (1979) 8 *Journal of Legal
  Studies* 103
  Economic Analysis of Law (6th edn, Aspen Law and Business, New York, 2002)
Pound, J., 'The Rise of the Political Model of Corporate Governance and
  Corporate Control' (1993) 68 NYU L Rev. 1003
Poutziouris, P., F. Chittenden and N. Michaelas, *The Financial Development of
  Smaller Private and Public SMEs* (Manchester Business School, Manchester,
  1999)
Power, M., *The Audit Explosion* (Demos, London, 1994)
  The Audit Society: Rituals of Verification (Oxford University Press, Oxford,
  1997)
  The Risk Management of Everything (Demos, London, 2004)
  Organised Uncertainty: Designing a World of Risk Management (Oxford
  University Press, Oxford, 2007)
Prangley, M., 'Providing Support to Management in a Highly Leveraged Market'
  (2007) *Recovery* (Summer) 26
Pratten, C. F., *Company Failure* (Institute of Chartered Accountants in England
  and Wales, London, 1991)
Prentice, D., 'The Effect of Insolvency on Pre-liquidation Transactions' in B. Pettet
  (ed.), *Company Law in Change* (Stevens & Sons, London, 1987)
  'Creditors' Interest and Directors' Duties' (1990) 10 OJLS 265
  'Directors, Creditors and Shareholders' in E. McKendrick (ed.), *Commercial
  Aspects of Trusts and Fiduciary Obligations* (Clarendon Press, Oxford, 1992)
  'Contracts and Corporate Insolvency Proceedings', paper given at SPTL
  Seminar on Insolvency Proceedings, Oxford, September 1995
  'Some Observations on the Law Relating to Preferences' in R. Cranston (ed.),
  Making Commercial Law (Clarendon Press, Oxford, 1997)
  'Corporate Personality, Limited Liability and the Protection of Creditors' in
  R. Grantham and C. Rickett (eds.), *Corporate Personality in the Twentieth
  Century* (Hart, Oxford, 1998)
  'Bargaining in the Shadow of the Enterprise Act 2002' (2004) 5 EBOR 153
Pugh, C., 'Duties of Care Owed to Mortgagors and Guarantors: The Hidden
  Liability' (1995) 11 IL&P 143
  '*Hollicourt* to Reduce Banks' Exposure under Section 127' (2001) 17 IL&P 53
Pugh, R., 'Turnaround of Dartington Group Limited' (2007) *Recovery* (Autumn) 20

Qi, L., 'The Rise of Pre-packaged Corporate Rescue on Both Sides of the Atlantic' (2007) 20 *Insolvency Intelligence* 129

Quo, S., 'Insolvency Law: A Comparative Analysis of the Preference Tests in the UK and Australia' (2007) 28 Co. Law. 355

R3, the Association of Business Recovery Professionals, 'The Moratorium Provisions for the Company Voluntary Arrangement Procedure in the Insolvency Bill 2000' (2000) 16 IL&P 77

Ninth Survey of Business Recovery in the UK (R3, London, 2001)

Ostrich's Guide to Business Survival (R3, London, 2002)

12th Survey, Corporate Insolvency in the United Kingdom (R3, London, 2004)

Rabin, R., 'Deterrence and the Tort System' in M. Friedman (ed.), *Sanctions and Rewards in the Legal System* (University of Toronto Press, Toronto, 1989)

Rafferty, C. and O. Gayle, 'Financial Services and Markets Act 2000: Considerations for the IP' (2007) *Recovery* (Summer) 35

Rajak, H., 'Company Rescue' (1993) 4 IL&P 111

Insolvency Law: Theory and Practice (Sweet & Maxwell, London, 1993)

'The Challenges of Commercial Reorganisation in Insolvency: Empirical Evidence from England' in J. S. Ziegel (ed.), *Current Developments in International and Comparative Corporate Insolvency Law* (Clarendon Press, Oxford, 1994)

'Can a Receiver be Negligent?' in B. Rider (ed.), *The Corporate Dimension: An Exploration of Developing Areas of Company and Commercial Law* (Jordans, Bristol, 1998) p. 129

'The Enterprise Act and Insolvency Law Reform' (2003) Co. Law. 3

Ramsay, I., 'Allocating Liability in Corporate Groups: An Australian Perspective' (1999) 13 Connecticut JIL 329

Ramsay, I. and B. Saunders, 'Litigation by Shareholders and Directors: An Empirical Study of the Statutory Derivative Action' [2006] 2 JCLS 397

Rasmussen, R., 'Debtor's Choice: A Menu Approach to Corporate Bankruptcy' (1992) 71 Texas L Rev. 51

'An Essay on Optimal Bankruptcy Rules and Social Justice' (1994) U Illinois L Rev. 1

'The Ex Ante Effects of Bankruptcy Reform on Investment Incentives' (1994) 72 Wash. ULQ 1159

Rawls, J., *A Theory of Justice* (Harvard University Press, Cambridge, Mass., 1971)

The Liberal Theory of Justice: A Critical Examination of the Principal Doctrines in 'A Theory of Justice' (Clarendon Press, Oxford, 1973)

Redstone, D., 'Customer Deposits (in the Twilight Zone)' (2008) *Recovery* (Spring) 17

Report of the Commission on the Bankruptcy Laws of the US, Part 1, HR Doc. No. 137, 93d Cong., 1st Sess. 85 (1973)

Report of the Committee on Consumer Credit (Lord Crowther, Chair) (Cmnd 4596, 1971)

Report of the Committee on the Financial Aspects of Corporate Governance (Cadbury Committee) (December 1992)

Report of the Review Committee on Insolvency Law and Practice (Cmnd 8558, 1982) (Cork Report)

Report of the Study Committee on Bankruptcy and Insolvency Legislation (Canada, 1970)

Richardson, P., 'Consumer Protection and the Trust' [1985] JBL 456

Rickett, C., 'Different Views on the Scope of the *Quistclose* Analysis: English and Antipodean Insights' (1991) 107 LQR 608

'Of Constructive Trusts and Insolvency' in F. Rose (ed.), *Restitution and Insolvency* (Lloyd's of London Press, London, 2000)

Ridgway, P., 'Corporation Tax in Insolvency: Part 3 – Equitable Set-off and Crown Debts' (2000) 13 *Insolvency Intelligence* 9

Riley, C., 'The Company Director's Duty of Care and Skill: The Case for an Onerous but Subjective Standard' (1999) 62 MLR 697

Rinze, J., 'Konzernrecht: Law on Groups of Companies in Germany' (1993) 14 Co. Law. 143

Robins, J., 'The Enterprise Act Has Failed to Earn Respect' (2005) *Finance Week* (25 May)

Roe, M., 'Commentary on "On the Nature of Bankruptcy": Bankruptcy, Priority and Economics' (1989) 75 Va. L Rev. 219

Roome, J., 'The Unwelcome Guest' (2004) *Recovery* (Summer) 30

Rosh, R., 'New York's Response to the "D & O" Insurance Crisis' (1989) 54 Brooklyn LR 1305

Rotherham, C., 'Charges Over Customers' Deposit Accounts' [1998] CLJ 260

Rubin, G. R. and D. Sugarman (eds.), *Law, Economy and Society: Essays in the History of English Law* (Professional Books, Abingdon, 1984)

Rumney, G. and R. Smith, 'Sorting Out the Bad Apples' (2005) *Recovery* (Winter) 36

Rusch, L. J., 'Bankruptcy Reorganisation Jurisprudence: Matters of Belief, Faith and Hope' (1994) 55 Montana L Rev. 16

Samuels, J., F. Wilkes and R. Brayshaw, *Management of Company Finance* (6th edn, International Thompson Business Press, London, 1995)

Sandel, M. J., *Liberalism and the Limits of Justice* (Cambridge University Press, Cambridge, 1982)

Sappideen, R., 'Ownership of the Large Corporation: Why Clothe the Emperor?' (1996–7) 7 King's College LJ 27

Sargeant, M., 'Business Transfers and Corporate Insolvencies: The Effect of TUPE' (1998) 14 IL&P 8

'More Flexibility for Insolvent Transfers: The Amended Acquired Rights Directive' (1999) 15 IL&P 6

'TUPE – The Final Round' [2006] JBL 549

Savarimuthu, A., '*Morphitis* in the Court of Appeal' (2005) 26 Co. Law. 245

Schermer, B. S., 'Response to Professor Gross: Taking the Interests of the Community into Account in Bankruptcy' (1994) 72 Wash. ULQ 1049

Schiller, C. and E. Braun, 'The New Insolvency Code' in J. Reuvid and R. Millar (eds.), *Doing Business with Germany* (Kogan Page, London, 1999)

Schmitthoff, C. M., 'A Consumers' Prepayment (Protection) Bill?' [1984] JBL 105

Schmitthoff, C. and F. Wooldridge (eds.), *Groups of Companies* (Sweet & Maxwell, London, 1991)

Schulte, R., 'Corporate Groups and the Equitable Subordination of Claims on Insolvency' (1997) 18 Co. Law. 2

Schwarcz, S., 'The Easy Case for the Priority of Secured Claims in Bankruptcy' (1997) 47 Duke LJ 425

Schwartz, A., 'Security Interests and Bankruptcy Priorities: A Review of Current Theories' (1981) 10 *Journal of Legal Studies* 1
 'A Theory of Loan Priorities' (1989) 18 *Journal of Legal Studies* 209
 'Taking the Analysis of Security Seriously' (1994) 80 Va. L Rev. 2073

Scott, J., 'Bankruptcy, Secured Debt and Optimal Capital Structure' (1977) 32 *Journal of Financial Law* 2

Scott, R., 'A Relational Theory of Secured Financing' (1986) 86 Colum. L Rev. 901

Sealy, L. S., *Company Law and Commercial Reality* (Sweet & Maxwell, London, 1984)
 'Directors' "Wider" Responsibilities: Problems, Conceptual, Practical and Procedural' (1987) 13 Monash LR 164
 'Personal Liability of Directors and Officers for Debts of Insolvent Corporations: A Jurisdictional Perspective (England)' in J. Ziegel (ed.), *Current Developments in International and Comparative Corporate Insolvency Law* (Clarendon Press, Oxford, 1994)
 'Corporate Rescue Procedures: Some Overseas Comparisons' in F. Macmillan (ed.), *Perspectives in Company Law* (Kluwer, London, 1995)
 'Mortgagees and Receivers: A Duty of Care Resurrected and Extended' [2000] CLJ 31

Sealy, L. S. and D. Milman, *Annotated Guide to the Insolvency Legislation*, Volumes I and II (10th edn, Thomson/Sweet & Maxwell, London, 2007)

Sears, T., 'Turbulence in the Travel Trade' (2008) *Recovery* (Spring) 28

Segal, N., 'Rehabilitation and Approaches other than Formal Insolvency Procedures' in R. Cranston (ed.), *Banks and Remedies* (Oxford University Press, Oxford, 1992) p. 133
 'An Overview of Recent Developments and Future Prospects in the UK' in J. Ziegel (ed.), *Current Developments in International and Comparative Corporate Insolvency Law* (Clarendon Press, Oxford, 1994)

'Corporate Recovery and Rescue: Mastering the Key Strategies Necessary for Successful Cross Border Workouts – Part I and Part II' (2000) 13 *Insolvency Intelligence* 17, 25

'Schemes of Arrangement and Junior Creditors – Does the US Approach to Valuations Provide the Answer?' (2007) 20 *Insolvency Intelligence* 49

Selvam, V., 'Revisiting the Justifications for Insolvency Set-off' (2004) 25 Co. Law. 343

'Recharacterisation in "True Sale" Securitizations' [2006] JBL 637

Sen, A. and B. Williams (eds.), *Utilitarianism and Beyond* (Cambridge University Press, Cambridge, 1982)

Shah, D., 'Undervalue Transactions and Preferences: The "Good Faith" Defence' (2007) 20 *Insolvency Intelligence* 76

Shanker, M., 'The Worthier Creditors (and a Cheer for the King)' (1975–6) 1 Canadian Bus. LJ 341

'The American Bankruptcy Preference Law: Perceptions of the Past, the Transition to the Present, and Ideas for the Future' in J. Ziegel (ed.), *Current Developments in International and Comparative Corporate Insolvency Law* (Clarendon Press, Oxford, 1994)

Sharp, A., 'The Collateral Directive – A New Way of Thinking About Security' (2004) 17 *Insolvency Intelligence* 145

Shavell, S., 'On Liability and Insurance' (1982) 13 Bell Journal of Economics 120

'Liability for Harm Versus Regulation of Safety' (1984) 13 *Journal of Legal Studies* 357

Economic Analysis of Accident Law (Harvard University Press, Cambridge, Mass., 1987)

Shaw, B., 'Occupational Pensions Trusts' (2008) *Recovery* (Autumn) 40

Shaw, P., 'Administrators: Peaceable Re-entry by a Landlord Revisited' [1999] Ins. Law. 254

Shillig, M., 'The Development of a New Concept of Creditor Protection for German GmbHs' (2006) 27 Co. Law. 348

Shimell, P., *The Universe of Risk* (Financial Times/Prentice Hall, London, 2002)

Shrubsall, V., 'Competitive Tendering, Out-sourcing and the Acquired Rights Directive' (1998) 61 MLR 85

Shuchman, P., 'An Attempt at a "Philosophy of Bankruptcy"' (1973) 21 UCLA L Rev. 403

Shulte, S., 'Enforcing Wrongful Trading as a Standard of Conduct for Directors and a Remedy for Creditors: The Special Case for Corporate Insolvency' (1999) 20 Co. Law. 80

Shupack, P., 'Solving the Puzzle of Secured Transactions' (1989) 41 Rutgers L Rev. 1067

Sidle, P., 'Whose Money is it Anyway?' (2005) *Recovery* (Autumn) 24

Sikka, P., 'Turkeys Don't Vote for Christmas, Do They?' (1999) *Insolvency Bulletin* 5 (June)

Simmons, M., 'Avoiding the *Pari Passu* Rule' (1996) 9 *Insolvency Intelligence* 9
  'Wrongful Trading' (2001) 14 *Insolvency Intelligence* 12
  'Enterprise Act and Plain English' (2004) 17 *Insolvency Intelligence* 76
  'Some Reflections on Administrations, Crown Preference and Ring Fenced Sums in the Enterprise Act' [2004] JBL 423
Simmons, M. and T. Smith, 'The Human Rights Act 1998: The Practical Impact on Insolvency' (2000) 16 IL&P 167
Sims, H. and N. Briggs, 'Enterprise Act 2002 – Corporate Wrinkles' (2004) 17 *Insolvency Intelligence* 49
Sinclair, D., 'Self-regulation Versus Command and Control' (1997) 20 *Law & Policy* 529
Skeel, D., 'The Past, Present and Future of Debtor-in-Possession Financing' (2004) 25 Cardozo LR 101
Smith, A. and M. Neill, 'The Insolvency Act 2000' (2001) 17 IL&P 84
Smith, C. and J. Warner, 'On Financial Contracting: An Analysis of Bond Covenants' (1979) 7 *Journal of Financial Economics* 117
Smith, D., 'Partners in Insolvency' (2007) *Recovery* 7 (Autumn)
Snaith, I., with assistance of F. Cownie, *The Law of Corporate Insolvency* (Waterlow, London, 1990)
Society of Practitioners of Insolvency, Eighth Survey, *Company Insolvency in the United Kingdom* (SPI, London, 1999)
Spahos, D., 'Lenders, Borrowing Groups of Companies and Corporate Guarantees: An Insolvency Perspective' [2001] JCLS 333
Spence, N., 'Personal Liability for Wrongful Trading' (2004) 17 *Insolvency Intelligence* 11
Spencer, J., 'The Commercial Realities of Reservation of Title Clauses' [1989] JBL 220
Stein, J., 'Rescue Operations in Business Crises' in K. J. Hopt and G. Teubner (eds.), *Corporate Governance and Directors' Liabilities: Legal, Economic, and Sociological Analyses on Corporate Social Responsibility* (De Gruyter, Berlin, 1985) p. 380
Stevens, R., 'Insolvency' in W. Swadling (ed.), *The Quistclose Trust: Critical Essays* (Hart Publishing, Oxford, 2004) p. 153
  'Security after the Enterprise Act' in J. Getzler and J. Payne (eds.), *Company Changes: Spectrum and Beyond* (Oxford University Press, Oxford, 2006) p. 153
Stevenson, M., 'The Enterprise Bill 2002 – A Move Towards a Rescue Culture?' (2002) 18 IL&P 155
Stewart, G., 'No Remedial Trust in Insolvency' (1998) (August) *Insolvency Practitioner* 8
  'Legal Update' (2001) *Recovery* (July) 8
  'The British Eagle has Landed' (2001) *Recovery* (December) 7

'Liquidation Expenses – Litigation' (2001) *Recovery* (July) 8

'Heresy in the House of Lords' (2002) *Recovery* (September) 6

'Liquidation Expenses – Provisional Liquidators' Remuneration' (2002) *Recovery* (Winter) 6

'Section 127 and Change of Position Defences' (2003) *Recovery* (Autumn) 6

'Legal Update – The Challenge of the *T & N* Case' (2006) *Recovery* (Spring) 7

Stewart, R. B., 'The Reformation of American Administrative Law' (1975) 99(2) Harv. L Rev. 1667

Stock, K., 'Australian Developments in the Law of Retention of Title' (2002) 15 *Insolvency Intelligence* 1

Stokes, M., 'Company Law and Legal Theory' in W. Twining (ed.), *Legal Theory and Common Law* (Blackwell, Oxford, 1986)

Stone, C. D., 'The Place of Enterprise Liability in the Control of Corporate Conduct' (1980) 90 Yale LJ 1

Stone, K. Van Wezel, 'Policing Employment Contracts Within the Nexus-of-Contracts Firm' (1993) 43 U Toronto LJ 353

'Labour Markets, Employment Contracts and Corporate Change' in J. McCahery, S. Picciotto, and C. Scott (eds.), *Corporate Control and Accountability* (Clarendon Press, Oxford, 1993)

Stubbs, R., 'Section 423 of the Insolvency Act in Practice' (2008) 21 *Insolvency Intelligence* 17

Stulz, R. and H. Johnson, 'An Analysis of Secured Debt' (1985) 14 *Journal of Financial Economics* 501

Sugarman, D. and G. Teubner (eds.), *Regulating Corporate Groups in Europe* (Nomos, Baden-Baden, 1990)

Sugden, R., *The Economics of Rights, Cooperation and Welfare* (Blackwell, Oxford, 1986)

Sullivan, T. A., E. Warren and J. L. Westbrook, *As We Forgive Our Debtors: Bankruptcy and Consumer Credit in America* (Oxford University Press, New York, 1989)

Summa, D., 'Credit Derivatives: An Untested Market' (2006) 3 *International Corporate Rescue* 249

Sutton, B. (ed.), *The Legitimate Corporation* (Blackwell, Oxford, 1993)

Swadling, W. (ed.), *The Quistclose Trust: Critical Essays* (Hart Publishing, Oxford, 2004)

Swain, C., 'A Move Towards a Stakeholder Society' (2003) IL&P 5

'He Who Pays the Piper Calls the Tune? Administrators' Remuneration under the New Administration Regime' (2006) 19 *Insolvency Intelligence* 33

Swain, V., 'Taking Care of Business' (1999) *Insolvency Bulletin* 9

Symes, C., 'The Protection of Wages When Insolvency Strikes' (1997) 5 Ins. LJ 196

Symposium, 'Contractual Freedoms in Corporate Law' (1988) 89 Colum. L Rev. 1385

Taffler, R., 'Forecasting Company Failure in the UK Using Discriminant Analysis and Financial Ratio Data' (1982) *Journal of the Royal Statistical Society*, Series A, 342

Taffler, R. and D. Citron, *Study* (City University, 1995)

Tashjian, E., R. Lease, J. McConnel *et al.*, 'Pre-packs: An Empirical Analysis' (1996) 40 *Journal of Financial Economics* 135

Tateossian, R., 'Briefing' (2000) 2 *Finance and Credit Law* 5

'The Future of Directors' Disqualification' (2000) *Insolvency Bulletin* 6

'The Scope of Section 166(5) Insolvency Act 1986: An Analysis' (2001) *Finance and Credit Law* 4

Telfer, T., 'Risk and Insolvent Trading' in R. Grantham and C. Rickett (eds.), *Corporate Personality in the Twentieth Century* (Hart, Oxford, 1998)

Tempest, M., 'Re-use of Company Names' (2006) *Recovery* (Summer) 25

Tett, R. and B. Jones, 'Hedge Funds – A Fad or Here to Stay?' (2007) *Recovery* (Summer) 22

Tett, R. and F. Paterson, 'World Class Administrators' (2005) *Recovery* (Summer) 24

Teubner, G., *Law as an Autopoietic System* (Blackwell, Oxford, 1993)

Teubner, G. and A. Febbrajo (eds.), *State, Law and Economy as Autopoietic Systems* (Giuffre, Milan, 1992)

Theobold, K., 'The Ferris Report' (1998) 14 IL&P 300

Thomas, K. and C. Ryan, 'Section 459, Public Policy and Freedom of Contract' (2001) 22 Co. Law. 199

Thompson, J. K., *Securitization* (OECD, Paris, 1995)

Todd, G., 'Administration Post-Enterprise Act – What Are the Options for Exits?' (2006) 19 *Insolvency Intelligence* 17

Todd, G. and S. Todd, 'Insolvency Practitioners have to be Bonded – Is it as Simple as it Seems?' (2006) 19 *Insolvency Intelligence* 129

Toms, D., 'Pensions: Another Ticking Time Bomb for Insolvency Practitioners' (2008) *Recovery* (Spring) 36

Townsend, J., 'Schemes of Arrangement and Asbestos Litigation: *In re Cape plc*' (2007) 70 MLR 837

Triantis, G., 'Mitigating the Collective Action Problem of Debt Enforcement through Bankruptcy Law: Bill C-22 and its Shadow' (1992) 20 Canadian Bus. LJ 242

'Secured Debt under Conditions of Imperfect Information' (1992) 21 *Journal of Legal Studies* 225

'The Interplay between Liquidation and Reorganisation in Bankruptcy: The Role of Screens, Gatekeepers and Guillotines' (1996) 16 *International Review of Law and Economics* 101

'Financial Slack Policy and the Law of Secured Transactions' (2000) 29 *Journal of Legal Studies* 35

Triantis, G. and R. Daniels, 'The Role of Debt in Interactive Corporate Governance' (1995) 83 Calif. L Rev. 1073

Tribe, J., 'Members' Voluntary Liquidations: A Declaration of Under Use' (2005) 26 Co. Law. 132

Trower, W., 'Bringing Human Rights Home to the Insolvency Practitioner' (2000) 13 *Insolvency Intelligence* 52

'Human Rights: Article 6 – The Reality and the Myth' [2001] Ins. Law. 48

Tucker, J. and J. Lean, 'Small Firm Finance and Public Policy' (2003) 10 *Journal of Small Business and Enterprise Development* 50

Tunc, A., 'The Fiduciary Duties of a Dominant Shareholder' in C. Schmitthoff and F. Wooldridge (eds.), *Groups of Companies* (Sweet & Maxwell, London, 1991)

Ulph, J., 'Equitable Proprietary Rights in Insolvency: The Ebbing Tide?' [1996] JBL 482

'Sale and Lease-back Agreements in a World of Title Relativity: *Michael Gerson (Leasing) Ltd v. Wilkinson and State Securities Ltd*' (2001) 64 MLR 481

Ulph, J. and T. Allen, 'Transactions at Undervalue, Purchasers and the Impact of the Human Rights Act 1998' [2004] JBL 1

United Nations Commission on International Trade Law (UNCITRAL), *Legislative Guide on Insolvency Law* (United Nations, New York, 2005)

Varollo, G. and J. Fukelstein, 'Fiduciary Obligations of Directors of the Financially Troubled Company' (1982) 48 *Business Lawyer* 239

Verrill, L., 'Attacking Antecedent Transactions' [1993] 12 JIBL 485

'The R3 Regulation Survey' (2004) *Recovery* (Autumn) 27

'ILA President's Column' (2007) *Insolvency Intelligence* 112

'The Use of LPA Receiverships' (2007) 20 *Insolvency Intelligence* 160

Verrill, L. and P. Elliot, 'Reflections on the *Powerhouse* Case' (2007) *Recovery* (Autumn) 28

Vilaplana, V., 'A Pre-pack Bankruptcy Primer' (1998) 44 *The Practical Lawyer* 33

Villiers, C., 'Employees as Creditors: A Challenge for Justice in Insolvency Law' (1999) 20 Co. Law. 222

Virgos, M. and F. Garcimartin, *The European Insolvency Regulation: Law and Practice* (Kluwer, The Hague, 2004)

Walker, D., *Guidelines for Disclosure and Transparency in Private Equity* (BVCA, London, 20 November 2007)

Walker, G., 'Sub-prime Loans, Inter-bank Markets and Financial Support' (2008) 29 Co. Law. 22

Walters, A., 'Foreshortening the Shadow: Maintenance, Champerty and the Funding of Litigation in Corporate Insolvency' (1996) 17 Co. Law. 165

'A Modern Doctrine of Champerty?' (1996) 112 LQR 560

'*Re Oasis Merchandising Services Ltd* in the Court of Appeal' (1997) 18 Co. Law. 214

'Anonymous Funders and Abuse of Process' (1998) 114 LQR 207

'Enforcing Wrongful Trading: Substantive Problems and Practical Disincentives' in B. Rider (ed.), *The Corporate Dimension: An Exploration of Developing Areas of Company and Commercial Law* (Jordans, Bristol, 1998)

'Round Up: Corporate Finance and Receivership' (1999) 20 Co. Law. 324

'Directors' Disqualification' (2000) 21 Co. Law. 90

'Directors' Duties: The Impact of the Directors' Disqualification Act 1986' (2000) 21 Co. Law. 110

'Round Up: Corporate Insolvency' (2000) 21 Co. Law. 262

'Staying Proceedings on Grounds of Champerty' [2000] Ins. Law. 16

'Bare Undertakings in Directors' Disqualification Proceedings: The Insolvency Act 2000, *Blackspur* and Beyond' (2001) 22 Co. Law. 290

'Directors' Disqualification after the Insolvency Act 2000: The New Regime' [2001] Ins. Law. 86

'*Re Floor Fourteen Ltd* in the Court of Appeal' (2001) 22 Co. Law. 215

'Wrongful Trading: Two Recent Cases' [2001] Ins. Law. 211

'Bare Undertakings in Disqualification Proceedings' (2002) 23 Co. Law. 123

'Recovering Costs of Litigation as a Liquidation Expense' (2003) 24 Co. Law. 84

'Corporate Restructuring under Sch. B1 of the Insolvency Act 1986' (2005) 26 Co. Law. 97

'The Impact of Employee Liabilities on the Administrator's Decision to Continue Trading' (2005) 26 Co. Law. 321

'Floating Charges and Liquidation Expenses' (2006) 27 Co. Law. 193

'Statutory Redistribution of Floating Charge Assets: Victory (Again) to Revenue and Customs' (2008) 29 Co. Law. 129

Walters, A. and M. Davis-White QC, *Directors' Disqualification and Bankruptcy Restrictions* (Thomson/Sweet & Maxwell, London, 2005)

Walters, A. and M. Seneviratne, *Complaints Handling in the Insolvency Practitioner Profession: A Report for the Insolvency Practices Council* (IPC, London, 2008)

Walton, P., 'The Landlord, his Distress, the Insolvent Tenant and the Stranger' (2000) 16 IL&P 47

'Pre-packaged Administrations – Trick or Treat?' (2006) 19 *Insolvency Intelligence* 113

'Pre-appointment Administration Fees – Papering Over the Crack in Pre-packs?' (2008) 21 *Insolvency Intelligence* 72

Walzer, M., *Spheres of Justice* (Basil Blackwell, Oxford, 1995)

Wardman, K., 'Directors and Employee Status: An Examination of Relevant Company Law and Employment Law Principles' (2003) 24 Co. Law. 139

Waring, A. and A. Glendon, *Managing Risk* (Thomson, London, 1998)

Warner, J. *et al.*, 'Stock Prices and Top Management Changes' (1988) *Journal of Financial Economics* 461

Warren, E., 'Bankruptcy Policy' (1987) 54 U Chic. L Rev. 775

'The Untenable Case for Repeal of Chapter 11' (1992) 102 Yale LJ 437

'Bankruptcy Policymaking in an Imperfect World' (1993) 92 Mich. L Rev. 336

Warren, E. and J. Westbrook, *The Law of Debtors and Creditors: Text, Cases and Problems* (Little, Brown, Boston, 1986)

'Contracting Out of Bankruptcy: An Empirical Intervention' (2005) 118 Harv. L Rev 1197

Webb, D., 'An Economic Evaluation of Insolvency Processes in the UK: Does the 1986 Insolvency Act Satisfy the Creditors' Bargain?' (1991) *Oxford Economic Papers* 144

Wedderburn, K. W., *Company Law Reform* (Fabian Society, London, 1965)

'Multinationals and the Antiquities of Company Law' (1984) 47 MLR 87

'The Social Responsibility of Companies' (1985) 15 Mel. ULR 4

Welby, R., 'Antecedent Recoveries and Litigation Funding – A Practical Perspective' (2006) *Recovery* (Winter) 32

Wessels, B., 'Europe Deserves a New Approach to Insolvency Proceedings' (2007) 4 *European Company Law* 253

Westbrook, J. L., 'A Functional Analysis of Executory Contracts' (1989) 74 Minn. L Rev. 227

'A Comparison of Bankruptcy Reorganisation in the US with Administration Procedure in the UK' (1990) 6 IL&P 86

'Global Insolvencies in a World of Nation States' in A. Clarke (ed.), *Current Issues in Insolvency Law* (Stevens, London, 1991)

'The Globalisation of Insolvency Reform' (1999) NZLR 401

'The Control of Wealth in Bankruptcy' (2004) 82 Texas L Rev. 795.

Westbrook, J. and E. Warren, 'Chapter 11: Conventional Wisdom and Reality' (University of Texas, Public Law Research Paper No. 125)

Weston, D., 'The London Rules and Debt Restructuring' (1992) Sol. Jo. 216

Wheeler, S., 'The Insolvency Act 1986 and ROTs' [1987] JBL 180

Reservation of Title Clauses (Oxford University Press, Oxford, 1991)

'Disqualification of Directors: A Broader View' in H. Rajak (ed.), *Insolvency Law: Theory and Practice* (Sweet & Maxwell, London, 1993)

'Capital Fractionalised: The Role of Insolvency Practitioners in Asset Distribution' in M. Cain and C. B. Harrington (eds.), *Lawyers in a Post Modern World: Translation and Transgression* (Open University Press, Buckingham, 1994)

'Empty Rhetoric and Empty Promises: The Creditors' Meeting' (1994) 21 *Journal of Law and Society* 350

'Directors' Disqualification: Insolvency Practitioners and the Decision-making Process' (1995) 15 *Legal Studies* 283

Wheeler, S. and G. Wilson, *Directors' Liabilities in the Context of Corporate Groups* (Insolvency Lawyers' Association, Oxfordshire, 1998)

White, J., 'The Recent Erosion of the Secured Creditor's Rights Through Cases, Rules and Statutory Changes in Bankruptcy Law' (1983) 53 Miss. LJ 389

'Efficiency Justifications for Personal Property Security' (1984) 37 Vand. L
    Rev. 473
White, M., 'Public Policy Toward Bankruptcy' (1980) 11 *Bell Journal of
    Economics* 550
'The Corporate Bankruptcy Decision' (1989) 3 *Journal of Economic Perspectives* 129
'Does Chapter 11 Save Economically Inefficient Firms?' (1994) 72 Wash.
    ULQ 1319
'The Cost of Corporate Bankruptcy: A US–European Comparison' in
    J. Bhandari and L. Weiss (eds.), *Corporate Bankruptcy: Economic and
    Legal Perspectives* (Cambridge University Press, Cambridge, 1996)
White Paper, *A Revised Framework for Insolvency Law* (Cmnd 9175, 1984)
    Our Competitive Future: Building the Knowledge Driven Economy (Cm 4176,
    December 1998)
    Enterprise, Skill and Innovation (2001)
    Productivity and Enterprise: Insolvency – A Second Chance (Cm 5234, July
    2001)
    Modernising Company Law (Cm 5553, 2002)
    Company Law Reform (Cm 6456, March 2005)
Wilding, J., 'Instructing Investigating Accountants' (1994) 7 *Insolvency
    Intelligence* 3
Wilkinson, A., A. Cohen and R. Sutherland, 'Creditors' Schemes of Arrangement
    and Company Voluntary Arrangements' in H. Rajak (ed.), *Insolvency Law:
    Theory and Practice* (Sweet & Maxwell, London, 1993)
Willcock, J., 'How the Banks Won the Battle for the Enterprise Bill' (2002)
    Recovery (June) 24
'Credit Panic Stokes Forensic Boom' (2007) *Recovery* (Winter) 17
Williams, C., 'Retention of Title: Some Recent Developments' (1991) 12 Co.
    Law. 54
Williams, C. and A. McGee, *A Company Director's Liability for Wrongful Trading*,
    ACCA Research Report 30 (London, 1992)
Williams, R., 'Disqualifying Directors: A Remedy Worse than the Disease?' [2007]
    7 JCLS 213
Wilson, J., *British Business History 1720–1994* (Manchester University Press,
    Manchester, 1995)
Winterborne, P., 'The Second Hand Cause of Action Market' (2001) 14 *Insolvency
    Intelligence* 65
Wishart, D., 'Models and Theories of Directors' Duties to Creditors' (1991) 14
    NZULR 323
    Company Law in Context (Oxford University Press, Auckland, 1994)
Wolff, R., *Understanding Rawls* (Princeton University Press, Princeton, N.J., 1977)
Wollaston, A., 'The Growing Importance of Debt in European Corporate
    Transactions' (2005) 18 *Insolvency Intelligence* 145

Wood, D., 'Can a Court Appointed Receiver Secure Assets Held Overseas?' (2008) *Recovery* (Spring) 30

World Bank, *Principles and Guidelines for Effective Insolvency and Creditors' Rights Systems* (World Bank, Washington D.C., 2001)

Worthington, S., *Proprietary Interests in Commercial Transactions* (Clarendon Press, Oxford, 1996)

'Floating Charges: Use and Abuse of Doctrinal Analysis' in J. Getzler and J. Payne (eds.), *Company Charge: Spectrum and Beyond* (Oxford University Press, Oxford, 2006) p. 25

Worthington, S. (ed.), *Commercial Law and Commercial Practice* (Hart, Oxford, 2003)

Wray, C., 'A Day in the Life of a Company Doctor' (2002) *Recovery* (September) 51

Wright, D., 'The Remedial Constructive Trust and Insolvency' in F. Rose (ed.), *Restitution and Insolvency* (Lloyd's of London Press, London, 2000)

Wruck, K., 'Financial Distress, Reorganisation and Organisational Efficiency' (1990) 27 *Journal of Financial Economics* 419

Zalman, D., 'The Unpaid Employee as Creditor' (1980) 6 Dalhouse LJ 148

Ziegel, J. S., 'Creditors as Corporate Stakeholders' (1993) 43 U Toronto LJ 511

'The Privately Appointed Receiver and the Enforcement of Security Interests: Anomaly or Superior Solution?' in Ziegel (ed.), *Current Developments in International and Comparative Corporate Insolvency Law* (Clarendon Press, Oxford, 1994)

INDEX

Lightning Source UK Ltd.
Milton Keynes UK
UKOW03f0826170414

230134UK00001B/13/P

English Skills
with Readings

Praise for *English Skills with Readings, 5th edition and English Skills, 7th edition*

"There can be no legitimate comparison between John Langan's McGraw-Hill developmental composition text series and any other texts available. Other texts are simply not as clear, precise, interesting, or comprehensive as *English Skills,* especially with the improvements made in the 7th edition."

Candace C. Mesa, Dixie College

"It is an outstanding text, good for discussion, individual work, or collaborative activities."

Patsy Krech, University of Memphis

"This text has great examples and activities. The writing is clear, the format appealing. I think it's a very useful textbook that students would enjoy using and that they would learn much from."

Janice S. Trollinger, Fort Valley State University

"The greatest strength of the previous edition of Langan's text is its organization and voice. I have found few [other] texts that offer the right combination of commonsense advice *and* helpful, sophisticated examples and exercises. This edition is even better. The topics are clear and up-to-date, and the new arrangement of important concepts makes the book easier to use than ever."

Kevin R. McGarvey, Cumberland County College

"The text is thorough, useful, well conceived, and well written."

Kurt Neumann, William Rainey Harper College

"The greatest strengths of this text are its flexibility for the instructor, accessibility for the student, and clear focus on the writing needs of developmental students."

Michael A. Orlando, Bergen Community College

"The strength of the entire text is its comprehensiveness: it has qualities of a skills text and English handbook, of a composition and research and library guide."

Russell J. Gaudio, Gateway Community College

"The emphasis on four principles of writing is excellent."

Francis N. Elmi, Manhattan Community College, City University of New York

"The updated and revised student models throughout the text contribute to an improved, timely, and very thorough textbook that will meet the needs of today's students. I can hardly wait to see the published copy."

Lola M. Richardson, Paine College

"Changing to this textbook is the single factor which has renewed my desire to teach this course."

Anneliese Homan, State Fair Community College

English Skills with Readings

Fifth Edition

John Langan
Atlantic Cape Community College

Boston   Burr Ridge, IL   Dubuque, IA   Madison, WI   New York   San Francisco   St. Louis
Bangkok   Bogotá   Caracas   Kuala Lumpur   Lisbon   London   Madrid   Mexico City
Milan   Montreal   New Delhi   Santiago   Seoul   Singapore   Sydney   Taipei   Toronto

McGraw-Hill Higher Education ⚛

*A Division of The **McGraw-Hill** Companies*

ENGLISH SKILLS WITH READINGS
Published by McGraw-Hill, an imprint of The McGraw-Hill Companies, Inc., 1221 Avenue of the Americas, New York, NY, 10020. Copyright © 2002, 1999, 1995, 1991, 1988 by The McGraw-Hill Companies, Inc. All rights reserved. No part of this publication may be reproduced or distributed in any form or by any means, or stored in a database or retrieval system, without the prior written consent of The McGraw-Hill Companies, Inc., including, but not limited to, in any network or other electronic storage or transmission, or broadcast for distance learning. Some ancillaries, including electronic and print components, may not be available to customers outside the United States.

This book is printed on acid-free paper.

1 2 3 4 5 6 7 8 9 0 DOC/DOC 0 9 8 7 6 5 4 3 2 1

ISBN 0-07-248003-3

Editorial director: *Phillip A. Butcher*
Senior editor: *Sarah Touborg*
Developmental editor II: *Alexis Walker*
Senior marketing manager: *David S. Patterson*
Senior project manager: *Pat Frederickson*
Senior production supervisor: *Lori Koetters*
Senior designer: *Jennifer McQueen*
Cover design: *Paul Turnbaugh*
Supplement producer: *Susan Lombardi*
Media producer: *Lance Gerhart*
Printer: *R. R. Donnelley & Sons Company*
Typeface: *11/13 Times Roman*
Compositor: *Electronic Publishing Services, Inc., TN*

Library of Congress Cataloging-in-Publication Data

Langan, John (date)
    English skills with readings / John Langan.—5th ed.
        p.   cm.
    Includes index.
    ISBN 0-07-248003-3 (student ed: alk. paper) — ISBN 0-07-248005-X (instructor's ed: alk. paper)
        1. English language—Rhetoric. 2. English language—Grammar. 3. College readers. I. Title.
PE1408.L3182 2002
808'.0427—dc21   2001030141

INTERNATIONAL EDITION ISBN 0-07-112121-8
Copyright © 2002. Exclusive rights by The McGraw-Hill Companies, Inc. for manufacture and export. This book cannot be re-exported from the country to which it is sold by McGraw-Hill. The International Edition is not available in North America.

www.mhhe.com

About the Author

John Langan has taught reading and writing at Atlantic Cape Community College near Atlantic City, New Jersey, for over twenty-five years. The author of a popular series of college textbooks on both subjects, he enjoys the challenge of developing materials that teach skills in an especially clear and lively way. Before teaching, he earned advanced degrees in writing at Rutgers University and in reading at Rowan University. He also spent a year writing fiction that, he says, "is now at the back of a drawer waiting to be discovered and acclaimed posthumously." While in school, he supported himself by working as a truck driver, machinist, battery assembler, hospital attendant, and apple packer. He now lives with his wife, Judith Nadell, near Philadelphia. Among his everyday pleasures are running, working on his Macintosh computer, and watching Philadelphia sports teams on TV. He also loves to read: newspapers at breakfast, magazines at lunch, and a chapter or two of a recent book ("preferably an autobiography") at night.

The Langan Series

Essay-Level

College Writing Skills, Fifth Edition
ISBN: 0-07-228322-X (Copyright © 2000)

College Writing Skills with Readings, Fifth Edition
ISBN: 0-07-238121-3 (Copyright © 2001)

Paragraph-Level

English Skills, Seventh Edition
ISBN: 0-07-238127-2 (Copyright © 2001)

English Skills with Readings, Fifth Edition
ISBN: 0-07-248003-3 (Copyright © 2002)

Sentence-Level

Sentence Skills: A Workbook for Writers, Form A, Sixth Edition
ISBN: 0-07-036672-1 (Copyright © 1998)

Sentence Skills: A Workbook for Writers, Form B, Sixth Edition
ISBN: 0-07-037127-X (Copyright © 1999)

Sentence Skills with Readings, Second Edition
ISBN: 0-07-238132-9 (Copyright © 2001)

Grammar Review

English Brushup, Second Edition
ISBN: 0-07-037108-3 (Copyright © 1998)

Reading

Reading and Study Skills, Seventh Edition
ISBN: 0-07-244599-8 (Copyright © 2002)

Contents

Readings Listed by Rhetorical Mode

Note: Some selections are listed more than once because they illustrate more than one rhetorical method of development.

Examples

Process

Comparison-Contrast

Persuasion

To the Instructor

Key Features of the Book

English Skills with Readings will help students learn and apply the basic principles of effective composition. It will also help them master essential reading skills. It is a nuts-and-bolts book based on a number of assumptions or beliefs about the writing process:

- *First of all,* English Skills with Readings *assumes that four principles in particular are keys to effective writing:* **unity, support, coherence, and sentence skills.** These four principles are highlighted on the inside front cover and reinforced throughout the book.

  - Part One focuses on the first three principles and to some extent on sentence skills; Part Five serves as a concise handbook of sentence skills.
  - The rest of the book shows how the four principles apply in different types of paragraph development (Part Two), in several-paragraph essays (Part Three), in specialized types of writing (Part Four), and in both paragraphs and essays (Part Six).

  The ongoing success of *English Skills with Readings* is evidence that the four principles are easily grasped, remembered, and followed by students.

- *The book also reflects a belief that, in addition to these four principles, there are other important factors in writing effectively.* The second chapter discusses *prewriting, rewriting, and editing.* Besides encouraging students to see *writing as a process,* the chapter also asks students to examine their *attitude toward writing,* to *write on what they know* about or can learn about, to consider keeping a *writing journal,* and to make *outlining* a part of the writing process.

- English Skills with Readings *assumes that the best way to begin writing is with personal experience.* After students have learned to support a point by providing material from their own experience, they are ready to develop an idea by drawing on their own reasoning abilities and on information in reports, articles, and books. In Parts Two and Three, students are asked to write on *both experiential and objective topics.*

- *The book also assumes that beginning writers are more likely to learn composition skills through lively, engaging, and realistic models than through materials remote from the common experiences that are part of everyday life.* For example, when a writer argues that proms should be banned, or catalogs ways to harass an instructor, or talks about why some teenagers take drugs, students will be more apt to remember and follow the writing principles that are involved.

- *A related assumption is that students are especially interested in and challenged by the writing of their peers.* After reading vigorous papers composed by other students and understanding the power that good writing can have, students will be more encouraged to aim for similar honesty, realism, and detail in their own work.

- *Another premise of* English Skills with Readings *is that mastery of the paragraph should precede work on the several-paragraph essay.* Thus Part One illustrates the basic principles of composition writing using paragraph models, and the assignments in Part Two aim at developing the ability to support ideas within a variety of paragraph forms. The essential principles of paragraph writing are then applied to the several-paragraph essays in Part Three.

- *Part Four in particular reflects the belief that an English text should provide help in specific writing situations.* The skills covered are (1) using the library and the Internet and (2) writing and documenting a research paper.

- *The grammar, punctuation, and usage skills that make up Part Five are explained clearly and directly, without unnecessary technical terms.* Here, as elsewhere, *abundant exercise material* is provided, especially for the mistakes that are most likely to interfere with clear communication.

- *A final assumption is that, since no two people will use an English text in exactly the same way, the material should be organized in a highly accessible manner.* Because each of the six parts of the book deals with a distinct area of writing, instructors can turn quickly and easily to the skills they want to present. At the same time, ideas for sequencing material are provided in a section titled "Using This Text" at the end of Chapter 1. And a detailed syllabus is provided in the Instructor's Manual.

I am very grateful for the ongoing popularity of *English Skills with Readings.* Instructors continue to say that the four bases really do help students learn to write effectively. And they continue to comment that students find the activities, assignments, model passages, and reading selections especially interesting and worthwhile.

Differences between This Book and *English Skills*

- Parts One to Three are essentially the same as the three rhetoric sections of *English Skills*. There are three omissions: the "Additional Paragraph Assignments" have been removed from the end of Part Two; and an assignment based on an article titled "Full Circle" has been taken out of Part Three. There is also one addition: "Writing an Exam Essay" is now included in Part Three.

- Part Four of *English Skills,* "Special Skills," has been reduced to two chapters on research skills, "Using the Library and the Internet" and "Writing a Research Paper," to help create space for the seventeen readings.

- As the title indicates, what is most different in this book is the inclusion of the seventeen reading selections by professional writers, along with detailed reading and writing apparatus following each selection.

The Readings

- The seventeen selections have been chosen for their content as much as for rhetorical mode. They are organized thematically into three groups: "Goals and Values," "Education and Self-Improvement," and "Human Groups and Society." Some selections reflect important contemporary concerns: for instance, "Let's Really Reform Our Schools," "Television Changed My Family Forever," and "What Good Families Are Doing Right." Some provide information many students may find helpful; examples are "Anxiety: Challenge by Another Name," "How They Get You to Do That," and "Dealing with Feelings." Some recount profoundly human experiences: "All the Good Things," "Rowing the Bus," "Adolescent Confusion," and "A Drunken Ride, a Tragic Aftermath." (A list on pages xiii–xv presents the readings by rhetorical mode.)

- Each reading begins with an overview that supplies background information where needed and stimulates interest in the piece.

- The ten reading comprehension questions that follow each selection give students practice in five key skills: understanding vocabulary in context, summarizing (by choosing an alternative title), determining the main idea, recognizing key supporting details, and making inferences. Reading educators agree that these are among the most crucial comprehension skills. A special chart in the Appendix enables students to track their progress as they practice these skills.

- Discussion questions following the reading comprehension questions deal with matters of content as well as aspects of structure, style, and tone. Through the questions on structure in particular, students will see that professional authors practice some of the same basic composing techniques (such as the use of transitions and emphatic order to achieve coherence) that they have been asked to practice in their own writing.

- Finally, two paragraph writing assignments and one essay writing assignment follow the discussion questions. The assignments range from personal narratives to expository and persuasive essays about issues in the world at large. Many assignments provide guidelines on how to proceed, including sample topic sentences or thesis statements and appropriate methods of development. In addition, six of the selections feature a fourth writing assignment requiring some simple Internet research.

When assigning a selection, instructors may find it helpful to ask students to read the overview as well as to answer the reading comprehension and discussion questions that follow the selection. Answers can then be gone over quickly in class. Through these activities, a writing instructor can contribute to the improvement of students' reading skills.

Changes in the Fifth Edition

Here is a list of what is new in the fifth edition of *English Skill with Readings:*

- The most substantial change in the book is its *far greater emphasis on prewriting and revising.*

  - A new opening chapter titled "The Writing Process" uses a model student essay to demonstrate how prewriting and revising are essential parts of the act of writing. The opening chapter of the book helps students see writing right from the start as both a skill and a process of discovery.

  - While Part One of the text continues to focus on four bases of effective writing—unity, support, coherence, and sentence skills—students also learn how prewriting and revising will help them achieve the four bases.

  - Some of the skills that deal with writing effective sentences (parallelism, consistent point of view, the use of specific and concise language, and sentence variety) have been moved from Part Five to a major new section on revising sentences in Part One, Chapter 5.

- Detailed prewriting and revising strategies are now part of many writing assignments that accompany the nine rhetorical patterns of essay development in Part Two.
- A second major change is the addition of the new Part Four, "Research Skills," made up of two chapters. The first chapter consists of a highly practical *guide to the library and the Internet.* This chapter illustrates how the author of a model research paper draws on the resources of the traditional library and the Internet in doing research. The second chapter includes a *model research paper* that examines a contemporary topic and that follows the latest MLA guidelines, including the citation of sources found on the Internet.
- An entirely new Chapter 44 presents *pointers and brief activities for ESL students.*
- As part of the book's *new design,* chapters in Parts One through Five are now numbered, making the text even easier to use.
- Throughout the book, particularly in Part Five, *student models and practice materials have been updated and revised.*
- *Six new selections* are now part of the seventeen selections in Part Six: "All the Good Things," by Sister Helen Mrosla; "Fifth Chinese Daughter," by Jade Snow Wong; "Tickets to Nowhere," by Andy Rooney; "How They Get You to Do That," by Janny Scott; "Dealing with Feelings," by Rudolf F. Verderber; and "Bullies in School," by Kathleen Berger. These six selections have been class-tested; they both engage the interest of students and make for interesting writing assignments.
- Six of the readings in Part Six now include *a writing assignment involving Internet research.*
- Finally, a new and more comprehensive *Annotated Instructor's Edition* consists of the student text complete with answers to all the activities and tests, followed by a helpful Instructor's Guide.

Learning Aids Accompanying the Book

Supplements for Instructors

- An *Annotated Instructor's Edition* (ISBN 0-07-248003-3) consists of the student text complete with answers to all activities and tests, followed by an Instructor's Guide featuring teaching suggestions and a model syllabus.
- The *Instructor's Manual* and *Test Bank* (ISBN 0-07-248004-1) includes the Instructor's Guide along with thirty-two supplementary activities and tests.

- An *Online Learning Center* (**www.mhhe.com/langan**) offers a host of instructional aids and additional resources for instructors, including a comprehensive computerized test bank, the Instructor's Manual and Test Bank, online resources for writing instructors, and more.

- An *Instructor's CD-ROM* (0-07-248007-6) offers all the above supplements and M.O.R.E. (McGraw-Hill Online Resources for English, also available online at **www.mhhe.com/english**) in a convenient offline format.

- *PageOut!* helps instructors create graphically pleasing and professional web pages for their courses, in addition to providing classroom management, collaborative learning, and content management tools. PageOut! is **FREE** to adopters of McGraw-Hill textbooks and learning materials. Learn more at **www.mhhe.com/pageout.**

- *WebWrite!* is an interactive peer-editing program that allows students to post papers, read comments from their peers and instructor, discuss, and edit online. To learn more, visit the online demo at **www.metatext.com/webwrite.**

Supplements for Students

- An *Online Learning Center* (**www.mhhe.com/langan**) offers a host of instructional aids and additional resources for students, including self-correcting exercises, writing activities for additional practice, a PowerPoint grammar tutorial, guides to doing research on the Internet and avoiding plagiarism, useful web links, and more.

- A *Student CD-ROM* (0-07-248009-2) offers all the resources of the Student's Online Learning Center and M.O.R.E. (McGraw-Hill Online Resources for English, also available online at **www.mhhe.com/english**) in a convenient offline format.

- *AllWrite!* 2.0 is an interactive, browser-based tutorial program that provides an online handbook, comprehensive diagnostic pretests and posttests, and extensive practice exercises in every area.

You can contact your local McGraw-Hill representative or consult McGraw-Hill's web site at **www.mhhe.com/english** for more information on the supplements that accompany *English Skills with Readings, 5th Edition.*

Acknowledgments

Reviewers who have contributed to this edition through their helpful comments include

David Basena, Bowie State University

Gail C. Caylor, Mesa Community College

Lillian Dailey, Cuyahoga Community College

Judith Rae Davis, Bergen Community College

Doug Dickston, Mt. Hood Community College

Michael M. Dinielli, Chaffey College

Ann D. Ecoff, Lambuth University

Francis N. Elmi, Manhattan Community College—City University of New York

Russell J. Gaudio, Gateway Community College

Patsy Krech, University of Memphis

Anneliese Homan, State Fair Community College

Nancy Kolk, Clinton Community College

Donna Lenhoff, Butte Community College

Kevin R. McGarvey, Cumberland County College

Candace C. Mesa, Dixie College

Robin Morris, Eastern Shore Community College

Kurt Neumann, William Rainey Harper College

Michael A. Orlando, Bergen Community College

Rebecca Peterson, Asbury College

Lola M. Richardson, Paine College

Barbara L. Tosi, Community College of Allegheny County—Boyce Campus

Janice S. Trollinger, Fort Valley State University

I am also grateful for help provided by Janet M. Goldstein, Beth Johnson, Carole Mohr, Susan Gamer, Pat Frederickson, Eliza Comodromos, and Paul Langan, as well as for the support of my McGraw-Hill editors: Sarah Touborg and Alexis Walker.

John Langan

Part One

Basic Principles of Effective Writing

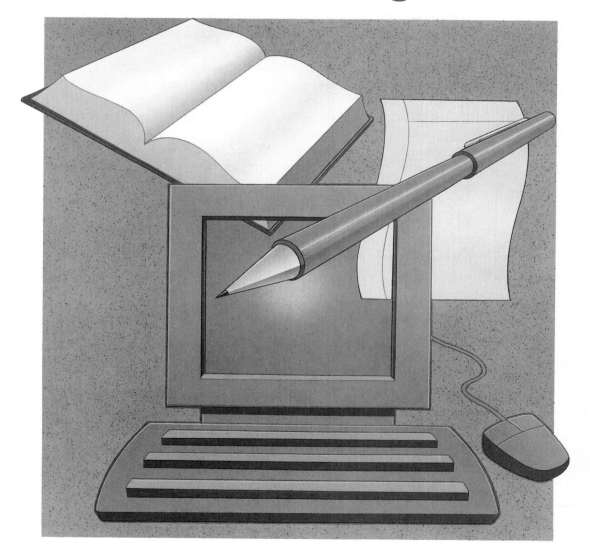

Preview

Part One begins, in Chapter 1, by introducing you to the basic principles of effective writing. You learn that what is most important in writing is to make a point and support that point. This chapter next provides an overview of how the book is organized. It then goes on to discuss the benefits of paragraph writing and two key ideas about writing. The first key idea is that writing is a skill that anyone can learn with practice. The second key idea is that one can often discover a subject in the very process of writing about it. Finally, the chapter presents journal writing and offers some suggestions on how to use the text.

Chapter 2, "The Writing Process," explains and illustrates the sequence of steps in writing an effective paragraph. You learn how prewriting, revising, and editing will help with every paper that you write.

Chapter 3, "The First and Second Steps in Writing," shows you, in detail, how to begin your paper with a point and provide specific evidence to support that point.

Chapter 4, "The Third Step in Writing," shows you how to organize and connect the specific evidence in a paper.

Chapter 5, "The Fourth Step in Writing," shows you how to revise so that your sentences flow smoothly and clearly and how to edit so that your sentences are error-free.

Chapter 6, "Four Bases for Evaluating Writing," explains how four bases—unity, support, coherence, and sentence skills—will help you evaluate and revise papers.

1 An Introduction to Writing

English Skills with Readings grows out of experiences I had when learning how to write. My early memories of writing in school are not pleasant. In the middle grades I remember getting back paper after paper on which the only comment was "Handwriting very poor." In high school, the night before a book report was due, I would work anxiously at a card table in my bedroom. I was nervous and sweaty because I felt out of my element, like a person who knows only how to open a can of soup being asked to cook a five-course meal. The act of writing was hard enough, and my feeling that I wasn't any good at it made me hate the process all the more.

Luckily, in college I had an instructor who changed my negative attitude about writing. During my first semester in composition, I realized that my instructor repeatedly asked two questions about any paper I wrote: "What is your point?" and "What is your support for that point?" I learned that sound writing consists basically of making a point and then providing evidence to support or develop that point. As I understood, practiced, and mastered these and other principles, I began to write effective papers. By the end of the semester, much of my uneasiness and bad feelings about writing had disappeared. I knew that competent writing is a skill that I or anyone can learn with practice. It is a nuts-and-bolts process consisting of a number of principles and techniques that can be studied and mastered. Further, I learned that while there is no alternative to the work required for competent writing, there is satisfaction to be gained through such work. I no longer feared or hated writing, for I knew I could work at it and be good at it.

English Skills explains in a clear and direct way the four basic principles you must learn to write effectively:

1 Start with a clearly stated point.
2 Provide logical, detailed support for your point.
3 Organize and connect your supporting material.
4 Revise and edit so that your sentences are effective and error-free.

Part One of this book explains each of these steps in detail and provides many practice materials to help you master them.

Understanding Point and Support

An Important Difference between Writing and Talking

In everyday conversation, you make all kinds of points, or assertions. You say, for example, "I hate my job"; "Sue's a really generous person"; or "That exam was unfair." The points that you make concern such personal matters as well as, at times, larger issues: "A lot of doctors are arrogant"; "The death penalty should exist for certain crimes"; "Tobacco and marijuana are equally dangerous."

The people you are talking with do not always challenge you to give reasons for your statements. They may know why you feel as you do, or they may already agree with you, or they simply may not want to put you on the spot; and so they do not always ask "Why?" But the people who *read* what you write may not know you, agree with you, or feel in any way obliged to you. If you want to communicate effectively with readers, you must provide solid evidence for any point you make. An important difference, then, between writing and talking is this: *In writing, any idea that you advance must be supported with specific reasons or details.*

Think of your readers as reasonable people. They will not take your views on faith, but they *are* willing to consider what you say as long as you support it. Therefore, remember to support with specific evidence any statement that you make.

Point and Support in a Paragraph

Suppose you and a friend are talking about jobs you have had. You might say about a particular job, "That was the worst one I ever had. A lot of hard work and not much money." For your friend, that might be enough to make your point, and you would not really have to explain your statement. But in writing, your point would have to be backed up with specific reasons and details.

Below is a paragraph, written by a student named Gene Hert, about his worst job. A *paragraph* is a short paper of 150 to 200 words. It usually consists of an opening point called a *topic sentence* followed by a series of sentences supporting that point.

My Job in an Apple Plant

Working in an apple plant was the worst job I ever had. First of all, the work was physically hard. For ten hours a night, I took cartons that rolled down a metal track and stacked them onto wooden skids in a tractor trailer. Each carton contained twenty-five pounds of bottled apple juice, and they came down the track almost nonstop. The second bad feature of the job was the pay. I was getting the minimum wage at that time, $3.65 an hour, plus a quarter extra for working the night shift. I had to work over sixty hours a week to get decent take-home pay. Finally, I hated the working conditions. We were limited to two ten-minute breaks and an unpaid half hour for lunch. Most of my time was spent outside on the loading dock in near-zero-degree temperatures. I was very lonely on the job because I had no interests in common with the other truck loaders. I felt this isolation especially when the production line shut down for the night, and I spent two hours by myself cleaning the apple vats. The vats were an ugly place to be on a cold morning, and the job was a bitter one to have.

Notice what the details in this paragraph do. They provide you, the reader, with a basis for understanding *why* the writer makes the point that is made. Through this specific evidence, the writer has explained and successfully communicated the idea that this job was his worst one.

The evidence that supports the point in a paragraph often consists of a series of reasons followed by examples and details that support the reasons. That is true of the paragraph above: three reasons are provided, with examples and details that back up those reasons. Supporting evidence in a paper can also consist of anecdotes, personal experiences, facts, studies, statistics, and the opinions of experts.

Activity 1

The paragraph on the apple plant, like almost any piece of effective writing, has two essential parts: (1) a point is advanced, and (2) that point is then supported. Taking a minute to outline the paragraph will help you understand these basic parts clearly. Add the words needed to complete the outline.

Point: Working in an apple plant is the worst job I ever had.

Reason 1: _____

    a.   Loaded cartons onto skids for ten hours a night

    b.   _____

Reason 2: _____

    a. _____

    b. Had to work sixty hours for decent take-home pay

Reason 3: _____

    a. Two ten-minute breaks and an unpaid lunch

    b. _____

    c. Loneliness on job

        (1) No interests in common with other workers

        (2) By myself for two hours cleaning the apple vats

Activity 2

See if you can complete the statements below.

1. An important difference between writing and talking is that in writing we absolutely must _____ any statement we make.

2. A _____ is made up of a point and a collection of specifics that support the point.

Activity 3

An excellent way to get a feel for the paragraph is to write one. Your instructor may ask you to do that now. The only guidelines you need to follow are the ones described here. There is an advantage to writing a paragraph right away, at a point where you have had almost no instruction. This first paragraph will give a quick sense of your needs as a writer and will provide a baseline—a standard of comparison that you and your instructor can use to measure your writing progress during the semester.

Here, then, is your topic: Write a paragraph on the best or worst job you have ever had. Provide three reasons why your job was the best or the worst, and give plenty of details to develop each of your three reasons.

Notice that the sample paragraph, "My Job in an Apple Plant," has the same format your paragraph should have. The author:

- states a point in his first sentence
- gives three reasons to support the point
- introduces each reason clearly with signal words (*First of all, Second,* and *Finally*)
- provides details that develop each of the three reasons

Write your paragraph on a separate sheet of paper. After completing the paragraph, hand it in to your instuctor.

An Overview: How the Book Is Organized

English Skills is divided into five parts. Each part will be discussed briefly below. Questions appear, not to test you but simply to introduce you to the book's central ideas and organization. Your instructor may ask you to fill in the answers or just to note the answers in your head.

Part One (Pages 1–157) A good way to get a quick sense of any part of a book is to look at the table of contents. Turn back to the contents at the start of this book (pages vii–xii) to answer the following questions:

- What is the title of Part One? _____

- "An Introduction to Writing" is the opening chapter of Part One. How many subheads are included in this chapter? _____

- Chapter 2 describes the steps in the writing process. Fill in the two missing steps:

  Step 1: _____

  Step 2: Writing a First Draft

  Step 3: _____

  Step 4: Editing

- The title of the third chapter in Part One is "The First and Second Steps in Writing." What are the first and second steps in writing?

  _____

  _____

- The title of the fourth chapter in Part One is "The Third Step in Writing." What is the third step in writing?

  _____

- The next chapter introduces the fourth step in writing, which includes all the skills involved in writing clear, error-free sentences. Most of these sentence skills are covered later in the book, where they can be easily referred to as needed. In which part of the book are sentence skills treated?

  _____

- The title of the final chapter in Part One is "Four Bases for Evaluating Writing." Fill in the first four subheads following the title.

Subhead 1. _____

Subhead 2. _____

Subhead 3. _____

Subhead 4. _____

Inside Front Cover   Turn now to the inside front cover. You will see there a *(fill in the missing word)* _____ of the four bases of effective writing. These four standards can be used as a guide for every paper that you write. They are summarized on the inside front cover for easy reference. If you follow them, you are almost sure to write effective papers.

Part Two (Pages 159–280)   The title of Part Two is

_____

Part Two, as the title explains, is concerned with different ways to develop paragraphs. Read the preview on page 160 and record here how many types of paragraph development are explained: _____.

Turn to the first method of paragraph development, "Providing Examples," on page 171. You will see that the chapter opens with a brief introduction followed by several paragraphs written by students. Then you will see a series of six *(fill in the missing word)* _____ to help you evaluate the descriptive paragraphs in terms of unity, support, and coherence. Finally, there is a series of writing topics that can be developed by means of description. The same format is used for each of the other methods of paragraph development in Part Two.

Part Three (Pages 281–308)   The title of Part Three is

_____

As the preview notes, in Part Two you were asked to write single paragraphs; in Part Three, you are asked to write papers of more than one *(fill in the missing word)* _____.

Part Four (Pages 309–351)   The title of Part Four is

_____

Part Four gives you advice on a number of important skills that are related to writing. You can refer to this part of the book whenever the need arises.

- Which chapter will give you information about two places to do research?

  _____

- Which chapter will help you with the stages of writing a paper that requires research?

  _____

Part Five (Pages 353–576)   The title of Part Five is

_____

Part Five is the longest part of the book. It gives you practice in skills needed to write clear and effective sentences. You will note from the table of contents that it contains a diagnostic test, the skills themselves, mastery tests, editing tests, and an achievement test. The skills are grouped into four sections:

"Grammar," "Mechanics," (*fill in the missing word*) "_____," and "Word Use."

Part Six (Pages 577–723)   The title of Part Six is

_____

Part Six contains a series of seventeen reading selections, along with activities that will help you improve both reading and writing skills. Turn to the first selection, "All the Good Things," on page 584. You will see that the selection begins with a short preview that gives you background information on the piece. Following the selection there are ten comprehension (*fill in the missing word*)

_____ to help you practice important reading skills. Then, after a series of discussion questions that have to do with both reading and writing, there are several writing assignments.

Inside Back Cover   On the inside back cover is an alphabetical list of (*fill in the missing words*) _____.
Your instructor may use these symbols in marking your papers. In addition, you can use the page numbers in the list for quick reference to a specific sentence skill.

Charts in the Book   In addition to the guides on the inside front and back covers, several charts have been provided in the book to help you take responsibility for your own learning.

- What are the names of the charts on pages 730–734?

_____

_____

_____

Benefits of Paragraph Writing

Paragraph writing offers at least three benefits. First of all, mastering the structure of the paragraph will help make you a better writer. For other courses, you'll often do writing that will be variations on the paragraph form—for example, exam answers, summaries, response papers, and brief reports. In addition, paragraphs serve as the basic building blocks of essays, the most common form of writing in college. The basic structure of the traditional paragraph, with its emphasis on a clear point and well-organized, logical support, will help you write effective essays and almost every kind of paper that you will have to do.

Second, the discipline of writing a paragraph will strengthen your skills as a reader and listener. You'll become more critically aware of other writers' and speakers' ideas and the evidence they provide—or fail to provide—to support those ideas.

Most important, paragraph writing will make you a stronger thinker. Writing a solidly reasoned paragraph requires mental discipline and close attention to a set of logical rules. Creating a paragraph in which there is an overall topic sentence supported by well-reasoned, convincing evidence is more challenging than writing a free-form or expressive paper. Such a paragraph obliges you to carefully sort out, think through, and organize your ideas. You'll learn to discover and express just what your ideas are and to develop those ideas in a sound and logical way. Traditional paragraph writing, in short, will train your mind to think clearly, and that ability will prove to be of value in every phase of your life.

Writing as a Skill

A sure way to wreck your chances of learning how to write competently is to believe that writing is a "natural gift" rather than a learned skill. People with such an attitude think that they are the only ones for whom writing is unbearably difficult. They feel that everyone else finds writing easy or at least tolerable. Such people typically say, "I'm not any good at writing" or "English was not one of my good subjects." They imply that they simply do not have a talent for writing, while others do. The result of this attitude is that people try to avoid writing, and when they do write, they don't try their best. Their attitude becomes a self-fulfilling prophecy: their writing fails chiefly because they have brainwashed themselves into thinking that they don't have the "natural talent" needed to write. Unless their attitude changes, they probably will not learn how to write effectively.

A realistic attitude about writing must build on the idea that *writing is a skill*. It is a skill like driving, typing, or cooking, and like any skill, it can be learned. If you have the determination to learn, this book will give you the extensive practice needed to develop your writing skills.

Many people find it difficult to do the intense, active thinking that clear writing demands. (Perhaps television has made us all so passive that the active thinking necessary in both writing and reading now seems harder than ever.) It is frightening to sit down before a blank sheet of paper or a computer screen and know that an hour later, nothing on it may be worth keeping. It is frustrating to discover how much of a challenge it is to transfer thoughts and feelings from one's head into words. It is upsetting to find that an apparently simple writing subject often turns out to be complicated. But writing is not an automatic process: we will not get something for nothing—and we should not expect to. For almost everyone, competent writing comes from plain hard work—from determination, sweat, and head-on battle. The good news is that the skill of writing can be mastered, and if you are ready to work, you will learn what you need to know.

Activity

To get a sense of just how you regard writing, read the following statements. Put a check (✓) beside those statements with which you agree. This activity is not a test, so try to be as honest as possible.

_____   1. A good writer should be able to sit down and write a paper straight through without stopping.

_____   2. Writing is a skill that anyone can learn with practice.

_____   3. I'll never be good at writing because I make too many mistakes in spelling, grammar, and punctuation.

_____   4. Because I dislike writing, I always start a paper at the last possible minute.

_____   5. I've always done poorly in English, and I don't expect that to change.

Now read the following comments about the five statements. The comments will help you see if your attitude is hurting or helping your efforts to become a better writer.

Comments

- Statement 1: *"A good writer should be able to sit down and write a paper straight through without stopping."*

  Statement 1 is not true. Writing is, in fact, a process. It is done not in one easy step but in a series of steps, and seldom at one sitting. If you cannot do a paper all at once, that simply means you are like most of the other people on the planet. It is harmful to carry around the false idea that writing should be easy.

- Statement 2: *"Writing is a skill that anyone can learn with practice."*

  Statement 2 is absolutely true. Writing is a skill, like driving or word processing, that you can master with hard work. If you want to learn to write, you can. It is as simple as that. If you believe this, you are ready to learn how to become a competent writer.

  Some people hold the false belief that writing is a natural gift, which some have and others do not. Because of this belief, they never make a truly honest effort to learn to write—and so they never learn.

- Statement 3: *"I'll never be good at writing because I make too many mistakes in spelling, grammar, and punctuation."*

  The first concern in good writing should be content—what you have to say. Your ideas and feelings are what matter most. You should not worry about spelling, grammar, or punctuation while working on content.

  Unfortunately, some people are so self-conscious about making mistakes that they do not focus on what they want to say. They need to realize that a paper is best done in stages, and that applying the rules can and should wait until a later stage in the writing process. Through review and practice, you will eventually learn how to follow the rules with confidence.

- Statement 4: *"Because I dislike writing, I always start a paper at the last possible minute."*

  This is all too common. You feel you are going to do poorly, and then behave in a way that ensures you *will* do poorly! Your attitude is so negative that you defeat yourself—not even allowing enough time to really try.

  Again, what you need to realize is that writing is a process. Because it is done in steps, you don't have to get it right all at once. If you allow yourself enough time, you'll find a way to make a paper come together.

- Statement 5: *"I've always done poorly in English, and I don't expect that to change."*

  How you may have performed in the *past* does not control how you can perform in the *present*. Even if you did poorly in English in high school, it is in your power to make English one of your best subjects in college. If you believe writing can be learned and then work hard at it, you *will* become a better writer.

In conclusion, your attitude is crucial. If you believe you are a poor writer and always will be, chances are you will not improve. If you realize you can become a better writer, chances are you *will* improve. Depending on how you allow yourself to think, you can be your own best friend or your own worst enemy.

Writing as a Process of Discovery

In addition to believing that writing is a natural gift, many people believe, mistakenly, that writing should flow in a simple, straight line from the writer's head onto the page. But writing is seldom an easy, one-step journey in which a finished paper comes out in a first draft. The truth is that *writing is a process of discovery* which involves a series of steps, and those steps are very often a zigzag journey. Look at the following illustrations of the writing process:

Seldom the Case

Starting point ———————————————————→ Finished paper

Usually the Case

Starting point ———⋁⋀⋀———⋀⋁⋀———⋁———→ Finished paper

Very often, writers do not discover just what they want to write about until they explore their thoughts in writing. For example, Gene Hert had been asked to write about a best or worst job. Only after he did some freewriting on good and bad jobs did he realize that the most interesting details centered on his job at an apple plant. He discovered his subject in the course of writing.

Another student, Rhonda, talking afterward about a paper she wrote, explained that at first her topic was how she relaxed with her children. But as she accumulated details, she realized after a page of writing that the words *relax* and *children* simply did not go together. Her details were really examples of how she *enjoyed* her children, not how she *relaxed* with them. She sensed that the real focus of her writing should be what she did by herself to relax, and then she thought suddenly that the best time of her week was Thursday after school. "A light clicked on in my head," she explained. "I knew I had my paper." Then it was a matter of detailing exactly what she did to relax on Thursday evenings. Her paper, "How I Relax," is on page 80.

The point is that writing is often a process of continuing discovery. As you write, you may suddenly switch direction or double back. You may be working on a topic sentence and realize suddenly that it could be your concluding thought.

Or you may be developing a supporting idea and then decide that it should be the main point of your paper. Chapter 2 will treat the writing process directly. What is important to remember here is that writers frequently do not know their exact destination as they begin to write. Very often they discover the direction and shape of a paper during the process of writing.

Keeping a Journal

Because writing is a skill, it makes sense that the more you practice writing, the better you will write. One excellent way to get practice in writing, even before you begin composing formal paragraphs, is to keep a daily or almost daily journal. Writing a journal will help you develop the habit of thinking on paper and will show you how ideas can be discovered in the process of writing. A journal can make writing a familiar part of your life and can serve as a continuing source of ideas for papers.

At some point during the day—perhaps during a study period after your last class of the day, or right before dinner, or right before going to bed—spend fifteen minutes or so writing in your journal. Keep in mind that you do not have to plan what to write about, or be in the mood to write, or worry about making mistakes as you write; just write down whatever words come out. You should write at least one page in each session.

You may want to use a notebook that you can easily carry with you for on-the-spot writing. Or you may decide to write on loose-leaf paper that can be transferred later to a journal folder on your desk. No matter how you proceed, be sure to date all entries.

Your instructor may ask you to make journal entries a specific number of times a week, for a specific number of weeks. He or she may have you turn in your journal every so often for review and feedback. If you are keeping the journal on your own, try to make entries three to five times a week every week of the semester. Your journal can serve as a source book of ideas for possible papers. More important, keeping a journal will help you develop the habit of thinking on paper, and it can help you make writing a familiar part of your life.

Activity

Following is an excerpt from one student's journal. (Sentence-skills mistakes have been corrected to improve readability.) As you read, look for a general point and supporting material that could be the basis for an interesting paper.

October 6

Today a woman came into our department at the store and wanted to know if we had any scrap lumber ten feet long. Ten feet! "Lady," I said, "anything we have that's ten feet long sure as heck isn't scrap." When the boss heard me say that, he almost canned me. My boss is a company man, down to his toe tips. He wants to make a big impression on his bosses, and he'll run us around like mad all night to make himself look good. He's the most ambitious man I've ever met. If I don't transfer out of Hardware soon, I'm going to go crazy on this job. I'm not ready to quit, though. The time is not right. I want to be here for a year and have another job lined up and have other things right before I quit. It's good the boss wasn't around tonight when another customer wanted me to carry a bookcase he had bought out to his car. He didn't ask me to help him—he <u>expected</u> me to help him. I hate that kind of "You're my servant" attitude, and I told him that carrying stuff out to cars wasn't my job. Ordinarily I go out of my way to give people a hand, but not guys like him. . . .

- If the writer of this journal is looking for an idea for a paper, he can probably find several in this single entry. For example, he might write a narrative supporting the point that "In my sales job I have to deal with some irritating customers." See if you can find another idea in this entry that might be the basis for an interesting paragraph. Write your point in the space below.

  _____

- Take fifteen minutes to prepare a journal entry right now on this day in your life. On a separate sheet of paper, just start writing about anything that you have said, heard, thought, or felt, and let your thoughts take you where they may.

Using This Text

Here is a suggested sequence for using this book if you are working on your own.

1   After completing this introduction, read the remaining five chapters in Part One and work through as many of the activities as you need to master the ideas in these chapters. By the end of Part One, you will have covered all the basic theory needed to write effective papers.

2   Turn to Part Five and take the diagnostic test. The test will help you determine what sentence skills you need to review. Study those skills one or two at a time while you continue to work on other parts of the book. These skills will help you write effective, error-free sentences.

3   What you do next depends on course requirements, individual needs, or both. You will want to practice at least several different kinds of paragraph development in Part Two. If your time is limited, be sure to include "Providing Examples," "Explaining a Process," "Comparing or Contrasting," and "Arguing a Position."

4   After you develop skill in writing effective paragraphs, go on to practice writing one or more of the several-paragraph essays described in Part Three.

5   Turn to Part Four as needed for help with projects that involve research.

6   Read at least one of the seventeen selections in Part Six every week, always being sure to work through the two sets of questions that follow each reading.

Remember that, for your convenience, the book includes the following:

- On the inside front cover, there is a checklist of the four basic steps in effective writing.
- On the inside back cover, there is a list of commonly used correction symbols.

Get into the habit of referring to these guides on a regular basis; they'll help you produce clearly thought-out, well-written papers.

English Skills with Readings will help you learn, practice, and apply the thinking and writing skills you need to communicate effectively. But the starting point must be your determination to do the work needed to become a strong writer. The ability to express yourself clearly and logically can open doors of opportunity for you, both in school and in your career. If you decide—*and only you can decide*—that you want such language power, this book will help you reach that goal.

2 The Writing Process

This chapter will explain and illustrate

- **the sequence of steps in writing an effective paragraph**
- **prewriting**
- **revising**
- **editing**

Chapter 1 introduced you to the paragraph form and some basics of writing. This chapter will explain and illustrate the sequence of steps in writing an effective paragraph. In particular, the chapter will focus on prewriting and revising—strategies that can help with every paper that you write.

For many people, writing is a process that involves the following steps:

1 Discovering a point—often through prewriting.
2 Developing solid support for the point—often through more prewriting.
3 Organizing the supporting material and writing it out in a first draft.
4 Revising and then editing carefully to ensure an effective, error-free paper.

Learning this sequence will help give you confidence when the time comes to write. You'll know that you can use prewriting as a way to think on paper and to discover gradually just what ideas you want to develop. You'll understand that there are four clear-cut goals to aim for in your writing—unity, support, organization, and error-free sentences. You'll realize that you can use revising to rework a paper until it is strong and effective. And you'll be able to edit a paper so that your sentences are clear and error-free.

Prewriting

If you are like many people, you may have trouble getting started writing. A mental block may develop when you sit down before a blank sheet of paper. You may not be able to think of an interesting topic or a point to make about your topic. Or you may have trouble coming up with specific details to support your point. And even after starting a paper, you may hit snags—moments when you wonder "What else can I say?" or "Where do I go next?"

The following pages describe five techniques that will help you think about and develop a topic and get words on paper: (1) freewriting, (2) questioning, (3) making a list, (4) clustering, and (5) preparing a scratch outline. These prewriting techniques help you think about and create material, and they are a central part of the writing process.

Technique 1: Freewriting

When you do not know what to write about a subject or when you are blocked in writing, freewriting sometimes helps. In *freewriting,* you write on your topic for ten minutes. You do not worry about spelling or punctuating correctly, about erasing mistakes, about organizing material, or about finding exact words. You just write without stopping. If you get stuck for words, you write "I am looking for something to say" or repeat words until something comes. There is no need to feel inhibited, since mistakes *do not count* and you do not have to hand in your paper.

Freewriting will limber up your writing muscles and make you familiar with the act of writing. It is a way to break through mental blocks about writing. Since you do not have to worry about mistakes, you can focus on discovering what you want to say about a subject. Your initial ideas and impressions will often become clearer after you have gotten them down on paper, and they may lead to other impressions and ideas. Through continued practice in freewriting, you will develop the habit of thinking as you write. And you will learn a technique that is a helpful way to get started on almost any paper.

Freewriting: A Student Model

Gene Hert's essay "My Job in an Apple Plant" on page 5 was written in response to an assignment to write a paper on the best or worst job he ever had. Gene began by doing some general freewriting and thinking about his jobs. Here is his freewriting:

> I have had good and bad jobs, that's for sure. It was great earning money for the first time. I shoveled snow for my neighbor, a friend of mine and I did the work and had snowball fights along the way. I remember my neighbor reaching into his pocket and pulling out several dollars and handing us the money, it was like magic. Then there was the lawnmowing, which was also a good job. I mowed my aunts lawn while she was away at work. Then I'd go sit by myself in her cool living room and have a coke she left in the refrigarator for me. And look through all her magazines. Then there was the apple plant job I had after high school. That was a worst job that left me totaly wiped out at the end of my shift. Lifting cartons and cartons of apple

juice for bosses that treated us like slaves. The cartons coming and coming all night long. I started early in the evening and finished the next morning. I still remember how tired I was. Driving back home the first time. That was a lonely job and a hard job and I don't eat apples anymore.

At this point, Gene read over his notes, and as he later commented, "I realized that I had several potential topics. I said to myself, 'What point can I make that I can cover in a paragraph? What do I have the most information about?' I decided to narrow my topic down to my awful job at the apple plant. I figured I would have lots of interesting details for that topic." Gene then did a more focused freewriting to accumulate details for a paragraph on his bad job:

> The job I remember most is the worst job I ever had. I worked in an apple plant, I put in very long hours and would be totaly beat after ten hours of work. All the time lifting cartons of apple juice which would come racing down a metal track. The guy with me was a bit lazy at times, and I would be one man doing a two-man job. The cartons would go into a tracter trailer, we would have to throw down wooden skids to put the cartons on, then wed have to move the metal track as we filled up the truck. There is no other job I have had that even compares to this job, it was a lot worse than it seems. The bosses treated us like slaves and the company paid us like slaves. I would work all night from 7 p.m. and drive home in the morning at 5 a.m. and be bone tired. I remember my arms and sholders were so tired after the first night. I had trouble turning the steering wheel of my father's car.

Comment: Notice that there are problems with spelling, grammar, and punctuation in Gene's freewriting. Gene was not worried about such matters, nor should he have been. At this stage, he just wanted to do some thinking on paper and get some material down on the page. He knew that this was a good first step, a good way of getting started, and that he would then be able to go on and shape that material.

You should take the same approach when freewriting: explore your topic without worrying at all about being "correct." Figuring out what you want to say and getting raw material down on the page should have all of your attention at this early stage of the writing process.

Activity

To get a sense of the freewriting process, take a sheet of paper and freewrite about different jobs you have had and what you liked or did not like about them. See how much material you can accumulate in ten minutes. And remember not to worry about "mistakes"; you're just thinking on paper.

Technique 2: Questioning

In *questioning*, you generate ideas and details by asking as many questions as you can think of about your subject. Such questions include *Why? When? Where? Who? How? In what ways?*

Here are questions that Gene Hert asked while further developing his paper:

Questioning: A Student Model

Questions	Answers
<u>What</u> did I hate about the job?	Very hard work. Poor pay. Mean bosses.
<u>How</u> was the work hard?	Nonstop cartons of apple juice. Cartons became very heavy.
<u>Why</u> was pay poor?	$3.65 an hour (minimum wage at the time). Only a quarter more for working the second shift. Only good money was in overtime—where you got time-and-a-half. No double time.
<u>How</u> were the bosses mean?	Yelled at some workers. Showed no appreciation. Created bad working conditions.
<u>In what ways</u> were working conditions bad?	Unheated truck in zero-degree weather. Floor of tractor trailer was cold steel. Breaks were limited—only two of them. Lonely job.

Comment: Asking questions can be an effective way of getting yourself to think about a topic from different angles. The questions can help you generate details about a topic and get ideas on how to organize those details. Notice how asking questions gives Gene a better sense of the different reasons why he hated the job.

Activity

To get a feel for the questioning process, use a sheet of paper to ask yourself a series of questions about your best and worst jobs. See how many details you can accumulate in ten minutes. And remember again not to be concerned about "mistakes," because you are just thinking on paper.

Technique 3: Making a List

In *making a list,* also known as *brainstorming*, you create a list of ideas and details that relate to your subject. Pile these items up, one after another, without trying to sort out major details from minor ones, or trying to put the details in any special order, or even trying to spell words correctly. Your goal is to accumulate raw material by making up a list of everything about your subject that occurs to you.

After freewriting and questioning, Gene made up the following list of details.

Making a List: A Student Model

> <u>Apple factory job—worst one I ever had</u>
>
> Bosses were mean
> Working conditions were poor
> Went to work at 5 P.M., got back at 7 A.M.
> Lifted cartons of apple juice for ten hours
> Cartons were heavy
> Only two ten-minute breaks a night
> Pay was only $3.65 an hour
> Just quarter extra for night shift
> Cost of gas money to and from work
> No pay for lunch break
> Had to work 60 hours for good take-home pay
> Loaded onto wooden skids in a truck
> Bosses yelled at some workers
> Temperature zero outside
> Floors of trucks ice-cold metal
> Nonstop pace
> Had to clean apple vats after work
> Slept, ate, and worked—no social life
> No real friends at work

Comment: One detail led to another as Gene expanded his list. Slowly but surely, more details emerged, some of which he could use in developing his paragraph. By the time he had finished his list, he was ready to plan an outline of his paragraph and then to write his first draft.

Activity

To get a sense of making a list, use a sheet of paper to list a series of details about one of the best or worst jobs you ever had. Don't worry about deciding whether the details are major or minor; instead, just get down as many details as you can think of in five or ten minutes.

Technique 4: Clustering

Clustering, also known as *diagramming* or *mapping*, is another strategy that can be used to generate material for a paper. This method is helpful for people who like to think in a visual way. In clustering, you use lines, boxes, arrows, and circles to show relationships among the ideas and details that occur to you.

Begin by stating your subject in a few words in the center of a blank sheet of paper. Then, as ideas and details occur to you, put them in boxes or circles around the subject and draw lines to connect them to each other and to the subject. Put minor ideas or details in smaller boxes or circles, and use connecting lines to show how they relate as well.

Keep in mind that there is no right or wrong way of clustering. It is a way to think on paper about how various ideas and details relate to one another. Below is an example of what Gene might have done to develop his ideas:

Clustering: A Student Model

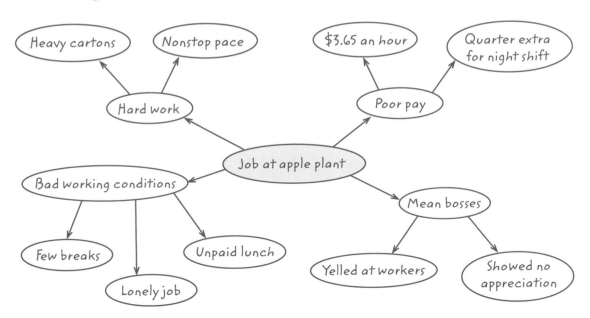

Comment: In addition to helping generate material, clustering often suggests ways to organize ideas and details.

Activity

Use clustering or diagramming to organize the details about a best or worst job that you created for the previous activity (page 20).

Technique 5: Preparing a Scratch Outline

A scratch outline can be the *single most helpful technique* for writing a good paper. A scratch outline often follows freewriting, questioning, making a list, or clustering, but it may also gradually emerge in the midst of these strategies. In fact, trying to make a scratch outline is a good way to see if you need to do more prewriting. If you cannot come up with a solid outline, then you know you need to do more prewriting to clarify your main point and its several kinds of support.

In a scratch outline, you think carefully about the point you are making, the supporting items for that point, and the order in which you will arrange those items. The scratch outline is a plan or blueprint to help you achieve a unified, supported, and well-organized composition.

Scratch Outline: A Student Model

In Gene's case, as he was working on his list of details, he suddenly realized what the plan of his paragraph could be. He could organize many of his details into one of three supporting groups: (1) the job itself, (2) the pay, and (3) the working conditions. He then went back to the list, crossed out items that he now saw did not fit, and numbered the items according to the group where they fit. Here is what Gene did with his list:

Apple factory job—worst one I ever had

~~Bosses were mean~~

3 Working conditions were poor

~~Went to work at 5 P.M., got back at 7 A.M.~~

1 Lifted cartons of apple juice for ten hours

1 Cartons were heavy

3 Only two ten-minute breaks a night

2 Pay was only $3.65 an hour

2 Just quarter extra for night shift

~~Cost of gas money to and from work~~

2 Had to work 60 hours for good take-home pay

1 Loaded onto wooden skids in a truck

~~Bosses yelled at some workers~~

3 Temperature zero outside

~~Floors of trucks ice-cold metal~~

1 Nonstop pace

3 No pay for lunch break

3 Had to clean apple vats after work

~~Slept, ate, and worked—no social life~~

3 No real friends at work

Under the list, Gene was now able to prepare his scratch outline:

The apple plant was my worst job.

1. Hard work

2. Poor pay

3. Poor working conditions

Comment: After all his prewriting, Gene was pleased. He knew that he had a promising paper—one with a clear point and solid support. He saw that he could organize the material into a paragraph with a topic sentence, supporting points, and vivid details. He was now ready to write the first draft of his paragraph, using his outline as a guide. Chances are that if you do enough prewriting and thinking on paper, you will eventually discover the point and support of your paragraph.

Activity

Create a scratch outline that could serve as a guide if you were to write a paragraph on your best or worst job experience.

Writing a First Draft

When you write a first draft, be prepared to put in additional thoughts and details that did not emerge during prewriting. And don't worry if you hit a snag. Just leave a blank space or add a comment such as "Do later" and press on to finish the paper. Also, don't worry yet about grammar, punctuation, or spelling. You don't want to take time correcting words or sentences that you may decide to remove later. Instead, make it your goal to state your main idea clearly and develop the content of your paper with plenty of specific details.

Writing a First Draft: A Student Model

Here is Gene's first draft, done in longhand:

> ~~The apple plant job was my worst.~~ Working in an apple plant was the worst job I ever had. The work was physicaly hard. For ~~a long time~~ ten hours a night, I stacked cartons that rolled down a metal track in a tracter trailer. Each carton had cans or bottles of apple juice, and they were heavy. At the same time, I had to keep a mental count of all the cartons I had loaded. The pay for the job was a bad feature. I was getting the minamum wage at that time plus a quarter extra for night shift. I had to work a lot to get a decent take-home pay. Working conditions were poor at the apple plant, we were limited to ~~short breaks~~ two ten-minute breaks. The truck-loading dock where I was most of the time was a cold and lonely place. Then by myself cleaning up. DETAILS!

Comment: After Gene finished the first draft, he was able to put it aside until the next day. You will benefit as well if you can allow some time between finishing a draft and starting to revise.

Activity

See if you can fill in the missing words in the following explanation of Gene's first draft.

1. Gene presents his _____ in the first sentence and then crosses it out and revises it right away to make it read smoothly and clearly.

2. Notice that he continues to accumulate specific supporting details as he writes the draft. For example, he crosses out and replaces "a long time" with the more specific _____; he crosses out and replaces "short breaks" with the more specific _____.

3. There are various misspellings—for example, _____. Gene doesn't worry about spelling at this point. He just wants to get down as much of the substance of his paper as possible.

4. There are various punctuation errors, especially the run-on and the fragment near the (*beginning, middle, end*) _____ of the paragraph.

5. Near the close of his paragraph, Gene can't think of added details to insert, so he simply prints "_____" as a reminder to himself for the next draft.

Revising

Revising is as much a stage in the writing process as prewriting, outlining, and doing the first draft. *Revising* means that you rewrite a paper, building upon what has already been done, in order to make it stronger. One writer has said about revision, "It's like cleaning house—getting rid of all the junk and putting things in the right order." It is not just "straightening up"; instead, you must be ready to roll up your sleeves and do whatever is needed to create an effective paper. Too many students think that a first draft *is* the paper. They start to become writers when they realize that revising a rough draft three or four times is often at the heart of the writing process.

Here are some quick hints that can help make revision easier. First, set your first draft aside for a while. You can then come back to it with a fresher, more objective point of view. Second, work from typed or printed text, preferably double-spaced so you'll have room to handwrite changes later. You'll be able to see the paper more impartially if it is typed than if you were just looking at your own familiar handwriting. Next, read your draft aloud. Hearing how your writing sounds will help you pick up problems with meaning as well as with style. Finally, as you do all these things, write additional thoughts and changes above the lines or in the margins of your paper. Your written comments can serve as a guide when you work on the next draft.

There are two stages to the revision process:

- Revising content
- Revising sentences

Revising Content

To revise the content of your paper, ask the following questions:

1 Is my paper **unified**?

- Do I have a main idea that is clearly stated at the beginning of my paragraph?
- Do all my supporting points truly support and back up my main idea?

2 Is my paper **supported**?

- Are there separate supporting points for the main idea?
- Do I have *specific* evidence for each supporting point?
- Is there *plenty of* specific evidence for the supporting points?

3 Is my paper **organized**?

- Do I have a clear method of organizing my paper?
- Do I use transitions and other connecting words?

The next two chapters (Chapters 3 and 4) will give you practice in achieving **unity**, **support**, and **organization** in your writing.

Revising Sentences

To revise individual sentences in your essay, ask the following questions:

1 Do I use *parallelism* to balance my words and ideas?
2 Do I have a *consistent point of view*?
3 Do I use *specific* words?
4 Do I use *active* verbs?

5   Do I use words effectively by *avoiding slang, clichés, pretentious language,* and *wordiness*?

6   Do I *vary my sentences* in length and structure?

Chapter 5 will give you practice in revising sentences.

Revising: A Student Model

For his second draft, Gene used a word-processing program on a computer. He then printed out a double-spaced version of his paragraph, leaving himself plenty of room for handwritten revisions. Here is Gene's second draft plus the handwritten changes and additions that became his third draft:

Working in an apple plant was the worst job I ever had. *First of all* The work was

physicaly hard. For ten hours a night, I stacked cartons that rolled down a

metal track in a tracter trailer. Each carton contained ~~bottles of~~ *25 pounds of bottled* apple juice,

and they came nonstop. *down the track* ~~At the same time, I had to keep a mental count of~~

~~all the cartons I had loaded.~~ The second bad feature ~~that made the job a~~

~~worst one~~ was the pay. I was getting the minamum wage at that time, $3.65

an hour. Plus *just* a quarter extra for night shift. I had to work ~~a lot of hours~~ *over sixty hours a week*

to get decent take-home pay. *Finally* I hated the working conditions. We were

limited to two ten-minute breaks and ~~the half hour for lunch was not paid~~ *an unpaid half hour for lunch*.

Most of my time was spent outside on the dock in *loading* ~~cold~~ *near-zero-degree* temperatures. And

I was very lonely on the job *because* I had nothing in common with the other

workers. ~~You~~ *I* felt this isolation especially when the production line shut

down for the night *, and* I had to clean the apple vats. The vats were ~~a bad~~ *an ugly* place

to be on a cold morning and the job was a ~~bad~~ *bitter* one to have.

Comment: Gene made his changes in longhand as he worked on the second draft. As you will see when you complete the activity below, his revision serves to make the paragraph more unified, supported, and organized.

Activity

Fill in the missing words.

1. To clarify the organization, Gene adds at the beginning of the first supporting point the transitional phrase "_____," and he sets off the third supporting point with the word "_____."

2. In the interest of (*unity, support, organization*) _____, he crosses out the sentence "_____." He realizes that this sentence is not a relevant detail to support the idea that the work was physically hard.

3. To add more (*unity, support, organization*) _____, he changes "a lot of hours" to "_____"; he changes "on the dock" to "_____"; he changes "cold temperatures" to "_____."

4. In the interest of eliminating wordiness, he removes the words "_____" from the sixth sentence.

5. To achieve parallelism, Gene changes "the half hour for lunch was not paid" to "_____."

6. For greater sentence variety, Gene combines two short sentences, beginning the second part of the sentence with the subordinating word "_____."

7. To create a consistent point of view, Gene changes "You felt this isolation" to "_____."

8. Finally, Gene replaces the somewhat vague "bad" in "The vats were a bad place to be on a cold morning, and the job was a bad one to have" with two more precise words: "_____" and "_____."

Editing

The last major stage in the writing process is editing—checking a paper for mistakes in grammar, punctuation, usage, and spelling. Editing as well as proofreading (checking a paper for typos and other careless errors) is explained in detail on pages 114–116.

Editing: A Student Model

After typing into his word-processing file all the revisions in his paragraph, Gene printed out another clean draft of the paper. He now turned his attention to editing changes, as shown below:

My Job in an Apple Plant

Working in an apple plant was the worst job I ever had. First of all, the

work was ~~physicaly~~ *physically* hard. For ten hours a night, I took cartons that rolled

down a metal track and stacked them onto wooden skids in a ~~tracter~~ *tractor* trailer.

Each carton contained ~~25~~ *twenty-five* pounds of bottled apple juice, and they came

down the track almost nonstop. The second bad feature of the job was the

pay. I was getting the ~~minamum~~ *minimum* wage at that time, $3.65 an hour. ~~P~~lus *, p* just

a quarter extra for working the night shift. I had to work over sixty hours a

week to get a decent take-home pay. Finally, I hated the working conditions.

We were limited to two ten-minute breaks and an unpaid half hour for

lunch. Most of my time was spent outside on the loading dock in near-zero-

degree temperatures. And I was very lonely on the job because I had no

interests in common with the other workers. I felt this isolation especially

when the production line shut down for the night, and I ~~had to clean~~ *spent two hours by myself cleaning* the

apple vats. The vats were an ugly place to be on a cold morning, and the

job was a bitter one to have.

Comment: Once again, Gene made his changes in longhand right on the print-out of his paper. To note these changes, complete the activity below.

Activity

Fill in the missing words.

1. As part of his editing, Gene checked and corrected the _____ of three words, *physically, tractor,* and *minimum.*

2. He added _____ to set off an introductory phrase ("First of all") and an introductory word ("Finally") and also to connect the two complete thoughts in the final sentence.

3. He corrected a fragment ("_____") by using a comma to attach it to the preceding sentence.

4. He realized that a number like "25" should be _____ as "twenty-five."

5. And since revision can occur at any stage of the writing process, including editing, Gene makes one of his details more vivid by adding the descriptive words "_____."

All that remained for Gene to do was to enter his corrections, print out the final draft of the paper, and proofread it for any typos or other careless errors. He was then ready to hand it in to his instructor.

Review Activities

You now have a good overview of the writing process, from prewriting to first draft to revising to editing. The remaining chapters in Part One will deepen your sense of the four goals of effective writing: unity, support, organization or coherence, and sentence skills.

To reinforce much of the information about the writing process that you have learned in this chapter, you can now work through the following activities:

1 Taking a writing inventory
2 Prewriting
3 Outlining
4 Revising

1 Taking a Writing Inventory

Activity

To evaluate your approach to the writing process, answer the questions below. This activity is not a test, so try to be as honest as possible. Becoming aware of your writing habits can help you make helpful changes in your writing.

1. When you start work on a paper, do you typically do any prewriting?

   _____ Yes   _____ Sometimes   _____ No

2. If so, which of the prewriting techniques do you use?

   _____ Freewriting   _____ Clustering

   _____ Questioning   _____ Scratch outline

   _____ List making   _____ Other (please describe)

3. Which prewriting technique or techniques work best for you or do you think will work best for you?

4. Many students have said they find it helpful to handwrite a first draft and then type that draft on a computer. They then print the draft out and revise it by hand. Describe your own way of drafting and revising a paper.

5. After you write the first draft of a paper, do you have time to set it aside for a while, so you can come back to it with a fresh eye?

6. How many drafts do you typically write when doing a paper?

7. When you revise, are you aware that you should be working toward a paper that is unified, solidly supported, and clearly organized? Has this chapter given you a better sense that unity, support, and organization are goals to aim for?

8. Do you revise a paper for the effectiveness of its sentences as well as for its content?

9. What (if any) information has this chapter given you about prewriting that you will try to apply in your writing?

10. What (if any) information has this chapter given you about revising that you will try to apply in your writing?

2 Prewriting

Activity

Below are examples of how the five prewriting techniques could be used to develop the topic "Inconsiderate Drivers." Identify each technique by writing F (for freewriting), Q (for questioning), L (for listing), C (for clustering), or SO (for the scratch outline) in the answer space.

_____

High beams on
Weave in and out at high speeds
Treat street like a trash can
Open car door onto street without looking
Stop on street looking for an address
Don't use turn signals
High speeds in low-speed zones
Don't take turns merging
Use horn when they don't need to
Don't give walkers the right of way
More attention to cell phone than the road

_____

What is one example of an inconsiderate driver?	A person who turns suddenly without signaling.
Where does this happen?	At city intersections or on smaller country roads.
Why is this dangerous?	You have to be alert and slow down yourself to avoid rear-ending the car in front.
What is another example of inconsideration on the road?	Drivers who come toward you at night with their high beams on.

_____   Some people are inconsiderate drivers.
1. In city:
   a. Stop in middle of street
   b. Turn without signaling
2. On highway:
   a. Leave high beams on
   b. Stay in passing lane
   c. Cheat during a merge
3. Both in city and on highway:
   a. Throw trash out of window
   b. Pay more attention to cell phone than to road

_____

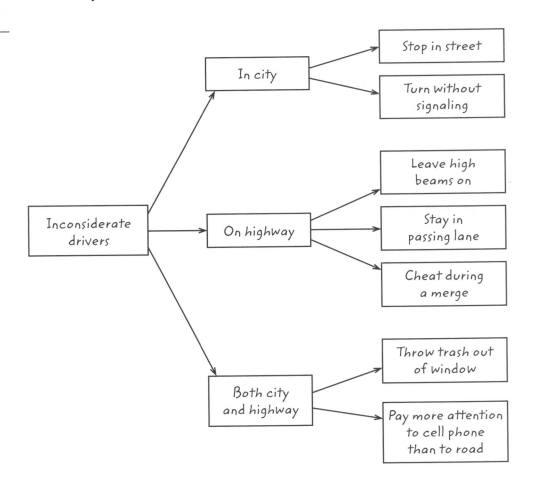

I was driving home last night after class and had three people try to blind me by coming at me with their high beams on. I had to zap them all with my high beams. Rude drivers make me crazy. The worst are the ones that use the road as a trash can. People who throw butts and cups and hamburger wrappings and other stuff out the car windows should be tossed into a trash dumpster. If word got around that this was the punishment maybe they would wise up. Other drivers do dumb things as well. I hate the person who will just stop in the middle of the street and try to figure out directions or look for a house address. Why don't they pull over to the side of the street? That hardly seems like too much to ask. Instead, they stop all traffic while doing their own thing. Then there are the people who keep what they want to do a secret. They're not going to tell you they plan to make a right- or left-hand turn. You've got to figure it out yourself when they suddenly slow down in front of you. Then there are all the people on their cell phones yakking away and not paying attention to their driving.

3 Outlining

As already mentioned (see page 23), outlining is central to writing a good paragraph. An outline lets you see, and work on, the bare bones of a paper, without the distraction of cluttered words and sentences. It develops your ability to think clearly and logically. Outlining provides a quick check on whether your paper will be *unified*. It also suggests right at the start whether your paper will be adequately *supported*. And it shows you how to plan a paper that is *well organized*.

The following series of exercises will help you develop the outlining skills so important to planning and writing a solid paragraph.

Activity 1

One key to effective outlining is the ability to distinguish between general ideas and specific details that fit under those ideas. Read each group of specific ideas below. Then circle the letter of the general idea that tells what the specific ideas have in common. Note that the general idea should not be too broad or too narrow. Begin by trying the example item, and then read the explanation that follows.

Example   *Specific ideas:* runny nose, coughing, sneezing, sore throat

The general idea is:

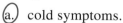

a.   cold symptoms.

b.   symptoms.

c.   throat problems.

Explanation: It is true that the specific ideas are all symptoms, but they have in common something even more specific—they are all symptoms of the common cold. Therefore, answer *b* is too broad; the correct answer is *a*. Answer *c* is too narrow because it doesn't cover all the specific ideas; it covers only the final item in the list ("sore throat").

1. *Specific ideas:* leaking toilet, no hot water, broken window, roaches
   The general idea is:

   a.   problems.

   b.   kitchen problems.

   c.   apartment problems.

2. *Specific ideas:* count to ten, take a deep breath, go for a walk
   The general idea is:

   a.   actions.

   b.   ways to calm down.

   c.   ways to calm down just before a test.

3. *Specific ideas:* putting sticky tape on someone's chair, putting a "kick me" sign on someone's back, putting hot pepper in someone's cereal
   The general idea is:

   a.   jokes.

   b.   practical jokes.

   c.   practical jokes played on teachers.

4. *Specific ideas:* going to bed earlier, eating healthier foods, reading for half an hour each day, trying to be kinder
   The general idea is:

   a.   resolutions.

   b.   problems.

   c.   solutions.

5. *Specific ideas:* money problems, family problems, relationship problems, health problems
   The general idea is:

   a.   poor grades.

   b.   causes of poor grades.

   c.   effects of poor grades.

Activity 2

In the following items, the specific ideas are given but the general ideas are unstated. Fill in each blank with a general heading that accurately describes the list provided.

Example

General idea: <u>Household Chores</u>

Specific ideas: washing dishes
preparing meals
taking out trash
dusting

1. *General idea:* _____

   Specific ideas: convenient work hours
short travel time to job
good pay
considerate boss

2. *General idea:* _____

   Specific ideas: greed
cowardice
selfishness
dishonesty

3. *General idea:* _____

   Specific ideas: order the invitations
get the bride's gown
rent the tuxedos
hire a photographer

4. *General idea:* _____

   Specific ideas: "Your mother stinks."
"Your father's a bum."
"You look like an ape."
"Your car is a real junk heap."

5. *General idea:* _____

   Specific ideas: "I like your dress."
"You look great in red."
"Your new haircut looks terrific."
"You did very well on the exam."

Activity 3

Major and minor ideas are mixed together in the two paragraphs outlined below.
Put the ideas in logical order by filling in the outlines.

1. *Topic sentence:* People can be classified by how they treat their cars.

   Seldom wax or vacuum car
   Keep every mechanical item in top shape
   Protective owners
   Deliberately ignore needed maintenance
   Indifferent owners
   Wash and polish car every week
   Never wash, wax, or vacuum car
   Abusive owners
   Inspect and service car only when required by state law

   a. _____
       (1) _____
       (2) _____
   b. _____
       (1) _____
       (2) _____
   c. _____
       (1) _____
       (2) _____

2. *Topic sentence:* Living with an elderly parent has many benefits.

   Advantages for elderly person
   Live-in baby-sitter
   Learn about the past
   Advantages for adult children
   Serve useful role in family
   Help with household tasks

Advantages for grandchildren

Stay active and interested in young people

More attention from adults

a. _____

   (1) _____

   (2) _____

b. _____

   (1) _____

   (2) _____

c. _____

   (1) _____

   (2) _____

Activity 4

Again, major and minor ideas are mixed together. In addition, in each outline one of the three major ideas is missing and must be added. Put the ideas in logical order by filling in the outlines that follow (summarizing as needed) and adding a third major idea.

1. *Topic sentence:* Extending the school day would have several advantages.

Help children academically

Parents know children are safe at the school

More time to spend on basics

Less pressure to cover subjects quickly

More time for extras like art, music, and sports

Help working parents

More convenient to pick up children at 4 or 5 P.M.

Teachers' salaries would be raised

a. _____

   (1) _____

   (2) _____

b. _____

    (1) _____

    (2) _____

c. _____

    (1) _____

    (2) _____

2. *Topic sentence:* By following certain hints about food, exercise, and smoking, you can increase your chances of dying young.

Don't ever walk if you can ride instead.

Choose foods such as bacon and lunch meats that are laced with nitrites and other preservatives.

Be very selective about what you eat.

If you begin to cough or feel short of breath, keep smoking.

If a friend invites you to play an outdoor sport, open a beer instead and head for your La-Z-Boy recliner.

Resist the urge to exercise.

Choose foods from one of four essential groups: fat, starch, sugar, and grease.

Smoke on a regular basis.

a. _____

    (1) _____

    (2) _____

b. _____

    (1) _____

    (2) _____

c. _____

    (1) _____

    (2) _____

Activity 5

Read the following two paragraphs. Then outline each one in the space provided. Write out the topic sentence in each case and summarize in a few words the primary and secondary supporting material that fits under the topic sentence.

1.   **Why I'm a Stay-at-Home Baseball Fan**

I'd much rather stay at home and watch ball games on television than go to the ballpark. First of all, it's cheaper to watch a game at home. I don't have to spend twelve dollars for a ticket and another eight dollars for a parking space. If I want some refreshments, I can have what's already in the refrigerator instead of shelling out another six dollars for a limp, lukewarm hot dog and a watery Coke. Also, it's more comfortable at home. I avoid a bumper-to-bumper drive to the ballpark and pushy crowds who want to go through the same gate I do. I can lie quietly on my living-room sofa instead of sitting on a hard stadium seat with noisy people all around me. Most of all, watching a game on television is more informative. Not only do I see all the plays that I might miss from my twelve-dollar seat, but I see some of them two and three times in instant replay. In addition, I get each play explained to me in glorious detail. If I were at the ballpark, I wouldn't know that the pitch our third baseman hit was a high and inside slider or that his grand-slam home run was a record-setting seventh in his career. The other fans can spend their money; put up with traffic, crowds, and hard seats; and guess at the plays. I'll take my baseball lying down—at home.

Topic sentence: _____

_____

a.   _____

  (1)   _____

  (2)   _____

b.   _____

  (1)   _____

  (2)   _____

c.   _____

  (1)   _____

  (2)   _____

2.

Why Teenagers Take Drugs

There are several reasons why teenagers take drugs. First of all, it is easy for young people to get drugs. Drugs are available almost anywhere, from a school cafeteria to a movie line to a football game. Teens don't have to risk traveling to the slums or dealing with shady types on street corners. It is also easy to get drugs because today's teens have spending money, which comes from allowances or earnings from part-time jobs. Teens can use their money to buy the luxuries they want—records, makeup, clothes, or drugs. Second, teens take drugs because the adolescent years are filled with psychological problems. For a teenager, one of these problems is the pressure of making important life decisions, such as choosing a career path. Another problem is establishing a sense of self. The teen years are the time when young people must become more independent from their parents and form their own values. The enormous mental pressures of these years can make some people turn to drugs. A final, and perhaps most important, reason why teenagers take drugs is peer pressure to conform. Teens often become very close to special friends, for one thing, and they will share a friend's interests, even if one interest is drugs. Teenagers also attend parties and other social events where it's all-important to be one of the crowd, to be "cool." Even the most mature teenager might be tempted to use drugs rather than risk being an outcast. For all these reasons, drugs are a major problem facing teenagers.

Topic sentence: _____

_____

a. _____

   (1) _____

   (2) _____

b. _____

   (1) _____

   (2) _____

c. _____

   (1) _____

   (2) _____

4 Revising

Activity 1

Listed in the box below are five stages in the process of composing a paragraph titled "Dangerous Places."

---

1. Prewriting (list)

2. Prewriting (freewriting, questioning, list, and scratch outline)

3. First draft

4. Revising (second draft)

5. Revising (final draft)

The five stages appear in scrambled order below and on the next page. Write the number 1 in the blank space in front of the first stage of development and number the remaining stages in sequence.

_____   There are some places where I never feel safe. For example, public rest rooms. The ~~dirt and graffiti~~ dirt on the floors and the graffiti scrawled on the walls ~~make the room seem dangerous~~ create a sense of danger. I'm also afraid in parking lots. ~~Late at night, I don't like walking in the lot After class, I don't like the parking lot.~~ When I leave my night class or the shopping mall late the walk to the car is scary. ~~Most parking lots have large lights which make me feel at least a little better.~~ I feel least safe in our laundry room. . . . It is a depressing place . . . Bars on the windows, . . . pipes making noises, . . . cement steps the only way out. . . .

_____   Dangerous Places
Highways
Cars—especially parking lots
Feel frightened in our laundry room
Big crowds—concerts, movies
Closed-in places
Bus and train stations
Airplane
Elevators and escalators

Dangerous Places

_____

There are some places where I never feel completely safe. For example, I seldom feel safe in public rest rooms. I worry that I'll suddenly be alone there and that someone will come in to mug me. The ugly graffiti often scrawled on the walls, along with the grime and dirt in the room and crumpled tissues and paper towels on the floor, add to my sense of unease and danger. I also feel unsafe in large, dark, parking lots. When I leave my night class a little late, or I am one of the few leaving the mall at 10 P.M., I dread the walk to my car. I am afraid that someone may be lurking behind another car, ready to mug me. And I fear that my car will not start, leaving me stuck in the dark parking lot. The place where I feel least safe is the basement laundry room in our apartment building. No matter what time I do my laundry, I seem to be the only person there. The windows are barred, and the only exit is a steep flight of cement steps. While I'm folding the clothes, I feel trapped. If anyone unfriendly came down those steps, I would have nowhere to go. The pipes in the room make sudden gurgles, clanks, and hisses, adding to my unsettledness. Places like public rest rooms, dark parking lots, and the basement laundry room give me the shivers.

_____

There are some places where I never feel completely safe. For example, I never feel safe in public rest rooms. If I'm alone there, I worry that someone will come in to rob and mug me. The dirt on the floors and the graffiti scrawled on the walls create a sense of danger. I feel unsafe in large, dark parking lots. When I leave my night class a little late or I leave the mall at 10 P.M., the walk to the car is scary. I'm afraid that someone may be behind a car. Also that my car won't start. Another place I don't feel safe is the basement laundry room in our apartment building. No matter when I do the laundry, I'm the only person there. The windows are barred and there are steep steps. I feel trapped when I fold the clothes. The pipes in the room make frightening noises such as hisses and clanks. Our laundry room and other places give me the shivers.

_____

Some places seem dangerous and unsafe to me. For example, last night I stayed till 10:15 after night class and walked out to parking lot alone. Very scary. Also, other places I go to every day, such as places in my apartment building. Also frightened by big crowds and public rest rooms.

Why was the parking lot scary?	What places in my building scare me?
Dark	Laundry room (especially)
Only a few cars	Elevators
No one else in lot	Lobby at night sometimes
Could be someone behind a car	Outside walkway at night
Cold	

2 Parking lots

3 Laundry room

1 Public rest rooms

Activity 2

The author of "Dangerous Places" in Activity 1 made a number of editing changes between the second draft and the final draft. Compare the two drafts and, in the spaces provided below, identify five of the changes.

1. _____

2. _____

3. _____

4. _____

5. _____

3 The First and Second Steps in Writing

This chapter will show you how to

- begin a paper by making a point of some kind
- provide specific evidence to support that point
- write a simple paragraph

Chapter 2 emphasized how prewriting and revising can help you become an effective writer. This chapter will focus on the first two steps in writing an effective paragraph:

1 Begin with a point.

2 Support the point with specific evidence.

Chapters 4 and 5 will then look at the third and fourth steps in writing:

3 Organize and connect the specific evidence (pages 79–96).

4 Write clear, error-free sentences (pages 97–130).

Step 1: Begin with a Point

Your first step in writing is to decide what point you want to make and to write that point in a single sentence. The point is commonly known as a *topic sentence.* As a guide to yourself and to the reader, put that point in the first sentence of your paragraph. Everything else in the paragraph should then develop and support in specific ways the single point given in the first sentence.

Activity

Read the two student paragraphs below about families today. Which paragraph clearly supports a single point? Which paragraph rambles on in many directions, introducing a number of ideas but developing none of them?

47

Paragraph A

Changes in the Family

Changes in our society in recent years have weakened family life. First of all, today's mothers spend much less time with their children. A generation ago, most households got by on Dad's paycheck, and Mom stayed home. Now many mothers work, and their children attend an after-school program, stay with a neighbor, or go home to an empty house. Another change is that families no longer eat together. In the past, Mom would be home and fix a full dinner—salad, pot roast, potatoes, and vegetables, with homemade cake or pie to top it off. Dinner today is more likely to be takeout food or TV dinners eaten at home, or fast food eaten out, with different members of the family eating at different times. Finally, television has taken the place of family conversation and togetherness. Back when there were traditional meals, family members would have a chance to eat together, talk with each other, and share events of the day in a leisurely manner. But now families are more likely to be looking at the TV set than talking to one another. Many homes even have several TV sets, which people watch in separate rooms. Clearly, modern life is a challenge to family life.

Paragraph B

The Family

Family togetherness is very important. However, today's mothers spend much less time at home than their mothers did, for several reasons. Most fathers are also home much less than they used to be. In previous times, families had to work together running a farm. Now children are left at other places or are home alone much of the time. Some families do find ways to spend more time together despite the demands of work. Another problem is that with parents gone so much of the day, nobody is at home to prepare wholesome meals for the family to eat together. The meals Grandma used to make would include pot roast and fried chicken, mashed potatoes, salad, vegetables, and delicious homemade desserts. Today's takeout foods and frozen meals can provide good nutrition. Some menu choices offer nothing but high-fat and high-sodium choices. People can supplement prepared foods by eating sufficient vegetables and fruit. Finally, television is also a big obstacle to togetherness. It sometimes seems that people are constantly watching TV and never talking to each other. Even when parents have friends over, it is often to watch something on TV. TV must be used wisely to achieve family togetherness.

Complete the following statement: Paragraph _____ is effective because it makes a clear, single point in the first sentence and goes on in the remaining sentences to support that single point.

Paragraph A starts with a point—that changes in our society in recent years have weakened family life—and then supports that idea with examples about mothers' working, families' eating habits, and television.

Paragraph B, on the other hand, does not make and support a single point. At first we think the point of the paragraph may be that "family togetherness is very important." But there is no supporting evidence showing how important family togetherness is. Instead, the line of thought in paragraph B swerves about like a car without a steering wheel. In the second sentence, we read that "today's mothers spend much less time at home than their mothers did, for several reasons." Now we think for a moment that this may be the main point and that the author will go on to list and explain some of those reasons. But the paragraph then goes on to comment on fathers, families in previous times, and families who find ways to spend time together. Any one of those ideas could be the focus of the paragraph, but none is. By now we are not really surprised at what happens in the rest of the paragraph. We are told about the absence of anyone "to prepare wholesome meals for the family," about what "the meals Grandma used to make" would be like, and about nutrition. The author then goes on to make a couple of points about how much people watch TV. The paragraph ends with yet another idea that does not support any previous point and that itself could be the point of a paragraph: "TV must be used wisely to achieve family togetherness." No single idea in this paragraph is developed, and the result for the reader is confusion.

In summary, while paragraph A is unified, paragraph B shows a complete lack of unity.

Step 2: Support the Point with Specific Evidence

The first essential step in writing effectively is to start with a clearly stated point. The second basic step is to support that point with specific evidence. Consider the supported point that you just read:

Point

Changes in our society in recent years have weakened family life.

Support

(1) Mothers
   (a) Most stayed home a generation ago
   (b) Most work now, leaving children at an after-school program, or with a neighbor, or in an empty house

(2) Eating habits
    (a) Formerly full homemade meals, eaten together
    (b) Now prepared foods at home or fast food out, eaten separately

(3) Television
    (a) Watching TV instead of conversing
    (b) Watching in separate rooms instead of being together

The supporting evidence is needed so that we can *see and understand for ourselves* that the writer's point is sound. The author of "Changes in the Family" has supplied specific supporting examples of how changes in our society have weakened family life. The paragraph has provided the evidence that is needed for us to understand and agree with the writer's point.

Now consider the following paragraph:

Good-Bye, Tony

I have decided not to go out with Tony anymore. First of all, he was late for our first date. He said that he would be at my house by 8:30, but he did not arrive until 9:30. Second, he was bossy. He told me that it would be too late to go to the new Jim Carrey comedy that I wanted to see, and that we would go instead to a new action film with Arnold Schwarzenegger. I told him that I didn't like violent movies, but he said that I could shut my eyes during the bloody parts. Only because it was a first date did I let him have his way. Finally, he was abrupt. After the movie, rather than suggesting a hamburger or a drink, he drove right out to a back road near Oakcrest High School and started necking with me. What he did a half hour later angered me most of all. He cut his finger on a pin I was wearing and immediately said we had to go right home. He was afraid the scratch would get infected if he didn't put Bactine and a Band-Aid on it. When he dropped me off, I said, "Good-bye, Tony," in a friendly enough way, but in my head I thought, "Good-bye <u>forever,</u> Tony."

The author's point is that she has decided not to go out with Tony anymore. See if you can summarize in the spaces below the three reasons she gives to support her decision:

Reason 1: _____

Reason 2: _____

Reason 3: _____

Notice what the supporting details in this paragraph do. They provide you, the reader, with a basis for understanding why the writer made the decision she did. Through specific evidence, the writer has explained and communicated her point successfully. The evidence that supports the point in a paragraph often consists of a series of reasons introduced by signal words (the author uses *First of all, Second,* and *Finally*) and followed by examples and details that support the reasons. That is true of the sample paragraph above: three reasons are provided, followed by examples and details that back up those reasons.

Activity

Both of the paragraphs that follow resulted from an assignment to "Write a paper that details your reasons for being in college." Both writers make the point that they have various reasons for attending college. Which paragraph then goes on to provide plenty of specific evidence to back up its point? Which paragraph is vague and repetitive and lacks the concrete details needed to show us exactly why the author decided to attend college?

Hint: Imagine that you've been asked to make a short film based on each paragraph. Which one suggests specific pictures, locations, words, and scenes you could shoot?

Paragraph A

Reasons for Going to College

I decided to attend college for various reasons. One reason is self-respect. For a long time now, I have had little self-respect. I spent a lot of time doing nothing, just hanging around or getting into trouble, and eventually I began to feel bad about it. Going to college is a way to start feeling better about myself. By accomplishing things, I will improve my self-image. Another reason for going to college is that things happened in my life that made me think about a change. For one thing, I lost the part-time job I had. When I lost the job, I realized I would have to do something in life, so I thought about school. I was in a rut and needed to get out of it but did not know how. But when something happens that is out of your control, then you have to make some kind of decision. The most important reason for college, though, is to fulfill my dream. I know I need an education, and I want to take the courses I need to reach the position that I think I can handle. Only by qualifying yourself can you get what you want. Going to college will help me fulfill this goal. These are the main reasons why I am attending college.

Paragraph B

Why I'm in School

There are several reasons I'm in school. First of all, my father's attitude made me want to succeed in school. One night last year, after I had come in at 3 A.M., my father said, "Mickey, you're a bum. When I look at my son, all I see is a good-for-nothing bum." I was angry, but I knew my father was right in a way. I had spent the last two years working at odd jobs at a pizza parlor and luncheonette, taking "uppers" and "downers" with my friends. That night, though, I decided I would prove my father wrong. I would go to college and be a success. Another reason I'm in college is my girlfriend's encouragement. Marie has already been in school for a year, and she is doing well in her computer courses. Marie helped me fill out my application and register for courses. She even lent me sixty-five dollars for textbooks. On her day off, she lets me use her car so I don't have to take the college bus. The main reason I am in college is to fulfill a personal goal: for the first time in my life, I want to finish something. For example, I quit high school in the eleventh grade. Then I enrolled in a government job-training program, but I dropped out after six months. I tried to get a high school equivalency diploma, but I started missing classes and eventually gave up. Now I am in a special program where I will earn my high school degree by completing a series of five courses. I am determined to accomplish this goal and to then go on and work for a degree in hotel management.

Complete the following statement: Paragraph _____ provides clear, vividly detailed reasons why the writer decided to attend college.

Paragraph B is the one that solidly backs up its point. The writer gives us specific reasons he is in school. On the basis of such evidence, we can clearly understand his opening point. The writer of paragraph A offers only vague, general reasons for being in school. We do not get specific examples of how the writer was "getting into trouble," what events occurred that forced the decision, or even what kind of job he or she wants to qualify for. We sense that the feeling expressed is sincere; but without particular examples we cannot really see why the writer decided to attend college.

The Importance of *Specific* Details

The point that opens a paper is a general statement. The evidence that supports a point is made up of specific details, reasons, examples, and facts.

Specific details have two key functions. First of all, details *excite the reader's interest*. They make writing a pleasure to read, for we all enjoy learning particulars about other people—what they do and think and feel. Second, details *support and explain a writer's point;* they give the evidence needed for us to see and understand a general idea. For example, the writer of "Good-Bye, Tony" provides details that make vividly clear her decision not to see Tony anymore. She specifies the exact time Tony was supposed to arrive (8:30) and when he actually arrived (9:30). She mentions the kind of film she wanted to see (a new Jim Carrey movie) and the one that Tony took her to instead (a violent movie). She tells us what she may have wanted to do after the movie (have a hamburger or a drink) and what Tony did instead (went necking); she even specifies the exact location of the place Tony took her (a back road near Oakcrest High School). She explains precisely what happened next (Tony "cut his finger on a pin I was wearing") and even mentions by name (Bactine and a Band-Aid) the treatments he planned to use.

The writer of "Why I'm in School" provides equally vivid details. He gives clear reasons for being in school (his father's attitude, his girlfriend's encouragement, and his wish to fulfill a personal goal) and backs up each reason with specific details. His details give us many sharp pictures. For instance, we hear the exact words his father spoke: "Mickey, you're a bum." He tells us exactly how he was spending his time ("working at odd jobs at a pizza parlor and luncheonette, taking 'uppers' and 'downers' with my friends"). He describes how his girlfriend helped him (filling out the college application, lending money and her car). Finally, instead of stating generally that "you have to make some kind of decision," as the writer of "Reasons for Going to College" does, he specifies that he has a strong desire to finish college because he dropped out of many schools and programs in the past: high school, a job-training program, and a high school equivalency course.

In both "Good-Bye, Tony" and "Why I'm in School," then, the vivid, exact details capture our interest and enable us to share in the writer's experience. We see people's actions and hear their words; the details provide pictures that make each of us feel "I am there." The particulars also allow us to understand each writer's point clearly. We are shown exactly why the first writer has decided not to see Tony anymore and exactly why the second writer is attending college.

Activity

Each of the five points below is followed by two attempts at support (*a* and *b*). Write S (for *specific*) in the space next to the one that succeeds in providing specific support for the point. Write X in the space next to the one that lacks supporting details.

1. My two-year-old son was in a stubborn mood today.

_____ a. When I asked him to do something, he gave me nothing but trouble. He seemed determined to make things difficult for me, for he had his mind made up.

_____ b. When I asked him to stop playing in the yard and come indoors, he looked me square in the eye and shouted "No!" and then spelled it out, "N . . . O!"

2. The prices in the amusement park were outrageously high.

_____ a. The food seemed to cost twice as much as it would in a super-market and was sometimes of poor quality. The rides also cost a lot, and so I had to tell the children that they were limited to a certain number of them.

_____ b. The cost of the log flume, a ride that lasts roughly three minutes, was ten dollars a person. Then I had to pay four dollars for an eight-ounce cup of Coke and six dollars for a hot dog.

3. My brother-in-law is accident-prone.

_____ a. Once he tried to open a tube of Krazy Glue with his teeth. When the cap came loose, glue squirted out and sealed his lips shut. They had to be pried open in a hospital emergency room.

_____ b. Even when he does seemingly simple jobs, he seems to get into trouble. This can lead to hilarious, but sometimes dangerous, results. Things never seem to go right for him, and he often needs the help of others to get out of one predicament or another.

4. The so-called "bargains" at the yard sale were junk.

_____ a. The tables were filled with useless stuff no one could possibly want. They were the kinds of things that should be thrown away, not sold.

_____ b. The "bargains" included two headless dolls, blankets filled with holes, scorched potholders, and a plastic Christmas tree with several branches missing.

5. The key to success in college is organization.

_____ a. Knowing what you're doing, when you have to do it, and so on is a big help for a student. A system is crucial in achieving an ordered approach to study. Otherwise, things become very disorganized, and it is not long before grades will begin to drop.

_____ b. Organized students never forget paper or exam dates, which are marked on a calendar above their desks. And instead of having to cram for exams, they study their clear, neat classroom and text-book notes on a daily basis.

Comments: The specific support for point 1 is answer *b*. The writer does not just tell us that the little boy was stubborn but provides an example that shows us. In particular, the detail of the son's spelling out "N . . . O!" makes his stubborn-ness vividly real for the reader. For point 2, answer *b* gives specific prices (ten dollars for a ride, four dollars for a Coke, and six dollars for a hot dog) to support the idea that the amusement park was expensive. For point 3, answer *a* vividly backs up the idea that the brother-in-law is accident-prone by detailing an accident with Krazy Glue. Point 4 is supported by answer *b*, which lists specific examples of useless items that were offered for sale—from headless dolls to a broken plastic Christmas tree. We cannot help agreeing with the writer's point that the items were not bargains but junk. Point 5 is backed up by answer *b*, which identifies two specific strategies of organized students: they mark important dates on calendars above their desks, and they take careful notes and study them on a daily basis.

In each of the five cases, the specific evidence enables us to *see for ourselves* that the writer's point is valid.

The Importance of *Adequate* Details

One of the most common and most serious problems in students' writing is inadequate development. You must provide *enough* specific details to support fully the point you are making. You could not, for example, submit a paragraph about your brother-in-law being accident-prone and provide only a single short example. You would have to add several other examples or provide an extended example of your brother-in-law's accident-proneness. Without such additional support, your paragraph would be underdeveloped.

At times, students try to disguise an undersupported point by using repetition and wordy generalities. You saw this, for example, in paragraph A ("Reasons for Going to College") on page 51. Be prepared to do the plain hard work needed to ensure that each of your paragraphs has full, solid support.

Activity

The following paragraphs were written on the same topic, and each has a clear opening point. Which one is adequately developed? Which one has few particulars and uses mostly vague, general, wordy sentences to conceal the fact that it is starved for specific details?

Paragraph A

Abuse of Public Parks

Some people abuse public parks. Instead of using the park for recreation, they go there, for instance, to clean their cars. Park caretakers regularly have to pick up the contents of dumped ashtrays and car litter bags. Certain juveniles visit parks with cans of spray paint to deface buildings, fences, fountains, and statues. Other offenders are those who dig up and cart away park flowers, shrubs, and trees. One couple were even arrested for stealing park sod, which they were using to fill in their lawn. Perhaps the most widespread offenders are the people who use park tables and benches and fireplaces but do not clean up afterward. Picnic tables are littered with trash, including crumpled bags, paper plates smeared with ketchup, and paper cups half-filled with stale soda. On the ground are empty beer bottles, dented soda cans, and sharp metal pop-tops. Parks are made for people, and yet—ironically—their worst enemy is "people pollution."

Paragraph B

Mistreatment of Public Parks

Some people mistreat public parks. Their behavior is evident in many ways, and the catalog of abuses could go on almost without stopping. Different kinds of debris are left by people who have used the park as a place for attending to their automobiles. They are not the only individuals who mistreat public parks, which should be used with respect for the common good of all. Many young people come to the park and abuse it, and their offenses can occur in any season of the year. The reason for their inconsiderate behavior is known only to themselves. Other visitors lack personal cleanliness in their personal habits when they come to the park, and the park suffers because of it. Such people seem to have the attitude that someone else should clean up after them. It is an undeniable fact that people are the most dangerous thing that parks must contend with.

Complete the following statement: Paragraph _____ provides an adequate number of specific details to support its point.

Paragraph A offers a series of detailed examples of how people abuse parks. Paragraph B, on the other hand, is underdeveloped. Paragraph B speaks only of "different kinds of debris," while paragraph A refers specifically to "dumped ashtrays and car litter bags"; paragraph B talks in a general way of young people abusing the park, while paragraph A supplies such particulars as "cans of spray paint" and defacing "buildings, fences, fountains, and statues." And there is no equivalent in paragraph B for the specifics in paragraph A about people who steal park property and litter park grounds. In summary, paragraph B lacks the full, detailed support needed to develop its opening point convincingly.

■ Review Activity

To check your understanding of the chapter so far, see if you can answer the following questions.

1. It has been observed: "To write well, the first thing that you must do is decide what nail you want to drive home." What is meant by *nail?*

2. How do you drive home the nail in the paper?

_____

3. What are the two reasons for using specific details in your writing?

    a. _____

    b. _____

Practice in Making and Supporting a Point

You now know the two most important steps in competent writing: (1) making a point and (2) supporting that point with specific evidence. The purpose of this section is to expand and strengthen your understanding of these two basic steps.

You will first work through a series of activities on *making* a point:

1 Identifying Common Errors in Topic Sentences
2 Understanding the Two Parts of a Topic Sentence
3 Selecting a Topic Sentence
4 Writing a Topic Sentence: I
5 Writing a Topic Sentence: II

You will then sharpen your understanding of specific details by working through a series of activities on *supporting* a point:

6 Recognizing Specific Details: I
7 Recognizing Specific Details: II
8 Providing Supporting Evidence
9 Identifying Adequate Supporting Evidence
10 Adding Details to Complete a Paragraph
11 Writing a Simple Paragraph

1 Identifying Common Errors in Topic Sentences

When writing a point, or topic sentence, people sometimes make mistakes that undermine their chances of producing an effective paper. One mistake is to substitute an announcement of the topic for a true topic sentence. Other mistakes include writing statements that are too broad or too narrow. Following are examples of all three errors, along with contrasting examples of effective topic sentences.

Announcement

My Ford Escort is the concern of this paragraph.

The statement above is a simple announcement of a subject, rather than a topic sentence expressing an idea about the subject.

Statement That Is Too Broad

Many people have problems with their cars.

The statement is too broad to be supported adequately with specific details in a single paragraph.

Statement That Is Too Narrow

My car is a Ford Escort.

The statement above is too narrow to be expanded into a paragraph. Such a narrow statement is sometimes called a *dead-end statement* because there is no place to go with it. It is a simple fact that does not need or call for any support.

Effective Topic Sentence

I hate my Ford Escort.

The statement above expresses an opinion that could be supported in a paragraph. The writer could offer a series of specific supporting reasons, examples, and details to make it clear why he or she hates the car.

Here are additional examples:

Announcements

The subject of this paper will be my apartment.

I want to talk about increases in the divorce rate.

Statements That Are Too Broad

The places where people live have definite effects on their lives.

Many people have trouble getting along with others.

Statements That Are Too Narrow

I have no hot water in my apartment at night.

Almost one of every two marriages ends in divorce.

Effective Topic Sentences

My apartment is a terrible place to live.

The divorce rate is increasing for several reasons.

Activity 1

For each pair of sentences below, write A beside the sentence that only *announces* a topic. Write OK beside the sentence that *advances an idea* about the topic.

1. _____ a. This paper will deal with flunking math.

   _____ b. I flunked math last semester for several reasons.

2. _____ a. I am going to write about my job as a gas station attendant.

   _____ b. Working as a gas station attendant was the worst job I ever had.

3. _____ a. Obscene phone calls are the subject of this paragraph.

   _____ b. People should know what to do when they receive an obscene phone call.

4. _____ a. In several ways, my college library is inconvenient to use.

   _____ b. This paragraph will deal with the college library.

5. _____ a. My paper will discuss the topic of procrastinating.

   _____ b. The following steps will help you stop procrastinating.

Activity 2

For each pair of sentences below, write TN beside the statement that is *too narrow* to be developed into a paragraph. Write OK beside the statement in each pair that could be developed into a paragraph.

1. _____ a. I do push-ups and sit-ups each morning.

   _____ b. Exercising every morning has had positive effects on my health.

2. _____ a. José works nine hours a day and then goes to school three hours a night.

   _____ b. José is an ambitious man.

3. _____ a. I started college after being away from school for seven years.

   _____ b. Several of my fears about returning to school have proved to be groundless.

4. _____ a. Parts of Walt Disney's *Bambi* make the movie frightening for children.

_____ b. Last summer I visited Disneyland in Anaheim, California.

5. _____ a. My brother was depressed yesterday for several reasons.

_____ b. Yesterday my brother had to pay fifty-two dollars for a motor tune-up.

Activity 3

For each pair of sentences below, write TB beside the statement that is *too broad* to be supported adequately in a short paper. Write OK beside the statement that makes a limited point.

1. _____ a. Professional football is a dangerous sport.

_____ b. Professional sports are violent.

2. _____ a. Married life is the best way of living.

_____ b. Teenage marriages often end in divorce for several reasons.

3. _____ a. Aspirin can have several harmful side effects.

_____ b. Drugs are dangerous.

4. _____ a. I've always done poorly in school.

_____ b. I flunked math last semester for several reasons.

5. _____ a. Computers are changing our society.

_____ b. Using computers to teach schoolchildren is a mistake.

2 Understanding the Two Parts of a Topic Sentence

As stated earlier, the point that opens a paragraph is often called a *topic sentence*. When you look closely at a point, or topic sentence, you can see that it is made up of two parts:

1 The *limited topic*

2 The writer's *attitude* toward the limited topic

The writer's attitude, point of view, or idea is usually expressed in one or more *key words*. All the details in a paragraph should support the idea expressed in the key words. In each of the topic sentences below, a single line appears under the topic and a double line under the idea about the topic (expressed in a key word or key words):

My girlfriend is very aggressive.

Highway accidents are often caused by absentmindedness.

The kitchen is the most widely used room in my house.

Voting should be required by law in the United States.

My pickup truck is the most reliable vehicle I have ever owned.

In the first sentence, the topic is *girlfriend*, and the key word that expresses the writer's idea about his topic is that his girlfriend is *aggressive*. In the second sentence, the topic is *highway accidents*, and the key word that determines the focus of the paragraph is that such accidents are often caused by *absentmindedness*. Notice each topic and key word or key words in the other three sentences as well.

Activity

For each point below, draw a single line under the topic and a double line under the idea about the topic.

1. Billboards should be abolished.
2. My boss is an ambitious man.
3. Politicians are often self-serving.
4. The apartment needed repairs.
5. Television commercials are often insulting.
6. My parents have rigid racial attitudes.
7. The middle child is often a neglected member of the family.
8. The language in many movies today is offensive.
9. Doctors are often insensitive.
10. Homeowners today are more energy-conscious than ever before.
11. My car is a temperamental machine.
12. My friend Debbie, who is only nineteen, is extremely old-fashioned.
13. Looking for a job can be a degrading experience.
14. The daily life of students is filled with conflicts.
15. Regulations in the school cafeteria should be strictly enforced.
16. The national speed limit should be raised.

17. Our vacation turned out to be a disaster.

18. The city's traffic-light system has both values and drawbacks.

19. Insects serve many useful purposes.

20. Serious depression often has several warning signs.

3 Selecting a Topic Sentence

Remember that a paragraph is made up of a topic sentence and a group of related sentences developing the topic sentence. It is also helpful to remember that the topic sentence is a *general* statement. The other sentences provide specific support for the general statement.

Activity

Each group of sentences below could be written as a short paragraph. Circle the letter of the topic sentence in each case. To find the topic sentence, ask yourself, "Which is a general statement supported by the specific details in the other three statements?"

Begin by trying the example item below. First circle the letter of the sentence you think expresses the main idea. Then read the explanation.

Example   a. If you stop carrying matches or a lighter, you can cut down on impulse smoking.

b. If you sit in no-smoking areas, you will smoke less.

c. You can behave in ways that will help you smoke less.

d. By keeping a record of when and where you smoke, you can identify the most tempting situations and then avoid them.

Explanation: Sentence *a* explains one way to smoke less. Sentences *b* and *d* also provide specific ways to smoke less. In sentence *c*, however, no one specific way is explained. The words *ways that will help you smoke less* refer only generally to such methods. Therefore, sentence *c* is the topic sentence; it expresses the author's main idea. The other sentences support that idea by providing examples.

1. a. "I couldn't study because I forgot to bring my textbook home."

   b. "I couldn't take the final because my grandmother died."

   c. Students give instructors some common excuses.

   d. "I couldn't come to class because I had a migraine headache."

2. a. Its brakes are badly worn.

   b. My old car is ready for the junk pile.

   c. Its floor has rusted through, and water splashes on my feet when the highway is wet.

   d. My mechanic says its engine is too old to be repaired, and the car isn't worth the cost of a new engine.

3. a. Tobacco is one of the most addictive of all drugs.

   b. Selling cigarettes ought to be against the law.

   c. Nonsmokers are put in danger by breathing the smoke from other people's cigarettes.

   d. Cigarette smoking kills many more people than all illegal drugs combined.

4. a. Part-time workers can be easily laid off.

   b. Most part-time workers get no fringe benefits.

   c. The average part-timer earns three dollars less an hour than a full-timer.

   d. Part-time workers have second-class status.

5. a. The last time I ate at the diner, I got food poisoning and was sick for two days.

   b. The city inspector found matches and mice in the diner's kitchen.

   c. Our town diner is a health hazard and ought to be closed down.

   d. The toilets in the diner often back up, and the sinks have only a trickle of water.

4 Writing a Topic Sentence: I

Activity

The following activity will give you practice in writing an accurate point, or topic sentence—one that is neither too broad nor too narrow for the supporting material in a paragraph. Sometimes you will construct your topic sentence after you have decided which details you want to discuss. An added value of this activity is that it shows you how to write a topic sentence that will exactly match the details you have developed.

1. *Topic sentence:* _____

_____

   a. When we brought a "welcome to the neighborhood" present, the family next door didn't even say thank you.

   b. The family never attends the annual block party.

   c. The family's children aren't allowed to play with other neighborhood kids.

   d. Our neighbors keep their curtains closed and never sit out in their yard.

2. *Topic sentence:* _____

_____

   a. Only about thirty people came to the dance, instead of the expected two hundred.

   b. The band arrived late and spent an hour setting up.

   c. There were at least three males at the dance to every female.

   d. An hour after the dance started, it ended because of a power failure.

3. *Topic sentence:* _____

_____

   a. We had to wait half an hour even though we had reserved a table.

   b. Our appetizer and main course arrived at the same time.

   c. The busboy ignored our requests for more water.

   d. The wrong desserts were served to us.

4. *Topic sentence:* _____

_____

   a. In early grades we had spelling bees, and I would be among the first to sit down.

   b. In sixth-grade English, my teacher kept me busy diagramming sentences on the board.

   c. In tenth grade we had to recite poems, and I always forgot my lines.

   d. In my senior year, my compositions had more red correction marks than anyone else's.

5. *Topic sentence:* _____

    _____

    a. The crowd scenes were crudely spliced from another film.
    b. Mountains and other background scenery were just painted cardboard cutouts.
    c. The "sync" was off, so that you heard voices even when the actors' lips were not moving.
    d. The so-called "monster" was just a spider that had been filmed through a magnifying lens.

5 Writing a Topic Sentence: II

Often you will start with a general topic or a general idea of what you want to write about. You may, for example, want to write a paragraph about some aspect of school life. To come up with a point about school life, begin by limiting your topic. One way to do this is to make a list of all the limited topics you can think of that fit under the general topic.

Activity

Following are five general topics and a series of limited topics that fit under them. Make a point out of *one* of the limited topics in each group.

Hint: To create a topic sentence, ask yourself, "What point do I want to make about _____ (*my limited topic*)?"

Example   Recreation
  • Movies
  • Dancing
  • TV shows
  • Reading
  • Sports parks

Your point: *Sports parks today have some truly exciting games.*

1. Your school
    • Instructor
    • Cafeteria

- Specific course
- Particular room or building
- Particular policy (attendance, grading, etc.)
- Classmate

Your point: _____

_____

2. Job
   - Pay
   - Boss
   - Working conditions
   - Duties
   - Coworkers
   - Customers or clients

   Your point: _____

   _____

3. Money
   - Budgets
   - Credit cards
   - Dealing with a bank
   - School expenses
   - Ways to get it
   - Ways to save it

   Your point: _____

   _____

4. Cars
   - First car
   - Driver's test
   - Road conditions
   - Accident
   - Mandatory speed limit
   - Safety problems

   Your point: _____

   _____

5. Sports
   - A team's chances
   - At your school
   - Women's team

- Recreational versus spectator
- Favorite team
- Outstanding athlete

Your point: _____

_____

6 Recognizing Specific Details: I

Specific details are examples, reasons, particulars, and facts. Such details are needed to support and explain a topic sentence effectively. They provide the evidence needed for readers to understand, as well as to feel and experience, a writer's point.

Here is a topic sentence followed by two sets of supporting sentences. Which set provides sharp, specific details?

Topic Sentence

Some poor people must struggle to make meals for themselves.

Set A

They gather up whatever free food they can find in fast-food restaurants and take it home to use however they can. Instead of planning well-balanced meals, they base their diet on anything they can buy that is cheap and filling.

Set B

Some make tomato soup by adding hot water to the free packets of ketchup they get at McDonald's. Others buy cans of cheap dog food and fry it like hamburger.

Set B provides specific details: instead of a general statement about "free food they find in fast-food restaurants and take . . . home to use however they can," we get a vivid detail we can see and picture clearly: "make tomato soup [from] free packets of ketchup." Instead of a general statement about how the poor will "base their diet on anything they can buy that is cheap and filling," we get exact and vivid details: "Others buy cans of cheap dog food and fry it like hamburger."

Specific details are often like the information we might find in a movie script. They provide us with such clear pictures that we could make a film of them if we wanted to. You would know just how to film the information given in set B. You would show a poor person breaking open a packet of ketchup from McDonald's and mixing it with water to make a kind of tomato soup. You would show someone opening a can of dog food and frying its contents like hamburger.

In contrast, the writer of set A fails to provide the specific information needed. If you were asked to make a film based on set A, you would have to figure out for yourself just what particulars you were going to show.

When you are working to provide specific supporting information in a paper, it might help to ask yourself, "Could someone easily film this information?" If the answer is "yes," you probably have good details.

Activity

Each topic sentence below is followed by two sets of supporting details (*a* and *b*). Write S (for *specific*) in the space next to the set that provides specific support for the point. Write G (for *general*) next to the set that offers only vague, general support.

1. *Topic sentence:* My roommate is messy.

    _____ a. He doesn't seem to mind that he can't find any clean clothes or dishes. He never puts anything back in its proper place; he just drops it wherever he happens to be. His side of the room looks as if a hurricane has gone through.

    _____ b. His coffee cup is covered inside with a thick layer of green mold. I can't tell you what color his easy chair is; it has disappeared under a pile of dirty laundry. When he turns over in bed, I can hear the crunch of cracker crumbs beneath his body.

2. *Topic sentence:* Roberta is very aggressive.

    _____ a. Her aggressiveness is apparent in both her personal and her professional life. She is never shy about extending social invitations. And while some people are turned off by her aggressive attitude, others are impressed by it and enjoy doing business with her.

    _____ b. When she meets a man she likes, she is quick to say, "Let's go out sometime. What's your phone number?" In her job as a furniture salesperson, she will follow potential customers out onto the sidewalk as she tries to persuade them to buy.

3. *Topic sentence:* Our new kitten causes us lots of trouble.

    _____ a. He has shredded the curtains in my bedroom with his claws. He nearly drowned when he crawled into the washing machine. And my hands look like raw hamburger from his playful bites and scratches.

    _____ b. He seems to destroy everything he touches. He's always getting into places where he doesn't belong. Sometimes he plays too roughly, and that can be painful.

4. *Topic sentence:* My landlord is softhearted.

_____ a. Even though he wrote them himself, he sometimes ignores the official apartment rules in order to make his tenants happy.

_____ b. Although the lease states "No pets," he brought my daughter a puppy after she told him how much she missed having one.

5. *Topic sentence:* The library is a distracting place to try to study.

_____ a. It's hard to concentrate when a noisy eight-person poker game is going on on the floor beside you. It's also distracting to overhear remarks like, "Hey, Baby, what's your mother's address? I want to send her a thank-you card for having such a beautiful daughter."

_____ b. Many students meet in the library to do group activities and socialize with one another. Others go there to flirt. It's easy to get more interested in all that activity than in paying attention to your studies.

7 Recognizing Specific Details: II

Activity

At several points in the following paragraphs you are given a choice of two sets of supporting details. Write S (for *specific)* in the space next to the set that provides specific support for the point. Write G (for *general*) next to the set that offers only vague, general support.

Paragraph 1

My daughter's boyfriend is a good-for-nothing young man. After knowing him for just three months, everyone in our family is opposed to the relationship. For one thing, Russell is lazy.

_____ a. He is always finding an excuse to avoid putting in an honest day's work. He never pitches in and helps with chores around our house, even when he's asked directly to do so. And his attitude about his job isn't any better. To hear him tell it, he deserves special treatment in the workplace. He thinks he's gone out of his way if he just shows up on time.

_____ b. After starting a new job last week, he announced this Monday that he wasn't going to work because it was his *birthday*—as if he were somebody special. And when my husband asked Russell to help put storm windows on the house next Saturday, Russell answered that he uses his weekends to catch up on sleep.

Another quality of Russell's which no one likes is that he is cheap.

_____ c. When my daughter's birthday came around, Russell said he would take her out to Baldoni's, a fancy Italian restaurant. Then he changed his mind. Instead of spending a lot of money on a meal, he said, he wanted to buy her a really nice pair of earrings. So my daughter cooked dinner for him at her apartment. But there was no present, not even a little one. He claims he's waiting for a jewelry sale at Macy's. I don't think my daughter will ever see that "really nice" gift.

_____ d. He makes big promises about all the nice things he's going to do for my daughter, but he never comes through. His words are cheap, and so is he. He's all talk and no action. My daughter isn't greedy, but it hurts her when Russell says he's going to take her someplace nice or give her something special and then nothing happens.

Worst of all, Russell is mean.

_____ e. Russell seems to get special pleasure from hurting people when he feels they have a weak point. I have heard him make remarks that to him were funny but were really very insensitive. You've got to wonder about someone who needs to be ugly to other people just for the sake of being powerful. Sometimes I want to let him know how I feel.

_____ f. When my husband was out of work, Russell said to him, "Well, you've got it made now, living off your wife." After my husband glared at him, he said, "Why're you getting sore? I'm just kidding." Sometimes he snaps at my daughter, saying things like "Don't make me wait—there are plenty of other babes who would like to take your place." At such times I want to blow off his head with a bazooka.

Everyone in the family is waiting anxiously for the day when my daughter will see Russell the way the rest of us see him.

Paragraph 2

Many adult children move back in with their parents for some period of time. Although living with Mom and Dad again has some advantages, there are certain problems that are likely to arise. One common problem is that children may expect their parents to do all the household chores.

_____ a. They never think that they should take on their share of work around the house. Not only do they not help with their parents' chores; they don't even take responsibility for the extra work that their presence creates. Like babies, they go through the house making a mess that the parents are supposed to clean up. It's as if they think their parents are their servants.

_____ b. They expect meals to appear on the table as if by magic. After they've eaten, they go off to work or play, never thinking about who's going to do the dishes. They drop their dirty laundry beside the washing machine, assuming that Mom will attend to it and return clean, folded clothes to their bedroom door. And speaking of their bedrooms: every day they await the arrival of Mom's Maid Service to make the bed, pick up the floor, and dust the furniture.

Another frequent problem is that parents forget their adult children are no longer adolescents.

_____ c. Parents like this want to know everything about their adult children's lives. They don't think their kids, even though they are adults, should have any privacy. Whenever they see their children doing anything, they want to know all the details. It's as though their children are still teenagers who are expected to report all their activities. Naturally, adult children get irritated when they are treated as if they were little kids.

_____ d. They may insist upon knowing far more about their children's comings and goings than the children want to share. For example, if such parents see their adult son heading out the door, they demand to know: "Where are you going? Who will you be with? What will you be doing? What time will you be back?" In addition, they may not let their adult child have any privacy. If their daughter and a date are sitting in the living room, for instance, they may join them there and start peppering the young man with questions about his family and his job, as if they were interviewing him for the position of son-in-law.

Finally, there may be financial problems when an adult child returns to live at home.

_____ e. Having an extra adult in the household creates extra expenses. But many adult children don't offer to help deal with those extra costs. Adult children often eat at home, causing the grocery bill to climb. They may stay in a formerly unused room, which now needs to be heated and lit. They produce extra laundry to be washed. They use the telephone, adding to the long-distance bill. For all these reasons, adult children should expect to pay a reasonable fee to their parents for room and board.

_____ f. It's expensive to have another adult living in the household. Adult children would be paying a lot of bills on their own if they weren't staying with their parents. It's only fair that they share the expenses at their parents' house. They should consider all the ways that their living at home is increasing their parents' expenses. Then they should insist on covering their share of the costs.

8 Providing Supporting Evidence

Activity

Provide three details that logically support each of the following points, or topic sentences. Your details can be drawn from your own experience, or they can be invented. In each case, the details should show in a specific way what the point expresses in only a general way. You may state your details briefly in phrases, or as complete sentences.

Example   The student had several ways of passing time during the dull lecture.

Shielded his eyes with his hand and dozed awhile.

Read the sports magazine he had brought to class.

Made an elaborate drawing on a page of his notebook.

1. I could tell I was coming down with the flu.

_____

_____

_____

2. The food at the cafeteria was terrible yesterday.

_____

_____

_____

3. I had car problems recently.

_____

_____

_____

4. When your money gets tight, there are several ways to economize.

   _____

   _____

   _____

5. Some people have dangerous driving habits.

   _____

   _____

   _____

9 Identifying Adequate Supporting Evidence

Activity

Two of the following paragraphs provide sufficient details to support their topic sentences convincingly. Write AD, for *adequate development,* beside those paragraphs. There are also three paragraphs that, for the most part, use vague, general, or wordy sentences as a substitute for concrete details. Write U, for *underdeveloped,* beside those paragraphs.

_____   1.

My Husband's Stubbornness

My husband's worst problem is his stubbornness. He simply will not let any kind of weakness show. If he isn't feeling well, he refuses to admit it. He will keep on doing whatever he is doing and will wait until the symptoms get almost unbearable before he will even hint that anything is the matter with him. Then things are so far along that he has to spend more time recovering than he would if he had a different attitude. He also hates to be wrong. If he is wrong, he will be the last to admit it. This happened once when we went shopping, and he spent an endless amount of time going from one place to the next. He insisted that one of them had a fantastic sale on things he wanted. We never found a sale, but the fact that this situation happened will not change his attitude. Finally, he never listens to anyone else's suggestions on a car trip. He always knows he's on the right road, and the results have led to a lot of time wasted getting back in the right direction. Every time one of these incidents happens, it only means that it is going to happen again in the future.

_____   2.   **Dangerous Games**

Because they feel compelled to show off in front of their friends, some teenagers play dangerous games. In one incident, police found a group of boys performing a dangerous stunt with their cars. The boys would perch on the hoods of cars going thirty-five or forty miles an hour. Then the driver would brake sharply, and the boy who flew the farthest off the car would win. Teenagers also drive their cars with the lights off and pass each other on hills or curves as ways of challenging each other. In addition to cars, water seems to tempt young people to invent dangerous contests. Some students dared each other to swim through a narrow pipe under a four-lane highway. The pipe carried water from a stream to a pond, and the swimmer would have to hold his or her breath for several minutes before coming out on the other side. Another contest involved diving off the rocky sides of a quarry. Because large stones sat under the water in certain places, any dive could result in a broken neck. But the students would egg each other on to go "rock diving." Playing deadly games like these is a horrifying phase of growing up for some teenagers.

_____   3.   **Attitudes toward Food**

As children, we form attitudes toward food that are not easily changed. In some families, food is love. Not all families are like this, but some children grow up with this attitude. Some families think of food as something precious and not to be wasted. The attitudes children pick up about food are hard to change in adulthood. Some families celebrate with food. If a child learns an attitude, it is hard to break this later. Someone once said: "As the twig is bent, so grows the tree." Children are very impressionable, and they can't really think for themselves when they are small. Children learn from the parent figures in their lives, and later from their peers. Some families have healthy attitudes about food. It is important for adults to teach their children these healthy attitudes. Otherwise, the children may have weight problems when they are adults.

_____   4.   **Qualities in a Friend**

There are several qualities I look for in a friend. A friend should give support and security. A friend should also be fun to be around. Friends can have faults, like anyone else, and sometimes it is hard to overlook them. But a friend can't be dropped because he or she has faults. A friend should stick to you, even in bad times. There is a saying that "a friend in need is a friend indeed." I believe this means that there are good friends and fair-weather friends. The second type is not a true friend. He or she is the kind of person who runs when there's trouble. Friends don't always last a lifetime. Someone you believed to be your best friend may lose contact with you if you move to a different area or go around with a different group of people. A friend should be generous and understanding. A friend does not have to be exactly like you. Sometimes friends are opposites, but they still like each other and get along. Since I am a very quiet person, I can't say that I have many friends. But these are the qualities I believe a friend should have.

_____ 5.   **A Dangerous Place**

We play touch football on a dangerous field. First of all, the grass on the field is seldom mowed. The result is that we have to run through tangled weeds that wrap around our ankles like trip wires. The tall grass also hides some gaping holes lurking beneath. The best players know the exact positions of all the holes and manage to detour around them like soldiers zigzagging across a minefield. Most of us, though, endure at least one sprained ankle per game. Another danger is the old baseball infield that we use as the last twenty yards of our gridiron. This area is covered with stones and broken glass. No matter how often we clean it up, we can never keep pace with the broken bottles hurled on the field by the teenagers we call the "night shift." These people apparently hold drinking parties every night in the abandoned dugout and enjoy throwing the empties out on the field. During every game, we try to avoid falling on especially big chunks of Budweiser bottles. Finally, encircling the entire field is an old, rusty chain-link fence full of tears and holes. Being slammed into the fence during the play can mean a painful stabbing by the jagged wires. All these dangers have made us less afraid of opposing teams than of the field where we play.

10 Adding Details to Complete a Paragraph

Activity

Each of the following paragraphs needs specific details to back up its supporting points. In the spaces provided, add a sentence or two of realistic details for each supporting point. The more specific you are, the more convincing your details are likely to be.

1.   **A Pushover Instructor**

We knew after the first few classes that the instructor was a pushover. First of all, he didn't seem able to control the class.

_____

_____

_____

In addition, he made some course requirements easier when a few
students complained.

_____

_____

_____

Finally, he gave the easiest quiz we had ever taken.

_____

_____

_____

2.

Helping a Parent in College

There are several ways a family can help a parent who is attending
college. First, family members can take over some of the household
chores that the parent usually does.

_____

_____

_____

Also, family members can make sure that the student has some quiet
study time.

_____

_____

_____

Last, families can take an interest in the student's problems and
accomplishments.

_____

_____

_____

11 Writing a Simple Paragraph

You know now that an effective paragraph does two essential things: (1) it makes
a point, and (2) it provides specific details to support that point. You have considered a number of paragraphs that are effective because they follow these two
basic steps or ineffective because they fail to follow them.

You are ready, then, to write a simple paragraph of your own. Choose one of the three assignments below, and follow carefully the guidelines provided.

Assignment 1

Turn back to the activity on page 72 and select the point for which you have the best supporting details. Develop that point into a paragraph by following these steps:

a If necessary, rewrite the point so that the first sentence is more specific or suits your purpose more exactly. For example, you might want to rewrite the second point so that it includes a specific time and place: "Dinner at the Union Building Cafeteria was terrible yesterday."

b Provide several sentences of information to develop each of your three supporting details fully. Make sure that all the information in your paragraph truly supports your point. As an aid, use the paragraph form on page 734.

c Use the words *First of all, Second,* and *Finally* to introduce your three supporting details.

d Conclude your paragraph with a sentence that refers to your opening point. This last sentence "rounds off" the paragraph and lets the reader know that your discussion is complete. For example, the "Changes in the Family" paragraph on page 48 begins with "Changes in our society in recent years have weakened family life." It closes with a statement that refers to, and echoes, the opening point: "Clearly, modern life is a challenge to family life."

e Supply a title based on your point. For instance, point 4 on page 73 might have the title "Ways to Economize."

Use the following list to check your paragraph for each of the above items:

Yes   *No*

____ ____   Do you begin with a point?

____ ____   Do you provide relevant, specific details that support the point?

____ ____   Do you use the words *First of all, Second,* and *Finally* to introduce your three supporting details?

____ ____   Do you have a closing sentence?

____ ____   Do you have a title based on your point?

____ ____   Are your sentences clear and free of obvious errors?

Assignment 2

In this chapter you have read two paragraphs (pages 51–52) on reasons for being in college. For this assignment, write a paragraph describing your own reasons for being in college. You might want to look first at the following list of common reasons students give for going to school. Write a check mark next to each reason that applies to you. If you have different reasons for being in college that are not listed here, add them to the list. Then select your three most important reasons for being in school and generate specific supporting details for each reason.

Before starting, reread paragraph B on page 52. *You must provide comparable specific details of your own.* Make your paragraph truly personal; do not fall back on vague generalities like those in paragraph A on page 51. As you work on your paragraph, use the checklist for Assignment 1 as a guide.

Apply in
My Case   *Reasons Students Go to College*

_____   To have some fun before getting a job

_____   To prepare for a specific career

_____   To please their families

_____   To educate and enrich themselves

_____   To be with friends who are going to college

_____   To take advantage of an opportunity they didn't have before

_____   To find a husband or wife

_____   To see if college has anything to offer them

_____   To do more with their lives than they've done so far

_____   To take advantage of Veterans Administration benefits or other special funding

_____   To earn the status that they feel comes with a college degree

_____   To get a new start in life

_____   Other: _____

Assignment 3

Write a paragraph about stress in your life. Choose three of the following stressful areas and provide specific examples and details to develop each area.

Stress at school
Stress at work
Stress at home
Stress with a friend or friends

Use the checklist for Assignment 1 as a guide while you are working on the paragraph.

4 The Third Step in Writing

> **This chapter will show you how to**
>
> - organize specific evidence in a paper by using a clear method of organization
> - connect the specific evidence by using transitions and other connecting words

You know from Chapter 3 that the first two steps in writing an effective paragraph are making a point and supporting the point with specific evidence. This chapter will deal with the third step. You'll learn the chief ways to organize and connect the supporting information in a paper.

Step 3: Organize and Connect the Specific Evidence

At the same time that you are generating the specific details needed to support a point, you should be thinking about ways to organize and connect those details. All the details in your paper must cohere, or stick together; when they do, your reader is able to move smoothly from one bit of supporting information to the next. This chapter will discuss the following ways to organize and connect supporting details: (1) common methods or organization, (2) transition words, and (3) other connecting words.

Common Methods of Organization: Time Order and Emphatic Order

Time order and emphatic order are common methods used to organize the supporting material in a paper. (You will learn more specialized methods of development in Part Two of the book.)

Time order simply means that details are listed as they occur in time. *First* this is done; *next* this; *then* this; *after* that, this; and so on. Here is a paragraph that organizes its details through time order.

How I Relax

The way I relax when I get home from school on Thursday night is, first of all, to put my three children to bed. Next, I run hot water in the tub and put in lots of perfumed bubble bath. As the bubbles rise, I undress and get into the tub. The water is relaxing to my tired muscles, and the bubbles are tingly on my skin. I lie back and put my feet on the water spigots, with everything but my head under the water. I like to stick my big toe up the spigot and spray water over the tub. After about ten minutes of soaking, I wash myself with scented soap, get out and dry myself off, and put on my nightgown. Then I go downstairs and make myself two ham, lettuce, and tomato sandwiches on white bread and pour myself a tall glass of iced tea with plenty of sugar and ice cubes. I carry these into the living room and turn on the television. To get comfortable, I sit on the couch with a pillow behind me and my legs under me. I enjoy watching <u>The Tonight Show</u> or a late movie. The time is very peaceful after a long, hard day of housecleaning, cooking, washing, and attending night class.

Fill in the missing words: "How I relax" uses the following words to help show time order: _____, _____, _____, _____, and _____.

Emphatic order is sometimes described as "save-the-best-till-last" order. It means that the most interesting or important detail is placed in the last part of a paper. (In cases where all the details seem equal in importance, the writer should impose a personal order that seems logical or appropriate to the details.) The last position in a paper is the most emphatic position because the reader is most likely to remember the last thing read. *Finally, last of all,* and *most important* are typical words showing emphasis. The following paragraph organizes its details through emphatic order.

The <u>National Enquirer</u>

There are several reasons why the <u>National Enquirer</u> is so popular. First of all, the paper is heavily advertised on television. In the ads, attractive-looking people say, with a smile, "I want to know!" as they scan the pages of the <u>Enquirer</u>. The ads reassure people that it's all right to want to read stories such as "Heartbreak for Jennifer Lopez" or "Prince's Fiancée in

New Royal Topless Scandal." In addition, the paper is easily available. In supermarkets, convenience stores, and drugstores, the <u>Enquirer</u> is always displayed in racks close to the cash register. As customers wait in line, they can't help being attracted to the paper's glaring headlines. Then, on impulse, customers will add the paper to their other purchases. Most of all, people read the <u>Enquirer</u> because they love gossip. We find other people's lives fascinating, especially if those people are rich and famous. We want to see and read about their homes, their clothes, and their friends, lovers, and families. We also take a kind of mean delight in their unflattering photos and problems and mistakes, perhaps because we envy them. Even though we may be ashamed of our interest, it's hard to resist buying a paper that promises "The Forbidden Love of Julia Roberts" or "Film Star Who Now Looks Like a Cadaver" or even "Hollywood Star Wars: Who Hates Whom and Why." The <u>Enquirer</u> knows how to get us interested and make us buy.

Fill in the missing words: The paragraph lists a total of _____ different reasons people read the *National Enquirer.* The writer of the paragraph feels that

the most important reason is _____.

He or she signals this reason by using the emphasis words _____.

Some paragraphs use a *combination of time order and emphatic order.* For example, "Good-Bye, Tony" on page 50 includes time order: it moves from the time Tony arrived to the end of the evening. In addition, the writer uses emphatic order, ending with her most important reason (signaled by the words *most of all*) for not wanting to see Tony anymore.

Transitions

Transitions, or *transition words,* are signal words that help readers follow the direction of the writer's thought. They show the relationship between ideas, connecting one thought to the next. They can be compared to road signs that guide travelers.

To see the value of transitions, look at the following pairs of examples. Write a check mark beside the example in each pair that is clearer to read and easier to understand.

1. _____ a. Our landlord recently repainted our apartment. He replaced our faulty air conditioner.

   _____ b. Our landlord recently repainted our apartment. Also, he replaced our faulty air conditioner.

2. _____ a. I turned on the power button. I carefully inserted a disk into the computer.

_____ b. I turned on the power button. Then I carefully inserted a disk into the computer.

3. _____ a. Moviegoers usually dislike film monsters. Audiences pitied King Kong and even shed tears at his death.

_____ b. Moviegoers usually dislike film monsters. However, audiences pitied King Kong and even shed tears at his death.

You should have checked the second example in each pair. The transitional words in those sentences—*Also, Then,* and *However*—make the relationship between the sentences clear. Like all effective transitions, they help connect the writer's thoughts.

In the following box are common transitional words and phrases, grouped according to the kind of signal they give readers. Note that certain words provide more than one kind of signal. In the paragraphs you write, you will most often use addition signals: words like *first of all, also, another,* and *finally* will help you move from one supporting reason or detail to the next.

Transitions

Addition signals: first of all, for one thing, second, the third reason, also, next, another, and, in addition, moreover, furthermore, finally, last of all

Time signals: first, then, next, after, as, before, while, meanwhile, now, during, finally

Space signals: next to, across, on the opposite side, to the left, to the right, in front, in back, above, below, behind, nearby

Change-of-direction signals: but, however, yet, in contrast, otherwise, still, on the contrary, on the other hand

Illustration signals: for example, for instance, specifically, as an illustration, once, such as

Conclusion signals: therefore, consequently, thus, then, as a result, in summary, to conclude, last of all, finally

Activity

1. Underline the three *addition* signals in the following paragraph:

   I am opposed to state-supported lotteries for a number of reasons. First of all, by supporting lotteries, states are supporting gambling. I don't see anything morally wrong with gambling, but it is a known cause of suffering for many people who do it to excess. The state should be concerned with relieving suffering, not causing it. Another objection I have to state lotteries is the kind of advertising they do on television. The commercials promote the lotteries as an easy way to get rich. In fact, the odds against getting rich are astronomical. Last, the lotteries take advantage of the people who can least afford them. Studies have shown that people with lower incomes are more likely to play the lottery than people with higher incomes. This is the harshest reality of the lotteries: the state is encouraging people of limited means not to save their money but to throw it away on a state-supported pipe dream.

2. Underline the four *time* signals in the following paragraph:

   It is often easy to spot bad drivers on the road because they usually make more than one mistake: they make their mistakes in series. First, for example, you notice that a man is tailgating you. Then, almost as soon as you notice, he has passed you in a no-passing zone. That's two mistakes already in a matter of seconds. Next, almost invariably, you see him speed down the road and pass someone else. Finally, as you watch in disbelief, glad that he's out of your way, he speeds through a red light or cuts across oncoming traffic in a wild left turn.

3. Underline the three *space* signals in the following paragraph:

   Standing in the burned-out shell of my living room was a shocking experience. Above my head were charred beams, all that remained of our ceiling. In front of me, where our television and stereo had once stood, were twisted pieces of metal and chunks of blackened glass. Strangely, some items seemed little damaged by the fire. For example, I could see the TV tuner knob and a dusty CD under the rubble. I walked through the gritty ashes until I came to what was left of our sofa. Behind the sofa had been a wall of family photographs. Now, the wall and the pictures were gone. I found only a waterlogged scrap of my wedding picture.

4. Underline the four *change-of-direction* signals in the following paragraph:

   In some ways, train travel is superior to air travel. People always marvel at the speed with which airplanes can zip from one end of the country to another. Trains, on the other hand, definitely take longer. But sometimes longer can be better. Traveling across the country by train allows you to experience the trip more completely. You get to see the cities and towns, mountains and prairies that too often pass by unnoticed when you fly. Another advantage of train travel is comfort. Traveling by plane means wedging yourself into a narrow seat with your knees bumping the back of the seat in front of you and being handed a "snack" consisting of a bag of ten roasted peanuts. In contrast, the seats on most trains are spacious and comfortable, permitting even the longest-legged traveler to stretch out and watch the scenery just outside the window. And when train travelers grow hungry, they can get up and stroll to the dining car, where they can order anything from a simple snack to a gourmet meal. There's no question that train travel is definitely slow and old-fashioned compared with air travel. However, in many ways it is much more civilized.

5. Underline the three *illustration* signals in the following selection:

Status symbols are all around us. The cars we drive, for instance, say something about who we are and how successful we have been. The auto makers depend on this perception of automobiles, designing their commercials to show older, well-established people driving Cadillacs and young, fun-loving people driving to the beach in sports cars. Television, too, has become something of a status symbol. Specifically, schoolchildren are often rated by their classmates according to the brand names of their clothing. Another example of a status symbol is the videocassette recorder. This device, not so long ago considered a novelty, is now as common as the television set itself. Being without a VCR today is like being without a record player in the seventies.

6. Underline the *conclusion* signal in the following paragraph:

A hundred years ago, miners used to bring caged canaries down into the mines with them to act as warning signals. If the bird died, the miner knew that the oxygen was running out. The smaller animal would be affected much more quickly than the miners. In the same way, animals are acting as warning signals to us today. Baby birds die before they can hatch because pesticides in the environment cause the adults to lay eggs with paper-thin shells. Fish die when lakes are contaminated with acid rain or poisonous mercury. The dangers in our environment will eventually affect all life on earth, including humans. Therefore, we must pay attention to these early warning signals. If we don't, we will be as foolish as a miner who ignored a dead canary—and we will die.

Other Connecting Words

In addition to transitions, there are three other kinds of connecting words that help tie together the specific evidence in a paper: *repeated words, pronouns,* and *synonyms.* Each will be discussed in turn.

Repeated Words

Many of us have been taught by English instructors—correctly so—not to repeat ourselves in our writing. On the other hand, repeating key words can help tie ideas together. In the paragraph that follows, the word *retirement* is repeated to remind readers of the key idea on which the discussion is centered. Underline the word the five times it appears.

> Oddly enough, retirement can pose more problems for the spouse than for the retired person. For a person who has been accustomed to a demanding job, retirement can mean frustration and a feeling of uselessness. This feeling will put pressure on the spouse to provide challenges at home equal to those of the workplace. Often, these tasks will disrupt the spouse's well-established routine. Another problem arising from retirement is filling up all those empty hours. The spouse may find himself or herself in the role of social director or tour guide, expected to come up with a new form of amusement every day. Without sufficient challenges or leisure activities, a person can become irritable and take out the resulting boredom and frustration of retirement on the marriage partner. It is no wonder that many of these partners wish their spouses would come out of retirement and do something—anything—just to get out of the house.

Pronouns

Pronouns (*he, she, it, you, they, this, that,* and others) are another way to connect ideas as you develop a paper. Using pronouns to take the place of other words or ideas can help you avoid needless repetition. (Be sure, though, to use pronouns with care in order to avoid the unclear or inconsistent pronoun references described in Chapters 27 and 28 of this book.) Underline the eight pronouns in the passage below, noting at the same time the words that the pronouns refer to.

> A professor of nutrition at a major university recently advised his students that they could do better on their examinations by eating lots of sweets. He told them that the sugar in cakes and candy would stimulate their brains to work more efficiently, and that if the sugar was eaten for only a month or two, it would not do them any harm.

Synonyms

Using synonyms—words that are alike in meaning—can also help move the reader from one thought to the next. In addition, the use of synonyms increases variety and interest by avoiding needless repetition of the same words. Underline the three words used as synonyms for *false ideas* in the following passage.

There are many false ideas about suicide. One wrong idea is that a person who talks about suicide never follows through. The truth is that about three out of every four people who commit suicide notify one or more other persons ahead of time. Another misconception is that a person who commits suicide is poor or downtrodden. Actually, poverty appears to be a deterrent to suicide rather than a predisposing factor. A third myth about suicide is that people bent on suicide will eventually take their lives one way or another, whether or not the most obvious means of suicide is removed from their reach. In fact, since an attempt at suicide is a kind of cry for help, removing a convenient means of taking one's life, such as a gun, shows people bent on suicide that someone cares enough about them to try to prevent it.

Activity

Read the selection below and then answer the questions about it that follow.

My Worst Experience of the Week

¹The registration process at State College was a nightmare. ²The night before registration officially began, I went to bed anxious about the whole matter, and nothing that happened the next day served to ease my tension. ³First, even though I had paid my registration fee early last spring, the people at the bursar's office had no record of my payment. ⁴And for some bizarre reason, they wouldn't accept the receipt I had. ⁵Consequently, I had to stand in line for two hours, waiting for someone to give me a slip of paper which stated that I had, in fact, paid my registration fee. ⁶The need for this new receipt seemed ludicrous to me, since all along I had proof that I had paid. ⁷I was next told that I had to see my adviser in the Law and Justice Department and that the department was in Corridor C of the Triad Building. ⁸I had no idea what or where the Triad was. ⁹But, finally, I found my way to the ugly gray-white building. ¹⁰Then I began looking for Corridor C. ¹¹When I found it, everyone there was a member of the Communications Department. ¹²No one seemed to know where Law and Justice had gone. ¹³Finally, one instructor said she thought Law and Justice was in Corridor A. ¹⁴"And where is Corridor A?" I asked. ¹⁵"I don't know," the teacher

answered. [16]"I'm new here." [17]She saw the bewildered look on my face and said sympathetically, "You're not the only one who's confused." [18]I nodded and walked numbly away. [19]I felt as if I were fated to spend the rest of the semester trying to complete the registration process, and I wondered if I would ever become an official college student.

Questions

1. How many times is the key word *registration* used? _____

2. Write here the pronoun that is used for *people at the bursar's office* (sentence 4): _____; *Corridor C* (sentence 11): _____; *instructor* (sentence 17): _____.

3. Write here the words that are used as a synonym for *receipt* (sentence 5):

   _____

   the words that are used as a synonym for *Triad* (sentence 9):

   _____

   the word that is used as a synonym for *instructor* (sentence 15).

   _____

■ ## Review Activity

Complete the following statements.

1. *Time order* means _____

   _____

2. *Emphatic order* means _____

   _____

3. _____ are signal words that help readers follow the direction of a writer's thought.

4. In addition to transitions, three other kinds of connecting words that help link sentences and ideas are repeated words, _____, and

   _____.

Practice in Organizing and Connecting Specific Evidence

You now know the third step in effective writing: organizing and connecting the specific evidence used to support the main point of a paper. This closing section will expand and strengthen your understanding of the third step in writing.

You will work through the following series of activities:

1 Organizing through Time Order
2 Organizing through Emphatic Order
3 Organizing through a Combination of Time Order and Emphatic Order
4 Identifying Transitions
5 Providing Transitions
6 Identifying Transitions and Other Connecting Words

1 Organizing through Time Order

Activity

Use time order to organize the scrambled list of sentences below. Write the number 1 beside the point that all the other sentences support. Then number each supporting sentence as it occurs in time.

_____ The table is right near the garbage pail.

_____ So you reluctantly select a gluelike tuna-fish sandwich, a crushed apple pie, and watery, lukewarm coffee.

_____ You sit at the edge of the table, away from the garbage pail, and gulp down your meal.

_____ Trying to eat in the cafeteria is an unpleasant experience.

_____ Suddenly you spot a free table in the center.

_____ With a last swallow of the lukewarm coffee, you get up and leave the cafeteria as rapidly as possible.

_____ Flies are flitting into and out of the pail.

_____ By the time it is your turn, the few things that are almost good are gone.

_____   There does not seem to be a free table anywhere.

_____   Unfortunately, there is a line in the cafeteria.

_____   The hoagies, coconut-custard pie, and iced tea have all disappeared.

_____   You hold your tray and look for a place to sit down.

_____   You have a class in a few minutes, and so you run in to grab something to eat quickly.

2 Organizing through Emphatic Order

Activity

Use emphatic order (order of importance) to arrange the following scrambled list of sentences. Write the number 1 beside the point that all the other sentences support. Then number each supporting sentence, starting with what seems to be the least important detail and ending with the most important detail.

_____   The people here are all around my age and seem to be genuinely friendly and interested in me.

_____   The place where I live has several important advantages.

_____   The schools in this neighborhood have a good reputation, so I feel that my daughter is getting a good education.

_____   The best thing of all about this area, though, is the school system.

_____   Therefore, I don't have to put up with public transportation or worry about how much it's going to cost to park each day.

_____   The school also has an extended day-care program, so I know my daughter is in good hands until I come home from work.

_____   First of all, I like the people who live in the other apartments near mine.

_____   Another positive aspect of this area is that it's close to where I work.

_____   That's more than I can say for the last place I lived, where people stayed behind locked doors.

_____   The office where I'm a receptionist is only a six-block walk from my house.

_____   In addition, I save a lot of wear and tear on my car.

3 Organizing through a Combination of Time Order and Emphatic Order

Activity

Use a combination of time and emphatic order to arrange the scrambled list of sentences below. Write the number 1 beside the point that all the other sentences support. Then number each supporting sentence. Paying close attention to transitional words and phrases will help you organize and connect the supporting sentences.

_____ I did not see the spider but visited my friend in the hospital, where he suffered through a week of nausea and dizziness because of the poison.

_____ We were listening to the radio when we discovered that nature was calling.

_____ As I got back into the car, I sensed, rather than felt or saw, a presence on my left hand.

_____ After my two experiences, I suspect that my fear of spiders will be with me until I die.

_____ The first experience was the time when my best friend received a bite from a black widow spider.

_____ I looked down at my hand, but I could not see anything because it was so dark.

_____ I had two experiences when I was sixteen that are the cause of my *arachnophobia*, a terrible and uncontrollable fear of spiders.

_____ We stopped the car at the side of the road, walked into the woods a few feet, and watered the leaves.

_____ My friend then entered the car, putting on the dashboard light, and I almost passed out with horror.

_____ I saw the bandage on his hand and the puffy swelling when the bandage was removed.

_____ Then it flew off my hand and into the dark bushes nearby.

_____ I sat in the car for an hour afterward, shaking and sweating and constantly rubbing the fingers of my hand to reassure myself that the spider was no longer there.

_____ But my more dramatic experience with spiders happened one evening when another friend and I were driving around in his car.

_____ Almost completely covering my fingers was a monstrous brown spider, with white stripes running down each of a seemingly endless number of long, furry legs.

_____ Most of all, I saw the ugly red scab on his hand and the yellow pus that continued oozing from under the scab for several weeks.

_____ I imagined my entire hand soon disappearing as the behemoth relentlessly devoured it.

_____   At the same time I cried out "Arghh!" and flicked my hand violently back and forth to shake off the spider.

_____   For a long, horrible second it clung stickily, as if intertwined for good among the fingers of my hand.

4 Identifying Transitions

Activity

Locate the major transitions used in the following two selections. Then write the transitions in the spaces provided. Mostly, you will find addition words such as *another* and *also*. You will also find several change-of-direction words such as *but* and *however*.

1.

Watching TV Football

Watching a football game on television may seem like the easiest thing in the world. However, like the game of football itself, watching a game correctly is far more complicated than it appears. First is the matter of the company. The ideal number of people depends on the size of your living room. Also, at least one of your companions should be rooting for the opposite team. There's nothing like a little rivalry to increase the enjoyment of a football game. Next, you must attend to the refreshments. Make sure to have on hand plenty of everyone's favorite drinks, along with the essential chips, dips, and pretzels. You may even want something more substantial on hand, like sandwiches or pizza. If you do, make everyone wait until the moment of kickoff before eating. Waiting will make everything taste much better. Finally, there is one last piece of equipment you should have on hand: a football. The purpose of this object is not to send lamps hurtling off tables or to smash the television screen, but to toss around—outside—during halftime. If your team happens to be getting trounced, you may decide not to wait until halftime.

a.   _____

b.   _____

c.   _____

d.   _____

e.   _____

f.   _____

2.

Avoidance Tactics

Sitting down to study for an exam or write a paper is hard, and so it is tempting for students to use one of the following five avoidance tactics in order to put the work aside. For one thing, students may say to themselves, "I can't do it." They adopt a defeatist attitude at the start and give up without a struggle. They could get help with their work by using such college services as tutoring programs and skills labs. However, they refuse even to try. A second avoidance technique is to say, "I'm too busy." Students may take on an extra job, become heavily involved in social activities, or allow family problems to become so time-consuming that they cannot concentrate on their studies. Yet if college really matters to a student, he or she will make sure that there is enough time to do the required work. Another avoidance technique is expressed by the phrase "I'm too tired." Typically, sleepiness occurs when it is time to study or go to class and then vanishes when the school pressure is off. This sleepiness is a sign of work avoidance. A fourth excuse is to say, "I'll do it later." Putting things off until the last minute is practically a guarantee of poor grades on tests and papers. When everything else seems more urgent than studying—watching TV, calling a friend, or even cleaning the oven—a student may simply be escaping academic work. Last, some students avoid work by saying to themselves, "I'm here and that's what counts." Such students live under the dangerous delusion that, since they possess a college ID, a parking sticker, and textbooks, the course work will somehow take care of itself. But once a student has a college ID in a pocket, he or she has only just begun. Doing the necessary studying, writing, and reading will bring real results: good grades, genuine learning, and a sense of accomplishment.

a. _____

b. _____

c. _____

d. _____

e. _____

f. _____

g. _____

h. _____

5 Providing Transitions

Activity

In the spaces provided, add logical transitions to tie together the sentences and ideas in the following paragraphs. Use the words in the boxes that precede each paragraph.

1.

however	a second	last of all
for one thing	also	on the other hand

Why School May Frighten a Young Child

Schools may be frightening to young children for a number of reasons. _____, the regimented environment may be a new and disturbing experience. At home, children may have been able to do what

they wanted when they wanted to do it. In school, _____, they are given a set time for talking, working, playing, eating, and even

going to the toilet. _____ source of anxiety may be the public method of discipline that some teachers use. Whereas at home children are scolded in private, in school they may be held up to embarrassment and ridiculed in front of their peers. "Bonnie," the teacher may say, "why are you the only one in the class who didn't do your homework?" Or, "David, why are you the only one who can't work quietly at your seat?" Children

may _____ be frightened by the loss of personal attention. Their little discomforts or mishaps, such as tripping on the stairs, may bring instant sympathy from a parent; in school, there is often no one to notice, or the teacher is frequently too busy to care and just says, "Go do your

work. You'll be all right." _____, a child may be scared by the competitive environment of the school. At home, one hopes, such

competition for attention is minimal. In school, _____, children may vie for the teacher's approving glance or tone of voice, or for stars on a paper, or for favored seats in the front row. For these and other reasons, it is not surprising that children may have difficulty adjusting to school.

2.

as a result	once	finally
second	when	first of all
	but	

Joining a Multicultural Club

One of the best things I've done in college is to join a multicultural club. _____, the club has helped me become friends with a diverse group of people. At any time in my apartment, I can have someone from Pakistan chatting about music to someone from Sweden, or someone from Russia talking about politics to someone from Uganda. _____ I watched a Mexican student give tacos to three students from China. They had never seen such a thing, but they liked it. A _____ benefit of the club is that it's helped me realize how similar people are.

_____ the whole club first assembled, we wound up having a conversation about dating and sex that included the perspectives of fifteen countries and six continents! It was clear we all shared the feeling that sex was fascinating. The talk lasted for hours, with many different persons describing the wildest or funniest experience they had had with the opposite sex. Only a few students, particularly those from the United States and Japan, seemed bashful. _____, the club has reminded me about the dangers of stereotyping. Before I joined the club, my only direct experience with people from China was when I ordered meals in the local Chinese restaurant. _____, I believed that most Chinese people ate lots of rice and worked in restaurants. _____ in the club, I met Chinese people who were soccer players, English majors, and math teachers. I've also seen Jewish and Muslim students—people who I thought would never get along—drop their preconceived notions and become friends. Even more than my classes, the club has been an eye-opener for me.

6 Identifying Transitions and Other Connecting Words

Activity

This activity will give you practice in identifying transitions and other connecting words that are used to help tie ideas together.

Section A—Transitions: Locate the transitional word or words in each sentence and write them in the spaces provided.

1. I decided to pick up a drop-add form from the registrar's office. However, I changed my mind when I saw the long line of students waiting there.

   _____

2. In England, drivers use the left-hand side of the road. Consequently, steering wheels are on the right side.

   _____

3. Crawling babies will often investigate new objects by putting them in their mouths. Therefore, parents should be alert for any pins, tacks, or other dangerous items on floors and carpets.

   _____

4. One technique that advertisers use is to have a celebrity endorse a product. The consumer then associates the star qualities of the celebrity with the product.

   _____

Section B—Repeated Words: In the space provided, write the repeated words.

5. We absorb radiation from many sources in our environment. Our color television sets and microwave ovens, among other things, give off low-level radiation.

   _____

6. Many researchers believe that people have weight set-points their bodies try to maintain. This may explain why many dieters return to their original weight.

   _____

7. At the end of the rock concert, thousands of fans held up Bic lighters in the darkened area. The sea of lighters signaled that the fans wanted an encore.

   _____

8. Establishing credit is important for a woman. A good credit history is often necessary when she is applying for a loan or charge account.

   _____

Section C—Synonyms: In the space provided, write in the synonym for the underlined word.

9. I checked my car's tires, oil, water, and belts before the trip. But the ungrateful machine blew a gasket about fifty miles from home.

    _____

10. Women's clothes, in general, use less material than men's clothes. Yet women's garments usually cost more than men's.

    _____

11. The temperance movement in this country sought to ban alcohol. Drinking liquor, movement leaders said, led to violence, poverty, prostitution, and insanity.

    _____

12. For me, apathy quickly sets in when the weather becomes hot and sticky. This listlessness disappears when the humidity decreases.

    _____

Section D—Pronouns: In the space provided, write in the word referred to by the underlined pronoun.

13. At the turn of the century, bananas were still an oddity in the United States. Some people even attempted to eat them with the skin on.

    _____

14. Canning vegetables is easy and economical. It can also be very dangerous.

    _____

15. There are a number of signs that appear when students are under stress. For example, they start to have trouble studying, eating, and even sleeping.

    _____

5 The Fourth Step in Writing

This chapter will show you how to

- revise so that your sentences flow smoothly and clearly
- edit so that your sentences are error-free

Step 4: Write Clear, Error-Free Sentences

Up to now this book has emphasized the first three steps in writing an effective paragraph: unity, support, and coherence. This chapter will focus on the fourth step of writing effectively: sentence skills. You'll learn how to revise a paragraph so that your sentences flow smoothly and clearly. Then you'll review how to edit a paragraph for mistakes in grammar, punctuation, and spelling.

Revising Sentences

The following strategies will help you to revise your sentences effectively.

- Use parallelism.
- Use a consistent point of view.
- Use specific words.
- Use concise wording.
- Vary your sentences.

Use Parallelism

Words in a pair or a series should have a parallel structure. By balancing the items in a pair or a series so that they have the same kind of structure, you will make a sentence clearer and easier to read. Notice how the parallel sentences that follow read more smoothly than the nonparallel ones.

Nonparallel (Not Balanced)	Parallel (Balanced)
I resolved to lose weight, to study more, and *watching* less TV.	I resolved to lose weight, to study more, and to watch less TV. (A balanced series of *to* verbs: *to lose, to study, to watch*)
A consumer group rates my car as noisy, expensive, and *not having much safety.*	A consumer group rates my car as noisy, expensive, and unsafe. (A balanced series of descriptive words: *noisy, expensive, unsafe*)
Lola likes wearing soft sweaters, eating exotic foods, and *to bathe* in Calgon bath oil.	Lola likes wearing soft sweaters, eating exotic foods, and bathing in Calgon bath oil. (A balanced series of *-ing* words: *wearing, eating, bathing*)
Single life offers more freedom of choice; *more security is offered by marriage.*	Single life offers more freedom of choice; marriage offers more security. (Balanced verbs and word order: *single life offers . . . ; marriage offers . . .*)

You need not worry about balanced sentences when writing first drafts. But when you rewrite, you should try to put matching words and ideas into matching structures. Such parallelism will improve your writing style.

Activity

Cross out and revise the unbalanced part of each of the following sentences.

Example   When Gail doesn't have class, she uses her time to clean house, ~~getting~~ *to get* her laundry done, and to buy groceries.

1. Lola plans to become a model, a lawyer, or to go into nursing.

2. Filling out an income tax form is worse than wrestling a bear or to walk on hot coals.

3. The study-skills course taught me how to take more effective notes, to read a textbook chapter, and preparing for exams.

4. The video store has sections devoted to comedy films, dramatic films, and films made in foreign countries.

5. Martha Grencher likes to water her garden, walking her fox terrier, and arguing with her husband.

6. Filled with talent and ambitious, Eduardo plugged away at his sales job.

7. When I saw my roommate with my girlfriend, I felt worried, angry, and embarrassment as well.

8. Cindy's cat likes sleeping in the dryer, lying in the bathtub, and to chase squirrels.

9. The bacon was fatty, grease was on the potatoes, and the eggs were cold.

10. People in the lobby munched popcorn, sipped sodas, and were shuffling their feet impatiently.

Use a Consistent Point of View

Consistency with Verbs

Do not shift verb tenses unnecessarily. If you begin writing a paper in the present tense, don't shift suddenly to the past. If you begin in the past, don't shift without reason to the present. Notice the inconsistent verb tenses in the following example:

The shoplifter *walked* quickly toward the front of the store. When a clerk *shouts* at him, he *started* to run.

The verbs must be consistently in the present tense:

The shoplifter *walks* quickly toward the front of the store. When a clerk *shouts* at him, he *starts* to run.

Or the verbs must be consistently in the past tense:

The shoplifter *walked* quickly toward the front of the store. When a clerk *shouted* at him, he *started* to run.

Activity

In each item, one verb must be changed so that it agrees in tense with the other verbs. Cross out the incorrect verb and write the correct form above each crossed-out verb.

Example   Kareem wanted to be someplace else when the dentist ~~carries~~ *carried* in a long needle.

1. I played my stereo and watched television before I decide to do some homework.

2. The hitchhiker stopped me as I walks from the turnpike rest station and said, "Are you on your way to San Jose?"

3. Some students attend all their classes in school and listen carefully during lectures, but they don't take notes. As a result, they often failed tests.

4. His parents stayed together for his sake; only after he graduates from college were they divorced.

5. In the movie, artillery shells exploded on the hide of the reptile monster. It just grinned, tosses off the shells, and kept eating people.

6. Several months a year, monarch butterflies come to live in a spot along the California coast. Thousands and thousands of them hang from the trees and fluttered through the air in large groups.

7. After waking up each morning, Harry stays in bed for a while. First he stretches and yawned loudly, and then he plans his day.

8. The salespeople at Biggs's Department Store are very helpful. When people asked for a product the store doesn't carry or is out of, the salesperson recommends another store.

9. Part-time workers at the company are the first to be laid off. They are also paid less, and they received no union representation.

10. Smashed cars, ambulances, and police cars blocked traffic on one side of the highway. On the other side, traffic slows down as drivers looked to see what happened.

Consistency with Pronouns

Pronouns should not shift point of view unnecessarily. When writing a paper, be consistent in your use of first-, second-, or third-person pronouns.

Type of Pronoun	Singular	Plural
First-person pronouns	I (my, mine, me)	we (our, us)
Second-person pronouns	you (your)	you (your)
Third-person pronouns	he (his, him) she (her) it (its)	they (their, them)

Note: Any person, place, or thing, as well as any indefinite pronoun like *one, anyone, someone,* and so on (page 427), is a third-person word.

For instance, if you start writing in the third person *she*, don't jump suddenly to the second person *you*. Or if you are writing in the first person *I*, don't shift unexpectedly to *one*. Look at the examples.

Inconsistent	*Consistent*
I enjoy movies like *The Return of the Vampire* that frighten *you*. (The most common mistake people make is to let *you* slip into their writing after they start with another pronoun.)	I enjoy movies like *The Return of the Vampire* that frighten me.
As soon as a person walks into Helen's apartment, *you* can tell that Helen owns a cat. (Again, *you* is a shift in point of view.)	As soon as a person walks into Helen's apartment, *he or she* can tell that Helen owns a cat. (See also the note on *his or her* references on pages 427–428.)

Activity

Cross out inconsistent pronouns in the following sentences and write the correct form of the pronoun above each crossed-out word. You may have to change the form of the verb as well.

Example   My dreams are always the kind that haunt ~~you~~ *me* the next day.

1. Whenever we take our children on a trip, you have to remember to bring snacks, tissues, and toys.

2. In our society, we often need a diploma before you are hired for a job.

3. I discovered that videotapes don't do well if you leave them in a hot car.

4. If a student organizes time carefully, you can accomplish a great deal of work.

5. Although I know you should watch your cholesterol intake, I can never resist an ear of corn dripping with melted butter.

6. A good conversationalist has the ability to make the person he is talking to feel as if they are the only other person in the room.

7. We never go to the Salad Bowl anymore, because you wait so long to be seated and the waiters usually make mistakes with the order.

8. I'm careful about talking to people on the subway because one can get into some really weird situations.

9. We can't afford to move right now, because you need not only the first month's rent but also an extra month's security deposit.

10. In my job as store manager, I'm supposed to be nice to the customer even if they are being totally unreasonable.

Use Specific Words

To be an effective writer, you must use specific words rather than general words. Specific words create pictures in the reader's mind. They help capture interest and make your meaning clear. Compare the following sentences:

General	Specific
The boy came down the street.	Theo ran down Woodlawn Avenue.
A bird appeared on the grass.	A blue jay swooped down onto the frost-covered lawn.
She stopped the car.	Jackie slammed on the brakes of her Lincoln.

The specific sentences create clear pictures in our minds. The details *show* us exactly what has happened.

Here are four ways to make your sentences specific.

1   Use exact names.

She loves her *car*.
Renée loves her *Honda*.

2   Use lively verbs.

The garbage truck *went* down Front Street.
The garbage truck *rumbled* down Front Street.

3   Use descriptive words (modifiers) before nouns.

A girl peeked out the window.
A *chubby six-year-old* girl peeked out the *dirty kitchen* window.

4   Use words that relate to the five senses: sight, hearing, taste, smell, and touch.

That woman is a karate expert.
That *tiny, silver-haired* woman is a karate expert. (*Sight*)

When the dryer stopped, a signal sounded.
When the *whooshing* dryer stopped, a *loud buzzer* sounded. (*Hearing*)

Lola offered me an orange slice.
Lola offered me a *sweet, juicy* orange slice. (*Taste*)

The real estate agent opened the door of the closet.
The real estate agent opened the door of the *cedar-scented* closet. (*Smell*)

I pulled the blanket around me to fight off the wind.
I pulled the *scratchy* blanket around me to fight off the *chilling* wind. (*Touch*)

Activity 1

This activity will give you practice in replacing vague, indefinite words with sharp, specific words. Add three or more specific words to replace the general word or words underlined in each sentence. Make changes in the wording of a sentence as necessary.

Example   My bathroom cabinet contains <u>many drugs</u>.
My bathroom cabinet contains aspirin, antibiotics, tranquilizers, and codeine cough medicine.

1. At the shopping center, we visited several stores.

   _____

   _____

2. Sunday is my day to take care of chores.

   _____

   _____

3. Lola enjoys various activities in her spare time.

   _____

   _____

4. I spent most of my afternoon doing homework.

   _____

   _____

5. We returned home from vacation to discover that several pests had invaded the house.

   _____

   _____

Activity 2

Again, you will practice changing vague, indefinite writing into lively, image-filled writing that helps capture the reader's interest and makes your meaning clear. With the help of the four methods described on page 103, add specific details to the sentences that follow. Note the examples.

Examples   The person got out of the car.
The elderly man painfully lifted himself out of the white Buick station wagon.

The fans enjoyed the victory.
Many of the fifty thousand fans stood, waved banners, and cheered wildly when Barnes scored the winning touchdown.

1. The lunch was not very good.

   _____

   _____

2. The animal ran away.

   _____

   _____

3. An accident occurred.

   _____

   _____

4. The instructor came into the room.

   _____

   _____

5. The machine did not work.

   _____

   _____

Use Concise Wording

Wordiness—using more words than necessary to express a meaning—is often a sign of lazy or careless writing. Your readers may resent the extra time and energy they must spend when you have not done the work needed to make your writing direct and concise.

Here are examples of wordy sentences:

Anne is of the opinion that the death penalty should be allowed.

I would like to say that my subject in this paper will be the kind of generous person that my father was.

Omitting needless words improves the sentences:

Anne supports the death penalty.

My father was a generous person.

The following box lists some wordy expressions that could be reduced to single words.

Wordy Form	Short Form
a large number of	many
a period of a week	a week
arrive at an agreement	agree
at an earlier point in time	before
at the present time	now
big in size	big
owing to the fact that	because
during the time that	while
five in number	five
for the reason that	because
good benefit	benefit
in every instance	always
in my own opinion	I think
in the event that	if
in the near future	soon
in this day and age	today
is able to	can
large in size	large
plan ahead for the future	plan
postponed until later	postponed
red in color	red
return back	return

Activity

Rewrite the following sentences, omitting needless words.

1. After a lot of careful thinking, I have arrived at the conclusion that drunken drivers should receive jail terms.

   _____

   _____

2. The movie that I went to last night, which was fairly interesting, I must say, was enjoyed by me and my girlfriend.

_____

_____

3. Owing to inclement weather conditions of wind and rain, we have decided not to proceed with the athletic competition about to take place on the baseball diamond.

_____

_____

4. Without any question, there should be a law making it a requirement for parents of young children to buckle the children into car seats for safety.

_____

_____

5. Beyond a doubt, the only two things you can rely or depend on would be the fact that death comes to everyone and also that the government will tax your yearly income.

_____

_____

Vary Your Sentences

One aspect of effective writing is to vary the kinds of sentences you write. If every sentence follows the same pattern, writing may become monotonous to read. This chapter explains four ways you can create variety and interest in your writing style. The first two ways involve coordination and subordination—important techniques for achieving different kinds of emphasis in writing.

The following are four methods you can use to make your sentences more varied and more sophisticated:

1 Add a second complete thought (coordination)
2 Add a dependent thought (subordination)
3 Begin with a special opening word or phrase
4 Place adjectives or verbs in a series

Revise by Adding a Second Complete Thought

When you add a second complete thought to a simple sentence, the result is a *compound* (or double) sentence. The two complete statements in a compound sentence are usually connected by a comma plus a joining, or *coordinating,* word (*and, but, for, or, nor, so, yet*).

Use a compound sentence when you want to give equal weight to two closely related ideas. The technique of showing that ideas have equal importance is called *coordination.* Following are some compound sentences. Each contains two ideas that the writer regards as equal in importance.

Bill has stopped smoking cigarettes, but he is now addicted to chewing gum.

I repeatedly failed the math quizzes, so I decided to drop the course.

Quincy turned all the lights off, and then he locked the office door.

Activity

Combine the following pairs of simple sentences into compound sentences. Use a comma and a logical joining word (*and, but, for, so*) to connect each pair.

Note: If you are not sure what *and, but, for,* and *so* mean, review pages 390–391.

Example   • The cars crept along slowly.
            • Visibility was poor in the heavy fog.
            The cars crept along slowly, for visibility was poor in the heavy fog.

            _____

1. • Lee thought she would never master the computer.
   • In two weeks she was using it comfortably.
   _____

   _____

2. • Vandals smashed the car's headlights.
   • They slashed the tires as well.
   _____

   _____

3. • I married at age seventeen.
   • I never got a chance to live on my own.
   _____

   _____

4. • Mold grew on my leather boots.
   • The closet was warm and humid.

   _____

   _____

5. • My father has a high cholesterol count.
   • He continues to eat red meat almost every day.

   _____

   _____

Revise by Adding a Dependent Thought

When you add a dependent thought to a simple sentence, the result is a complex sentence.* A dependent thought begins with a word or phrase like one of the following:

Dependent Words		
after	if, even if	when, whenever
although, though	in order that	where, wherever
as	since	whether
because	that, so that	which, whichever
before	unless	while
even though	until	who, whoever
how	what, whatever	whose

A *complex* sentence is used to emphasize one idea over another. Look at the following complex sentence:

Although I lowered the thermostat, my heating bill remained high.

---

*The two parts of a complex sentence are sometimes called an *independent clause* and a *dependent clause*. A *clause* is simply a word group that contains a subject and a verb. An independent clause expresses a complete thought and can stand alone. A dependent clause does not express a complete thought in itself and "depends on" the independent clause to complete its meaning. Dependent clauses always begin with a dependent, or subordinating, word.

The idea that the writer wants to emphasize here—*my heating bill remained high*—is expressed as a complete thought. The less important idea—*Although I lowered my thermostat*—is subordinated to this complete thought. The technique of giving one idea less emphasis than another is called *subordination*.

Following are other examples of complex sentences. In each case, the part starting with the dependent word is the less emphasized part of the sentence.

> Even though I was tired, I stayed up to watch the horror movie.
>
> Before I take a bath, I check for spiders in the tub.
>
> When Vera feels nervous, she pulls on her earlobe.

Activity

Use logical subordinating words to combine the following pairs of simple sentences into sentences that contain a dependent thought. Place a comma after a dependent statement when it starts the sentence.

Example   • Our team lost.
             • We were not invited to the tournament.

    Because our team lost, we were not invited to the tournament.

_____

1. • I receive my degree in June.
   • I will begin applying for jobs.

_____

_____

2. • Lola doesn't enjoy cooking.
   • She often eats at fast-food restaurants.

_____

_____

3. • I sent several letters of complaint.
   • The electric company never corrected my bill.

_____

_____

4. • Neil felt his car begin to skid.
   • He took his foot off the gas pedal.

_____

_____

5. • The final exam covered sixteen chapters.
    • The students complained.

_____

_____

Revise by Beginning with a Special Opening Word or Phrase

Among the special openers that can be used to start sentences are (1) *-ed* words, (2) *-ing* words, (3) *-ly* words, (4) *to* word groups, and (5) prepositional phrases. Here are examples of all five kinds of openers:

-ed *word*
Tired from a long day of work, Sharon fell asleep on the sofa.

-ing *word*
Using a thick towel, Mel dried his hair quickly.

-ly *word*
Reluctantly, I agreed to rewrite the paper.

to *word group*
To get to the church on time, you must leave now.

Prepositional phrase
With Fred's help, Martha planted the evergreen shrubs.

Activity

Combine the simple sentences into one sentence by using the opener shown at the left and omitting repeated words. Use a comma to set off the opener from the rest of the sentence.

Example   *-ing* word   • The toaster refused to pop up.
            • It buzzed like an angry hornet.
            Buzzing like an angry hornet, the toaster refused
            to pop up.

-ed word
1. • Nate dreaded the coming holidays.
   • He was depressed by his recent divorce.

   _____

   _____

-ing word
2. • The star player glided down the court.
   • He dribbled the basketball like a pro.

   _____

   _____

-ly word
3. • I waited in the packed emergency room.
   • I was impatient.

   _____

   _____

to word
group
4. • The little boy likes to annoy his parents.
   • He pretends not to hear them.

   _____

   _____

Prepositional
phrase
5. • People must wear rubber-soled shoes.
   • They must do this in the gym.

   _____

   _____

Revise by Placing Adjectives or Verbs in a Series

Various parts of a sentence may be placed in a series. Among these parts are adjectives (descriptive words) and verbs. Here are examples of both in a series.

Adjectives

The *black, smeary* newsprint rubbed off on my *new butcher-block* table.

Verbs

The quarterback *fumbled* the ball, *recovered* it, and *sighed* with relief.

Activity

Combine the simple sentences in each group into one sentence by using adjectives or verbs in a series and by omitting repeated words. In most cases, use a comma between the adjectives or verbs in a series.

Example   • Before Christmas, I made fruitcakes.
　　　　　　• I decorated the house.
　　　　　　• I wrapped dozens of toys.

　　　　　　Before Christmas, I made fruitcakes, decorated the house, and

　　　　　　wrapped dozens of toys.

1. • My lumpy mattress was giving me a cramp in my neck.
   • It was causing pains in my back.
   • It was making me lose sleep.

   _____

   _____

2. • Lights appeared in the fog.
   • The lights were flashing.
   • The lights were red.
   • The fog was soupy.
   • The fog was gray.

   _____

   _____

3. • Before going to bed, I locked all the doors.
   • I activated the burglar alarm.
   • I slipped a kitchen knife under my mattress.

   _____

   _____

4. • Lola picked sweater hairs off her coat.
   • The hairs were fuzzy.
   • The hairs were white.
   • The coat was brown.
   • The coat was suede.

   _____

   _____

5. • The contact lens fell onto the floor.
   • The contact lens was thin.
   • The contact lens was slippery.
   • The floor was dirty.
   • The floor was tiled.

_____

_____

Editing Sentences

After revising sentences in a paragraph so that they flow smoothly and clearly, you need to edit the paragraph for mistakes in grammar, punctuation, mechanics, usage, and spelling. Even if a paragraph is otherwise well-written, it will make an unfavorable impression on readers if it contains such mistakes. To edit a paragraph, check it against the agreed-upon rules or conventions of written English—simply called *sentence skills* in this book. Here are the most common of these conventions:

1   Write complete sentences rather than fragments.
2   Do not write run-ons.
3   Use verb forms correctly.
4   Make sure that subject, verbs, and pronouns agree.
5   Eliminate faulty modifiers.
6   Use pronoun forms correctly.
7   Use capital letters where needed.
8   Use the following marks of punctuation correctly: apostrophe, quotation marks, comma, semicolon, colon, hyphen, dash, parentheses.
9   Use correct manuscript form.
10   Eliminate slang, clichés, and pretentious words.
11   Check for possible spelling errors.
12   Eliminate careless errors.

These sentence skills are treated in detail in Part Five of this book, and they can be referred to easily as needed. Both the list of sentence skills on the inside front cover and the correction symbols on the inside back cover include page references so that you can turn quickly to any skill you want to check.

Hints for Editing

Here are hints that can help you edit the next-to-final draft of a paper for sentence-skills mistakes:

1   Have at hand two essential tools: a good dictionary (see page 500) and a grammar handbook (you can use the one in this book on pages 361–549).

2   Use a sheet of paper to cover your paragraph so that you will expose only one sentence at a time. Look for errors in grammar, spelling, and typing. It may help to read each sentence out loud. If a sentence does not read clearly and smoothly, chances are something is wrong.

3   Pay special attention to the kinds of errors you tend to make. For example, if you tend to write run-ons or fragments, be especially on the lookout for those errors.

4   Try to work on a typewritten or word-processed draft, where you'll be able to see your writing more objectively than you can on a handwritten page; use a pen with colored ink so that your corrections will stand out.

A Note on Proofreading

Proofreading means checking the final, edited draft of your paragraph closely for typos and other careless errors. A helpful strategy is to read your paper backward, from the last sentence to the first. This helps keep you from getting caught up in the flow of the paper and missing small mistakes. Here are six helpful proofing symbols:

Proofing Symbol	*Meaning*	*Example*
⌃	insert missing letter or word	beleve
⟋	omit	in the the meantime
∼	reverse order of words or letters	once a upon time
#	add space	alltogether #
‿	close up space	foot ball
cap, lc	Add a capital (or a lowercase) letter	cap My persian Cat lc

If you make too many corrections, retype the page or enter corrections into your word processor file and reprint the page.

Activity

In the spaces at the bottom, write the numbers of the ten word groups that contain fragments or run-ons. Then, in the spaces between the lines, edit by making the necessary corrections. One is done for you as an example.

¹Two groups of researchers have concluded that "getting cold" has little to do with "catching a cold." ²When the experiment was done for the first time, ³Researchers exposed more than four hundred people to the cold virus. ⁴Then divided those people into three groups. ⁵One group, wearing winter coats, sat around in ten-degree temperatures the second group was placed in sixty-degree temperatures. ⁶With the third group staying in a room. ⁷Where it was eighty degrees. ⁸The number of people who actually caught cold was the same. ⁹In each group. ¹⁰Other researchers repeated this experiment ten years later. ¹¹This time they kept some subjects cozy and warm they submerged others in a tank filled with water. ¹²Whose temperature had been lowered to seventy-five degrees. ¹³They made others sit around in their underwear in forty-degree temperatures. ¹⁴The results were the same, the subjects got sick at the same rate. ¹⁵Proving that people who get cold do not always get colds.

1. _____   2. _____   3. _____   4. _____   5. _____
6. _____   7. _____   8. _____   9. _____   10. _____

Note: A series of editing tests appears on pages 558–570. You will probably find it most helpful to take these tests after reviewing the sentence skills in Part Five.

Practice in Revising Sentences

You now know the fourth step in effective writing: revising and editing sentences. You also know that practice in *editing* sentences is best undertaken after you have worked through the sentence skills in Part Five. The focus in this closing section, then, will be on *revising* sentences—using a variety of methods to ensure that your sentences flow smoothly and are clear and interesting. You will work through the following series of review tests:

1 Using parallelism.
2 Using a consistent point of view.
3 Using specific words.
4 Using concise wording.
5 Varying your sentences.

Using Parallelism

■ Review Test 1

Cross out the unbalanced part of each sentence. In the space provided, revise the unbalanced part so that it matches the other item or items in the sentence. The first one is done for you as an example.

1. Our professor warned us that he would give surprise tests, ~~the assignment of term papers~~, and allow no makeup exams.
   assign term papers

2. Making a big dinner is a lot more fun than to clean up after it.
   _____

3. The street-corner preacher stopped people walking by, was asking them questions, and handed them a pamphlet.
   _____

4. My teenage daughter enjoys shopping for new clothes, to try different cosmetics, and reading beauty magazines.
   _____

5. Fantastic special effects are part of the "Star Wars" movies, but dialogue that is believable is not.
   _____

6. While you're downtown, please pick up the dry cleaning, return the library books, and the car needs washing too.
   _____

7. I want a job that pays high wages, provides a complete benefits package, and offering opportunities for promotion.
   _____

8. As the elderly woman climbed the long staircase, she breathed hard and was grabbing the railing tightly.
   _____

9. I fell into bed at the end of the hard day, grateful for the sheets that were clean, soft pillow, and cozy blanket.
   _____

10. Ray's wide smile, clear blue eyes, and expressing himself earnestly all make him seem honest, even though he is not.
    _____

■ **Review Test 2**

Cross out the unbalanced part of each sentence. In the space provided, revise the unbalanced part so that it matches the other item or items in the sentence.

1. The neighborhood group asked the town council to repair the potholes and that a traffic light be installed.

    _____

2. Pesky mosquitoes, humidity that is high, and sweltering heat make summer an unpleasant time for me.

    _____

3. The afternoon mail brought advertisements that were unwanted, bills I couldn't pay, and magazines I didn't like.

    _____

4. Our house has a broken garage door, shutters that are peeling, and a crumbling chimney.

    _____

5. My car needed the brakes replaced, the front wheels aligned, and recharging of the battery.

    _____

6. I had to correct my paper for fragments, misplaced modifiers, and there were apostrophe mistakes.

    _____

7. We do not want to stay home during our vacation, but a trip is not something we can afford.

    _____

8. Stumbling out of bed, a cup of coffee that he drinks, and listening to the weather report make up Roy's early-morning routine.

    _____

9. Having a headache, my stomach being upset, and a bad case of sunburn did not put me in a good mood for the evening.

    _____

10. The Gray Panthers is an organization that not only aids older citizens but also providing information for their families.

    _____

Using a Consistent Point of View

■ Review Test 1

Change verbs as needed in the following passage so that they are consistently in the past tense. Cross out each incorrect verb and write the correct form above it, as shown in the example. You will need to make nine corrections.

Late one rainy night, Mei Ling woke to the sound of steady dripping. When she got out

splashed

of bed to investigate, a drop of cold water ~~splashes~~ onto her arm. She looks up just in time

to see another drop form on the ceiling, hang suspended for a moment, and fall to the

carpet. Stumbling to the kitchen, Mei Ling reaches deep into one of the cabinets and lifts

out a large roasting pan. As she did so, pot lids and baking tins clattered out and crash onto

the counter. Mei Ling ignored them, stumbled back to the bedroom, and places the pan on

the floor under the drip. But a minute after sliding her icy feet under the covers, Mei Ling

realized she is in trouble. The sound of each drop hitting the metal pan echoed like a

gunshot in the quiet room. Mei Ling feels like crying, but she finally thought of a solution.

She got out of bed and returns a minute later with a thick bath towel. She lined the pan with

the towel and crawls back into bed.

■ **Review Test 2**

Cross out the inconsistent pronouns in the following sentences and revise by writing the correct form of the pronoun above each crossed-out word.

Example   I dislike waitressing, for ~~you~~ can never count on a fair tip.

(I written above)

1. My kitchen is so narrow that one can't open the refrigerator without turning sidewise first.

2. Wanting relief from her headaches, Carla asked her doctor if acupuncture could really do you any good.

3. I love Jell-O because one can eat about five bowls of it and still not feel full.

4. As we entered the house, you could hear someone giggling in the hallway.

5. I hate going to the supermarket because you always have trouble finding a parking space there.

6. In this company, a worker can take a break only after a relief person comes to take your place.

7. Sometimes the Bradleys take the turnpike route, but it costs you five dollars in tolls.

8. As we sat in class waiting for the test results, you could feel the tension.

9. My brother doesn't get enough regular exercise, even though he knows exercise is good for you.

10. My favorite subject is abnormal psychology because the case studies make one seem so normal by comparison.

Using Specific Words

■ Review Test 1

Revise the following sentences, replacing vague, indefinite words with sharp, specific ones.

1. When I woke up this morning, I had *several signs of a cold.*

   _____

   _____

2. Lin brought *lots of reading materials* to keep her busy in the hospital waiting room.

   _____

   _____

3. To succeed in school, a student must possess *certain qualities.*

   _____

   _____

4. The table at the wedding reception was full of *a variety of appetizers.*

   _____

   _____

5. As I grew older and less stupid, I realized that money cannot buy *certain things.*

   _____

   _____

■ Review Test 2

With the help of the methods described on page 103 and summarized below, add specific details to the sentences that follow.

1 Use exact names.
2 Use lively verbs.
3 Use descriptive words (modifiers) before nouns.
4 Use words that relate to the senses—sight, hearing, taste, smell, touch.

1. The crowd grew restless.

   _____

   _____

2. I relaxed.

   _____

   _____

3. The room was cluttered.

   _____

   _____

4. The child threw the object.

   _____

   _____

5. The driver was angry.

   _____

   _____

Using Concise Wording

■ **Review Test 1**

Rewrite the following sentences, omitting needless words.

1. There was this one girl in my class who rarely if ever did her homework.

   _____

   _____

2. Judging by the looks of things, it seems to me that it will probably rain very soon.

   _____

   _____

3. Seeing as how the refrigerator is empty of food, I will go to the supermarket in the very near future.

   _____

   _____

4. In this day and age it is almost a certainty that someone you know will be an innocent victim of criminal activity.

   _____

   _____

5. In my personal opinion it is correct to say that the spring season is the most beautiful period of time in the year.

   _____

   _____

■ **Review Test 2**

Rewrite the following sentences, omitting needless words.

1. Workers who are on a part-time basis are attractive to a business because they do not have to be paid as much as full-time workers for a business.

   _____

   _____

2. During the time that I was sick and out of school, I missed a total of three math tests.

   _____

   _____

3. The game, which was scheduled for later today, has been canceled by the officials because of the rainy weather.

   _____

   _____

4. At this point in time, I am quite undecided and unsure about just which classes I will take during this coming semester.

   _____

   _____

5. An inconsiderate person located in the apartment next to mine keeps her radio on too loud a good deal of the time, with the result being that it is disturbing to everyone in the neighboring apartments.

   _____

   _____

Varying Your Sentences

■ **Review Test 1**

Using coordination, subordination, or both, combine each of the following groups of simple sentences into one longer sentence. Omit repeated words. Various combinations are possible, so for each group, try to find the combination that flows most smoothly and clearly.

1. • My grandmother is eighty-six.
   • She drives to Florida alone every year.
   • She believes in being self-reliant.

   _____

   _____

2. • They left twenty minutes early for class.
   • They were late anyway.
   • The car overheated.

   _____

   _____

3. • John failed the midterm exam.
   • He studied harder for the final.
   • He passed it.

   _____

   _____

4. • A volcano erupts.
   • It sends tons of ash into the air.
   • This creates flaming orange sunsets.

   _____

   _____

5. • A telephone rings late at night.
   • We answer it fearfully.
   • It could bring tragic news.

   _____

   _____

■ **Review Test 2**

Using coordination, subordination, or both, combine each of the following groups of simple sentences into two longer sentences. Omit repeated words. Various combinations are possible, so for each group, try to find the combination that flows most smoothly and clearly.

1. • Wendy pretended not to overhear her coworkers.
   • She couldn't stop listening.
   • She felt deeply embarrassed.
   • They were criticizing her work.

   _____

   _____

   _____

2. • Tony got home from the shopping mall.
   • He discovered that his rented tuxedo did not fit.
   • The jacket sleeves covered his hands.
   • The pants cuffs hung over his shoes.

   _____

   _____

   _____

3. • The boys waited for the bus.
   • The wind shook the flimsy shelter.
   • They shivered with cold.
   • They were wearing thin jackets.

   _____

   _____

   _____

4. • The engine almost started.
   • Then it died.
   • I realized no help would come.
   • I was on a lonely road.
   • It was very late.

   _____

   _____

   _____

5. • Gary was leaving the store.
   • The shoplifting alarm went off.
   • He had not stolen anything.
   • The clerk had forgotten to remove the magnetic tag.
   • The tag was on a shirt Gary had bought.

   _____

   _____

   _____

■ **Review Test 3**

Part A: Combine the simple sentences into one sentence by using the opener shown in the margin and omitting repeated words. Use a comma to set off the opener from the rest of the sentence.

-ed word

1. • We were exhausted from four hours of hiking.
    • We decided to stop for the day.

    _____

    _____

-ing word

2. • Gus was staring out the window.
    • He didn't hear the instructor call on him.

    _____

    _____

-ly word

3. • Nobody saw the thieves steal our bikes.
    • This was unfortunate.

    _____

    _____

to word
group

4. • Wayne rented a limousine for the night.
    • He wanted to make a good impression.

    _____

    _____

Prepositional
phrase

5. • Joanne goes online to visit her friends.
    • She does this during her lunch breaks.

    _____

    _____

Part B: Combine the simple sentences in each group into one sentence by using adjectives or verbs in a series and by omitting repeated words. In most cases, use a comma between the adjectives or verbs in a series.

6. The photographer waved a teddy bear at the baby.
   He made a funny face.
   He quacked like a duck.

   _____

   _____

7. The bucket held a bunch of daisies.
   The bucket was shiny.
   The bucket was aluminum.
   The daisies were fresh.
   The daisies were white.

   _____

   _____

8. Amy poured herself a cup of coffee.
   She pulled her hair back into a ponytail.
   She opened her textbook.
   She sat down at her desk.
   She fell asleep.

   _____

   _____

9. The box in the dresser drawer was stuffed with letters.
   The box was cardboard.
   The dresser drawer was locked.
   The letters were faded.
   The letters were about love.

   _____

   _____

10. The boy asked the girl to dance.
    The boy was short.
    The boy was self-confident.
    The girl was tall.
    The girl was shy.

   _____

   _____

6 Four Bases for Revising Writing

This chapter will show you how to evaluate a paragraph for

- unity
- support
- coherence
- sentence skills

In the preceding chapters, you learned four essential steps in writing an effective paragraph. The box below shows how these steps lead to four standards, or bases, you can use in revising a paper.

Four Steps ⟶	*Four Bases*
1 If you make one point and stick to that point,	your writing will have *unity*.
2 If you back up the point with specific evidence,	your writing will have *support*.
3 If you organize and connect the specific evidence,	your writing will have *coherence*.
4 If you write clear, error-free sentences,	your writing will demonstrate effective *sentence skills*.

This chapter will discuss the four bases—unity, support, coherence, and sentence skills—and will show how these four bases can be used to evaluate and revise a paragraph.

Base 1: Unity

Understanding Unity

The following two paragraphs were written by students on the topic "Why Students Drop Out of College." Read them and decide which one makes its point more clearly and effectively, and why.

Paragraph A

Why Students Drop Out

Students drop out of college for many reasons. First of all, some students are bored in school. These students may enter college expecting nonstop fun or a series of fascinating courses. When they find out that college is often routine, they quickly lose interest. They do not want to take dull required courses or spend their nights studying, and so they drop out. Students also drop out of college because the work is harder than they thought it would be. These students may have made decent grades in high school simply by showing up for class. In college, however, they may have to prepare for two-hour exams, write fifteen-page term papers, or make detailed presentations to a class. The hard work comes as a shock, and students give up. Perhaps the most common reason students drop out is that they are having personal or emotional problems. Younger students, especially, may be attending college at an age when they are also feeling confused, lonely, or depressed. These students may have problems with roommates, family, boyfriends, or girlfriends. They become too unhappy to deal with both hard academic work and emotional troubles. For many types of students, dropping out seems to be the only solution they can imagine.

Paragraph B

Student Dropouts

There are three main reasons students drop out of college. Some students, for one thing, are not really sure they want to be in school and lack the desire to do the work. When exams come up, or when a course requires a difficult project or term paper, these students will not do the required studying or research. Eventually, they may drop out because their grades are so poor they are about to flunk out anyway. Such students sometimes come back to school later with a completely different attitude about school. Other students drop out for financial reasons. The pressures of paying tuition, buying textbooks, and possibly having to support themselves can be overwhelming. These students can often be helped by the school because financial aid is available, and some schools offer work-study programs. Finally, students drop out because they have personal problems. They cannot concentrate on their courses because they are unhappy at home, they are lonely, or they are having trouble with boyfriends or girlfriends. Instructors should suggest that such troubled students see counselors or join support groups. If instructors would take a more personal interest in their students, more students would make it through troubled times.

Activity

Fill in the blanks: Paragraph _____ makes its point more clearly and effectively because _____

_____

_____

Comment: Paragraph A is more effective because it is *unified*. All the details in paragraph A are *on target;* they support and develop the single point expressed in the first sentence—that there are many reasons students drop out of college.

On the other hand, paragraph B contains some details irrelevant to the opening point—that there are three main reasons students drop out. These details should be omitted in the interest of paragraph unity. Go back to paragraph B and cross out the sections that are off target—the sections that do not support the opening idea.

You should have crossed out the following sections: "Such students sometimes . . . attitude about school"; "These students can often . . . work-study programs"; and "Instructors should suggest . . . through troubled times."

The difference between these two paragraphs leads us to the first base, or standard, of effective writing: *unity*. To achieve unity is to have all the details in your paper related to the single point expressed in the topic sentence, the first sentence. Each time you think of something to put in, ask yourself whether it relates to your main point. If if does not, leave it out. For example, if you were writing about a certain job as the worst job you ever had and then spent a couple of sentences talking about the interesting people that you met there, you would be missing the first and most essential base of good writing.

Checking for Unity

To check a paper for unity, ask yourself these questions:

1 Is there a clear opening statement of the point of the paper?
2 Is all the material on target in support of the opening point?

Base 2: Support

Understanding Support

The following student paragraphs were written on the topic "A Quality of Some Person You Know." Both are unified, but one communicates more clearly and effectively. Which one, and why?

Paragraph A

My Quick-Tempered Father

My father is easily angered by normal everyday mistakes. One day my father told me to wash the car and cut the grass. I did not hear exactly what he said, and so I asked him to repeat it. Then he went into a hysterical mood and shouted, "Can't you hear?" Another time he asked my mother to go to the store and buy groceries with a fifty-dollar bill, and he told her to spend no more than twenty dollars. She spent twenty-two dollars. As soon as he found out, he immediately took the change from her and told her not to go anywhere else for him; he did not speak to her the rest of the day. My father even gives my older brothers a hard time with his irritable moods. One day he told them to be home from their dates by midnight; they came home at 12:15. He informed them that they were grounded for three weeks. To my father, making a simple mistake is like committing a crime.

Paragraph B

My Generous Grandfather

My grandfather is the most generous person I know. He gave up a life of his own in order to give his children everything they wanted. Not only did he give up many years of his life to raise his children properly, but he is now sacrificing many more years to his grandchildren. His generosity is also evident in his relationship with his neighbors, his friends, and the members of his church. He has been responsible for many good deeds and has always been there to help all the people around him in times of trouble. Everyone knows that he will gladly lend a helping hand. He is so generous that you almost have to feel sorry for him. If one day he suddenly became selfish, it would be earthshaking. That's my grandfather.

Activity

Fill in the blanks: Paragraph _____ makes its point more clearly and effectively

because _____

_____

_____

Comment: Paragraph A is more effective, for it offers specific examples that show us the father in action. We see for ourselves why the writer describes the father as quick-tempered.

Paragraph B, on the other hand, gives us no specific evidence. The writer of paragraph B tells us repeatedly that the grandfather is generous but never shows us examples of that generosity. Just how, for instance, did the grandfather sacrifice his life for his children and grandchildren? Did he hold two jobs so that his son could go to college, or so that his daughter could have her own car? Does he give up time with his wife and friends to travel every day to his daughter's house to baby-sit, go to the store, and help with the dishes? Does he wear threadbare suits and coats and eat Hamburger Helper and other inexpensive meals (with no desserts) so that he can give money to his children and toys to his grandchildren? We want to see and judge for ourselves whether the writer is making a valid point about the grandfather, but without specific details we cannot do so. In fact, we have almost no picture of him at all.

Consideration of these two paragraphs leads us to the second base of effective writing: *support.* After realizing the importance of specific supporting details, one student writer revised a paper she had done on a restaurant job as the worst job she ever had. In the revised paper, instead of talking about "unsanitary conditions in the kitchen," she referred to such specifics as "green mold on the bacon" and "ants in the potato salad." All your papers should include many vivid details!

Checking for Support

To check a paper for support, ask yourself these questions:

1 Is there *specific* evidence to support the opening point?
2 Is there *enough* specific evidence?

Base 3: Coherence

Understanding Coherence

The following two paragraphs were written on the topic "The Best or Worst Job You Ever Had." Both are unified and both are supported. However, one communicates more clearly and effectively. Which one, and why?

Paragraph A

Pantry Helper

My worst job was as a pantry helper in one of San Diego's well-known restaurants. I had an assistant from three to six in the afternoon who did little but stand around and eat the whole time she was there. She would listen for the sound of the back door opening, which was a sure sign the boss was coming in. The boss would testily say to me, "You've got a lot of things to do here, Alice. Try to get a move on." I would come in at two o'clock to relieve the woman on the morning shift. If her day was busy, that meant I would have to prepare salads, slice meat and cheese, and so on. Orders for sandwiches and cold platters would come in and have to be prepared. The worst thing about the job was that the heat in the kitchen, combined with my nerves, would give me an upset stomach by seven o'clock almost every night. I might be going to the storeroom to get some supplies, and one of the waitresses would tell me she wanted a bacon, lettuce, and tomato sandwich on white toast. I would put the toast in and head for the supply room, and a waitress would holler out that her customer was in a hurry. Green flies would come in through the torn screen in the kitchen window and sting me. I was getting paid only $3.60 an hour. At five o'clock, when the dinner rush began, I would be dead tired. Roaches scurried in all directions whenever I moved a box or picked up a head of lettuce to cut.

Paragraph B

My Worst Job

The worst job I ever had was as a waiter at the Westside Inn. First of all, many of the people I waited on were rude. When a baked potato was hard inside or a salad was flat or their steak wasn't just the way they wanted it, they blamed me, rather than the kitchen. Or they would ask me to light their cigarettes, or chase flies from their tables, or even take their children to the bathroom. Also, I had to contend not only with the customers but with the kitchen staff as well. The cooks and busboys were often undependable and surly. If I didn't treat them just right, I would wind up having to apologize to customers because their meals came late or their water glasses weren't filled. Another reason I didn't like the job was that I was always moving. Because of the constant line at the door, as soon as one group left, another would take its place. I usually had only a twenty-minute lunch break and a ten-minute break in almost nine hours of work. I think I could have put up with the job if I had been able to pause and rest more often. The last and most important reason I hated the job was my boss. She played favorites, giving some of the waiters and waitresses the best-tipping repeat customers and preferences on holidays. She would hover around during my break to make sure I didn't take a second more than the allotted time. And even when I helped out by working through a break, she never had an appreciative word but would just tell me not to be late for work the next day.

Activity

Fill in the blanks: Paragraph _____ makes its point more clearly and effectively because _____

_____

_____

Comment: Paragraph B is more effective because the material is organized clearly and logically. Using emphatic order, the writer gives us a list of four reasons why the job was so bad: rude customers, an unreliable kitchen staff, constant motion, and—most of all—an unfair boss. Further, the writer includes transitional words that act as signposts, making movement from one idea to the next easy to follow. The major transitions are *First of all, Also, Another reason,* and *The last and most important reason.*

While paragraph A is unified and supported, the writer does not have any clear and consistent way of organizing the material. Partly, emphatic order is used, but this is not made clear by transitions or by saving the most important reason for last. Partly, time order is used, but it moves inconsistently from two to seven to five o'clock.

These two paragraphs lead us to the third base of effective writing: *coherence.* The supporting ideas and sentences in a composition must be organized so that they cohere, or "stick together." As has already been mentioned, key techniques for tying material together are a clear method of organization (such as time order or emphatic order), transitions, and other connecting words.

Checking for Coherence

To check a paper for coherence, ask yourself these questions:

1 Does the paper have a clear method of organization?

2 Are transitions and other connecting words used to tie the material together?

Base 4: Sentence Skills

Understanding Sentence Skills

Two versions of a paragraph are given below. Both are unified, supported, and organized, but one version communicates more clearly and effectively. Which one, and why?

Paragraph A

Falling Asleep Anywhere

[1]There are times when people are so tired that they fall asleep almost anywhere. [2]For example, there is a lot of sleeping on the bus or train on the way home from work in the evenings. [3]A man will be reading the newspaper, and seconds later it appears as if he is trying to eat it. [4]Or he will fall asleep on the shoulder of the stranger sitting next to him. [5]Another place where unplanned naps go on is the lecture hall. [6]In some classes, a student will start snoring so loudly that the professor has to ask another student to shake the sleeper awake. [7]A more embarrassing situation occurs when a student leans on one elbow and starts drifting off to sleep. [8]The weight of the head pushes the elbow off the desk, and this momentum carries the rest of the body along. [9]The student wakes up on the floor with no memory of getting there. [10]The worst place to fall asleep is at the wheel of a car. [11]Police reports are full of accidents that occur when people lose consciousness and go off the road. [12]If the drivers are lucky, they are not seriously hurt. [13]One woman's car, for instance, went into a river. [14]She woke up in four feet of water and thought it was raining. [15]When people are really tired, nothing will stop them from falling asleep—no matter where they are.

Paragraph B

"Falling Asleep Anywhere"

[1]There are times when people are so tired that they fall asleep almost anywhere. [2]For example, on the bus or train on the way home from work. [3]A man will be reading the newspaper, seconds later it appears as if he is trying to eat it. [4]Or he will fall asleep on the shoulder of the stranger sitting next to him. [5]Another place where unplanned naps go on are in the lecture hall. [6]In some classes, a student will start snoring so loudly that the professor has to ask another student to shake the sleeper awake. [7]A more embarrassing situation occurs when a student leans on one elbow and starting to drift off to sleep. [8]The weight of the head push the elbow off the

desk, and this momentum carries the rest of the body along. [9]The student wakes up on the floor with no memory of getting there. [10]The worst time to fall asleep is when driving a car. [11]Police reports are full of accidents that occur when people conk out and go off the road. [12]If the drivers are lucky they are not seriously hurt. [13]One womans car, for instance, went into a river. [14]She woke up in four feet of water. [15]And thought it was raining. [16]When people are really tired, nothing will stop them from falling asleep— no matter where they are.

Activity 1

Fill in the blanks: Paragraph _____ makes its point more clearly and effectively because _____

_____

_____

Comment: Paragraph A is more effective because it incorporates *sentence skills,* the fourth base of competent writing.

Activity 2

See if you can identify the ten sentence-skills mistakes in paragraph B. Do this, first of all, by going back and underlining the ten spots in paragraph B that differ in wording or punctuation from paragraph A. Then try to identify the ten sentence-skills mistakes by circling what you feel is the correct answer in each of the ten statements below.

Note: Comparing paragraph B with the correct version may help you guess correct answers even if you are not familiar with the names of certain skills.

1. The title should not be set off with
    a. capital letters.
    b. quotation marks.

2. In word group 2, there is a
    a. missing comma.
    b. missing apostrophe.
    c. sentence fragment.
    d. dangling modifier.

3. In word group 3, there is a
    a. run-on.
    b. sentence fragment.
    c. mistake in subject-verb agreement.
    d. mistake involving an irregular verb.

4. In word group 5, there is a
   a. sentence fragment.
   b. spelling error.
   c. run-on.
   d. mistake in subject-verb agreement.

5. In word group 7, there is a
   a. misplaced modifier.
   b. dangling modifier.
   c. mistake in parallelism.
   d. run-on.

6. In word group 8, there is a
   a. nonstandard English verb.
   b. run-on.
   c. comma mistake.
   d. missing capital letter.

7. In word group 11, there is a
   a. mistake involving an irregular verb.
   b. sentence fragment.
   c. slang phrase.
   d. mistake in subject-verb agreement.

8. In word group 12, there is a
   a. missing apostrophe.
   b. missing comma.
   c. mistake involving an irregular verb.
   d. sentence fragment.

9. In word group 13, there is a
   a. mistake in parallelism.
   b. mistake involving an irregular verb.
   c. missing apostrophe.
   d. missing capital letter.

10. In word group 15, there is a
    a. missing quotation mark.
    b. mistake involving an irregular verb.
    c. sentence fragment.
    d. mistake in pronoun point of view.

Comment: You should have chosen the following answers:

1. b   2. c   3. a   4. d   5. c
6. a   7. c   8. b   9. c   10. c

Part Five of this book explains these and other sentence skills. You should review all the skills carefully. Doing so will ensure that you know the most important rules of grammar, punctuation, and usage—rules needed to write clear, error-free sentences.

Checking for Sentence Skills

Sentence skills and the other bases of effective writing are summarized in the following chart and on the inside front cover of the book.

A Summary of the Four Bases of Effective Writing

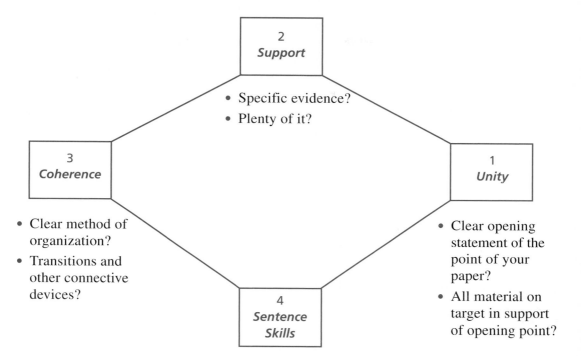

- Fragments eliminated? (page 369)
- Run-ons eliminated? (385)
- Correct verb forms? (400)
- Subject and verb agreement? (418)
- Faulty parallelism and faulty modifiers eliminated? (97, 443, 447)
- Faulty pronouns eliminated? (425, 432)
- Capital letters used correctly? (457)
- Punctuation marks where needed?
  - (a) Apostrophe (469)
  - (b) Quotation marks (478)
  - (c) Comma (485)
  - (d) Semicolon; colon (496–497)
  - (e) Hyphen; dash (497–498)
  - (f) Parentheses (499)
- Correct paper format? (452)
- Needless words eliminated? (105)
- Effective word choices? (529)
- Possible spelling errors checked? (509)
- Careless errors eliminated through proofreading? (114–116, 166, 558)
- Sentences varied? (107)

Practice in Using the Four Bases

You are now familiar with four bases, or standards, of effective writing: unity, support, coherence, and sentence skills. In this closing section, you will expand and strengthen your understanding of the four bases as you work through the following activities:

1 Evaluating Scratch Outlines for Unity
2 Evaluating Paragraphs for Unity
3 Evaluating Paragraphs for Support
4 Evaluating Paragraphs for Coherence
5 Revising Paragraphs for Coherence
6 Evaluating Paragraphs for All Four Bases:
   Unity, Support, Coherence, and Sentence Skills

1 Evaluating Scratch Outlines for Unity

The best time to check a paper for unity is at the outline stage. A scratch outline, as explained on page 23, is one of the best techniques for getting started with a paper.

Look at the following scratch outline that one student prepared and then corrected for unity:

I had a depressing weekend.
1.   Hay fever bothered me
2.   Had to pay seventy-seven-dollar car bill
3.   ~~Felt bad~~
4.   Boyfriend and I had a fight
5.   ~~Did poorly in my math test today as a result~~
6.   My mother yelled at me unfairly

Four reasons support the opening statement that the writer was depressed over the weekend. The writer crossed out "Felt bad" because it was not a reason for her depression. (Saying that she felt bad is only another way of saying that she was depressed.) She also crossed out the item about the math test because the point she is supporting is that she was depressed over the weekend.

Activity

In each outline, cross out the items that do not support the opening point. These items must be omitted in order to achieve paragraph unity.

1. The cost of raising a child keeps increasing.
   a. School taxes get higher every year.
   b. A pair of children's sneakers now costs over $100.
   c. Overpopulation is a worldwide problem.
   d. Providing nutritious food is more costly because of inflated prices.
   e. Children should work at age sixteen.

2. My father's compulsive gambling hurt our family life.
   a. We were always short of money for bills.
   b. Luckily, my father didn't drink.
   c. My father ignored his children to spend time at the racetrack.
   d. Gamblers' Anonymous can help compulsive gamblers.
   e. My mother and father argued constantly.

3. There are several ways to get better mileage in your car.
   a. Check air pressure in tires regularly.
   b. Drive at no more than fifty-five miles per hour.
   c. Orange and yellow cars are the most visible.
   d. Avoid jackrabbit starts at stop signs and traffic lights.
   e. Always have duplicate ignition and trunk keys.

4. My swimming instructor helped me overcome my terror of the water.
   a. He talked with me about my fears.
   b. I was never good at sports.
   c. He showed me how to hold my head under water and not panic.
   d. I held on to a floating board until I was confident enough to give it up.
   e. My instructor was on the swimming team at his college.

5. Fred Wilkes is the best candidate for state governor.
   a. He has fifteen years' experience in the state senate.
   b. His son is a professional football player.
   c. He has helped stop air and water pollution in the state.
   d. His opponent has been divorced.
   e. He has brought new industries and jobs to the state.

2 Evaluating Paragraphs for Unity

Activity

Each of the following five paragraphs contains sentences that are off target—sentences that do not support the opening point—and so the paragraphs are not unified. In the interest of paragraph unity, such sentences must be omitted.

Cross out the irrelevant sentences and write the numbers of those sentences in the spaces provided. The number of spaces will tell you the number of irrelevant sentences in each paragraph.

1.

A Kindergarten Failure

[1]In kindergarten I experienced the fear of failure that haunts many schoolchildren. [2]My moment of panic occurred on my last day in kindergarten at Charles Foos Public School in Riverside, California. [3]My family lived in California for three years before we moved to Omaha, Nebraska, where my father was a personnel manager for Mutual of Omaha. [4]Our teacher began reading a list of names of all those students who were to line up at the door in order to visit the first-grade classroom. [5]Our teacher was a pleasant-faced woman who had resumed her career after raising her own children. [6]She called off every name but mine, and I was left sitting alone in the class while everyone else left, the teacher included. [7]I sat there in absolute horror. [8]I imagined that I was the first kid in human history who had flunked things like crayons, sandbox, and sliding board. [9]Without getting the teacher's permission, I got up and walked to the bathroom and threw up into a sink. [10]Only when I ran home in tears to my mother did I get an explanation of what had happened. [11]Since I was to go to a parochial school in the fall, I had not been taken with the other children to meet the first-grade teacher at the public school. [12]My moment of terror and shame had been only a misunderstanding.

The numbers of the irrelevant sentences: _____   _____

2.

How to Prevent Cheating

[1]Instructors should take steps to prevent students from cheating on exams. [2]To begin with, instructors should stop reusing old tests. [3]A test that has been used even once is soon known on the student grapevine. [4]Students will check with their friends to find out, for example, what was on Dr. Thompson's biology final last term. [5]They may even manage to find

a copy of the test itself, "accidentally" not turned in by a former student of Dr. Thompson's. 6Instructors should also take some commonsense precautions at test time. 7They should make students separate themselves— by at least one seat—during an exam, and they should watch the class closely. 8The best place for the instructor to sit is in the rear of the room, so that a student is never sure if the instructor is looking at him or her. 9Last of all, instructors must make it clear to students that there will be stiff penalties for cheating. 10One of the problems with our school systems is a lack of discipline. 11Instructors never used to give in to students' demands or put up with bad behavior, as they do today. 12Anyone caught cheating should immediately receive a zero for the exam. 13A person even suspected of cheating should be forced to take an alternative exam in the instructor's office. 14Because cheating is unfair to honest students, it should not be tolerated.

The numbers of the irrelevant sentences: _____   _____

3.   **Other Uses for Cars**

1Many people who own a car manage to turn the vehicle into a trash can, a clothes closet, or a storage room. 2People who use their cars as trash cans are easily recognized. 3Empty snack bags, hamburger wrappers, pizza cartons, soda cans, and doughnut boxes litter the floor. 4On the seats are old cassette tapes with their innards hanging out, blackened fruit skins, crumpled receipts, crushed cigarette packs, and used tissues. 5At least the trash stays in the car, instead of adding to the litter on our highways. 6Other people use a car as a clothes closet. 7The car contains several pairs of shoes, pants, or shorts, along with a suit or dress that's been hanging on the car's clothes hanger for over a year. 8Sweaty, smelly gym clothes will also find a place in the car, a fact passengers quickly discover. 9The world would be better off if people showed more consideration of others. 10Finally, some people use a car as a spare garage or basement. 11In the backseats or trunks of these cars are bags of fertilizer, beach chairs, old textbooks, chainsaws, or window screens that have been there for months. 12The trunk may also contain an extra spare tire, a dented hubcap, a gallon container of window washer fluid, and old stereo equipment. 13If apartments offered more storage space, probably fewer people would resort to using their cars for such storage purposes. 14All in all, people get a lot more use out of their cars than simply the miles they travel on the road.

The numbers of the irrelevant sentences: _____   _____   _____

4.   **Why Adults Visit Amusement Parks**

[1]Adults visit amusement parks for several reasons. [2]For one thing, an amusement park is a place where it is acceptable to "pig out" on junk food. [3]At the park, everyone is drinking soda and eating popcorn, ice cream, or hot dogs. [4]No one seems to be on a diet, and so buying all the junk food you can eat is a guilt-free experience. [5]Parks should provide stands where healthier food, such as salads or cold chicken, would be sold. [6]Another reason people visit amusement parks is to prove themselves. [7]They want to visit the park that has the newest, scariest ride in order to say that they went on the Parachute Drop, the seven-story Elevator, the Water Chute, or the Death Slide. [8]Going on a scary ride is a way to feel courageous and adventurous without taking much of a risk. [9]Some rides, however, can be dangerous. [10]Rides that are not properly inspected or maintained have killed people all over the country. [11]A final reason people visit amusement parks is to escape from everyday pressures. [12] When people are poised at the top of a gigantic roller coaster, they are not thinking of bills, work, or personal problems. [13]A scary ride empties the mind of all worries—except making it to the bottom alive. [14]Adults at an amusement park may claim they have come for their children, but they are there for themselves as well.

The numbers of the irrelevant sentences: _____   _____   _____

5.   **A Dangerous Cook**

[1]When my friend Tom sets to work in the kitchen, disaster often results. [2]Once he tried to make toasted cheese sandwiches for us by putting slices of cheese in the toaster along with the bread; he ruined the toaster. [3]Unfortunately, the toaster was a fairly new one that I had just bought for him three weeks before, on his birthday. [4]On another occasion, he had cut up some fresh beans and put them in a pot to steam. [5]I was really looking forward to the beans, for I eat nothing but canned vegetables in my dormitory. [6]I, frankly, am not much of a cook either. [7]The water in the Teflon pan steamed away while Tom was on the telephone, and both the beans and the Teflon coating in the pan were ruined. [8]Finally, another time Tom made spaghetti for us, and the noodles stuck so tightly together that we had to cut off slices with a knife and fork. [9]In addition, the meatballs were burned on the outside but almost raw inside. [10]The tomato sauce, on the other hand, turned out well. [11]For some reason, Tom is very good at making meat and vegetable sauces. [12]Because of Tom's kitchen mishaps, I never eat at his place without an Alka-Seltzer in my pocket, or without money in case we have to go out to eat.

The numbers of the irrelevant sentences: _____   _____   _____

_____   _____

3 Evaluating Paragraphs for Support

Activity

The five paragraphs that follow lack sufficient supporting details. In each paragraph, identify the spot or spots where more specific details are needed.

1.

Chicken: Our Best Friend

¹Chicken is the best-selling meat today for a number of good reasons. ²First of all, its reasonable cost puts it within everyone's reach. ³Chicken is popular, too, because it can be prepared in so many different ways. ⁴It can, for example, be cooked by itself, in spaghetti sauce, or with noodles and gravy. ⁵It can be baked, boiled, broiled, or fried. ⁶Chicken is also convenient. ⁷Last and most important, chicken has a high nutritional value. ⁸Four ounces of chicken contain twenty-eight grams of protein, which is almost half the recommended daily dietary allowance.

Fill in the blanks: The first spot where supporting details are needed occurs after sentence number _____. The second spot occurs after sentence number _____

2.

A Car Accident

¹I was on my way home from work when my terrible car accident took place. ²As I drove my car around the curve of the expressway exit, I saw a number of cars ahead of me, backed up because of a red light at the main road. ³I slowly came to a stop behind a dozen or more cars. ⁴In my rearview mirror, I then noticed a car coming up behind me that did not slow down or stop. ⁵I had a horrible, helpless feeling as I realized the car would hit me. ⁶I knew there was nothing I could do to signal the driver in time, nor was there any way I could get away from the car. ⁷Minutes after the collision, I picked up my glasses, which were on the seat beside me. ⁸My lip was bleeding, and I got out a tissue to wipe it. ⁹The police arrived quickly, along with an ambulance for the driver of the car that hit me. ¹⁰My car was so damaged that it had to be towed away. ¹¹Today, eight years after the accident, I still relive the details of the experience whenever a car gets too close behind me.

Fill in the blank: The point where details are needed occurs after sentence number _____.

3.
Tips on Bringing Up Children

¹In some ways, children should be treated as mature people. ²For one thing, adults should not use baby talk with children. ³Using real words with children helps them develop language skills more quickly. ⁴Baby talk makes children feel patronized, frustrated, and confused, for they want to understand and communicate with adults by learning their speech. ⁵So animals should be called cows and dogs, not "moo-moos" and "bow-wows." ⁶Second, parents should be consistent when disciplining children. ⁷For example, if a parent tells a child, "You cannot have dessert unless you put away your toys," it is important that the parent follow through on the warning. ⁸By being consistent, parents will teach children responsibility and give them a stable center around which to grow. ⁹Finally, and most important, children should be allowed and encouraged to make simple decisions. ¹⁰Parents will thus be helping their children prepare for the complex decisions that they will have to deal with in later life.

Fill in the blank: The spot where supporting details are needed occurs after sentence number _____.

4.
Being on TV

¹People act a little strangely when a television camera comes their way. ²Some people behave as if a crazy puppeteer were pulling their strings. ³Their arms jerk wildly about, and they begin jumping up and down for no apparent reason. ⁴Often they accompany their body movements with loud screams, squeals, and yelps. ⁵Another group of people engage in an activity known as the cover-up. ⁶They will be calmly watching a sports game or other televised event when they realize the camera is focused on them. ⁷The camera operator can't resist zooming in for a close-up of these people. ⁸Then there are those who practice their funny faces on the unsuspecting public. ⁹They take advantage of the television time to show off their talents, hoping to get that big break that will carry them to stardom. ¹⁰Finally, there are those who pretend they are above reacting for the camera. ¹¹They wipe an expression from their faces and appear to be interested in something else. ¹²Yet if the camera stays on them long enough, they will slyly check to see if they are still being watched. ¹³Everybody's behavior seems to be slightly strange in front of a TV camera.

Fill in the blanks: The first spot where supporting details are needed occurs after sentence number _____. The second spot occurs after sentence number _____.

5. **Culture Conflict**

¹I am in a constant tug-of-war with my parents over conflicts between their Vietnamese culture and American culture. ²To begin with, my parents do not like me to have American friends. ³They think that I should spend all my time with other Vietnamese people and speak English only when necessary. ⁴I get into an argument whenever I want to go to a fast-food restaurant or a movie at night with my American friends. ⁵The conflict with my parents is even worse when it comes to plans for a career. ⁶My parents want me to get a degree in science and then go on to medical school. ⁷On the other hand, I think I want to become a teacher. ⁸So far I have been taking both science and education courses, but soon I will have to concentrate on one or the other. ⁹The other night my father made his attitude about what I should do very clear. ¹⁰The most difficult aspect of our cultural differences is the way our family is structured. ¹¹My father is the center of our family, and he expects that I will always listen to him. ¹²Although I am twenty-one years old, I still have a nightly curfew at an hour which I consider insulting. ¹³Also, I am expected to help my mother perform certain household chores that I've really come to hate. ¹⁴My father expects me to live at home until I am married to a Vietnamese man. ¹⁵When that happens, he assumes I will obey my husband just as I obey him. ¹⁶I do not want to be a bad daughter, but I want to live like my American female friends.

Fill in the blanks: The first spot where supporting details are needed occurs after sentence number _____. The second spot occurs after sentence number _____. The third spot occurs after sentence number _____.

4 Evaluating Paragraphs for Coherence

Activity

Answer the questions about coherence that follow each of the two paragraphs below.

1. **Why I Bought a Handgun**

¹I bought a handgun to keep in my house for several reasons. ²Most important, I have had a frightening experience with an obscene phone caller. ³For several weeks, a man has called me once or twice a day, sometimes as late as three in the morning. ⁴As soon as I pick up the phone, he whispers something obscene or threatens me by saying, "I'll get you." ⁵I decided to buy a gun because crime is increasing in my neighborhood.

⁶One neighbor's house was burglarized while she was at work; the thieves not only stole her appliances but also threw paint around her living room and slashed her furniture. ⁷Not long after this incident, an elderly woman from the apartment house on the corner was mugged on her way to the supermarket. ⁸The man grabbed her purse and threw her to the ground, breaking her hip. ⁹Buying a gun was my response to listening to the nightly news. ¹⁰It seemed that every news story involved violence of some kind—rapes, murders, muggings, and robberies. ¹¹I wondered if some of the victims in the stories would still be alive if they had been able to frighten off the criminal with a gun. ¹²As time passed, I became more convinced that I should keep a gun in the house.

a.   The paragraph should use emphatic order. Write 1 before the reason that seems slightly less important than the other two, 2 before the second-most-important reason, and 3 before the most important reason.

_____ Obscene phone caller

_____ Crime increase in neighborhood

_____ News stories about crime

b.   Before which of the three reasons should the transitional words *First of all*

be added? _____

c.   Before which of the three reasons could the transition *In addition* be

added? _____

d.   Which words show emphasis in sentence 2? _____

e.   In sentence 8, to whom does the pronoun *her* refer? _____

f.   How often does the key word *gun* appear in the paragraph? _____

g.   What is a synonym for *burglarized* in sentence 6? _____

2.   **Apartment Hunting**

¹Apartment hunting is a several-step process. ²Visit and carefully inspect the most promising apartments. ³Check each place for signs of unwanted guests such as roaches or mice. ⁴Make sure that light switches and appliances work and that there are enough electrical outlets. ⁵Turn faucets on and off and flush the toilet to be sure that the plumbing works smoothly. ⁶Talk to the landlord for a bit to get a sense of him or her as a person. ⁷If a problem develops after you move in, you want to know that a decent and capable person will be there to handle the matter. ⁸Find out what's available that matches your interests. ⁹Your town newspaper and local real estate offices can provide you with a list of apartments for rent. ¹⁰Family and friends may be able to give you leads. ¹¹And your school may have a housing office that

keeps a list of approved apartments for rent. [12]Decide just what you need. [13]If you can afford no more than $400 a month, you need to find a place that will cost no more than that. [14]If you want a location that's close to work or school, you must take that factor into account. [15]If you plan to cook, you want a place with a workable kitchen. [16]By taking these steps, you should be ready to select the apartment that is best for you.

a. The paragraph should use time order. Write 1 before the step that should come first, 2 before the intermediate step, and 3 before the final step.

_____ Visit and carefully inspect the most promising apartments.

_____ Decide just what you need.

_____ Find out what's available that matches your interests.

b. Before which of three steps could the transitional words *The first step is to* be added? _____

c. Before which step could the transitional words *After you have decided what you are looking for, the next step is to* be added? _____

d. Before which step could the transitional words *The final step* be added? _____

e. To whom does the pronoun *him or her* in sentence 6 refer to? _____

f. What is a synonym for *landlord* in sentence 7? _____

g. What is a synonym for *apartment* in sentence 13? _____

5 Revising Paragraphs for Coherence

The two paragraphs in this section begin with a clear point, but in each case the supporting material that follows the point is not coherent. Read each paragraph and the comments that follow it on how to organize and connect the supporting material. Then do the activity for the paragraph.

Paragraph 1

A Difficult Period

Since I arrived in the Bay Area in midsummer, I have had the most difficult period of my life. I had to look for an apartment. I found only one place that I could afford, but the landlord said I could not move in until it was painted. When I first arrived in San Francisco, my thoughts were to stay with my father and stepmother. I had to set out looking for a job so that I could afford my own place, for I soon realized that my stepmother was not at all happy having me live with them. A three-week search led to a job shampooing rugs for a housecleaning company. I painted the apartment myself, and at least that problem was ended. I was in a hurry to get settled because I was starting school at the University of San Francisco in September. A transportation problem developed because my stepmother insisted that I return my father's bike, which I was using at first to get to school. I had to rely on a bus that often arrived late, with the result that I missed some classes and was late for others. I had already had a problem with registration in early September. My counselor had made a mistake with my classes, and I had to register all over again. This meant that I was one week late for class. Now I'm riding to school with a classmate and no longer have to depend on the bus. My life is starting to order itself, but I must admit that at first I thought it was hopeless to stay here.

Comments on Paragraph 1:   The writer of this paragraph has provided a good deal of specific evidence to support the opening point. The evidence, however, needs to be organized. Before starting the paragraph, the writer should have decided to arrange the details by using time order. He or she could then have listed in a scratch outline the exact sequence of events that made for such a difficult period.

Activity 1

Here is a list of the various events described by the writer of paragraph 1. Number the events in the correct time sequence by writing 1 in front of the first event that occurred, 2 in front of the second event, and so on.

Since I arrived in the Bay Area in midsummer, I have had the most difficult period of my life.

_____ I had to search for an apartment I could afford.

_____ I had to find a job so that I could afford my own place.

_____ My stepmother objected to my living with her and my father.

_____ I had to paint the apartment before I could move in.

_____ I had to find an alternative to unreliable bus transportation.

_____ I had to register again for my college courses because of a counselor's mistake.

Your instructor may now have you rewrite the paragraph on separate paper. If so, be sure to use time signals such as *first, next, then, during, when, after,* and *now* to help guide your reader from one event to the next.

Paragraph 2

Childhood Cruelty

When I was in grade school, my classmates and I found a number of excuses for being cruel to a boy named Andy Poppovian. Sometimes Andy gave off a strong body odor, and we knew that several days had passed since he had taken a bath. Andy was very slow in speaking, as well as very careless in personal hygiene. The teacher would call on him during a math or grammar drill. He would sit there silently for so long before answering that she sometimes said, "Are you awake, Andy?" Andy had long fingernails that he never seemed to cut, with black dirt caked under them. We called him "Poppy," or we accented the first syllable in his name and mispronounced the rest of it and said to him, "How are you today, POP-o-van?" His name was funny. Other times we called him "Popeye," and we would shout at him. "Where's your spinach today, Popeye?" Andy always had sand in the corners of his eyes. When we played tag at recess, Andy was always "it" or the first one who was caught. He was so physically slow that five guys could dance around him and he wouldn't be able to touch any of them. Even when we tried to hold a regular conversation with him about sports or a teacher, he was so slow in responding to a question that we got bored talking with him. Andy's hair was always uncombed, and it was often full of white flakes of dandruff. Only when Andy died suddenly of spinal meningitis in seventh grade did some of us begin to realize and regret our cruelty toward him.

Comments on Paragraph 2:   The writer of this paragraph provides a number of specifics that support the opening point. However, the supporting material has not been organized clearly. Before writing this paragraph, the author should have (1) decided to arrange the supporting evidence by using emphatic order and (2) listed in a scratch outline the reasons for the cruelty to Andy Poppovian and the supporting details for each reason. The writer could also have determined which reason to use in the emphatic final position of the paper.

Activity 2

Create a clear outline for paragraph 2 by filling in the scheme below. The outline is partially completed.

When I was in grade school, my classmates and I found a number of excuses for being cruel to a boy named Andy Poppovian.

Reason   1. *Funny name* _____

Details   a. _____

                      b. _____

                      c. _____

Reason	2.	*Physically slow* _____
Details		a. _____
		b. *Five guys could dance around him* _____
Reason	3.	_____
Details		a. _____
		b. *In regular conversation* _____
Reason	4.	_____
Details		a. _____
		b. *Sand in eyes* _____
		c. _____
		d. _____

Your instructor may have you rewrite the paragraph on separate paper. If so, be sure to introduce each of the four reasons with transitions such as *First, Second, Another reason,* and *Finally.* You may also want to use repeated words, pronouns, and synonyms to help tie your sentences together.

6 Evaluating Paragraphs for All Four Bases: Unity, Support, Coherence, and Sentence Skills

Activity

In this activity, you will evaluate paragraphs in terms of all four bases: unity, support, coherence, and sentence skills. Evaluative comments follow each paragraph below. Circle the letter of the statement that best applies in each case.

1.   **Drunk Drivers**

People caught driving while drunk—even first offenders—should be jailed. Drunk driving, first of all, is more dangerous than carrying around a loaded gun. In addition, a jail term would show drivers that society will no longer tolerate such careless and dangerous behavior. Finally, severe penalties might encourage solutions to the problem of drinking and driving. People who go out for a good time and intend to have several drinks would always designate one person, who would stay completely sober, as the driver.

a.   The paragraph is not unified.

b.   The paragraph is not adequately supported.

c.   The paragraph is not well organized.

d.   The paragraph does not show a command of sentence skills.

e.   The paragraph is well written in terms of the four bases.

2.   **A Frustrating Moment**

A frustrating moment happened to me several days ago. When I was shopping. I had picked up a tube of crest toothpaste and a jar of noxema skin cream. After the cashier rang up the purchases, which came to $4.15. I handed her $10. Then got back my change, which was only $0.85. I told the cashier that she had made a mistake. Giving me change for $5 instead of $10. But she insist that I had only gave her $5, I became very upset and demand that she return the rest of my change. She refused to do so instead she asked me to step aside so she could wait on the next customer. I stood very rigid, trying not to lose my temper. I simply said to her, I'm not going to leave here, Miss, without my change for $10. Giving in at this point a bell was rung and the manager was summoned. After the situation was explain to him, he ask the cashier to ring off her register to check for the change. After doing so, the cashier was $5 over her sale receipts. Only then did the manager return my change and apologize for the cashier mistake.

a.   The paragraph is not unified.

b.   The paragraph is not adequately supported.

c.   The paragraph is not well organized.

d.   The paragraph does not show a command of sentence skills.

e.   The paragraph is well written in terms of the four bases.

3.   **Asking Girls Out**

There are several reasons I have trouble asking girls to go out with me. I have asked some girls out and have been turned down. This is one reason that I can't talk to them. At one time I was very shy and quiet, and people sometimes didn't even know I was present. I can talk to girls now as friends, but as soon as I want to ask them out, I usually start to become quiet, and a little bit of shyness comes out. When I finally get the nerve up, the girl will turn me down, and I swear that I will never ask another one out again. I feel sure I will get a refusal, and I have no confidence in myself. Also, my friends mock me, though they aren't any better than I am. It can become discouraging when your friends get on you. Sometimes I just stand there and wait to hear what line the girl will use. The one they use a lot is "We like you as a friend, Ted, and it's better that way." Sometimes I want to have the line put on a tape recorder, so they won't have to waste their breath on me. All my past experiences with girls have been just as bad. One girl used me to make her old boyfriend jealous. Then when she succeeded, she started going out with him again. I had a bad experience when I took a girl to the prom. I spent a lot of money on her. Two days later, she told me that she was going steady with another guy. I feel that when I meet a girl I have to be sure I can trust her. I don't want her to turn on me.

a.   The paragraph is not unified.

b.   The paragraph is not adequately supported.

c.   The paragraph is not well organized.

d.   The paragraph does not show a command of sentence skills.

e.   The paragraph is well written in terms of the four bases.

4.   **A Change in My Writing**

A technique in my present English class has corrected a writing problem that I've always had. In past English courses, I had major problems with commas in the wrong places, bad spelling, capitalizing the wrong words, sentence fragments, and run-on sentences. I never had any big problems with unity, support, or coherence, but the sentence skills were another matter. They were like little bugs that always appeared to infest my writing. My present instructor asked me to rewrite papers, just concentrating on sentence skills. I thought that the instructor was crazy because I didn't feel that rewriting would do any good. I soon became certain that my instructor was out of his mind, for he made me rewrite my first paper four times. It was very frustrating, for I became tired of doing the same paper over and over. I wanted to belt my instructor against the wall when I'd show him each new draft and he'd find skills mistakes and say, "Rewrite." Finally, my papers began to improve and the sentence skills began to fall into place. I was able to see them and correct them before turning in a paper, whereas I couldn't before. Why or how this happened I don't know, but I think that rewriting helped a lot. It took me most of the semester, but I stuck it out and the work paid off.

a.   The paragraph is not unified.

b.   The paragraph is not adequately supported.

c.   The paragraph is not well organized.

d.   The paragraph does not show a command of sentence skills.

e.   The paragraph is well written in terms of the four bases.

5.   **Luck and Me**

I am a very lucky man, though the rest of my family has not always been lucky. Sometimes when I get depressed, which is too frequently, it's hard to see just how lucky I am. I'm lucky that I'm living in a country that is free. I'm allowed to worship the way I want to, and that is very important to me. Without a belief in God a person cannot live with any real certainty in life. My relationship with my wife is a source of good fortune for me. She gives me security, and that's something I need a lot. Even with these positive realities in my life, I still seem to find time for insecurity, worry, and, worst of all, depression. At times in my life I have had bouts of terrible luck. But overall, I'm a very lucky guy. I plan to further develop the positive aspects of my life and try to eliminate the negative ones.

a.   The paragraph is not unified.

b.   The paragraph is not adequately supported.

c.   The paragraph is not well organized.

d.   The paragraph does not show a command of sentence skills.

e.   The paragraph is well written in terms of the four bases.

Part Two

Paragraph Development

Preview

Part Two introduces you to paragraph development and gives you practice in the following common types of paragraph development:

Providing Examples

Explaining a Process

Examining Cause and Effect

Comparing or Contrasting

Defining a Term

Dividing and Classifying

Describing a Scene or Person

Narrating an Event

Arguing a Position

After a brief explanation of each type of paragraph development, student paragraphs illustrating each type are presented, followed by questions about those paragraphs. The questions relate to the standards of effective writing described in Part One. You are then asked to write your own paragraph. In each case, writing assignments progress from personal-experience topics to more formal and objective topics; some topics require simple research, and the last assignment in each section asks you to write with a specific purpose and audience in mind. At times, points or topic sentences for development are suggested, so that you can concentrate on (1) making sure your evidence is on target in support of your opening idea, (2) providing plenty of specific supporting details to back up your point, and (3) organizing your supporting material clearly.

7 Introduction to Paragraph Development

Nine Patterns of Paragraph Development

Traditionally, writing has been divided into the following patterns of development:

- Exposition

  Examples   Comparison and contrast

  Process   Definition

  Cause and effect   Division and classification

- Description
- Narration
- Argumentation

In *exposition*, the writer provides information about and explains a particular subject. Patterns of development within exposition include giving *examples*, detailing a *process* of doing or making something, analyzing *causes and effects*, *comparing* and *contrasting*, *defining* a term or concept, and *dividing* something into parts or *classifying* it into categories.

In addition to exposition, three other patterns of development are common: description, narration, and argumentation. A *description* is a verbal picture of a person, place, or thing. In *narration*, a writer tells the story of something that happened. Finally, in *argumentation*, a writer attempts to support a controversial point or defend a position on which there is a difference of opinion.

The pages ahead present individual chapters on each pattern. You will have a chance, then, to learn nine different patterns or methods for organizing material in your papers. Each pattern has its own internal logic and provides its own special strategies for imposing order on your ideas. As you practice each pattern, you should remember two points:

- *Point 1:* While each paragraph that you write will involve one predominant pattern, very often one or more additional patterns may be involved as well. For instance, the "Good-Bye, Tony" paragraph that you have already read (page 50) presents a series of causes leading to an effect—that the writer will not go out with Tony again. But the writer also presents examples to explain each of the causes (Tony was late, he was bossy, he was abrupt). And there is an element of narration, as the writer presents examples that occur from the beginning to the end of the date.

- *Point 2:* No matter which pattern or patterns you use, each paragraph will probably involve some form of argumentation. You will advance a point and then go on to support your point. To convince the reader that your point is valid, you may use a series of examples, or narration, or description, or some other pattern of organization. Among the paragraphs you will read in Part Two, one writer supports the point that a certain pet shop is depressing by providing a number of descriptive details. Another writer labels a certain experience in his life as heartbreaking and then uses a narrative to demonstrate the truth of his statement. A third writer advances the opinion that good horror movies can be easily distinguished from bad horror movies and then supplies comparative information about both to support her claim. Much of your writing, in short, will have the purpose of persuading your reader that the idea you have advanced is valid.

The Progression in Each Chapter

After each type of paragraph development is explained, student papers illustrating that type are presented, followed by questions about the paragraphs. The questions relate to unity, support, and coherence—principles of effective writing explained earlier in this book. You are then asked to write your own paragraph. In most cases, the first assignment is fairly structured and provides a good deal of guidance for the writing process. The other assignments offer a wide choice of writing topics. The fourth assignment always requires some simple research, and the fifth assignment requires writing with a specific purpose and for a specific audience.

Important Considerations in Paragraph Development

Before you begin work on particular types of paragraphs, there are several general considerations about writing to keep in mind. They will be discussed in turn.

Knowing Your Subject

Whenever possible, try to write on a subject that interests you. You will then find it easier to put more time into your work. Even more important, try to write on a subject that you already know something about. If you do not have direct experience with the subject, you should at least have indirect experience—knowledge gained through thinking, prewriting, reading, or talking about the subject.

If you are asked to write on a topic about which you have no experience or knowledge, you should do whatever research is required to gain the information you need. Chapter 18, "Using the Library and the Internet," will show you how to look up relevant information. Without direct or indirect experience, or the information you gain through research, you may not be able to provide the specific evidence needed to develop whatever point you are trying to make. Your writing will be starved for specifics.

Knowing Your Purpose and Audience

The three most common purposes of writing are to inform, to persuade, and to entertain. As already noted, much of the writing you do in this book will involve some form of argumentation or persuasion. You will advance a point or thesis and then support it in a variety of ways. To some extent, also, you will write papers to inform—to provide readers with information about a particular subject. And since, in practice, writing often combines purposes, you might find yourself at times providing vivid or humorous details in order to entertain your readers as well.

Your audience will be primarily your instructor and sometimes other students. Your instructor is really a symbol of the larger audience you should see yourself writing for—an audience of educated adults who expect you to present your ideas in a clear, direct, organized way. If you can learn to write to persuade or inform such a general audience, you will have accomplished a great deal.

It will also be helpful for you to write some papers for a more specific audience. By so doing, you will develop an ability to choose words and adopt a tone of voice that is just right for a given purpose and a given group of people. In this part of the book, then, there is an assignment at or near the end of each chapter that asks you to write with a very specific purpose in mind and for a very specific audience.

You will be asked, for example, to imagine yourself as an employee writing a description of a new job opening at your workplace, as a graduate of a local high school advising a counselor there about a drug problem, as an aide at a day-care center preparing instructions for children, as an apartment tenant complaining to a landlord about neighbors, or as a travel agent providing suggestions for different kinds of family vacations. Through these and other assignments, you will learn how to adjust your style and tone of voice to a given writing situation.

Using a Computer

If you don't yet write on a computer, it's time to start. In today's world, word processing is an essential mechanical skill, just as effective writing is a vital communication skill.

The computer can be a real aid in the writing process. You can quickly add or delete anything, from a word to an entire section. You can "cut" material and "paste" it elsewhere in seconds. A word-processing program makes it easy to set margins, space lines, and number pages. It can also help you check your spelling, your grammar, and to some extent your style. And at any point during your work, you can print out one or more copies of your text.

Word processing is not hard to learn. Just as you don't need to know how a car works to drive one, you don't need to understand how a computer functions to use it. With a few simple keystrokes under your belt, you can begin. You do not even need to own your own computer. Nearly every college has at least one computer center, complete with rows of computers and staff members to provide assistance. Free classes in word processing may be available as well.

Tips on Using a Computer

- If you are using your school's computer center, allow yourself enough time. You may have to wait for a computer or printer to be free. In addition, you may need several sessions at the computer and printer to complete your paper.

- Every word-processing program allows you to "save" your writing by hitting one or more keys. Save your work frequently as you work on a draft. Work that is saved is preserved by the computer. Work that is not saved is lost when the file you are working on is closed, when the computer is turned off—or if there's a power or system failure.

- Keep your work in two places—the hard drive or disk you are working on and a backup disk. At the end of each session with the computer, copy your work onto the backup disk. Then if the hard drive or working disk becomes damaged, you'll have the backup copy.

- Print out your work at least at the end of every session. Then you'll not only have your most recent draft to work on away from the computer; you'll also have a copy in case something should happen to your disks.

- Work in single spacing so you can see as much of your writing on the screen at one time as possible. Just before you print out your work, change to double spacing.

- Before making major changes in a paper, create a copy of your file. For example, if your file is titled "Worst Job," create a file called "Worst Job 2." Then make all your changes in that file. If the changes don't work out, you can always go back to the original file.

Ways to Use a Computer at Each Stage of the Writing Process

Following are some ways to make word processing a part of your writing. Note that the sections that follow correspond to the stages of the writing process described in Chapter 2, pages 17–45.

Prewriting

If you're a fast typist, many kinds of prewriting will go well on the computer. With freewriting in particular, you can get ideas onto the screen almost as quickly as they occur to you. A passing thought that could be productive is not likely to get lost. You may even find it helpful, when freewriting, to dim the screen of your monitor so that you can't see what you're typing. If you temporarily can't see the screen, you won't have to worry about grammar or spelling or typing errors (all of which do not matter in prewriting); instead, you can concentrate on getting down as many ideas and details as possible about your subject.

After any initial freewriting, questioning, and list-making on a computer, it's often very helpful to print out a hard copy of what you've done. With a clean printout in front of you, you'll be able to see everything at once and revise and expand your work with handwritten comments in the margins of the paper.

If you have prepared a list of items, you may be able to turn that list into an outline right on the screen. Delete the ideas you feel should not be in your paper (saving them at the end of the file in case you change your mind), and add any new ideas that occur to you. Then use the cut and paste functions to shuffle the supporting ideas around until you find the best order for your paper.

Word processing also makes it easy for you to experiment with the wording of the point of your paper. You can try a number of versions in a short time. After you have decided upon the version that works best, you can easily delete the other versions—or simply move them to a temporary "leftover" section at the end of the paper.

Writing Your First Draft

Like many writers, you may want to write out your first draft by hand and then type it into the computer for revision. Even as you type your handwritten draft, you may find yourself making some changes and improvements. And once you have a draft on the screen, or printed out, you will find it much easier to revise than a handwritten draft.

If you feel comfortable composing directly on the screen, you can benefit from the computer's special features. For example, if you have written an anecdote in your freewriting that you plan to use in your paper, simply copy the story from your freewriting file and insert it where it fits in your paper. You can refine it then or later. Or if you discover while typing that a sentence is out of place, cut it out from where it is and paste it wherever you wish. And if while writing you realize that an earlier sentence can be expanded, just move your cursor back to that point and type in the added material.

Revising

It is during revision that the virtues of word processing really shine. All substituting, adding, deleting, and rearranging can be done easily within an existing file. All changes instantly take their proper places within the paper, not scribbled above the line or squeezed into the margin. You can concentrate on each change you want to make, because you never have to type from scratch or work on a messy draft. You can carefully go through your paper to check that all your supporting evidence is relevant and to add new support here and there where needed. Anything you decide to eliminate can be deleted in a keystroke. Anything you add can be inserted precisely where you choose. If you change your mind, all you have to do is delete or cut and paste. Then you can sweep through the paper focusing on other changes, such as improving word choice, increasing sentence variety, eliminating wordiness, and so on.

If you are like many students, you will find it convenient to print out a hard copy of your file at various points throughout the revision. You can then revise in longhand—adding, crossing out, and indicating changes—and later quickly make those changes in the document.

Editing and Proofreading

Editing and proofreading also benefit richly from word processing. Instead of crossing out or whiting out mistakes, or rewriting an entire paper to correct numerous errors, you can make all necessary changes within the most recent draft. If you find editing or proofreading on the screen hard on your eyes, print out a copy. Mark any corrections on that copy, and then transfer them to the final draft.

If the word-processing package you're using includes spelling and grammar checks, by all means use them. The spell-check function tells you when a word is not in the computer's dictionary. Keep in mind, however, that the spell-check cannot tell you how to spell a name correctly or when you have mistakenly used, for example, *their* instead of *there*. To a spell-check, *Thank ewe four the compliment* is as correct as *Thank you for the compliment*. Also use the grammar check with caution. Any errors it doesn't uncover are still your responsibility.

A word-processed paper, with its clean appearance and attractive formatting, looks so good that you may think it is in better shape than it really is. Do not be fooled by your paper's appearance. Take sufficient time to review your grammar, punctuation, and spelling carefully.

Even after you hand in your paper, save the computer file. Your teacher may ask you to do some revising, and then the file will save you from having to type the paper from scratch.

Using Peer Review

In addition to having your instructor as an audience for your writing, you will benefit by having another student in your class as an audience. On the day a paper is due, or on a day when you are writing papers in class, your instructor may ask you to pair up with another student. That student will read your paper, and you will read his or her paper.

Ideally, read the other paper aloud while your partner listens. If that is not practical, read it in a whisper while he or she looks on. As you read, both you and your partner should look and listen for spots where the paper does not read smoothly and clearly. Check or circle the trouble spots where your reading snags.

Your partner should then read your paper, marking possible trouble spots while doing so. Then each of you should do three things:

1 Identification

On a separate sheet of paper, write at the top the title and author of the paper you have read. Under it, put your name as the reader of the paper.

2 Scratch Outline

"X-ray" the paper for its inner logic by making up a scratch outline. The scratch outline need be no more than twenty words or so, but it should show clearly the logical foundation on which the essay is built. It should identify and summarize the overall point of the paper and the three areas of support for the point.

Your outline can look as follows.

Point: _____

Support:

1. _____

2. _____

3. _____

For example, here is a scratch outline of the paper on page 195 about a new puppy in the house:

Point: A new puppy can have drastic effects on a house.

Support:

1. Keeps family awake at night

2. Destroys possessions

3. Causes arguments

3 Comments

Under the outline, write the heading "Comments." Here is what you should comment on:

• Look at the spots where your reading of the paper snagged: Are words missing or misspelled? Is there a lack of parallel structure? Are there mistakes with punctuation? Is the meaning of a sentence confused? Try to figure out what the problems are and suggest ways of fixing them.

- Are there spots in the paper where you see problems with *unity*, *support*, or *organization*? (You'll find it helpful to refer to the checklist on the inside front cover of this book.) If so, offer comments. For example, you might say, "More details are needed in the first supporting paragraph," or "Some of the details in the last supporting paragraph don't really back up your point."
- Finally, make note of something you really liked about the paper, such as good use of transitions or an especially realistic or vivid specific detail.

After you have completed your evaluation of the paper, give it to your partner. Your instructor may provide you with the option of rewriting a paper in light of this feedback. Whether or not you rewrite, be sure to hand in the peer evaluation form with your paper.

Doing a Personal Review

1 While you're writing and revising an essay, you should be constantly evaluating it in terms of *unity, support,* and *organization.* Use as a guide the detailed checklist on the inside front cover of this book.

2 After you've finished the next-to-final draft of an essay, check it for the *sentence skills* listed on the inside front cover. It may also help to read the paper out loud. If a given sentence does not sound right—that is, if it does not read clearly and smoothly—chances are something is wrong. Then revise or edit as needed until your paper is complete.

8 Providing Examples

In our daily conversations, we often provide *examples*—that is, details, particulars, specific instances—to explain statements that we make. Consider the several statements and supporting examples in the box below:

Statement	Examples
The A&P was crowded today.	There were at least four carts waiting at each of the checkout counters, and it took me forty-five minutes to get through a line.
The corduroy shirt I bought is poorly made.	When I washed it, the colors began to fade, one button cracked and another fell off, a shoulder seam opened, and the sleeves shrank almost two inches.
My son Peter is unreliable.	If I depend on him to turn off a pot of beans in ten minutes, the family is likely to eat burned beans. If I ask him to turn down the thermostat before he goes to bed, the heat is likely to stay on all night.

In each case, the examples help us *see for ourselves* the truth of the statement that has been made. In paragraphs, too, explanatory examples help the audience fully understand a point. Lively, specific examples also add interest to a paper.

In this chapter, you will be asked to provide a series of examples to support a topic sentence. Providing examples to support a point is one of the most common and simplest methods of paragraph development. First read the paragraphs ahead; they all use examples to develop their points. Then answer the questions that follow.

Paragraphs to Consider

Inconsiderate Drivers

[1]Some people are inconsiderate drivers. [2]In the city, they will at times stop right in the middle of the street while looking for a certain home or landmark. [3]If they had any consideration for the cars behind them, they would pull over to the curb first. [4]Other drivers will be chatting on their cell phones and then slow down unexpectedly at a city intersection to make a right or left turn. [5]The least they could do is use their turn signals to let those behind them know in advance of their intention. [6]On the highway, a common example of inconsiderateness is night drivers who fail to turn off their high beams, creating glare for cars approaching in the other direction. [7]Other rude highway drivers move to the second or passing lane and then stay there, making it impossible for cars behind to go around them. [8]Yet other drivers who act as if they have special privileges are those who do not wait their turn in bottleneck situations where the cars in two lanes must merge alternately into one lane. [9]Perhaps the most inconsiderate drivers are those who throw trash out their windows, creating litter that takes away some of the pleasure of driving and that must be paid for with everyone's tax dollars.

Office Politics

[1]Office politics is a destructive game played by several types of people. [2]For instance, two supervisors may get into a conflict over how to do a certain job. [3]Instead of working out an agreement like adults, they carry on a power struggle that turns the poor employees under them into human Ping-Pong balls being swatted between two angry players. [4]Another common example of office politics is the ambitious worker who takes credit for other people's ideas. [5]He or she will chat in a "friendly" fashion with inexperienced employees, getting their ideas about how to run the office more smoothly. [6]Next thing you know, Mr. or Ms. Idea-Stealer is having a closed-door session with the boss and getting promotion points for his or her "wonderful creativity." [7]Yet another illustration of office politics is the spy. [8]This employee acts very buddy-buddy with other workers, often dropping little comments about things he or she doesn't like in the workplace. [9]The spy encourages people to talk about their problems at work, how they don't like their boss, the pay, and the working conditions. [10]Then the spy goes straight back and repeats all he or she has heard to the boss, and the employees get blamed for their "poor attitude." [11]A final example of office politics is people who gossip. [12]Too often, office politics can turn a perfectly fine work situation into a stressful one.

An Egotistical Neighbor

[1]I have an egotistical neighbor named Alice. [2]If I tell Alice how beautiful her dress is, she will take the time to tell me the name of the store where she bought it, the type of material that was used in making it, and the price. [3]Alice is also egotistical when it comes to her children. [4]Because they are hers, she thinks they just have to be the best children on the block. [5]I am wasting my time by trying to tell her I have seen her kids expose themselves on the street or take things from parked cars. [6]I do not think parents should praise their children too much. [7]Kids have learned how to be good at home and simply awful when they are not at home. [8]Finally, Alice is quick to describe the furnishings of her home for someone who is meeting her for the first time. [9]She tells how much she paid for the paneling in her dining room. [10]She mentions that she has three color television sets and that they were bought at an expensive furniture store. [11]She lets the person know that the stereo set in her living room cost more than a thousand dollars, and that she has such a large collection of CDs that she would not be able to play them all in one week. [12]Poor Alice is so self-centered that she never realizes how boring she can be.

■ Questions

About Unity

1. Which two sentences in "An Egotistical Neighbor" are irrelevant to the point that Alice is egotistical? (*Write the sentence numbers here.*)

   _____   _____

About Support

2. In "Inconsiderate Drivers," how many examples are given of inconsiderate drivers?

   _____ two   _____ four   _____ six   _____ seven

3. After which sentence in "Office Politics" are specific details needed?

   _____

About Coherence

4. What are the four transition words or phrases that are used to introduce each new example in "Office Politics"?

   _____   _____   _____   _____

5. What two transition words are used to introduce examples in "An Egotistical Neighbor"?

   _____   _____

6. Which paragraph clearly uses emphatic order to organize its details, saving for last what the writer regards as the most important example?

_____

Developing an Examples Paragraph

Development through Prewriting

Backing up your statements with clear, specific illustrations is the key to a successful examples paragraph. When Charlene, the writer of "Office Politics," was assigned an examples paragraph, she at first did not know what to write about.

Then her teacher made a suggestion. "Imagine yourself having lunch with some friends," the teacher said. "You're telling them *how* you feel about something and *why*. Maybe you're saying, 'I am so mad at my boyfriend!' or 'My new apartment is really great.' You wouldn't stop there—you'd continue by saying what your boyfriend does that is annoying, or in what way your apartment is nice. In other words, you'd be making a general point and backing it up with examples. That's what you need to do in this paper."

That night, Charlene was on the telephone with her brother. She was complaining about the office where she worked. "Suddenly I realized what I was doing," Charlene said. "I was making a statement—I hate the politics in my office—and giving examples of those politics. I knew what I could write about!"

Charlene began preparing to write her paragraph by freewriting. She gave herself ten minutes to write down everything she could think of on the subject of politics in her office. This is what she wrote:

> Of all the places I've ever worked this one is the worst that way. Can't trust anybody there—everybody's playing some sort of game. Worst one of all is Bradley and the way he pretends to be friendly with people. Gets them to complain about Ms. Bennett and Mr. Hankins and then runs back to them and reports everything. He should realize that people are catching on to his game and figuring out what a jerk he is. Melissa steals people's ideas and then takes credit for them. Anything to get brownie points. She's always out for herself first, you can tell. Then there's all the gossip that goes on. You think you're in a soap opera or something, and it's kind of fun in a way but it also is very distracting people always talking about each other and worrying about what they say about you. And people talk about our bosses a lot. Nobody knows why Ms. Bennett and Mr. Hankins hate each other so much but they each want the workers on their side. You do something one boss's way, but then the other boss appears and is angry that you're not doing it another way. You don't know what to do at times to keep people happy.

Charlene read over her freewriting and then spent some time asking questions about her paragraph. "Exactly what do I want my point to be?" she asked. "And exactly how am I going to support that point?" Keeping those points in mind, she worked on several scratch outlines and wound up with the following:

Office politics are ruining the office.
1. Bradley reports people's complaints.
2. Melissa steals ideas.
3. People gossip.
4. Ms. Bennett and Mr. Hankins make workers choose sides.

Working from this outline, she then wrote the following first draft:

My office is being ruined by office politics. It seems like everybody is trying to play some sort of game to get ahead and don't care what it does to anybody else. One example is Bradley. Although he pretends to be friendly with people he isn't sincere. What he is trying to do is get them to complain about their bosses. Once they do, he goes back to the bosses and tells them what's been said and gets the worker in trouble. I've seen the same kind of thing happen at two other offices where I've worked. Melissa is another example of someone who plays office politics games. She steals other people's ideas and takes the credit for them. I had a good idea once to save paper. I told her we ought to use E-mail to send office memos instead of typing them on paper. She went to Ms. Bennett and pretended the idea was hers. I guess I was partly to blame for not acting on the idea myself. And Ms. Bennett and Mr. Hankins hate each other and try to get us to take sides in their conflict. Then there is all the gossip that goes on. People do a lot of backbiting, and you have to be very careful about your behavior or people will start talking about you. All in all, office politics is really a problem where I work.

Development through Revising

After completing her first draft, Charlene put it aside until the next day. When she reread it, this was her response:

"I think the paragraph would be stronger if I made it about office politics in general instead of just politics in my office. The things I was writing about happen in many offices, not just in mine. And our instructor wants us to try some third-person writing. Also, I need to make better use of transitions to help the reader follow as I move from one example to another."

With these thoughts in mind, Charlene began revising her paper, and after several drafts she produced the paragraph that appears on page 172.

Writing an Examples Paragraph

■ **Writing Assignment 1**

The assignment here is to complete an unfinished paragraph (in the box), which has as its topic sentence, "My husband Roger is a selfish person." Provide the supporting details needed to develop the examples of Roger's selfishness. The first example has been done for you.

A Selfish Person

My husband Roger is a selfish person. For one thing, he refuses to move out of the city, even though it is a bad place to raise the children. *We inherited some money when my parents died, and it might be enough for a down payment on a small house in a nearby town. But Roger says he would miss his buddies in the neighborhood.*

_____

Also, when we go on vacation, we always go where Roger wants to go. _____

_____

_____

Another example of Roger's selfishness is that he always spends any budget money that is left over. _____

_____

_____

_____

Finally, Roger leaves all the work of caring for the children to me.

_____

_____

_____

_____

Prewriting

a On a separate piece of paper, jot down a couple of answers for each of the following questions:

- What specific vacations did the family go on because Roger wanted to go? Write down particular places, length of stay, time of year. What vacations has the family never gone on (for example, to visit the wife's relatives), even though the wife wanted to?
- What specific items has Roger bought for himself (rather than for the whole family's use) with leftover budget money?
- What chores and duties involved in the everyday caring for the children has Roger never done?

Note: Your instructor may ask you to work with one or two other students in generating the details needed to develop the three examples in the paragraph. The groups may then be asked to read their details aloud, with the class deciding which details are the most effective for each example.

Here and in general in your writing, try to generate *more* supporting material than you need. You are then in a position to choose the most convincing details for your paper.

b Read over the details you have generated and decide which sound most effective. Jot down additional details as they occur to you.

c Take your best details, reshape them as needed, and use them to complete the paragraph about Roger.

Revising

Read over the paragraph you have written. Ask yourself these questions:

- Do the examples I have provided really support the idea that Roger is selfish?
- Are there enough examples to make my point about Roger and have people agree with me?
- Have I checked my paper for spelling and other sentence skills, as listed on the inside front cover of the book?

Continue revising your work until you can answer "yes" to all these questions.

■ Writing Assignment 2

Write an examples paragraph about one quality of a person you know well. The person might be a member of your family, a friend, a roommate, a boss or supervisor, a neighbor, an instructor, or someone else. Here is a list of descriptive qualities that you might consider choosing from. Feel free to choose another quality that does not appear here.

Honest	Hardworking	Jealous
Bad-tempered	Supportive	Materialistic
Ambitious	Suspicious	Sarcastic
Prejudiced	Open-minded	Self-centered
Considerate	Lazy	Spineless
Argumentative	Independent	Good-humored
Softhearted	Stubborn	Cooperative
Energetic	Flirtatious	Self-disciplined
Patient	Irresponsible	Sentimental
Reliable	Stingy	Defensive
Generous	Trustworthy	Dishonest
Persistent	Aggressive	Insensitive
Shy	Courageous	Unpretentious
Sloppy	Compulsive	Tidy

Prewriting

a   Select the individual you will write about and the quality of this person that you will focus on. For example, you might choose your cousin and her quality of self-discipline. This will be the point of your paper.

b   Make a list of examples that will support your point. Such a list about the self-disciplined cousin might look like this:

Exercises every day for forty-five minutes
Never lets herself watch TV until homework is done
Keeps herself on a strict budget
Organizes her school papers in color-coordinated notebooks
Eats no more than one dessert every week
Balances her checkbook the day her statement arrives

c   Read over your list and see how you might group the items into categories. The list above, for example, could be broken into three categories: schoolwork, fitness, and money.

Exercises every day for forty-five minutes (fitness)

Never lets herself watch TV until homework is done (schoolwork)

Keeps herself on a strict budget (money)

Organizes her school papers in color-coordinated notebooks (schoolwork)

Eats no more than one dessert every week (fitness)

Balances her checkbook the day her bank statement arrives (money)

d   Prepare a scratch outline made up of the details you've generated, with those details grouped into appropriate categories.

1. <u>Self-disciplined about fitness</u>
    A. Exercises every day for forty-five minutes
    B. Eats no more than one dessert every week

2. <u>Self-disciplined about schoolwork</u>
    A. Never lets herself watch TV until homework is done
    B. Organizes her school papers in color-coordinated notebooks

3. <u>Self-disciplined about money</u>
    A. Keeps herself on a strict budget
    B. Balances her checkbook the day her bank statement arrives

e   Write the topic sentence of your paragraph. You should include the name of the person you're writing about, your relationship to that person, and the specific quality you are focusing on. For example, you might write, "Keisha, a schoolmate of mine, is very flirtatious," or "Stubbornness is Uncle Carl's outstanding characteristic." And a topic sentence for the paragraph about the self-disciplined cousin might be: "My cousin Mari is extremely self-disciplined."

Remember to focus on only *one* characteristic. Also remember to focus on a *specific* quality, not a vague, general quality. For instance, "My English instructor is a nice person" is too general.

f   Now you have a topic sentence and an outline and are ready to write the first draft of your paragraph. Remember, as you flesh out the examples, that your goal is not just to *tell* us about the person but to *show* us the person by detailing his or her words, actions, or both. In preparation for this writing assignment, you might want to go back and reread the examples provided in "An Egotistical Neighbor."

Revising

It's hard to criticize your own work honestly, especially right after you've done it. If at all possible, put your paragraph away for a day or so and then return to it. Better yet, wait a day and then read it aloud to a friend whose judgment you trust.

Read the paragraph with these questions in mind:

- Does my topic sentence clearly state whom I am writing about, what that person's relationship is to me, and what quality of that person I am going to focus on?
- Do the examples I provide truly show that my subject has the quality I'm writing about?
- Have I provided enough specific details to solidly support my point that my subject has a certain quality?
- Have I organized the details in my paragraph into several clearly defined categories?
- Have I used transitional words such as *also, in addition, for example,* and *for instance* to help the reader follow my train of thought?
- Have I checked my paper for sentence skills, as listed on the inside front cover of the book?

Continue revising your work until you and your reader can answer "yes" to all these questions.

■ Writing Assignment 3

Write a paragraph that uses examples to develop one of the following statements or a related statement of your own.

1. _____ is a distracting place to try to study.
2. The daily life of a student is filled with conflicts.
3. Abundant evidence exists that the United States has become a health-conscious nation.
4. Despite modern appliances, many household chores are still drudgery.
5. One of my instructors, _____, has some good (*or* unusual) teaching techniques.
6. Wasted electricity is all around us.
7. Life in the United States is faster-paced today than ever before.

8. Violence on television is widespread.

9. Today, some people are wearing ridiculous fashions.

10. Some students here at _____ do not care about learning (*or* are overly concerned about grades).

Be sure to choose examples that truly support your topic sentence. They should be relevant facts, statistics, personal experiences, or incidents you have heard or read about. Organize your paragraph by listing several examples that support your point. Save the most vivid, most convincing, or most important example for last.

■ Writing Assignment 4

Write a paragraph with this topic sentence: "The diet of the average American is unhealthy." Using strategies described in the chapter on the library and the Internet (pages 311–328), research the topic. Your reading will help you think about just how to proceed with the paper.

■ Writing Assignment 5

Imagine that you are a television critic for a daily newspaper. Your job is to recommend to viewers, every day, the programs most worth watching. You've decided that there is nothing particularly good on TV today. Therefore, your plan is to write a one-paragraph article about TV commercials, supporting this point: "Television advertisements are more entertaining than the programs they interrupt." To prepare for this article, spend some time watching television, taking detailed notes on several ads. Decide on two or three ways in which the ads are entertaining; these ways will be the main supporting points in your outline. Then choose at least one ad to use as a specific example to illustrate each of those points. Here are some entertaining qualities that may be seen in ads:

Humor

Cleverness

Music

Drama

Emotion

Suspense

Beauty

9 Explaining a Process

Every day we perform many activities that are *processes*—that is, series of steps carried out in a definite order. Many of these processes are familiar and automatic: for example, tying shoelaces, changing bed linen, using a vending machine, and starting a car. We are thus seldom aware of the sequence of steps making up each activity. In other cases, such as when we are asked for directions to a particular place, or when we try to read and follow the directions for a new table game, we may be painfully conscious of the whole series of steps involved in the process.

In this section, you will be asked to write a process paragraph—one that explains clearly how to do or make something. To prepare for this assignment, you should first read the student process papers below and then respond to the questions that follow.

Note: In process writing, where you are often giving instruction to the reader, the pronoun *you* can appropriately be used. Two of the model paragraphs here use *you*—as indeed does much of this book, which gives instruction on how to write effectively. As a general rule, though, do not use *you* in your writing.

Paragraphs to Consider

Sneaking into the House at Night

¹The first step I take is bringing my key along with me. ²Obviously, I don't want to have to knock on the door at 1:30 in the morning and rouse my parents out of bed. ³Second, I make it a point to stay out past midnight. ⁴If I come in before then, my father is still up, and I'll have to face his disapproving look. ⁵All I need in my life is for him to make me feel guilty. ⁶Trying to make it as a college student is as much as I'm ready to handle. ⁷Next, I am careful to be very quiet upon entering the house. ⁸This involves lifting the front door up slightly as I open it, so that it does not creak. ⁹It also means treating the floor and steps to the second floor like a minefield, stepping carefully over the spots that squeak. ¹⁰When I'm upstairs, I stop briefly in the bathroom without turning on the light. ¹¹Finally, I tiptoe to my room, put my clothes in a pile on a chair, and slip quietly into bed. ¹²With my careful method of sneaking into the house at night, I have avoided some major hassles with my parents.

How to Harass an Instructor

¹There are several steps you can take to harass an instructor during a class. ²First of all, show up late, so that you can interrupt the beginning of the instructor's presentation. ³Saunter in nonchalantly and try to find a seat next to a friend. ⁴In a normal tone of voice, speak some words of greeting to your friends as you sit down, and scrape your chair as loudly as possible while you make yourself comfortable in it. ⁵Then just sit there and do anything but pay attention. ⁶When the instructor sees that you are not involved in the class, he or she may pop a quick question, probably hoping to embarrass you. ⁷You should then say, in a loud voice, "I DON'T KNOW THE ANSWER." ⁸This declaration of ignorance will throw the instructor off guard. ⁹If the instructor then asks you why you don't know the answer, say, "I don't even know what page we're on" or "I thought the assignment was boring, so I didn't do it." ¹⁰After the instructor calls on someone else, get up loudly from your seat, walk to the front of the classroom, and demand to be excused for an emergency visit to the washroom. ¹¹Stay there at least fifteen minutes and take your time coming back. ¹²If the instructor asks you where you've been when you reenter the room, simply ignore the question and go to your seat. ¹³Flop into your chair, slouching back and extending your legs as far out as possible. ¹⁴When the instructor informs you of the assignment that the class is working on, heave an exaggerated sigh and very slowly open up your book and start turning the pages. ¹⁵About a half hour before class is over, begin to look at the clock every few minutes. ¹⁶Ten minutes before dismissal time, start noisily packing up your books and papers. ¹⁷Then get up and begin walking to the door a couple of minutes before the class is supposed to end. ¹⁸The instructor will look at you and wonder whether it wouldn't have been better to go into business instead of education.

Dealing with Verbal Abuse

¹If you are living with a man who abuses you verbally with criticism, complaints, and insults, you should take steps to change your situation. ²First, realize that you are not to blame for his abusive behavior. ³This may be difficult for you to believe. ⁴Years of verbal abuse have probably convinced you that you're responsible for everything that's wrong with your relationship. ⁵But that is a lie. ⁶If your partner is verbally abusive, it is his responsibility to learn why he chooses to deal with his problems by saying nasty things. ⁷Perhaps he observed his father treating his mother that same way. ⁸Maybe he never learned any more positive ways to deal with negative emotions, like anger, fear, or disappointment. ⁹Steps two and three need to be done one right after the other. ¹⁰Step two is for you to announce that you will no longer tolerate being verbally abused. ¹¹State that you are a

person who deserves respect and civil behavior, and that you will accept no less. ¹²Next, offer to go with him to talk to a counselor who will help both of you learn new ways to communicate. ¹³While he learns to express his feelings without attacking you, you can learn to stand up for yourself and express your feelings clearly. ¹⁴If he refuses to take responsibility for changing his abusive behavior, then you must consider step four: to leave him. ¹⁵You were not put here on earth to have your self-concept demolished by serving as someone else's verbal punching-bag.

■ Questions

About Unity

1. Which paragraph lacks an opening topic sentence?

   _____

2. Which two sentences in "Sneaking into the House at Night" should be eliminated in the interest of paragraph unity? *(Write the sentence numbers here.)*

   _____   _____

About Support

3. After which sentence in "How to Harass an Instructor" are supporting details (examples) needed?

   _____

4. Summarize the four steps in the process of dealing with verbal abuse.

   a. _____

   b. _____

   c. _____

   d. _____

About Coherence

5. Do these paragraphs use time order or emphatic order?

   _____

6. Which transition words introduce the first, second, and third steps in "Sneaking into the House at Night"?

   _____   _____   _____

Developing a Process Paragraph

Development through Prewriting

To be successful, a process essay must explain clearly each step of an activity. The key to preparing to write such an essay is thinking through the activity as though you're doing it for the first time. Selma is the author of "Dealing with Verbal Abuse." As she considered possible topics for her paper, she soon focused on a situation in her own life: living with an abusive man. Selma had not known how to change her situation. But with the help of a counselor, she realized there were steps she could take—a process she could follow. She carried out that process and finally left her abusive partner. Remembering this, Selma decided to write about how to deal with abuse.

She began by making a list of the steps she followed in coping with her own abusive relationship. This is what she wrote:

Tell him you won't accept any more abuse.

Open your own checking account.

Apply for credit cards in your own name.

Offer to go with him to counseling.

Realize you're not to blame.

Learn to stand up for yourself.

Go into counseling yourself if he won't do it.

Call the police if he ever becomes violent.

Leave him if he refuses to change.

Next, she numbered the steps in the order in which she had performed them. She crossed out some items she realized weren't really part of the process of dealing with verbal abuse.

2 Tell him you won't accept any more abuse.

~~Open your own checking account.~~

~~Apply for credit cards in your own name.~~

3 Offer to go with him to counseling.

1 Realize you're not to blame.

5 Learn to stand up for yourself.

4 Go into counseling yourself if he won't do it.

~~Call the police if he ever becomes violent.~~

6 Leave him if he refuses to change.

Then Selma grouped her items into four steps. Those steps were (1) realize you're not to blame; (2) tell the abuser you won't accept more abuse; (3) get into counseling, preferably with him; and (4) if necessary, leave him.

Selma was ready to write her first draft. Here it is:

Some people think that "abuse" has to mean getting punched and kicked, but that's not so. Verbal abuse can be as painful inside as physical abuse is on the outside. It can make you feel worthless and sad. I know because I lived with a verbally abusive man for years. Finally I found the courage to deal with the situation. Here is what I did. With the help of friends, I finally figured out that I wasn't to blame. I thought it was my fault because that's what he always told me—that if I wasn't so stupid, he wouldn't criticize and insult me. When I told him I wanted him to stop insulting and criticizing me, he just laughed at me and told me I was a crybaby. One of my friends suggested a counselor, and I asked Harry to go talk to him with me. We went together once but Harry wouldn't go back. He said he didn't need anyone to tell him how to treat his woman. I wasn't that surprised because Harry grew up with a father who treated his mother like dirt and his mom just accepts it to this day. Even after Harry refused to go see the counselor, though, I kept going. The counselor helped me see that I couldn't make Harry change, but I was still free to make my own choices. If I didn't want to live my life being Harry's verbal punching bag, and if he didn't want to change, then I would have to. I told Harry that I wasn't going to live that way anymore. I told him if he wanted to work together on better ways to communicate, I'd work with him. But otherwise, I would leave. He gave me his usual talk about "Oh, you know I don't really mean half the stuff I say when I'm mad." I said that wasn't a good enough excuse, and that I did mean what I was saying. He got mad all over again and called me every name in the book. I stuck around for a little while after that but then realized "This is it. I can stay here and take this or I can do what I know is right for me." So I left. It was a really hard decision but it was the right one. Harry may be angry at me forever but I know now that his anger and his verbal abuse is his problem, not mine.

Development through Revising

After Selma had written her first draft, she showed it to a classmate for her comments. Here is what the classmate wrote in response:

In order for this to be a good process essay, I think you need to do a couple of things.

First, although the essay is based on what you went through, I think it's too much about your own experience. I'd suggest you take yourself out of it and just write about how any person could deal with any verbally abusive situation. Otherwise this paper is about you and Harry, not the process.

Second, you need a clear topic sentence that tells the reader what process you're going to explain.

Third, I'd use transitions like 'first' and 'next' to make the steps in the process clearer. I think the steps are all there, but they get lost in all the details about you and Harry.

When Selma reread her first draft, she agreed with her classmate's suggestions. She then wrote the version of "Dealing with Verbal Abuse" that appears on page 184.

Writing a Process Paragraph

■ Writing Assignment 1

Choose one of the topics below to write about in a process paper.

How to feed a family on a budget

How to break up with a boyfriend or girlfriend

How to balance a checkbook

How to change a car or bike tire

How to get rid of house or garden pests, such as mice, roaches, or wasps

How to play a simple game like checkers, ticktacktoe, or an easy card game

How to shorten a skirt or pants

How to meet new people, for either dating or friendship

How to plant a garden

How to deal with a nosy person

How to fix a leaky faucet, a clogged drain, or the like

How to build a campfire or start a fire in a fireplace

How to study for an important exam

How to conduct a yard or garage sale

How to wash dishes efficiently, clean a bathroom, do laundry, or the like

Prewriting

a Begin by freewriting on your topic for ten minutes. Do not worry about spelling, grammar, organization, or other matters of form. Just write whatever comes into your head regarding the topic. Keep writing for more than ten minutes if ideas keep coming to you. This freewriting will give you a base of raw material to draw from during the next phase of your work on the paragraph. After freewriting, you should have a sense of whether there is enough material available for you to write a process paragraph about the topic. If so, continue as explained below. If there is not enough material, choose another topic and freewrite about *it* for ten minutes.

b Write a clear, direct topic sentence stating the process you are going to describe. For instance, if you are going to describe a way to study for major exams, your topic sentence might be "My study-skills instructor has suggested a good way to study for major exams." Or you can state in your topic sentence the process and the number of steps involved: "My technique for building a campfire involves four main steps."

c List all the steps you can think of that may be included in the process. Don't worry, at this point, about how each step fits or whether two steps overlap. Here, for example, is the list prepared by the author of "Sneaking into the House at Night":

Quiet on stairs
Come in after Dad's asleep
House is freezing at night
Bring key
Know which steps to avoid
Lift up front door
Late dances on Saturday night
Don't turn on bathroom light
Avoid squeaky spots on floor
Get into bed quietly

d Number your items in the order in which they occur; strike out items that do not fit in the list; add others that come to mind. The author of "Sneaking into the House at Night" did this step as follows:

~~Quiet on stairs~~
2 Come in after Dad's asleep
~~House is freezing at night~~
1 Bring key
5 Know which steps to avoid
3 Lift up front door
~~Late dances on Saturday night~~
6 Don't turn on bathroom light

4 Avoid squeaky spots on floor

8 Get into bed quietly

7 Undress quietly

e Use your list as a guide to write the first draft of your paper. As you write, try to think of additional details that will support your opening sentence. Do not expect to finish your paper in one draft. After you complete your first rough draft, in fact, you should be ready to write a series of drafts as you work toward the goals of unity, support, and coherence.

Revising

After you have written the first draft of your paragraph, set it aside for a while if you can. Then read it out loud, either to yourself or (better yet) to a friend or class-mate who will be honest with you about how it sounds. You (or you and your friend) should keep these points in mind:

- An effective process paper describes a series of activities in a way that is clear and easy to follow. Are the steps in this paper described in a clear, logical way? Have you used transitions such as *first, next, also, then, after, now, during,* and *finally* to make the paper move smoothly from one step to another?

- Does the paragraph explain every necessary step so that a reader could perform the task described?

- Can you answer "yes" to other questions about unity, support, and coherence on the inside front cover of this book?

- Is the point of view consistent? For example, if you begin by writing "This is how I got rid of mice" (first person), do not switch to "You must buy the right traps" (second person). Write your paragraph either from the first-person point of view (using *I* and *we*) or from the second-person point of view (*you*)—do not jump back and forth between the two.

- Have you corrected any sentence-skills mistakes that you noticed while reading the paper out loud? Have you checked the paper carefully for sentence skills, including spelling, as listed on the inside front cover of the book?

Continue revising your work until you and your reader can answer "yes" to all these questions.

■ Writing Assignment 2

Write a paragraph about one of the following processes. For this assignment, you will be working with more general topics than those in Writing Assignment 1. In fact, many of the topics are so broad that entire books have been written about them. A big part of your task, then, will be to narrow the topic down enough so that it can be covered in one paragraph. Then you'll have to invent your own steps for the process. In addition, you'll need to make decisions about how many steps to include and the order in which to present them.

How to break a bad habit such as smoking, overeating, or excess drinking
How to improve a course you have taken
How to make someone you know happy
How to discipline a child
How to improve the place where you work
How to show appreciation to others
How to make someone forgive you
How to make yourself depressed
How to get over a broken relationship
How to procrastinate
How to flirt

Prewriting

a   Choose a topic that appeals to you. Then ask yourself, "How can I make this broad, general topic narrow enough to be covered in a paragraph?" A logical way to proceed would be to think of a particular time you have gone through this process. For instance, if the general topic is "How to decorate economically," you might think about a time you decorated your own apartment.

b   Write a topic sentence about the process you are going to describe. Your topic sentence should clearly reflect the narrowed-down topic you have chosen. If you chose the topic described in step *a*, for example, your topic sentence could be "I made my first apartment look nice without spending a fortune."

c   Make a list of as many different items as you can think of that concern your topic. Don't worry about repeating yourself, about putting them in order, about whether details are major or minor, or about spelling. Simply make a list of everything about your topic that occurs to you. Here, for instance, is a list of items generated by the student writing about decorating her apartment on a budget:

Bought pretty towels and used them as wall hangings
Trimmed overgrown shrubs in front yard
Used old mayonnaise jars for vases to hold flowers picked in the yard
Found an old oriental rug at a yard sale

Painted mismatched kitchen chairs in bright colors

Kept dishes washed and put away

Bought a slipcover for a battered couch

Used pink lightbulbs

Hung pretty colored sheets over the windows

d Next, decide what order you will present your items in and number them. (As in the example of "decorating an apartment," there may not be an order that the steps *must* be done in. If that is the case, you'll need to make a decision about a sequence that makes sense, or that you followed yourself.) As you number your items, strike out items that do not fit in the list and add others that you think of, like this:

6 Bought pretty towels and used them as wall hangings

~~Trimmed overgrown shrubs in front yard~~

7 Used old mayonnaise jars for vases to hold flowers picked in the yard

4 Found an old oriental rug at a yard sale

2 Painted mismatched kitchen chairs in bright colors

~~Kept dishes washed and put away~~

1 Bought a slipcover for a battered couch

8 Used pink lightbulbs

5 Hung pretty colored sheets over the windows

3 Built bookshelves out of cinder blocks and boards

e Referring to your list of steps, write the first draft of your paper. Add additional steps as they occur to you.

Revising

If you can, put your first draft away for a day or so and then return to it. Read it out loud to yourself or, better yet, to a friend who will give you honest feedback.

Here are questions to ask yourself as you read over your first draft and the drafts to follow:

- Have I included a clear topic sentence that tells what process I will be describing?
- Have I included all the essential information so that anyone reading my paper could follow the same process?
- Have I made the sequence of steps easy to follow by using transitions like *first, second, then, next, during,* and *finally*?

- Can I answer "yes" to other questions about unity, support, and coherence found on the inside front cover of the book?
- Have I corrected sentence-skills mistakes, including spelling?

Continue revising your work until you can answer "yes" to all these questions.

■ Writing Assignment 3

Everyone is an expert at something. Write a process paragraph on some skill that you can perform very well. The skill might be, for example, refereeing a game, fishing for perch, painting a room, putting up a tent, making an ice-cream soda, becoming a long-distance runner, or tuning a car engine. Your topic sentence should be a general statement that summarizes in some way the process described, such as the following:

> Building a good deck requires time and care.
>
> Getting my four-year-old to bed at night is a lengthy process.
>
> You can create a beautiful centerpiece for your Thanksgiving table using a pumpkin and dried flowers.

■ Writing Assignment 4

Write a process paragraph on how to succeed at a job interview. Using strategies described in the chapter on the library and the Internet (pages 311–328), research the topic. Your reading will help you think about how to proceed with the paper.

Condense the material you have found into three, four, or five basic steps. Choose the steps, tips, and pointers that seem most important to you or that recur most often in the material. Remember that you are reading only to obtain background information for your paper. Do not copy material or repeat someone else's words or phrases in your own work.

■ Writing Assignment 5

Option 1:   Imagine that you have a part-time job helping out in a day-care center. The director, who is pleased with your work and wants to give you more responsibility, has put you in charge of a group activity (for example, an exercise session, an alphabet lesson, or a valentine-making project). But before you actually begin the activity, the director wants to see a summary of how you would go about it. What advance preparation would be needed, and what exactly would you be doing throughout the time of the project? Write a paragraph explaining the steps you would follow in conducting the activity.

Option 2:   Alternatively, write an explanation you might give to one of the children of how to do a simple classroom task—serving juice and cookies, getting ready for nap time, watering a plant, putting toys or other classroom materials away, or any other task you choose. Explain each step of the task in a way that a child would understand.

10 Examining Cause and Effect

What caused Pat to drop out of school? Why are soap operas so popular? Why does our football team do so poorly each year? How has retirement affected Dad? What effects does divorce have on children? Every day we ask such questions and look for answers. We realize that situations have causes and also effects—good or bad. By examining causes and effects, we seek to understand and explain things.

In this section, you will be asked to do some detective work by examining the causes of something or the effects of something. First read the three paragraphs that follow and answer the questions about them. All three paragraphs support their opening points by explaining a series of causes or a series of effects.

Paragraphs to Consider

New Puppy in the House

[1]Buying a new puppy can have significant effects on a household. [2]For one thing, the puppy keeps the entire family awake for at least two solid weeks. [3]Every night when the puppy is placed in its box, it begins to howl, yip, and whine. [4]Even after the lights go out and the house quiets down, the puppy continues to moan. [5]A second effect is that the puppy tortures the family by destroying material possessions. [6]Every day something different is damaged. [7]Family members find chewed belts and shoes, gnawed table legs, and ripped sofa cushions leaking stuffing. [8]In addition, the puppy often misses the paper during the paper-training stage of life, thus making the house smell like the public restroom at a city bus station. [9]Maybe the most serious problem, though, is that the puppy causes family arguments. [10]Parents argue with children about who is supposed to feed and walk the dog. [11]Children argue about who gets to play with the puppy first. [12]Everyone argues about who left socks and shoes around for the puppy to find. [13]These continual arguments, along with the effects of sleeplessness and the loss of valued possessions, can really disrupt a household. [14]Only when the puppy gets a bit older does the household settle back to normal.

My Car Accident

[1]Several factors caused my recent car accident. [2]First of all, because a heavy snow and freezing rain had fallen the day before, the road that I was driving on was hazardous. [3]The road had been plowed but was dangerously icy in spots where dense clusters of trees kept the early-morning sun from hitting the road and melting the ice. [4]Second, despite the slick patches, I was stupidly going along at about fifty miles an hour instead of driving more cautiously. [5]I have a daredevil streak in my nature and sometimes feel I want to become a stock-car racer after I finish school, rather than an accountant as my parents want me to be. [6]A third factor contributing to my accident was a dirty green Chevy van that suddenly pulled onto the road from a small intersecting street about fifty yards ahead of me. [7]The road was a sheet of ice at that point, but I was forced to apply my brake and also swing my car into the next lane. [8]Unfortunately, the fourth and final cause of my accident now came into play. [9]The rear of my Honda Civic was heavy because I had a set of barbells in the backseat. [10]I was selling this fairly new weight-lifting set to someone at school, since the weights had failed to build up my muscles immediately and I had gotten tired of practicing with them. [11]The result of all the weight in the rear was that after I passed the van, my car spun completely around on the slick road. [12]For a few horrifying, helpless moments, I was sliding down the highway backward at fifty miles an hour, with no control whatsoever over the car. [13]Then, abruptly, I slid off the road, thumping into a huge snowbank. [14]I felt stunned for a moment but then also relieved. [15]I saw a telephone pole about six feet to the right of me and realized that my accident could have been disastrous.

Why I Stopped Smoking

[1]For one thing, I realized that my cigarette smoke bothered others, irritating people's eyes and causing them to cough and sneeze. [2]They also had to put up with my stinking smoker's breath. [3]Also, cigarettes are a messy habit. [4]Our house was littered with ashtrays piled high with butts, matchsticks, and ashes, and the children were always knocking them over. [5]Cigarettes are expensive, and I estimated that the carton a week that I was smoking cost me about $1,060 a year. [6]Another reason I stopped was that the message about cigarettes being harmful to health finally got through to me. [7]I'd known they could hurt the smoker—in fact, a heavy smoker I know from work is in Eagleville Hospital now with lung cancer. [8]But when I realized what secondhand smoke could do to my wife and children, causing them bronchial problems and even increasing their risk of cancer, it really bothered me. [9]Cigarettes were also inconvenient. [10]Whenever I smoked, I would have to drink something to wet my dry throat, and that meant I had to keep going to the bathroom all the time. [11]I sometimes seemed to spend whole weekends doing nothing but smoking, drinking, and going to the

bathroom. ^{12}Most of all, I resolved to stop smoking because I felt exploited. ^{13}I hated the thought of wealthy, greedy corporations making money off my sweat and blood. ^{14}The rich may keep getting richer, but—at least as regards cigarettes—with no thanks to me.

■ Questions

About Unity

1. Which two sentences in "My Car Accident" do not support the opening idea and so should be omitted? (*Write the sentence numbers here.*)

   _____   _____

2. Which of the above paragraphs lacks a topic sentence?

   _____

About Support

3. How many separate causes are given in "Why I Stopped Smoking"?

   _____ four   _____ six   _____ seven   _____ eight

4. How many effects of bringing a new puppy into the house are given in "New Puppy in the House"?

   _____ one   _____ two   _____ three   _____ four

About Coherence

5. What transition words or phrases are used to introduce the four reasons listed in "My Car Accident"?

   _____   _____   _____   _____

6. In "New Puppy in the House," what words signal the effect that the author feels may be the most important?

   _____

Developing a Cause-and-Effect Paragraph

Development through Prewriting

In order to write a good cause-and-effect paragraph, you must clearly define an effect (*what* happened) and the contributing causes (*why* it happened). In addition, you will need to provide details that support the causes and effects you're writing about.

Jerome is the student author of "Why I Stopped Smoking." As soon as the topic occurred to him, he knew he had his *effect* (he had stopped smoking). His next task was to come up with a list of *causes* (reasons he had stopped). He decided to make a list of all the reasons for his quitting smoking that he could think of. This is what he came up with:

Annoyed others
Messy
Bad for health
Expensive

Taking his list, Jerome then jotted down details that supported each of those reasons:

<u>Annoyed others</u>
Bad breath
Irritates eyes
Makes other people cough
People hate the smell

<u>Messy</u>
Ashtrays, ashes, butts everywhere
Messes up my car interior

<u>Bad for health</u>
Marco in hospital with lung cancer
Secondhand smoke dangerous to family
My morning cough

<u>Expensive</u>
Carton a week costs more than $1,000 a year
Tobacco companies getting rich off me

Jerome then had an effect and four causes with details to support them. On the basis of this list, he wrote a first draft:

My smoking annoyed other people, making them cough and burning their eyes. I bothered them with my smoker's breath. Nonsmokers usually hate the smell of cigarettes and I got embarrassed when nonsmokers visited my house. I saw them wrinkle their noses in disgust at the smell. It is a messy habit. My house was full of loaded ashtrays that the kids were always knocking over. My car was messy too. A guy from work, Marco, who has smoked for years, is in the hospital now with lung cancer. It doesn't look like he's going to make it. Secondhand smoke is bad for people too and

I worried it would hurt my wife and kids. Also I realized I was coughing once in a while. The price of cigarettes keeps going up and I was spending too much on smokes. When I see things in the paper about tobacco companies and their huge profits it made me mad.

Development through Revising

The next day, Jerome traded first drafts with his classmate Roger. This is what Roger had to say about Jerome's work:

> The biggest criticism I have is that you haven't used many transitions to tie your sentences together. Without them, the paragraph sounds like a list, not a unified piece of writing.
>
> Is one of your reasons more important than the others? If so, it would be good if you indicated that.
>
> You could add a little more detail in several places. For instance, how could secondhand smoke hurt your family? And how much were you spending on cigarettes?

As Jerome read his own paper, he realized he wanted to add one more reason to his paragraph: the inconvenience to himself. "Maybe it sounds silly to write about always getting drinks and going to the bathroom, but that's one of the ways that smoking takes over your life that you never think about when you start," he said. Using Roger's comments and his own new idea, he produced the paragraph that appears on page 196.

Writing a Cause-and-Effect Paragraph

■ Writing Assignment 1

Choose one of the three topic sentences and brief outlines below. Each is made up of three supporting points (causes or effects). Your task is to turn the topic sentence and outline into a cause or effect paragraph.

Option 1

Topic sentence: There are several reasons why some high school graduates are unable to read.

(1) Failure of parents (*cause*)

(2) Failure of schools (*cause*)

(3) Failure of students themselves (*cause*)

Option 2

Topic sentence: Attending college has changed my personality in positive ways.

(1) More confident (*effect*)

(2) More knowledgeable (*effect*)

(3) More adventurous (*effect*)

Option 3

Topic sentence: Living with roommates (or family) makes attending college difficult.

(1) Late-night hours (*cause*)

(2) More temptations to cut class (*cause*)

(3) More distractions from studying (*cause*)

Prewriting

a After you've chosen the option that appeals to you most, jot down all the details you can think of that might go under each of the supporting points. Use separate paper for your lists. Don't worry yet about whether you can use all the items— your goal is to generate more material than you need. Here, for example, are some of the details generated by the author of "New Puppy in the House" to back up her supporting points:

Topic sentence: Having a new puppy disrupts a household.

1. Keeps family awake
   a. Whines at night
   b. Howls
   c. Loss of sleep
2. Destroys possessions
   a. Chews belts and shoes
   b. Chews furniture
   c. Tears up toys it's supposed to fetch
3. Has accidents in house
   a. Misses paper
   b. Disgusting clean-up
   c. Makes house smell bad
4. Causes arguments
   a. Arguments about walking dog
   b. Arguments about feeding dog
   c. Arguments about who gets to play with dog
   d. Arguments about vet bills

b Now go through the details you have generated and decide which are most effective. Strike out the ones you decide are not worth using. Do other details occur to you? If so, jot them down as well.

c Now you are ready to write your paragraph. Begin the paragraph with the topic sentence you chose. Make sure to develop each of the supporting points from the outline into a complete sentence, and then back it up with the best of the details you have generated.

Revising

Review your paragraph with these questions in mind:

- Have I begun the paragraph with the topic sentence provided?
- Is each supporting point stated in a complete sentence?
- Have I provided effective details to back up each supporting point?
- Have I used transitions such as *in addition, another thing,* and *also* to make the relationships between the sentences clear?
- Have I proofread the paragraph for sentence skills errors, including spelling?

Revise your paragraph until you are sure the answer to each question is "yes."

■ Writing Assignment 2

Most of us find it easy to criticize other people, but we may find it harder to give compliments. In this assignment, you will be asked to write a one-paragraph letter praising someone. The letter may be to a person you know (for instance, a parent, relative, or friend); to a public figure (an actor, politician, religious leader, sports star, and so on); or to a company or organization (for example, the people who manufactured a product you own, a newspaper, a government agency, or a store where you shop).

Prewriting

a The fact that you are writing this letter indicates that its recipient has had an *effect* on you: you like, admire, or appreciate the person or organization. Your job will be to put into words the *causes*, or reasons, for this good feeling. Begin by making a list of reasons for your admiration. Here, for example, are a few reasons a person might praise an automobile manufacturer:

My car is dependable.

The price was reasonable.

I received prompt action on a complaint.

The car is well-designed.

The car dealer was honest and friendly.

The car has needed little maintenance.

Reasons for admiring a parent might include these:

You are patient with me.

You are fair.

You have a great sense of humor.

You encourage me in several ways.

I know you have made sacrifices for me.

Develop your own list of reasons for admiring the person or organization you've chosen.

b Now that you have a list of reasons, you need details to back up each reason. Jot down as many supporting details as you can for each reason. Here is what the writer of a letter to the car manufacturer might do:

My car is dependable.
Started during last winter's coldest days when neighbors' cars wouldn't start
Has never stranded me anywhere

The price was reasonable.
Compared with other cars in its class, it cost less
Came standard with more options than other cars of the same price

I received prompt action on a complaint.
When I complained about rattle in door, manufacturer arranged for
a part to be replaced at no charge

The car is well-designed.
Controls are easy to reach
Dashboard gauges are easy to read

The car dealer was honest and friendly.
No pressure, no fake "special deal only today" prices

The car has needed little maintenance.
Haven't done anything but regular tune-ups and oil changes

c Next, select from your list the three or four reasons that you can best support with effective details. These will make up the body of your letter.

d For your topic sentence, make the positive statement you wish to support. For example, the writer of the letter to the car manufacturer might begin like this: "I am a very satisfied owner of a 1998 Meteor."

e Now combine your topic sentence, reasons, and supporting details, and write a draft of your letter.

Revising

If possible, put your letter aside for a day. Then read it aloud to a friend. As you and he or she listen to your words, you should both keep these questions in mind:

- Is my topic sentence a positive statement that is supported by the details?
- Do I clearly state several different reasons why I like or admire the person or organization I'm writing to?
- Do I support each of those reasons with specific evidence?
- Have I linked my sentences together with transitional words and phrases?
- Is my letter free of sentence-skills mistakes, including spelling errors?

Continue revising your work until you and your reader can answer "yes" to all these questions.

■ Writing Assignment 3

What do you do to keep yourself well and fit? Do you eat or avoid certain foods? Do you exercise? Write a paragraph explaining in detail one or more healthy habits you've adopted and the results each has had. For instance, if you jog several times a week, tell where and when you jog and for how long, and then explain what you think are the effects. Give specific examples and descriptive details from your experience to illustrate each effect. Below are a couple of sample topic sentences for this assignment.

> Adding a few hours of jogging to my weekly schedule has had several very positive effects.
>
> The discipline I have used over the past year to stick to a healthy diet has had some good results.

Feel free to use a tongue-in-cheek approach. For example, you might want to use a topic sentence like the following:

> I have managed to avoid becoming overly thin and muscular by giving up all exercise and including plenty of chocolate in my diet.

Even with humor, however, you must support your topic sentence with specific details. For instance, one supporting detail for the above topic sentence might be the point that giving up exercise leaves you plenty of time for homework in your health sciences class.

■ Writing Assignment 4

Investigate the reasons behind a current news event. For example, you may want to discover the causes of one of the following:

> A labor strike or some other protest
>
> A military action by our or some other government
>
> A murder or some other act of violence
>
> A tax increase
>
> A traffic accident, a fire, a plane crash, or some other disastrous event

Research the reasons for the event by reading current newspapers (especially big-city dailies that are covering the story in detail), reading weekly newsmagazines (such as *Time* and *Newsweek*), watching television shows and specials, or consulting an Internet news source.

Decide on the major cause or causes of the event and their specific effects. Then write a paragraph explaining in detail the causes and effects. Below is a sample topic sentence for this assignment.

> The rape and murder that occurred recently on X Street have caused much fear and caution throughout the neighborhood.

Note how this topic sentence uses general words (*fear, caution*) that can summarize specific supporting details. Support for the word *caution,* for example, might include specific ways in which people in the neighborhood are doing a better job of protecting themselves.

■ Writing Assignment 5

Option 1:   Assume that there has been an alarming increase in drug abuse among the students at the high school you attended. What might be the causes of this increase? Spend some time thinking and freewriting about several possible causes. Then, as a concerned member of the community, write a letter to the high school guidance counselor explaining the reasons for the increased drug abuse. Your purpose is to provide information the counselor may be able to use in dealing with the problem.

Option 2:   Your roommate has been complaining that it's impossible to succeed in Mr. X's class because the class is too stressful. You volunteer to attend the class and see for yourself. Afterward, you decide to write a letter to the instructor calling attention to the stressful conditions and suggesting concrete ways to deal with them. Write this letter, explaining in detail the causes and effects of stress in the class.

11 Comparing or Contrasting

Comparison and contrast are two everyday thought processes. When we *compare* two things, we show how they are similar; when we *contrast* two things, we show how they are different. We might compare or contrast two brand-name products (for example, Nike versus Adidas running shoes), two television shows, two instructors, two jobs, two friends, or two courses of action we could take in a given situation. The purpose of comparing or contrasting is to understand each of the two things more clearly and, at times, to make judgments about them.

In this section, you will be asked to write a paper of comparison or contrast. First, however, you must learn the two common methods of developing a comparison or contrast paragraph. Read the two paragraphs that follow and try to explain the difference in the two methods of development.

Paragraphs to Consider

My Senior Prom

[1]My senior prom was nothing like what I expected it to be. [2]From the start of my senior year, I had pictured getting dressed in a sleek silvery slip dress that my aunt would make and that would cost $200 in any store. [3]No one else would have a gown as attractive as mine. [4]I imagined my boyfriend coming to the door with a lovely deep-red corsage, and I pictured myself happily inhaling its perfume all evening long. [5]I saw us setting off for the evening in his brother's 2000 BMW convertible. [6]We would make a flourish as we swept in and out of a series of parties before the prom. [7]Our evening would be capped by a delicious shrimp dinner at the prom and by dancing close together into the early morning hours. [8]The prom was held on May 15, 2000, at the Pony Club on Black Horse Pike. [9]However, because of sickness in her family, my aunt had no time to finish my gown and I had to buy an ugly pink one off the discount rack at the last minute. [10]My corsage of red roses looked terrible on my pink gown, and I do not remember its having any scent. [11]My boyfriend's brother was out of town, and I stepped outside and saw the stripped-down Chevy that he used at the races on weekends. [12]We went to one party where I drank a lot of wine that made me sleepy and upset my stomach. [13]After we arrived at the prom, I did not have much more to eat than a roll and some celery sticks. [14]Worst of all, we left early without dancing because my boyfriend and I had had a fight several days before, and at the time we did not really want to be with each other.

205

Day versus Evening Students

¹As a part-time college student who has taken both day and evening courses, I have observed notable differences between day and evening students. ²First of all, day and evening students differ greatly in age, styles, and interests. ³The students in my daytime classes are all about the same age, with similar clothing styles and similar interests. ⁴Most are in their late teens to early twenties, and whether male or female, they pretty much dress alike. ⁵Their uniform consists of jeans, a T-shirt, running shoes, a baseball cap, and maybe a gold earring or two. ⁶They use the same popular slang, talk about the same movies and TV shows, and know the same musical artists. ⁷But students in my evening courses are much more diverse. ⁸Some are in their late teens, but most range from young married people in their twenties and thirties to people my grandparents' age. ⁹Generally, their clothing is more formal than the day students'. ¹⁰They are dressed for the workplace, not for a typical college classroom. ¹¹Many of the women wear skirts or dresses; the men often wear dress shirts or sweaters. ¹²And they are more comfortable talking about their mortgages or work schedules or child care than about what was on TV last night. ¹³Day and evening students also have very different responsibilities. ¹⁴For day students, college and a part-time job are generally the only major responsibilities. ¹⁵They have plenty of time to study and get assignments done. ¹⁶However, evening students lead much more complicated lives than most day students. ¹⁷They may come to campus after putting in a nine-to-five day at work. ¹⁸Most have children to raise or grandchildren to baby-sit for. ¹⁹When they miss a class or hand in an assignment late, it's usually because of a real problem, such as a sick child or an important deadline at work. ²⁰Finally, day and evening students definitely have different attitudes toward school. ²¹Day students often seem more interested in the view out the window or the cute classmate in the next row than in what the instructor is saying. ²²They doze, draw cartoons, whisper, and write notes instead of paying attention. ²³Evening students sit up straight, listen hard, and ask the instructor lots of questions. ²⁴They obviously are there to learn, and they don't want their time wasted. ²⁵In short, day students and night students are as different as . . . day and night.

Complete this comment: The difference in the methods of contrast in the two paragraphs is that

_____

_____

_____

Compare your answer with the following explanation of the two methods of development used in comparison or contrast paragraphs.

Methods of Development

There are two common methods, or formats, of development in a comparison or contrast paper. One format presents the details *one side at a time*. The other presents the details *point by point*. Each format is explained below.

One Side at a Time

Look at the outline of "My Senior Prom":

Topic sentence: My senior prom was nothing like what I had expected it to be.

A. Expectations (<u>first half of paper</u>)
   1. Dress (expensive, silver)
   2. Corsage (deep red, fragrant)
   3. Car (BMW convertible)
   4. Parties (many)
   5. Dinner (shrimp)
   6. Dancing (all night)
B. Reality (<u>second half of paper</u>)
   1. Dress (cheap, pink)
   2. Corsage (wrong color, no scent)
   3. Car (stripped-down Chevy)
   4. Parties (only one)
   5. Dinner (roll and celery)
   6. Dancing (none because of quarrel)

When you use the one-side-at-a-time method, follow the same order of points of contrast or comparison for each side, as in the outline above. For example, both the first half of the paper and the second half begin with the topic of what dress would be worn. Then both sides go on to the corsage, the car, and so on.

Point by Point

Now look at the outline of "Day versus Evening Students":

Topic sentence: There are notable differences between day and night students.

A. Age and related interests and tastes in clothing
   1. Youthful nature of day students
   2. Older nature of evening students
B. Amount of responsibilities
   1. Lighter responsibilities of day students
   2. Heavier responsibilities of evening students

C. Attitude toward school
    1. Casual attitude of day students
    2. Serious attitude of evening students

The outline shows how the two kinds of students are contrasted point by point. First, the writer contrasts the ages, clothing styles, and interests of the young day-time students and the older evening students. Next, the writer contrasts the limited responsibilities of the daytime students with the heavier responsibilities of the evening students. Finally, the writer contrasts the casual attitude toward school of the daytime students and the serious attitude of the evening students.

When you begin a comparison or contrast paper, you should decide right away which format you are going to use: one side at a time or point by point. An outline is an essential step in helping you decide which format will be more workable for your topic. Keep in mind, however, that an outline is just a guide, not a permanent commitment. If you later feel that you've chosen the wrong format, you can reshape your outline to the other format.

Activity

Complete the partial outlines provided for the two paragraphs that follow.

1.

How My Parents' Divorce Changed Me

In the three years since my parents' divorce, I have changed from a spoiled brat to a reasonably normal college student. Before the divorce, I expected my mother to wait on me. She did my laundry, cooked and cleaned up after meals, and even straightened up my room. My only response was to complain if the meat was too well done or if the sweater I wanted to wear was not clean. In addition, I expected money for anything I wanted. Whether it was a portable CD player or my own pager, I expected Mom to hand over the money. If she refused, I would get it from Dad. However, he left when I was fifteen, and things changed. When Mom got a full-time job to support us, I was the one with the free time to do housework. Now, I did the laundry, started the dinner, and cleaned not only my own room but also the rest of the house. Also, I no longer asked her for money, since I knew there was none to spare. Instead, I got a part-time job on weekends to earn my own spending money. Today, I have my own car that I am paying for, and I am putting myself through college. Things have been hard sometimes, but I am glad not to be that spoiled kid any more.

Topic sentence: In the three years since my parents' divorce, I have changed from a spoiled brat to a reasonably normal college student.

   a. Before the divorce

      (1) _____

      (2) _____

   b. After the divorce

      (1) _____

      (2) _____

Complete the following statement: Paragraph 1 uses the _____
method of development.

  2.   **Good and Bad Horror Movies**

     A good horror movie is easily distinguishable from a bad one. A good horror movie, first of all, has both male and female victims. Both sexes suffer terrible fates at the hands of monsters and maniacs. Therefore, everyone in the audience has a chance to identify with the victim. Bad horror movies, on the other hand, tend to concentrate on women, especially half-dressed ones. These movies are obviously prejudiced against half the human race. Second, a good horror movie inspires compassion for its characters. For example, the audience will feel sympathy for the victims in the horror classics about the Wolfman, played by Lon Chaney, Jr., and also for the Wolfman himself, who is shown to be a sad victim of fate. In contrast, a bad horror movie encourages feelings of aggression and violence in viewers. For instance, in the Halloween films, the murders are seen from the murderer's point of view. The effect is that the audience stalks the victims along with the killer and feels the same thrill he does. Finally, every good horror movie has a sense of humor. In <u>Alien</u>, as a crew member is coughing and choking just before the horrible thing bursts out of his chest, a colleague chides him, "The food ain't <u>that</u> bad, man." Humor provides relief from the horror and makes the characters more human. A bad horror movie, though, is humorless and boring. One murder is piled on top of another, and the characters are just cardboard figures. Bad horror movies may provide cheap thrills, but the good ones touch our emotions and live forever.

Topic sentence: A good horror movie is easily distinguished from a bad one.

   a. Kinds of victims

      (1) _____

      (2) _____

b.   Effect on audience

  (1) _____

  (2) _____

c.   Tone

  (1) _____

  (2) _____

Complete the following statement: Paragraph 1 uses the _____
method of development.

Additional Paragraphs to Consider

Read these additional paragraphs of comparison or contrast and then answer the
questions that follow.

My Broken Dream

¹When I became a police officer in my town, the job was not as I had
dreamed it would be. ²I began to dream about being a police officer at
about age ten. ³I could picture myself wearing a handsome blue uniform
with an impressive-looking badge on my chest. ⁴I could also picture myself
driving a powerful patrol car through town and seeing everyone stare at
me with envy. ⁵But most of all, I dreamed of wearing a gun and using all
the equipment that "TV cops" use. ⁶I just knew everyone would be proud
of me. ⁷I could almost hear the guys on the block saying, "Boy, Steve made
it big. ⁸Did you hear he's a cop?" ⁹I dreamed of leading an exciting life,
solving big crimes, and meeting lots of people. ¹⁰I just knew that if I became
a cop, everyone in town would look up to me. ¹¹However, when I actually
did become a police officer, I soon found out that the reality was different.
¹²My first disappointment came when I was sworn in and handed a well-
used, baggy uniform. ¹³My disappointment continued when I was given
a badge that looked like something pulled out of a Cracker Jack box.
¹⁴I was assigned a beat-up old junker and told that it would be my patrol
car. ¹⁵It had a striking resemblance to a car that had lost in a demolition
derby at a stock-car raceway. ¹⁶Disappointment seemed to continue.
¹⁷I soon found out that I was not the envy of all my friends. ¹⁸When I drove
through town, they acted as if they had not seen me, despite the gun and
nightstick at my side. ¹⁹I was told I was crazy doing this kind of job by
people I thought would look up to me. ²⁰My job was not as exciting as

I had dreamed it would be, either. [21]Instead of solving robberies and murders every day, I found that I spent a great deal of time comforting a local resident because a neighborhood dog had watered his favorite bush.

Two Views on Toys

[1]Children and adults have very different preferences. [2]First, there is the matter of taste. [3]Adults pride themselves on taste, while children ignore the matter of taste in favor of things that are fun. [4]Adults, especially grandparents, pick out tasteful toys that go unused, while children love the cheap playthings advertised on television. [5]Second, of course, there is the matter of money. [6]The new games on the market today are a case in point. [7]Have you ever tried to lure a child away from some expensive game in order to get him or her to play with an old-fashioned game or toy? [8]Finally, there is a difference between an adult's and a child's idea of what is educational. [9]Adults, filled with memories of their own childhood, tend to be fond of the written word. [10]Today's children, on the other hand, concentrate on anything electronic. [11]These things mean much more to them than to adults. [12]Next holiday season, examine the toys that adults choose for children. [13]Then look at the toys the children prefer. [14]You will see the difference.

Mike and Helen

[1]Like his wife, Helen, Mike has a good sense of humor. [2]Also, they are both short, dark-haired, and slightly pudgy. [3]Unlike Helen, Mike tends to hold a grudge. [4]He is slow to forget a cruel remark, a careless joke, or an unfriendly slight. [5]Mike enjoys swimming, camping, and tennis, but Helen is an indoor type. [6]Both Mike and Helen can be charming when they want to be, and they seem to handle small crises in a calm, cool way. [7]A problem such as an overflowing washer, a stalled car, or a sick child is not a cause for panic; they seem to take such events in stride. [8]In contrast to Helen, though, Mike tends to be disorganized. [9]He is late for appointments and unable to keep important documents—bank records, receipts, and insurance papers—where he can find them.

■ Questions

About Unity

1. Which paragraph lacks a topic sentence?

_____

2. Which paragraph has a topic sentence that is too broad?

_____

About Support

3. Which paragraph contains almost no specific details?

_____

4. Which paragraph provides the most complete support?

_____

About Coherence

5. What method of development (one side at a time or point by point) is used in "My Broken Dream"?

_____

In "Two Views in Toys"?

_____

6. Which paragraph offers specific details but lacks a clear, consistent method of development?

_____

Developing a Comparison or Contrast Paragraph

Development through Prewriting

Gayle, the author of "My Senior Prom," had little trouble thinking of a topic for her comparison or contrast paragraph.

"My instructor said, 'You might compare or contrast two individuals, jobs you've had, or places you've lived,'" Gayle said. "Then he added, 'Or you might compare or contrast your expectations of a situation with the reality.' I immediately thought of my prom—boy, were my expectations different from the reality! I had thought it would be the high point of my senior year, but instead it was a total disaster."

Because she is a person who likes to think visually, Gayle started her preparations for her paragraph by clustering. She found this a helpful way to "see" the relationships between the points she was developing. Her diagram looked like this:

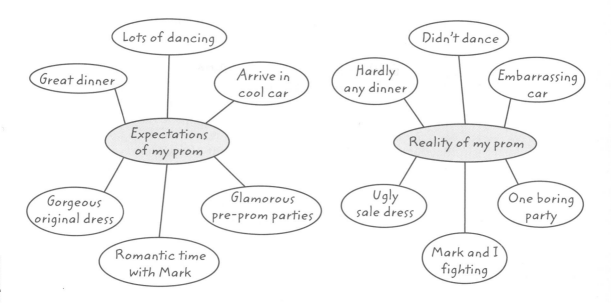

Taking a detail first from the "Expectations" part of the diagram, then one from the "Reality" portion, then another from "Expectations," and so on, Gayle began to write her paragraph using a point-by-point format:

> My senior prom was nothing like what I expected. First of all, I expected to be wearing a beautiful dress that my aunt would make for me. But because she couldn't finish it in time, I had to buy an ugly one at the last minute. Second, I thought I'd have a wonderful romantic evening with my boyfriend. But we'd been fighting that week and by the time the prom came around we were barely speaking. I thought we'd have a great time stopping in at lots of parties before the prom, but we went to only one and I left with an upset stomach.

Gayle stopped here, because she wasn't satisfied with the way the paragraph was developing. "I wanted the reader to picture the way I had imagined my prom, and I didn't like interrupting that picture with the reality of the evening. So I decided to try the one-side-at-a-time approach instead." Here is Gayle's first draft:

> My senior prom was nothing like what I expected. I imagined myself wearing a beautiful, expensive-looking dress that my aunt would make. I thought my boyfriend and I would have a wonderful romantic evening together. We'd dance all through the night and we would cruise around

in my boyfriend's brother's hot car. We would stop in at a lot of fun pre-prom parties, I thought, and we'd have a delicious shrimp dinner at the prom itself. But instead my uncle had a gall-bladder attack that they thought might be a heart attack and my aunt went to the hospital with him instead of finishing my dress. I had to go to the mall at the last minute and buy an ugly dress that nobody else had wanted off the sale rack. Mark and I had been fighting all week. Because he's in track and has a part-time job too we don't have much time together and still he wants to go out on Saturdays with his guy friends. So by the night of the prom we were hardly speaking to each other. We went to only one party before the prom and I left it feeling sick. And the restaurant was so crowded and noisy that I hardly got anything to eat. Because we were angry at each other, we didn't dance at all. And instead of his brother's luxury car, we had to use a stripped-down racing car.

Development through Revising

Gayle's instructor reviewed the first drafts of students who wanted his feedback. Here are his comments on Gayle's work:

> All this is very promising, but some of your details are out of order—for example, you mention the pre-prom parties after the dance itself. Be sure to follow the evening's sequence of events.
>
> More descriptive details are needed! For instance, what was your "beautiful" dress supposed to look like, and what did the "ugly" one you ended up with look like?
>
> You include some unnecessary information: for example, the details of your uncle's illness. Everything in your paragraph should support your topic sentence.

Taking her instructor's suggestions (and remembering a few more details she wanted to include), Gayle wrote the version of her paragraph that appears on page 205.

Writing a Comparison or Contrast Paragraph

■ Writing Assignment 1

Write a comparison or contrast paragraph on one of the topics below:

Two holidays	Two jobs
Two instructors	Two characters in the same movie or TV show
Two children	
Two kinds of eaters	Two homes
Two drivers	Two neighborhoods
Two coworkers	Two cartoon strips
Two members of a team (or two teams)	Two cars
	Two friends
Two singers or groups	Two crises
Two pets	Two bosses or supervisors
Two parties	Two magazines

Prewriting

a Choose your topic, the two subjects you will write about.

b Decide whether your paragraph will *compare* the two subjects (discuss their similarities) or *contrast* them (discuss their differences). Students most often choose to write about differences. For example, you might write about how a musical group you enjoy differs from a musical group you dislike. You might discuss important differences between two employers you have had or between two neighborhoods you've lived in. You might contrast a job you've had in a car factory with a white-collar job you've had as a receptionist.

c Write a direct topic sentence for your paragraph. Here's an example: "My job in a car-parts factory was very different from my job as a receptionist."

d Come up with at least three strong points to support your topic sentence. If you are contrasting two jobs, for example, your points might be that they differed greatly (1) in their physical setting, (2) in the skills they required, and (3) in the people they brought you into contact with.

e Use your topic sentence and supporting points to create a scratch outline for your paragraph. For the jobs paragraph, the outline would look like this:

Topic sentence: My job in a car-parts factory was very different from my job as a receptionist.

1. The jobs differed in physical setting.
2. The jobs differed in the skills they required.
3. The jobs differed in the people they brought me into contact with.

f   Under each of your supporting points, jot down as many details as occur to you. Don't worry yet about whether the details all fit perfectly or whether you will be able to use them all. Your goal is to generate a wealth of material to draw on. An example:

<u>Topic sentence:</u> My job in a car-parts factory was very different from my job as a receptionist.

1.   <u>The jobs differed in physical setting.</u>
Factory loud and dirty
Office clean and quiet
Factory full of machines, hunks of metal, tools
Office full of desks, files, computers
Factory smelled of motor oil
Office smelled of new carpet
Windows in factory too high and grimy to look out of
Office had clean windows onto street

2.   <u>The jobs differed in the skills and behavior they required.</u>
Factory required physical strength
Office required mental activity
Didn't need to be polite in factory
Had to be polite in office
Didn't need to think much for self in factory
Constantly had to make decisions in office

3.   <u>The jobs differed in the people they brought me into contact with.</u>
In factory, worked with same crew every day
In office, saw constant stream of new customers
Most coworkers in factory had high-school education or less
Many coworkers and clients in office well educated
Coworkers in factory spoke variety of languages
Rarely heard anything but English in office

g   Decide which format you will use to develop your paragraph: one side at a time or point by point. Either is acceptable; it is up to you to decide which you prefer. The important thing is to be consistent: whichever format you choose, be sure to use it throughout the entire paragraph.

h   Write the first draft of your paragraph.

Revising

Put your writing away for a day or so. You will return to it with a fresh perspective and a better ability to critique what you have done.

Reread your work with these questions in mind:

- Does my topic sentence make it clear what two things I am comparing or contrasting?
- Have I compared or contrasted the subjects in at least three important ways?
- Have I provided specific details that effectively back up my supporting points?
- If I have chosen the point-by-point format, have I consistently discussed a point about one subject, then immediately discussed the same point about the other subject before moving on to the next point?
- If I have chosen the one-side-at-a-time format, have I discussed every point about one of my subjects, then discussed the same points *in the same order* about the second subject?
- Have I used appropriate transitions, such as *first*, *in addition*, *also*, and *another way*, to help the reader follow my train of thought?
- Have I carefully proofread my paragraph, using the list on the inside front cover of the book, and corrected all sentence-skills mistakes, including spelling?

Continue revising your work until you can answer "yes" to all these questions.

■ Writing Assignment 2

Write a paragraph in which you compare or contrast your life in the real world with your life in an imagined "perfect world." Your paragraph may be humorous or serious.

Prewriting

a   As your "real life" and "ideal life" are too broad for a paragraph, decide on three specific areas to focus on. You might select from any of the areas below, or others you think of yourself.

Work

Money

Romance

Physical location

Personal appearance

Friends

Possessions

Housing

Talents

b Write the name of one of your three areas (for example, "Work"), across the top of a page. Divide the page into two columns. Label one column "real world" and the other "perfect world." Under "real world," write down as many details as you can think of describing your real-life work situation. Under "perfect world," write down details describing what your perfect work life would be like. Repeat the process on separate pages for your other two major areas.

c Write a topic sentence for your paragraph. Here's an example: "In my perfect world, my life would be quite different in the areas of work, money, and housing."

d Decide which approach you will take: one side at a time or point by point.

e Write a scratch outline that reflects the format you have selected. The outline for a point-by-point format would look like this:

Topic sentence: In my perfect world, my life would be quite different in the areas of work, money, and housing.

1. Work
    a. Real-life work
    b. Perfect-world work
2. Money
    a. Real-life money
    b. Perfect-world money
3. Housing
    a. Real-life housing
    b. Perfect-world housing

The outline for a one-side-at-a-time format would look like this:

Topic sentence: In my perfect world, my life would be quite different in the areas of work, money, and housing.

1. Real life
    a. Work
    b. Money
    c. Housing
2. Perfect world
    a. Work
    b. Money
    c. Housing

f Drawing from the three pages of details you generated in step *b*, complete your outline by jotting down your strongest supporting details for each point.

g Write the first draft of your paragraph.

Revising

Reread your paragraph, and then show it to a friend who will give you honest feedback. You should both review it with these questions in mind:

- Does the topic sentence make it clear what three areas of life are being compared or contrasted?
- Does the paragraph follow a consistent format: point by point or one side at a time?
- Does the paragraph provide specific details that describe both the "real life" situation and the "perfect world" situation?
- Does the paragraph include transitional words and phrases that make it easy to follow?
- Have all sentence-skills mistakes, including spelling, been corrected?

Continue revising your work until you and your reader can answer "yes" to all these questions.

■ Writing Assignment 3

Write a contrast paragraph on one of the fifteen topics below.

Neighborhood stores versus a shopping mall

Driving on an expressway versus driving on country roads

People versus *Us* (or any other two popular magazines)

Camping in a tent versus camping in a recreational vehicle

Working parents versus stay-at-home parents

Shopping at a department store versus shopping on the Internet

A used car versus a new one

Recorded music versus live music

PG-rated movies versus R-rated movies

News in a newspaper versus news on television or on the Internet

Yesterday's toys versus today's toys

Fresh food versus canned or frozen food

The locker room of a winning team after a game versus the locker room of a losing team

An ad on television versus an ad for the same product in a magazine

Amateur sports teams versus professional teams

Follow the directions for prewriting and rewriting given in Writing Assignment 2.

■ Writing Assignment 4

Television talk shows share certain features, but they also differ in significant ways. Write a paragraph contrasting two talk shows. In preparation, watch two different talk shows, taking notes on various aspects of the shows. Then arrange the details of your notes into a few categories, such as the performance of the hosts, the types of guests, and the behavior of their audiences. Use your notes to help you decide on a point of view to take in your topic sentence, which might be similar to this one:

> While *(fill in the name of show 1)* _____ aims to help its viewers, *(fill in the name of show 2)* _____ is more interested in satisfying viewers' desire for dramatic conflict.

Once you decide on your topic sentence, use only those details that support it. Then decide which method of organization you will use, and prepare a brief outline. Be sure to use transition words and to edit the next-to-final draft carefully.

■ Writing Assignment 5

Imagine that you are living in an apartment building in which new tenants are making life unpleasant for you. Write a letter of complaint to your landlord comparing and contrasting life before and after the tenants arrived. You might want to focus on one or more of the following:

Noise

Trash

Safety hazards

Parking situation

12 Defining a Term

In talking with other people, we sometimes offer informal definitions to explain just what we mean by a particular term. Suppose, for example, we say to a friend, "Karen can be so clingy." We might then expand on our idea of "clingy" by saying, "You know, a clingy person needs to be with someone every single minute. If Karen's best friend makes plans that don't include her, she becomes hurt. And when she dates someone, she calls him several times a day and gets upset if he even goes to the grocery store without her. She hangs on to people way too tightly." In a written definition, we make clear in a more complete and formal way our own personal understanding of a term. Such a definition typically starts with one meaning of a term. The meaning is then illustrated with a series of examples or a story.

In this section, you will be asked to write a paragraph that begins with a one-sentence definition; that sentence will be the topic sentence. The three student papers below are all examples of definition paragraphs. Read them and then answer the questions that follow.

Paragraphs to Consider

Luck

¹Luck is putting $1.75 into a vending machine and getting the money back with your snack. ²It is an instructor's decision to give a retest on a test on which you first scored thirty. ³Luck refers to moments of good fortune that happen in everyday life. ⁴It is not going to the dentist for two years and then going and finding out that you do not have any cavities. ⁵It is calling up a plumber to fix a leak on a day when the plumber has no other work to do. ⁶Luck is finding a used car for sale at a good price at exactly the time when your car rolls its last mile. ⁷It is driving into a traffic bottleneck and choosing the lane that winds up moving most rapidly. ⁸Luck is being late for work on a day when your boss arrives later than you do. ⁹It is having a new checkout aisle at the supermarket open up just as your cart arrives. ¹⁰The best kind of luck is winning a new wide-screen TV on a chance for which you paid only a quarter.

Disillusionment

[1]Disillusionment is the feeling we have when one of our most cherished beliefs is stolen from us. [2]I learned about disillusionment firsthand the day Mr. Keller, our eighth-grade teacher, handed out the grades for our class biology projects. [3]I had worked hard to assemble what I thought was the best insect collection any school had ever seen. [4]For weeks, I had set up homemade traps around our house, in the woods, and in vacant lots. [5]At night, I would stretch a white sheet between two trees, shine a lantern on it, and collect the night-flying insects that gathered there. [6]With my own money, I had bought killing jars, insect pins, gummed labels, and display boxes. [7]I carefully arranged related insects together, with labels listing each scientific name and the place and date of capture. [8]Slowly and painfully, I wrote and typed the report that accompanied my project at the school science fair. [9]In contrast, my friend Eddie did almost nothing for his project. [10]He had his father, a doctor, build an impressive maze complete with live rats and a sign that read, "You are the trainer." [11]A person could lift a little plastic door, send a rat running through the maze, and then hit a button to release a pellet of rat food as a reward. [12]This exhibit turned out to be the most popular one at the fair. [13]I felt sure that our teacher would know that Eddie could not have built it, and I was certain that my hard work would be recognized and rewarded. [14]Then the grades were finally handed out, and I was crushed. [15]Eddie had gotten an A-plus, but my grade was a B. [16]I suddenly realized that honesty and hard work don't always pay off in the end. [17]The idea that life is not fair, that sometimes it pays to cheat, hit me with such force that I felt sick. [18]I will never forget that moment.

A Mickey Mouse Course

[1]A Mickey Mouse course is any college course that is so easy that even Mickey Mouse could achieve an A. [2]A student who is taking a heavy schedule, or who does not want four or five especially difficult courses, will try to sandwich in a Mickey Mouse course. [3]A student can find out about such a course by consulting other students, since word of a genuine Mickey Mouse course spreads like wildfire. [4]Or a student can study the college master schedule for telltale course titles like The Art of Pressing Wildflowers, History of the Comic Book, or Watching Television Creatively. [5]In an advanced course such as microbiology, though, a student had better be prepared to spend a good deal of time during the semester on the course. [6]Students in a Mickey Mouse course can attend classes while half-asleep, hungover, or wearing Walkman earphones or a blindfold; they will still pass. [7]The course exams (if there are any) would not challenge a five-year-old. [8]The course lectures usually consist of information that anyone with common sense knows anyway. [9]Attendance may be required, but

participation or involvement in the class is not. [10]The main requirement for passing is that a student's body is there, warming a seat in the classroom. [11]There are no difficult labs or special projects, and term papers are never mentioned. [12]Once safely registered for such a course, all the students have to do is sit back and watch the credits accumulate on their transcripts.

■ Questions

About Unity

1. Which paragraph places its topic sentence within the paragraph rather than, more appropriately, at the beginning?

   _____

2. Which sentence in "A Mickey Mouse Course" should be omitted in the interest of paragraph unity? *(Write the sentence number here.)* _____

About Support

3. Which two paragraphs develop their definitions through a series of short examples?

   _____

   _____

4. Which paragraph develops its definition through a single extended example?

   _____

About Coherence

5. Which paragraph uses emphatic order, saving its best detail for last?

   _____

6. Which paragraph uses time order to organize its details?

   _____

Developing a Definition Paragraph

Development through Prewriting

When Harry, the author of "Disillusionment," started working on his assignment, he did not know what he wanted to write about. He looked around the house for inspiration. His two-year-old twins racing around the room made him think about defining "energy." The fat cat asleep on a sunny windowsill suggested that he might write about "laziness" or "relaxation." Still not sure of a topic, he looked over his notes from that day's class. His instructor had jotted a list of terms on the blackboard, saying, "Maybe you could focus on what one of these words has meant in your own life." Harry looked over the words he had copied down: *honesty, willpower, faith, betrayal, disillusionment*—"When I got to the word 'disillusionment,' the eighth-grade science fair flashed into my mind," Harry said. "That was a bitter experience that definitely taught me what disillusionment was all about."

Because the science fair had occurred many years before, Harry had to work to remember it well. He decided to try the technique of questioning himself to come up with the details of what had happened. Here are the questions Harry asked himself and the answers he wrote:

<u>When did I learn about disillusionment?</u>
When I was in eighth grade

<u>Where did it happen?</u>
At the school science fair

<u>Who was involved?</u>
Me, Eddie Loomis and his father, and Mr. Keller

<u>What happened?</u>
I had worked very hard on my insect collection. Eddie had done almost nothing but he had a rat maze that his father had built. I got a B on my project while Eddie got an A+.

<u>Why was the experience so disillusioning?</u>
I thought my hard work would be rewarded. I was sure Mr. Keller would recognize that I had put far more effort into my project than Eddie had. When Eddie won, I learned that cheating can pay off and that honest work isn't always rewarded.

<u>How did I react?</u>
I felt sick to my stomach. I wanted to confront Mr. Keller and Eddie and make them see how unfair the grades were. But I knew I'd just look like a poor loser, so I didn't do anything.

<u>On the basis of this experience, how would I define disillusionment?</u>
It's finding out that something you really believed in isn't true.

Drawing from the ideas generated by his self-questioning, Harry wrote the following draft of his paragraph:

Disillusionment is finding out that one of your most important beliefs isn't true. I learned about disillusionment at my eighth-grade science fair. I had worked very hard on my project, an insect collection. I was sure it would get an A. I had worked so hard on it, even spending nights outside making sure it was very good. My friend Eddie also did a project, but he barely worked on his at all. Instead, he had his father build a maze for a rat to run through. The trainer lifted a little plastic door to let the rat into the maze, and if he completed the maze, the trainer could release a pellet of food for it to eat. It was a nice project, but the point is that Eddie hadn't made it. He just made things like the banner that hung over it. Mr. Keller was our science teacher. He gave Eddie an A+ and me just a B. So that really taught me about disillusionment.

Development through Revising

The next day, Harry's teacher divided the class up into groups of three. The groups reviewed each member's paragraph. Harry was grouped with Curtis and Jocelyn. After reading through Harry's paper several times, the group had the following discussion:

"My first reaction is that I want to know more about your project," said Jocelyn. "You give details about Eddie's, but not many about your own. What was so good about it? You need to show us, not just tell us. Also, you said that you worked very hard, but you didn't show us how hard."

"Yeah," said Harry. "I remember my project clearly, but I guess the reader has to know what it was like and how much effort went into it."

Curtis said, "I like your topic sentence, but when I finished the paragraph I wasn't sure what 'important belief' you'd learned wasn't true. What would you say that belief was?"

Harry thought a minute. "I'd believed that honest hard work would always be rewarded. I found out that it doesn't always happen that way, and that cheating can actually win."

Curtis nodded. "I think you need to include that in your paper."

Jocelyn added, "I'd like to read how you felt or reacted after you saw your grade, too. If you don't explain that, the paragraph ends sort of abruptly."

Harry agreed with his classmates' suggestions. After he had gone through several revisions, he produced the version that appears on page 222.

Writing a Definition Paragraph

■ Writing Assignment 1

Write a paragraph that defines the term *TV addict*. Base your paragraph on the topic sentence and three supporting points provided below.

Topic sentence: Television addicts are people who will watch all the programs they can, for as long as they can, without doing anything else.

(1) TV addicts, first of all, will watch anything on the tube, no matter how bad it is. . . .

(2) In addition, addicts watch more hours of TV than normal people do. . . .

(3) Finally, addicts feel that TV is more important than other people or any other activities that might be going on. . . .

Prewriting

a   Generate as many examples as you can for each of the three qualities of a TV addict. You can do this by asking yourself the following questions:

- What are some truly awful shows that I (or TV addicts I know) watch just because the television is turned on?
- What are some examples of the large amounts of time that I (or TV addicts I know) watch television?
- What are some examples of ways that I (or TV addicts I know) neglect people or give up activities in order to watch TV?

Write down every answer you can think of for each question. At this point, don't worry about writing full sentences or even about grammar or spelling. Just get your thoughts down on paper.

b   Look over the list of examples you have generated. Select the strongest examples you have thought of. You should have at least two or three for each quality. If not, ask yourself the questions in step *a* again.

c   Write out the examples you will use, this time expressing them in full, grammatically correct sentences.

d   Start with the topic sentence and three points provided in the assignment. Fill in the examples you've generated to support each point and write a first draft of your paragraph.

Revising

Put your first draft away for a day or so. When you come back to it, reread it critically, asking yourself these questions:

- Have I used the topic sentence and the three supporting points that were provided?
- Have I backed up each supporting point with at least two examples?
- Does each of my examples truly illustrate the point that it backs up?
- Have I used appropriate transitional language (*another, in addition, for example*) to tie my thoughts together?
- Have I proofread my paragraph and corrected any sentence-skills mistakes, including spelling?

Keep revising your paragraph until you can answer "yes" to each question.

■ Writing Assignment 2

Write a paragraph that defines one of the following terms. Each term refers to a certain kind of person.

Know-it-all	Clown	Workaholic
Charmer	Jellyfish	Showoff
Loser	Leader	Control freak
Lazybones	Nerd	Mother hen
Snob	Good neighbor	Toady
Con artist	Optimist	Fusspot
Fair-weather friend	Pessimist	
Good sport	Pack rat	

Prewriting

a Write a topic sentence for your definition paragraph. This is a two-part process:

- *First,* place the term in a class, or category. For example, if you are writing about a certain kind of person, the general category is *person*. If you are describing a type of friend, the general category is *friend*.
- *Second,* describe what you consider the special feature or features that set your term apart from other members of its class. For instance, say what *kind* of person you are writing about or what *type* of friend.

In the following topic sentence, try to identify three things: the term being defined, the class it belongs to, and the special feature that sets the term apart from other members of the class.

A chocoholic is a person who craves chocolate.

The term being defined is *chocoholic*. The category it belongs to is *person*. The words that set *chocoholic* apart from any other person are *craves chocolate*.

Below is another example of a topic sentence for this assignment. It is a definition of *whiner*. The class, or category, is underlined: A whiner is a type of person. The words that set the term *whiner* apart from other members of the class are double-underlined.

A whiner is a <u>person</u> who <u><u>feels wronged by life</u></u>.

In the following sample topic sentences, underline the class and double-underline the special features.

A clotheshorse is a <u>person</u> who <u><u>needs new clothes to be happy</u></u>.
The class clown is a <u>student</u> who <u><u>gets attention through silly behavior</u></u>.
A worrywart is a <u>person</u> who <u><u>sees danger everywhere</u></u>.

b Develop your definition by using one of the following methods:

Examples. Give several examples that support your topic sentence.

Extended example. Use one longer example to support your topic sentence.

Contrast. Support your topic sentence by contrasting what your term *is* with what it is *not*. For instance, you may want to define a *fair-weather friend* by contrasting his or her actions with those of a true friend.

c Once you have created a topic sentence and decided how to develop your paragraph, make a scratch outline. If you are using a contrast method of development, remember to present the details one side at a time or point by point (see page 207).

d Write a first draft of your paragraph.

Revising

As you revise your paragraph, keep these questions in mind:

• Does my topic sentence (1) place my term in a class and (2) name some special features that set it apart from its class?

- Have I made a clear choice to develop my topic sentence through either several examples, one extended example, or contrast?
- If I have chosen to illustrate my topic through contrast, have I consistently followed either a point-by-point or a one-side-at-a-time format?
- Have I used appropriate transitions (*another, in addition, in contrast, for example*) to tie my thoughts together?
- Is my paragraph free of sentence-skills and spelling errors?

Continue revising your work until you can answer "yes" to all these questions.

■ Writing Assignment 3

Write a paragraph that defines one of the abstract terms below.

Arrogance	Family	Persistence
Assertiveness	Fear	Practicality
Class	Freedom	Rebellion
Common sense	Gentleness	Responsibility
Conscience	Innocence	Self-control
Curiosity	Insecurity	Sense of humor
Danger	Jealousy	Shyness
Depression	Nostalgia	Violence
Escape	Obsession	

As a guide in writing your paper, use the suggestions for prewriting and rewriting in Writing Assignment 2. Remember to place your term in a class or category and to describe what *you* feel are the distinguishing features of that term.

After writing your topic sentence, check that it is complete and correct by doing the following:

- Single-underline the category of the term you're defining.
- Double-underline the term's distinguishing characteristic or characteristics.

Here are three sample topic sentences:

Laziness is the trait of resisting all worthwhile work as much as possible.
Jealousy is the feeling of wanting a possession or quality that someone else has.
A family is a group whose members are related to one another in some way.

■ Writing Assignment 4

Since it affects all of us to some degree, *stress* is a useful word to explore. Write a paragraph defining that word. Organize your paragraph in one of the ways listed below:

- Use a series of examples (see page 171) of stress.
- Use narration (see page 257) to provide one longer example of stress: Create a hypothetical person (or use a real person) and show how this person's typical morning or day illustrates your definition of *stress*.

Using strategies described in the chapter on the library and the Internet (pages 311–328), research the topic of stress. Your reading will help you think about how to proceed with the paper.

Hints: Do not simply write a series of general, abstract sentences that repeat and reword your definition. If you concentrate on providing specific support, you will avoid the common trap of getting lost in a maze of generalities.

Make sure your paper is set firmly on the four bases: unity, support, coherence, and sentence skills. Edit the next-to-final draft of the paragraph carefully for sentence-skills errors, including spelling.

■ Writing Assignment 5

Option 1:   Imagine that at the place where you work, one employee has just quit, creating a new job opening. Since you have been working there for a while, your boss has asked you to write a description of the position. That description, a detailed definition of the job, will be sent to employment agencies. These agencies will be responsible for interviewing candidates. Choose any position you know about, and write a paragraph defining it. First state the purpose of the job, and then list its duties and responsibilities. Finally, describe the qualifications for the position. Below is a sample topic sentence for this assignment.

Purchasing-department secretary is a <u>position</u> in which someone <u>provides a variety of services to the purchasing-department managers.</u>

In a paragraph with the topic sentence above, the writer would go on to list and explain the various services the secretary must provide.

Option 2:   Alternatively, imagine that a new worker has been hired, and your boss has asked you to explain "team spirit" to him or her. The purpose of your explanation will be to give the newcomer an idea of the kind of teamwork that is expected in this workplace. Write a paragraph that defines in detail what your boss means by *team spirit*. Use examples or one extended example to illustrate each of your general points about team spirit.

13 Dividing and Classifying

If you were doing the laundry, you might begin by separating the clothing into piles. You would then put all the whites in one pile and all the colors in another. Or you might classify the laundry, not according to color, but according to fabric—putting all cottons in one pile, polyesters in another, and so on. *Classifying* is the process of taking many things and separating them into categories. We generally classify to better manage or understand many things. Librarians classify books into groups (novels, travel, health, etc.) to make them easier to find. A scientist sheds light on the world by classifying all living things into two main groups: animals and plants.

Dividing, in contrast, is taking one thing and breaking it down into parts. We often divide, or analyze, to better understand, teach, or evaluate something. For instance, a tinkerer might take apart a clock to see how it works; a science text might divide a tree into its parts to explain their functions. A music reviewer may analyze the elements of a band's performance—for example, the skill of the various players, rapport with the audience, selections, and so on.

In short, if you are classifying, you are sorting *numbers of things* into categories. If you are dividing, you are breaking *one thing* into parts. It all depends on your purpose—you might classify flowers into various types or divide a single flower into its parts.

In this section, you will be asked to write a paragraph in which you classify a group of things into categories according to a single principle. To prepare for this assignment, first read the paragraphs below, and then work through the questions and the activity that follow.

Paragraphs to Consider

Types of E-Mail

[1]As more and more people take advantage of e-mailing, three categories of e-mail have emerged. [2]One category of e-mail is junk mail. [3]When most people sign on to their computers, they are greeted with a flood of get-rich-quick schemes, invitations to pornographic websites, and ads for a variety of unwanted products. [4]E-mail users quickly become good at hitting the "delete" button to get rid of this garbage. [5]The second category that clogs most people's electronic mailbox is forwarded mail, most

of which also gets deleted without being read. [6]The third and best category of e-mail is genuine personal e-mail from genuine personal friends. [7]Getting such real, thoughtful e-mail can almost make up for the irritation of the other two categories.

Studying for a Test

[1]Phase 1 of studying for a test, often called the "no problem" phase, runs from the day the test is announced to approximately forty-eight hours before the dreaded exam is passed out. [2]During phase 1, the student is carefree, smiling, and kind to helpless animals and small children. [3]When asked by classmates if he or she has studied for the test yet, the reply will be an assured "No problem." [4]During phase 1, no actual studying takes place. [5]Phase 2 is entered two days before the test. [6]For example, if the test is scheduled for 9 A.M. Friday, phase 2 begins at 9 A.M. Wednesday. [7]During phase 2, again, no actual studying takes place. [8]Phase 3, the final phase, is entered twelve hours before "zero hour." [9]This is the cram phase, characterized by sweaty palms, nervous twitches, and confused mental patterns. [10]For a test at nine o'clock on Friday morning, a student begins exhibiting these symptoms at approximately nine o'clock on Thursday night. [11]Phase 3 is also termed the "shock" phase, since the student is shocked to discover the imminence of the exam and the amount of material to be studied. [12]During this phase, the student will probably be unable to sleep and will mumble meaningless phrases like "$a^2 + c^2$." [13]This phase will not end until the exam is over. [14]If the cram session has worked, the student will fall gratefully asleep that night. [15]On waking up, he or she will be ready to go through the whole cycle again with the next test.

Three Kinds of Dogs

[1]A city walker will notice that most dogs fall into one of three categories. [2]First there are the big dogs, which are generally harmless and often downright friendly. [3]They walk along peacefully with their masters, their tongues hanging out and big goofy grins on their faces. [4]Apparently they know they're too big to have anything to worry about, so why not be nice? [5]Second are the spunky medium-sized dogs. [6]When they see a stranger approaching, they go on alert. [7]They prick up their ears, they raise their hackles, and they may growl a little deep in their throats. [8]"I could tear you up," they seem to be saying, "but I won't if you behave yourself." [9]Unless the walker leaps for their master's throat, these dogs usually won't do anything more than threaten. [10]The third category is made up of the shivering neurotic little yappers whose shrill barks could shatter glass and whose needle-like little teeth are eager to sink into a friendly outstretched hand. [11]Walkers always wonder about these dogs—don't they know that anyone who really wanted to could squash them under their feet like bugs?

[12]Apparently not, because of all the dogs a walker meets, these provide the most irritation. [13]Such dogs are only one of the potential hazards that the city walker encounters.

■ Questions

About Unity

1. Which paragraph lacks a topic sentence?

   _____

2. Which sentence in "Three Kinds of Dogs" should be eliminated in the interest of paragraph unity? *(Write the sentence number here.)* _____

About Support

3. Which of the three phases in "Studying for a Test" lacks specific details?

   _____

4. After which sentence in "Types of E-Mail" are supporting details needed? *(Write the sentence number here.)* _____

About Coherence

5. Which paragraph uses emphatic order to organize its details?

   _____

6. Which words in the emphatic-order paragraph signal the most important detail?

   _____

Activity

This activity will sharpen your sense of the classifying process. In each of the ten groups, cross out the one item that has not been classified on the same basis as the other three. Also, indicate in the space provided the single principle of classification used for the remaining three items. Note the examples.

Examples   Water
      a. Cold
      b. ~~Lake~~
      c. Hot
      d. Lukewarm
      Unifying principle:
      Temperature

Household pests
a. ~~Mice~~
b. Ants
c. Roaches
d. Flies
Unifying principle:
Insects

1. Eyes
   a. Blue
   b. Nearsighted
   c. Brown
   d. Hazel
   Unifying principle:

   _____

2. Mattresses
   a. Double
   b. Twin
   c. Queen
   d. Firm
   Unifying principle:

   _____

3. Zoo animals
   a. Flamingo
   b. Peacock
   c. Polar bear
   d. Ostrich
   Unifying principle:

   _____

4. Vacation
   a. Summer
   b. Holiday
   c. Seashore
   d. Weekend
   Unifying principle:

   _____

5. Books
   a. Novels
   b. Biographies
   c. Boring
   d. Short stories
   Unifying principle:

   _____

6. Wallets
   a. Leather
   b. Plastic
   c. Stolen
   d. Fabric
   Unifying principle:

   _____

7. Newspaper
   a. Wrapping garbage
   b. Editorials
   c. Making paper planes
   d. Covering floor while painting
   Unifying principle:

   _____

8. Students
   a. First-year
   b. Transfer
   c. Junior
   d. Sophomore
   Unifying principle:

   _____

9. Exercise
   a. Running
   b. Swimming
   c. Gymnastics
   d. Fatigue
   Unifying principle:

   _____

10. Leftovers
    a. Cold chicken
    b. Feed to dog
    c. Reheat
    d. Use in a stew
    Unifying principle:

    _____

Developing a Division-Classification Paragraph

Development through Prewriting

Marcus walked home from campus to his apartment, thinking about the assignment to write a division-classification paragraph. As he strolled along his familiar route, his observations made him think of several possibilities. "First I thought of writing about the businesses in my neighborhood, dividing them into the ones run by Hispanics, Asians, and African-Americans," he said. "When I stopped in at my favorite coffee shop, I thought about dividing the people who hang out there. There is a group of old men who meet to drink coffee and play cards, and there are students like me, but there didn't seem to be a third category and I wasn't sure two was enough. As I continued walking home, though, I saw Mr. Enriquez and his big golden retriever, and some lady with two nervous little dogs that acted as if they wanted to eat me, and the newsstand guy with his mutt that's always guarding the place, and I thought 'Dogs! I can classify different types of dogs.'"

But how would he classify them? Thinking further, Marcus realized that he thought of dogs as having certain personalities depending on their size. "I know there are exceptions, of course, but since this was going to be a lighthearted, even comical paragraph, I thought it would be OK if I exaggerated a bit." He wrote down his three categories:

Big dogs

Medium-sized dogs

Small dogs

Under each division, then, he wrote down as many characteristics as he could think of:

<u>Big dogs</u>

calm

friendly

good-natured

dumb

lazy

<u>Medium-sized dogs</u>
- spunky
- energetic
- ready to fight
- protective
- friendly if they know you

<u>Small dogs</u>
- nervous
- trembling
- noisy
- yappy
- snappy
- annoying

Marcus then wrote a topic sentence: "Dogs seem to fall into three categories." Using that topic sentence and the scratch outline he'd just produced, he wrote the following paragraph:

> Most dogs seem to fall into one of three categories. First there are the big dumb friendly dogs. They give the impression of being sweet but not real bright. One example of this kind of dog is Lucy. She's a golden retriever belonging to a man in my neighborhood. Lucy goes everywhere with Mr. Enriquez. She doesn't even need a leash but just follows him. Dogs like Lucy never bother anybody. She just lies at Mr. Enriquez's feet when he stops to talk to anyone. The guy who runs the corner newsstand I pass every day has a spunky medium-sized dog. Once the dog knows you he's friendly and even playful. But he's always on the lookout for a stranger who might mean trouble. For a dog who's not very big he can make himself look pretty fierce if he wants to. Then there are my least favorite kind of dogs. Little nervous yappy ones. My aunt used to have a Chihuahua like that. It knew me for nine years and still went crazy shaking and yipping at me every time we met. She loved that dog but I can't imagine why. If I had a dog it would definitely come from category 1 or 2.

Development through Revising

Marcus traded his first draft with a fellow student, Rachel, and asked her to give him feedback. Here are the comments Rachel wrote on his paper:

This is a change in point of view—you haven't been using "you" before.

Is this the beginning of a second category? That's not clear.

Not a complete sentence.

Another change in point of view—you've gone from writing in the third person to "you" to "me."

Most dogs seem to fall into three categories. First there are the big dumb friendly dogs. They give the impression of being sweet but not real bright. One example of this kind of dog is Lucy, a golden retriever belonging to a man in my neighborhood. Lucy goes everywhere with Mr. Enriquez. She doesn't even need a leash but just follows him everywhere. Lucy never bothers you. She just lies at Mr. Enriquez's feet when he stops to talk to anyone. The guy who runs the corner newsstand I pass every day has a spunky medium-sized dog. Once the dog knows you he's friendly and even playful. But he's always on the lookout for a stranger who might mean trouble. For a dog who's not very big he can make himself look pretty fierce if he wants to scare you. Then there are my least favorite kind of dogs. Little nervous yappy ones. My aunt used to have a Chihuahua like that. It knew me for nine years and still went crazy shaking and yipping at me every time we met. She loved that dog but I can't imagine why. If I had a dog it would definitely come from category 1 or 2.

Marcus—I think you need to make your three categories clearer. Your first one is OK—"big dogs," which you say are friendly—but categories 2 and 3 aren't stated as clearly.

It's distracting to have your point of view change from third person to "you" to "me."

Since you're trying to divide and classify all dogs, I'm not sure it's a good idea to talk only about three individual dogs. This way it sounds as if you're just describing those three dogs instead of putting them into three groups.

When Marcus considered Rachel's comments and reread his own paragraph, he agreed with what she had written. "I realized it was too much about three particular dogs and not enough about the categories of dogs," he said. "I decided to revise it and focus on the three classes of dogs."

Marcus then wrote the version that appears on page 232.

Writing a Division-Classification Paragraph

■ Writing Assignment 1

Below are four options to develop into a classification paragraph. Each one presents a topic to classify into three categories. Choose one option to develop into a paragraph.

Option 1

Supermarket shoppers

(1)   Slow, careful shoppers

(2)   Average shoppers

(3)   Hurried shoppers

Option 2

Eaters

(1)   Very conservative eaters

(2)   Typical eaters

(3)   Adventurous eaters

Option 3

Types of housekeepers

(1)   Never clean

(2)   Clean on a regular basis

(3)   Clean constantly

Option 4

Attitudes toward money

(1)   Tightfisted

(2)   Reasonable

(3)   Extravagant

Prewriting

a Begin by doing some freewriting on the topic you have chosen. For five or ten minutes, simply write down everything that comes into your head when you think about "types of housekeepers, "attitudes toward money," or whichever option you choose. Don't worry about grammar, spelling, or organization—just write.

b Now that you've "loosened up your brain" a little, try asking yourself questions about the topic and writing down your answers. If you are writing about supermarket shoppers, for instance, you might ask questions like these:

How do the three kinds of shoppers prepare for their shopping trip?

How many aisles will each kind of shopper visit?

What do the different kinds of shoppers bring along with them—lists, calculators, coupons, etc.?

How long does each type of shopper spend in the store?

Write down whatever answers occur to you for these and other questions. Again, do not worry at this stage about writing correctly. Instead, concentrate on getting down all the information you can think of that supports your three points.

c Reread the material you have accumulated. If some of the details you have written make you think of even better ones, add them. Select the details that best support your three points. Number them in the order you will present them.

d Restate your topic as a grammatically complete topic sentence. For example, if you're writing about eaters, your topic sentence might be "Eaters can be divided into three categories." Turn each of your three supporting points into a full sentence as well.

e Using your topic sentence and three supporting sentences and adding the details you have generated, write the first draft of your paragraph.

Revising

Put away your work for a day or so. Reread it with a critical eye, asking yourself these questions:

- Does my paragraph include a complete topic sentence and three supporting points?
- Have I backed up each supporting point with strong, specific details?
- Does my paragraph hang together in terms of unity, support, and coherence?
- Have I edited my paragraph and corrected sentence-skills mistakes, including spelling errors?

Continue revising your work until you can answer "yes" to all these questions.

■ Writing Assignment 2

Write a classification paragraph on one of the following topics:

Instructors	Drivers
Sports fans	Mothers or fathers
Restaurants	Women's or men's magazines
Attitudes toward life	Presents
Commercials	Neighbors
Employers	Rock, pop, rap, or country singers
Jobs	Houseguests
Bars	Baseball, basketball, football, or hockey players
Family get-togethers	Cars
First dates	

Prewriting

a Classify members of the group you are considering writing about into three categories. Remember: *You must use a single principle of division when you create your three categories.* For example, if your topic is "School courses" and you classify them into easy, moderate, and challenging, your basis for classification is "degree of difficulty." It would not make sense to have as a fourth type "foreign language" (the basis of such a categorization would be "subject matter") or "early morning" (the basis of that classification would be "time of day the classes meet"). You *could* categorize school courses on the basis of subject matter or time of day they meet, for almost any subject can be classified in more than one way. In a single paper, however, you must choose *one* basis for classification and stick to it.

b Once you have a satisfactory three-part division, spend at least five minutes freewriting about each of your three points. Don't be concerned yet with grammar, spelling, or organization. Just write whatever comes into your mind about each of the three points.

c Expand your topic into a fully stated topic sentence.

d At this point, you have all three elements of your paragraph: the topic sentence, the three main points, and the details needed to support each point. Now weave them all together in one paragraph.

Revising

Do not attempt to revise your paragraph right away. Put it away for a while, if possible until the next day. When you reread it, try to be as critical of it as you would be if someone else had written it. As you go over the work, ask yourself these questions:

- Have I divided my topic into three distinct parts?
- Is each of those three parts based on the same principle of division?
- Have I given each of the three parts approximately equal weight? In other words, have I spent about the same amount of time discussing each part?
- Have I provided effective details to back up each of my three points?
- Does my paragraph satisfy the requirements of unity, coherence, and support?
- Have I edited my paragraph for sentence-skills mistakes, including spelling?

Continue revising until you are sure the answer to each question is "yes."

■ Writing Assignment 3

There are many ways you could classify your fellow students. Pick out one of your courses and write a paragraph in which you classify the students in that class according to one underlying principle. You may wish to choose one of the classification principles below.

Attitude toward the class	Punctuality
Participation in the class	Attendance
Method of taking notes in class	Level of confidence
Performance during oral reports, speeches, presentations, lab sessions	

If you decide, for instance, to classify students according to their attitude toward class, you might come up with these three categories:

Students actually interested in learning the material
Students who know they need to learn the material, but don't want to overdo it
Students who find the class a good opportunity to catch up with lost sleep

Of course, you may use any other principle of classification that seems appropriate. Follow the steps listed under "Prewriting" and "Rewriting" for Writing Assignment 2.

■ Writing Assignment 4

Write a review of a restaurant by analyzing its (1) food, (2) service, and (3) atmosphere. For this assignment, you should visit a restaurant, take a notebook with you, and write down observations about such elements as:

Quantity of food you receive	Attitude of the servers
Taste of the food	Efficiency of the servers
Temperature of the food	Decor
Freshness of the ingredients	Level of cleanliness
How the food is presented (garnishes, dishes, and so on)	Noise level and music, if any

Feel free to write about details other than those listed above. Just be sure each detail fits into one of your three categories: food, service, or atmosphere.

For your topic sentence, rate the restaurant by giving it from one to five stars, on the basis of your overall impression. Include the restaurant's name and location in your topic sentence. Here are some examples:

Guido's, an Italian restaurant downtown, deserves three stars.

The McDonald's on Route 70 merits a four-star rating.

The Circle Diner in Westfield barely earns a one-star rating.

■ Writing Assignment 5

Imagine that you are a travel agent and someone has asked you for suggestions for family vacations. Write a paragraph classifying vacations for families into three or more types, for example, vacations in theme parks, in national parks, or in cities. For each type, include an explanation with one or more examples (see page 171).

14 Describing a Scene or Person

When you describe something or someone, you give your readers a picture in words. To make this "word picture" as vivid and real as possible, you must observe and record specific details that appeal to your readers' senses (sight, hearing, taste, smell and touch). More than any other type of writing, a descriptive paragraph needs sharp, colorful details.

Here is a description in which only the sense of sight is used:

A rug covers the living-room floor.

In contrast, here is a description rich in sense impressions:

A thick, reddish-brown shag rug is laid wall to wall across the living-room floor. The long, curled fibers of the shag seem to whisper as you walk through them in your bare feet, and when you squeeze your toes into the deep covering, the soft fibers push back at you with a spongy resilience.

Sense impressions include sight (*thick, reddish-brown shag rug; laid wall to wall; walk through them in your bare feet; squeeze your toes into the deep covering; push back*), hearing (*whisper*), and touch (*bare feet, soft fibers, spongy resilience*). The sharp, vivid images provided by the sensory details give us a clear picture of the rug and enable us to share the writer's experience.

In this section, you will be asked to describe a person, place, or thing for your readers by using words rich in sensory details. To prepare for the assignment, first read the three paragraphs ahead and then answer the questions that follow.

Paragraphs to Consider

My Teenage Son's Room

[1]I push open the door with difficulty. [2]The doorknob is loose and has to be jiggled just right before the catch releases from the doorjamb. [3]Furthermore, as I push at the door, it runs into a basketball shoe lying on the floor. [4]I manage to squeeze in through the narrow opening. [5]I am

immediately aware of a pungent odor in the room, most of which is coming from the closet, to my right. 6That's the location of a white wicker clothes hamper, heaped with grass-stained jeans, sweat-stained T-shirts, and smelly socks. 7But the half-eaten burrito, lying dried and unappetizing on the bedside table across the room, contributes a bit of aroma, as does the glass of curdled sour milk sitting on the sunny windowsill. 8To my left, the small wire cage on Greg's desk is also fragrant, but pleasantly. 9From its nest of sweet-smelling cedar chips, the gerbil peers out at me with its bright eyes, its tiny claws scratching against the cage wall. 10The floor around the wastebasket that is next to the desk is surrounded by what appears to be a sprinkling of snowballs. 11They're actually old wadded-up school papers, and I can picture Greg sitting on his bed, crushing them into balls and aiming them at the "basket" of the trash can. 12I glance at the bed across from the desk and chuckle because pillows stuffed under the tangled nest of blankets make it look as if someone is still sleeping there, though I know Greg is in history class right now. 13I step carefully through the room, trying to walk through the obstacle course of science-fiction paperbacks, a wristwatch, assorted CD cases, and the radio with a wire coat hanger for an antenna. 14I leave everything as I find it, but tape a note to Greg's door saying, "Isn't it about time to clean up?"

A Depressing Place

1The pet shop in the mall is a depressing place. 2A display window attracts passersby who stare at the prisoners penned inside. 3In the right-hand side of the window, two puppies press their forepaws against the glass and attempt to lick the human hands that press from the outside. 4A cardboard barrier separates the dogs from several black-and-white kittens piled together in the opposite end of the window. 5Inside the shop, rows of wire cages line one wall from top to bottom. 6At first, it is hard to tell whether a bird, hamster, gerbil, cat, or dog is locked inside each cage. 7Only an occasional movement or a clawing, shuffling sound tells visitors that living creatures are inside. 8Running down the center of the store is a line of large wooden perches that look like coatracks. 9When customers pass by, the parrots and mynas chained to these perches flutter their clipped wings in a useless attempt to escape. 10At the end of this center aisle is a large plastic tub of dirty, stagnant-looking water containing a few motionless turtles. 11The shelves against the left-hand wall are packed with all kinds of pet-related items. 12The smell inside the entire shop is an unpleasant mixture of strong chemical deodorizers, urine-soaked newspapers, and musty sawdust. 13Because so many animals are crammed together, the normally pleasant, slightly milky smell of the puppies and kittens is sour and strong. 14The droppings inside the uncleaned birdcages give off a dry, stinging odor. 15Visitors hurry out of the shop, anxious to feel fresh air and sunlight. 16The animals stay on.

Karla

¹Karla, my brother's new girlfriend, is a catlike creature. ²Framing her face is a layer of sleek black hair that always looks just-combed. ³Her face, with its wide forehead, sharp cheekbones, and narrow, pointed chin, resembles a triangle. ⁴Karla's skin is a soft, velvety brown. ⁵Her large brown eyes slant upward at the corners, and she emphasizes their angle with a sweep of maroon eye shadow. ⁶Karla's habit of looking sidelong out of the tail of her eye makes her look cautious, as if she were expecting something to sneak up on her. ⁷Her nose is small and flat. ⁸The sharply outlined depression under it leads the observer's eye to a pair of red-tinted lips. ⁹With their slight upward tilt at the corners, Karla's lips make her seem self-satisfied and secretly pleased. ¹⁰One reason Karla may be happy is that she recently was asked to be in a local beauty contest. ¹¹Her long neck and slim body are perfectly in proportion with her face. ¹²Karla manages to look elegant and sleek no matter how she is standing or sitting, for her body seems to be made up of graceful angles. ¹³Her slender hands are tipped with long, polished nails. ¹⁴Her narrow feet are long, too, but they appear delicate even in flat-soled running shoes. ¹⁵Somehow, Karla would look perfect in a cat's jeweled collar.

■ Questions

About Unity

1. Which paragraph lacks a topic sentence?

   _____

2. Which sentence in the paragraph about Karla should be omitted in the interest of paragraph unity? (*Write the sentence number here.*) _____

About Support

3. Label as *sight*, *touch*, *hearing*, or *smell* all the sensory details in the following sentences taken from the three paragraphs. The first one is done for you as an example.

   a. From its nest of sweet-smelling cedar chips, the gerbil peers out at me
   smell
   sight   *sight*   *hearing*
   with its bright eyes, its tiny claws scratching against the cage wall.

   b. Because so many animals are crammed together, the normally pleasant,

   slightly milky smell of the puppies and kittens is sour and strong.

   c. Her slender hands are tipped with long, polished nails.

    d.   That's the location of a white wicker clothes hamper, heaped with grass-
stained jeans, sweat-stained T-shirts, and smelly socks.

4. After which sentence in "A Depressing Place" are specific details needed?
_____

About Coherence

5. Spatial signals (*above, next to, to the right*, and so on) are often used to help organize details in a descriptive paragraph. List four space signals that appear in "My Teenage Son's Room":

_____ _____ _____ _____

6. The writer of "Karla" organizes the details by observing Karla in an orderly way. Which of Karla's features is described first? _____ Which is described last? _____ Check the method of spatial organization that best describes the paragraph:

_____ Interior to exterior

_____ Near to far

_____ Top to bottom

Developing a Descriptive Paragraph

Development through Prewriting

When Victor was assigned a descriptive paragraph, he thought at first of describing his own office at work. He began by making a list of details he noticed while looking around the office:

    adjustable black chair

    beige desk

    piles of papers

    computer

    pictures of Marie and kids on desk

    desk calendar

But Victor quickly became bored. Here is how he describes what happened next:

"As I wrote down what I saw in my office, I was thinking, 'What a drag.' I gave up and worked on something else. Later that evening I told my wife that I was going to write a boring paragraph about my boring office. She started laughing at me. I said 'What's so funny?' and she said, 'You're so certain that a writing assignment has to be boring that you deliberately chose a subject that bores you. How about writing about something you care about?' At first I was annoyed, but then I realized she was right. When I hear 'assignment' I automatically think 'pain in the neck' and just want to get it over with."

Victor's attitude is not uncommon. Many students who are not experienced writers don't take the time to find a topic that interests them. They grab the one closest at hand and force themselves to write about it just for the sake of completing the assignment. Like Victor, they ensure that they (and probably their instructors as well) will be bored with the task.

In Victor's case, he decided that this assignment would be different. That evening as he talked with his son, Mikey, he remembered a visit the two had made to a mall a few days earlier. Mikey had asked Victor to take him to the pet store. Victor had found the store a very unpleasant place. "As I remembered the store, I recalled a lot of descriptive details—sounds, smells, sights," Victor said. "I realized not only that would it be easier to describe a place like that than my bland, boring office, but that I would actually find it an interesting challenge to make a reader see it through my words. For me to realize writing could be enjoyable was a real shock!"

Now that Victor had his subject, he began making a list of details about the pet shop. Here is what he wrote:

Sawdust, animal droppings on floor

Unhappy-looking puppies and kittens

Dead fish floating in tanks

Screech of birds

Chained parrots

Tanks full of dirty water

Strong urine smell

No place for animals to play

Bored-looking clerks

Animals scratching cages for attention

As he looked over his list of details, the word that came to mind was "depressing." He decided his topic sentence would be "The pet store in the mall is depressing." He then wrote this first draft:

The pet store in the mall is depressing. There are sawdust and animal droppings all over the floor. Sad-looking puppies and kittens scratch on their cages for attention. Dead fish and motionless turtles float in tanks of stagnant water. The loud screeching of birds is everywhere, and parrots with clipped wings try to escape when customers walk too near. Everywhere there is the smell of animal urine that has soaked the sawdust and newspapers. The clerks, who should be cleaning the cages, stand around talking to each other and ignoring the animals.

Development through Revising

The next day Victor's instructor asked to see the students' first drafts. This is what she wrote in response to Victor's:

This is a very good beginning. You have provided some strong details that appeal to the reader's senses of smell, hearing, and sight.

In your next draft, organize your paragraph by using spatial order. In other words, describe the room in some logical physical order—maybe from left to right, or from the front of the store to its back. Such an organization mirrors the way a visitor might move through the store.

I encourage you to become even more specific in your details. For instance, in what way did the puppies and kittens seem sad? As you work on each sentence, ask yourself if you can add more descriptive details to paint a more vivid picture in words.

In response to his teacher's suggestion about a spatial order method of organization, Victor rewrote the paragraph, beginning with the display window that attracts visitors, then going on to the store's right-hand wall, the center aisle, and the left-hand wall. He ended the paragraph with a sentence that brought the reader back outside the shop. Thinking about the shop in this way enabled Victor to remember and add a number of new specific details as well. He then wrote the version of "A Depressing Place" that appears on page 244.

Writing a Descriptive Paragraph

■ Writing Assignment 1

Write a paragraph describing a certain person's room. Use as your topic sentence "I could tell by looking at the room that a _____ lived there." There are many kinds of people who could be the focus for such a paragraph. You can select any one of the following, or think of another type of person.

Photographer	Music lover	Carpenter
Cook	TV addict	Baby
Student	Camper	Cat or dog lover
Musician	Computer expert	World traveler
Hunter	Cheerleader	Drug addict
Slob	Football player	Little boy or girl
Outdoors person	Actor	Alcoholic
Doctor	Prostitute	Inline skater

Prewriting

a After choosing a topic, spend a few minutes making sure it will work. Prepare a list of all the details you can think of that support the topic. For example, a student who planned to describe a soccer player's room made this list:

soccer balls

shin guards

posters of professional soccer teams

soccer trophies

shirt printed with team name and number

autographed soccer ball

medals and ribbons

photos of player's own team

sports clippings

radio that looks like soccer ball

soccer socks

soccer shorts

If you don't have enough details, then choose another type of person. Check your new choice with a list of details before committing yourself to the topic.

b You may want to use other prewriting techniques, such as freewriting or questioning, to develop more details for your topic. As you continue prewriting, keep the following in mind:

• Everything in the paragraph should support your point. For example, if you are writing about a soccer player's room, every detail should serve to show that the person who lives in that room plays and loves soccer. Other details—for example, the person's computer, tropical fish tank, or daily "to-do" list—should be omitted.

- Description depends on the use of specific rather than general descriptive words. For example:

General	Specific
Mess on the floor	The obstacle course of science-fiction paperbacks, a wristwatch, assorted CD cases, and the radio with a wire coat hanger for an antenna
Ugly turtle tub	Large plastic tub of dirty, stagnant-looking water containing a few motionless turtles
Bad smell	Unpleasant mixture of strong chemical deodorizers, urine-soaked newspapers, and musty sawdust
Nice skin	Soft, velvety brown skin

Remember that you want your readers to experience the room vividly. Your words should be as detailed as a clear photograph, giving readers a real feel for the room. Appeal to as many senses as possible. Most of your description will involve the sense of sight, but you may be able to include details about touch, hearing, and smell as well.

- Spatial order is a good way to organize a descriptive paragraph. Move as a visitor's eye might move around the room, from right to left or from larger items to smaller ones. Here are a few transition words of the sort that show spatial relationships.

to the left	across from	on the opposite side
to the right	above	nearby
next to	below	

Such transitions will help prevent you—and your reader—from getting lost as the description proceeds.

c   Before you write, see if you can make a scratch outline based on your list. Here is one possible outline of the paragraph about the soccer player's room. Note that the details are organized according to spatial order—from the edges of the room in toward the center.

<u>Topic sentence:</u> I could tell by looking at the room that a soccer player lived there.

1. Walls
2. Bookcase
3. Desk
4. Chair
5. Floor

d Then proceed to write a first draft of your paragraph.

Revising

Read your descriptive paragraph slowly out loud to a friend. Ask the friend to close his or her eyes and try to picture the room as you read. Read it aloud a second time. Ask your friend to answer these questions:

- Does every detail in the paragraph support the topic sentence? Here's one way to find out: Ask your friend to imagine omitting the key word or words (in the case of our example, "soccer player") in your topic sentence. Would readers know what word should fit in that empty space?
- Are the details specific and vivid rather than general?
- Has the writer included details that appeal to as many senses as possible?
- Does the paragraph follow a logical spatial order?
- Has the writer used transitions (such as *on top of, beside, to the left of*) to help the reader follow that order?

Continue revising your work until you and your reader can answer "yes" to all these questions.

In the later drafts of your paragraph, edit carefully for sentence-skills mistakes, including spelling. Refer to the checklist of these skills on the inside front cover of this book.

■ Writing Assignment 2

Write a paragraph describing a specific person. Select a dominant impression of the person, and use only details that will convey that impression. You might want to write about someone who falls into one of these categories.

TV or movie personality	Coworker
Instructor	Clergyman or clergywoman
Employer	Police officer
Child	Store owner or manager

Older person   Bartender
Close friend   Joker
Enemy   Neighbor

Prewriting

a Reread the paragraph about Karla that appears earlier in this chapter. Note the dominant impression that the writer wanted to convey: that Karla is a catlike person. Having decided to focus on that impression, the writer included only details that contributed to her point. Similarly, you should focus on one dominant aspect of your subject's appearance, personality, or behavior.

Once you have chosen the person you will write about and the impression you plan to portray, put that information into a topic sentence. Here are some examples of topic sentences that mention a particular person and the dominant impression of that person:

Kate gives the impression of being permanently nervous.

The old man was as faded and brittle as a dying leaf.

The child was an angelic little figure.

Our high school principal resembled a cartoon drawing.

The TV newscaster seems as synthetic as a piece of Styrofoam.

Our neighbor is a fussy person.

The rock singer seemed to be plugged into some special kind of energy source.

The drug addict looked as lifeless as a corpse.

My friend Jeffrey is a slow, deliberate person.

The owner of that grocery store seems burdened with troubles.

b Make a list of the person's qualities that support your topic sentence. Write quickly; don't worry if you find yourself writing down something that doesn't quite fit. You can always edit the list later. For now, just write down all the details that occur to you that support the dominant impression you want to convey. Include details that involve as many senses as possible (sight, sound, hearing, touch, smell). For instance, here's a list one writer jotted down to support the sentence "The child was an angelic little figure":

soft brown ringlets of hair

pink cheeks

wide shining eyes

shrieking laugh

joyful smile

starched white dress

white flowers in hair

c Edit your list, striking out details that don't support your topic sentence and adding others that do. The author of the paragraph on an angelic figure crossed out one detail from the original list and added a new one:

soft brown ringlets of hair

pink cheeks

wide shining eyes

~~shrieking laugh~~

joyful smile

starched white dress

white flowers in hair

sweet singing voice

d Decide on a spatial order of organization. In the example above, the writer ultimately decided to describe the child from head to toe.

e Make a scratch outline for your paragraph, based on the organization you have chosen.

f Then proceed to write a first draft of your paragraph.

Revising

Put your paragraph away for a day or so if at all possible. When you read it and your later drafts, ask yourself these questions:

- Does my topic sentence clearly state my dominant impression of my subject?
- If I left out the key words in my topic sentence (the words that state my dominant impression), would a reader know what idea fits there?
- Does every detail support my topic sentence?
- Are the details I have included specific rather than vague and general?
- Have I used a logical spatial organization that helps my reader follow my description?
- Have I checked my paper for sentence skills, as listed on the inside front cover of the book?

Continue revising your work until you can answer "yes" to all these questions.

■ Writing Assignment 3

Write a paragraph describing an animal you have spent some time with—a pet, a friend's pet, an animal you've seen in a park or zoo or even on television. Write a paragraph about how the animal looks and behaves. Select details that support a dominant impression of your subject. Once you decide on the impression you wish to convey, compose a topic sentence, such as either of those below, that summarizes the details you will use.

> The appearance of a gorilla named Koko gives no hint of the animal's intelligence and gentleness.
>
> A cute squirrel who has taken up residence in my backyard exhibits surprising agility and energy.

Remember to provide colorful, detailed descriptions to help your readers picture the features and behavior you are writing about. Note the contrast in the two items below.

> *Lacks rich descriptive details:* The squirrel was gray and enjoyed our deck.
>
> *Includes rich descriptive details:* On our deck, the young gray squirrel dug a hole in the dirt in a planter full of marigolds and then deposited an acorn in the hole, his fluffy tail bobbing enthusiastically all the while.

■ Writing Assignment 4

Visit a place you have never gone to before and write a paragraph describing it. You may want to visit:

A restaurant

A classroom, a laboratory, an office, a workroom, or some other room in your school

A kind of store you ordinarily don't visit: for example, a hardware store, toy store, record shop, gun shop, or sports shop, or a particular men's or women's clothing store

A bus terminal, train station, or airport

A place of worship

A park, vacant lot, or street corner

You may want to jot down details about the place while you are there or very soon after you leave. Again, decide on a dominant impression you want to convey of the place, and use only those details which will support that impression. Follow the notes on prewriting, writing, and revising for Writing Assignment 2.

■ Writing Assignment 5

Option 1:   Imagine that you are an interior designer. A new dormitory is going to be built on campus, and you have been asked to create a sample dormitory room for two students. Write a paragraph describing your design of the room, telling what it would include and how it would be arranged. In your prewriting for this assignment, you might list all the relevant student needs you can think of, such as a good study space, storage space, and appropriate lighting and colors. Then put all of the parts together so that they work well as a whole. Use a spatial order in your paragraph to help readers "see" your room. Begin with the following topic sentence or something like it:

> My design for a dormitory room offers both efficiency and comfort for two students.

Feel free to use a less-than-serious tone.

Option 2:   Alternatively, write a paragraph describing your design of another type of room, including any of the following:

Child's bedroom	Kitchen
Schoolroom	Porch
Restaurant	Bakery

15 Narrating an Event

At times we make a statement clear by relating in detail something that has happened. In the story we tell, we present the details in the order in which they happened. A person might say, for example, "I was embarrassed yesterday," and then go on to illustrate the statement with the following narrative:

> I was hurrying across campus to get to a class. It had rained heavily all morning, so I was hopscotching my way around puddles in the pathway. I called to two friends ahead to wait for me, and right before I caught up to them, I came to a large puddle that covered the entire path. I had to make a quick choice of either stepping into the puddle or trying to jump over it. I jumped, wanting to seem cool, since my friends were watching, but didn't clear the puddle. Water splashed everywhere, drenching my shoe, sock, and pants cuff, and spraying the pants of my friends as well. "Well done, Dave!" they said. My embarrassment was all the greater because I had tried to look so casual.

The speaker's details have made his moment of embarrassment vivid and real for us, and we can see and understand just why he felt as he did.

In this section, you will be asked to tell a story that illustrates or explains some point. The paragraphs below all present narrative experiences that support a point. Read them and then answer the questions that follow.

Paragraphs to Consider

Heartbreak

¹Bonnie and I had gotten engaged in August, just before she left for college at Penn State. ²A week before Thanksgiving, I drove up to see her as a surprise. ³When I knocked on the door of her dorm room, she was indeed surprised, but not in a pleasant way. ⁴She introduced me to her roommate, who looked uncomfortable and quickly left. ⁵I asked Bonnie how classes were going, and at the same time I tugged on the sleeve of my heavy sweater in order to pull it off. ⁶As I was slipping it over my head, I noticed a large photo on the wall—of Bonnie and a tall guy laughing together. ⁷It was decorated with paper flowers and a yellow ribbon, and on the ribbon was written "Bonnie and Blake." ⁸"What's going on?" I said.

⁹I stood there stunned and then felt an anger that grew rapidly. ¹⁰"Who is Blake?" I asked. ¹¹Bonnie laughed nervously and said, "What do you want to hear about—my classes or Blake?" ¹²I don't really remember what she then told me, except that Blake was a sophomore math major. ¹³I felt a terrible pain in the pit of my stomach, and I wanted to rest my head on someone's shoulder and cry. ¹⁴I wanted to tear down the sign and run out, but I did nothing. ¹⁵Clumsily I pulled on my sweater again. ¹⁶My knees felt weak, and I barely had control of my body. ¹⁷I opened the room door, and suddenly more than anything I wanted to slam the door shut so hard that the dorm walls would collapse. ¹⁸Instead, I managed to close the door quietly. ¹⁹I walked away understanding what was meant by a broken heart.

Losing My Father

¹Although my father died ten years ago, I felt that he'd been lost to me four years earlier. ²Dad had been diagnosed with Alzheimer's disease, an illness that destroys the memory. ³He couldn't work any longer, but in his own home he got along pretty well. ⁴I lived hundreds of miles away and wasn't able to see my parents often. ⁵So when my first child was a few weeks old, I flew home with the baby to visit them. ⁶After Mom met us at the airport, we picked up Dad and went to their favorite local restaurant. ⁷Dad was quiet, but kind and gentle as always, and he seemed glad to see me and his new little grandson. ⁸Everyone went to bed early. ⁹In the morning, Mom left for work. ¹⁰I puttered happily around in my old bedroom. ¹¹I heard Dad shuffling around in the kitchen, making coffee. ¹²Eventually I realized that he was pacing back and forth at the foot of the stairs as if he were uneasy. ¹³I called down to him, "Everything all right there? ¹⁴I'll be down in a minute." ¹⁵"Fine!" he called back, with a forced-sounding cheerfulness. ¹⁶Then he stopped pacing and called up to me, "I must be getting old and forgetful. ¹⁷When did you get here?" ¹⁸I was surprised, but made myself answer calmly. ¹⁹"Yesterday afternoon. ²⁰Remember, Mom met us at the airport, and then we went to The Skillet for dinner." ²¹"Oh, yes," he said. ²²"I had roast beef." ²³I began to relax. ²⁴But then he continued, hesitantly, "And . . . who are you?" ²⁵My breath stopped as if I'd been punched in the stomach. ²⁶When I could steady my voice, I answered, "I'm Laura; I'm your daughter. ²⁷I'm here with my baby son, Max." ²⁸"Oh," is all he said. ²⁹"Oh." ³⁰And he wandered into the living room and sat down. ³¹In a few minutes I joined him and found him staring blankly out the window. ³²He was a polite host, asking if I wanted anything to eat, and if the room was too cold. ³³I answered with an aching heart, mourning for his loss and for mine.

A Frustrating Job

¹Working as a baby-sitter was the most frustrating job I ever had. ²I discovered this fact when my sister asked me to stay with her two sons for the evening. ³I figured I would get them dinner, let them watch a little TV, and then put them to bed early. ⁴The rest of the night I planned to watch TV and collect an easy twenty dollars. ⁵It turned out to be anything but easy. ⁶First, right before we were about to sit down for a pizza dinner, Rickie let the parakeet out of its cage. ⁷This bird is really intelligent and can repeat almost any phrase. ⁸The dog started chasing it around the house, so I decided to catch it before the dog did. ⁹Rickie and Jeff volunteered to help, following at my heels. ¹⁰We had the bird cornered by the fireplace when Rickie jumped for it and knocked over the hamster cage. ¹¹Then the bird escaped again, and the hamsters began scurrying around their cage like crazy creatures. ¹²The dog had disappeared by this point, so I decided to clean up the hamsters' cage and try to calm them down. ¹³While I was doing this, Rickie and Jeff caught the parakeet and put it back in its cage. ¹⁴It was time to return to the kitchen and eat cold pizza. ¹⁵But upon entering the kitchen, I discovered why the dog had lost interest in the bird chase. ¹⁶What was left of the pizza was lying on the floor, and tomato sauce was dripping from the dog's chin. ¹⁷I cleaned up the mess and then served chicken noodle soup and ice cream to the boys. ¹⁸Only at nine o'clock did I get the kids to bed. ¹⁹I then returned downstairs to find that the dog had thrown up pizza on the living-room rug. ²⁰When I finished cleaning the rug, my sister returned. ²¹I took the twenty dollars and told her that she should get someone else next time.

■ Questions

About Unity

1. Which paragraph lacks a topic sentence?

   _____

   Write a topic sentence for the paragraph.

   _____

   _____

2. Which sentence in "A Frustrating Job" should be omitted in the interest of

   paragraph unity? (Write the sentence number here.) _____

About Support

3. What is for you the best (most real and vivid) detail or image in the paragraph "Heartbreak"?

   _____

   _____

   What is the best detail or image in "Losing My Father"?

   _____

   _____

   What is the best detail or image in "A Frustrating Job"?

   _____

   _____

4. Which two paragraphs include the actual words spoken by the participants?

   _____

   _____

About Coherence

5. Do the three paragraphs use time order or emphatic order to organize details?

   _____

6. What are four transition words used in "A Frustrating Job"?

   _____   _____   _____   _____

Developing a Narrative Paragraph

Development through Prewriting

Gary's instructor was helping her students think of topics for their narrative paragraphs. "A narrative is simply a story that illustrates a point," she said. "That point is often about an emotion you felt. Looking at a list of emotions may help you think of a topic. Ask yourself what incident in your life has made you feel any of these emotions."

The instructor then jotted these feelings on the board:

Anger

Embarrassment

Jealousy

Amusement

Confusion

Thankfulness

Loneliness

Sadness

Terror

Relief

As Gary looked over the list, he thought of several experiences in his life. "The word 'angry' made me think about a time when I was a kid. My brother took my skateboard without permission and left it in the park, where it got stolen. 'Amused' made me think of when I watched my roommate, who claimed he spoke Spanish, try to bargain with a street vendor in Mexico. He got so flustered that he ended up paying even more than the vendor had originally asked for. When I got to 'sad,' though, I thought about when I visited Bonnie and found out she was dating some-one else. 'Sad' wasn't a strong enough word, though—I was heartbroken. So I decided to write about heartbreak."

Gary's first step was to do some freewriting. Without worrying about spelling or grammar, he simply wrote down everything that came into his mind concerning his visit to Bonnie. Here is what he came up with:

I hadn't expected to see Bonnie until Christmas. We'd got engaged just before she went off to college. The drive to Penn State took ten hours each way and that seemed like to much driving for just a weekend visit. But I realized I had a long weekend over thanksgiving I decided to surprise her. I think down deep I knew something was wrong. She had sounded sort of cool on the phone and she hadn't been writing as often. I guess I wanted to convince myself that everything was OK. We'd been dating since we were 16 and I couldn't imagine not being with her. When I knocked at her dorm door I remember how she was smiling when she opened the door. Her expression changed to one of surprise. Not happy surprise. I hugged her and she sort of hugged me back but like you'd hug your brother. Another girl was in the room. Bonnie said, "This is Pam," and Pam shot out of the room like I had a disease. Everything seemed wrong and confused. I started taking off my sweater and then I saw it. On a bulletin board was this photo of Bonnie with Blake, the guy she had been messing around with. They broke up about a year later, but by then I never wanted to see Bonnie again. I couldn't believe Bonnie would start seeing somebody else when we were planning to get married. It had even been her idea to get engaged. Before she left for college. Later on I realized that wasn't the first dishonest thing she'd done. I got out of there as quick as I could.

Development through Revising

Gary knew that the first, freewritten version of his paragraph needed work. Here are the comments he made after he reread it the following day:

> "Although my point is supposed to be that my visit to Bonnie was heartbreaking, I didn't really get that across. I need to say more about how the experience felt.
>
> "I've included some information that doesn't really support my point. For instance, what happened to Bonnie and Blake later isn't important here. Also, I think I spend too much time explaining the circumstances of the visit. I need to get more quickly to the point where I arrived at Bonnie's dorm.
>
> "I think I should include more dialogue, too. That would make the reader feel more like a witness to what really happened."

With this self-critique in mind, Gary revised his paragraph until he had produced the version that appears on page 257.

Writing a Narrative Paragraph

Writing Assignment 1

Write a paragraph about an experience in which a certain emotion was predominant. The emotion might be fear, pride, satisfaction, embarrassment, or any of these:

Frustration	Sympathy	Shyness
Love	Bitterness	Disappointment
Sadness	Violence	Happiness
Terror	Surprise	Jealousy
Shock	Nostalgia	Anger
Relief	Loss	Hate
Envy	Silliness	Nervousness

The experience you write about should be limited in time. Note that the three paragraphs presented in this chapter all detail experiences that occurred within relatively short periods. One writer describes a heartbreaking surprise he received the day he visited his girlfriend; another describes the loss of her father; the third describes a frustrating night of baby-sitting.

A good way to bring an event to life for your readers is to include some dialogue, as the writers of two of the three paragraphs in this chapter have done. Words that you said, or that someone else said, help make a situation come alive. First, though, be sure to check the section on quotation marks on pages 478–484.

Prewriting

a Begin by freewriting. Think of an experience or event that caused you to feel a certain emotion strongly. Then spend ten minutes writing freely about the experience. Do not worry at this point about such matters as spelling or grammar or putting things in the right order. Instead, just try to get down all the details you can think of that seem related to the experience.

b This preliminary writing will help you decide whether your topic is promising enough to develop further. If it is not, choose another emotion and repeat step *a*. If it does seem promising, do two things:

- First, write your topic sentence, underlining the emotion you will focus on. For example, "My first day in kindergarten was one of the <u>scariest</u> days of my life."
- Second, make up a list of all the details involved in the experience. Then number these details according to the order in which they occurred.

c Referring to your list of details, write a rough draft of your paragraph. Use time signals such as *first, then, after, next, while, during,* and *finally* to help connect details as you move from the beginning to the middle to the end of your narrative. Be sure to include not only what happened but also how you felt about what was going on.

Revising

Put your first draft away for a day or so. When you return to it, read it over, asking yourself these questions:

- Does my topic sentence clearly state what emotion the experience made me feel?
- Have I included some dialogue to make the experience come alive?
- Have I explained how I felt as the experience occurred?
- Have I used time order to narrate the experience from beginning to end?
- Have I used time signals to connect one detail to the next?
- Have I checked my paper for sentence skills, including spelling, as listed on the inside front cover of the book?

Continue revising your work until you can answer "yes" to all these questions.

■ Writing Assignment 2

Narrate a real-life event you have witnessed. Listed below are some places where interesting personal interactions often happen. Think of an event that you saw happen at one of these places, or visit one of them and take notes on an incident to write about.

The traffic court or small-claims court in your area

The dinner table at your or someone else's home

A waiting line at a supermarket, unemployment office, ticket counter, movie theater, or cafeteria

A doctor's office

An audience at a movie, concert, or sports event

A classroom

A restaurant

A student lounge

Prewriting

a   Decide what point you will make about the incident. What one word or phrase characterizes the scene you witnessed? Your narration of the incident will emphasize that characteristic.

b   Write your topic sentence. The topic sentence should state where the incident happened as well as your point about it. Here are some possibilities:

I witnessed a *heartwarming* incident at Burger King yesterday.

Two fans at last week's baseball game got into a *hilarious* argument.

The scene at our family dinner table Monday was one of complete *confusion*.

A *painful* dispute went on in Atlantic County small-claims court yesterday.

c   Use the questioning technique to remind yourself of details that will make your narrative come alive. Ask yourself questions like these and write down your answers:

Whom was I observing?

How were they dressed?

What were their facial expressions like?

What tones of voice did they use?

What did I hear them say?

d Drawing details from the notes you have written, write the first draft of your paragraph. Remember to use time signals such as *then, after that, during, meanwhile,* and *finally* to connect one sentence to another.

Revising

After you have put your paragraph away for a day, read it to a friend who will give you honest feedback. You and your friend should consider these questions:

- Does the topic sentence make a general point about the incident?
- Do descriptions of the appearance, tone of voice, and expressions of the people involved paint a clear picture of the incident?
- Is the sequence of events made clear by transitional words such as *at first, later,* and *then*?

Continue revising your work until you and your reader can answer "yes" to all these questions. Then check to make sure your paragraph is free of sentence-skills mistakes, including spelling errors. Use the list on the inside front cover of this book.

■ Writing Assignment 3

Write an account of a memorable personal experience. Make sure that your story has a point, expressed in the first sentence of the paragraph. If necessary, tailor your narrative to fit your purpose. Use time order to organize your details (*first* this happened; *then* this; *after that*, this; *next*, this; and so on). Concentrate on providing as many specific details as possible so that the reader can really share your experience. Try to make it as vivid for the reader as it was for you when you first experienced it.

Use one of the topics below or a topic of your own choosing. Regardless, remember that your story must illustrate or support a point stated in the first sentence of your paper.

The first time you felt grown-up

A major decision you made

A moment you knew you were happy

Your best or worst date

A time you took a foolish risk

An argument you will never forget

An incident that changed your life

A time when you did or did not do the right thing

Your best or worst holiday or birthday, or some other special occasion

A time you learned a lesson or taught a lesson to someone else

An occasion of triumph in sports or some other area

You may want to refer to the suggestions for prewriting and rewriting in Writing Assignment 1.

■ Writing Assignment 4

Write a paragraph that shows, through some experience you have had, the truth or falsity of a popular belief. You might write about any one of the following statements or some other popular saying.

Every person has a price.

Haste makes waste.

Don't count your chickens before they're hatched.

A bird in the hand is worth two in the bush.

It isn't what you know, it's who you know.

Borrowing can get you into trouble.

What you don't know won't hurt you.

A promise is easier made than kept.

You never really know people until you see them in an emergency.

If you don't help yourself, nobody will.

An ounce of prevention is worth a pound of cure.

Hope for the best but expect the worst.

Never give advice to a friend.

You get what you pay for.

A stitch in time saves nine.

A fool and his money are soon parted.

There is an exception to every rule.

Nice guys finish last.

Begin your narrative paragraph with a topic sentence that expresses your agreement or disagreement with a popular saying or belief, for example:

"Never give advice to a friend" is not always good advice, as I learned after helping a friend reunite with her boyfriend.

My sister learned recently that it is easier to make a promise than to keep one.

Refer to the suggestions for prewriting and revising on page 263. Remember that the purpose of your story is to support your topic sentence. Omit details from the experience you're writing about that don't support your topic sentence. Also, feel free to use made-up details that will strengthen your support.

■ Writing Assignment 5

Imagine that a younger brother or sister, or a young friend, has to make a difficult decision of some kind. Perhaps he or she must decide how to prepare for a job interview, whether or not to get help with a difficult class, or what to do about a coworker who is taking money from the cash register. Narrate a story from your own experience (or that of someone you know) that will teach a younger person something about the decision he or she must make. In your paragraph, include a comment or two about the lesson your story teaches. Write about any decision young people often face, including any of those already mentioned or those listed below.

Should he or she save a little from a weekly paycheck?

Should he or she live at home or move to an apartment with some friends?

How should he or she deal with a group of friends who are involved with drugs, stealing, or both?

16 Arguing a Position

Most of us know someone who enjoys a good argument. Such a person usually challenges any sweeping statement we might make. "Why do you say that?" he or she will ask. "Give your reasons." Our questioner then listens carefully as we cite our reasons, waiting to see if we really do have solid evidence to support our point of view. Such a questioner may make us feel a bit nervous, but we may also appreciate the way he or she makes us think through our opinions.

The ability to advance sound and compelling arguments is an important skill in everyday life. We can use argument to get an extension on a term paper, obtain a favor from a friend, or convince an employer that we are the right person for a job. Understanding persuasion based on clear, logical reasoning can also help us see through the sometimes faulty arguments advanced by advertisers, editors, politicians, and others who try to bring us over to their side.

In this section, you will be asked to argue a position and defend it with a series of solid reasons. In a general way, you are doing the same thing with all the paragraph assignments in the book: making a point and then supporting it. The difference here is that, in a more direct and formal manner, you will advance a point about which you feel strongly and seek to persuade others to agree with you.

Paragraphs to Consider

Let's Ban Proms

[1]While many students regard proms as peak events in high school life, I believe that high school proms should be banned. [2]One reason is that even before the prom takes place, it causes problems. [3]Teenagers are separated into "the ones who were asked" and "the ones who weren't." [4]Being one of those who weren't asked can be heartbreaking to a sensitive young person. [5]Another pre-prom problem is money. [6]The price of the various items needed can add up quickly to a lot of money. [7]The prom itself can be unpleasant and frustrating, too. [8]At the beginning of the evening, the girls enviously compare dresses while the boys sweat nervously inside their rented suits. [9]During the dance, the couples who have gotten together only to go to the prom have split up into miserable singles. [10]When the prom draws to a close, the popular teenagers drive off happily to other parties while the less popular ones head home, as usual. [11]Perhaps the main reason proms

should be banned, however, is the drinking and driving that go on after the prom is over. ¹²Teenagers pile into their cars on their way to "after-proms" and pull out the bottles and cans stashed under the seat. ¹³By the time the big night is finally over, at 4 or 5 A.M., students are trying to weave home without encountering the police or a roadside tree. ¹⁴Some of them do not make it, and prom night turns into tragedy. ¹⁵For all these reasons, proms have no place in our schools.

Bashing Men

¹Our culture now puts down men in ways that would be considered very offensive if the targets were women. ²For instance, men are frequently portrayed in popular culture as bumbling fools. ³The popular TV show <u>The Simpsons</u>, for instance, shows the father, Homer, as a total idiot, dishonest and childish. ⁴His son, Bart, is equally foolish; but the mother, Marge, and the sister, Lisa, are levelheaded and responsible. ⁵Little children love the "Berenstain Bears" books, which are supposed to teach lessons about subjects including honesty, bad habits, and going to the doctor. ⁶In every book, while the mother bear gives her cubs good advice, the father bear acts stupidly and has to be taught a lesson along with the kids. ⁷In addition, society teaches us to think of men as having no value in a family other than to contribute money. ⁸Popular stars like Madonna go on national TV and proclaim that their babies don't need a father because they are financially independent women. ⁹Families on welfare are denied benefits if the children's father stays in the home—apparently if he isn't bringing in money, the family is better off without him. ¹⁰The welfare system is deeply flawed in other ways as well. ¹¹And women tell each other men-bashing jokes that would be considered sexist and offensive if they were directed at women. ¹²Here's one: "Question: A woman has a flat tire. ¹³Santa Claus, Oprah Winfrey, and a decent man all stop to help her. ¹⁴Who actually changes the tire?" ¹⁵The answer: "Oprah, of course. ¹⁶The other two are fictional characters." ¹⁷Women deserve to be treated with respect, but that doesn't mean men should be put down.

Living Alone

¹Living alone is quite an experience. ²People who live alone, for one thing, have to learn to do all kinds of tasks by themselves. ³They must learn—even if they have had no experience—to change fuses, put up curtains and shades, temporarily dam an overflowing toilet, cook a meal, and defrost a refrigerator. ⁴When there is no father, husband, mother, or wife to depend on, a person can't fall back on the excuse, "I don't know how to do that." ⁵Those who live alone also need the strength to deal with people. ⁶Alone, singles must face noisy neighbors, unresponsive landlords,

dishonest repair people, and aggressive bill collectors. 7Because there are no buffers between themselves and the outside world, people living alone have to handle every visitor—friendly or unfriendly—alone. 8Finally, singles need a large dose of courage to cope with occasional panic and unavoidable loneliness. 9That weird thump in the night is even more terrifying when there is no one in the next bed or the next room. 10Frightening weather or unexpected bad news is doubly bad when the worry can't be shared. 11Even when life is going well, little moments of sudden loneliness can send shivers through the heart. 12Struggling through such bad times taps into reserves of courage that people may not have known they possessed. 13Facing everyday tasks, confronting all types of people, and handling panic and loneliness can shape singles into brave, resourceful, and more independent people.

■ Questions

About Unity

1. The topic sentence in "Living Alone" is too broad. Circle the topic sentence below that states accurately what the paragraph is about.

   a.   Living alone can make one a better person.

   b.   Living alone can create feelings of loneliness.

   c.   Living alone should be avoided.

2. Which sentence in "Bashing Men" should be eliminated in the interest of paragraph unity? (*Write the sentence number here.*) _____

3. How many reasons are given to support the topic sentence in each paragraph?

   a.   In "Let's Ban Proms" ____ one   ____ two   ____ three   ____ four

   b.   In "Bashing Men"   ____ one   ____ two   ____ three   ____ four

   c.   In "Living Alone"   ____ one   ____ two   ____ three   ____ four

4. After which sentence in "Let's Ban Proms" are more specific details needed?

   _____

About Coherence

5. Which paragraph uses a combination of time and emphatic order to organize its details? _____

6. What are the three main transition words in "Living Alone"?

   _____   _____   _____

Activity

Complete the outline below of "Bashing Men." Summarize in a few words the supporting material that fits under the topic sentence: After *1, 2,* and *3,* write in the three main points of support for the topic sentence. In the spaces after the numbers, write in the examples used to support those three main points. Two items have been done for you as examples.

Topic sentence: It's become more and more acceptable to bash men, acting as though they are less deserving of respect than women.

1. _____

    a. _____

    b. Berenstain Bears

2. _____

    a. _____

    b. Welfare benefits cut off if father in home

3. _____

    a. _____

Developing an Argument Paragraph

Development through Prewriting

Yolanda is the student author of "Let's Ban Proms." She decided on her topic after visiting her parents' home one weekend and observing her younger brother's concern about his upcoming prom.

"I really felt bad for Martin as I saw what he was going through," Yolanda said. "He's usually a happy kid who enjoys school. But this weekend he wasn't talking about his track meets or term papers or any of the things he's usually chatting about. Instead he was all tied up in knots about his prom. The girl he'd really wanted to go with had already been asked, and so friends had fixed him up with a girl he barely knew who didn't have a date either. Neither of them was excited about being together, but they felt that they just 'had' to go. And now he's worried about how to afford renting a tux, and how will he get a cool car to go in, and all that stuff. It's shaping up to be a really stressful, expensive evening. When I was in high school, I saw a lot of bad things associated with the prom, too. I hate to see young kids feeling pressured to attend an event that is fun for only a few."

Yolanda began prewriting by making a list of all the negative aspects of proms. This is what she came up with:

Drinking after prom

Car accidents (most important!)

Competition for dates

Preparation for prom cuts into school hours

Rejection of not being asked

Waste of school money

Going with someone you don't like

Separates popular from unpopular

Expensive

Bad-tempered chaperones

Next, Yolanda numbered the details in the order she was going to present them. She also struck out details she decided not to use:

6   Drinking after prom

7   Car accidents (most important!)

3   Competition for dates

~~Preparation for prom cuts into school hours~~

1   Rejection of not being asked

~~Waste of school money~~

4   Going with someone you don't like

5   Separates popular from unpopular

2   Expensive

~~Bad-tempered chaperones~~

Drawing from these notes, Yolanda wrote the following first draft of her paragraph:

In my opinion, high school proms should be banned. First, they cause unhappiness by separating students into "the ones who were asked" and "the ones who weren't." Proms are also expensive, as anyone who has attended one knows. The competition for dates can damage previously strong friendships. Many couples get together only in order to have a date for the prom and do not enjoy each other's company. After the prom, too, the kids are separated into "more popular" and "less popular" groups, with the popular ones going to after-prom parties. The biggest reason to ban proms, though, is the prom-night drinking that commonly occurs. Teenagers hide liquor in their cars and then try to drive home drunk. Some of them do not make it. For all these reasons, proms should be banned.

Development through Revising

Yolanda's instructor reviewed her first draft and made these comments:

> The order of your paragraph could be made stronger. Although you make good use of emphatic order (by ending with "the biggest reason to ban proms"), it's less clear that the paragraph is also organized according to time—in other words, you move from before the prom starts to during the prom to after it. Better use of transitional language will make the organization more clear.
>
> Also, you could make the paragraph more alive by including concrete details and illustrations. Your main points would be stronger with such support.

With these comments in mind, Yolanda revised her paragraph until she produced the version that appears on page 269.

Writing an Argument Paragraph

■ **Writing Assignment 1**

Develop an argument paragraph based on one of the following statements:

1. Condoms should (*or* should not) be made available in schools.
2. _____ (*name a specific athlete*) is the athlete most worthy of admiration in his *or* her sport.
3. Television is one of the best (*or* worst) inventions of this century.
4. _____ make the best (*or* worst) pets.
5. Cigarette and alcohol advertising should (*or* should not) be banned.
6. Teenagers make poor parents.
7. _____ is one public figure today who can be considered a hero.
8. This college needs a better _____ (cafeteria *or* library *or* student center *or* grading policy *or* attendance policy).

Prewriting

a   Make up brief outlines for any three of the eight statements above. Make sure you have three separate and distinct reasons for each statement. Below is an example of a brief outline for a paragraph making another point.

Large cities should outlaw passenger cars.
1.   Cut down on smog and pollution
2.   Cut down on noise
3.   Make more room for pedestrians

b   Decide, perhaps through discussion with your instructor or classmates, which of your outlines is the most promising for development into a paragraph. Make sure your supporting points are logical by asking yourself in each case, "Does this item truly support my topic sentence?"

c   Do some prewriting. Prepare a list of all the details you can think of that might actually support your point. Don't limit yourself; include more details than you can actually use. Here, for example, are details generated by the writer of "Living Alone":

Deal with power failures	Noisy neighbors
Nasty landlords	Develop courage
Scary noises at night	Do all the cooking
Spiders	Home repairs
Bill collectors	Obscene phone calls
Frightening storms	Loneliness

d   Decide which details you will use to develop your paragraph. Number the details in the order in which you will present them. Because presenting the strongest reason last (emphatic order) is the most effective way to organize an argument paragraph, be sure to save your most powerful reason for last. Here is how the author of "Living Alone" made decisions about details:

1   Deal with power failures

4   Nasty landlords

7   Scary noises at night

~~Spiders~~

6   Bill collectors

8   Frightening storms

5   Noisy neighbors

10 Develop courage

2   Do all the cooking

3   Home repairs

~~Obscene phone calls~~

9   Loneliness

e Write the first draft of your paragraph. As you write, develop each reason with specific details. For example, in "Living Alone," notice how the writer makes the experience of living alone come alive with phrases like "That weird thump in the night" or "little moments of sudden loneliness can send shivers through the heart."

Revising

- Put your paragraph away for a day or so. When you reread it, imagine that your audience is a jury that will ultimately render a verdict on your argument. Have you presented a convincing case? If you were on the jury, would you be favorably impressed with this argument?

- As you work on subsequent drafts of your paragraph, keep in mind unity, support, and coherence.

- Edit the next-to-final draft of your paper for sentence-skills mistakes, including spelling. Use the list on the inside front cover of this book.

■ ## Writing Assignment 2

Write a paragraph in which you take a stand on one of the controversial points below. Support the point with three reasons.

Students should not be required to attend high school.

All handguns should be banned.

Homosexuals should not be allowed in the armed forces.

The death penalty should exist for certain crimes.

Abortion should be legal.

Federal prisons should be coed, and prisoners should be allowed to marry.

Parents of girls under eighteen should be informed if their daughters receive birth-control aids.

The government should set up centers where sick or aged persons can go voluntarily to commit suicide.

Any woman on welfare who has more than two illegitimate children should be sterilized.

Parents should never hit their children.

Prewriting

a   As a useful exercise to help you begin developing your argument, your instructor might give class members a chance to "stand up" for what they believe in. One side of the front of the room should be designated *strong agreement* and the other side *strong disagreement,* with an imaginary line representing varying degrees of agreement or disagreement in between. As the class stands in front of the room, the instructor will read one value statement at a time from the list above, and students will move to the appropriate spot, depending on their degree of agreement or disagreement. Some time will be allowed for students, first, to discuss with those near them the reasons they are standing where they are, and second, to state to those at the other end of the scale the reasons for their position.

b   Begin your paragraph by writing a sentence that expresses your attitude toward one of the value statements above, for example, "I feel that prostitution should be legalized."

c   Outline the reason or reasons you hold the opinion that you do. Your support may be based on your own experience, the experience of someone you know, or logic. For example, an outline of a paragraph based on one student's logic looked like this:

I feel that prostitution should be legalized for the following reasons:
1.   Prostitutes would then have to pay their fair share of income tax.
2.   Government health centers would administer regular checkups. This would help prevent the spread of AIDS and venereal disease.
3.   Prostitutes would be able to work openly and independently and would not be controlled by pimps and gangsters.
4.   Most of all, prostitutes would be less looked down upon—an attitude that is psychologically damaging to those who may already have emotional problems.

Another outline, based on experience, proceeded as follows:

The experiences of a former prostitute I know show that prostitution should not be legalized.

1. The attention Linda received as a prostitute prevented her from seeing and working on her personal problems.
2. She became bitter toward all men, suspecting them all of wanting to exploit her.
3. She developed a negative self-image and felt that no one could love her.

d Write a first draft of your paragraph, providing specific details to back up each point in your outline.

Revising

Put your paragraph away for a while, ideally at least a day. Ask a friend whose judgment you trust to read and critique it. Your friend should consider each of these questions as he or she reads:

- Does the topic sentence clearly state the author's opinion on a controversial subject?
- Does the paragraph include at least three separate and distinct reasons that support the author's argument?
- Is each of the three reasons backed up by specific, relevant evidence?
- Has the author saved the most powerful reason for last?
- Is the paragraph free of spelling errors and the other sentence-skills mistakes listed on the inside front cover of the book?

Continue revising your work until you and your reader can answer "yes" to all these questions.

■ Writing Assignment 3

Where do you think it is best to bring up children—in the country, the suburbs, or the city? Write a paragraph in which you argue that one of those three environments is best for families with young children. Your argument should cover two types of reasons: (1) the advantages of living in the environment you've chosen and (2) the disadvantages of living in the other places. Use the following, or something much like it, for your topic sentence:

For families with young children, (*the country, a suburb,* or *the city*) _____ is the best place to live.

For each reason you advance, include at least one persuasive example. For instance, if you argue that the cultural life in the city is one important reason to live there, you should explain in detail just how going to a science museum is interesting and helpful to children. After deciding on your points of support, arrange them in a brief outline, saving your strongest point for last. In your paragraph, introduce each of your reasons with an addition transition, such as *first of all, another, also,* and *finally.*

■ Writing Assignment 4

Write a paper in which you use research findings to help support one of the following statements.

Wearing seat belts in automobiles should be mandatory.

Many people do not need vitamin pills.

Disposable cans and bottles should be banned.

Everyone should own a pet.

Mandatory retirement ages should be abolished.

Cigarettes should be illegal.

Penalties against drunken drivers should be sharply increased.

Advertising should not be permitted on Saturday morning cartoon shows.

Using strategies described in the chapter on the library and the Internet (pages 311–328), research the topic you have chosen. Reading material on your topic will help you think about that topic. See if you can then organize your paper in the form of three reasons that support the topic. Put these reasons into a scratch outline, and use it as a guide in writing your paragraph. Here is an example:

Wearing seat belts should be mandatory.
1. Seat belts are now comfortable and easy to use . . .
2. A seat-belt law would be easy to enforce . . .
3. Seat belts would save lives . . .

Note that statistics (on how many lives could be saved) would support the last reason. Do not hesitate to cite studies and other data in a limited way; they make your argument more objective and compelling.

■ Writing Assignment 5

Imagine that you have finally met Mr. or Ms. Right—but your parents don't approve of him or her. Specifically, they are against your doing one of the the following:

Continuing to see this person

Going steady

Moving in together

Getting married at the end of the school year

Write a letter to your parents explaining in detail why you have made your choice. Do your best to convince them that it is a good choice.

Part Three

Essay Development

Preview

Part Three moves from the single-paragraph paper to the several-paragraph essay. The differences between a paragraph and an essay are explained and then illustrated with a paragraph that has been expanded into an essay. You are shown how to begin an essay, how to tie its supporting paragraphs together, and how to conclude it. Three student essays are presented, along with questions to increase your understanding of the essay form. Finally, directions on how to plan an essay are followed by guidelines for writing an exam essay, and then by a series of essay writing assignments.

17 Writing the Essay

What Is an Essay?

Differences between an Essay and a Paragraph

An essay is simply a paper of several paragraphs, rather than one paragraph, that supports a single point. In an essay, subjects can and should be treated more fully than they would be in a single-paragraph paper.

The main idea or point developed in an essay is called the *thesis statement* or *thesis sentence* (rather than, as in a paragraph, the *topic sentence*). The thesis statement appears in the introductory paragraph, and it is then developed in the supporting paragraphs that follow. A short concluding paragraph closes the essay.

The Form of an Essay

The diagram on the next page shows the form of an essay.

Introductory Paragraph

> Introduction
> Thesis statement
> Plan of development:
> Points 1, 2, 3

The *introduction* attracts the reader's interest.

The *thesis statement* (or *thesis sentence*) states the main idea advanced in the paper.

The *plan of development* is a list of points that support the thesis. The points are presented in the order in which they will be developed in the paper.

First Supporting Paragraph

> Topic sentence (point 1)
> Specific evidence

The *topic sentence* advances the first supporting point for the thesis, and the *specific evidence* in the rest of the paragraph develops that first point.

Second Supporting Paragraph

> Topic sentence (point 2)
> Specific evidence

The *topic sentence* advances the second supporting point for the thesis, and the *specific evidence* in the rest of the paragraph develops that second point.

Third Supporting Paragraph

> Topic sentence (point 3)
> Specific evidence

The *topic sentence* advances the third supporting point for the thesis, and the *specific evidence* in the rest of the paragraph develops that third point.

Concluding Paragraph

> Summary, conclusion,
> or both

A *summary* is a brief restatement of the thesis and its main points. A *conclusion* is a final thought or two stemming from the subject of the paper.

A Model Essay

Gene, the writer of the paragraph on working in an apple plant (page 5), later decided to develop his subject more fully. Here is the essay that resulted.

My Job in an Apple Plant

Introductory paragraph

[1]In the course of working my way through school, I have taken many jobs I would rather forget. [2]I have spent nine hours a day lifting heavy automobile and truck batteries off the end of an assembly belt. [3]I have risked the loss of eyes and fingers working a punch press in a textile factory. [4]I have served as a ward aide in a mental hospital, helping care for brain-damaged men who would break into violent fits at unexpected moments. [5]But none of these jobs was as dreadful as my job in an apple plant. [6]The work was physically hard; the pay was poor; and, most of all, the working conditions were dismal.

First supporting paragraph

[7]First, the job made enormous demands on my strength and energy. [8]For ten hours a night, I took cartons that rolled down a metal track and stacked them onto wooden skids in a tractor trailer. [9]Each carton contained twelve heavy bottles of apple juice. [10]A carton shot down the track about every fifteen seconds. [11]I once figured out that I was lifting an average of twelve tons of apple juice every night. [12]When a truck was almost filled, I or my partner had to drag fourteen bulky wooden skids into the empty trailer nearby and then set up added sections of the heavy metal track so that we could start routing cartons to the back of the empty van. [13]While one of us did that, the other performed the stacking work of two men.

Second supporting paragraph

[14]I would not have minded the difficulty of the work so much if the pay had not been so poor. [15]I was paid the minimum wage at that time, $3.65 an hour, plus just a quarter extra for working the night shift. [16]Because of the low salary, I felt compelled to get as much overtime pay as possible. [17]Everything over eight hours a night was time-and-a-half, so I typically worked twelve hours a night. [18]On Friday I would sometimes work straight through until Saturday at noon—eighteen hours. [19]I averaged over sixty hours a week but did not take home much more than $180.

Third supporting paragraph

[20]But even more than the low pay, what upset me about my apple plant job was the working conditions. [21]Our humorless supervisor cared only about his production record for each night and tried to keep the assembly line moving at breakneck pace. [22]During work I was limited to two ten-minute breaks and an unpaid half hour for lunch. [23]Most of my time was spent outside on the truck loading dock in near-zero-degree temperatures. [24]The steel floors of the trucks were like ice; the quickly penetrating cold made my feet feel like stone. [25]I had no shared interests with the man I loaded cartons with, and so I had to work without companionship on the

job. [26]And after the production line shut down and most people left, I had to spend two hours alone scrubbing clean the apple vats, which were coated with a sticky residue.

Concluding paragraph

[27]I stayed on the job for five months, all the while hating the difficulty of the work, the poor money, and the conditions under which I worked. [28]By the time I quit, I was determined never to do such degrading work again.

Important Points about the Essay

Introductory Paragraph

An introductory paragraph has certain purposes or functions and can be constructed using various methods.

Purposes of the Introduction

An introductory paragraph should do three things:

1 Attract the reader's *interest*. Using one of the suggested methods of introduction described below can help draw the reader into your paper.

2 Present a *thesis sentence*—a clear, direct statement of the central idea that you will develop in your paper. The thesis statement, like a topic sentence, should have a keyword or keywords reflecting your attitude about the subject. For example, in the essay on the apple plant job, the keyword is *dreadful*.

3 Indicate a *plan of development*—a preview of the major points that will support your thesis statement, listed in the order in which they will be presented. In some cases, the thesis statement and plan of development may appear in the same sentence. In some cases, also, the plan of development may be omitted.

Activity

1. In "My Job in an Apple Plant," which sentences are used to attract the reader's interest?

    _____ sentences 1 to 3   _____ 1 to 4   _____ 1 to 5

2. The thesis in "My Job in an Apple Plant" is presented in

    _____ sentence 4   _____ sentence 5   _____ sentence 6

3. Is the thesis followed by a plan of development?

    _____ Yes   _____ No

4. Which words in the plan of development announce the three major supporting points in the essay? Write them below.

a. _____

b. _____

c. _____

Common Methods of Introduction

Here are some common methods of introduction. Use any one method, or a combination of methods, to introduce your subject in an interesting way.

1 **Broad statement.** Begin with a broad, general statement of your topic and narrow it down to your thesis statement. Broad, general statements ease the reader into your thesis statement by providing a background for it. In "My Job in an Apple Plant," Gene writes generally on the topic of his worst jobs and then narrows down to a specific worst job.

2 **Contrast.** Start with an idea or situation that is the opposite of the one you will develop. This approach works because your readers will be surprised, and then intrigued, by the contrast between the opening idea and the thesis that follows it. Here is an example of a "contrast" introduction:

> When I was a girl, I never argued with my parents about differences between their attitudes and mine. My father would deliver his judgment on an issue, and that was usually the end of the matter. Discussion seldom changed his mind, and disagreement was not tolerated. But the situation is different with today's parents and children. My husband and I have to contend with radical differences between what our children think about a given situation and what we think about it. We have had disagreements with all three of our daughters, Stephanie, Diana, and Giselle.

3 **"Relevance."** Explain the importance of your topic. If you can convince your readers that the subject applies to them in some way, or is something they should know more about, they will want to continue reading. The introductory paragraph of "Sports-Crazy America" (page 291) provides an example of a "relevance" introduction.

4 **Anecdote.** Use an incident or brief story. Stories are naturally interesting. They appeal to a reader's curiosity. In your introduction, an anecdote will grab the reader's attention right away. The story should be brief and should be related to your central idea. The incident in the story can be something that

happened to you, something that you may have heard about, or something that you have read about in a newspaper or magazine. Here is an example of a paragraph that begins with a story:

The husky man pushes open the door of the bedroom and grins as he pulls out a .38 revolver. An elderly man wearing thin pajamas looks at him and whimpers. In a feeble effort at escape, the old man slides out of his bed and moves to the door of the room. The husky man, still grinning, blocks his way. With the face of a small, frightened animal, the old man looks up and whispers, "Oh, God, please don't hurt me." The grinning man then fires four times. The television movie cuts now to a soap commercial, but the little boy who has been watching the set has begun to cry. Such scenes of direct violence on television must surely be harmful to children for a number of psychological reasons.

5   *Questions.*   Ask your readers one or more questions. These questions catch the readers' interest and make them want to read on. Here is an example of a paragraph that begins with questions:

What would happen if we were totally honest with ourselves? Would we be able to stand the pain of giving up self-deception? Would the complete truth be too much for us to bear? Such questions will probably never be answered, for in everyday life we protect ourselves from the onslaught of too much reality. All of us cultivate defense mechanisms that prevent us from seeing, hearing, or feeling too much. Included among such defense mechanisms are rationalization, reaction formation, and substitution.

Note, however, that the thesis itself must not be a question.

6   *Quotation.*   A quotation can be something you have read in a book or an article. It can also be something that you have heard: a popular saying or proverb ("Never give advice to a friend"); a current or recent advertising slogan ("Just do it"); a favorite expression used by your friends or family ("My father always says . . ."). Using a quotation in your introductory paragraph lets you add someone else's voice to your own. Here is an example of a paragraph that begins with a quotation:

"Evil," wrote Martin Buber, "is lack of direction." In my school days as a fatherless boy, with a mother too confused by her own life to really care for me, I strayed down a number of dangerous paths. Before my eighteenth birthday, I had been a car thief, a burglar, and a drug dealer.

Supporting Paragraphs

Most essays have three supporting points, developed in three separate paragraphs. (Some essays will have two supporting points; others, four or more.) Each of the supporting paragraphs should begin with a topic sentence that states the point to be detailed in that paragraph. Just as the thesis provides a focus for the entire essay, the topic sentence provides a focus for each supporting paragraph.

Activity

1. What is the topic sentence for the first supporting paragraph of "My Job in an Apple Plant"? (*Write the sentence number here.*) _____

2. What is the topic sentence for the second supporting paragraph? _____

3. What is the topic sentence for the third supporting paragraph? _____

Transitional Sentences

In paragraphs, transitions and other connective devices (pages 81–87) are used to help link sentences. Similarly, in an essay *transitional sentences* are used to help tie the supporting paragraphs together. Such transitional sentences usually occur near the end of one paragraph or the beginning of the next.

In "My Job in an Apple Plant," the first transitional sentence is:

I would not have minded the difficulty of the work so much if the pay had not been so poor.

In this sentence, the keyword *difficulty* reminds us of the point of the first supporting paragraph, while *pay* tells us the point to be developed in the second supporting paragraph.

Activity

Here is the other transitional sentence in "My Job in an Apple Plant":

But even more than the low pay, what upset me about my apple plant job was the working conditions.

Complete the following statement: In the sentence above, the keywords _____ echo the point of the second supporting paragraph, and the keywords _____ announce the topic of the third supporting paragraph.

Concluding Paragraph

The concluding paragraph often summarizes the essay by briefly restating the thesis and, at times, the main supporting points. Also, the conclusion brings the paper to a natural and graceful end, sometimes leaving the reader with a final thought on the subject.

Activity

1. Which sentence in the concluding paragraph of "My Job in an Apple Plant" restates the thesis and supporting points of the essay? _____

2. Which sentence contains the concluding thought of the essay? _____

Essays to Consider

Read the three student essays below and then answer the questions that follow.

Giving Up a Baby

[1]As I awoke, I overheard a nurse say, "It's a lovely baby boy. [2]How could a mother give him up?" [3]"Be quiet," another voice said. [4]"She's going to wake up soon." [5]Then I heard the baby cry, but I never heard him again. [6]Three years ago, I gave up my child to two strangers, people who wanted a baby but could not have one. [7]I was in pain over my decision, and I can still hear the voices of people who said I was selfish or crazy. [8]But the reasons I gave up my child were important ones, at least to me.

[9]I gave up my baby, first of all, because I was very young. [10]I was only seventeen, and I was unmarried. [11]Because I was so young, I did not yet feel the desire to have and raise a baby. [12]I knew that I would be a child raising a child and that, when I had to stay home to care for the baby, I would resent the loss of my freedom. [13]I might also blame the baby for that loss. [14]In addition, I had not had the experiences in life that would make me a responsible, giving parent. [15]What could I teach my child, when I barely knew what life was all about myself?

[16]Besides my age, another factor in my decision was the problems my parents would have. [17]I had dropped out of high school before graduation, and I did not have a job or even the chance of a job, at least for a while. [18]My parents would have to support my child and me, possibly for years. [19]My mom and dad had already struggled to raise their family and were not well off financially. [20]I knew I could not burden them with an unemployed teenager and her baby. [21]Even if I eventually got a job, my parents would have to help raise my child. [22]They would have to be full-time baby-sitters

while I tried to make a life of my own. [23]Because my parents are good people, they would have done all this for me. [24]But I felt I could not ask for such a big sacrifice from them.

[25]The most important factor in my decision was, I suppose, a selfish one. [26]I was worried about my own future. [27]I didn't want to marry the baby's father. [28]I realized during the time I was pregnant that we didn't love each other. [29]My future as an unmarried mother with no education or skills would certainly have been limited. [30]I would be struggling to survive, and I would have to give up for years my dreams of getting a job and my own car and apartment. [31]It is hard to admit, but I also considered the fact that, with a baby, I would not have the social life most young people have. [32]I would not be able to stay out late, go to parties, or feel carefree and irresponsible, for I would always have an enormous responsibility waiting for me at home. [33]With a baby, the future looked limited and insecure.

[34]In summary, thinking about my age, my responsibility to my parents, and my own future made me decide to give up my baby. [35]As I look back today at my decision, I know that it was the right one for me at the time.

Sports-Crazy America

[1]Almost all Americans are involved with sports in some way. [2]They may play basketball or volleyball or go swimming or skiing. [3]They may watch football or basketball games on the high school, college, or professional level. [4]Sports may seem like an innocent pleasure, but it is important to look under the surface. [5]In reality, sports have reached a point where they play too large a part in daily life. [6]They take up too much media time, play too large a role in the raising of children, and give too much power and prestige to athletes.

[7]The overemphasis on sports can be seen most obviously in the vast media coverage of athletic events. [8]It seems as if every bowl game play-off, tournament, trial, bout, race, meet, or match is shown on one television channel or another. [9]On Saturday and Sunday, a check of TV Guide will show almost forty sports programs on network television alone, and many more on cable stations. [10]In addition, sports make up about 30 percent of local news at six and eleven, and network world news shows often devote several minutes to major American sports events. [11]Radio offers a full roster of games and a wide assortment of sports talk shows. [12]Furthermore, many daily newspapers such as USA Today are devoting more and more space to sports coverage, often in an attempt to improve circulation. [13]The newspaper with the biggest sports section is the one people will buy.

[14]The way we raise and educate our children also illustrates our sports mania. [15]As early as age six or seven, kids are placed in little leagues, often to play under screaming coaches and pressuring parents. [16]Later, in high school, students who are singled out by the school and by the community are not those who are best academically but those who are best athletically.

17And college sometimes seems to be more about sports than about learning. 18The United States may be the only country in the world where people often think of their colleges as teams first and schools second. 19The names Penn State, Notre Dame, and Southern Cal mean "sports" to the public.

20Our sports craziness is especially evident in the prestige given to athletes in the United States. 21For one thing, we reward them with enormous salaries. 22In 1995, for example, baseball players averaged over $1,000,000 a year; the average annual salary in the United States is $25,000. 23Besides their huge salaries, athletes receive the awe, the admiration, and sometimes the votes of the public. 24Kids look up to a Kobe Bryant or a Roger Clemens as a true hero, while adults wear the jerseys and jackets of their favorite teams. 25Ex-players become senators and congressmen. 26And an athlete like Mia Hamm or Tiger Woods needs to make only one commercial for advertisers to see the sales of a product boom.

27Americans are truly mad about sports. 28Perhaps we like to see the competitiveness we experience in our daily lives acted out on playing fields. 29Perhaps we need heroes who can achieve clear-cut victories in the space of only an hour or two. 30Whatever the reason, the sports scene in this country is more popular than ever.

An Interpretation of Lord of the Flies

1Modern history has shown us the evil that exists in human beings. 2Assassinations are common, governments use torture to discourage dissent, and six million Jews were exterminated during World War II. 3In Lord of the Flies, William Golding describes a group of schoolboys shipwrecked on an island with no authority figures to control their behavior. 4One of the boys soon yields to dark forces within himself, and his corruption symbolizes the evil in all of us. 5First, Jack Merridew kills a living creature; then, he rebels against the group leader; and finally, he seizes power and sets up his own murderous society.

6The first stage in Jack's downfall is his killing of a living creature. 7In Chapter 1, Jack aims at a pig but is unable to kill. 8His upraised arm pauses "because of the enormity of the knife descending and cutting into living flesh, because of the unbearable blood," and the pig escapes. 9Three chapters later, however, Jack leads some boys on a successful hunt. 10He returns triumphantly with a freshly killed pig and reports excitedly to the others, "I cut the pig's throat." 11Yet Jack twitches as he says this, and he wipes his bloody hands on his shorts as if eager to remove the stains. 12There is still some civilization left in him.

13After the initial act of killing the pig, Jack's refusal to cooperate with Ralph shows us that this civilized part is rapidly disappearing. 14With no adults around, Ralph has made some rules. 15One is that a signal fire must be kept burning. 16But Jack tempts the boys watching the fire to go hunting, and the fire goes out. [17]Another rule is that at a meeting, only the person holding a special seashell has the right to speak. [18]In Chapter 5, another boy is speaking when Jack rudely tells him to shut up. [19]Ralph accuses Jack of breaking the rules. [20]Jack shouts: "Bollocks to the rules! We're strong—we hunt! If there's a beast, we'll hunt it down! We'll close in and beat and beat and beat—!" [21]He gives a "wild whoop" and leaps off the platform, throwing the meeting into chaos. [22]Jack is now much more savage than civilized.

[23]The most obvious proof of Jack's corruption comes in Chapter 8, when he establishes his own murderous society. [24]Insisting that Ralph is not a "proper chief" because he does not hunt, Jack asks for a new election. [25]After he again loses, Jack announces, "I'm going off by myself. . . . Anyone who wants to hunt when I do can come too." [26]Eventually, nearly all the boys join Jack's "tribe." [27]Following his example, they paint their faces like savages, sacrifice to "the beast," brutally murder two of their schoolmates, and nearly succeed in killing Ralph as well. [28]Jack has now become completely savage—and so have the others.

[29]Through Jack Merridew, then, Golding shows how easily moral laws can be forgotten. [30]Freed from grown-ups and their rules, Jack learns to kill living things, defy authority, and lead a tribe of murdering savages. [31]Jack's example is a frightening reminder of humanity's potential for evil. [32]The "beast" the boys try to hunt and kill is actually within every human being.

■ Questions

1. In which essay does the thesis statement appear in the last sentence of the introductory paragraph?

   _____

2. In the essay on *Lord of the Flies,* which sentence of the introductory paragraph contains the plan of development? _____

3. Which method of introduction is used in "Giving Up a Baby"?

   a. General to narrow   c. Incident or story

   b. Stating importance of topic   d. Questions

4. Complete the following brief outline of "Giving Up a Baby":
   I gave up my baby for three reasons:

   a. _____

   b. _____

   c. _____

5. Which *two* essays use a transitional sentence between the first and second supporting paragraphs?

   _____

6. *Complete the following statement:* Emphatic order is shown in the last supporting paragraph of "Giving Up a Baby" with the words *most important factor;* in the last supporting paragraph of "Sports-Crazy America" with the words _____; and in the last supporting paragraph of "An Interpretation of *Lord of the Flies*" with the words _____.

7. Which essay uses time order as well as emphatic order to organize its three supporting paragraphs? _____

8. List four major transitions used in the supporting paragraphs of "An Interpretation of *Lord of the Flies.*"

   a. _____   c. _____

   b. _____   d. _____

9. Which *two* essays include a sentence in the concluding paragraph that summarizes the three supporting points?

   _____

   _____

10. Which essay includes two final thoughts in its concluding paragraph?

   _____

Planning the Essay

Outlining the Essay

When you write an essay, planning is crucial for success. You should plan your essay by outlining in two ways:

1 Prepare a scratch outline. This should consist of a short statement of the thesis followed by the main supporting points for the thesis. Here is Gene's scratch outline for his essay on the apple plant:

Working at an apple plant was my worst job.
   1.   Hard work
   2.   Poor pay
   3.   Bad working conditions

Do not underestimate the value of this initial outline—or the work involved in achieving it. Be prepared to do a good deal of plain hard thinking at this first and most important stage of your paper.

2 Prepare a more detailed outline. The outline form that follows will serve as a guide. Your instructor may ask you to submit a copy of this form either before you actually write an essay or along with your finished essay.

Form for Planning an Essay

To write an effective essay, use a form like the one that follows.

Introduction

Opening remarks

Thesis statement _____

_____

Plan of development

Body

Topic sentence 1 _____

_____

Specific supporting evidence

Topic sentence 2 _____

_____

Specific supporting evidence

Topic sentence 3 _____

_____

Specific supporting evidence

Conclusion

Summary, closing remarks, or both

Writing an Exam Essay

Examination essays are among the most common types of writing that you will do in college. An exam essay includes one or more questions to which you must respond in detail, writing your answers in a clear, well-organized manner. This chapter describes five basic steps needed to prepare adequately for an essay test and to take the test. It is assumed, however, that you are already doing two essential things: first, attending class regularly and taking notes on what happens in class; second, reading your textbook and other assignments and taking notes on them. If you are not consistently going to class, reading your text, and taking notes in both cases, perhaps you should be asking yourself and talking with others (counselors, instructors, friends) about your feelings on being in school.

To write an effective exam essay, follow these five steps:

Step 1: Try to anticipate the probable questions on the exam.
Step 2: Prepare and memorize an informal outline answer for each question.
Step 3: Read exam directions and questions carefully, and budget your time.
Step 4: Prepare a brief outline before answering an essay question.
Step 5: Write a clear, well-organized essay.

Each step will be described on the pages that follow.

Step 1: Anticipate Probable Questions

Anticipating probable questions is not as hard as you might think. Because exam time is limited, the instructor can give you only several questions to answer. He or she will—reasonably enough—focus on questions dealing with the most important aspects of the subject. You can probably guess most of them if you make up a list of ten or more likely questions.

Your class notes are one key. What topics and ideas did your instructor spend a good deal of time on? Similarly, in your textbook, what ideas are emphasized? Usually the keys to the most important ideas are headings and subheadings, definitions and examples, enumerations, and ideas marked by emphasis signals. Also, take advantage of any study guides that may have been given out, any questions that you may have been given on quizzes, and any reviews that your instructor may have provided in class. You should, then, be able to determine the most important areas of the subject and make up questions that cover them.

Step 2: Prepare and Memorize an Informal Outline Answer and Keywords for Each Question

First, write out each question you have made up and, under it, list the main points that need to be discussed. Put important supporting information in parentheses after each main point. You now have an informal outline that you can memorize. The following suggestions will help you memorize this material.

Six Aids to Memorization

1 ***Intend to remember.*** The first aid to memory is intending to remember. This bit of advice appears to be so obvious that many people overlook its value. But if you have made the decision to remember something, and you then work at mastering it, you will remember. Anyone can have a bear-trap memory by working at it; no one is born with a naturally poor memory.

2 ***Overlearn.*** Overlearning is a second memory aid. If you study a subject beyond the time needed for perfect recall, you will increase the length of time that you will remember it. The method of repeated self-testing used the principle of overlearning; you can also apply this principle by going over several times a lesson you have already learned perfectly.

3 ***Space memory work.*** Spacing memory work over several sessions, rather than a single long one, is the third aid. Just as with physical exercise, five two-hour sessions spaced over several days are more helpful than ten hours all at once. The spaced sessions allow material time to "sink in." (Psychologists would say that it "transfers from short-term to long-term memory.") Spacing the sessions also helps you "lock in" material you have studied in the first session but have begun to forget. Studies show that forgetting occurs most rapidly soon after learning ends—but that review within a day or two afterward prevents much memory loss.

4 ***Study before bedtime.*** A fourth aid in memorizing material is studying just before going to bed. Do not watch a late movie or allow any other interference between studying and sleep. Then be sure to review the material immediately when you get up in the morning. Set your clock a half hour earlier than usual so that you will have time to do this. The review in the morning will help "lock in" the material that you have studied the night before and that your mind has worked over during the night.

continued

---

5 **Use keywords as "hooks."** A fifth helpful tool is using keywords in an outline as "hooks." Reduce your outline of a passage to a few keywords and memorize those words. The keywords you master will then serve as "hooks" that will help you pull back entire ideas into your memory.

6 **Use memory formulas.** Sixth and finally, another tool is using memory formulas to help you recall points under a main idea, items in a list, steps in a procedure, or other things arranged in a series. For example, you might remember the four methods used in behavior therapy (extinction, reinforcement, desensitization, and imitation) by writing down the first letter in each word (*e r d i*) and remembering the letters by forming an easily recalled catchphrase ("Ellen's rolling dice inside") or rearranging them to form an easily recalled word (*r i d e*). The letters serve as hooks that help you pull in words that are often themselves hooks for entire ideas.

Next, identify *keywords* in your outline. Circle one keyword in each entry in your outline.

As an additional memory aid, try combining the initial letters of your keywords to form a *catchword* or *catchphrase*—something you will be able to recall immediately.

Test yourself repeatedly on your outline, keywords, and catchword or catchphrase.

An Illustration of Step 2

One class was given a day to prepare for an essay exam. The students were told that the essay topic would be "Describe six aids to memory." One student, Teri, made up the following outline answer.

Six Memory Aids
1. (Intend) to remember (personal decision is crucial)
2. (Overlearn) (helps you remember longer)
3. (Space) memory work (several sessions rather than one long session)
4. Time before (bed) as a study period (no interference; review the next morning)
5. Use (keywords) as "hooks" (help pull whole ideas into memory)
6. Memory (formulas) (letters serve as hooks to help you remember items in a series)
IOSßKF (I often see Bill kicking footballs.)

Activity

See whether you can complete the following explanation of what Teri has done in preparing for the essay exam.

First, Teri wrote down the heading and numbered the different items under it.

Also, in parentheses beside each point she added _____.

_____. Next, she circled a keyword for each hint and wrote below her outline the first _____ of each keyword. She then used the first letter in each keyword to make up a catchphrase she could remember easily.

Finally, she _____ herself repeatedly until she could recall the keywords the letters stood for and the main points the keywords represented.

Step 3: Look at the Exam Carefully and Budget Your Time

First, read all test directions carefully. This point seems obvious, but people are often so anxious at the start of a test that they fail to read the instructions, and so they never understand clearly and completely just what they must do.

Second, read all the essay questions carefully, first noting the *direction word* or *words* in each question that tell you just what to do. For example, *enumerate,* or *list,* means "number 1, 2, 3, and so on"; *illustrate* means "explain by giving examples"; *compare* means "give similarities"; *contrast* means "give differences"; *summarize* means "give a condensed account of the main ideas."

Finally, budget your time, depending on the point value of each question and its difficulty for you. Write in the margin of the test the approximate time you give yourself to answer each question. This way you will not end the exam with too little time to respond to a question that you know you can answer.

An Illustration of Step 3

When Teri received the exam, she circled the direction word *Describe,* which she knew meant "Explain in detail." She also jotted "30" in the margin when the instructor said that students would have a half hour to write their answers.

Step 4: Prepare a Brief Outline before Answering an Essay Question

Too many students make the mistake of anxiously and blindly starting to write. Instead, you should first jot down the main points you want to discuss in an answer. (Use the margin of the exam or a separate piece of scratch paper.) Then decide how you will order the points in your essay. Write *1* in front of the first point, *2* beside the second, and so on. You now have an informal outline to guide you as you write your essay answer.

If there is a question on an exam which is similar to the questions you anticipated and outlined at home, quickly write down the catchphrase that calls back the content of your outline. Below the catchphrase, write the keywords represented by each letter in it. The keywords, in turn, will remind you of the ideas they represent. If you have prepared properly, this step will take only a minute or so, and you will have before you the guide you need to write a focused, supported, organized answer.

An Illustration of Step 4

Teri first recited her catchphrase to herself, using it as a guide to write down her memory formula (IOSBKF) at the bottom of the test sheet. The letters in the formula helped her call into memory the keywords in her study outline, and she wrote down those words. Then in parentheses beside each word she added the supporting points she remembered.

By investing only a couple of minutes, Teri was able to reconstruct her study outline and give herself a clear and solid guide to use in writing her answer.

Step 5: Write a Clear, Well-Organized Essay

If you have followed the suggestions to this point, you have done all the preliminary work needed to write an effective essay. Be sure not to wreck your chances of getting a good grade by writing carelessly. Instead, as you prepare your response, keep in mind the principles of good writing: unity, support, coherence, and clear, error-free sentences.

First, start your essay with a sentence that clearly states what your paper will be about. Then make sure that everything in your paper relates to your opening statement.

Second—although you must obviously take time limitations into account—provide as much support as possible for each of your main points.

Third, use transitions to guide your reader through your answer. Words such as *first, next, then, however,* and *finally* make it easy for the reader to follow your train of thought.

Last, leave time to edit your essay for sentence-skills mistakes you may have made while you concentrated on writing your answer. Look for words omitted, mis-written, or misspelled (if it is possible, bring a dictionary with you); look for awkward phrasings or misplaced punctuation marks; and look for whatever else may prevent the reader from understanding your thought. Cross out any mistakes and make your corrections neatly above the errors. To make a short insertion, use a *caret* (∧) and write the insertion above the line. For longer insertions—if you want to change or add to some point—insert an asterisk at the appropriate spot, put another asterisk at the bottom of the page, and add the corrected or additional material there.

An Illustration of Step 5

Read through Teri's answer, reproduced here, and then do the activity that follows.

3024	There are six aids to memory. One aid is to intend to remember. An important part of success is making the ~~decison~~ *decision* that you are truly
	going to remember something. A second aid is overlearning. ~~Studing~~
	Studying a lesson several more times after you know it will help you
	remember it longer. Also, space study over several sessions rather than *just*∧
	one long one.* Another aid is to study just before bedtime and not
	watch TV or do anything else after study. The mind ~~ad~~ absorbs the
	material during the night. ~~The most~~ You should then review the material
	the next morning. A fifth memory aid is *to*∧ use keywords as hooks. For
	example, the keyword "bed" helped me remember the entire idea
	about the value of studying right before sleep. A final aid to memory is
	memory formulas. I used the catchphrase "I often see Bill kicking
	footballs" and IOSBKF to recall the first letters of the six memory aids.
	*You need time in between for material to "sink in."

Activity

The following sentences comment on Teri's essay. Fill in the missing word or words in each case.

1. Teri begins with a sentence that clearly states what her paper _____. Always begin with such a clear signal!

2. The six transitions that Teri used to guide her reader, and herself, through the six points of her answer are:

    _____   _____   _____

    _____   _____   _____

3. Notice the various _____ that Teri made when writing and proof-reading her paper. She neatly crossed out miswritten or unwanted words; she

    used her _____ after she had finished her essay to correct a misspelled word; she used insertion signs, or carets (∧), to add omitted words; and she used an asterisk (*) to add an omitted detail.

Essay Writing Assignments

Hints: Keep the following points in mind when writing an essay on any of the topics below.

1 Your first step must be to plan your essay. Prepare both a scratch outline and a more detailed outline, as explained on the preceding pages.

2 While writing your essay, use the checklist below to make sure your essay touches all four bases of effective writing.

Base 1: Unity

_____ Clearly stated thesis in the introductory paragraph of your paper

_____ All the supporting paragraphs on target in backing up your thesis

Base 2: Support

_____ Three separate supporting points for your thesis

_____ *Specific* evidence for each of the three supporting points

_____ *Plenty* of specific evidence for each supporting point

Base 3: Coherence

_____ Clear method of organization

_____ Transitions and other connecting words

_____ Effective introduction and conclusion

Base 4: Sentence Skills

_____ Clear, error-free sentences (use the checklist on the inside front cover of this book)

■ 1 Your House or Apartment

Write an essay on the advantages *or* disadvantages (not both) of the house or apartment where you live. In your introductory paragraph, describe briefly the place you plan to write about. End the paragraph with your thesis statement and a plan of development. Here are some suggestions for thesis statements:

> The best features of my apartment are its large windows, roomy closets, and great location.
>
> The drawbacks of my house are its unreliable oil burner, tiny kitchen, and old-fashioned bathroom.
>
> An inquisitive landlord, sloppy neighbors, and platoons of cockroaches came along with our rented house.
>
> My apartment has several advantages, including friendly neighbors, lots of storage space, and a good security system.

■ 2 A Big Mistake

Write an essay about the biggest mistake you made within the past year. Describe the mistake and show how its effects have convinced you that it was the wrong thing to do. For instance, if you write about "taking a full-time job while going to school" as your biggest mistake, show the problems it caused. (You might discuss such matters as low grades, constant exhaustion, and poor performance at work, for example.)

To get started, make a list of all the things you did last year that, with hindsight, now seem to be mistakes. Then pick out the action that has had the most serious consequences for you. Make a brief outline to guide you as you write, as in the examples below.

<u>Thesis</u>: Separating from my husband was the worst mistake I made last year.
1.   Children have suffered
2.   Financial troubles
3.   Loneliness

<u>Thesis</u>: Buying a used car to commute to school was the worst mistake of last year.
1.   Unreliable—late for class or missed class
2.   Expenses for insurance, repairs
3.   Led to an accident

■   3   A Valued Possession

Write an essay about a valued material possession. Here are some suggestions:

Car	Appliance
Portable radio	Cassette deck
TV set	Photograph album
Piece of furniture	Piece of clothing
Piece of jewelry	Stereo system (car or home)
Camera	Piece of hobby equipment

In your introductory paragraph, describe the possession: tell what it is, when and where you got it, and how long you have owned it. Your thesis statement should center on the idea that there are several reasons this possession is so important to you. In each of your supporting paragraphs, provide details to back up one of the reasons.

For example, here is a brief outline of an essay written about a leather jacket:

1.   It is comfortable.
2.   It wears well.
3.   It makes me look and feel good.

■   4   Summarizing a Selection

Write an essay in which you summarize three of the Internet search techniques described on pages 320–326. *Summarizing* involves condensing material by highlighting main points and key supporting details. You can eliminate minor details and most examples given in the original material. You should avoid using the exact language in the original material; put the ideas into your own words.

The introductory paragraph of the essay and suggested topic sentences for the supporting paragraphs are provided below. In addition to developing the supporting paragraphs, you should write a brief conclusion for the essay.

Introductory Paragraph

Using the Internet for Research

Most of us love "surfing the Net." Where else could we so easily find the location and ticket prices of every concert within a hundred miles, up-to-the-minute news and sports scores, or a roomful of friendly people to chat with on a moment's notice? The Internet, however, is much more than an amusement park. Knowledgeable students have learned that it is also an invaluable source of information for papers and projects. There are three ways in which the Internet can be particularly helpful to students doing research papers. These are . . . *(Complete this sentence with the three uses of the Internet you decide to write about.)*

Suggested Topic Sentences for the Supporting Paragraphs (Choose Any Three)

First of all, the Internet can help students find books on a topic. . . .

In addition, students can use the Internet to locate periodical articles on a topic. . . .

Internet search directories are useful in several ways. . . .

Internet search engines are also a valuable research tool. . . .

Finally, students using the Internet should know how to evaluate what they find there. . . .

■ 5 Single Life

Write an essay on the advantages or drawbacks of single life. To get started, make a list of all the advantages and drawbacks you can think of. Advantages might include:

Fewer expenses
Fewer responsibilities
More personal freedom
More opportunities to move or travel

Drawbacks might include:

Parental disapproval
Being alone at social events
No companion for shopping, movies, and so on
Sadness at holiday time

After you make up two lists, select the thesis for which you feel you have more supporting material. Then organize your material into a scratch outline. Be sure to include an introduction, a clear topic sentence for each supporting paragraph, and a conclusion.

Alternatively, write an essay on the advantages or drawbacks of married life. Follow the directions given above.

■ 6 Influences on Your Writing

Are you as good a writer as you want to be? Write an essay analyzing the reasons you have become a good writer or explaining why you are not as good as you'd like to be. Begin by considering some factors that may have influenced your writing ability.

Your family background: Did you see people writing at home? Did your parents respect and value the ability to write?

Your school experience: Did you have good writing teachers? Did you have a history of failure or success with writing? Was writing fun, or was it a chore? Did your school emphasize writing?

Social influences: How did your school friends do at writing? What were your friends' attitudes toward writing? What feelings about writing did you pick up from TV or the movies?

You might want to organize your essay by describing the three greatest influences on your skill (or your lack of skill) as a writer. Show how each of these has contributed to the present state of your writing.

■ 7 A Major Decision

All of us come to various crossroads in our lives—times when we must make an important decision about which course of action to follow. Think about a major decision you had to make (or one you are planning to make). Then write an essay on the reasons for your decision. In your introduction, describe the decision you have reached. Each of the body paragraphs that follow should fully explain one of the reasons for your decision. Here are some examples of major decisions that often confront people:

Enrolling in or dropping out of college

Accepting or quitting a job

Getting married or divorced

Breaking up with a boyfriend or girlfriend

Having a baby

Moving away from home

Student papers on this topic include the essay on page 290 and the paragraphs on pages 51–52.

■ 8 Reviewing a TV Show or Movie

Write an essay about a television show or movie you have seen very recently. The thesis of your essay will be that the show (or movie) has both good and bad features. (If you are writing about a TV series, be sure that you evaluate only one episode.)

In your first supporting paragraph, briefly summarize the show or movie. Don't get bogged down in small details here; just describe the major characters briefly and give the highlights of the action.

In your second supporting paragraph, explain what you feel are the best features of the show or movie. Listed below are some examples of good features you might write about:

Suspenseful, ingenious, or realistic plot

Good acting

Good scenery or special effects

Surprise ending

Good music

Believable characters

In your third supporting paragraph, explain what you feel are the worst features of the show or movie. Here are some possibilities:

Far-fetched, confusing, or dull plot

Poor special effects

Bad acting

Cardboard characters

Unrealistic dialogue

Remember to cover only a few features in each paragraph; do not try to include everything.

■ 9 Good Qualities

We are often quick to point out a person's flaws, saying, for example, "That instructor is conceited," "My boss has no patience," or "My sister is lazy." We are usually equally hard on ourselves; we constantly analyze our own faults. We rarely, though, spend as much time thinking about another person's, or our own, good qualities. Write an essay on the good qualities of a particular person. The person might be an instructor, a job supervisor, a friend, a relative, some other person you know well, or even yourself.

■ 10 Your High School

Imagine that you are an outside consultant called in as a neutral observer to examine the high school you attended. After your visit, you must send the school board a five-paragraph letter in which you describe the most striking features (good, bad, or a combination of both) of the school and the evidence for each of these features.

In order to write the letter, you may want to think about the following features of your high school:

Attitude of the teachers, student body, or administration

Condition of the buildings, classrooms, recreational areas, and so on

Curriculum

How classes are conducted

Extracurricular activities

Crowded or uncrowded conditions

Be sure to include an introduction, a clear topic sentence for each supporting paragraph, and a conclusion.

Part Four

Research
Skills

Preview

Part Four presents skills that will help you with writing projects requiring research. "Using the Library and the Internet" provides basic information about these two sources. It explains how a college library and the Internet are organized and shows how you can use them to decide on a topic and find material on that topic. "Writing a Research Paper" then guides you through the process of writing the paper itself. It describes six steps to follow, from selecting a topic through using an appropriate format and method of documentation, and it includes a model research paper.

18 Using the Library and the Internet

This chapter provides the basic information you need to use your college library and the Internet with confidence. You will learn that for most research topics there are two basic steps you should take:

1 Find books on your topic.
2 Find articles on your topic.

You will learn, too, that while using the library is the traditional way of doing such research, a home computer with an online service and Internet access now enables you to investigate any topic.

Using the Library

Most students seem to know that libraries provide study space, word-processing facilities, and copying machines. They are also aware of a library's reading area, which contains recent copies of magazines and newspapers. But the true heart of a library is the following: a *main desk,* the library's *catalog or catalogs of holdings, book stacks,* and the *periodicals storage area.* Each of these will be discussed on the pages that follow.

Main Desk

The main desk is usually located in a central spot. Check at the main desk to see if there is a brochure that describes the layout and services of the library. You might also ask if the library staff provides tours of the library. If not, explore your library to find each of the areas described below.

Activity

Make up a floor plan of your college library. Label the main desk, catalog or catalogs, book stacks, and periodicals area.

Library Catalog

The *library catalog* will be your starting point for almost any research project. The *catalog* is a list of all the holdings of the library. It may still be an actual card catalog: a file of cards alphabetically arranged in drawers. More likely, however, the catalog is computerized and can be accessed on computer terminals located at different spots in the library. And increasingly, local and college libraries can be accessed online, so you may be able to check their book holdings on your home computer.

Finding a Book—Author, Title, and Subject

Whether you use an actual file of cards, use a computer terminal, or visit your library's holdings online, it is important for you to know that there are three ways to look up a book. You can look it up according to *author, title,* or *subject.* For example, suppose you wanted to see if the library has the book *Amazing Grace,* by Jonathan Kozol. You could check for the book in any of three ways:

1 You could do an *author* search and look it up under *Kozol, Jonathan.* An author is always listed under his or her last name.

2 You could do a *title* search and look it up under *Amazing Grace.* Note that you always look up a book under the first word in the title, excluding the words *A, An,* or *The.*

3 If you know the subject that the book deals with—in this case, "poor children"— you could do a *subject* search and look it up under *Poor children.*

Here is the author entry in a computerized catalog for Kozol's book *Amazing Grace:*

Author:	Kozol, Jonathan
Title:	Amazing Grace
Publisher:	New York: Crown, 1995
LC Subjects:	1. Poor children— New York (N.Y.) 2. Racism and racial segregation— New York (N.Y.) 3. Children of minorities— New York (N.Y.) 4. AIDS, asthma, illnesses of children.
Call Number:	362.709 Koz
Material:	Book
Location:	Cherry Hill
Status:	Available

Note that in addition to giving you the publisher (Crown) and year of publication (1995), the entry also tells you the *call number*—where to find the book in the library. If the computerized catalog is part of a network of libraries, you may also learn at what branch or location the book is available. If the book is not at your library, you can probably arrange for an interlibrary loan.

Using Subject Headings to Research a Topic

Generally if you are looking for a particular book, it is easier to search by *author* or *title.* On the other hand, if you are researching a topic, then you should search by *subject.*

The subject section performs three valuable functions:

- It will give you a list of books on a given topic.
- It will often provide related topics that might have information on your subject.
- It will suggest to you more limited topics, helping you narrow your general topic.

Chances are you will be asked to do a research paper of about five to fifteen pages. You do not want to choose a topic so broad that it could be covered only by an entire book or more. Instead, you want to come up with a limited topic that can be adequately supported in a relatively short paper. As you search the subject section, take advantage of ideas that it might offer on how you can narrow your topic.

Activity

Part A: Answer the following questions about your library's catalog.

1. Is your library's catalog an actual file of cards in drawers, or is it computerized?

_____

2. Which type of catalog search will help you research and limit a topic?

_____

Part B: Use your library's catalog to answer the following questions.

1. What is the title of one book by Alice Walker?

_____

2. What is the title of one book by George Will?

_____

3. Who is the author of *The Making of the President?* (Remember to look up the title under *Making*, not *The.*)

_____

4. Who is the author of *Angela's Ashes?* _____

5. List two books and their authors dealing with the subject of adoption:

   a. _____

   _____

   b. _____

   _____

6. Look up a book titled *The Road Less Traveled* or *Passages* or *The American Way of Death* and give the following information:

   a. Author _____

   b. Publisher _____

   c. Date of publication _____

   d. Call number _____

   e. Subject headings: _____

7. Look up a book written by Barbara Tuchman or Russell Baker or Bruce Catton and give the following information:

   a. Title _____

   b. Publisher _____

   c. Date of publication _____

   d. Call number _____

   e. Subject headings: _____

Book Stacks

The *book stacks* are the library shelves where books are arranged according to their call numbers. The *call number*, as distinctive as a social security number, always appears on the catalog entry for any book. It is also printed on the spine of every book in the library.

If your library has open stacks (ones that you are permitted to enter), here is how to find a book. Suppose you are looking for *Amazing Grace*, which has the call number HV[875] / N48 / K69 in the Library of Congress system. (Libraries using the Dewey decimal system have call letters made up entirely of numbers rather than letters and numbers. However, you use the same basic method to locate a book.) First, you go to the section of the stacks that holds the H's. After you locate the H's, you look for the HV's. After that, you look for HV875. Finally, you look for HV875 / N48 /K69, and you have the book.

If your library has *closed stacks* (ones you are not permitted to enter), you will have to write down the title, author, and call number on a request form. (Such forms will be available near the card catalog or computer terminals.) You'll then give the form to a library staff person, who will locate the book and bring it to you.

Activity

Use the book stacks to answer one of the following sets of questions. Choose the questions that relate to the system of classifying books used by your library.

Library of Congress System (letters and numbers)

1. Books in the BF21 to BF833 area deal with
   a. philosophy.   c. psychology.
   b. sociology.   d. history.
2. Books in the HV580 to HV5840 area deal with which type of social problem?
   a. Drugs   c. White-collar crime
   b. Suicide   d. Domestic violence
3. Books in the PR4740 to PR 4757 area deal with
   a. James Joyce.   c. George Eliot.
   b. Jane Austen.   d. Thomas Hardy.

Dewey Decimal System (numbers)

1. Books in the 320 area deal with:
   a. self-help.   c. science.
   b. divorce.   d. politics.
2. Books in the 636 area deal with:
   a. animals.   c. marketing.
   b. computers.   d. senior citizens.
3. Books in the 709 area deal with
   a. camping.   c. art.
   b. science fiction.   d. poetry.

Periodicals

The first step in researching a topic is to check for relevant books; the second step is to locate relevant periodicals. *Periodicals* (from the word *periodic*, which means "at regular periods") are magazines, journals, and newspapers. Periodicals often contain recent information about a given subject, or very specialized information about a subject, which may not be available in a book.

The library's catalog lists the periodicals that it holds, just as it lists its book holdings. To find articles in these periodicals, however, you will need to consult a *periodicals index.* Three indexes widely used in libraries are *Readers' Guide to Periodical Literature, Magazine Index Plus,* and *EBSCOhost.*

Readers' Guide to Periodical Literature

The old-fashioned way to do research is to use the familiar green volumes of the *Readers' Guide,* found in just about every library. They list articles published in more than two hundred popular magazines, such as *Newsweek, Health, People, Ebony, Redbook,* and *Popular Science.* Articles appear alphabetically under both subject and author. For example, if you wanted to learn the names of articles published on the subject of child abuse within a certain time span, you would look under the heading "Child abuse."

Here is a typical entry from the *Guide:*

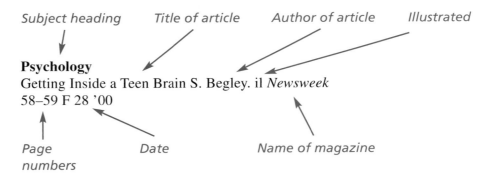

Note the sequence in which information about the article is given:

1 Subject heading.
2 Title of the article. In some cases, there will be bracketed words [ ] after the title that help make clear just what the article is about.
3 Author (if it is a signed article). The author's first name is always abbreviated.
4 Whether the article has a bibliography (*bibl*) or is illustrated with pictures (*il*). Other abbreviations sometimes used are shown in the front of the *Readers' Guide.*

5 Name of the magazine. A short title like *Time* is not abbreviated, but longer titles are. For example, the magazine *Popular Science* is abbreviated *Pop Sci.* Refer to the list of magazines in the front of the index to identify abbreviations.

6 Page numbers on which the article appears.

7 Date when the article appeared. Dates are abbreviated: for example, *Mr* stands for *March*, *Ag* for *August*, *O* for *October*. Other abbreviations are shown in the front of the *Guide*.

The *Readers' Guide* is published in monthly supplements. At the end of a year, a volume is published covering the entire year. You will see in your library large green volumes that say, for instance, *Readers' Guide 1998* or *Readers' Guide 2000*. You will also see the small monthly supplements for the current year.

The drawback of *Readers' Guide* is that it gives you only a list of articles; you must then go to your library's catalog to see if the library actually has copies of the magazines that contain those articles. If you're lucky and it does, you must take the time to locate the relevant issue, and then to read and take notes on the articles or make copies of them.

Readers' Guide is also available in a much more useful form on CD-ROM (compact disc, read-only memory). Using a computer terminal that accesses the CD-ROM, you can quickly search for articles on a given subject. You do this by typing into a box provided a keyword or phrase that will enable the computer to search for articles on your subject.

Magazine Index Plus

Magazine Index Plus is a computerized file that lists articles published over the last several years in about four hundred general-interest magazines, in addition to the *New York Times*. Once again, by sitting at a computer terminal and typing in a keyword or keywords for your subject, you can rapidly locate relevant articles.

EBSCOhost

Many libraries now provide an online computer search service such as *InfoTrac, Dialog,* or *EBSCOhost*. Sitting at a terminal and using *EBSCOhost,* for instance, you will be able to use keywords to quickly search many hundreds of periodicals for full-text articles on your subject. When you find articles that are relevant for your purpose, you can either print them off using a library printer (libraries may charge you about ten cents a page) or e-mail those articles to your home computer and run them off on your own printer. Obviously, if an online resource is available, that is the way you should conduct your research.

Activity 1

At this point in the chapter, you now know the two basic steps in researching a topic in the library. What are the steps?

1. _____

_____

2. _____

_____

Activity 2

1. Look up a recent article about Internet shopping using one of your library's periodicals indexes and fill in the following information:

   a. Name of the index you used _____

   b. Article title _____

   c. Author (if given) _____

   d. Name of magazine _____

   e. Pages _____   f.   Date _____

2. Look up a recent article about violence in schools using one of your library's periodicals indexes and fill in the following information:

   a. Name of the index you used _____

   b. Article title _____

   c. Author (if given) _____

   d. Name of magazine _____

   e. Pages _____   f.   Date _____

Specialized Indexes

Either through CD-ROM or online, your library will make available to you a number of specialized indexes. Your instructors may expect you to consult one or more of these indexes to obtain more specialized and professional information on a given subject. Listed here are representative indexes.

General
Biography Index
Humanities Index

New York Times Index
Social Sciences Index
Speech Index

Art/Literature

Art Index
Book Review Index
MLA Index
Music Index
New York Times Book Review Index

Business

Business Periodicals Index

Education

Education Index
ERIC

History/Political Science

Historical Abstracts
Public Affairs Information Service

Philosophy/Religion

Religion Index

Sciences

Applied Science and Technology Index
Biological Abstracts
Environment Index

Women's and Ethnic Studies

Hispanic American Periodicals Index
Index to Periodical Articles by and about Blacks
Women's Resources International

Using the Internet

The *Internet* is dramatic proof that a computer revolution has occurred in our lives. It is a giant network that connects computers at tens of thousands of educational, scientific, government, and commercial agencies around the world. Existing within the Internet is the World Wide Web, a global information system which got its name because countless individual websites contain *links* to other sites, forming a kind of web.

To use the Internet, you need a personal computer with a *modem*—a device that sends or receives electronic data over a telephone line for no more than the cost of a local telephone call. You also need to subscribe to an online service provider such as America Online or Earthlink. If you have an online service as well as a printer for your computer, you can do a good deal of your research for a paper at home. As you would in a library, you should proceed by searching for books and articles on your topic.

Before you begin searching the Internet on your own, though, take the time to learn whether your local or school library is online. If it is, visit its online address to find out exactly what sources and databases it has available. You may be able to do all your research using the online resources available through your library. If, on the other hand, your library's resources are limited, you can turn on your own to the Internet to search for material on any topic, as explained on the pages that follow.

Find Books on Your Topic

To find current books on your topic, go online and type in the address of one of the large commercial online booksellers:

Amazon at *www.amazon.com.*
Barnes and Noble Books at *www.bn.com*

The easy-to-use search facilities of both Amazon and Barnes and Noble are free, and you are under no obligation to buy books from them.

In some cases, you may not have to type the *www.* (for *World Wide Web*); the search program you are using may provide it for you. Note, by the way, that *.com* in the two addresses above is simply an abbreviation for *commercial*, referring to a business. Common abbreviations and examples are shown in the box on the next page.

Abbreviation	What It Indicates	Examples
.com	commercial organization; business	*www.mhhe.com* (McGraw-Hill Higher Education)
.edu	educational institution	*www.atlantic.edu* (Atlantic Cape Community College)
.gov	government agency	*www.whitehouse.gov* (President of the United States)
		www.usps.gov (United States Postal Service)
.mil	military agency	*www.defenselink.mil* (United States Department of Defense)
.net	Internet service provider; commercial organization	*www.earthlink.net* (Earthlink Network)
.org	nonprofit organization	*www.redcross.org* (American Red Cross)
		www.pbs.org (Public Broadcasting System)

Use the "Browse Subjects" Box

After you arrive at the Amazon or Barnes and Noble website (or the online library site of your choice), go to the "Browse Subjects" or "Keywords" box. You'll then get a list of categories where you might locate books on your general subject. For example, if your assignment was to report on the development of the modern telescope, you would notice that one of the subject listings is "science and nature." Upon choosing "science and nature," you would get several subcategories, one of which is "astronomy." Clicking on that will offer you still more subcategories, including one called "telescopes." When you choose that, you would get a list of recent books on the topic of telescopes. You could then click on each title for information about each book. All this browsing and searching can be done very easily and will help you research your topic quickly.

Use the "Keyword" Box

If your assignment is to prepare a paper on some aspect of photography, type in the word "photography" in the keyword search box. You'll then get a list of books on that subject. Just looking at the list may help you narrow your subject and decide on a specific topic you might want to develop. For instance, one student typed in "photography" as her keyword on Barnes and Noble's site and got back a list of thirteen thousand books on the subject. Considering just part of that list helped her realize that she wanted to write on some aspect of photography during the U.S. Civil War. She typed "Civil War Photography" and got back a list of twenty-six titles. After looking at information about those books, she was able to decide on a limited topic for her paper.

A Note on the Library of Congress

The commercial bookstore sites described are especially quick and easy to use. But you should know that to find additional books on your topic, you can also visit the Library of Congress website (*www.loc.gov*). The Library of Congress, in Washington, D.C., has copies of all books published in the United States. Its online catalog contains about twelve million entries. You can browse this catalog by subject or search by keywords. The search form permits you to check just those books that interest you and then print the list or e-mail it to yourself. Clicking on "Full Record" provides publication information about a book, as well as its call numbers. You can then try to find the book in your college library or through an interlibrary loan.

Other Points to Note

Remember that at any time, you can use your printer to quickly print out information presented on the screen. (For example, the student planning a paper on photography in the Civil War could print out a list of the twenty-six books, along with sheets of information about individual books.) You could then go to your library knowing just what books you want to borrow. If your own local or school library is accessible online, you can visit in advance to find out whether it has the books you want. Also, if you have time and money and if some of the books are available in paperback, you may want to purchase them from the online bookstore, which typically ships books in two to three days.

Find Articles on Your Topic

There are many online sources that will help you find articles on your subject. Following are descriptions of some of them.

A Resource for Magazines and Newspaper Articles

One online research resource that you can use at home is Electric Library; it's available at *www.elibrary.com*. Chances are you may get a free thirty-day trial subscription, or you'll be able to enroll on a monthly basis at a modest cost. Electric Library contains millions of newspaper and magazine articles as well as many thousands of book chapters and television and radio transcripts. After typing in one or more keywords, you'll get long lists of articles that may relate to your subject. When you then click on a given title, the full text of the article appears. If it fits your needs, you can print it out right away on your printer. Very easily, then, you can research a full range of magazine and newspaper articles.

For instance, one student wanted to write about the general topic of earthquakes. He typed in the keyword "earthquakes" and indicated that he wanted to see sixty documents. (In Electric Library, the user can indicate how many documents he or she wishes to see; the documents are ranked by the number of times the search term appears in each document.) In return, he got four magazine articles, four book excerpts, forty-seven newspaper articles, and five radio transcripts. Reading through the titles of these documents helped him decide that he would focus his research on the science of predicting earthquakes. When he typed in the keywords "predicting earthquakes" and asked for thirty documents, he received a variety of newspaper and magazine articles, book excerpts, and radio transcripts dealing specifically with that topic.

Here are three other good sources for magazine and newspaper articles.

America Online Newspaper Directory at *www.aol.com/directories/newspaper/html*

The Internet Public Library at *www.ipl.org/reading/news* and *www.ipl.org/reading/serials*

The Magazine Rack at *www.magazine-rack.com*

Search Directories and Search Engines

A number of search directories and search engines will help you find information quickly on the Internet; the box below shows some popular ones and their addresses.

About *(www.about.com)*

AltaVista *(www.altavista.com)*

Ask Jeeves *(www.askjeeves.com)*

Excite *(www.excite.com)*

Go *(www.go.com)*

Google *(www.google.com)*

Lycos *(www.lycos.com)*

Northern Light *(www.northernlight.com)*

Refdesk *(www.refdesk.com)*

Yahoo! *(www.yahoo.com)*

A *search directory* organizes websites by categories. For example, on the next page is a picture of Yahoo's opening screen, also known as its *home page*. (Websites change their home pages all the time, so what appears on your computer screen may differ from what you see here.) You'll see that there are a number of subject areas you might visit, ranging from "Arts & Humanities" to "Society & Culture," depending on the area you want to research.

Each category is presented as a *link*—a stepping-stone that will take you to other sites. Typically, a link shows up as an underlined word or phrase that is a different color from the type elsewhere on the page. When you click on a link, you're automatically transported to a related site. There you are often presented with a more detailed list of websites and pages to choose from. As you move from link to link, you move from the general topic to more specific aspects of the topic.

If, for instance, you felt you wanted to do a research paper on some aspect of animals, you could click on the category "animals." Doing so would bring up more than fifty subcategories, including "Marine Life," "Animal Rights," "Veterinary Medicine," and "Prehistoric Animals." Let's say you wanted to explore possible topics in the area of marine life. Simply click on that item and you get a list of fourteen subgroupings, including "Squids," "Public Aquariums," "Underwater Photography," "Sharks," and "Jellyfish." In other words, Yahoo or any other search directory can help you discover a limited topic that you might want to research.

A *search engine* uses keywords to comb through the vast amount of information on the Web for sites or articles on particular topics. You activate a search engine by typing in a keyword or keywords that tell the engine what to look for. It then provides you with a list of "hits," or links, to sites or pages that contain your keywords. For example, a student planning a paper on threatened extinction of animal species first typed the words "animal species extinction" into the Search box on the Yahoo home page and within seconds got back a list of five website matches. Each of these sites brought up many individual articles on the extinction and animal species. The student was also given the option of learning about Web page matches. When he clicked on this option, he was given a list of 13,353 different articles he could access!

The overwhelming amount of information helped him realize that his research topic was far too broad, and he decided then to narrow his topic to extinction and the peregrine falcon. He typed in those keywords, which resulted in 689 Web page matches. As he read those articles and printed out the most relevant ones, he was able to further narrow his research.

Very often your challenge with searches will be getting too much information rather than too little. Most search engines include a *help* feature that will provide you with suggestions on ways to limit your search. Also, you might try another search engine. It may pitch a subject in a different way and give you other ideas for exploring your subject.

Auctions   Messenger   Check Email  YAHOO!   What's New   Personalize   Help

new! **Tournament Pick'em**
Men's – Women's

Free Cell Phone and Accessories + No Credit Card Needed

Yahoo! Mail
free from anywhere

[Search] advanced search

Y! Shopping Depts: Books, CDs, Computers, DVDs **Stores**: Handspring, LuxuryFinder, The Company Store, and more

Shop Auctions · Classifieds · **PayDirect** · Shopping · Travel · Yellow Pgs · Maps Media **Finance**/Quotes · News · Sports · Weather
Connect **Careers** · Chat · Clubs · Experts · GeoCities · Greetings · **Mail** · Members · Messenger · Mobile · Personals · People Search
Personal Addr Book · Briefcase · Calendar · **My Yahoo!** · Photos Fun Games · Kids · Movies · Music · **Radio** · TV **more...**

Yahoo! Auctions – Bid, buy, or sell anything!
Categories
· Antiques   · Computers   · Longaberger   · Scooters
· Cameras   · Electronics   · PlayStation 2 · Dale Earnhardt
· Coins   · Sports Cards · MP3 Players   · State Quarters
· Comic Books   · Stamps   · WWF   · Palm Pilots
Got Something to Sell? Auction it Now!

In the News
· Ground controller tried to abort Kuwait bombing
· Bush backs off pledge to regulate carbon dioxide emissions
· U.S. bans EU meat imports over foot-and-mouth disease
more...

Marketplace
· Tax Center – forms, tips, online filing and more
· Y! Careers – find a job, post your resume
· Y! Autos – buy, sell, maintain & worship
· Y! Travel – plan your spring break

Broadcast Events
· 9pm ET : Avalanche vs. Devils
· 10pm : Blazers vs. Sonics
more...

Inside Yahoo!
· new! Play free Tournament Pick'em
· Planning a party? Send an invite
· Play free Fantasy Baseball
· Y! Games – backgammon, euchre, hearts, chess, pinochle

Arts & Humanities
Literature, Photography...

Business & Economy
B2B, Finance, Shopping, Jobs...

Computers & Internet
Internet, WWW, Software, Games...

Education
College and University, K-12...

Entertainment
Cool Links, Movies, Humor, Music...

Government
Elections, Military, Law, Taxes...

Health
Medicine, Diseases, Drugs, Fitness...

News & Media
Full Coverage, Newspapers, TV...

Recreation & Sports
Sports, Travel, Autos, Outdoors...

Reference
Libraries, Dictionaries, Quotations...

Regional
Countries, Regions, US States...

Science
Animals, Astronomy, Engineering...

Social Science
Archaeology, Economics, Languages...

Society & Culture
People, Environment, Religion...

Make Yahoo! your home page

How to Suggest a Site – Company Info – Copyright Policy – Terms of Service – Contributors – Jobs – Advertising

All the information, including categories and subcategories and related sites and pages, may seem overwhelming at first. But the very process of considering all of this information can help you think actively and creatively about just what you want your topic to be and how to limit that topic.

Additional Internet Pointers

1 *Creating bookmarks.* When you find a helpful website that you may want to visit again, save its address. The program you are using will probably have a "Bookmark" or "Favorite Places" option. With the click of a mouse, you can "bookmark" a site. You will then be able to return to it simply by clicking on its name, rather than having to remember and type an address.

2 ***Evaluating Internet sources.*** Keep in mind that the quality and reliability of information you find on the Internet may vary widely. Anyone with a bit of computer know-how can create a website and post information there. That person may be a Nobel prize winner, a high school student, or a crackpot. Be careful, then, to look closely at your electronic source:

- *Electronic address:* Who is sponsoring the website? Is it an organization, a business, a government agency, a lobbying group, or an individual? Does the sponsor have reason to push a single point of view? If so, use this material with caution.
- *Author:* What credentials (if any) does the author have? Do these credentials qualify the author to provide information on the topic? Does the author provide an e-mail address so that you can request more information?
- *Internal evidence:* Does the author refer to studies or to other authors you can investigate? If the author does not name other sources or points of view, the information may be opinionated and one-sided.
- *Date:* Is the information cited recent and up-to-date? Check at the top or bottom of the document for copyright date, publication date, revision date, or all three. Having these dates will help you decide whether the material is recent enough for your purposes.

Practice in Using the Library and the Internet

Activity

Use your library or the Internet to research a subject that interests you. Select one of the following areas, or (with your instructor's permission) one of your own choice:

Assisted suicide	Computer use and carpal tunnel syndrome
Interracial adoptions	Noise control
Best job prospects today	Animals nearing extinction
Sexual harassment	Animal rights movement
Home schooling	Antigay violence
Greenhouse effect	Drug treatment programs for adolescents
Nursing home costs	Fertility drugs
Pro-choice movement today	Witchcraft today
Pro-life movement today	New treatments for AIDS
Attention deficit disorder (ADD)	Mind-body medicine

Drinking water pollution	Habitat for Humanity
Problems of retirement	Hazardous substances in the home
Cremation	Teenage fathers
Road rage	Gambling and youth
Prenatal care	Nongraded schools
Acid rain	Earthquake forecasting
New aid for the handicapped	Ethical aspects of hunting
New remedies for allergies	Vegetarianism
Censorship on the Internet	Recent consumer frauds
New prison reforms	Stress reduction in the workplace
Drug treatment programs	Global warming
Sudden infant death syndrome (SIDS)	Everyday addictions
New treatments for insomnia	Toxic waste disposal
Organ donation	Self-help groups
Child abuse	Telephone crimes
Voucher system in schools	Date rape
Food poisoning (salmonella)	Heroes for today
Alzheimer's disease	Eating disorders
Holistic healing	Surrogate mothers
Adoptions: Open records or closed?	Computer crime

Research the topic first through a subject search in your library's catalog or that of an online bookstore. Then research the topic through a periodicals index (print or online), or an online search directory or search engine. On a separate sheet of paper, provide the following information:

1. Topic
2. Three books that either cover the topic directly or at least in some way touch on the topic. Include these items:

   Author

   Title

   Place of publication

   Publisher

   Date of publication

3. Three articles on the topic published in 1996 or later. Include these items:

Title of article

Author (if given)

Title of magazine

Date

Page or pages (if given)

4. Finally, include a paragraph describing just how you went about researching your topic. In addition, include a photocopy or printout of one of the three articles.

19 Writing a Research Paper

The process of writing a research paper can be divided into six steps:

1 Select a topic that you can readily research.

2 Limit your topic and make the purpose of your paper clear.

3 Gather information on your limited topic.

4 Plan your paper and take notes on your limited topic.

5 Write the paper.

6 Use an acceptable format and method of documentation.

This chapter explains and illustrates each of these steps and then provides a model research paper.

Step 1: Select a Topic That You Can Readily Research

Researching at a Local Library

First of all, do a *subject* search of your library's catalog (as described on page 313) and see whether there are several books on your general topic. For example, if you initially choose the broad topic of "divorce," try to find at least three books on the topic of divorce. Make sure that the books are actually available on the library shelves.

Next, go to a *periodicals index* in your library (see pages 316–319) to see if there are a fair number of magazine, newspaper, or journal articles on your subject. For instance, when Sarah Hughes, author of the model research paper "Divorce Mediation," visited her local library, she found a CD-ROM index called *Magazine Index Plus* (see page 317), which indexes all the articles published over a three- to four-year period in over four hundred popular magazines. When Sarah typed in the search term "divorce," *Magazine Index Plus* came back with hundreds of "hits"—titles, locations, and brief descriptions of articles about divorce. The index also marked those articles that were in magazines available in Sarah's library.

Researching on the Internet

If you have access to the Internet on a home or library computer, you can use it to determine if resources are available for your topic.

The first step is to go to the *subjects* section of a large online bookseller or library catalog to find relevant books. (Don't worry—you don't have to buy the books; you're just browsing for information.) As mentioned in Chapter 18, two of the largest online booksellers are Barnes and Noble and Amazon.

Sarah Hughes checked out both Barnes and Noble *(www.bn.com)* and Amazon *(www.amazon.com)*. "Both sites were easy to use," she reported. "All I had to do to get started was look at their 'browse subject' options and click on the subjects that seemed most relevant.

"At Barnes and Noble, the category I clicked on first was called 'Parenting and Families.' Under that was a bunch of subcategories, including one on 'Divorce.' I clicked on 'Divorce' and that brought up a list of 733 books! I spent some time scrolling through those titles and saw that there were lots of different themes: mostly 'how to survive your own divorce' books, but also books on all kinds of other topics, like 'how to keep sane while your boyfriend is going through a divorce' and 'how to stay involved in your children's lives when you're not living with them.' Others were about all kinds of emotional, legal, and financial aspects of divorce. There were clearly plenty of divorce-related books available, but I still didn't know what my paper's focus was going to be." At this point Sarah was feeling frustrated. She would return to Barnes and Noble a little later, but first she decided to try something else: searching online for newspaper and magazine articles.

There are several ways to determine if magazine or newspaper articles on your topic are available online. Your Internet service provider (such as America Online) has a built-in "engine" that allows you to search the Internet for any topic you like. When you type in a keyword or keywords related to your topic, you'll get back a listing of sources, or "hits," on the Internet. Sarah relates her experience searching the Internet in this way:

"First I typed in the word 'divorce' in the keyword box," she said. "I got more than a hundred thousand hits! When I looked at the first twenty or thirty sites, I saw that most of them were useless to me—they were advertisements from divorce lawyers, or information about divorce law in one particular state, etc. Now I was *really* frustrated. How was I ever going to narrow this topic down?"

Sarah turned to her instructor, asking how she could find magazine and newspaper articles about divorce. Her instructor recommended Electric Library, an online research service that the college subscribed to. (See more about Electric Library on pages 322–323.) This is what happened next: "I typed in the search word 'divorce,' clicked on the newspaper and magazine icons to indicate where I wanted to search, and asked to see 150 documents—the maximum number Electric

Library offers," says Sarah. "In a few seconds I was looking at headlines of 150 recent articles about divorce. I started clicking and reading, skimming each article for its main ideas, and finally I felt I was making some progress. I noticed the title of a *USA Today* article—'A Kinder, Gentler Divorce?'—that really grabbed my attention. I read it carefully and came across a phrase I hadn't heard before: 'divorce mediation.' In that article, I learned that divorce mediation helps people divorce without becoming bitter enemies in the process. To me, it definitely sounded like a topic worth exploring. So I went back to the Electric Library search box and typed in 'divorce mediation,' asking for 30 articles. I began to read them and realized I had struck gold. I'd narrowed the huge topic of 'divorce' down to a much more specific one. Now I was beginning to have a focus."

Encouraged, Sarah returned to Barnes and Noble and asked to see books on "divorce mediation." That brought up a manageable list of just 41 books. As Sarah clicked on their titles, she instantly saw on the screen information about those books—the titles and authors, reviews, sometimes even summaries and tables of contents. Reading about those books helped Sarah narrow her focus even further: she decided that her paper would be about the advantages of divorce mediation over traditional divorce. With that idea in mind, she was able to choose ten books that sounded most relevant to her paper. She went to her local library and found six of those books, then bought one more that was available in paperback at a nearby bookstore. (If you find relevant books in your online search that your local library does not own, ask your research librarian if he or she can obtain them from another library through an interlibrary loan program.)

However you choose to do your research, the outcome is the same: If both books and articles are available, pursue your topic. Otherwise, you may have to choose another topic. You cannot write a paper on a topic for which research materials are not readily available.

Step 2: Limit Your Topic and Make the Purpose of Your Paper Clear

A research paper should *thoroughly* develop a *limited* topic. It should be narrow and deep rather than broad and shallow. Therefore, as you read through books and articles on your general topic, look for ways to limit the topic.

For instance, as Sarah read through materials on the general topic "divorce," she chose to limit her paper to divorce mediation. Furthermore, she decided to limit it even more by focusing on the advantages of mediated divorce over more traditional adversarial divorce. The general topic "violence in the media" might be narrowed to instances of copycat crimes inspired by movies or TV. After doing some reading on protests against the death penalty, you might decide to limit your paper to cases in which executed people were later proved innocent. The broad subject "learning disabilities" could be reduced to the widespread use of the drug Ritalin or possible causes of dyslexia. "AIDS" might be limited to federal funding to fight the disease; "personal debt" could be narrowed to the process an individual goes through in declaring bankruptcy.

The subject headings in your library's catalog and periodicals index will give you helpful ideas about how to limit your subject. For example, under the subject heading "Divorce" in the book file at Sarah's library were titles suggesting many limited directions for research: helping children cope with divorce, cooperative parenting after a divorce, the financial toll of divorce, fathers and custody rights. Under the subject heading "Divorce" in the library's periodicals index were sub-headings and titles of many articles which suggested additional limited topics that a research paper might explore: how women can learn more about family finances in the event of a divorce, how parents can move past their own pain to focus on children's welfare, becoming a divorce mediator, divorce rates in second marriages. The point is that *subject headings and related headings, as well as book and article titles, may be of great help to you in narrowing your topic.* Take advantage of them.

Do not expect to limit your topic and make your purpose clear all at once. You may have to do quite a bit of reading as you work out the limited focus of your paper. Note that many research papers have one of two general purposes. Your purpose might be to make and defend a point of some kind. (For example, your purpose in a paper might be to provide evidence that gambling should be legalized.) Or, depending on the course and the instructor, your purpose might simply be to present information about a particular subject. (For instance, you might be asked to write a paper describing the most recent scientific findings about what happens when we dream.)

Step 3: Gather Information on Your Limited Topic

After you have a good sense of your limited topic, you can begin gathering information that is relevant to it. A helpful way to proceed is to sign out the books that you need from your library. In addition, make copies of all relevant articles from magazines, newspapers, or journals. If your library has an online periodicals database, you may be able to print those articles out.

In other words, take the steps needed to get all your important source materials together in one place. You can then sit and work on these materials in a quiet, unhurried way in your home or some other place of study.

Step 4: Plan Your Paper and Take Notes on Your Limited Topic

Preparing a Scratch Outline

As you carefully read through the material you have gathered, think constantly about the specific content and organization of your paper. Begin making decisions about exactly what information you will present and how you will arrange it. Prepare a scratch outline for your paper that shows both its thesis and the areas of support for the thesis. It may help to try to plan at least three areas of support.

Thesis: _____

Support: 1. _____

2. _____

3. _____

Here, for example, is the brief outline that Sarah Hughes prepared for her paper on divorce mediation:

<u>Thesis:</u>   Divorce mediation is an alternative to the painful, expensive process of a traditional divorce.

<u>Support:</u>   1. Saves time and money

2. Produces less hostility

3. Produces more acceptable agreement between ex-spouses

Taking Notes

With a tentative outline in mind, you can begin taking notes on the information that you expect to include in your paper. Write your notes on four- by six-inch or five- by eight-inch cards, on sheets of loose-leaf paper, or in a computer file. The notes you take should be in the form of *direct quotations, summaries in your own words,* or both. (At times you may also *paraphrase*—use an equal number of your own words in place of someone else's words. Since most research involves condensing information, you will summarize much more than you will paraphrase.)

A *direct quotation* must be written *exactly* as it appears in the original work. But as long as you don't change the meaning, you may omit words from a quotation if they are not relevant to your point. Show such an omission with three bracketed spaced periods (known as an *ellipsis)* in place of the deleted words:

Original Passage

If you choose to follow the traditional path through this adversarial system, you will each hire lawyers who will fight on your behalf like ancient knights, charging each other with lances. Each knight, highly skilled in the intricacies of jousting but untrained in other ways to resolve conflict, will try to win by seizing for his client as much booty (children and property) as possible.

Direct Quotation with Ellipses

"[Y]ou will each hire lawyers who will fight on your behalf like ancient knights, charging each other with lances. Each knight [. . .] will try to win by seizing for his client as much booty (children and property) as possible."

(Note that the capital letter in brackets shows that the word was capitalized by the student, but did not begin the sentence in the original source. Similarly, the brackets around the three periods indicate that the student inserted these ellipses.)

In a *summary*, you condense the original material by expressing it in your own words. Summaries may be written as lists, as brief paragraphs, or both. Following is one of Sarah Hughes's summary note cards:

Abusive spouse

If there has been a recent history of physical abuse, mediation should not be attempted. If the abuse has been mental/verbal, mediation may not be successful if abused partner is very intimidated.

Butler/Walker, 46–47

Keep in mind the following points about your research notes:

- Write on only one side of each card or sheet of paper.
- Write only one kind of information, from one source, on any one card or sheet. For example, the sample card above has information on only one idea (abusive spouse) from one source (Butler/Walker).

- At the top of each card or sheet, write a heading that summarizes its content. This will help you organize the different kinds of information that you gather.
- Identify the source and page number at the bottom.

Whether you quote or summarize, be sure to record the exact source and page from which you take each piece of information. In a research paper, you must document all information that is not common knowledge or a matter of historical record. For example, the birth and death dates of Dr. Martin Luther King, Jr., are established facts and do not need documenting. On the other hand, the number of adoptions granted to single people in 2000 is a specialized fact that should be documented. As you read several sources on a subject, you will develop a sense of what authors regard as generally shared or common information and what is more specialized information that must be documented.

A Note on Plagiarism

If you do not document information that is not your own, you will be stealing. The formal term is *plagiarizing*—using someone else's work as your own, whether you borrow a single idea, a sentence, or an entire essay. Plagiarism is a direct violation of academic ethics; if you pass someone else's work off as your own, you risk being failed or even expelled. Also, plagiarism undermines the money, time, and energy you have spent in school, cheating you out of an education.

With the accessibility of the Internet—especially websites targeting students—comes new temptation to plagiarize. But just remember that those sites are just as accessible to your instructor as they are to you. Many writing instructors are aware of these Internet "resources" and can spot "recycled" work.

If you use another person's material, *you must acknowledge your source.* When you cite a source properly, you give credit where it is due, you provide your readers with a way to locate the original material on their own, and you demonstrate that your work is carefully researched.

Step 5: Write the Paper

After you have finished reading and note-taking, you should have a fairly clear idea of the plan of your paper. Make a *final outline* and use it as a guide to write your first full draft. If your instructor requires an outline as part of your paper, you should prepare either a *topic outline*, which contains your thesis plus supporting words and phrases; or a *sentence outline,* which contains all complete sentences. In the model paper shown on pages 342–352, a topic outline appears on page 343. You will note that roman numerals are used for first-level headings, capital letters for second-level headings, and arabic numerals for third-level headings.

In your *introduction,* include a thesis statement expressing the purpose of your paper and indicate the plan of development that you will follow. The section on writing an introductory paragraph for an essay (pages 286–288) is also appropriate for the introductory section of a research paper.

As you move from *introduction* to *main body* to *conclusion,* strive for unity, support, and coherence so that your paper will be clear and effective. Repeatedly ask, "Does each of my supporting paragraphs develop the thesis of my paper?" Use the checklist on the inside front cover of this book to make sure that your paper touches all four bases of effective writing.

Step 6: Use an Acceptable Format and Method of Documentation

Format

The model paper on pages 342–352 shows acceptable formats for a research paper, including the style recommended by the Modern Language Association (MLA). Be sure to note carefully the comments and directions set in small print in the margins of each page.

Documentation of Sources

You must tell the reader the sources (books, articles, and so on) of the borrowed material in your paper. Whether you quote directly or summarize ideas in your own words, you must acknowledge your sources. In the past, you may have used footnotes and a bibliography to cite your sources. Here you will learn a simplifed and widely accepted documentation style used by the Modern Language Association.

Citations within a Paper

When citing a source, you must mention the author's name and the relevant page number. The author's name may be given either in the sentence you are writing or in parentheses following the sentence. Here are two examples:

Paula James, the author of <u>The Divorce Mediation Handbook</u>, has witnessed the divorce process from both sides—actually, <u>three</u> sides. First, she went through a traditional divorce herself. In her words, "we simply turned our destinies over to our two attorneys. [. . .] Many thousands of dollars later we were divorced, but with resentment and distrust and no idea of how we would jointly raise our child" (xvi).

> As the authors of <u>The Divorce Mediation Answer Book</u> say, a mediated agreement is "future focused. In mediation, as contrasted to litigation, each of you is empowered to control your own future, and since you have shared in the negotiation process, you are more likely to abide by the agreement" (Butler and Walker 5).

There are several points to note about citations within the paper:

- When an author's name is provided within the parentheses, only the last name is given.
- There is no punctuation between the author's name and the page number.
- The parenthetical citation is placed after the borrowed material but before the period at the end of the sentence.
- If you are using more than one work by the same author, include a shortened version of the title within the parenthetical citation. For example, suppose you were using two books by Paula James and you included a second quotation from her book *The Divorce Mediation Handbook*. Your citation within the text would be:

> (James, <u>Handbook</u> 39).

Note that a comma separates the author's last name from the abbreviated title and page number.

Citations at the End of a Paper

Your paper should end with a list of "Works Cited" which includes all the sources actually used in the paper. (Don't list any other sources, no matter how many you have read.) Look at "Works Cited" in the model research paper (page 352) and note the following points:

- The list is organized alphabetically according to the authors' last names. (If no author is given, the entry is alphabetized by title.) Entries are not numbered.
- Entries are double-spaced, with no extra space between entries.
- After the first line of each entry, there is a half-inch indentation for each additional line in the entry.
- Use the abbreviation *qtd. in* when citing a quotation from another source. For example, a quotation from Lynn Jacob on page 3 of the paper is from a work written not by her but by Ann Field. The citation is therefore handled as follows:

> As pointed out by Lynn Jacob, president of the Academy of Family Mediators, "the legal system is designed so that the more the couples fight, the more money the lawyers earn" (qtd. in Field 136).

Model Entries for a List of "Works Cited"

Model entries of "Works Cited" are given below. Use these entries as a guide when you prepare your own list.

Book by One Author

Nuland, Sherwin B. <u>How We Die: Reflections on Life's Final Chapter</u>. New

York: Vintage, 1995.

Note that the author's name is reversed.

In addition, when citing *any* book, always provide the full title, which you should copy from the inside title page. Include any subtitle by placing a colon after the main title and then copying the subtitle, word for word.

Two or More Entries by the Same Author

---. <u>The Mysteries Within: A Surgeon Reflects on Medical Myths</u>. New York:

Simon & Schuster, 2000.

If you cite two or more entries by the same author (in the example above, a second book by Sherwin B. Nuland is cited), do not repeat the author's name. Instead, begin with a line made up of three hyphens followed by a period. Then give the remaining information as usual. Arrange the works by the same author alphabetically by title. The words *A, An,* and *The* are ignored in alphabetizing by title.

Book by Two or More Authors

Baxandall, Rosalyn, and Elizabeth Ewen. <u>Picture Windows: How the</u>

<u>Suburbs Happened</u>. New York: Basic Books, 2000.

For a book with two or three authors, give all the authors' names but reverse only the first name. For a book with more then three authors, cite only the first author's name, followed by a comma and the phrase *et al.*

Magazine Article

Chin, Paula. "You Were a Good Man, Charlie Brown." <u>People</u> 28 Feb. 2000:

52–59.

Write the date of the issue as follows: day, month (abbreviated in most cases to three or four letters), and year, followed by a colon. The final number or numbers refer to the pages of the issue on which the article appears.

Newspaper Article

Zoroya, Gregg. "A Hunger for Heroes." <u>USA Today</u> 28 Feb. 2000: D1–2.

The final letter and number refer to pages 1 and 2 of section D.

If the article is not printed on consecutive pages, simply list the first page, followed by a plus sign "+" (in that case, the above example would read "D1+").

In addition, when citing newspaper titles, omit the introductory *The* (for example, *Boston Globe*, not *The Boston Globe*).

Editorial

"Drugs and Preschoolers." Editorial. <u>Philadelphia Inquirer</u> 28 Feb.

2000: A10.

List an editorial as you would any signed or unsigned article, but indicate the nature of the piece by adding *Editorial* or *Letter* after the article's title.

Selection in an Edited Collection

Feist, Raymond E. "The Wood Boy." <u>Legends: Short Novels by the Masters of Modern Fantasy</u>. Ed. Robert Silverberg. New York: Tor Books, 1998. 176–211.

Revised or Later Edition

Davis, Mark H. <u>Social Psychology</u>. 4th ed. New York: McGraw-Hill, 2000.

Note: The abbreviations *Rev. ed., 2nd ed., 3rd ed.,* and so on, are placed right after the title.

Chapter or Section in a Book by One Author

Secunda, Victoria. "A New Sense of Family." <u>Losing Your Parents, Finding Yourself: The Defining Turning Point of Adult Life</u>. New York: Hyperion, 2000. 242–59.

Pamphlet

<u>Heart and Stroke Facts</u>. New York: American Heart Association, 2000.

Television Program

"Not As Private As You Think." <u>60 Minutes</u>. Narr. Lesley Stahl. Prod. Rome
Hartman. CBS. 13 Aug. 2000.

Film

<u>Music of the Heart</u>. Dir. Wes Craven. Miramax, 1999.

Sound Recording

Chapman, Tracy. "Speak the Word." <u>Telling Stories</u>. Elektra Entertainment,
2000.

Videocassette

"To the Moon." <u>Nova</u>. Narr. Liev Schrieber. Videocassette. PBS Video, 1999.

Personal Interview

Anderson, Robert B. Personal interview. 17 Sept. 2000.

Online Source in a Reference Database

"Heredity." <u>Britannica Online</u>. Sept. 1999. Encyclopaedia Britannica.
2 Mar. 2000 <http://www.britannica.com/bcom/eb/article/4/0,
5716,120934,00.html#Article>.

The first date refers to the online publication date; the second refers to the exact
day when the student researcher accessed the information and should *not* be followed by a period.

Online Article

Ehrenreich, Barbara. "Will Women Still Need Men?" <u>Time Online</u> 21 Feb.
2000. 15 Apr. 2000 <http://www.time.com/time/reports/v21/live/
men_mag.html>.

Activity

On a separate sheet of paper, convert the information in each of the following references into the correct form for a list of "Works Cited." Use the appropriate model above as a guide.

1. An article by Alex Yannis titled "In New League, Women Get Payoff and Payday" on page D5 of the April 13, 2001 issue of the *New York Times.*

2. An article by Nancy Franklin titled "Nonsense and Sensibility" on pages 96–97 of the March 6, 2000 issue of the *New Yorker.*

3. A book by Francis McInerney and Sean White called *Futurewealth: Investing in the Second Great Wave of Technology* and published in New York by St. Martin's in 2000.

4. A book by Ellen N. Junn and Chris Boyatzis titled *Child Growth and Development* and published in a seventh edition by McGraw-Hill in New York in 2000.

5. An article by Melinda Liu and Leila Abboud titled "Generation Superpower" dated April 11, 2001 and found on April 12, 2001 at <http://www.msnbc.com/news/557986.asp> in the online version of *Newsweek.*

Model Paper

Option 1: Model Title Page

The title should begin about one-third of the way down the page. Center the title. Double-space between lines of the title and your name. Also center and double-space the instructor's name and the date.

While the *MLA Handbook* does not require a title page or an outline for a paper, your instructor may ask you to include one or both. Here is a model title page.

Divorce Mediation: A Better Alternative

by

Sarah Hughes

English 101

Professor Martinez

8 March 2001

Option 2: Model First Page with Top Heading

Double-space between lines. Leave a one-inch margin on all sides.

Papers written in MLA style use the simple format shown below. There is no title page or outline.

½ inch

1 inch

Hughes 1

Sarah Hughes

Professor Martinez

English 101

8 March 2001

Divorce Mediation: A Better Alternative

Divorce is never easy. Even if two people both want to part, ending a marriage is a painful experience. In order to become divorced, most people go through a process that increases this pain. Starting with the lawsuit that one partner has to file against the other, the two take on the roles of enemies. . . .

Model Outline Page

After the title page, number all pages in upper-right corner—a half-inch from the top. Place your name before the page number. Use small Roman numerals on outline pages. Use arabic numbers on pages following the outline.

The word *Outline* (without underlining or quotation marks) is centered one inch from the top. Double-space between lines. Leave a one-inch margin on all sides.

— Use this format if your instructor asks you to submit an outline of your paper. —

Hughes i

Outline

Thesis: Divorce mediation offers several advantages over the traditional process of divorce.

I.   Introduction
   A.   Traditional divorce
      1.   Casts divorcing couple in the role of enemies
      2.   Expensive and painful
   B.   Mediation
      1.   Description of mediation process
      2.   Growing popularity of mediation

II.   Advantages of mediation in terms of money and time
   A.   Traditional divorce
      1.   Lawyers' fees charged for every step
      2.   Lawyers' and courts' involvement slows process down
   B.   Mediation
      1.   Mediators' fees lower than lawyers'
      2.   Couple controls costs of case
      3.   Mediated divorces completed more quickly

III.   Emotional benefits of mediation
   A.   Traditional divorce
      1.   Pits clients against one another
      2.   Produces hostility and distrust
   B.   Mediation encourages clients to work cooperatively

IV.   Advantages of mediation in terms of divorce agreement
   A.   Traditional divorce leaves clients with attorney-negotiated agreement that may not work well for them
   B.   Mediation creates agreement that both clients can live with

V.   Who shouldn't use mediation

VI.   Conclusion

Hughes 1

Divorce Mediation: A Better Alternative

Divorce is never easy. Even if two people both want to break up, ending a marriage is a painful experience. In order to become divorced, most people go through a process that increases this pain. Starting with the lawsuit that one partner files against the other, the two take on the roles of enemies. As author Paula James describes it,

> You will each hire lawyers who will fight on your behalf like ancient knights, charging each other with lances. Each knight [. . .] will try to win by seizing for his client as much booty (children and property) as possible. You will stand on the sidelines wringing your hands while you watch the battle—and, of course, pay your knight a high hourly fee. One peculiarity of this battle is that the wounds inflicted don't appear on the other warrior; they appear on you, your spouse, and your children. (3)

But there is an alternative to this traditional, ugly divorce process. It is called divorce mediation. Couples who use divorce mediation find that it saves them time and money, it produces less hostility, and it leaves them with an agreement they can respect.

What is divorce mediation? According to a 1997 article in USA Today, it is a process in which "the couple, rather than a judge, decides who gets the kids, the house, the cars, and other marital assets. The mediator serves as coach, counselor, consensus builder and occasional referee" (Valente B7). That mediator, who is usually a lawyer or a therapist, helps the couple hammer out a divorce agreement they both find acceptable. This is done in as few or as

---

Margin notes (left column):

Double-space between lines of the text. Leave a one-inch margin all the way around the page. Your name and the page number should be typed one-half inch from the top of the page.

Source is identified by name.

Direct quotations of five typed lines or more are indented ten spaces from the left margin. Quotation marks are not used.

The bracketed spaced periods (ellipsis) show that material from the original source has been omitted.

Only the page number is needed, as the author has already been named in the text.

Thesis, followed by plan of development.

Citation for a signed newspaper article. The letter and number refer to section B, page 7.

Hughes 2

many meetings as necessary. Each spouse will probably hire a personal lawyer to review the agreement before it is made final. But the spouses, not "hired gun" lawyers, are responsible for creating it. During the process, the mediator doesn't favor one partner over the other. Instead the mediator maintains, in the words of the lawyer and mediator Gary Friedman, an attitude of "positive neutrality." Friedman explains the term by saying, "While I am largely neutral as to outcome [. . .] I am not neutral as to process. On the contrary, I am actively engaged in trying to ensure that each party takes responsibility for him- or herself, and making sure that all decisions are sound for both of them" (26).

Once the couple is satisfied with the agreement, it is filed in court and approved by a judge in a brief hearing. In many states, the couple does not even need to attend that hearing. Couples can thus complete a divorce without ever seeing the inside of a courtroom.

There are no official statistics to tell how many divorcing couples use mediation, but it is definitely becoming a popular option. According to the Academy of Family Mediators in Boston, the number of mediators has jumped in recent years from just 100 to over 3,600 (Valente B7). And courts in twenty-five states now <u>require</u> couples involved in child-custody disputes to work with a mediator (Field 136).

One practical advantage of mediation is that it is less expensive and less time-consuming. In a traditional divorce, after each partner retains a lawyer and sets the divorce machine in motion, costs mount up quickly. A lawyer's fee "may range from $125 to $500 per hour [. . .] for each spouse" ("Avoiding the War"). The lawyers bill their clients

---

Margin notes:

Source is identified by name and area of expertise

This typical citation is made up of the author's last name and the relevant page number. "Works Cited" then provides full information about the source.

Citation for an on-line source. No page number is given because the online document does not provide one.

Hughes 3

for every phone call made, every letter written, every hearing attended, every meeting held to iron out another wrinkle in the process. In addition, when people divorce, they must make decisions about countless details. Even if the spouses are not far apart in their thinking, those decisions take time. If the husband and wife are deeply divided, the bills can become staggering. According to Field, "An uncontested, amiable divorce may cost $5,000 per partner and drag on for more than a year. [. . .] A warring duo [. . .] could wind up spending $30,000 apiece, and the case might span an entire Presidential administration" (136). The couple's financial welfare is not the top concern of courts and attorneys. As pointed out by Lynn Jacob, president of the Academy of Family Mediators, "the legal system is designed so that the more the couples fight, the more money the lawyers earn" (qtd. in Field 136).

By contrast, mediation costs are far more reasonable. Most mediators charge between $100 and $350 an hour (Friedman 19). Because both spouses are present for all mediating sessions, they are in control of how high the costs mount. Although there is no "typical" divorce, it is clear that mediated divorces tend to be much less expensive than others. In Friedman's experience, a mediated divorce in which there is "substantial disagreement" costs between $2,000 and $5,000 (19). Ken Waldron, a mediator with the Madison (Wisconsin) Center for Divorce Mediation, estimates that most mediated divorces end up costing one-half to one-third less than an attorney-negotiated divorce (Schuetz 10). Mediator Paula James

The abbreviation *qtd.* means *quoted.* The quoted material is not capitalized because the student has blended it into a sentence with an introductory phrase.

Quotation marks acknowledge that the phrase is copied from the previous citation.

Hughes 4

describes mediated divorces as costing "a fraction" of attorney-negotiated ones (60).

Second, mediated divorces are finalized much more quickly than divorces fought out in the courts. Couples divorcing in the traditional way spend a long time going through the following cycle: meet with attorney, wait for attorney to talk with spouse's attorney, wait for spouse's attorney to talk with spouse, wait for spouse's attorney to return with response. Mediating couples don't have to do any of that. They also don't have the ordeal of endless hearings, court delays, and their attorneys' own schedule problems. Mediating couples can do a large part of the work of their divorce agreement outside their meetings with the mediator. Most mediating couples really want to get their agreement finished, for both financial and emotional reasons. Because they have the guidance of a professional to help them work through difficult points, they tend to work efficiently. According to an article by Meg Lundstrum in <u>Business Week</u>, most mediated divorces are completed in four to eight sessions, or six to twenty-four hours (228). Gary Friedman's estimate is about the same: four to six meetings spaced over a period of two to three months (18). A typical mediation center advertising online, Divorce Solutions of New York, N.Y., says, "The entire divorce process takes approximately 2–3 months, as opposed to 2–3 years in the adversarial process" ("Mediation: How It Works").

Citation for an online source. →

A third important point is that mediated divorces leave less hostility behind them. It's true that a divorce produces feelings of grief, anger, and frustration for almost everyone. But mediation can help people deal with these feelings. By contrast, an attorney-fought

divorce seems designed to make the splitting partners hate each

other as much as possible. Before she wrote <u>The Divorce Mediation</u>

<u>Handbook</u>, Paula James had witnessed the divorce process from both

sides—actually, <u>three</u> sides. First, she went through a traditional

divorce herself. In her words, "we simply turned our destinies over

to our two attorneys. [. . .] Many thousands of dollars later we were

divorced, but with resentment and distrust and no idea of how we

would jointly raise our child" (xvi).

Later, James became an attorney herself and represented clients

in traditional divorces. She describes how she and her colleagues

routinely dug for dirt about possible affairs, alcohol abuse, shady

business dealings, child neglect, and any other personal weaknesses

they could use as ammunition in court. By the end of such an ordeal,

she writes, couples were "deeply in debt, very angry, and distrustful

of one another" (10).

Finally, James began working as a divorce mediator. As a mediator

she works with many clients who may no longer be the best of friends

but who want to remain on decent terms with their ex-spouses, for

their own sake as well as for the sake of any children. One such client,

Terri, expressed the feelings of many people who want a mediated

divorce. She called James after having talked with an attorney. Terri

was horrified by the attorney's fee ($5,000 to start) and what he told

her. " 'He said that Eli and I are now adversaries, that I must do

everything I can to protect myself from him and to get as much

money as possible . . . ,' Terri said. 'That's not what I want. I'm sorry

Single
quotation
marks are
used for a
quotation
within a
quotation.

Hughes 6

that our marriage hasn't worked out, but I'm not trying to take Eli to the cleaners' " (10). Terri and Eli then started working with James. By listening carefully to them both, and stepping in occasionally to help them explain their fears and priorities rather than attack one another, James helped Terri and Eli work out an agreement in a short time and for a reasonable fee. "They left my office looking more relaxed than when they had entered," she reported (15). According to the Divorce Law Information Service Center's home page, "In family law disputes, mediation is often preferred over litigation because it facilitates future communication between the parties which is necessary when the future of the children is at stake."

In the long run, the biggest advantage of mediated divorce is that it helps couples develop an agreement they will be willing to live with. As the authors of The Divorce Mediation Answer Book say, a mediated agreement is "future focused. In mediation, as contrasted to litigation, each of you is empowered to control your own future, and since you have shared in the negotiation process, you are more likely to abide by the agreement" (Butler and Walker 5). Attorney-negotiated agreements tend to fall into rigid, traditional patterns: she gets the house; he gets the car; the kids spend every other weekend and six weeks in the summer with him. But mediated agreements are generally more creative and in tune with the divorcing couple's lives. One couple described in the Cosmopolitan article, Vivian and Bill, had been fighting bitterly over the mail-order business they had built together. Each insisted that he or she should take over the business entirely.

Quoted from an on-line source. Since the source has been named in the text, no further citation is necessary.

Without lawyers, judges, or formal courtroom rules to get in the way, the mediator got Vivian and Bill to agree on a general plan whereby one spouse would keep the business, buy out the other, and lend him or her enough money to start a new venture. Then he instructed them to calculate their company's net worth. Finally, the material helped them realize on their own that Vivian, who'd had more contact with overseas suppliers, should keep the business; Bill, who was more aggressive, would do better taking the loan and launching a new product line. (Field 137)

Once they are used to the idea, most couples like the idea of creating an agreement that really works for them. In the words of Paula James, "[The divorcing couple] aren't ignorant children who must be silenced while their lawyers do the talking" (xvii).

Although mediation has clear advantages, it is not right for everyone. Most mediation experts agree with Butler and Walker, who say that mediation "would not be an appropriate way to negotiate a fair settlement" if one of the divorcing partners feels unable or too frightened to stand up to the other. Examples are situations characterized by "intimidation or fear of violence," "a recent history of domestic violence or child abuse," or "severe intellectual or emotional limitations" (6). In such cases, it is probably best for the weaker partner if an attorney does his or her negotiating.

In conclusion, while divorce is never a pleasant experience, divorce mediation can save a couple time and money, help them keep a civil relationship, and produce an agreement that they both feel is

Brackets indicate that the words inside them were supplied by the student and did not appear in the original source.

The conclusion provides a summary and restates the thesis.

Hughes 8

reasonable. According to the Academy of Family Mediators, 70 to 90 percent of couples are satisfied with the terms of their mediated divorces (Lundstrum 228). This high figure shows that mediation is a more civilized and respectful way to achieve a divorce than the traditional courtroom method.

A mediating couple, Sam and Jane, said it best:

> [Sam said,] "I really do appreciate your help. This was a lot easier than I thought it would be."
>
> Jane smiled. "We both thought we were going to end up in a huge fight. Doing it this way was so much better." (Qtd. in James xi)

Works cited should be double-spaced. Titles of books, magazines, and the like should be underlined.

Include the date you accessed a Web source—in this case, February 18, 2000.

Works Cited

"Avoiding the War." Divorce Mediation Services. 18 Feb. 2000

<http://www.divorcewithoutwar.com/avoiding.htm>.

Butler, Carol A., and Dolores D. Walker. <u>The Divorce Mediation</u>

<u>Answer Book</u>. New York: Kodansha America, 1999.

<u>The Divorce Law Information Center Home Page</u>. The Divorce Law

Information Center. 18 Feb. 2000

<http://www.divorcelawinfo.com/mediation/intromed.htm>.

Field, Ann. "Divorce Mediation and Other (Cheap) Ways to Split."

<u>Cosmopolitan</u> Aug. 1995: 136–37.

Friedman, Gary J. <u>A Guide to Divorce Mediation</u>. New York: Workman,

1993.

James, Paula. <u>The Divorce Mediation Handbook</u>. San Francisco: Jossey-

Bass, 1997.

Lundstrom, Meg. "A Way to 'Take the War' Out of Divorce." <u>Business</u>

<u>Week</u> 16 Nov. 1998: 228.

"Mediation: How It Works." <u>Divorce Solutions Home Page</u>. Mar. 1999.

18 Feb. 2000 <http://www.divorcesolutions.com/mediation.html>.

Schuetz, Lisa. "Mediation Offers an Alternative When Dealing with

Divorce." <u>Wisconsin State Journal</u> 31 May 1998: 10.

Valente, Judith. "A Kinder, Gentler Divorce?" <u>USA Today</u> 25 Aug.

1997: B7.

Three of the above sources (*The Divorce Law Information Center Home Page* and the articles "Avoiding the War" and "Mediation: How It Works") are online. By going online and typing the letters after *www.* in each citation, you can access any of the sources. For example, you could type *divorcewithoutwar.com/avoiding.htm* to call up the first online article cited.

Part Five

Handbook of
Sentence Skills

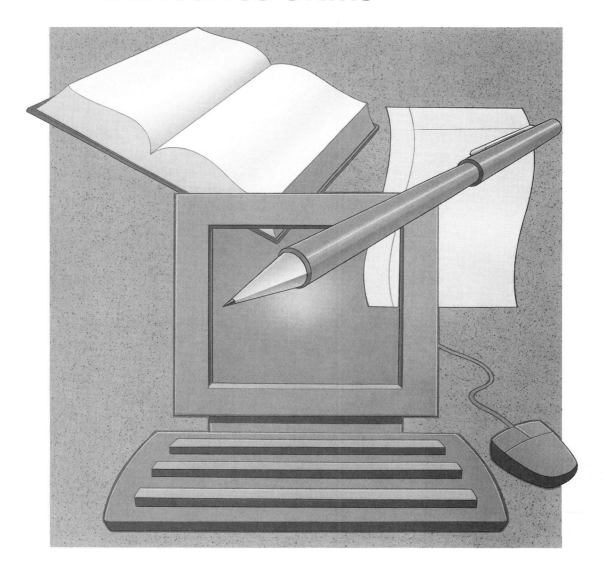

Preview

As explained in Part One, there are four steps, or bases, in effective writing. Part Five is concerned with the fourth step: the ability to write clear, error-free sentences. First a diagnostic test is provided so that you can check your present understanding of important sentence skills. Then the skills themselves appear under the general headings "Grammar," "Mechanics," "Punctuation," and "Word Use." Then there is a chapter that presents pointers and brief activities for ESL students. Next come mastery tests and then editing tests that reinforce many basic writing skills and give you practice in editing and proofreading. Closing out Part Five is an achievement test that helps you measure your improvement in important sentence skills.

Sentence-Skills Diagnostic Test

Part 1

This test will help you check your knowledge of important sentence skills. Certain parts of the following word groups are underlined. Write X in the answer space if you think a mistake appears at the underlined part. Write C in the answer space if you think the underlined part is correct.

A series of headings ("Fragments," "Run-Ons," and so on) will give you clues to the mistakes to look for. However, you do not have to understand the label to find a mistake. What you are checking is your own sense of effective written English.

Fragments

_____ 1. Until his mother called him twice. Barry did not get out of bed. He had stayed up too late the night before.

_____ 2. After I slid my aching bones into the hot water of the tub, I realized there was no soap. I didn't want to get out again.

_____ 3. I spent two hours on the phone yesterday. Trying to find a garage to repair my car. Eventually I had to have the car towed to a garage in another town.

_____ 4. Sweating under his heavy load. Brian staggered up the stairs to his apartment. He felt as though his legs were crumbling beneath him.

_____ 5. I love to eat and cook Italian food, especially lasagna and ravioli. I make everything from scratch.

_____ 6. One of my greatest joys in life is eating desserts. Such as blueberry cheesecake and vanilla cream puffs. Almond fudge cake makes me want to dance.

Run-Ons

_____ 7. He decided to stop smoking, for he didn't want to die of lung cancer.

_____ 8. The window shade snapped up like a gunshot her cat leaped four feet off the floor.

_____ 9. Billy is the meanest little kid on his block, he eats only the heads of animal crackers.

_____ 10. He knew he had flunked the driver's exam, he ran over a stop sign.

_____ 11. My first boyfriend was five years <u>old. We</u> met every day in the playground sandbox.

_____ 12. The store owner watched the shopper <u>carefully, she</u> suspected him of stealing from her before.

Standard English Verbs

_____ 13. Jed <u>tows</u> cars away for a living and is ashamed of his job.

_____ 14. You <u>snored</u> like a chain saw last night.

_____ 15. When I was about to finish work last night, a man <u>walk</u> into the restaurant and ordered two dozen hamburgers.

_____ 16. Charlotte <u>react</u> badly whenever she gets caught in a traffic jam.

Irregular Verbs

_____ 17. I <u>gived</u> a twenty-dollar bill to the cashier and waited for my change.

_____ 18. I had <u>eaten</u> so much food at the buffet dinner that I went into the bathroom just to loosen my belt.

_____ 19. When the mud slide started, the whole neighborhood <u>began</u> going downhill.

_____ 20. Juan has <u>rode</u> the bus to school for two years while saving for a car.

Subject-Verb Agreement

_____ 21. There <u>is</u> long lines at the checkout counter.

_____ 22. The little girl <u>have</u> a painful ear infection.

_____ 23. One of the crooked politicians <u>was</u> jailed for a month.

_____ 24. The cockroaches behind my stove <u>gets</u> high on Raid.

Consistent Verb Tense

_____ 25. My brother and I played video games for an hour before we <u>start</u> to do homework.

_____ 26. The first thing Jerry does every day is weigh himself. The scale <u>informs</u> him what kind of meals he can eat that day.

_____ 27. Sandy eats a nutritional breakfast, <u>skips</u> lunch, and then enjoys a big dinner.

_____ 28. His parents stayed together for his sake; only after he <u>graduates</u> from college were they divorced.

Pronoun Agreement, Reference, and Point of View

_____ 29. I get my hair cut by a barber who talks to <u>you</u> constantly.

_____ 30. I enjoy movies like *The Return of the Vampire* that frighten <u>me</u>.

_____ 31. Every guest at the party dressed like <u>their</u> favorite cartoon character.

_____ 32. Persons camping in those woods should watch <u>their</u> step because of wild dogs.

_____ 33. Angry because he had struck out, Tony hurled the baseball bat at the fence and broke <u>it</u>.

_____ 34. I love Parmesan cheese, but <u>it</u> does not always agree with me.

Pronoun Types

_____ 35. Alfonso and <u>me</u> take turns driving to work.

_____ 36. No one is a better cook than <u>she</u>.

Adjectives and Adverbs

_____ 37. Bonnie ran <u>quick</u> up the steps, taking them two at a time.

_____ 38. Larry is <u>more better</u> than I am at darts.

Misplaced Modifiers

_____ 39. He swatted the wasp that stung him <u>with a newspaper</u>.

_____ 40. Charlotte returned the hamburger <u>that was spoiled</u> to the supermarket.

_____ 41. Jamal test-drove a car at the dealership <u>with power windows and a sunroof</u>.

_____ 42. I adopted a dog from a junkyard <u>which is very close to my heart</u>.

Dangling Modifiers

_____ 43. <u>Tapping a pencil on the table</u>, Ms. Garcia asked for the students' attention.

_____ 44. <u>Flunking out of school</u>, my parents demanded that I get a job.

_____ 45. <u>While I was waiting for the bus</u>, rain began to fall.

_____ 46. <u>Braking the car suddenly</u>, the shopping bags tumbled onto the floor.

Faulty Parallelism

_____ 47. Jeff enjoys hunting for rabbits, socializing with friends, and <u>to read the comics</u>.

_____ 48. The recipe instructed me to chop onions, to peel carrots, and <u>to boil a pot of water</u>.

_____ 49. When I saw my roommate with my girlfriend, I felt worried, angry, and <u>embarrassment as well</u>.

_____ 50. Frances enjoys shopping for new clothes, <u>trying different cosmetics</u>, and reading beauty magazines.

Capital Letters

_____ 51. Sitting in the hot, stuffy classroom, I couldn't stop thinking about a cold <u>pepsi</u>.

_____ 52. During <u>july</u>, Frank's company works a four-day week.

_____ 53. A woman screamed, "<u>He's</u> stolen my purse!"

_____ 54. On <u>Summer</u> days I like to sit in the backyard and sunbathe.

Apostrophe

_____ 55. The <u>Wolfman's</u> bite is worse than his bark.

_____ 56. <u>Clydes</u> quick hands reached out to break his son's fall.

_____ 57. I'll be with you shortly if <u>youll</u> just wait a minute.

_____ 58. We <u>didn't</u> leave the rude waiter any tip.

Quotation Marks

_____ 59. Mark Twain once said, "<u>The</u> more I know about human beings, the more I like my dog."

_____ 60. Say something tender to me, "<u>whispered Tony to Lola.</u>"

_____ 61. "I hate that commercial, <u>he muttered.</u>"

_____ 62. "If you don't leave soon," he warned, "<u>you'll be late for work.</u>"

Comma

_____ 63. My favorite sandwich includes <u>turkey tomatoes lettuce and mayonnaise</u> on whole-wheat bread.

_____ 64. Although I have a black belt in <u>karate</u> I decided to go easy on the demented bully who had kicked sand in <u>my face.</u>

_____ 65. All the tree branches, <u>which were covered with ice,</u> glittered like diamonds.

_____ 66. We could always tell when our instructor felt <u>disorganized for</u> his shirt would not be tucked into his pants.

_____ 67. You, <u>my man,</u> are going to get yours.

_____ 68. His father <u>shouted</u> "Why don't you go out and get a job?"

Commonly Confused Words

_____ 69. Some stores will accept your credit cards but not <u>you're</u> money.

_____ 70. Since he's lost weight, most of Max's clothes are <u>to</u> big for him.

_____ 71. <u>They're</u> planning to trade in their old car.

_____ 72. <u>Its</u> important to get this job done properly.

_____ 73. Will you <u>except</u> this job if it's offered to you, or keep looking for something better?

_____ 74. <u>Who's</u> the culprit who left the paint can on the table?

Effective Word Choice

_____ 75. Because the school was flooded, the dance had to be <u>postponed until a later date</u>.

_____ 76. The movie was a <u>real bomb</u>, so we left early.

_____ 77. The victims of the car accident were shaken but <u>none the worse for wear</u>.

_____ 78. Anne is <u>of the opinion that</u> the death penalty should be abolished.

Answers are on page 727.

Part 2 (Optional)

Do Part 2 at your instructor's request. This second part of the test will provide more detailed information about skills you need to know. On separate paper, number and correct all the items you have marked with an X. For example, suppose you had marked the following word groups with an X. (Note that these examples are not taken from the test.)

  4. <u>If football games disappeared entirely from television.</u> I would not even miss them. Other people in my family would perish.

  7. The kitten suddenly saw her reflection in the <u>mirror, she</u> jumped back in surprise.

15. I wanted to get close enough to see the tag on the stray <u>dogs</u> collar.

29. When we go out to a <u>restaurant we</u> always order something we would not cook for ourselves.

Here is how you should write your corrections on a separate sheet of paper.

  4. television, I

  7. mirror, and

15. dog's

29. restaurant, we

There are over forty corrections to make in all.

20 Subjects and Verbs

The basic building blocks of English sentences are subjects and verbs. Understanding them is an important first step toward mastering a number of sentence skills.

Every sentence has a subject and a verb. Who or what the sentence speaks about is called the <u>subject</u>; what the sentence says about the subject is called the <u>verb</u>.

> The <u>children</u> <u>laughed</u>.
> Several <u>branches</u> <u>fell</u>.
> Most <u>students</u> <u>passed</u> the test.
> That <u>man</u> <u>is</u> a crook.

A Simple Way to Find a Subject

To find a subject, ask *who* or *what* the sentence is about. As shown below, your answer is the subject.

> *Who* is the first sentence about? <u>Children</u>
> *What* is the second sentence about? Several <u>branches</u>
> *Who* is the third sentence about? Most <u>students</u>
> *Who* is the fourth sentence about? That <u>man</u>

A Simple Way to Find a Verb

To find a verb, ask what the sentence *says about* the subject. As shown below, your answer is the verb.

> What does the first sentence *say about* the children? They <u>laughed</u>.
> What does the second sentence *say about* the branches? They <u>fell</u>.
> What does the third sentence *say about* the students? They <u>passed</u>.
> What does the fourth sentence *say about* that man? He <u>is</u> (a crook).

A second way to find the verb is to put *I, you, we, he, she, it,* or *they* (whichever form is appropriate) in front of the word you think is a verb. If the result makes sense, you have a verb. For example, you could put *they* in front of *laughed* in the first sentence above, with the result, *they laughed,* making sense. Therefore you know that *laughed* is a verb. You could use *they* or *he,* for instance, to test the other verbs as well.

Finally, it helps to remember that most verbs show action. In the sentences already considered, the three action verbs are *laughed, fell,* and *passed.* Certain other verbs, known as *linking verbs,* do not show action. They do, however, give information about the subject. In "That man is a crook," the linking verb *is* tells us that the man is a crook. Other common linking verbs include *am, are, was, were, feel, appear, look, become,* and *seem.*

Activity

In each of the following sentences, draw one line under the subject and two lines under the verb.

1. A sudden thunderstorm ended the baseball game.
2. Small stones pinged onto the windshield.
3. The test directions confused the students.
4. Cotton shirts feel softer than polyester ones.
5. The fog rolled into the cemetery.
6. Yoko invited her friends to dinner.
7. A green fly stung her on the ankle.
8. Every other night, garbage trucks rumble down my street on their way to the river.
9. The elderly man sat for a few minutes on the park bench.
10. With their fingers, the children drew pictures on the steamed window.

More about Subjects and Verbs

1 A pronoun (a word like *he, she, it, we, you,* or *they* used in place of a noun) can serve as the subject of a sentence. For example:

> He seems like a lonely person.
> They both like to gamble.

Without a surrounding context (so that we know who *He* or *They* refers to), such sentences may not seem clear, but they *are* complete.

2 A sentence may have more than one verb, more than one subject, or several subjects and verbs:

> My heart skipped and pounded.
> The radio and tape player were stolen from the car.
> Dave and Ellen prepared the report together and presented it to the class.

3 The subject of a sentence never appears within a prepositional phrase. A *prepositional phrase* is simply a group of words that begins with a preposition. Following is a list of common prepositions:

about	before	by	inside	over
above	behind	during	into	through
across	below	except	of	to
among	beneath	for	off	toward
around	beside	from	on	under
at	between	in	onto	with

Cross out prepositional phrases when you are looking for the subject of a sentence.

> ~~Under my pillow~~ I found a quarter left by the tooth fairy.
> One ~~of the yellow lights at the school crossing~~ began flashing.
> The comics pages ~~of the newspaper~~ have disappeared.
> ~~In spite of my efforts~~, Bob dropped out of school.
> ~~During a rainstorm~~, I sat in my car reading magazines.

4 Many verbs consist of more than one word. Here, for example, are some of the many forms of the verb *smile*.

smile	smiled	should smile
smiles	were smiling	will be smiling
does smile	have smiled	can smile
is smiling	had smiled	could be smiling
are smiling	had been smiling	must have smiled

Notes

a   Words like *not, just, never, only,* and *always* are not part of the verb, although they may appear within the verb.

> Larry <u>did</u> not <u>finish</u> the paper before class.
> The road <u>was</u> just <u>completed</u> last week.

b   No verb preceded by *to* is ever the verb of a sentence.

> My car suddenly <u>began</u> to sputter on the freeway.
> I <u>swerved</u> to avoid a squirrel on the road.

c   No -*ing* word by itself is ever the verb of a sentence. (It may be part of the verb, but it must have a helping verb in front of it.)

> They <u>leaving</u> early for the game. (not a sentence, because the verb is not complete)
> They <u>are leaving</u> early for the game. (a sentence)

Activity

Draw a single line under the subjects and a double line under the verbs in the following sentences. Be sure to include all parts of the verb.

1. A burning odor from the wood saw filled the room.
2. At first, sticks of gum always feel powdery on your tongue.
3. Vampires and werewolves are repelled by garlic.
4. Three people in the long bank line looked impatiently at their watches.
5. The driving rain had pasted wet leaves all over the car.
6. She has decided to buy a condominium.
7. The trees in the mall were glittering with tiny white lights.
8. The puppies slipped and tumbled on the vinyl kitchen floor.
9. Tony and Lola ate at Pizza Hut and then went to a movie.
10. We have not met our new neighbors in the apartment building.

■ Review Test

Draw a single line under subjects and a double line under verbs. Crossing out prepositional phrases may help to find the subjects.

1. A cloud of fruit flies hovered over the bananas.
2. Candle wax dripped onto the table and hardened into pools.
3. Nick and Fran are both excellent Frisbee players.
4. The leaves of my dying rubber plant resembled limp brown rags.
5. During the first week of vacation, Ken slept until noon every day.
6. They have just decided to go on a diet together.
7. Psychology and word processing are my favorite subjects.
8. The sofa in the living room has not been cleaned for over a year.
9. The water stains on her suede shoes did not disappear with brushing.
10. Fred stayed in bed too long and, as a result, arrived late for work.

21 Sentence Sense

What Is Sentence Sense?

As a speaker of English, you already possess the most important of all sentence skills. You have *sentence sense*—an instinctive feel for where a sentence begins, where it ends, and how it can be developed. You learned sentence sense automatically and naturally, as part of learning the English language, and you have practiced it through all the years that you have been speaking English. It is as much a part of you as your ability to speak and understand English is a part of you.

Sentence sense can help you recognize and avoid fragments and run-ons, two of the most common and most serious sentence-skills mistakes in written English. Sentence sense will also help you to place commas, spot awkward and unclear phrasing, and add variety to your sentences.

You may ask, "If I already have this 'sentence sense,' why do I still make mistakes in punctuating sentences?" One answer could be that your past school experiences in writing were unrewarding or unpleasant. English courses may have been a series of dry writing topics and heavy doses of "correct" grammar and usage, or they may have given no attention at all to sentence skills. For any of these reasons, or perhaps for other reasons, the instinctive sentence skills you practice while *speaking* may turn off when you start *writing*. The very act of picking up a pen may shut down your natural system of language abilities and skills.

Turning On Your Sentence Sense

Chances are that you don't *read a paper aloud* after you write it, or you don't do the next best thing: read it "aloud" in your head. But reading aloud is essential to turn on the natural language system within you. By reading aloud, you will be able to hear the points where your sentences begin and end. In addition, you will be able to pick up any trouble spots where your thoughts are not communicated clearly and well.

The activities that follow will help you turn on and rediscover the enormous language power within you. You will be able to see how your built-in sentence sense can guide your writing just as it guides your speaking.

Activity

Each item that follows lacks basic punctuation. There is no period to mark the end of one sentence and no capital letter to mark the start of the next. Read each item aloud (or in your head) so that you "hear" where each sentence begins and ends. Your voice will tend to drop and pause at the point of each sentence break. Draw a light slash mark (/) at every point where you hear a break. Then go back and read the item a second time. If you are now sure of each place where a split occurs, insert a period and change the first small letter after it to a capital. Minor pauses are often marked in English by commas; these are already inserted. Part of item 1 is done for you as an example.

1. I take my dog for a walk on Saturdays in the big park by the lake,/I do this very early in the morning before children come to the park that way I can let my dog run freely he jumps out the minute I open the car door and soon sees the first innocent squirrel then he is off like a shot and doesn't stop running for a least half an hour.

2. Lola hates huge tractor trailers that sometimes tailgate her Honda Civic the enormous smoke-belching machines seem ready to swallow her small car she shakes her fist at the drivers, and she rips out a lot of angry words recently she had a very satisfying dream she broke into an army supply depot and stole a bazooka she then became the first person in history to murder a truck.

3. When I sit down to write, my mind is blank all I can think of is my name, which seems to me the most boring name in the world often I get sleepy and tell myself I should take a short nap other times I start daydreaming about things I want to buy sometimes I decide I should make a telephone call to someone I know the piece of paper in front of me is usually still blank when I leave to watch my favorite television show.

4. One of the biggest regrets of my life is that I never told my father I loved him I resented the fact that he had never been able to say the words "I love you" to his children even during the long period of my father's illness, I remained silent and unforgiving then one morning he was dead, with my words left unspoken a guilt I shall never forget tore a hole in my heart I determined not

to hold in my feelings with my daughters they know they are loved, because I both show and tell them this all people, no matter who they are, want to be told that they are loved.

5. Two days ago, Greg killed seven flying ants in his bedroom he also sprayed a column of ants forming a colony along the kitchen baseboard yesterday he picked the evening newspaper off the porch and two black army ants scurried onto his hand this morning, he found an ant crawling on a lollipop he had left in his shirt pocket if any more insects appear, he is going to call Orkin Pest Control he feels like the victim in a Hitchcock movie called *The Ants* he is half afraid to sleep the darkness may be full of tiny squirming things waiting to crawl all over him.

Summary: Using Sentence Sense

You probably did well in locating the end stops in these selections—proving to yourself that you *do* have sentence sense. This instinctive sense will help you deal with fragments and run-ons, perhaps the two most common sentence-skills mistakes.

Remember the importance of *reading your paper aloud.* By reading aloud, you turn on the natural language skills that come from all your experience of speaking English. The same sentence sense that helps you communicate effectively in speaking will help you communicate effectively in writing.

22 Fragments

Introductory Project

Every sentence must have a subject and a verb and must express a complete thought. A word group that lacks a subject or a verb and that does not express a complete thought is a fragment. Underline the statement in each numbered item that you think is *not* a complete sentence.

1. Because I could not sleep. I turned on my light and read.
2. Calling his dog's name. Todd walked up and down the street.
3. My little sister will eat anything. Except meat, vegetables, and fruit.
4. The reporter turned on her laptop computer. Then began to type quickly.

Understanding the answers: Read and complete each explanation.

1. *Because I could not sleep* is not a complete sentence. The writer does not complete the _____ by telling us what happened because he could not sleep. Correct the fragment by joining it to the sentence that follows it:

   Because I could not sleep, I turned on my light and read.

2. *Calling his dog's name* is not a complete sentence. This word group has no _____ and no verb, and it does not express a complete thought. Correct the fragment by adding it to the sentence that follows it:

   Calling his dog's name, Todd walked up and down the street.

3. *Except meat, vegetables, and fruit* is not a complete sentence. Again, the word group has no subject and no _____, and it does not express a complete thought. Correct the fragment by adding it to the sentence that comes before it:

   My little sister will eat anything except meat, vegetables, and fruit.

4. *Then began to type quickly* is not a complete sentence. This word group has no _____. One way to correct the fragment is to add the subject *she:*

   Then she began to type quickly.

Answers are on page 728.

What Are Fragments?

Every sentence must have a subject and a verb and must express a complete thought. A word group that lacks a subject or a verb and does not express a complete thought is a *fragment*. The most common types of fragments are:

1 Dependent-word fragments

2 *-ing* and *to* fragments

3 Added-detail fragments

4 Missing-subject fragments

Once you understand what specific kinds of fragments you write, you should be able to eliminate them from your writing. The following pages explain all four types of fragments.

Dependent-Word Fragments

Some word groups that begin with a dependent word are fragments. Here is a list of common dependent words:

Dependent Words		
after	if, even if	when, whenever
although, though	in order that	where, wherever
as	since	whether
because	that, so that	which, whichever
before	unless	while
even though	until	who, whoever
how	what, whatever	whose

Whenever you start a sentence with one of these words, you must be careful that a fragment does not result.

The word group beginning with the dependent word *After* in the example below is a fragment.

After I learned the price of new cars. I decided to keep my old Buick.

A *dependent statement*—one starting with a dependent word like *After*—cannot stand alone. It depends on another statement to complete the thought. "After I learned the price of new cars" is a dependent statement. It leaves us hanging. We expect to find out—in the same sentence—*what happened after* the writer learned the price of new cars. When a writer does not follow through and complete a thought, a fragment results.

To correct the fragment, simply follow through and complete the thought:

After I learned the price of new cars, I decided to keep my old Buick.

Remember, then, that *dependent statements by themselves are fragments.* They must be attached to a statement that makes sense standing alone.

Here are two other examples of dependent-word fragments:

My daughter refused to stop smoking. <u>Unless I quit also.</u>

Tommy made an appointment. <u>Which he did not intend to keep.</u>

"Unless I quit also" is a fragment; it does not make sense standing by itself. We want to know—in the same statement—*what would not happen unless* the writer quit also. The writer must complete the thought. Likewise, "Which he did not intend to keep" is not in itself a complete thought. We want to know in the same statement what *which* refers to.

Correcting a Dependent-Word Fragment

In most cases you can correct a dependent-word fragment by attaching it to the sentence that comes after it or the sentence that comes before it:

After I learned the price of new cars, I decided to keep my old Buick.
(The fragment has been attached to the sentence that comes after it.)

My daughter refused to quit smoking unless I quit also.
(The fragment has been attached to the sentence that comes before it.)

Tommy made an appointment which he did not intend to keep.
(The fragment has been attached to the sentence that comes before it.)

Another way of connecting a dependent-word fragment is simply to eliminate the dependent word by rewriting the sentence:

I learned the price of new cars and decided to keep my old Buick.

She wanted me to quit also.

He did not intend to keep it.

Do not use this method of correction too frequently, however, for it may cut down on interest and variety in your writing style.

Notes

1   Use a comma if a dependent-word group comes at the beginning of a sentence (see also page 487):

After I learned the price of new cars, I decided to keep my old Buick.

However, do not generally use a comma if the dependent-word group comes at the end of a sentence:

My daughter refused to stop smoking unless I quit also.

Tommy made an appointment which he did not intend to keep.

2   Sometimes the dependent words *who, that, which,* or *where* appear not at the very start, but near the start, of a word group. A fragment often results:

The town council decided to put more lights on South Street. <u>A place where several people have been mugged.</u>

"A place where several people have been mugged" is not in itself a complete thought. We want to know in the same statement *where the place was* that several people were mugged. The fragment can be corrected by attaching it to the sentence that comes before it:

The town council decided to put more lights on South Street, a place where several people have been mugged.

Activity 1

Turn each of the following dependent-word groups into a sentence by adding a complete thought. Put a comma after the dependent-word group if a dependent word starts the sentence.

Examples   Although I arrived in class late

Although I arrived in class late, I still did well on the test.

The little boy who plays with our daughter

The little boy who plays with our daughter just came down with German measles.

1. Because the weather is bad

2. If I lend you twenty dollars

_____

_____

3. The car that we bought

_____

_____

4. Since I was tired

_____

_____

5. Before the instructor entered the room

_____

_____

Activity 2

Underline the dependent-word fragment or fragments in each item. Then correct each fragment by attaching it to the sentence that comes before or the sentence that comes after it—whichever sounds more natural. Put a comma after the dependent-word group if it starts the sentence.

1. When my neighbor and I both use our cordless telephones. We hear one another's conversations. One of us needs to get a different phone.

_____

_____

2. Bill always turns on the radio in the morning to hear the news. He wants to be sure that World War III has not started. Before he gets on with his day.

_____

_____

3. Although Mr. Simon is over eighty years old. He walks briskly to work every day. He seems like a much younger man. Since he is so active and involved in life.

_____

_____

4. My dog ran in joyous circles on the wide beach. Until she found a dead fish. Before I had a chance to drag her away. She began sniffing and nudging the smelly remains.

_____

_____

_____

5. When the air conditioner broke down. The temperature was over ninety degrees. I then found an old fan. Which turned out to be broken also.

_____

_____

_____

-ing and *to* Fragments

When an *-ing* word appears at or near the start of a word group, a fragment may result. Such fragments often lack a subject and part of the verb. Underline the word groups in the examples below that contain *-ing* words. Each is a fragment.

Example 1

I spent almost two hours on the phone yesterday. Trying to find a garage to repair my car. Eventually I had to have it towed to a garage in another town.

Example 2

Maggie was at first very happy with the blue sports car she had bought for only five hundred dollars. Not realizing until a week later that the car averaged seven miles per gallon of gas.

Example 3

He looked forward to the study period at school. It being the only time he could sit unbothered and dream about his future. He imagined himself as a lawyer with lots of money and women to spend it on.

People sometimes write *-ing* fragments because they think the subject in one sentence will work for the next word group as well. Thus, in the first example, the writer thinks that the subject *I* in the opening sentence will also serve as the subject for "Trying to find a garage to repair my car." But the subject must actually be *in* the sentence.

Correcting *-ing* Fragments

1 Attach the *-ing* fragment to the sentence that comes before it or the sentence that comes after it, whichever makes sense. Example 1 could read: "I spent almost two hours on the phone yesterday, trying to find a garage to repair my car."

2 Add a subject and change the *-ing* verb part to the correct form of the verb. Example 2 could read: "She did not realize until a week later that the car averaged seven miles per gallon of gas."

3 Change *being* to the correct form of the verb *be (am, are, is, was, were)*. Example 3 could read: "It was the only time he could sit unbothered and dream about his future."

Correcting *to* Fragments

When *to* appears at or near the start of a word group, a fragment sometimes results:

> I plan on working overtime. To get this job finished. Otherwise, my boss may get angry at me.

The second word group is a fragment and can be corrected by adding it to the preceding sentence:

> I plan on working overtime to get this job finished.

Activity 1

Underline the *-ing* fragment in each of the items that follow. Then make it a sentence by rewriting it, using the method described in parentheses.

Example   A thunderstorm was brewing. A sudden breeze shot through the windows. <u>Driving the stuffiness out of the room.</u>
(Add the fragment to the preceding sentence.)

A sudden breeze shot through the windows, driving the stuffiness out of the room.

(In the example, a comma is used to set off "driving the stuffiness out of the room," which is extra material placed at the end of the sentence.)

1. Sweating under his heavy load. Brian staggered up the stairs to his apartment. He felt as though his legs were crumbling beneath him.
   (Add the fragment to the sentence that comes after it.)

   _____

   _____

2. He works 10 hours a day. Then going to class for 2½ hours. It is no wonder he writes fragments.
   (Connect the fragment by adding the subject *he* and changing *going* to the proper form of the verb, *goes.)*

   _____

   _____

3. Charlotte loved the movie *Gone with the Wind,* but Clyde hated it. His chief objection being that it lasted four hours.
   (Correct the fragment by changing *being* to the proper verb form, *was.)*

   _____

   _____

Activity 2

Underline the *-ing* or *to* fragment or fragments in each item. Then rewrite each item, using one of the methods of correction described on pages 374–375.

1. A mysterious package arrived on my porch yesterday. Bearing no return address. I half expected to find a bomb inside.

   _____

   _____

2. Jack bundled up and went outside on the bitterly cold day. To saw wood for his fireplace. He returned half frozen with only two logs.

   _____

   _____

3. Looking tired and drawn. The little girl's parents sat in the waiting room. The operation would be over in a few minutes.

   _____

   _____

4. Sighing with resignation. Jill switched on her television set. She knew that the picture would be snowy and crackling with static. Her house being in a weak reception area.

_____

_____

_____

5. Jabbing the ice with a screwdriver. Luis attempted to speed up the defrosting process in his freezer. However, he used too much force. The result being a freezer compartment riddled with holes.

_____

_____

_____

Added-Detail Fragments

Added-detail fragments lack a subject and a verb. They often begin with one of the following words:

also	except	including
especially	for example	such as

See if you can locate and underline the one added-detail fragment in each of the examples that follow:

Example 1

I love to cook and eat Italian food. Especially spaghetti and lasagna. I make everything from scratch.

Example 2

The class often starts late. For example, yesterday at a quarter after nine instead of at nine sharp. Today the class started at five after nine.

Example 3

He failed a number of courses before he earned his degree. Among them, English I, Economics, and General Biology.

People often write added-detail fragments for much the same reason they write *-ing* fragments. They think the subject and verb in one sentence will serve for the next word group as well. But the subject and verb must be in *each* word group.

Correcting Added-Detail Fragments

1   Attach the fragment to the complete thought that precedes it. Example 1 could read: "I love to cook and eat Italian food, especially spaghetti and lasagna."

2   Add a subject and a verb to the fragment to make it a complete sentence. Example 2 could read: "The class often starts late. For example, yesterday it began at a quarter after nine instead of at nine sharp."

3   Change words as necessary to make the fragment part of the preceding sentence. Example 3 could read: "Among the courses he failed before he earned his degree were English I, Economics, and General Biology."

Activity 1

Underline the fragment in each of the items below. Then make it a sentence by rewriting it, using the method described in parentheses.

Example   I am always short of pocket money. Especially for everyday items like magazines and sodas. Luckily my friends often have change.
(Add the fragment to the preceding sentence.)

I am always short of pocket money, especially for everyday items

like magazines and sodas.

1. There are many little things wrong with this apartment. For example, defective lights and leaking faucets. The landlord is not good about making repairs.
(Correct the fragment by adding the subject and verb *it has.*)

_____

_____

2. I could feel Bill's anger building. Like a land mine ready to explode. I was silent because I didn't want to be the one to set it off.
(Add the fragment to the preceding sentence.)

_____

_____

3. We went on vacation without several essential items. Among other things, our sneakers and sweat jackets.
(Correct the fragment by adding the subject and verb *we forgot.*)

_____

_____

Activity 2

Underline the added-detail fragment in each item. Then rewrite that part of the item needed to correct the fragment. Use one of the three methods of correction described above.

1. It's always hard for me to get up for work. Especially on Monday after a holiday weekend. However, I always wake up early on free days.

_____

_____

_____

2. Tony has enormous endurance. For example, the ability to run five miles in the morning and then play basketball all afternoon.

_____

_____

_____

3. A counselor gives you a chance to talk about your problems. With your family or the boss at work. You learn how to cope better with life.

_____

_____

_____

4. Fred and Martha do most of their shopping through mail-order catalogs. Especially the J. C. Penney catalog.

_____

_____

_____

5. One of my greatest joys in life is eating desserts. Such as cherry cheesecake and vanilla cream puffs. Almond fudge cake makes me want to dance.

_____

_____

_____

Missing-Subject Fragments

In each example below, underline the word group in which the subject is missing.

Example 1

The truck skidded on the rain-slick highway. But missed a telephone pole on the side of the road.

Example 2

Michelle tried each of the appetizers on the table. And then found that, when the dinner arrived, her appetite was gone.

People write missing-subject fragments because they think the subject in one sentence will apply to the next word group as well. But the subject, as well as the verb, must be in *each* word group to make it a sentence.

Correcting Missing-Subject Fragments

1 Attach the fragment to the preceding sentence. Example 1 could read: "The truck skidded on the rain-slick highway but missed a telephone pole on the side of the road."

2 Add a subject (which can often be a pronoun standing for the subject in the preceding sentence). Example 2 could read: "She then found that, when the dinner arrived, her appetite was gone."

Activity

Underline the missing-subject fragment in each item. Then rewrite that part of the item needed to correct the fragment. Use one of the two methods of correction described above.

1. I tried on an old suit hanging in our basement closet. And discovered, to my surprise, that it was too tight to button.

   _____

   _____

   _____

2. When Mary had a sore throat, friends told her to gargle with salt water. Or suck on an ice cube. The worst advice she got was to avoid swallowing.

    _____

    _____

3. One of my grade-school teachers embarrassed us with her sarcasm. Also, seated us in rows from the brightest student to the dumbest. I can imagine the pain the student in the last seat must have felt.

    _____

    _____

    _____

A Review: How to Check for Fragments

1 Read your paper aloud from the *last* sentence to the *first.* You will be better able to see and hear whether each word group you read is a complete thought.

2 If you think a word group is a fragment, ask yourself: Does this contain a subject and a verb and express a complete thought?

3 More specifically, be on the lookout for the most common fragments:
- Dependent-word fragments (starting with words like *after, because, since, when,* and *before)*
- *-ing* and *to* fragments (*-ing* or *to* at or near the start of a word group)
- Added-detail fragments (starting with words like *for example, such as, also,* and *especially)*
- Missing-subject fragments (a verb is present but not the subject)

■ **Review Test 1**

Turn each of the following word groups into a complete sentence. Use the spaces provided.

Example   With sweaty palms

With sweaty palms, I walked in for the job interview.

Even when it rains

The football teams practice even when it rains.

1. When the alarm sounded

   _____

   _____

2. In order to save some money

   _____

   _____

3. Were having a party

   _____

   _____

4. To pass the course

   _____

   _____

5. Geraldo, who is very impatient

   _____

   _____

6. During the holiday season

   _____

   _____

7. The store where I worked

   _____

   _____

8. Before the movie started

   _____

   _____

9. Down in the basement

   _____

   _____

10. Feeling very confident

    _____

    _____

■ Review Test 2

1. _____

2. _____

3. _____

4. _____

5. _____

6. _____

7. _____

8. _____

9. _____

10. _____

11. _____

12. _____

13. _____

14. _____

15. _____

16. _____

17. _____

18. _____

19. _____

20. _____

Each word group in the student paragraph below is numbered. In the space provided, write C if a word group is a *complete sentence;* write F if it is a *fragment.* You will find seven fragments in the paragraph.

A Disastrous First Date

1My first date with Donna was a disaster. 2I decided to take her to a small Italian restaurant. 3That my friends told me had reasonable prices. 4I looked over the menu and realized I could not pronounce the names of the dishes. 5Such as "veal piccata" and "fettucini Alfredo." 6Then, I noticed a burning smell. 7The candle on the table was starting to blacken. 8And scorch the back of my menu. 9Trying to be casual, I quickly poured half my glass of water onto the menu. 10When the waiter returned to our table. 11He asked me if I wanted to order some wine. 12I ordered a bottle of Blue Nun. 13The only wine that I had heard of and could pronounce. 14The waiter brought the wine, poured a small amount into my glass, and waited. 15I said, "You don't have to stand there. We can pour the wine ourselves." 16After the waiter put down the wine bottle and left. 17Donna told me I was supposed to taste the wine. 18Feeling like a complete fool. 19I managed to get through the dinner. 20However, for weeks afterward, I felt like jumping out of a tenth-story window.

On separate paper, correct the fragments you have found. Attach each fragment to the sentence that comes before or after it, or make whatever other change is needed to turn the fragment into a sentence.

■ Review Test 3

Underline the two fragments in each item. Then rewrite the item in the space provided, making the changes needed to correct the fragments.

Example   The people at the diner save money. By watering down the coffee. Also, using the cheapest grade of hamburger. Few people go there anymore.

The people at the diner save money by watering down the coffee.

Also, they use the cheapest grade of hamburger. . . .

1. Gathering speed with enormous force. The plane was suddenly in the air. Then it began to climb sharply. And several minutes later leveled off.

_____

_____

_____

2. Before my neighbors went on vacation. They asked me to watch their house. I agreed to check the premises once a day. Also, to take in their mail.

_____

_____

_____

3. Running untouched into the end zone. The halfback raised his arms in triumph. Then he slammed the football to the ground. And did a little victory dance.

_____

_____

_____

4. It's hard to keep up with bills. Such as the telephone, gas, and electricity. After you finally mail the checks. New bills seem to arrive a day or two later.

_____

_____

_____

5. While a woman ordered twenty pounds of cold cuts. Customers at the deli counter waited impatiently. The woman explained that she was in charge of a school picnic. And apologized for taking up so much time.

_____

_____

_____

■ Review Test 4

Write quickly for five minutes about what you like to do in your leisure time. Don't worry about spelling, punctuation, finding exact words, or organizing your thoughts. Just focus on writing as many words as you can without stopping.

After you have finished, go back and make whatever changes are needed to correct any fragments in your writing.

23 Run-Ons

Introductory Project

A run-on occurs when two sentences are run together with no adequate sign given to mark the break between them. Shown below are four run-ons and four correctly marked sentences. See if you can complete the statement that explains how each run-on is corrected.

1. He is the meanest little kid on his block he eats only the heads of animal crackers. *Run-on*

   He is the meanest little kid on his block. He eats only the heads of animal crackers. *Correct*

   The run-on has been corrected by using a _____ and a capital letter to separate the two complete thoughts.

2. Fred Grencher likes to gossip about other people, he doesn't like them to gossip about him. *Run-on*

   Fred Grencher likes to gossip about other people, but he doesn't like them to gossip about him. *Correct*

   The run-on has been corrected by using a joining word, _____, to connect the two complete thoughts.

3. The chain on my bike likes to chew up my pants, it leaves grease marks on my ankle as well. *Run-on*

   The chain on my bike likes to chew up my pants; it leaves grease marks on my ankles as well. *Correct*

   The run-on has been corrected by using a _____ to connect the two closely related thoughts.

4. The window shade snapped up like a gunshot, her cat leaped four feet off the floor. *Run-on*

   When the window shade snapped up like a gunshot, her cat leaped four feet off the floor. *Correct*

   The run-on has been corrected by using the subordinating word _____ to connect the two closely related thoughts.

Answers are on page 728.

What Are Run-Ons?

A *run-on* is two complete thoughts that are run together with no adequate sign given to mark the break between them.[*] Some run-ons have no punctuation at all to mark the break between the thoughts. Such run-ons are known as *fused sentences:* they are fused, or joined together, as if they were only one thought.

Fused Sentences

My grades are very good this semester my social life rates only a C.

Our father was a madman in his youth he would do anything on a dare.

In other run-ons, known as *comma splices,* a comma is used to connect, or "splice" together, the two complete thoughts. However, a comma alone is *not enough* to connect two complete thoughts. Some stronger connection than a comma alone is needed.

Comma Splices

My grades are very good this semester, my social life rates only a C.

Our father was a madman in his youth, he would do anything on a dare.

Comma splices are the most common kind of run-on. Students sense that some kind of connection is needed between two thoughts and so put a comma at the dividing point. But the comma alone is not sufficient: a stronger, clearer mark is needed between the two thoughts.

A Warning about Words That Can Lead to Run-Ons:
People often write run-ons when the second complete thought begins with one of the following words:

I	we	there	now
you	they	this	then
he, she, it		that	next

Remember to be on the alert for run-ons whenever you use one of these words in writing a paper.

*Notes:
1 Some instructors feel that the term *run-ons* should be applied only to fused sentences, not to comma splices. But for many other instructors, and for our purposes in this book, the term *run-on* applies equally to fused sentences and comma splices. The bottom line is that you do not want either fused sentences or comma splices in your writing.
2 Some instructors refer to each complete thought in a run-on as an *independent clause.* A *clause* is simply a group of words having a subject and a verb. A clause may be *independent* (expressing a complete thought and able to stand alone) or *dependent* (not expressing a complete thought and not able to stand alone). A run-on is two independent clauses that are run together with no adequate sign given to mark the break between them.

Correcting Run-Ons

Here are four common methods of correcting a run-on:

1 Use a period and a capital letter to break the two complete thoughts into separate sentences.

My grades are very good this semester. My social life rates only a C.
Our father was a madman in his youth. He would do anything on a dare.

2 Use a comma plus a joining word (*and, but, for, or, nor, so, yet*) to connect the two complete thoughts.

My grades are very good this semester, but my social life rates only a C.
Our father was a madman in his youth, for he would do anything on a dare.

3 Use a semicolon to connect the two complete thoughts.

My grades are very good this semester; my social life rates only a C.
Our father was a madman in his youth; he would do anything on a dare.

4 Use subordination.

Although my grades are very good this semester, my social life rates only a C.
Because my father was a madman in his youth, he would do anything on a dare.

The following pages will give you practice in all four methods of correcting a run-on. The use of subordination is explained on pages 109–111.

Method 1: Period and a Capital Letter

One way of correcting a run-on is to use a period and a capital letter at the break between the two complete thoughts. Use this method especially if the thoughts are not closely related or if another method would make the sentence too long.

Activity 1

Locate the split in each of the following run-ons. Each is a *fused sentence*—that is, each consists of two sentences that are fused, or joined together, with no punctuation at all between them. Reading each fused sentence aloud will help you "hear" where a major break or split in the thought occurs. At such a point, your voice will probably drop and pause.

Correct the run-on by putting a period at the end of the first thought and a capital letter at the start of the next thought.

Example   Martha Grencher shuffled around the apartment in her slippers. her
husband couldn't stand their slapping sound on the floor.

1. A felt-tip pen is easy to ruin just leave it lying around without its cap.
2. Phil cringed at the sound of the dentist's drill it buzzed like a fifty-pound mosquito.
3. Last summer no one swam in the lake a little boy had dropped his pet piranhas into the water.
4. A horse's teeth never stop growing they will eventually grow outside the horse's mouth.
5. Sue's doctor told her he was an astrology nut she did not feel good about learning that.
6. Ice water is the best remedy for a burn using butter is like adding fat to a flame.
7. In the apartment the air was so dry that her skin felt parched the heat was up to eighty degrees.
8. My parents bought me an ant farm it's going to be hard to find tractors that small.
9. Lobsters are cannibalistic this is one reason they are hard to raise in captivity.
10. Julia placed an egg timer next to the phone she did not want to talk more than three minutes on her long-distance calls.

Activity 2

Locate the split in each of the following run-ons. Some of the run-ons are fused sentences, and some are *comma splices*—run-ons spliced, or joined together, with only a comma. Correct each run-on by putting a period at the end of the first thought and a capital letter at the start of the next thought.

1. A bird got into the house through the chimney we had to catch it before our cat did.
2. Some so-called health foods are not so healthy, many are made with oils that raise cholesterol levels.

3. We sat only ten feet from the magician, we still couldn't see where all the birds came from.

4. Jerome needs only five hours of sleep each night his wife needs at least seven.

5. Our image of dentistry will soon change dentists will use lasers instead of drills.

6. Gale entered her apartment and jumped with fright someone was leaving through her bedroom window.

7. There were several unusual hairstyles at the party one woman had bright green braids.

8. Todd saves all his magazines, once a month, he takes them to a nearby nursing home.

9. The doctor seemed to be in a rush, I still took time to ask all the questions that were on my mind.

10. When I was little, my brother tried to feed me flies, he told my they were raisins.

Activity 3

Write a second sentence to go with each of the sentences that follow. Start the second sentence with the word given in italics. Your sentences can be serious or playful.

Example   *She*   Jackie works for the phone company. <u>She climbs telephone</u> <u>poles in all kinds of weather.</u>

It   1. The alarm clock is unreliable. _____

He   2. My uncle has a peculiar habit. _____

Then   3. Lola studied for the math test for two hours. _____

It   4. I could not understand why the car would not start. _____

There   5. We saw all kinds of litter on the highway. _____

Method 2: Comma and a Joining Word

A second way of correcting a run-on is to use a comma plus a joining word to connect the two complete thoughts. Joining words (also called *conjunctions*) include *and, but, for, or, nor, so,* and *yet.* Here is what the four most common joining words mean:

and   in addition to, along with

His feet hurt from the long hike, and his stomach was growling.

(*And* means "in addition": His feet hurt from the long hike; *in addition,* his stomach was growling.)

but   however, except, on the other hand, just the opposite

I remembered to get the cocoa, but I forgot the marshmallows.

(*But* means "however": I remembered to get the cocoa; *however,* I forgot the marshmallows.)

for   because, the reason why, the cause of something

She was afraid of not doing well in the course, for she had always had bad luck with English before.

(*For* means "because" or "the reason why": She was afraid of not doing well in the course; *the reason why* was that she had always had bad luck with English before.)

Note: If you are not comfortable using *for,* you may want to use *because* instead of *for* in the activities that follow. If you do use *because*, omit the comma before it.

so   as a result, therefore

The windshield wiper was broken, so she was in trouble when the rain started.

(*So* means "as a result": The windshield wiper was broken; *as a result,* she was in trouble when the rain started.)

Activity 1

Insert the joining word *(and, but, for, so)* that logically connects the two thoughts in each sentence.

1. The couple wanted desperately to buy the house, _____ they did not qualify for a mortgage.

2. A lot of men today get their hair styled, _____ they use perfume and other cosmetics as well.

3. Clyde asked his wife if she had any bandages, _____ he had just sliced his finger with a paring knife.

4. The computer's mouse was not behaving correctly, _____ Rita took it apart and cleaned it.

5. The restaurant was beautiful, _____ the food was overpriced.

Activity 2

Add a complete, closely related thought to go with each of the following statements. Use a comma plus the italicized joining word when you write the second thought.

Example   *for*   Lola spent the day walking barefoot, *for the heel of one of her shoes had come off.*

but   1. She wanted to go to the party _____

_____

and   2. Tony washed his car in the morning _____

_____

so   3. The day was dark and rainy _____

_____

for   4. I'm not going to eat in the school cafeteria anymore _____

_____

but   5. I asked my brother to get off the telephone _____

_____

Method 3: Semicolon

A third method of correcting a run-on is to use a semicolon to mark the break between two thoughts. A *semicolon* (;) is made up of a period above a comma and is sometimes called a *strong comma*. The semicolon signals more of a pause than a comma alone but not quite the full pause of a period.

Semicolon Alone: Here are some earlier sentences that were connected with a comma plus a joining word. Notice that a semicolon alone, unlike a comma alone, can be used to connect the two complete thoughts in each sentence:

> A lot of men today get their hair styled; they use perfume and other cosmetics as well.
>
> She was afraid of not doing well in the course; she had always had bad luck with English before.
>
> The restaurant was beautiful; the food was overpriced.

The semicolon can add to sentence variety. For some people, however, the semicolon is a confusing mark of punctuation. Keep in mind that if you are not comfortable using it, you can and should use one of the first two methods of correcting a run-on.

Activity

Insert a semicolon where the break occurs between the two complete thoughts in each of the following run-ons.

Example   I missed the bus by seconds;there would not be another for half an hour.

1. I spend eight hours a day in a windowless office it's a relief to get out into the open air after work.
2. The audience howled with laughter the comedian enjoyed a moment of triumph.
3. It rained all week parts of the highway were flooded.
4. Tony never goes to a certain gas station anymore he found out that the service manager overcharged him for a valve job.
5. The washer shook and banged with its unbalanced load then it began to walk across the floor.

Semicolon with a Transitional Word: A semicolon is sometimes used with a transitional word and a comma to join two complete thoughts.

> We were short of money; therefore, we decided not to eat out that weekend.
>
> The roots of a geranium have to be crowded into a small pot; otherwise, the plants may not flower.
>
> I had a paper to write; however, my brain had stopped working for the night.

Following is a list of common transitional words (also known as *adverbial conjunctions).* Brief meanings are given for the words.

Transitional Word	Meaning
however	but
nevertheless	but
on the other hand	but
instead	as a substitute
meanwhile	in the intervening time
otherwise	under other conditions
indeed	in fact
in addition	and
also	and
moreover	and
furthermore	and
as a result	in consequence
thus	as a result
consequently	as a result
therefore	as a result

Activity 1

Choose a logical transitional word from the list in the box and write it in the space provided. Put a semicolon *before* the connector and a comma *after* it.

Example   Exams are over _____*; however,*_____ I still feel tense and nervous.

  1. I did not understand her point _____ I asked her to repeat it.

2. Janis spent several minutes trying to pry open the case of her new CD _____ she didn't succeed until she attacked it with a hammer.

3. Post offices are closed for today's holiday _____ no mail will be delivered.

4. Mac and Alana didn't have a fancy wedding _____ they used their money for a nice honeymoon.

5. I had to skip lunch _____ I would have been late for class.

Activity 2

Punctuate each sentence by using a semicolon and a comma.

Example   My brother's asthma was worsening; as a result, he quit the soccer team.

1. My brother ate an entire pizza for supper in addition he had a big chunk of pound cake for dessert.

2. The man leaned against the building in obvious pain however no one stopped to help him.

3. Our instructor was absent therefore the test was postponed.

4. I had no time to type up the paper instead I printed it out neatly in black ink.

5. Lola loves the velvety texture of cherry Jell-O moreover she loves to squish it between her teeth.

Method 4: Subordination

A fourth method of joining related thoughts is to use subordination. *Subordination* is a way of showing that one thought in a sentence is not as important as another thought.

Here are three earlier sentences that have been recast so that one idea is subordinated to (made less important than) the other idea:

When the window shade snapped up like a gunshot, her cat leaped four feet off the floor.

Because it rained all week, parts of the highway were flooded.

Although my grades are very good this year, my social life rates only a C.

Notice that when we subordinate, we use dependent words like *when, because,* and *although.* Here is a brief list of common dependent words:

Common Dependent Words		
after	before	unless
although	even though	until
as	if	when
because	since	while

Subordination is explained on pages 109–111.

Activity

Choose a logical dependent word from the box above and write it in the space provided.

Example _____*Because*_____ I had so much to do, I never even turned on the TV last night.

1. _____ we emerged from the darkened theater, it took several minutes for our eyes to adjust to the light.

2. _____ "All Natural" was printed in large letters on the yogurt carton, the fine print listing the ingredients told a different story.

3. I can't study for the test this weekend _____ my boss wants me to work overtime.

4. _____ the vampire movie was over, my children were afraid to go to bed.

5. _____ you have a driver's license and two major credit cards, that store will not accept your check.

A Review: How to Check for Run-Ons

1   To see if a sentence is a run-on, read it aloud and listen for a break marking two complete thoughts. Your voice will probably drop and pause at the break.

2   To check an entire paper, read it aloud from the *last* sentence to the *first*. Doing so will help you hear and see each complete thought.

3   Be on the lookout for words that can lead to run-on sentences:

I	he, she, it	they	this	next
you	we	there	that	then

4   Correct run-on sentences by using one of the following methods:

- Period and capital letter
- Comma and joining word *(and, but, for, or, nor, so, yet)*
- Semicolon
- Subordination

■ **Review Test 1**

Some of the run-ons that follow are fused sentences, having no punctuation between the two complete thoughts; others are comma splices, having only a comma between the two complete thoughts. Correct the run-ons by using one of the following three methods:

- Period and capital letter
- Comma and joining word
- Semicolon

Do not use the same method of correction for every sentence.

Example   Three people did the job, I could have done it alone.
                                              but

1. The impatient driver tried to get a jump on the green light he kept edging his car into the intersection.

2. The course on the history of UFOs sounded interesting, it turned out to be very dull.

3. That clothing store is a strange place to visit you keep walking up to dummies that look like real people.

4. Everything on the menu of the Pancake House sounded delicious they wanted to order the entire menu.

5. Chung pressed a cold washcloth against his eyes, it helped relieve his headache.

6. Marc used to be a fast-food junkie now he eats only vegetables and sunflower seeds.

7. I knew my term paper was not very good, I placed it in a shiny plastic cover to make it look better.

8. The boy smiled joyously, his silver braces flashed in the sun.

9. My boss does not know what he is doing half the time then he tries to tell me what to do.

10. In the next minute, 100 people will die, over 240 babies will be born.

■ Review Test 2

Correct each run-on by using subordination. Choose from among the following dependent words:

after	before	unless
although	even though	until
as	if	when
because	since	while

Example   My eyes have been watering all day, I can tell the pollen count is high.
Because my eyes have been watering all day, I can tell the pollen count is high.

1. There are a number of suits and jackets on sale, they all have very noticeable flaws.

_____

_____

2. Rust has eaten a hole in the muffler, my car sounds like a motorcycle.

    _____

    _____

3. I finished my household chores, I decided to do some shopping.

    _____

    _____

4. The power went off for an hour during the night, all the clocks in the house must be reset.

    _____

    _____

5. Self-cleaning public toilets are available, few American cities have installed them.

    _____

    _____

■ Review Test 3

There are two run-ons in each passage. Correct them by using the following methods.

- Period and capital letter
- Comma and one of these joining words: *and, but,* or *so*
- One of these dependent words: *although, because,* or *when*

1. The dog raced into the house it was happy to be among people. Its owner bent down to pet it he drew back in disgust. The dog had rolled in something with a horrible smell.

    _____

    _____

    _____

2. Small feet were admired in ancient China, some female infants had their feet tightly bound. The feet then grew into a tiny, deformed shape. The women could barely walk their feet were crippled for life.

    _____

    _____

    _____

3. Davie insisted on dressing himself for nursery school. It was a cold winter day, he put on shorts and a tank top. He also put on cowboy boots over his bare feet. He liked his image in the mirror his mother made him change.

_____

_____

_____

4. A stimulating scent such as peppermint can help people concentrate better. The idea has practical applications, studies have shown that students do better on tests when peppermint is in the air. Maybe scented air could improve students' performance, it might help office workers be more alert, too.

_____

_____

_____

■ Review Test 4

Write quickly for five minutes about what you did this past weekend. Don't worry about spelling, punctuation, finding exact words, or organizing your thoughts. Just focus on writing as many words as you can without stopping.

After you have finished, go back and make whatever changes are needed to correct any run-ons in your writing.

24 Standard English Verbs

Answers are on page 728.

Introductory Project

Underline what you think is the correct form of the verb in each of the sentences below:

As a boy, he (enjoy, enjoyed) watching nature shows on television.

He still (enjoy, enjoys) watching such shows today as an adult.

When my car was new, it always (start, started) in the morning.

Now it (start, starts) only sometimes.

A couple of years ago, when Alice (cook, cooked) dinner, you needed an antacid tablet.

Now, when she (cook, cooks), neighbors invite themselves over to eat with us.

On the basis of the above examples, see if you can complete the following statements:

1. The first example in each pair refers to a (past, present) action, and the regular verb ends in _____.

2. The second example in each pair refers to a (past, present) action, and the regular verb ends in _____.

Answers are on page 728.

Many people have grown up in communities where nonstandard verb forms are used in everyday life. Such forms include *I thinks, he talk, it done, we has, you was,* and *she don't.* Community dialects have richness and power but are a drawback in college and the world at large, where standard English verb forms must be used. Standard English helps ensure clear communication among English-speaking people everywhere, and it is especially important in the world of work.

This chapter compares community dialect and standard English forms of one regular verb and three common irregular verbs.

Regular Verbs: Dialect and Standard Forms

The chart below compares community dialect (nonstandard) and standard English forms of the regular verb *smile*.

Smile

Community Dialect (Do not use in your writing)		Standard English (Use for clear communication)	
Present tense			
I smiles	we smiles	I smile	we smile
you smiles	you smiles	you smile	you smile
he, she, it smile	they smiles	he, she, it smiles	they smile
Past tense			
I smile	we smile	I smiled	we smiled
you smile	you smile	you smiled	you smiled
he, she, it smile	they smile	he, she, it smiled	they smiled

One of the most common nonstandard forms results from dropping the endings of regular verbs. For example, people might say, "David never *smile* anymore" instead of "David never *smiles* anymore." Or they will say, "Before he lost his job, David *smile* a lot," instead of, "Before he lost his job, David *smiled* a lot." To avoid such nonstandard usage, memorize the forms shown above for the regular verb *smile*. Then use the activities that follow to help make a habit of including verb endings when you write.

Present Tense Endings

The verb ending -*s* or -*es* is needed with a regular verb in the present tense when the subject is *he, she, it,* or any *one person* or *thing.* Consider the following examples of present tense endings.

He	He yell*s*.
She	She throw*s* things.
It	It really anger*s* me.
One person	Their son storm*s* out of the house.
One person	Their frightened daughter crouch*es* behind the bed.
One thing	At night the house shake*s*.

Activity 1

All but one of the ten sentences that follow need -*s* or -*es* verb endings. Cross out the nonstandard verb forms and write the standard forms in the spaces provided. Mark the one sentence that needs no change with a *C* for *correct.*

Example   ___wants___ Dana always ~~want~~ the teacher's attention.

_____   1. That newspaper print nothing but bad news.

_____   2. Don't eat a fish that smell funny.

_____   3. Claire plan to enter the contest.

_____   4. Whole-wheat bread taste better to me than rye bread.

_____   5. Bob weaken his lungs by smoking so much.

_____   6. The sick baby scream whenever her mother puts her down.

_____   7. You make me angry sometimes.

_____   8. Troy run faster than anybody else on the track team.

_____   9. She live in a rough section of town.

_____ 10. Martha like mystery novels better than romances.

Activity 2

Rewrite the short passage below, adding present -*s* or -*es* verb endings wherever needed.

Terri work in a big office downtown. Her cubicle sit right next to another worker's. This worker drive Terri crazy. He make more noise than you can imagine. Every day he bring a bag of raw carrots to work. The crunching noise fill the air. After he eat the carrots, he chew gum. He pop it so loud it sound like gunfire.

_____

_____

_____

_____

_____

Past Tense Endings

The verb ending *-d* or *-ed* is needed with a regular verb in the past tense.

A midwife deliver*ed* my baby.
The visitor puzzl*ed* over the campus map.
The children watch*ed* cartoons all morning.

Activity 1

All but one of the ten sentences that follow need *-d* or *-ed* verb endings. Cross out the nonstandard verb forms and write the standard forms in the spaces provided. Mark the one sentence that needs no change with a *C*.

Example ____*failed*____ Yesterday I ~~fail~~ a chemistry quiz.

_____ 1. Lily carefully color her mouth with red lipstick.

_____ 2. The Vietnamese student struggle with the new language.

_____ 3. The sick little boy start to cry again.

_____ 4. The tired mother turned on the TV for him.

_____ 5. I miss quite a few days of class early in the semester.

_____ 6. The weather forecaster promise blue skies, but rain began early this morning.

_____ 7. Sam attempt to put out the candle flame with his finger.

_____ 8. However, he end up burning himself.

_____ 9. On the bus, Yolanda listen to music through the headphones of her Walkman.

_____ 10. As the photographer was about to take a picture of the smiling baby, a sudden noise frighten the child and made her cry.

Activity 2

Rewrite the short passage on the next page, adding past tense *-d* or *-ed* verb endings wherever needed.

I smoke for two years and during that time suffer no real side effects. Then my body attack me. I start to have trouble falling asleep, and I awaken early every morning. My stomach digest food very slowly, so that at lunchtime I seem to be still full with breakfast. My lips and mouth turn dry, and I swallow water constantly. Also, mucus fill my lungs and I cough a lot. I decide to stop smoking when my wife insist I take out more life insurance for our family.

_____

_____

_____

_____

_____

_____

Three Common Irregular Verbs: Dialect and Standard Forms

The following charts compare community dialect and standard English forms of the common irregular verbs *be, have,* and *do. (*For more on irregular verbs, see pages 409–417.)

Be

Community Dialect (Do not use in your writing)		Standard English (Use for clear communication)	
Present tense			
I be (or is)	we be	I am	we are
you be	you be	you are	you are
he, she, it be	they be	he, she, it is	they are
Past tense			
I were	we was	I was	we were
you was	you was	you were	you were
he, she, it were	they was	he, she, it was	they were

Have

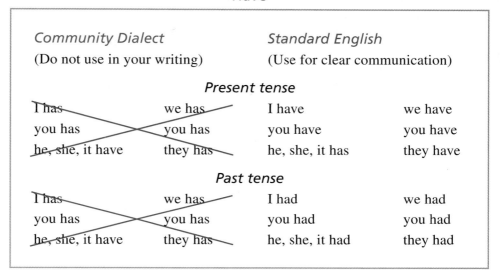

Community Dialect		Standard English	
(Do not use in your writing)		(Use for clear communication)	

Present tense

I has	we has	I have	we have
you has	you has	you have	you have
he, she, it have	they has	he, she, it has	they have

Past tense

I has	we has	I had	we had
you has	you has	you had	you had
he, she, it have	they has	he, she, it had	they had

Do

Community Dialect		Standard English	
(Do not use in your writing)		(Use for clear communication)	

Present tense

I does	we does	I do	we do
you does	you does	you do	you do
he, she, it do	they does	he, she, it does	they do

Past tense

I done	we done	I did	we did
you done	you done	you did	you did
he, she, it done	they done	he, she, it did	they did

Note: Many people have trouble with one negative form of *do*. They will say, for example, "He don't agree" instead of "He doesn't agree," or they will say, "The door don't work," instead of "The door doesn't work." Be careful to avoid the common mistake of using *don't* instead of *doesn't*.

Activity 1

Underline the standard form of *be, have,* or *do.*

1. Crystal (have, has) such a nice singing voice that she often sings solos at our choir concerts.
2. The children (is, are) ready to go home.
3. Whenever we (do, does) the laundry, our clothes are spotted with blobs of undissolved detergent.
4. Rod and Arlene (was, were) ready to leave for the movies when the baby began to wail.
5. Our art class (done, did) the mural on the wall of the cafeteria.
6. If I (have, has) the time later, I will help you set up your new laser printer.
7. Jesse (be, is) the best Ping-Pong player in the college.
8. My mom always goes to the same hair stylist because she (do, does) Mom's hair just the way Mom likes.
9. The mice in our attic (have, has) chewed several holes in our ceiling.
10. The science instructor said that the state of California (be, is) ready for a major earthquake any day.

Activity 2

Fill in each blank with the standard form of *be, have,* or *do.*

1. My car _____ a real personality.
2. I think it _____ almost human.
3. On cold mornings, it _____ not want to start.
4. Like me, the car _____ a problem dealing with freezing weather.
5. I don't want to get out of bed, and my car _____ not like leaving the garage.
6. Also, we _____ the same feeling about rainstorms.
7. I hate driving to school in a downpour, and so _____ the car.
8. When the car _____ stopped at a light, it stalls.
9. The habits my car _____ may be annoying.
10. But they _____ understandable.

■ **Review Test 1**

Underline the standard verb form.

1. Alex (argue, <u>argues</u>) just to hear himself talk.
2. Manuel and Yvonne (<u>do</u>, does) their grocery shopping first thing in the morning when the store is nearly empty.
3. The cheap ballpoint pen (leak, <u>leaked</u>) all over the lining of my pocketbook.
4. Dan (climb, <u>climbed</u>) up on the roof to see where the water was coming in.
5. If you (has, <u>have</u>) any trouble with the assignment, give me a call.
6. As soon as she gets home from work, Missy (boil, <u>boils</u>) some water to make tea.
7. My daughter often (watch, <u>watches</u>) TV after the rest of the family is in bed.
8. Two of the players (was, <u>were</u>) suspended from the league for ten games for using drugs.
9. Jeannie (<u>has</u>, have) only one eye; she lost the other years ago after falling on some broken glass.
10. I remember how my wet mittens (use, <u>used</u>) to steam on the hot school radiator.

■ **Review Test 2**

Cross out the two nonstandard verb forms in each sentence below. Then write the standard English verbs in the spaces provided.

Example ___*is*___ When our teacher ~~be~~ angry, his eyelid ~~begin~~ to twitch.
   ___*begins*___

_____

_____   1. My mother work for the local newspaper; she take classified ads over the phone.

_____   2. Last week the city tow away my car; this morning I paid sixty dollars and pick

_____   it up from the towing company.

_____   3. When my wife be late for work, she rush around the house like a speeded-up

_____   cartoon character.

_____   4. Henry love to go camping until two thieves in the campground remove his

_____   cooler, stove, and sleeping bag from his tent.

_____

_____   5. If the baby have a bad cold, I takes her into a steamy bathroom for a while to

_____   ease her breathing.

_____   6. Although my little girls knows they shouldn't tease the cat, they often dresses

_____   up the animal in doll clothes.

_____   7. When my brothers watches their favorite *Star Trek* reruns, they knows

_____   exactly what Captain Kirk is going to say next.

_____   8. The hot, sweaty children jumps into the cool water of the pool and splashes

_____   around like a couple of happy seals.

_____   9. I show the receipt to the manager to prove that the clerk had accidentally

_____   overcharge me.

_____   10. As far as our son be concerned, oatmeal taste like soggy cardboard.

_____

25 Irregular Verbs

Introductory Project

You may already have a sense of which common English verbs are regular and which are not. To test yourself, fill in the past tense and past participle of the verbs below. Five are regular verbs and so take *-d* or *-ed* in the past tense and past participle. (The item at the top is an example.) Five are irregular verbs and will probably not sound right when you try to add *-d* or *-ed*. Write *I* for *irregular* in front of these verbs. Also, see if you can write in their irregular verb forms.

Present	Past	Past Participle
shout	*shouted*	*shouted*
1. crawl	_____	_____
2. bring	_____	_____
3. use	_____	_____
4. do	_____	_____
5. give	_____	_____
6. laugh	_____	_____
7. go	_____	_____
8. scare	_____	_____
9. dress	_____	_____
10. see	_____	_____

Answers are on page 728.

A Brief Review of Regular Verbs

Every verb has four principal parts: present, past, past participle, and present participle. These parts can be used to build all the verb tenses (the times shown by a verb).

The past and past participle of a regular verb are formed by adding *-d* or *-ed* to the present. The *past participle* is the form of the verb used with the helping verbs *have, has,* or *had* (or some form of *be* with passive verbs). The *present participle* is formed by adding *-ing* to the present. Here are the principal forms of some regular verbs:

Present	Past	Past Participle	Present Participle
crash	crashed	crashed	crashing
shiver	shivered	shivered	shivering
kiss	kissed	kissed	kissing
apologize	apologized	apologized	apologizing
tease	teased	teased	teasing

Most verbs in English are regular.

List of Irregular Verbs

Irregular verbs have irregular forms in the past tense and past participle. For example, the past tense of the irregular verb *know* is *knew;* the past participle is *known.*

Almost everyone has some degree of trouble with irregular verbs. When you are unsure about the form of a verb, you can check the following list of irregular verbs. (The present participle is not shown on this list, because it is formed simply by adding *-ing* to the base form of the verb.) Or you can check a dictionary, which gives the principal parts of irregular verbs.

Present	Past	Past Participle
arise	arose	arisen
awake	awoke *or* awaked	awoken *or* awaked
be (am, are, is)	was (were)	been
become	became	become
begin	began	begun
bend	bent	bent
bite	bit	bitten
blow	blew	blown
break	broke	broken
bring	brought	brought
build	built	built
burst	burst	burst
buy	bought	bought
catch	caught	caught
choose	chose	chosen
come	came	come
cost	cost	cost
cut	cut	cut
do (does)	did	done
draw	drew	drawn
drink	drank	drunk
drive	drove	driven
eat	ate	eaten
fall	fell	fallen
feed	fed	fed
feel	felt	felt
fight	fought	fought
find	found	found
fly	flew	flown
freeze	froze	frozen
get	got	got *or* gotten
give	gave	given
go (goes)	went	gone
grow	grew	grown

Present	Past	Past Participle
have (has)	had	had
hear	heard	heard
hide	hid	hidden
hold	held	held
hurt	hurt	hurt
keep	kept	kept
know	knew	known
lay	laid	laid
lead	led	led
leave	left	left
lend	lent	lent
let	let	let
lie	lay	lain
lose	lost	lost
make	made	made
meet	met	met
pay	paid	paid
ride	rode	ridden
ring	rang	rung
run	ran	run
say	said	said
see	saw	seen
sell	sold	sold
send	sent	sent
shake	shook	shaken
shrink	shrank	shrunk
shut	shut	shut
sing	sang	sung
sit	sat	sat
sleep	slept	slept
speak	spoke	spoken
spend	spent	spent
stand	stood	stood
steal	stole	stolen

Present	Past	Past Participle
stick	stuck	stuck
sting	stung	stung
swear	swore	sworn
swim	swam	swum
take	took	taken
teach	taught	taught
tear	tore	torn
tell	told	told
think	thought	thought
wake	woke *or* waked	woken *or* waked
wear	wore	worn
win	won	won
write	wrote	written

Activity 1

Cross out the incorrect verb form in each of the following sentences. Then write the correct form of the verb in the space provided.

Example   _drew_ The little boy ~~drawed~~ on the marble table with permanent ink.

_____ 1. Tomatoes were once thought to be poisonous, and they were growed only as ornamental shrubs.

_____ 2. On the last day of swim class, every student swimmed the whole length of the pool.

_____ 3. My cats have tore little holes in all my good wool sweaters.

_____ 4. The pipes in the bathroom freezed last winter, and they burst when they thawed.

_____ 5 Every time my telephone has rang today, there has been bad news on the line.

_____ 6. Only seven people have ever knowed the formula for Coca-Cola.

_____ 7. Amy blowed up animal-shaped balloons for her son's birthday party.

_____ 8. I shaked the bottle of medicine before I took a teaspoonful of it.

_____ 9. While waiting for the doctor to arrive, I sitted in a plastic chair for over two hours.

_____ 10. The pile of bones on the plate showed how much chicken the family had ate.

Activity 2

For each of the italicized verbs, fill in the three missing forms in the following order:

> **a** Present tense, which takes an *-s* ending when the subject is *he, she, it,* or any *one person* or *thing* (see pages 401–402)
>
> **b** Past tense
>
> **c** Past participle—the form that goes with the helping verb *have, has,* or *had*

Example   My uncle likes to *give* away certain things. He *(a)* __*gives*__ old, threadbare clothes to the Salvation Army. Last year he *(b)* __*gave*__ me a worthless television set whose picture tube was burned out. He has *(c)* __*given*__ away stuff that a junk dealer would reject.

1. I like to *freeze* Hershey bars. A Hershey bar *(a)* _____ in half an hour. Once I *(b)* _____ a bottle of Pepsi. I put it in the freezer to chill and then forgot about it. Later I opened the freezer and discovered that it had *(c)* _____ and exploded.

2. Natalie *speaks* French. She *(a)* _____ German too. Her grandmother *(b)* _____ both languages and taught them to her. Since she was a baby, Natalie has *(c)* _____ them both as well as she speaks English.

3. An acquaintance of mine is a shoplifter, although he knows it's wrong to *steal*. He *(a)* _____ candy bars from supermarkets. Last month he *(b)* _____ a Sony Walkman and was caught by a detective. He has *(c)* _____ pants and shirts by wearing several layers of clothes out of a store.

4. I *go* to parties a lot. Often Camille *(a)* _____ with me. She *(b)* _____ with me just last week. I have *(c)* _____ to parties every Friday for the past month.

5. My brother likes to *throw* things. Sometimes he *(a)* _____ socks into his bureau drawer. In high school he *(b)* _____ footballs while quarterbacking the team. And he has *(c)* _____ Frisbees in our backyard for as long as I can remember.

6. I would like to *see* a UFO. I spend hours looking at the night sky, hoping to *(a)* _____ one. A neighbor of ours claims he *(b)* _____ one last month. But he says he has *(c)* _____ the Abominable Snowman, too.

7. I often *lie* down for a few minutes after a hard day's work. Sometimes my cat *(a)* _____ down near me. Yesterday was Saturday, so I *(b)* _____ in bed all morning. I probably would have *(c)* _____ in bed all afternoon, but I wanted to get some planting done in my vegetable garden.

8 I *do* not understand the assignment. It simply *(a)* _____ not make sense to me. I was surprised to learn that Shirley *(b)* _____ understand it. In fact, she had already *(c)* _____ the assignment.

9. I often find it hard to *begin* writing a paper. The assignment that I must do *(a)* _____ to worry me while I'm watching television, but I seldom turn off the set. Once I waited until the late movie had ended before I *(b)* _____ to write. If I had *(c)* _____ earlier, I would have gotten a decent night's sleep.

10. Martha likes to *eat*. She *(a)* _____ as continuously as some people smoke. Once she *(b)* _____ a large pack of cookies in half an hour. Even if she has *(c)* _____ a heavy meal, she often starts munching snacks right afterward.

■ Review Test 1

Underline the correct verb in the parentheses.

1. As I began my speech, my hands (shaked, shook) so badly I nearly dropped my notes.

2. Chico came into the gym and (began, begun) to practice on the parallel bars.

3. Over half the class has (taken, took) this course on a pass-fail basis.

THE LEARNING CENTRE
CITY & ISLINGTON COLLEGE
444 CAMDEN ROAD
LONDON N7 0SP
TEL: 020 7700 8642

4. Even though my father (teached, taught) me how to play baseball, I never enjoyed any part of the game.

5. Because I had (lended, lent) him money, I had a natural concern about what he did with it.

6. The drugstore clerk (gave, gived) him the wrong change.

7. Lola (brang, brought) a sweatshirt with her, for she knew the mountains got cold at night.

8. My sister (was, be) at school when a stranger came asking for her at our home.

9. The mechanic (did, done) an expensive valve job on my engine without getting my permission.

10. The basketball team has (broke, broken) the school record for most losses in one year.

11. Someone (leaved, left) his or her books in the classroom.

12. That jacket was (tore, torn) during the football game.

13. If I hadn't (threw, thrown) away the receipt, I could have gotten my money back.

14. I would have (become, became) very angry if you had not intervened.

15. As the flowerpot (fell, falled) from the windowsill, the little boy yelled, "Bombs away!"

■ Review Test 2

Write short sentences that use the form requested for the following irregular verbs.

Example   Past of *grow* ___I grew eight inches in one year.___

1. Past of *know* _____

_____

2. Past participle of *take* _____

_____

3. Past of *give* _____

_____

4. Past participle of *write* _____

_____

5. Past of *bring* _____

_____

6. Past participle of *speak* _____

_____

7. Past of *begin* _____

_____

8. Past of *go* _____

_____

9. Past participle of *see* _____

_____

10. Past of *drive* _____

_____

26 Subject-Verb Agreement

Introductory Project

As you read each pair of sentences below, write a check mark beside the sentence that you think uses the underlined word correctly.

There <u>was</u> too many people talking at once. _____
There <u>were</u> too many people talking at once. _____

The onions in that spaghetti sauce <u>gives</u> me heartburn. _____
The onions in that spaghetti sauce <u>give</u> me heartburn. _____

The mayor and her husband <u>attends</u> our church. _____
The mayor and her husband <u>attend</u> our church. _____

Everything <u>seem</u> to slow me down when I'm in a hurry. _____
Everything <u>seems</u> to slow me down when I'm in a hurry. _____

Answers are on page 728.

A verb must agree with its subject in number. A *singular subject* (one person or thing) takes a singular verb. A *plural subject* (more than one person or thing) takes a plural verb. Mistakes in subject-verb agreement are sometimes made in the situations listed below (each situation is explained on the following pages):

1   When words come between the subject and the verb
2   When a verb comes before the subject
3   With compound subjects
4   With indefinite pronouns

Words between Subject and Verb

Words that come between the subject and the verb do not change subject-verb agreement. In the sentence

The tomatoes in this salad are brown and mushy.

the subject (tomatoes) is plural, and so the verb (are) is plural. The words *in this salad* that come between the subject and the verb do not affect subject-verb agreement.

To help find the subject of certain sentences, you should cross out prepositional phrases (see page 363):

Nell, ~~with her three dogs close behind,~~ runs around the park every day.
The seams ~~in my new coat~~ have split after only two wearings.

Activity

Underline the correct verb form in the parentheses.

1. The decisions of the judge (seem, seems) questionable.
2. The flakes in this cereal (taste, tastes) like sawdust.
3. The woman with the dark sunglasses (is, are) our mayor.
4. Many people in Europe (speak, speaks) several languages.
5. A hamburger with a double order of french fries (is, are) my usual lunch.
6. That silk flower by the candles (look, looks) real.
7. One of my son's worst habits (is, are) leaving an assortment of dirty plates on the kitchen counter.

8. The rust spots on the back of Emily's car (need, needs) to be cleaned with a special polish.

9. The collection of medicine bottles in my parents' bathroom (overflow, overflows) the cabinet shelves.

10. A tired-looking student in my classes often (sleep, sleeps) through most of the lectures.

Verb before Subject

A verb agrees with its subject even when the verb comes *before* the subject. Words that may precede the subject include *there, here,* and, in questions, *who, which, what,* and *where.*

On Glen's doorstep were two police officers.
There are many pizza places in our town.
Here is your receipt.
Where are they going to sleep?

If you are unsure about the subject, look at the verb and ask *who* or *what.* With the first example above, you might ask, "*Who* were on the doorstep?" The answer, *police officers,* is the subject.

Activity

Write the correct form of the verb in the space provided.

is, are   1. What _____ your middle name?

was, were   2. Among the guests _____ a private detective.

do, does   3. Where _____ you go when you want to be alone?

is, are   4. There _____ many hungry people in American cities.

rest, rests   5. In that grave _____ the bones of my great-grandfather.

was, were   6. There _____ too many people in the room for me to feel comfortable.

is, are   7. Why _____ the lights turned off?

stand, stands   8. Across the street _____ the post office.

is, are   9. Here _____ the tickets for tonight's game.

was, were   10. Stuffed into the mailbox _____ ten pieces of junk mail and three ripped magazines.

Compound Subjects

Subjects joined by *and* generally take a plural verb.

Maple syrup and sweet butter taste delicious on pancakes.
Fear and ignorance have a lot to do with hatred.

When subjects are joined by *either . . . or, neither . . . nor, not only . . . but also,* the verb agrees with the subject closer to the verb.

Either the Oak Ridge Boys or Mary Chapin Carpenter deserves the award for the best country album of the year.

The nearer subject, *Mary Chapin Carpenter,* is singular, and so the verb is singular.

Activity

Write the correct form of the verb in the space provided.

stays, stay 1. Our cats and dog _____ at a neighbor's house when we go on vacation.

Is, Are 2. _____ the birthday cake and ice cream ready to be served?

holds, hold 3. Staples and Scotch tape _____ all our old photo albums together.

was, were 4. Rent and car insurance _____ my biggest expenses last month.

wants, want 5. Neither the students nor the instructor _____ to postpone the final exam till after the holidays.

is, are 6. An egg and a banana _____ required for the recipe.

was, were 7. Owning a car and having money in my pocket _____ the chief ambitions of my adolescence.

visits, visit 8. My aunt and uncle from Ireland _____ us every other summer.

was, were 9. Before they saw a marriage therapist, Peter and Jenny _____ planning to get divorced.

acts, act 10. Not only the landlady but also her children _____ unfriendly to us.

Indefinite Pronouns

The following words, known as *indefinite pronouns*, always take singular verbs:

(-one *words*)	(-body *words*)	(-thing *words*)	
one	nobody	nothing	each
anyone	anybody	anything	either
everyone	everybody	everything	neither
someone	somebody	something	

Note: *Both* always takes a plural verb.

Activity

Write the correct form of the verb in the space provided.

is, are

1. Everybody at my new school _____ friendly.

feel, feels

2. Neither of those mattresses _____ comfortable.

knows, know

3. Nobody in my family _____ how to swim.

needs, need

4. Each of the children _____ some attention.

sounds, sound

5. Something about Robbie's story _____ suspicious.

pitches, pitch

6. If each of us _____ in, we can finish this job in an hour.

was, were

7. Everybody in the theater _____ getting up and leaving before the movie ended.

provides, provide

8. Neither of the restaurants _____ facilities for the handicapped.

likes, like

9. No one in our family _____ housecleaning, but we all take a turn at it.

steals, steal

10. Someone in our neighborhood _____ vegetables from people's gardens.

■ Review Test 1

Underline the correct verb in parentheses.

1. Lettuce in most of the stores in our area now (costs, cost) almost three dollars a head.
2. Nobody in the class of fifty students (understands, understand) how to solve the equation on the blackboard.
3. The packages in the shopping bag (was, were) a wonderful mystery to the children.
4. My exercise class of five students (meets, meet) every Thursday afternoon.
5. Anyone who (steals, steal) my purse won't find much inside it.
6. Business contacts and financial backing (is, are) all that I need to establish my career as a dress designer.
7. Each of those breakfast cereals (contains, contain) a high proportion of sugar.
8. The serious look in that young girl's eyes (worries, worry) me.
9. All the cars on my block (has, have) to be moved one day a month for street cleaning.
10. Some people (know, knows) more about their favorite TV characters than they do about the members of their own family.

■ Review Test 2

Each of the following passages contains *two* mistakes in subject-verb agreement. Find these two mistakes and cross them out. Then write the correct form of each verb in the space provided.

1. Few people recalls seeing baby pigeons. The reason is simple. Baby pigeons in the nest eats a huge amount of food each day. Upon leaving the nest, they are close to the size of their parents.

   a. _____

   b. _____

2. Everything in the mall stores are on sale today. Customers from all over are crowding the aisles. There is terrific bargains in many departments.

   a. _____

   b. _____

3. All the neighbors meets once a year for a block party. Everyone talks and dances far into the night. Huge bowls of delicious food sits on picnic tables. Afterward, everyone goes home and sleeps all day.

   a. _____

   b. _____

4. The members of the swimming team paces nervously beside the pool. Finally, an official blows a whistle. Into the pool dive a swimmer with thick, tan arms. He paddles quickly through the water.

   a. _____

   b. _____

4. When Lin Soo comes home from school each day, her work is just beginning. The members of her family all works in their small restaurant. Nobody rest until the last customer is served. Only then do Lin Soo and her brother start their homework.

   a. _____

   b. _____

27 Pronoun Agreement and Reference

Introductory Project

Read each pair of sentences below. Then write a check mark beside the sentence that you think uses the underlined word or words correctly.

Someone in my neighborhood lets their dog run loose. _____

Someone in my neighborhood lets his or her dog run loose. _____

After Tony reviewed his notes with Bob, he passed the exam with ease.

_____

After reviewing his notes with Bob, Tony passed the exam with ease.

_____

Answers are on page 728.

Pronouns are words that take the place of nouns (persons, places, or things). In fact, the word *pronoun* means "for a noun." Pronouns are shortcuts that keep you from unnecessarily repeating words in writing. Here are some examples of pronouns:

> Shirley had not finished *her* paper. (*Her* is a pronoun that takes the place of *Shirley's.*)
>
> Tony swung so heavily on the tree branch that *it* snapped. (*It* replaces *branch.*)
>
> When the three little pigs saw the wolf, *they* pulled out cans of Mace. (*They* is a pronoun that takes the place of *pigs.*)

This section presents rules that will help you avoid two common mistakes people make with pronouns. The rules are as follows:

1   A pronoun must agree in number with the word or words it replaces.

2   A pronoun must refer clearly to the word it replaces.

Pronoun Agreement

A pronoun must agree in number with the word or words it replaces. If the word a pronoun refers to is singular, the pronoun must be singular; if that word is plural, the pronoun must be plural. (Note that the word a pronoun refers to is also known as the *antecedent.*)

Barbara agreed to lend me (her) Willie Nelson CDs.

People walking the trail must watch (their) step because of snakes.

In the first example, the pronoun *her* refers to the singular word *Barbara;* in the second example, the pronoun *their* refers to the plural word *People.*

Activity

Write the appropriate pronoun *(their, they, them, it)* in the blank space in each of the following sentences.

Example   I lifted the pot of hot potatoes carefully, but ____*it*____ slipped out of my hand.

1. People should try to go into a new situation with _____ minds open, not with opinions already firmly formed.

2. Fred never misses his daily workout; he believes _____ keeps him healthy.

3. Sometimes, in marriage, partners expect too much from _____ mates.

4. For some students, college is often their first experience with an undisciplined learning situation, and _____ are not always ready to accept the responsibility.

5. Our new neighbors moved in three months ago, but I have yet to meet _____.

Indefinite Pronouns

The following words, known as *indefinite pronouns,* are always singular.

(-one words)	*(-body words)*	
one	nobody	each
anyone	anybody	either
everyone	everybody	neither
someone	somebody	

If a pronoun in a sentence refers to one of the above singular words, the pronoun should be singular.

Each father felt that (his) child should have won the contest.

One of the women could not find (her) purse.

Everyone must be in (his) seat before the instructor takes the roll.

In each example, the circled pronoun is singular because it refers to one of the special singular words.

Note: The last example is correct if everyone in the class is a man. If everyone in the class is a woman, the pronoun would be *her.* If the class has both women and men, the pronoun form would be *his or her:*

Everyone must be in his or her seat before the instructor takes the roll.

Some writers follow the traditional practice of using *his* to refer to both women and men. Many now use *his or her* to avoid an implied sexual bias. To avoid using *his* or the somewhat awkward *his or her,* a sentence can often be rewritten in the plural:

Students must be in their seats before the instructor takes the roll.

Activity

Underline the correct pronoun.

1. Someone has blocked the parking lot exit with (his or her, their) car.
2. Everyone in the women's group has volunteered some of (her, their) time for the voting drive.
3. Neither of the men arrested as terrorists would reveal (his, their) real name.
4. Not one of the women coaches will be returning to (her, their) job next year.
5. Each of the president's advisers offered (his or her, their) opinion about the airline strike.

Pronoun Reference

A sentence may be confusing and unclear if a pronoun appears to refer to more than one word, or if the pronoun does not refer to any specific word. Look at this sentence:

Joe almost dropped out of high school, for he felt *they* emphasized discipline too much.

Who emphasized discipline too much? There is no specific word that *they* refers to. Be clear:

Joe almost dropped out of high school, for he felt *the teachers* emphasized discipline too much.

Here are sentences with other kinds of faulty pronoun reference. Read the explanations of why they are faulty and look carefully at how they are corrected.

Faulty	*Clear*
June told Margie that *she* lacked self-confidence.	June told Margie, "You lack self-confidence."
(*Who* lacked self-confidence: June or Margie? Be clear.)	(Quotation marks, which can sometimes be used to correct an unclear reference, are explained on pages 478–484.)
Nancy's mother is a hairdresser, but Nancy is not interested in *it*.	Nancy's mother is a hairdresser, but Nancy is not interested in becoming one.
*(There is no specific word that *it* refers to. It would not make sense to say, "Nancy is not interested in hairdresser.")	
Ron blamed the police officer for the ticket, *which* was foolish.	Foolishly, Ron blamed the police officer for the ticket.
(Does *which* mean that the officer's giving the ticket was foolish, or that Ron's blaming the officer was foolish? Be clear.)	

Activity

Rewrite each of the following sentences to make the vague pronoun reference clear. Add, change, or omit words as necessary.

Example   Our cat was friends with our hamster until he bit him.
<u>Until the cat bit the hamster, the two were friends.</u>

1. Maria's mother let her wear her new earrings to school.

2. When I asked why I failed my driver's test, he said I drove too slowly.

3. Dad ordered my brother to paint the garage because he didn't want to do it.

4. Herb dropped his psychology courses because he thought they assigned too much reading.

5. I love Parmesan cheese on veal, but it does not always digest well.

■ Review Test 1

Cross out the pronoun error in each sentence and write the correction in the space provided at the left. Then circle the letter that correctly describes the type of error that was made.

Examples

his (or her) Each player took ~~their~~ position on the court.

Mistake in: ⓐ pronoun agreement.   b. pronoun reference.

the store I was angry when ~~they~~ wouldn't give me cash back when I returned the sweater I had bought.

Mistake in: a. pronoun agreement.   ⓑ pronoun reference.

_____ 1. Dan asked Mr. Sanchez if ~~he~~ could stay an extra hour at work today.

Mistake in: a. pronoun agreement.   b. pronoun reference.

_____ 2. Both the front door and the back door of the abandoned house had fallen off ~~its~~ hinges.

Mistake in: a. pronoun agreement.   b. pronoun reference.

_____ 3. I've been taking cold medicine, and now ~~it~~ is better.

Mistake in: a. pronoun agreement.   b. pronoun reference.

_____ 4. Norm was angry when ~~they~~ raised the state tax on cigarettes.

Mistake in: a. pronoun agreement.   b. pronoun reference.

_____ 5. Every one of those musicians who played for two hours in the rain truly earned ~~their~~ money last night.

Mistake in: a. pronoun agreement.   b. pronoun reference.

_____ 6. An annual flu shot is a good idea; ~~they~~ will help children and older people stay healthy.

Mistake in: a. pronoun agreement.   b. pronoun reference.

_____ 7. Each of the beauty queens is asked a thought-provoking question and then judged on ~~their~~ answer.

Mistake in: a. pronoun agreement.   b. pronoun reference.

_____ 8. Indira could not believe that ~~they~~ had changed the immigration laws again.

Mistake in: a. pronoun agreement.   b. pronoun reference.

_____   9. At the dental office, I asked ~~him~~ if it was really necessary to take X rays of my mouth again.

Mistake in: a. pronoun agreement.   b. pronoun reference.

_____   10. Every ant in the bustling anthill has ~~their~~ own job to do that helps support the entire community.

Mistake in: a. pronoun agreement.   b. pronoun reference.

■ **Review Test 2**

Underline the correct word in parentheses.

1. Cindy is the kind of woman who will always do (their, her) best.
2. Hoping to be first in line when (they, the ushers) opened the doors, we arrived two hours early for the concert.
3. If a person really wants to appreciate good coffee, (he or she, they) should drink it black.
4. My children are hooked on science fiction stories because (they, the stories) allow readers to escape to other worlds.
5. Lois often visits the reading center in school, for she finds that (they, the tutors) give her helpful instruction.
6. Nobody seems to know how to add or subtract without (his or her, their) pocket calculator anymore.
7. As the room got colder, everybody wished for (his or her, their) coat.
8. Each of my brothers has had (his, their) apartment broken into.
9. If someone is going to write a composition, (he or she, they) should prepare at least one rough draft.
10. My wife and I both need thick glasses, so I imagine our children won't escape (it, needing glasses).

28 Pronoun Types

This chapter describes some common types of pronouns: subject and object pronouns, possessive pronouns, and demonstrative pronouns.

Subject and Object Pronouns

Pronouns change their form depending on the purpose they serve in a sentence. In the box that follows is a list of subject and object pronouns.

Subject Pronouns	Object Pronouns
I	me
you	you *(no change)*
he	him
she	her
it	it *(no change)*
we	us
they	them

Subject Pronouns

Subject pronouns are subjects of verbs.

> *She* is wearing blue nail polish on her toes. (*She* is the subject of the verb *is wearing*)
>
> *They* ran up three flights of steps. (*They* is the subject of the verb *ran*).
>
> *We* children should have some privacy too. (*We* is the subject of the verb *should have.*)

Rules for using subject pronouns, and several kinds of mistakes people sometimes make with subject pronouns, are explained below.

Rule 1:   Use a subject pronoun in spots where you have a compound (more than one) subject.

Incorrect	*Correct*
Sally and *me* are exactly the same size.	Sally and *I* are exactly the same size.
Her and *me* share our wardrobes with each other.	*She* and *I* share our wardrobes with each other.

Hint: If you are not sure what pronoun to use, try each pronoun by itself in the sentence. The correct pronoun will be the one that sounds right. For example, "her shares her wardrobe" does not sound right. "She shares her wardrobe" does.

Rule 2:   Use a subject pronoun after forms of the verb *be*. Forms of *be* include *am, are, is, was, were, has been,* and *have been.*

It was *I* who called you a minute ago and then hung up.

It may be *they* entering the diner.

It was *he* who put the white tablecloth into the washing machine with a red sock.

The sentences above may sound strange and stilted to you because they are seldom used in conversation. When we speak with one another, forms such as "It was me," "It may be them," and "It is her" are widely accepted. In formal writing, however, the grammatically correct forms are still preferred.

Hint: To avoid having to use the subject pronoun form after *be,* you can simply reword a sentence. Here is how the preceding examples could be reworded:

I was the one who called you a minute ago and then hung up.

They may be the ones entering the diner.

He put the white tablecloth into the washing machine with a red sock.

Rule 3:   Use subject pronouns after *than* or *as*. The subject pronoun is used because a verb is understood after the pronoun.

Mark can hold his breath longer than *I* (can). (The verb *can* is understood after *I*.)

Her thirteen-year-old daughter is as tall as *she* (is). (The verb *is* is understood after *she*.)

You drive much better than *he* (drives). (The verb *drives* is understood after *he.*)

Hint: Avoid mistakes by mentally adding the "missing" verb at the end of the sentence.

Object Pronouns

Object pronouns *(me, him, her, us, them)* are the objects of verbs or prepositions. (*Prepositions* are connecting words like *for, at, about, to, before, by, with,* and *of.* See also page 363.)

Lee pushed *me.* (*Me* is the object of the verb *pushed.*)

We dragged *them* all the way home. (*Them* is the object of the verb *dragged.*)

She wrote all about *us* in her diary. (*Us* is the object of the preposition *about.*)

Vera passed a note to *him* as she walked to the pencil sharpener. (*Him* is the object of the preposition *to.*)

People are sometimes uncertain about which pronoun to use when two objects follow the verb.

Incorrect	*Correct*
I argued with his sister and *he.*	I argued with his sister and *him.*
The cashier cheated Rick and *I.*	The cashier cheated Rick and *me.*

Hint: If you are not sure which pronoun to use, try each pronoun by itself in the sentence. The correct pronoun will be the one that sounds right. For example, "I argued with he" does not sound right; "I argued with him" does.

Activity

Underline the correct subject or object pronoun in each of the following sentences. Then show whether your answer is a subject or an object pronoun by circling S or O in the margin. The first one is done for you as an example.

(S) O   1. Darcy and (<u>she</u>, her) kept dancing even after the band stopped playing.

S   O   2 The letters Mom writes to Estelle and (I, me) are always typed in red.

S   O   3. Pilar is good at bowling, but her little sister is even better than (she, her).

S   O   4. Their relay team won because they practiced more than (we, us).

S   O   5. (We, Us) choir members get to perform for the governor.

S   O   6. The rest of (they, them) came to the wedding by train.

S   O   7. (She, Her) and Sammy got divorced and then remarried.

S   O   8. Since we were both taking a tough statistics course, it was a long, hard semester for my best friend and (me, I).

S   O   9. Tony and (he, him) look a lot alike, but they're not even related.

S   O   10. Our neighbors asked Rosa and (I, me) to help with their parents' surprise party.

Possessive Pronouns

Possessive pronouns show ownership or possession.

Using a small branch, Stu wrote *his* initials in the wet cement.
The furniture is *mine,* but the car is *hers*.

Here is a list of possessive pronouns:

my, mine	our, ours
your, yours	your, yours
his	their, theirs
her, hers	
its	

Note: A possessive pronoun *never* uses an apostrophe. (See also page 473.)

Incorrect	*Correct*
That earring is *her's.*	That earring is *hers*.
The orange cat is *theirs'.*	The orange cat is *theirs*.

Activity

Cross out the incorrect pronoun form in each of the sentences below. Write the correct form in the space at the left.

Example   ___*ours*___ The house with the maroon shutters is ~~ours'~~.

_____ 1. A porcupine has no quills on it's belly.

_____ 2. The PowerBook on that table is theirs'.

_____ 3. You can easily tell which team is ours' by when we cheer.

_____ 4. My dog does not get along with her's.

_____ 5. Grandma's silverware and dishes will be yours' when you get married.

Demonstrative Pronouns

Demonstrative pronouns point to or single out a person or thing. There are four demonstrative pronouns:

this	these
that	those

Generally speaking, *this* and *these* refer to things close at hand; *that* and *those* refer to things farther away. These four pronouns are commonly used in the role of demonstrative adjectives as well.

> *This* milk has gone sour.
> My son insists on saving all *these* hot rod magazines.
> I almost tripped on *that* roller skate at the bottom of the steps.
> *Those* plants in the corner don't get enough light.

Note: Do not use *them, this here, that there, these here,* or *those there* to point out. Use only *this, that, these,* or *those.*

Activity

Cross out the incorrect form of the demonstrative pronoun and write the correct form in the space provided.

Example   ___*Those*___   ~~Those there~~ tires look worn.

_____ 1. This here child has a high fever.

_____ 2. These here pants I'm wearing are so tight I can hardly breathe.

_____ 3. Them kids have been playing in the alley all morning.

_____ 4. That there umpire won't stand for any temper tantrums.

_____ 5. I save them old baby clothes for my daughter's dolls.

■ Review Test

Underline the correct word in the parentheses.

1. If I left dinner up to (he, him), we'd have Cheerios every night.
2. The vase on my dresser belonged to my grandmother, and the candlesticks on the windowsill were (hers', hers) as well.
3. My boyfriend offered to drive his mother and (I, me) to the mall to shop for his birthday present.
4. (Them, Those) little marks on the floor are scratches, not crumbs.
5. I took a picture of my brother and (I, me) looking into the hallway mirror.
6. When Lin and (she, her) drove back from the airport, they talked so much that they missed their exit.
7. (That there, That) orange juice box says "Fresh," but the juice is made from concentrate.
8. Eliot swears that he dreamed about (she, her) and a speeding car the night before Irina was injured in a car accident.
9. The waitress brought our food to the people at the next table and gave (theirs, theirs') to us.
10. Since it was so hot out, Lana and (he, him) felt they had a good excuse to study at the beach.

29 Adjectives and Adverbs

Adjectives

What Are Adjectives?

Adjectives describe nouns (names of persons, places, or things) or pronouns.

> Ernie is a *rich* man. (The adjective *rich* describes the noun *man.*)
> He is also *generous*. (The adjective *generous* describes the pronoun *he.*)
> Our *gray* cat sleeps a lot. (The adjective *gray* describes the noun *cat.*)
> She is *old*. (The adjective *old* describes the pronoun *she.*)

Adjectives usually come before the word they describe (as in *rich man* and *gray cat*). But they also come after forms of the verb *be (is, are, was, were,* and so on). They also follow verbs such as *look, appear, seem, become, sound, taste,* and *smell.*

> That speaker was *boring*. (The adjective *boring* describes the speaker.)
> The Petersons are *homeless*. (The adjective *homeless* describes the Petersons.)
> The soup looked *good*. (The adjective *good* describes the soup.)
> But it tasted *salty*. (The adjective *salty* describes the pronoun *it.*)

Using Adjectives to Compare

For all one-syllable adjectives and some two-syllable adjectives, add *-er* when comparing two things and *-est* when comparing three or more things.

> My sister's handwriting is *neater* than mine, but Mother's is the *neatest.*
> Canned juice is sometimes *cheaper* than fresh juice, but frozen juice is often the *cheapest.*

For some two-syllable adjectives and all longer adjectives, add *more* when comparing two things and *most* when comparing three or more things.

Typing something is *more efficient* than writing it out by hand, but the *most efficient* way to write is on a computer.

Jeans are generally *more comfortable* than slacks, but sweat pants are the *most comfortable* of all.

You can usually tell when to use *more* and *most* by the sound of a word. For example, you can probably tell by its sound that "carefuller" would be too awkward to say and that *more careful* is thus correct. In addition, there are many words for which both *-er* or *-est* and *more* or *most* are equally correct. For instance, either "a more fair rule" or "a fairer rule" is correct.

To form negative comparisons, use *less* and *least.*

When kids called me "Dum-dum," I tried to look *less* hurt than I felt.

They say men gossip *less* than women do, but I don't believe it.

Suzanne is the most self-centered, *least* thoughtful person I know.

Points to Remember about Comparing

Point 1:   Use only one form of comparison at a time. In other words, do not use both an *-er* ending and *more* or both an *-est* ending and *most.*

Incorrect	*Correct*
My Southern accent is always *more stronger* after I visit my family in Georgia.	My Southern accent is always *stronger* after I visit my family in Georgia.
My *most luckiest* day was the day I met my wife.	My *luckiest* day was the day I met my wife.

Point 2:   Learn the irregular forms of the words shown below.

	Comparative (for Comparing Two Things)	*Superlative (for Comparing Three or More Things)*
bad	worse	worst
good, well	better	best
little (in amount)	less	least
much, many	more	most

Do not use both *more* and an irregular comparative or *most* and an irregular superlative.

Incorrect

It is *more better* to stay healthy than to have to get healthy.

Yesterday I went on the *most best* date of my life—and all we did was go on a picnic.

Correct

It is *better* to stay healthy than to have to get healthy.

Yesterday I went on the *best* date of my life—and all we did was go on a picnic.

Activity

Add to each sentence the correct form of the word in the margin.

bad   *Examples* The _____*worst*_____ scare I ever had was the time when I thought my son was on an airplane that had crashed.

wonderful   The day of my divorce was even _*more wonderful*_ than the day of my wedding.

good   1. The Grammy awards are given to the _____ recording artists of each year.

popular   2. Vanilla ice cream is even _____ than chocolate ice cream.

bad   3. One of the _____ things you can do to people is ignore them.

light   4. A pound of feathers is no _____ than a pound of stones.

little   5. The _____ expensive way to accumulate a wardrobe is to buy used clothing whenever possible.

Adverbs

What Are Adverbs?

Adverbs—which usually end in *-ly*—describe verbs, adjectives, or other adverbs.

The referee *suddenly* stopped the fight. (The adverb *suddenly* describes the verb *stopped*.)

Her yellow rosebushes are *absolutely* beautiful. (The adverb *absolutely* describes the adjective *beautiful*.)

The auctioneer spoke so *terribly* fast that I couldn't understand him. (The adverb *terribly* describes the adverb *fast*.)

A Common Mistake with Adverbs and Adjectives

People often mistakenly use an adjective instead of an adverb after a verb.

Incorrect	*Correct*
I jog *slow*.	I jog *slowly*.
The nervous witness spoke *quiet*.	The nervous witness spoke *quietly*.
The first night I quit smoking, I wanted a cigarette *bad*.	The first night I quit smoking, I wanted a cigarette *badly*.

Activity

Underline the adjective or adverb needed. (Remember that adjectives describe nouns, and adverbs describe verbs, adjectives, or other adverbs.)

1. During a quiet moment in class, my stomach rumbled (loud, loudly).
2. I'm a (slow, slowly) reader, so I have to put aside more time to study than some of my friends.
3. Thinking no one was looking, the young man (quick, quickly) emptied his car's ashtray onto the parking lot.
4. The kitchen cockroaches wait (patient, patiently) in the shadows; at night they'll have the place to themselves.
5. I hang up the phone (immediate, immediately) whenever the speaker is a recorded message.

Well and *Good*

Two words that are often confused are *well* and *good*. *Good* is an adjective; it describes nouns. *Well* is usually an adverb; it describes verbs. *Well* (rather than *good)* is also used to refer to a person's health.

Activity

Write *well* or *good* in each of the sentences that follow.

1. I could tell by the broad grin on Della's face that the news was _____.
2. They say my grandfather sang so _____ that even the wind stopped to listen.
3. The food at the salad bar must not have been too fresh, because I didn't feel _____ after dinner.

4. When I want to do a really _____ job of washing the floor, I do it on my hands and knees.

5. The best way to get along _____ with our boss is to stay out of his way.

■ Review Test

Underline the correct word in the parentheses.

1. In Egypt, silver was once (more valued, most valued) than gold.
2. The doctor predicted that Ben would soon be (good, well) enough to go home.
3. The (little, less) coffee I drink, the better I feel.
4. Light walls make a room look (more large, larger) than dark walls do.
5. One of the (unfortunatest, most unfortunate) men I know is a millionaire.
6. The moth's (continuous, continuously) thumping against the screen got on my nerves.
7. The Amish manage (good, well) without radios, telephones, or television.
8. When the store owner caught the little boys stealing, he scolded them (bad, badly) and called their parents.
9. It is (good, better) to teach people to fish than to give them fish.
10. Today a rocket can reach the moon more (quick, quickly) than it took a stage-coach to travel from one end of England to the other.

30 Misplaced Modifiers

Introductory Project

Because of misplaced words, each of the sentences below has more than one possible meaning. In each case, see if you can explain the intended meaning and the unintended meaning. Also, circle the words that you think create the confusion because they are misplaced.

1. The sign in the restaurant window reads, "Wanted: Young Man—To Open Oysters with References."

   Intended meaning: _____

   _____

   Unintended meaning: _____

   _____

2. Clyde and Charlotte decided to have two children on their wedding day.

   Intended meaning: _____

   _____

   Unintended meaning: _____

   _____

3. The students no longer like the math instructor who failed the test.

   Intended meaning: _____

   _____

   Unintended meaning: _____

   _____

Answers are on page 728.

What Misplaced Modifiers Are
and How to Correct Them

Modifiers are descriptive words. *Misplaced modifiers* are words that, because of awkward placement, do not describe the words the writer intended them to describe. Misplaced modifiers often obscure the meaning of a sentence. To avoid them, place words as close as possible to what they describe.

Misplaced Words	*Correctly Placed Words*
Tony bought an old car from a crooked dealer *with a faulty transmission.* (The *dealer* had a faulty transmission?)	Tony bought an old car with a faulty transmission from a crooked dealer. (The words describing the old car are now placed next to "car.")
I *nearly* earned a hundred dollars last week. (You just missed earning a hundred dollars, but in fact earned nothing?)	I earned nearly a hundred dollars last week. (The meaning—that you earned a little under a hundred dollars—is now clear.)
Bill yelled at the howling dog *in his underwear.* (The *dog* wore underwear?)	Bill, in his underwear, yelled at the howling dog. (The words describing Bill are placed next to "Bill.")

Activity

Underline the misplaced word or words in each sentence. Then rewrite the sentence, placing related words together and thereby making the meaning clear.

Examples   The suburbs <u>nearly</u> had five inches of rain.

The suburbs had nearly five inches of rain.

We could see the football stadium <u>driving across the bridge.</u>

Driving across the bridge, we could see the football stadium.

1. I saw mountains of uncollected trash walking along the city streets.

    _____

    _____

2. I almost had a dozen job interviews after I sent out my résumé.

    _____

    _____

3. The child stared at the movie monster with huge, innocent eyes.

_____

_____

4. Joanne decided to live with her grandparents while she attended college to save money.

_____

_____

5. Charlotte returned the hamburger to the supermarket that was spoiled.

_____

_____

6. Roger visited the old house still weak with the flu.

_____

_____

7. The phone almost rang fifteen times last night.

_____

_____

8. My uncle saw a kangaroo at the window under the influence of whiskey.

_____

_____

9. We decided to send our daughter to college on the day she was born.

_____

_____

10. Fred always opens the bills that arrive in the mailbox with a sigh.

_____

_____

■ Review Test

Write *M* for *misplaced modifier* or *C* for *correct* in front of each sentence.

_____ 1. Rita found it difficult to mount the horse underline{wearing tight jeans.}

_____ 2. Rita, wearing tight jeans, found it difficult to mount the horse.

_____ 3. I noticed a crack in the window underline{walking into the delicatessen.}

_____ 4. Walking into the delicatessen, I noticed a crack in the window.

_____   5. The biology teacher told us there would be a pop quiz <u>with an evil grin.</u>

_____   6. With an evil grin, the biology teacher told us there would be a pop quiz.

_____   7. I <u>almost</u> caught a hundred lightning bugs.

_____   8. I caught almost a hundred lightning bugs.

_____   9. In a secondhand store, Willie found a television set that had been stolen from me last month.

_____   10. Willie found a television set in a secondhand store <u>that had been stolen from me last month.</u>

_____   11. Willie found, in a secondhand store, a television set that had been stolen from me last month.

_____   12. In his shrillest voice, the reporter yelled a question at the departing mayor.

_____   13. The reporter yelled a question at the departing mayor <u>in his shrillest voice.</u>

_____   14. The president was quoted on the *NBC Evening News* as saying that the recession was about to end.

_____   15. The president was quoted as saying that the recession was about to end <u>on the *NBC Evening News.*</u>

31 Dangling Modifiers

Introductory Project

Because of dangling words, each of the sentences below has more than one possible meaning. In each case, see if you can explain the intended meaning and the unintended meaning.

1. While smoking a pipe, my dog sat with me by the crackling fire.

   Intended meaning: _____

   Unintended meaning: _____

2. Looking at the leather-skirted woman, his sports car went through a red light.

   Intended meaning: _____

   Unintended meaning: _____

3. After baking for several hours, Grandmother removed the beef pie from the oven.

   Intended meaning: _____

   Unintended meaning: _____

Answers are on page 728.

What Dangling Modifiers Are and How to Correct Them

A modifier that opens a sentence must be followed immediately by the word it is meant to describe. Otherwise, the modifier is said to be *dangling*, and the sentence takes on an unintended meaning. For example, in the sentence

> While smoking a pipe, my dog sat with me by the crackling fire.

the unintended meaning is that the *dog* was smoking the pipe. What the writer meant, of course, was that *he,* the writer, was smoking the pipe. The dangling modifier could be corrected by placing *I,* the word being described, directly after the opening modifier and revising as necessary:

> While smoking a pipe, *I sat with* my dog by the crackling fire.

The dangling modifier could also be corrected by placing the subject within the opening word group:

> While *I was* smoking my pipe, my dog sat with me by the crackling fire.

Here are other sentences with dangling modifiers. Read the explanations of why they are dangling and look carefully at how they are corrected.

Dangling	*Correct*
Swimming at the lake, a rock cut Sue's foot. (*Who* was swimming at the lake? The answer is not *rock* but *Sue.* The subject *Sue* must be added.)	Swimming at the lake, Sue cut her foot on a rock. *Or:* When Sue was swimming at the lake, she cut her foot on a rock.
While eating my sandwich, five mosquitoes bit me. (*Who* is eating the sandwich? The answer is not *five mosquitoes,* as it unintentionally seems to be, but *I.* The subject *I* must be added.)	While *I* was eating my sandwich, five mosquitoes bit me. *Or:* While eating my sandwich, *I* was bitten by five mosquitoes.
Getting out of bed, the tile floor was so cold that Yoko shivered all over. (*Who* got out of bed? The answer is not *tile floor* but *Yoko.* The subject *Yoko* must be added.)	Getting out of bed, *Yoko* found the tile floor so cold that she shivered all over. *Or:* When *Yoko* got out of bed, the tile floor was so cold that she shivered all over.

Dangling	*Correct*
To join the team, a C average or better is necessary.	To join the team, *you* must have a C average or better.
(*Who* is to join the team? The answer is not *C average* but *you.* The subject *you* must be added.)	*Or:* For *you* to join the team, a C average or better is necessary.

The preceding examples make clear the two ways of correcting a dangling modifier. Decide on a logical subject and do one of the following:

1   Place the subject *within* the opening word group.

   When Sue was swimming at the lake, she cut her foot on a rock.

Note: In some cases an appropriate subordinating word such as *When* must be added, and the verb may have to be changed slightly as well.

2   Place the subject right *after* the opening word group.

   Swimming at the lake, Sue cut her foot on a rock.

Activity

Ask *Who?* as you look at the opening words in each sentence. The subject that answers the question should be nearby in the sentence. If it is not, provide the logical subject by using either method of correction described above.

Example   While sleeping at the campsite, a Frisbee hit Derek on the head.

   While Derek was sleeping at the campsite, a Frisbee hit him on the head.

   or   *While sleeping at the campsite, Derek was hit on the head by a Frisbee.*

1. Watching the horror movie, goose bumps covered my spine.

   _____

   _____

2. After putting on a corduroy shirt, the room didn't seem as cold.

   _____

   _____

3. Flunking out of school, my parents demanded that I get a job.

_____

_____

4. Covered with food stains, my mother decided to wash the tablecloth.

_____

_____

5. Joining several college clubs, Antonio's social life became more active.

_____

_____

6. While visiting the Jungle Park Safari, a baboon scrambled onto the hood of their car.

_____

_____

7. Under attack by beetles, Charlotte sprayed her roses with insecticide.

_____

_____

8. Standing at the ocean's edge, the wind coated my glasses with a salty film.

_____

_____

9. Braking the car suddenly, my shopping bags tumbled off the seat.

_____

_____

10. Using binoculars, the hawk was clearly seen following its prey.

_____

_____

■ Review Test

Write *D* for *dangling* or *C* for *correct* in the blank next to each sentence. Remember that the opening words are a dangling modifier if they have no nearby logical subject to modify.

_____ 1. Advertising in the paper, Ian's car was quickly sold.

_____ 2. By advertising in the paper, Ian quickly sold his car.

_____ 3. After painting the downstairs, the house needed airing to clear out the fumes.

_____ 4. After we painted the downstairs, the house needed airing to clear out the fumes.

_____ 5. Frustrated by piles of homework, Wanda was tempted to watch television.

_____ 6. Frustrated by piles of homework, Wanda's temptation was to watch television.

_____ 7. After I waited patiently in the bank line, the teller told me I had filled out the wrong form.

_____ 8. After waiting patiently in the bank line, the teller told me I had filled out the wrong form.

_____ 9. When dieting, desserts are especially tempting.

_____ 10. When dieting, I find desserts especially tempting.

_____ 11. Looking through the telescope, I saw a brightly lit object come into view.

_____ 12. As I was looking through the telescope, a brightly lit object came into view.

_____ 13. Looking through the telescope, a brightly lit object came into my view.

_____ 14. Tossed carelessly over the arm of a chair, Mildred saw her new raincoat slide onto the floor.

_____ 15. Mildred saw her new raincoat, which had been tossed carelessly over the arm of a chair, slide onto the floor.

32 Paper Format

When you hand in a paper for any of your courses, probably the first thing you will be judged on is its format. It is important, then, that you do certain things to make your papers look attractive, neat, and easy to read.

Here are guidelines to follow in preparing a paper for an instructor:

1 Use full-size theme or typewriter paper, 8½ by 11 inches.

2 Leave wide margins (1 to 1½ inches) on all four sides of each page. In particular, do not crowd the right-hand or bottom margin. The white space makes your paper more readable; also, the instructor has room for comments.

3 If you write by hand:

   a Use a pen with blue or black ink (*not* a pencil).

   b Be careful not to overlap letters or to make decorative loops on letters. On narrow-ruled paper, write only on every other line.

   c Make all your letters distinct. Pay special attention to *a, e, i, o,* and *u*— five letters that people sometimes write illegibly.

   d Keep your capital letters clearly distinct from small letters. You may even want to print all the capital letters.

   e Make commas, periods, and other punctuation marks firm and clear. Leave a slight space after each period.

4 Center the title of your paper on the first line of page 1. Do *not* put quotation marks around the title, do not underline it, and do not put a period after it. Capitalize all the major words in a title, including the first word. Short connecting words within a title like *of, for, the, in,* and *to* are not capitalized. Skip a line between the title and the first line of your text.

5 Indent the first line of each paragraph about five spaces (half an inch) from the left-hand margin.

6 When you type or word-process, use double-spacing between lines. Also double-space after a period.

7 Whenever possible, avoid breaking (hyphenating) words at the end of lines. If you must break a word, break only between syllables (see page 501). Do not break words of one syllable.

8 Write your name, the date, and the course number where your instructor asks for them.

     Also keep in mind these important points about the *title* and *first sentence* of your paper:

9 The title should simply be several words that tell what the paper is about. It should usually *not* be a complete sentence. For example, if you are writing a paper about one of the most frustrating jobs you have ever had, the title could be just "A Frustrating Job."

10 Do not rely on the title to help explain the first sentence of your paper. The first sentence must be independent of the title. For instance, if the title of your paper is "A Frustrating Job," the first sentence should *not* be "It was working as a baby-sitter." Rather, the first sentence might be "Working as a baby-sitter was the most frustrating job I ever had."

Activity 1

Identify the mistakes in format in the following lines from a student theme. Explain the corrections in the spaces provided. One correction is provided as an example.

	"an unpleasant dining companion"
	My little brother is often an unpleasant dining companion. Last
	night was typical. For one thing, his appearance was disgusting.
	His shoes were not tied, and his shirt was unbuttoned and han-
	ging out of his pants, which he had forgotten to zip up. Traces
	of his afternoon snack of grape juice and chocolate cookies were

1. *Hyphenate only between syllables.* _____

2. _____

3. _____

4. _____

5. _____

6. _____

Activity 2

As already stated, a title should tell in several words (but *not* a complete sentence) what a paper is about. Often a title can be based on the topic sentence—the sentence that expresses the main idea of the paper. Following are five topic sentences from student papers. Write a suitable and specific title for each paper, basing the title on the topic sentence. (Note the example.)

Example   <u>Compromise in a Relationship</u>

Learning how to compromise is essential to a good relationship.

1. *Title:* _____
   Some houseplants are dangerous to children and pets.

2. *Title:* _____
   A number of fears haunted me when I was a child.

3. *Title:* _____
   You don't have to be a professional to take good photographs if you keep a few guidelines in mind.

4. *Title:* _____
   My husband is compulsively neat.

5. *Title:* _____
   There are a number of drawbacks to having a roommate.

Activity 3

As has already been stated, you must *not* rely on the title to help explain your first sentence. In four of the five sentences that follow, the writer has, inappropriately, used the title to help explain the first sentence.

Rewrite these four sentences so that they stand independent of the title. Write *Correct* under the one sentence that is independent of the title.

Example   *Title:* My Career Plans
             First sentence: They have changed in the last six months.
             Rewritten: <u>My career plans have changed in the last six months.</u>

1. *Title:* Contending with Dogs
   First sentence: This is the main problem in my work as a mail carrier.

   Rewritten : _____

   _____

2. *Title:* Study Skills
First sentence: They are necessary if a person is to do well in college.

Rewritten : _____

_____

3. *Title:* Summer Vacation
First sentence: Contrary to popular belief, a summer vacation can be the most miserable experience of the year.

Rewritten : _____

_____

4. *Title:* My Wife and the Sunday Newspaper
First sentence: My wife has a peculiar way of reading it.

Rewritten : _____

_____

5. *Title:* Cell Phones
First sentence: Many motorists have learned the hard way just how dangerous these handy tools can be.

Rewritten : _____

_____

■ Review Test

In the space provided, rewrite the following sentences from a student paper. Correct the mistakes in format.

	"disciplining our children"
	My husband and I are becoming experts in disciplining our child-
	ren. We have certain rules that we insist upon, and if there are
	any violations, we are swift to act. When our son simply doesn't
	do what he is told to do, he must write that particular action
	twenty times. For example, if he doesn't brush his teeth, he
	writes, "I must brush my teeth." If a child gets home after the

33 Capital Letters

Introductory Project

Items 1–13: You probably know a good deal about the uses of capital letters. Answering the questions below will help you check your knowledge.

1. Write the full name of a person you know: _____

2. In what city and state were you born? _____

3. What is your present street address? _____

4. Name a country where you would like to travel: _____

5. Name a school that you attended: _____

6. Give the name of a store where you buy food: _____

7. Name a company where someone you know works: _____

8. What day of the week gives you the best chance to relax? _____

9. What holiday is your favorite? _____

10. What brand of toothpaste do you use? _____

11. Write the brand name of a candy or gum you like: _____

12. Name a song or a television show you enjoy: _____

13. Write the title of a magazine you read: _____

Items 14–16: Three capital letters are needed in the lines below. Underline the words that you think should be capitalized. Then write them, capitalized, in the spaces provided.

the masked man reared his silvery-white horse, waved good-bye, and rode out of town. My heart thrilled when i heard someone say, "that was the Lone Ranger. You don't see his kind much, anymore."

14. _____ 15. _____ 16. _____

Answers are on page 728.

Main Uses of Capital Letters

Capital letters are used with:

1 The first word in a sentence or direct quotation

2 Names of persons and the word *I*

3 Names of particular places

4 Names of days of the week, months, and holidays

5 Names of commercial products

6 Names of organizations such as religious and political groups, associations, companies, unions, and clubs

7 Titles of books, magazines, newspapers, articles, stories, poems, films, television shows, songs, papers that you write, and the like

Each use is illustrated on the pages that follow.

First Word in a Sentence or Direct Quotation

The panhandler touched me and asked, "Do you have any change?"

(Capitalize the first word in the sentence.)

(Capitalize the first word in the direct quotation.)

"If you want a ride," said Tawana, "get ready now. Otherwise, I'm going alone."

(*If* and *Otherwise* are capitalized because they are the first words of sentences within a direct quotation. But *get* is not capitalized because it is part of the first sentence within the quotation.)

Names of Persons and the Word *I*

Last night I ran into Tony Curry and Lola Morrison.

Names of Particular Places

Charlotte graduated from Fargone High School in Orlando, Florida. She then moved with her parents to Bakersfield, California, and worked for a time there at Alexander's Gift House. Eventually she married and moved with her husband to the Naval Reserve Center in Atlantic County, New Jersey. She takes courses two nights a week at Stockton State College. On weekends she and her family often visit the nearby Wharton State Park and go canoeing on the

Mullica River. She does volunteer work at Atlantic City Hospital in connection with the First Christian Church. In addition, she works during the summer as a hostess at Convention Hall and the Holiday Inn.

But: Use small letters if the specific name of a place is not given.

Charlotte sometimes remembers her unhappy days in high school and at the gift shop where she worked after graduation. She did not imagine then that she would one day be going to college and doing volunteer work for a church and a hospital in the community where she and her husband live.

Names of Days of the Week, Months, and Holidays

I was angry at myself for forgetting that Sunday was Mother's Day.

During July and August, Fred works a four-day week, and he has Mondays off.

Bill still has a scar on his ankle from a cherry bomb that exploded near him on a Fourth of July and a scar on his arm where he stabbed himself with a fishhook on a Labor Day weekend.

But: Use small letters for the seasons—summer, fall, winter, spring.

Names of Commercial Products

Clyde uses Scope mouthwash, Certs mints, and Dentyne gum to drive away the taste of the Marlboro cigarettes and White Owl cigars that he always smokes.

My sister likes to play Monopoly and Sorry; I like chess and poker; my brother likes Scrabble, baseball, and table tennis.

But: Use small letters for the *type* of product (mouthwash, mints, gum, cigarettes, and so on).

Names of Organizations Such as Religious and Political Groups, Associations, Companies, Unions, and Clubs

Fred Grencher was a Lutheran for many years but converted to Catholicism when he married. Both he and his wife, Martha, are members of the Democratic Party. Both belong to the American Automobile Association. Martha works part time as a refrigerator salesperson at Sears. Fred is a mail carrier and belongs to the Postal Clerks' Union.

Tony met Lola when he was a Boy Scout and she was a Campfire Girl; she asked him to light her fire.

Titles of Books, Magazines, Newspapers, Articles, Stories, Poems, Films, Television Shows, Songs, Papers That You Write, and the Like

On Sunday Lola read the first chapter of *I Know Why the Caged Bird Sings,* a book required for her writing course. She looked through her parents' copy of the *New York Times.* She then read an article titled "Thinking about a Change in Your Career" and a poem titled "Some Moments Alone" in *Cosmopolitan* magazine. At the same time she played an old Beatles album, *Abbey Road.* In the evening she watched *60 Minutes* on television and a movie, *Sudden Impact,* starring Clint Eastwood. Then from 11 P.M. to midnight she worked on a paper titled "Uses of Leisure Time in Today's Culture" for her sociology class.

Activity

Cross out the words that need capitals in the following sentences. Then write the capitalized forms of the words in the spaces provided. The number of spaces tells you how many corrections to make in each case.

Example   I brush with ~~crest~~ toothpaste but get cavities all the time. ___*Crest*___

1. A spokesperson for general motors announced that the prices of all chevrolets will rise next year.

    _____   _____   _____

2. In may 2000 mario's family moved here from brownsville, Texas.

    _____   _____   _____

3. The mild-mannered reporter named clark kent said to the Wolfman, "you'd better think twice before you mess with me, Buddy."

    _____   _____   _____

4. While watching television, Spencer drank four pepsis, ate an entire package of ritz crackers, and finished a bag of oreo cookies.

    _____   _____   _____

5. A greyhound bus almost ran over Tony as he was riding his yamaha to a friend's home in florida.

    _____   _____   _____

6. Before I lent my polaroid camera to Janet, I warned her, "be sure to return it by friday."

    _____   _____

7. Before christmas George took his entire paycheck, went to sears, and bought a twenty-inch zenith color television.

_____   _____   _____

8. On their first trip to New York City, Fred and Martha visited the empire State Building and Times square. They also saw the New York mets play at Shea Stadium.

_____   _____   _____

9. Clyde was listening to Tina Turner's recording of "Proud mary," Charlotte was reading an article in *Reader's digest* titled "let's Stop Peddling Sex," and their son was watching *sesame Street.*

_____   _____   _____   _____

10. When a sign for a howard johnson's rest stop appeared on the turnpike, anita said, "let's stop here and stretch our legs for a bit."

_____   _____   _____   _____

Other Uses of Capital Letters

Capital letters are also used with:

1 Names that show family relationships
2 Titles of persons when used with their names
3 Specific school courses
4 Languages
5 Geographic locations
6 Historical periods and events
7 Races, nations, and nationalities
8 Opening and closing of a letter

Each use is illustrated on the pages that follow.

Names That Show Family Relationships

I got Mother to baby-sit for me.
I went with Grandfather to the church service.
Uncle Carl and Aunt Lucy always enclose twenty dollars with birthday cards.

But: Do not capitalize words like *mother, father, grandmother, aunt,* and so on, when they are preceded by a possessive word (*my, your, his, her, our, their*).

I got my mother to baby-sit for me.

I went with my grandfather to the church service.

My uncle and aunt always enclose twenty dollars with birthday cards.

Titles of Persons When Used with Their Names

I wrote to Senator Grabble and Congresswoman Punchie.

Professor Snorrel sent me to Chairperson Ruck, who sent me to Dean Rappers.

He drove to Dr. Helen Thompson's office after the cat bit him.

But: Use small letters when titles appear by themselves, without specific names.

I wrote to my senator and my congresswoman.

The professor sent me to the chairperson, who sent me to the dean.

He drove to the doctor's office after the cat bit him.

Specific School Courses

I got an A in both Accounting I and Small Business Management, but I got a C in Human Behavior.

But: Use small letters for general subject areas.

I enjoyed my business courses but not my psychology or language courses.

Languages

She knows German and Spanish, but she speaks mostly American slang.

Geographic Locations

I grew up in the Midwest. I worked in the East for a number of years and then moved to the West Coast.

But: Use small letters for directions.

A new high school is being built at the south end of town.

Because I have a compass in my car, I know that I won't be going east or west when I want to go north.

Historical Periods and Events

Hector did well answering an essay question about the Second World War, but he lost points on a question about the Great Depression.

Races, Nations, and Nationalities

The research study centered on African Americans and Hispanics.

They have German knives and Danish glassware in the kitchen, an Indian wood carving in the bedroom, Mexican sculptures in the study, and an Oriental rug in the living room.

Opening and Closing of a Letter

Dear Sir:

Dear Madam:

Sincerely yours,

Truly yours,

Note: Capitalize only the first word in a closing.

Activity

Cross out the words that need capitals in the following sentences. Then write the capitalized forms of the words in the spaces provided. The number of spaces tells you how many corrections to make in each case.

1. Although my grandfather spoke german and polish, my mother never learned either language.

   _____ _____

2. The chain letter began, "dear friend—You must mail twenty copies of this letter if you want good luck."

   _____ _____

3. Tomorrow in our history class, dr. connalley will start lecturing on the civil war.

   _____ _____ _____ _____

4. aunt Sarah and uncle Hal, who are mormons, took us to their church services when we visited them in the midwest.

_____   _____   _____   _____

5. While visiting san francisco, Liza stopped in at a buddhist temple and talked to a chinese nun there.

_____   _____   _____   _____

Unnecessary Use of Capitals

Many errors in capitalization are caused by using capitals where they are not needed.

Activity

Cross out the incorrectly capitalized words in the following sentences. Then write the correct forms of the words in the spaces provided. The number of spaces tells you how many corrections to make in each sentence.

1. The old man told the Cabdriver, "I want to go out to the Airport, and don't try to cheat me."

_____   _____

2. When I see Nike Ads that say, "Just do it," I always think, "Why should a Sneaker tell Me what to do?"

_____   _____   _____

3. A front-page Newspaper story about the crash of a commercial Jet has made me nervous about my Overseas trip.

_____   _____   _____

4. During a Terrible Blizzard in 1888, People froze to Death on the streets of New York.

_____   _____   _____   _____

5. I asked the Bank Officer at Citibank, "How do I get an identification Card to use the automatic teller machines?"

_____   _____   _____

■ Review Test 1

Cross out the words that need capitals in the following sentences. Then write the capitalized forms of the words in the spaces provided. The number of spaces tells you how many corrections to make in each sentence.

1. wanda and i agreed to meet on saturday before the football game.

   _____ _____ _____

2. Between Long island and the atlantic Ocean lies a long, thin sandbar called fire island.

   _____ _____ _____ _____

3. When I'm in the supermarket checkout line, it seems as if every magazine on display has an article called "how You Can Lose Twenty pounds in two weeks."

   _____ _____ _____ _____

4. At the bookstore, each student received a free sample pack of bayer aspirin, arrid deodorant, and pert shampoo.

   _____ _____ _____

5. "can't you be quiet?" I pleaded. "do you always have to talk while I'm watching *general hospital* on television?"

   _____ _____ _____ _____

6. On father's day, the children drove home and took their parents out to dinner at the ramada inn.

   _____ _____ _____ _____

7. I will work at the holly Day School on mondays and fridays for the rest of september.

   _____ _____ _____ _____

8. glendale bank, where my sister Amber works, is paying for her night course, business accounting I.

   _____ _____ _____

9. I subscribe to one newspaper, the *daily planet,* and two magazines, *people* and *glamour.*

   _____ _____ _____ _____

10. On thanksgiving my brother said, "let's hurry and eat so i can go watch the football game on our new sony TV."

    _____ _____ _____ _____

■ Review Test 2

On separate paper,

1. Write seven sentences demonstrating the seven main uses of capital letters.
2. Write eight sentences demonstrating the eight additional uses of capital letters.

34 Numbers and Abbreviations

Numbers

1 Spell out numbers that can be expressed in one or two words. Otherwise, use numerals—the numbers themselves.

During the past five years, over twenty-five barracuda have been caught in the lake.

The parking fine was ten dollars.

In my grandmother's attic are eighty-four pairs of old shoes.

But

Each year about 250 baby trout are added to the lake.

My costs after contesting a parking fine in court were $135.

Grandmother has 382 back copies of *Reader's Digest* in her attic.

2 Be consistent when you use a series of numbers. If some numbers in a sentence or paragraph require more than two words, then use numerals throughout the selection:

During his election campaign, State Senator Mel Grabble went to 3 county fairs, 16 parades, 45 cookouts, and 112 club dinners, and delivered the same speech 176 times.

3 Use numerals for dates, times, addresses, percentages, and parts of a book.

The letter was dated April 3, 1872.

My appointment was at 6:15. (*But:* Spell out numbers before *o'clock*. For example: The doctor didn't see me until seven o'clock.)

He lives at 212 West 19th Street.

About 20 percent of our class dropped out of school.

Turn to page 179 in Chapter 8 and answer questions 1–10.

Activity

Cross out the mistakes in numbers and write the corrections in the spaces provided.

1. Pearl Harbor was attacked on December the seventh, nineteen forty-one.

   _____

   _____

2. When the 2 children failed to return from school, over 50 people volunteered to search for them.

   _____

   _____

3. At 1 o'clock in the afternoon last Thursday, an earthquake destroyed at least 20 buildings in the town.

   _____

   _____

Abbreviations

While abbreviations are a helpful time-saver in note-taking, you should avoid most abbreviations in formal writing. Listed below are some of the few abbreviations that can be used acceptably in compositions. Note that a period is used after most abbreviations.

1 Mr., Mrs., Ms., Jr., Sr., Dr. when used with proper names:

   Mr. Tibble   Dr. Stein   Ms. O'Reilly

2 Time references:

   A.M. or a.m.   P.M. or p.m.   B.C. or A.D.

3 First or middle name in a signature:

   R. Anthony Curry   Otis T. Redding   J. Alfred Prufrock

4 Organizations and common terms known primarily by their initials:

   FBI   UN   CBS   FM   VCR

Activity

Cross out the words that should not be abbreviated and correct them in the spaces provided.

1. On a Sat. morning I will never forget, Jan. 15, 2000, at ten min. after eight o'clock, I came downstairs and discovered that I had been robbed.

   _____   _____   _____

2. For six years I lived at First Ave. and Gordon St. right next to Shore Memorial Hosp., in San Fran., Calif.

   _____   _____   _____   _____   _____

3. Before her biol. and Eng. exams, Linda was so nervous that her doc. gave her a tranq.

   _____   _____   _____   _____

■ Review Test

Cross out the mistakes in numbers and abbreviations and correct them in the spaces provided.

1. At three-fifteen P.M., an angry caller said a bomb was planted in a bus stat. locker.

   _____   _____

2. Page eighty-two is missing from my chem. book.

   _____   _____

3. Martha has over 200 copies of *People* mag.; she thinks they may be worth money someday.

   _____   _____

4. When I was eight yrs. old, I owned three cats, two dogs, and 4 rabbits.

   _____   _____

5. Approx. half the striking workers returned to work on Nov. third, two thousand one.

   _____   _____   _____

35 Apostrophe

Introductory Project

1. Larry's motorcycle
   my sister's boyfriend
   Grandmother's shotgun
   the men's room

   What is the purpose of the *'s* in the examples above?

   _____

2. They didn't mind when their dog bit people, but now they're leashing him because he's eating all their garden vegetables.

   What is the purpose of the apostrophe in *didn't, they're,* and *he's?*

   _____

3. I used to believe that vampires lived in the old coal bin of my cellar.
   The vampire's whole body recoiled when he saw the crucifix.

   Fred ate two baked potatoes.
   One baked potato's center was still hard.

   In each of the sentence pairs above, why is the *'s* used in the second sentence but not in the first?

   _____

   _____

Answers are on pages 728–729.

The two main uses of the apostrophe are:

1 To show the omission of one or more letters in a contraction

2 To show ownership or possession

Each use is explained on the pages that follow.

Apostrophe in Contractions

A *contraction* is formed when two words are combined to make one word. An apostrophe is used to show where letters are omitted in forming the contraction. Here are two contractions:

have + not = haven't (*o* in *not* has been omitted)

I + will = I'll (*wi* in *will* has been omitted)

The following are some other common contractions:

I	+ am	= I'm	it	+ is	= it's
I	+ have	= I've	it	+ has	= it's
I	+ had	= I'd	is	+ not	= isn't
who	+ is	= who's	could	+ not	= couldn't
do	+ not	= don't	I	+ would	= I'd
did	+ not	= didn't	they	+ are	= they're

Note: Will + not has an unusual contraction, won't.

Activity 1

Combine the following words into contractions. One is done for you.

1. we   + are   = ___we're___   6. you   + have = _____

2. are   + not   = _____   7. has   + not = _____

3. you   + are   = _____   8. who   + is   = _____

4. they   + have   = _____   9. does + not = _____

5. would + not   = _____   10. there + is   = _____

Activity 2

Write the contractions for the words in parentheses. One is done for you.

1. (Are not) _____*Aren't*_____ you coming with us to the concert?

2. (I am) _____ going to take the car if (it is) _____ all right with you.

3. (There is) _____ an extra bed upstairs if (you would) _____ like to stay here for the night.

4. (I will) _____ give you the name of the personnel director, but there (is not) _____ much chance that (he will) _____ speak to you.

5. Denise (should not) _____ complain about the cost of food if (she is) _____ not willing to grow her own by planting a backyard garden.

Note: Even though contractions are common in everyday speech and in written dialogue, it is usually best to avoid them in formal writing.

Apostrophe to Show Ownership or Possession

To show ownership or possession, we can use such words as *belongs to, possessed by, owned by,* or (most commonly) *of.*

the jacket that *belongs to* Tony
the grades *possessed by* James
the gas station *owned by* our cousin
the footprints *of* the animal

But often the quickest and easiest way to show possession is to use an apostrophe plus *s* (if the word is not a plural ending in *-s*). Thus we can say:

Tony's jacket
James's grades
our cousin's gas station
the animal's footprints

Points to Remember

1   The *'s* goes with the owner or possessor (in the examples given, *Tony, James, cousin, the animal*). What follows is the person or thing possessed (in the examples given, *the jacket, grades, gas station, footprints*).

2   When *'s* is handwritten, there should always be a break between the word and the *'s*.

    Tony's   not   *Tony's*

    Yes   No

3   A singular word ending in *-s* (such as *James* in the earlier example) also shows possession by adding an apostrophe plus *s* (*James's*).

Activity 1

Rewrite the italicized part of each of the sentences below, using *'s* to show possession. Remember that the *'s* goes with the owner or possessor.

Example   *The toys belonging to the children* filled an entire room.
               The children's toys
               _____

1.   *The new sunglasses belonging to Elena* have been stolen.

      _____

2.   *The visit of my cousin* lasted longer than I wanted it to.

      _____

3.   *The owner of the pit bull* was arrested after the dog attacked a child.

      _____

4.   *The prescription of a doctor* is needed for the pills.

      _____

5.   *The jeep owned by Dennis* was recalled because of an engine defect.

      _____

6.   Is this *the hat of somebody?*

      _____

7.   The broken saddle produced a sore on *the back of the horse.*

      _____

8. *The cords coming from the computer* were so tangled they looked like spaghetti.

_____

9. *The energy level possessed by the little boy* is much higher than hers.

_____

10. *The foundation of the house* is crumbling.

_____

Activity 2

Add *'s* to each of the following words to make them the possessors or owners of something. Then write sentences using the words. Your sentences can be serious or playful. One is done for you.

1. parakeet __*parakeet's*__   *The parakeet's cage needs cleaning.*

_____

2. instructor _____   _____

_____

3. Lola _____   _____

_____

4. store _____   _____

_____

5. mother _____   _____

_____

Apostrophe versus Possessive Pronouns

Do not use an apostrophe with possessive pronouns. They already show owner-ship. Possessive pronouns include *his, hers, its, yours, ours,* and *theirs.*

Incorrect	*Correct*
The bookstore lost its' lease.	The bookstore lost its lease.
The racing bikes were theirs'.	The racing bikes were theirs.
The change is your's.	The change is yours.
His' problems are ours', too.	His problems are ours, too.
His' skin is more sunburned than her's.	His skin is more sunburned than hers.

Apostrophe versus Simple Plurals

When you want to make a word plural, just add an -*s* at the end of the word. Do *not* add an apostrophe. For example, the plural of the word *movie* is *movies,* not *movie's* or *movies'*. Look at this sentence:

Lola adores Tony's broad shoulders, rippling muscles, and warm eyes.

The words *shoulders, muscles,* and *eyes* are simple plurals, meaning *more than one shoulder, more than one muscle, more than one eye.* The plural is shown by adding only an -*s*. On the other hand, the *'s* after *Tony* shows possession—that Tony owns the shoulders, muscles, and eyes.

Activity

In the space provided under each sentence, add the one apostrophe needed and explain why the other word or words ending in *s* are simple plurals.

Example   Karens tomato plants are almost six feet tall.

Karens: _Karen's, meaning "belonging to Karen"_

plants: _simple plural meaning "more than one plant"_

1. The restaurants reputation brought hungry diners from miles around.

   restaurants: _____

   diners: _____

2. Phils job—slaughtering pigs—was enough to make him a vegetarian.

   Phils: _____

   pigs: _____

3. As Tinas skill at studying increased, her grades improved.

   Tinas: _____

   grades: _____

4. When I walked into my doctors office, there were six people waiting who also had appointments.

   doctors: _____

   appointments: _____

5. I asked the music store clerk for several blank cassette tapes and Lauryn Hills new CD.

   tapes: _____

   Hills: _____

6. After six weeks without rain, the nearby streams started drying up, and the lakes water level fell sharply.

   weeks: _____

   streams: _____

   lakes: _____

7. Rebeccas hooded red cloak makes her look like a fairy-tale character, but her heavy black boots spoil the effect.

   Rebeccas: _____

   boots: _____

8. When the brakes failed on Eriks truck, he narrowly avoided hitting several parked cars and two trees.

   brakes: _____

   Eriks: _____

   cars: _____

   trees: _____

9. My familys favorite breakfast is bacon, eggs, and home-fried potatoes.

   familys: _____

   eggs: _____

   potatoes: _____

10. My parents like Floridas winters, but they prefer to spend their summers back home in Maine.

   Floridas: _____

   winters: _____

   summers: _____

Apostrophe with Plural Words Ending in -s

Plurals that end in -s show possession simply by adding the apostrophe (rather than an apostrophe plus s):

My *parents'* station wagon is ten years old.

The *students'* many complaints were ignored by the high school principal.

All the *Boy Scouts'* tents were damaged by the hailstorm.

Activity

In each sentence, cross out the one plural word that needs an apostrophe. Then write the word correctly, with the apostrophe, in the space provided.

Example   _soldiers'_   All the ~~soldiers~~ rifles were cleaned for inspection.

1. My parents car was stolen last night.

   _____

2. The transit workers strike has just ended.

   _____

3. Two of our neighbors homes are up for sale.

   _____

4. The door to the ladies room is locked.

   _____

5. When students gripes about the cafeteria were ignored, many started to bring their own lunches.

   _____

■ Review Test 1

In each sentence, cross out the two words that need apostrophes. Then write the words correctly in the spaces provided.

1. The contestants face fell when she learned that all she had won was a years supply of Ajax cleanser.

   _____   _____

2. Weve been trying for weeks to see that movie, but theres always a long line.

   _____   _____

3. Freds car wouldnt start until the baby-faced mechanic replaced its spark plugs and points.

   _____   _____

4. The citys budget director has trouble balancing his own familys checkbook.

   _____   _____

5. Taking Dianes elderly parents to church every week is one example of Pauls generous behavior.

   _____   _____

6. Heres a checklist of points to follow when youre writing your class reports.

   _____   _____

7. The curious child dropped his sisters makeup into the bedrooms hot-air vent.

   _____   _____

8. The cats babies are under my chair again; I cant find a way to keep her from bringing them near me.

   _____   _____

9. Because of a family feud, Julie wasnt invited to a barbecue at her only cousins house.

   _____   _____

10. Phyllis grade was the highest in the class, and Kevin grade was the lowest.

    _____   _____

■ Review Test 2

Make the following words possessive and then use at least five of them in a not-so-serious paragraph that tells a story. In addition, use at least three contractions in the paragraph.

mugger	restaurant	Tony	student
New York	sister	children	vampire
skunk	Jay Leno	boss	Oprah Winfrey
customer	bartender	police car	yesterday
instructor	someone	mob	Chicago

36 Quotation Marks

Introductory Project

Read the following scene and underline all the words enclosed within quotation marks. Your instructor may also have you dramatize the scene, with one person reading the narration and two persons acting the two speaking parts—the young man and the old woman. The two speakers should imagine the scene as part of a stage play and try to make their words seem as real and true-to-life as possible.

An old woman in a Rolls-Royce was preparing to back into a parking space. Suddenly a small sports car appeared and pulled into the space. "That's what you can do when you're young and fast," the young man in the car yelled to the old woman. As he strolled away, laughing, he heard a terrible crunching sound. "What's that noise?" he said. Turning around, he saw the old woman backing repeatedly into his small car and crushing it. "You can't do that, old lady!" he yelled.

"What do you mean, I can't?" she chuckled, as metal grated against metal. "This is what you can do when you're old and rich."

1. On the basis of the above passage, what is the purpose of quotation marks?

   _____

2. Do commas and periods that come after a quotation go inside or outside the quotation marks?

   _____

Answers are on page 729.

The two main uses of quotation marks are:

1 To set off the exact words of a speaker or a writer
2 To set off the titles of short works

Each use is explained on the pages that follow.

Quotation Marks to Set Off Exact Words of a Speaker or Writer

Use quotation marks when you want to show the exact words of a speaker or a writer.

"Say something tender to me," whispered Lola to Tony.
(Quotation marks set off the exact words that Lola spoke to Tony.)

Mark Twain once wrote, "The more I know about human beings, the more I like my dog."
(Quotation marks set off the exact words that Mark Twain wrote.)

"The only dumb question," the instructor said, "is the one you don't ask."
(Two pairs of quotation marks are used to enclose the instructor's exact words.)

Sharon complained, "I worked so hard on this paper. I spent two days getting information in the library and two days writing it. Guess what grade I got on it."
(Note that the end quotation marks do not come until the end of Sharon's speech. Place quotation marks before the first quoted word of a speech and after the last quoted word. As long as no interruption occurs in the speech, do not use quotation marks for each new sentence.)

Punctuation Hint: In the four examples above, notice that a comma sets off the quoted part from the rest of the sentence. Also observe that commas and periods at the end of a quotation always go *inside* quotation marks.
    Complete the following statements explaining how capital letters, commas, and periods are used in quotations. Refer to the four examples as guides.

1. Every quotation begins with a _____ letter.
2. When a quotation is split (as in the sentence above about dumb questions), the second part does not begin with a capital letter unless it is a _____ sentence.

3. _____ are used to separate the quoted part of a sentence from the rest of the sentence.

4. Commas and periods that come at the end of a quotation should go _____ the quotation marks.

The answers are *capital, new, Commas,* and *inside.*

Activity 1

Place quotation marks around the exact words of a speaker or writer in the sentences that follow.

1. The health-food store clerk said, Sucking on zinc lozenges can help you get over a cold.
2. How are you doing in school? my uncle always asks me.
3. An epitaph on a tombstone in Georgia reads, I told you I was sick!
4. Dave said, Let's walk faster. I think the game has already started.
5. Mark Twain once said, The man who doesn't read good books has no advantage over the man who can't.
6. Thelma said, My brother is so lazy that if opportunity knocked, he'd resent the noise.
7. It's extremely dangerous to mix alcohol and pills, Dr. Wilson reminded us. The combination could kill you.
8. Ice-cold drinks! shouted the vendor selling lukewarm drinks.
9. Be careful not to touch the fence, the guard warned. It's electrified.
10. Just because I'm deaf, Lynn said, many people treat me as if I were stupid.

Activity 2

1. Write a sentence in which you quote a favorite expression of someone you know. Identify the relationship of the person to you.

   Example   One of my father's favorite expressions is, "Don't sweat the small stuff."

   _____

   _____

   _____

   _____

2. Write a quotation that contains the words *Tony asked Lola.* Write a second quotation that includes the words *Lola replied.*

_____

_____

_____

_____

3. Copy a sentence or two that interest you from a book or magazine. Identify the title and author of the work.

Example In *Night Shift*, Stephen King writes, "I don't like to sleep with one leg sticking out. Because if a cool hand ever reached out from under the bed and grasped my ankle, I might scream."

_____

_____

_____

_____

Indirect Quotations

An indirect quotation is a rewording of someone else's comments, rather than a word-for-word direct quotation. The word *that* often signals an indirect quotation. Quotation marks are *not* used with indirect quotations.

Direct Quotation	Indirect Quotation
Fred said, "The distributor cap on my car is cracked." (Fred's exact spoken words are given, so quotation marks are used.)	Fred said that the distributor cap on his car was cracked. (We learn Fred's words indirectly, so no quotation marks are used.)
Sally's note to Jay read, "I'll be working late. Don't wait up for me." (The exact words that Sally wrote in the note are given, so quotation marks are used.)	Sally left a note for Jay saying she would be working late and he should not wait up for her. (We learn Sally's words indirectly, so no quotation marks are used.)

Activity

Rewrite the following sentences, changing words as necessary to convert the sentences into direct quotations. The first one is done for you as an example.

1. The instructor told everyone to take out a pen and sheet of paper.
   The instructor said, "Take out a pen and sheet of paper."

2. A student in the front row asked if this was a test.

   _____

3. The instructor replied that it was more of a pop quiz.

   _____

4. She added that anyone who did the homework would find it easy.

   _____

5. The student groaned that he was a dead man.

   _____

Quotation Marks to Set Off Titles of Short Works

Titles of short works are usually set off by quotation marks, while titles of long works are underlined. Use quotation marks to set off the titles of such short works as articles in books, newspapers, or magazines; chapters in a book; short stories; poems; and songs.

On the other hand, you should underline the titles of books, newspapers, magazines, plays, movies, record albums, and television shows.

Quotation Marks	*Underlines*
the article "The Mystique of Lawyers"	in the book <u>Verdicts on Lawyers</u>
the article "Getting a Fix on Repairs"	in the newspaper the <u>New York Times</u>
the article "Animal Facts and Fallacies"	in the magazine <u>Reader's Digest</u>
the chapter "Why Do Men Marry?"	in the book <u>Passages</u>
the story "The Night the Bed Fell"	in the book <u>A Thurber Carnival</u>
the poem "A Prayer for My Daughter"	in the book <u>Poems of W.B. Yeats</u>
the song "Beat It"	in the album <u>Thriller</u>
	the television show <u>Dateline NBC</u>
	the movie <u>Gone with the Wind</u>

Note: In printed works, titles of books, newspapers, and so on are set off by italics—slanted type that looks *like this*—instead of being underlined.

Activity

Use quotation marks or underlines as needed.

1. Whenever Gina sees the movie The Sound of Music, the song near the end, Climb Every Mountain, makes her cry.

2. No advertising is permitted in Consumer Reports, a nonprofit consumer magazine.

3. I printed out an article titled Too Much Homework? from the online version of Time to use in my sociology report.

4. Maddie's favorite television show is The Simpsons, and her favorite movie is Titanic.

5. Our instructor gave us a week to buy the textbook titled Personal Finance and to read the first chapter, Work and Income.

6. Every holiday season, our family watches the movie A Christmas Carol on television.

7. Looking around to make sure no one he knew saw him, Bob bought the newest National Enquirer in order to read the story called Man Explodes on Operating Table.

8. Edgar Allan Poe's short story The Murders in the Rue Morgue and his poem The Raven are in a paperback titled Great Tales and Poems of Edgar Allan Poe.

9. When Ling got her TV Guide, she read an article called Who Will Oscar Smile Upon? and thumbed through the listings to read the preview for Ally McBeal.

10. The night before his exam, he discovered with horror that the chapter Becoming Mature was missing from Childhood and Adolescence, the psychology text that he had bought secondhand.

Other Uses of Quotation Marks

1 Quotation marks are used to set off special words or phrases from the rest of a sentence:

Many people spell the words "a lot" as *one* word, "alot," instead of correctly spelling them as two words.

I have trouble telling the difference between "their" and "there."

Note: In printed works, *italics* are often used to set off special words or phrases. That is usually done in this book, for example.

2   Single quotation marks are used to mark off a quotation within a quotation.

The instructor said, "Know the chapter titled 'Status Symbols' in *Adolescent Development* if you expect to pass the test."

Lola said, "One of my favorite Mae West lines is 'I used to be Snow White, but I drifted.' "

■ Review Test 1

Insert quotation marks or underlines where needed in the sentences that follow.

1. Don't you ever wash your car? Lola asked Tony.

2. When the washer tilted and began to buzz, Martha shouted, Let's get rid of that blasted machine!

3. Take all you want, read the sign above the cafeteria salad bar, but please eat all you take.

4. After scrawling formulas all over the board with lightning speed, my math instructor was fond of asking, Any questions now?

5. Move that heap! the truck driver yelled. I'm trying to make a living here.

6. I did a summary of an article titled Aspirin and Heart Attacks in the latest issue of Time.

7. Writer's block is something that happens to everyone at times, the instructor explained. You simply have to keep writing to break out of it.

8. A passenger in the car ahead of Clyde threw food wrappers and empty cups out the window. That man, said Clyde to his son, is a human pig.

9. If you are working during the day, said the counselor, the best way to start college is with a night course or two.

10. I told the dentist that I wanted Novocain. Don't be a sissy, he said. A little pain won't hurt. I told him that a little pain wouldn't hurt him, but it would bother me.

■ Review Test 2

Go through the comics section of a newspaper to find a comic strip that amuses you. Be sure to choose a strip in which two or more characters are speaking to each other. Write a full description that will enable people who have not read the comic strip to visualize it clearly and appreciate its humor. Describe the setting and action in each panel, and enclose the words of the speakers in quotation marks.

37 Comma

Introductory Project

Commas often (though not always) signal a minor break, or pause, in a sentence. Each of the six pairs of sentences below illustrates one of the six main uses of the comma. Read each pair of sentences aloud and place a comma wherever you feel a slight pause occurs.

1. a. Frank's interests are Maria television and sports.
   b. My mother put her feet up sipped some iced tea and opened the newspaper.
2. a. Although the Lone Ranger used lots of silver bullets he never ran out of ammunition.
   b. To remove the cap of the aspirin bottle you must first press down on it.
3. a. Kitty Litter and Dredge Rivers Hollywood's leading romantic stars have made several movies together.
   b. Sarah who is my next-door neighbor just entered the hospital with an intestinal infection.
4. a. The wedding was scheduled for four o'clock but the bride changed her mind at two.
   b. Verna took three coffee breaks before lunch and then she went on a two-hour lunch break.
5. a. Lola's mother asked her "What time do you expect to get home?"
   b. "Don't bend over to pat the dog" I warned "or he'll bite you."
6. a. Roy ate seventeen hamburgers on July 29 1992 and lived to tell about it.
   b. Roy lives at 817 Cresson Street Detroit Michigan.

Answers are on page 729.

485

Six Main Uses of the Comma

Commas are used mainly as follows:

1 To separate items in a series
2 To set off introductory material
3 Before and after words that interrupt the flow of thought in a sentence
4 Before two complete thoughts connected by *and, but, for, or, nor, so, yet*
5 To set off a direct quotation from the rest of a sentence
6 For certain everyday material

Each use is explained on the pages that follow.

You may find it helpful to remember that the comma often marks a slight pause, or break, in a sentence. Read aloud the sentence examples given for each use, and listen for the minor pauses, or breaks, that are signaled by commas.

Comma between Items in a Series

Use commas to separate items in a series.

Do you drink tea with milk, lemon, or honey?

Today the dishwasher stopped working, the garbage bag split, and the refrigerator turned into an icebox.

The television talk shows enraged him so much he did not know whether to laugh, cry, or throw up.

Reiko awoke from a restless, nightmare-filled sleep.

Notes

a The final comma in a series is optional, but it is often used.

b A comma is used between two descriptive words in a series only if *and* inserted between the words sounds natural. You could say:

Reiko awoke from a restless *and* nightmare-filled sleep.

But notice in the following sentence that the descriptive words do not sound natural when *and* is inserted between them. In such cases, no comma is used.

Wanda drove a shiny blue Corvette. (A shiny *and* blue Corvette doesn't sound right, so no comma is used.)

Activity

Place commas between items in a series.

1. Superman believes in truth justice and the American way.
2. Jerry opened his textbook made sure his pencil was sharpened and fell asleep with his head on the desk.
3. Felipe added white wine mushrooms salt pepper and oregano to his spaghetti sauce.
4. Baggy threadbare jeans feel more comfortable than pajamas to me.
5. Carmen grabbed a tiny towel bolted out of the bathroom and ran toward the ringing phone.

Comma after Introductory Material

Use a comma to set off introductory material.

> After punching the alarm clock with his fist, Bill turned over and went back to sleep.
>
> Looking up at the sky, I saw a man who was flying faster than a speeding bullet.
>
> Holding a baited trap, Clyde cautiously approached the gigantic mousehole.
>
> In addition, he held a broom in his hand.
>
> Also, he wore a football helmet in case a creature should leap out at his head.

Notes

a If the introductory material is brief, the comma is sometimes omitted. In the activities here, you should use the comma.

b A comma is also used to set off extra material at the end of a sentence. Here are two sentences where this comma rule applies:

> A sudden breeze shot through the windows, driving the stuffiness out of the room.
>
> I love to cook and eat Italian food, especially spaghetti and lasagna.

Activity

Place commas after introductory material.

1. When the president entered the room became hushed.

2. Feeling brave and silly at the same time Tony volunteered to go on stage and help the magician.

3. While I was eating my tuna sandwich the cats circled my chair like hungry sharks.

4. Because my parents died when I was young I have learned to look after myself. Even though I am now independent I still carry a special loneliness within me.

5. At first putting extra hot pepper flakes on the pizza seemed like a good idea. However I felt otherwise when flames seemed about to shoot out of my mouth.

Comma around Words Interrupting the Flow of Thought

Use commas before and after words or phrases that interrupt the flow of thought in a sentence.

My brother, a sports nut, owns over five thousand baseball cards.

That game show, at long last, has been canceled.

The children used the old Buick, rusted from disuse, as a backyard clubhouse.

Usually you can "hear" words that interrupt the flow of thought in a sentence. However, if you are not sure that certain words are interrupters, remove them from the sentence. If it still makes sense without the words, you know that the words are interrupters and the information they give is nonessential. Such nonessential information is set off with commas. In the sentence

Dody Thompson, who lives next door, won the javelin-throwing competition.

the words *who lives next door* are extra information, not needed to identify the subject of the sentence, *Dody Thompson.* Put commas around such nonessential information. On the other hand, in the sentence

The woman who lives next door won the javelin-throwing competition.

the words *who lives next door* supply essential information—information needed for us to identify the woman being spoken of. If the words were removed from the sentence, we would no longer know who won the competition. Commas are *not* used around such essential information.

Here is another example:

Wilson Hall, which the tornado destroyed, was ninety years old.

Here the words *which the tornado destroyed* are extra information, not needed to identify the subject of the sentence, *Wilson Hall.* Commas go around such nonessential information. On the other hand, in the sentence

The building which the tornado destroyed was ninety years old.

the words *which the tornado destroyed* are needed to identify the building. Commas are *not* used around such essential information.

As noted above, however, most of the time you will be able to "hear" words that interrupt the flow of thought in a sentence and will not have to think about whether the words are essential or nonessential.

Activity

Use commas to set off interrupting words.

1. On Friday my day off I went to get a haircut.
2. Dracula who had a way with women is Tony's favorite movie hero. He feels that the Wolfman on the other hand showed no class in handling women.
3. Many people forget that Franklin Roosevelt one of our most effective presidents was disabled.
4. Mowing the grass especially when it is six inches high is my least favorite job.
5. A jar of chicken noodle soup which was all there was in the refrigerator did not make a very satisfying meal.

Comma between Complete Thoughts

Use a comma between two complete thoughts connected by *and, but, for, or, nor, so, yet.*

The wedding was scheduled for four o'clock, but the bride changed her mind at two.

We could always tell when our instructor felt disorganized, for his shirt would not be tucked in.

Rich has to work on Monday nights, so he tapes the TV football game on his VCR.

Notes

a The comma is optional when the complete thoughts are short.

Grace's skin tans and Mark's skin freckles.

Her soda was watery but she drank it anyway.

The day was overcast so they didn't go swimming.

b Be careful not to use a comma in sentences having *one* subject and a *double* verb. The comma is used only in sentences made up of two complete thoughts (two subjects and two verbs). In the following sentence, there is only one subject (*Kevin*) with a double verb (*will go* and *forget*). Therefore, no comma is needed:

Kevin will go partying tonight and forget all about tomorrow's exam.

Likewise, the following sentence has only one subject (*Rita*) and a double verb (*was* and *will work*); therefore, no comma is needed:

Rita was a waitress at the Holiday Inn last summer and probably will work there this summer.

Activity

Place a comma before a joining word that connects two complete thoughts (two subject-verb combinations). Remember, do *not* place a comma within sentences that have only one subject and a double verb.

1. The oranges in the refrigerator were covered with blue mold and the potatoes in the cupboard felt like sponges.
2. All the slacks in the shop were on sale but not a single pair was my size.
3. Martha often window-shops in the malls for hours and comes home without buying anything.
4. Tony left the dentist's office with his mouth still numb from Novocain and he talked with a lisp for two hours.
5. The whole family searched the yard inch by inch but never found Mom's missing wedding ring.
6. The car squealed down the entrance ramp and sped recklessly out onto the freeway.
7. The dancers in the go-go bar moved like wound-up Barbie dolls and the men in the audience sat as motionless as stones.

8. The aliens in the science fiction film visited our planet in peace but we greeted them with violence.

9. I felt like shouting at the gang of boys but didn't dare open my mouth.

10. Lenny claims that he wants to succeed in college but he has missed classes all semester.

Comma with Direct Quotations

Use a comma to set off a direct quotation from the rest of a sentence.

His father shouted, "Why don't you go out and get a job?"

"Our modern world has lost a sense of the sacredness of life," the speaker said.

"No," said Celia to Jerry. "I won't go to the roller derby with you."

"Can anyone remember," wrote Emerson, "when the times were not hard and money not scarce?"

Note: Commas and periods at the end of a quotation go inside quotation marks. See also page 479.

Activity

Use commas to set off quotations from the rest of the sentence.

1. Hassan came to the door and called out "Welcome to my home!"

2. My partner on the dance floor said "Don't be so stiff. You look as if you swallowed an umbrella."

3. The question on the anatomy test read "What human organ grows faster than any other, never stops growing, and always remains the same size?"

4. The student behind me whispered "The skin."

5. "My stomach hurts" Bruce said "and I don't know whether it was the hamburger or the math test."

Comma with Everyday Material

Use a comma with certain everyday material.

Persons Spoken To

Tina, go to bed if you're not feeling well.

Cindy, where did you put my shoes?

Are you coming with us, Owen?

Dates

March 4, 2000, is when Martha buried her third husband.

Addresses

Tony's grandparents live at 183 Roxborough Avenue, Cleveland, Ohio 44112.

Note: No comma is used to mark off the zip code.

Openings and Closings of Letters

Dear Santa,

Dear Larry,

Sincerely yours,

Truly yours,

Note: In formal letters, a colon is used after the opening: Dear Sir: *or* Dear Madam:

Numbers

The dishonest dealer turned the used car's odometer from 98,170 miles to 39,170 miles.

Activity

Place commas where needed.

1. I expected you to set a better example for the others Mike.
2. Janet with your help I passed the test.
3. The movie stars Kitty Litter and Dredge Rivers were married on September 12 2000 and lived at 3865 Sunset Boulevard Los Angeles California for one month.
4. They received 75000 congratulatory fan letters and were given picture contracts worth $3000000 in the first week of their marriage.
5. Kitty left Dredge on October 12 2000 and ran off with their marriage counselor.

■ Review Test 1

Insert commas where needed. In the space provided below each sentence, summarize briefly the rule that explains the use of the comma or commas.

1. The best features of my new apartment are its large kitchen its bay windows and its low rent.

   _____

2. Because we got in line at dawn we were among the first to get tickets for the concert.

   _____

3. "When will someone invent a telephone" Lola asked "that will ring only at convenient moments?"

   _____

4. Without opening his eyes Simon stumbled out of bed and opened the door for the whining dog.

   _____

5. I think Roger that you had better ask someone else for your $2500 loan.

   _____

6. Hot dogs are the most common cause of choking deaths in children for a bite-size piece can easily plug up a toddler's throat.

   _____

7. Tax forms though shortened and revised every year never seem to get any simpler.

   _____

8. Sandra may decide to go to college full-time or she may start by enrolling in a couple of evening courses.

   _____

9. I remember how with the terrible cruelty of children we used to make fun of the retarded girl who lived on our street.

   _____

10. Although that old man on the corner looks like a Skid Row bum he is said to have a Swiss bank account.

   _____

■ Review Test 2

Insert commas where needed.

1. My dog who is afraid of the dark sleeps with a night-light.
2. "Although men have more upper-body strength" said the lecturer "women are more resistant to fatigue."

3. The hot dogs at the ball park tasted delicious but they reacted later like delayed time bombs.

4. Janice attended class for four hours worked at the hospital for three hours and studied at home for two hours.

5. The patient as he gasped for air tried to assure the hospital clerk that he had an insurance card somewhere.

6. George and Ida sat down to watch the football game with crackers sharp cheese salty pretzels and two frosty bottles of beer.

7. Although I knew exactly what was happening the solar eclipse gave me a strong feeling of anxiety.

8. The company agreed to raise a senior bus driver's salary to $38000 by January 1 2003.

9. Even though King Kong was holding her at the very top of the Empire State Building Fay Wray kept yelling at him "Let me go!"

10. Navel oranges which Margery as a little girl called belly-button oranges are her favorite fruit.

■ Review Test 3

On separate paper, write six sentences, each demonstrating one of the six main comma rules.

38 Other Punctuation Marks

Introductory Project

Each of the sentences below needs one of the following punctuation marks:

;   —   -   ( )   :

See if you can insert the correct mark in each sentence. Each mark should be used once.

1. The following holiday plants are poisonous and should be kept away from children and pets holly, mistletoe, and poinsettias.
2. The freeze dried remains of Annie's canary were in the clear bottle on her bookcase.
3. William Shakespeare 1564–1616 married a woman eight years his senior when he was eighteen.
4. Grooming in space is more difficult than on Earth no matter how much astronauts comb their hair, for instance, it still tends to float loosely around their heads.
5. I opened the front door, and our cat walked in proudly with a live bunny hanging from his mouth.

Answers are on page 729.

Colon (:)

Use the colon at the end of a complete statement to introduce a list, a long quotation, or an explanation.

List
The following were my worst jobs: truck loader in an apple plant, assembler in a battery factory, and attendant in a state mental hospital.

Long Quotation
Thoreau explains in *Walden:* "I went to the woods because I wished to live deliberately, to front only the essential facts of life, and see if I could not learn what it had to teach, and not, when I came to die, discover that I had not lived."

Explanation
There are two softball leagues in our town: the fast-pitch league and the lob-pitch league.

Activity

Place colons where needed.

1. Foods that are high in cholesterol include the following eggs, butter, milk, cheese, shrimp, and well-marbled meats.

2. All the signs of the flu were present hot and cold spells, heavy drainage from the sinuses, a bad cough, and an ache through the entire body.

3. In his book *Illiterate America,* Jonathan Kozol has written "Twenty-five million American adults cannot read the poison warnings on a can of pesticide, a letter from their child's teacher, or the front page of a daily paper. An additional 35 million read only at a level which is less than equal to the full survival needs of our society. Together, these 60 million people represent more than one-third of the entire adult population."

Semicolon (;)

The main use of the semicolon is to mark a break between two complete thoughts, as explained on page 392. Another use of the semicolon is to mark off items in a series when the items themselves contain commas. Here are some examples:

Winning prizes at the national flower show were Roberta Collins, Alabama, azaleas; Sally Hunt, Kentucky, roses; and James Weber, California, Shasta daisies.

The following books must be read for the course: *The Color Purple,* by Alice Walker; *In Our Time,* by Ernest Hemingway; and *Man's Search for Meaning,* by Victor Frankl.

Activity

Place semicolons where needed.

1. The specials at the restaurant today are eggplant Parmesan, for $5.95 black beans and rice, for $4.95 and chicken potpie, for $6.95.
2. The top of the hill offered an awesome view of the military cemetery thousands of headstones were ranged in perfect rows.
3. Lola's favorite old movies are *To Catch a Thief,* starring Cary Grant and Grace Kelly *Animal Crackers,* a Marx Brothers comedy and *The Wizard of Oz,* with Judy Garland.

Dash (—)

A dash signals a pause longer than a comma but not as complete as a period. Use a dash to set off words for dramatic effect:

I didn't go out with him a second time—once was more than enough.

Some of you—I won't mention you by name—cheated on the test.

It was so windy that the VW passed him on the highway—overhead.

Notes

a The dash can be formed on a keyboard by striking the hyphen twice (--). In handwriting, the dash is as long as two letters would be.

b Be careful not to overuse dashes.

Activity

Place dashes where needed.

1. Riding my bike, I get plenty of exercise especially when dogs chase me.
2. I'm advising you in fact, I'm telling you not to bother me again.
3. The package finally arrived badly damaged.

Hyphen (-)

1 Use a hyphen with two or more words that act as a single unit describing a noun.

The fast-talking salesman was so good that he went into politics. (*Fast* and *talking* combine to describe the salesman.)

I both admire and envy her well-rounded personality.

When the dude removed his blue-tinted shades, Lonnell saw the spaced-out look in his eyes.

2 Use a hyphen to divide a word at the end of a line of writing or typing. When you need to divide a word at the end of a line, divide it between syllables. Use your dictionary to be sure of correct syllable divisions (see also page 501).

When Josh lifted up the hood of his Toyota, he realized that one of the radiator hoses had broken.

Notes

a Do not divide words of one syllable.

b Do not divide a word if you can avoid doing so.

Activity

Place hyphens where needed.

1. High flying jets and gear grinding trucks are constant sources of noise pollution in our neighborhood.
2. When Linda turned on the porch light, ten legged creatures scurried every where over the crumb filled floor.
3. Fred had ninety two dollars in his pocket when he left for the supermarket, and he had twenty two dollars when he got back.

Parentheses ( )

Parentheses are used to set off extra or incidental information from the rest of a sentence:

> The section of that book on the medical dangers of abortion (pages 35 to 72) is outdated.

> Yesterday at Hamburger House (my favorite place to eat), the guy who makes french fries asked me to go out with him.

Note: Do not use parentheses too often in your writing.

Activity

Add parentheses where needed.

1. Certain sections of the novel especially Chapter 5 made my heart race with suspense.
2. Did you hear that George Linda's first husband just got remarried?
3. Sigmund Freud 1856–1939 was the founder of psychoanalysis.

■ Review Test

At the appropriate spot, place the punctuation mark shown in the margin.

;

1. Efra's savings have dwindled to nothing she's been borrowing from me to pay her rent.

—

2. There's the idiot I'd know him anywhere who dumped trash on our front lawn.

-

3. Today's two career couples spend more money on eating out than their parents did.

:

4. Ben Franklin said "If a man empties his purse into his head, no man can take it away from him. An investment in knowledge always pays the best interest."

( )

5. One-fifth of our textbook pages 401–498 consists of footnotes and a bibliography.

39 Using the Dictionary

The dictionary is a valuable tool. To take advantage of it, you need to understand the main kinds of information that a dictionary gives about a word. Look at the information provided for the word *murder* in the following entry from the *American Heritage Dictionary of the English Language:**

Spelling and syllabication   *Pronunciation*   *Part of speech*

mur•der (mûr′dər) *n.* The unlawful killing of one human being by another, esp. with premeditated malice. —*v.* **1.** To kill (a human being) unlawfully. **2.** To mar or spoil by ineptness: *murder the English language.* **3.** *Slang.* To defeat decisively. [< OE *morthor.*] — **mur′der•er** *n.* — **mur′der•ess** *n.*

Meanings

Other forms of the word

Spelling

The first bit of information, in the boldface (heavy-type) entry itself, is the spelling of *murder.* You probably already know the spelling of *murder,* but if you didn't, you could find it by pronouncing the syllables in the word carefully and then looking it up in the dictionary.

Use your dictionary to correct the spelling of the following words:

compatable _____   insite _____

althogh _____   troble _____

aksident _____   untill _____

embelish _____   easyer _____

systimatise _____   prepostrous _____

shedule _____   comotion _____

attenshun _____   Vasaline _____

wierd _____   fatel _____

hurryed _____   busines _____

alright _____   jenocide _____

fony _____   poluted _____

kriterion _____   perpose _____

hetirosexual _____   chalange _____

Syllabication

The second bit of information that the dictionary gives, also in the boldface entry, is the syllabication of *murder*. Note that a dot separates the syllables.

Use your dictionary to mark the syllable divisions in the following words. Also indicate how many syllables are in each word.

j i t t e r   (_____ syllables)

m o t i v a t e   (_____ syllables)

o r a n g u t a n   (_____ syllables)

i n c o n t r o v e r t i b l e   (_____ syllables)

Noting syllable divisions will enable you to *hyphenate* a word: divide it at the end of one line of writing and complete it at the beginning of the next line. You can correctly hyphenate a word only at a syllable division, and you may have to check your dictionary to make sure of the syllable divisions.

Pronunciation

The third bit of information in the dictionary entry is the pronunciation of *murder:* (murder). You already know how to pronounce *murder,* but if you didn't, the information within the parentheses would serve as your guide. Use your dictionary to complete the following exercises that relate to pronunciation.

Vowel Sounds

You will probably use the pronunciation key in your dictionary mainly as a guide to pronouncing different vowel sounds (vowels are the letters *a, e, i, o,* and *u*). Here is a part of the pronunciation key in the *American Heritage Dictionary:*

ă pat / ā way / ĕ pet / ē bee / ĭ pit / ī pie

This key tells you, for example, that the sound of the short *a* is like the *a* in *pat,* the sound of the long *a* is like the *a* in *way,* and the sound of the short *e* is like the *e* in *pet.*

Now look at the pronunciation key in your own dictionary. The key is probably located in the front of the dictionary or at the bottom of alternate pages. What common word in the key tells you how to pronounce each of the following sounds?

ī _____   ŭ _____

ŏ _____   oŏ _____

ō _____   oō _____

(Note that a long vowel always has the sound of its own name.)

The Schwa (ə)

The symbol ə looks like an upside-down e. It is called a *schwa,* and it stands for the unaccented sound in such words as *ago, item, easily, gallop,* and *circus.* More approximately, it stands for the sound *uh*—like the *uh* that speakers sometimes make when they hesitate. Perhaps it would help to remember that *uh,* as well as ə, could be used to represent the schwa sound.

Here are some of the many words in which the schwa sound appears: *imitation (im-uh-tā′shuhn or im-ə-tā′shən); elevate (el′uh-vāt or el′ə-vāt); horizon (huh-rī′zuhn or hə-rī′zən).* Open your dictionary to any page, and you will almost surely be able to find three words that make use of the schwa in the pronunciation in parentheses after the main entry.

In the spaces below, write three words that make use of the schwa, and their pronunciations.

1. _____   (_____)

2. _____   (_____)

3. _____   (_____)

Accent Marks

Some words contain both a primary accent, shown by a heavy stroke (′), and a secondary accent, shown by a lighter stroke (′). For example, in the word *controversy* (kon′trə vûr′se), the stress, or accent, goes chiefly on the first syllable (*kon′*), and, to a lesser extent, on the third syllable (*vûr′*).

Use your dictionary to add stress marks to the following words:

preclude (pri klo͞od)

atrophy (at rə fē)

inveigle (in vā gəl)

ubiquitous (yo͞o bik wi təs)

prognosticate (prog nos ti kāt)

Full Pronunciation

Use your dictionary to write the full pronunciation (the information given in parentheses) for each of the following words.

1. inveigh _____

2. diatribe _____

3. raconteur _____

4. panacea _____

5. esophagus _____

6. cesarean _____

7. clandestine _____

8. vicarious _____

9. quiescent _____

10. parsimony _____

11. penchant _____

12. antipathy _____

13. capricious _____

14. schizophrenia _____

15. euphemism _____

16. internecine _____

17. amalgamate _____

18. quixotic _____

19. laissez-faire _____

20. antidisestablishmentarianism (This word is probably not in a paperback dictionary, but if you can say *establish* and if you break the rest of the word into individual syllables, you should be able to pronounce it.)

_____

Now practice pronouncing each word. Use the pronunciation key in your dictionary as an aid to sounding out each syllable. *Do not* try to pronounce a word all at once; instead, work on mastering *one syllable at a time.* When you can pronounce each of the syllables in a word successfully, then say them in sequence, add the accent, and pronounce the entire word.

Parts of Speech

The next bit of information that the dictionary gives about *murder* is *n.* This abbreviation means that the meanings of *murder* as a noun will follow.

Use your dictionary if necessary to fill in the meanings of the following abbreviations:

v. = _____   sing. = _____

adj. = _____   pl. = _____

Principal Parts of Irregular Verbs

Murder is a regular verb and forms its principal parts by adding *-ed, -ed,* and *-ing* to the stem of the verb. When a verb is irregular, the dictionary lists its principal parts. For example, with *give* the present tense comes first (the entry itself, *give*). Next comes the past tense (*gave*), and then the past participle (*given*)—the form of the verb used with such helping words as *have, had,* and *was.* Then comes the present participle (*giving*)—the *-ing* form of the verb.

Look up the principal parts of the following irregular verbs and write them in the spaces provided. The first one has been done for you.

Present	Past	Past Participle	Present Participle
tear	*tore*	*torn*	*tearing*
go			
know			
steal			

Plural Forms of Irregular Nouns

The dictionary supplies the plural forms of all irregular nouns. (Regular nouns like *murder* form the plural by adding *-s* or *-es*). Give the plurals of the following nouns. If two forms are shown, write down both.

analysis _____

dictionary _____

criterion _____

activity _____

thesis _____

Meanings

When a word has more than one meaning, the meanings are numbered in the dictionary, as with the verb *murder*. In many dictionaries, the most common meanings of a word are presented first. The introductory pages of your dictionary will explain the order in which meanings are presented.

Use the sentence context to try to explain the meaning of the underlined word in each of the following sentences. Write your definition in the space provided. Then look up and record the dictionary meaning of the word. Be sure to select the meaning that fits the word as it is used in the sentence.

1. I spend an <u>inordinate</u> amount of time watching television.

Your definition: _____

Dictionary definition: _____

2.   I appreciated her <u>candid</u> remark that my pants were so baggy they made me look like a clown.

   Your definition: _____

   Dictionary definition: _____

3.   The FBI <u>squelched</u> the terrorists' plan to plant a bomb in the White House.

   Your definition: _____

   Dictionary definition: _____

4.   One of the <u>cardinal</u> rules in our house was, "Respect other people's privacy."

   Your definition: _____

   Dictionary definition: _____

5.   A special <u>governor</u> prevents the school bus from traveling more than fifty-five miles an hour.

   Your definition: _____

   Dictionary definition: _____

Etymology

Etymology refers to the origin and historical development of a word. Such information is usually enclosed in brackets and is more likely to be present in a hardbound desk dictionary than in a paperback one. Good desk dictionaries include the following:

> *American Heritage Dictionary of the English Language*
> *Random House College Dictionary*
> *Webster's New Collegiate Dictionary*
> *Webster's New World Dictionary*

A good desk dictionary will tell you, for example, that the word *berserk* derives from the name of a tribe of Scandanavian warriors who would work themselves into a frenzy during battle. The word is now a general term to describe someone whose actions are frenzied or crazed.

See if your dictionary says anything about the origins of the following words.

bikini _____

_____

_____

_____

sandwich _____

_____

_____

_____

tantalize _____

_____

_____

breakfast _____

_____

_____

_____

Usage Labels

As a general rule, use only standard English words in your writing. If a word is not standard English (as is the case, for example, with the third meaning of *murder* as a verb), your dictionary will probably give it a usage label like one of the following: *informal, nonstandard, slang, vulgar, obsolete, archaic, rare.*

Look up the following words and record how your dictionary labels them. Remember that a recent hardbound desk dictionary will always be the best source of information about usage.

flunk _____

tough (meaning "unfortunate, too bad") _____

creep (meaning "an annoying person") _____

ain't _____

scam _____

Synonyms

A *synonym* is a word that is close in meaning to another word. Using synonyms helps you avoid unnecessary repetition of the same word in a paper. A paperback dictionary is not likely to give you synonyms for words, but a good desk dictionary will. (You might also want to own a *thesaurus,* a book that lists synonyms and antonyms. An *antonym* is a word approximately opposite in meaning to another word.)

Consult a desk dictionary that gives synonyms for the following words, and write the synonyms in the spaces provided.

heavy _____

escape _____

necessary _____

40 Improving Spelling

Poor spelling often results from bad habits developed in early school years. With work, you can correct such habits. If you can write your name without misspelling it, there is no reason why you can't do the same with almost any word in the English language. Following are six steps you can take to improve your spelling.

Step 1: Use the Dictionary

Get into the habit of using the dictionary. When you write a paper, allow yourself time to look up the spelling of all those words you are unsure about. Do not overlook the value of this step just because it is such a simple one. By using the dictionary, you can probably make yourself a 95 percent better speller.

Step 2: Keep a Personal Spelling List

Keep a list of words you misspell, and study these words regularly. Use the chart on page 732 as a starter. When you accumulate additional words, write them on the back page of a frequently used notebook or on a separate sheet of paper titled "Personal Spelling List."

To master the words on your list, do the following:

1 Write down any hint that will help you remember the spelling of a word. For example, you might want to note that *occasion* is spelled with two *c's* and one *s,* or that *all right* is two words, not one word.

2 Study a word by looking at it, saying it, and spelling it. You may also want to write out the word one or more times, or "air-write" it with your finger in large, exaggerated motions.

3 When you have trouble spelling a long word, try to break the word into syllables and see whether you can spell the syllables. For example, *inadvertent* can be spelled easily if you can hear and spell in turn its four syllables: *in ad ver tent*. And *consternation* can be spelled easily if you hear and spell in turn its four syllables: *con ster na tion*. Remember, then: try to see, hear, and spell long words syllable by syllable.

4 Keep in mind that review and repeated self-testing are the keys to effective learning. When you are learning a series of words, go back after studying each new word and review all the preceding ones.

Step 3: Master Commonly Confused Words

Master the meanings and spellings of the commonly confused words on pages 519–528. Your instructor may assign twenty words at a time for you to study and may give you a series of quizzes until you have mastered the words.

Step 4: Understand Basic Spelling Rules

Explained briefly here are three rules that may improve your spelling. While exceptions sometimes occur, the rules hold true most of the time.

Rule 1: *Changing y to i*   When a word ends in a consonant plus *y*, change *y* to *i* when you add an ending (but keep the *y* before *-ing*).

try + ed = tried	easy + er = easier
defy + es = defies	carry + ed = carried
ready + ness = readiness	penny + less = penniless

Rule 2: *Final Silent e*   Drop a final *e* before an ending that starts with a vowel (the vowels are *a, e, i, o,* and *u*).

create + ive = creative	believe + able = believable
nerve + ous = nervous	share + ing = sharing

Keep the final *e* before an ending that starts with a consonant.

extreme + ly = extremely	life + less = lifeless
hope + ful = hopeful	excite + ment = excitement

Rule 3: *Doubling a Final Consonant*   Double the final consonant of a word when all three of the following are true:

a   The word is one syllable or is accented on the last syllable.
b   The word ends in a single consonant preceded by a single vowel.
c   The ending you are adding starts with a vowel.

shop + er = shopper	thin + est = thinnest
equip + ed = equipped	submit + ed = submitted
swim + ing = swimming	drag + ed = dragged

Activity

Combine the following words and endings by applying the three rules above.

1. worry   + ed   = _____
2. write   + ing = _____
3. marry   + es   = _____
4. run   + ing = _____
5. terrify + ed   = _____
6. dry   + es   = _____
7. forget   + ing = _____
8. care   + ful   = _____
9. control + ed   = _____
10. debate + able = _____

Step 5: Study a Basic Word List

Study the spellings of the words in the following list. They are five hundred of the words most often used in English. Your instructor may assign twenty-five or fifty words for you to study at a time and give you a series of quizzes until you have mastered the list.

Five Hundred Basic Words

ability	all right	another	automobile
absent	almost	answer	autumn
accept	a lot	anxious	avenue
accident	already	appetite	awful
ache	also	apply	awkward
across	although	approach	back
address	always	approve	balance
advertise	amateur	argue	bargain
advice	American	around	beautiful
after	among	arrange	because
again	amount	attempt	become **50**
against	angry **25**	attention	been
agree	animal	August	before

begin	choose	disease	fight
being	church	distance	flower
believe	cigarette	doctor **125**	forehead
between	citizen	does	foreign
bicycle	city	dollar	forty
black	close	don't	forward
blue	clothing	doubt	found
board	coffee	down	fourteen
borrow	collect	dozen	Friday
bottle	college	during	friend
bottom	color	each	from
brake	come	early	gallon
breast	comfortable **100**	earth	garden
breathe	company	easy	general
brilliant	condition	education	get
brother	conversation	eight	good
building	copy	either	grammar
bulletin	daily	empty	great **175**
bureau	danger	English	grocery
business	daughter	enough	grow
came	daybreak	entrance	guess
can't	dear	evening	half
careful **75**	death	everything	hammer
careless	December	examine	hand
cereal	decide	except	handkerchief
certain	deed	exercise	happy
chair	dentist	exit	having
change	deposit	expect **150**	head
charity	describe	fact	heard
cheap	did	factory	heavy
cheat	died	family	high
cheek	different	far	himself
chicken	dinner	February	hoarse
chief	direction	few	holiday
children	discover	fifteen	home

hospital	light	needle	part
house	listen	neither	peace
however	little	never	pear **300**
hundred	loaf	newspaper	pencil
hungry	loneliness	nickel	penny
husband	long	niece	people
instead	lose	night	perfect
intelligence **200**	made	ninety	period
interest	making	noise	person
interfere	many	none	picture
interrupt	March	not	piece
into	marry	nothing	pillow
iron	match	November **275**	place
itself	matter	now	plain
January	may	number	please
July	measure	ocean	pocket
June	medicine	o'clock	policeman
just	men	October	possible
kindergarten	middle	offer	post office
kitchen	might	often	potato
knock	million	old	power
knowledge	minute	omit	prescription
labor	mistake **250**	once	president
laid	Monday	one	pretty
language	money	only	probably
last	month	operate	promise
laugh	more	opinion	psychology
learn	morning	opportunity	public **325**
led	mother	optimist	pursue
left	mountain	original	put
leisure	mouth	ought	quart
length	much	ounce	quarter
lesson **225**	must	overcoat	quick
letter	nail	pain	quiet
life	near	paper	quit

quite	since	tenant	understand
quiz	sister	tenth	United States
raise	sixteenth	than	until
read	sleep	Thanksgiving	upon
ready	smoke	that	used
really	soap	theater	usual
reason	soldier	them	valley
receive	something **375**	there	value
recognize	sometimes	they	variety
refer	soul	thing	vegetable
religion	soup	thirteen	very
remember	south	this	view
repeat	stamp	though	villain **450**
resource	state	thousand	visitor
restaurant	still	thread	voice
ribbon	stockings	three	vote
ridiculous	straight	through	wage
right **350**	street	Thursday	wagon
said	strong	ticket	waist
same	student	time	wait
sandwich	studying	tired	wake
Saturday	such	today	walk
say	suffer	together **425**	warm
school	sugar	tomorrow	warning
scissors	suit	tongue	Washington
season	summer	tonight	watch
see	Sunday	touch	water
sentence	supper	toward	wear
September	sure	travel	weather
service	sweet	trouble	Wednesday
seventeen	take	trousers	week
several	teach	truly	weigh
shoes	tear **400**	twelve	welcome
should	telegram	uncle	well
sight	telephone	under	went

were	whose	won't	wrong
what	wife	work	year
whether **475**	window	world	yesterday
which	winter	worth	yet
while	without	would	young
white	woman	writing	your
whole	wonder	written	you're **500**

Note: Two spelling mistakes that students often make are to write *a lot* as one word (*alot*) and to write *all right* as one word (*alright*). Do not write either *a lot* or *all right* as one word.

Step 6: Use Electronic Aids

There are three electronic aids that may help your spelling. First, most *electronic typewriters* can be set to beep automatically when you misspell a word. They include built-in dictionaries that will then give you the correct spelling. Second, *electronic spell-checks* are pocket-size devices that look much like the pocket calculators you may use in math class. Electronic spellers can be found in almost any electronics store. The checker includes a tiny keyboard. You type out the word the way you think it is spelled, and the checker quickly provides you with the correct spelling of related words. Finally, *a computer with a spell-checker* as part of its word processing program will identify incorrect words and suggest correct spellings. If you know how to write on the computer, you will have little trouble learning how to use the spell-check feature.

41 Vocabulary Development

A good vocabulary is a vital part of effective communication. A command of many words will make you a better writer, speaker, listener, and reader. Studies have shown that students with a strong vocabulary, and students who work to improve a limited vocabulary, are more successful in school. And one research study found that *a good vocabulary, more than any other factor, was common to people enjoying successful careers.* This section will describe three ways of developing your word power: (1) regular reading, (2) vocabulary wordsheets, and (3) vocabulary study books. You should keep in mind from the start, however, that none of the approaches will help unless you truly decide that vocabulary development is an important goal. Only when you have this attitude can you begin doing the sustained work needed to improve your word power.

Regular Reading

Through reading a good deal, you will learn words by encountering them a number of times in a variety of sentences. Repeated exposure to a word in context will eventually make it a part of your working language.

You should develop the habit of reading a daily newspaper and one or more weekly magazines like *Time, Newsweek,* or even *People,* as well as monthly magazines suited to your interests. In addition, you should try to read some books for pleasure. This may be especially difficult at times when you also have textbook reading to do. Try, however, to redirect a regular half hour to one hour of your recreational time to reading books, rather than watching television, listening to music, or the like. Doing so, you may eventually reap the rewards of an improved vocabulary *and* discover that reading can be truly enjoyable. If you would like some recommendations, ask your instructor for a copy of the "List of Interesting Books" in the Instructor's Manual that accompanies *English Skills with Readings.*

Vocabulary Wordsheets

Vocabulary wordsheets are another means of vocabulary development. Whenever you read, you should mark off words that you want to learn. After you have accumulated a number of words, sit down with a dictionary and look up basic information about each of them. Put this information on a wordsheet like the one shown below. Be sure also to write down a sentence in which each word appears. A word is always best learned not in a vacuum but in the context of surrounding words.

Study each word as follows. To begin with, make sure you can correctly pronounce the word and its derivations. (Pages 501–504 explain the dictionary pronunciation key that will help you pronounce each word properly.) Next, study the main meanings of the word until you can say them without looking at them. Finally, spend a moment looking at the example of the word in context. Follow the same process with the second word. Then, after testing yourself on the first and the second words, go on to the third word. After you learn each new word, remember to continue to test yourself on all the words you have studied. Repeated self-testing is a key to effective learning.

Activity

In your reading, locate four words that you would like to master. Enter them in the spaces on the vocabulary wordsheet below and fill in all the needed information. Your instructor may then check your wordsheet and perhaps give you a quick oral quiz on selected words.

You may receive a standing assignment to add five words a week to a wordsheet and to study the words. Note that you can create your own wordsheets using loose-leaf paper, or your instructor may give you copies of the wordsheet that appears below.

Vocabulary Wordsheet

1. Word: _____formidable_____   Pronunciation: _____(fôr′ mi də bəl)_____

   Meanings: _____1. feared or dreaded_____

   _____2. extremely difficult_____

   _____

   Other forms of the word: _formidably   formidability_

   Use of the word in context: _Several formidable obstacles stand between_
   Matt and his goal.

2. Word: _____   Pronunciation: _____

   Meanings: _____

   _____

   _____

   Other forms of the word: _____

   Use of the word in context: _____

   _____

3. Word: _____ Pronunciation: _____

   Meanings: _____

   _____

   _____

   Other forms of the word: _____

   Use of the word in context: _____

   _____

4. Word: _____ Pronunciation: _____

   Meanings: _____

   _____

   _____

   Other forms of the word: _____

   Use of the word in context: _____

   _____

5. Word: _____ Pronunciation: _____

   Meanings: _____

   _____

   _____

   Other forms of the word: _____

   Use of the word in context: _____

   _____

Vocabulary Study Books

A third way to increase your word power is to use vocabulary study books. Many vocabulary books and programs are available. The best are those that present words in one or more contexts and then provide several reinforcement activities for each word. These books will help you increase your vocabulary if you have the determination required to work with them on a regular basis.

42 Commonly Confused Words

Introductory Project

Circle the five words that are misspelled in the following passage. Then see if you can write the correct spellings in the spaces provided.

You're mind and body are not as separate as you might think. Their is a lot of evidence, for instance, that if you believe a placebo (a substance with no medicine) will help you, than it will. One man is said too have recovered rapidly from an advanced case of cancer after only one dose of a drug that he believed was highly effective. Its not clear just how placebos work, but they do show how closely the mind and body are related.

1. _____

2. _____

3. _____

4. _____

5. _____

Answers are on page 729.

Homonyms

The commonly confused words on the following pages have the same sounds but different meanings and spellings; such words are known as *homonyms*. Complete the activity for each set of homonyms, and check off and study the words that give you trouble.

all ready   completely prepared
already   previously; before

> We were *all ready* to start the play, but the audience was still being seated.
>
> I have *already* called the police.

Fill in the blanks: I am _____ for the economics examination because I have _____ studied the chapter three times.

brake   stop; the stopping device in a vehicle
break   come apart

> His car bumper has a sticker reading, "I *brake* for animals."
>
> "I am going to *break* up with Bill if he keeps seeing other women," said Rita.

Fill in the blanks: When my car's emergency _____ slipped, the car rolled back and demolished my neighbor's rose garden, causing a _____ in our good relations with each other.

coarse   rough
course   part of a meal; a school subject; direction; certainly (as in *of course*).

> By the time the waitress served the customers the second *course* of the meal, she was aware of their *coarse* eating habits.

Fill in the blanks: Ted felt that the health instructor's humor was too _____ for his taste and was glad when he finished the _____.

hear   perceive with the ear
here   in this place

> "The salespeople act as though they don't see or *hear* me, even though I've been standing *here* for fifteen minutes," the woman complained.

Fill in the blanks: "Did you _____ about the distinguished visitor who just came into town and is staying _____ at this very hotel?"

hole   an empty spot
whole   entire

"I can't believe I ate the *whole* pizza," moaned Ralph. "I think it's going to make a *hole* in my stomach lining."

Fill in the blanks: The _____ time I was at the party I tried to conceal the _____ I had in my pants.

its   belonging to it
it's   shortened form of *it is* or *it has*

The car blew *its* transmission (the transmission belonging to it, the car).
It's (it has) been raining all week and *it's* (it is) raining now.

Fill in the blanks: _____ hot and unsanitary in the restaurant kitchen I work in, and I don't think the restaurant deserves _____ good reputation.

knew   past form of *know*
new   not old

"I had *new* wallpaper put up," said Sarah.
"I *knew* there was some reason the place looked better," said Bill.

Fill in the blanks: Lola _____ that getting her hair cut would give her face a _____ look.

know   to understand
no   a negative

"I don't *know* why my dog Fang likes to attack certain people," said Martha. "There's *no* one thing the people have in common."

Fill in the blanks: I _____ of _____ way to tell whether that politician is honest or not.

pair   set of two
pear   fruit

"What a great *pair* of legs Tony has," said Lola to Vonnie. Tony didn't hear her, for he was feeling very sick after munching on a green *pear.*

Fill in the blanks: In his lunch box was a _____ of

_____s.

passed   went by; succeeded in; handed to
past   time before the present; beyond, as in "We worked past closing time."

Someone *passed* him a wine bottle; it was the way he chose to forget his unhappy *past.*

Fill in the blanks: I walked _____ the instructor's office but was afraid to ask her whether or not I had _____ the test.

peace   calm
piece   part

Nations often risk world *peace* by fighting over a *piece* of land.

Fill in the blanks: Martha did not have any _____ until she gave her dog a _____ of meat loaf.

plain   simple
plane   aircraft

The *plain,* unassuming young man on the *plane* suddenly jumped up with a grenade in his hand and announced, "We're all going to Tibet."

Fill in the blanks: The game-show contestant opened the small box wrapped in _____ brown paper and found inside the keys to his own jet

_____.

principal   main; a person in charge of a school
principle   law, standard, or rule

Pete's high school *principal* had one *principal* problem: Pete. This was because there were only two *principles* in Pete's life: rest and relaxation.

Fill in the blanks: The _____ reason she dropped out of school was that she believed in the _____ of complete freedom of choice.

Note: It might help to remember that the *e* in *principle* is also in *rule*—the meaning of *principle.*

right   correct; opposite of *left*
write   put words on paper

If you have the *right* course card, I'll *write* your name on the class roster.

Fill in the blanks: Eddie thinks I'm weird because I _____ with both my _____ and my left hand.

than   used in comparisons
then   at that time

When we were kids, my friend Elaine had prettier clothes *than* I did. I really envied her *then.*

Fill in the blanks: Marge thought she was better _____ the rest of us, but _____ she got the lowest grade on the history test.

Note: It might help to remember that th*e*n (with an *e*) is also a tim*e* signal.

their   belonging to them
there   at that place; neutral word used with verbs like *is, are, was, were, have,*
           and *had*
they're   shortened form of *they are*

Two people own that van over *there* (at that place). *They're* (they are) going to move out of *their* apartment (the apartment belonging to them) and into the van, in order to save money.

Fill in the blanks: _____ not going to invite us to _____ table because _____ is no room for us to sit down.

threw   past form of *throw*
through   from one side to the other; finished

The fans *threw* so much litter onto the field that the teams could not go *through* with the game.

Fill in the blanks: When Mr. Jefferson was _____ screaming about the violence on television, he _____ the newspaper at his dog.

to	verb part, as in *to smile;* toward, as in "I'm going *to* heaven"
too	overly, as in "The pizza was *too* hot"; also, as in "The coffee was hot, *too.*"
two	the number 2

Tony drove *to* the park *to* be alone with Lola. (The first *to* means "toward"; the second *to* is a verb part that goes with *be.)*

Tony's shirt is *too* tight, *too.* (The first *too* means "overly"; the second *too* means "also.")

You need *two* hands (2 hands) to handle a Whopper.

Fill in the blanks: _____ times tonight, you have been _____ ready _____ make assumptions without asking questions first.

wear	to have on
where	in what place

Fred wanted to *wear* his light pants on the hot day, but he didn't know *where* he had put them.

Fill in the blanks: Exactly _____ on my leg should I _____ this elastic bandage?

weather	atmospheric conditions
whether	if it happens that; in case; if

Some people go on vacations *whether* or not the *weather* is good.

Fill in the blanks: I always ask Bill _____ or not we're going to have a storm, for his bad knee can feel rainy _____ approaching.

whose	belonging to whom
who's	shortened form of *who is* and *who has*

Who's the instructor *whose* students are complaining?

Fill in the blanks: _____ the guy _____ car I saw you in?

your   belonging to you
you're   shortened form of *you are*

> *You're* (meaning "you are") not going to the fair unless *your* brother (the brother belonging to you) goes with you.

Fill in the blanks: _____ going to have to put aside individual differences and play together for the sake of _____ team.

Other Words Frequently Confused

Following is a list of other words that people frequently confuse. Complete the activities for each set of words, and check off and study the words that give you trouble.

a, an   Both *a* and *an* are used before other words to mean, approximately, "one."

Generally you should use *an* before words starting with a vowel (*a, e, i, o, u*):

> an ache   an experiment   an elephant   an idiot   an ox

Generally you should use *a* before words starting with a consonant (all other letters):

> a Coke   a brain   a cheat   a television   a gambler

Fill in the blanks: The girls had _____ argument over _____ former boyfriend.

accept (ăk sĕpt′)   receive; agree to
except (ĕk sĕpt′)   exclude; but

> "I would *accept* your loan," said Bill to the bartender, "*except* that I'm not ready to pay 25 percent interest."

Fill in the blanks: _____ for the fact that she can't _____ any criticism, Lori is a good friend.

advice (ăd vīs′)   noun meaning "an opinion"
advise (ăd vīz′)   verb meaning "to counsel, to give advice"

I *advise* you to take the *advice* of your friends and stop working so hard.

Fill in the blanks: I _____ you to listen carefully to any

_____ you get from your boss.

affect (uh fĕkt′)   verb meaning "to influence"
effect (i fĕkt′)   verb meaning "to bring about something"; noun meaning
                     "result"

The full *effects* of marijuana and alcohol on the body are only partly known;
however, both drugs clearly *affect* the brain in various ways.

Fill in the blanks: The new tax laws go into _____ next month,

and they are going to _____ your income tax deductions.

among   implies three or more
between   implies only two

We had to choose from *among* fifty shades of paint but *between* only two
fabrics.

Fill in the blanks: The layoff notices distributed _____ the

unhappy workers gave them a choice _____ working for another

month at full pay and leaving immediately with two weeks' pay.

beside   along the side of
besides   in addition to

I was lucky I wasn't standing *beside* the car when it was hit.
Besides being unattractive, these uniforms are impractical.

Fill in the blanks: _____ the alarm system hooked up to the door,

our neighbors keep a gun _____ their beds.

desert (dĕz′ərt)   stretch of dry land; (dĭ zûrt′) to abandon one's post or duty
dessert (dĭ zûrt′)   last part of a meal

Sweltering in the *desert,* I was tormented by the thought of an icy *dessert.*

Fill in the blanks: After their meal, they carried their _____
into the living room so that they would not miss the start of the old

_____ movie about Lawrence of Arabia.

fewer   used with things that can be counted
less   refers to amount, value, or degree

There were *fewer* than seven people in all my classes today.
I seem to feel *less* tired when I exercise regularly.

Fill in the blanks: With _____ people driving large cars, we are importing _____ oil than we used to.

loose (lo͞os)   not fastened; not tight-fitting
lose (lo͞oz)   misplace; fail to win

Phil's belt is so *loose* that he always looks ready to *lose* his pants.

Fill in the blanks: At least once a week our neighbors _____ their dog; it's because they let him run _____.

quiet (kwī′ ĭt)   peaceful
quite (kwīt)   entirely; really; rather

After a busy day, the children are now *quiet,* and their parents are *quite* tired.

Fill in the blanks: The _____ halls of the church become _____ lively during square-dance evenings.

though (thō)   despite the fact that
thought (thôt)   past form of *think*

Even *though* she worked, she *thought* she would have time to go to school.

Fill in the blanks: Yoshiko _____ she would like the job, but even _____ the pay was good, she hated the traveling involved.

■ **Review Test 1**

Underline the correct word in the parentheses. Don't try to guess. If necessary, look back at the explanations of the words.

1. Please take my (advice, advise) and (where, wear) something warm and practical, rather (than, then) something fashionable and flimsy.
2. Glen felt that if he could (loose, lose) twenty pounds, the (affect, effect) on his social life might be dramatic.

3. (Their, There, They're) going to show seven horror films at (their, there, they're) Halloween festival; I hope you'll be (their, there, they're).

4. (Your, You're) going to have to do (a, an) better job on (your, you're) final exam if you expect to pass the (coarse, course).

5. Those (to, too, two) issues are (to, too, two) hot for any politician (to, too, two) handle.

6. Even (though, thought) the (brakes, breaks) on my car were worn, I did not have (quiet, quite) enough money to get them replaced (right, write) away.

7. (Accept, Except) for the fact that my neighbor receives most of his mail in (plain, plane) brown wrappers, he is (know, no) stranger (than, then) anyone else in this rooming house.

8. Because the Randalls are so neat and fussy, (its, it's) hard (to, too, two) feel comfortable when (your, you're) in (their, there, they're) house.

9. (Whose, Who's) the culprit who left the paint can on the table? The paint has ruined a (knew, new) tablecloth, and (its, it's) soaked (threw, through) the linen and (affected, effected) the varnish.

10. I would have been angry at the car that (passed, past) me at ninety miles an hour on the highway, (accept, except) that I (knew, new) it would not get (passed, past) the speed trap (to, too, two) miles down the road.

■ Review Test 2

On a separate paper, write short sentences using the ten words shown below.

their	principal
its	except
you're	past
too	through
then	who's

43 Effective Word Choice

Introductory Project

Write a check mark beside the sentence in each pair that makes more effective use of words.

1. I flipped out when Faye broke our date. _____

   I got very angry when Faye broke our date. _____

2. Doctors as dedicated as Dr. Curtin are few and far between. _____

   Doctors as dedicated as Dr. Curtin are rare. _____

3. Yesterday I ascertained that Elena and Wes broke up. _____

   Yesterday I found out that Elena and Wes broke up. _____

Now see if you can circle the correct number in each case:

Pair (1, 2, 3) contains a sentence with slang.

Pair (1, 2, 3) contains a sentence with a cliché.

Pair (1, 2, 3) contains a sentence with a pretentious word.

Answers are on page 729.

Choose your words carefully when you write. Always take the time to think about your word choices rather than simply using the first word that comes to mind. You want to develop the habit of selecting words that are appropriate and exact for your purposes. One way you can show sensitivity to language is by avoiding slang, clichés, and pretentious words.

Slang

We often use slang expressions when we talk because they are so vivid and colorful. However, slang is usually out of place in formal writing. Here are some examples of slang expressions:

My girlfriend *got straight* with me by saying she wanted to see other men.
Rick spent all Saturday *messing around* with his stereo.
My boss keeps *riding* me about coming to work late.
The tires on the Corvette make the car look like *something else.*
The crowd was *psyched up* when the game began.

Slang expressions have a number of drawbacks: they go out of date quickly, they become tiresome if used excessively in writing, and they may communicate clearly to some readers but not to others. Also, the use of slang can be a way of evading the specific details that are often needed to make one's meaning clear in writing. For example, in "The tires on the Corvette make the car look like something else," the writer has not provided the specific details about the tires necessary for us to understand the statement clearly. In general, then, you should avoid slang in your writing. If you are in doubt about whether an expression is slang, it may help to check a recently published hardbound dictionary.

Activity

Rewrite the following sentences, replacing the italicized slang words with more formal ones.

Example   The movie was *a real bomb,* so we cut out early.
            The movie was terrible, so we left early.
_____

1. My roommate told me he was going to quit school and *hit the road*, but later he admitted he was just *messing with my mind*.

_____

_____

2. The car was a *steal* until the owner *jacked up* the price.

_____

_____

3. If the instructor stops *hassling* me, I am going to *get my act together* in the course.

_____

_____

Clichés

A *cliché* is an expression that has been worn out through constant use. Some typical clichés are listed below:

Clichés	
all work and no play	saw the light
at a loss for words	short but sweet
better late than never	sigh of relief
drop in the bucket	singing the blues
easier said than done	taking a big chance
had a hard time of it	time and time again
in the nick of time	too close for comfort
in this day and age	too little, too late
it dawned on me	took a turn for the worse
it goes without saying	under the weather
last but not least	where he (she) is coming from
make ends meet	word to the wise
on top of the world	work like a dog
sad but true	

Clichés are common in speech but make your writing seem tired and stale. Also, clichés—like slang—are often a way of evading the specific details that you must work to provide in your writing. You should, then, avoid clichés and try to express your meaning in fresh, original ways.

Activity

Underline the cliché in each of the following sentences. Then substitute specific, fresh words for the trite expression.

Example   I passed the test <u>by the skin of my teeth.</u>
              I barely passed the test.

1. Hal decided not to eat anything because he was feeling under the weather.

   _____

2. Judy doesn't make any bones about her ambition.

   _____

3. I met with my instructor to try to iron out the problems in my paper.

   _____

Pretentious Words

Some people feel they can improve their writing by using fancy, elevated words rather than simple, natural words. They use artificial and stilted language that more often obscures their meaning than communicates it clearly.

Here are some unnatural-sounding sentences:

I comprehended her statement.

While partaking of our morning meal, we engaged in an animated conversation.

I am a stranger to excessive financial sums.

Law enforcement officers directed traffic when the lights malfunctioned.

The same thoughts can be expressed more clearly and effectively by using plain, natural language, as below:

I understood what she said.

While eating breakfast, we had a lively talk.

I have never had much money.

Police officers directed traffic when the lights stopped working.

Activity

Cross out the pretentious words in each sentence. Then substitute clear, simple language for the artificial words.

Example   The manager ~~reproached~~ me for my ~~tardiness~~.
           The manager criticized me for being late.
_____

1. One of Colleen's objectives in life is to accomplish a large family.

   _____

   _____

2. Upon entering our residence, we detected smoke in the atmosphere.

   _____

   _____

3. I am not apprehensive about the test, which encompasses five chapters of the book.

   _____

   _____

■ Review Test

Certain words are italicized in the following sentences. In the space provided, identify the words as *slang* (S), *clichés* (C), or *pretentious words* (PW). Then rewrite the sentences, replacing the words with more effective diction.

_____   1. We're *psyched* for tonight's concert, which is going to be *totally awesome.*

             _____

             _____

_____   2. Getting good grades in college is sometimes *easier said than done.*

             _____

             _____

_____   3. I *availed myself* of the chance to *participate in* the computer course.

             _____

             _____

_____   4. The victims of the car accident were shaken but *none the worse for wear.*

             _____

             _____

_____   5. My roommate *pulled an all-nighter* and almost *conked out* during the exam.

_____

_____

_____   6. Be sure to *deposit* your trash in the appropriate *receptacle*.

_____

_____

_____   7. Fred has to *work like a dog* in his advanced math class.

_____

_____

_____   8. My sister's constant criticism *drives me up the wall*.

_____

_____

_____   9. Everyone in our family *congregates* at Miriam's house for the annual Thanksgiving *repast*.

_____

_____

_____   10. Carlos *totally lost it* when the clerk told him that she didn't have any blue shirts in his size.

_____

_____

44 ESL Pointers

This section covers rules that most native speakers of English take for granted but that are useful for speakers of English as a second language (ESL).

Articles

An *article* is a noun marker—it signals that a noun will follow. There are two kinds of articles: indefinite and definite. The indefinite articles are *a* and *an*. Use *a* before a word that begins with a consonant sound:

> **a c**arrot, **a p**ig, **a u**niform
>
> (*A* is used before *uniform* because the *u* in that word sounds like the consonant *y* plus *u,* not a vowel sound.)

Use *an* before a word beginning with a vowel sound:

> **an e**xcuse, **an o**nion, **an h**onor
>
> (*Honor* begins with a vowel because the *h* is silent.)

The definite article is *the*.

> **the** lemon, **the** fan

An article may come right before a noun:

> **a** circle, **the** summer

Or an article may be separated from the noun by words that describe the noun:

> **a** large circle, **the** long hot summer.

Note: There are various other noun markers, including quantity words (*a few, many, a lot of*), numerals (*one, ten, 120*), demonstrative adjectives (*this, these*), adjectives (*my, your, our*), and possessive nouns (*Vinh's, the school's*).

Articles with Count and Noncount Nouns

To know whether to use an article with a noun and which article to use, you must recognize count and noncount nouns. (A *noun* is a word used to name something—a person, place, thing, or idea.)

Count nouns name people, places, things, or ideas that can be counted and made into plurals, such as *window, table,* and *principal* (*one window, two tables, three principals*).

Noncount nouns refer to things or ideas that cannot be counted and therefore cannot be made into plurals, such as *weather, anger,* and *happiness.* The box below lists and illustrates common types of noncount nouns.

Common Noncount Nouns

Abstractions and emotions: joy, humor, patience, mercy, curiosity

Activities: soccer, gardening, reading, writing, searching

Foods: sugar, spaghetti, fudge, chicken, lettuce

Gases and vapors: air, nitrogen, oxygen, smoke, steam

Languages and areas of study: Laotian, German, social studies, calculus, biology

Liquids: coffee, gasoline, soda, milk, water

Materials that come in bulk or mass form: lumber, soil, dust, detergent, hay

Natural occurrences: gravity, hail, snow, thunder, rust

Other things that cannot be counted: clothing, furniture, homework, machinery, money, news, transportation, vocabulary, work

---

The quantity of a noncount noun can be expressed with a word or words called a *qualifier,* such as *some, more, a unit of,* and so on. In the following two examples, the qualifiers are shown in *italic* type, and the noncount nouns are shown in **boldface** type.

I hear *a little* **anger** in your voice.

The pea soup had gotten thick overnight, so Kala added *more* **water** to it.

Some words can be either count or noncount nouns, depending on whether they refer to one or more individual items or to something in general:

The yearly **rains** in India are called monsoons.

(This sentence refers to individual rains; *rains* in this case is a count noun.)

Rain is something that farmers cannot live without.

(This sentence refers to rain in general; in this case, *rain* is a noncount noun.)

Using *a* or *an* with Nonspecific Singular Count Nouns

Use *a* or *an* with singular nouns that are nonspecific. A noun is nonspecific when the reader doesn't know its specific identity.

A penguin cannot fly; it uses its "wings" to "fly" through the water.

(The sentence refers to any penguin, not a specific one.)

There was **a** fire today in our neighborhood.

(The reader isn't familiar with the fire. This is the first time it is mentioned.)

Using *the* with Specific Nouns

In general, use *the* with all specific nouns—specific singular, plural, and noncount nouns. A noun is specific—and therefore requires the article *the*—in the following cases:

- When it has already been mentioned once

  There was a fire today in our neighborhood. **The** fire destroyed the Smiths' garage.

  (*The* is used with the second mention of *fire*.)

- When it is identified by a word or phrase in the sentence

  The lights in the bathroom do not work.

  (*Lights* is identified by the words *in the bathroom*.)

- When its identity is suggested by the general context

  The coffee at Billy's Diner always tastes a week old.

  (*Coffee* is identified by the words *at Billy's Diner.*)

- When it is unique

  Scientists warn that there is a growing hole in **the** ozone layer.

  (Earth has only one ozone layer.)

- When it comes after a superlative adjective (*best, biggest, wisest*)

  Many of **the** best distance runners come from East Africa.

Omitting Articles

Omit articles with nonspecific plurals and nonspecific noncount nouns. Plurals and noncount nouns are nonspecific when they refer to something in general.

Lights were on all over the empty house.

Coffee should be stored in the refrigerator or freezer if possible.

Runners from Kenya, Ethiopia, and Tanzania often win world-class races.

Using *the* with Proper Nouns

Proper nouns name particular people, places, things, or ideas and are always capitalized. Most proper nouns do not require articles; those that do, however, require *the*. Following are general guidelines about when and when not to use *the*.

Do not use *the* for most singular proper nouns, including names of the following:

- *People and animals* (Rosa Parks, Skipper)
- *Continents, states, cities, streets, and parks* (Asia, North Dakota, San Diego, Rodeo Boulevard, Fairmount Park)
- *Most countries* (Thailand, Argentina, England)
- *Individual bodies of water, islands, and mountains* (Lake Tahoe, Prince Edward Island, Mount Saint Helens)

Use *the* for the following types of proper nouns:

- *Plural proper nouns* (the Jacksons, the United Arab Emirates, the Great Lakes, the Appalachian Mountains)
- *Names of large geographic areas, deserts, oceans, seas, and rivers* (the Northeast, the Gobi Desert, the Indian Ocean, the Mediterranean Sea, the Thames River)
- *Names with the format* "the _____ of _____" (the king of Sweden, the Gulf of Aden, the University of New Hampshire)

Activity

Underline the correct form of the noun in parentheses.

1. (A telephone, Telephone) is found in almost every American home.

2. Today Kim bought (a used car, the used car).

3. (The car, A car) Kim bought is four years old but in very good condition.

4. Thick (fog, fogs) blocked the plane's approach to the airport.

5. My grandparents and cousins all live in (New Jersey, the New Jersey).

6. Adults should have (patience, the patience) when dealing with children.

7. (Indian Ocean, The Indian Ocean) lies between the east coast of Africa and the west coast of Australia.

8. Cats are known for having a great deal of (curiosity, the curiosity).

9. Through the ages, (wine, the wine) has been made out of many fruits other than grapes, such as apples and blueberries.

10. (Water, The water) in the barrel outside is for watering the vegetable garden.

Subjects and Verbs

Avoiding Repeated Subjects

In English, a particular subject can be used only once in a word group with a subject and a verb. Don't repeat a subject in the same word group by following a noun with a pronoun.

> Incorrect: My *friend she* is a wonderful cook.
>
> Correct: My **friend** is a wonderful cook.
>
> Correct: **She** is a wonderful cook.

Even when the subject and verb are separated by several words, the subject cannot be repeated in the same word group.

> Incorrect: The *flowers* that are blooming in the yard *they* are called snapdragons.
>
> Correct: The **flowers** that are blooming in the yard **are called** snapdragons.

Including Pronoun Subjects and Linking Verbs

Some languages may omit a pronoun as a subject, but in English, every sentence other than a command must have a subject. (In a command, the subject *you* is understood: [**You**] Hand in your papers now.)

Incorrect: The party was a success. *Was* lots of fun.

Correct: The party was a success. **It was** lots of fun.

Every English sentence must also have a verb, even when the meaning of the sentence is clear without the verb.

Incorrect: Rosa's handwriting very neat.

Correct: Rosa's handwriting **is** very neat.

Including *There* and *Here* at the Beginning of Sentences

Some English sentences begin with *there* or *here* plus a linking verb (usually a form of *to be: is, are,* and so on). In such sentences, the verb comes before the subject.

There are oranges in the refrigerator.

(The subject is the plural noun *oranges*, so the plural verb *are* is used.)

Here is the book you wanted.

(The subject is the singular noun *book*, so the singular verb *is* is used.)

In sentences like those above, remember not to omit *there* or *here*.

Incorrect: *Are* many good reasons to quit smoking.

Correct: **There are** many good reasons to quit smoking.

Not Using the Progressive Tense of Certain Verbs

The progressive tenses are made up of forms of *be* plus the *-ing* form of the main verb. They express actions or conditions still in progress at a particular time.

Iris **will be running** for student-body president this year.

However, verbs for mental states, the senses, possession, and inclusion are normally not used in the progressive tense.

Incorrect: I **am loving** chocolate.

Correct: I **love** chocolate.

Incorrect: Sonia **is having** a lovely singing voice.

Correct: Sonia **has** a lovely singing voice.

Common verbs not generally used in the progressive tense are listed in the box below.

Common Verbs Not Generally Used in the Progressive

Thoughts, attitudes and desires: agree, believe, imagine, know, like, love, prefer, think, understand, want, wish

Sense perceptions: hear, see, smell, taste

Appearances: appear, seem, look

Possession: belong, have, own, possess

Inclusion: contain, include

Using Gerunds and Infinitives after Verbs

A *gerund* is the *-ing* form of a verb that is used as a noun:

Complaining is my cousin's favorite activity.

(*Complaining* is the subject of the sentence.)

An *infinitive* is *to* plus the basic form of the verb (the form in which the verb is listed in the dictionary), as in **to eat.** The infinitive can function as an adverb, an adjective, or a noun.

We decided **to eat** dinner on the porch.

(*To eat dinner on the porch* functions as an adverb that describes the verb *decided.*)

Simon built a shelf **to hold** his compact disk collection.

(*To hold his compact disk collection* functions as an adjective describing the noun *shelf.*)

To have good friends is a blessing.

(*To have good friends* functions as a noun—the subject of the verb *is.*)

Some verbs can be followed by only a gerund or only an infinitive; other verbs can be followed by either. Examples are given in the following lists. There are many others; watch for them in your reading.

Verb + gerund (*dislike + studying*)
Verb + preposition + gerund (*insist + on + paying*)

Some verbs can be followed by a gerund but not by an infinitive. In many cases, there is a preposition (such as *for, in,* or *of*) between the verb and the gerund. Following are some verbs and verb-preposition combinations that can be followed by gerunds but not by infinitives:

admit	deny	look forward to
apologize for	discuss	postpone
appreciate	dislike	practice
approve of	enjoy	suspect of
avoid	feel like	talk about
be used to	finish	thank for
believe in	insist on	think about

Incorrect: Sometimes I *enjoy to eat* by myself in a restaurant.
Correct: Sometimes I **enjoy eating** by myself in a restaurant.

Incorrect: Do you *feel like to dance*?
Correct: Do you **feel like dancing**?

Verb + infinitive (*agree + to leave*)

Following are common verbs that can be followed by an infinitive but not by a gerund:

agree	decide	manage
arrange	expect	refuse
claim	have	wait

Incorrect: I *agreed taking* Grandma shopping this afternoon.
Correct: I **agreed to take** Grandma shopping this afternoon.

Verb + noun or pronoun + infinitive (*cause + them + to flee*)

Below are common verbs that are first followed by a noun or pronoun and then by an infinitive, not a gerund.

cause	force	remind
command	persuade	warn

Incorrect: The queen *commanded the prince obeying.*

Correct: The queen **commanded the prince to obey.**

Following are common verbs that can be followed either by an infinitive alone or by a noun or pronoun and an infinitive:

ask	need	want
expect	promise	would like

Jerry **would like to join** the army.

Jerry's parents **would like him to go** to college.

Verb + gerund or infinitive (*begin + packing* or *begin + to pack*)

Following are verbs that can be followed by either a gerund or an infinitive:

begin	hate	prefer
continue	love	start

The meaning of each of the verbs above remains the same or almost the same whether a gerund or an infinitive is used.

I prefer **eating** dinner early.

I prefer **to eat** dinner early.

With the verbs below, the gerunds and the infinitives have very different meanings.

forget	remember	stop

Nadia **stopped to put on** makeup.

(She interrupted something to put on makeup.)

Nadia **stopped putting on** makeup.

(She discontinued putting on makeup.)

Activity

Underline the correct form in parentheses.

1. The police officer (she gave, gave) me a ticket for speeding.

2. The telephone never stops ringing. (Is, It is) driving me crazy.

3. (Are paints and crayons, There are paints and crayons) in that cupboard.

4. That book (contains, is containing) photos of our wedding.

5. My midterm math grade persuaded me (getting, to get) a tutor.

6. After walking in the hot sun, we (very thirsty, were very thirsty).

7. The little girl (talked about to become, talked about becoming) a famous scientist.

8. Lucia (expects earning, expects to earn) a B in the class.

9. The pigeons on the sidewalk (pick up, they pick up) crumbs of food that people drop.

10. For lunch today I (want, am wanting) a big salad.

Adjectives

Following the Order of Adjectives in English

Adjectives describe nouns and pronouns. In English, an adjective usually comes directly before the word it describes or after a linking verb (a form of *be* or a "sense" verb such as *look*, *seem* and *taste*), in which case it modifies the subject. In each of the following two sentences, the adjective is **boldfaced** and the noun it describes is *italicized*.

That is a **bright** *light.*

That *light* is **bright.**

When more than one adjective modifies the same noun, the adjectives are usually stated in a certain order, though there are often exceptions. Following is the typical order of English adjectives:

Typical Order of Adjectives in a Series

1 **An article or another noun marker:** a, an, the, Joseph's, this, three, your

2 **Opinion adjective:** exciting, plain, annoying, difficult

3 **Size:** enormous, huge, petite, tiny

4 **Shape:** circular, short, round, square

5 **Age:** newborn, recent, old, new, young

6 **Color:** pink, yellow, orange, white

7 **Nationality:** Italian, Chinese, Guatemalan, Russian

8 **Religion:** Buddhist, Catholic, Jewish, Muslim

9 **Material:** plastic, silver, cement, cotton

10 **Noun used as an adjective:** school (as in *school bus*), closet (as in *closet shelf*), birthday (as in *birthday party*)

Here are some examples of the order of adjectives:

> **an interesting old** story
> **the long orange cotton** dress
> **your elderly Hungarian** cousin
> **Rafael's friendly little black** dog

In general, use no more than two or three adjectives after the article or other noun marker. Numerous adjectives in a series can be awkward: **the lovely little old Methodist stone** church.

Using the Present and Past Participles as Adjectives

The present participle ends in *-ing*. Past participles of regular verbs end in *-ed* or *-d*; a list of the past participles of many common irregular verbs appears on pages 411–413. Both types of participles may be used as adjectives. A participle used as an adjective may come before the word it describes:

> It was a **boring** *lecture.*

A participle used as an adjective may also follow a linking verb and describe the subject of the sentence:

> The *lecture* was **boring.**

While both present and past participles of a particular verb may be used as adjectives, their meanings differ. Use the present participle to describe whoever or whatever causes a feeling:

> a **surprising** *conversation*
> (The conversation *caused* the surprise.)

Use the past participle to describe whoever or whatever experiences the feeling:

> the **surprised** *waitress*
> (The waitress *is* surprised.)

Here are two more sentences that illustrate the differing meanings of present and past participles.

> The mystery movie was **frightening.**
> The audience was **frightened.**
> (The movie caused the fear; the audience experienced the fear.)

Following are pairs of present and past participles with similar distinctions:

annoying / annoyed	exhausting / exhausted
boring / bored	fascinating / fascinated
confusing / confused	tiring / tired
depressing / depressed	surprising / surprised
exciting / excited	

Activity

Underline the correct form in parentheses.

1. It was so windy that we had to use stones to hold down the (yellow big plastic, big yellow plastic) tablecloth on the picnic table.

2. At the party, Julie sang a(n) (Vietnamese old, old Vietnamese) song.

3. For her party, the little girl asked if her mother would buy her a (beautiful long velvet, beautiful velvet long) dress.

4. The long walk home from the supermarket left Mira feeling (exhausting, exhausted).

5. The constant barking of our neighbor's dog is very (annoying, annoyed).

Prepositions Used for Time and Place

In English, the use of prepositions is often not based on their common meanings, and there are many exceptions to general rules. As a result, correct use of prepositions must be learned gradually through experience. Following is a chart showing how three of the most common prepositions are used in some customary references to time and place:

Use of *On*, *In*, and *At* to Refer to Time and Place

Time

On *a specific day:* on Saturday, on June 12, on your birthday

In *a part of a day:* in the morning, in the daytime (but *at* night)

In *a month or a year:* in November, in 1492

In *a period of time:* in a minute, in a couple of days, in a while

At *a specific time:* at 10:00 A.M., at dawn, at sunset, at dinnertime

Place

On *a surface:* on the dresser, on the porch, on the roof

In *a place that is enclosed:* in my bedroom, in the hallway, in the drawer

At *a specific location:* at the pool, at the bar, at the racetrack

---

Activity

Underline the correct preposition in parentheses.

1. Your next appointment is (on, at) Tuesday.

2. Class begins (on, at) 9 A.M.

3. I love to relax (on, in) a whirlpool bathtub.

4. Sonia is moving to Florida (in, at) a month.

5. The children's birthday party was held (on, at) the bowling alley.

■ Review Test

Underline the correct form in parentheses.

1. When I looked out the window, I was surprised by the deep (snow, snows).

2. (Are, There are) cockroaches in the kitchen.

3. When she did not get the job she wanted, Laura felt (depressing, depressed) for a few days.

4. Owls hunt (at, in) night and sleep most of the day.

5. Larry (postponed to go, postponed going) on vacation because he broke his foot.

6. My English teacher wears a (silver small, small silver) ring in his ear.

7. Marta (has, is having) a very bad cold.

8. (On, In) Valentine's Day, friends and lovers send each other affectionate cards.

9. (Turkey is, Turkeys are) the traditional main course at Thanksgiving dinner.

10. Before the camera was invented, (the paintings, paintings) were the only way to record how people look.

45 Combined Mastery Tests

Fragments and Run-Ons

■ Combined Mastery Test 1

The word groups below are numbered 1 through 20. In the space provided for each, write C if a word group is a complete sentence, write F if it is a fragment, and write RO if it is a run-on. Then correct the errors.

1. _____

2. _____

3. _____

4. _____

5. _____

6. _____

7. _____

8. _____

9. _____

10. _____

11. _____

12. _____

13. _____

14. _____

15. _____

16. _____

17. _____

18. _____

19. _____

20. _____

[1]I had a frightening dream last night, I dreamed that I was walking high up on an old railroad trestle. [2]It looked like the one I used to walk on recklessly. [3]When I was about ten years old. [4]At that height, my palms were sweating, just as they did when I was a boy. [5]I could see the ground out of the corners of my eyes, I felt a swooning, sickening sensation. [6]Suddenly, I realized there were rats below. [7]Thousands upon thousands of rats. [8]They knew I was up on the trestle, they were laughing. [9]Because they were sure they would get me. [10]Their teeth glinted in the moonlight, their red eyes were like thousands of small reflectors. [11]That almost blinded my sight. [12]Sensing that there was something even more hideous behind me. [13]I kept moving forward. [14]Then I realized that I was coming to a gap in the trestle. [15]There was no way I could stop or go back I would have to cross over that empty gap. [16]I leaped out in despair. [17]Knowing I would never make it. [18]And felt myself falling helplessly down to the swarm of rejoicing rats. [19]I woke up bathed in sweat. [20]Half expecting to find a rat in my bed.

Score Number correct _____ × 5 = _____ percent	

Fragments and Run-Ons

■ Combined Mastery Test 2

The word groups below are numbered 1 through 20. In the space provided for each, write C if a word group is a complete sentence, write F if it is a fragment, and write RO if it a run-on. Then correct the errors.

1. _____

2. _____

3. _____

4. _____

5. _____

6. _____

7. _____

8. _____

9. _____

10. _____

11. _____

12. _____

13. _____

14. _____

15. _____

16. _____

17. _____

18. _____

19. _____

20. _____

[1]My sister asked my parents and me to give up television for two weeks. [2]As an experiment for her psychology class. [3]We were too embarrassed to refuse, we reluctantly agreed. [4]The project began on Monday morning. [5]To help us resist temptation. [6]My sister unplugged the living room set. [7]That evening the four of us sat around the dinner table much longer than usual, we found new things to talk about. [8]Later we played board games for several hours, we all went to bed pleased with ourselves. [9]Everything went well until Thursday evening of that first week. [10]My sister went out after dinner. [11]Explaining that she would be back about ten o'clock. [12]The rest of us then decided to turn on the television. [13]Just to watch the network news. [14]We planned to unplug the set before my sister got home. [15]And pretend nothing had happened. [16]We were settled down comfortably in our respective chairs, unfortunately, my sister walked in at that point and burst out laughing. [17]"Aha! I caught you," she cried. [18]She explained that part of the experiment was to see if we would stick to the agreement. [19]Especially during her absence. [20]She had predicted we would weaken, it turned out she was right.

| **Score** Number correct _____ × 5 = _____ percent |

Verbs

■ **Combined Mastery Test 3**

Each sentence contains a mistake involving (1) standard English or irregular verb forms, (2) subject-verb agreement, or (3) consistent verb tense. Circle the letter that identifies the mistake. Then cross out the incorrect verb and write the correct form in the space provided.

_____   1. One of my apartment neighbors always keep the radio on all night.
Mistake in: a. Subject-verb agreement   b. Verb tense

_____   2. The more the instructor explained the material and the more he wroted on the board, the more confused I got.
Mistake in: a. Irregular verb form   b. Verb tense

_____   3. I grabbed the last carton of skim milk on the supermarket shelf, but when I checks the date on it, I realized it was not fresh.
Mistake in: a. Subject-verb agreement   b. Verb tense

_____   4. This morning my parents argued loudly, but later they apologized to each other and embrace.
Mistake in: a. Subject-verb agreement   b. Verb tense

_____   5. When the bell rang, Mike takes another bite of his sandwich and then prepared for class.
Mistake in: a. Irregular verb form   b. Verb tense

_____   6. Someone called Marion at the office to tell her that her son had been bit by a stray dog.
Mistake in: a. Irregular verb form   b. Verb tense

_____   7. Because I had throwed away the sales slip, I couldn't return the microwave.
Mistake in: a. Irregular verb form   b. Verb tense

_____   8. My dog and cat usually ignores each other, but once in a while they fight.
Mistake in: a. Subject-verb agreement   b. Verb tense

_____   9. From the back of our neighborhood bakery comes some of the best smells in the world.
Mistake in: a. Subject-verb agreement   b. Verb tense

_____   10. The cost of new soles and heels are more than those old shoes are worth.
Mistake in: a. Subject-verb agreement   b. Verb tense

Score   Number correct _____ × 5 = _____ percent

Verbs

■ Combined Mastery Test 4

Each sentence contains a mistake involving (1) standard English or irregular verb forms, (2) subject-verb agreement, or (3) consistent verb tense. Circle the letter that identifies the mistake. Then cross out the incorrect verb and write the correct form in the space provided.

_____ 1. My friend's bitter words had stinged me deeply.

    Mistake in: a. Irregular verb form   b. Verb tense

_____ 2. After she poured the ammonia into the bucket, Karen reels backward because the strong fumes made her eyes tear.

    Mistake in: a. Subject-verb agreement   b. Verb tense

_____ 3. Flying around in space is various pieces of debris from old space satellites.

    Mistake in: a. Subject-verb agreement   b. Verb tense

_____ 4. Eileen watched suspiciously as a strange car drived back and forth in front of her house.

    Mistake in: a. Irregular verb form   b. Verb tense

_____ 5. Both crying and laughing helps us get rid of tension.

    Mistake in: a. Subject-verb agreement   b. Verb tense

_____ 6. All my clothes were dirty, so I stayed up late and washes a load for tomorrow.

    Mistake in: a. Subject-verb agreement   b. Verb tense

_____ 7. McDonald's has selled enough hamburgers to reach to the moon.

    Mistake in: a. Irregular verb form   b. Verb tense

_____ 8. When Chen peeled back the bedroom wallpaper, he discovered another layer of wallpaper and uses a steamer to get that layer off.

    Mistake in: a. Subject-verb agreement   b. Verb tense

_____ 9. Rosie searched for the fifty-dollar bill she had hid somewhere in her dresser.

    Mistake in: a. Irregular verb form   b. Verb tense

_____ 10. The realistic yellow tulips on the gravestone is made of a weather-resistant fabric.

    Mistake in: a. Subject-verb agreement   b. Verb tense

Score   Number correct _____ × 5 = _____ percent

Capital Letters and Punctuation

■ Combined Mastery Test 5

Each of the following sentences contains an error in capitalization or punctuation. Refer to the box below and write, in the space provided, the letter identifying the error. Then correct the error.

a. missing capital letter	c. missing quotation marks
b. missing apostrophe	d. missing comma

_____ 1. Maggie's aerobics class has been canceled this week so she's decided to go running instead.

_____ 2. "One of the striking differences between a cat and a lie, wrote Mark Twain, "is that a cat has only nine lives."

_____ 3. My uncles checks are printed to look like Monopoly money.

_____ 4. Did you know someone is turning the old school on ninth Street into a restaurant named Home Economics?

_____ 5. My parents always ask me where Im going and when I'll be home.

_____ 6. She doesn't talk about it much, but my aunt has been a member of alcoholics Anonymous for ten years.

_____ 7. The sweating straining horses neared the finish line.

_____ 8. Whenever he gave us the keys to the car, my father would say, Watch out for the other guy."

_____ 9. If you're going to stay up late be sure to turn down the heat before going to bed.

_____ 10. I decided to have a glass of apple juice rather than order a pepsi.

Score   Number correct _____ × 5 = _____ percent

Capital Letters and Punctuation

■ Combined Mastery Test 6

Each of the following sentences contains an error in capitalization or punctuation. Refer to the box below and write, in the space provided, the letter identifying the error. Then correct the error.

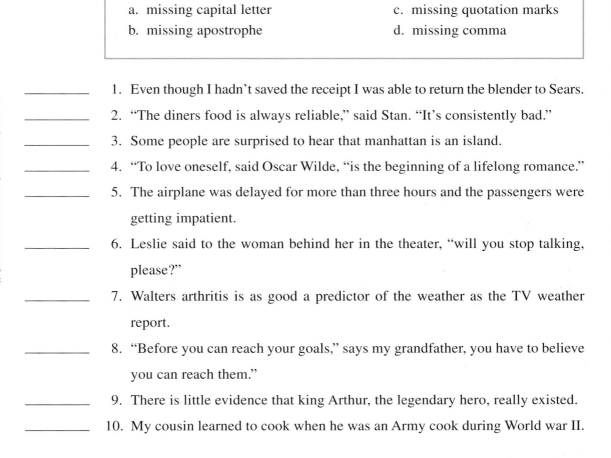

> a. missing capital letter
> b. missing apostrophe
>
> c. missing quotation marks
> d. missing comma

_____ 1. Even though I hadn't saved the receipt I was able to return the blender to Sears.

_____ 2. "The diners food is always reliable," said Stan. "It's consistently bad."

_____ 3. Some people are surprised to hear that manhattan is an island.

_____ 4. "To love oneself, said Oscar Wilde, "is the beginning of a lifelong romance."

_____ 5. The airplane was delayed for more than three hours and the passengers were getting impatient.

_____ 6. Leslie said to the woman behind her in the theater, "will you stop talking, please?"

_____ 7. Walters arthritis is as good a predictor of the weather as the TV weather report.

_____ 8. "Before you can reach your goals," says my grandfather, you have to believe you can reach them."

_____ 9. There is little evidence that king Arthur, the legendary hero, really existed.

_____ 10. My cousin learned to cook when he was an Army cook during World war II.

Score   Number correct _____ × 5 = _____ percent

Word Use

■ Combined Mastery Test 7

Each of the following sentences contains a mistake identified in the left-hand margin. Underline the mistake and then correct it in the space provided.

Slang

1. Because Nicole has a lot of pull at work, she always has first choice of vacation time.

_____

Wordiness

2. Truthfully, I've been wishing that the final could be postponed to a much later date sometime next week.

_____

Cliché

3. Kate hoped her friends would be green with envy when they saw her new boyfriend.

_____

Pretentious language

4. Harold utilizes old coffee cans to water his houseplants.

_____

Adverb error

5. The sled started slow and then picked up speed as the icy hill became steeper.

_____

Error in comparison

6. When the weather is dry, my sinus condition feels more better.

_____

Confused word

7. If you neglect your friends, their likely to become former friends.

_____

Confused word

8. She's the neighbor who's dog is courting my dog.

_____

Confused word

9. If you don't put cans, jars, and newspapers on the curb for recycling, the township won't pick up you're garbage.

_____

Confused word

10. "Its the most economical car you can buy," the announcer said.

_____

> ***Score***   Number correct _____ × 5 = _____ percent

Word Use

■ **Combined Mastery Test 8**

Each of the following sentences contains a mistake identified in the left-hand margin. Underline the mistake and then correct it in the space provided.

Slang

1. After coming in to work late all last week, Sheila was canned.

_____

Wordiness

2. At this point in time, I'm not really sure what my major will be.

_____

Cliché

3. Jan and Alan knew they could depend on their son in their hour of need.

_____

Pretentious language

4. I plan to do a lot of comparison shopping before procuring a new dryer.

_____

Adverb error

5. The children sat very quiet as their mother read the next chapter of *Charlie and the Chocolate Factory*.

_____

Error in comparison

6. The respectfuller you treat people, the more they are likely to deserve your respect.

_____

Confused word

7. The dog has lost its' flea collar.

_____

Confused word

8. "My advise to you," said my grandmother, "is to focus on your strengths, not your fears."

_____

Confused word

9. The principle advantage of the school cafeteria is that it's three blocks from a Wendy's.

_____

Confused word

10. My parents mean well, but there goals for me aren't my goals.

_____

> ***Score***   Number correct _____ × 5 = _____ percent

46 Editing Tests

The twelve editing tests in this chapter will give you practice in revising for sentence-skills mistakes. Remember that if you don't edit carefully, you run the risk of sabotaging much of the work you have put into a paper. If readers see too many surface flaws, they may assume you don't place much value on what you have to say, and they may not give your ideas a fair hearing. Revising to eliminate sentence-skills errors is a basic part of clear, effective writing.

In half of the tests, the spots where errors occur have been underlined; your job is to identify and correct each error. In the rest of the tests, you must locate as well as identify and correct the errors.

Following are hints that can help you edit the next-to-final draft of a paper for sentence-skills mistakes:

Editing Hints

1 Have at hand two essential tools: a good dictionary (see page 500) and a grammar handbook (you can use Chapter 5 and Part Five of this book).

2 Use a sheet of paper to cover your essay so that you will expose only one sentence at a time. Look for errors in grammar, spelling, and typing. It may help to read each sentence out loud. If a sentence does not read clearly and smoothly, chances are something is wrong.

3 Pay special attention to the kinds of errors you yourself tend to make. For example, if you tend to write run-ons or fragments, be especially on the lookout for those errors.

4 Proofreading symbols that may be of particular help are the following:

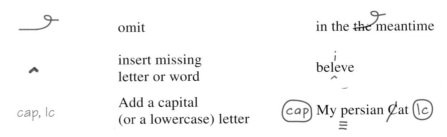

⟋	omit	in the ~~the~~ meantime
^	insert missing letter or word	bel^eve
cap, lc	Add a capital (or a lowercase) letter	(cap) My persian Cat (lc)

■ **Editing Test 1**

Identify the five mistakes in paper format in the student paper that follows. From the box below, choose the letters that describe the five mistakes and write those letters in the spaces provided.

---

a. The title should not be underlined.
b. The title should not be set off in quotation marks.
c. There should not be a period at the end of a title.
d. All the major words in a title should be capitalized.
e. The title should be a phrase, not a complete sentence.
f. The first line of a paper should stand independent of the title.
g. A line should be skipped between the title and the first line of the paper.
h. The first line of a paragraph should be indented.
i. The right-hand margin should not be crowded.
j. Hyphenation should occur only between syllables.

"my candy apple adventure"

It was the best event of my day. I loved the sweetness that filled my mouth as I bit into the sugary coating. With my second bite, I munched contentedly on the apple underneath. Its crunchy tartness was the perfect balance to the smooth sweet-ness of the outside. Then the apple had a magical effect on me. Suddenly I remembered when I was seven years old, walking through the county fairgrounds, holding my father's hand. We stopped at a refreshment stand, and he bought us each a candy apple. I had never had one before, and I asked him what it was. "This is a very special fruit," he said. "If you ever feel sad, all you have to do is eat a candy apple, and it will bring you sweetness." Now, years later, his words came back to me, and as I ate my candy apple, I felt the world turn sweet once more.

---

1. _____   2. _____   3. _____   4. _____   5. _____

■ Editing Test 2

Identify the sentence-skills mistakes at the underlined spots in the paragraph that follows. From the box below, choose the letter that describes each mistake and write it in the space provided. The same mistake may appear more than once.

a. fragment	d. apostrophe mistake
b. run-on	e. faulty parallelism
c. mistake in subject-verb agreement	

Looking Out for Yourself

It's sad but true: "If you don't look out for yourself, no one else will." For example, some people have a false idea about the power of a college <u>degree, they</u> think that once they <u>possesses</u> the degree, the world will be waiting on their doorstep. In fact, nobody is likely to be on their doorstep unless, through advance planning, they <u>has</u> prepared themselves for a career. <u>The kind in which good job opportunities exist.</u> Even after a person has landed a job, however, a healthy amount of self-interest is needed. People who hide in corners or <u>with hesitation</u> to let others know about their skills <u>doesn't</u> get promotions or raises. <u>Its</u> important to take credit for a job well done, whether the job involves writing a report, <u>organized the office filing system,</u> or calming down an angry customer. Also, people should feel free to ask the boss for a raise. <u>If they work hard and really deserve it.</u> Those who look out for themselves get the <u>rewards, people</u> who depend on others to help them along get left behind.

1. _____   2. _____   3. _____   4. _____   5. _____

6. _____   7. _____   8. _____   9. _____   10. _____

■ Editing Test 3

Identify the sentence-skills mistakes at the underlined spots in the paragraph that follows. From the box below, choose the letter that describes each mistake and write it in the space provided. The same mistake may appear more than once.

a. fragment	e. missing commas around an interrupter
b. run-on	f. mistake with quotation marks
c. mistake in verb tense	g. apostrophe mistake
d. mistake in irregular verb	

Deceptive Appearances

Appearances can be deceptive. While looking through a library window yesterday, I saw a neatly groomed woman walk by. Her clothes were skillfully <u>tailored her</u> makeup was
₁ perfect. <u>Then thinking no one was looking she</u> crumpled a piece of paper in her hand.
₂ <u>And tossed it into a nearby hedge.</u> Suddenly she no longer <u>looks</u> attractive to me. On
₃ ₄ another occasion, I started talking to a person in my psychology class named Eric. Eric seemed to be a great person. He always got the class laughing with his <u>jokes, on</u> the days
₅ when Eric was absent, I think even the professor missed his lively personality. Eric asked me <u>"if I wanted to get a Coke in the cafeteria,"</u> and I felt happy he had <u>chose</u> me to be
₆ ₇ a friend. <u>While we were sitting in the cafeteria.</u> Eric took out an envelope with several
₈ kinds of pills inside. "Want one?" he asked. "They're uppers." I didn't want <u>one, I</u> felt
₉ disappointed. <u>Erics</u> terrific personality was the product of the pills he took.
₁₀

1. _____   2. _____   3. _____   4. _____   5. _____

6. _____   7. _____   8. _____   9. _____   10. _____

■ Editing Test 4

Identify the sentence-skills mistakes at the underlined spots in the paragraph that follows. From the box below, choose the letter that describes each mistake and write it in the space provided. The same mistake may appear more than once.

a. fragment	e. apostrophe mistake
b. run-on	f. dangling modifier
c. irregular verb mistake	g. missing quotation marks
d. missing comma after introductory words	

A Horrifying Moment

The most horrifying moment of my life occurred in the dark hallway of my building. <u>Which led to my apartment.</u>¹ Though the hallway light was <u>out I</u>² managed to find my apartment door. However, I could not find the keyhole with my door key. I then pulled a book of matches from my pocket. <u>Trying to strike a match,</u>³ the entire book of matches <u>bursted</u>⁴ into flames. I flicked the matches away but not before my coat sleeve <u>catched</u>⁵ fire. Within seconds, my arm was like a torch. <u>Struggling to unsnap the buttons of my coat,</u>⁶ flames began to sear my skin. I was quickly going into shock. <u>And began screaming in pain.</u>⁷ A <u>neighbors</u>⁸ door opened and a voice cried out, <u>My God!</u>⁹ I was pulled through an apartment and put under a bathroom shower, which extinguished the flames. I suffered third-degree burns on my <u>arm, I</u>¹⁰ felt lucky to escape with my life.

1. _____   2. _____   3. _____   4. _____   5. _____

6. _____   7. _____   8. _____   9. _____   10. _____

■ Editing Test 5

Identify the sentence-skills mistakes at the underlined spots in the paragraph that follows. From the box below, choose the letter that describes each mistake and write it in the space provided. The same mistake may appear more than once.

a. fragment	e. faulty parallelism
b. run-on	f. apostrophe mistake
c. missing capital letter	g. missing quotation mark
d. mistake in subject-verb agreement	h. missing comma after introductory words

Why I Didn't Go to Church

In my boyhood years, I almost never attended church. There was an unwritten code that the guys on the corner was not to be seen in churches'. Although there was many days
<u>1</u>   <u>2</u>   <u>3</u>
when I wanted to attend a church, I felt I had no choice but to stay away. If the guys had heard I had gone to church, they would have said things like, "hey, angel, when are you
<u>4</u>
going to fly? With my group of friends, its amazing that I developed any religious feeling
<u>5</u>   <u>6</u>
at all. Another reason for not going to church was my father. When he was around the house he told my mother, "Mike's not going to church. No boy of mine is a sissy." My
<u>7</u>
mother and sister went to church, I sat with my father and read the Sunday paper or
<u>8</u>
watching television. I did not start going to church until years later. When I no longer hung
<u>9</u>   <u>10</u>
around with the guys on the corner or let my father have power over me.

1. _____   2. _____   3. _____   4. _____   5. _____

6. _____   7. _____   8. _____   9. _____   10. _____

■ Editing Test 6

Identify the sentence-skills mistakes at the underlined spots in the paragraph that follows. From the box below, choose the letter that describes each mistake and write it in the space provided. The same mistake may appear more than once.

a. fragment	f. missing comma between two complete thoughts
b. run-on	
c. faulty parallelism	g. missing comma after introductory words
d. missing apostrophe	
e. missing quotation mark	h. misspelled word

Anxiety and the Telephone

Not many of us would want to do without our <u>telephone but</u> there are times when the

¹

phone is a source of anxiety. For example, you might be walking up to your front door.

<u>When you hear the phone ring.</u> You struggle to find your key, to unlock the door, and

²

<u>getting</u> to the phone quickly. You know the phone will stop ringing the instant you pick up

³

<u>the receiver, then</u> you wonder if you missed the call that would have made you a <u>millionare</u>

⁴   ⁵

or introduced you to the love of your life. Another time, you may have called in sick to

work with a phony excuse. All day long, <u>youre</u> afraid to leave the house in case the boss

⁶

<u>calls back. And asks himself why you were feeling well enough to go out.</u> In addition, you

⁷

worry that you might unthinkingly pick up the phone and say in a cheerful voice, <u>"Hello,</u>

⁸

completely <u>forgeting</u> to use your fake cough. In cases like <u>these having</u> a telephone is more

⁹   ¹⁰

of a curse than a blessing.

1. _____   2. _____   3. _____   4. _____   5. _____

6. _____   7. _____   8. _____   9. _____   10. _____

■ Editing Test 7

See if you can locate and correct the ten sentence-skills mistakes in the following passage. The mistakes are listed in the box below. As you locate each mistake, write the number of the word group containing that mistake. Use the spaces provided. Then (on separate paper) correct the mistakes.

5 fragments	_____	_____	_____	_____	_____
5 run-ons	_____	_____	_____	_____	_____

Family Stories

[1]When I was little, my parents invented some strange stories to explain everyday events to me, my father, for example, told me that trolls lived in our house. [2]When objects such as scissors or pens were missing. [3]My father would look at me and say, "The trolls took them." [4]For years, I kept a flashlight next to my bed. [5]Hoping to catch the trolls in the act as they carried away our possessions. [6]Another story I still remember is my mother's explanation of pussy willows. [7]After the fuzzy gray buds emerged in our backyard one spring. [8]I asked Mom what they were. [9]Pussy willows, she explained, were cats who had already lived nine lives, in this tenth life, only the tips of the cats' tails were visible to people. [10]All the tails looked alike. [11]So that none of the cats would be jealous of the others. [12]It was also my mother who created the legend of the birthday fairy, this fairy always knew which presents I wanted. [13]Because my mother called up on a special invisible telephone. [14]Children couldn't see these phones, every parent had a direct line to the fairy. [15]My parents' stories left a great impression on me, I still feel a surge of pleasure when I think of them.

■ Editing Test 8

See if you can locate and correct the ten sentence-skills mistakes in the following passage. The mistakes are listed in the box below. As you locate each mistake, write the number of the word group containing that mistake. Use the spaces provided. Then (on separate paper) correct the mistakes.

1 fragment _____	2 missing commas between items
1 run-on _____	in a series _____ _____
1 nonstandard verb _____	2 apostrophe mistakes _____ _____
1 missing comma around	1 capital letter mistake _____
an interrupter _____	1 homonym mistake _____

Search for the Perfect Pajama Bottoms

¹I met a strange character in my job as an Orderly at a state mental hospital. ²Jacks illness was such that it led to strange behavior. ³Jack, a middle-aged man spent most of the day obsessed with pajama bottoms. ⁴He seemed to think that someone might have a better pair of pajama bottoms than his. ⁵He would sneak into other patients rooms. ⁶And steal there pajama bottoms. ⁷Other times, he would undress a distracted patient to try on his pajamas. ⁸He would try them on find they were not perfect and discard them. ⁹Some days, I'd come upon three or four patients with no pajama bottoms on, I'd know Jack was on the prowl again. ¹⁰He were tireless in his search for the perfect pair of pajama bottoms. ¹¹It was clearly a search that would never end in success.

■ Editing Test 9

See if you can locate and correct the ten sentence-skills mistakes in the following passages. The mistakes are listed in the box below. As you locate each mistake, write the number of the word group containing that mistake. Use the spaces provided. Then (on separate paper) correct the mistakes.

2 fragments _____ _____	1 missing comma after introductory
1 run-on _____	words _____
1 irregular verb mistake _____	2 apostrophe mistakes _____ _____
1 missing comma between	1 faulty parallelism _____
items in a series _____	1 missing quotation mark _____

Fred's Funeral

¹Sometimes when Fred feels undervalued and depression, he likes to imagine his own funeral. ²He pictures all the people who will be there. ³He hears their hushed words sees their tears, and feels their grief. ⁴He glows with warm sadness as the minister begins a eulogy by saying, Fred Grencher was no ordinary man . . . " ⁵As the minister talks on Freds eyes grow moist. ⁶He laments his own passing and feels altogether appreciated and wonderful.

Feeding Time

⁷Recently I was at the cat house in the zoo. ⁸Right before feeding time. ⁹The tigers and lions were lying about on benches and little stands. ¹⁰Basking in the late-afternoon sun. ¹¹They seemed tame and harmless. ¹²But when the meat was brung in, a remarkable change occurred. ¹³All the cats got up and moved toward the food. ¹⁴I was suddenly aware of the rippling muscles' of their bodies and their large claws and teeth. ¹⁵They seemed three times bigger, I could feel their power.

■ Editing Test 10

See if you can locate and correct the ten sentence-skills mistakes in the following passage. The mistakes are listed in the box below. As you locate each mistake, write the number of the word group containing that mistake. Use the spaces provided. Then (on separate paper) correct the mistakes.

---

1 run-on _____   2 missing commas around

1 mistake in subject-verb   an interrupter _____ _____

   agreement _____   1 missing comma between items

1 missing comma after   in a series _____

   introductory words _____   2 apostrophe mistakes _____ _____

            2 missing quotation marks _____ _____

Walking Billboards

¹Many Americans have turned into driving, walking billboards. ²As much as we all claim to hate commercials on television we dont seem to have any qualms about turning ourselves into commercials. ³Our car bumpers for example advertise lake resorts underground caverns, and amusement parks. ⁴Also, we wear clothes marked with other peoples initials and slogans. ⁵Our fascination with the names of designers show up on the backs of our sneakers, the breast pockets of our shirts, and the right rear pockets of our blue jeans. ⁶And we wear T-shirts filled with all kinds of advertising messages. ⁷For instance, people are willing to wear shirts that read, "Dillon Construction," "Nike," or even I Got Crabs at Ed's Seafood Palace. ⁸In conclusion, we say we hate commercials, we actually pay people for the right to advertise their products.

■ Editing Test 11

See if you can locate and correct the ten sentence-skills mistakes in the following passage. The mistakes are listed in the box below. As you locate each mistake, write the number of the word group containing that mistake. Use the spaces provided. Then (on separate paper) correct the mistakes.

3 fragments _____	1 mistake in pronoun point
_____ _____	of view _____
2 run-ons _____ _____	1 dangling modifier _____
1 irregular verb mistake _____	1 missing comma between two
1 faulty parallelism _____	complete thoughts _____

Too Many Cooks

¹The problem in my college dining hall was the succession of incompetent cooks who were put in charge. ²During the time I worked there, I watched several cooks come and go. ³The first of these was Irving. ⁴He was skinny and greasy like the undercooked bacon he served for breakfast. ⁵Irving drank, by late afternoon he begun to sway as he cooked. ⁶Once, he looked at the brightly colored photograph on the orange juice machine. ⁷And asked why the TV was on. ⁸Having fired Irving, Lonnie was hired. ⁹Lonnie had a soft, round face that resembled the Pillsbury Doughboy's but he had the size and temperament of a large bear. ¹⁰He'd wave one paw and growl if you entered the freezers without his permission. ¹¹He also had poor eyesight. ¹²This problem caused him to substitute flour for sugar and using pork for beef on a regular basis. ¹³After Lonnie was fired, Enzo arrived. ¹⁴Because he had come from Italy only a year or two previously. ¹⁵He spoke little English. ¹⁶In addition, Enzo had trouble with seasoning and spices. ¹⁷His vegetables were too salty, giant bay leaves turned up in everything. ¹⁸Including the scrambled eggs. ¹⁹The cooks I worked for in the college dining hall would have made Julia Child go into shock.

■ Editing Test 12

See if you can locate and correct the ten sentence-skills mistakes in the following passage. The mistakes are listed in the box below. As you locate each mistake, write the number of the word group containing that mistake. Use the spaces provided. Then (on separate paper) correct the mistakes.

2 fragments _____ _____	1 missing comma between two
2 run-ons _____ _____	complete thoughts _____
1 mistake in pronoun	1 missing quotation mark _____
point of view _____	1 missing comma between items in
1 apostrophe mistake _____	a series _____
	1 misspelled word _____

My Ideal Date

¹Here are the ingredients for my ideal date, first of all, I would want to look as stunning as possible. ²I would be dressed in a black velvet jumpsuit. ³That would fit me like a layer of paint. ⁴My accessories would include a pair of red satin spike heels a diamond hair clip, and a full-length black mink coat. ⁵My boyfriend, Tony, would wear a sharply tailored black tuxedo, a white silk shirt, and a red bow tie. ⁶The tux would emphasize Tony's broad shoulders and narrow waist, and you would see his chest muscles under the smooth shirt fabric. ⁷Tony would pull up to my house in a long, shiney limousine, then the driver would take us to the most exclusive and glittery nightclub in Manhattan. ⁸All eyes would be on us as we entered and photographers would rush up to take our picture for *People* magazine. ⁹As we danced on the lighted floor of the club, everyone would step aside to watch us perform our moves. ¹⁰After several bottles of champagne, Tony and I would head for the top floor of the World Trade Center. ¹¹As we gazed out over the light's of the city, Tony would hand me a small velvet box containing a fifty-carat ruby engagement ring. ¹²And ask me to marry him. ¹³I would thank Tony for a lovely evening and tell him gently, "Tony, I don't plan to marry until I'm thirty.

Sentence-Skills Achievement Test

Part 1

This test will help you measure your improvement in important sentence skills. Certain parts of the following word groups are underlined. Write X in the answer space if you think a mistake appears at the underlined part. Write C in the answer space if you think the underlined part is correct.

The headings ("Fragments," Run-Ons," and so on) will give you clues to the mistakes to look for.

Fragments

_____ 1. After a careless driver hit my motorcycle, I decided to buy a car. At least I would have more protection against other careless drivers.

_____ 2. I was never a good student in high school. Because I spent all my time socializing with my group of friends. Good grades were not something that my group really valued.

_____ 3. The elderly couple in the supermarket were not a pleasant sight. Arguing with each other. People pretended not to notice them.

_____ 4. Using a magnifying glass, the little girls burned holes in the dry leaf. They then set some tissue paper on fire.

_____ 5. My brother and I seldom have fights about what to watch on television. Except with baseball games. I get bored watching this sport.

_____ 6. My roommate and I ate, talked, danced, and sang at a fish-fry party the other night. Also, we played cards until 3 A.M. As a result, we both slept until noon the next day.

Run-Ons

_____ 7. She decided to quit her high-pressured job, she didn't want to develop heart trouble.

_____ 8. His car's wheels were not balanced properly, for the car began to shake when he drove over forty miles an hour.

_____ 9. I got through the interview without breaking out in a sweat <u>mustache, I</u> also managed to keep my voice under control.

_____ 10. The craze for convenience in our country has gone too <u>far. There</u> are drive-in banks, restaurants, and even churches.

_____ 11. My most valued possession is my stoneware <u>cooker, I</u> can make entire meals in it at a low cost.

_____ 12. The shopping carts outside the supermarket seemed welded <u>together, Rita</u> could not separate one from another.

Standard English Verbs

_____ 13. I am going to borrow my father's car if he <u>agree</u>.

_____ 14. For recreation he sets up hundreds of dominoes, and then he <u>knocks</u> them over.

_____ 15. He <u>stopped</u> taking a nap after supper because he then had trouble sleeping at night.

_____ 16. There was no bread for sandwiches, so he <u>decided</u> to drive to the store.

Irregular Verbs

_____ 17. I learned that Dennis had <u>began</u> to see someone else while he was still going out with me.

_____ 18. That woman has never <u>ran</u> for political office before.

_____ 19. I <u>knowed</u> the answer to the question, but I was too nervous to think of it when the instructor called on me.

_____ 20. They had <u>ate</u> the gallon of natural vanilla ice cream in just one night.

Subject-Verb Agreement

_____ 21. Her watchband <u>have</u> to be fixed.

_____ 22. There <u>is</u> two minutes left in the football game.

_____ 23. He believes films that feature violence <u>is</u> a disgrace to our society.

_____ 24. The plastic slipcovers that she bought <u>have</u> begun to crack.

Consistent Verb Tense

_____ 25. Myra wanted to watch the late movie, but she was so tired she <u>falls</u> asleep before it started.

_____ 26. When the mailman arrived, I <u>hoped</u> the latest issue of *People* magazine would be in his bag.

_____ 27. Juan ran down the hall without looking and <u>trips</u> over the toy truck lying on the floor.

_____ 28. Debbie enjoys riding her bike in the newly built park, which <u>features</u> a special path for bikers and runners.

Pronoun Agreement, Reference, and Point of View

_____ 29. At the Saturday afternoon movie we went to, children were making so much noise that <u>you</u> could not relax.

_____ 30. We did not return to the amusement park, for <u>we</u> had to pay too much for the rides and meals.

_____ 31. Drivers should check the oil level in <u>their</u> cars every three months.

_____ 32. At the hospital, I saw mothers with tears in their eyes wandering down the hall, hoping that <u>her</u> child's operation was a success.

_____ 33. Sharon's mother was overjoyed when <u>Sharon</u> became pregnant.

_____ 34. You must observe all the rules of the game, even if you do not always agree with <u>it</u>.

Pronoun Types

_____ 35. Nancy and <u>her</u> often go to singles bars.

_____ 36. No one in the class is better at computers than <u>he</u>.

Adjectives and Adverbs

_____ 37. The little girl spoke so <u>quiet</u> I could hardly hear her.

_____ 38. Lola looks <u>more better</u> than Gina in a leather coat.

Misplaced Modifiers

_____ 39. I saw sharks <u>scuba-diving</u>.

_____ 40. <u>With a mile-wide grin,</u> Betty turned in her winning raffle ticket.

_____ 41. I bought a beautiful blouse in a local store <u>with long sleeves and French cuffs</u>.

_____ 42. I first spotted the turtle <u>playing tag on the back lawn</u>.

Dangling Modifiers

_____ 43. <u>When seven years old,</u> Jeff's father taught him to play ball.

_____ 44. <u>Running across the field,</u> I caught the Frisbee.

_____ 45. <u>Turning on the ignition,</u> the car backfired.

_____ 46. <u>Looking at my watch,</u> a taxi nearly ran me over.

Faulty Parallelism

_____ 47. Much of my boyhood was devoted to getting into rock fights, crossing railway trestles, and <u>the hunt for rats in drainage tunnels.</u>

_____ 48. I put my books in my locker, changed into my gym clothes, and <u>hurried to the playing field.</u>

_____ 49. Ruth begins every day with warm-up exercises, a half-hour run, and <u>taking a hot shower.</u>

_____ 50. In the evening I plan to write a paper, <u>to watch a movie,</u> and to read two chapters in my biology text.

Capital Letters

_____ 51. When the can of <u>drano</u> didn't unclog the sink, Hal called a plumber.

_____ 52. I asked Cindy, "<u>what</u> time will you be leaving?"

_____ 53. I have to get an allergy shot once a <u>Week.</u>

_____ 54. Mother ordered a raincoat from the catalog on <u>Monday,</u> and it arrived four days later.

Apostrophe

_____ 55. I asked the clerk if the store had Stevie <u>Wonders</u> latest CD.

_____ 56. <u>He's</u> failing the course because he doesn't have any confidence in his ability to do the work.

_____ 57. Clyde was incensed at the dentist who charged him fifty dollars to fix his <u>son's</u> tooth.

_____ 58. I <u>cant</u> believe that she's not coming to the dance.

Quotation Marks

_____ 59. <u>"Don't forget to water the grass, my sister said.</u>

_____ 60. Martha said to Fred at bedtime, "Why is it that men's pajamas always have such baggy <u>bottoms?" "You</u> look like a circus clown in that flannel outfit."

_____ 61. The red sign on the door <u>read, "Warning</u>—open only in case of an emergency."

_____ 62. "I can't stand that commercial," said Sue. <u>"Do you mind if I turn off the television?"</u>

Comma

_____ 63. Hard-luck Sam needs a <u>loan, a good-paying job, and</u> someone to show an interest in him.

_____ 64. Even though I was <u>tired I</u> agreed to go shopping with my parents.

_____ 65. <u>Power, not love or money, is</u> what most politicians want.

_____ 66. The heel on one of Lola's shoes came <u>off, so</u> she spent the day walking barefoot.

_____ 67. "Thank goodness I'm almost <u>done</u>" I said aloud with every stroke of the broom.

_____ 68. I hated to ask <u>Anita who is a very stingy person to</u> lend me the money.

Commonly Confused Words

_____ 69. To succeed in the job, you must learn how to control <u>your</u> temper.

_____ 70. Fortunately, I was not driving very fast when my car lost <u>it's</u> brakes.

_____ 71. Put your packages on the table over <u>their.</u>

_____ 72. There are <u>too</u> many steps in the math formula for me to understand it.

_____ 73. The counseling center can <u>advise</u> you on how to prepare for an interview.

_____ 74. <u>Who's</u> white Eldorado is that in front of the house?

Effective Word Use

_____ 75. The teacher called to discuss Ron's <u>social maladjustment difficulties.</u>

_____ 76. I thought the course would be a <u>piece of cake,</u> but a ten-page paper was required.

_____ 77. When my last class ended, I felt <u>as free as a bird.</u>

_____ 78. Spike gave away his television <u>owing to the fact that</u> it distracted him from studying.

Part 2 (Optional)

Do Part 2 at your instructor's request. This second part of the test will provide more detailed information about your improvement in sentence skills. On separate paper, number and correct all the items you have marked with an X. For example, suppose you had marked the word groups below with an X. (Note that these examples are not taken from the test.)

4. <u>If football games disappeared entirely from television.</u> I would not even miss them. Other people in my family would perish.

7. The kitten suddenly saw her reflection in the <u>mirror, she</u> jumped back in surprise.

15. The tree in my <u>cousins</u> front yard always sheds its leaves two weeks before others on the street.

29. When we go out to a <u>restaurant we</u> always order something we would not cook for ourselves.

Here is how you should write your corrections on a separate sheet of paper.

4. television, I
7. mirror, and
15. cousin's
29. restaurant, we

There are over forty corrections to make in all.

Part Six

Seventeen
Reading Selections

Preview

This book assumes that writing and reading are closely connected skills—so that practicing one helps the other, and neglecting one hurts the other. Part Six will enable you to work on becoming a better reader as well as a stronger writer. Following an introductory section that offers a series of tips on effective reading, there are seventeen reading selections. Each selection begins with an overview that supplies background information about the piece. After the selection are ten questions to give you practice in key reading comprehension skills. A set of discussion questions is also provided, both to deepen your understanding of the selection and to point out basic writing techniques used in the essay. Then come several writing assignments, along with guidelines to help you think about the assignments and get started working on them.

Introduction
to the
Readings

The reading selections in Part Six will help you find topics for writing. Some of the selections provide helpful practical information. For example, you'll learn how to discuss problems openly with others and how to avoid being manipulated by clever ads. Other selections deal with thought-provoking aspects of contemporary life. One article, for instance, argues that friendship may be the most important ingredient for health in a stressful world; another dramatizes in a vivid and painful way the tragedy that can result when teenagers drink and drive. Still other selections are devoted to a celebration of human goals and values; one essay, for example, reminds us of the power that praise and appreciation can have in our daily lives. The varied subjects should inspire lively class discussions as well as serious individual thought. The selections should also provide a continuing source of high-interest material for a wide range of writing assignments.

The selections serve another purpose as well. They will help develop reading skills with direct benefits to you as a writer. First, through close reading, you will learn how to recognize the main idea or point of a selection and how to identify and evaluate the supporting material that develops the main idea. In your writing, you will aim to achieve the same essential structure: an overall point followed by detailed and valid support for that point. Second, close reading will help you explore a selection and its possibilities thoroughly. The more you understand about what is said in a piece, the more ideas and feelings you may have about writing on an assigned topic or a related topic of your own. A third benefit of close reading is becoming more aware of authors' stylistic devices—for example, their introductions and conclusions, their ways of presenting and developing a point, their use of transitions, their choice of language to achieve a particular tone. Recognizing these devices in other people's writing will help you enlarge your own range of writing techniques.

The Format of Each Selection

Each selection begins with a short overview that gives helpful background information. The selection is then followed by two sets of questions.

- First, there are ten reading comprehension questions to help you measure your understanding of the material. These questions involve several important reading skills: understanding vocabulary in context, recognizing a subject or topic, determining the thesis or main idea, identifying key supporting points, and making inferences. Answering the questions will enable you and your instructor to check quickly your basic understanding of a selection. More significantly, as you move from one selection to the next, you will sharpen your reading skills as well as strengthen your thinking skills—two key factors in making you a better writer.
- Following the comprehension questions are several discussion questions. In addition to dealing with content, these questions focus on structure, style, and tone.

Finally, several writing assignments accompany each selection. Many of the assignments provide guidelines on how to proceed, including suggestions for prewriting and appropriate methods of development. When writing your responses to the readings, you will have opportunities to apply all the methods of development presented in Part Two of this book.

How to Read Well: Four General Steps

Skillful reading is an important part of becoming a skillful writer. Following are four steps that will make you a better reader—both of the selections here and in your reading at large.

1 Concentrate as You Read

To improve your concentration, follow these tips. First, read in a place where you can be quiet and alone. Don't choose a spot where a TV or stereo is on or where friends or family are talking nearby. Next, sit in an upright position when you read. If your body is in a completely relaxed position, sprawled across a bed or nestled in an easy chair, your mind is also going to be completely relaxed. The light muscular tension that comes from sitting in an upright chair promotes concentration and keeps your mind ready to work. Finally, consider using your index finger (or a pen) as a pacer while you read. Lightly underline each line of print with your index finger as you read down a page. Hold your hand slightly above the page and move your finger at a speed that is a little too fast for comfort. This pacing with your index finger, like sitting upright on a chair, creates a slight physical tension that will keep your body and mind focused and alert.

2 Skim Material before You Read It

In skimming, you spend about two minutes rapidly surveying a selection, looking for important points and skipping secondary material. Follow this sequence when skimming:

- Begin by reading the overview that precedes the selection.
- Then study the title of the selection for a few moments. A good title is the shortest possible summary of a selection; it often tells you in several words what a selection is about. For example, the title "People Need People" suggests that you're going to read about how people depend on each other to deal with their lives.
- Next, form a basic question (or questions) out of the title. For instance, for the selection titled "People Need People," you might ask, "Why do people need people?" or "What can people do to make life easier for others?" Forming questions out of the title is often a key to locating a writer's main idea—your next concern in skimming.
- Read the first two or three paragraphs and the last two or three paragraphs in the selection. Very often a writer's main idea, *if* it is directly stated, will appear in one of these paragraphs and will relate to the title. For instance, in "People Need People," the author states in the third paragraph that "a society that fosters connectedness to others—such as traditional Japanese society—may be healthier, in a real sense, than a culture as individualistic as our own."
- Finally, look quickly at the rest of the selection for other clues to important points. Are there any subheads you can relate in some way to the title? Are there any words the author has decided to emphasize by setting them off in *italic* or **boldface** type? Are there any major lists of items signaled by words such as *first, second, also, another,* and so on?

3 Read the Selection Straight Through with a Pen Nearby

Don't slow down or turn back; just aim to understand as much as you can the first time through. Place a check or star beside answers to basic questions you formed from the title, and beside other ideas that seem important. Number lists of important points 1, 2, 3. . . . Circle words you don't understand. Put question marks in the margin next to passages that are unclear and that you will want to reread.

4 Work with the Material

Go back and reread passages that were not clear the first time through. Look up words that block your understanding of ideas and write their meanings in the margin. Also, reread carefully the areas you identified as most important; doing so will enlarge your understanding of the material. Now that you have a sense of the whole, prepare a short outline of the selection by answering the following questions on a sheet of paper:

- What is the main idea?
- What key points support the main idea?
- What seem to be other important points in the selection?

By working with the material in this way, you will significantly increase your understanding of a selection. Effective reading, just like effective writing, does not happen all at once. Rather, it is a process. Often you begin with a general impression of what something means, and then, by working at it, you move to a deeper level of understanding of the material.

How to Answer the Comprehension Questions: Specific Hints

Several important reading skills are involved in the ten reading comprehension questions that follow each selection. The skills are:

- Understanding vocabulary in context
- Summarizing the selection by providing a title for it
- Determining the main idea
- Recognizing key supporting details
- Making inferences

The following hints will help you apply each of these reading skills:

- ***Vocabulary in context.*** To decide on the meaning of an unfamiliar word, consider its context. Ask yourself, "Are there any clues in the sentence that suggest what this word means?"
- ***Subject or title.*** Remember that the title should accurately describe the *entire* selection. It should be neither too broad nor too narrow for the material in the

selection. It should answer the question "What is this about?" as specifically as possible. Note that you may at times find it easier to do the "title" question *after* the "main idea" question.

- **Main idea.** Choose the statement that you think best expresses the main idea or thesis of the entire selection. Remember that the title will often help you focus on the main idea. Then ask yourself, "Does most of the material in the selection support this statement?" If you can answer *Yes* to this question, you have found the thesis.

- **Key details.** If you were asked to give a two-minute summary of a selection, the major details are the ones you would include in that summary. To determine the key details, ask yourself, "What are the major supporting points for the thesis?"

- **Inferences.** Answer these questions by drawing on the evidence presented in the selection and on your own common sense. Ask yourself, "What reasonable judgments can I make on the basis of the information in the selection?"

On page 733 is a chart on which you can keep track of your performance as you answer the ten questions for each selection. The chart will help you identify reading skills you may need to strengthen.

Goals and Values

All the Good Things

Sister Helen Mrosla

Sometimes the smallest things we do have the biggest impact. A teacher's impulsive idea, designed to brighten a dull Friday-afternoon class, affected her students more than she ever dreamed. Sister Helen Mrosla's moment of classroom inspiration took on a life of its own, returning to visit her at a most unexpected time. Her account of the experience reminds us of the human heart's endless hunger for recognition and appreciation.

He was in the first third-grade class I taught at Saint Mary's School in Morris, Minnesota. All thirty-four of my students were dear to me, but Mark Eklund was one in a million. He was very neat in appearance but had that happy-to-be-alive attitude that made even his occasional mischievousness delightful. 1

Mark talked incessantly. I had to remind him again and again that talking without permission was not acceptable. What impressed me so much, though, was his sincere response every time I had to correct him for misbehaving—"Thank you for correcting me, Sister!" I didn't know what to make of it at first, but before long I became accustomed to hearing it many times a day. 2

One morning my patience was growing thin when Mark talked once too often, and then I made a novice teacher's mistake. I looked at him and said, "If you say one more word, I am going to tape your mouth shut!" 3

It wasn't ten seconds later when Chuck blurted out, "Mark is talking again." I hadn't asked any of the students to help me watch Mark, but since I had stated the punishment in front of the class, I had to act on it. 4

I remember the scene as if it had occurred this morning. I walked to my desk, very deliberately opened my drawer, and took out a roll of masking tape. Without saying a word, I proceeded to Mark's desk, tore off two pieces of tape and made a big X with them over his mouth. I then returned to the front of the room. As I glanced at Mark to see how he was doing, he winked at me. 5

That did it! I started laughing. The class cheered as I walked back to Mark's desk, removed the tape, and shrugged my shoulders. His first words were, "Thank you for correcting me, Sister." 6

At the end of the year I was asked to teach junior-high math. The years flew by, and before I knew it Mark was in my classroom again. He was more handsome than ever and just as polite. Since he had to listen carefully to my instruction in the "new math," he did not talk as much in ninth grade as he had talked in the third. 7

One Friday, things just didn't feel right. We had worked hard on a new concept all week, and I sensed that the students were frowning, frustrated with themselves—and edgy with one another. I had to stop this crankiness before it got out of hand. So I asked them to list the names of the other students in the room on two sheets of paper, leaving a space after each name. Then I told them to think of the nicest thing they could say about each of their classmates and write it down. **8**

It took the remainder of the class period to finish the assignment, and as the students left the room, each one handed me the papers. Charlie smiled. Mark said, "Thank you for teaching me, Sister. Have a good weekend." **9**

That Saturday, I wrote down the name of each student on a separate sheet of paper, and I listed what everyone else had said about that individual. **10**

On Monday I gave each student his or her list. Before long, the entire class was smiling. "Really?" I heard whispered. "I never knew that meant anything to anyone!" "I didn't know others liked me so much!" **11**

No one ever mentioned those papers in class again. I never knew if the students discussed them after class or with their parents, but it didn't matter. The exercise had accomplished its purpose. The students were happy with themselves and one another again. **12**

That group of students moved on. Several years later, after I returned from a vacation, my parents met me at the airport. As we were driving home, Mother asked me the usual questions about the trip—the weather, my experiences in general. There was a slight lull in the conversation. Mother gave Dad a sideways glance and simply said, "Dad?" My father cleared his throat as he usually did before something important. "The Eklunds called last night," he began. "Really?" I said. "I haven't heard from them in years. I wonder how Mark is." **13**

Dad responded quietly. "Mark was killed in Vietnam," he said. "The funeral is tomorrow, and his parents would like it if you could attend." To this day I can still point to the exact spot on I-494 where Dad told me about Mark. **14**

I had never seen a serviceman in a military coffin before. Mark looked so handsome, so mature. All I could think at that moment was, Mark, I would give all the masking tape in the world if only you would talk to me. **15**

The church was packed with Mark's friends. Chuck's sister sang "The Battle Hymn of the Republic." Why did it have to rain on the day of the funeral? It was difficult enough at the graveside. The pastor said the usual prayers, and the bugler played taps. One by one those who loved Mark took a last walk by the coffin and sprinkled it with holy water. **16**

I was the last one to bless the coffin. As I stood there, one of the soldiers who had acted as pallbearer came up to me. "Were you Mark's math teacher?" he asked. I nodded as I continued to stare at the coffin. "Mark talked about you a lot," he said. **17**

After the funeral, most of Mark's former classmates headed to Chuck's farmhouse for lunch. Mark's mother and father were there, obviously waiting for me. "We want to show you something," his father said, taking a wallet out of his pocket. "They found this on Mark when he was killed. We thought you might recognize it." **18**

Opening the billfold, he carefully removed two worn pieces of notebook paper that had obviously been taped, folded and refolded many times. I knew without looking that the papers were the ones on which I had listed all the good **19** things each of Mark's classmates had said about him. "Thank you so much for doing that," Mark's mother said. "As you can see, Mark treasured it."

Mark's classmates started to gather around us. Charlie smiled rather sheepishly   20 and said, "I still have my list. It's in the top drawer of my desk at home." Chuck's wife said, "Chuck asked me to put his list in our wedding album." "I have mine too," Marilyn said. "It's in my diary." Then Vicki, another classmate, reached into her pocketbook, took out her wallet, and showed her worn and frazzled list to the group. "I carry this with me at all times," Vicki said without batting an eyelash. "I think we all saved our lists."

That's when I finally sat down and cried. I cried for Mark and for all his friends   21 who would never see him again.

■ Reading Comprehension Questions

1. The word *incessantly* in "Mark talked incessantly. I had to remind him again and again that talking without permission was not acceptable" (paragraph 2) means

   a. slowly.

   b. quietly.

   c. constantly.

   d. pleasantly.

2. The word *edgy* in "We had worked hard on a new concept all week, and I sensed that the students were frowning, frustrated with themselves—and edgy with one another. I had to stop this crankiness before it got out of hand" (paragraph 8) means

   a. funny.

   b. calm.

   c. easily annoyed.

   d. dangerous.

3. Which of the following would be the best alternative title for this selection?

   a. Talkative Mark

   b. My Life as a Teacher

   c. More Important Than I Knew

   d. A Tragic Death

4. Which sentence best expresses the main idea of the selection?

   a. Although Sister Helen sometimes scolded Mark Eklund, he appreciated her devotion to teaching.

   b. When a former student of hers died, Sister Helen discovered how important one of her assignments had been to him and his classmates.

    c.   When her students were cranky one day, Sister Helen had them write down something nice about each of their classmates.

    d.   A pupil whom Sister Helen was especially fond of was tragically killed while serving in Vietnam.

5. Upon reading their lists for the first time, Sister Helen's students

    a.   were silent and embarrassed.

    b.   were disappointed.

    c.   pretended to think the lists were stupid, although they really liked them.

    d.   smiled and seemed pleased.

6. In the days after the assignment to write down something nice about one another,

    a.   students didn't mention the assignment again.

    b.   students often brought their lists to school.

    c.   Sister Helen received calls from several parents complaining about the assignment.

    d.   Sister Helen decided to repeat the assignment in every one of her classes.

7. According to Vicki,

    a.   Mark was the only student to have saved his list.

    b.   Vicki and Mark were the only students to have saved their lists.

    c.   Vicki, Mark, Charlie, Chuck, and Marilyn were the only students to have saved their lists.

    d.   all the students had saved their lists.

8. The author implies that

    a.   she was surprised to learn how much the lists had meant to her students.

    b.   Mark's parents were jealous of his affection for Sister Helen.

    c.   Mark's death shattered her faith in God.

    d.   Mark's classmates had not stayed in touch with one another over the years.

9. *True or false?* _____ The author implies that Mark had gotten married.

10. We can conclude that when Sister Helen was a third-grade teacher, she

    a.   was usually short-tempered and irritable.

    b.   wasn't always sure how to discipline her students.

    c.   didn't expect Mark to do well in school.

    d.   had no sense of humor.

■ Discussion Questions

About Content

1. What did Sister Helen hope to accomplish by asking her students to list nice things about one another?

2. At least some students were surprised by the good things others wrote about them. What does this tell us about how we see ourselves and how we communicate our views of others?

3. "All the Good Things" has literally traveled around the world. Not only has it been reprinted in numerous publications, but many readers have sent it out over the Internet for others to read. Why do you think so many people love this story? Why do they want to share it with others?

About Structure

4. This selection is organized according to time. What three separate time periods does it cover? What paragraphs are included in the first time period? The second? The third?

5. Paragraph 8 includes a cause-and-effect structure. What part of the paragraph is devoted to the cause? What part is devoted to the effect? What transition word signals the break between the cause and the effect?

6. What does the title "All The Good Things" mean? Is this a good title for the essay? Why or why not?

About Style and Tone

7. Sister Helen is willing to let her readers see her weaknesses as well as her strengths. Find a place in the selection in which the author shows herself as less than perfect.

8. What does Sister Helen accomplish by beginning her essay with the word "he"? What does that unusual beginning tell the reader?

9. How does Sister Helen feel about her students? Find evidence that backs up your opinion.

10. Sister Helen comments on Mark's "happy-to-be-alive" attitude. What support does she provide that makes us understand what Mark was like?

■ Writing Assignments

Assignment 1: Writing a Paragraph

Early in her story, Sister Helen refers to a "teacher's mistake" that forced her to punish a student in front of the class. Write a paragraph about a time you gave in to pressure to do something because others around you expected it. Explain what the situation was, just what happened, and how you felt afterward. Here are two sample topic sentences:

> Even though I knew it was wrong, I went along with some friends who shoplifted at the mall.

> Just because my friends did, I made fun of a kid in my study hall who was a slow learner.

Assignment 2: Writing a Paragraph

Sister Helen's students kept their lists for many years. What souvenir of the past have you kept for a long time? Why? Write a paragraph describing the souvenir, how you got it, and what it means to you. Begin with a topic sentence such as this:

> I've kept a green ribbon in one of my dresser drawers for over ten years because it reminds me of an experience I treasure.

Assignment 3: Writing an Essay

It's easy to forget to let others know how much they have helped us. Only after one of the students died did Sister Helen learn how important the list of positive comments had been to her class. Write an essay about someone to whom you are grateful and explain what that person has done for you. In your thesis statement, introduce the person and describe his or her relationship to you. Also include a general statement of what that person has done for you. Your thesis statement can be similar to any of these:

> My brother Roy has been an important part of my life.

> My best friend Ginger helped me through a major crisis.

> Mrs. Morrison, my seventh-grade English teacher, taught me a lesson for which I will always be grateful.

Use freewriting to help you find interesting details to support your thesis statement. You may find two or three separate incidents to write about, each in a paragraph of its own. Or you may find it best to use several paragraphs to give a detailed narrative of one incident or two or three related events. (Note how Sister Helen uses several separate "scenes" to tell her story.) Whatever your approach, use some dialogue to enliven key parts of your essay. (Review the reading to see how Sister Helen uses dialogue throughout her essay.)

Alternatively, write an essay about three people to whom you are grateful. In that case, each paragraph of the body of your essay would deal with one of those people. The thesis statement in such an essay might be similar to this:

> There are three people who have made a big difference in my life.

Rowing the Bus

Paul Logan

There is a well-known saying that goes something like this: All that is necessary in order for evil to triumph is for good people to do nothing. Even young people are forced to face cruel behavior and to decide how they will respond to it. In this essay, Paul Logan looks back at a period of schoolyard cruelty in which he was both a victim and a participant. With unflinching honesty, he describes his behavior then and how it helped to shape the person he has become.

When I was in elementary school, some older kids made me row the bus. Rowing meant that on the way to school I had to sit in the dirty bus aisle littered with paper, gum wads, and spitballs. Then I had to simulate the motion of rowing while the kids around me laughed and chanted, "Row, row, row the bus." I was forced to do this by a group of bullies who spent most of their time picking on me. 1

I was the perfect target for them. I was small. I had no father. And my mother, though she worked hard to support me, was unable to afford clothes and sneakers that were "cool." Instead she dressed me in outfits that we got from "the bags"—hand-me-downs given as donations to a local church. 2

Each Wednesday, she'd bring several bags of clothes to the house and pull out musty, wrinkled shirts and worn bell-bottom pants that other families no longer wanted. I knew that people were kind to give things to us, but I hated wearing clothes that might have been donated by my classmates. Each time I wore something from the bags, I feared that the other kids might recognize something that was once theirs. 3

Besides my outdated clothes, I wore thick glasses, had crossed eyes, and spoke with a persistent lisp. For whatever reason, I had never learned to say the "s" sound properly, and I pronounced words that began with "th" as if they began with a "d." In addition, because of my severely crossed eyes, I lacked the hand and eye coordination necessary to hit or catch flying objects. 4

As a result, footballs, baseballs, soccer balls and basketballs became my enemies. I knew, before I stepped onto the field or court, that I would do something clumsy or foolish and that everyone would laugh at me. I feared humiliation so much that I became skillful at feigning illnesses to get out of gym class. Eventually I learned how to give myself low-grade fevers so the nurse would write me an excuse. It worked for a while, until the gym teachers caught on. When I did have to play, I was always the last one chosen to be on any team. In fact, team captains did everything in their power to make their opponents get stuck with me. 5

When the unlucky team captain was forced to call my name, I would trudge over to the team, knowing that no one there liked or wanted me. For four years, from second through fifth grade, I prayed nightly for God to give me school days in which I would not be insulted, embarrassed, or made to feel ashamed.

I thought my prayers were answered when my mother decided to move during   6
the summer before sixth grade. The move meant that I got to start sixth grade in a different school, a place where I had no reputation. Although the older kids laughed and snorted at me as soon as I got on my new bus—they couldn't miss my thick glasses and strange clothes—I soon discovered that there was another kid who received the brunt of their insults. His name was George, and everyone made fun of him. The kids taunted him because he was skinny; they belittled him because he had acne that pocked and blotched his face; and they teased him because his voice was squeaky. During my first gym class at my new school, I wasn't the last one chosen for kickball; George was.

George tried hard to be friends with me, coming up to me in the cafeteria   7
on the first day of school. "Hi. My name's George. Can I sit with you?" he asked with a peculiar squeakiness that made each word high-pitched and raspy. As I nodded for him to sit down, I noticed an uncomfortable silence in the cafeteria as many of the students who had mocked George's clumsy gait during gym class began watching the two of us and whispering among themselves. By letting him sit with me, I had violated an unspoken law of school, a sinister code of childhood that demands there must always be someone to pick on. I began to realize two things. If I befriended George, I would soon receive the same treatment that I had gotten at my old school. If I stayed away from him, I might actually have a chance to escape being at the bottom.

Within days, the kids started taunting us whenever we were together. "Who's   8
your new little buddy, Georgie?" In the hallways, groups of students began mumbling about me just loud enough for me to hear, "Look, it's George's ugly boyfriend." On the bus rides to and from school, wads of paper and wet chewing gum were tossed at me by the bigger, older kids in the back of the bus.

It became clear that my friendship with George was going to cause me several   9
more years of misery at my new school. I decided to stop being friends with George. In class and at lunch, I spent less and less time with him. Sometimes I told him I was too busy to talk; other times I acted distracted and gave one-word responses to whatever he said. Our classmates, sensing that they had created a rift between George and me, intensified their attacks on him. Each day, George grew more desperate as he realized that the one person who could prevent him from being completely isolated was closing him off. I knew that I shouldn't avoid him, that he was feeling the same way I felt for so long, but I was so afraid that my life would become the hell it had been in my old school that I continued to ignore him.

Then, at recess one day, the meanest kid in the school, Chris, decided he had had   10
enough of George. He vowed that he was going to beat up George and anyone else who claimed to be his friend. A mob of kids formed and came after me. Chris led the way and cornered me near our school's swing sets. He grabbed me by my

shirt and raised his fist over my head. A huge gathering of kids surrounded us, urging him to beat me up, chanting "Go, Chris, go!"

"You're Georgie's new little boyfriend, aren't you?" he yelled. The hot blast 11 of his breath carried droplets of his spit into my face. In a complete betrayal of the only kid who was nice to me, I denied George's friendship.

"No, I'm not George's friend. I don't like him. He's stupid," I blurted out. 12 Several kids snickered and mumbled under their breath. Chris stared at me for a few seconds and then threw me to the ground.

"Wimp. Where's George?" he demanded, standing over me. Someone 13 pointed to George sitting alone on top of the monkey bars about thirty yards from where we were. He was watching me. Chris and his followers sprinted over to George and yanked him off the bars to the ground. Although the mob quickly encircled them, I could still see the two of them at the center of the crowd, looking at each other. George seemed stoic, staring straight through Chris. I heard the familiar chant of "Go, Chris, go!" and watched as his fists began slamming into George's head and body. His face bloodied and his nose broken, George crumpled to the ground and sobbed without even throwing a punch. The mob cheered with pleasure and darted off into the playground to avoid an approaching teacher.

Chris was suspended, and after a few days, George came back to school. I 14 wanted to talk to him, to ask him how he was, to apologize for leaving him alone and for not trying to stop him from getting hurt. But I couldn't go near him. Filled with shame for denying George and angered by my own cowardice, I never spoke to him again.

Several months later, without telling any students, George transferred to 15 another school. Once in a while, in those last weeks before he left, I caught him watching me as I sat with the rest of the kids in the cafeteria. He never yelled at me or expressed anger, disappointment, or even sadness. Instead he just looked at me.

In the years that followed, George's silent stare remained with me. It was there 16 in eighth grade when I saw a gang of popular kids beat up a sixth-grader because, they said, he was "ugly and stupid." It was there my first year in high school, when I saw a group of older kids steal another freshman's clothes and throw them into the showers. It was there a year later, when I watched several seniors press a wad of chewing gum into the hair of a new girl on the bus. Each time that I witnessed another awkward, uncomfortable, scared kid being tormented, I thought of George, and gradually his haunting stare began to speak to me. No longer silent, it told me that every child who is picked on and taunted deserves better, that no one— no matter how big, strong, attractive, or popular—has the right to abuse another person.

Finally, in my junior year when a loudmouthed, pink-skinned bully named 17 Donald began picking on two freshmen on the bus, I could no longer deny George. Donald was crumpling a large wad of paper and preparing to bounce it off the back of the head of one of the young students when I interrupted him.

"Leave them alone, Don," I said. By then I was six inches taller and, after 18 two years of high-school wrestling, thirty pounds heavier than I had been in my freshman year. Though Donald was still two years older than me, he wasn't much bigger. He stopped what he was doing, squinted, and stared at me.

"What's your problem, Paul?"   19

I felt the way I had many years earlier on the playground when I watched the   20
mob of kids begin to surround George.

"Just leave them alone. They aren't bothering you," I responded quietly.   21

"What's it to you?" he challenged. A glimpse of my own past, of rowing the   22
bus, of being mocked for my clothes, my lisp, my glasses, and my absent father
flashed in my mind.

"Just don't mess with them. That's all I am saying, Don." My fingertips were   23
tingling. The bus was silent. He got up from his seat and leaned over me, and I rose
from my seat to face him. For a minute, both of us just stood there, without a
word, staring.

"I'm just playing with them, Paul," he said, chuckling. "You don't have to go   24
psycho on me or anything." Then he shook his head, slapped me firmly on the chest
with the back of his hand, and sat down. But he never threw that wad of paper.
For the rest of the year, whenever I was on the bus, Don and the other troublemakers were noticeably quiet.

Although it has been years since my days on the playground and the school   25
bus, George's look still haunts me. Today, I see it on the faces of a few scared kids
at my sister's school—she is in fifth grade. Or once in a while I'll catch a glimpse
of someone like George on the evening news, in a story about a child who
brought a gun to school to stop the kids from picking on him, or in a feature
about a teenager who killed herself because everyone teased her. In each school,
in almost every classroom, there is a George with a stricken face, hoping that
someone nearby will be strong enough to be kind—despite what the crowd says—
and brave enough to stand up against people who attack, tease or hurt those who
are vulnerable.

If asked about their behavior, I'm sure the bullies would say, "What's it to you?   26
It's just a joke. It's nothing." But to George and me, and everyone else who has
been humiliated or laughed at or spat on, it is everything. No one should have
to row the bus.

■ Reading Comprehension Questions

1. The word *simulate* in "Then I had to simulate the motion of rowing while the
   kids around me laughed and chanted, 'Row, row, row the bus'" (paragraph 1)
   means

   a. sing.

   b. ignore.

   c. imitate.

   d. release.

2. The word *rift* in "I decided to stop being friends with George. . . . Our class-mates, sensing that they had created a rift between George and me, intensified their attacks on him" (paragraph 9) means

    a. friendship.

    b. agreement.

    c. break.

    d. joke.

3. Which of the following would be the best alternative title for this selection?

    a. A Sixth-Grade Adventure

    b. Children's Fears

    c. Dealing with Cruelty

    d. The Trouble With Busing

4. Which sentence best expresses the main idea of the selection?

    a. Although Paul Logan was the target of other students' abuse when he was a young boy, their attacks stopped as he grew taller and stronger.

    b. When Logan moved to a different school, he discovered that another student, George, was the target of more bullying than he was.

    c. Logan's experience of being bullied and his shame at how he treated George eventually made him speak up for someone else who was teased.

    d. Logan is ashamed that he did not stand up for George when George was being attacked by a bully on the playground.

5. When Chris attacked George, George reacted by

    a. fighting back hard.

    b. shouting for Logan to help him.

    c. running away.

    d. accepting the beating.

6. Logan finally found the courage to stand up for abused students when he saw

    a. Donald about to throw paper at a younger student.

    b. older kids throwing a freshman's clothes into the shower.

    c. seniors putting bubble gum in a new student's hair.

    d. a gang beating up a sixth-grader whom they disliked.

7. *True or false?* _____ After Logan confronted Donald on the bus, Donald began picking on Logan as well.

8. *True or false?* _____ The author suggests that his mother did not care very much about him.

9. The author implies that, when he started sixth grade at a new school,

   a.   he became fairly popular.

   b.   he decided to try out for athletic teams.

   c.   he was relieved to find a kid who was more unpopular than he.

   d.   he was frequently beaten up.

10. We can conclude that

   a.   the kids who picked on George later regretted what they had done.

   b.   George and the author eventually talked together about their experience in sixth grade.

   c.   the author thinks kids today are kinder than they were when he was in sixth grade.

   d.   the author is a more compassionate person now because of his experience with George.

■ Discussion Questions

About Content

1. Logan describes a number of incidents involving students' cruelty to other students. Find at least three such incidents. What do they seem to have in common? Judging from such incidents, what purpose does cruel teasing seem to serve?

2. Throughout the essay, Paul Logan talks about cruel but ordinary school behavior. But in paragraph 25, he briefly mentions two extreme and tragic consequences of such cruelty. What are those consequences, and why do you think he introduces them? What is he implying?

About Structure

3. Overall, the author uses narration to develop his points. Below, write three time transitions he uses to advance his narration.

_____   _____   _____

4. Logan describes the gradual change within him that finally results in his standing up for a student who is being abused. Where in the narrative does Logan show how internal changes may be taking place within him? Where in the narrative does he show that his reaction to witnessing bullying has changed?

5. Paul Logan titled his selection "Rowing the Bus." Yet very little of the essay actually deals with the incident the title describes. Why do you think Logan chose that title?

About Style and Tone

6. Paul Logan backs up his point "I was the perfect target for them" (paragraph 2) with solid support. Identify two of the several details that support that point, and write a summary of each below.

   _____

   _____

7. Good descriptive writing involves the reader's senses. Give examples of how Logan appeals to our senses in paragraphs 1–4 of "Rowing the Bus."

   Sight _____

   Smell _____

   Hearing _____

8. What is Logan's attitude towards himself regarding his treatment of George? Find three phrases that reveal his attitude and write them here.

■ Writing Assignments

Assignment 1: Writing a Paragraph

Logan writes, " In each school, in almost every classroom, there is a George with a stricken face." Think of a person who filled the role of George in one of your classes. Then write a descriptive paragraph about that person, explaining why he or she was a target and what form the teasing took. Be sure to include a description of your own thoughts and actions regarding the student who was teased. Your topic sentence might be something like one of these:

> A girl in my fifth-grade class was a lot like George in "Rowing the Bus."
>
> Like Paul Logan, I suffered greatly in elementary school from being bullied.

Try to include details that appeal to two or three of the senses.

Assignment 2: Writing a Paragraph

Paul Logan feared that his life at his new school would be made miserable if he continued being friends with George. So he ended the friendship, even though he felt ashamed of doing so. Think of a time when you have wanted to do the right thing but felt that the price would be too high. Maybe you knew a friend was doing something dishonest and wanted him to stop but were afraid of losing his friendship. Or perhaps you pretended to forget a promise you had made because you decided it was too difficult to keep. Write a paragraph describing the choice you made and how you felt about yourself afterward.

Assignment 3: Writing an Essay

Logan provides many vivid descriptions of incidents in which bullies attack other students. Reread these descriptions, and consider what they teach you about the nature of bullies and bullying. Then write an essay that supports the following main idea:

> Bullies seem to share certain qualities.

Identify two or three qualities; then discuss each in a separate paragraph. You may use two or three of the following as the topic sentences for your supporting paragraphs, or come up with your own supporting points:

> Bullies are cowardly.
>
> Bullies make themselves feel big by making other people feel small.
>
> Bullies cannot feel very good about themselves.
>
> Bullies are feared but not respected.
>
> Bullies act cruelly in order to get attention.

Develop each supporting point with one or more anecdotes or ideas from any of the following: your own experience, your understanding of human nature, and "Rowing the Bus."

Fifth Chinese Daughter

Jade Snow Wong

Wave after wave of immigrants come to the United States, determined that their children will enjoy this country's freedom and prosperity. Their hard work and dreams rarely prepare them for a harsh reality: along with the wonderful opportunities in this country, their children are going to absorb unfamiliar—and to them, sometimes shocking—American values and customs. In this selection from her autobiography, *Fifth Chinese Daughter*, Jade Snow Wong describes what happened when her new American lifestyle first clashed with her parents' traditional Chinese expectations.

By the time I was graduating from high school, my parents had done their best 1
to produce an intelligent, obedient daughter, who would know more than the
average Chinatown girl and should do better than average at a conventional job,
her earnings brought home to them in repayment for their years of child support.
Then, they hoped, she would marry a nice Chinese boy and make him a good wife,
as well as an above-average mother for his children. Chinese custom used to decree
that families should "introduce" chosen partners to each other's children. The
groom's family should pay handsomely to the bride's family for rearing a well-bred
daughter. They should also pay all bills for a glorious wedding banquet for several
hundred guests. Then the bride's family could consider their job done. Their daughter belonged to the groom's family and must henceforth seek permission from all
persons in his home before returning to her parents for a visit.

But having been set upon a new path, I did not oblige my parents with the 2
expected conventional ending. At fifteen, I had moved away from home to work
for room and board and a salary of twenty dollars per month. Having found that
I could subsist independently, I thought it regrettable to terminate my education.
Upon graduating from high school at the age of sixteen, I asked my parents to assist
me in college expenses. I pleaded with my father, for his years of encouraging me
to be above mediocrity in both Chinese and American studies had made me wish
for some undefined but brighter future.

My father was briefly adamant. He must conserve his resources for my oldest 3
brother's medical training. Though I desired to continue on an above-average
course, his material means were insufficient to support that ambition. He added
that if I had the talent, I could provide for my own college education. When he
had spoken, no discussion was expected. After his edict, no daughter questioned.

But this matter involved my whole future—it was not simply asking for per- 4
mission to go to a night church meeting (forbidden also). Though for years I had
accepted the authority of the one I honored most, his decision that night embittered
me as nothing ever had. My oldest brother had so many privileges, had incurred
unusual expenses for luxuries which were taken for granted as his birthright, yet
these were part of a system I had accepted. Now I suddenly wondered at my
father's interpretation of the Christian code: was it intended to discriminate
against a girl after all, or was it simply convenient for my father's economics and
cultural prejudice? Did a daughter have any right to expect more than a fate of
obedience, according to the old Chinese standard? As long as I could remember,
I had been told that a female followed three men during her lifetime: as a girl,
her father; as a wife, her husband; as an old woman, her son.

My indignation mounted against that tradition and I decided then that my 5
past could not determine my future. I knew that more education would prepare
me for a different expectation than my other female schoolmates, few of whom
were to complete a college degree. I, too, had my father's unshakable faith in the
justice of God, and I shared his unconcern with popular opinion.

So I decided to enter junior college, now San Francisco's City College, because 6
the fees were lowest. I lived at home and supported myself with an after-school job
which required long hours of housework and cooking but paid me twenty dollars

per month, of which I saved as much as possible. The thrills derived from reading and learning, in ways ranging from chemistry experiments to English compositions, from considering new ideas of sociology to the logic of Latin, convinced me that I had made a correct choice. I was kept in a state of perpetual mental excitement by new Western subjects and concepts and did not mind long hours of work and study. I also made new friends, which led to another painful incident with my parents, who had heretofore discouraged even girlhood friendships.

The college subject which had most jolted me was sociology. The instructor   7
fired my mind with his interpretation of family relationships. As he explained to our class, it used to be an economic asset for American farming families to be large, since children were useful to perform agricultural chores. But this situation no longer applied and children should be regarded as individuals with their own rights. Unquestioning obedience should be replaced with parental understanding. So at sixteen, discontented as I was with my parents' apparent indifference to me, those words of my sociology professor gave voice to my sentiments. How old-fashioned was the dead-end attitude of my parents! How ignorant they were of modern thought and progress! The family unit had been China's strength for centuries, but it had also been her weakness, for corruption, nepotism, and greed were all justified in the name of the family's welfare. My new ideas festered; I longed to release them.

One afternoon on a Saturday, which was normally occupied with my house-   8
work job, I was unexpectedly released by my employer, who was departing for a country weekend. It was a rare joy to have free time and I wanted to enjoy myself for a change. There had been a Chinese-American boy who shared some classes with me. Sometimes we had found each other walking to the same 8:00 A.M. class. He was not a special boyfriend, but I had enjoyed talking to him and had confided in him some of my problems. Impulsively, I telephoned him. I knew I must be breaking rules, and I felt shy and scared. At the same time, I was excited at this newly found forwardness, with nothing more purposeful than to suggest another walk together.

He understood my awkwardness and shared my anticipation. He asked me to   9
"dress up" for my first movie date. My clothes were limited but I changed to look more graceful in silk stockings and found a bright ribbon for my long black hair. Daddy watched, catching my mood, observing the dashing preparations. He asked me where I was going without his permission and with whom.

I refused to answer him. I thought of my rights! I thought he surely would   10
not try to understand. Thereupon Daddy thundered his displeasure and forbade my departure. I found a new courage as I heard my voice announce calmly that I was no longer a child, and if I could work my way through college, I would choose my own friends. It was my right as a person.

My mother heard the commotion and joined my father to face me; both   11
appeared shocked and incredulous. Daddy at once demanded the source of this unfilial, non-Chinese theory. And when I quoted my college professor, reminding him that he had always felt teachers should be revered, my father denounced that professor as a foreigner who was disregarding the superiority of our Chinese culture,

with its sound family strength. My father did not spare me; I was condemned as an ingrate for echoing dishonorable opinions which should only be temporary whims, yet nonetheless inexcusable.

The scene was not yet over. I completed my proclamation to my father, who had never allowed me to learn how to dance, by adding that I was attending a movie, unchaperoned, with a boy I met at college.   12

My startled father was sure that my reputation would be subject to whispered innuendos. I must be bent on disgracing the family name; I was ruining my future, for surely I would yield to temptation. My mother underscored him by saying that I hadn't any notion of the problems endured by parents of a young girl.   13

I would not give in. I reminded them that they and I were not in China, that I wasn't going out with just anybody but someone I trusted! Daddy gave a roar that no man could be trusted, but I devastated them in declaring that I wished the freedom to find my own answers.   14

Both parents were thoroughly angered, scolded me for being shameless, and predicted that I would some day tell them I was wrong. But I dimly perceived that they were conceding defeat and were perplexed at this breakdown of their training. I was too old to beat and too bold to intimidate.   15

■ Reading Comprehension Questions

1. The word *incurred* in "My oldest brother had so many privileges, had incurred unusual expenses for luxuries which were taken for granted as his birth-right . . ." (paragraph 4) means

   a.   acquired.

   b.   avoided.

   c.   promised.

   d.   given away.

2. The word *innuendos* in "My startled father was sure that my reputation would be subject to whispered innuendos" (paragraph 13) means

   a.   compliments.

   b.   answers.

   c.   facts.

   d.   negative suggestions.

3. Which of the following would be the best alternative title for this selection?

   a.   Family Life in China

   b.   A Domineering Father

   c.   A Clash of Cultures

   d.   Teenage Rebellion

4. Which sentence best expresses the article's main point?

   a.   Traditional Chinese parents want their daughters to submit to the authority of the men in their lives.

   b.   A college sociology course encouraged the author to see her parents as unreasonably old-fashioned.

   c.   Traditional Chinese families expect unquestioning obedience from their daughters.

   d.   The author and her parents came into conflict when she began to reject traditional Chinese values for modern American ones.

5. *True or false?* _____ The author's father forbade her to attend college.

6. Jade Snow Wong

   a.   had grown up in China.

   b.   felt scared but also excited about calling a boy who shared some classes with her.

   c.   had fallen in love with a boy she sometimes walked to class with.

   d.   received a full scholarship to attend college.

7. In college, the author was especially struck by her sociology instructor's interpretation of

   a.   traditional American values.

   b.   American farming families.

   c.   corruption, nepotism, and greed.

   d.   modern family relationships.

8. We can infer from the essay that the

   a.   author's parents were Christians.

   b.   author was a below-average student.

   c.   author majored in sociology in college.

   d.   author never married.

9. We can conclude that the author's parents

   a.   felt sons should be prepared for careers and daughters for marriage.

   b.   did not love her.

   c.   expected her to work for a few years, then marry an American boy.

   d.   were secretly happy that their daughter was so spirited.

10. In the last paragraph of the reading, the author implies that
   a.   she eventually told her parents she had been wrong and they had been right.
   b.   her mother actually wanted her to be more independent.
   c.   her parents had no desire to intimidate her.
   d.   as a child, she had been beaten when she disobeyed.

■ Discussion Questions

About Content

1. What did the selection teach you about traditional Chinese views of men's and women's roles? How did Wong's views differ from those traditional views?

2. The main drama of the reading stems from the differences between Wong and her father. Yet Wong also mentions ways in which she and her father are similar. What are those ways? Find passages that indicate those similarities.

3. Wong writes that her parents "were perplexed at this breakdown of their training" (paragraph 15). What didn't they understand? Was their lack of understanding due to their cultural background, or are all parents apt to have this problem? Why or why not?

4. What were Wong's parents' expectations for her future? What can you infer about Wong's own hopes for her future? What had happened to make Wong's expectations different?

About Structure

5. As she begins her essay, Wong immediately introduces the contrast between her parents' thinking and her own. How many paragraphs does she use to introduce that conflict? What transitional word does she use to make the contrast evident?

6. Read the final two sentences in paragraph 3 and the final sentence in paragraph 16. How are the two places alike in structure? How are they different in content? How do this similar structure and contrast in content emphasize Wong's main point?

About Style and Tone

7. Although Wong is describing her struggle against her father's authority, she reveals her own respect and even affection for him. How and where does she indicate these positive feelings?

8. Even though she does not quote her father directly, Wong describes his speech in ways that give the reader a clear idea of his manner of speaking. For instance, the observation that after her father had spoken "no discussion was expected" (paragraph 3) tells us he spoke in a dictatorial tone. Find other instances in which Wong gives descriptions that help us understand her father's way of speaking.

■ Writing Assignments

Assignment 1: Writing a Paragraph

Wong held a difficult after-school job to earn money to finance her college education. What actions have you taken in order to get something you wanted badly? Perhaps you worked hard to develop an athletic skill, buy a car, rent your own apartment, or become a stronger student. Write a paragraph about an important goal you've had, or have now, and how you have worked to achieve it. Your supporting details should make it clear just what you had to do in order to accomplish your goal. Your topic sentence might be similar to either of these:

> During my second semester in college, I found ways to raise my grades.
>
> Last summer, I managed to train successfully for a fall ten-mile run.

Assignment 2: Writing a Paragraph

As a college student, you—like Wong—undoubtedly recognize the value of a college education. Write a paragraph in which you support the point "There are several benefits of going to college." For example, here's one benefit you could use as a supporting detail:

> Managers respect workers with college degrees more than those who haven't gone beyond high school.

For each benefit you mention, include a brief explanation and at least one specific example, as in the example below. It begins with one supporting detail. Next is a brief explanation, which is then followed by an example.

> On the job, people respect workers with college degrees more than those who haven't gone beyond high school. Managers assume that college graduates are more knowledgeable and skilled. Although my cousin James is an intelligent man and a hard worker, for example, he is still a warehouse laborer after fifteen years on the job. Whenever he's applied for a promotion, he's been passed over in favor of someone with a college degree.

Assignment 3: Writing an Essay

Children often resent the household rules and parental ideas they must live under. However, when they grow up, they often decide that at least some such rules and ideas were appropriate. In an essay, contrast your point of view then and now on one or more parental rules or guidelines.

Here are some sample thesis statements for such an essay:

Now that I have kids of my own, I expect them to live by rules that I resented when I was their age.

Although I thought my parents were too strict when I was younger, I now believe that many of their ideas made sense.

Each paragraph in the body of your essay should describe one parental idea or rule you used to resist. Illustrate your previous resistance to each by describing at least one specific incident, confrontation, or conversation. Then explain why your attitude toward each idea or rule has changed. To help you think about why parents make the rules they do and the effects on their families, read "What Good Families Are Doing Right" on page 617.

Assignment 4: Writing an Essay Using Internet Research

At the end of her essay, Jade Snow Wong comments that her parents "were conceding defeat" because she was "too old to beat and too bold to intimidate." Many parents resort to corporal punishment—beating or spanking—when their young children disobey. Is this kind of punishment a good way to discipline a child? Do some research on the Internet and write an essay explaining what experts have discovered about the effectiveness of corporal punishment.

To access the Internet, use the very helpful search engine Google (*www.google.com*) or one of the other search engines listed on pages 323–325 of this book. Try one of the following phrases or some related phrase:

effects of corporal punishment on children

parents spanking children good or bad

corporal punishment children discipline home

You may, of course, use one or two words such as "punishment" or "corporal punishment," but they will bring up too many items. As you proceed, you'll develop a sense of how to "track down" and focus a topic by adding more information to your search words and phrases.

Adolescent Confusion

Maya Angelou

In this selection from her highly praised autobiographical work, *I Know Why the Caged Bird Sings,* Maya Angelou writes with honesty, humor, and sensitivity about her sexual encounter with a neighborhood boy. Angelou captures some of the confused feelings about sex we all experience when we are growing up; she is frightened but curious, outwardly aggressive yet inwardly shy, calculating and innocent at the same time. Angelou's outrageous plan for finding out what it is like to be a "real woman" may seem shocking. But her candor makes us respond to her account with understanding and delight.

1   A classmate of mine, whose mother had rooms for herself and her daughter in a ladies' residence, had stayed out beyond closing time. She telephoned me to ask if she could sleep at my house. Mother gave her permission, providing my friend telephoned her mother from our house.

2   When she arrived, I got out of bed and we went to the upstairs kitchen to make hot chocolate. In my room we shared mean gossip about our friends, giggled over boys, and whined about school and the tedium of life. The unusualness of having someone sleep in my bed (I'd never slept with anyone except my grandmothers) and the frivolous laughter in the middle of the night made me forget simple courtesies. My friend had to remind me that she had nothing to sleep in. I gave her one of my gowns, and without curiosity or interest I watched her pull off her clothes. At none of the early stages of undressing was I in the least conscious of her body. And then suddenly, for the briefest eye span, I saw her breasts. I was stunned.

3   They were shaped like light-brown falsies in the five-and-ten-cent store, but they were real. They made all the nude paintings I had seen in museums come to life. In a word, they were beautiful. A universe divided what she had from what I had. She was a woman.

4   My gown was too snug for her and much too long, and when she wanted to laugh at her ridiculous image I found that humor had left me without a promise to return.

5   Had I been older I might have thought that I was moved by both an esthetic sense of beauty and the pure emotion of envy. But those possibilities did not occur to me when I needed them. All I knew was that I had been moved by looking at a woman's breasts. So all the calm and casual words of Mother's explanation a few weeks earlier and the clinical terms of Noah Webster did not alter the fact that in a fundamental way there was something queer about me.

I somersaulted deeper into my snuggery of misery. After a thorough self-   6
examination, in the light of all I had read and heard about dykes and bulldaggers,
I reasoned that I had none of the obvious traits—I didn't wear trousers, or have
big shoulders or go in for sports, or walk like a man or even want to touch a
woman. I wanted to be a woman, but that seemed to me to be a world to which
I was to be eternally refused entrance.

What I needed was a boyfriend. A boyfriend would clarify my position to the   7
world and, even more important, to myself. A boyfriend's acceptance of me would
guide me into that strange and exotic land of frills and femininity.

Among my associates, there were no takers. Understandably the boys of my   8
age and social group were captivated by the yellow- or light-brown-skinned girls,
with hairy legs and smooth little lips, whose hair "hung down like horses' manes."
And even those sought-after girls were asked to "give it up or tell where it is." They
were reminded in a popular song of the times, "If you can't smile and say yes,
please don't cry and say no." If the pretties were expected to make the supreme
sacrifice in order to "belong," what could the unattractive female do? She who
had been skimming along on life's turning but never-changing periphery had to
be ready to be a "buddy" by day and maybe by night. She was called upon to be
generous only if the pretty girls were unavailable.

I believe most plain girls are virtuous because of the scarcity of opportunity   9
to be otherwise. They shield themselves with an aura of unavailableness (for
which after a time they begin to take credit) largely as a defense tactic.

In my particular case, I could not hide behind the curtain of voluntary goodness.   10
I was being crushed by two unrelenting forces: the uneasy suspicion that I might
not be a normal female and my newly awakening sexual appetite.

I decided to take matters into my own hands. (An unfortunate but apt phrase.)   11

Up the hill from our house, and on the same side of the street, lived two   12
handsome brothers. They were easily the most eligible young men in the neighborhood. If I was going to venture into sex, I saw no reason why I shouldn't make
my experiment with the best of the lot. I didn't really expect to capture either
brother on a permanent basis, but I thought if I could hook one temporarily I
might be able to work the relationship into something more lasting.

I planned a chart for seduction with surprise as my opening ploy. One evening   13
as I walked up the hill suffering from youth's vague malaise (there was simply
nothing to do), the brother I had chosen came walking directly into my trap.

"Hello, Marguerite." He nearly passed me.   14

I put the plan into action. "Hey." I plunged, "Would you like to have a sexual   15
intercourse with me?" Things were going according to the chart. His mouth hung
open like a garden gate. I had the advantage and so I pressed it.

"Take me somewhere."   16

His response lacked dignity, but in fairness to him I admit that I had left him   17
little chance to be suave.

He asked, "You mean, you're going to give me some trim?"   18

I assured him that that was exactly what I was about to give him. Even as the   19
scene was being enacted, I realized the imbalance in his values. He thought I was
giving him something, and the fact of the matter was that it was my intention

to take something from him. His good looks and popularity had made him so inordinately conceited that they blinded him to that possibility.

We went to a furnished room occupied by one of his friends, who understood   20
the situation immediately and got his coat and left us alone. The seductee quickly turned off the lights. I would have preferred them left on, but didn't want to appear more aggressive than I had been already—if that was possible.

I was excited rather than nervous, and hopeful instead of frightened. I had   21
not considered how physical an act of seduction would be. I had anticipated long soulful tongued kisses and gentle caresses. But there was no romance in the knee which forced my legs, nor in the rub of hairy skin on my chest.

Unredeemed by shared tenderness, the time was spent in laborious gropings,   22
pullings, yankings, and jerkings.

Not one word was spoken.   23

My partner showed that our experience had reached its climax by getting up   24
abruptly, and my main concern was how to get home quickly. He may have sensed that he had been used, or his lack of interest may have been an indication that I was less than gratifying. Neither possibility bothered me.

Outside on the street we left each other with little more than "OK, see you   25
around."

Thanks to Mr. Freeman nine years before, I had had no pain of entry to   26
endure, and because of the absence of romantic involvement neither of us felt much had happened.

At home I reviewed the failure and tried to evaluate my new position. I had   27
had a man. I had been had. Not only didn't I enjoy it, but my normality was still a question.

What happened to the moonlight-on-the-prairie feeling? Was there something   28
so wrong with me that I couldn't share a sensation that made poets gush out rhyme after rhyme, that made Richard Arlen brave the Arctic wastes and Veronica Lake betray the entire free world?

There seemed to be no explanation for my private infirmity, but being a   29
product (is "victim" a better word?) of the Southern Negro upbringing, I decided that I "would understand it all better by and by." I went to sleep.

Three weeks later, having thought very little of the strange and strangely   30
empty night, I found myself pregnant.

■ ## Reading Comprehension Questions

1. The word *malaise* in "I walked up the hill suffering from youth's vague malaise" (paragraph 13) means

   a. patience.

   b. pleasure.

   c. ambition.

   d. uneasiness.

2. The word *inordinately* in "His good looks and popularity had made him so inordinately conceited" (paragraph 19) means

    a.   timidly.

    b.   excessively.

    c.   unexpectedly.

    d.   unknowingly.

3. Which of the following would be the best alternative title for this selection?

    a.   A Wasted Life

    b.   The Story of a Teenage Pregnancy

    c.   The Pain and Confusion of Growing Up

    d.   A Handsome Young Man

4. Which sentence best expresses the main idea of the selection?

    a.   Teenage girls feel more insecure about sex than teenage boys do.

    b.   A sexual experience is the first step toward adulthood.

    c.   Maya Angelou's innocence led her to a joyless experience with sex and an unplanned pregnancy.

    d.   Women who are sexually aggressive often become pregnant.

5. In the days following her sexual experience, the author

    a.   talked to her mother about her feelings.

    b.   wrote about the incident.

    c.   asked her classmates for advice.

    d.   virtually ignored what had happened.

6. The author chose the boy she did to experiment with because

    a.   he had shown some interest in her.

    b.   she wanted to start with one of the two most eligible boys in the neighborhood.

    c.   she knew he would be kind to her.

    d.   she had a crush on him.

7. The author expected that

    a.   having a boyfriend would help her become a woman.

    b.   she would feel guilty about her actions.

    c.   she would no longer be plain.

    d.   she would probably get pregnant.

8. The author implies that

   a.   she would become a homosexual.

   b.   she had little sense of right and wrong.

   c.   she had little idea of what love, sex, or femininity really mean.

   d.   none of the girls she knew had had a sexual experience.

9. *True or false?* _____ The author implies that she had discussed the facts of womanhood with her mother.

10. The author implies that

    a.   she wanted the boy to marry her.

    b.   she was raped as a child.

    c.   the boy's lack of tenderness was expected.

    d.   the movies had taught her the facts of life.

■ Discussion Questions

About Content

1. For what reasons did Angelou decide she needed a boyfriend?

2. In what ways did Angelou's actual experience differ from what she expected it to be? Find passages in the selection that describe (a) Angelou's expectations and (b) the reality of the experience.

3. What was the young man's reaction to Angelou's seduction? What does his reaction reveal about him?

About Structure

4. A narrative selection most often focuses on a single event. But this selection is developed through two narratives. What are the two narratives? Why does Angelou include both?

5. Within her narratives, Angelou uses contrast to develop her paragraphs. For example, she contrasts her body and her classmate's body, and the "pretties" and "unattractive females." Find two other areas of contrast and write them below:

   _____

   _____

6. Paragraph 23 consists of just one sentence: "Not one word was spoken." What effect does Angelou achieve by making this paragraph so short?

About Style and Tone

7. Angelou enlivens her narrative with humor. Find two places where she touches on the humorous side of her experience and write the paragraph numbers here:

    _____   _____

8. Find two other places where the tone is quite serious.

    _____   _____

■ Writing Assignments

Assignment 1: Writing a Paragraph

Most teenagers are, at times, as impulsive and unthinking as Angelou was. Write a narrative about a time during your teenage years when you did something impulsively, with little regard for the possible consequences—something which you later regretted. You may have committed this act because you, like Angelou, wanted to know about something or because you were pressured into it by others.

Assignment 2: Writing a Paragraph

Because of her confusion and insecurity, Angelou acted without consulting anyone else about her problem. Pretend that the young Maya has come to you with her doubts and her plan to seduce a boy. What advice would you give her? In a paragraph written in the form of a letter to Maya, explain what you would say to her.

Assignment 3: Writing an Essay

Many teenagers face the problem of whether or not to engage in premarital sex. If a teenager stopped to think before becoming involved in a sexual relationship, what should he or she think about? What should be considered before a person gets involved? Write an essay on three potential problems a teenager should think about before becoming involved sexually with someone. Discuss each potential problem in a separate paragraph. Your thesis might be similar to this: "A teenager who is thinking about getting involved in a sexual relationship should think seriously about several potential problems first."

You may want to write about some of the following: possibility of pregnancy, parents' feelings, feeling used by the other person, sexually transmitted diseases, feelings of guilt and worry, feeling pressured by a partner.

Assignment 4: Writing an Essay Using Internet Research

Adolescence is often a time of curiosity and confusion about one's sexual identity. As shown by Maya Angelou's experience, this combination can lead to unwise choices about sexual behavior. Can sex education programs help adolescents make better choices? Use the Internet to find out what sort of sex education programs are offered in schools and communities and how effective they are. Then write an essay describing three elements that seem to make a sex education program work well.

To access the Internet, use the very helpful search engine Google (*www. google.com*) or one of the other search engines listed on pages 323–325 of this book. Try one of the following phrases or some related phrase:

> adolescents and sex education that works
>
> successful sex education programs for adolescents

You may, of course, use a simple phrase such as "sex education," but that will bring up too many items. As you proceed, you'll develop a sense of how to "track down" and focus a topic by adding more information to your search words and phrases.

Tickets to Nowhere

Andy Rooney

Who doesn't love a "get rich quick" story? We eagerly read the accounts of lucky people who've become wealthy overnight just by buying the right lottery ticket. The hope that we might do the same keeps many of us "investing" in the lottery week after week. But the syndicated columnist Andy Rooney thinks there's another lottery story that also deserves our attention.

1   Things never went very well for Jim Oakland. He dropped out of high school because he was impatient to get rich, but after dropping out he lived at home with his parents for two years and didn't earn a dime.

2   He finally got a summer job working for the highway department holding up a sign telling oncoming drivers to be careful of the workers ahead. Later that same year, he picked up some extra money putting fliers under the windshield wipers of parked cars.

3   Things just never went very well for Jim, and he was twenty-three before he left home and went to Florida hoping his ship would come in down there. He

never lost his desire to get rich; but first he needed money for the rent, so he took a job near Fort Lauderdale for $4.50 an hour servicing the goldfish aquariums kept near the cashier's counter in a lot of restaurants.

Jim was paid in cash once a week by the owner of the goldfish business, and the first thing he did was go to the little convenience store near where he lived and buy $20 worth of lottery tickets. He was really determined to get rich.   4

A week ago, the lottery jackpot in Florida reached $54 million. Jim woke up nights thinking what he could do with $54 million. During the days, he day-dreamed about it. One morning he was driving along the main street in the boss's old pickup truck with six tanks of goldfish in back. As he drove past a BMW dealer, he looked at the new models in the window.   5

He saw the car he wanted in the showroom window, but unfortunately he didn't see the light change. The car in front of him stopped short and Jim slammed on his brakes. The fish tanks slid forward. The tanks broke, the water gushed out, and the goldfish slithered and flopped all over the back of the truck. Some fell off into the road.   6

It wasn't a good day for the goldfish or for Jim, of course. He knew he'd have to pay for the tanks and 75 cents each for the fish, and if it weren't for the $54 million lottery, he wouldn't have known which way to turn. He had that lucky feeling.   7

For the tanks and the dead goldfish, the boss deducted $114 of Jim's $180 weekly pay. Even though he didn't have enough left for the rent and food, Jim doubled the amount he was going to spend on lottery tickets. He never needed $54 million more.   8

Jim had this system. He took his age and added the last four digits of the tele-phone number of the last girl he dated. He called it his lucky number . . . even though the last four digits changed quite often and he'd never won with his sys-tem. Everyone laughed at Jim and said he'd never win the lottery.   9

Jim put down $40 on the counter that week and the man punched out his tickets. Jim stowed them safely away in his wallet with last week's tickets. He never threw away his lottery tickets until at least a month after the drawing just in case there was some mistake. He'd heard of mistakes.   10

Jim listened to the radio all afternoon the day of the drawing. The people at the radio station he was listening to waited for news of the winning numbers to come over the wires and, even then, the announcers didn't rush to get them on. The station manager thought the people running the lottery ought to pay to have the winning numbers broadcast, just like any other commercial announcement.   11

Jim fidgeted while they gave the weather and the traffic and the news. Then they played more music. All he wanted to hear were those numbers.   12

"Well," the radio announcer said finally, "we have the lottery numbers some of you have been waiting for. You ready?" Jim was ready. He clutched his ticket with the number 274802.   13

"The winning number," the announcer said, "is 860539. I'll repeat that. 860539." Jim was still a loser.   14

I thought that, with all the human interest stories about lottery winners, we ought to have a story about one of the several million losers.   15

■ Reading Comprehension Questions

1. The word *gushed* in "The tanks broke, the water gushed out, and the goldfish slithered and flopped all over the back of the truck" (paragraph 6) means
   a. dripped slowly.
   b. steamed.
   c. poured.
   d. held.

2. The word *digits* in "He took his age and added the last four digits of the telephone number of the last girl he dated" (paragraph 9) means
   a. letters.
   b. single numbers.
   c. rings.
   d. area codes.

3. Which of the following would be the best alternative title for this selection?
   a. A $54 Million Jackpot
   b. An Unnecessary Accident
   c. Foolish Dreams
   d. Moving to Florida

4. Which sentence best expresses the main idea of the selection?
   a. Everyone dreams of winning the lottery.
   b. The more money you invest in lottery tickets, the better your chances of winning.
   c. Jim Oakland's dreams of getting rich by winning the lottery were unrealistic.
   d. Jim Oakland is a very unlucky man.

5. *True or false?* ____ Jim dropped out of school because he was offered a good-paying job in Florida.

6. When Jim lost money as a result of his accident with the goldfish, he
   a. put himself on a strict budget.
   b. spent even more on lottery tickets.
   c. got a second job.
   d. moved back in with his parents to save money.

7. Jim never threw away his lottery tickets
   a. at all.
   b. until his next paycheck.

    c.   until at least a month after the drawing.

    d.   so that he could write off his losses on his tax return.

8. We can infer from paragraphs 6–7 that

    a.   Jim's daydreams about getting rich made him careless.

    b.   the driver in front of Jim should have gotten a ticket.

    c.   the brakes on Jim's pickup truck were faulty.

    d.   Jim slammed on his brakes because he'd suddenly realized that he'd never win the lottery.

9. In paragraph 9, the author suggests that Jim

    a.   was good in math.

    b.   did not date very often.

    c.   never told anyone about his dreams of winning the lottery.

    d.   never dated the same girl for very long.

10. Andy Rooney suggests that

    a.   although few people win the lottery, it's still worth trying.

    b.   most of what the public hears about lotteries shows how harmful they are.

    c.   Jim Oakland gave up playing the lottery after losing the $54 million jackpot.

    d.   playing the lottery harms far more people than it helps.

■ Discussion Questions

About Content

1. Jim Oakland seemed to feel that lotteries were entirely good. Andy Rooney takes a more negative view. What is your opinion? On balance, are lotteries good or bad? On what are you basing your opinion?

2. Do you know anyone like Jim, someone who depends on luck more than on hard work or ability? If so, why do you think this person relies so much on luck? How lucky has he or she been?

3. What would be the good points of suddenly winning a large amount of money? What might be the downside? All in all, would you prefer to win or to earn the money you have? Why?

About Structure

4. As Rooney's piece went on, did you think that it was going to be about Jim Oakland winning the lottery—or losing it? What details contributed to your expectations?

About Style and Tone

5. At only one point in the essay does Rooney use a direct quotation. What is that point? Why do you think he chooses to dramatize that moment with the speaker's exact words?

6. One meaning of *irony* is a contradiction between what might be expected and what really happens. Rooney uses this type of irony in an understated way to contrast Oakland's goal with his actions. For instance, in paragraph 1, he states that Oakland was "impatient to get rich." In the same sentence he states, "he lived at home with his parents for two years and didn't earn a dime." Find one other spot in the selection where Rooney uses irony and write its paragraph number here. _____

7. Rooney refers to himself only one time in the essay, in the final paragraph. Why do you think he chooses to refer to "I" at that point? What is the effect?

8. How do you think Rooney feels about Jim? Does he admire his continued optimism about striking it rich? Does he think Jim is a bad person? Find passages in the essay that support your opinion about how Rooney regards Jim.

■ Writing Assignments

Assignment 1: Writing a Paragraph

Write a paragraph about a time when you had good luck. Perhaps you found a twenty-dollar bill, or you happened to meet the person you are currently dating or are married to, or you were fortunate enough to find a job you like. Provide plenty of detail to let readers know why you consider your experience so fortunate. Your topic sentence may begin like this:

A time I had incredibly good luck was the day that _____.

Assignment 2: Writing a Paragraph

As Andy Rooney describes him, Jim is a man who has relied on luck to make good things happen in his life, rather than on hard work or realistic planning. Do you know someone who drifts along in life, hoping for a lucky break but doing little to make it happen? Write a paragraph describing how this person goes about his or her life. Introduce that person in your topic sentence, as in these examples:

My sister's former husband relies on luck, not work or planning, to get ahead in life.

Instead of studying, my roommate hopes that luck will be enough to help her pass her classes.

Then give several specific examples of the person's behavior. Conclude by providing a suggestion about what this person might do in order to take the responsibility of creating his or her own "good luck."

Alternatively, write a paragraph about a person who plans logically and works hard to achieve his or her goals.

Assignment 3: Writing an Essay

Rooney uses just one example—Jim Oakland's story—to suggest the general point that people should not count on the lottery to make them rich. Write an essay in which you, like Rooney, defend an idea that many oppose or have given little thought to. Perhaps you will argue that high schools should distribute birth-control devices to students or that alcohol should be banned on your college campus.

Develop your essay by describing in detail the experiences of one person. Your three supporting paragraphs may be organized by time order, describing the person's experience from an early to a later point; or they may be organized as a list—for example, showing how the person's experience affected him or her in three different ways. In your conclusion, make it clear, as Rooney does, that the one person you're writing about is intended to illustrate a general point.

Here is a sample outline for one such essay:

Thesis statement: Alcoholic beverages should be banned on this campus.

Topic sentence 1: Drinking affected Beverly's academic life.

Topic sentence 2: Drinking also affected Beverly's social life.

Topic sentence 3: Finally, drinking jeopardized Beverly's work life.

Conclusion: Many students, like Beverly, have their lives damaged and even ruined by alcohol.

What Good Families Are Doing Right

Delores Curran

It isn't easy to be a successful parent these days. Pressured by the conflicting demands of home and workplace, confused by changing moral standards, and drowned out by their offspring's rock music and television, today's parents seem to be facing impossible odds in their struggle to raise healthy families. Yet some parents manage to "do it all"—and even remain on speaking terms with their children. How do they do it? Delores Curran's survey offers some significant suggestions; her article could serve as a recipe for a successful family.

1. I have worked with families for fifteen years, conducting hundreds of seminars, workshops, and classes on parenting, and I meet good families all the time. They're fairly easy to recognize. Good families have a kind of visible strength. They expect problems and work together to find solutions, applying common sense and trying new methods to meet new needs. And they share a common shortcoming—they can tell me in a minute what's wrong with them, but they aren't sure what's right with them. Many healthy families with whom I work, in fact, protest at being called *healthy.* They don't think they are. The professionals who work with them do.

2. To prepare the book on which this article is based, I asked respected workers in the fields of education, religion, health, family counseling, and voluntary organizations to identify a list of possible traits of a healthy family. Together we isolated fifty-six such traits, and I sent this list to five hundred professionals who regularly work with families—teachers, doctors, principals, members of the clergy, scout directors, YMCA leaders, family counselors, social workers—asking them to pick the fifteen qualities they most commonly found in healthy families.

3. While all of these traits are important, the one most often cited as central to close family life is communication: The healthy family knows how to talk—and how to listen.

4. "Without communication you don't know one another," wrote one family counselor. "If you don't know one another, you don't care about one another, and that's what the family is all about."

5. "The most familiar complaint I hear from wives I counsel is 'He won't talk to me' and 'He doesn't listen to me,'" said a pastoral marriage counselor. "And when I share this complaint with their husbands, they don't hear *me,* either."

6. "We have kids in classes whose families are so robotized by television that they don't know one another," said a fifth-grade teacher.

7. Professional counselors are not the only ones to recognize the need. The phenomenal growth of communication groups such as Parent Effectiveness Training,

Parent Awareness, Marriage Encounter, Couple Communication, and literally hundreds of others tells us that the need for effective communication—the sharing of deepest feelings—is felt by many.

Healthy families have also recognized this need, and they have, either instinctively or consciously, developed methods of meeting it. They know that conflicts are to be expected, that we all become angry and frustrated and discouraged. And they know how to reveal those feelings—good and bad—to each other. Honest communication isn't always easy. But when it's working well, there are certain recognizable signs or symptoms, what I call the hallmarks of the successfully communicating family. 8

The Family Exhibits a Strong Relationship between the Parents

According to Dr. Jerry M. Lewis—author of a significant work on families, *No Single Thread*—healthy spouses complement, rather than dominate, each other. Either husband or wife could be the leader, depending on the circumstances. In the unhealthy families he studied, the dominant spouse had to hide feelings of weakness while the submissive spouse feared being put down if he or she exposed a weakness. 9

Children in the healthy family have no question about which parent is boss. Both parents are. If children are asked who is boss, they're likely to respond, "Sometimes Mom, sometimes Dad." And, in a wonderful statement, Dr. Lewis adds, "If you ask if they're comfortable with this, they look at you as if you're crazy—as if there's no other way it ought to be." 10

My survey respondents echo Dr. Lewis. One wrote, "The healthiest families I know are ones in which the mother and father have a strong, loving relationship. This seems to flow over to the children and even beyond the home. It seems to breed security in the children and, in turn, fosters the ability to take risks, to reach out to others, to search for their own answers, become independent and develop a good self-image." 11

The Family Has Control over Television

Television has been maligned, praised, damned, cherished, and even thrown out. It has more influence on children's values than anything else except their parents. Over and over, when I'm invited to help families mend their communication ruptures, I hear "But we have no time for this." These families have literally turned their "family-together" time over to television. Even those who control the quality of programs watched and set "homework-first" regulations feel reluctant to intrude upon the individual's right to spend his or her spare time in front of the set. Many families avoid clashes over program selection by furnishing a set for each family member. One of the women who was most desperate to establish a better sense of communication in her family confided to me that they owned nine sets. Nine sets for seven people! 12

Whether the breakdown in family communication leads to excessive viewing   13
or whether too much television breaks into family lives, we don't know. But we
do know that we can become out of one another's reach when we're in front of
a TV set. The term *television widow* is not humorous to thousands whose spouses
are absent even when they're there. One woman remarked, "I can't get worried
about whether there's life after death. I'd be satisfied with life after dinner."

In family-communication workshops, I ask families to make a list of phrases   14
they most commonly hear in their home. One parent was aghast to discover that
his family's most familiar comments were "What's on?" and "Move." In families
like this one, communication isn't hostile—it's just missing.

But television doesn't have to be a villain. A 1980 Gallup Poll found that the   15
public sees great potential for television as a positive force. It can be a tremendous device for initiating discussion on subjects that may not come up elsewhere,
subjects such as sexuality, corporate ethics, sportsmanship, and marital fidelity.

Even very bad programs offer material for values clarification if family mem-   16
bers view them together. My sixteen-year-old son and his father recently watched
a program in which hazardous driving was part of the hero's characterization. At
one point, my son turned to his dad and asked, "Is that possible to do with that
kind of truck?"

"I don't know," replied my husband, "but it sure is dumb. If that load   17
shifted . . ." With that, they launched into a discussion on the responsibility of
drivers that didn't have to originate as a parental lecture. Furthermore, as the
discussion became more engrossing to them, they turned the sound down so that
they could continue their conversation.

Parents frequently report similar experiences; in fact, this use of television was   18
recommended in the widely publicized 1972 Surgeon General's report as the most
effective form of television gatekeeping by parents. Instead of turning off the set,
parents should view programs with their children and make moral judgments and
initiate discussion. Talking about the problems and attitudes of a TV family can
be a lively, nonthreatening way to risk sharing real fears, hopes, and dreams.

The Family Listens and Responds

"My parents say they want me to come to them with problems, but when I do,   19
either they're busy or they only half-listen and keep on doing what they were
doing—like shaving or making a grocery list. If a friend of theirs came over to talk,
they'd stop, be polite, and listen," said one of the children quoted in a *Christian
Science Monitor* interview by Ann McCarroll. This child put his finger on the most
difficult problem of communicating in families: the inability to listen.

It is usually easier to react than to respond. When we react, we reflect our   20
own experiences and feelings; when we respond, we get into the other person's
feelings. For example:

Tom, age seventeen: "I don't know if I want to go to college. I don't think I'd do
very well there."
Father: "Nonsense. Of course you'll do well."

That's reacting. This father is cutting off communication. He's refusing either 21 to hear the boy's fears or to consider his feelings, possibly because he can't accept the idea that his son might not attend college. Here's another way of handling the same situation:

Tom: "I don't know if I want to go to college. I don't think I'd do very well there."
Father: "Why not?"
Tom: "Because I'm not that smart."
Father: "Yeah, that's scary. I worried about that, too."
Tom: "Did you ever come close to flunking out?"
Father: "No, but I worried a lot before I went because I thought college would be full of brains. Once I got there, I found out that most of the kids were just like me."

This father has responded rather than reacted to his son's fears. First, he 22 searched for the reason behind his son's lack of confidence and found it was fear of academic ability (it could have been fear of leaving home, of a new environment, of peer pressure, or of any of a number of things); second, he accepted the fear as legitimate; third, he empathized by admitting to having the same fear when he was Tom's age; and, finally, he explained why his, not Tom's, fears turned out to be groundless. He did all this without denigrating or lecturing.

And that's tough for parents to do. Often we don't want to hear our children's 23 fears, because those fears frighten us; or we don't want to pay attention to their dreams because their dreams aren't what we have in mind for them. Parents who deny such feelings will allow only surface conversation. It's fine as long as a child says, "School was OK today," but when she says, "I'm scared of boys," the parents are uncomfortable. They don't want her to be afraid of boys, but since they don't quite know what to say, they react with a pleasant "Oh, you'll outgrow it." She probably will, but what she needs at the moment is someone to hear and understand her pain.

In Ann McCarroll's interviews, she talked to one fifteen-year-old boy who said 24 he had *"some* mother. Each morning she sits with me while I eat breakfast. We talk about anything and everything. She isn't refined or elegant or educated. She's a terrible housekeeper. But she's interested in everything I do, and she always listens to me—even if she's busy or tired."

That's the kind of listening found in families that experience real commu- 25 nication. Answers to the routine question, "How was your day?" are heard with the eyes and heart as well as the ears. Nuances are picked up and questions are asked, although problems are not necessarily solved. Members of a family who really listen to one another instinctively know that if people listen to you, they are interested in you. And that's enough for most of us.

The Family Recognizes Unspoken Messages

Much of our communication—especially our communication of feelings—is non- 26 verbal. Dr. Lewis defines *empathy* as "someone responding to you in such a way that you feel deeply understood." He says, "There is probably no more important dimension in all of human relationships than the capacity for empathy. And healthy families teach empathy." Their members are allowed to be mad, glad, and sad. There's no crime in being in a bad mood, nor is there betrayal in being happy while someone else is feeling moody. The family recognizes that bad days and good days attack everyone at different times.

27 Nonverbal expressions of love, too, are the best way to show children that parents love each other. A spouse reaching for the other's hand, a wink, a squeeze on the shoulder, a "How's-your-back-this-morning?" a meaningful glance across the room—all these tell children how their parents feel about each other.

28 The most destructive nonverbal communication in marriage is silence. Silence can mean lack of interest, hostility, denigration, boredom, or outright war. On the part of a teen or preteen, silence usually indicates pain, sometimes very deep pain. The sad irony discovered by so many family therapists is that parents who seek professional help when a teenager becomes silent have often denied the child any other way of communicating. And although they won't permit their children to become angry or to reveal doubts or to share depression, they do worry about the withdrawal that results. Rarely do they see any connection between the two.

29 Healthy families use signs, symbols, body language, smiles, and other gestures to express caring and love. They deal with silence and withdrawal in a positive, open way. Communication doesn't mean just talking or listening; it includes all the clues to a person's feelings—his bearing, her expression, their resignation. Family members don't have to say, "I'm hurting," or, "I'm in need." A quick glance tells that. And they have developed ways of responding that indicate caring and love, whether or not there's an immediate solution to the pain.

The Family Encourages Individual Feelings and Independent Thinking

30 Close families encourage the emergence of individual personalities through open sharing of thoughts and feelings. Unhealthy families tend to be less open, less accepting of differences among members. The family must be Republican, or Bronco supporters, or gun-control advocates, and woe to the individual who says, "Yes, but . . . ."

31 Instead of finding differing opinions threatening, the healthy family finds them exhilarating. It is exciting to witness such a family discussing politics, sports, or the world. Members freely say, "I don't agree with you," without risking ridicule or rebuke. They say, "I think it's wrong . . ." immediately after Dad says, "I think it's right. . ."; and Dad listens and responds.

32 Give-and-take gives children practice in articulating their thoughts at home so that eventually they'll feel confident outside the home. What may seem to be verbal rambling by preteens during a family conversation is a prelude to sorting out their thinking and putting words to their thoughts.

33 Rigid families don't understand the dynamics of give-and-take. Some label it disrespectful and argumentative; others find it confusing. Dr. John Meeks, medical director of the Psychiatric Institute of Montgomery County, Maryland, claims

that argument is a way of life with normally developing adolescents. "In early adolescence they'll argue with parents about anything at all; as they grow older, the quantity of argument decreases but the quality increases." According to Dr. Meeks, arguing is something adolescents need to do. If the argument doesn't become too bitter, they have a good chance to test their own beliefs and feelings. "Incidentally," says Meeks, "parents can expect to 'lose' most of these arguments, because adolescents are not fettered by logic or even reality." Nor are they likely to be polite. Learning how to disagree respectfully is a difficult task, but good families work at it.

Encouraging individual feelings and thoughts, of course, in no way presumes 34 that parents permit their children to do whatever they want. There's a great difference between permitting a son to express an opinion on marijuana and allowing him to use it. That his opinion conflicts with his parents' opinion is OK as long as his parents make sure he knows their thinking on the subject. Whether he admits it or not, he's likely at least to consider their ideas if he respects them.

Permitting teenagers to sort out their feelings and thoughts in open discussions 35 at home gives them valuable experience in dealing with a bewildering array of situations they may encounter when they leave home. Cutting off discussion of behavior unacceptable to us, on the other hand, makes our young people feel guilty for even thinking about values contrary to ours and ends up making those values more attractive to them.

The Family Recognizes Turn-Off Words and Put-Down Phrases

Some families deliberately use hurtful language in their daily communication. 36 "What did you do all day around here?" can be a red flag to a woman who has spent her day on household tasks that don't show unless they're not done. "If only we had enough money" can be a rebuke to a husband who is working as hard as he can to provide for the family. "Flunk any tests today, John?" only discourages a child who may be having trouble in school.

Close families seem to recognize that a comment made in jest can be insulting. 37 A father in one of my groups confided that he could tease his wife about every-thing but her skiing. "I don't know why she's so sensitive about that, but I back off on it. I can say anything I want to about her cooking, her appearance, her mothering—whatever. But not her skiing."

One of my favorite exercises with families is to ask them to reflect upon 38 phrases they most like to hear and those they least like to hear. Recently, I invited seventy-five fourth- and fifth-graders to submit the words they most like to hear from their mothers. Here are the five big winners:

> *"I love you."*
> *"Yes."*
> *"Time to eat."*
> *"You can go."*
> *"You can stay up late."*

And on the children's list of what they least like to hear from one another are 39 the following:

"I'm telling."
"Mom says!"
"I know something you don't know."
"You think you're so big."
"Just see if I ever let you use my bike again."

It can be worthwhile for a family to list the phrases members like most and 40 least to hear, and post them. Often parents aren't even aware of the reaction of their children to certain routine comments. Or keep a record of the comments heard most often over a period of a week or two. It can provide good clues to the level of family sensitivity. If the list has a lot of "shut ups" and "stop its," that family needs to pay more attention to its relationships, especially the role that communication plays in them.

The Family Interrupts, but Equally

When Dr. Jerry M. Lewis began to study the healthy family, he and his staff video- 41 taped families in the process of problem solving. The family was given a question, such as, "What's the main thing wrong with your family?" Answers varied, but what was most significant was what the family actually did: who took control, how individuals responded or reacted, what were the put-downs, and whether some members were entitled to speak more than others.

The researchers found that healthy families expected everyone to speak 42 openly about feelings. Nobody was urged to hold back. In addition, these family members interrupted one another repeatedly, but no one person was interrupted more than anyone else.

Manners, particularly polite conversational techniques, are not hallmarks of 43 the communicating family. This should make many parents feel better about their family's dinner conversation. One father reported to me that at their table people had to take a number to finish a sentence. Finishing sentences, however, doesn't seem all that important in the communicating family. Members aren't sensitive to being interrupted, either. The intensity and spontaneity of the exchange are more important than propriety in conversation.

The Family Develops a Pattern of Reconciliation

"We know how to break up," one man said, "but who ever teaches us to make 44 up?" Survey respondents indicated that there is indeed a pattern of reconciliation in healthy families that is missing in others. "It usually isn't a kiss-and-make-up situation," explained one family therapist, "but there are certain rituals developed over a long period of time that indicate it's time to get well again. Between husband and wife, it might be a concessionary phrase to which the other is expected to respond in kind. Within a family, it might be that the person who stomps off to his or her room voluntarily reenters the family circle, where something is said to make him or her welcome."

When I asked several families how they knew a fight had ended, I got remark- 45 ably similar answers from individuals questioned separately. "We all come out of our rooms," responded every member of one family. Three members of another family said, "Mom says, 'Anybody want a Pepsi?'" One five-year-old scratched his head and furrowed his forehead after I asked him how he knew the family fight was over. Finally, he said, "Well, Daddy gives a great big yawn and says, 'Well . . .'" This scene is easy to visualize, as one parent decides that the unpleasantness needs to end and it's time to end the fighting and to pull together again as a family.

Why have we neglected the important art of reconciling? "Because we have 46 pretended that good families don't fight," says one therapist. "They do. It's essential to fight for good health in the family. It gets things out into the open. But we need to learn to put ourselves back together—and many families never learn this."

Close families know how to time divisive and emotional issues that may cause 47 friction. They don't bring up potentially explosive subjects right before they go out, for example, or before bedtime. They tend to schedule discussions rather than allow a matter to explode, and thus they keep a large measure of control over the atmosphere in which they will fight and reconcile. Good families know that they need enough time to discuss issues heatedly, rationally, and completely—and enough time to reconcile. "You've got to solve it right there," said one father. "Don't let it go on and on. It just causes more problems. Then when it's solved, let it be. No nagging, no remembering."

The Family Fosters Table Time and Conversation

Traditionally, the dinner table has been a symbol of socialization. It's probably the 48 one time each day that parents and children are assured of uninterrupted time with one another.

Therapists frequently call upon a patient's memory of the family table during 49 childhood in order to determine the degree of communication and interaction there was in the patient's early life. Some patients recall nothing. Mealtime was either so unpleasant or so unimpressive that they have blocked it out of their memories. Therapists say that there is a relationship between the love in a home and life around the family table. It is to the table that love or discord eventually comes.

But we are spending less table time together. Fast-food dining, even within 50 the home, is becoming a way of life for too many of us. Work schedules, individual organized activities, and television all limit the quantity and quality of mealtime interaction. In an informal study conducted by a church group, 68 percent of the families interviewed in three congregations saw nothing wrong with watching television while eating.

Families who do a good job of communicating tend to make the dinner meal 51 an important part of their day. A number of respondents indicated that adults in the healthiest families refuse dinner business meetings as a matter of principle and discourage their children from sports activities that cut into mealtime hours. "We know which of our swimmers will or won't practice at dinnertime," said a coach, with mixed admiration. "Some parents never allow their children to miss dinners. Some don't care at all." These families pay close attention to the number of times they'll be able to be together in a week, and they rearrange schedules to be sure of spending this time together.

The family that wants to improve communication should look closely at its atti- 52 tudes toward the family table. Are family table time and conversation important? Is table time open and friendly or warlike and sullen? Is it conducive to sharing more than food—does it encourage the sharing of ideas, feelings, and family intimacies?

We all need to talk to one another. We need to know we're loved and appre- 53 ciated and respected. We want to share our intimacies, not just physical intimacies but all the intimacies in our lives. Communication is the most important element of family life because it is basic to loving relationships. It is the energy that fuels the caring, giving, sharing, and affirming. Without genuine sharing of ourselves, we cannot know one another's needs and fears. Good communication is what makes all the rest of it work.

■ Reading Comprehension Questions

1. The word *aghast* in "One parent was aghast to discover that his family's most familiar comments were 'What's on?' and 'Move'" (paragraph 14) means

   a. horrified.

   b. satisfied.

   c. curious.

   d. amused.

2. The word *engrossing* in "as the discussion became more engrossing to them, they turned the sound down so that they could continue their conversation" (paragraph 17) means

   a. disgusting.

   b. intellectual.

   c. foolish.

   d. interesting.

3. Which of the following would be the best alternative title for this selection?

   a. Successful Communication

   b. How to Solve Family Conflicts

   c. Characteristics of Families

   d. Hallmarks of the Communicating Family

4. Which sentence best expresses the article's main point?

    a.   Television can and often does destroy family life.

    b.   More American families are unhappy than ever before.

    c.   A number of qualities mark the healthy and communicating family.

    d.   Strong families encourage independent thinking.

5. *True or false?* _____ According to the article, healthy families have no use for television.

6. Healthy families

    a.   never find it hard to communicate.

    b.   have no conflicts with each other.

    c.   know how to reveal their feelings.

    d.   permit one of the parents to make all final decisions.

7. The author has found that good families frequently make a point of being together

    a.   in the mornings.

    b.   after school.

    c.   during dinner.

    d.   before bedtime.

8. *True or false?* _____ The article implies that the most troublesome nonverbal signal is silence.

9. The article implies that

    a.   verbal messages are always more accurate than nonverbal ones.

    b.   in strong families, parents practice tolerance of thoughts and feelings.

    c.   parents must avoid arguing with their adolescent children.

    d.   parents should prevent their children from watching television.

10. From the article, we can conclude that

    a.   a weak marital relationship often results in a weak family.

    b.   children should not witness a disagreement between parents.

    c.   children who grow up in healthy families learn not to interrupt other family members.

    d.   parents always find it easier to respond to their children than to react to them.

■ Discussion Questions

About Content

1. What are the nine hallmarks of a successfully communicating family? Which of the nine do you feel are most important?

2. How do good parents control television watching? How do they make television a positive force instead of a negative one?

3. In paragraph 20, the author says, "It is usually easier to react than to respond." What is the difference between the two terms *react* and *respond?*

4. Why, according to Curran, is a "pattern of reconciliation" (paragraph 44) crucial to good family life? Besides those patterns mentioned in the essay, can you describe a reconciliation pattern you have developed with friends or family?

About Structure

5. What is the thesis of the selection? Write here the number of the paragraph in which it is stated: _____

6. What purpose is achieved by Curran's introduction (paragraphs 1–2)? Why is a reader likely to feel that her article will be reliable and worthwhile?

7. Curran frequently uses dialogue or quotations from unnamed parents or children as the basis for her examples. The conversation related in paragraphs 16–17 is one instance. Find three other dialogues used to illustrate points in the essay and write the numbers below:

Paragraph(s) _____

Paragraph(s) _____

Paragraph(s) _____

About Style and Tone

8. Curran enlivens the essay by using some interesting and humorous remarks from parents, children, and counselors. One is the witty comment in paragraph 5 from a marriage counselor: "And when I share this complaint with their husbands, they don't hear *me,* either." Find two other places where the author keeps your interest by using humorous or enjoyable quotations, and write the numbers of the paragraphs here:

_____   _____

■ Writing Assignments

Assignment 1: Writing a Paragraph

Write a definition paragraph on the hallmarks of a *bad* family. Your topic sentence might be, "A bad family is one that is _____, _____, and _____."

To get started, you should first reread the features of a good family explained in the selection. Doing so will help you think about what qualities are found in a bad family. Prepare a list of as many bad qualities as you can think of. Then go through the list and decide on the qualities that seem most characteristic of a bad family.

Assignment 2: Writing a Paragraph

Curran tells us five phrases that some children say they most like to hear from their mothers (paragraph 38). When you were younger, what statement or action of one of your parents (or another adult) would make you especially happy—or sad? Write a paragraph that begins with a topic sentence like one of the following:

> A passing comment my grandfather once made really devastated me.
>
> When I was growing up, there were several typical ways my mother treated me that always made me sad.
>
> A critical remark by my fifth-grade teacher was the low point of my life.
>
> My mother has always had several lines that make her children feel very pleased.

You may want to write a narrative that describes in detail the particular time and place of a statement or action. Or you may want to provide three or so examples of statements or actions and their effect on you.

To get started, make up two long lists of childhood memories involving adults—happy memories and sad memories. Then decide which memory or memories you could most vividly describe in a paragraph. Remember that your goal is to help your readers see for themselves why a particular time was sad or happy for you.

Assignment 3: Writing an Essay

In light of Curran's description of what healthy families do right, examine your own family. Which of Curran's traits of communicative families fit your family? Write an essay pointing out three things that your family is doing right in creating a communicative climate for its members. Or, if you feel your family could work harder at communicating, write the essay about three specific ways your family could improve. In either case, choose three of Curran's nine "hallmarks of the successfully communicating family" and show how they do or do not apply to your family.

In your introductory paragraph, include a thesis statement as well as a plan of development that lists the three traits you will talk about. Then present these traits in turn in three supporting paragraphs. Develop each paragraph by giving specific examples of conversations, arguments, behavior patterns, and so on, that illustrate how your family communicates. Finally, conclude your essay with a summarizing sentence or two and a final thought about your subject.

Education and
Self-Improvement

Do It Better!

Ben Carson, M.D., with Cecil Murphey

If you suspect that you are now as "smart" as you'll ever be, then read the following selection. Taken from the book *Think Big,* it is about Dr. Ben Carson, who was sure he was "the dumbest kid in the class" when he was in fifth grade. Carson tells how he turned his life totally around from what was a sure path of failure. Today he is a famous neurosurgeon at the Johns Hopkins University Children's Center in Baltimore, Maryland.

"Benjamin, is this your report card?" my mother asked as she picked up the folded white card from the table.   1

"Uh, yeah," I said, trying to sound casual. Too ashamed to hand it to her, I had dropped it on the table, hoping that she wouldn't notice until after I went to bed.   2

It was the first report card I had received from Higgins Elementary School since we had moved back from Boston to Detroit, only a few months earlier.   3

I had been in the fifth grade not even two weeks before everyone considered me the dumbest kid in the class and frequently made jokes about me. Before long I too began to feel as though I really was the most stupid kid in fifth grade. Despite Mother's frequently saying, "You're smart, Bennie. You can do anything you want to do," I did not believe her.   4

No one else in school thought I was smart, either.   5

Now, as Mother examined my report card, she asked, "What's this grade in reading?" (Her tone of voice told me that I was in trouble.) Although I was embarrassed, I did not think too much about it. Mother knew that I wasn't doing well in math, but she did not know I was doing so poorly in every subject.   6

While she slowly read my report card, reading everything one word at a time, I hurried into my room and started to get ready for bed. A few minutes later, Mother came into my bedroom.   7

"Benjamin," she said, "are these your grades?" She held the card in front of me as if I hadn't seen it before.   8

"Oh, yeah, but you know, it doesn't mean much."   9

"No, that's not true, Bennie. It means a lot."   10

"Just a report card."   11

"But it's more than that."   12

Knowing I was in for it now, I prepared to listen, yet I was not all that interested. 13
I did not like school very much and there was no reason why I should. Inasmuch as
I was the dumbest kid in the class, what did I have to look forward to? The others
laughed at me and made jokes about me every day.

"Education is the only way you're ever going to escape poverty," she said. "It's 14
the only way you're ever going to get ahead in life and be successful. Do you
understand that?"

"Yes, Mother," I mumbled.   15

"If you keep on getting these kinds of grades you're going to spend the rest 16
of your life on skid row, or at best sweeping floors in a factory. That's not the kind
of life that I want for you. That's not the kind of life that God wants for you."   17

I hung my head, genuinely ashamed. My mother had been raising me and my
older brother, Curtis, by herself. Having only a third-grade education herself, she
knew the value of what she did not have. Daily she drummed into Curtis and me
that we had to do our best in school.

"You're just not living up to your potential," she said. "I've got two mighty 18
smart boys and I know they can do better."

I had done my best—at least I had when I first started at Higgins Elementary 19
School. How could I do much when I did not understand anything going on in our
class?

In Boston we had attended a parochial school, but I hadn't learned much 20
because of a teacher who seemed more interested in talking to another female
teacher than in teaching us. Possibly, this teacher was not solely to blame—perhaps
I wasn't emotionally able to learn much. My parents had separated just before we
went to Boston, when I was eight years old. I loved both my mother and father and
went through considerable trauma over their separating. For months afterward,
I kept thinking that my parents would get back together, that my daddy would
come home again the way he used to, and that we could be the same old family
again—but he never came back. Consequently, we moved to Boston and lived
with Aunt Jean and Uncle William Avery in a tenement building for two years
until Mother had saved enough money to bring us back to Detroit.

Mother kept shaking the report card at me as she sat on the side of my bed. 21
"You have to work harder. You have to use that good brain that God gave you,
Bennie. Do you understand that?"

"Yes, Mother." Each time she paused, I would dutifully say those words.   22

"I work among rich people, people who are educated," she said. "I watch how 23
they act, and I know they can do anything they want to do. And so can you." She
put her arm on my shoulder. "Bennie, you can do anything they can do—only you
can do it better!"

Mother had said those words before. Often. At the time, they did not mean 24
much to me. Why should they? I really believed that I was the dumbest kid in fifth
grade, but of course, I never told her that.

"I just don't know what to do about you boys," she said. "I'm going to talk 25
to God about you and Curtis." She paused, stared into space, then said (more to
herself than to me), "I need the Lord's guidance on what to do. You just can't
bring in any more report cards like this."

As far as I was concerned, the report card matter was over.   26

The next day was like the previous ones—just another bad day in school,   27
another day of being laughed at because I did not get a single problem right in
arithmetic and couldn't get any words right on the spelling test. As soon as I came
home from school, I changed into play clothes and ran outside. Most of the boys
my age played softball, or the game I liked best, "Tip the Top."

We played Tip the Top by placing a bottle cap on one of the sidewalk cracks.   28
Then taking a ball—any kind that bounced—we'd stand on a line and take turns
throwing the ball at the bottle top, trying to flip it over. Whoever succeeded got
two points. If anyone actually moved the cap more than a few inches, he won five
points. Ten points came if he flipped it into the air and it landed on the other side.

When it grew dark or we got tired, Curtis and I would finally go inside and   29
watch TV. The set stayed on until we went to bed. Because Mother worked long
hours, she was never home until just before we went to bed. Sometimes I would
awaken when I heard her unlocking the door.

Two evenings after the incident with the report card, Mother came home   30
about an hour before our bedtime. Curtis and I were sprawled out, watching TV.
She walked across the room, snapped off the set, and faced both of us. "Boys,"
she said, "you're wasting too much of your time in front of that television. You
don't get an education from staring at television all the time."

Before either of us could make a protest, she told us that she had been praying   31
for wisdom. "The Lord's told me what to do," she said. "So from now on, you will
not watch television, except for two preselected programs each week."

"Just *two* programs?" I could hardly believe she would say such a terrible   32
thing. "That's not—"

"And *only* after you've done your homework. Furthermore, you don't play   33
outside after school, either, until you've done all your homework."

"Everybody else plays outside right after school," I said, unable to think of   34
anything except how bad it would be if I couldn't play with my friends. "I won't
have any friends if I stay in the house all the time—"

"That may be," Mother said, "but everybody else is not going to be as successful   35
as you are—"

"But, Mother—"   36

"This is what we're going to do. I asked God for wisdom, and this is the answer   37
I got."

I tried to offer several other arguments, but Mother was firm. I glanced at   38
Curtis, expecting him to speak up, but he did not say anything. He lay on the floor,
staring at his feet.

"Don't worry about everybody else. The whole world is full of 'everybody   39
else,' you know that? But only a few make a significant achievement."

The loss of TV and play time was bad enough. I got up off the floor, feeling   40
as if everything was against me. Mother wasn't going to let me play with my
friends, and there would be no more television—almost none, anyway. She was
stopping me from having any fun in life.

"And that isn't all," she said. "Come back, Bennie."   41

I turned around, wondering what else there could be.   42

"In addition," she said, "to doing your homework, you have to read two 43
books from the library each week. Every single week."

"Two books? Two?" Even though I was in fifth grade, I had never read a 44
whole book in my life.

"Yes, two. When you finish reading them, you must write me a book report 45
just like you do at school. You're not living up to your potential, so I'm going to
see that you do."

Usually Curtis, who was two years older, was the more rebellious. But this time 46
he seemed to grasp the wisdom of what Mother said. He did not say one word.

She stared at Curtis. "You understand?" 47

He nodded. 48

"Bennie, is it clear?" 49

"Yes, Mother." I agreed to do what Mother told me—it wouldn't have 50
occurred to me not to obey—but I did not like it. Mother was being unfair and
demanding more of us than other parents did.

The following day was Thursday. After school, Curtis and I walked to the local 51
branch of the library. I did not like it much, but then I had not spent that much
time in any library.

We both wandered around a little in the children's section, not having any 52
idea about how to select books or which books we wanted to check out.

The librarian came over to us and asked if she could help. We explained that 53
both of us wanted to check out two books.

"What kind of books would you like to read?" the librarian asked. 54

"Animals," I said after thinking about it. "Something about animals." 55

"I'm sure we have several that you'd like." She led me over to a section of 56
books. She left me and guided Curtis to another section of the room. I flipped
through the row of books until I found two that looked easy enough for me to
read. One of them, *Chip, the Dam Builder*—about a beaver—was the first one I had
ever checked out. As soon as I got home, I started to read it. It was the first book
I ever read all the way through even though it took me two nights. Reluctantly I
admitted afterward to Mother that I really had liked reading about Chip.

Within a month I could find my way around the children's section like someone 57
who had gone there all his life. By then the library staff knew Curtis and me and
the kind of books we chose. They often made suggestions. "Here's a delightful
book about a squirrel," I remember one of them telling me.

As she told me part of the story, I tried to appear indifferent, but as soon as 58
she handed it to me, I opened the book and started to read.

Best of all, we became favorites of the librarians. When new books came in 59
that they thought either of us would enjoy, they held them for us. Soon I became
fascinated as I realized that the library had so many books—and about so many
different subjects.

After the book about the beaver, I chose others about animals—all types of 60
animals. I read every animal story I could get my hands on. I read books about
wolves, wild dogs, several about squirrels, and a variety of animals that lived in
other countries. Once I had gone through the animal books, I started reading
about plants, then minerals, and finally rocks.

My reading books about rocks was the first time the information ever became 61 practical to me. We lived near the railroad tracks, and when Curtis and I took the route to school that crossed by the tracks, I began paying attention to the crushed rock that I noticed between the ties.

As I continued to read more about rocks, I would walk along the tracks, 62 searching for different kinds of stones, and then see if I could identify them.

Often I would take a book with me to make sure that I had labeled each stone 63 correctly.

"Agate," I said as I threw the stone. Curtis got tired of my picking up stones 64 and identifying them, but I did not care because I kept finding new stones all the time. Soon it became my favorite game to walk along the tracks and identify the varieties of stones. Although I did not realize it, within a very short period of time, I was actually becoming an expert on rocks.

Two things happened in the second half of fifth grade that convinced me of 65 the importance of reading books.

First, our teacher, Mrs. Williamson, had a spelling bee every Friday afternoon. 66 We'd go through all the words we'd had so far that year. Sometimes she also called out words that we were supposed to have learned in fourth grade. Without fail, I always went down on the first word.

One Friday, though, Bobby Farmer, whom everyone acknowledged as the 67 smartest kid in our class, had to spell "agriculture" as his final word. As soon as the teacher pronounced his word, I thought, *I can spell that word.* Just the day before, I had learned it from reading one of my library books. I spelled it under my breath, and it was just the way Bobby spelled it.

If I can spell "agriculture," I'll bet I can learn to spell any other word in the 68 *world. I'll bet I can learn to spell better than Bobby Farmer.*

Just that single word, "agriculture," was enough to give me hope. 69

The following week, a second thing happened that forever changed my life. 70 When Mr. Jaeck, the science teacher, was teaching us about volcanoes, he held up an object that looked like a piece of black, glass-like rock. "Does anybody know what this is? What does it have to do with volcanoes?"

Immediately, because of my reading, I recognized the stone. I waited, but 71 none of my classmates raised their hands. I thought, *This is strange. Not even the smart kids are raising their hands.* I raised my hand.

"Yes, Benjamin," he said. 72

I heard snickers around me. The other kids probably thought it was a joke, 73 or that I was going to say something stupid.

"Obsidian," I said. 74

"That's right!" He tried not to look startled, but it was obvious he hadn't 75 expected me to give the correct answer.

"That's obsidian," I said, "and it's formed by the supercooling of lava when it 76 hits the water." Once I had their attention and realized I knew information no other student had learned, I began to tell them everything I knew about the subject of obsidian, lava, lava flow, supercooling, and compacting of the elements.

When I finally paused, a voice behind me whispered, "Is that Bennie Carson?" 77

"You're absolutely correct," Mr. Jaeck said and he smiled at me. If he had announced that I'd won a million-dollar lottery, I couldn't have been more pleased and excited.   78

"Benjamin, that's absolutely, absolutely right," he repeated with enthusiasm in his voice. He turned to the others and said, "That is wonderful! Class, this is a tremendous piece of information Benjamin has just given us. I'm very proud to hear him say this."   79

For a few moments, I tasted the thrill of achievement. I recall thinking, *Wow, look at them. They're all looking at me with admiration. Me, the dummy! The one everybody thinks is stupid. They're looking at me to see if this is really me speaking.*   80

Maybe, though, it was I who was the most astonished one in the class. Although I had been reading two books a week because Mother told me to, I had not realized how much knowledge I was accumulating. True, I had learned to enjoy reading, but until then I hadn't realized how it connected with my schoolwork. That day—for the first time—I realized that Mother had been right. Reading is the way out of ignorance, and the road to achievement. I did not have to be the class dummy anymore.   81

For the next few days, I felt like a hero at school. The jokes about me stopped. The kids started to listen to me. *I'm starting to have fun with this stuff.*   82

As my grades improved in every subject, I asked myself, "Ben, is there any reason you can't be the smartest kid in the class? If you can learn about obsidian, you can learn about social studies and geography and math and science and everything."   83

That single moment of triumph pushed me to want to read more. From then on, it was as though I could not read enough books. Whenever anyone looked for me after school, they could usually find me in my bedroom—curled up, reading a library book—for a long time, the only thing I wanted to do. I had stopped caring about the TV programs I was missing; I no longer cared about playing Tip the Top or baseball anymore. I just wanted to read.   84

In a year and a half—by the middle of sixth grade—I had moved to the top of the class.   85

■ Reading Comprehension Questions

1. The word *trauma* in "I loved both my mother and father and went through considerable trauma over their separating. For months afterward, I kept thinking that my parents would get back together, . . . but he never came back" (paragraph 20) means

   a. love.

   b. knowledge.

   c. distance.

   d. suffering.

2. The word *acknowledged* in "One Friday, though, Bobby Farmer, whom everyone acknowledged as the smartest kid in our class, had to spell 'agriculture' as his final word" (paragraph 67) means

   a. denied.

   b. recognized.

   c. forgot.

   d. interrupted.

3. Which of the following would be the best alternative title for this selection?

   a. The Importance of Fifth Grade

   b. The Role of Parents in Education

   c. The Day I Surprised My Science Teacher

   d. Reading Changed My Life

4. Which sentence best expresses the main idea of this selection?

   a. Children who grow up in single-parent homes may spend large amounts of time home alone.

   b. Because of parental guidance that led to a love of reading, the author was able to go from academic failure to success.

   c. Most children do not take school very seriously, and they suffer as a result.

   d. Today's young people watch too much television.

5. Bennie's mother

   a. was not a religious person.

   b. spoke to Bennie's teacher about Bennie's poor report card.

   c. had only a third-grade education.

   d. had little contact with educated people.

6. To get her sons to do better in school, Mrs. Carson insisted that they

   a. stop watching TV.

   b. finish their homework before playing.

   c. read one library book every month.

   d. all of the above.

7. *True or false?* _____ Bennie's first experience with a library book was discouraging.

8. We can conclude that Bennie Carson believed he was dumb because

   a. in Boston he had not learned much.

   b. other students laughed at him.

   c.   he had done his best when he first started at Higgins Elementary School, but still got poor grades.

   d.   all of the above.

9.   We can conclude that the author's mother believed

   a.   education leads to success.

   b.   her sons needed to be forced to live up to their potential.

   c.   socializing was less important for her sons than a good education.

   d.   all of the above.

10.   From paragraphs 70–80, we can infer that

   a.   Bennie thought his classmates were stupid because they did not know about obsidian.

   b.   Mr. Jaeck knew less about rocks than Bennie did.

   c.   this was the first time Bennie had answered a difficult question correctly in class.

   d.   Mr. Jaeck thought that Bennie had taken too much class time explaining about obsidian.

■ Discussion Questions

About Content

1.   How do you think considering himself the "dumbest kid in class" affected Bennie's schoolwork?

2.   The author recalls his failure in the classroom as an eight-year-old child by writing, "Perhaps I wasn't emotionally able to learn much." Why does he make this statement? What do you think parents and schools can do to help children through difficult times?

3.   How did Mrs. Carson encourage Bennie to make school—particularly reading—a priority in his life? What effect did her efforts have on Bennie's academic performance and self-esteem?

4.   As a child, Carson began to feel confident about his own abilities when he followed his mother's guidelines. How might Mrs. Carson's methods help adult students build up their own self-confidence and motivation?

About Structure

5.   What is the main order in which the details of this selection are organized—time order or listing order? Locate and write below three of the many transitions that are used as part of that time order or listing order.

_____   _____   _____

6. In paragraph 65, Carson states, "Two things happened in the second half of fifth grade that convinced me of the importance of reading books." What two transitions does Carson use in later paragraphs to help readers recognize those two events? Write those two transitions here:

_____   _____

About Style and Tone

7. Instead of describing his mother, Carson reveals her character through specific details of her actions and words. Find one paragraph in which this technique is used, and write its number here: _____. What does this paragraph tell us about Mrs. Carson?

8. Why do you suppose Carson italicizes sentences in paragraphs 67, 68, 71, 80, and 82? What purpose do the italicized sentences serve?

■ Writing Assignments

Assignment 1: Writing a Paragraph

The reading tells about some of Carson's most important school experiences, both positive and negative. Write a paragraph about one of your most important experiences in school. To select an event to write about, try asking yourself the following questions:

Which teachers or events in school influenced how I felt about myself?

What specific incidents stand out in my mind as I think back to elementary school?

To get started, you might use freewriting to help you remember and record the details. Then begin your draft with a topic sentence similar to one of the following:

A seemingly small experience in elementary school encouraged me greatly.

If not for my sixth-grade teacher, I would not be where I am today.

My tenth-grade English class was a turning point in my life.

Use concrete details—actions, comments, reactions, and so on—to help your readers see what happened.

Assignment 2: Writing a Paragraph

Reading helped Bennie, and it can do a lot for adults, too. Most of us, however, don't have someone around to make us do a certain amount of personal reading every week. In addition, many of us don't have as much free time as Bennie and Curtis had. How can adults find time to read more? Write a paragraph listing several ways adults can add more reading to their lives.

To get started, simply write down as many ways as you can think of—in any order. Here is an example of a prewriting list for this paper:

> Situations in which adults can find extra time to read:
> Riding to and from work or school
> In bed at night before turning off the light
> While eating breakfast or lunch
> Instead of watching some TV
> In the library

Feel free to use items from the list above, but see if you can add at least one or two of your own points as well. Use details such as descriptions and examples to emphasize and dramatize your supporting details.

Assignment 3: Writing an Essay

Mrs. Carson discovered an effective way to boost her children's achievement and self-confidence. There are other ways as well. Write an essay whose thesis statement is "There are several ways parents can help children live up to their potential." Then, in the following paragraphs, explain and illustrate two or three methods parents can use. In choosing material for your supporting paragraphs, you might consider some of these areas, or think of others on your own:

Assigning regular household "chores" and rewarding a good job

Encouraging kids to join an organization that fosters achievement: Scouts, Little League, religious group, or neighborhood service club

Going to parent-teacher conferences at school and then working more closely with children's teachers—knowing when assignments are due, etc.

Giving a child some responsibility for an enjoyable family activity, such as choosing decorations or food for a birthday party

Setting up a "Wall of Fame" in the home where children's artwork, successful schoolwork, etc. can be displayed

Setting guidelines (as Mrs. Carson did) for use of leisure time, homework time, and the like

Draw on examples from your own experiences or from someone else's—including those of Bennie Carson, if you like.

Anxiety: Challenge by Another Name

James Lincoln Collier

What is your basis for making personal decisions? Do you aim to rock the boat as little as possible, choosing the easy, familiar path? There is comfort in sticking with what is safe and well-known, just as there is comfort in eating mashed potatoes. But James Lincoln Collier, author of numerous articles and books, decided soon after leaving college not to live a mashed-potato sort of life. In this essay, first published in *Reader's Digest,* he tells how he learned to recognize the marks of a potentially exciting, growth-inducing experience, to set aside his anxiety, and to dive in.

1 Between my sophomore and junior years at college, a chance came up for me to spend the summer vacation working on a ranch in Argentina. My roommate's father was in the cattle business, and he wanted Ted to see something of it. Ted said he would go if he could take a friend, and he chose me.

2 The idea of spending two months on the fabled Argentine pampas* was exciting. Then I began having second thoughts. I had never been very far from New England, and I had been homesick my first weeks at college. What would it be like in a strange country? What about the language? And besides, I had promised to teach my younger brother to sail that summer. The more I thought about it, the more the prospect daunted me. I began waking up nights in a sweat.

3 In the end I turned down the proposition. As soon as Ted asked somebody else to go, I began kicking myself. A couple of weeks later I went home to my old summer job, unpacking cartons at the local supermarket, feeling very low. I had turned down something I wanted to do because I was scared, and I had ended up feeling depressed. I stayed that way for a long time. And it didn't help when I went back to college in the fall to discover that Ted and his friend had had a terrific time.

4 In the long run that unhappy summer taught me a valuable lesson out of which I developed a rule for myself: *do what makes you anxious, don't do what makes you depressed.*

5 I am not, of course, talking about severe states of anxiety or depression, which require medical attention. What I mean is that kind of anxiety we call stage fright, butterflies in the stomach, a case of nerves—the feelings we have at a job interview, when we're giving a big party, when we have to make an important presentation at the office. And the kind of depression I am referring to is that downhearted feeling of the blues, when we don't seem to be interested in anything, when we can't get going and seem to have no energy.

---

*A vast plain in south-central South America.

I was confronted by this sort of situation toward the end of my senior year. As graduation approached, I began to think about taking a crack at making my living as a writer. But one of my professors was urging me to apply to graduate school and aim at a teaching career. 6

I wavered. The idea of trying to live by writing was scary—a lot more scary than spending a summer on the pampas, I thought. Back and forth I went, making my decision, unmaking it. Suddenly, I realized that every time I gave up the idea of writing, that sinking feeling went through me; it gave me the blues. 7

The thought of graduate school wasn't what depressed me. It was giving up on what deep in my gut I really wanted to do. Right then I learned another lesson. To avoid that kind of depression meant, inevitably, having to endure a certain amount of worry and concern. 8

The great Danish philosopher Søren Kierkegaard believed that anxiety always arises when we confront the possibility of our own development. It seems to be a rule of life that you can't advance without getting that old, familiar, jittery feeling. 9

Even as children we discover this when we try to expand ourselves by, say, learning to ride a bike or going out for the school play. Later in life we get butterflies when we think about having that first child, or uprooting the family from the old hometown to find a better opportunity halfway across the country. Any time, it seems, that we set out aggressively to get something we want, we meet up with anxiety. And it's going to be our traveling companion, at least part of the way, in any new venture. 10

When I first began writing magazine articles, I was frequently required to interview big names—people like Richard Burton, Joan Rivers, sex authority William Masters, baseball great Dizzy Dean. Before each interview I would get butterflies and my hands would shake. 11

At the time, I was doing some writing about music. And one person I particularly admired was the great composer Duke Ellington. On stage and on television, he seemed the very model of the confident, sophisticated man of the world. Then I learned that Ellington still got stage fright. If the highly honored Duke Ellington, who had appeared on the bandstand some ten thousand times over thirty years, had anxiety attacks, who was I to think I could avoid them? 12

I went on doing those frightening interviews, and one day, as I was getting onto a plane for Washington to interview columnist Joseph Alsop, I suddenly realized to my astonishment that I was looking forward to the meeting. What had happened to those butterflies? 13

Well, in truth, they were still there, but there were fewer of them. I had benefited, I discovered, from a process psychologists call "extinction." If you put an individual in an anxiety-provoking situation often enough, he will eventually learn that there isn't anything to be worried about. 14

Which brings us to a corollary to my basic rule: *you'll never eliminate anxiety by avoiding the things that caused it.* I remember how my son Jeff was when I first began to teach him to swim at the lake cottage where we spent our summer vacations. He resisted, and when I got him into the water he sank and sputtered and wanted to quit. But I was insistent. And by summer's end he was splashing around like a puppy. He had "extinguished" his anxiety the only way he could— by confronting it. 15

The problem, of course, is that it is one thing to urge somebody else to take on those anxiety-producing challenges; it is quite another to get ourselves to do it. 16

Some years ago I was offered a writing assignment that would require three months of travel through Europe. I had been abroad a couple of times on the usual "If it's Tuesday this must be Belgium"* trips, but I hardly could claim to know my way around the continent. Moreover, my knowledge of foreign languages was limited to a little college French. 17

I hesitated. How would I, unable to speak the language, totally unfamiliar with local geography or transportation systems, set up interviews and do research? It seemed impossible, and with considerable regret I sat down to write a letter begging off. Halfway through, a thought—which I subsequently made into another corollary to my basic rule—ran through my mind: *you can't learn if you don't try.* So I accepted the assignment. 18

There were some bad moments. But by the time I had finished the trip I was an experienced traveler. And ever since, I have never hesitated to head for even the most exotic of places, without guides or even advance bookings, confident that somehow I will manage. 19

The point is that the new, the different, is almost by definition scary. But each time you try something, you learn, and as the learning piles up, the world opens to you. 20

I've made parachute jumps, learned to ski at forty, flown up the Rhine in a balloon. And I know I'm going to go on doing such things. It's not because I'm braver or more daring than others. I'm not. But I don't let the butterflies stop me from doing what I want. Accept anxiety as another name for challenge, and you can accomplish wonders. 21

■ Reading Comprehension Questions

1. The word *daunted* in "The more I thought about [going to Argentina], the more the prospect daunted me. I began waking up nights in a sweat" (paragraph 2) means

   a.   encouraged.

   b.   interested.

   c.   discouraged.

   d.   amused.

2. The word *corollary* in "Which brings us to a corollary to my basic rule: *you'll never eliminate anxiety by avoiding the things that caused it*" (paragraph 15) means

   a.   an idea that follows from another idea.

   b.   an idea based on a falsehood.

---

*Reference to a film comedy about a group of American tourists who visited too many European countries in too little time.

    c.   an idea that creates anxiety.

    d.   an idea passed on from one generation to another.

3. Which of the following would be the best alternative title for this selection?

    a.   A Poor Decision

    b.   Don't Let Anxiety Stop You

    c.   Becoming a Writer

    d.   The Courage to Travel

4. Which sentence best expresses the main idea of the selection?

    a.   The butterflies-in-the-stomach type of anxiety differs greatly from severe states of anxiety or depression.

    b.   Taking on a job assignment that required traveling helped the author get over his anxiety.

    c.   People learn and grow by confronting, not backing away from, situations that make them anxious.

    d.   Anxiety is a predictable part of life that can be dealt with in positive ways.

5. When a college friend invited the writer to go with him to Argentina, the writer

    a.   turned down the invitation.

    b.   accepted eagerly.

    c.   was very anxious about the idea but went anyway.

    d.   did not believe his friend was serious.

6. *True or false?* _____ As graduation approached, Collier's professor urged him to try to make his living as a writer.

7. *True or false?* _____ The philosopher Søren Kierkegaard believed that anxiety occurs when we face the possibility of our own development.

8. "Extinction" is the term psychologists use for

    a.   the inborn tendency to avoid situations that make one feel very anxious.

    b.   a person's gradual loss of confidence.

    c.   the natural development of a child's abilities.

    d.   the process of losing one's fear by continuing to face the anxiety-inspiring situation.

9. The author implies that

    a.   it was lucky he didn't take the summer job in Argentina.

    b.   his son never got over his fear of the water.

c.   Duke Ellington's facing stage fright inspired him.

d.   one has to be more daring than most people to overcome anxiety.

10. The author implies that

a.   anxiety may be a signal that one has an opportunity to grow.

b.   he considers his three-month trip to Europe a failure.

c.   facing what makes him anxious has eliminated all depression from his life.

d.   he no longer has anxiety about new experiences.

■ Discussion Questions

About Content

1. Collier developed the rule "Do what makes you anxious; don't do what makes you depressed." How does he distinguish between feeling anxious and feeling depressed?

2. In what way does Collier believe that anxiety is positive? How, according to him, can we eventually overcome our fears? Have you ever gone ahead and done something that made you anxious? How did it turn out?

About Structure

3. Collier provides a rule and two corollary rules that describe his attitude toward challenge and anxiety. Below, write the location of that rule and its corollaries.

   Collier's rule: paragraph _____
   First corollary: paragraph _____
   Second corollary: paragraph _____

   How does Collier emphasize the rule and its corollaries?

4. Collier uses several personal examples in his essay. Find three instances of these examples and explain how each helps Collier develop his main point.

About Style and Tone

5. In paragraph 3, Collier describes the aftermath of his decision not to go to Argentina. He could have just written, "I worked that summer." Instead he writes, "I went home to my old summer job, unpacking cartons at the local supermarket." Why do you think he provides that bit of detail about his job? What is the effect on the reader?

6. Authors often use testimony by authorities to support their points. Where in Collier's essay does he use such support? What do you think it adds to his piece?

7. In the last sentence of paragraph 10, Collier refers to anxiety as a "traveling companion." Why do you think he uses that image? What does it convey about his view of anxiety?

8. Is Collier just telling about a lesson he has learned for himself, or is he encouraging his readers to do something? How can you tell?

■ Writing Assignments

Assignment 1: Writing a Paragraph

Collier explains how his life experiences made him view the term *anxiety* in a new way. Write a paragraph in which you explain how a personal experience of yours has given new meaning to a particular term. Following are some terms you might wish to consider for this assignment:

> Failure
>
> Friendship
>
> Goals
>
> Homesickness
>
> Maturity
>
> Success

Here are two sample topic sentences for this assignment:

> I used to think of failure as something terrible, but thanks to a helpful boss, I now think of it as an opportunity to learn.
>
> The word *creativity* has taken on a new meaning for me ever since I became interested in dancing.

Assignment 2: Writing a Paragraph

The second corollary to Collier's rule is "you can't learn if you don't try." Write a paragraph using this idea as your main idea. Support it with your own experience, someone else's experience, or both. One way of developing this point is to compare two approaches to a challenge: One person may have backed away from a frightening opportunity while another person decided to take on the challenge. Or you could write about a time when you learned something useful by daring to give a new experience a try. In that case, you might discuss your reluctance to take on the new experience, the difficulties you encountered, and your eventual success. In your conclusion, include a final thought about the value of what was learned.

Listing a few skills you have learned will help you decide on the experience you wish to write about. To get you started, below is a list of things adults often need to go to some trouble to learn.

Driving with a stick shift

Taking useful lecture notes

Knowing how to do well on a job interview

Asking someone out on a date

Making a speech

Standing up for your rights

Assignment 3: Writing an Essay

Collier describes three rules he follows when facing anxiety. In an essay, write about one or more rules, or guidelines, that you have developed for yourself through experience. If you decide to discuss two or three such guidelines, mention or refer to them in your introductory paragraph. Then go on to discuss each in one or more paragraphs of its own. Include at least one experience that led you to develop a given guideline, and tell how it has helped you at other times in your life. You might end with a brief summary and an explanation of how the guidelines as a group have helped. If you decide to focus on one rule, include at least two or three experiences that help to illustrate your point.

To prepare for this assignment, spend some time freewriting about the rules or guidelines you have set up for yourself. Continue writing until you feel you have a central idea for which you have plenty of interesting support. Then organize that support into a scratch outline, such as this one:

Thesis: I have one rule that keeps me from staying in a rut: Don't let the size of a challenge deter you; instead, aim for it by making plans and taking steps.

Topic sentence 1: I began to think about my rule one summer in high school when a friend got the type of summer job that I had only been thinking about.

Topic sentence 2: After high school, I began to live up to my rule when I aimed for a business career and entered college.

Topic sentence 3: My rule is also responsible for my having the wonderful boyfriend [OR girlfriend OR job] I now have.

Old before Her Time

Katherine Barrett

Most of us wait for our own advanced years to learn what it is like to be old. Patty Moore decided not to wait. At the age of twenty-six, she disguised herself as an eighty-five-year-old woman. What she learned suggests that to be old in our society is both better and worse than is often thought. This selection may give you a different perspective on the older people in your life—on what they are really like inside and on what life is really like for them.

1   This is the story of an extraordinary voyage in time, and of a young woman who devoted three years to a singular experiment. In 1979, Patty Moore—then aged twenty-six—transformed herself for the first of many times into an eighty-five-year-old woman. Her object was to discover firsthand the problems, joys, and frustrations of the elderly. She wanted to know for herself what it's like to live in a culture of youth and beauty when your hair is gray, your skin is wrinkled, and no men turn their heads as you pass.

2   Her time machine was a makeup kit. Barbara Kelly, a friend and professional makeup artist, helped Patty pick out a wardrobe and showed her how to use latex to create wrinkles and wrap Ace bandages to give the impression of stiff joints. "It was peculiar," Patty recalls, as she relaxes in her New York City apartment. "Even the first few times I went out, I realized that I wouldn't have to act that much. The more I was perceived as elderly by others, the more 'elderly' I actually became. . . . I imagine that's just what happens to people who really are old."

3   What motivated Patty to make her strange journey? It was partly her career—as an industrial designer, Patty often focuses on the needs of the elderly. But the roots of her interest are also deeply personal. Extremely close to her own grandparents—particularly her maternal grandfather, now ninety—and raised in a part of Buffalo, New York, where there was a large elderly population, Patty always drew comfort and support from the older people around her. When her own marriage ended in 1979 and her life seemed to be falling apart, she dove into her "project" with all her soul. In all, she donned her costume more than two hundred times in fourteen states. Here is the remarkable story of what she found.

4   Columbus, Ohio, May 1979. Leaning heavily on her cane, Pat Moore stood alone in the middle of a crowd of young professionals. They were all attending a gerontology conference, and the room was filled with animated chatter. But no one was talking to Pat. In a throng of men and women who devoted their working lives to the elderly, she began to feel like a total nonentity. "I'll get us all some coffee," a young man told a group of women next to her. "What about me?" thought Pat. "If I were young, they would be offering me coffee, too." It was a bitter thought at the end of a disappointing day—a day that marked Patty's

first appearance as "the old woman." She had planned to attend the gerontology conference anyway, and almost as a lark decided to see how professionals would react to an old person in their midst.

Now, she was angry. All day she had been ignored . . . counted out in a way 5 she had never experienced before. She didn't understand. Why didn't people help her when they saw her struggling to open a heavy door? Why didn't they include her in conversations? Why did the other participants seem almost embarrassed by her presence at the conference—as if it were somehow inappropriate that an old person should be professionally active?

And so, eighty-five-year-old Pat Moore learned her first lesson: The old are 6 often ignored. "I discovered that people really do judge a book by its cover," Patty says today. "Just because I looked different, people either condescended to me or totally dismissed me. Later, in stores, I'd get the same reaction. A clerk would turn to someone younger and wait on her first. It was as if he assumed that I—the older woman—could wait because I didn't have anything better to do."

New York City, October 1979. Bent over her cane, Pat walked slowly toward the 7 edge of the park. She had spent the day sitting on a bench with friends, but now dusk was falling and her friends had all gone home. She looked around nervously at the deserted area and tried to move faster, but her joints were stiff. It was then that she heard the barely audible sound of sneakered feet approaching and the kids' voices. "Grab her, man." "Get her purse." Suddenly an arm was around her throat and she was dragged back, knocked off her feet.

She saw only a blur of sneakers and blue jeans, heard the sounds of mocking 8 laughter, felt fists pummeling her—on her back, her legs, her breasts, her stomach. "Oh, God," she thought, using her arms to protect her head and curling herself into a ball. "They're going to kill me. I'm going to die. . . ."

Then, as suddenly as the boys attacked, they were gone. And Patty was left 9 alone, struggling to rise. The boy's punches had broken the latex makeup on her face, the fall had disarranged her wig, and her whole body ached. (Later she would learn that she had fractured her left wrist, an injury that took two years to heal completely.) Sobbing, she left the park and hailed a cab to return home. Again the thought struck her: What if I really lived in the gray ghetto? . . . What if I couldn't escape to my nice safe home . . . ?

Lesson number two: the fear of crime is paralyzing. "I really understand now 10 why the elderly become homebound," the young woman says as she recalls her ordeal today. "When something like this happens, the fear just doesn't go away. I guess it wasn't so bad for me. I could distance myself from what happened . . . and I was strong enough to get up and walk away. But what about someone who is really too weak to run or fight back or protect herself in any way? And the elderly often can't afford to move if the area in which they live deteriorates, becomes unsafe. I met people like this, and they were imprisoned by their fear. That's when the bolts go on the door. That's when people starve themselves because they're afraid to go to the grocery store."

New York City, February, 1980. It was a slushy, gray day, and Pat had laboriously 11 descended four flights of stairs from her apartment to go shopping. Once outside, she struggled to hold her threadbare coat closed with one hand and manipulate her cane with the other. Splotches of snow made the street difficult for anyone to navigate, but for someone hunched over, as she was, it was almost impossible. The curb was another obstacle. The slush looked ankle-deep—and what was she to do? Jump over it? Slowly, she worked her way around to a drier spot, but the crowds were impatient to move. A woman with packages jostled her as she rushed past, causing Pat to nearly lose her balance. If I really were old, I would have fallen, she thought. Maybe broken something. On another day, a woman had practically knocked her over by letting go of a heavy door as Pat tried to enter a coffee shop. Then there were the revolving doors. How could you push them without strength? And how could you get up and down stairs, on and off a bus, without risking a terrible fall?

Lesson number three: If small, thoughtless deficiencies in design were corrected,   12 life would be so much easier for older people. It was no surprise to Patty that the "built" environment is often inflexible. But even she didn't realize the extent of the problems, she admits. "It was a terrible feeling. I never realized how difficult it is to get off a curb if your knees don't bend easily. Or the helpless feeling you get if your upper arms aren't strong enough to open a door. You know, I just felt so vulnerable—as if I was at the mercy of every barrier or rude person I encountered."

Fort Lauderdale, Florida, May 1980. Pat met a new friend while shopping, and   13 they decided to continue their conversation over a sundae at a nearby coffee shop. The woman was in her late seventies, "younger" than Pat, but she was obviously reaching out for help. Slowly, her story unfolded. "My husband moved out of our bedroom," the woman said softly, fiddling with her coffee cup and fighting back tears. "He won't touch me anymore. And when he gets angry at me for being stupid, he'll even sometimes . . . " The woman looked down, too embarrassed to go on. Pat took her hand. "He hits me; . . . he gets so mean." "Can't you tell anyone?" Pat asked. "Can't you tell your son?" "Oh, no!" the woman almost gasped. "I would never tell the children; they absolutely adore him."

Lesson number four: Even a fifty-year-old marriage isn't necessarily a good   14 one. While Pat met many loving and devoted elderly couples, she was stunned to find others who had stayed together unhappily—because divorce was still an anathema in their middle years. "I met women who secretly wished their husbands dead, because after so many years they just ended up full of hatred. One woman in Chicago even admitted that she deliberately angered her husband because she knew it would make his blood pressure rise. Of course, that was pretty extreme. . . ."

Patty pauses thoughtfully and continues. "I guess what really made an impres-   15 sion on me, the real eye-opener, was that so many of these older women had the same problems as women twenty, thirty, or forty—problems with men . . . problems with the different roles that are expected of them. As a 'young woman' I, too, had just been through a relationship where I spent a lot of time protecting someone by covering up his problems from family and friends. Then I heard this woman in Florida saying that she wouldn't tell her children their father beat her because she didn't want to disillusion them. These issues aren't age-related. They affect everyone."

Clearwater, Florida, January 1981. She heard the children laughing, but she 16 didn't realize at first that they were laughing at her. On this day, as on several others, Pat had shed the clothes of a middle-income woman for the rags of a bag lady. She wanted to see the extremes of the human condition, what it was like to be old and poor, and outside traditional society as well. Now, tottering down the sidewalk, she was most concerned with the cold, since her layers of ragged clothing did little to ease the chill. She had spent the afternoon rummaging through garbage cans, loading her shopping bags with bits of debris, and she was stiff and tired. Suddenly, she saw that four little boys, five or six years old, were moving up on her. And then she felt the sting of the pebbles they were throwing. She quickened her pace to escape, but another handful of gravel hit her and the laughter continued. They're using me as a target, she thought, horror-stricken. They don't even think of me as a person.

Lesson number five: Social class affects every aspect of an older person's 17 existence. "I found out that class is a very important factor when you're old," says Patty. "It was interesting. That same day, I went back to my hotel and got dressed as a wealthy woman, another role that I occasionally took. Outside the hotel, a little boy of about seven asked if I would go shelling with him. We walked along the beach, and he reached out to hold my hand. I knew he must have a grand-mother who walked with a cane, because he was so concerned about me and my footing. 'Don't put your cane there, the sand's wet,' he'd say. He really took responsibility for my welfare. The contrast between him and those children was really incredible—the little ones who were throwing pebbles at me because they didn't see me as human, and then the seven-year-old taking care of me. I think he would have responded to me the same way even if I had been dressed as the middle-income woman. There's no question that money does make life easier for older people, not only because it gives them a more comfortable lifestyle, but because it makes others treat them with greater respect."

New York City, May 1981. Pat always enjoyed the time she spent sitting on 18 the benches in Central Park. She'd let the whole day pass by, watching young children play, feeding the pigeons and chatting. One spring day she found herself sitting with three women, all widows, and the conversation turned to the few available men around. "It's been a long time since anyone hugged me," one woman complained. Another agreed. "Isn't that the truth. I need a hug, too." It was a favorite topic, Pat found—the lack of touching left in these women's lives, the lack of hugging, the lack of men.

In the last two years, she found out herself how it felt to walk down Fifth 19 Avenue and know that no men were turning to look after her. Or how it felt to look at models in magazines or store mannequins and know that those gorgeous clothes were just not made for her. She hadn't realized before just how much casual attention was paid to her because she was young and pretty. She hadn't realized it until it stopped.

Lesson number six: You never grow old emotionally. You always need to feel 20 loved. "It's not surprising that everyone needs love and touching and holding," says Patty. "But I think some people feel that you reach a point in your life when you accept that those intimate feelings are in the past. That's wrong. These women were still interested in sex. But more than that, they—like everyone—needed to be hugged and touched. I'd watch two women greeting each other on the street and just holding onto each other's hands, neither wanting to let go. Yet, I also saw that there are people who are afraid to touch an old person; . . . they were afraid to touch me. It's as if they think old age is a disease and it's catching. They think that something might rub off on them."

New York City, September 1981. He was a thin man, rather nattily dressed, 21 with a hat that he graciously tipped at Pat as he approached the bench where she sat. "Might I join you?" he asked jauntily. Pat told him he would be welcome and he offered her one of the dietetic hard candies that he carried in a crumpled paper bag. As the afternoon passed, they got to talking . . . about the beautiful buds on the trees and the world around them and the past. "Life's for the living, my wife used to tell me," he said. "When she took sick, she made me promise her that I wouldn't waste a moment. But the first year after she died, I just sat in the apartment. I didn't want to see anyone, talk to anyone or go anywhere. I missed her so much." He took a handkerchief from his pocket and wiped his eyes, and they sat in silence. Then he slapped his leg to break the mood and change the subject. He asked Pat about herself, and described his life alone. He belonged to a "senior center" now, and went on trips and had lots of friends. Life did go on. They arranged to meet again the following week on the same park bench. He brought lunch—chicken salad sandwiches and decaffeinated peppermint tea in a thermos—and wore a carnation in his lapel. It was the first date Patty had had since her marriage ended.

Lesson number seven: Life does go on . . . as long as you're flexible and open 22 to change. "That man really meant a lot to me, even though I never saw him again," says Patty, her eyes wandering toward the gray wig that now sits on a wig-stand on the top shelf of her bookcase. "He was a real old-fashioned gentleman, yet not afraid to show his feelings—as so many men my age are. It's funny, but at that point I had been through months of self-imposed seclusion. Even though I was in a different role, that encounter kind of broke the ice for getting my life together as a single woman."

In fact, while Patty was living her life as the old woman, some of her young 23 friends had been worried about her. After several years, it seemed as if the lines of identity had begun to blur. Even when she wasn't in makeup, she was wearing unusually conservative clothing, she spent most of her time with older people, and she seemed almost to revel in her role—sometimes finding it easier to be in costume than to be a single New Yorker.

But as Patty continued her experiment, she was also learning a great deal 24 from the older people she observed. Yes, society often did treat the elderly abysmally; . . . they were sometimes ignored, sometimes victimized, sometimes poor and frightened, but so many of them were survivors. They had lived through two world wars, through the Depression, and into the computer age. "If there was one lesson to learn, one lesson that I'll take with me into my old age, it's that you've got to be flexible," Patty says. "I saw my friend in the park, managing after the loss of his wife, and I met countless other people who picked themselves up after something bad—or even something catastrophic—happened. I'm not worried about them. I'm worried about the others who shut themselves away. It's funny, but seeing these two extremes helped me recover from the trauma in my own life, to pull my life together."

Today, Patty is back to living the life of a single thirty-year-old, and she rarely dons her costumes anymore. "I must admit, though, I do still think a lot about aging," she says. "I look in the mirror and I begin to see wrinkles, and then I realize that I won't be able to wash those wrinkles off." Is she afraid of growing older? "No. In a way, I'm kind of looking forward to it," she smiles. "I know it will be different from my experiment. I know I'll probably even look different. When they aged Orson Welles in *Citizen Kane* he didn't resemble at all the Orson Welles of today." 25

But Patty also knows that in one way she really did manage to capture the feeling of being old. With her bandages and her stooped posture, she turned her body into a kind of prison. Yet inside she didn't change at all. "It's funny, but that's exactly how older people always say they feel," says Patty. "Their bodies age, but inside they are really no different from when they were young." 26

■ Reading Comprehension Questions

1. The word *nonentity* in "But no one was talking to Pat. In a throng of men and women who devoted their working lives to the elderly, she began to feel like a total nonentity. . . . All day she had been ignored" (paragraphs 4–5) means

   a. expert.

   b. nobody.

   c. experiment.

   d. leader.

2. The word *abysmally* in "society often did treat the elderly abysmally; . . . they were sometimes ignored, sometimes victimized, sometimes poor and frightened" (paragraph 24) means

   a. politely.

   b. absentmindedly.

   c. very badly.

   d. angrily.

3. Which of the following would be the best alternative title for this selection?

   a. How Poverty Affects the Elderly

   b. Similarities Between Youth and Old Age

   c. One Woman's Discoveries about the Elderly

   d. Violence against the Elderly

4. Which sentence best expresses the main idea of the selection?

   a.   The elderly often have the same problems as young people.

   b.   Pat Moore dressed up like an elderly woman over two hundred times.

   c.   By making herself appear old, Pat Moore learned what life is like for the elderly in the United States.

   d.   Elderly people often feel ignored in a society that glamorizes youth.

5. *True or false?* _____ As they age, people need others less.

6. Pat Moore learned that the elderly often become homebound because of the

   a.   high cost of living.

   b.   fear of crime.

   c.   availability of in-home nursing care.

   d.   lack of interesting places for them to visit.

7. One personal lesson Pat Moore learned from her experiment was that

   a.   she needs to start saving money for her retirement.

   b.   by being flexible she can overcome hardships.

   c.   she has few friends her own age.

   d.   her marriage could have been saved.

8. From paragraph 2, we can infer that

   a.   behaving like an old person was difficult for Moore.

   b.   many older people wear Ace bandages.

   c.   people sometimes view themselves as others see them.

   d.   Barbara Kelly works full-time making people look older than they really are.

9. The article suggests that fifty years ago

   a.   young couples tended to communicate better than today's young couples.

   b.   divorce was less acceptable than it is today.

   c.   verbal and physical abuse was probably extremely rare.

   d.   the elderly were treated with great respect.

10. We can conclude that Pat Moore may have disguised herself as an elderly woman over two hundred times in fourteen states because

   a.   she and her friend Barbara Kelly continuously worked at perfecting Moore's costumes.

   b.   her company made her travel often.

c. she was having trouble finding locations with large numbers of elderly people.

d. she wanted to see how the elderly were seen and treated all over the country, rather than in just one area.

■ Discussion Questions

About Content

1. Why did Pat Moore decide to conduct her experiment? Which of her discoveries surprised you?

2. Using the information Moore learned from her experiment, list some of the things that could be done to help the elderly. What are some things you personally could do?

3. How do the elderly people Moore met during her experiment compare with the elderly people you know?

4. Lesson number seven in the article is "Life does go on . . . as long as you're flexible and open to change" (paragraph 22). What do you think this really means? How might this lesson apply to situations and people you're familiar with—in which people either were or were not flexible and open to change?

About Structure

5. Most of the selection is made up of a series of Pat Moore's experiences and the seven lessons they taught. Find the sentence used by the author to introduce those experiences and lessons, and write that sentence here:

_____

6. The details of paragraph 21 are organized in time order, and the author has used a few time transition words to signal time relationships. Find two of those time words, and write them here:

_____   _____

About Style and Tone

7. What device does the author use to signal that she is beginning a new set of experiences and the lesson they taught? How does she ensure that the reader will recognize what each of the seven lessons is?

8. Do you think Barrett is objective in her treatment of Patty Moore? Or does the author allow whatever her feelings might be for Moore to show in her writing? Find details in the article to support your answer.

■ Writing Assignment

Assignment 1: Writing a Paragraph

In her experiment, Moore discovered various problems faced by the elderly. Choose one of these areas of difficulty and write a paragraph in which you discuss what could be done in your city to help solve the problem. Following are a few possible topic sentences for this assignment:

> Fear of crime among the elderly could be eased by a program providing young people to accompany them on their errands.

> The courthouse and train station in our town need to be redesigned to allow easier access for the elderly.

> Schools should start adopt-a-grandparent programs, which would enrich the emotional lives of both the young and the old participants.

Assignment 2: Writing a Paragraph

What did you learn from the selection, or what do you already know, about being older in our society that might influence your own future? Write a paragraph in which you list three or four ways in which you plan to minimize or avoid some of the problems often faced by elderly people. For instance, you may decide to do whatever you can to remain as healthy and strong as possible throughout your life. That might involve quitting smoking and incorporating exercise into your schedule. Your topic sentence might simply be: "There are three important ways in which I hope to avoid some of the problems often faced by the elderly."

Assignment 3: Writing an Essay

Lesson number seven in Barrett's article is "Life does go on . . . as long as you're flexible and open to change" (paragraph 22). Think about one person of any age whom you know well (including yourself). Write an essay in which you show how being (or not being) flexible and open to change has been important in that person's life. Develop your essay with three main examples.

In preparation for writing, think of several key times in your subject's life. Select three times in which being flexible or inflexible had a significant impact on that person. Then narrate and explain each of those times in a paragraph of its own. Here are two possible thesis statements for this essay:

> My grandmother generally made the most of her circumstances by being flexible and open to change.

> When I was a teenager, I could have made life easier for myself by being more flexible and open to change.

Your conclusion for this essay might summarize the value of being flexible or the problems of being inflexible, or both, for the person you are writing about.

Assignment 4: Writing an Essay Using Internet Research

As Patty Moore studied the elderly people around her, she recognized that some were "survivors"—people who adapted successfully to the challenges of aging—and some were not. What can people do, both mentally and physically, to make their later years active and happy? Use the Internet to see what some experts have suggested. Then write an essay on three ways that people can cope well with old age.

To access the Internet, use the very helpful search engine Google (*www.google.com*) or one of the other search engines listed on pages 323–325 of this book. Try one of the following phrases or some related phrase:

growing older and keeping active and happy

happy healthy aging

elderly people and healthy living

You may, of course, use a simple phrase such as "growing older," but that will bring up too many items. As you proceed, you'll develop a sense of how to "track down" and focus a topic by adding more information to your search words and phrases.

Let's Really Reform Our Schools

Anita Garland

A few years back, a National Commission on Excellence in Education published *A Nation at Risk,* in which the commission reported on a "rising tide of mediocrity" in our schools. Other studies have pointed to students' poor achievement in science, math, communication, and critical thinking. What can our schools do to improve students' performance? Anita Garland has several radical ideas, which she explains in this selection. As you read it, think about whether or not you agree with her points.

American high schools are in trouble. No, that's not strong enough. American high
schools are disasters. "Good" schools today are only a rite of passage for American
kids, where the pressure to look fashionable and act cool outweighs any concern
for learning. And "bad" schools—heaven help us—are havens for the vicious and
corrupt. There, metal detectors and security guards wage a losing battle against
the criminals that prowl the halls.

Desperate illnesses require desperate remedies. And our public schools are
desperately ill. What is needed is no meek, fainthearted attempt at "curriculum
revision" or "student-centered learning." We need to completely restructure our
thinking about what schools are and what we expect of the students who attend
them.

The first change needed to save our schools is the most fundamental one. Not
only must we stop *forcing* everyone to attend school; we must stop *allowing* the
attendance of so-called students who are not interested in studying. Mandatory
school attendance is based upon the idea that every American has a right to basic
education. But as the old saying goes, your rights stop where the next guy's begin.
A student who sincerely wants an education, regardless of his or her mental or
physical ability, should be welcome in any school in this country. But "students"
who deliberately interfere with other students' ability to learn, teachers' ability
to teach, and administrators' ability to maintain order should be denied a place
in the classroom. They do not want an education. And they should not be allowed
to mark time within school walls, waiting to be handed their meaningless diplomas
while they make it harder for everyone around them to either provide or receive
a quality education.

By requiring troublemakers to attend school, we have made it impossible to deal
with them in any effective way. They have little to fear in terms of punishment.
Suspension from school for a few days doesn't improve their behavior. After all,
they don't want to be in school anyway. For that matter, mandatory attendance
is, in many cases, nothing but a bad joke. Many chronic troublemakers are absent
so often that it is virtually impossible for them to learn anything. And when they
are in school, they are busy shaking down other students for their lunch money
or jewelry. If we permanently banned such punks from school, educators could
turn their attention away from the troublemakers and toward those students who
realize that school is a serious place for serious learning.

You may ask, "What will become of these young people who aren't in school?"
But consider this: What is becoming of them now? They are not being educated.
They are merely names on the school records. They are passed from grade to grade,
learning nothing, making teachers and fellow students miserable. Finally they are
bumped off the conveyor belt at the end of twelfth grade, oftentimes barely
literate, and passed into society as "high school graduates." Yes, there would be
a need for alternative solutions for these young people. Let the best thinkers of
our country come up with some ideas. But in the meanwhile, don't allow our
schools to serve as a holding tank for people who don't want to be there.

Once our schools have been returned to the control of teachers and genuine
students, we could concentrate on smaller but equally meaningful reforms. A
good place to start would be requiring students to wear school uniforms. There

would be cries of horror from the fashion slaves, but the change would benefit everyone. If students wore uniforms, think of the mental energy that could be redirected into more productive channels. No longer would young girls feel the need to spend their evenings laying out coordinated clothing, anxiously trying to create just the right look. The daily fashion show that currently absorbs so much of students' attentions would come to a halt. Kids from modest backgrounds could stand out because of their personalities and intelligence, rather than being tagged as losers because they can't wear the season's hottest sneakers or jeans. Affluent kids might learn they have something to offer the world other than a fashion statement. Parents would be relieved of the pressure to deal with their offspring's constant demands for wardrobe additions.

7   Next, let's move to the cafeteria. What's for lunch today? How about a Milky Way bar, a bag of Fritos, a Coke, and just to round out the meal with a vegetable, maybe some french fries. And then back to the classroom for a few hours of intense mental activity, fueled on fat, salt, and sugar. What a joke! School is an institution of education, and that education should be continued as students sit down to eat. Here's a perfect opportunity to teach a whole generation of Americans about nutrition, and we are blowing it. School cafeterias, of all places, should demonstrate how a healthful, low-fat, well-balanced diet produces healthy, energetic, mentally alert people. Instead, we allow school cafeterias to dispense the same junk food that kids could buy in any mall. Overhaul the cafeterias! Out with the candy, soda, chips, and fries! In with the salads, whole grains, fruits, and vegetables!

8   Turning our attention away from what goes on during school hours, let's consider what happens after the final bell rings. Some school-sponsored activities are all to the good. Bands and choirs, foreign-language field trips, chess or skiing or drama clubs are sensible parts of an extracurricular plan. They bring together kids with similar interests to develop their talents and leadership ability. But other common school activities are not the business of education. The prime example of inappropriate school activity is in competitive sports between schools.

9   Intramural sports are great. Students need an outlet for their energies, and friendly competition against one's classmates on the basketball court or baseball diamond is fun and physically beneficial. But the wholesome fun of sports is quickly ruined by the competitive team system. School athletes quickly become the campus idols, encouraged to look down on classmates with less physical ability. Schools concentrate enormous amounts of time, money, and attention upon their teams, driving home the point that competitive sports are the *really* important part of school. Students are herded into gymnasiums for "pep rallies" that whip up adoration of the chosen few and encourage hatred of rival schools. Boys' teams are supplied with squads of cheerleading girls . . . let's not even get into what the subliminal message is *there*. If communities feel they must have competitive sports, let local businesses or even professional teams organize and fund the programs. But school budgets and time should be spent on programs that benefit more than an elite few.

10   Another school-related activity that should get the ax is the fluff-headed, money-eating, misery-inducing event known as the prom. How in the world did the schools of America get involved in this showcase of excess? Proms have to be the

epitome of everything that is wrong, tasteless, misdirected, inappropriate, and just plain sad about the way we bring up our young people. Instead of simply letting the kids put on a dance, we've turned the prom into a bloated nightmare that ruins young people's budgets, their self-image, and even their lives. The pressure to show up at the prom with the best-looking date, in the most expensive clothes, wearing the most exotic flowers, riding in the most extravagant form of transportation, dominates the thinking of many students for months before the prom itself. Students cling to doomed, even abusive romantic relationships rather than risk being dateless for this night of nights. They lose any concept of meaningful values as they implore their parents for more, more, more money to throw into the jaws of the prom god. The adult trappings of the prom—the slinky dresses, emphasis on romance, slow dancing, nightclub atmosphere—all encourage kids to engage in behavior that can have tragic consequences. Who knows how many unplanned pregnancies and alcohol-related accidents can be directly attributed to the pressures of prom night? And yet, not going to the prom seems a fate worse than death to many young people—because of all the hype about the "wonder" and "romance" of it all. Schools are not in the business of providing wonder and romance, and it's high time we remembered that.

We have lost track of the purpose of our schools. They are not intended to   11 be centers for fun, entertainment, and social climbing. They are supposed to be institutions for learning and hard work. Let's institute the changes suggested here—plus dozens more—without apology, and get American schools back to business.

■ Reading Comprehension Questions

1. The word *affluent* in "Kids from modest backgrounds could stand out because of their personalities and intelligence. . . . Affluent kids might learn they have something to offer the world other than a fashion statement" (paragraph 6) means

    a. intelligent.

    b. troubled.

    c. wealthy.

    d. poor.

2. The word *implore* in "They lose any concept of meaningful values as they implore their parents for more, more, more money to throw into the jaws of the prom god" (paragraph 10) means

    a. ignore.

    b. beg.

    c. pay.

    d. obey.

3. Which of the following would be the best alternative title for this selection?

    a. America's Youth

    b. Education of the Future

    c. Social Problems of Today's Students

    d. Changes Needed in the American School System

4. Which sentence best expresses the main idea of the selection?

    a. Excesses such as the prom and competitive sports should be eliminated from school budgets.

    b. Major changes are needed to make American schools real centers of learning.

    c. Attendance must be voluntary in our schools.

    d. The best thinkers of our country must come up with ideas on how to improve our schools.

5. Garland believes that mandatory attendance at school

    a. gives all students an equal chance at getting an education.

    b. allows troublemakers to disrupt learning.

    c. is cruel to those who don't really want to be there.

    d. helps teachers maintain control of their classes.

6. Garland is against school-sponsored competitive sports because she believes that

    a. exercise and teamwork should not have a role in school.

    b. they overemphasize the importance of sports and athletes.

    c. school property should not be used in any way after school hours.

    d. they take away from professional sports.

7. We can infer that Garland believes

    a. teens should not have dances.

    b. proms promote unwholesome values.

    c. teens should avoid romantic relationships.

    d. proms are even worse than mandatory education.

8. The author clearly implies that troublemakers

    a. are not intelligent.

    b. really do want to be in school.

    c. should be placed in separate classes.

    d. don't mind being suspended from school.

9. *True or false?* _____ We can conclude that the author feels that teachers and genuine students have lost control of our schools.

10. The essay suggests that the author would also oppose
    a. school plays.
    b. serving milk products in school cafeterias.
    c. the selection of homecoming queens.
    d. stylish school uniforms.

■ Discussion Questions

About Content

1. What reforms does Garland suggest in her essay? Think back to your high school days. Which of the reforms that Garland suggests do you think might have been most useful at your high school?

2. Garland's idea of voluntary school attendance directly contradicts the "stay in school" campaigns. Do you agree with her idea? What do you think might become of students who choose not to attend school?

3. At the end of her essay, Garland writes, "Let's institute the changes suggested here—plus dozens more." What other changes do you think Garland may have in mind? What are some reforms you think might improve schools?

About Structure

4. The thesis of this essay can be found in the introduction, which is made up of the first two paragraphs. Find the thesis statement and write it here:

    _____

    _____

5. The first point on Garland's list of reforms is the elimination of mandatory (that is, required) education. Then she goes on to discuss other reforms. Find the transition sentence which signals that she is leaving the discussion about mandatory education and going on to other needed changes. Write that sentence here:

    _____

    _____

6. What are two transitional words that Garland uses to introduce two of the other reforms?

    _____   _____

About Style and Tone

7. Garland uses some colorful images to communicate her ideas. For instance, in paragraph 5 she writes, "Finally [the troublemakers] are bumped off the conveyor belt at the end of twelfth grade, oftentimes barely literate, and passed into society as 'high school graduates.'" What does the image of a conveyor belt imply about schools and about the troublemakers? What do the quotation marks around *high school graduates* imply?

8. Below are three other colorful images from the essay. What do the italicized words imply about today's schools and students?

> . . . don't allow our schools to serve as a *holding tank* for people who don't want to be there. (paragraph 5)

> A good place to start would be requiring students to wear school uniforms. There would be cries of horror from the *fashion slaves* . . . (paragraph 6)

> Students are *herded* into gymnasiums for "pep rallies" that whip up adoration of the chosen few . . . (paragraph 9)

9. To convey her points, does the author use a formal, straightforward tone or an informal, impassioned tone? Give examples from the essay to support your answer.

■ Writing Assignments

Assignment 1: Writing a Paragraph

Write a persuasive paragraph in which you agree or disagree with one of Garland's suggested reforms. Your topic sentence may be something simple and direct, like these:

> I strongly agree with Garland's point that attendance should be voluntary in our high schools.

> I disagree with Garland's point that high school students should be required to wear uniforms.

Alternatively, you may want to develop your own paragraph calling for reform in some other area of American life. Your topic sentence might be like one of the following:

> We need to make radical changes in our treatment of homeless people.

> Strong new steps must be taken to control the sale of guns in our country.

> Major changes are needed to keep television from dominating the lives of our children.

Assignment 2: Writing a Paragraph

If troublemakers were excluded from schools, what would become of them? Write a paragraph in which you suggest two or three types of programs that trouble-makers could be assigned to. Explain why each program would be beneficial to the troublemakers themselves and society in general. You might want to include in your paragraph one or more of the following:

Apprentice programs

Special neighborhood schools for troublemakers

Reform schools

Work-placement programs

Community service programs

Assignment 3: Writing an Essay

Garland suggests ways to make schools "institutions for learning and hard work." She wants to get rid of anything that greatly distracts students from their education, such as having to deal with troublemakers, overemphasis on fashion, and interschool athletics. When you were in high school, what tended most to divert your attention from learning? Write an essay explaining in full detail the three things that interfered most with your high school education. You may include any of Garland's points, but present details that apply specifically to you. Organize your essay by using emphatic order—in other words, save whatever interfered most with your education for the last supporting paragraph.

It is helpful to write a sentence outline for this kind of essay. Here, for example, is one writer's outline for an essay titled "Obstacles to My High School Education."

Thesis: There were three main things that interfered with my high school education.

Topic sentence 1: Concern about my appearance took up too much of my time and energy.
a. Since I was concerned about my looking good, I spent too much time shopping for clothes.
b. In order to afford the clothes, I worked twenty hours a week, which cut drastically into my study time.
c. Spending even more time on clothes, I fussed every evening over what I would wear to school the next day.

Topic sentence 2: Cheerleading was another major obstacle to my academic progress in high school.
a. I spent many hours practicing in order to make the cheerleading squad.

b.   Once I made the squad, I had to spend even more time practicing and then attending games.
c.   Once when I didn't make the squad, I was so depressed for a while that I couldn't study, and this had serious consequences.

Topic sentence 3: The main thing that interfered with my high school education was my family situation.
a.   Even when I had time to study, I often found it impossible to do so at home, since my parents often had fights that were noisy and upsetting.
b.   My parents showed little interest in my school work, giving me little reason to work hard for my classes.
c.   When I was in eleventh grade, my parents divorced; this was a major distraction for me for a long time.

To round off your essay with a conclusion, you may simply want to restate your thesis and main supporting points.

As an alternative to the above assignment, you can write about current obstacles to your college education.

How They Get You to Do That

Janny Scott

So you think you're sailing along in life, making decisions based on your own preferences? Not likely! Janny Scott brings together the findings of several researchers to show how advertisers, charitable organizations, politicians, employers, and even your friends get you to say "yes" when you should have said "no"—or, at least, "Let me think about that."

The woman in the supermarket in a white coat tenders a free sample of "lite" cheese. A car salesman suggests that prices won't stay low for long. Even a penny will help, pleads the door-to-door solicitor. Sale ends Sunday! Will work for food.   1

The average American exists amid a perpetual torrent of propaganda. Everyone, it sometimes seems, is trying to make up someone else's mind. If it isn't an athletic shoe company, it's a politician, a panhandler, a pitchman, a boss, a billboard company, a spouse.   2

The weapons of influence they are wielding are more sophisticated than ever, 3
researchers say. And they are aimed at a vulnerable target—people with less and
less time to consider increasingly complex issues.

As a result, some experts in the field have begun warning the public, tipping 4
people off to precisely how "the art of compliance" works. Some critics have taken
to arguing for new government controls on one pervasive form of persuasion—
political advertising.

The persuasion problem is "the essential dilemma of modern democracy," 5
argue social psychologists Anthony Pratkanis and Elliot Aronson, the authors of
Age of Propaganda: The Everyday Use and Abuse of Persuasion.

As the two psychologists see it, American society values free speech and public 6
discussion, but people no longer have the time or inclination to pay attention.
Mindless propaganda flourishes, they say; thoughtful persuasion fades away.

The problem stems from what Pratkanis and Aronson call our "message-dense 7
environment." The average television viewer sees nearly 38,000 commercials a
year, they say. The average home receives 216 pieces of junk mail annually and a
call a week from telemarketing firms.

Bumper stickers, billboards and posters litter the public consciousness. Athletic 8
events and jazz festivals carry corporate labels. As direct selling proliferates, workers
patrol their offices during lunch breaks, peddling chocolate and Tupperware to
friends.

Meanwhile, information of other sorts multiplies exponentially. Technology 9
serves up ever-increasing quantities of data on every imaginable subject, from
home security to health. With more and more information available, people have
less and less time to digest it.

"It's becoming harder and harder to think in a considered way about anything," 10
said Robert Cialdini, a persuasion researcher at Arizona State University in
Tempe. "More and more, we are going to be deciding on the basis of less and less
information."

Persuasion is a democratic society's chosen method for decision making and 11
dispute resolution. But the flood of persuasive messages in recent years has
changed the nature of persuasion. Lengthy arguments have been supplanted by
slogans and logos. In a world teeming with propaganda, those in the business of
influencing others put a premium on effective shortcuts.

Most people, psychologists say, are easily seduced by such shortcuts. Humans 12
are "cognitive misers," always looking to conserve attention and mental energy—
which leaves them at the mercy of anyone who has figured out which shortcuts
work.

The task of figuring out shortcuts has been embraced by advertising agencies, 13
market researchers, and millions of salespeople. The public, meanwhile, remains
in the dark, ignorant of even the simplest principles of social influence.

As a result, laypeople underestimate their susceptibility to persuasion, psychol- 14
ogists say. They imagine their actions are dictated simply by personal preferences.
Unaware of the techniques being used against them, they are often unwittingly
outgunned.

As Cialdini tells it, the most powerful tactics work like jujitsu: They draw their 15 strength from deep-seated, unconscious psychological rules. The clever "compliance professional" deliberately triggers these "hidden stores of influence" to elicit a predictable response.

One such rule, for example, is that people are more likely to comply with a 16 request if a reason—no matter how silly—is given. To prove that point, one researcher tested different ways of asking people in line at a copying machine to let her cut the line.

When the researcher asked simply, "Excuse me, I have five pages. May I use the 17 Xerox machine?" only 60 percent of those asked complied. But when she added nothing more than, "because I have to make some copies," nearly everyone agreed.

The simple addition of "because" unleashed an automatic response, even 18 though "because" was followed by an irrelevant reason, Cialdini said. By asking the favor in that way, the researcher dramatically increased the likelihood of getting what she wanted.

Cialdini and others say much of human behavior is mechanical. Automatic 19 responses are efficient when time and attention are short. For that reason, many techniques of persuasion are designed and tested for their ability to trigger those automatic responses.

"These appeals persuade not through the give-and-take of argument and 20 debate," Pratkanis and Aronson have written. ". . . They often appeal to our deepest fears and most irrational hopes, while they make use of our most simplistic beliefs."

Life insurance agents use fear to sell policies, Pratkanis and Aronson say. Parents 21 use fear to convince their children to come home on time. Political leaders use fear to build support for going to war—for example, comparing a foreign leader to Adolf Hitler.

As many researchers see it, people respond to persuasion in one of two 22 ways: If an issue they care about is involved, they may pay close attention to the arguments; if they don't care, they pay less attention and are more likely to be influenced by simple cues.

Their level of attention depends on motivation and the time available. As David 23 Boninger, a UCLA psychologist, puts it, "If you don't have the time or motivation, or both, you will pay attention to more peripheral cues, like how nice somebody looks."

Cialdini, a dapper man with a flat Midwestern accent, describes himself as an 24 inveterate sucker. From an early age, he said recently, he had wondered what made him say yes in many cases when the answer, had he thought about it, should have been no.

So in the early 1980s, he became "a spy in the wars of influence." He took a 25 sabbatical and, over a three-year period, enrolled in dozens of sales training programs, learning firsthand the tricks of selling insurance, cars, vacuum cleaners, encyclopedias, and more.

He learned how to sell portrait photography over the telephone. He took a 26 job as a busboy in a restaurant, observing the waiters. He worked in fund-raising, advertising, and public relations. And he interviewed cult recruiters and members of bunco squads.

By the time it was over, Cialdini had witnessed hundreds of tactics. But he   27
found that the most effective ones were rooted in six principles. Most are not new,
but they are being used today with greater sophistication on people whose fast-
paced lifestyle has lowered their defenses.

Reciprocity. People have been trained to believe that a favor must be repaid   28
in kind, even if the original favor was not requested. The cultural pressure to
return a favor is so intense that people go along rather than suffer the feeling of
being indebted.

Politicians have learned that favors are repaid with votes. Stores offer free   29
samples—not just to show off a product. Charity organizations ship personalized
address labels to potential contributors. Others accost pedestrians, planting paper
flowers in their lapels.

Commitment and Consistency. People tend to feel they should be consistent—   30
even when it no longer makes sense. While consistency is easy, comfortable, and
generally advantageous, Cialdini says, "mindless consistency" can be exploited.

Take the "foot in the door technique." One person gets another to agree to   31
a small commitment, like a down payment or signing a petition. Studies show that
it then becomes much easier to get the person to comply with a much larger
request.

Another example Cialdini cites is the "lowball tactic" in car sales. Offered a   32
low price for a car, the potential customer agrees. Then at the last minute, the
sales manager finds a supposed error. The price is increased. But customers tend
to go along nevertheless.

Social Validation. People often decide what is correct on the basis of what   33
other people think. Studies show that is true for behavior. Hence, sitcom laugh
tracks, tip jars "salted" with a bartender's cash, long lines outside nightclubs,
testimonials, and "man on the street" ads.

Tapping the power of social validation is especially effective under certain   34
conditions: When people are in doubt, they will look to others as a guide; and when
they view those others as similar to themselves, they are more likely to follow their
lead.

Liking. People prefer to comply with requests from people they know and like.   35
Charities recruit people to canvass their friends and neighbors. Colleges get alum-
ni to raise money from classmates. Sales training programs include grooming tips.

According to Cialdini, liking can be based on any of a number of factors. Good-   36
looking people tend to be credited with traits like talent and intelligence. People
also tend to like people who are similar to themselves in personality, background,
and lifestyle.

Authority. People defer to authority. Society trains them to do so, and in many   37
situations deference is beneficial. Unfortunately, obedience is often automatic,
leaving people vulnerable to exploitation by compliance professionals, Cialdini says.

As an example, he cites the famous ad campaign that capitalized on actor 38
Robert Young's role as Dr. Marcus Welby, Jr., to tout the alleged health benefits
of Sanka decaffeinated coffee.

An authority, according to Cialdini, need not be a true authority. The trappings 39
of authority may suffice. Con artists have long recognized the persuasive power
of titles like doctor or judge, fancy business suits, and expensive cars.

Scarcity. Products and opportunities seem more valuable when the supply is 40
limited.

As a result, professional persuaders emphasize that "supplies are limited." 41
Sales end Sunday and movies have limited engagements—diverting attention from
whether the item is desirable to the threat of losing the chance to experience it
at all.

The use of influence, Cialdini says, is ubiquitous. 42

Take the classic appeal by a child of a parent's sense of consistency: "But you 43
said . . ." And the parent's resort to authority: "Because I said so." In addition,
nearly everyone invokes the opinions of like-minded others—for social validation—
in vying to win a point.

One area in which persuasive tactics are especially controversial is political 44
advertising—particularly negative advertising. Alarmed that attack ads might be
alienating voters, some critics have begun calling for stricter limits on political ads.

In Washington, legislation pending in Congress would, among other things, 45
force candidates to identify themselves at the end of their commercials. In that
way, they might be forced to take responsibility for the ads' contents and be
unable to hide behind campaign committees.

"In general, people accept the notion that for the sale of products at least, there 46
are socially accepted norms of advertising," said Lloyd Morrisett, president of the
Markle Foundation, which supports research in communications and information
technology.

"But when those same techniques are applied to the political process—where 47
we are judging not a product but a person, and where there is ample room for
distortion of the record or falsification in some cases—there begins to be more
concern," he said.

On an individual level, some psychologists offer tips for self-protection. 48

- Pay attention to your emotions, says Pratkanis, an associate professor of psy- 49
  chology at UC Santa Cruz: "If you start to feel guilty or patriotic, try to figure
  out why." In consumer transactions, beware of feelings of inferiority and the
  sense that you don't measure up unless you have a certain product.

- Be on the lookout for automatic responses, Cialdini says. Beware foolish 50
  consistency. Check other people's responses against objective facts. Be skeptical
  of authority, and look out for unwarranted liking for any "compliance professionals."

Since the publication of his most recent book, *Influence: The New Psychology* 51
of Modern Persuasion, Cialdini has begun researching a new book on ethical uses

of influence in business—addressing, among other things, how to instruct sales-people and other "influence agents" to use persuasion in ways that help, rather than hurt, society.

"If influence agents don't police themselves, society will have to step in to   52
regulate . . . the way information is presented in commercial and political settings,"
Cialdini said. "And that's a can of worms that I don't think anybody wants to get
into."

■ Reading Comprehension Questions

1. The word *wielding* in "The weapons of influence they are wielding are more sophisticated than ever" (paragraph 3) means
   a. handling effectively.
   b. giving up.
   c. looking for.
   d. demanding.

2. The word *peripheral* in "As David Boninger . . . puts it, 'If you don't have the time or motivation, or both, you will pay attention to more peripheral cues, like how nice someone looks'" (paragraph 23) means
   a. important.
   b. dependable.
   c. minor.
   d. attractive.

3. Which of the following would be the best alternative title for this selection?
   a. Automatic Human Responses
   b. Our Deepest Fears
   c. The Loss of Thoughtful Discussion
   d. Compliance Techniques

4. Which sentence best expresses the selection's main point?
   a. Americans are bombarded by various compliance techniques, the dangers of which can be overcome through understanding and legislation.
   b. Fearful of the effects of political attack ads, critics are calling for strict limits on such ads.
   c. With more and more messages demanding our attention, we find it harder and harder to consider any one subject really thoughtfully.
   d. The persuasion researcher Robert Ciandini spent a three-year sabbatical learning the tricks taught in dozens of sales training programs.

5. *True or false?* _____ According to the article, most laypeople think they are more susceptible to persuasion than they really are.

6. According to the article, parents persuade their children to come home on time by appealing to the children's sense of

    a.   fair play.

    b.   guilt.

    c.   humor.

    d.   fear.

7. When a visitor walks out of a hotel and a young man runs up, helps the visitor with his luggage, hails a cab, and then expects a tip, the young man is depending on which principle of persuasion?

    a.   Reciprocity

    b.   Commitment and consistency

    c.   Social validation

    d.   Liking

8. An inference that can be drawn from paragraph 49 is that

    a.   Anthony Pratkanis is not a patriotic person.

    b.   one compliance technique involves appealing to the consumer's patriotism.

    c.   people using compliance techniques never want consumers to feel inferior.

    d.   consumers pay too much attention to their own emotions.

9. One can infer from the selection that

    a.   the actor Robert Young was well-known for his love of coffee.

    b.   Sanka is demonstrably better for one's health than other coffees.

    c.   the actor Robert Young was also a physician in real life.

    d.   the TV character Marcus Welby, Jr., was trustworthy and authoritative.

10. We can conclude that to resist persuasive tactics, a person must

    a.   buy fewer products.

    b.   take time to question and analyze.

    c.   remain patriotic.

    d.   avoid propaganda.

■ Discussion Questions

About Content

1. What unusual method did Robert Cialdini employ to learn more about compliance techniques? Were you surprised by any of the ways he used his time during that three-year period? Have you ever been employed in a position in which you used one or more compliance techniques?

2. What are the six principles that Cialdini identifies as being behind many persuasion tactics? Describe an incident in which you were subjected to persuasion based on one or more of these principles.

3. In paragraph 16, we learn that "people are more likely to comply with a request if a reason—no matter how silly—is given." Do you find that to be true? Have you complied with requests that, when you thought about them later, were backed up with silly or weak reasons? Describe such an incident. Why do you think such requests work?

4. In paragraphs 44–47, the author discusses persuasive tactics in political advertising. Why might researchers view the use of such tactics in this area as "especially controversial"?

About Structure

5. What is the effect of Janny Scott's introduction to the essay (paragraphs 1–2)? On the basis of that introduction, why is a reader likely to feel that the selection will be worth his or her time?

6. Which of the following best describes the conclusion of the selection?
   a. It just stops.
   b. It restates the main point of the selection.
   c. It focuses on possible future occurrences.
   d. It presents a point of view that is the opposite of views in the body of the selection.

   Is this conclusion effective? Why or why not?

About Style and Tone

7. Why might Robert Cialdini have identified himself to the author as an "inveterate sucker"? How does that self-description affect how you regard Cialdini and what he has to say?

8. The author writes, "People defer to authority. Society trains them to do so; and in many situations deference is beneficial." Where does the author himself use the power of authority to support his own points? In what situations would you consider authority to be beneficial?

■ Writing Assignments

Assignment 1: Writing a Paragraph

According to the article, "laypeople underestimate their susceptibility to persuasion. . . . They imagine their actions are dictated simply by personal preferences. Unaware of the techniques being used against them, they are often unwittingly outgunned." After having read the selection, do you believe that statement is true of you? Write a paragraph in which you either agree with or argue against the statement. Provide clear, specific examples of ways in which you are or are not influenced by persuasion.

Your topic sentence might be like either of these:

After reading "How They Get You to Do That," I recognize that I am more influenced by forms of persuasion than I previously thought.

Many people may "underestimate their susceptibility to persuasion," but I am not one of those people.

Assignment 2: Writing a Paragraph

Think of an advertisement—on TV, or radio, in print, or on a billboard—that you have found especially memorable. Write a paragraph in which you describe it. Provide specific details that make your reader understand why you remember it so vividly. Conclude your paragraph by indicating whether or not the advertisement persuaded you to buy or do what it was promoting.

Assignment 3: Writing an Essay

Robert Cialdini identifies "social validation" as a strong persuasion technique. Social validation involves people's need to do what they hope will get approval from the crowd, rather than thinking for themselves. The essay provides several examples of social validation, such as laughing along with a laugh track and getting in a long line to go to a nightclub.

Choose a person you know for whom the need for social validation is very strong. Write an essay about that person and the impact the need for social validation has in several areas of his or her life. Develop each paragraph with colorful, persuasive examples of the person's behavior. (You may wish to write about an invented person, in which case, feel free to use humorous exaggeration to make your points.)

Here is a possible outline for such an essay:

Thesis statement: My cousin Nina has a very strong need for social validation.

Topic sentence 1: Instead of choosing friends because of their inner qualities, Nina chooses them on the basis of their popularity.

Topic sentence 2: Nina's wardrobe has to be made up of the newest and most popular styles.

Topic sentence 3: Instead of having any real opinions of her own, Nina adopts her most popular friend's point of view as her own.

End your essay with a look into the future of a person whose life is ruled by the need for social validation.

Alternatively, write about the most independent thinker you know, someone who tends to do things his or her way without worrying much about what others say.

Dealing with Feelings

Rudolph F. Verderber

Do you hide your feelings, no matter how strong they are, letting them fester inside? Or do you lash out angrily at people who irritate you? If either of these descriptions fits you, you may be unhappy with the results of your actions. Read the following excerpt from the college text-book *Communicate!* Sixth Edition (Wadsworth), to discover what the author recommends as a better approach to dealing with your emotions.

An extremely important aspect of self-disclosure is the sharing of feelings. We all experience feelings such as happiness at receiving an unexpected gift, sadness about the breakup of a relationship, or anger when we believe we have been taken advantage of. The question is whether to disclose such feelings, and if so, how. Self-disclosure of feelings usually will be most successful not when feelings are withheld or displayed but when they are described. Let's consider each of these forms of dealing with feelings.

Withholding Feelings

Withholding feelings—that is, keeping them inside and not giving any verbal or nonverbal clues to their existence—is generally an inappropriate means of dealing with feelings. Withholding feelings is best exemplified by the good poker player who develops a "poker face," a neutral look that is impossible to decipher. The look is the same whether the player's cards are good or bad. Unfortunately, many people use poker faces in their interpersonal relationships, so that no one knows whether they hurt inside, are extremely excited, and so on. For instance, Doris feels very nervous when Candy stands over her while Doris is working on her report. And when Candy says, "That first paragraph isn't very well written," Doris begins to seethe, yet she says nothing—she withholds her feelings.

Psychologists believe that when people withhold feelings, they can develop physical problems such as ulcers, high blood pressure, and heart disease, as well as psychological problems such as stress-related neuroses and psychoses. Moreover, people who withhold feelings are often perceived as cold, undemonstrative, and not much fun to be around.

Is withholding ever appropriate? When a situation is inconsequential, you may well choose to withhold your feelings. For instance, a stranger's inconsiderate behavior at a party may bother you, but because you can move to another part of the room, withholding may not be detrimental. In the example of Doris seething at Candy's behavior, however, withholding could be costly to Doris.

Displaying Feelings

Displaying feelings means expressing those feelings through a facial reaction, body response, or spoken reaction. Cheering over a great play at a sporting event, booing the umpire at a perceived bad call, patting a person on the back when the person does something well, or saying, "What are you doing?" in a nasty tone of voice are all displays of feelings.   5

Displays are especially appropriate when the feelings you are experiencing are positive. For instance, when Gloria does something nice for you, and you experience a feeling of joy, giving her a big hug is appropriate; when Don gives you something you've wanted, and you experience a feeling of appreciation, a big smile or an "Oh, thank you, Don" is appropriate. In fact, many people need to be even more demonstrative of good feelings. You've probably seen the bumper sticker "Have you hugged your kid today?" It reinforces the point that you need to display love and affection constantly to show another person that you really care.   6

Displays become detrimental to communication when the feelings you are experiencing are negative—especially when the display of a negative feeling appears to be an overreaction. For instance, when Candy stands over Doris while she is working on her report and says, "That first paragraph isn't very well written," Doris may well experience resentment. If Doris lashes out at Candy by screaming, "Who the hell asked you for your opinion?" Doris's display no doubt will hurt Candy's feelings and short-circuit their communication. Although displays of negative feelings may be good for you psychologically, they are likely to be bad for you interpersonally.   7

Describing Feelings

Describing feelings—putting your feelings into words in a calm, nonjudgmental way—tends to be the best method of disclosing feelings. Describing feelings not only increases chances for positive communication and decreases chances for short-circuiting lines of communication; it also teaches people how to treat you. When you describe your feelings, people are made aware of the effect of their behavior. This knowledge gives them the information needed to determine whether they should continue or repeat that behavior. If you tell Paul that you really feel flattered when he visits you, such a statement should encourage Paul to visit you again; likewise, when you tell Cliff that you feel very angry when he borrows your jacket without asking, he is more likely to ask the next time he borrows a jacket. Describing your feelings allows you to exercise a measure of control over others' behavior toward you.   8

Describing and displaying feelings are not the same. Many times people think they are describing when in fact they are displaying feelings or evaluating.   9

If describing feelings is so important to communicating effectively, why don't more people do it regularly? There seem to be at least four reasons why many people don't describe feelings.   10

1. Many people have a poor vocabulary of words for describing the various 11 feelings they are experiencing. People can sense that they are angry; however, they may not know whether what they are feeling might best be described as annoyed, betrayed, cheated, crushed, disturbed, furious, outraged, or shocked. Each of these words describes a slightly different aspect of what many people lump together as anger.

2. Many people believe that describing their true feelings reveals too much 12 about themselves. If you tell people when their behavior hurts you, you risk their using the information against you when they want to hurt you on purpose. Even so, the potential benefits of describing your feelings far outweigh the risks. For instance, if Pete has a nickname for you that you don't like and you tell Pete that calling you by that nickname really makes you nervous and tense, Pete may use the nickname when he wants to hurt you, but he is more likely to stop calling you by that name. If, on the other hand, you don't describe your feelings to Pete, he is probably going to call you by that name all the time because he doesn't know any better. When you say nothing, you reinforce his behavior. The level of risk varies with each situation, but you will more often improve a relationship than be hurt by describing feelings.

3. Many people believe that if they describe feelings, others will make them 13 feel guilty about having such feelings. At a very tender age we all learned about "tactful" behavior. Under the premise that "the truth sometimes hurts" we learned to avoid the truth by not saying anything or by telling "little" lies. Perhaps when you were young your mother said, "Don't forget to give Grandma a great big kiss." At that time you may have blurted out, "Ugh—it makes me feel yucky to kiss Grandma. She's got a mustache." If your mother responded, "That's terrible—your grandma loves you. Now you give her a kiss and never let me hear you talk like that again!" then you probably felt guilty for having this "wrong" feeling. But the point is that the thought of kissing your grandma made you feel "yucky" whether it should have or not. In this case what was at issue was the way you talked about the feelings—not your having the feelings.

4. Many people believe that describing feelings causes harm to others or to a 14 relationship. If it really bothers Max when his girlfriend, Dora, bites her fingernails, Max may believe that describing his feelings to Dora will hurt her so much that the knowledge will drive a wedge into their relationship. So it's better for Max to say nothing, right? Wrong! If Max says nothing, he's still going to be bothered by Dora's behavior. In fact, as time goes on, Max will probably lash out at Dora for others things because he can't bring himself to talk about the behavior that really bothers him. The net result is that not only will Dora be hurt by Max's behavior, but she won't understand the true source of his feelings. By not describing his feelings, Max may well drive a wedge into their relationship anyway.

If Max does describe his feelings to Dora, she might quit or at least try to quit 15 biting her nails; they might get into a discussion in which he finds out that she doesn't want to bite them but just can't seem to stop, and he can help her in her efforts to stop; or they might discuss the problem and Max may see that it is a small thing really and not let it bother him as much. The point is that in describing feelings the chances of a successful outcome are greater than they are in not describing them.

To describe your feelings, first put the emotion you are feeling into words. Be 16 specific. Second, state what triggered the feeling. Finally, make sure you indicate that the feeling is yours. For example, suppose your roommate borrows your jacket without asking. When he returns, you describe your feelings by saying, "Cliff, I [indication that the feeling is yours] get really angry [the feeling] when you borrow my jacket without asking [trigger]." Or suppose that Carl has just reminded you of the very first time he brought you a rose. You describe your feelings by saying, "Carl, I [indication that the feeling is yours] get really tickled [the feeling] when you remind me about that first time you brought me a rose [trigger]."

You may find it easiest to begin by describing positive feelings: "I really feel 17 elated knowing that you were the one who nominated me for the position" or "I'm delighted that you offered to help me with the housework." As you gain success with positive descriptions, you can try negative feelings attributable to environmental factors: "It's so cloudy; I feel gloomy" or "When the wind howls through the cracks, I really get jumpy." Finally, you can move to negative descriptions resulting from what people have said or done: "Your stepping in front of me like that really annoys me" or "The tone of your voice confuses me."

■ Reading Comprehension Questions

1. The word *detrimental* in "For instance, a stranger's inconsiderate behavior at a party may bother you, but because you can move to another part of the room, withholding may not be detrimental" (paragraph 4) means

   a. useful.

   b. private.

   c. helpless.

   d. harmful.

2. The word *wedge* in "Max may believe that describing his feelings to Dora will hurt her so much that the knowledge will drive a wedge into their relationship" (paragraph 14) means

   a. something that divides.

   b. loyalty.

   c. friendship.

   d. many years.

3. Which of the following would be the best alternative title for this selection?

   a.   Effective Communication

   b.   Negative Feelings

   c.   The Consequences of Withholding Feelings

   d.   Emotions: When and How to Express Them

4. Which sentence best expresses the article's main point?

   a.   Everyone has feelings.

   b.   There are three ways to deal with feelings; describing them is most useful for educating others about how you want to be treated.

   c.   Withholding feelings means not giving verbal or nonverbal clues that might reveal those feelings to others.

   d.   Psychologists have studied the manner in which people deal with their feelings.

5. You are most likely to create physical problems for yourself by

   a.   withholding your feelings.

   b.   displaying your positive feelings.

   c.   describing your positive feelings.

   d.   describing your negative feelings.

6. The author uses the term "describing your feelings" to refer to

   a.   keeping your feelings inside.

   b.   giving a nonverbal response to feelings.

   c.   putting your feelings into words calmly.

   d.   telling "little" lies.

7. Shouting angrily at a person who has stepped in front of you in line is an example of

   a.   withholding feelings.

   b.   displaying feelings.

   c.   describing feelings.

   d.   self-disclosing.

8. From the reading, we can conclude that describing feelings

   a.   is usually easy for people.

   b.   is often a good way to solve problems.

   c.   should be done only for positive feelings.

   d.   should make you feel guilty.

9. Which sentence can we infer is an example of describing a feeling?

   a. Although Mrs. Henderson hates going to the mountains, she says nothing as her husband plans to go there for their vacation.

   b. Neil calls Joanna the day after their date and says, "I want you to know how much I enjoyed our evening together. You're a lot of fun."

   c. Raoul jumps out of his seat and yells joyfully as the Packers make a touchdown.

   d. Peggy's office-mate chews gum noisily, cracking and snapping it. Peggy shrieks, "How inconsiderate can you be? You're driving me crazy with that noise!"

10. *True or false?* _____ We can infer that people who describe their feelings tend to be physically healthier than those who withhold them.

■ Discussion Questions

About Content

1. What is the difference between describing feelings and expressing them? How might Doris describe her feelings to Candy after Candy says, "That first paragraph isn't very well written" (paragraph 2)?

2. Why do you think Verderber emphasizes describing feelings over the other two methods of dealing with feelings?

3. What are some examples from your own experience of withholding, expressing or displaying, and describing feelings? How useful was each?

About Structure

4. What method of introduction does Verderber use in this selection?

   a. Broad to narrow

   b. Anecdote

   c. Beginning with a situation opposite to the one he will describe

   d. Question

   Is his introduction effective? Why or why not?

5. Verderber divides the body of his essay into three parts: first about withholding feelings, second about displaying feelings, and finally about describing feelings. He further divides the third part by introducing a list. What is that list about? How many items does he include in it?

6. What devices does the author use to emphasize the organization of his essay?

7. How many examples does Verderber provide for withholding feelings? Displaying feelings? Describing feelings?

About Style and Tone

8. What type of evidence does the author use to back up his points throughout the selection? What other types of support might he have used?

■ Writing Assignments

Assignment 1: Writing a Paragraph

Write a paragraph about a time when you withheld or displayed feelings, but describing them would have been a better idea. Your topic sentence might be something like either of these:

> An argument I had with my boyfriend recently made me wish that I had described my feelings rather than displaying them.
>
> Withholding my feelings at work recently left me feeling frustrated and angry.

Then narrate the event, showing how feelings were withheld or displayed and what the result was. Conclude your paragraph by contrasting what really happened with what *might* have happened if feelings had been described.

Assignment 2: Writing a Paragraph

"Dealing with Feelings" lists and discusses several ways to cope with emotions. Write a paragraph in which you present three ways to do something else. Your tone may be serious or humorous. You might write about three ways to do one of the following:

> Cut expenses
> Meet people
> Get along with a difficult coworker
> Ruin a party
> Embarrass your friends
> Lose a job

Here is a possible topic sentence for this assignment:

> To ruin a party, you must follow three simple steps.

Assignment 3: Writing an Essay

At one time or another, you have probably used all three methods of communicating described by Verderber: withholding, displaying, and describing. Write an essay that describes a situation in which you have used each of those methods. In each case, narrate the event that occurred. Then explain why you responded as you did and how you ended up feeling about your response. Finish your essay with some conclusion of your own about dealing with feelings.

Here's a sample outline for such an essay:

<u>Thesis statement:</u> At different times, I have withheld my feelings, displayed my feelings, and described my feelings.

<u>Topic sentence 1:</u> Dealing with a rude store clerk, I withheld my feelings.

<u>Topic sentence 2:</u> When another driver cut me off in traffic, I displayed my feelings.

<u>Topic sentence 3:</u> When my mother angered me by reading a letter I'd left lying on the dining-room table, I described my feelings.

<u>Conclusion:</u> When it comes to dealing with people I care about, describing my feelings works better than withholding or displaying them.

Human Groups and Society

Television Changed My Family Forever

Linda Ellerbee

We have all heard people complain that television is too violent, that too many programs are mediocre, and so on. But it can be argued that one of television's greatest disadvantages is simply that it takes "center stage" in our living rooms. One way to evaluate that argument is to consider what life was like before TV sets took their place in American homes. The television producer and writer Linda Ellerbee remembers well what life was like then—and what it was like after her family bought a television set. In this selection from her book *Move On,* she details some of the differences.

Santa Claus brought us a television for Christmas. See, said my parents, television doesn't eat people. Maybe not. But television changes people. Television changed my family forever. We stopped eating dinner at the dining-room table after my mother found out about TV trays. We kept the TV trays behind the kitchen door and served ourselves from pots on the stove. Setting and clearing the dining-room table used to be my job; now, setting and clearing meant unfolding and wiping our TV trays, then, when we'd finished, wiping and folding our TV trays. Dinner was served in time for one program and finished in time for another. During dinner we used to talk to one another. Now television talked to us. If you had something you absolutely had to say, you waited until the commercial, which is, I suspect, where I learned to speak in thirty-second bursts. For a future writer, it was good practice in editing my thoughts. For a little girl, it was lonely as hell. Once in a while, I'd pass our dining-room table and stop, thinking I heard our ghosts sitting around talking to one another, saying stuff. 1

Before television, I would lie in bed at night listening to my parents come upstairs, enter their bedroom and say things to one another that I couldn't hear, but it didn't matter; their voices rocked me to sleep. My first memory, the first one ever, was of my parents and their friends talking me to sleep when we were living in Bryan and my bedroom was right next to the kitchen. I was still in my crib then. From the kitchen I could hear them, hear the rolling cadence of their speech, the rising and falling of their voices and the sound of chips. 2

"Two pair showing."
"Call?"
"Check."
"Call?"
"Call." Clink.
"I raise." Clink. Clink.
"See your raise and raise you back." Clink clink clink.
"Call." Clink Clink.
"I'm in." Clink.
"I'm out."
"Let's see 'em."

It was a song to me, a lullaby. Now Daddy went to bed right after the weather   3
and Mama stayed up to see Jack Paar (later she stayed up to see Steve Allen and
Johnny Carson and even Joey Bishop, but not David Letterman). I went to sleep
alone, listening to voices in my memory.

Daddy stopped buying Perry Mason books. Perry was on television and that   4
was so much easier for him, Daddy said, because he could never remember which
Perry Mason books he'd read and was always buying the wrong ones by mistake,
then reading them all the way to the end before he realized he'd already read
them. Television fixed that, he said, because although the stories weren't as good
as the stories in the books, at least he knew he hadn't already read them. But it had
been Daddy and Perry who'd taught me how fine it could be to read something
you liked twice, especially if you didn't know the second time wasn't the first time.
My mother used to laugh at Daddy. She would never buy or read the same book
again and again. She had her own library card. She subscribed to magazines and
belonged to the Book-of-the-Month Club. Also, she hated mystery stories. Her
favorite books were about doctors who found God and women who found doctors.
Her most favorite book ever was *Gone With the Wind,* which she'd read before
I was born. Read it while she vacuumed the floor, she said. Read it while she'd
ironed shirts. Read it while she'd fixed dinner and read it while she'd washed up.
Mama sure loved that book. She dropped Book-of-the-Month after she discovered
As the World Turns. Later, she stopped her magazine subscriptions. Except for *TV
Guide.* I don't know what she did with her library card. I know what she didn't do
with it.

Mom quit taking me to the movies about this time, not that she'd ever take   5
me to the movies very often after Mr. Disney let Bambi's mother get killed, which
she said showed a lack of imagination. She and Daddy stopped going to movies,
period. Daddy claimed it was because movies weren't as much fun after Martin
broke up with Lewis, but that wasn't it. Most movies he cared about seeing would
one day show up on television, he said. Maybe even Martin and Lewis movies. All
you had to do was wait. And watch.

After a while, we didn't play baseball anymore, my daddy and I. We didn't   6
go to baseball games together, either, but we watched more baseball than ever.
That's how Daddy perfected The Art of Dozing to Baseball. He would sit down in
his big chair, turn on the game and fall asleep within five minutes. That is, he

appeared to be asleep. His eyes were shut. He snored. But if you shook him and said, Daddy, you're asleep, he'd open his eyes and tell you what the score was, who was up and what the pitcher ought to throw next. The Art of Dozing to Baseball. I've worked at it myself, but have never been able to get beyond waking up in time to see the instant replay. Daddy never needed instant replay and, no, I don't know how he did it; he was a talented man and he had his secrets.

Our lives began to seem centered around, and somehow measured by, tele-   7
vision. My family believed in television. If it was on TV, it must be so. Calendars were tricky and church bells might fool you, but if you heard Ed Sullivan's voice you knew it was Sunday night. When four men in uniforms sang that they were the men from Texaco who worked from Maine to Mexico, you knew it was Tuesday night. Depending on which verse they were singing, you knew whether it was seven o'clock or eight o'clock on Tuesday night. It was the only night of the week I got to stay up until eight o'clock. My parents allowed this for purely patriotic reasons. If you didn't watch Uncle Milty on Tuesday nights, on Wednesday mornings you might have trouble persuading people you were a real American and not some commie pinko foreigner from Dallas. I wasn't crazy about Milton Berle, but I pretended I was; an extra hour is an extra hour, and if the best way to get your daddy's attention is to watch TV with him, then it was worth every joke Berle could steal.

Television was taking my parents away from me, not all the time, but enough,   8
I believed. When it was on, they didn't see me, I thought. Take holidays. Although I was an only child, there were always grandparents, aunts, uncles, and cousins enough to fill the biggest holiday. They were the best times. White linen and old silver and pretty china. Platters of turkey and ham, bowls of cornbread dressing and sweet potatoes and ambrosia. Homemade rolls. Glass cake stands holding pineapple, coconut, angel food, and devil's food cakes, all with good boiled icing. There was apple pie with cheese. There were little silver dishes with dividers for watermelon pickles, black olives, and sliced cranberry jelly. There was all the iced tea you'd ever want. Lord, it was grand. We kids always finished first (we weren't one of those families where they make the kids eat last and you never get a drumstick). After we ate, we'd be excused to go outside, where we'd play. When we decided the grown-ups had spent enough time sitting around the table after they'd already finished eating, which was real boring, we'd go back in and make as much noise as we could, until finally four or five grown-ups would come outside and play with us because it was just easier, that's all. We played hide-and-seek or baseball or football or dodgeball. Sometimes we just played ball. Sometimes we just played. Once in a while, there would be fireworks, which were always exciting ever since the Christmas Uncle Buck shot off a Roman candle and set the neighbor's yard on fire, but that was before we had a television.

Now, holiday dinners began to be timed to accommodate the kickoff, or once   9
in a while the halftime, depending on how many games there were to watch; but on Thanksgiving or New Year's there were always games so important they absolutely could not be missed under any circumstances, certainly not for something as inconsequential as being "it" and counting to ten while you pretended not to see six children climb into the backseat of your car.

"Ssshhh, not now, Linda Jane. The Aggies have the ball."

"But you said . . . you promised . . . ."

"Linda Jane, didn't your daddy just tell you to hush up? We can't hear the television for you talking."

■ Reading Comprehension Questions

1. The word *cadence* in "From the kitchen I could . . . hear the rolling cadence of their speech, the rising and falling of their voices and the sound of chips. 'Two pair showing.' 'Call?' 'Check.' 'Call?' Clink" (paragraph 2) means

   a. loud anger.

   b. distance.

   c. silence.

   d. rhythmic flow.

2. The word *inconsequential* in "on Thanksgiving or New Year's there were always games so important they absolutely could not be missed . . . , certainly not for something as inconsequential as being 'it'" (paragraph 9) means

   a. unimportant.

   b. serious.

   c. noisy.

   d. physically demanding.

3. Which of the following would be the best alternative title for this selection?

   a. The Effects of Television on Children

   b. How Television Hurt My Childhood

   c. Television and Reading

   d. Advantages and Disadvantages of Television

4. Which sentence best expresses the main idea of the selection?

   a. After they bought a television set, Ellerbee's parents stopped reading.

   b. The Ellerbees enjoyed a wide variety of television shows.

   c. Holidays at the Ellerbee household were centered on television.

   d. Television changed Ellerbee's family for the worse.

5. Although Ellerbee and her father were baseball fans, after they got a television set they

   a. no longer attended baseball games.

   b. refused to watch baseball on TV.

   c. began to watch Milton Berle instead of baseball.

   d. preferred football to baseball.

6. Ellerbee says she may have learned to edit her thoughts and speak quickly because

   a. the mystery books she read taught her to communicate rapidly.

   b. she often gave short reports on baseball games to her father.

   c. her parents thought children should spend more time reading than talking.

   d. she was allowed to speak freely only during television commercials.

7. After the author's parents bought a TV set, holiday dinners were

   a. no longer fancy meals.

   b. timed according to the football games being broadcast.

   c. delayed until the children were finished playing outside.

   d. times when the children and adults enjoyed lingering at the table together.

8. In paragraph 4, the author implies that

   a. her mother was silly for liking *Gone with the Wind*.

   b. television had tempted her mother away from an activity she had once loved.

   c. her mother often reread books about doctors.

   d. book clubs are a poor source for good books.

9. Ellerbee implies that

   a. her parents bought a TV set in order to spend less time talking together.

   b. television's effects on her family must have been unusual.

   c. once her family had a TV set, her parents paid too little attention to her.

   d. good television shows bring adults and children closer together.

10. Ellerbee implies that television made her family more

    a. efficient.

    b. inactive.

    c. close.

    d. energetic.

■ Discussion Questions

About Content

1. How did television change the Ellerbee family's lives?

2. The reader can learn quite a bit about Ellerbee's parents from the descriptions in her essay. What kind of person do you think Ellerbee's father was? Her mother? Give evidence from the reading to support your points.

3. Ellerbee writes, "Our lives began to seem centered around, and somehow measured by, television" (paragraph 7). In what ways was that so? When, if ever, do you center your life on television?

4. We often think of television as something that children watch too much, but Ellerbee writes that it was her parents who watched too much TV. As a result, television made Ellerbee's childhood lonely. How might her parents have spent more active time with her without giving up television altogether? What activities did you and your parents share? If you have children, what activities do you and they share?

About Structure

5. "Television Changed My Family Forever" is basically a list of ways in which TV changed the author's family. After the introduction, for instance, paragraph 1 is about how TV changed the Ellerbees' dinnertime. Paragraphs 2–3 are about how TV changed her parents' interaction with each other and with their friends. Below, write what paragraphs 4, 5, and 6 are about.

Paragraph 4 is about _____

Paragraph 5 is about _____

Paragraph 6 is about _____

6. In discussing the changes television made in her life, Ellerbee contrasts what her life was like without television and what her life was like with television. Which two time words does she use in paragraphs 2–3 to contrast those two time periods? Write those words here:

_____   _____

About Style and Tone

7. Irony is an inconsistency between what might be expected to happen and what really happens. How does Ellerbee use irony in the very first sentence of her essay?

8. Ellerbee concludes her essay with some dialogue. How does this dialogue support her thesis?

■ Writing Assignments

Assignment 1: Writing a Paragraph

Ellerbee writes, "Television was taking my parents away from me." Write a paragraph in which you describe at least three ways parents can make a special effort to spend active time with their children. You can include ways that are suggested by Ellerbee's essay (such as sitting around the table at dinnertime), or any other way that appeals to you, or both.

Assignment 2: Writing a Paragraph

Although Ellerbee's mother and father were once eager readers, they stopped reading when they bought a television set. Unfortunately, watching television has replaced reading in many households. Write a paragraph in which you discuss several ways reading might be encouraged among adults and children.

Assignment 3: Writing an Essay

Ellerbee points out some of the ways in which television can interfere with family communication. However, many people defend television, citing educational children's programs and inexpensive entertainment among its benefits. Make a list of the benefits you see in television. Then write an essay in which you defend television by citing several of its most important benefits. For each positive point you list, explain why it is beneficial and include one or more examples.

Alternatively, you can write an essay in which you criticize television. In preparation, list the disadvantages you see in television. Choose at least three of the most persuasive disadvantages to use in your essay. For each negative point you list, explain why it is a disadvantage and include one or more examples.

Assignment 4: Writing an Essay Using Internet Research

Develop Assignment 3 with the help of Internet research. Use the very helpful search engine Google (*www.google.com*) or one of the other search engines listed on pages 323–325 of this book. Try one of the following phrases:

> advantages and disadvantages of television viewing
>
> benefits and drawbacks of television viewing

Note that if you typed in just "television," you would get over seven million entries! If you typed "benefits of television," you would get about half a million entries. If you typed "drawbacks of television," you would get over 50,000 entries. But if you type "advantages and disadvantages of television viewing," you get a more limited and workable 3,000 entries. As you proceed, you'll develop a sense of how to "track down" and focus a topic by adding more information to your search words and phrases.

Rudeness at the Movies

Bill Wine

When you're at a movie theater, do loud conversations, the crinkling of candy wrappers, and the wailing of children make you wish you'd gone bowling instead? Do you cringe when your fellow viewers announce plot twists moments before they happen? If so, you'll find a comrade in suffering in the film critic and columnist Bill Wine, who thinks people have come to feel far too at home in theaters. In the following essay, which first appeared as a newspaper feature story, Wine wittily describes what the moviegoing experience all too often is like these days.

Is this actually happening or am I dreaming?　　　　　　　　　　　　　　　　1

　　I am at the movies, settling into my seat, eager with anticipation at the　　2
prospect of seeing a long-awaited film of obvious quality. The theater is absolutely
full for the late show on this weekend evening, as the reviews have been ecstatic
for this cinema masterpiece.

　　Directly in front of me sits a man an inch or two taller than the Jolly Green　　3
Giant. His wife, sitting on his left, sports the very latest in fashionable hairdos, a
gathering of her locks into a shape that resembles a drawbridge when it's open.

　　On his right, a woman spritzes herself liberally with perfume that her popcorn-　　4
munching husband got her for Valentine's Day, a scent that should be renamed
"Essence of Elk."

　　The row in which I am sitting quickly fills up with members of Cub Scout Troop　　5
432, on an outing to the movies because rain has canceled their overnight hike.
One of the boys, demonstrating the competitive spirit for which Scouts are
renowned worldwide, announces to the rest of the troop the rules in the Best
Sound Made from an Empty Good-n-Plenty's Box contest, about to begin.

　　Directly behind me, a man and his wife are ushering three other couples into　　6
their seats. I hear the woman say to the couple next to her: "You'll love it. You'll
just love it. This is our fourth time and we enjoy it more and more each time. Don't
we, Harry? Tell them about the pie-fight scene, Harry. Wait'll you see it. It comes
just before you find out that the daughter killed her boyfriend. It's great."

　　The woman has more to say—much more—but she is drowned out at the　　7
moment by the wailing of a six-month-old infant in the row behind her. The baby
is crying because his mother, who has brought her twins to the theater to save
on baby-sitting costs, can change only one diaper at a time.

　　Suddenly, the lights dim. The music starts. The credits roll. And I panic.　　8

I plead with everyone around me to let me enjoy the movie. All I ask, I wail, is to be able to see the images and hear the dialogue and not find out in advance what is about to happen. Is that so much to expect for six bucks, I ask, now engulfed by a cloud of self-pity. I begin weeping unashamedly. 9

Then, as if on cue, the Jolly Green Giant slumps down in his seat, his wife removes her wig, the Elk lady changes her seat, the Scouts drop their candy boxes on the floor, the play-by-play commentator takes out her teeth, and the young mother takes her two bawling babies home. 10

Of course I am dreaming, I realize, as I gain a certain but shaky consciousness. I notice that I am in a cold sweat. Not because the dream is scary, but from the shock of people being that cooperative. 11

I realize that I have awakened to protect my system from having to handle a jolt like that. For never—NEVER—would that happen in real life. Not on this planet. 12

I used to wonder whether I was the only one who feared bad audience behavior more than bad moviemaking. But I know now that I am not. Not by a long shot. The most frequent complaint I have heard in the last few months about the moviegoing experience has had nothing to do with the films themselves. 13

No. What folks have been complaining about is the audience. Indeed, there seems to be an epidemic of galling inconsiderateness and outrageous rudeness. 14

It is not that difficult to forgive a person's excessive height, or malodorous perfume, or perhaps even an inadvisable but understandable need to bring very young children to adult movies. 15

But the talking: that is not easy to forgive. It is inexcusable. Talking—loud, constant, and invariably superfluous—seems to be standard operating procedure on the part of many movie patrons these days. 16

It is true, I admit, that after a movie critic has seen several hundred movies in the ideal setting of an almost-empty screening room with no one but other politely silent movie critics around him, it does tend to spoil him for the packed-theater experience. 17

And something is lost viewing a movie in almost total isolation—a fact that movie distributors acknowledge with their reluctance to screen certain audience-pleasing movies for small groups of critics. Especially with comedies, the infectiousness of laughter is an important ingredient of movie-watching pleasure. 18

But it is a decidedly uphill battle to enjoy a movie—no matter how suspenseful or hilarious or moving—with nonstop gabbers sitting within earshot. And they come in sizes, ages, sexes, colors and motivations of every kind. 19

Some chat as if there is no movie playing. Some greet friends as if at a picnic. Some alert those around them to what is going to happen, either because they have seen the film before, or because they are self-proclaimed experts on the predictability of plotting and want to be seen as prescient geniuses. 20

Some describe in graphic terms exactly what is happening as if they were doing the commentary for a sporting event on radio. ("Ooh, look, he's sitting down. Now he's looking at that green car. A banana—she's eating a banana.") Some audition for film critic Gene Shalit's job by waxing witty as they critique the movie right before your very ears. 21

And all act as if it is their constitutional or God-given right. As if their admission 22
price allows them to ruin the experience for anyone and everyone else in the
building. But why?

Good question. I wish I knew. Maybe rock concerts and ball games—both envi- 23
ronments which condone or even encourage hootin' and hollerin'—have conditioned
us to voice our approval and disapproval and just about anything else we can spit
out of our mouths at the slightest provocation when we are part of an audience.

But my guess lies elsewhere. The villain, I'm afraid, is the tube. We have seen 24
the enemy and it is television.

We have gotten conditioned over the last few decades to spending most of 25
our screen-viewing time in front of a little box in our living rooms and bedrooms.
And when we watch that piece of furniture, regardless of what is on it—be it
commercial, Super Bowl, soap opera, funeral procession, prime-time sitcom,
Shakespeare play—we chat. Boy, do we chat. Because TV viewing tends to be an
informal, gregarious, friendly, casually interruptible experience, we talk whenever
the spirit moves us. Which is often.

All of this is fine. But we have carried behavior that is perfectly acceptable in 26
the living room right to our neighborhood movie theater. And that *isn't* fine. In fact,
it is turning lots of people off to what used to be a truly pleasurable experience:
sitting in a jammed movie theater and watching a crowd-pleasing movie. And
that's a first-class shame.

Nobody wants Fascist-like ushers, yet that may be where we're headed of 27
necessity. Let's hope not. But something's got to give.

Movies during this Age of Television may or may not be better than ever. 28
About audiences, however, there is no question.

They are worse. 29

■ Reading Comprehension Questions

1. The word *ecstatic* in "The theater is absolutely full . . . as the reviews have
   been ecstatic for this cinema masterpiece" (paragraph 2) means

   a. clever.

   b. disappointing.

   c. a little confusing.

   d. very enthusiastic.

2. The word *malodorous* in "It is really not that difficult to forgive a person's . . .
   malodorous perfume" (paragraph 15) means

   a. pleasant.

   b. expensive.

   c. bad-smelling.

   d. hard-to-smell.

3. Which of the following would be the best alternative title for this selection?
   a. Television-Watching Behavior
   b. Today's Movie Audiences
   c. Modern Films
   d. The Life of a Movie Critic

4. Which sentence best expresses the main idea of the selection?
   a. Ushers should now make movie audiences keep quiet.
   b. People talk while they watch television or sports.
   c. Rude audiences are ruining movies for many.
   d. Films have changed in recent years.

5. The author states that in his dream
   a. he had come to the movies with a friend.
   b. he wore a tall hat and sat in front of a person shorter than he is.
   c. the Cub Scouts were making noises with empty candy boxes.
   d. the popcorn was too salty.

6. *True or false?* _____ The experience that Wine describes in the first ten paragraphs of this article really happened.

7. The most frequent complaint the author has heard about movies is
   a. they are too long.
   b. they are too expensive.
   c. the audiences are too noisy.
   d. the audiences arrive too late.

8. The author suggests that watching television
   a. has affected the behavior of movie audiences.
   b. should be done in silence.
   c. is more fun than seeing movies in a theater.
   d. is a good model for watching movies in theaters.

9. From the selection, we can conclude that the author feels
   a. films aren't as good as they used to be.
   b. teenagers are the rudest members of movie audiences.
   c. talking during a movie is much more common now than it used to be.
   d. tall people should be seated in the back of a theater.

10. In paragraph 27, the author implies that unless audiences become quieter,

    a.   movie theaters will be closed.

    b.   everyone will watch less television.

    c.   movies will get worse.

    d.   ushers will have to force talkers to be quiet or leave.

■ Discussion Questions

About Content

1. According to Wine, what are some possible causes for people's rude behavior at movies? Of these, which does Wine consider the most likely cause?

2. Do you agree with Wine's theory about why some people are rude at the movies? Why or why not? What might theater operators and other audience members do to control the problem?

3. Have you noticed the problem of noisy audiences in a movie theater? If so, what exactly have you experienced? What, if anything, was done about the problems you encountered?

About Structure

4. Wine writes about a problem. Write here the paragraphs in which Wine presents details that explain and illustrate what that problem is: paragraphs _____ to _____.

5. Wine discusses reasons for the problem he writes about. Write here the paragraphs in which he discusses those reasons: paragraphs _____ to _____.

6. Wine suggests one possible but unwelcome solution for the problem he writes about. Write here the number of the paragraph in which he mentions that solution: _____.

About Style and Tone

7. Wine provides exaggerated descriptions of audience members—for example, he refers to the tall man sitting in front of him as "an inch or two taller than the Jolly Green Giant." Find two other examples of this humorous exaggeration.

_____

_____

Besides making readers smile, why might Wine have described the audience in this way?

_____

_____

8. Wine tends to use informal wording and sentence structure. In paragraphs 22–26, for instance, find two examples of his informal wording.

_____

_____

In the same paragraphs, find an example of his informal sentence structure.

_____

■ Writing Assignments

Assignment 1: Writing a Paragraph

Which do you prefer—watching a movie on your VCR at home or seeing it in a movie theater? Drawing on your own experiences, write a paragraph in which you explain why you prefer one viewing location over the other. Provide a strong example or two for each of your reasons. For instance, below is one reason with a specific example to support it.

> *Reason:* One reason I prefer going to a movie theater is that it is definitely more peaceful than watching a film at home.
>
> *Supporting example:* For instance, when I tried watching *Titanic* at home the other night, I had to check on a crying baby or a fussy toddler every ten minutes. Can you imagine what it is like just as two pairs of lips on the screen are getting close enough to meet, to hear, "Mommy, my tummy hurts." If I go out to the movies, I leave my kids and their diapers in the care of my husband or mother.

Assignment 2: Writing a Paragraph

Using exaggeration and humor, Wine gives his impressions of people's looks and behavior at a movie theater. Write a paragraph describing your impressions of people's looks and behavior at a specific event or place. For instance, you might describe how people look and act at a rock concert, in an elevator, in a singles' hangout, or in a library. Like Wine, use colorful descriptions and quotations. Your topic sentence might be similar to the following:

> How people behave on an elevator reveals some key personal qualities.

Try listing ideas to develop your supporting details. For example, below is a list of possible supporting points for the topic sentence above.

Shy people tend to avoid eye contact.

Very friendly people smile and may say something.

Helpful people will keep the elevator from leaving when they see someone rushing toward it.

A romantic couple won't notice anyone else on the elevator.

Impatient people may push the number of their floor more than once.

Assignment 3: Writing an Essay

Rudeness, unfortunately, is not limited to the movie theater. We have all observed rude behavior in various places we often go to. Write an essay on this topic. You might use one of the following thesis statements:

> Rude behavior is all too common in several places I often go to.
>
> A common part of life at my neighborhood supermarket is the rude behavior of other shoppers.

In an essay with the first central point, you could write about three places where you have seen rude behavior. Develop each paragraph with one or more vivid examples.

In an essay on the second central point, you would need to come up with two or three general types of rude behavior to write about. Below is one student's outline for an essay with that topic sentence.

> <u>Central idea:</u> A common part of life at my neighborhood supermarket is the rude behavior of other shoppers.
>
> (1) Getting in the way of other shoppers
>   Blocking the aisle with a cart
>   Knocking things down and not picking them up
>   "Parking" in front of all the free samples
>
> (2) Misplacing items
>   Putting unwanted frozen food on a shelf instead of back in a freezer
>   Putting unwanted meat on a shelf instead of in a refrigerated section
>
> (3) Unreasonably making others wait at the checkout line
>   Bringing a bulging cartload to the express line
>   Keeping a line waiting while running to get "just one more thing" (instead of stepping out of line)
>   Keeping a line waiting while deciding what not to buy to keep the total price down (instead of keeping track while shopping)

Bullies in School

Kathleen Berger

How serious a problem is bullying in schools? Is it a rite of passage, a normal part of childhood that every kid has to go through? Should adults intervene, or is the bully-victim relationship something children need to work out for themselves? And what influences create a bully or a victim? In this selection, Kathleen Berger reports on the work of a researcher who has come up with some surprising—even alarming—findings about bullies. Read it and see if the researcher's conclusions correspond with what you have observed or experienced.

Bullying was once commonly thought to be an unpleasant but normal part of children's play, not to be encouraged, of course, but of little consequence in the long run. However, developmental researchers who have looked closely at the society of children consider bullying to be a very serious problem, one that harms both the victim and the aggressor, sometimes continuing to cause suffering years after the child has grown up.

One leading researcher in this area is Dan Olweus, who has studied bullying in his native country of Norway and elsewhere for twenty-five years. The cruelty, pain, and suffering that he has documented in that time are typified by the examples of Linda and Henry:

> Linda was systematically isolated by a small group of girls, who pressured the rest of the class, including Linda's only friend, to shun her. Then the ringleader of the group persuaded Linda to give a party, inviting everyone. Everyone accepted; following the ringleader's directions, no one came. Linda was devastated, her self-confidence "completely destroyed."

> Henry's experience was worse. Daily, his classmates called him "Worm," broke his pencils, spilled his books on the floor, and mocked him whenever he answered a teacher's questions. Finally, a few boys took him to the bathroom and made him lie, face down, in the urinal drain. After school that day he tried to kill himself. His parents found him unconscious, and only then learned about his torment.

Following the suicides of three other victims of bullying, the Norwegian government asked Olweus in 1983 to determine the extent and severity of the problem. After concluding a confidential survey of nearly all of Norway's 90,000 school-age children, Olweus reported that the problem was widespread and serious; that teachers and parents were "relatively unaware" of specific incidents of bullying; and that even when adults noticed bullying, they rarely intervened. Of all the children Olweus surveyed, 9 percent were bullied "now and then"; 3 percent were victims once a week or more; and 7 percent admitted that they themselves sometimes deliberately hurt other children, verbally or physically.

As high as these numbers may seem, they are equaled and even exceeded in   4
research done in other countries. For instance, a British study of eight- to nine-year-
olds found that 17 percent were victims of regular bullying and that 13 percent
were bullies. A study of middle-class children in a university school in Florida found
that 10 percent were "extremely victimized." Recently, American researchers have
looked particularly at sexual harassment, an aspect of childhood bullying ignored
by most adults. Fully a third of nine- to fifteen-year-old girls say they have experienced sexual teasing and touching sufficiently troubling that they wanted to avoid
school, and, as puberty approaches, almost every boy who is perceived as homosexual by his peers is bullied, sometimes mercilessly.

Researchers define bullying as repeated, systematic efforts to inflict harm on   5
a particular child through physical attack (such as hitting, punching, pinching, or
kicking), verbal attack (such as teasing, taunting, or name-calling), or social attack
(such as deliberate social exclusion or public mocking). Implicit in this definition
is the idea of an unbalance of power: victims of bullying are in some way weaker
than their harassers and continue to be singled out for attack, in part because they
have difficulty defending themselves. In many cases, this difficulty is compounded
by the fact that the bullying is being carried out by a group of children. In
Olweus's research, at least 60 percent of bullying incidents involved group attacks.

As indicated by the emphasis given to it, the key word in the preceding defi-   6
nition of bullying is "repeated." Most children experience isolated attacks or social
slights from other children and come through them unscathed. But when a child
must endure such shameful experiences again and again—being forced to hand
over lunch money, or to drink milk mixed with detergent, or to lick someone's
boots, or to be the butt of insults and practical jokes, with everyone watching and
no one coming to the child's defense—the effects can be deep and long-lasting. Not
only are bullied children anxious, depressed, and underachieving during the months
and years of their torment, but even years later, they have lower self-esteem as
well as painful memories.

The picture is somewhat different, but often more ominous, for bullies. Contrary   7
to the public perception that bullies are actually insecure and lonely, at the peak
of their bullying they usually have friends who abet, fear, and admire them, and
they seem brashly unapologetic about the pain they have inflicted, as they often
claim, "all in fun." But their popularity and school success fade over the years, and
especially if they are boys, they run a high risk of ending up in prison. In one lon-
gitudinal study done by Olweus, by age twenty-four, two-thirds of the boys who
had been bullies in the second grade were convicted of at least one felony, and
one-third of those who had been bullies in the sixth through the ninth grades
were already convicted of three or more crimes, often violent ones. International
research likewise finds that children who are allowed to regularly victimize other
children are at high risk of becoming violent offenders as adolescents and adults.

Unfortunately, bullying during middle childhood seems to be universal: it occurs   8
in every nation that has been studied, is as much a problem in small rural schools
as in large urban ones, and is as prevalent among well-to-do majority children as
among poor immigrant children. Also quite common, if not universal, is the "profile"

of bullies and their victims. Contrary to popular belief, victims are not distinguished by their external traits: they are no more likely to be fat, skinny, or homely, or to speak with an accent, than nonvictims are. But they usually are "rejected" children, that is, children who have few friends because they are more anxious and less secure than most children and are unable or unwilling to defend themselves. They also are more often boys than girls and more often younger children.

Bullies have traits in common as well, some of which can be traced to their   9
upbringing. The parents of bullies often seem indifferent to what their children do outside the home but use "power-assertive" discipline on them at home. These children are frequently subjected to physical punishment, verbal criticism, and displays of dominance meant to control and demean them, thereby giving them a vivid model, as well as a compelling reason, to control and demean others. Boys who are bullies are often above average in size, while girls who are bullies are often above average in verbal assertiveness. These differences are reflected in bullying tactics: boys typically use force or the threat of force; girls often mock or ridicule their victims, making fun of their clothes, behavior, or appearance, or revealing their most embarrassing secrets.

What can be done to halt these damaging attacks? Many psychologists have   10
attempted to alter the behavior patterns that characterize aggressive or rejected children. Cognitive interventions seem particularly fruitful: some programs teach social problem-solving skills (such as how to use humor or negotiation to reduce a conflict); others help children reassess their negative assumptions (such as the frequent, fatalistic view of many rejected children that nothing can protect them, or the aggressive child's typical readiness to conclude that accidental slights are deliberate threats); others tutor children in academic skills, hoping to improve confidence and short-circuit the low self-esteem that might be at the root of both victimization and aggression.

These approaches sometimes help individuals. However, because they target   11
one child at a time, they are piecemeal, time-consuming, and costly. Further, they have to work against habits learned at home and patterns reinforced at school, making it hard to change a child's behavior pattern. After all, bullies and their admirers have no reason to learn new social skills if their current attitudes and actions bring them status and pleasure. And even if rejected children change their behavior, they still face a difficult time recovering accepted positions in the peer group and gaining friends who will support and defend them. The solution to this problem must begin, then, by recognizing that the bullies and victims are not acting in isolation but, rather, are caught up in a mutually destructive interaction within a particular social context.

Accordingly, a more effective intervention is to change the social climate within   12
the school, so that bully-victim cycles no longer spiral out of control. That this approach can work was strikingly demonstrated by a government-funded awareness campaign that Olweus initiated for every school in Norway. In the first phase of the campaign, community-wide meetings were held to explain the problem; pamphlets were sent to all parents to alert them to the signs of victimization (such

as a child's having bad dreams, having no real friends, and coming home from school with damaged clothes, torn books, or unexplained bruises); and videotapes were shown to all students to evoke sympathy for victims.

The second phase of the campaign involved specific actions within the schools. 13 In every classroom, students discussed reasons for and ways to mediate peer conflicts, to befriend lonely children, and to stop bullying attacks whenever they saw them occur. Teachers were taught to be proactive, organizing cooperative learning groups so that no single child could be isolated, halting each incident of name-calling or minor assault as soon as they noticed it, and learning how to see through the bully's excuses and to understand the victim's fear of reprisal. Principals were advised that adequate adult supervision during recess, lunch, and bathroom breaks distinguished schools where bullying was rare from those where bullying was common.

If bullying incidents occurred despite such measures, counselors were urged to 14 intervene, talking privately and seriously with bullies and their victims, counseling their parents, and seeking solutions that might include intensive therapy with the bully's parents to restructure family discipline, reassigning the bully to a different class, grade, or even school, and helping the victim strengthen skills and foster friendships.

Twenty months after this campaign began, Olweus resurveyed the children 15 in forty-two schools. He found that bullying had been reduced overall by more than 50 percent, with dramatic improvement for both boys and girls at every grade level. Developmental researchers are excited because results such as these, in which a relatively simple, cost-effective measure has such a decided impact on a developmental problem, are rare. Olweus concludes, "It is no longer possible to avoid taking action about bullying problems at school using lack of awareness as an excuse. . . . it all boils down to a matter of will and involvement on the part of the adults." Unfortunately, at the moment, Norway is the only country to have mounted a nationwide attack to prevent the problem of bullying. Many other school systems, in many other nations, have not even acknowledged the harm caused by this problem, much less shown the "will and involvement" to stop it.

■ Reading Comprehension Questions

1. The word *compounded* in ". . . victims of bullying . . . continue to be singled out for attack, in part because they have difficulty defending themselves. In many cases, this difficulty is compounded by the fact that the bullying is being carried out by a group of children" (paragraph 5) means

   a.   reduced.

   b.   increased.

   c.   solved.

   d.   forgiven.

2. The word *unscathed* in "Most children experience isolated attacks . . . from other children and come through them unscathed. But when a child must endure such shameful experiences again and again . . . the effects can be deep and long-lasting" (paragraph 6) means

    a.   unharmed.

    b.   unpleasant.

    c.   unknown.

    d.   uncertain.

3. Which of the following would be the best alternative title for the selection?

    a.   Bullies: Why Do They Act That Way?

    b.   The Pain of Being Bullied

    c.   Bullies in Norway

    d.   Bullying: A Problem Too Serious to Ignore

4. Which sentence best expresses the selection's main point?

    a.   Certain types of children are inclined to become either bullies or victims.

    b.   To combat the problem of bullying in Norway, a researcher designed an innovative program for all of its schools.

    c.   Researchers consider bullying a very serious problem, one that harms both victims and bullies.

    d.   Researchers have concluded that bullying is a very serious problem that can be solved only by changing the social climate in which it develops.

5. One thing many bullies have in common is that they

    a.   are harshly punished at home.

    b.   have few friends.

    c.   are often apologetic after they've acted in a bullying way.

    d.   are often from poor immigrant families.

6. *True or false?* _____ Victims of bullies tend to be physically unattractive.

7. Parents of a bully

    a.   are usually anxious to stop their child's bullying behavior.

    b.   were often victims of bullies themselves.

    c.   often seem unconcerned about their child's behavior away from home.

    d.   actively encourage their child to be a bully.

8. A study done by Dan Olweus of what happens in later years to boys who are bullies showed that

    a.   a high proportion become teachers.

    b.   a high percentage end up in prison.

   c.   they have trouble finding and keeping jobs.

   d.   their suicide rate is higher than average.

9. Boy and girl bullies

   a.   differ: girls tend to mock their victims, while boys are more likely to use force.

   b.   bully their victims in just about the same ways.

   c.   differ: girls tend to be bigger than average, while boys are more verbally assertive than average.

   d.   differ: girls tend to use force on their victims, while boys are more likely to mock them.

10. If a teacher witnessed an incident of bullying, we can infer that Olweus (the designer of the Norwegian program) would advise him or her to

   a.   ignore it, letting the students involved settle the matter themselves.

   b.   privately encourage the victim to fight back.

   c.   transfer the victim to another class.

   d.   immediately confront the bully.

■ Discussion Questions

About Content

1. Olweus describes two specific incidents of bullying, involving Linda and Henry. Did those incidents remind you of anything that ever occurred at your own school? Who were the bullies? Who were the victims? Describe the incident. What, if any, role did you play in such events?

2. What are some of the measures Olweus recommends be taken in a school and community to stop bullying? Do you think such measures would have been helpful in your school? If you are a parent, would you support such programs in your child's school?

3. Olweus concludes that bullying is a very serious problem, with effects that carry over for years into the lives of both bullies and victims. Do you agree? Or do you think Olweus is exaggerating the problem?

4. Olweus reports that, although bullying is a widespread and serious problem, most teachers and parents are "relatively unaware" of bullying going on. How can this be? What is it about the dynamics of the relationship between bully and victim that can make it both a serious problem and one that is nearly invisible to adults?

About Structure

5. What combination of methods does Berger use to introduce this selection?

   a.   Broad to narrow; quotation.

   b.   Anecdote; question.

   c.   Beginning with opposite; anecdotes.

   d.   Quotation; question.

   Is this introduction effective? Why or why not?

6. This selection can be divided be into five parts. Fill in the following blanks to show which paragraphs are included in each part:

   (1) Berger's introduction of the topic: paragraph _____

   (2) Two examples of bullying typical of the consequences Olweus reports on: paragraph _____

   (3) Findings of Olweus's government-sponsored study and other research: paragraphs _____ to _____

   (4) Ways to halt bullying: paragraphs _____ to _____

   (5) Olweus's follow-up study and the author's brief conclusion: paragraph _____

About Style and Tone

7. Find three places in the selection where statistics are cited. Why would a selection like this use so many statistics? What do statistics accomplish that anecdotes cannot?

8. The author's tone can be described as a combination of

   a.   horror and fear.

   b.   concern and objectivity.

   c.   bewilderment and pleading.

   d.   curiosity and excitement.

   Find examples in the selection that illustrate this tone.

■ Writing Assignments

Assignment 1: Writing a Paragraph

Write a paragraph describing a bully you have been acquainted with. Focus on three aspects of the person: his or her appearance, actions, and effects on others. Help your reader vividly imagine the bully by providing concrete details that illustrate each aspect. Your topic sentence might be similar to this:

In junior high school, I became familiar with a bully and the pain he caused one student.

Assignment 2: Writing a Paragraph

The social aspect of school is hard for many students, even if they are not victims of bullies. Write a paragraph about another reason or reasons that school was difficult for you or for people you observed. Was it the pressure to wear a certain kind of clothing? Be involved in sports? Use drugs and drink? Become sexually active? Hang out with a "cool" crowd? Provide details that help your reader understand how difficult pressures at school can be.

Assignment 3: Writing an Essay

Think of a time when you were on the giving end or the receiving end of an act of bullying. (The incident could fall into any of the categories mentioned in paragraph 5 of the reading—a physical, verbal, or social attack.) If you cannot think of an incident that involved you, think of one that you witnessed. Write an essay describing the incident. In your essay, be sure to cover the following points: How did the bully behave? How did the victim respond? And how did any onlookers react to what was going on? For an example of one author's clear, detailed narrative of such an incident, read Paul Logan's essay "Rowing the Bus" (page 590).

Assignment 4: Writing an Essay Using Internet Research

Victims of bullying often need help for two reasons. They have to stand up to the bullies who are tormenting them, and they also have to deal with negative feelings about themselves. Use the Internet to research methods recommended by experts for helping victims of bullying. Then write an essay that describes in detail three methods that can help victims cope with their own negative self-image or with the bullies themselves.

To access the Internet, use the very helpful search engine Google (*www.google.com*) or one of the other search engines listed on pages 323–325 of this book. Try one of the following phrases or some related phrase:

coping with bullies

victims of bullying

bullies and coping and victims

You may, of course, use a single keyword such as "bullies," but that will bring up too many items. By using a phrase such as one of the above, you can begin to limit your search. As you proceed, you'll develop a sense of how to "track down" and focus a topic by adding more information to your search words and phrases.

People Need People

S. Leonard Syme

"People who need people," says the song, "are the luckiest people in the world." Recent studies indicate that they are also among the healthiest. We don't know exactly why strong family and community ties should help the body's immune system fight disease, but evidence that they do is growing rapidly. In the following article, written for *American Health* magazine, a medical doctor prescribes friendship as the key to a long and healthy life.

1   Between 1970 and 1980, according to the United States census, the number of men living alone rose 92.3 percent; the figure for women went up 50.6 percent. Loneliness is apparently becoming a more common aspect of American life, and this may have serious effects on health and well-being.

2   It's long been known, for example, that widowers and widows do not live as long as married men and women. Several investigators, including my own group at the University of California, Berkeley, have been attempting to study this issue in more detail.

3   The latest research has gone beyond the traditional measures of loneliness—such as marital status—to look at the more subtle influence of social networks on health. So far, this work suggests that a society that fosters connectedness to others—such as traditional Japanese society—may be healthier, in a real sense, than a culture as individualistic as our own.

4   A colleague of mine, Lisa Berkman, Ph.D., did a study that shows how all kinds of people can suffer physically from a lack of social support. In 1974 she examined the records of seven thousand people in Alameda County, California, who had been randomly chosen for interviews about their lives and social relationships a decade earlier.

5   Berkman was able to classify these people in terms of their social support networks, ranging from the relatively isolated to those who were extensively involved with others. She then went to the state health department and examined the death rates in this group over nine years. Sure enough, those who were more isolated had death rates two to three times higher during this period than those with more extensive social ties. The more such ties, the lower the death rate. This finding was true for both sexes and all ages, social classes, and races. Further, the findings were independent of such other factors as smoking, alcohol consumption, physical activity, obesity, eating patterns, and use of health services.

Our first thought was that those who were more isolated were sick already and   6
that was the reason they had a higher death rate. But we could find no evidence
that this was true. While I was convinced that prior ill health did not explain the
findings, I nevertheless was anxious for some more supportive evidence. Just a few
months ago that confirmation came through. Data are now in from a ten-year study
at the University of Michigan that followed 2,754 adults in Tecumseh, Michigan,
and asked the question, "Does the social network affect physical health?"

The researchers, James House, Ph.D., and his colleagues, carefully measured   7
the participants' health at the beginning of the study to rule out the possibility
that people might become isolated because they were already sick. They then
looked at their subjects' personal relationships and group activities—and their
health—for a decade. The result: those with the least social contacts had two to
four times the mortality rate of the well-connected.

The Surprising Japanese: Urban, Stressed—and Healthy

Consider these findings along with our research on Japanese immigrants. It is said   8
that many of our health problems are traceable to such modern evils as industrialization, pollution, and so on. Japan, however, offers a striking exception. It is
highly industrialized, has a high level of technology, is one of the most urbanized
nations in the world, and suffers from urban pollution that is at least equal to
ours. Cigarette smoking and high blood pressure are also common in Japan. And
if you've visited their large cities, you know the pace of life is at least as frantic
as ours.

Yet Japan now has the highest life expectancy in the world, with one of the   9
lowest reported rates of heart disease. Why?

The easiest explanation would be that the Japanese have a favorable genetic   10
makeup. This is plausible, but the evidence does not entirely support this idea.
Instead, something about their lifestyle seems to hold the key. When Japanese
people move to California, those who adopt Western ways exhibit a disease pattern very much like that of other Westerners. Those who retain Japanese ways
have lower disease rates, as if they were still in Japan. Because Hawaii is not as
Westernized as California, Japanese there generally remained healthier than those
on the mainland—though not as healthy as those in Japan.

We did a study of twelve thousand Japanese men, some in the San Francisco   11
Bay Area, some in Hawaii, and some in the southwestern area of Japan, from
which most of the Japanese immigrants came. My colleague Michael Marmot,
Ph.D., found very low rates of heart disease among Japanese in the Bay Area who
grew up in Japanese neighborhoods, whose childhood friends were Japanese,
who attended Japanese-language schools in addition to English-language schools,
and who returned to Japan for more schooling. He also found low disease rates
among those who, as adults, kept their ties to the Japanese community.

In contrast, those Japanese who became Westernized—both as children and 12 as adults—had coronary heart disease rates five times higher, even after we had taken into account the usual risk factors of diet, serum cholesterol, smoking, and blood pressure. The Japanese who retained their community ties—and their health—often ate Western foods, had high serum cholesterol levels, smoked cigarettes, and had high blood pressure. It is possible that their intimate community bonds protected them.

It is one thing to talk about staying involved with the Japanese community. 13 It is another to explain precisely what this means. I now believe that the special characteristic of Japanese culture is the importance of social ties and social supports.

To the Japanese one's very identity is bound up with one's group. In Western 14 society individualism is far more predominant. The American hero is the cowboy who stands alone and follows his convictions no matter what others think and no matter what the cost. John F. Kennedy's book *Profiles in Courage* tells the stories of eight American public figures who stood up for their beliefs, even though others thought they were wrong and tried to pressure them to change their minds. A Japanese colleague told me that in Japan these heroes would be considered mentally ill.

In Japan, people often go through school with the same friends, graduate 15 together, and work together in the same company for much of their lives. They value their social networks so highly that, whenever possible, employers try to move work groups together. The famous Quality Control Circle, considered the key to Japan's incredible productivity, is a stable working team.

Why Moss Can Be Beautiful

Another important feature of Japanese life is the concept of the native place—a 16 place you come from and a place to which you will return after you retire. You *can* go home again. It is a place to which you return all your life and where people know you and keep track of you.

How many Americans have a native place? Perhaps the simplest way to 17 describe the difference in the Japanese and American approaches to life is in terms of the Japanese saying, "A rolling stone gathers no moss." Since moss is a beautiful and treasured thing, a stone without moss is not much of a stone. To acquire moss, you must have the patience to stay put.

In the United States this saying is meant in exactly the opposite way—it's best 18 to keep moving on, so that moss doesn't dirty your slick surface. Moss is a sure sign that you're not a go-getter.

But moving on breaks old ties and exacts a high cost. From these studies it 19 seems that, for reasons not yet understood, people with more stable social bonds have better health than those who are more isolated. Social ties seem to buffer us from the effects of disease risk factors.

Disease rates go up with certain changes in life—particularly events that cause 20 social disruption, such as the death of a spouse or some other loved one, job changes, loss of a job, and moving. When social ties are interrupted or broken, the rates of many diseases rise: coronary heart disease, cancer, arthritis, strokes, accidents, mental illness, upper respiratory ailments, infections of wisdom teeth, and so on. Since the effects are so wide-ranging, it seems that interrupted social ties affect the body's defense systems, so that a person becomes more susceptible to a number of conditions. The particular disease one gets may be tied to such specific risk factors as serum cholesterol, blood pressure, smoking, viruses, and air pollution.

What we are seeing, in effect, is that loneliness is a health hazard. The idea 21 is not a new one, but the data have never been as persuasive as they are now. The evidence forces us to look for positive ways to fight loneliness—and illness.

Yes, married people have lower rates of disease than those who are widowed, 22 divorced, or single. We cannot explain this in terms of clear physical differences—in age, weight, physical activity, or standard heart disease risk factors—between the single and the wed.

Even owning a pet—an easy remedy for loneliness—can have an effect on 23 health. Pet owners, according to one study, have better survival rates after heart attacks than those who don't own an animal.

Hard Times Make Fast Friends

Human companionship can be more important than comfort, safety, or affluence 24 in determining the quality of a person's life. For years people have told me that the best times in their lives were when they were involved closely with others. And it does not seem to matter whether the situation was pleasant or miserable.

Linda Nilson, Ph.D., a sociologist at UCLA, reports that residents in communities 25 struck by natural disasters (tornadoes, hurricanes, floods, earthquakes) do *not* panic, loot, and suffer psychological breakdowns. They generally keep their heads, care for one another, share scarce resources, and reach an emotional high as they pull together to face the common challenges of survival and rebuilding.

Many people actually feel better about themselves and their neighbors, she 26 adds, after going through a disaster. They are proud of the way they handled the crisis and touched by the generosity of others, and they look on their part in the common recovery effort as the most meaningful work of their lives. Nilson notes that in no case on record in the United States have authorities had to declare martial law in a natural disaster area—and she has analyzed more than one hundred reports of responses to such disasters over the past sixty years.

Well, what shall we make of all this? What are the practical implications for how 27 we live our lives to preserve our health? Exhortations to "be friendly" or "smile" won't be enough, and neither will singing forty choruses of "Up with People." But it should certainly be possible to make it easier for people to work together and be together if they choose to.

Educational campaigns should not just teach people to look for the seven signs 28 of cancer, but also give them information they can use to make healthy decisions for themselves and their families: Is this move necessary? What are the real costs of this promotion? What groups can I join that will share my interests and generate intellectual and social excitement?

More and more, people are coming together voluntarily to support one 29 another, almost in opposition to social and institutional trends. The results achieved by self-help groups, such as Alcoholics Anonymous and Gamblers Anonymous, are impressive; so are those of the support groups for people in particular situations, such as those recovering from cancer operations, going through divorce, or moving to a new city. It seems that, whatever the self-help group's philosophy, being in a group is itself therapeutic.

All of us could learn from these examples. But it shouldn't take a common 30 problem like alcoholism or gambling—or a natural disaster—to draw people together. We need to recognize the importance of community, of touching other people, in our daily existence. Our health, our lives, may depend on it.

■ Reading Comprehension Questions

1. The word *buffer* in "Social ties seem to buffer us from . . . disease risk factors" (paragraph 19) means
   a. free.
   b. weaken.
   c. frighten.
   d. protect.

2. The word *therapeutic* in "being in a group is itself therapeutic" (paragraph 29) means
   a. necessary.
   b. harmful.
   c. healing.
   d. unusual.

3. Which of the following would be the best alternative title for this selection?
   a. Living Longer in the United States
   b. The Value of Human Companionship
   c. The Self-Help Group
   d. Aging in Japanese Society

4. Which sentence best expresses the main idea of the selection?
   a. Many of our health problems are caused by industrialization and pollution.
   b. People are healthier and live longer when they have good social contacts.
   c. The Japanese have a genetic makeup that helps them live longer.
   d. Disease rates increase when people make changes in their lives.

5. Researchers found that people in areas hit by natural disasters
   a. helped each other.
   b. panicked immediately.
   c. usually resorted to looting.
   d. often isolated themselves from other people.

6. *True or false?* _____ Married people have lower rates of disease than those who are widowed, divorced, or single.

7. People who live alone
   a. are usually unemployed, divorced women.
   b. have lower serum cholesterol levels.
   c. have higher death rates.
   d. eat and smoke more than married people.

8. The author implies that
   a. a person's health does not suffer because he or she has few social contacts.
   b. sickness isolates people from other people.
   c. in Japan, the individual's rights are not as important as the group's.
   d. cigarette smoking and high blood pressure are uncommon in Japan.

9. The author implies that
   a. Japan has less pollution and industrialization than the United States.
   b. the pace of life is slower in Japan than in the United States.
   c. Hawaii's climate is healthier for the Japanese than Japan's climate.
   d. the Japanese do not consider the American cowboy as their kind of hero.

10. *True or false?* _____ The author implies that many Americans do not have the concept of a native place.

■ Discussion Questions

About Content

1. What characteristics of Japanese society prevent loneliness?

2. Why do disasters and hard times cause people to "reach an emotional high" (paragraph 25)? Why do many people feel better about each other after such times?

3. Do you think that college students generally have a strong sense of connectedness to others? When do you feel most lonely? What techniques have you learned to combat this feeling?

About Structure

4. Besides paragraph 1, locate two other paragraphs where the author uses statistics to make a point:

   _____   _____

5. Find three change-of-direction signals used in paragraphs 8–12 and write them below:

   _____

   _____

   _____

6. This essay contrasts American isolation with the Japanese sense of community. In paragraphs 8 to 18, does Syme use mainly a point-by-point or a one-side-at-a-time contrast?

About Style and Tone

7. Why does Syme use questions to begin the concluding section of the essay (paragraphs 27–30)? What is his persuasive purpose in his concluding paragraphs?

8. For what audience might this essay have been intended: scholars, psychologists, teachers, students, or the general public? How can you tell?

◼ Writing Assignments

Assignment 1: Writing a Paragraph

Write a paragraph contrasting two times in your life: a time when you had few human contacts and a time when you had many.

To get started, you might make up two lists: (1) happy times when you had especially close connections with other people; (2) lonely times when you seemed to lack even a single person who cared about you. You might, for example, have felt particularly happy when you were with a group of close friends at some time in high school; you might have felt neglected during a time of trouble between your parents. Choose those two times for which you have the sharpest memory of details. Then freewrite for five or ten minutes about each of them, putting down on paper whatever comes into mind.

Next, decide which method of development to use: point-by-point or one-side-at-a-time. If you choose one-side-at-a-time, you might use an outline like this:

Happy time:

a. Situation (when and where)

b. Your thoughts and feelings

c. Why the time ended

Sad time:

a. Situation (when and where)

b. Your thoughts and feelings

c. Why the time ended

Once you have your outline, you should be ready to work on the first draft of your paper. You may also find it helpful to look over the general guidelines on pages 215–217 while writing your paragraph.

Assignment 2: Writing a Paragraph

The Japanese have a concept of a "native place," a place where each person is from and where he or she feels truly at home. In a less formal way, most of us also have a place where we feel "at home." We can turn to such a place to replenish ourselves and restore our peace of mind. In a paragraph, identify your special place and describe it in detail. Your topic sentence might read: " _____ is a special place where I feel relaxed and at home." Use only those details that add to the dominant impression of comfort and ease.

Assignment 3: Writing an Essay

Americans may not often belong to large, stable communities, but our personal relationships can keep us from feeling isolated. What do you especially value about the people who are close to you? You may prefer such time-honored qualities as loyalty and openness. You may also delight in more unusual traits, like a wacky sense of humor, a shared interest in an unusual pastime, or a love of friendly arguments. Examine your friends and family to determine which aspects of their personalities you particularly enjoy. Then write an essay describing three of the qualities you most appreciate in your personal relationships.

Remember to list in your thesis statement the three qualities you select. Each characteristic, in turn, will provide the subject for one of your three topic sentences. Use examples from your friends, your family, or both to support your topic sentences.

Here is one student's outline for this essay.

Thesis: Three of the qualities I most appreciate in my personal relationships are shared interests, honesty, and a sense of humor.

Topic sentence 1: Sharing special interests with my friends and family has been one source of great pleasure for me.

a. My friend Jon and I have listened to rock music together for years.

b. My father and I love going to baseball games together.

c. Lately, a couple of friends and I have enjoyed discussing Stephen King's books.

<u>Topic sentence 2:</u> I also highly value honesty in my personal relationships.

a. I know I can count on my sister to give me honest evaluations of outfits I wear.
b. I hope that my friends will speak about their true preferences for how to spend an evening.
c. I am pleased that my good friends and my family do not agree with my opinions just to be polite.

<u>Topic sentence 3:</u> Finally, I especially value humor in my personal relationships.

a. I like to be able to laugh with my friends after a hard day of work.
b. I look forward to my friend Nelson's practical jokes.
c. My sister and I are better friends than we would be if we could not tease each other.

A Drunken Ride, a Tragic Aftermath

Theresa Conroy and Christine M. Johnson

Have you ever sat behind the wheel of your car after drinking? Have you ever assured yourself, "I haven't had too much. I'm still in control"? If you have, you're not alone. The large number of arrests for drunk driving proves that plenty of drivers who have been drinking thought they were capable of getting home safely. After all, who would get into a car with the intention of killing himself or herself or others? Yet killing is exactly what many drunk drivers do. If all drivers could read the following selection—a newspaper report on one tragic accident—perhaps the frequent cautions about drinking and driving would have some impact. Read the article and see if you agree.

1   When Tyson Baxter awoke after that drunken, tragic night—with a bloodied head, broken arm, and battered face—he knew that he had killed his friends.

2   "I knew everyone had died," Baxter, eighteen, recalled. "I knew it before anybody told me. Somehow, I knew."

3   Baxter was talking about the night of Friday, September 13, the night he and seven friends piled into his Chevrolet Blazer after a beer-drinking party. On Street Road in Upper Southampton, he lost control, rear-ended a car, and smashed into two telephone poles. The Blazer's cab top shattered, and the truck spun several times, ejecting all but one passenger.

Four young men were killed. 4

Tests would show that Baxter and the four youths who died were legally 5 intoxicated.

Baxter says he thinks about his dead friends on many sleepless nights at the 6 Abraxas Drug and Alcohol Rehabilitation Center near Pittsburgh, where, on December 20, he was sentenced to be held after being found delinquent on charges of vehicular homicide.

"I drove them where they wanted to go, and I was responsible for their lives," 7 Baxter said recently from the center, where he is undergoing psychological treatment. "I had the keys in my hand, and I blew it."

The story of September 13 is a story about the kind of horrors that drinking 8 and driving is spawning among high school students almost everywhere, . . . about parents who lost their children in a flash and have filled the emptiness with hatred, . . . about a youth whose life is burdened with grief and guilt because he happened to be behind the wheel.

It is a story that the Baxter family and the dead boys' parents agreed to tell 9 in the hope that it would inspire high school students to remain sober during this week of graduation festivities—a week that customarily includes a ritual night of drunkenness.

It is a story of the times. 10

The evening of September 13 began in high spirits as Baxter, behind the wheel 11 of his gold Blazer, picked up seven high school chums for a drinking party for William Tennent High School students and graduates at the home of a classmate. Using false identification, according to police, the boys purchased one six-pack of beer each from a Warminster Township bar.

The unchaperoned party, attended by about fifty teenagers, ended about 12 10:30 P.M. when someone knocked over and broke a glass china cabinet. Baxter and his friends decided to head for a fast-food restaurant. As Baxter turned onto Street Road, he was trailed by a line of cars carrying other partygoers.

Baxter recalled that several passengers were swaying and rocking the high- 13 suspension vehicle. Police were unable to determine the vehicle's exact speed, but, on the basis of the accounts of witnesses, they estimated it at fifty-five miles per hour—ten miles per hour over the limit.

"I thought I was in control," Baxter said. "I wasn't driving like a nut; I was just 14 . . . driving. There was a bunch of noise, just a bunch of noise. The truck was really bouncing.

"I remember passing two [cars]. That's the last I remember. I remember a big 15 flash, and that's it."

Killed in that flash were: Morris "Marty" Freedenberg, sixteen, who landed 16 near a telephone pole about thirty feet from the truck, his face ripped from his skull; Robert Schweiss, eighteen, a Bucks County Community College student, whose internal organs were crushed when he hit the pavement about thirty feet from the truck; Brian Ball, seventeen, who landed near Schweiss, his six-foot-seven-inch frame stretched three inches when his spine was severed; and Christopher

Avram, seventeen, a premedical student at Temple University, who landed near the curb about ten feet from the truck.

Michael Serratore, eighteen, was thrown fifteen feet from the truck and landed   17
on the lawn of the CHI Institute with his right leg shattered. Baxter, who sailed about ten feet after crashing through the windshield of the Blazer, lost consciousness after hitting the street near the center lane. About five yards away, Paul Gee Jr., eighteen, lapsed into a coma from severe head injuries.

John Gahan, seventeen, the only passenger left in the Blazer, suffered a broken   18
ankle.

Brett Walker, seventeen, one of several Tennent students who saw the carnage   19
after the accident, would recall later in a speech to fellow students: "I ran over [to the scene]. These were the kids I would go out with every weekend.

"My one friend [Freedenberg], I couldn't even tell it was him except for his   20
eyes. He had real big, blue eyes. He was torn apart so bad . . . ."

Francis Schweiss was waiting up for his son, Robert, when he received a telephone   21
call from his daughter, Lisa. She was already at Warminster General Hospital.

"She said Robbie and his friends were in a bad accident and Robbie was not   22
here" at the hospital, Schweiss said. "I got in my car with my wife; we went to the scene of the accident."

There, police officers told Francis and Frances Schweiss that several boys had   23
been killed and that the bodies, as well as survivors, had been taken to Warminster General Hospital.

"My head was frying by then," Francis Schweiss said. "I can't even describe   24
it. I almost knew the worst was to be. I felt as though I were living a nightmare. I thought, 'I'll wake up. This just can't be.' "

In the emergency room, Francis Schweiss recalled, nurses and doctors were   25
scrambling to aid the injured and identify the dead—a difficult task because some bodies were disfigured and because all the boys had been carrying fake drivers' licenses.

A police officer from Upper Southampton was trying to question friends of   26
the dead and injured—many of whom were sobbing and screaming—in an attempt to match clothing with identities.

When the phone rang in the Freedenberg home, Robert Sr. and his wife, Bobbi,   27
had just gone upstairs to bed; their son Robert Jr. was downstairs watching a movie on television.

Bobbi Freedenberg and her son picked up the receiver at the same time. It was   28
from Warminster General . . . . There had been a bad accident . . . . The family should get to the hospital quickly.

Outside the morgue about twenty minutes later, a deputy county coroner told   29
Rob Jr., twenty-two, that his brother was dead and severely disfigured; Rob decided to spare his parents additional grief by identifying the body himself.

Freedenberg was led into a cinderblock room containing large drawers resem-   30
bling filing cabinets. In one of the drawers was his brother, Marty, identifiable only by his new high-top sneakers.

"It was kind of like being taken through a nightmare," Rob Jr. said. "That's 31 something I think about every night before I go to sleep. That's hell . . . .That whole night is what hell is all about for me."

As was his custom, Morris Ball started calling the parents of his son's friends after 32 Brian missed his 11:00 P.M. curfew.

The first call was to the Baxters' house, where the Baxters' sixteen-year-old 33 daughter, Amber, told him about the accident.

At the hospital, Morris Ball demanded that doctors and nurses take him to his 34 son. The hospital staff had been unable to identify Brian—until Ball told them that his son wore size fourteen shoes.

Brian Ball was in the morgue. Lower left drawer. 35

"He was six foot seven, but after the accident he measured six foot ten, 36 because of what happened to him," Ball said. "He had a severed spinal cord at the neck. His buttocks were practically ripped off, but he was lying down and we couldn't see that. He was peaceful and asleep.

"He was my son and my baby. I just can't believe it sometimes. I still can't 37 believe it. I still wait for him to come home."

Lynne Pancoast had just finished watching the 11:00 P.M. news and was curled up 38 in her bed dozing with a book in her lap when the doorbell rang. She assumed that one of her sons had forgotten his key, and she went downstairs to let him in.

A police light was flashing through the window and reflecting against her 39 living room wall; Pancoast thought that there must be a fire in the neighborhood and that the police were evacuating homes.

Instead, police officers told her there had been a serious accident involving 40 her son, Christopher Avram, and that she should go to the emergency room at Warminster General.

At the hospital she was taken to an empty room and told that her son was dead. 41

Patricia Baxter was asleep when a Warminster police officer came to the house 42 and informed her that her son had been in an accident.

At the hospital, she could not immediately recognize her own son lying on a bed 43 in the emergency room. His brown eyes were swollen shut, and his straight brown hair was matted with blood that had poured from a deep gash in his forehead.

While she was staring at his battered face, a police officer rushed into the 44 room and pushed her onto the floor—protection against the hysterical father of a dead youth who was racing through the halls, proclaiming that he had a gun and shouting, "Where is she? I'm going to kill her. I'm going to kill him. I'm going to kill his mother."

The man, who did not have a gun, was subdued by a Warminster police officer 45 and was not charged.

Amid the commotion, Robert Baxter, a Lower Southampton highway patrol 46 officer, arrived at the hospital and found his wife and son.

"When he came into the room, he kept going like this," Patricia Baxter said, 47
holding up four fingers. At first, she said, she did not understand that her husband
was signaling that four boys had been killed in the accident.

After Tyson regained consciousness, his father told him about the deaths.   48

"All I can remember is just tensing up and just saying something," Tyson Baxter   49
said. "I can remember saying, 'I know.'

"I can remember going nuts."   50

In the days after the accident, as the dead were buried in services that Tyson Baxter   51
was barred by the parents of the victims from attending, Baxter's parents waited
for him to react to the tragedy and release his grief.

"In the hospital he was nonresponsive," Patricia Baxter said. "He was home   52
for a month, and he was nonresponsive.

"We never used to do this, but we would be upstairs and listen to see if Ty   53
responded when his friends came to visit," she said. "But the boy would be silent.
That's the grief that I felt. The other kids showed a reaction. My son didn't."

Baxter said, however, that he felt grief from the first, that he would cry in the   54
quiet darkness of his hospital room and, later, alone in the darkness of his bedroom.
During the day, he said, he blocked his emotions.

"It was *just* at night. I thought about it all the time. It's still like that."   55

At his parents' urging, Baxter returned to school on September 30.   56

"I don't remember a thing," he said of his return. "I just remember walking   57
around. I didn't say anything to anybody. It didn't really sink in."

Lynne Pancoast, the mother of Chris Avram, thought it was wrong for Baxter   58
to be in school, and wrong that her other son, Joel, a junior at William Tennent,
had to walk through the school halls and pass the boy who "killed his brother."

Morris Ball said he was appalled that Baxter "went to a football game while   59
my son lay buried in a grave."

Some William Tennent students said they were uncertain about how they   60
should treat Baxter. Several said they went out of their way to treat him normally,
others said they tried to avoid him, and others declined to be interviewed on the
subject.

The tragedy unified the senior class, according to the school principal, Kenneth   61
Kastle. He said that after the accident, many students who were friends of the
victims joined the school's Students Against Driving Drunk chapter.

Matthew Weintraub, seventeen, a basketball player who witnessed the   62
bloody accident scene, wrote to President Reagan and detailed the grief among
the student body. He said, however, that he experienced a catharsis after reading the letter at a student assembly and, as a result, did not mail it.

"And after we got over the initial shock of the news, we felt as though we   63
owed somebody something," Weintraub wrote. "It could have been us and maybe
we could have stopped it, and now it's too late . . . .

"We took these impressions with us as we then visited our friends who had   64
been lucky enough to live. One of them was responsible for the accident; he was
the driver. He would forever hold the deaths of four young men on his conscience.

Compared with our own feelings of guilt, [we] could not begin to fathom this boy's emotions. He looked as if he had a heavy weight upon his head and it would remain there forever."

About three weeks after the accident, Senator H. Craig Lewis (D., Bucks) 65 launched a series of public forums to formulate bills targeting underage drinking. Proposals developed through the meetings include outlawing alcohol ads on radio and television, requiring police to notify parents of underage drinkers, and creating a tamperproof driver's license.

The parents of players on William Tennent's 1985–1986 boys' basketball team, 66 which lost Ball and Baxter because of the accident, formed the Caring Parents of William Tennent High School Students to help dissuade students from drinking.

Several William Tennent students, interviewed on the condition that their 67 names not be published, said that, because of the accident, they would not drive after drinking during senior week, which will be held in Wildwood, N.J., after graduation June 13.

But they scoffed at the suggestion that they curtail their drinking during the 68 celebrations.

"We just walk [after driving to Wildwood]," said one youth. "Stagger is more 69 like it."

"What else are we going to do, go out roller skating?" an eighteen-year-old 70 student asked.

"You telling us we're not going to drink?" one boy asked. "We're going to 71 drink very heavily. I want to come home retarded. That's senior week. I'm going to drink every day. Everybody's going to drink every day."

Tyson Baxter sat at the front table of the Bucks County courtroom on December 72 20, his arm in a sling, his head lowered, and his eyes dry. He faced twenty counts of vehicular homicide, four counts of involuntary manslaughter, and two counts of driving under the influence of alcohol.

Patricia Ball said she told the closed hearing that "it was Tyson Baxter who 73 killed our son. They used the car as a weapon. We know they killed our children as if it were a gun. They killed our son.

"I really could have felt justice [was served] if Tyson Baxter was the only one 74 who died in that car," she said in an interview, "because he didn't take care of our boys."

Police officers testified before Bucks County President Judge Isaac S. Garb that 75 tests revealed that the blood-alcohol levels of Baxter and the four dead boys were above the 0.10 percent limit used in Pennsylvania to establish intoxication.

Baxter's blood-alcohol level was 0.14 percent, Ball's 0.19 percent, Schweiss's 76 0.11 percent, Avram's 0.12 percent, and Freedenberg's 0.38 percent. Baxter's level indicated that he had had eight or nine drinks—enough to cause abnormal bodily functions such as exaggerated gestures and to impair his mental faculties, according to the police report.

After the case was presented, Garb invited family members of the dead teens 77 to speak.

In a nine-page statement, Bobbi Freedenberg urged Garb to render a decision 78
that would "punish, rehabilitate, and deter others from this act."

The parents asked Garb to give Baxter the maximum sentence, to prohibit him 79
from graduating, and to incarcerate him before Christmas Day. (Although he will
not attend formal ceremonies, Baxter will receive a diploma from William Tennent
this week.)

After hearing from the parents, Garb called Baxter to the stand. 80

"I just said that all I could say was, 'I'm sorry; I know I'm totally responsible 81
for what happened,'" Baxter recalled. "It wasn't long, but it was to the point."

Garb found Baxter delinquent and sentenced him to a stay at Abraxas 82
Rehabilitation Center—for an unspecified period beginning December 23—and
community service upon his return. Baxter's driver's license was suspended by the
judge for an unspecified period, and he was placed under Garb's jurisdiction until
age twenty-one.

Baxter is one of fifty-two Pennsylvania youths found responsible for fatal 83
drunken-driving accidents in the state in 1985.

Reflecting on the hearing, Morris Ball said there was no legal punishment that 84
would have satisfied his longings.

"They can't bring my son back," he said, "and they can't kill Tyson Baxter." 85

Grief has forged friendships among the dead boys' parents, all of whom blame 86
Tyson Baxter for their sons' deaths. Every month they meet at each other's homes,
but they seldom talk about the accident.

Several have joined support groups to help them deal with their losses. Some 87
said they feel comfortable only with other parents whose children are dead.

Bobbi Freedenberg said her attitude had worsened with the passage of time. 88
"It seems as if it just gets harder," she said. "It seems to get worse."

Freedenberg, Schweiss, and Pancoast said they talk publicly about their sons' 89
deaths in hopes that the experience will help deter other teenagers from
drunken driving.

Schweiss speaks each month to the Warminster Youth Aid Panel—a group of 90
teenagers who, through drug use, alcohol abuse, or minor offenses, have run
afoul of the law.

"When I talk to the teens, I bring a picture of Robbie and pass it along to 91
everyone," Schweiss said, wiping the tears from his cheeks. "I say, 'He was with
us last year.' I get emotional and I cry. . . .

"But I know that my son helps me. I firmly believe that every time I speak, 92
he's right on my shoulder."

When Pancoast speaks to a group of area high school students, she drapes her 93
son's football jersey over the podium and displays his graduation picture.

"Every time I speak to a group, I make them go through the whole thing 94
vicariously," Pancoast said. "It's helpful to get out and talk to kids. It sort of helps
keep Chris alive. . . . When you talk, you don't think."

At Abraxas, Baxter attended high school classes until Friday. He is one of three youths there who supervise fellow residents, who keep track of residents' whereabouts, attendance at programs, and adherence to the center's rules and regulations. 95

Established in Pittsburgh in 1973, the Abraxas Foundation provides an alternative to imprisonment for offenders between sixteen and twenty-five years old whose drug and alcohol use has led them to commit crimes. 96

Licensed and partially subsidized by the Pennsylvania Department of Health, the program includes work experience, high school education, and prevocational training. Counselors conduct individual therapy sessions, and the residents engage in peer-group confrontational therapy sessions. 97

Baxter said his personality had changed from an "egotistical, arrogant" teenager to someone who is "mellow" and mature. 98

"I don't have quite the chip on my shoulder. I don't really have a right to be cocky anymore," he said. 99

Baxter said not a day went by that he didn't remember his dead friends. 100

"I don't get sad. I just get thinking about them," he said. "Pictures pop into my mind. A tree or something reminds me of the time. . . . Sometimes I laugh. . . . Then I go to my room and reevaluate it like a nut," he said. 101

Baxter said his deepest longing was to stand beside the graves of his four friends. 102

More than anything, Baxter said, he wants to say good-bye. 103

"I just feel it's something I *have* to do, . . . just to talk," Baxter said, averting his eyes to hide welling tears. "Deep down I think I'll be hit with it when I see the graves. I know they're gone, but they're not gone." 104

■ Reading Comprehension Questions

1. The word *fathom* in "Compared with our own feelings of guilt, [we] could not begin to fathom this boy's emotions" (paragraph 64) means

   a. choose.

   b. understand.

   c. mistake.

   d. protest.

2. The word *dissuade* in "The parents . . . formed the Caring Parents of William Tennent High School Students to help dissuade students from drinking" (paragraph 66) means

   a. discourage.

   b. delay.

   c. organize.

   d. frighten.

3. Which of the following would be the best alternative title for this selection?
   a. The Night of September 13
   b. A Fatal Mistake: Teenage Drinking and Driving
   c. The Agony of Parents
   d. High School Drinking Problems

4. Which sentence best expresses the main idea of the selection?
   a. Teenagers must understand the dangers and consequences of drinking and driving.
   b. Tyson Baxter was too drunk to drive that night.
   c. The Abraxas Foundation is a model alternative program to imprisonment for teenagers.
   d. Teenagers are drinking more than ever before.

5. The hospital had trouble identifying the boys because
   a. officials could not find their families.
   b. the boys all had false licenses and some of their bodies were mutilated.
   c. there weren't enough staff members on duty at the hospital that night.
   d. everyone was withholding information.

6. Tyson Baxter feels that
   a. the judge's sentence was unfair.
   b. he will never graduate from high school.
   c. he is responsible for the whole accident.
   d. he should not be blamed for the accident.

7. *True or false?* _____ Because of the accident, all the seniors promised that they would not drink during senior week.

8. The authors imply that the parents of the dead boys felt that
   a. Tyson should not be punished.
   b. their boys shared no blame for the accident.
   c. Tyson should have come to the boys' funerals.
   d. Tyson should be allowed to attend graduation.

9. The authors imply that most of the parents' anger has been toward
   a. school officials.
   b. Senator H. Craig Lewis.
   c. their local police.
   d. Tyson Baxter.

10. The authors imply that Tyson
   a.   behaved normally after the accident.
   b.   will always have a problem with alcohol.
   c.   no longer thinks about his dead friends.
   d.   is benefiting from his time at Abraxas.

■ Discussion Questions

About Content

1. Why do the authors call their narrative "a story of the times"?

2. Exactly why did four teenagers die in the accident? To what extent were their deaths the driver's fault? Their own fault? Society's fault?

3. What effect has the accident had on other Tennent students? In view of the tragedy, can you explain the reluctance of the Tennent students to give up drinking during "senior week"?

4. How would you describe the attitude of Tyson Baxter after the accident? How would you characterize the attitude of the parents? Whose attitude, if any, seems more appropriate under the circumstances?

About Structure

5. The lead paragraphs in a newspaper article such as this one are supposed to answer questions known as the *five W's:* who, what, where, when, and why.

   Which paragraphs in the article answer these questions? _____

6. The authors *do not* use transitional words to move from one section of their article to the next. How, then, do they manage to keep their narrative organized and clear?

About Style and Tone

7. Why do the authors use so many direct quotations in their account of the accident? How do these quotations add to the effectiveness of the article?

8. What seems to be the authors' attitude toward Tyson Baxter at the end of the piece? Why do you think they end with Tyson's desire to visit his dead friends' graves? What would have been the effect of ending with Lynne Pancoast's words in paragraph 94?

■ Writing Assignments

Assignment 1: Writing a Paragraph

While drunk drivers come in all ages, a large percentage of them are young. Write a paragraph explaining what you think would be one or more *effective* ways of dramatizing to young people the dangers of drunk driving. Keep in mind that the young are being cautioned all the time, and that some of the warnings are so familiar that they probably don't have any impact.

What kind of caution or cautions would make young people take notice? Develop one approach in great detail or suggest several approaches for demonstrating the dangers of drunk driving to the young.

Assignment 2: Writing a Paragraph

Tyson Baxter's friends might still be alive if he had not been drunk when he drove. But there is another way their deaths could have been avoided—they might have refused to get into the car. Such a refusal would not have been easy; one does not, after all, want to embarrass a person who has given you a ride to some event. At the same time, it may be absolutely necessary to make such a refusal. Write a paragraph suggesting one or more ways to turn down a ride from a driver who may be drunk.

Assignment 3: Writing an Essay

A number of letters to the editor followed the appearance of "A Drunken Ride, a Tragic Aftermath." Here are some of them:

> To the Editor:
>
> I am deeply concerned by the June 8 article, "A Drunken Ride, a Tragic Aftermath," not because of the tragedy it unfolds, but because of the tragedy that is occurring as a result.
>
> It is an injustice on the part of the parents whose children died to blame Tyson Baxter so vehemently for those deaths. (I lost my best friend in a similar accident eight years ago, and I haven't forgotten the pain or the need to blame.) All the youths were legally intoxicated. None of them refused to go with Mr. Baxter, and I submit that he did not force them to ride with him.
>
> Yes, Mr. Baxter is guilty of drunk driving, but I would like the other parents to replace Mr. Baxter with their sons and their cars and ask themselves again where the blame lies.
>
> Tyson Baxter did not have the intent to kill, and his car was not the weapon. All these boys were Mr. Baxter's friends. The weapon used to kill them was alcohol, and in a way each boy used it on himself.
>
> If we are to assign blame it goes far beyond one drunk eighteen-year-old.

The answer lies in our society and its laws—laws about drinking and driving, and laws of parenting, friendship, and responsibility. Why, for instance, didn't the other youths call someone to come get them, or call a taxi, rather than choose to take that fatal ride?

These parents should be angry and they should fight against drunk driving by making people aware. But they shouldn't continue to destroy the life of one boy whose punishment is the fact that he survived.

Elizabeth Bowen
Philadelphia

To the Editor:

I could not believe the attitude of the parents of the boys who were killed in the accident described in the June 8 article "A Drunken Ride, a Tragic Aftermath." Would they really feel that justice was done if Tyson Baxter were dead, too?

Tyson Baxter is not the only guilty person. All the boys who got into the vehicle were guilty, as well as all the kids at the party who let them go. Did any of the parents question their children earlier that fateful night as to who would be the "designated driver" (or did they think their sons would never go out drinking)?

How would those parents feel if their son happened to be the one behind the wheel?

I do not want to lessen the fact that Tyson Baxter was guilty (a guilt he readily admits to and will carry with him for a lifetime). However, should he have to carry his own guilt and be burdened with everyone else's guilt as well?

Andrea D. Colantti
Philadelphia

To the Editor:

Reading the June 8 article about the tragic aftermath of the drunken-driving accident in which high school students were killed and injured, I was aware of a major missing element. That element is the role of individual responsibility.

While we cannot control everything that happens to us, we can still manage many of the events of our lives. Individual responsibility operates at two levels. First is the accountability each person has for his own actions. To drink, or not to drink. To drink to excess, or to remain sober. To ride with someone who has been drinking, or to find another ride.

Second is the responsibility to confront those who are drinking or using drugs and planning to drive. To talk to them about their alcohol or drug consumption, to take their keys, call a cab, or do whatever else a friend would do.

The toughest, most punitive laws will not prevent people from drinking and driving, nor will they rectify the results of an accident. The only things we can actually control are our personal choices and our responses.

Don't drink and drive. Don't ride with those that do. Use your resources to stop those who try.

Gregory A. Gast
Willow Grove

To the Editor:

After reading the June 8 article about the tragic accident involving the students from William Tennent High School, my heart goes out to the parents of the boys who lost their lives. I know I can't begin to understand the loss they feel. However, even more so, my heart goes out to them for their inability to forgive the driver and their ability to wish him dead.

I certainly am not condoning drunk driving; in fact, I feel the law should be tougher.

But how can they be so quick to judge and hate this boy, when all their sons were also legally drunk, some more so than the driver, and any one of them could have easily been the driver himself? They all got into the car knowingly drunk and were noisily rocking the vehicle. They were all teenagers, out for a night of fun, never thinking of the consequences of drunk driving.

I would view this differently had the four dead boys been in another car, sober, and hit by a drunk driver. However, when you knowingly enter a car driven by someone who is drunk and are drunk yourself, you are responsible for what happens to you.

Tyson Baxter, the driver, needs rehabilitation and counseling. He will live with this for the rest of his life. The parents of the four boys who died need to learn about God, who is forgiving, and apply that forgiveness to a boy who desperately needs it. He could have easily been one of their sons.

Debbie Jones
Wilmington

To the Editor:

The June 8 article "A Drunken Ride, a Tragic Aftermath" missed an important point. The multiple tragedy was a double—a perhaps needless—tragedy because the young men were not belted into their seats when the Blazer crashed.

All of those who were killed and severely injured had been thrown out of the vehicle; the only one left inside suffered a broken ankle. Had all been properly belted, all or most would probably have survived with similar minor injuries.

As much as this article points up the dangers of drunken driving, it also points up the absolute need for a mandatory seat-belt law strictly enforced. Two other points reinforce this. With eight people, the Blazer was overloaded by a factor of two. Also, Tyson Baxter, the driver, stated that his passengers were bouncing about and making the vehicle rock, a dangerous situation even when the driver is stone cold sober; being belted in puts a real damper on this sort of thing.

Roy West
Philadelphia

These letters make apparent a difference of opinion about how severely Tyson Baxter should be punished. Write an essay in which, in an introductory paragraph, you advance your judgment about the appropriate punishment for Tyson Baxter. Then provide three supporting paragraphs in which you argue and defend your opinion. You may use or add to ideas stated in the article or the letters, but think through the ideas yourself and put them into your own words.

Assignment 4: Writing an Essay Using Internet Research

The tragic deaths of Tyson Baxter's four friends highlight the problem of drinking and driving. But what can be done to get drunken drivers off the road? Use the Internet to research the topic. Then write an essay that explains three ways to get intoxicated drivers off the road. These could include ways to prevent people from drinking and driving in the first place, or ways to keep a person convicted of drunken driving from doing it again.

To access the Internet, use the very helpful search engine Google (*www. google.com*) or one of the other search engines listed on pages 323–325 of this book. Try one of the following phrases or some related phrase:

keeping drunk drivers off the road

drunk drivers and prevention

successful prevention programs for drunk driving

As you proceed, you'll develop a sense of how to "track down" and focus a topic by adding more information to your search words and phrases.

THE LEARNING CENTRE
CITY & ISLINGTON COLLEGE
444 CAMDEN ROAD
LONDON N7 0SP
TEL: 020 7700 8642

Appendix

Answers and Charts

Preview

This Appendix provides answers for the Sentence-Skills Diagnostic Test on pages 355–359 and for the Introductory Projects in Part Five. It also contains four useful charts: an assignment chart, a spelling list, and a reading comprehension chart, to be filled in by the student, and a general form for planning a paragraph.

Answers to Sentence-Skills Diagnostic Test and Introductory Projects

Sentence-Skills Diagnostic Test (pages 355–359)

Fragments

1. X
2. C
3. X
4. X
5. C
6. X

Run-Ons

7. C
8. X
9. X
10. X
11. C
12. X

Standard English Verbs

13. C
14. C
15. X
16. X

Irregular Verbs

17. X
18. C
19. C
20. X

Subject-Verb Agreement

21. X
22. X
23. C
24. X

Consistent Verb Tense

25. X
26. C
27. C
28. X

Pronoun Agreement, Reference, and Point of View

29. X
30. C
31. X
32. C
33. X
34. C

Pronoun Types

35. X
36. C

Adjectives and Adverbs

37. X
38. X

Misplaced Modifiers

39. X
40. C
41. X
42. X

Dangling Modifiers

43. C
44. X
45. C
46. X

Faulty Parallelism

47. X
48. C
49. X
50. C

Capital Letters

51. X
52. X
53. C
54. X

Apostrophe

55. C
56. X
57. X
58. C

Quotation Marks

59. C
60. X
61. X
62. C

Comma

63. X
64. X
65. C
66. X
67. C
68. X

Commonly Confused Words

69. X
70. X
71. C
72. X
73. X
74. C

Effective Word Use

75. X
76. X
77. X
78. X

Introductory Projects

Fragments (page 369)

1. thought
2. subject
3. verb
4. subject

Run-Ons (page 385)

1. period
2. *but*
3. semicolon
4. *When*

Standard English Verbs (page 400)

enjoyed . . . enjoys; started . . . starts;
cooked . . . cooks

1. past . . . *-ed*
2. present . . . *-s*

Irregular Verbs (page 409)

1. crawled, crawled (regular)
2. brought, brought (irregular)
3. used, used (regular)
4. did, done (irregular)
5. gave, given (irregular)
6. laughed, laughed (regular)
7. went, gone (irregular)
8. scared, scared (regular)
9. dressed, dressed (regular)
10. saw, seen (irregular)

Subject-Verb Agreement (page 418)

The second sentence in each pair is correct.

Pronoun Agreement and Reference (page 425)

The second sentence in each pair is correct.

Misplaced Modifiers (page 443)

1. Intended: A young man with references is wanted to open oysters.
   Unintended: The oysters have references.
2. Intended: On their wedding day, Clyde and Charlotte decided they would have two children.
   Unintended: Clyde and Charlotte decided to have two children who would appear on the day of their wedding.
3. Intended: The students who failed the test no longer like the math instructor.
   Unintended: The math instructor failed the test.

Dangling Modifiers (page 447)

1. Intended: My dog sat with me as I smoked a pipe.
   Unintended: My dog smoked a pipe.
2. Intended: He looked at a leather-skirted woman.
   Unintended: His sports car looked at the woman.
3. Intended: A beef pie baked in the oven for several hours.
   Unintended: Grandmother baked in the oven.

Capital Letters (page 457)

All the answers to questions 1 to 13 should be in capital letters.

14. The   15. I   16. That

Apostrophe (page 469)

1. The purpose of the *'s* is to show possession (Larry owns the motorcycle, the boyfriend belongs to the sister, Grandmother owns the shotgun, the room belongs to the men).
2. The purpose of the apostrophe is to show the omission of one or more letters in a contraction—two words shortened to form one word.

3. In each of the second sentences, the *'s* shows possession: the body of the vampire; the center of the baked potato. In each of the first sentences, the *s* is used to form a simple plural: more than one vampire; more than one potato.

Quotation Marks (page 478)

1. The purpose of quotation marks is to set off the exact words of a speaker. (The words that the young man actually spoke aloud are set off with quotation marks, as are the words that the old woman spoke aloud.)
2. Commas and periods go inside quotation marks.

Comma (page 485)

1. a. Frank's interests are Maria, television, and sports.
   b. My mother put her feet up, sipped some iced tea, and opened the newspaper.
2. a. Although the Lone Ranger used lots of silver bullets, he never ran out of ammunition.
   b. To remove the cap of the aspirin bottle, you must first press down on it.
3. a. Kitty Litter and Dredge Rivers, Hollywood's leading romantic stars, have made several movies together.
   b. Sarah, who is my next-door neighbor, just entered the hospital with an intestinal infection.
4. a. The wedding was scheduled for four o'clock, but the bride changed her mind at two.
   b. Verna took three coffee breaks before lunch, and then she went on a two-hour lunch break.
5. a. Lola's mother asked her, "What time do you expect to get home?"
   b. "Don't bend over to pat the dog," I warned, "or he'll bite you."
6. a. Roy ate seventeen hamburgers on July 29, 1992, and lived to tell about it.
   b. Roy lives at 817 Cresson Street, Detroit, Michigan.

Other Punctuation Marks (page 495)

1. pets: holly
2. freeze-dried
3. Shakespeare (1564–1616)
4. Earth; no
5. proudly—with

Commonly Confused Words (page 519)

Your mind and body . . . *There* is a lot of evidence . . .
then it will . . . said *to* have . . . *It's* not clear

Effective Word Choice (page 529)

1. "Flipped out" is slang.
2. "Few and far between" is a cliché.
3. "Ascertained" is a pretentious word.

Charts

Assignment Chart

Use this chart to record daily or weekly assignments in your writing class. You might want to print writing assignments and their due dates in capital letters so that they stand out clearly.

Date Given	Assignment	Date Due

Date Given	Assignment	Date Due

Spelling List

Enter here the words that you misspelled in your papers (note the examples). If you add to and study this list regularly, you will not repeat the same mistakes in your writing.

Incorrect Spelling	Correct Spelling	Points to Remember
alright	all right	two words
ocasion	occasion	two "c"s

Reading Comprehension Chart

Write an X through the numbers of any questions you missed while answering the comprehension questions for each selection in Part Six, Seventeen Reading Selections. Then write in your comprehension score. To calculate your score for each reading, give yourself 10 points for each item that is *not* X'd out. The chart will make clear any skill question you get wrong repeatedly, so that you can pay special attention to that skill in the future.

Selection	Vocabulary in Context	Subject or Title	Thesis or Main Idea	Key Details	Inferences	Comprehension Score
Mrosla	1 2	3	4	5 6 7	8 9 10	%
Logan	1 2	3	4	5 6 7	8 9 10	%
Wong	1 2	3	4	5 6 7	8 9 10	%
Angelou	1 2	3	4	5 6 7	8 9 10	%
Rooney	1 2	3	4	5 6 7	8 9 10	%
Curran	1 2	3	4	5 6 7	8 9 10	%
Carson	1 2	3	4	5 6 7	8 9 10	%
Collier	1 2	3	4	5 6 7 8	9 10	%
Barrett	1 2	3	4	5 6 7	8 9 10	%
Garland	1 2	3	4	5 6 7	8 9 10	%
Scott	1 2	3	4	5 6 7	8 9 10	%
Verderber	1 2	3	4	5 6 7	8 9 10	%
Ellerbee	1 2	3	4	5 6 7	8 9 10	%
Wine	1 2	3	4	5 6 7	8 9 10	%
Berger	1 2	3	4	5 6 7 8 9	10	%
Syme	1 2	3	4	5 6 7	8 9 10	%
Conroy/ Johnson	1 2	3	4	5 6 7	8 9 10	%

Form for Planning a Paragraph

To write an effective paragraph, first prepare an outline. Often (though not always) you may be able to use a form like the one below.

Topic sentence: _____

_____

_____

Support (1): _____

_____

Details:

Support (2): _____

_____

Details:

Support (3): _____

_____

Details:

Acknowledgments

Maya Angelou, "Adolescent Confusion" (editor's title). Excerpt from *I Know Why the Caged Bird Sings* by Maya Angelou, copyright ©1969 by Maya Angelou. Used by permission of Random House, Inc. and Virago Press.

Katherine Barrett, "Old before Her Time." From *Ladies' Home Journal* magazine. Copyright 1983 by Meredith Corporation. All rights reserved. Used with the permission of *Ladies' Home Journal.*

Kathleen Stassen Berger and Ross A. Thompson, "Bullies in School." Excerpt from *The Developing Person through the Life Span* by Kathleen Stassen Berger and Ross A. Thompson, ©1998 by Worth Publishers. Used with permission.

Ben Carson, M.D., with Cecil Murphey, "Do It Better!" Excerpt from *Think Big,* copyright ©1992 by Benjamin Carson, M.D. Used by permission of Zondervan Publishing House.

James Lincoln Collier, "Anxiety: Challenge by Another Name." Originally published in *Reader's Digest,* December 1986. Reprinted by permission of the author.

Theresa Conroy and Christine M. Johnson, "A Drunken Ride, A Tragic Aftermath." From *The Philadelphia Inquirer.* Copyright ©1986, The Philadelphia Inquirer. Reprinted by permission.

Delores Curran, "What Good Families Are Doing Right," from *McCall's,* March 1983. Reprinted by permission.

Linda Ellerbee, "Television Changed My Family Forever." From *Move On,* copyright 1991 by Linda Ellerbee. Reprinted by permission of International Creative Management, Inc.

Anita Garland, "Let's Really Reform Our Schools." Copyright ©1994. Reprinted by permission of the author.

Paul Logan, "Rowing the Bus." Copyright ©1997. Reprinted by permission of the author.

Sister Helen Mrosla, "All the Good Things." Originally published in *Reader's Digest,* October 1991. Reprinted by permission.

Andy Rooney, "Tickets to Nowhere." Originally published in the *San Francisco Chronicle,* Sept. 25, 1988. ©Tribune Media Services, Inc. All Rights Reserved. Reprinted with permission.

Janny Scott, "How They Get You to Do That." Originally published in the *Los Angeles Times,* July 23, 1992. Copyright 1992, Los Angeles Times. Reprinted by permission.

S. Leonard Syme, "People Need People," from *American Health* (July–August 1982). Reprinted by permission of S. Leonard Syme.

Rudolph F. Verderber, "Dealing with Feelings." Excerpt from *Communicate, 6th Edition,* by Rudolph F. Verderber, ©1990. Reprinted with permission of Wadsworth, an imprint of the Wadsworth Group, a division of Thomson Learning.

Bill Wine, "Rudeness at the Movies." Copyright 1989. Reprinted by permission of the author.

Jade Snow Wong, "Fifth Chinese Daughter." Excerpt from Jade Snow Wong's *Fifth Chinese Daughter,* ©1989 by University of Washington Press. Reprinted by permission of University of Washington Press.

Yahoo!® home page. Reproduced with permission of Yahoo! Inc. ©2000 by Yahoo! Inc. YAHOO! and the YAHOO! logo are trademarks of Yahoo! Inc.

Index